International Directory of
COMPANY
HISTORIES

International Directory of
COMPANY HISTORIES

VOLUME 19

Editor
Tina Grant

ST. JAMES PRESS

AN IMPRINT OF GALE

DETROIT • NEW YORK • TORONTO • LONDON

STAFF

Tina Grant, *Editor*

Miranda H. Ferrara, *Project Manager*
Nicolet V. Elert, Jay P. Pederson, *Contributing Editors*
Peter M. Gareffa, *Managing Editor, St. James Press*

The paper used in this publication meets the minimum
requirements of American National Standard for Information Sciences—
Permanence Paper for Printed Library Materials, ANSI Z39.48-1984.

Library of Congress Catalog Number: 89-190943

British Library Cataloguing in Publication Data

International directory of company histories. Vol. 19
I. Tina Grant
338.7409

ISBN 1-55862-353-1

Printed in the United States of America
Published simultaneously in the United Kingdom

St. James Press is an imprint of Gale

Cover photograph: Trading at Hong Kong's unified stock exchange.
(courtesy Hong Kong Trade Development Council)

10 9 8 7 6 5 4 3 2 1

CONTENTS _____

Company Histories

PREFACE

The St. James Press series *The International Directory of Company Histories (IDCH)* is intended for reference use by students, business people, librarians, historians, economists, investors, job candidates, and others who seek to learn more about the historical development of the world's most important companies. To date, *IDCH* has covered over 3,000 companies in nineteen volumes.

Inclusion Criteria

Most companies chosen for inclusion in *IDCH* have achieved a minimum of US$100 million in annual sales and are leading influences in their industries or geographical locations. Companies may be publicly held, private, or non-profit. State-owned companies that are important in their industries and that may operate much like public or private companies also are included. Wholly owned subsidiaries and divisions are profiled if they meet the requirements for inclusion. Entries on companies that have had major changes since they were last profiled may be selected for updating.

The *IDCH* series highlights 10% private and non-profit companies, and features updated entries on approximately 25 companies per volume.

Entry Format

Each entry begins with the company's legal name, the address of its headquarters, its telephone and fax numbers, and its web site. A statement of public, private, state, or parent ownership follows. A company with a legal name in both English and the language of its headquarters country is listed by the English name, with the native-language name in parentheses.

The company's founding or earliest incorporation date, the number of employees, and the most recent sales figures available follow. Sales figures are given in local currencies with equivalents in U.S. dollars. For some private companies, sales figures are estimates. The entry lists the exchanges on which a company's stock is traded, as well as the company's principal Standard Industrial Classification codes.

Entries also contain a *Company Perspectives* box which provides a short summary of the company's mission, goals, and ideals, a list of *Principal Subsidiaries*, *Principal Divisions*, *Principal Operating Units*, and articles for *Further Reading*.

American spelling is used throughout *IDCH*, and the word "billion" is used in its U.S. sense of one thousand million.

Sources

Entries have been compiled from publicly accessible sources both in print and on the Internet such as general and academic periodicals, books, annual reports, and material supplied by the companies themselves.

Cumulative Indexes

IDCH contains two indexes: the **Index to Companies**, which provides an alphabetical index to companies discussed in the text as well as companies profiled, and the **Index to Industries**, which allows researchers to locate companies by their principal industry. Both indexes are cumulative and specific instructions for using them are found immediately preceding each index.

Suggestions Welcome

Comments and suggestions from users of *IDCH* on any aspect of the product as well as suggestions for companies to be included or updated are cordially invited. Please write:

The Editor
International Directory of Company Histories
St. James Press
835 Penobscot Building
Detroit, Michigan 48226-4094

A.B.	Aktiebolaget (Sweden)
A.G.	Aktiengesellschaft (Germany, Switzerland)
A.S.	Atieselskab (Denmark)
A.S.	Aksjeselskap (Denmark, Norway)
A.Ş.	Anomin Şirket (Turkey)
B.V.	Besloten Vennootschap met beperkte, Aansprakelijkheid (The Netherlands)
Co.	Company (United Kingdom, United States)
Corp.	Corporation (United States)
G.I.E.	Groupement d'Intérêt Economique (France)
GmbH	Gesellschaft mit beschränkter Haftung (Germany)
H.B.	Handelsbolaget (Sweden)
Inc.	Incorporated (United States)
KGaA	Kommanditgesellschaft auf Aktien (Germany)
K.K.	Kabushiki Kaisha (Japan)
LLC	Limited Liability Company (Middle East)
Ltd.	Limited (Canada, Japan, United Kingdom, United States)
N.V.	Naamloze Vennootschap (The Netherlands)
OY	Osakeyhtiöt (Finland)
PLC	Public Limited Company (United Kingdom)
PTY.	Proprietary (Australia, Hong Kong, South Africa)
S.A.	Société Anonyme (Belgium, France, Switzerland)
SpA	Società per Azioni (Italy)

DA	Algerian dinar		M$	Malaysian ringgit
A$	Australian dollar		Dfl	Netherlands florin
Sch	Austrian schilling		NZ$	New Zealand dollar
BFr	Belgian franc		N	Nigerian naira
Cr	Brazilian cruzado		NKr	Norwegian krone
C$	Canadian dollar		RO	Omani rial
RMB	Chinese renminbi		P	Philippine peso
DKr	Danish krone		Esc	Portuguese escudo
E£	Egyptian pound		SRls	Saudi Arabian riyal
Fmk	Finnish markka		S$	Singapore dollar
FFr	French franc		R	South African rand
DM	German mark		W	South Korean won
HK$	Hong Kong dollar		Pta	Spanish peseta
Rs	Indian rupee		SKr	Swedish krona
Rp	Indonesian rupiah		SFr	Swiss franc
IR£	Irish pound		NT$	Taiwanese dollar
L	Italian lira		B	Thai baht
¥	Japanese yen		£	United Kingdom pound
W	Korean won		$	United States dollar
KD	Kuwaiti dinar		B	Venezuelan bolivar
LuxFr	Luxembourgian franc		K	Zambian kwacha

International Directory of
COMPANY
HISTORIES

Advance Publications Inc.

950 Fingerboard Road
Staten Island, New York 10305
U.S.A.
(718) 981-1234
Fax: (718) 981-5679

Private Company
Incorporated: 1924 as Staten Island Advance Company
Employees: 24,000
Sales: $5.35 billion (estimated, 1996)
SICs: 2711 Newspapers; 2721 Periodicals

Family owned and operated, Advance Publications Inc. is a multibillion dollar international communications empire that publishes newspapers, magazines, books, and electronic media. It is the second-largest publishing concern in the United States. The founder, Samuel I. Newhouse, built his success on hard work, innovative business methods, and the help of Newhouse family members, who took over the company after the founder's death and continued his idiosyncratic organizational system.

The Beginnings of an Empire

Solomon Neuhaus—later called Samuel I. Newhouse and finally just S.I. Newhouse—was born in 1895 in New York City. He was the oldest of eight children born to recent immigrants from Eastern Europe. Financial success eluded the first generation, the suspender business of the father having failed in 1905. After graduating in 1908 from eighth grade in Bayonne, New Jersey, Newhouse briefly attended a business school in New York City. He carried bundles of newspapers across the Hudson River to earn money for the fare to and from business school. This was Newhouse's first newspaper job. Newhouse earned no money the first month he was employed by Judge Hyman Lazarus, a city magistrate who operated a law office, Lazarus & Brenner, in Bayonne. After showing his worth as an office assistant that first month, Newhouse was given $2.00 a week.

Starting a steady rise in the firm, Newhouse became the accountant, real estate manager, and general troubleshooter for Lazarus. The judge had acquired 51 percent of the *Bayonne Times* in payment of a debt. It seemed at first to be a losing proposition, but Lazarus hoped to stem the losses until he could sell the newspaper, which he had moved into the same building as the law firm. To that end Lazarus gave Newhouse responsibility for the business aspect of the *Times*. Newhouse concentrated on increasing both advertising revenues and subscriptions, and the paper showed a profit within a year.

By 1916 Newhouse, at the age of 21, was earning $30,000 a year for his myriad responsibilities with Lazarus & Brenner, as well as with the newspaper, where he now worked for a percentage of the profits. This same year he finished his study of law at New Jersey College and passed the bar examination in New Jersey. After losing his first and only trial, a debt-collection case, Newhouse paid his client the disputed amount out of his own pocket and retired from trial law.

When the United States entered World War I in 1917, Newhouse, as the sole source of support of his family, was exempt from conscription and concentrated on building up the *Bayonne Times,* which enjoyed increased circulation as people sought to learn the latest war news. Newhouse devoted much of his free time to learning about the newspaper business, which impressed him as a feasible way to make his fortune. His model was William Randolph Hearst.

Despite Newhouse's lofty ambitions, his first step in this direction was less than successful. With borrowed money from his family, along with his own savings, Newhouse went into partnership with Lazarus to buy The Fitchburg Daily News Company of Fitchburg, Massachusetts, for $15,000. Newhouse took pains to make the new paper a going concern, but faced with antagonism directed toward him as both an outsider and a Jew, he decided within a year to sell the property to Frank L. Hoyt, publisher of the competing *Fitchburg Sentinel.* Persuading Hoyt of the benefits inherent in owning a newspaper monopoly, Newhouse was able to turn a profit on even this first, relatively unsuccessful newspaper deal.

Strong Growth in the 1920s and 1930s

By 1922 Newhouse was ready for another acquisition and with Lazarus bought 51 percent of the stock of *The Staten*

Island Advance for $98,000. In 1923 the circulation of the *Advance* rose 50 percent, and the number of pages had doubled with additional advertising. In November of that year the *Advance*'s masthead listed S.I. Newhouse as publisher.

The Staten Island Advance proved to be the foundation of the publishing empire Newhouse established in the 1920s. In 1924 Newhouse, along with St. John Mclean and William Wolfe, bought out Judge Lazarus's interest in the *Advance* and incorporated the Staten Island Advance Company, renamed Staten Island Advance Corporation shortly thereafter. Newhouse owned 60 percent of the new company, and his two partners split the rest. Although the business consisted of just one newspaper at the time, its stated purpose was "to engage in, conduct, manage, and transact the business of publishing, selling, binding, and distribution of books, journals, magazines, newspapers, periodicals, and all other kinds of publications" and to collect and distribute "news and press reports and dispatches and information of every sort and kind by any and all means." Newhouse would fulfill this stated purpose with the help of associates: Charles Goldman, the legal representative of the firm; Louis Glickman, the accountant, whose tax advice convinced Newhouse of the wisdom of reinvesting profits in newspaper acquisitions; and Louis Hochstein, whose editorial expertise was to guide many Newhouse concerns starting with the *Advance*.

Staten Island proved to be a good place to own a newspaper in the 1920s, a decade of intense land speculation and business activity. Many newspaper stands were at first reluctant to carry the *Advance*, but Newhouse increased circulation by adopting a Brooklyn newspaper's home-delivery system, and by 1928 he had made enough to buy out his two partners in the company for $198,000. By this time Lazarus had died, and Newhouse, no longer associated with the *Bayonne Times*, had married Mitzi Epstein. The Newhouses had two sons, Samuel I. (Si) Newhouse, Jr., in 1927, and Donald E. Newhouse in 1929. Despite the challenge to the *Advance* by the *Staten Islander* and a politically motivated libel suit, Newhouse was able not only to prosper during good times but to survive the stock market crash of 1929 and the Great Depression. Newhouse had invested his company's profits in the newspaper, not in stocks; thus, in 1932 the bank account of the *Advance* stood at close to $400,000. Staten Island Advance Corporation did not lay off or cut the pay of any employees.

When Newhouse learned in 1932 that Victor, Bernard, and Joseph Ridder were willing to sell their 51 percent of shares in the *Long Island Press*, his cash-rich position made it easy to acquire that newspaper. Newhouse's younger brother Norman became the managing editor of the *Advance*, and Hochstein was made the managing editor of the *Press*. This purchase was to bring Newhouse into conflict with the newly organized American Newspaper Guild, when, in 1934, the *Press* became the first newspaper in U.S. history to be picketed by its editorial workers. Labor problems continued at the Long Island paper throughout the 1930s, and New York City mayor Fiorello LaGuardia was twice called in to arbitrate. The issue for Newhouse was control. Later Newhouse—quoted by the November 27, 1989, issue of *Barron's*—would say, "I refuse to stand by passively and allow any union to 'bust' me." He continued, "As I learned at the *Advance* nearly 40 years before,

to yield to others the controls that are vital to your own security is suicide."

Despite these labor problems, Newhouse was able to acquire six newspapers during the 1930s. The first of these acquisitions, in 1935, was a 51 percent share in the *Newark Ledger* of Newark, New Jersey. For this newspaper Newhouse used the recently developed technique of market survey to help shape the newspaper to a new, affluent suburban readership. When Newhouse bought as a package the *North Shore Journal* in Flushing, New York, and the *Long Island Star* in Long Island City, New York, in 1938 for $250,000, he combined the two into the *Long Island Star-Journal,* and by merging physical operations he was able to make a profitable enterprise out of two unprofitable newspapers. Newhouse repeated this merger strategy when he bought the *Newark Star-Eagle* and merged it with the *Newark Ledger* to form the *Newark Star-Ledger* in 1939. The same year he acquired the *Syracuse Herald* of Syracuse, New York, for $1 million and combined it with the *Syracuse Journal* (a property he picked up at about the same time from Hearst Corporation for $900,000) to form the *Syracuse Herald-Journal.* To help offset the cost, 428 *Journal* employees were fired immediately. In 1942 Newhouse bought for $1.3 million the only remaining Syracuse newspaper, the morning *Post-Standard,* establishing a highly profitable monopoly during World War II, even with shortages of newsprint and other supplies.

In the 1940s Newhouse acquired the remaining 49 percent of shares in Long Island Daily Press Publishing Company, purchased half of the Jersey City, New Jersey, *Jersey Journal,* and bought all three newspapers in Harrisburg, Pennsylvania. Operating out of a car with a telephone, Newhouse, with the help of the trains, managed to visit most of the newspapers he owned on an almost weekly basis, making informal notes as he visited the operations and maintaining a wealth of information in his head.

It was also during the 1940s that Newhouse was labeled a "literary *chiffonier*" (French for ragpicker) by critic A.J. Liebling of *The New Yorker,* reflecting Newhouse's reputation for picking up and turning around small, undistinguished newspapers that were in financial difficulty or plagued by family squabbles. Indeed, the *Jersey Journal* was one such transaction involving a dispute between Walter Dear and his nephew, Albert Dear. In this case Newhouse, after buying almost half the paper from Walter Dear in 1945, was able to acquire only after lengthy litigation the remaining shares from Albert Dear in 1951. In 1947 Newhouse acquired the Patriot Company, publisher of the *Patriot* and the *Evening News* in Harrisburg, Pennsylvania. A socially prominent former Newhouse employee, Edwin Russell, acted as a front man for Staten Island Advance Corporation in convincing the owner, Annie McCormick, to sell the company to Newhouse.

Postwar Years

In 1949 Staten Island Advance Corporation became Advance Publications Inc., and in the 1950s Newhouse established a new reputation as a major competitor in newspaper publishing. With the purchase of the *Portland Oregonian* in 1950, he paid a record $5.6 million. The *Oregonian* was a prestige newspaper, considered one of the best in the northwestern

United States. Before expanding his operations beyond the Northeast, Newhouse made sure his brother Theodore (Ted) Newhouse would agree to fly to Portland once a month to report on the *Oregonian*. This was in line with Newhouse's oft-stated policy of family control.

Newhouse was ready to pay a record price for a newspaper because of his unique way of assessing a paper's value. Rather than follow the industry rule that a newspaper should be valued at approximately 10 percent of its net earnings, Newhouse considered possible earnings based on its potential market. Because of his policy of retaining earnings, Newhouse was able to buy without borrowing.

When Newhouse bought the *St. Louis Globe-Democrat* in 1955, paying $6.5 million, he added another jewel to his newspaper group (to use a term preferred by Newhouse). Newhouse disliked the term ''chain'' because he felt that it suggested that the parent company imposed some degree of editorial uniformity on its properties. In fact, Advance allowed its newspapers a notable amount of editorial latitude. The publisher of Advance's Birmingham, Alabama, paper in 1962 was an unabashed racist, while Newhouse himself was staunchly liberal. Newhouse's papers varied as much in quality as in editorial standpoint. This policy was unlike that of most other chain publishers. Newhouse, as quoted in *The New York Times* (August 1979), was ''not interested in molding the nation's opinion.''

This policy of local autonomy helped in the purchase of the *St. Louis Globe-Democrat*, as E. Lansing Ray, the conservative owner, was convinced that the paper would continue with its long-held editorial policies. It also persuaded the Hanson family to sell the *Birmingham News* and the *Huntsville Times* in Alabama to Newhouse in 1955 for $18.7 million. In fact, because of Newhouse's attention to business operations rather than editorial stance, his papers took a wide range of positions. For example, one paper, the *Newark Star-Ledger,* supported right-wing senator Joseph McCarthy during his ascendancy, while other Newhouse papers attacked McCarthy. Although Newhouse did not invent local autonomy, Advance was the first major newspaper chain to practice it.

The 1959 purchase of Condé Nast Publications for $5 million was supposedly suggested by Mitzi Newhouse, S.I. Newhouse's wife. According to Newhouse, ''She asked for a fashion magazine and I went out and got her *Vogue*.'' Condé Nast published not only *Vogue* but also *Glamour, House & Garden,* and *Young Bride's*. As far back as the 1924 statement of Advance's purpose, Newhouse had a declared intention of publishing magazines. By buying another magazine publisher, Street & Smith, which also published women's magazines, and merging it with Condé Nast, Newhouse became a major publisher of magazines as well as newspapers. He also ran a national news service in Washington, D.C., and radio stations in Portland, Oregon, and Syracuse, New York.

Despite labor problems that were to begin in 1959 with a stereotypers' strike at the *Oregonian* and an American Newspaper Guild strike at the *St. Louis Globe-Democrat,* Newhouse was able to continue expanding his operations throughout the 1960s, beginning with acquisitions of portions of the *Denver Post* and of three newspapers in Springfield, Massachusetts. In

1961 Newhouse established a newspaper monopoly in Portland with his purchases of the *Oregon Journal* for $8 million. In 1962 Advance paid $42 million for the Times-Picayune Publishing Company in New Orleans, Louisiana. Newhouse borrowed money outside his family for the first time to make this purchase, but now, with both the New Orleans newspapers, the morning *Times-Picayune* and the evening *States-Item,* Newhouse owned more newspapers than any other U.S. publisher. The $15 million that Newhouse donated to Syracuse University for a school of communications indicated his new stature in publishing. When the S.I. Newhouse School of Public Communications was opened in 1964, President Lyndon Johnson gave the dedication speech.

Increased media attention meant increased media criticism, and in

Increased media attention meant increased media criticism, and in 1966 this came with the publication of John A. Lent's *Newhouse, Newspapers, Nuisances: Highlights in the Growth of a Communications Empire,* which concentrated on Newhouse's dealings with labor unions. Given that Newhouse operated, according to the November 27, 1989 issue of *Barron's,* ''not only one of the most powerful, but one of the most secretive family businesses in America,'' the public curiosity was understandable. Nevertheless, Newhouse preferred to work his deals discreetly, and as a private corporation Advance could maintain a very low profile.

Newhouse continued to make acquisitions throughout the remainder of the 1960s, expanding further into the southeastern United States with the purchase of two Alabama newspapers, the *Mobile Register* and the *Mobile Press,* and of the *Mississippi Press-Register,* all in 1966. Newhouse's largest deal of the decade turned out to be his acquisition of the *Cleveland Plain Dealer* for $54.2 million in 1967, breaking his own record for the highest price ever paid for a newspaper and again requiring a bank loan. This gave Advance 22 newspapers in 16 cities that produced each day more than 3.2 million papers and grossed almost $500 million a year.

In the 1970s Newhouse seemed to be slowing down. Advance bought 49 percent of a massive paper mill in Catawba, South Carolina, in 1970. In 1971 Advance bought both the *Bayonne Times,* the paper at which Newhouse had started his career, and the *Newark Evening News.* He merged the *Times* into the *Jersey Journal,* and within one year shut down the *Evening News,* which he had purchased for $20 million. Newhouse still had one massive newspaper deal left in him, however. In 1976 he purchased for $305 million Booth Newspapers, publisher of eight papers in Michigan, as well as *Parade* magazine, a syndicated Sunday newspaper magazine supplement.

As he built his empire, Newhouse organized his businesses to minimize taxes. Advance Publications served as the central holding company, publishing *The Staten Island Advance* and owning the Long Island Daily Press Publishing Company. From there the various companies owned varying shares of other companies, making it possible for one company to loan money to another and allowing a cash-rich company to reduce its surplus earnings. In addition, the way Newhouse had set up stock holdings in Advance made it difficult, if not impossible, for him to lose control. Newhouse owned all 1,000 shares of common stock, including the 10 shares of Class A stock that carried voting privileges. The 3,500 shares of preferred stock were all owned by family members.

With S.I. Newhouse's death in 1979, this arrangement was to provide the opening for an Internal Revenue Service (IRS) tax suit that threatened the financial position of Advance throughout the 1980s. Valuing all stock at $187.25 a share, the family filed an inheritance tax return with a liability of $48 million. The IRS found the common stock more valuable than the preferred and demanded $1 billion.

After the Founder's Death: Advance in the 1980s and 1990s

With Newhouse's death the leadership of Advance became diffused among his surviving two brothers, Norman and Ted, and his two sons, Samuel I. Jr. (Si) and Donald. During Newhouse's lifetime the organizational structure had been decidedly imprecise. When *Business Week* inquired in 1976 what titles his two brothers held, Newhouse responded, "I couldn't really tell you." Instead of titles the family members had regional or special responsibilities. Si oversaw the magazines and Donald the Eastern newspapers, while Norman handled Midwestern and Southern newspapers; Ted took care of Western and Massachusetts properties. In addition, Newhouse nephew Richard Diamond led *The Staten Island Advance,* while nephew Robert Miron oversaw the Syracuse, New York, broadcasting headquarters.

In the years following Newhouse's death, his family, jointly headed by Si and Donald, oversaw a rapid growth of Advance largely by managing the company's existing assets. Si and Donald, however, made some major changes. The first was in 1980, when they paid $70 million to RCA Corporation for Random House publishing, the leading general-interest book publisher at the time, thus acquiring the third type of media listed in Advance's statement of purpose. By selling its five television stations to the Times Mirror Company for $82 million, the Newhouses were also able to finance their expansion into cable television systems, becoming the eighth-largest cable operator in the United States in 1981.

Of the $700 million worth of communications purchases made by the Newhouses in the 1980s, only one was a newspaper, New Jersey's *Trenton Times.* The greatest amount of activity had been in magazines, with the start-ups of such magazines as *Self* in 1982 and *Vanity Fair* in 1983; the purchases of *Gentleman's Quarterly* and, in London, *Tatler, World of Interiors;* and the buying of minority shares of *The Face* and *Arena.* Perhaps the most notable acquisition was the *New Yorker* for $200 million in 1983. Si Newhouse continued the family policy of allowing publications considerable editorial liberty while eschewing conventional corporate planning. "There is no particular global view about what Condé Nast should be," Si Newhouse told the *New York Times* in September 1989. "We think pragmatically."

The Newhouse style of business continued to make money but drew criticism. Pointing to the purchases of Crown Publishing and a variety of British publishers, *Barron's* commented that "the family-style decision-making that produced such re-

markable results when buying local newspapers from disgruntled heirs may not work so well when evaluating international publishing acquisitions." The sale for $200 million of Random House's college publishing division—usually the most steadily profitable part of publishing—to McGraw-Hill was questioned. Newhouse was also charged with lowering the overall quality of American journalism.

As the 1980s were particularly good years for newspaper publishers, so cable television was a good growth industry in the 1990s, and Advance would take important steps toward becoming a major player in the cable industry. Also, in 1990 the long-standing litigation with the IRS was settled in the Newhouses' favor. The judge ruled that the total tax liability would be approximately $48 million, close to the amount that the Newhouses claimed. By 1996 *Forbes* magazine listed Si and Donald Newhouse as sharing a fortune worth at least $9 billion.

Advance continued its moderate pace of acquisition in the 1990s. In 1993 Condé Nast purchased Knapp Publications, whose periodicals included *Architectural Digest* and *Bon Appetit.* Also that year the company bought the electronic publishing division of Bantam Doubleday Dell. In 1994 Advance acquired 25 percent of the computer and multimedia magazine *Wired.* In 1995 Random House made an agreement with Planeta Internacional to distribute its Spanish-language books throughout the U.S. and Canada. Planeta was the number one book publisher in Spanish-speaking countries. Also in 1995 Advance purchased American City Business Journals for $269 million. At the time of the purchase, American City Business Journals owned 28 weekly business newspapers, three motor sports magazines, and an advertising firm. Meanwhile, Random House continued to be a good investment for Advance, enjoying a record year in 1996 with best-sellers from Oprah Winfrey, Michael Chrichton, Colin Powell, and Pope John Paul II.

Advance made several moves in the 1990s to establish itself as a cable television and entertainment powerhouse. In 1993 the company offered $500 million to back QVC's bid to purchase Paramount, though QVC later lost their bid to Viacom. In 1994 Newhouse Broadcasting Corp. combined its cable operations with Time Warner to create Time Warner Entertainment-Advance-Newhouse. Robert Miron, then president of the Newhouse cable division, told *Broadcasting & Cable* that they had been looking to pair with a larger company. "What we lacked was size, certain geographical strengths and a really proficient technical expertise," said Miron. "We did not want to be a seller, although day-to-day control was not a key issue." Time Warner was to handle day-to-day management of the joint operation. The ownership was divided on the basis of the number of subscribers, giving Advance one-third and Time Warner two-thirds of the new company. To establish a greater market share in an area it already served, Time Warner Entertainment-Advance-Newhouse agreed to trade cable stations with Cox Communications Inc., which gave them Cox's Myrtle Beach area cable system and a smaller system near Waco, Texas.

In 1996 Advance began a new service on the World Wide Web to provide regional news from Advance's three New Jersey newspapers—*The Star-Ledger* of Newark, *The Times* of Trenton, and *The Jersey Journal* of Jersey City—and from Advance's News 12 New Jersey, New Jersey's only state-wide,

24-hour television station. Offered for free, the new service was titled *New Jersey Online* (http://www.nj.com). It was affiliated with Newhouse Newspapers New Media and supported entirely by advertising revenue. Advance was originally resistant to the on-line venture but was eventually persuaded by people at America Online that the future of news distribution required a move in that direction. *New Jersey Online*'s intent, as described by Susan Mernit in the paper's "Frequently Asked Question" site, "is to be the Internet's World Wide Web destination and resource for people who live and work in and are interested in New Jersey." Three of the on-line paper's productions—*NJO Weather,* the *Yuckiest Site on the Internet,* and *RockHall,* Advance-owned *Cleveland Plain Dealer*'s Rock Hall of Fame site—were selected as a "Cool Site of the Day," a well-known and sought-after designation on the internet.

Principal Subsidiaries

Condé Nast Publications, Inc.; Parade Publications, Inc.; Random House, Inc.

Further Reading

Foisie, Geoffrey and Rich Brown, "Time Warner Entertainment: A Big MSO Gets Bigger," *Broadcasting & Cable,* September 19, 1994, p. 12.

Hunter, Jeannine F., "Cox Communications May Swap Myrtle Beach, S.C., System to Time Warner," *Knight-Ridder/Tribune Business News,* March 28, 1996, p. 3280137.

Lent, John A., *Newhouse, Newspapers, Nuisances: Highlights in the Growth of a Communications Empire,* New York: Exposition Press, 1966.

Mahar, Maggie, "All in the Family," *Barron's,* November 27, 1989.

Meeker, Richard H., *Newspaperman: S.I. Newhouse and the Business of News,* New Haven, Connecticut: Ticknor & Fields, 1983.

"The Newspaper Collector," *Time,* July 27, 1962.

"S.I. Newhouse and Sons: America's Most Profitable Publisher," *Business Week,* January 26, 1976.

—Wilson B. Lindauer
updated by Terry Bain

AK Steel Holding Corporation

703 Curtis Street
Middletown, Ohio 45043
U.S.A.
(513) 425-5000
Fax: (513) 425-2676
Web site: http://www.aksteel.com

Public Company
Incorporated: 1899 as The American Rolling Mill
   Company
Employees: 5,800
Sales: $2.3 billion (1996)
Stock Exchanges: New York
SICs: 3312 Blast Furnaces and Steel Mills; 6719 Holding
   Companies Not Elsewhere Classified

AK Steel Holding Corporation is the controlling body for numerous steel production companies throughout the United States, including its own namesake, AK Steel Corporation. AK Steel manufactures and sells value-added hot-rolled and cold-rolled steel flat carbon steel. AK then sells its product to other manufacturers, such as the construction, automotive, and appliance industries. AK Steel Holding Corp. also possesses a 50 percent interest in Southwestern Ohio Steel and an almost 50 percent interest in Nova Steel Processing. Sixteen percent of AK Steel is owned by Japan's Kawasaki Steel, with whom AK Steel entered into a joint venture in 1989.

The Early Years

The history of AK Steel Holding Corporation itself (incorporated in 1994) is extremely short, yet the company's roots actually date back to the late 1800s. In 1899, the American Rolling Mill Company was created to engage in the production of rolled steel, mainly for other manufacturers to use in their own products. After 20 years of successful production, the company had laid plans for and broken ground at the site of a new manufacturing facility at Middletown, Ohio. The facility, dubbed Middletown Works, remained in operation into the 1990s as one of AK Steel's two principle production plants.

The company's second production plant was erected in Ashland, Kentucky, 11 years later. The facility was named Ashland Works and joined Middletown in the production of both coated and uncoated rolled steel. The plants produced the company's custom-engineered, low-carbon steel products through two different processes. Both hot and cold flat rolling procedures were used to create the company's high-strength steel sheets.

The American Rolling Mill Company continued to operate its steel mills under that name for almost 30 years after Ashland was constructed. Then in 1948, the company adopted the acronym ''ARMCO,'' and soon thereafter, changed its formal name to Armco Steel Corporation.

Acquisitions in the 1950s through the 1970s

After realizing a decent amount of success with the Middletown and Ashland production centers, Armco began to purchase additional steel facilities in the 1950s. These purchases were added to the company's existing holdings, subsequently adopting both the Armco name and business procedures. This practice continued for two decades, as Armco expanded its operational base both geographically and throughout the steel industry itself. Geographic expansion enabled the company to distribute its finished product to a wider base of customers more easily, while expansion in the steel industry gave the company more market share.

In 1978, Armco Steel Corporation changed its name to Armco Inc., which more accurately reflected the company's few non-steel holdings that had been added during Armco's acquisition phase. The original steel mill holdings, Middletown and Ashland Works, were placed in a newly-formed group called the Eastern Steel Division. The company then left its Ohio-based headquarters location and moved to New Jersey in 1985, believing that the new location was more well suited to serve the majority of its holdings' and customers' needs.

By the end of the 1980s, Armco Inc. was continuing to gain market share and increase annual sales, in an industry which many felt was prone to low profitability. Sales figures were hovering near the $1 billion mark, and the company began exploring options for future growth. In 1989, Armco entered into a limited partnership with the Kawasaki Steel Corporation of Japan, merging portions of each company to form the Armco Steel Company, L.P. Another partnership formed by Armco was with the Japanese steel maker Itochu Corporation, a deal which gave Armco an almost 50 percent share of Nova Steel Processing, one of the company's present-day operating divisions.

The Early 1990s: AK Steel Holding Corp. is Born

Entering the 1990s, Armco's annual sales had surpassed the $1 billion mark, with 1991 sales reaching $1.3 billion. Unfortunately, however, the company was not as profitable as its sales figures might indicate. Armco was realizing first-hand what analysts had been preaching for years, which was that the steel industry required such a large output of operating expenses that achieving a high profit was incredibly difficult. Armco had found itself with approximately $600 million in debt and negative equity, and made the decision that it was time to make moves to turn its situation around.

Armco began searching for a new management head to give the company some direction and build a new era of profitability in the 1990s. The company finally persuaded Tom Graham to come out of retirement and lead Armco Steel Company's redirection efforts. In 1992, at the age of 65, Graham had spent almost 45 years working in the management of different steel companies around the United States. Earlier in his life, Graham had spent substantial time at J & L Steel, U.S. Steel, and Washington Steel. When he came to Armco, he brought with him another ex-U.S. Steel and Washington Steel coworker, Richard M. Wardrop, Jr.

Graham and Wardrop immediately set about the task of turning Armco's financial situation around. First came an extensive evaluation of the company's holdings, which resulted in the divestiture of more than ten of the company's subsidiaries and operating divisions. These operations either lacked efficiency in production or profit potential, and were relinquished in an effort to lower Armco's operating costs and subsequently boost earnings. Another notable change which occurred within the first year of Graham's tenure was the replacement of a whopping 75 of the company's top executives and managers.

Next, the newly-restructured Armco worked on improving its actual operations and service. The quality of the company's finished steel product was improved upon first, in order to increase its ability to market and sell the steel to its customers, such as the construction, automotive, and large appliance industries. Then came an improvement in Armco's service, with an emphasis on increasing the company's ability to deliver its products to buyers on time.

Meanwhile, Armco had also acquired a new subsidiary, Cyclops Industries, a producer of specialty steel products. In 1993, Armco again moved its corporate executive offices, this time from New Jersey to Pittsburgh, Pennsylvania. The following year, the limited partnership between Armco and Kawasaki was altered slightly and AK Steel Holding Corporation was finally born. Its main operating division became AK Steel Corp., at which steel production continued as normal. AK Steel Holding Corporation was then taken public later that same year, and the sale of common and preferred shares of its stock helped the company earn $654 million. The money was used to pay off

AK's debt, leaving the company's balance sheet clear and in excellent financial condition.

The End of the Century and Beyond

After relocating its corporate offices again—this time from Pittsburgh back to Middletown, Ohio—AK Steel entered 1995 with high hopes for strong financial success. However, profits throughout the entire steel industry dropped, which briefly signaled problems through a turn of events. But despite difficulties in the industry, AK Steel still managed to achieve an estimated $146 million on sales of $2.26 billion. As a result of this success, the Regis ICM Small Company Mutual Fund increased its holdings in AK Steel, noting the fact that the company was averaging annual growth rates in the realm of 15 percent and above.

Graham then made the risk-laden decision to forge ahead with plans to construct a brand-new, state of the art steel production facility in Rockport, Indiana. The cost of building the new manufacturing site was estimated at $1.1 billion. Right away, many analysts and industry experts criticized the decision, some in awe of the fact that a company that had just rescued itself from massive debt would choose to put itself back into that position again. Immediately, comparisons were drawn between AK Steel and competitor Inland Steel, who had built its own $1 billion steel facility in a joint venture with Nippon Steel in the beginning of the 1990s. Inland's complex was completed in 1993, and four years later had still not earned a good return on its cost. Some thought that AK Steel should take a hint from Inland's situation and reconsider its plan.

But Graham insisted that the addition of a newer and more efficient production facility was important to AK Steel's future. He cited increased efficiency and lower energy consumption as factors that would aid in lowering AK Steel's operating costs if the new Rockport site was erected. Also, the new facility would be equipped to produce 80-inch-wide rolls of carbon steel, whereas all existing mills were capable only of producing rolls with a width of 72 inches. Graham believed that this would increase the demand for AK Steel's finished product, because it would allow auto makers to save money through elimination of the necessity to weld together two pieces of steel.

In 1997, Graham retired once again at the age of 70. Wardrop took his place at the head of the company with the intent to continue not only Graham's plans for the new facility, but also the business practices that had helped AK Steel recover in the beginning of the decade. Approaching the end of the century, AK Steel's future would be determined by the success of its new facility, once constructed, as well as by the company's ability to innovate and increase the distribution of its product.

Principal Divisions

AK Steel Corp.; Cyclops Industries; Southwestern Ohio Steel (50%); Nova Steel Processing (50%).

Further Reading

AK Steel Holding Corporation Historical Timeline, Middletown, Ark.: Steel Holding Corp., 1994.
Rudnitsky, Howard, "A Throw of the Dice," *Forbes,* February 10, 1997, p. 47.

—Laura E. Whiteley

Alfa, S.A. de C.V.

Avenida Gomez Morin 1111
San Pedro, Garza Garcia, Nuevo Leon 66220
Mexico
(528) 335-9781, (528) 335-9228
Fax: (528) 335-9781, (528) 335-9588

Public Company
Incorporated: 1974 as Grupo Industrial Alfa, S.A. de
   C.V.
Employees: 23,412
Sales: 27.83 billion pesos (US $3.64 billion, 1996)
Stock Exchanges: Mexico City
SICs: 1011 Iron Ores; 2011 Meat Packing Plants; 2033
   Natural Processed & Imitation Cheese; 2099 Food
   Preparations, Not Elsewhere Classified; 2273 Carpets
   & Rugs; 2821 Plastic Materials, Synthetic Resins &
   Nonvulcanizable Elastomers; 2824 Manmade Organic
   Fibers, Except Cellulosic; 3312 Steel Works, Blast
   Furnaces (Including Coke Ovens) & Rolling Mills;
   3316 Cold-Rolled Steel Sheet, Strip & Bars; 3317
   Steel Pipe and Tubes; 3714 Motor Vehicle Parts &
   Accessories; 4813 Telephone Communications,
   Except Radiotelephone; 5211 Lumber & Other
   Building Materials Dealers; 6719 Offices of Holding
   Companies, Not Elsewhere Classified

Alfa, S.A. de C.V. is a holding company for subsidiaries
engaged in telecommunications services and in producing, marketing, and distributing petrochemicals, synthetic fibers, steel
and steel products, refrigerated foods, auto parts, carpets and
rugs, mattresses, and building supplies. It is the largest of the
four holding companies that constitute the Monterrey Group,
which encompasses the holdings of the extended Garza Sada
family, Mexico's wealthiest. Although Alfa suffered near-bankruptcy in the economic crisis of 1982 and lost money in the peso
devaluation of 1994, it remained among the largest industrial
enterprises in Mexico.

Alfa Before 1980

The Monterrey Group empire derived from the founding in
Monterrey of Cerveceria Cuauhtemoc, a brewery, in 1890 by
Isaac Garza Garza, his brother-in-law, Francisco Sada
Muguerza, and two others. In 1936 the family holdings, already
vast, were divided into two separate industrial groups. One of
these, Valores Industriales S.A. (Visa), established Hojalata y
Laminas S.A. (Hylsa) to make steel sheet for the bottletops of
its beverages during World War II, when the United States cut
steel supplies to Mexico to meet its own needs. Hylsa became
the largest privately run steelmaker in Mexico, a fully integrated
complex with activities ranging from mining and processing
iron ore to finished products. In 1957 it patented HyL, a system
of direct reduction known as fire sponging.

After Eugenio Garza Sada, head of the Monterrey Group,
was murdered in 1973 in what was described as an abortive
kidnapping by left-wing terrorists, the family empire broke into
four parts. Bernardo Garza Sada, a nephew of Eugenio, became
chairman of Grupo Industrial Alfa, S.A., which inherited Hylsa
and many other industrial enterprises, including Empaques de
Carton Titan, a packaging company founded in 1926; Nylon de
Mexico (synthetic fibers), founded in 1952; and Polioles (chemicals), founded in 1962. "There is no falling out," one source
explained to the *New York Times*. "But there was a real problem
as to who would be next 'supreme,' so they juggled the shares
within the family and divided the group."

Under Bernardo Garza Sada's leadership Alfa diversified
from its base into petrochemicals, synthetic fibers, capital machinery, farm equipment, television sets, and tourism. It also
took a quarter share in Grupo Televisa, which virtually monopolized Mexican television broadcasting. Its assets grew from
$315 million to $1.5 billion between 1974 and 1978, its sales
from $194 million to $836 million, and its income from $21
million to $83 million. In 1978 Alfa was the only Mexican
company in the Fortune 500 list of the biggest companies
outside the United States, except for state-owned Petroleos de
Mexico (Pemex). Himself a graduate of the Massachusetts Institute of Technology, Garza Sada staffed top management with
graduates of MIT, Harvard, and the University of Pennsylvania's Wharton School of Business. One observer said they

"always picked the kid with the Harvard MBA over the guy who really knew the business. The Alfa man had to look good on paper."

Although Alfa formed joint ventures with Hercules and American Petrofina to produce polyester, Du Pont to produce other synthetic fibers, Ford to turn out aluminum cylinder heads, and Hitachi to make electric motors, it insisted on control. "We manage these ventures, *always*," Garza Sada told *Forbes* in 1979. "We demand that!" Alfa received $2.4 billion in loans from more than 130 foreign creditors and was planning to invest $3.5 billion by the end of 1984, almost three-fifths of it in money to be borrowed, mostly from sources outside Mexico. It was not only the leading private firm in Mexico but in all of Latin America. By 1980 it had 157 subsidiaries in 39 branches of the economy.

In retrospect, following Alfa's near-bankruptcy in 1982, Alfa's success bred arrogance. Many of the lower-management people had no practical experience, while the experienced upper management took charge of firms about which they knew very little. The company unwisely abandoned its prudent traditional policy of only integrating firms that had similar or complementary products. One observer said that Alfa "bought businesses like someone would buy candies for their children." A foreign bank representative recalled, "They were on the same kind of roll that the Mexican government was on then. Oil prices would know no limit. Grupo Alfa profits would know no limit."

Restructuring in the 1980s

As an era of high prices for Mexico's oil exports suddenly came to an end, in late 1981 Alfa dropped its projection of earnings for the year from $80 million to $2 million. By the end of the year it was predicting a $60 million loss and it finally reported an actual loss of $120 million. Before the year was out the government had extended Alfa an emergency aid package of 12 billion pesos ($480 million). In 1982 the Mexican economy hit the rocks. Largely because of the collapse of the peso and heavy interest obligations, Alfa lost $233 million and suspended principal as well as interest payments. In July 1982 it presented a restructuring plan that called for it to sell one-fourth of its assets over a five-year period. The corporate staff was slashed from 4,000 to 1,000, and later to 400. Manufacturing ventures in television sets, bicycles, and tractors were sold.

Eventually, in 1986, Alfa paid off about five dozen foreign banks in stock. Under a complex arrangement, the creditor banks forgave $920 million in Alfa's debt in return for 45 percent of its stock. A 15-member board was named to govern the company, of which nine would be named jointly by the foreign banks and the Garza Sada family. A five-year voting trust for the stock was formed under which 16 percent of the Garza Sada family stock would be held with the 45 percent of the bank stock. The creditors also were paid $25 million by Alfa and $200 million in Mexican government debt.

Alfa also was required to divest itself of an undisclosed number of companies that were not part of its core business. By the end of 1988 it had sold most of its food, and all of its tourism, real estate, and electric home-appliance holdings, retaining only two dozen subsidiaries. "There are no family

members in important executive positions," *Business Latin America* wrote, "and this has contributed to a more professional and predictable management style."

The settlement of Alfa's debt left unresolved Hylsa's own debt, which in 1988 reached $1.2 billion to 68 lenders, including about $300 million in overdue interest. About 70 percent of the foreign lenders agreed to exchange about $639 million of the debt for about $385 million in debt owed by Mexico itself and about $69 million in cash. In addition, foreign lenders who were owed $273 million and Mexican banks holding about $301 million in Hylsa debt agreed to stretch out the loan repayments over 15 years and received 21 percent of Hylsa's common stock. The agreements allowed Hylsa to spend as much as $165 million over the next five years in capital expenditures, thereby giving it the opportunity to continue trying to compete in a crowded industry.

Alfa celebrated the restructuring of its debts with an elaborate outdoor mass on a Monterrey baseball field in 1988, attended by 10,000 employees. The company recorded the most profitable year of its history in 1988. Operating income was a record $425 million and special gains related to the debt restructuring and the peso's stabilization against the dollar added $575 million more. Alfa did so well that the Garza Sada family was able to buy back much of the equity it had surrendered to its creditors.

Alfa in the Early 1990s

The early 1990s were not as good a period for Alfa, as world demand for petrochemicals and steel slowed. In 1993 the company had revenues of 8.56 billion pesos ($2.5 billion), but operating income fell to 444 million pesos ($130 million). That year it sold its 51 percent stake in one of the Monterrey Group's oldest holdings, the paper and packaging subsidiary Empaques de Carton Titan.

When Dionisio Garza Medina, a nephew of Bernardo Garza Sada, became chairman in 1994, he fired half of Alfa's middle managers and focused on restoring higher profitability to the company's three main business sectors: steel, petrochemicals, and food. Hylsa (now Hylsamex) and Sigma Alimentos, the food subsidiary, received their own separate stock listings to reduce their dependence on the parent company. "If you look at the profile of our strategy," Garza Medina told a *Wall Street Journal* reporter, "we are going from a commodity company into more value-added products," with higher profit margins. He also said Alfa would enter retailing by opening 25 home-improvement stores over the next five years.

The collapse of the peso in late 1994 took a heavy toll on Alfa, as on other Mexican enterprises. Net sales rose to 14.21 billion pesos ($4.06 billion), but the company lost 2.16 billion pesos ($617 million). In 1995 Alfa returned to profitability, with net income of 2.09 billion pesos ($307 million) on net sales of 21.52 billion pesos ($3.16 billion). This was followed in 1996 by net income of 3.06 billion pesos ($400 million) on net sales of 27.83 billion pesos ($3.64 billion). Alfa's total debt was 18.5 billion pesos ($2.7 billion). The net worth of Bernardo Garza Sada and his family was estimated at $1.5 billion in 1996.

Alfa in 1996

Hylsamex's revenues accounted for nearly one-third of Alfa's in 1995 (and 35 percent in 1996), but its net income in 1995 was only 12 percent of the group's total. This company was involved in the entire steelmaking process from mining iron ore to manufacturing and distributing steel products. A low-cost steel producer that invested $982 million between 1990 and 1996 to modernize its facilities, it had the most diversified product line in Mexico's steel industry and was making products for use in the construction, auto parts, and home appliance industries. It held 48 percent of the cold-rolled sheet market, 44 percent of the small-diameter pipe market, and 38 percent of the galvanized-sheet market in 1995. A new flat-steel minimill was opened that year.

Sigma Alimentos, S.A. de C.V. (formerly Salumni, S.A. de C.V.), which distributed Oscar Mayer and its own brand of packaged meat and other food products, enjoyed 36 percent of domestic market share in processed meats in 1995. Its distribution network included 50 refrigerated warehouses and a fleet of more than 800 refrigerated vehicles, including 570 delivery trucks. A frozen food plant and a cheese manufacturing facility were under construction. Sigma was planning to make frozen Mexican food for both the domestic and U.S. markets. This subsidiary accounted for 12 percent of Alfa's revenues in 1996.

Alfa's subsidiary Alpex, S.A. de C.V. was engaged in the manufacture of petrochemicals and synthetic fibers for use primarily as raw materials in the textile, food, beverage, packaging, construction, and automotive industries. It was also engaged in the manufacture of raw materials used in the production of polyester fibers and polymer products and in the manufacture of specialty chemical products. Its own subsidiaries included Petrocel, S.A.; Nylon de Mexico, S.A. (60 percent); and Polioles, S.A. de C.V. (51 percent). Alpex was Alfa's biggest subsidiary, accounting for 44.5 percent of the parent company's revenues in 1996.

Versax, S.A. de C.V. was an Alfa subsidiary engaged in the production of aluminum cylinder heads and in three other industries: carpets and rugs, mattresses, and building supplies. Another important subsidiary was Dinamica, S.A., which acted as the service group for the holding company.

In 1996 Alfa formed a joint venture with Valores Industriales, Bancomer (Mexico's second largest bank), and AT&T to enter the Mexican long distance telephone market in competition against Telefonos de Mexico. Alfa took a 26 percent interest in the company, Alestra, with Visa and Bancomer holding 25 percent and AT&T holding the remaining 49 percent. Alestra began long distance operations in Monterrey and Queretaro at the beginning of 1997 under the AT&T name. Alfa's stake was held through its subsidiary AlfaTelecom, S.A. de C.V.

In all, Alfa was operating ten petrochemical and synthetic fiber plants in 1995, seven steel plants and a service center, six refrigerated-food plants, two carpet and rug plants, two mattress plants, an aluminum cylinder-head plant, and two building supplies retail stores. It operated more than 70 distribution centers. Alfa was a party to 11 joint ventures with foreign companies.

Principal Subsidiaries

AlfaTelecom, S.A. de C.V.; Alpex, S.A. de C.V,; Dinamica, S.A. de C.V.; Hylsamex, S.A. de C.V.; Sigma Alimentos, S.A. de C.V.; Versax, S.A. de C.V.

Further Reading

Blumenthal, Karen, ''Hylsa's Debt of $1.2 Billion Is Restructured,'' *Wall Street Journal,* May 4, 1988, p. 4.

''Buoyant Domestic Sales Boost Grupo Alfa,'' *El Financiero* (English-language weekly edition), February 24-March 2, 1997, pp. 17, 25.

Camp, Roderic, *Entrepreneurs and Politics in Twentieth-CenturyMexico,* New York: Oxford University Press, 1989, pp. 208–219.

''The Chosen Instruments,'' *Forbes,* October 29, 1979, pp. 44–49, 52.

Moffett, Matt, ''Mexico Conglomerate Cuts Costs and Learns There's Life After Debt,'' *Wall Street Journal,* July 26, 1989, pp. Al, A8.

Much, Marilyn, ''Mexico: The Long Road Back,'' *Industry Week,* August 8, 1983, pp. 37–38.

Pratt, Lawrence, ''Alfa of Mexico Stops Paying Debt Principal,'' *Wall Street Journal,* April 28, 1982, pp. 1, 31.

Riding, Alan, ''Monterrey Group: A Family of Wealth and Symbol of Economic Independence,'' *New York Times,* October 21, 1974, p. 53.

Stockton, William, ''Banks To Get Stake in Mexico's Alfa,'' *New York Times,* December 11, 1986, p. D10.

Torres, Craig, ''Mexican Conglomerate Alfa, As It Cuts Operations, May Face Hostile Investor,'' *Wall Street Journal,* August 25, 1994, p. A8.

—Robert Halasz

Amcor Limited

Southgate Tower East
40 City Road
South Melbourne
Victoria, 3205
Australia
(61-3) 694-9000
Fax: (61-3) 686-2924

Public Company
Incorporated: 1926 as Australian Paper Manufacturers
   Ltd.
Employees: 25,300
Sales: A$6.42 billion (1996)
Stock Exchanges: Australia NASDAQ
SICs: 2657 Folding Paperboard Boxes; 3411 Metal Cans;
   3085 Plastics Bottles; 2676 Sanitary Paper Products;
   3089 Plastics Products Not Elsewhere Classified

Headquartered in Australia, Amcor Limited manufactures and sells a diverse assortment of paper, plastic, and metal packaging materials. Amcor products are used in the creation of paper wrappings, corrugated and solid fiber containers, rigid plastic containers, plastic bags and tubes, and cans for processed foods. Amcor also has substantial interests in pulp, paper, and other forest products, in tissue and personal-care markets, and in the trading and distribution of paper and packaging products. The company has operations located in 14 countries throughout the world, with its headquarters office in Melbourne, the capital of Victoria, Australia. Amcor adopted its current name in May 1986, and its major period of expansion and acquisition has taken place since that time.

The Early Years

Amcor began as a paper making business called the Australian Paper Manufacturers Ltd. (APM). The origins of APM—although it was not incorporated under this name until 1926—can be traced back to the 1860s and to some of the earliest Australian ventures in paper making. The 1860s were years of rapid industrial growth in Australia's New South Wales and neighboring Victoria. The gold rushes initiated not only rising prosperity, but also an explosion in the area's population and available labor force. Furthermore, the introduction of a governmental protection policy for manufacturers in Victoria created a climate in which factories exploded in number. The paper making industry was no exception to this trend.

In 1864, the Collingwood Mill at Liverpool, New South Wales, was constructed for the Australian Paper Company. Four years later in Melbourne, Samuel Ramsden built his own mill and began production with the Number One Paper Machine. In 1871, William Fieldhouse erected Melbourne Number Two Paper Machine adjacent to Ramsden's mill; this operation was subsequently purchased by Ramsden. By the time a new entity—the Australian Paper Mills Company—was formed and registered in 1895, mills had been combined in Melbourne, Broadford, and Geelong. The company's capital was A$214,000 and its output was approximately 730 tons per year. The following year, it became the Australian Paper Mills Company Ltd.

Meanwhile, in the New South Wales capital of Sydney, John Thomson Brown had started a business of his own, trading in meat, grain, and farming and household goods. In 1885 David Henry Dureau became Brown's Melbourne partner. Their company would later play an important role in APM/Amcor's future. Brown and Dureau's company thrived, and was incorporated as Brown & Dureau, Ltd. in 1910. Over the years, as general commission agents, Brown and Dureau handled a wide range of goods.

In the first two decades of the 1900s, the Australian Paper Mills Company Ltd. entered a period of expansion as Australia's overseas trade doubled since the turn of the century. In 1920, the Australian Paper Mills Company Ltd. combined forces with Sydney Paper Mills Ltd. to form the Australian Paper and Pulp Company Ltd. This entity then merged with the Cumberland Paper Board Mills Ltd. in 1926, and the operating company of APM was finally formed. This company would continue to function under that name for years to come, and into the 1990s as the pulp and paper making arm of Amcor.

The War Years: The 1930s and Beyond

In 1936, an agreement was signed between APM and the Victorian Forest Commission covering the procurement of wood pulp. Later that year, the 1936 Wood Pulp Agreement Act was passed by the Victorian parliament and led to the establishment of the Maryvale pulp mill. This pilot mill began semi-commercial production of eucalyptus kraft pulp in March of 1938, and the main mill started commercial production the following year.

The year 1939 saw the outbreak of World War II and the worst bush fires in Victoria's history. APM's mill buildings survived, but the majority of its prime pulp wood source was destroyed. The company found, however, that fire-killed timber could still be used for pulping. This was fortunate, as the advent of the war brought about drastic changes in APM's operations: imports ceased abruptly, price controls were imposed by the federal government, a war-time profits tax was imposed, and Australian industries were required to provide military equipment to meet defense needs. Within two years, 70 percent of APM's total production was directed toward the manufacture of ammunitions and war equipment. During this period, the company demonstrated its strength as an innovator, supplying purified cellulose for the manufacture of smokeless cordite and other propellants for the Allied forces. APM also developed special papers and boards to resist moisture penetration for the troops fighting in tropical regions.

War-time conditions also prompted APM to increase its self-sufficiency. For example, before the war began, 80 percent of APM's total pulp requirements were imported, compared to times during and after the war, when 80 percent of its necessary raw materials were derived from local sources. Also, the war demanded self-sufficiency in fuel; in 1946, the company acquired a controlling interest in Maddingley Brown Coal Pty. Ltd. This acquisition, combined with the purchase of further coal-bearing land, soon produced 10,000 tons of coal per week and supplied all of the Victorian mills as well as other commercial and public enterprises.

Although APM was designated a ''protected'' industry by the Australian federal government during the war, the company nevertheless saw 25 percent of its work force enlist. Therefore, it recruited women to work in the mills. The company still operated with a decreased staff, but despite this and other hardships—such as a coal strike in New South Wales and further bush fires in 1944—the company managed to continue the expansion of its mills. Production grew dramatically from 92,000 tons in 1938, to 131,000 tons in 1942.

Toward the end of the war, APM's managing director, Sir Herbert Gepp, set up a Post-war Planning Committee to win back freedom from government control and the war-time profit tax, and to prepare a case for reasonable tariff protection against the inevitable resurgence of competitive imports. The committee also discussed APM's future strategy, which was to include the extension of operations in wrapping paper and board; expansion into converting operations, such as the manufacturing of cartons and containers from APM's paper and board; and the manufacture of allied products such as cellophane and tissues.

Post-World War II Diversification Efforts

War time had resulted in major reorganizations, both financial and administrative. The development of public relations at APM was changed, and a new emphasis on industrial relations was adopted. The company still possessed a monopoly on the country's wrapping paper and board markets, and was firmly established in mainland Australia as the country's largest paper and pulp company. In the 1950s, APM initiated a foray into the corrugated packaging industry in which it was later to make significant acquisitions. Before 1940, there were four Australian companies operating in the corrugated packaging field; J. Fielding & Co. was the earliest, installing the first corrugator in 1914 at Buckingham Street in Sydney to produce the corrugating medium for packaging. In 1950, APM bought the first 96-inch corrugator, with plans to install it on the Springvale wastepaper recycling site, but instead sold it to Fieldings.

The 1960s saw APM extend its interests to the production of other paper products. In 1963, it established the jointly owned Kimberly-Clark Australia Ltd., in partnership with the Kimberly-Clark Corporation of the United States. The subsidiary produced all kinds of tissue products.

It was in the 1970s that Brown & Dureau, Ltd. took on a significant role in the history of APM/Amcor. Brown & Dureau acquired the Eastern Tool Company, Lukey Mufflers, and Angus Hill Holdings, which would later form the nucleus of Amcor's automotive division. In 1975 Stan Wallis became the deputy managing director of APM, which marked the beginning of many years of strong leadership for the company. Under Wallis, APM began a process of diversification in the late 1970s. One of the most important acquisitions was that of Brown & Dureau in the financial year 1978–1979. This purchase brought APM substantial interests in the fields of international trading, automotive, retailing, and aviation.

Acquisitions in the 1980s

In the following decade, more major acquisitions for APM included the Ingram Corporation Ltd. and Edwards Dunlop & Co. Ltd., a paper merchant and stationery manufacturer, respectively. From these acquisitions grew the merchanting, stationery and designer products division. During the same period, APM acquired 40 percent of James Hardie Containers, manufacturers of corrugated fiber boxes for packaging food and drink.

In 1982, APM acquired Containers Packaging, the fourth major wholly-owned subsidiary. That same year, New Zealand Forest Products (NZFP)—that country's leading forestry group—formed a joint venture company with APM, allocating 50 percent of the shares to each corporation, and called it Anfor. This was set up to develop a corrugated box plant in Hong Kong, with NZFP supplying liner board and APM supplying the corrugating medium to make boxes to be sold to Chinese, South Korean, and Japanese customers.

In 1986, APM bought the balance of James Hardie Containers and an era of rationalization began. During this time period, plants were acquired from Reed Corrugated Containers, J. Fielding & Co., Tasman U.E.B., United Packages, Corrugated Paper, Fibreboard Containers, Fibre Containers, J. Gadsden Paper Products, Tasmanian Fibre Containers, and Cardboard Containers. Also in 1986, the company adopted the name of Amcor Limited, in order to better reflect the company's emerging diversity in its holdings.

Near the middle to end of the decade, Stan Wallis embarked on an ambitious program of capital investment in import-substituting plants, and in reopening existing plants to supply growing export markets. But not all of Stan Wallis's plans were successful. In April 1987, a possible merger between NZFP and Amcor was announced. The proposed merger would have covered only the pulp and paper production and marketing of the two companies, thus stopping short of a full merger of operations. But in August 1987, Amcor received the New Zealand Commerce Commission's decision: the merger would not go ahead.

The principal reason for the commission's rejection was that the proposed new entity would have a virtual monopoly of the manufacture and import of kraft paper and paperboard in New Zealand. The same obstacle did not impede Fletcher Challenge, Amcor's main domestic rival. Amcor promptly sold its 11 percent stake in NZFP to the Rada Corporation, which some thought was a defense against a Fletcher Challenge takeover. In 1986-1987 Kiwi Packaging of New Zealand also became a wholly owned subsidiary of Amcor, running five corrugating plants and two sheet plants.

Amcor then turned its eyes to offshore investment opportunities. In 1988, the year following the failed merger with NZFP, the group announced it was concentrating on overseas business expansion; as evidence, it switched Don B. Macfarlane to the newly-created post of general manager of international business development. According to Amcor, the creation of Macfarlane's new post signified its commitment to a structured and systematic approach to expansion outside Australia.

Throughout the decade, Amcor's packaging division established two plants: one at Smithfield, New South Wales; and another at Scoresby, Victoria. In the financial year 1988–1989 it bought 46 percent of Sydney's Universal Containers. During the 1980s Amcor's key objectives were to broaden its range of activities, particularly into packaging; to restructure its core pulp and paper businesses and integrate forward into paper converting in Australia; and to commence major overseas expansion. In June 1989, Amcor bought Twinpak, the largest plastics containers producer in Canada with 13 plants spread across the country. The acquisition accounted for a significant proportion of the 32 percent increase in containers packaging sales in the financial year 1989–1990.

In 1989 Amcor appointed a new chairman, Sir Brian Inglis. He replaced Alan Skurrie, who had held the office for five years and had an association of more than 55 years with Amcor. Amcor's 1989–1990 annual report recorded expenditure during the five years through June 1990 of A$2 billion on capital equipment and acquisitions. The company's commitment to growth was clear. Yet for all the ambition of the program, funding for Amcor's investments came principally from internal cash flow, as well as from the sale of assets and some borrowing. The program was financially conservative.

It was at that time that Sunclipse Incorporated was acquired, which was a California-based corrugated box manufacturer and distributor of packaging products. Amcor Packaging (Europe)

Ltd. was another development, constituting Amcor's first direct investment in the United Kingdom—a corrugated box plant on a greenfield site in Cambridgeshire. A 49 percent share in SACOC, a French corrugated box manufacturer, was also acquired near the turn of the decade.

The 1990s and Beyond

After setting out to diversify in the 1980s, paper accounted for only 19 percent of Amcor's 1990 sales, compared with 57 percent a decade earlier. Much of this diversification was achieved through acquisitions, which typified almost all of the company's activity in the 1980s and 1990s. In June 1990 Amcor Fibre Packaging was formed to manage the group's international corrugated box manufacturing and related activities. It included APM Packaging, Kiwi Packaging, Sunclipse, Amcor Packaging (Europe), SACOC, and Anfor. At that time, in total, it had the capacity to manufacture almost one million tons per year of corrugated products, accounting for more than half of the capacity of others outside Australia.

The following year, Amcor's Containers Packaging subsidiary added New Zealand Can Ltd. to its holdings for A$45 million. Amcor also purchased an eventual 42 percent stake in Spicers Paper Ltd., an Australian stationary producer, and a 49 percent portion of Willander Holdings, another corrugated box manufacturer that was stationed in the United Kingdom.

1993 saw Amcor make moves to consolidate its rapidly expanding holdings into three main divisions. Its Containers Packaging division was mainly responsible for the production of plastic and metal containers for food packaging; Amcor Fibre Packaging dealt with the company's corrugated cardboard products; and the Amcor Paper Group division was responsible for the manufacture of paper, stationary, paperboard, and coated paper products. In the wake of numerous acquisitions that year, Amcor also began to sell off operations that either deviated from the above categories, or that were generally unprofitable. Divestitures included the company's games division (including Amcor's rights to ''Scrabble''), Amidale Industries Ltd./Croxley Collins Olympic N.Z., and Petersen Contact Stationers. Amcor also purchased almost 20 new holdings in 1993 and 1994.

In 1994, Amcor also began operations at a new paper mill in Prewitt, New Mexico in the United States. This mill, dubbed the McKinley Paper Company, was constructed to be a cost-effective operation and was strategically positioned to service the market in Southern California and surrounding areas. The McKinley location immediately received high accolades from Amcor's top Australian-based executives due to its high-quality production and efficient operations, as well as to its intelligent geographic placement and ability to serve the surrounding market.

Internationally, Amcor continued its expansion-through-acquisitions plan, making 12 substantial purchases and selling 4 of its holdings in 1995. The company increased its revenue that year by over A$1 billion from its 1994 figures. Activity in 1996 followed suit, as the company again consolidated its holdings with new purchases and the divestiture of inconsistent and unprofitable operations.

Entering the end of the century, Amcor was positioning itself for continued future success. Major challenges facing the company would be the ability to adapt to vastly increasing public awareness of environmental issues, and also the ability to continue its trend of becoming even more competitive at the international level. Amcor's focus on the second goal was obvious, however, after the company had spent almost the entire span of the 1990s acquiring holdings on a global level that would help position it for growth and success.

Principal Subsidiaries

Amcor Plantations Pty. Ltd.; Australian Paper Ltd.; Amcor Insurances Pte. Ltd.; Amcor Investments Pty. Ltd.; Anneckum Pty. Ltd. (93%); Brown & Dureau Pty. Ltd.; Brown & Dureau Building Materials Pty. Ltd.; Cellulose Australia Ltd.; Containers Pty. Ltd.; Australian Paper Chase Pty. Ltd.; Maryvale Project Leasing Pty. Ltd.; Micabank Pty. Ltd.; Multix Pty. Ltd.; Advance Packaging Pty. Ltd. (46%); Amcor Trading (Japan) Ltd. (49%); CapVision International Co. Ltd. (HK) (50%); Kimberly-Clark Australia Pty. Ltd. (50%); Pinegro Products Pty. Ltd. (50%); Rota Die International Pty. Ltd. (49%); S.G. Sociedade Grafica, S.A. (36%); Spicers Paper Ltd. (42%); Zac's Packs Pty. Ltd. (46%).

Principal Divisions

Containers Packaging; Amcor Fibre Packaging; Amcor Paper Group.

Further Reading

"Cardboard is Gold in McKinley County," *New Mexico Business Journal,* October 1994, p. 66.
"McKinley Paper Co.: New Mexico's First Mill Will Tap the Lucrative L.A. market," *Pulp & Paper,* September 1993, p. 72.
Sinclair, E.K., *The Spreading Tree: A History of APM and AMCOR 1844–1989,* Sydney: Allen & Unwin, 1991.

—Mary Scott
—updated by Laura E. Whiteley

Arnoldo Mondadori Editore S.p.A.

Via Arnoldo Mondadori 1
20090 Segrate
Milan
Italy
(02) 7542 2044
Fax: (02) 7542 2748
Web site: http://www.mondadori.com

Public Company
Incorporated: 1912 as La Sociale di A. Mondadori & C.
Employees: 5,235
Sales: L 2,194.7 billion (1996)
Stock Exchanges: Milan Rome Turin Trieste Florence
   Genoa
SICs: 2721 Periodicals: Publishing, or Publishing and
   Printing; 2731 Books: Publishing, or Publishing and
   Printing; 2741 Miscellaneous Publishing; 7311
   Advertising

Arnoldo Mondadori Editore S.p.A. is one of the largest publishing companies in Italy. Its holdings include books, magazines, advertising agencies, printing activities, direct marketing, stationery, school supplies, and a host of small publishing companies and imprints.

The Early Years

Arnoldo Mondadori was the son of a poor craftsman in the northern Italian city of Ostiglia near Mantua. Before going to work for a small printing company in his town, Mondadori held various jobs, including a stint at the local cinema. In a community with an illiteracy rate of almost 40 percent, one of his responsibilities was reading aloud the titles of silent films for audiences. At the age of 16 he was hired as a pressman at Ostiglia's small printing and stationery concern, Fratelli Manzoli. Two years later, in 1907, Arnoldo Mondadori borrowed enough money to take over the company. He changed its name to La Sociale. The new name reflected Mondadori's

espousal of humanitarian and socialist reform movements active in Italy at this time, as well as his own ideal view of the press as a diffuser of culture. That same year the company, previously limited to the printing of posters, letterheads, and pamphlets, began publishing *Luce!,* a magazine subtitled *Giornale Popolare Istruttivo.*

In 1911 Mondadori bought a new press and published his first two books, *Aia Madama* and *Nullino e Stellina* by Tomaso Monicelli, an ex-socialist who had moved toward a nationalist position. Arnoldo Mondadori married Monicelli's sister, Andreina, in 1913.

La Sociale di A. Mondadori & C. was incorporated in 1912 as a limited stock partnership with 15 employees. Stock was held almost entirely by the Mondadori family. At that time the press initiated a series of children's books called La Lampada. The company's capital grew from L 75,000 in 1913 to L 400,000 the following year, and the staff more than doubled. Already Mondadori set about competing actively with the two Milan-based publishers, Sonzogno and Fratelli Treves, that shared a monopoly on book publishing in northern Italy.

The company grew rapidly during World War I. In 1915 the town of Ostiglia granted Mondadori a site measuring 2,000 square meters adjacent to the railway line. New equipment was purchased. The number of employees at the new plant reached 100.

In 1916 the death of Mondadori's former competitor, Emilio Treves, left available a catalog of authors that included many of the most prestigious names in contemporary Italian literature, among them Gabriele D'Annunzio, Luigi Pirandello, and Grazia Deledda. The acquisition in 1917 of the Franchini printing plant in the city of Verona put Mondadori in a position to sign on many of Treves's authors and to attract important new clients, including the Italian military. Mondadori also contracted to produce several illustrated magazines for the Third Army.

In 1921 Mondadori consolidated all printing activities at Verona. The old Franchini plant was replaced by a new press that covered almost 100,000 square feet of land. Employees numbered 250, and Mondadori at this time created a separate magazine department. Fiction magazines were especially popular, and in the early 1920s Mondadori introduced Italy's first monthly women's magazine, *La Donna,* and *Le Grazie,* a fiction magazine. By this time Mondadori magazines also served the Italian immigrant communities that had developed in North and South America. The bi-weekly *Girogirotondo* sold 30,000 copies in Argentina alone. Other popular ventures were film and theatrical magazines.

In 1923 publishing management was also established in Milan. Building on the newly literate readership of common Italians, Mondadori initiated several series and brought out a children's encyclopedia, the *Enciclopedia dei Ragazzi,* modeled on English and American counterparts and sold in weekly issues. The first Italian gravure magazine was published by Mondadori in 1925.

The decade of the 1920s was characterized by three major innovations for Mondadori: the company published its first textbook in 1926, its first popular paperback in 1927, and, in 1929, the so-called *giallo* or detective thriller. The series *I gialli di Mondadori* was packaged in a soft yellow jacket; today the word *giallo* is an Italian genre term for mysteries or thrillers in print, radio, or film.

In 1930, with the *Libri Azzurri* (Blue Books) series, Mondadori introduced its first Italian translations of foreign authors in accessible paperback form—six years before the appearance of Penguin books in the United Kingdom. Other series of translations in paperback included *Biblioteca Romantica*—a collection of 50 masterpieces of 17th- and 18th-century fiction—and "*i Romanzi della Palma.*" Mondadori's translators included Cesare Pavese and Eugenio Montale.

Another important foreign acquisition for Mondadori's list was the Walt Disney Company's cartoon character Mickey Mouse, who, endearing himself to Italians under the name Topolino, appeared in a weekly series in 1935. This success was repeated shortly after by Donald Duck (Paperino) in the first Disney story conceived and produced in Italy by agreement with the U.S. company. *Grazia,* the first mass-circulation women's weekly, was introduced in the late 1930s, and the weekly news magazine *Tempo* began publishing under the direction of Arnoldo Mondadori's son, Alberto. Alberto Mondadori was eldest of the founder's children, who included

another son, Giorgio, and two daughters, Laura and Cristina. All were to play an important part in the company's future development.

World War II in Europe had a devastating effect on Mondadori. Mondadori was compelled to transfer its editorial offices to the town of Arona in 1942. When the Fascist government fell and German troops occupied Italy in 1943, the plant at Verona was confiscated and its equipment dismantled and in large part shipped off to Germany. The Milan headquarters later sustained severe bomb damage, and the offices at Arona came under the control of the Fascist party commissars.

From 1943 to 1945 Arnoldo Mondadori went into exile at Lugano, Switzerland, but continued to maintain contact with his editors and authors. With the help of his son, Alberto—who spoke English and other languages—the publisher acquired rights to the work of U.S. authors Ernest Hemingway and William Faulkner, which later helped the company regain its position after the war ended.

Postwar Developments

With funds from the U.S. Marshall Plan, Mondadori launched a postwar recovery and replaced its bomb-damaged Verona plant. The new facility was much larger and included modern equipment capable of newspaper publishing. In 1950 the company published *Epoca,* a new large-format illustrated news weekly modeled on *Time* and *Life.*

Italy's economy began a period of tremendous growth in the postwar years. Mondadori introduced direct marketing with the first Italian book club, Club degli Editori. In 1958 Alberto Mondadori founded Il Saggiatore, an imprint of Mondadori that specialized in philosophy and intellectual works. The project was initiated with 150 employees and intentions of publishing 100 new titles each year. Il Saggiatore brought out the likes of Jean-Paul Sartre and Claude Levi-Strauss in Italian translations, but the company was plagued with financial problems. In 1967 Alberto Mondadori broke from the parent company, and two years later a bankrupt Il Saggiatore was reassumed by Arnoldo Mondadori Editore.

The younger son, Giorgio Mondadori—who in 1944 had joined the company at the age of 27—was a more effective manager. After overseeing the rebuilding of the Verona plant, he turned to a program of diversification. This included Mondadori's entrance into industrial activity with the establishment in 1961 of Auguri Mondadori S.p.A., a stationery and greeting card operation with a huge plant at Caselle di Sommacampagna near Verona and the building of Cartiere Ascoli Piceno, a papermaker that opened its plant at Marino del Tronto in 1964. Giorgio Mondadori also directed the building of the company's present headquarters at Segrate, a vast, modern edifice designed by the architect Oscar Niemeyer.

In 1960 the company had annual gross profits of L 16 billion and employed 2,279 workers. During the decade that followed, the company founded by Arnoldo Mondadori profited from his friendship with two captains of the Italian banking industry, Raffaele Mattioli and Enrico Cuccia. Mondadori preferred stock was listed on the Milan stock exchange in 1965. Five years later annual gross sales stood at L 71 billion. The company employed 4,988 people and was ranked first in the Italian publishing industry in gross sales.

Publishing expansion in the 1960s included the founding of *Panorama,* which first appeared as a monthly in 1962 and became a weekly in 1967. In 1963 Mondadori initiated its *Enciclopedia della Scienza e della Tecnica,* a 15-volume work whose authors included several Nobel prize winners. Mondadori's practice of putting inexpensive works of literature on newsstands continued with the introduction of the Oscar series of highly successful fiction paperbacks.

The decade that followed brought difficulties. The family patriarch, Arnoldo Mondadori, died in 1971, leaving the company to his four children. The second son, Giorgio Mondadori, took over as president of the publishing empire in 1968. A few years later Mondadori administration was moved from Milan to the new headquarters at Segrate. During the 1970s expansion of industrial activity continued with the acquisition of two new printing plants in Vicenza, San Donato Milanese, and the establishment of a new plant at Cles. In 1975 yet another was acquired in Toledo, Spain.

In 1975, spurred on by the purchase of the top-selling Italian daily *Corriere della Sera* by Mondadori's competitor Rizzoli, the company joined in founding what would be its first daily newspaper, *la Repubblica.* The newspaper was founded as a joint venture by Mondadori and *L'Espresso,* the top news weekly competing with Mondadori's *Panorama* magazine. A holding company, Editoriale L'Espresso, was formed, with 50 percent of the capital, L 1 billion, shared by Mondadori and the *L'Espresso* group, which included the new newspaper's editors Eugenio Scalfari and Carlo Caracciolo.

Giorgio Mondadori held the chairmanship of Mondadori until 1976, when his sisters, Cristina and Laura Mondadori, joined in forcing their brother Giorgio from the company. He was succeeded as chairman by Mario Formenton, husband of Cristina, the youngest Mondadori daughter.

Meanwhile, *la Repubblica* was quickly gaining in stature and sales, thanks in part to its outspoken editorial positions on the political events of the decade. The newspaper opposed negotiations with the leftist terrorists who kidnapped and assassinated Italian statesman Aldo Moro in 1978. Competition from the largest Italian daily, *Corriere della Sera,* was later handicapped by the implication of *Corriere's* parent, Rizzoli Publishing, in the political scandals of the early 1980s. By virtue of its editorial independence, *la Repubblica* was widely seen as a bastion of integrity. Already by 1979 *la Repubblica* was no longer losing money and had begun to command an appreciable market share. Shortly thereafter the new paper began showing increasing profits.

The late 1970s and early 1980s brought a period of decline for the Mondadori group. The economic boom years of the postwar era were drawing to a close in Italy. In 1975 the company suffered from a falloff in its advertising and publicity revenues. The signal event of this period, which set the stage for the acrimonious boardroom battles at the end of the decade, was Mondadori's entrance into the television market, with the creation of the Italian network Retequattro. Guided by Mario Formenton in 1978, Mondadori established Gestione Pub-

blicitaria Editoriale (Gpe), an advertising agency for 18 local channels. Two years later the company entered directly into broadcasting activity with a second enterprise, Telemond, which bought and resold television programming. In 1982 the companies were reconstituted as the network Retequattro.

The ill-fated venture occurred in an unfamiliar market environment dominated by two major competitors. First was the state-owned radio and television network, which had in 1976 relinquished the monopoly on television programming it held since 1954. The second was media baron Silvio Berlusconi's Fininvest Group, which was at the time amassing a vast empire of small local stations. Retequattro's managers withheld from such expansion in the mistaken belief that a law would shortly be passed impeding the growth of national monopolies in television. Late in 1982, with the acquisition of the Italian channel Italia 1 by Fininvest, Retequattro found itself in a low position in audience ratings. Retequattro was unable to compete effectively with the maverick Berlusconi.

At the same time, Mondadori was involved in a program of expansion in its other sectors. Daily newspaper activity increased with the introduction of four provincial papers published by a subsidiary, Editoriale Le Gazzette. In addition, the Mondadori group reached an agreement with the Canadian Harlequin group in 1981 for the publication in Italy of its romance novels and in 1983 acquired another papermaking concern, Cartiera F.A. Marsoni of Treviso.

Internal Conflicts during the 1980s

At the end of 1983 Mario Formenton turned the failing Retequattro over to Leonardo Forneron Mondadori, the son of Laura Mondadori, who had legally been given his grandfather's family name. Leonardo Mondadori had worked in the company since 1972 and had successfully directed the book publishing activity. Initially the younger manager improved the network, but the losses had already become too great, and in late 1984 Mario Formenton sought a buyer for Retequattro.

The situation in 1984 was one of near emergency for Mondadori, with Retequattro losing L 10 billion each month. The network was eventually sold to Fininvest, but the losses had been too great. The consolidated balance of the company in 1984 showed losses of L 10.7 billion. Salvaging the company required a recapitalization of the order of at least L 50 billion.

With help from associates in the financial world, Mario Formenton and Leonardo Mondadori created a holding company, AME Finanziaria (AMEF), in 1985. To create the new company, the two families contributed just over 50 percent in Mondadori shares, while the other partners contributed capital. Since the Mondadori shares constituted a majority in the holding company, the family remained in control of both AMEF and the recapitalization of Mondadori, the ailing publishing empire. AMEF's partners included Carlo De Benedetti, who had been in contact with Mondadori as a shareholder of the Editoriale l'Espresso group that founded the daily *la Repubblica.* De Benedetti held approximately 17 percent of AMEF. Silvio Berlusconi held 9 percent.

At Arnoldo Mondadori Editore, Mario Formenton was still president, and his nephew Leonardo Mondadori was promoted to vice-president. As managing director, Franco Tatò guided the restructuring of the company. In 1985 profits rose to L 25 billion as opposed to L 10 billion in 1984; in 1986 profits tripled to L 75 billion. When, in 1987, Mondadori reported profits of L 100 billion, it was evident that the company was out of danger and that the rescue program, with the recapitalization from AMEF, had been a success. It also proved that, despite the losses of the Retequattro venture, Mondadori was a basically healthy company. In 1987, however, Mario Formenton died prematurely. Former managing director and vice-president Sergio Polillo was brought in to fill his place but only after a bitter struggle over the succession, which opposed Leonardo Mondadori to his aunt, Cristina, and her son, Luca Formenton.

The loss of Mario Formenton triggered a series of events that eventually catapulted the company into national news. With the two branches of the family in conflict, the shareholder Carlo De Benedetti achieved a position of considerable influence. During this period the skilled financier struck a deal with the Formenton family by which he retained right of first refusal if they ever decided to sell their shares. Then, aligned with the Formentons at the Mondadori 1988 shareholders' assembly, De Benedetti successfully exploited a technicality in the relationship between the publishing group and the AMEF holding company to emerge in a majority position. Together the Formentons and De Benedetti voted to exclude the founder's grandson from the board of Mondadori. Embittered, Leonardo left the family business to found his own publishing house, Leonardo Editore.

Under De Benedetti's guidance, the Mondadori group continued to thrive. The group acquired a stake in Elemond, which controlled the prestigious Einaudi publishing house. In April 1989 De Benedetti arranged an important agreement whereby *la Repubblica* shareholders Eugenio Scalfari and Carlo Caracciolo sold their 51.85 percent share in Editoriale L'Espresso to Mondadori for L 407 billion. As part of the deal, Caracciolo was nominated president of Mondadori, and Scalfari became a member of the board of directors. With *la Repubblica* and Editoriale L'Espresso added to its interests, Mondadori was now worth L 2.3 trillion and was by far the largest publishing company in Italy.

Conflict developed again in 1989, the 100th anniversary of Arnoldo Mondadori's birth. Silvio Berlusconi had acquired more shares of AMEF and sided with Leonardo Mondadori to wield majority power in the decision making. Berlusconi's interest in Mondadori emerged when he blocked a move by Carlo De Benedetti to merge his holding company Compagnie Industriali Riunite S.p.A. (CIR) and AMEF.

By December 1989, fearful of their loss of influence on the board of Mondadori, the Formentons struck a deal to sell their AMEF shares to Berlusconi, effectively reuniting with their cousin Leonardo Mondadori. The move immediately set off a furor in the financial world and in the media, where the contestants carried out a bruising and highly publicized battle for control. On one side was Berlusconi, allied with the two families of Mondadori and in control of AMEF and therefore of the ordinary capital of Mondadori. On the other side was Carlo De Benedetti, joined by the *la Repubblica* editors Scalfari and Caracciolo, with 51 percent of the privileged capital of Mondadori. By the end of the year, the contest was transformed into a complicated legal struggle that turned on the validity of De Benedetti's agreement with the Formentons, which granted him first option on the Formenton's shares should they ever decide to sell.

For 156 days Silvio Berlusconi claimed control of Mondadori. The 1989 annual report listed Berlusconi as president and Luca Formenton as vice-president. The report described recent developments: a new division called "business and information" comprising business publishing and a computer software company, Mondadori Informatica; an agreement reached with *Fortune* for publication of an Italian edition; and the divestment of Mondadori's papermaking activities. But the victory was short-lived.

The deal between Berlusconi and the Formentons was contested in the courts and, in June 1990, arbitrators ruled in favor of De Benedetti. Judges assigned Giacinto Spizzico, an 81-year-old business lawyer, to the post of president. The office of vice-president was shared by Fedele Confaloniere, formerly managing director of Fininvest, and Luigi Vita Samory, a lawyer appointed by the courts. Two men also filled the post of managing director: Carlo Caracciolo and the court-appointed Antonio Coppi, a former executive of the Rizzoli publishing house. The new general director was a former executive of Carlo De Benedetti's CIR holding company, Corrado Passera.

In January 1991 this ruling was nullified in the Rome Court of Appeals without, however, significantly altering the balance of power between De Benedetti and Berlusconi. De Benedetti's original agreement with the Formentons was found to be in violation of the AMEF charter. A negotiated settlement was reached in May 1991 whereby Berlusconi and the Mondadori-Formenton families retained control of Mondadori's advertising agency and book and magazine publishing interests. De Benedetti controlled the Repubblica-Espresso group plus 15 local newspapers.

Meanwhile, events between 1989 and 1991 were traumatic for Mondadori. In spite of the contest for power already under way, 1988 was a strong year for the company, which reported a net profit of L 103 billion. In 1989 this figure was reduced by half, partly owing to losses in advertising.

The 1990s: Stagnant Economic Growth and Increased Market Share

Though the early and mid-1990s were slow economic years for Italy, Mondadori managed to retain and broaden its role as market leader. While cost-cutting efforts were aimed at increasing the Modadori profit margin, strategic acquisitions garnered the company a consistent gain in market share, from a leading 20 percent in 1990 to a dominating 29.3 percent in 1995. Leonardo Mondadori summed up the company's ability to succeed during economic stagnation: "We're never satisfied with where we are. We're always looking for something new. And even if we don't grow, others are declining, so we appear bigger."

In 1995, in an effort to cut costs and increase efficiency, Mondadori reduced the number of its printing plants, and in 1996 it completed its new central book warehouse in Verona. The new warehouse was expected to increase distribution capacity from 23 million to 40 million copies, which represented an increase in the number of titles that could be warehoused from 4,000 to 30,000.

Pope John Paul II astonished the religious publishing community in 1994 by choosing a lay publisher, Mondadori, as the worldwide publisher of his book *Crossing the Threshold of Hope.* Mondadori transferred these rights to various publishers around the world, and the book was published in more than 20 languages. More than one million copies were sold in 1994 in Italy alone (compared with Mondadori's second best-seller, Gabriel Garcia Marquez's *Of Love and Other Demons,* which sold 200,000 Italian copies in 1994).

In 1996 Mondadori book titles were put on a computer network that provided statistical sales data from Italian bookshops. This network allowed for better planning of distribution and reprinting of their books. Also in 1996 Mondadori launched *Pagine Utili Mondadori,* a directory meant to challenge the Italian Yellow Pages (*Pagine Gialle*), which had previously enjoyed a market monopoly. *Pagine Utili* was to take advantage of Pagine Gialle's weaknesses, mainly a low 17 percent market penetration, a difficult-to-use product, and a monopolistic pricing policy. Though its strategy of lower pricing and more targeted listings seemed well developed, *Pagine Utili*'s initial advertising volume was lower than estimated. This was partly the result of the competition's privatization and its adoption of more aggressive and competitive policies aimed at thwarting the Mondadori entry.

Though Mondadori has made the creation of "New Media" (such as CD-ROMs and on-line magazines) one of its primary goals, growth in the Italian computer software market was relatively slow. Still, sales of Mondadori's New Media were L 6 billion in 1996. One of the most remarkable areas of growth in 1996 was that of advertisement, which had been previously stagnant. Thanks to a growth of 9.2 percent in advertising sales in daily newspapers, Mondadori showed an overall advertising sales growth of 7.7 percent in 1996.

In looking toward the future, Mondadori formed an executive committee on July 18, 1996, and granted it administrative authority over the company. This included authorization to make investments and disposals, as well as the power to approve strategic policy and development programs. Following the resignation of Paolo Forlin as vice-chairman and managing director of Arnoldo Mondadori Editore S.p.A., the members of the executive committee consisted of Leonardo Mondadori (chairman), Marina Berlusconi, Fedele Confalonieri, and Ubaldo Livolsi.

Principal Subsidiaries

Auguri di Mondadori S.r.l.; Artes Graficas Toledo S.A. (Spain); Club degli Editori S.p.A.; Editiones Grijalbo S.A. (Spain); Elemonde S.p.A.; Giulio Einaudi Editore S.p.A; Monadori Espuna S.A. (Spain); Mondadori Business Information S.p.A.; Mondadori Informatica S.p.A.; Mondadori Pubblicita S.p.A.; Mondadori Video S.p.A.; Riccardo Ricciardi Editore S.p.A.; Sperling & Kupfer Editori S.p.A.; Stock Libri S.p.A.; Verkerke Reproduletres N.V. (Netherlands).

Further Reading

Arnoldo Mondadori Editore, *Arnoldo Mondadori Editore S.p.A.: Facts and Images 1987,* Segrate: Mondadori, 1988.
——, *Arnoldo Mondadori Editore S.p.A.: Facts and Images 1988,* Segrate: Mondadori, 1989.
"How Mondadori Keeps Its Italian Market Leadership," *Publisher's Weekly,* August 21, 1995, p. 12.
Lottman, Herbert R., "Gala Italian Launch for Pope's Book," *Publisher's Weekly,* October 24, 1994, p. 12.
——, "Mondadori Up, Rizzoli Down, in '94 Results," *Publisher's Weekly,* April 17, 1995, p. 17.
Mondadori, Mimma, *Tipografia in Paradiso,* Milan: Mondadori, 1984.
Pansa, Giampaolo, L'Intrigo, Milan: Sperling & Kupfer, 1990.
Turnai, Giuseppe, and Delfina Rattazi, *Mondadori: la grande sfida,* Milan: RCS Rizzoli, 1990.

—Paul Conrad
updated by Terry Bain

Ashland Inc.

1000 Ashland Drive
Russel, Kentucky 41169
U.S.A.
(606) 329-3333
Fax: (606) 329-5274
Web site: http://www.ashland.com

Public Company
Incorporated: 1924 as Ashland Refining Company
Employees: 36,100
Sales: $13.13 billion (1996)
Stock Exchanges: New York
SICs: 2821 Plastics Materials & Resins; 2869 Industrial
    Organic Chemicals, Not Elsewhere Classified; 2911
    Petroleum Refining

Ashland Inc. occupies a middle position in the oil industry—far smaller than the major international players but large enough to remain a powerful competitor in its own region. Its traditional emphasis has been on oil refining, an area in which it has long enjoyed a reputation for excellence. Unlike most of the world's great oil concerns, Ashland has never owned significant amounts of crude oil. In the 1990s Ashland became more involved with chemicals and road construction but remained primarily a refiner and distributor of oil products.

Company Origins

The history of Ashland Inc. begins with J. Fred Miles and the founding in 1910 of Swiss Drilling Company, an Oklahoma corporation. Miles had been raised in Oklahoma and worked in the oil business from his youth. After gathering a store of capital, he created Swiss Drilling with two other men to explore and operate new wells.

During this period Standard Oil had an overwhelming presence in the industry, and, as a result, the U.S. government ordered a breakup of the company in 1911. The years immediately following the breakup, Standard Oil's near-monopoly were

challenging in the oil business, and Miles found that he could not survive on the low prices offered for Oklahoma crude. In 1916 he moved his operations to the new fields then opening in eastern Kentucky, where, with the help of some powerful financiers in Chicago and in Cleveland, Ohio, he obtained control of nearly 200,000 acres of oil land. Two years later the energetic Miles incorporated Swiss Oil Company in Lexington, Kentucky, with a group of backers that included the Insulls and the Armours of Chicago, with Miles serving as general manager and J.I. Lamprecht of Cleveland as president. Swiss Oil was soon one of the leading oil concerns in the state of Kentucky.

By the early 1920s a postwar depression and the early exhaustion of key oil wells had thrust Swiss Oil into a precarious financial condition. Despite the company's difficulties, Fred Miles was eager to expand its operations into refining, and in 1923 he hired the services of young Paul Blazer to select, buy, and operate the most advantageously located and outfitted refinery obtainable in the area. Blazer had gone into the oil-trading business after college and then picked up valuable experience as a partner in a Lexington refinery, from which he had just resigned when Miles made him the head of Swiss Oil's new division, Ashland Refining Company, in 1924. Blazer selected for his refinery an existing facility at Cattletsburg, Kentucky, on the Ohio River near the West Virginia border and just upstream from Ashland, where Blazer set up his modest offices. The Cattletsburg refinery had a capacity of 1,000 barrels per day and, after a program of extensive repairs, was soon operating profitably.

Blazer's choice of Cattletsburg was excellent because of several factors that would prove critical in the company's long-term success. In general, a refining operation that had access to its own local crude-oil supplies would do well in the eastern Kentucky region. Swiss Oil, though not a terribly successful company, did own a substantial amount of the region's crude and could therefore supply its new subsidiary with most of its needs. Ashland was thus able to sell regionally refined petroleum products, such as gasoline and motor oil, more cheaply than competitors who were forced to transport their crude or finished products from the Atlantic seaboard, the Mississippi River, or the Gulf of Mexico. The Cattletsburg site promised ready access to hundreds of miles of navigable rivers, by means of which Ashland could both receive crude and deliver product to the greater Ohio River basin. Until the introduction of pipelines, river freight was unmatched as an economic carrier of oil, and Ashland remained dependent on its river barges and terminals for the delivery of much of its refined product. These factors gave Ashland an early advantage over its much larger rivals and allowed the company to achieve a firm and lasting position as regional leader.

Success during the Depression and World War II

By 1926 Ashland's gross sales were $3 million a year, and Paul Blazer had confirmed his reputation as an outstanding refinery manager. J. Fred Miles had been eased out of Swiss Oil when the company required a bailout by one of its investors, and it was not long before the Ashland subsidiary was outperforming its parent company. Blazer steadily improved the refinery's operation and expanded sales of its products, and in 1929 he convinced Swiss Oil's board of directors to authorize Ashland's purchase of $400,000 worth of marketing companies in the area. Despite the onset of the Great Depression, this was followed by the 1930 acquisition of Tri-State Refining Company over the West Virginia border. Tri-State had a sizable refinery and its own team of gas stations and trucks, giving Ashland the makings of an integrated refining and marketing organization in the eastern Kentucky region. While inexpensive, river transport was continually threatened with the imposition of federal tolls that would largely negate its economy. Thus, in 1931, Ashland took the first in a long series of steps intended to lessen its dependence on river transportation of its crude supplies. When Ashland bought the Cumberland Pipeline Company for $420,000 in 1931, it facilitated shipment of crude from the Atlantic seaboard, as well as from its Kentucky fields. This opening to the sea would become vital when Ashland grew dependent upon Middle Eastern oil arriving by tanker.

So skilled an operator was Blazer that Ashland continued to turn a profit in the worst Depression years. Ashland was now the staff upon which leaned the ailing Swiss Oil, and in 1936, when it became apparent that the latter could not sustain the two companies, they were merged and Blazer elected president and chief executive officer of the new Ashland Oil & Refining Company. The combined companies showed a 1936 net profit of $677,583 on sales of $4.8 million, good results at any time but remarkable in the Depression era. Blazer forged ahead with new investments, joining Standard Oil Company (Ohio) in a pipeline from fields in southern Illinois and adding a costly new unit to the Cattlesburg refinery. By the time the United States

entered World War II in 1941, Ashland had nearly doubled its sales to $8 million.

During World War II the petroleum industry came under fairly tight government control. Like all the other oil companies, big and small, Ashland benefited mightily from the rapid increase in demand for the entire spectrum of petroleum products, which were needed for everything from gasoline to rubber boots to explosives. With government assistance Ashland built a new facility at Cattlesburg for the refining of 100-octane aviation fuel, and within four years it had doubled and redoubled company revenues to $35 million in 1945. The following years saw an inevitable recession as the war machine was dismantled, but it soon became apparent that postwar America was about to indulge its love affair with the automobile as never before. From the remote mountain towns of West Virginia to the streets of Cincinnati, Ohio, the postwar economy moved on wheels powered by oil, and Ashland remained the region's most economical supplier of that oil.

Postwar Growth

In 1948 Ashland took a major step when it merged with Cleveland-based Allied Oil Company, a fuel-oil broker with sales slightly in excess of Ashland's. Allied had been started in 1925 by Floyd R. Newman and W.W. Vandeveer with the support of Blazer. The combined companies had revenue in that year of $100 million. Ashland's new Allied division was directed by Rex Blazer, nephew of Ashland's president and a former marketing executive at Allied. The merger extended Ashland's marketing area to Cleveland and as far west as Chicago, and, to make use of its new sales opportunities, Ashland soon added a trio of other acquisitions—Aetna Oil Company, a Louisville, Kentucky, refiner and distributor; Frontier Oil Company, of Buffalo, New York; and Freedom-Valvoline Oil Company, the Pennsylvania maker of Valvoline motor oil. The latter was already a well-known brand name and under Ashland's ownership has since become one of the most widely distributed motor oils in the world. By the time these purchases were completed in 1950, Ashland was the 19th-largest oil company in the United States and for the first time was listed on the New York Stock Exchange.

Sales in 1955 topped $250 million, though net income was only $10 million. In contrast to its early years, Ashland as a mature company tended to earn rather low levels of net income, which Blazer attributed to two basic factors. First, the company had far outstripped its limited sources of crude oil and never had much success as a prospector. This meant that it would never enjoy the extraordinary profits brought in by big oil strikes and that its crude-oil expense would always be somewhat higher than for a fully integrated oil concern. Second, Ashland also sold more refined products than it made, supplementing its own production with purchases of refined goods for resale, which necessarily resulted in a diminished margin. Such a policy also meant that Ashland's refineries were kept running at or near capacity, a clear gain in efficiency over plants forced to cut back or work on shorter, more costly runs. Added to its advantageous system of waterway transport and freedom from the advertising expense associated with operation of a high-profile, branded chain of gas stations, Ashland's refining efficiency offset its lack of crude and enabled the company to earn a steady if unspectacular return on investment.

In 1957, after heading Ashland Oil for 22 years, Blazer retired as the chief executive. His nephew Rex Blazer took over the top management spot, while Everett Wells, a longtime associate of the senior Blazer, became the new president. The year before these changes, Ashland entered a new field with the purchase of the R.J. Brown Company of St. Louis, Missouri, a diversified manufacturer of petrochemicals. A great number of useful chemicals are derived from petroleum, and the oil industry as a whole was expanding rapidly into this new and largely unexplored area. Ashland steadily increased its petrochemical holdings, in 1962 buying United Carbon Company of Houston, Texas, makers of carbon black, and in 1966 adding Archer Daniels Midland Chemicals Company for $65 million. At that point Ashland formed a new operating subsidiary, Ashland Chemical Company, to oversee the workings of its manifold chemical interests.

The early 1960s were also notable for Ashland's 1962 purchase of the Central Louisiana pipeline system from Humble Oil & Refining. Central Louisiana was a major pipeline, gathering most of the oil produced in greater Louisiana and the Gulf of Mexico fields, and its acquisition by Ashland largely relieved the company of its worries about a steady supply of crude oil, made worse by the intermittent threat of new user tolls on the waterways. The net effect of these acquisitions was to boost Ashland's sales sharply, from $490 million in 1963 to $723 million three years later, elevating the company from the status of an independent to what might be called a "mini-major" oil firm. The robust U.S. economy had much to do with Ashland's prosperity, of course, as more citizens relied on the automobile.

Changes in the 1970s and 1980s

In 1969 Ashland had entered the coal business and soon became one of the top-ten coal producers in the country. It also took advantage of its refineries' asphalt by-products to gain a leading place among the nation's road-construction firms. The result of such diversification was a gradual lessening of Ashland's dependence on oil refining for its sales dollar. By 1971 refining and marketing of oil accounted for only 57 percent of Ashland's $1.4 billion in revenue, with Ashland Chemical providing another 25 percent and its other holdings chipping in the remainder. This apparent balance was somewhat misleading, however; Ashland continued to rely on its refining and marketing divisions for the bulk of its net income, as the growing chemical business proved to be a sluggish moneymaker. Refining capacity reached 350,000 barrels per day in 1973, and, as always, Ashland's crude production was less than 20 percent of that figure, forcing the company to join the mounting number of U.S. oil refiners dependent upon Middle Eastern crude for their survival.

In 1970 shareholders approved changing the company's name from Ashland Oil & Refining to Ashland Oil, Inc. That same year Ashland consolidated most of its Canadian interests with those of Canadian Gridoil Limited to form Ashland Oil Canada Limited. Domestically Ashland acquired Union Carbide Petroleum Company and Empire State Petroleum, and

these were consolidated with other exploration and production activities into Ashland Exploration, Inc.

In the mid-1970s Ashland became entangled in its first of a series of legal controversies. In 1976 chief executive officer Orin Atkins, a lawyer who had served in that position since 1965, agreed in response to a shareholder suit to repay Ashland some $175,000 in funds he was said to have spent improperly. The previous year, 1975, Ashland had been fined by the Securities and Exchange Commission for illegally contributing more than $700,000 to several political campaigns.

Ashland's problems with meeting its own needs for crude oil became increasingly pronounced as the company continued to expand its refining and marketing operations. The 1973 OPEC embargo and ensuing energy crisis had effectively raised the stakes in the oil-exploration game. After the early 1970s only those companies willing and able to mount massive drilling campaigns would be likely to reap the benefits of crude-oil supplies. Ashland was simply not big enough to join the majors in their exorbitant outlays, and Ashland therefore got out of the production business entirely. Sale of most of its oil leases, equipment, and reserves netted Ashland about $1.5 billion by 1980, but it also left the company wholly dependent upon outside sources of crude, primarily in the Middle East. In 1975 all construction activities were consolidated, and Ashland Coal, Inc., was formed in anticipation of the increasing potential of coal in the national energy market. Ashland took a comprehensive review of all segments of its operations to determine necessary changes. As an initial step in this strategy to maximize return on existing assets, the company sold its 79 percent interest in Ashland Oil Canada.

In 1981 Atkins was forced out as chairman and chief executive officer by a group of executives who brought to light illegal payments Atkins had made to government officials in Middle East countries, most notably Oman. He was replaced in both positions by John R. Hall. In June 1988 two former Ashland employees won a wrongful-discharge suit against the company. The employees, a former vice-president for oil supply and a former vice-president for government relations, had accused Ashland of firing them in 1983 for refusing to cover up the illegal payments. The jury awarded the plaintiffs $70.85 million, $1.25 million of which was to be paid by Hall personally. The plaintiffs ultimately settled out of court for $25 million.

On July 13, 1988, Atkins was arrested by customs agents at John F. Kennedy International Airport and accused of selling company documents to the National Iranian Oil Company (NIOC). Atkins denied the charges. The papers Atkins allegedly peddled related to an ongoing, $283 million billing dispute between Ashland and NIOC. In 1989 Ashland settled the case with a $325 million payment to NIOC. The company's public image was not helped by a 1988 spill of four million gallons of diesel fuel into the Ohio River, although Ashland was credited with a prompt, candid response.

In the meantime, Ashland sales skyrocketed along with the price of oil. Hall watched revenue hit an all-time peak of $9.5 billion in 1981, but Ashland found itself squeezed by the high cost of crude, and net income actually dropped into a net loss during the first part of 1982, when a spreading recession only made matters worse. Atkins had also saddled Ashland with an unusually high debt ratio when, in 1981, he used the receipts from the oil-drilling asset sale to buy United States Filter Corporation and Integon Corporation for $661 million. Integon, an insurance holding company, hardly matched the range of Ashland's other interests and in due time was sold to reduce debt. Once the recession had eased by 1983, Ashland's earnings again picked up, and the company's future brightened.

Scurlock Oil Company, a crude-oil gathering, transporting, and marketing firm, was acquired in 1982, thereby aiding Ashland in a shift from foreign to domestic crude-oil sources. In 1982 more than 20 corporate staff departments were brought together to form Ashland Services Company, a division that would cut overhead and also provide cost-effective services to the corporation and to its divisions and subsidiaries.

Restructuring and Acquisitions: Ashland in the 1990s

Ashland began the 1990s with a strong financial position. In 1992 Ashland surpassed $10 billion in sales for the first time, and it also established itself as the leading distributor of chemicals and solvents in North America by acquiring the majority of Unocal's chemical distribution business. Though refining profits were largely disappointing during the early 1990s, Ashland's chemical profits remained a boon for the company. Operating income from chemicals increased to $47 million in the last three months of 1994 compared to $28 million the year before.

Several important developments occurred in 1994. Ashland's Valvoline division purchased Zerex, the nation's number two antifreeze. Ashland also acquired Eurobase (Italy) and ACT Inc. (Pennsylvania), both companies that produced chemicals used in the creation of semiconductors. Also that year Ashland began a new multi-well oil exploration in Nigeria and made a promising discovery in the first well sunk.

In an effort to have the name of the company reflect Ashland's increasingly diversified business, shareholders approved the name change from Ashland Oil, Inc., to Ashland Inc. in 1995. At the same time, the company began to shore up its nonrefining business segments to minimize the effect of its weak refining margins. According to Paul W. Chellgren, the company's president and chief operating officer, Ashland's strategy was to become an "integrated, but diversified company" by adding value to its petroleum products rather than by increasing volume. In 1996 Ashland chairman and chief executive officer John Hall announced his retirement, and Chellgren succeeded him in both positions.

In early 1997 Ashland announced plans to consolidate operations of Arch Mineral and Ashland Coal, thus creating the fifth-largest coal producer in the United States. Also in early 1997 Ashland was the first to be granted foreign trade subzone status at Akron-Canton Regional Airport in Ohio (known as "Foreign Trade Zone 181"). This status allowed Ashland to import crude oil to its Canton refinery and Lima storage facility without paying duties and tariffs. The subzone status was designed to protect those companies who imported oil not in its finished state (such as crude oil) and that diminished in volume once the oil had been processed into products such as asphalt, diesel fuel, or home heating oil. Tariffs on foreign crude were 2.5 cents a barrel in 1997. Not having to pay the fee saved Ashland more than $250,000 a year at its Canton facility. To further enhance efficiency and increase profitability, Ashland Inc. and Marathon Oil Co. announced in May 1997 a plan to merge their refining and marketing operations, with Marathon holding 62 percent of ownership and Ashland 38 percent. Ashland Chemical was expected to be the largest customer of the joint venture.

In the late 1990s Ashland was a highly diversified energy company, with extensive coal and petrochemical holdings to complement its core of oil refining and marketing. It was the nation's leading designer and builder of roadways through its APAC subsidiaries, which laid more than 13 million tons of asphalt in fiscal 1996. Oil remained the centerpiece of Ashland's corporate structure, however. Still relying on cheap river transport for much of its outgoing freight, Ashland delivered gasoline and related petroleum products to a large network of wholesalers and Ashland-affiliated gas stations. Ashland itself operated 742 SuperAmerica retail gasoline-grocery outlets in 1996 (SuperAmerica Group's 1996 sales were $1.9 billion). Added to these was the $1.2 billion in sales generated by the Valvoline, Inc., subsidiary, Ashland's nationally recognized brand name. Combined oil activities thus still provided well over half of the company's revenue and earnings, as Ashland continued to fill a narrow niche between international oil giant and regional independent.

Principal Subsidiaries

Ashland Petroleum Company; SuperAmerica Group, Inc.; Valvoline, Inc.; Ashland Chemical, Inc.; APAC, Inc.; Arch Mineral Corporation (50%); Ashland Coal, Inc. (54%); Ashland Services Company.

Further Reading

Butters, Jamie, "Kentucky Merger Threatens to Subordinate One Company to the Other," *Knight-Ridder/Tribune Business News,* May 19, 1997, p 519B1012.
"Environmental Accident Ushers in NovAlert," *Occupational Hazards,* March 1994, p. 99.
Fan, Aliza, "Ashland to Stay True to Solid Reputation," *The Oil Daily,* January 30, 1995, p. 1.
Kovski, Alan, "Ashland, Lyondell Gain on Chemicals, Slip Back on Poor Results in Refining," *The Oil Daily,* January 24, 1995, p. 3.
——, "Marathon, Ashland Put Proposal in Writing to Combine Refining, Marketing Operations," *The Oil Daily,* May 16, 1997, p. 1.
Sachdev, Ameet, "Ashland Inc. to Sell Shares in Exploration Unit," *Knight-Ridder/Tribune Business News,* January 31, 1997, p. 131B1290.
——, "Ashland Oil to Seek a Partner for Refinery Business," *Knight-Ridder/Tribune Business News,* December 10, 1996, p. 1210B0939.
Scott, Otto, *Buried Treasure: The Story of Arch Mineral,* Washington, D.C.: Braddock Communications, 1989.
——, *The Exception: The Story of Ashland Oil & Refining Company,* New York: McGraw-Hill Book Company, 1968.

—Jonathan Martin
—updated by Terry Bain

AVON

Avon Products, Inc.

9 West 57th Street
New York, New York 10019-2683
U.S.A.
(212) 282-7000
Web site: http://www.avon.com

Public Company
Incorporated: 1886 as the California Perfume Company
Employees: 33,700
Sales: $4.81 billion (1996)
Stock Exchanges: New York
SICs: 5963 Direct Selling Establishments; 2844 Toilet
   Preparations; 5122 Drugs, Proprietaries, and Sundries;
   3961 Costume Jewelry; 3999 Manufacturing
   Industries Not Elsewhere Classified

The oldest beauty company in the United States, Avon Products, Inc. has grown from a modest line of perfumes sold door-to-door to one of the world's leading brand of cosmetics. It manufactures and sells cosmetics, fragrances, toiletries, and accessories, and has recently begun offering sportswear for women. Avon employs a unique direct-selling method, which was greatly responsible for its incredible success in the 1950s and 1960s, when women were easily found in the home for sales purposes. After unsuccessful efforts at diversification into the health-care service industry left the company with massive debts in the 1970s, Avon began to refocus on its roots: beauty products and direct selling. Today, Avon's products are sold through catalogs as well as directly to customers by its sales representatives. Avon products are sold in more than 130 countries by two million representatives, making Avon the number one direct sales company in the world.

Early Years as the California Perfume Company

The beginnings of Avon Products, Inc. can be traced to the mid-1880s, when a door-to-door book salesman named David H. McConnell attempted to bolster declining sales by offering small samples of perfume to housewives who would listen to his sales pitch. It soon became clear, however, that his customers were more interested in the perfume, and McConnell left the bookselling business to create an entire line of perfumes to be sold door-to-door. He brewed the perfume in a pantry-sized space in New York City, naming the product line the "Little Dot Perfume Set," which consisted of five scents: white rose, violet, lily of the valley, heliotrope, and hyacinth. His endeavor was named the California Perfume Company, in an effort to invoke images of the beauty and excitement of that state.

McConnell's intent was to build a business around quickly-used products sold directly to the consumer, through use of the national network of sales agents he had organized during his years as a bookseller. The nation's first Avon Lady was Mrs. P. F. E. Albee of Winchester, New Hampshire, the wife of a U. S. senator. Within the first six months of operation, Albee had assembled a solid base of 100 salespeople and their customers; within 12 years, Albee had recruited and trained nearly 5,000 representatives.

In addition to new scents, other products were quickly added to the California Perfume Company's product line. Popular early items included spot remover, Witch Hazel Cream, machine oil, mending cement, Almond Cream Balm, food flavorings, Tooth Tablet, and carpet cleaner. In 1896, ten years after the company was conceived, McConnell hired Adolf Goetting, a noted perfumer who had been in the business for 25 years. The following year, a new laboratory was built in Suffern, New York, and the first illustrated catalog was produced. By the company's 20th year, its product line had expanded to include more than 100 items, and in 1914 the company's rapid expansion was marked by the opening of an office in Montreal, Canada.

The Early 1900s: Avon is Born

The first products in the California Perfume Company's line of Avon Products—a toothbrush, cleanser, and vanity set—appeared in 1920. The Avon name was inspired by the area around the Suffern lab, which McConnell thought resembled the countryside of William Shakespeare's home, Stratford-on-

Avon, England. Never wavering from its strategy of door-to-door sales and catalogs filled with low-cost home and beauty products, the company surpassed the $2 million sales mark in 1926, the year of its 40th anniversary.

By the end of the 1920s, the company was doing business in 48 of the United States and in Canada. During this time, thousands of female sales representatives, under Albee's supervision, were partaking in one of the first opportunities for American women to experience a degree of economic freedom without upsetting their culturally-accepted role as homemakers. The company launched three-week sales campaigns and a "specials" strategy in 1932. Five years later, in 1937, McConnell died and was replaced by his son, David H. McConnell Jr., who headed the company for the next seven years. Under his supervision, the company's growth remained steady. In 1939, the California Perfume Company was renamed Avon Products, due to that product line's immense popularity and success.

During World War II, cosmetic production slowed while nearly half of the staff in the Suffern lab devoted themselves to wartime production of such things as insect repellent, pharmaceuticals, and paratrooper kits. In 1944, W. Van Alan Clark replaced McConnell as the company's chairman. The new Avon then instituted several changes during the 1950s, the most notable of which was its entry into overseas markets and the rapid expansion of its sales force.

Post-War Expansion in the 1950s and Beyond

Following the war, many more housewives began seeking extra income and work that did not interfere with family life. In the early 1950s, the Avon sales force almost quadrupled in size. Sales representatives' territories were downsized by several hundred homes, a strategy which enabled more representatives to be added and sales to increase sixfold over the following 12 years. Avon advertisements appeared on television for the first time, including the famous slogan, "Ding Dong, Avon Calling," which was first televised in 1954. That same year, Avon opened offices in Venezuela and Puerto Rico, marking its first venture into what would become a very lucrative Latin American market. It also penetrated the European market in 1957 with the institution of Avon Cosmetics, Ltd. in the United Kingdom.

Under the leadership of W. Van Alan Clark, Avon also saw changes such as the rapid expansion of foreign sales and Avon's listing on the New York Stock Exchange in 1964. Clark was replaced by J. A. Ewald in 1966, who was followed by W. Hicklin a year later. Under Hicklin, the traditional three-week sales cycle was changed to two weeks to improve sales. The three-week campaign was still used overseas, particularly in Asia, a market which was entered by Avon in 1969 through the opening of operations in Japan. Japan has remained one of Avon's key foreign markets, along with Brazil, Mexico, and the United Kingdom.

The 1970s presented Avon with its greatest challenges in the company's history. Though sales topped $1 billion in 1972, and its profitable costume-jewelry line—begun in 1971—had made Avon the world's biggest jewelry manufacturer in just five years, Avon's growth stalled in 1973. The company was hit hard by a recession and the mass entry of women into the workforce. The direct-selling system, Avon's innovation and strength, was nearly toppled by social changes that management had not anticipated. The status of the U.S. dollar reduced the company's international profits; recession and inflation crippled its high-sales decanter products line; in 1975, about 25,000 Avon Ladies quit; and Avon products were outpaced by retail cosmetic firms offering jazzier products to women with new attitudes. All of these factors converged and led to troubled times—and Avon's eventual restructuring.

In response to these hardships, the most visible change Avon made was to become more sensitive to its market. Sales representatives began to follow women into the workplace, where about 25 percent of Avon's sales are made today, and new businesses such as direct-mail women's apparel were tested. Changes were also made to the cosmetics product line and its overall pricing, as a result of market studies. Fred Fusee, who had advanced through the manufacturing side of Avon to become its chairman in 1972, was replaced in 1975 by David W. Mitchell, whose years with Avon had been spent in marketing. Mitchell worked to solidify Avon's presence in the beauty business via consumer and product research, product development, and promotion. Avon's image was overhauled to give it a more contemporary appeal, advertising time was more than tripled, and sales were revamped.

In 1979, Avon made another strategic move to update its product offerings through the purchase of Tiffany & Company, the upmarket jeweler, for $104 million. The Tiffany purchase set the tone for the next decade: diversification through acquisition. This included an ill-fated billion-dollar plunge into the health-care industry, and a later entry into the prestige-fragrance market.

The 1980s: Diversification Through Acquisition

In 1983, Hicks Waldron, who had previously helped turn around General Electric, left his post at R. J. Reynolds to become Avon's chairman. Shortly before Waldron's appointment, Avon had purchased Mallinckrodt, a chemical and hospital supply company. Waldron followed this purchase with the acquisition of Foster Medical Corporation in 1984. Initially thriving in the home and health-care equipment field, Foster became the fastest-growing division of Avon. Just as the company began to celebrate its success, however, Foster was devastated by Medicare cost-containment efforts. At the same time, Tiffany's profits were steadily declining—in part because customers had become alienated by the introduction of lower-priced merchandise—and the Tiffany subsidiary was sold in 1984.

Avon then tried to focus on health care for the elderly with the 1985 acquisitions of the Retirement Inns of America and The Mediplex Group, both of which were nursing home operations. Unfortunately, only 15 percent of Avon's sales came from its health care holdings that year. This failure, combined with the fact that annual profits overall were about half of what they were in 1979, caused Waldron to rethink his strategy and abandon the diversification plan. Mallinckrodt was sold in early 1986 and Foster in 1988, both at a great loss to Avon, and plans to sell the remaining health-care divisions were announced. The company sold Retirement Inns of America in 1989 and The Mediplex Group in 1990. Avon's brief health-care industry foray left it $1.1 billion in debt.

Diversification into prestige fragrances later proved to be a more stable endeavor. First came a joint venture with Liz Claiborne in 1985, followed by the acquisitions of Parfums Stern and Giorgio, Inc. in 1987. Parfums Stern, which produced Oscar de la Renta, Perry Ellis, and other designer perfumes, was a chief competitor of Liz Claiborne, and before long, Claiborne dissolved its agreement with Avon. Strapped for cash, Avon then sold Parfums Stern in early 1990. Giorgio remained a top-selling national brand well into the 1990s, however, and under the parentage of Avon introduced several new products in the Giorgio line.

The 1990s and Beyond

Waldron retired in 1989, and his successor, James E. Preston, immediately faced several takeover attempts. Avon fought off a bid by Amway Corporation in partnership with Irwin L. Jacobs, a Minneapolis, Minnesota-based raider who then launched a takeover attempt himself. While these efforts receded in the early-1990s, a new suitor appeared in the form of the Chartwell Association, an investment group which included the chief financial officer of Mary Kay Cosmetics. Interestingly, the Avon sales force proved to be the greatest deterrent to these takeover bids; in massive letter-writing campaigns, the sales representatives told aggressors that they will be unwilling to work for them.

In 1990, Avon continued to focus on rejuvenating its domestic sales figures, while selling approximately 40 percent of Avon Japan to the Japanese public for $218 million in revenues. Meanwhile, the company entered further into the business of selling items in the United States through direct-mail means, using full-color catalogs to promote its products. These measures helped the company increase 1990 sales to $3.45 billion, marking an increase of over $150 million from the previous year.

As Avon began to stand on firmer ground financially, it was able to focus once again on expanding its scope worldwide. The early 1990s were spent establishing sales headquarters and networks in other countries, while also continuing to boost sales in the United States. Avon entered the sales market in Poland in 1992 through the recruitment and training of more representatives to work in direct sales capacities there. The company also entered the Russian market in 1993. Annual sales broke the $4 billion mark that year, and the per-share price of Avon's stock rose to over $32. The company also began selling its product on the internet, taking advantage of the increasing popularity of the information superhighway.

In 1994, Avon sold off its Giorgio product line, which was becoming a less important asset as time went on. The company instead focused on promoting products carrying its own name. It further strengthened its standing in the foreign market in 1995 with the addition of a sales office in India, and the acquisition of Justin (Pty) Ltd. in South Africa, the country's second largest direct-selling cosmetics company. 1995 sales topped off at almost $4.5 billion.

Expansion continued as Avon also began selling sportswear and apparel for women in its direct-mail catalogs, after finalizing a joint venture with fashion designer Diane Von Furstenberg to introduce a line of moderately-priced casual wear. Avon tied the addition in with the company's corporate sponsorship of the 1996 Summer Olympics in Atlanta, Georgia, and a multi-million dollar advertising campaign that named sports figures such as Jackie Joyner-Kersee as "Just Another Avon Lady." Also in 1996, Avon introduced "Lifedesigns," a corporation developed to offer goal-setting and management seminars to women. Early the following year, Avon also purchased Discovery Toys, Inc., a direct-sales marketer of educational toy products for children. Discovery Toys continued operations separate from those of Avon, with the hope that Avon's immense global sales network would help the small company attain higher sales and thus contribute to its new parent's yearly revenues.

Entering the end of the century trimmed of its unwieldy diversification into the health-care industry, Avon made great strides in expanding business in its areas of strength. The company has continued to hire sales representatives throughout the world to sell products directly to consumers, while also working to expand its direct-mail business. With sales figures increasing each year, and a more concrete conceptualization of its spectrum of business, Avon remained a world leader with the potential to achieve future growth.

Principal Subsidiaries

Cosmeticos Avon S.A.C.I. (Argentina); Avon Cosmetics Australia Proprietary Limited (Australia); Avon Products Pty. Limited (Australia); Avon Cosmetics Vertriebsgesellschaft m.b.h. (Austria); Arlington Limited (Bermuda); Stratford Insurance Co., Ltd. (Bermuda); Productos Avon Bolivia Ltda. (Bolivia); Avon Cosmeticos, Ltda. (Brazil); Avon Canada, Inc. (Canada); Avon Direct Inc. (Canada); Cosmeticos Avon S.A. (Chile); Compagnia de Ventra Directa Seller Chile S.A. (Chile); Avon Products (Guangzhau) Ltd. (China) (60%); CS Avon Cosmetics, Spol. sr. o (Czech Republic); Avon Capital Corp.; Avon Diversified Services, Inc.; Avon International Operations, Inc.; Avon-Lomalinda, Inc.; Avon-Mirabella, Inc.; Marbella Dominicana; Manila Manufacturing Co.; Productos Avon S.A. (Dominican Republic); Productos Avon Ecuador S.A. (Ecuador); Productos Avon, S.A. (El Salvador); Avon S.A. (France); Avon Cosmetics GmbH (Germany); Productos Avon de Guatemala, S.A. (Guatamala); Productos Avon, S.A. (Honduras); Avon Cosmetics (FEBO) Limited (Hong Kong); Avon Cosmetics Hungary KFT (Hungary); Avon Service Center, Inc.; P.T. Avon Indonesia (Indonesia) (85%); Albee Dublin Finance Company

(Ireland); Avon Limited (Ireland); Avon Cosmetics S.p.A. (Italy); Avon Products Company Limited (Japan, 66%); Live & Life Company Limited (Japan); Avon Cosmetics (Malaysia) Sendirian Berhad (Malaysia); Avon Cosmetics, S.A. de C.V. (Mexico); Avonova, S.A. de C.V. (Mexico) (49%); M.I. Holdings Inc.; Avon International Finance N.V. (Netherlands Antilles); Avon Americas, Ltd.; Avon Overseas Capital Corp.; Avon Cosmetics Limited (New Zealand); Productos Avon S.A. (Peru); Productos Avon S.A. (Panama); Productos De Bellesa, S.A. (Peru); Avon Cosmetics, Inc. (Philippines); Avon Products Mfg., Inc. (Philippines); Beautifont Products, Inc. (Phillipines); Avon Cosmetics Polska Sp. z o.o (Poland); Avon Cosmeticos, Lda. (Portugal); Avon Cosmetics Spal s r.o (Slovak Republic); Avon Beauty Products Company (Russia); Justin (Pty) Ltd. (South Africa); Avon Cosmetics, S.A. (Spain) (75%); Avon Cosmetics (Taiwan) Ltd. (Taiwan); Avon Products Limited (Taiwan); Avon Cosmetics (Thailand) Ltd. (Thailand); California Manufacturing Co. Ltd. (Thailand); Eczacibasi Avon Kosmetik Urunleri Sanayi ve Ticaret A.S. (Turkey) (50%); Avon Cosmetics Limited (U.K.); Avon European Holdings Ltd. (U.K.); Avon Cosmetics de Venezuela, C.A.; Discovery Toys, Inc.

Further Reading

The Greatest Beauty Story Ever Told, New York: Avon Products, 1986.
Hayes, Linda, "The Changes in Avon's Makeup Aren't Just Cosmetic," *Fortune,* August 13, 1979.
Kleinfield, Sonny, *Staying at the Top,* New York: New American Library Books, 1986.

—Carol I. Keeley
—updated by Laura E. Whiteley

✕AYDIN

Aydin Corp.

P.O. Box 349
Horsham, Pennsylvania 19044
U.S.A.
(215) 657-7510
Fax: (215) 657-3830
Web site: http://www.aydin.com

Public Company
Incorporated: 1967
Employees: 1,400
Sales: $116.6 million (1996)
Stock Exchanges: New York
SICs: 3575 Computer Terminals; 3577 Computer
   Peripheral Equipment, Not Elsewhere Classified; 3661
   Telephone and Telegraph Apparatus; 3663 Radio and
   Television Broadcasting and Communications Equip-
   ment; 3812 Search, Detection, Navigation, Guidance,
   Aeronautical and Nautical Systems and Instruments

A world class provider of products and systems for the acqui-sition and distribution of information over electronic communica-tions media, Aydin Corp. operates predominantly in the electron-ics manufacturing industry. The company develops, manufactures, and sells a wide range of military and commercial telecommunications equipment, including microwave transmis-sion equipment and systems military applications. The company also provides airborne equipment and systems to gather critical information and terminals to receive and analyze this data on the ground. In addition Aydin installs turnkey telecom systems, selling cathode-ray-tube monitors and workstations, developing radars, and selling software for applications such as radar simula-tion and air-traffic control systems. Turkish-born Ayhan Hakimoglu guided the company from its inception until 1996.

Rocky Start, 1967–1972

Incorporated in 1967, Aydin established executive offices in an industrial park in Fort Washington, Pennsylvania, near Philadelphia. By 1969 Aydin was designing, manufacturing, and selling electronics products and systems for ultimate use in the aerospace and data communications fields. In addition, the company designed, manufactured, and sold electronically-controlled machine tools and electrohydraulic and pneumatic equipment and systems; was engaged in sheet- and strip-steel forming and processing and manufactured steel storage racks and storage handling systems.

The vast array of products Aydin offered came through acquisition. Aydin acquired ten firms in its first two years of operation. By 1970 the company owned property in Pennsylva-nia and California and leased property in seven states. It went public in 1968, raising about $1.5 million from the sale of common stock to reduce debt and pay for new equipment and new-product introduction. Proceeds from the sale of 15-year convertible subordinated debentures in 1969 came to more than $3 million.

Unfortunately, Aydin's acquisitions proved to be ill-ad-vised. In 1968 the company lost $2.8 million on $19.7 million of sales. After a profitable 1969, it lost $4.1 million in 1970 on revenues of $16.1 million and $4.9 million in 1971 on revenues of $15.6 million. Its common stock, which climbed to $52 a share in 1969, fell as low as 25 cents a share in 1972. Aydin did not climb out of the red until 1972, when it earned $415,000 on revenues of $22.2 million. The company's profitability came from streamlining. By 1972, Aydin had sold four of its nonelec-tronic businesses and discontinued other operations, enabling it to take a charge against income of about $6 million before taxes. Subsequently, the company concentrated its efforts on the areas of microwave and satellite equipment and display terminal sys-tems. In 1974 it organized an international sales network, with headquarters in Brussels, Belgium, to market its products in Europe, the Middle East, Asia, and Africa.

Growing Prosperity, 1976–1983

By 1976 microwave communications equipment was Aydin's largest line of business, accounting for 39 percent of its $42.4 million in revenues. Its products in this field included high-power microwave transmitters, used in satellite earth sta-tions, and troposcatter terminals, used to reflect microwave signals by bouncing them off a layer of the atmosphere called the troposphere. Aydin also manufactured microwave radio sets or systems installed in repeater towers of microwave line-of-sight networks. Aydin's data communications business, including systems used in the space shuttle, cruise missile, and F-15 airplane, generated 30 percent of the company's dollar volume in 1976. Its digital color display terminals, used mainly by electric utilities for power dispatch and control, accounted for 17 percent of revenue. The remaining 14 percent came from support components: precision-fabricated electronic cabinets, high-quality printed circuit boards, and miscellaneous vinyl components.

Aydin lost some luster when sales dropped in 1978 and it was found in 1979 to have violated federal securities law by inflating its 1975 profits. Nevertheless, the company grew rapidly in this period. Its net sales rose from $47.4 million in 1978 to $102.9 million in 1980, and its net profit grew from $2.7 million to $7.3 million in this period.

The company's new products as well as its overseas expansion contributed to growth in the late 1970s. Introduced in 1977, Aydin's Model 5216 display computer was generating significant business in varied government programs, including the cruise missile mission-planning system. About 40 percent of the company's sales were in overseas markets. By late 1979 Aydin had a backlog of about $135 million, including $73.5 million in subcontracts from a subsidiary of Litton Industries for troposcatter equipment earmarked for Saudi Arabia's army, and $23 million for a communications system for the Egyptian national railway. To accommodate the company's growth, Aydin constructed a new facility in San Jose, California in 1979 to house its microwave division, and by the end of the year was about 40 percent physically located in the San Francisco Bay area.

After experiencing a growth in revenue of 60 percent in 1980, Aydin's sales volume slumped to $100.4 million in 1981, but its net profit remained a comfortable $6.3 million. In a *New York Times* interview that year, Hakimoglu conceded that small orders "come on a more regular basis, so they are more stable," but indicated the company would continue going after major contracts, such as a military communications system in Saudi Arabia that would bring in $100 million worth of business.

The company bolstered its financial position by focusing on nuclear-fusion electronics, a field it entered in 1977. This sector accounted for $15 million of Aydin's sales in 1980. To enhance the company's position in the field, it purchased the fusion-electronics unit of Gulton Industries in 1981. By 1982 the company had also entered into the manufacture of radar subassemblies. Also in that year, Aydin became a partner in a Turkish manufacturing joint venture called Havelsan-Aydin and received a contract from Western Union to provide up to 24 earth stations.

Although reduced federal funds for the fusion-electronics field in 1982 threw off Aydin's predictions, the company's sales rebounded in 1982, reaching $124.3 million. The company's net profit rose to $10.3 million, and its backlog of business to $192 million, including $100 million in troposcatter systems for an unidentified Middle Eastern country and an unidentified South American country. Telecommunications accounted for 59 percent of sales in 1982. Color display terminals and computers accounted for another 29 percent and included sales of Patriot, the first high-resolution color monitor made in the United States.

Big-Ticket Defense Contracts, 1984–1990

Aydin's sales grew to a record $153 million in 1983 and its profit to an all-time high of $15.8 million, but the following year saw an abrupt halt to its growth. Hakimoglu blamed the company's downturn to a drop in international orders caused by a surge in the value of the dollar and the decline in oil prices that made oil-exporting countries no longer viable buyers.

Aydin then redirected its efforts toward the federal government, including developing tactical air-defense radar systems for the military. The company, for example, built the airborne data-communications equipment for the Patriot missile.

By 1986 the company's efforts to focus on marketing its products in the United States paid off. Sales to the U.S. government reached 44 percent of the 1986 total of $136.9 million and included equipment and systems on board almost every major missile, aircraft, or weapons systems in the world. Aydin also enjoyed an 80 percent market share of color displays to the electric utilities. Telecommunications accounted for 57 percent of sales in 1986; computer equipment and systems for 35 percent; and radars, electronic warfare, and support components to 8 percent. U.S. industrial clients accounted for 28 percent and overseas sales for another 28 percent. Six company divisions were outside Philadelphia (with head offices having moved from Fort Washington to Horsham) and three in San Jose; a subsidiary was in Great Britain.

In 1987 Aydin won a five-year, $94-million Air Force contract to provide a system to train pilots and test airborne radar warning and electronic countermeasures. Delivery of this AN/MST-TIA multiple-threat emitter simulator began in 1990. As the Reagan Administration's military buildup continued, 1987 sales by Aydin to U.S. government agencies came to 61 percent of the total. Revenues reached an apex of $170 million in 1988. With the cold war coming to an end, revenues sank to $142 million in 1990. Nevertheless, Aydin's backlog reached a record $311 million as the company signed a contract with the Turkish government for a set of mobile radar complexes expected to contribute $200 million in sales over a six-year period. The Havelsen-Aydin joint venture was expected to provide about $86 million of this total.

Difficulties in the 1990s

By 1992 Aydin's backlog of work had fallen to $175 million, and sales to the U.S. military came to only 27 percent of the total, compared to 54 percent for exports, including 34 percent to the Turkish government alone. Aydin created a new business segment: environmental consultation, remediation, and remediation equipment. It also planned to step up sales efforts in its foreign and software businesses.

The company suffered a blow in 1993, when the army fined it $2 million for faking test results showing that a battlefield radio system Aydin built worked under high temperature conditions. This system was used extensively during the Persian Gulf War and was found to be so deficient that soldiers had to hook up air conditioning units to them in the field and wear cold weather gear to operate them. Two company managers were convicted on multiple felony counts of conspiracy and making false statements in connection with the fraudulent tests. It cost Aydin $9.4 million to settle a suit brought by the federal government and the company incurred a $5 million net loss for the year. The company also received bad publicity when Hakimoglu sued two Atlantic City casinos in 1993, alleging that they caused him to lose $8 million by getting him drunk.

Sales remained flat from 1993 to 1995, ranging between $140 million and $142 million. The company earned $5 million in 1994 and $3.9 million in 1995. In 1995 the Turkish subsidiary accounted for no less than 82 percent of net income. That year sales to U.S. government agencies came to 32 percent of the total and export sales to 41 percent. A new division, Aydin Telecom, was formed in 1994 to manufacture, market, and sell digital wireless telephony equipment and systems, digital telephony networks for video cable systems, network access equipment, satellite modems, TDMA next-generation equipment transcoders, and multiplexers.

Aydin announced in mid-1995 that the company was being put up for sale. There were no immediate developments, but in May 1996 the electronic manufacturing concern EA Industries Inc. announced it had purchased 11.7 percent of the common stock from Hakimoglu for $10.75 million. Hakimoglu resigned as chairman and chief executive officer of Aydin and was replaced by I. Gary Bard, who had previously served two stints as an Aydin executive. Aydin and EA Industries subsequently held merger talks that ended in October 1996 without an agreement. EA said it had made "a fair and reasonable offer," but Aydin described the proposal as "inadequate." In an interview with the *Philadelphia Business Journal* shortly after assuming the helm, Bard said, "What you're seeing now represents a culmination of the past poor judgments. Aydin in the past has not done well for a high-technology company. I think its investments have been made in the wrong direction."

Bard went on to blame the company's poor earnings on bad management, which he said over the years had focused too much attention on technology without considering whether there were specific markets that would want specific products. He also said the company had made a mistake by using its reserves to buy back stock and thus raise the price of its shares instead of investing the money in product. He said that he planned to increase market research, focusing first on the question of whether there is demand before creating a supply. A good part of future investment and marketing, he indicated, would be in the telecommunications area. Bard said one potential growth area was vehicle-tracking technology, which allows organizations to put a device in cars that will permit the vehicle location to be tracked.

Aydin's stock fell to a year-long low in September on the news that company president Donald S. Taylor had resigned. Bard said that he and Taylor had been unable to see the company's future from the same perspective and that the company charter would probably be modified to eliminate the need for a president. Aydin ended 1996 with sharply reduced net sales of $116.6 million, of which U.S. government agencies accounted for 33 percent, export and foreign sales for 41 percent, and U.S. commercial and industrial business for 26 percent. Aydin lost $14.8 million during the year.

Principal Subsidiaries

Aydin, S.A. (Argentina, 19%); Aydin Europe Limited (Great Britain); Aydin Foreign Sales Limited (Guam); Aydin Investments, Inc.; Aydin Zailim ve Elektronik Sanayi A.S. (Turkey).

Further Reading

"Aydin Corporation," *Modern Data,* September 1975, p. 22.
"Aydin Corp. (AYD)," *Wall Street Transcript,* June 8, 1987, pp. 85795–85796.
"Aydin May Find Last Year's Act Tough to Follow," *New York Times,* August 17, 1981, p. 4D.
Campanella, Frank W., "Better Account?" *Barron's,* November 19, 1979, pp. 58–59, 62.
"Multiple Threat Emitter Simulator Ready for Delivery to Air Force," *Aviation Week and Space Technology,* October 22, 1990, p. 62.
Stets, Dan, "Aydin Says It's for Sale," *Philadelphia Inquirer,* July 4, 1995, pp. 1C–2C.
Troxell, Thomas N., Jr., "Operating Results of Aydin Beamed toward Fresh Advance," *Barron's,* October 1, 1977, pp. 37–38.
——, "Record Display," *Barron's,* March 4, 1983, pp. 49–50.
Turner, Dan, "San Jose Firm Fined $2 Million for Faking Tests," *San Francisco Chronicle,* January 8, 1994, pp. 15A–16A.
Webber, Maura, "The Man Who Would Save Aydin Rose through Ranks," *Philadelphia Business Journal,* September 6, 1995, p. 1B.

—Robert Halasz

Banco Itaú S.A.

Rua Boa Vista 176
CEP 01-092-900
01013 Sao Paulo, SP
Brazil
(55) 11 237 3000
Fax: (55) 11 277 1044
Web site: http://www.itau.com.br

Public Company
Incorporated: 1944 as Banco Central de Crédito
Employees: 31,368
Total Assets: R$35.06 billion (1996)
Stock Exchanges: Brazil
SICs: 6000 Depository Institutions; 6021 National
   Commercial Banks; 6211 Security Brokers & Dealers

Headquartered in Brazil's financial capital of Sao Paulo, Banco Itaú S.A. ranks second only to Banco Bradesco S.A. among the nation's largest nongovernmental financial institutions. Although not the biggest of Brazil's banks, it was, in 1996, one of the few ever to have been listed among *Euromoney's* ranking of "The World's 100 Best Banks." By the mid-1990s, Itaú boasted more than 1,800 branches in 455 cities; more than 7,700 automated teller machines (ATMs); and an innovative telebanking network. With more than 16.7 million checking, savings, and mutual fund accounts, Itaú claims an estimated 11 percent of the Brazilian retail banking market. Its operations are segmented into four primary groups: Itaúcorp is dedicated to serving corporate accounts; Itaú "Empresas" deals with mid-sized firms; branch banks offer nationwide access to individual accounts via ATM, telephone, and personal service; and Itaú Private Bank offers portfolio management to wealthy individuals. Banco Itaú's Itaúseg insurance subsidiary holds an eight percent share of the nation's insurance market.

Itaú is the lead affiliate of Investimentos Itaú S.A., also known as Itaúsa, one of Brazil's most profitable private sector conglomerates. The parent company ranks among *Fortune* magazine's ranking of the world's 500 largest corporations.

Itaúsa's interests include insurance, building materials, chemicals, electronics, and real estate, as well as banking.

Origins in 1940s

Banco Itaú was founded in Sao Paulo January 2, 1945 as Banco Central de Crédito. It was then as small as the law allowed, with only ten million cruzeiros (US $513,000) in capital. But growth came quickly. Over the course of its first decade-and-a-half in business, Banco Central de Crédito expanded to rank among Brazil's 75 largest banks, having more than 30 branch outlets and doubling its capital by 1953. The institution changed its name to Banco Federal de Crédito that year to reflect its augmented stature.

This period in the bank's history was played out against an environment of political and economic instability. The near-dictatorship of Getzlio Vargas in the 1930s and early 1940s yielded to an experiment in democracy from 1945 to 1960. The nation enjoyed robust industrial growth and expansion of infrastructure during Juscelino Kubitschek de Oliveira's term in office in the late 1950s, when Brazil's GNP rose six percent to seven percent annually. But that growth was financed in large part by a spiraling national debt, which almost doubled from 1956 to 1961 and sent the nation on an inflationary roller coaster ride that would reign almost continuously through the remainder of the 20th century.

By the early 1960s, triple-digit annual percentage rates of inflation, rapid currency devaluation, and a flat gross domestic product had forced the nation's banks to "index" many transactions to the rate of inflation. For example, savings accounts would guarantee a return of a given number of percentage points above inflation, instead of a particular interest rate.

From the outset, Banco Federal de Crédito concentrated its operations in Brazil's urban areas, especially those in the southeast. This strategy would prove wise, for the nation experienced a profound population shift from the outlying areas to the cities in the last half of the 20th century. By the early 1980s, substantially more than two-thirds of the country's people were urbanites. The bank's "hometown," Sao Paulo, would grow to become one of the world's most populous cities.

Company Perspectives:

Banco Itaú's corporate objectives are "to be the leading bank in performance, recognized as being sound and reliable, standing out because of its aggressive use of marketing, its advanced technology and its highly capable staff, committed to total quality and to customer satisfaction."

Mergers and Acquisitions in the 1960s and 1970s

Itaú's growth to prominence among Brazil's financial institutions was, in large part, due to its participation in a long period of consolidation in the banking industry. Following a major reorganization in the late 1950s and early 1960s, Banco Federal de Crédito pursued several mergers and acquisitions that expanded both its capitalization and its geographical reach. The program began with a 1964 union with Banco Itaú to form Banco Federal Itaú S.A. Two years later, the group added Banco Sul Americano S.A. This marriage not only lengthened the bank's name to Banco Federal Itaú Sul Americano S.A. but also brought its total roster of branches to more than 180 and increased its capital to US $6.7 million. A 1969 merger with Banco da América catapulted the growing institution into Brazil's top ten, with nearly 275 branches and US $14.8 million in capital.

A military *coup d'état* in 1964 ushered in a period of government-led economic planning that brought about "the Brazilian miracle" of the late 1960s and early 1970s. Under the Castelo Branco administration from 1964 to 1966, the country entered an exceptional era of rising standards of living, low inflation, and economic expansion. This trend continued into the early 1970s despite a series of political crises.

Following the acquisitions of Banco Aliança S.A. and Banco Português do Brasil S.A. in the early 1970s, the institution shortened its name to the more manageable and memorable Banco Itaú S.A. in 1973. A 1974 union with Banco União Comercial made it Brazil's second largest nongovernmental bank, with 561 branch locations throughout the country.

1980s Bring Renewed Economic Challenges

Bank patrons countered rampant inflation in the early 1980s by making daily transfers of funds to accounts with higher yields. Along with many of Brazil's leading banks, Itaú made its services more accessible to accommodate the increased number of transactions, more than tripling the number of branch outlets from the mid-1970s to the mid-1990s.

In an effort to combat inflation without slowing economic growth, Brazil's Sarney administration ratified the "Cruzado Plan" in 1986. This strategy embraced a new fixed rate currency, the cruzado, as well as price and wage freezes. The government even limited banking hours to just five midday hours to hinder activity. These new imperatives forced many Brazilian banks to rationalize heretofore generous staffing levels. Tens, if not hundreds, of thousands of bank employees were put out of work. Due in part to its acquisition of Banco Pinto de

Mahalhãhes in 1985, Itaú bucked this trend for a brief period. Its employment levels actually rose from 74,700 in 1986 to 84,200 in 1988. But in the years to come, the bank reduced its employee roster by more than half, to less than 32,000 by 1996.

New Frontiers in the 1990s

Technology helped increase the productivity, efficiency, and service quotient of the workers who remained. Investment in automation began in 1979 and by the early 1990s Itaú's electronic services included telebanking via the Itaúfone, Itaúfax, and Bankfone networks and Itaú Bankline for online computer commerce. The institution's vast series of more than 7,700 ATMs included nearly 800 machines installed on customers' premises. By 1996, substantially more than half of Itaú's total teller transactions were made through one of these self-service outlets.

The 1990s also brought international expansion at Itaú. Aided by the creation of the Mercosur free-trade zone, the company created a subsidiary in neighboring Argentina in 1994 and announced plans to open 35 branches there. The bank also launched subsidiaries in Europe and Grand Cayman as well as a branch outlet in New York City by mid-decade. Affiliations with some of the world's largest and most influential banks helped raise Banco Itaú's presence on the world stage and diversify its activities from the core retail banking. The institution forged a joint venture investment bank in Brazil with U.S.-based Bankers Trust New York Corp. in 1995 and purchased Banco Frances y Brasiliero from France's Credit Lyonnais for US $335 million that same year. In 1997, Itaúsa merged its insurance company Itaú Seguros (Itaúseg) with Banco Itaú, thereby giving the banking subsidiary an eight percent share of the Brazilian insurance industry.

In mid-1995, Brazilian President Fernando Henrique Cardoso launched a new strategy to restrain inflation. Known as the Real Plan, this program tied the value of the Brazilian dollar to that of the U.S. dollar. The plan succeeded in cutting annual inflation rates from nearly 1,800 percent in 1989 to about ten percent by the end of 1996. The news was not so good for some Brazilian banks dependent on "the float"—described by *Institutional Investor's* Bill Hinchberger as "the high interest earned by investing non-interest-paying deposits and other low-cost money in high-yielding government bonds—for profits." Bank failures and reorganizations cost the government an estimated R $30 billion (US $30 billion) in 1994 and 1995.

Itaú had indeed relied on the float. According to analysis by Baring Securities quoted in Hinchberger's 1994 article, more than two-fifths of Itaú's 1993 revenues were generated via the strategy—more than the bank's credit revenues. But with US $20.5 billion in assets in 1995, Banco Itaú remained one of the nation's most well-capitalized institutions. Furthermore, *Moody's* rating service has called Itaú "the most efficient of the large banks," and Thomson BankWatch Inc. praised it as "among the best capitalized in the [Brazilian] banking system." In 1996, it was ranked among *The Banker's* Top 500 Banks worldwide and Top 100 Latin institutions.

Principal Subsidiaries

Banco Francês e Brasileiro S.A.; Itau Bank, Ltd. (Cayman); Itaú Corretora S.A.; Itauleasing S.A.; Banco Itaú Argentina S.A.; Itaú Capitalização S.A.; Itaú Bankers Trust S.A. (54%); Banco Itaú Europa S.A. (35%); Credicard S.A. (33%); Itauprevidência S.A.

Further Reading

"Banco Itaú Takes Over Control of Itaúseg," *South American Business Information,* April 18, 1997, n.p.

Brandao, Ignacio de Loyola, *Itau, 50 Anos,* Sao Paulo, SP, Brasil: DBA - Dorea Books and Art, 1995.

"Brazil's Banking Reform: Three in One," *The Economist,* June 6, 1964, pp. 1156–1157.

Fischer, Rodolfo Henrique, *Banco Itau, A Strategic Analysis,* MIT: thesis, 1990.

Hieronymus, William, "An Awful Lot of Queueing in Brazil," *Euromoney,* March 1986, pp. 62–63.

Kraus, James R., "BT Forming Alliance with Credit Lyonnais," *American Banker,* July 6, 1995, pp. 1–2.

——, "BT Teams Up with Brazil's Banco Itau To Launch Investment Bank in Sao Paulo," *American Banker,* May 22, 1995, p. 6.

Lake, David, "Banco Itau Creates Hardware and Software To Handle Complex Transactions in Brazil," *American Banker,* December 19, 1988, pp. 10–11.

Moffett, Matt, "Brazil's Banks Return from Near Collapse," *The Wall Street Journal,* March 7, 1997, p. A8.

Robinson, Danielle, "How Safe Are Brazil's Banks?," *Euromoney,* September 1995, pp. 121–123.

Rubenstein, Ed, "And for Our Next Crisis," *Economist,* April 20, 1996, p. 65.

Sieniawski, Michael, "Banking in Booming Brazil," *Burroughs Clearing House,* December 1960, pp. 44–46, 94–96.

Taylor, Robert, "Cardoso's Next Battle," *The Banker,* January 1997, pp. 59–60.

—April Dougal Gasbarre

"Leading the retread industry worldwide"

Bandag, Inc.

2905 North Highway 61
Muscatine, Iowa 52761-5886
U.S.A.
(319) 262-1400
Fax: (319) 262-1284
Web site: http://www.bandag.com

Public Company
Incorporated: 1957
Employees: 2,591
Sales: $769 million (1996)
Stock Exchanges: New York; Midwest
SICs: 3011 Tires & Inner Tubes; 3559 Special Industry
  Machinery, Not Elsewhere Classified

Bandag, Inc. is the leading supplier of rubber used by its franchisees for the retreading of tires, mostly for trucks and buses. The company manufactures precured tread rubber, equipment, and supplies for the retreading of tires by means of a patented "cold" bonding process. During the early 1990s Bandag outstripped 31 other automotive parts companies in profitability, with a five-year average return on equity of 30.2 percent. The company and its licensees had 1,383 franchisees worldwide in more than 120 countries in 1996.

Early Developments, 1957–1970

Roy J. Carver of Muscatine, Iowa, was the owner of a family manufacturing firm named Carver Pump Co. when, on a business trip to West Germany in 1957, he learned about the "cold-cure" tire-retreading process invented by Bernhard Nowak. This process cured tire treads in one step and bonded them to old tire casings in another step. Because it employed temperatures lower than those used in other retreading processes, the casings were less likely to be damaged, thereby allowing durability greater than that of conventional recaps and thus cutting cost per mile. Carver, who had learned the tire business by changing flats in his father's shop, was an entrepreneur willing to take a flyer on any number of schemes, and he bought the

U.S. rights to the process from Nowak. The Bandag name combined Nowak's initials (BAN) with "D" for his home town (Darmstadt) and "AG" for the German abbreviation for "incorporated." (It also, probably not coincidentally, approximated "bandage.")

Back in Muscatine, Carver opened Bandag in a dilapidated former sauerkraut plant. He found that, given the usual problems with a start-up business, particularly one involving technical innovations, tire retreading was no easy road to riches. Carver nearly bankrupted the family pump company to develop the Nowak method commercially. "More than once it was a case of 'get some money or fold camp,'" a company executive later told a *Financial World* reporter. This man remembered asking suppliers for loans payable with notes that converted to Bandag stock, adding that those who held on to the notes eventually became millionaires.

One technical problem was finding a way to apply uniform pressure on tire casings when retreads were being bonded to them. Carver himself came up with a solution by inventing a flexible rubber envelope capable of fitting over tires of any size. Another problem was solved when his research-and-development engineer formulated a more effective rubber-gum mixture to replace the bonding cement holding together the casing and retread. Carver received U.S. patents on the cold-recapping process during 1961–1962.

By fiscal 1963 (ending May 31, 1963) Bandag had turned the corner to profitability, earning $32,024 in net income on net sales of $1,910,187. These figures rose steadily, and by 1968, when the company went public, its facilities included three plants in Muscatine and a fourth in Shawinigan, Quebec. In that year Bandag had net income of $1.3 million on net sales of $13.5 million and marketed about one-quarter of its shares of common stock at $12 a share. Soon three other plants were opened, in Oxford, North Carolina; in Abilene, Texas; and in Lanklaar, Belgium.

Impressive Growth in the 1970s

By 1971 Bandag held about ten percent of the U.S. truck tire-retreading market and had a worldwide network of more

Company Perspectives:

"Our mission is to be the market leader in every market served by offering our customers clearly outstanding and unique products and services. As the market leader, we are dedicated to constantly and forever improving quality, service and customer satisfaction. We believe that continually improving the system of production and delivery of services and products will improve quality and reduce costs. This ultimately will enhance our competitive position, resulting in outstanding long-term growth and profitability."

than 500 franchised dealers, with some one-third of its sales being made abroad. The company sold its franchisees precured rubber and auxiliary supplies and equipment to retread worn tires in their own shops. It also was manufacturing and selling buffers, pressure chambers, and other equipment used by its franchisees.

In 1973 Bandag entered into the business of distributing and remanufacturing replacement parts for the heavy-duty vehicle industry by acquiring three companies for stock. One of these was Master Processing, manufacturers of specialty rubber compounds and high-technology industrial hoses. Eight other companies were subsequently acquired by 1978. In December 1973 Bandag also established a subsidiary, Heavy Duty Parts, Inc., to sell replacement parts for trucks and buses through its own distribution network. That year Bandag's net sales reached $95.1 million. During the first half of the 1970s the company achieved a five-year annual sales growth rate of 32 percent and annual earnings growth rate of 43 percent. It commanded about 75 percent of the cold-rubber market and was retreading the tires on about 20 percent of all U.S. trucks in 1975. That year its sales came to $169.9 million and its earnings amounted to $19 million.

Although passenger tires were accounting for only three to four percent of its business, in 1976 Bandag launched a national television advertising campaign with a 30-second commercial running on all three national networks. This attempt to carve out a share of the passenger car, pickup, or van retreading market was not successful. In 1980 Bandag held less than one percent of the passenger car tire-retreading market.

Bandag's profits dipped in 1977, when it earned $18.4 million on revenues of $200.1 million, but the company maintained that this was due to its policy that year of encouraging its franchisees to reduce their inventories. The following year brought a new surge in sales and profits, partly because of the rise in popularity of radial tires, a retreading market in which Bandag characterized itself as dominant. The company treated its shareholders well, raising the dividend each year after 1976, when payments were first made.

By 1980 Bandag was the world's largest producer of tread rubber and retreading equipment. It held an estimated 20 percent of the retreading market and one-third of the bus and truck retreading market. This sector of its business was being carried

on by eight manufacturing plants (including one in South Africa) and about 1,000 franchised dealers, of which some 250 of them were abroad in 92 countries. The company also maintained 16 off-road tire-retreading centers in the United States. Heavy Duty Parts was selling more than 60,000 different items and had 43 distribution centers in the United States. Company revenues in 1980 totaled $337 million and net earnings rose to $27.4 million, both records. Heavy Duty Parts, however, while accounting for about one-fifth of sales, was contributing only two percent of profits.

Reorganization in the 1980s

Roy Carver had been leaving management to his subordinates, enjoying the good life as he flew around the world in his white Lear jet. He also owned two yachts, a 25,000-acre ranch in Belize, and a villa on the French Riviera. When he suddenly died of a heart attack in 1981, there were no succession plans, but his widow, who controlled most of the estate's 43 percent of the company shares, backed her youngest son, Martin. The 32-year-old business school graduate was duly elected chairman and chief executive officer.

Martin Carver later recalled, "Top management didn't welcome me with open arms. I was surprised by the level of resistance I got. It was fierce." This opposition was understandable, for Carver promptly fired the managers hired to carry out a plan to diversify Bandag that he called "kind of stupid" and refocused the company on its core business of retreading tires. He also sacked the president, taking the title himself, eliminated employment contracts, which he said made people lazy, and recalled executive cars. In December 1981 Bandag sold Heavy Duty Parts for $11.5 million in cash and securities. The unprofitable two off-the-road retreading subsidiaries, which accounted for about five percent of company sales, were sold in 1982 for $2.5 million, principally in cash. In 1984 Master Processing was sold to a privately held company for an undisclosed sum, and the Empex Hose division was sold for $3.6 million.

By 1984 Bandag held about 40 percent of the U.S. truck retreading market and 70 percent of the radial retreading truck and bus market. High-quality radial retreads were selling for only about 30 percent of the price of a new tire and yet were said to perform much the same. Specialty rubber compounds and industrial hoses accounted for less than ten percent of company sales. Return on equity averaged 22 percent in the first half of the 1980s. A stock repurchase program reduced shares outstanding by 40 percent between 1982 and 1990. The Carver family further solidified its grip on the firm by distributing shares of a new Class B common stock, with ten times the voting power of the old shares, in 1987. The action immediately raised the Carver family's voting power from 37 to 65 percent of the total. Bandag's stock price rose tenfold between the early 1980s and the early 1990s.

By the end of the 1980s Bandag had doubled the size of its dealer force and held nearly 50 percent of the U.S. truck tire-retreading market. Carver's style of management won him widespread recognition. He expected managers to know the names of all of their workers, regardless of how many they supervised. Carver himself visited every Bandag dealer in the

United States. A Formula Ford driver in his youth, he set a world land speed record for diesel trucks in a specially prepared vehicle to promote Bandag's retreads. *Financial World* gave him an award in 1989, the year he vowed to make Bandag "the best company in the world." That year the company achieved a 41 percent return on equity, with net income of $75.9 million on revenues of $535 million. Forty-two percent of its sales were abroad.

Developments in the 1990s

During this period Bandag shook up its European franchising network, replacing exclusive distributors who charged high prices and never worried much about volume with aggressive new entrepreneurs paying about $150,000 apiece for their units who even made "house calls" in $60,000 Mercedes trucks filled with tires and equipment. By 1992 Bandag's share of Western Europe's retread market had risen from five to 20 percent. That year the company's stock reached an all-time high and was split 2 for 1.

For the first time since 1977, Bandag's sales and profits dipped in 1993, although only slightly. Carver blamed the problem on the high costs of developing a tougher, higher-priced new retread called the Eclipse, molded to curve onto tire casings in a relaxed state. Initially forecast to account for half of company sales by 1995, the Eclipse was slow to reach the market and was only being produced by the Muscatine and Oxford plants by that year. European earnings continued to be disappointing despite the company's larger market share. Net sales rebounded to $650.6 million and net income totaled $94 million in 1994, levels surpassed once again in 1995.

In 1992 Carver adopted for Bandag the total-quality management principles developed by the late Edwards Deming. This formula included long-range planning, statistical monitoring of process control to make manufacturing more predictable, just-in-time delivery of inventory, greater responsibility of individual workers for their output, and more attention to customer needs. Among the changes was a pay plan that eliminated bonuses for executives, managers, and salespeople. "The concern is that if I'm working my butt off, I should get paid more than a slacker," Carver told *Financial World.* "But a system that's well designed will not have slackers."

Bandag's revenues rose from $755.3 million in 1995 to $769 million in 1996, but its net income fell from $97 million to $81.6 million. Carver attributed this development to soft sales trends and higher operating expenses. One of the company's problems was a legal dispute with Treadco, the largest U.S. tire retreader and formerly Bandag's largest franchisee. This company was in the process of terminating its 26 franchises. In addition, Tredcor, Bandag's largest franchisee in South Africa, did not renew its roughly 30 franchise contracts because of disputes over pricing and its marketing of a competing retread. During the year Bandag introduced a new tire-management system and two new product lines.

Of Bandag's 1996 revenues, tread rubber, cushion gum, and retreading supplies constituted 91 percent. Sales in the United States accounted for 64 percent and European sales accounted for 17 percent. About 50 European franchisees were retreading tires using the Vakuum Vulk Method, another cold-process precured retreading system for which Bandag owned worldwide rights. The company was manufacturing precured tread rubber, cushion gum, and related supplies in manufacturing plants that it owned in the United States, Belgium, Brazil, Canada, Indonesia, Malaysia, Mexico, New Zealand, and South Africa. It was also manufacturing pressure chambers, tire-casing analyzers, buffers, tire builders, tire-handling systems, and other items of equipment used in the Bandag and Vakuum Vulk retreading methods.

At the close of 1996 Bandag had no long-term debt. As of March 1997 the Carver family owned shares of common stock constituting 75 percent of the votes entitled to be cast in the election of directors and other corporate matters.

Principal Subsidiaries

Bandag A.G. (Switzerland); Bandag B.V. (Netherlands); Bandag de Mexico, S.A. de C.V. (Mexico); Bandag do Brasil Ltda. (Brazil); Bandag Canada Ltd. (Canada); Bandag Europe N.V. (Belgium); Bandag Incorporated of S.A. (Proprietary) Limited (South Africa); Bandag Licensing Corporation; Bandag New Zealand Limited (New Zealand); VV-System AG (Switzerland).

Further Reading

"Bandag Gets a Bounce Out of Retreads," *Business Week,* May 22, 1971, pp. 44–45.

"Bandag Incorporated," *Wall Street Transcript,* August 10, 1981, pp. 62,610–62,611.

"Bandag Profits Rebound as Dealer Orders Mount," *Barron's,* October 2, 1978, p. 41.

"Breaking into European Markets by Breaking the Rules," *Business Week,* January 20, 1992, pp. 88–89.

Byrne, Harlan S., "Bandag Inc.," *Barron's,* January 29, 1990, pp. 60–61.

——, "Bandag Inc.," *Barron's,* April 26, 1993, pp. 40–41.

Croghan, Lore, "Hot Cars and Cold Rubber," *Financial World,* March 28, 1995, pp. 52, 54, 58.

Fierman, Jacquelyn, "How to Make Money in Mature Markets," *Fortune,* November 25, 1985, p. 48.

"Financial World's Silver Winners," *Financial World,* April 4, 1989, p. 74.

Gray, Ralph, "Bandag Put Its Retreads into National TV Spotlight," *Advertising Age,* April 5, 1976, p. 12.

Lazo, Shirley A., "Bandag Keeps Its Payout String Alive," *Barron's,* November 18, 1996, p. 70.

Miller, Joe, "Retread Giant Got Start in Iowa River Town," *Rubber & Plastics News,* October 9, 1995, pp. 44–45.

Pacey, Margaret D., "Brad Ragan vs. Bandag," *Barron's,* March 24, 1975, pp. 11, 18, 20.

Simon, Ruth, "Minding the Store," *Business Week,* November 4, 1985, pp. 208–209.

Troxell, Thomas N., Jr., "Bandag's Sure Grip," *Barron's,* June 9, 1980, pp. 56–57.

Walser, Clarke L., "Bandag, Incorporated," *Wall Street Today,* March 16, 1970, pp. 19,927–19,928.

—Robert Halasz

BBN Corp.

150 Cambridge Park Drive
Cambridge, Massachusetts 02140 U.S.A.
(617) 873-2000
Fax: (617) 873-5011
Web site: http://www.bbn.com

Public Company
Incorporated: 1953 as Bolt Beranek & Newman, Inc.
Employees: 2,000
Sales: $234.3 million (1996)
Stock Exchanges: New York Boston Cincinnati Midwest
    Pacific Philadelphia
SICs: 3812 Search, Detection, Navigation, Guidance,
    Aeronautical & Nautical Systems & Instruments; 7372
    Prepackaged Software; 7373 Computer Integrated
    Systems Design; 8711 Engineering Services; 8731
    Commercial Physical & Biological Research; 8748
    Business Consulting Services, Not Elsewhere
    Classified

BBN Corp. is a leading provider of Internet services and networking services and solutions to businesses and other organizations and a provider of a range of contract research, development, and consulting services to governmental and other organizations. Known as Bolt Beranek & Newman, Inc. until November 1995, the company first gained recognition for its research and development of computer technologies.

BBN's strategy is to capitalize on its extensive internetworking experience and unique capabilities by offering Internet services with global reach, as well as Internet and intranet business applications solutions. BBN's objective is to create a growing, recurring service revenue base by providing high-bandwidth managed access with managed security and value-added services. Through its research and development activities under government contracts, BBN's strategy is to leverage its advanced network and related technologies into Internet offerings.

Private Company, 1948–1961

Bolt Beranek & Newman began in 1948 as a partnership of two Massachusetts Institute of Technology (MIT) professors: physicist Richard H. Bolt and communications engineer Leo L. Beranek, who had received a consulting contract for the acoustic design of the hall to be built for the United Nations General Assembly. Robert A. Newman, an MIT graduate student in architecture, joined the two shortly after the partnership was established. BBN, which was incorporated in 1953, soon won research contracts in other fields. In the 1950s it was hired by the federal government to seek ways of keeping jet engines quiet enough so that airplanes could land near residential areas. In studying this problem, the company invented a measurement called the "perceived noise decibel" that was still being used in the 1980s.

Other federal contracts followed, because BBN had a reputation for doing the job on time and without cost overruns. The company was hired by the National Aeronautical and Space Administration (NASA) to measure the vibration of the Mercury space capsule during its launch. Later, it was chosen to analyze the famous 18-minute gap in one of the White House tapes involved in the Watergate investigation and also a tape of the assassination of President John F. Kennedy that included gunfire noises, from which BBN concluded that four rather than three bullets had been fired. Much of its work was for the military, including research on reducing submarine noise underwater and devising software for battlefield simulations and communications and computer networks. The firm also was engaged in biomedical technology.

In 1960 BBN was leasing 56,000 square feet of laboratory space in Cambridge, Massachusetts, and smaller facilities in Los Angeles and in Downers Grove, Illinois. The firm had 189 employees and earned $183,756 on a little more than $2 million in income in fiscal 1960 (the year ended June 30, 1960). It made its initial public offering of stock in 1961, seeking to sell 160,000 shares—90,000 for its own account—at $12 a share. Beranek remained the company's president and chief executive officer until 1967, and Bolt was its chairman until 1976.

Computing Pioneer in the 1960s

In the late 1950s BBN devised a time-sharing system for computers when they were still scarce and expensive, forming a subsidiary called Telcomp to market the system. Telcomp was the first company to sell computer time shares. One of its clients was Massachusetts General Hospital, which used the system for keeping medical records. Telcomp, which was sold in 1971, also placed time-share terminals in six high schools in the Boston area. BBN also was credited with inventing electronic mail, designing the first modem for connecting to computers through a telephone line and demonstrating the first computer-based communication system in 1964.

During this period, while under contract with the Department of Defense, BBN also developed packet switching, a method for making computer-to-computer interactions more reliable and efficient. Out of this development work in 1968 BBN created ARPAnet, the largest, fastest packet-switching network in the world, connecting more than 100 computers of different makes and thousands of terminals in a massive data-communications network. Designed to ensure that government and military communications would continue even if telephone lines were knocked out in a nuclear war, ARPAnet was a forerunner of the Internet system.

On the basis of its expertise in underwater acoustical research, BBN also became a contender in marine science. In 1967 BBN and the steamship line Moore and McCormack Co. Inc. created a subsidiary to explore such commercial possibilities in ocean science and technology as the development and operation of stable floating platforms for research or mineral exploration. Two years later it acquired Moore & McCormack's share of the venture for $500,000 and another Moore & McCormack subsidiary for $3.5 million. Under the auspices of BBN-Geosciences Corp., a subsidiary, marine research grew to account, in the mid-1970s, for as much as one-quarter of corporate revenue from continuing services.

By 1970 BBN had raised its annual sales to $18.8 million. Its office and laboratory space in Cambridge had expanded to 120,000 square feet, and it was also leasing space in New York City, San Francisco, two southern California sites, Downers Grove, East Orange, New Jersey, and Arlington, Virginia. It also held a minority interest in a West German company. However, its net income came to only $252,300 in fiscal 1970, and most of its revenues were coming from consulting and research rather than from the products its brainpower had helped to develop.

Seeking Commercial Rewards in the 1970s

In 1973 the company formed Telenet Communications Corp. to exploit the commercial potential of packet switching. Unfortunately, this venture proved to be ahead of its time. Telenet generated too little cash for BBN to expand the network, which was necessary to win more business. The parent company's interest in Telenet was reduced to 37 percent in 1976 and about 25 percent in 1978. When Telenet was acquired by General Telephone & Electronics Corp. the following year, BBN received payment in GTE stock, which it sold in 1981 for $15.1 million.

A finance-oriented entrepreneur within BBN, Stephen R. Levy, became its president in 1976. Sales increased from $30.2 million in fiscal 1978 to $37.7 million in 1979 and $46.9 million in 1980, but net income fluctuated wildly, from a deficit of $397,000 in 1978 to a profit of $10.1 million in 1979 but only $2.9 million in 1980. In fiscal 1980, 84 percent of company revenues came from consulting, research, and development services in acoustics and computer-science systems and software. Office and laboratory space in Cambridge now totaled 313,000 square feet. Officers and directors held 24 percent of the outstanding shares of common stock in September 1980, while financier George Soros and two of his companies held a combined 17 percent.

By this time BBN was transforming itself from contract work, mostly for the government, to the development and exploitation of a gradually broadening stream of products to be designed, manufactured, and marketed by BBN subsidiaries. Three such subsidiaries were formed between 1978 and 1980. BBN Computer was designing, manufacturing, and selling the high-performance communications multiprocessor Pluribus and packet-switching C/30 and a time-sharing system, C/70, to help computer programmers design software. Manufacture of these products was in Cambridge and Hong Kong. BBN Instruments was producing and marketing a line of accelerometers, portable noise monitors, and digital vibration analyzers. BBN Information Management specialized in software packages, including an electronic-mail system called Infomail.

This corporate structure insulated laboratory researchers from commercial pressures in order to combat poor morale, which had led some of BBN's stars to move to other think tanks. Computer technology accounted for 57 percent of company revenues in fiscal 1979 and acoustics for 43 percent.

Still Dependent on the Military in the 1980s

BBN Instruments was sold in 1983 to Vibro-Meter Corp. for an undisclosed sum of cash. Later that year Wang Laboratories Inc. contracted BBN to design and build a system linking computers over telephone lines for a 199-city network, using its latest packet-switching technology. In 1984 BBN established a $3.1 million limited partnership to pay for development of a systems program to integrate advanced database management and graphics functions for scientists and engineers. The following year the company developed a special microprocessor, dubbed the butterfly chip, to coordinate the problem-solving efforts of parallel processing. The largest of these systems was capable of running 60 million instructions per second and cost about $1.2 million. It was used by various government agencies in robot control, artificial intelligence, vision processing, and battle management for the Navy.

Some of these ventures had to be abandoned because of heavy competition from other companies or poor marketing and servicing. Packet switching remained BBN's main field of activity, accounting for half of company revenues and two-thirds of profits in fiscal 1987, when about 75 percent of its revenue came from the federal government. This dependence on the military became a major problem with the end of the Cold War. The company lost $25.1 million on revenues of $291.6 million in fiscal 1989—down from its peak of $305 million the previous year—and $34.8 million on revenues of $261.9 million in fiscal 1990. At the end of the latter year its long-term debt had reached $84.7 million. The price of company stock fell from nearly $19 a share in July 1988 to under $8 in May 1989.

Focusing on the Internet in the 1990s

BBN became profitable again in fiscal 1990 and 1991, but it had to cut costs sharply to do so. In 1991 it merged its unprofitable Advanced Computers Inc. unit into other company divisions, suspending development of its next-generation parallel-processing computer, code named Coral. Parallel processing had never brought in revenue of more than $10 million to $12 million a year to the company, despite its potential and high profile. BBN already had significantly downsized the division in 1990 after selling only 14 of its recently developed TC2000 machines to the commercial real-time computing market.

Despite its problems making high technology pay, BBN was excited in the early 1990s by the progress it was making on speech-recognition software. Using Unix computer language, its software could recognize spoken words by processing the sounds into a computer language, follow up a spoken query by searching a data base, and respond with a written answer on the computer screen. This work was being funded by the Department of Defense for the military's automated system for routing and keeping track of personnel and supplies.

In fiscal 1993 BBN's revenues fell by $25 million, and it incurred a loss of $32.3 million. When revenues dropped to $196 million the following year, BBN held its loss to $7.8 million, but only by cutting its work force from 3,200 to 1,600. In 1994 Levy resigned as chief executive officer, turning the job over to George H. Conrades, a highly regarded former IBM executive who had been head of that company's domestic operations. Conrades had been called in to manage LightStream Corp., a joint venture with Ungermann-Bass, Inc. created in 1992 to manufacture and market asynchronous transfer mode (ATM) products, which enable computer networks to carry much more data at faster speeds and can also carry voice and video. LightStream, in which BBN held 80 percent, was sold to Cisco Systems Inc. in 1994 for $120 million.

Conrades brought in a new management team and established three subsidiaries: BBN Software Products, for data-analysis software; BBN Hark Systems, for speech-recognition systems; and BBN Planet, to manage Internet access. A retired Navy admiral was recruited for the company's research-and-development arm, Systems and Technologies, to direct maritime warfare-related programs.

The Internet became BBN's chief focus. Used by an estimated 20 million people in mid-1994, this system, originally mainly for nonprofit communications among academics and researchers, was a natural outgrowth of ARPAnet, the military communications system BBN had devised as a precursor of the Internet. BBN had, in 1993, acquired Nearnet, the New England Internet services provider, from the Massachusetts Institute of Technology. The following year it purchased BARRnet, the largest Internet access provider in the San Francisco area, from Stanford University. Before the end of 1994 BBN also acquired SURAnet, the leading Internet access provider in the Southeast,

bringing the number of its Internet customers to more than 1,100 and making it the largest provider of Internet access and security services to corporations and institutions.

In July 1995 AT&T Corp. bought a minority share of BBN Planet, shortly after concluding a partnership agreement by which BBN Planet would provide a broad array of Internet services to AT&T clients. BBN thus became one of the nation's "backbone" Internet service providers, like IBM Global Network, MCI, and Sprint. As such it was operating trunk telephone lines connecting major regions of the United States and owned major regional computer networks that stored and sent data for its clients. The transaction also gave BBN access to AT&T's fiber-optic network. A January 1996 report by a Cambridge research firm concluded that BBN/AT&T provided the "best security, soup-to-nuts management, and leading ideas for private and guaranteed real-time Internets."

BBN Planet also won a five-year, $55-million contract from America Online, Inc. in March 1995 for 50,000 modems. In October 1996 this transaction was widened into the company's largest contract, a $340-million, four-year pact to provide America Online with 280,000 modems and provisions for additional telecommunications circuits from local and interexchange carriers. In January 1997 the agreement was enhanced further, with BBN set to deliver a minimum of 400,000 modems and associated services over the life of the contract, now valued at $500 million.

BBN's speech-recognition effort also was yielding fruit in 1995. Its software was licensed by IBM to be included in a hardware and software package that automatically answered and directed large number of calls. In addition, AT&T licensed its software as part of a new "virtual call center" for Avis Inc. by which customers would be able to reserve rental cars by telephone, speaking to a computer. With net income of $64.8 million in fiscal 1995, BBN was again an investor favorite, its stock climbing to a high of $40.75 a share during the year, from a low of $4.25 a share in 1993. The company officially shed the Bolt Beranek & Newman name in November 1995, becoming the BBN Corp.

In order to raise more funds for its Internet network, BBN sold all but 15 percent of BBN Domain Corp., a unit making software for pharmaceutical and manufacturing firms, to ABS Capital Partners in 1996 for $36 million in cash. The sale raised BBN's capital for investment in Internet-related activities to $150 million, according to a spokesperson. In June 1996 BBN sold 2.4 million shares of its common stock to private and institutional investors at $22.08 a share, raising $53 million more. This sum was to be used to expand BBN's network infrastructure and distribution channels and to develop value-added services to major corporate accounts.

As part of a company reorganization, the Hark Systems subsidiary was merged into the parent company in April 1996 and the Planet subsidiary in September 1996. The reorganization left BBN with two divisions: BBN Planet, accounting for $73 million in revenues in fiscal 1996, and BBN Systems and Technologies, accounting for the remaining (before intercompany eliminations) $164 million. BBN ended the fiscal year with a loss of $56.6 million, mainly because of investment in

Internet-related services. Management warned that it expected to incur substantial operating losses in fiscal 1997, principally as a result of its continuing investment in Internet businesses. Its long-term debt was $82 million at the end of fiscal 1996.

In fiscal 1996, 55 percent of BBN's revenues were derived from contracts and subcontracts involving the United States government and its agencies, compared to 70 percent in fiscal 1995 and 80 percent in fiscal 1994. Almost all of this work was being done by the Systems and Technologies division. BBN's headquarters remained in Cambridge, where it occupied a 15-acre complex of about 15 buildings, partly owned by the company. BBN was also leasing office space at 18 other domestic locations and in two foreign countries.

Principal Subsidiaries

BBN Advanced Computers Inc.; BBN Canada Ltd. (Canada); BBN Certificate Services Inc.; BBN Instruments Corp.; BBN International Corp.; BBN International Sales Corp. (U.S. Virgin Islands); BBN Manufacturing H.K. Ltd. (Hong Kong); BBN Securities Corp.; BBN U.K. Ltd. (Great Britain); Bolt Beranek and Newman Corp.; Parlance Corp.; Realtech Corp.

Principal Divisions

BBN Planet; BBN Systems and Technologies.

Further Reading

Churbuck, David, "Genius Unrewarded," *Forbes,* March 2, 1992, pp. 98–99.

Guterl, Fred V., "The Education of BBN," *Business Month,* August 1987, pp. 36–37, 40–41.

McCloy, Andrew P., "BBN Raises $90 Million for Internet Network," *Boston Business Journal,* July 5, 1996, p. 3.

McCright, John S., "New BBN Still Waits for Profits," *Boston Business Journal,* August 14, 1995, p. 3.

Rifkin, Glenn, "Computers That Hear and Respond," *New York Times,* August 14, 1991, pp. D1, D5.

——, "It's Not I.B.M. and It's Not Big, But He's Got Big Ideas," *New York Times,* February 27, 1994, Sec. 3, p. 8.

Underhill, Roland D., "Bolt, Beranek & Newman," *Wall Street Transcript,* March 16, 1981, pp. 60,898–60,899.

Veronis, Nicholas, "Good Times Rolling Downhill for BBN," *Boston Business Journal,* May 8, 1989, p. 1 and continuation.

Zuckerman, Laurence, "Innovator Is Leaving the Shadows for the Limelight," *New York Times,* July 17, 1995, p. D5.

—Robert Halasz

Belden Inc.

7701 Forsyth Boulevard #800
St. Louis, Missouri 63105
U.S.A.
(314) 854-8000
Fax: (314) 983-5294
Web site: http://www.belden.com

Public Company
Incorporated: 1902 as Belden Manufacturing Company
Employees: 4,000
Sales: $667.4 million (1996)
Stock Exchanges: New York
SICs: 3357 Drawing & Insulating Nonferrous Wire

Belden Inc. is a leader in the design and manufacturing of wire, cable, and cord products. Belden serves four primary markets: computers, audio/visual, industrial, and electrical. Computer products, accounting for 34 percent of sales, include shielded and unshielded twisted pair cables, coaxial cables, fiber optic cables, and flat cables used in computer networking, peripheral equipment connections, and internal computer wiring. For the audio/visual market, representing 25 percent of sales with customers in the broadcast, music, and entertainment industries, sports and entertainment stadiums and arenas, airports, convention centers and other public facilities, televisions, production and sound studios, and public address systems, Belden's products include CATV coaxial and composite cables, microphone and musical instrument cables, digital video/audio cables, 50 ohm transmission cables, and deflection wire. Products for the industrial market, including such processes as factory automation, instrumentation and control systems, robotics, and fire alarm and security systems, include specialized industrial cables, aluminum and steel armored data cables, and instrumentation and control cables, and make up 16 percent of Belden's sales. The electrical market, with applications including electronic equipment, floor care products, power tools, large and small appliances, electric motor leads, power distribution, and internal wiring for fixtures and equipment, provides 25 percent of Belden's sales, with products including appliance and power supply cords, and lead and hook-up wire.

Founded in 1902, Belden was operated as an unincorporated division of Cooper Industries between 1981 and 1993 but has been public again since 1993. The company, led by C. Baker Cunningham, who previously led Cooper's tool, hardware, and automotive division, posted sales of $667 million and net income of $55 million in 1996.

Recognizing a Need in 1902

Belden was founded by Joseph C. Belden in Chicago in 1902. Belden had been working as a purchasing agent for Kellogg Switchboard & Supply Company of Chicago but was finding it difficult to locate the high-quality, silk-wrapped magnetic wire needed for telephone coils. Recognizing the need for this product, Belden, then 26, decided to go into business for himself, selling shares in the company, called Belden Manufacturing Company, to 11 investors for $25,000 in start-up capital. Belden served as the company's president until 1939.

The wiring of America was just getting underway, and Belden quickly found a market for his product. However, in order to protect itself from fluctuations in demand, the company began to expand its product line. An initial foray into supply silk-wound wire frames for ladies' hats proved less successful given caprices of fashion, and Belden quickly found two new markets—the nascent automotive and electrical appliance industries—for the company's wire products. Belden's early commitment to quality helped the company become a leading source of wiring and cables for these industries. Early customers included Thomas Edison and Lee De Forest, creator of the radio vacuum tube. By the end of the century's first decade, the company had achieved sales of $350,000.

Belden was already establishing its reputation for innovative product development, with strong research and development efforts and a quick recognition of market opportunities. The increasing use of electricity demanded better insulation capacities, and in 1910, Belden introduced its enamel insulation, marketing under the trade name Beldenamel, which would become an industry standard and open the way for such wire

---

Company Perspectives:

"Belden's strategy for the future is fairly simple. We intend to generate sustained increases in revenues and improve profitability. Revenue growth should come from three sources: market growth, market penetration and acquisitions. Market growth will be fueled by the creation of the information superhighway, conversion to digitalized broadcast technology, expanded and improved CATV systems, added automation by industry and general economic growth. Market penetration should result primarily from new product introductions that provide innovative solutions to the increasingly stringent technological demands of data, audio and video signal transmission and from expanded sales and distribution coverage. Consolidation of the global wire and cable industry appears to be occurring. Belden plans to be an active participant in that process. Improved profitability will be attained through increased manufacturing efficiency, effective utilization of assets and more sophisticated process controls that allow higher throughput and higher yields."

---

refinements as fine and ultra-fine magnet wire. At the same time, Belden also introduced rubber-covered wire products. The new additions to the Belden line helped the company nearly triple its sales to $900,000 by 1913.

Belden next expanded operations to include plastic manufacturing capabilities, primarily to supply bakelite housings and other products for the electrical markets. However, the outbreak of World War I provided the company's strongest growth, as Belden supplied wire and cables for such support units as motorized transport and field communications for the war effort. The company also began receiving orders from England and Russia for enameled copper wire—Belden later discovered that its products were used for developing and installing wireless radio communications, bringing the company into a new market. After the war, Belden continued to supply both the aviation and radio markets. Meanwhile, the company had a two-year backlog of orders from its domestic customers.

When commercial radio broadcasting began in the 1920s, Belden's low tension cables, aerial wire, and magnet wire found strong demand. The company also began selling parts to jobbers in the radio industry, beginning the company's distribution arm. In the late 1920s, Belden entered another market with the development of a molded rubber plug. By then, orders for the company's expanded product line were outstripping its production capacity, and in 1928 the company opened its second plant, in Richmond, Indiana, which would later become the site of the company's Electronic Division. In that year, also, the company started producing for the automotive aftermarket. Four years later, Belden signed a distribution agreement with the recently formed National Automotive Parts Association.

Despite the Depression, Belden's diversified product line and its expansion into the replacement parts market helped the company continue to grow. In 1939, with sales of $4.9 million,

and a net income of $378,000, the company went public, listing on the Midwest Stock Exchange. Joe Belden died in 1939; replacing him was Whipple Jacobs, who had started in the company's cost department as a temporary clerk earning $9.10 a week in 1914. Whipple led Belden into the World War II era, during which, Belden, already a major military supplier, converted much of its production to supply the war effort. Belden also began introducing new forms of wire insulation using such recently developed chemical compounds as vinyl, nylon, and neoprene, further expanding the Belden family of products with Beldure, Nylclad, Formvar, Beldfoil and other brand names. Belden also introduced the first solderable enamel compound, replacing its Beldenamel with the Celenamel trademark. During the postwar years, Belden continued to supply the electric product markets but also expanded into the new and growing fields of radar, sonar, and electronics. Whipple stepped down as president, and Charles S. Craigmile, who had started with the company as an electrical engineer in 1915, was named in his place.

Growth through the 1970s

Belden began its shift toward the television and data processing markets as these industries began their commercial growth in the 1950s. Belden's sales continued to grow steadily, and it continued to add capacity to its Chicago and Richmond plants. By 1965, the company's sales had grown to $53 million. In that year, Robert W. Hawkinson became the company's president. Hawkinson, who joined Belden in 1945 as an engineer after serving as a fighter-bomber captain in the Army Air Forces during the Second World War, would lead Belden through its next growth phase.

That era began in 1966, when Belden changed its name to Belden Corporation and built a plant in Franklin, North Carolina—its first new plant since 1938. Over the next three years, the company constructed two more plants, one in Pontotoc, Mississippi, and a 170,000-square-foot site in Jena, Louisiana. The company also went on an acquisition binge, acquiring Complete-Reading Electric Co., a distributor of electrical motor parts, in 1967. The following year, Belden acquired Southern Electric Sales Co., based in Dallas, which distributed electrical wire, insulating material, and replacement parts, and Insulation & Copper Sales, a Detroit-based distributor of magnet wire, lead wire, and associated products. Capping the expansion of Belden's distribution business, which gave the company 16 warehouse distribution centers, was the 1969 stock-swap acquisition of Electrical Specialty Co. of San Francisco, adding that company's electrical wire, insulating materials, industrial plastics, and shop equipment distribution facilities. Meanwhile, Belden was also expanding its production capacity, with the acquisition of General Wire & Cable Co. Ltd. of Canada and that company's two manufacturing plants. At the same time, Belden moved to consolidate its research and development operations, building the company's Technical Research Center in Geneva, Illinois. Among the products Belden developed during this period was its Duofoil brand of coaxial cables for master antenna and cable television systems.

By 1970, sales had topped $100 million, and the company began listing on the New York Stock Exchange. Helping to fuel this growth was a stepping up of its activity in the automotive aftermarket, which itself was growing rapidly with the steady increases in car sales of the period. During the 1970s, the company continued to expand its production capacity, adding a 75,000-square-foot automotive aftermarket facility to its Jena plant, while adding new plants in Dumas, Arkansas, and Monticello, Kentucky. The company also moved to improve its profits by exiting the low-margin commodity market, discontinuing production of heavy wire and closing its original Chicago plant. By 1978, the company's sales had grown to $240 million, earning profits of $8.8 million.

Reemerging in the 1990s

Belden's stock price, however, had not kept pace with its revenue growth. By 1980, the company had become the target of a hostile takeover, and Belden found refuge in a merger with Crouse-Hinds Co.. The following year, when Crouse-Hinds itself became a takeover target, another white knight appeared, and Belden found itself a subsidiary of Cooper Industries. Belden served Cooper as a source of cash flow to fuel Cooper's expansion into other industries; meanwhile, Belden began positioning itself toward the international market, while also expanding heavily in the booming computer industry. In 1993, Cooper spun off Belden as an independent, publicly-traded company with annual sales of $300 million.

Within three years, Belden would more than double its annual sales, a growth fueled in large part by sales of the company's network cable products. The company's international sales to Canada, Europe, and Latin America were also becoming a strong source of revenue, nearing 25 percent of annual sales by the mid-1990s. After moving its headquarters to St. Louis in 1994, the company prepared for a new string of acquisitions. In March 1995, Belden acquired American Electric Cordsets, based in Bensenville, Illinois, adding the $24 million company to its newly formed Cord Products Division.

Two months later, Belden purchased rival Pope Cable and Wire B.V., based in Venlo, the Netherlands, for $50 million, adding that company's $112 million in annual sales and strengthening Belden's position in Europe. A year later, Belden acquired the wire division of Alpha Wire Corp., based in Elizabeth, New Jersey, further positioning Belden to achieve a strong share of the ongoing networking products boom. Meanwhile, Belden began preparing for expansion into the growing Asian and Pacific Rim markets, while extending its Latin American reach as well. With the new market for internet and corporate intranet products just beginning to explode in the mid-1990s, Belden's history of quickly shifting its focus to emerging technologies and markets continued to serve the company well.

Principal Divisions

Belden Wire and Cable; Cord Products Division.

Further Reading

De Young, Garrett H., " 'You Must Know Your Strengths,' " *Photonics Spectra,* August 1989, p. 52.

Galarza, Pablo, "Belden Inc., St. Louis, Mo., Cashing in as Technology Lifts Wire Demand," *Investor's Business Daily,* June 16, 1994, p. A6.

"High Operating Rates Prove Boon to Belden, Wire Maker," *Barron's,* August 7, 1978, p. 39.

Manor, Robert, "Local Newcomer Soars on Market," *St. Louis Post-Dispatch,* July 11, 1994, p. 4.

Mehlman, William, "Investors Responding Slowly to Altered Belden Image," *Insiders' Chronicle,* April 6, 1979, p. 1.

"Strong Demand Puts Belden Operations in High Gear," *Barron's,* September 25, 1972, p. 29.

"Wire and Cable Maker Belden Set to String Up an Earnings Comeback," *Barron's,* December 15, 1969, p. 26.

—M. L. Cohen

Belk Stores Services, Inc.

2801 West Tyvola Road
Charlotte, North Carolina 28217
U.S.A.
(704) 377-4251
Fax: (704) 342-4320
Web site: http://www.belk.com

Private Company
Incorporated: 1891 as Belk Brothers Company
Employees: 1,450
Sales: $1.7 billion (1996)
SICs: 5311 Department Stores; 5632 Women's Accessory
and Specialty Stores.

Still operated by descendants of the founding Belk brothers, Belk Stores Services, Inc. (BSS) is one of the few large family-owned retail entities remaining in the United States. Over its more than one hundred years in business, BSS has evolved from a budget-minded variety store into one of the nation's leading department stores. BSS provides merchandising, centralized buying, data processing, market research, legal planning, training, importing and private label procurement services to Belk Corp., a $2 billion confederation of 14 department store partnerships controlled by the Belk family. Stores in this unorthodox retail conglomeration are located in 14 largely southern states. Though many of the affiliated stores are wholly or partially owned by members of the Belk clan, they are not considered a chain. Thomas Belk Sr., who led the company from 1980 until his death early in 1997, cited this corporate strategy as one of the organization's strengths, noting in a September 1995 interview for *WWD* that "Unlike J.C. Penney or Sears, which tend to be the same everywhere, all of our stores are different, by catering to the community and the personality of the people there."

Late 19th-Century Origins

In 1888 William Henry Belk opened a small bargain store in Monroe, North Carolina. The store, New York Racket, was financed with a loan from a local widow, Belk's savings, and goods on consignment. The goods' prices were clearly marked and not negotiated with customers, an idea that was just becoming accepted in retailing. Within seven months, Belk had gone from being over $4,000 in debt to earning a $3,300 profit.

The founder approached his brother, John Belk, in 1891, to become a partner in the prospering store. Thus the Belk Brothers Company was formed. A second store was opened in 1893 in Chester, South Carolina. A third opened in Union, South Carolina, in 1894, and the following year, William Belk moved to Charlotte, North Carolina, to open the company's fourth store. His brother John remained to manage the Monroe store until his death in 1928. The brothers' stores were doing so well by 1895 that other merchants even began to copy its straight-talking slogans like "Cheap Goods Sell Themselves" and "The Cheapest Store on Earth."

William Belk's success resulted from some retailing ideas that were innovative for the time. In 1897 he combined the purchasing power of the four stores, plus two others in which the brothers had no financial interest, and formed a loose cooperative buying network. This allowed them to purchase goods in bulk quantity at favorable prices. All purchases and sales were cash. Belk also made extensive use of advertising. The brothers opened a store in Greensboro, North Carolina, in 1899.

Rapid Expansion After Turn of the Century

In the early 1900s, Charlotte was a boom town, expanding along with the textile industry and was the state's largest city by 1910. That year, Belk sales approached $1 million, and a new five-story building was unveiled to house the Charlotte store. The company's greatest expansion followed World War I, as the southern economy received a boost. Cotton prices went up, and soldiers came home. Between 1918 and 1920, Belk stores' total sales more than doubled to $12 million a year. In 1920 Will Leggett—John Belk's nephew by marriage—opened a store with the Belks in Burlington, North Carolina. His brother, Fred Leggett, opened a store in Danville, Virginia, that same year— the Belk-Leggett. The Belk brothers often added managers' names to their own on new stores.

Company Perspectives:

"The mission of Belk corporations and their stores is to be the leader in their markets in selling merchandise that meets customers' needs for fashion, quality, value and selection; to offer superior customer service; and to make a reasonable profit. Reflecting the beliefs of the founders of the various Belk corporations, Belk stores want their customers to have a feeling of confidence that they will receive honest and fair treatment, that they will get full value for every dollar, and that they will be satisfied in every respect so that they will want to shop with Belk stores again. Belk stores have a responsibility to the people who make their growth and success possible. They are committed to maintaining relationships of integrity, honesty, and fairness with customers, associates, vendors, other business partners, stockholders, and with all people in every community they serve."

Boom days and postwar prosperity gave way to recession, however, and the Belks retrenched, not opening any stores between 1922 and 1925. In 1925, however, they opened three more stores and three again in 1926. In 1927 the Belks and the Leggett brothers agreed that the Leggetts would own 80 percent of the stores they opened, with Belk Brothers Company owning the remaining 20 percent. In the past, the Belks had always owned the majority of their stores. This arrangement formed the foundation of Belk's unusual organizational scheme.

Opportunistic Growth During the Great Depression

The years between 1910 and 1930 were prosperous for retailing. Competition, however, began to creep up on the Belks. Then the stock market crash of 1929 slowed Belk's sales growth, but stores stayed open. Belk took advantage of other companies' misfortune by acquiring defunct stores, netting 22 stores in 1930 and 1931. In 1934 Belk opened a record 27 stores, expanding geographically into Tennessee and Georgia in the process. By 1938 Charlotte was again a booming southern city and the Belks's headquarters store there expanded. This location evolved into the organization's operational headquarters, consolidating purchasing, assistance with taxes and merchandise distribution, and other services for all affiliated stores. By 1938 Belk was doing business in 162 locations in seven states.

In response to growing competition from such national chains as J.C. Penney, Montgomery Ward, and Sears Roebuck, which were thriving in larger cities, Belk stores were remodeled and expanded. Belk Stores Association had formed in the 1920s, gathering the new store managers for quarterly meetings. By the late 1930s, the group was too large feasibly organize meetings four times a year, so it gathered at annual conventions. Belk Buying Service was formally set up in 1940. World War II defense spending enhanced the economy, and by the war's end, sales were two-and-one-half times what they had been in 1941. This helped pay off Depression debts and feed expansion. The Belks opened 25 stores in 1945 alone and achieved a net increase of more than 60 stores between the end of World War

II and the close of the decade. In 1952 founder William Belk died at the age of 89. He had worked as the head of the company right up to his death.

Second Generation of Managers in the Postwar Era

After Belk's death, his son Henry took his place. The founder's other sons, John and Tom, were also active in the company. Six months after his father's death, Henry opened the company's first shopping center store in Florida. This store marked a dramatic break from Belk traditions: a New York design firm created a fancy interior, music was played, and merchandise was displayed for self-service. This contrasted sharply with the Belk stores' trademark features of spare, no-nonsense decor, and an army of well-trained sales clerks. Henry opened several more stores afterward without consulting his family, and by 1955 legal disputes were brewing among family members and other shareholders. Although lawsuits were filed, they eventually were dropped. Later that year, Belk Stores Services, Inc., was established to make a formal organization out of what had long been an operating entity. The BSS board then elected John Belk as president, leaving Henry to his Florida pursuit, the Belk-Lindsey Company. Though BSS cut all ties with Henry's chain of department stores in November 1955, family feuding would continue throughout the next four decades. John would later advance to chairman of BSS, with Tom as president.

By this time, the Belks' private-label business was thriving. By 1959 it accounted for a major share of the buying office's inventory. In the late 1950s, the Belks department stores had nearly peaked in the South, with 325 stores in 16 states. In 1956 Belk acquired its only viable competitor in the region, the Efird department stores.

Modernization Program Begins in 1960s

During the 1960s, the company had to adjust to a changing retail environment in the South. Stores that could once count on their reputations as local institutions found themselves in the midst of a highly mobile population that was attracted to the offerings of big-city stores. The largely autonomous and divergent stores making up the Belk group were not prepared to compete. A more mobile society, newly popular shopping centers, and the South's expanding economy presented BSS with the task of uniting its network of stores.

In 1958 there were 380 stores in 17 states. By 1963 the stores were, for the first time, presented to the public as a unit, instead of the string of independent operations they had been. Change was still slow, however. At a time when more buyers were using credit, 87 percent of Belk's sales were still cash. In 1967 extensive meetings were held by BSS and its long-range planning committees to chart the company's future.

Meanwhile, more stores were added to the fold: 14 opened in 1969 and 16 in 1970. The new stores were larger and used modern management techniques, such as computerized payrolls and centralized personnel departments. As planning and coordination gained in importance, so did BSS's role. By assuming more leadership, it accelerated the changes as the stores moved from budget to fashion merchandise. Expansion continued—

between 1972 and 1975, more than 50 stores were opened. Several of the company's signature downtown stores were closed in favor of stores in the prospering outlying malls. Credit and data processing systems were centralized and upgraded. Another change was Belk's pursuit of upscale brand names. Estee Lauder, a brand of cosmetics, was aggressively wooed until it was added to product lines in 1975. Even Belk stores in smaller towns upgraded their look and merchandise. This served to add new customers to an already loyal clientele.

Under the direction of President and CEO Thomas Belk beginning in 1980, the company succeeded in making the transition to meeting the demand of style-conscious shoppers of the 1970s and 1980s, as opposed to the previous demand for thrift, durability, and value. For example, Belk hosted its first fashion buying show in New York in 1983, and within four years, representatives from the nation's top fashion lines were competing for representation in the show. This further consolidated buying and proved Belk's place in the fashion retail market. Marking the change from bargain chain to fashion stores was top designer Oscar de la Renta's appearance at a grand re-opening of a Belk store in 1986. Though some stores retained the small-town, bargain-budget flavor of Belk's founder's vision, others moved to suburban malls and shopping centers. The company celebrated its 100th birthday in 1988 while opening a huge new BSS office complex in Charlotte. The company would later close its New York office and consolidate buying operations at the new facility.

The 1990s and Beyond

Though the retail industry in general and the department store segment in particular were disrupted by recession, competition from mega-discounters, mergers, and multi-billion-dollar bankruptcies in the early 1990s, one observer characterized Belk Stores as "a rock of stability." The company achieved this constancy through a series of well-considered divestments and acquisitions. In an effort to focus on its strongest markets, the company sold a few stores in marginal markets, maintaining its strongholds in North and South Carolina. Hot on the heels of

rumors that longtime affiliate Leggett Stores Inc. was negotiating a merger with Dillard Department Stores Inc., Belk's parent company purchased a controlling interest in the Virginia-based chain in the fall of 1996. The addition of Leggett's more than 40 stores increased Belk Corp.'s amalgamation of stores by nearly 20 percent and, perhaps more importantly, ensured the continuation of Leggett's long-running affiliation with Belk Stores Services.

Belk Stores withstood an unplanned management transition in January 1997, when 71-year-old Thomas Belk died following gall bladder surgery. His three sons, Thomas M. "Tim" Belk Jr., H.W. McKay Belk, and John R. Belk shared the title of president and divided merchandising and operating responsibilities among themselves. Strategies for the future included cost reduction, consolidation of operations with a special focus on inventory management, and a continuing emphasis on the customer.

Further Reading

"Battling Belks: Maul in the Family," *Business North Carolina,* December 1993, pp. 14–15.

"Belk Corp. buying Majority Stake in Leggett Chain," *Daily News Record,* September 16, 1996, p. 13.

Blueweiss, Herbert, "Belk's . . . Beginning the Next 100 Years," *Daily News Record,* January 16, 1989, p. 48.

Covington, Howard, *Belk: A Century of Retail Leadership,* Chapel Hill: University of North Carolina Press, 1988.

Lee, Georgia, "Tom Belk: After Drought, Women's Seeing Revival," *WWD,* September 13, 1995, p. 18.

Lee, Georgia and David Moin, "Thomas M. Belk, 71 Belk Stores President, Dies in Charlotte," *WWD,* January 28, 1997, pp. 1–2.

Palmieri, Jean E., "Many Department Stores Still Clicking; Belk," *Daily News Record,* January 17, 1990, p. 10.

"Three Belk Brothers Promoted," *Daily News Record,* March 3, 1997, p. 2.

—Carol I. Keeley
—updated by April D. Gasbarre

Besnier SA

10-20, rue Alolph Beck
53089 Laval Cedex 09
France
43 59 40 52
Fax: 43 59 42 61
Web site: http://www.plante.fr/webs/besnier

Private Company
Incorporated: 1933
Employees: 12,000
Sales: FFr 24 billion (1993 est.)
SICs: 2022 Cheese, Natural & Processed; 5143 Dairy
    Products, Except Dried or Canned; 2020 Dairy
    Products

Besnier SA is France's largest dairy products producer and one of the largest dairy products producers in Europe. Besnier's primary business is in cheese making, selling its products under the company's renowned President label, but also under such brand names as Lepetit, Claudel, Lactel, Valmont, and Jean Jacques. The company also owns approximately two-thirds of famed Société des Caves et des Producteurs Reunis de Roquefort, the world's leading producer of Roquefort cheese. Best known for its brie and Camembert, Besnier produces more than 100 types of cheese, butter, and milk products. Besnier's products reach some 100 countries; the company operates some 60 plants in France and ten in foreign countries. Its U.S. operations are based in Belmont, Wisconsin, where the company produces President label Camembert, brie, and feta, and in Turlock, California, where the company produces brie, Gouda, Edam, and feta. A private company, Besnier is owned 100 percent by the Besnier family. Michel Besnier, son of the company's founder, continues to lead the family business.

Besnier's annual milk collection is more than five billion liters, primarily of cow's milk, but also includes 135 million liters of sheep's milk and 30 million liters of goat's milk per year. From this, Besnier produces one billion liters of milk, 127,000 tons of butter, 365,000 tons of cheese, and 215,000 tons of fresh dairy products, including cream and yogurt. Besnier last reported revenues of FFr 24 billion (US $4.5 billion) in 1993, of which approximately 25 percent came from foreign sales. Earnings for that year were reported at FFr 443 million. Since then, the company has continued its aggressive expansion-by-acquisition drive, started during the 1970s and stepped up in the 1980s, consolidating its position in France with the 1996 acquisition of Marcillat, a cheese with FFr 600 in sales, and expanding into Eastern Europe with the formation of a joint venture with Ukraine's Nikolaiev and the acquisition of 83 percent of Poland's Polser.

A Small Family Business into the 1960s

Besnier was founded as a single plant in Laval, in the Loire Valley region of France, by Andre Besnier, a former cooper by trade. In 1955, Andre's son, Michel, who had started with the family business as a delivery boy, took over the dairy company's operations. Besnier remained a small, single-plant operation until well into the 1960s. But after a flood destroyed the factory's entire dairy production in 1966, Michel Besnier became determined to protect the company from such calamities in the future by expanding its operations to multiple plants and diversifying the company's dairy products. As a first step, in 1968, Besnier created its own brand, the President label, which, in many parts of the world, would become synonymous with French cheese. The following year, the company opened a second plant, in Mayenne, adding to its cheese production capacity. By then, however, Michel Besnier was already preparing to take a new direction in an ambitious plan to build the family's business. In 1969, Besnier made the first of a long string of acquisitions, buying the cheese maker Bourdon, based in the Normandy region.

That first acquisition made Besnier hungry for more. In 1973, the company acquired a cheese making plant in Charchigné from Preval and followed that acquisition with the purchase of the Buquet cheese dairies. The following year, Besnier solidified its position in the Normandy region, the traditional center of Camembert cheese production, by forming the Société Laiterière de Normandie with rival Bridel. At the same time, the company expanded its own Camembert production with the acquisitions of Groupement Laitier du Perche and of Laiteries Prairies de l'Orne. One year later, Besnier expanded again, adding brie to its product line with the purchase of cheese producer Renault of Doué la Fontaine. Another takeover followed in 1976, when Besnier acquired Stenval Sud.

By 1978, Besnier was thriving; in that year, the company built a new, state-of-the-art production facility in Donfront. The capacity of the new plant, located on 18 acres in the heart of Normandy, was reported to be three times larger than that of the company's principal competitors of the time. With production levels reaching up to 400,000 units of Camembert per day, the Donfront factory was among the largest soft-cheese plants in the world. Meanwhile, the company's line was augmented with the Lepetit brand name. Then, in 1979, Besnier expanded its butter production unit, building a butter plant in Isigny le Buat.

Besnier started the next decade strongly. In 1980, the company acquired the cheese making group Atlalait and that group's six plants in the Loire and Deux-Sèvres, building on the company's position in western France. In that year, Besnier also moved into eastern France, with the takeover of the Jean Lincet cheese dairy. By then, foreign demand was building for Camembert and other French soft cheeses. In response, Besnier established a small plant in the United States, in Belmont, Wisconsin in 1981, which focused on supplying soft cheeses to the U.S. market. The company also began industrial production in Villalba, Spain in 1983.

By then, Besnier's sales had swelled to more than FFr 5 billion per year. The company's takeover drive continued, with the acquisition of Martin Collet in 1982, and the acquisition, between 1982 and 1985, of six cheeses from Claudel Roustand Galac. To fuel further expansion, however, Besnier set its sights on acquiring a larger cheese operation. When the Société de Collecte des Prodicteurs de Preval (SCPP) went bankrupt in 1982, Besnier purchased that group's 34 percent stake in the FFr 3 billion-per-year Preval dairy operation. Besnier claimed that its purchase also gave it the right to exercise an option to buy an additional 24 percent of Preval from majority stakeholder Union Laitière Normande (ULN). More than twice Besnier's size at the time, with annual turnover of some FFr 10 billion, the ULN denied Besnier's action to exercise the option. Despite threatening legal action, Besnier lost that takeover bid.

The Preval setback proved to be a rarity in Besnier's aggressive expansion. The company completed its acquisition of Claudel Roustand Galac in 1985. That group had been a subsidiary of Nestlé, of Switzerland; its acquisition by Besnier had given Nestlé a 20 percent share of Besnier. In 1987, however, Nestlé agreed to sell its stake back to Michel Besnier, once again giving him complete control over the family business. With the 1985 acquisition of the Picault dairy operations, based in Normandy, and the cheese dairy plant of Moreau, based in the Ardennes region, the Besnier family business was worth some FFr 8.8 billion by 1987. Profits were also soaring, jumping from FFr 60 million in 1986 to FFr 194 million in 1987. Exports had grown to represent more than 25 percent of the company's sales, with approximately 60 percent of export sales going to neighboring European countries. Besnier also boosted its U.S. presence in 1987 with the opening of a larger plant in Turlock, California, which enabled the company to add fresh milk products, including cream and yogurt, to the U.S. market.

Eyeing the European Union of the 1990s

By the late 1980s, Besnier had built the family business into a dairy empire of some 36 plants, processing more than two billion liters of milk per year into more than 400 products under the President, Lepetit, Claudel, Lactel, and other branded and private label names. Sales in 1988 had risen to FFr 9.7 billion, and profits had nearly doubled to FFr 378 million. Besnier's growth during the previous two decades had been impressive, but it proved to be just the beginning. By the early years of the 1990s, Besnier would more than double its sales.

With the creation of the European common market looming in 1992, Besnier moved to consolidate its position in France while simultaneously stepping up its expansion into foreign countries, the better to compete with the European dairy giants. The next phase of the company's expansion began in 1989. In that year Besnier made a number of smaller acquisitions, including that of Hugerot, of the Aube region of France, and the acquisition of the milk production operations of Valmont, a subsidiary of the Perrier group. The Valmont acquisition also helped confirm Michel Besnier's reputation for transforming the failing operations of some of its acquisitions into profitable additions to the Besnier group. Also in 1989, the company expanded into the Los Angeles market, with the acquisition of the small fresh dairy operation, Atlantis, while the company deepened its European presence with the purchase of Laiterie Ekabe, of Luxembourg, and the formation of a partnership to bring the company into the Catalonia region of Spain. Another partnership, with a Belgian dairy cooperative, led to the formation of SA Laiterie Walhorn Molkerel.

Besnier, however, reserved its biggest move for 1990. In that year, the company outmaneuvered its larger competitors, including Sodiaal, ULN, and Bongrain as well as a number of foreign competitors, to purchase the Bridel dairy company, another family business described as the patriarch of the French Camembert industry and Besnier's fiercest competitor. The purchase, for an estimated FFr 2 billion, catapulted Besnier to the top of the French dairy industry, giving the company total annual revenues of more than FFr 17 billion. The combined operations gave Besnier a large share of the French dairy market, with 16 percent of cheese products, 24 percent of milk, and 24 percent of the country's butter production. In January 1991, Besnier reinforced its position with the acquisition of another family-controlled cheese producer, Girod, based in Saint-Julien-en-Genevois, adding that company's FFr 240 million in sales. Three months later, Besnier outmaneuvered its competitors again, acquiring the Jean-Jacques fresh dairy operations and the rest of the Valmont dairy operations from the troubled Perrier group, which had been forced to recall all of its bottled water after the water had been found to contain traces of benzene. These purchases helped raise Besnier's turnover to some FFr 22 billion by the end of that year.

By October of 1992, Besnier caused a new stir in the French dairy industry. After Nestlé's takeover of Perrier in the beginning of 1992, the Swiss company announced its intentions of selling off another Perrier subsidiary, the renowned Caves de

Roquefort, the leading maker (with 80 percent of world production) of the famous French blue cheese. Again, Besnier outran its competitors, paying Nestlé FFr 863 million for 57 percent of Caves de Roquefort. The remaining shares of the Roquefort operation continued to be controlled by French bank Crédit Agricole. To finance the Roquefort acquisition, Besnier set up a subsidiary unit, Société pour le Financement de l'Industrie Laitière (SOFIL), which increased its participation in Roquefort to 69.5 percent in 1993. Besnier's acquisition spree in the 1990s, however, had brought the company heavily into debt, with FFr 2.5 billion owed even before the Roquefort acquisition. To finance its debt without going public, Besnier sold 40 percent of SOFIL to three French banks—Crédit Lyonnais, Banque Nationale de Paris, and Société Generale—raising as much as FFr 800 million in capital.

After the Roquefort acquisition, Besnier slowed the pace of its purchases. Turning to consolidating the company's operations and improving the profitability of its recent operations, Besnier also sold off the Roquefort subsidiary, Sorrento, based in Buffalo, New York, to Kraft Foods. The lull did not last long, however. By the end of 1993, Besnier had made several new investments, including the acquisition of small (FFr 60 million) cheese producer Rousel, based in Puy-de-Dome, near Chamalieres, and a 51 percent controlling interest in Alsace Lorraine-based Unicoolait (Union des Cooperatives Laitières), a group of 820 cheese producers in the region with FFr 550 million in sales. Besnier was also maneuvering toward another major purchase. In January of 1993, he stepped up his stake in Fromageries Bel, the maker of the worldwide top-selling processed cheese product La Vache Qui Rit (Laughing Cow) with FFr 6.8 billion in 1991 sales. Besnier's share increased to eight percent, giving him slightly more than five percent of the voting rights in the company. By the beginning of 1994, however, Besnier had extended his share of Bel's voting rights to 20.57 percent. Bel's main shareholder and chairman, Robert Fievet, was then 84 years old; at the same time, succession issues were beginning to present themselves to the Bel founding family and controllers of the majority of that company's voting rights.

Besnier adopted a wait-and-see attitude, making no secret of its interest in eventually adding Bel to the Besnier fold.

With FFr 24 billion in annual sales in 1993, Besnier was not only France's largest dairy products group, it had also become one of the largest in Europe, behind industry leader Nestlé. As the French dairy industry moved closer to consolidation, Besnier began focusing on new product development, introducing, among others, its own emmental cheese. In 1995, the company expanded its U.S. operation, building a 60,000-square-foot facility in Belmont, Wisconsin. The following year, the company made its first move to expand into the reviving Eastern European market. In April 1996, Besnier created a joint venture in the Ukraine with Nikolaiev. Four months later, Besnier entered Poland with the 83 percent purchase of that country's Polser dairy. Meanwhile, questions about the possible successor to Michel Besnier, who turned 67 in 1996, were answered as Besnier began grooming son Emmannuel, 26, to take over the company's operations.

Principal Subsidiaries

SOFIL (60%); Caves de Roquefort (66%); Besnier America; Besnier International.

Further Reading

''French Cheese Move in Poland,'' *East European Markets,* August 30, 1996.

Dawkins, William, ''Roquefort Returns to the French Cheeseboard,'' *Financial Times,* October 3, 1992, p. 12.

Herzog, Karen, ''French Connection: Wisconsin Village Says 'Oui' to Cheese,'' *Milwaukee Journal Sentinel,* September 8, 1996, Food Sec., p. 1.

''How a French Connection Found a Taste for the UK,'' *Grocer,* January 15, 1994.

Mans, Jack, ''C'est le Brie,'' *Dairy Foods,* January 1996, p. 49.

—M.L. Cohen

BFGoodrich

The BFGoodrich Company

4020 Kinross Lakes Parkway
Richfield, Ohio 44286
U.S.A.
(330) 659-7600
Fax: (330) 659-7906
Web site: http://www.bfgoodrich.com

Public Company
Incorporated: 1870 as Goodrich, Tew & Company
Employees: 14,160
Sales: $2.2 billion (1996)
Stock Exchanges: New York
SICs: 2800 Chemicals and Allied Products

With operations in eight countries, the BFGoodrich Company manufactures and supplies a wide range of systems and component parts for the aerospace industry, and provides maintenance, repair, and overhaul services on commercial, regional, business, and general aviation aircraft. The company also manufactures specialty plastics and specialty additives products for a variety of end-user applications. In addition, it produces chlor-alkali and olefins products. BFGoodrich has manufacturing operations and aircraft service centers in eight countries. Throughout most of its history Goodrich built its business on rubber production, gaining a reputation among U.S. tire makers as a leader in product development and innovation. In the early 20th century Goodrich used its experience in the rubber industry to diversify into chemicals and plastics, and it spearheaded the development of synthetic rubber technology during World War II. The company prospered during the postwar era but faced difficulties when the U.S. auto industry's decline in the 1970s curtailed the demand for tires. Convinced that its future lay in chemicals and plastics, the company's directors embarked on a long and often difficult restructuring plan. Goodrich finally divested itself of its tire business in 1987, emerging as a leaner, more profitable company. The company continues to strengthen its aerospace and specialty chemicals business groups.

Company Origins

Benjamin Franklin Goodrich followed a circuitous route into the rubber industry. Born in Ripley, New York in 1841, Good-

rich pursued an education in medicine and served as an assistant surgeon in the Union Army during the U.S. Civil War. After the war Goodrich pursued a career in business and entered into a real estate partnership with John P. Morris of New York City. In 1869 the partners found themselves investors in a small operation called the Hudson River Rubber Company. They soon acquired full ownership of the company and Goodrich took over as its president.

Goodrich was not impressed with the company's prospects in New York and he considered moving it west, where a growing population and economy offered plenty of opportunities for expansion. After listening to a stranger praise a canal town in Ohio called Akron, he investigated it for himself. Akron's citizens were as anxious to attract business as Goodrich was to develop it. After his visit a group of 19 potential investors sent George T. Perkins back to New York with Goodrich to examine his operations there. The group received a favorable report, and it loaned Goodrich the money he needed to move west. On December 31, 1870, Goodrich formed the partnership of Goodrich, Tew & Company with his brother-in-law Harvey W. Tew and the Akron investors. After completing a two-story factory on the banks of the Ohio Canal, Goodrich was in business as the first rubber company west of the Allegheny Mountains.

Goodrich experienced a shaky start during its first decade. The company's first product was a cotton-covered firehose designed to withstand the high pressures and low temperatures that often caused leather hoses to burst. While the firehose was a welcome innovation among the nation's firefighters, poor financing led to several reorganizations within the company. George W. Crouse, one of the original Akron investors, finally stabilized the company's finances with an additional loan in 1880, and it was incorporated in the state of Ohio as The B.F. Goodrich Company.

Goodrich died in 1888, just a few years before the bicycle craze of the 1890s revolutionized his company and the rubber industry. Among the company's early products had been the solid-band tire used on bicycles of the 1880s. The invention of the pneumatic tire in 1890 greatly increased the comfort of bicycle riding, and Goodrich began turning out bicycle tires to keep pace with the popularity of this recreation. The introduction of cord tires, which increased the speed of bicycles, and the adaptation of pneumatic tires to horse-drawn buggies expanded the nation's rubber markets further. Goodrich increased its capacity with each addition to its tire demand, and company engineers cooperated with independent inventors to find new applications for company products.

The most important of these joint efforts was a contribution Goodrich made to the nation's infant automobile industry. In 1897 Alexander Winton of Cleveland, Ohio, organized the Winton Motor Car Company to market his horseless carriages. He asked Goodrich to develop a pneumatic tire strong enough to handle its high speeds and heavier loads. Goodrich responded with the first pneumatic tires for automobiles, beginning a long partnership with the auto industry that became the foundation for the company's profits for the next 70 years.

Early Commitment to Research and Development

From very early in its history Goodrich committed itself to research and development in rubber technology. Under the aegis of Goodrich's son, Charles Cross Goodrich, the company opened the rubber industry's first experimental research laboratory in 1895. Arthur H. Marks, one of Goodrich's engineers, was responsible for several breakthroughs in the processing of crude rubber. In its natural form, crude rubber is very sensitive to changes in temperature, becoming hard and brittle when cooled, and soft and tacky when heated. Vulcanization, a process first discovered by Charles Goodyear in 1839, mixes crude rubber with sulfur and heat to convert it to a durable material unaffected by changes in climate. At the turn of the century, Arthur Marks pioneered a procedure for devulcanizing vulcanized rubber, thus enabling producers to reclaim crude rubber from manufactured goods for re-use. Marks also developed methods for speeding vulcanization by adding certain organic chemical accelerators to the process. The use of such compounds reduced the time necessary for vulcanization by as much as 75 percent.

Goodrich continued to apply the latest technology to its tire production. In 1910 it introduced the first cord tire for use on U.S. automobiles. This tire, which reduced fuel consumption and increased the comfort of the ride, was developed in Silvertown, England, and marketed there as the Palmer Cord. Goodrich purchased the patent rights for it in the United States and sold it to U.S. consumers as the Silvertown Cord. Other innovations in Goodrich's tire manufacturing included the use of other organic compounds to resist deterioration by heat, oxidation, and flexing; and carbon black, a coloring pigment that improved the tires' resistance to abrasion.

World War I and Product Diversification

Goodrich's success in its tire business led it into product diversification. By the time of World War I, it was producing rubber for consumer goods such as shoes, boots, tennis balls, and waterproof clothing, and for industrial goods such as belting for power transmission and for mechanical conveyors. Goodrich also expanded into chemical production. One of its first products in this field was Vulcalock, an adhesive capable of bonding rubber to metal and used to protect pipes and storage tanks from the corrosive materials they often contained. In 1926 a Goodrich engineer developed a method for plasticizing polyvinyl chloride (PVC), turning this waste chemical compound into the material recognized today as vinyl. Goodrich marketed its PVC products under the brand names Geon and Koroseal, applying them to such varied uses as floor tiles, garden hoses, and electrical insulation. Goodrich also grew with the nation's aviation industry, producing airplane tires and the first airplane de-icers, important devices used in the achievement of all-weather flying.

The automobile and aviation industries, along with the rubber demand created by World War I, powered Goodrich's expansion through the first 30 years of the 20th century. In 1912 Goodrich re-incorporated as a New York company and increased its production capacity by acquiring the Diamond Rubber Company, which owned plants adjacent to Goodrich's in Akron.

Great Depression Setbacks

On the eve of the Great Depression, Goodrich acquired two more rubber companies, the Hood Rubber Company of Watertown, Massachusetts, and the Miller Rubber Company of Akron. The Depression, however, brought the company its first setbacks since the 1870s. The slowed U.S. economy reduced rubber demand, and Goodrich incurred over $24 million in net losses between 1930 and 1933. The depression also affected the company's labor relations with its 15,000 employees in Akron. The United Rubber Workers union (URW) was formed in 1934, and in 1936 national labor leader John Lewis came to Akron to rally union support. His visit sparked a five-week strike at the plants of Goodrich, Goodyear, and Firestone, temporarily shutting down the nation's three largest rubber producers.

World War II and Recovery

Recovery for Goodrich came with the nation's preparations for World War II. At the time of the war's outbreak in Europe, the United States was importing 97 percent of its crude rubber from Southeast Asia. Japanese expansion in the Pacific threatened this supply, while German advances in Europe and Africa interrupted supply routes through the Suez Canal and the Mediterranean Sea. In cooperation with the nation's rubber companies, the U.S. government began an intensive stockpiling and conservation effort. It also committed itself to developing synthetic rubber technology.

The rubber industry had known how to make synthetic rubber since the late 1930s. In 1937 Goodrich opened a pilot plant for producing butadiene-copolymer synthetic rubber, and within two years it was using synthetic rubber in some of its commercial products. As long as crude rubber supplies were cheap and plentiful, however, synthetic rubber remained an expensive alternative. In 1939 John L. Collyer took over as Goodrich's president after having spent ten years working for a British rubber company. Collyer returned to the United States convinced of its need to develop synthetic rubber production before it was drawn into the European conflict. Under his direction Goodrich introduced in June 1940 the first passenger-car tire in the United States to contain synthetic rubber. Called Ameripol—for its use of a polymer of American materials—this tire was more expensive than one made of natural rubber, but it gained rapid consumer acceptance because it outlasted conventional tires. After Collyer's appearance before a Senate Military Affairs Committee hearing on national preparedness, the federal government announced plans to build its own synthetic rubber plants. Goodrich cooperated with this effort, building and operating three such plants for wartime production in Port Neches and Borger, Texas, and in Louisville, Kentucky. These plants had a combined capacity of 165,000 tons per year, making Goodrich the nation's leading synthetic rubber manufacturer by the war's end.

Postwar Return to the Consumer Market

Goodrich avoided any postwar interruptions in its growth by quickly converting to meet consumer demand. The U.S. auto industry's return to peacetime production kept the demand for tires high, and Goodrich met this demand by introducing the first 100 percent synthetic rubber tire in 1945. Two years later it developed the tubeless puncture-sealing tire that increased motorists' protection from blow-outs. The company's LifeSaver and Safetyliner tubeless tires gained wide popularity in the early 1950s, and by 1955 tubeless tires became standard equipment on new cars. Ten years later Goodrich brought another innovation to U.S. drivers, the first radial tires for passenger cars. The radial dramatically changed the U.S. tire industry by increasing tire life by up to 50 percent, and like its tubeless predecessor, it ultimately became standard equipment on U.S. cars.

Goodrich further diversified its production in the postwar era. Continuing a long tradition of research and development, it opened a new research center in Brecksville, Ohio, in 1948. B.F. Goodrich Chemical Company, a subsidiary founded in 1943, took over the company's wartime plants and built new ones in Marietta and Avon Lake, Ohio, and in Calvert City, Kentucky. Production of Goodrich's Geon and Koroseal plastic products expanded into overseas markets with joint ventures in Britain and Japan. By 1955 Goodrich was manufacturing goods in five different areas, including tires, chemicals and plastics, footwear and flooring, industrial products, and sponge rubber goods. It had operations in 21 nations on six continents, and in 1966 its sales reached a record $1 billion.

Challenges of 1960s and 1970s

Goodrich's fortunes declined, however, when a 1967 strike began a decade of rocky labor relations and interrupted production. In April 1967 the URW walked off of jobs at Goodrich, Firestone, and Uniroyal, and the resulting strike stalled rubber production in Akron for 86 days. That strike, along with a six-month work stoppage at one of the company's chemical plants, cost Goodrich a 27.6 percent decrease in its profits from the previous year. Three years later Goodrich was once again facing serious losses because of strikes in the rubber and related industries. The URW walked out on Goodrich plants for five weeks, while strikes by the Teamsters Union and General Motors workers also hurt the nation's tire markets. Goodrich's net income in 1970 dropped by $22 million. Continued hard times in the nation's auto and rubber industries brought Goodrich back to the bargaining table in 1976. A 141-day URW strike stopped production in all of Goodrich's domestic tire plants and finally required the intercession of U.S. Labor Secretary W. J. Usery, Jr. to settle it.

These crippling experiences with labor disputes and the stagnation of the U.S. auto industry convinced Goodrich that its future was not in tires. In 1971 Goodrich's net income had fallen to $1.7 million from a high of $48.6 million in 1966.

Plastics and Aerospace Instead of Tires

Ready for a drastic change, the company handed its reins to a rubber industry outsider in 1972. O. Pendleton Thomas, a former oil executive with the Atlantic Richfield Company, shook up Goodrich by having chemicals and plastics replace tires as the foundation of the company's business. At the time Thomas took over, Goodrich's position among U.S. tiremakers had fallen to a weak fourth and the industry showed no signs of improving. The success of radials had cut consumer demand for replacement tires, while the oil crisis had lessened the U.S. taste for new cars. Thomas streamlined Goodrich's tire operations by closing unprofitable plants and retail outlets and concentrating on certain product niches, such as high-performance replacement tires. By maximizing profits in its tire business, he developed the capital necessary to increase the capacity of Goodrich's chemical and plastics production. In 1976 Thomas changed The B.F. Goodrich Company's name to The BFGoodrich Company.

Thomas's program of retrenchment and redeployment allowed his successor, John D. Ong, to develop Goodrich's chemicals business in the 1980s. Goodrich had long been the nation's number-one producer of PVC, the versatile plastic used primarily in the construction industry, as well as a producer of specialty chemicals used in products ranging from cosmetics to floor polishes. Like its tire division, Goodrich's chemical production had been hurt by the petroleum shortages and sluggish national economy of the 1970s, but when Ong took over in 1979, he maintained the course set by Thomas. The acquisition in 1979 of Tremco Inc., a producer of roofing products and construction sealants, strengthened Goodrich's position in specialty chemicals markets. Ong also announced plans to double Goodrich's PVC production by the mid-1980s, and he sank millions into the development of a plant in Convent, Louisiana. This project backfired, however, when the nation's housing industry went into its worst slump in 36 years and PVC demand plummeted. Goodrich suddenly found itself plagued by an overcapacity in its chemical production, and the company ended 1982 with a $32.8 million loss.

Goodrich's tailspin in the early 1980s led to the most dramatic changes in its history. Taking a record loss of $354.6 million in 1985, the company sold off the Louisiana plant into which it had sunk so much capital. In 1986 Ong merged Goodrich's tire division with Uniroyal, which had just fought a costly takeover battle with corporate raider Carl Icahn. The jointly owned Uniroyal-Goodrich Tire Company looked good on paper for both companies, combining Goodrich's replacement tire business with Uniroyal's original equipment market to make it the nation's second largest tire producer. Unfortunately, the relationship faltered, and in December 1987 Goodrich sold its interest in the venture for $225 million to an investment group that had already bought out Uniroyal. Shortly thereafter, Goodrich sold off its 38-acre factory complex in Akron, ending its nearly century-long association with the U.S. tire industry. In 1988 Goodrich acquired Tramco Incorporated, a provider of maintenance and repair services for commercial aircraft.

Strategic Moves in the 1990s

With the full divestiture of its tire business, Goodrich became a company devoted solely to the production of chemicals, plastics, and aerospace goods. The recovery of its PVC business and the wise investment of capital gained from its tire division sale had in the early 1990s stabilized the company. But in 1993 chief executive John D. Ong sold off the PVC business, to the concern of investors, in favor of emphasizing the company's other chemical businesses.

Some analysts were skeptical of these strategic turns. Writer Zachary Schiller of *Business Week,* for example, noted that "The company has produced an average annual return on equity of just 1.4 percent since Ong became CEO in 1979, compared with an average of 14.4 percent for the companies in the Standard & Poors Industrials index." Moreover, the companies in the S&P index posted a 5.4 percent annual gain, but Goodrich's sales fell an average of 3.5 percent per year, wrote Schiller. Stock lagged at 44, not even close to its 1989 height of 69.

Ong, however, noted for his willingness to change course, pushed into aerospace, although the industry had been sluggish for more than a decade. He built on Goodrich's aircraft parts and servicing business. Using proceeds from the sale of PVC, BFGoodrich acquired in 1993 Cleveland Pneumatic Co., a landing gear maker that complemented Goodrich's wheel-and-brake business, and Rosemount Aerospace, which made sensors that measure flight and data (speed and temperature, for example). That same year also marked the additions of the Landing Gear Division and Landing Gear Services Division, and Sanncor Industries.

Ong persisted with his current business mix, pointing out that the company was now positioned for growth opportunities. By 1994 the specialty chemical business started to show improvement, and the aerospace business held promise. The aircraft wheel-and-brake business gradually grew into aircraft parts and servicing. The following year BFGoodrich acquired QSI, Inc. in Greenville, South Carolina. In 1995 purchases included Hoskins Aviation and de-icing product lines and associated technology from Lucas Aerospace.

By 1996 BFGoodrich reported that earnings in 1996 were significantly higher than in the past three years. For the second year in a row, BFGoodrich Aerospace and BFGoodrich Specialty Chemical set records for sales and operating income. The growing demand for replacement products and service proved advantageous to the aerospace division, which also benefited from the upturn in new commercial aircraft production. BFGoodrich Specialty Chemicals acquired five businesses and increased manufacturing capacity at existing facilities. Moreover, three new plants were seen as the base for further expansion in Europe and Asia.

In the mid-1990s, Ong reflected on the last decade that took BFGoodrich from a struggling company that manufactured commodity products and sold them in highly cyclical markets to a streamlined organization focused on specialty businesses. He noted that the company's inclination for risk-taking lay within the BFGoodrich structure rather than outside. By late 1996 BFGoodrich shares reached "historic, 126-year highs" and trade at levels once thought unlikely, Ong said. He added that after challenges rocked corporate America in the 1980s and 1990s, BFGoodrich started reaching goals. Ong noted that market capitalization at the end of 1996 had increased by about 100 percent from the time the new BFGoodrich came into being at the end of 1993.

As Ong was slated to retire in 1997, David L. Burner was tapped to succeed him. Meanwhile BFGoodrich remained focused on growth and improved returns as an aerospace and specialty chemicals company. Acquisitions that complemented and strengthened its current businesses remained on the forefront. Businesses not central to the strategy were ripe for divestment, as in the 1996 sale of Tremco to RPM, Inc., with the proceeds invested in the expansion of aerospace and specialty chemicals. BFGoodrich anticipated growth in sales and earnings in 1997 and 1998, excluding special items. Continuing expansion of current business worldwide and strategic acquisitions were expected to sustain growth.

Principal Divisions

BFGoodrich Aerospace; BFGoodrich Specialty Chemicals.

Further Reading

B.F. Goodrich Story: Nine Stories Celebrating One Hundred Twenty-Five Years, Akron Ohio: B.F. Goodrich Corporate Communications, 1995.

Collyer, John Lyon, *The B.F. Goodrich Story of Creative Enterprise: 1870–1952,* New York: The Newcomen Society in North America, 1952.

Deutsch, Claudia H., "Goodrich Finally Gets It Right," *The New York Times,* March 12, 1989.

"Goodrich's Cash Cow Starts to Deliver," *Business Week,* November 14, 1977.

Ong, John D., *The BFGoodrich Company: A Proud Heritage, An Exciting Future,* New York: Newcomen Society of the United States, 1995.

Schiller, Zachary, "Goodrich: From Tires to PVC to Chemicals to Aerospace," *Business Week,* July 18, 1994, pp. 86–87.

—Timothy J. Shannon
—udpated by Catherine Hamrick

Bird Corporation

1077 Pleasant Street
Norwood, Massachusetts 02062
U.S.A.
(617) 551-0656
Fax: (617) 762-6586

Public Company
Incorporated: 1795 as Bird
Employees: 174 (1995)
Sales: $51.96 million (1996)
Stock Exchanges: NASDAQ
SICs: 2952 Asphalt Felts and Coatings; 5033 Roofing,
   Siding & Insulation

Bird Corporation (Bird), which began its third century of business in 1995, is best known for making asphalt roofing shingles and vinyl siding, popular items in the American construction market. After expanding into window fabrication and environmental services, Bird refocused itself in the mid-1990s and sold these operations. Its remaining business unit was devoted totally to the production of commercial and residential asphalt and roll roofing materials, which were marketed through independent wholesalers and retail building materials outlets. Bird's main geographic market was the northeastern United States; its base of operations remained near the site of its original paper plant in Massachusetts.

Early History

In 1995 Bird celebrated its 200th anniversary, proudly announcing that it was one of the ten oldest existing companies in the United States. The company opened for business during George Washington's second term as president, when George Bird obtained a license to build waterwheels on the Charles River in Needham and Dover (only a few miles from Boston) and set up a small paper mill. At first production was limited to five reams of handmade paper per day. However, by 1812 Bird had established his reputation as a maker of quality paper, and his company was chosen to produce the rag paper on which

currency for the new nation was printed. Bird opened a second plant on the Neponset River in East Walpole, Massachusetts, in 1817. Bird's son, Francis, joined the company in 1833 and the business continued to expand steadily, aided by the introduction of new products made with newly developed machinery.

The late 1800s brought great changes for the growing company. When Charles Sumner Bird graduated from Harvard and joined the company in 1877, the company took the name ''Bird and Son,'' which it would keep for the next 100 years. Charles Bird remained the guiding force at the company for the next 50 years. An eccentric character filled with energy and enthusiasm, he would spend half of his day dressed in overalls and working in the mill, and the other half in his starched shirt learning the details of running the business. He also spent many evenings at home, performing experiments in his kitchen.

These experiments proved a lifesaver when the main Bird mill was destroyed by a terrible fire in 1880, closely followed by the worst flood in Massachusetts history. The only equipment still usable could produce only coarse paper, rather than the fine writing paper on which Bird's reputation had been built. Charles Bird retreated to his kitchen table, and within months three new Bird products were on the market. ''Neponset Black Waterproof Building Paper'' was a tarred paper that quickly became popular for building New England barns. ''Neponset Red Rope Roofing Paper'' and ''Neponset Paroid Roofing Paper'' soon followed. In one of the original American recycling activities, Bird salvaged wood resins and discarded rope from ships in the Boston harbor to produce these papers.

As a result, the company emerged from this crisis even stronger than before as it celebrated the beginning of its second century. Having been driven by disaster to manufacture the first felt-based asphalt roofing product on the market, Bird then made this product a mainstay of the company. Asphalt shingles as introduced in 1895 remained virtually unchanged and in widespread use for almost a century. The company also began to expand outside of the rural areas of New England into the Midwest, South, and Canada, and to market more new products, such as corrugated boxes.

Company Perspectives:

"Over the long term we have found that we prosper when we insist on the highest quality products, produced in the most cost effective, modern facilities, designed and delivered to our customers with their needs in mind, by people totally dedicated to these simple principles."

A new plant was built in East Walpole in 1904 for production of roofing materials and served as the company's headquarters for more than 75 years. A highlight of the building was a machine invented by Charles Bird himself to heat and dry rag material more quickly. Bird also imported a German papermaking screen and began to manufacture it at his plant, giving birth to the now-defunct Bird Industrial Group.

Along with the technological innovations he instituted during his half century in charge of the family business, Charles Bird was also a pioneer in the area of employee relations. Between 1900 and 1925, Bird became one of the first American companies to offer an eight-hour workday (as opposed to the standard twelve-hour day of that time), an employee suggestion box, an employee credit union, paid employee vacations, and a benefit association to provide income for sick or disabled employees.

Prosperity and a Rude Awakening in the 1930s–1970s

The great guiding figure of the company, Charles Sumner Bird, ended his fifty years of management in 1927 on the brink of the Great Depression in which his creative approach to crisis would have been welcome. Nevertheless, the company managed to stay financially sound through the 1930s, even acquiring several faltering companies along the way. When World War II began, Bird once again was flexible enough to adapt its roofing and paper technology and create new products. It began to manufacture shell casings and waterproof shipping cartons for sale to the government. Following World War II, Bird was buoyed by the postwar housing boom and continued to expand its line of building materials. In 1964, it introduced a new product at the New York World's Fair: vinyl siding. This product quickly became extremely popular and Bird earned record profits year after year into the 1970s.

However, the economic expansion of the previous thirty years came to a crashing halt with one unforeseen event: the Arab oil embargo of the mid-1970s. Suddenly the price of asphalt—the essential ingredient of Bird's shingle production—rose dramatically, and soon afterward the national housing boom stopped short. As the decade ended, Bird had to report that it earned no profit in 1980, an occurrence unheard of in its 186-year history. To add to its difficulties, Bird also began to face competition from foreign manufacturers, and the first of 550 asbestos-related liability cases was filed against it.

In order to survive, Bird had to reexamine its entire approach to business. It was time to move from production that was so dependent on asphalt and felt-based products. At the same time, the plant built in 1904 had become outdated, as had much of the machinery in general use by the roofing industry.

Back to Basics in the 1980s

As it entered the 1980s, Bird experimented with a number of new business operations and invested $15 million in a state-of-the-art computerized facility, designed to produce shingles with refinements such as fiberglass matting and improved coatings. In the Bird tradition, the plant was built around an existing facility near the site of the original paper mill. But, at the same time, the company changed its name from "Bird and Son" to "Bird Inc." in 1983 to show it had become a modernized company.

New operations included an environmental services company based in Texas and vinyl building products and window fabrication manufacturing based in Kentucky. Initially these operations were promising, with the environmental services business quadrupling between 1989 and 1992. Bird was chosen to clean up a dumping area behind a Texas refinery and Bird celebrated in 1990 by once again changing its name, this time to its current name, Bird Corporation.

However, Bird entered the 1990s with serious financial difficulties brewing. Although its sales continued to grow, its earnings dropped each year, from $5.18 million in 1991 to the company's low point, a net loss of over $28 million in 1993. George Haufler, CEO at the time, sold peripheral operations such as Bird's municipal sludge disposal business in order to focus on more promising operations such as the industrial resource recovery business. However, Haufler was forced to step aside in late 1993 after he was diagnosed with lung cancer. Joseph Vecchiolla, who had joined Bird earlier that year as vice-president and chief financial officer, was named president and chief operating officer. With a background in finance and operations management, Vecchiolla had been brought into the company in a conscious strategy of succession planning.

Vecchiolla inherited the company's management just as the worst financial year in Bird's history was almost over. The joint venture to fabricate vinyl replacement windows, just formed the previous year, was blamed for the bulk of 1993's $28 million in losses. Bird was forced to enter into a $65 million refinancing agreement and the company was restructured to concentrate on its housing products operations.

In 1994 Bird began to jettison major operations in order to regain its financial footing. It sold its distribution businesses (located in New England, New York, Kentucky, Texas, Louisiana, and Arizona) to Cameron Ashley Inc., allowing it to pay off $23 million of its debt. The company ended 1994 with a net loss of $3.68 million, a major improvement over the previous year.

In March of 1995 Bird sold its vinyl building products manufacturing operation (including the ill-fated vinyl replacement window venture) to Jannock, Inc. for $47.5 million, again using the sale proceeds to reduce its debt. That November, Bird also sold all of its holdings in its Texas hydrocarbon waste recycling center, effecting its total withdrawal from the environmental services industry. Nevertheless, Bird still sustained a net loss for 1995, slightly over $12 million.

As a result of these divestitures, Bird's manufacturing operations were reduced to one primary unit by the end of 1995: the Housing Group, which manufactured and sold asphalt roofing products from the home base in Norwell, Massachusetts. Facilities at this location included a roofing manufacturing facility, a granule plant, a quarry, an asphalt plant, and a private landfill. Vecchiolla retained a position as chairman of the board of directors, and Richard Maloof, former president of the Roofing Division, began to serve as president and chief operating officer in May 1995.

Bird's board of directors soon decided the best course of action would be for the company to merge with another corporation and it entered into an agreement to be acquired by CertainTeed Corporation, another manufacturer of roofing materials and a subsidiary of the French company, Saint-Gobain Corporation (Compagnie de Saint Gobain). Vecchiolla explained the reasoning behind the merger: "Bird has enjoyed a rich and innovative history since its founding over 200 years ago. However, during the past year it became apparent that greater progress could be made if Bird became part of a larger, financially strong organization with similar goals and philosophies." It was hoped that the merger would strengthen Bird's remaining core operations.

The announcement of the planned merger in March 1996 set an unexpected chain of events in motion. Bird was one of three companies which already controlled over half of the national market for asphalt shingles. The U.S. Justice Department viewed the planned merger as having potential anti-competitive results and immediately launched an investigation of the industry's leading companies, including Bird. By May 1996 CertainTeed had terminated its agreement with Bird. No reason was given by CertainTeed for dropping the $50 million transaction, but a spokeswoman implied that the investigation "could have influenced the decision," according to the *Wall Street Journal.* Bird's stock value fell 32 percent as soon as the termination was announced. Shortly afterward, the Justice Department dropped the investigation without taking action against anyone in the roofing industry. However, the merger with CertainTeed was not revived.

Surprisingly, Bird weathered this rather chaotic episode by reporting its first profitable year since 1992 with net earnings of $2.3 million in 1996. Bird's management was encouraged by the return to profitability in 1996 and believed that the company had completed its financial and operational turnaround and reemerged with a strong position in the industry.

Further Reading

"Bird Chairman Announces New President and Issues Personal Statement," *PR Newswire,* November 4, 1993.

"Bird Corporation Agrees to Merge with CertainTeed Corporation," *PR Newswire,* March 15, 1996.

"Bird Corporation Announces Sale of Hydrocarbon Waste Recycling Center Joint Venture to GTS Duratek, Inc.," *PR Newswire,* November 30, 1995.

"Bird Corporation Announces Successful Close of Distribution Businesses Sale to Cameron Ashley Inc.," *PR Newswire,* August 23, 1994.

"Bird Corporation—Department of Justice Closes Antitrust Investigation," *PR Newswire,* October 9, 1996.

"Bird Corporation Reports $28.3 Million 1993 Loss," *PR Newswire,* March 11, 1994.

"Bird Corporation Sells Municipal Sludge Business to Browning-Ferris Industries," *PR Newswire,* July 22, 1993.

The Bird Heritage: An American Success Story, Norwell, Mass.: Bird Inc., 1987.

"Bird Shares Fall 32 Percent on Termination of Acquisition Pact by CertainTeed," *Wall Street Journal* (Eastern Edition), May 6, 1996, p. B8.

Hage, David, "Corporate Reincarnation; Converting to New Business Lines," *U.S. News & World Report,* June 15, 1992, p. 43.

Hower, Wendy, et al., "Bird, Inc. Reorganization, Merger Plan with Newly-Formed Bird Corporation," *Boston Business Journal,* June 25, 1990, p. 36.

"Justice Has Begun Probe of Pricing in Asphalt Shingles," *Wall Street Journal* (Eastern Edition), April 25, 1996, p. A10.

"Richard C. Maloof Named to Bird Corporation Board," *PR Newswire,* December 6, 1994.

"Vecchiolla Named Director of Bird Corporation," *PR Newswire,* December 3, 1993.

—Gerry Azzata

Blessings Corp.

200 Enterprise Drive
Newport News, Virginia 23603
U.S.A.
(757) 887-2100
Fax: (757) 887-3787

Public Company
Incorporated: 1944 as Associated Baby Services, Inc.
Employees: 475
Sales: $158.1 million (1996)
Stock Exchanges: American
SICs: 3081 Unsupported Plastics Film and Sheet

Blessings Corp. produces plastics film products for health care, agricultural, and industrial applications. These include materials used by makers of disposal baby diapers and feminine hygiene products. Kimberley-Clark Corp. alone accounted for nearly 45 percent of Blessings' total sales in 1996.

Private Company Until 1962

General Diaper Service, the precursor of Blessings, was founded in 1932 by Morris A. Bonoff. Bonoff, whose father owned a laundry service, needed some way to support his family in the depths of the Depression and asked himself what he might do that no one else wanted to do and that someone might pay for. Picking up dirty diapers, washing them, and returning them to the customer was the answer for someone already steeped in the laundry trade. Shortly afterward, Bonoff launched *Baby Talk,* said to be the first baby magazine in the United States. The business was incorporated in Delaware in 1944 as Associated Baby Services, Inc. by a group of diaper-service operators led by Bonoff. The company began manufacturing disposable products in 1954. Net sales rose from $8.3 million in fiscal 1957 to $9.9 million in fiscal 1960 and 1961; net income increased from $132,014 in 1957 to $189,222 in 1961.

In 1962, when Associated Baby Services first offered shares of common stock to the public, the company and its subsidiaries operated diaper, laundry, dry-cleaning, and linen-supply services, publishing *Baby Talk,* and making disposable-diaper products. The diaper service ran out of 10 plants in 10 states. Laundry and linen-rental service divisions serviced the metropolitan areas of New Orleans and Houston, providing sheets, pillow cases, towels, table linens, uniforms, and other textile items to commercial and industrial establishments. The company operated 337 vehicles and was leasing a plant in Bound Brook, New Jersey, for the production of disposable items such as diapers and underpads for hospitals and nursing homes. These were constructed as a three-ply sandwich of plastics-film backing, absorbent material, and nonwoven facing. Corporate headquarters was in New York City. Bonoff served as both president and chairman.

The Pampers Challenge, 1966–1972

By 1965, when it had a circulation of more than 800,000, *Baby Talk,* was the leading monthly publication in the United States edited specifically for expectant mothers and was said to be making a handsome profit. Company sales reached $14.4 million in fiscal 1965 and net income $646,000. However, the business—and 400 others in the United States—faced devastation with the introduction in 1966 of Pampers disposable paper diapers by Procter & Gamble and, subsequently, similar products by competitors such as Kimberley-Clark and Scott Paper Co., at a cost of only about 10 percent more than (cotton) cloth diapers.

As the nation's largest diaper service by 1969, Associated Baby Services had the most to lose by a stampede to paper products. By then the company was operating 21 local services in 25 metropolitan areas of 11 states, handling 6 million diapers weekly. Of its net sales of nearly $27 million and pretax profits of $2.6 million in fiscal 1970 (the year ended April 25, 1970), diaper services accounted for 58 percent and 79 percent, respectively. Nevertheless, Associated Baby Services expressed confidence that its cloth-diaper business would continue to grow because so many mothers were switching from hand washing. Moreover, disposable diapers posed a pollution threat to communities with sewage problems and were thought to contribute more than cloth to baby rash. During 1969 and 1970 the company acquired local diaper services routes throughout the country as owners of such routes retired or decided to sell out.

Associated Baby Services was not neglecting its other businesses, however. The linen and laundry services in New Orleans and Houston accounted for 18 percent of 1970 sales, with the former showing impressive growth. Disposable products (including disposal diapers), was the fastest-growing sector of the company, accounting for 17 percent of 1970 sales. These products, made at three company plants, included materials for hospitals and other health-care facilities, plastic film to produce waterproof backing on disposable products, as well as packaging and wrapping material, and disposable head-rest covers and paper slippers for the transportation market. *Baby Talk* contributed about 5 percent to total company revenues. Associated Baby Services' disposable diapers (sold by its deliverymen), bed pads, surgical gowns, pillowcases, and similar items were being sold under the trade name ''Blessings.'' In 1972 the company changed its name to Blessings.

As part of its effort to diversify, Associated Baby Services acquired Preferred Dental & Supply Co., a mail-order firm, in 1970. By late 1973 Blessings had added to its activities the development and assembly of high-precision automatic machinery for sewing paper and fabrics, both for its own use and for customers. A subsidiary, Acme Automatic Disposables Co., and a division, Automatic Thread Control Co., were moved to Bound Brook from New York City that year. A new plant for the Edison Plastics Co. subsidiary in South Plainfield, New Jersey, was brought into production in September 1972.

Deemphasizing Baby Diapers, 1975–1984

In spite of its growing scope of activities, Blessings' net income dwindled to $1.4 million in fiscal 1973 and $1.1 million in fiscal 1974. The following year the company incurred a loss of $4.4 million after taking a charge of $5.2 million to write off to goodwill ''certain activities which had not attained their assigned earnings quota,'' according to a company spokesperson. That year David Lewis, a paper-company executive, was brought in as president, and two years later he succeeded Bonoff as chairman and chief executive officer. Lewis liquidated Preferred Dental & Supply, which was losing $400,000 a year, in 1976. He also decided *Baby Talk* was overstaffed and fired all but three of its about two dozen employees.

By April 1977 Williamson-Dickie Manufacturing Co. of Fort Worth, Texas, owned almost 30 percent of Blessings' common stock. That year this company—primarily a maker of work clothes—raised its stake in Blessings to 58 percent by offering other shareholders $3 in cash and a $9 subordinated sinking-fund debenture, due in 1992 and bearing 10 percent annual interest, for each share of stock. Blessings remained a separate company, however, and its stock continued to be traded on the American Stock Exchange. It moved its headquarters from New York City to Piscataway, New Jersey, in 1978.

Blessings opened a factory in Washington, Georgia, for its plastic films division, expanding it in 1980 and again in 1983.

The company sold its New Orleans and Houston linen services in 1979 for $4.7 million. In 1980 it still processed 6 million baby diapers a week in 24 plants, using a proprietary 13-step process and employing about 400 trucks for pickup and delivery. It also processed thousands of adult ''Geri-Pads'' for incontinent patients in nursing homes. The Edison Plastics Co. subsidiary manufactured thin-gauge plastic films for industry and agriculture. Founded in 1978, the GeriCare Division was manufacturing cotton adult and baby diapers for use by its own units and for sale to others. *Baby Talk* continued to be sold to department stores, diaper services, dairies, and firms in the infant market, usually for free distribution to customers and prospects. Net sales rose from $48.2 million in fiscal 1977 to $53.7 million in fiscal 1980.

In 1982 Blessings was still the country's largest diaper service, with 28 percent of the nation's $120-million market. However, although this segment of its business accounted for half of company sales, it contributed only one-third to net income.

Edison Plastics, more profitable, controlled 70 percent of the $8.5-million-a-year market for plastic outer shields for hospital bedpans and more than 80 percent of the $5-million-a-year market for plastic sanitary pads. GeriCare ($9 million in sales), sold its lines to linen-supply and textile companies for use in hospitals and nursing homes.

Lewis, who told a *Forbes* reporter in 1983 that his company's future was not in baby diapers but ''at the other end of the age span,'' made good on this belief later that year, when he negotiated the sale of this sector of Blessings' business to Sketchley, a British company, for $13 million. The transaction was completed in March 1984. ''We were on both sides of the street,'' James P. Luke, the company's chief financial officer, explained to a *Barron's* reporter. ''We chose to go with disposables.''

Primarily Plastic Films, 1985–1994

In 1985 Blessings earned $5.3 million on revenues of $63.6 million. Forty percent of its plastics sales were to disposable-diaper makers, chiefly Kimberley-Clark, maker of the Huggies brand diaper. The Edison Plastics division, which also made plastic liners for surgical instrument holders, sanitary napkins, and other high-quality plastic-sheet products, accounted for about three-quarters of revenues. The publishing subsidiary accounted for 7 percent and Geri-Care for 17 percent.

A plant for the production of polyethylene and polypropylene, built in McAlester, Oklahoma, opened in late 1985. Geri-Care added a factory in Union City, New Jersey, in 1987, and in Medley, Florida, in 1989. The publishing division was sold to Parenting Unlimited, an investment group, in 1987. The following year the company acquired Advanced Compounding, a manufacturer of specialized plastic materials in Cheshire, Connecticut, from RW Technology Inc.

Geri-Care, making reusable cloth diapers that linen services rented to nursing homes, saw its future tied to the growth of the population 75 years or older. Lewis said that in addition to the perhaps 900,000 residents of nursing homes who were incontinent, perhaps another 11 million adults in the United States suffered from the malady but were not institutionalized. In an attempt to reach that market, Blessings introduced a disposable adult diaper bearing the brand name Confidence in 1985, but sales proved catastrophically small.

Lewis stepped down at the end of 1987 and was succeeded as president and chief executive officer by Ivan E. Backer, corporate vice-president and general manager of the Edison Plastics division. The following year Blessings rejected a proposal by Williamson-Dickie to buy the remaining shares in the company at $18.75 a share. Also in 1989, Blessings acquired a Newport News, Virginia, plant manufacturing polypropylene film and sheets from a division of Chicago-based Industrial Coating Group Inc. for about $2.5 million. In 1991 the company completed a new technical and commercial development center adjacent to the plant at a cost of nearly $9 million. A $5 million expansion of the Georgia plant also was completed that year, in which Blessings had net income of $9.6 million on revenues of $111 million.

Blessings Since 1994

In 1994 Blessings sold its Geri-Care Products division for a small after-tax gain. This segment of its business had accounted for 12 percent of its sales but only five percent of its profits in 1993. That year the company shut down its Advanced Compounding division and moved its head offices to Newport News. Also in 1994, Blessings purchased a 60 percent interest in Nacional de Envases Plasticos, S.A. de C.V. (NEPSA), a Mexican-based plastic-films processor and maker and its associated firms, in exchange for 200,000 share of common stock and about $41 million in cash. With three factories in the Mexico City metropolitan area, NEPSA was the leading Mexican manufacturer of extruded, printed, and converted plastic films and also was printing point-of-purchase messages on its products for a variety of packaging and uses.

Blessings was ranked among the top 100 small U.S. companies by *Forbes* in 1992, with a five-year average return on equity—profits divided by net worth—of 17.2 percent. It set new records for revenues and net income every year between 1988 and 1994. The purchase of NEPSA, however, raised Blessings' long-term debt from $8 million to $28 million, and the collapse of the Mexican peso at the end of 1994 took a toll on this subsidiary's earnings.

In 1994 Blessings earned a record $11.9 million on sales of $151 million, but in 1995 the company's net income slid to $5.9 million on revenues of $156 million, and its stock dropped to below $10 a share, compared to a high of about $17 in 1994. Earnings for 1996 were lower again—$5 million on revenues of $158.1 million. Management blamed high raw-material costs, product development, increased competition in the health-care market, and the impact of Mexico's monetary problems on NEPSA. In February 1997 Blessings announced it would suspend its cash dividend in the first quarter of the year and would buy back up to 10 percent of its stock to increase the value, still under $10 a share. The company's long-term debt was $36.4 million in mid-1996.

Principal Subsidiaries

ASPEN Industrial, S.A. de C.V. (Mexico); Edison Exports, Inc. FSC Limited (Jamaica); Edison Plastics International, Inc.; Hermes Industrial, S.A. de C.V. (Mexico, 60%); Mexicana de Tintas, S.A. (Mexico, 60%); Nacional de Envases Plasticos, S.A. de C.V. (Mexico, 60%); Plastihul, S.A. de C.V. (Mexico, 60%); Servicios Profesionales Vigo (Mexico, 60%).

Further Reading

"Blessings Corporation," *Stock Market Magazine,* November 1973, pp. 13–15.

Jones, John Wayne, "Associated Baby Services Is Set to Pin Down Record High Earnings," *Barron's,* December 21, 1970, pp. 17, 20.

Krewatch, Mark, "Blessings Corp. Will Buy Back up to 10 Percent of Its Stock," *Knight-Ridder Tribune Business News,* February 7, 1997, p. 207B1105.

Kuseski, Allen R., "Associated Baby Services," *Wall Street Transcript,* December 9, 1968, p. 15148.

Rohmann, Laura, "Up from the Cradle," *Forbes,* July 4, 1983, pp. 69, 72.

Weiss, Gary, "Formula for Growth," *Barron's,* September 8, 1986, pp. 15, 24.

—Robert Halasz

British Steel

British Steel plc

9 Albert Embankment
London SE1 7SN
United Kingdom
(+44) 171-735-7654
Fax: (+44) 171-587-1142
Web site: http://www.britishsteel.co.uk

Public Company
Incorporated: 1967 as the British Steel Corporation
Employees: 53,900
Sales: $10.75 billion (1996)
Stock Exchanges: London New York Toronto
SICs: 3320 Iron and Steel Foundries; 5051 Metals
  Service Centers and Offices

British Steel plc is the third largest steel producer in the world and the largest steel producer in Europe. More than 50 percent of the company's sales are to overseas markets, making the company one of the top ten exporters in the United Kingdom. British Steel has more than 70 sales and distribution companies located in over 75 countries around the world. The company's steel products are used in construction, transportation, automobiles, domestic appliances, engineering, energy, aerospace, and packaging.

Over 14 million tons of steel are produced each year by more than 15 operating units, some of them leaders in their fields. British Steel Engineering Steels, for example, is the largest manufacturer of engineering steels in Europe. British Steel Tinplate is one of Europe's major suppliers of steel-based products used to produce food, beverage, household and industrial packaging. British Steel Tubes and Pipes is the largest supplier in the United Kingdom in the manufacture of welded steel tubes. British Steel Special Sections is the largest manufacturer of custom-designed hot and cold rolled special sections. The company is also heavily involved in recycling, with every plant a recycling at least 40 percent, and all new steel produced by British Steel contains some recycled steel.

Early History and Development

The company is the successor, by way of the state-owned British Steel Corporation (BSC), of the leading private steel companies that survived the Depression of the 1920s and 1930s and World War II. Under the Labour government of 1945 to 1951 these companies first profited from the large compensation payments they received for giving up their coal-mining interests to the state and then were nationalized themselves, on the grounds that they formed an oligopoly with the power to restrict output, raise prices, and prevent technical progress. The Iron and Steel Corporation of Great Britain was established in 1950 as a state holding company for their shares, but the steelmasters retained the initiative, mainly through a boycott organized by the British Iron and Steel Federation (BISF), the industry's trade association, which they controlled.

In autumn 1951 a new Conservative government suspended the corporation's activities after eight months of largely ineffective existence. Between 1953 and 1963 an Iron and Steel Holding and Realisation Agency sold off 16 of the 17 nationalized firms, mostly to the former shareholders. At the same time an Iron Steel Board was given the negative powers of fixing maximum prices for products sold in the United Kingdom and approving or rejecting any investment of over £100,000. Price control was nothing new, having begun on a more modest scale in 1932, with the result by the 1950s that losses during low points of the economic cycle could not be offset by higher profits in more prosperous times. The companies' reluctance to invest intensified, and the Iron and Steel Board—or rather the taxpayers who financed it—became the major source of new investment funds.

During the 1950s and 1960s the British steel industry lost its historic advantages of cheap coal and plentiful iron ore, the industry's basic raw materials. Coal prices rose by 134 percent between 1950 and 1967, and the domestic iron ore industry was neglected in favor of ore from new fields overseas. Rearmament, from 1950 onwards, caused the company to retain old plants, instead of investing in costly new plants, in the attempt to keep up with demand. Between 1945 and 1960 total crude steel production in the United Kingdom doubled in volume, an increase largely attributable to such technical innovations as oxygen-based production and continuous casting. The claim that the industry had now been taken out of politics was belied by the events of 1958 and 1959, when the Conservative prime minister, Harold Macmillan, sanctioned not the single extra strip mill the industry wanted, but two, one at Llanwern in Wales and another at Ravenscraig in Scotland, both subsidized from public funds and neither able to operate at full capacity.

However, the British steel industry's problems were not all due to the government or the companies. It faced new rivals, especially in Japan, as well as old ones, in France, West Germany, Belgium, and Luxembourg, which were now protected by the European Coal and Steel Community and some of which were blessed with deep-water harbors taking in high-grade ores. In addition, there was a general fall in the rate of growth of world demand for steel from about 1960, leading to declining prices and profits for the steel industry worldwide, a scramble to dispose of surplus output at the lowest sustainable prices, and a worldwide steel glut which lasted until 1969. The British industry in particular continued to be marked by a cautious attitude learned in the 1920s and never shaken off and by the refusal of the individual firms to cooperate with one another in anything that might threaten their own identities. The steel industry faced the 1960s with a fragmented structure based on investment decisions which, apart from the establishment of the Ravenscraig mill, had been made in the 1930s.

Re-Nationalization under Labour in the Mid-1960s

In 1964 the Labour Party returned to office with a commitment to re-nationalize steel. The BISF's response was the Benson report, which concluded that the industry needed to go over entirely to the basic oxygen process, to build extra capacity in much larger plants, to site them near the coasts (for raw materials supplies), and to shed 65 percent of existing plant space and 100,000 workers. These proposals gave the government new ammunition, since in spite of the companies' claims that they could provide most of the necessary capital from their falling profits, it was clear that the industry alone could not hope to finance these developments. The nationalized British Steel Corporation (BSC) began operations on July 28, 1967, just when new orders were at their lowest level in five years, and in a period of mergers among companies in France, Germany, and Japan. At its inception BSC was the second largest steel company in the noncommunist world, endowed with the assets of the 14 crude steel companies, whose output exceeded 475,000 tons. They employed 268,500 people and included Richard Thomas & Baldwins, a company that had remained in state ownership since 1951.

BSC faced some formidable problems. First, since compensation to the former owners was based on stock market values, and not—as in private mergers and acquisitions—on net assets or future profitability, the shareholders received about £350 million more than the assets were worth. A later Conservative government recognized the loss to BSC and wrote off that amount of its debt in 1972. In addition, the 14 companies' return on capital had fallen from 15 percent in 1956 to 3.7 percent, making them unable to carry out the Benson plan they had commissioned, and the sorry state of their assets was bound to damage BSC's profitability for some time to come. Also, 10 percent of crude steel production and about 30 percent of finished steel production remained in the private sector, leaving BSC with the generally less profitable bulk steel and lower-quality finished steel business. As the private firms were effectively subsidized through the controls on BSC's pricing of crude steel sold to them, they could concentrate resources on technical advances which allowed higher productivity, giving them about a third of the market for finished steel, with only a quarter of total capacity, by the late 1970s. In this respect BSC was unlike its major rivals abroad, which were diversified within steel and across other sectors. Finally, BSC's capital consisted of £834 million, to be repaid to the Treasury at a fixed rate of interest, regardless of its profit cycle. Between 1967 and 1980 BSC's interest payments were equivalent to 73 percent of its losses. A private-sector company in the same situation would not have been burdened with interest payments.

Unlike other public corporations BSC had been given the freedom to decide organizational questions for itself. Its structure was regionally based until 1970, divided into six product divisions until 1976, configured on a different geographical basis until 1980, and then redivided into different product divisions with numerous profit centers within them and linked to a new system of mostly self-financing local bonus schemes for the workers.

One unique aspect of BSC's organization was the presence of worker-directors, first on the boards of the regional groups, then on the boards of the product divisions, and lastly, after 1976, on the main board. The steel industry had long enjoyed a comparably good record in industrial relations. The relatively few strikes in the industry's history had usually been over demarcation among the trade unions, of which there were 17 in the industry in 1967, and among which the Iron and Steel Trades Confederation (ISTC) was dominant, containing half of the 80 percent of the work force which belonged to unions. It was the ISTC that felt most threatened by change, since it would tend to cut into the union's base among the less skilled workers. The part-time worker-directors were appointed after consultations with these unions and with the Trades Union Congress (TUC), the national labor federation. Since the management retained its monopoly of information and authority, the influence of these unelected representatives was minimal, ceasing altogether with their abolition in 1983, three years after the defeat of the national steelworkers' strike had signaled the end of the trade unions' influence in the company. In 1970 and 1971 the new Conservative government at first considered various ways of breaking up or partially privatizing BSC, then decided to continue with the status quo while raising the corporation's borrowing limits and giving some flexibility on pricing. BSC later announced that with British steel prices held below European Community levels from 1967 to 1975 the losses amounted to about £780 million, representing another indirect subsidy to the private sector, in this case to steel consumers.

BSC in the 1970s

The corporation initiated its "heritage program" in 1971 and 1972 to develop the strengths and overcome the weaknesses of the assets inherited from the private companies, in particular the low productivity of blast furnaces, which was due to inefficient cooling and the use of such low-grade material as coking coal with a high sulfur content. By 1973 BSC had invested £764 million in this program and in such new projects as Anchor III, the construction of a new plant at the Appleby-Frodingham complex in Scunthorpe, Lincolnshire, on the site of abandoned ironstone workings. At the nearby port of Immingham, a terminal was built to accommodate 100,000-ton vessels bringing foreign ore for the furnaces. The opening of the plant only three years after the scheme was authorized seemed to bode well for BSC's increased efficiency, and helped accelerate the trend whereby imported ores rose from 55 percent of the total used in the United Kingdom in 1967 to 85 percent in 1974.

By 1973 British steel consumption had exceeded 18 million tons a year. The 10-year development strategy started in 1973 envisaged concentration of resources on five inherited sites, and on a new sixth complex in Teesside. Some £3 billion—half from BSC, half from the taxpayers—were to be spent on raising capacity and on shutting down older plants, with the loss of at least 50,000 jobs—in other words, a slightly revised version of the BISF's Benson report. BSC also did something that the steelmasters had never done; it created a subsidiary, BSC (Industry) Ltd. in 1975, to invest in new non-steel ventures in areas where its closure program would hit hardest.

The development strategy committed the government, BSC, and the country to the largest capital investment program in British history. Also in 1973, the United Kingdom joined the European Community, where excess capacity in steel was already at the highest level in the world and where BSC could no longer rely on an eight percent tariff to keep European imports out. Then came a worldwide slump, caused by the Arab oil embargo and the ensuing energy crisis. The collapse of demand for steel during 1975 caused BSC to accelerate its closure program, after a public fight over the issue with the Labour government and, in 1977, to give up the 10-year strategy in favor of aiming for 30 million tons by 1982.

Operating under Conservative Policies in the 1980s

The Conservative government elected in 1979 at first announced that no more money would be available for BSC. Then in 1980, when BSC's losses rose to £545 million, the government increased its borrowing limit once again, while the board announced that 60,000 jobs would be cut within 12 months. The 13-week national strike which followed, the first in the steel industry since 1926, cut deeper into BSC's profits as imports rose to fill the gap it caused.

In 1980 and 1981 the Conservative government abolished the BSC's statutory duties to promote the supply of iron and steel and to further the public interest, took new powers to direct

BSC's use of its assets, and wrote off a total of £5 billion of debts. In the next few years BSC regained some lost ground and beat European records for closing plants and making cuts in the work force, but by 1982 British customers' demand for steel was down to just over 12 million tons, and BSC's share of this market went below 50 percent for the first time. The majority of the private steelmakers also sought state aid and received about £50 million in 1982—more in later years. They also benefitted from the "Phoenix" series of joint ventures with BSC, starting in 1981, since they were financed mainly out of public funds.

British Steel plc, the Late-1980s and 1990s

In 1986 the chairmanship of BSC passed to Robert Scholey, who had spent his entire career in the industry and whose father was a director of one of the pre-1967 private steel firms. In 1987, with Scholey's full support, the government announced its intention to privatize BSC and the company became British Steel plc in 1988, just before demand for steel began to fall. The new company undertook to keep all five of its main plants open until the end of 1994, subject to market conditions.

British Steel plc's first 18 months were certainly eventful. The company carried out the fourth overhaul of its production structure since 1967, ending up with five divisions—general steels, strip products, stainless steels, distribution, and diversified activities. The company then won the contract to supply rails for the Channel Tunnel, was fined by the European Commission—along with five other steel companies—for participating in an illegal cartel to fix stainless steel prices, acquired the Mannstädt division of the German steel firm Klöckner-Werke, and announced that the hot strip mill at Ravenscraig would be shut down in 1991. It replaced national pay bargaining with divisional and local talks to reinforce the emphasis on productivity and increased total payments to the directors of the company by 78 percent.

State versus Private Ownership of British Steel

The pendulum of ownership of British Steel often leads to discussion of its management, yet the act of nationalizing the company seems to have made little difference to its operations. Even BSC's huge investment program might have been carried out by a public board aiding private firms, as in the 1960s, although BSC's second chairman, Sir Monty Finniston, told the House of Commons Select Committee on Nationalized Industries in 1977 that "we would have done nothing if we were in the private sector, absolutely nothing." At the same time the company's history reveals that the act of privatizing did not automatically improve its efficiency or contribute to its economic growth.

Steel production is repeatedly affected by changes in the world economy. Supplies of coal and iron ore are subject to enormous fluctuations in price and volume. The industry has fixed capital costs. Steel is a raw material, with construction accounting for 18.5 percent of British Steel's sales in 1989 and 1990; the motor industry accounting for 14.6 percent of sales; and other manufacturers providing further sales. Fluctuations in the steel industry's economic conditions depend on the demand for its customers' products, not for steel itself. Government intervention, to control prices, protect jobs, promote regional development, and secure self-sufficiency, has been pervasive but inconsistent. Steel production has displayed long-term tendencies toward alternating crises of under- and over-production, in what has generally been a four-yearly cycle. The postwar history of the British steel industry has displayed all of these features, and apparently would have done so regardless of ownership.

The company's improved results in the late 1980s, both in and out of state ownership, were due—at least in part—to the growth of the British economy, to the global fall in the prices of raw materials, and to favorable movements on the foreign exchange markets since 1985. Post-tax profit, declared in June 1990 after BSC's first full year in the private sector, was £565 million.

In 1990 iron ore and coal prices moved upwards again, while sales of steel in the United Kingdom fell by approximately 10 percent, and the company's own pre-tax profits fell by 27 percent. The company decided to shut down the Clydesdale seamless tube works, and the chairman stated that running five big integrated plants put the company at a competitive disadvantage.

Foreign Expansion Signals Growth in the 1990s

In 1993 the economy in the United Kingdom began to advance and so did demand for steel. By 1994, the company had returned to profitability after two years of heavy losses. In 1995, British Steel announced plans to expand its operations in Latin America, central Europe, and Asia, in the expectation that demand for steel from these emerging markets would persist into the next century. For example, the British Steel Track Products Ltd. unit, which supplies rails and railway infrastructure, was involved in projects in several countries in Latin America, including Brazil, Colombia, and Paraguay. In 1996, the company sold 6,000 tons of rails to Latin America, chiefly in fulfillment of a $3 million contract to supply rails to Peru's state-owned Empresa Nacional de Ferrocarriles. Plans for 1997 included selling 10,000 to 15,000 tons of rails for Brazil's Sao Paulo subway.

In 1997, British Steel built its first steelmaking facility outside the United Kingdom, in Tuscaloosa, Alabama. The unit,

Tuscaloosa Steel, is located on the banks of the Black Warrior River, and produces plate in coil and cut length form used in the construction, transportation, and energy industries. Some 800,000 tons were expected to be produced annually. In nearby Mobile, British Steel invested in two Direct Reduction Iron units that would produce feedstock for the Tuscaloosa plant and another company unit, Trico Steel, based in Decatur. Trico was British Steel's first steelmaking joint venture in the United States. Its 25 percent stake was part of a $450 million project that produced high quality, light-gauge, hot rolled coil.

In addition to expanding in overseas markets and investing in joint ventures, British Steel seeks to maintain profitability by selling units. In 1997, the company sold British Steel Forgings, the unit that supplied forged and machined components to the automotive and aerospace industries, to United Engineering Forgings Ltd.

Principal Subsidiaries

European Electrical Steels Limited; Avesta Sheffield AB; Trico Steel Company.

Principal Operating Units

Sections Plates and Commercial Steels; British Steel Engineering Steels; British Steel Strip Products; British Steel Tubes and Pipes; British Steel Track Products and Engineering.

Further Reading

Abromeit, Heidrun, *British Steel*, Leamington Spa: Berg Publishers, 1986.
Bryer, R. A., et al., *Accounting for British Steel*, Aldershot: Gower Publishing, 1982.
Heal, David W., *The Steel Industry in Post-War Britain*, London: David & Charles, 1974.
Ovenden, Keith, *The Politics of Steel*, London: Macmillan, 1978.
Vaizey, John, *The History of British Steel*, London: Weidenfeld & Nicolson, 1974.
World Beaters, London: British Steel plc.

—Patrick Heenan
—updated by Dorothy Kroll

Burr-Brown Corporation

6730 South Tucson Boulevard, #BC-7
Tucson, Arizona 85706
U.S.A.
(520) 746-1111
Fax: (520) 889-1510

Public Company
Incorporated: 1956 as Burr-Brown Research Corp.
Employees: 1,900
Sales: $269 million (1995)
Stock Exchanges: NASDAQ
SICs: 3674 Semiconductors & Related Devices

Burr-Brown Corporation designs, manufactures, and sells a broad line of microelectronic components, especially high-performance integrated circuits (standard analog and mixed-signal) used in the processing of electronic signals. For example, its integrated circuits help guide robots in Japanese automotive assembly lines and help control locomotive engines in Germany. Burr-Brown products are found in numerous areas: industrial and process control, test and measurement, medical and scientific instrumentation, medical imaging, digital audio and video, telecommunications, personal computers, and multimedia systems. The company's manufacturing and technical facilities are located in Tucson, Arizona; Atsugi, Japan; and Livingston, Scotland. Its worldwide sales organization markets the company's products in 45 countries.

Humble Beginnings

Burr-Brown began in 1956 in founder Tom Brown's 400-square-foot garage in Tucson, Arizona, and from its founding it was concerned with the manufacture and sales of microelectronic components. That year it incorporated in the state of Arizona as Burr-Brown Research Corp.

With the help of two employees, Brown, who was a real estate developer, was able to market his first analog products. First-year sales totaled a modest $1,600 dollars, but within a

year Brown moved his operations to a 1,200-square-foot building, and sales grew to $7,200. As sales increased, the company continued to move into larger facilities, and in 1965 Brown bought ten acres near the Tucson airport so that he could create a permanent location for his growing business. His first building there, a 22,000-square-foot structure, housed more than 150 employees.

By the early seventies Burr-Brown was a major presence in the Tucson area. It was, in fact, only the second major high-tech manufacturing firm to establish its headquarters in the city (Hughes Aircraft had come to Tucson in 1951). This presence in the city was reflected by the company's new buildings. In 1970 Burr-Brown constructed near the airport a second building, this one with 52,000 square feet of space for production and management. That year sales topped $6.6 million, and the number of employees rose to 300. By 1975 it became necessary to expand the Tucson facility with a third building (until it was constructed, the company leased space around the airport). During the 1970s sales increased at a rate of about 25 percent a year, and by 1980 Burr-Brown was operating in Tucson in 94,000 square feet of space. Sales had surpassed $50 million. At this time in its history, Burr-Brown was making more per working minute ($2,300) than it made in its first year of operation.

During this period of expansion Burr-Brown also began to sell its products overseas. It first entered the international market in 1961. A decade later it established a subsidiary in the United Kingdom, and four years later it created a Japanese subsidiary. By 1979, 50 percent of sales were outside the United States.

Growth and Expansion during the 1980s

Burr-Brown experienced healthy growth during the early and mid-1980s, a time when many other companies in the industry "were forced into cutbacks, layoffs and even bankruptcy," wrote Kathie Price in *The Arizona Republic*. "The catalysts for Burr-Brown's success," she said, were "in its choice of products and markets." The strategy, one initiated by Tom Brown years before when he was starting out in his garage, was to locate "profits in such small-volume computer compo-

Company Perspectives:

The company excels in the design and manufacturing of ICs (integrated circuits) used in signal processing associated with the measurement and interpretation of "real world" phenomena such as sound, pressure, temperature, distance, and light. By combining specialized design and application knowledge with advanced semiconductor process technology, the company creates products which are highly proprietary in nature. The high value-added content of these products makes them more resistant to redesign in customer systems and less susceptible to second sourcing and commodity pricing that often affect digital ICs.

Historically Burr-Brown has developed a very strong position in the stable industrial process control and test and instrumentation markets, which are characterized by long product-life cycles and high margins. The company will continue to emphasize these markets in order to protect its position and expand market share.

The company has been able to leverage capabilities developed in these more traditional markets to penetrate very large, fast-growing markets, such as communications and computers and multimedia, for which high performance analog and mixed-signal products are particularly well suited. Increased emphasis on cost-effective solutions to customer applications in these markets benefit profitability in all markets. By pursuing this strategy, the company intends to accelerate total revenue growth while expanding overall profit margins.

nents as circuit boards, integrated circuits, digital-to-analog converters that change digital (numeric) signals to analog (sound wave) signals and personal-computer instrumentation.''

Also important to the growth of Burr-Brown was Jim Burns, who was hired in 1971 to oversee the daily operations of the manufacturing facility. Burns had spent 11 years as a Motorola manager before joining the company. Burns won praise from his employees and outsiders alike for keeping Burr-Brown competitive in the global market. His attitude was simple. Burns said, ''We saw that more than half the population of the world was outside the United States. We just believed the market was there.'' He also refrained from bashing foreign competition. ''Should we punish the Japanese,'' Burns asked, ''for having good old American values?'' His approach for Burr-Brown was to ''look for niches with minimum competition.'' ''It might not be something special,'' Burns explained, ''but a market area that's fragmented or where the competition is weak.'' Rather than challenge giant corporations with greater resources, Burns used a cooperative approach with larger companies. Burr-Brown was able to find solutions for difficult problems that larger companies could not.

Burr-Brown's early entry into the Japanese market made it possible for it to develop parts for new Japanese products. In 1978, for example, it helped Sony with its compact-disc player. Burr-Brown's integrated circuits converted digital signals to analog signals in these electronic devices; in so doing they produced tone qualities from compact disks that surpassed those in tapes and records.

Another aspect of Burns's approach helped Burr-Brown succeed in the Japanese market. Burns believed in the simple method of listening carefully to the customer's problem and then searching for solutions. At the time the compact disc was developed, for example, there was not a single chip on which to put the new technology. As a result, Burr-Brown used existing technology to create a multiple-component integrated circuit. ''We did that,'' Burns said, ''rather than say no and have the Japanese later figure out how to do it on a single chip.'' Not many years later, in 1983, Burr-Brown developed a single integrated circuit, or chip, for the compact disc.

In 1983 Burr-Brown incorporated in the state of Delaware, and the company changed its name from Burr-Brown Research Corp. to Burr-Brown Corporation. In March of the following year Burr-Brown went public, abandoning its long-standing policy of reinvesting profits back into the company. One reason for this change was that a major competitor, Analog Devices of Norwood, Massachusetts, was beginning to overtake Burr-Brown. When Tom Brown realized that Analog was outpacing them, he decided the company needed an infusion of new capital—something that going public would bring it. The change proved a boon to Burr-Brown. The year it went public, Burr-Brown reached $66 million in sales, a company record. Burr-Brown also wanted to increase its presence in the lucrative European market, and soon after it became a public company, it was able to build a new manufacturing plant in Scotland. In 1986 a technical facility was built thirty miles from Tokyo. By 1987, 65 percent of sales were in international markets. But despite continued growth, Burr-Brown's profits were not always high. Costs in the construction of new facilities and the consolidation of divisions affected the bottom line in some years.

Because of its notable successes, Burr-Brown's visibility in Arizona continued to be high. In 1984 the company was named ''Arizona's Growth Company of the Year'' by the Phoenix chapter of the Association for Corporate Growth. Much later, in 1995, it was at the top of the list for Arizona Inc. ''Best of Business'' ranking. But elsewhere—and, in particular, Silicon Valley—Burr-Brown's visibility remained low. Dan Hutcheson, president of VLSI Research Inc., was quoted as saying that it was tough for Burr-Brown to be isolated in Arizona ''because there's not this electronics infrastructure where you can go out and mingle with your customer every day.'' Even so, Hutcheson said, Burr-Brown by the 1990s had ''a nice, stable work force with a good work ethic.''

Innovation and Innovators: Growth through the 1990s

Two other key factors—new product development and skilled engineers—have led to Burr-Brown's success over the years. At Burr-Brown new-product development strategy has been based on a twelve-year life span, with each new product designed to return that investment within five years. This strategy was one reason for Burr-Brown's remarkable annual growth rates in the 1970s, which reached as high as 50 percent. In the early 1980s, 25 to 35 new products a year were introduced. New products were also a contributing factor in the company's record sales during the 1980s.

Finding skilled engineers was simplified by Burr-Brown's location near the University of Arizona in Tucson and Arizona State University in Phoenix. The University of Edinburgh supplied many of the engineers needed at the Scotland facility. Some of Burr-Brown's engineers have been recognized within the industry. Jerry Graeme, for example, received the 1994 ''Innovator of the Year'' award by *EDN* magazine. In his 25 years with the company, Graeme designed more than 25 linear integrated circuits, received 8 patents, and developed more than 300 applications for operational amplifiers. The same year another engineer, Greg Waterfall, received the ''Test Engineer of the Year'' award from *Test & Measurement World*. Burr-Brown anticipated more than $220 million in lifetime sales from products that will use the test method Waterfall developed. The importance of Burr-Brown's talented engineers was underscored when three engineers left in 1984 to start their own company. As a result, Jim Burns, then president and chairman of the board, set up a corporate development program to help ''intrapreneurs'' who developed new ideas within the company.

By the late 1990s Burr-Brown made more than 1,500 microelectronic components and had more than 25,000 buyers around the world. Among its better known customers were AT&T, Canon, General Electric, Hewlett-Packard, Hughes Network Systems, Nokia, Northern Telecom, Sony, and Toshiba. With Syrus Madavi as the chief executive officer and John Carter as the chief financial officer, Burr-Brown saw cutting costs and micromanaging the details of the company as urgent for its continued

growth and success. This management team was also committed to continuing the company's tradition of finding niches in a changing marketplace. For example, Burr-Brown, which was producing chips for Sony camcorders, hoped that the introduction of digital versatile disks (DVDs) would soon provide a major market for Burr-Brown's microelectronic components.

Principal Subsidiaries

Intelligent Instrumentation Inc.; Power Convertibles Corp.

Further Reading

Bruner, Richard, ''Burr-Brown Changes Market Strategy,'' *Electronic News,* February 10, 1997, p. 25.
''Chip Maker Opens Facility in Japan,'' *Arizona Republic,* October 23, 1986.
''Fired Up,'' *Arizona Republic,* January 29, 1984, pp. E1–2.
Haber, Carol, ''Street-Wise,'' *Electronic News,* September 5, 1994.
Mogollon, Carlos David, ''Burr-Brown's Stock Rising,'' *Tucson Citizen,* May 29, 1995, pp. 1, 6.
Munday, Michael F. and Janet Mitchell, *Tucson at Tomorrow's Frontier,* Tucson, Arizona: Tucson Economic Development Corporation, 1989, pp. 67–68.
Price, Kathie, ''Foreign Attitude,'' *Arizona Republic,* August 11, 1986, pp. C1–2.
Sprout, Alison L., ''A High-Powered Home Office,'' *Fortune,* September 19, 1994, p. 230.
Western, Ken, ''No. 1 Burr-Brown Corp. High-Tech Company Tops 'Best' List, Steps Out of Shadows,'' *Arizona Republic,* May 5, 1996.

—Vita Richman

CalMat Co.

3200 San Fernando Road
Los Angeles, California 90065
U.S.A.
(213) 258-2777
Fax: (213) 258-5920
Web site: http://www.calmat.com

Public Company
Incorporated: 1891 as California Portland Cement Co.
Employees: 1,776
Sales: $407.2 million (1996)
Stock Exchanges: New York Midwest Pacific
SICs: 1442 Construction Sand and Gravel; 2951 Asphalt
Paving Mixtures and Blocks; 3273 Ready-Mixed
Concrete; 6512 Operators of Nonresidential Buildings;
6531 Real Estate Agents and Managers; 6552 Land
Subdividers and Developers, Except Cemeteries

CalMat Co. is a major producer, manufacturer, distributor, and seller of construction materials: aggregates (crushed rock, sand, and gravel), hot-mix asphalt, and ready-mixed concrete in California, Arizona, and New Mexico. It also owns, leases, and manages industrial and office buildings, owns and leases undeveloped real property, and sells real property. The company was established in 1984 by the merger of California Portland Cement Co. and Conrock Co.

Predecessor Companies to 1950

California Portland Cement Co., based in Los Angeles, was founded in 1891. It began operating in San Diego County in 1926. The company was paying dividends by 1927 and continued paying them throughout the Great Depression. In 1947, the year it began selling a minority of its common stock to the public, California Portland Cement was manufacturing and selling Portland, plastic, and oil-well cements under the trade name Colton. It also was manufacturing scale rock, sand, and lime products. It owned a deposit of limestone and siliceous

materials, along with a cement mill and lime mill, near Colton, California, and raw-materials deposits in other locations. The company added a second cement plant at Rillito, Arizona, (near Tucson) in 1948.

Consolidated Rock Products Co., also based in Los Angeles, was incorporated in 1929 to consolidate the business and properties of Reliance Rock Co. with Union Rock Co. and its subsidiaries. These predecessors had been engaged in business as far back as 1909. The combined company and its subsidiaries manufactured, sold, and distributed crushed rock, gravel, and sand for use in construction. In 1930 it owned and operated 23 producing plants in southern California, plus sand, gravel, and rock deposits, a private railroad, four warehouses, and more than 225 automatic self-dumping motor trucks. That year it lost $620,259 on net sales of $4.3 million. Consolidated Rock Products continued to lose money throughout the decade. Its sales dropped as low as $1.5 million in 1934, and it was in bankruptcy between 1935 and 1938. The company returned to profitability in 1941, but the initial reorganization plan apparently failed to resolve all its problems, for it was again in bankruptcy during 1944–45.

Growth and Development, 1950–1984

California Portland Cement added a third plant at Mojave, California, in 1956. Despite profit downturns in 1952 and 1958, net income rose steadily through the decade, coming to nearly $7.3 million in both fiscal 1959 and 1960. In 1961 the company formed a subsidiary, Arizona Sand & Rock Co., to manufacture prestressed concrete and ready-mixed concrete in Phoenix as well as to excavate rock and sand. During the early 1960s California Portland Cement completed a new $23.6-million unit at Colton. At the end of 1964, when it was one of the three biggest cement producers in the West, the company had capacity of 14 million barrels of cement, of which 6.5 million barrels were at Mojave, 4.5 million at Colton, and the remaining 3 million at Rillito. In fiscal 1965 the firm had net income of $6.7 million on revenues of $40.3 million.

California Portland Cement's net income fell from its 1959 peak to as low as $5.7 million in fiscal 1967. During the latter years of the decade it began correcting this situation by branching into new fields. The company founded Spancrete of California, a manufacturer of prestressed concrete hollow-cored slabs and rectangular beams at Irwindale, California, in 1966. It formed Colton Industrial Park Co., a developer of properties not required for cement operations, in 1969, and Calport Financial Corp. to finance, develop, and construct low-cost housing in 1970. In 1969 it acquired 54 percent of State Exploration Co. (later renamed Statex Petroleum, Inc.), an oil-and-gas exploration company. Net income topped the previous 1959 peak in 1969 and reached $9.5 million on sales of $64.8 million in fiscal 1971.

By 1950 Consolidated Rock Products was producing cement and cement blocks and ready-mixed concrete as well as rock, sand, and gravel, and its railway had been replaced by a conveyor plant. By 1968 the company was southern California's top supplier of a broad range of basic construction materials. It had a network of 48 plants and service yards. Consolidated Rock Products earned $2.9 million on sales volume of nearly $50 million that year. It renamed itself Conrock Co. in 1972.

California Portland Cement branched into a new field in 1974, when it incorporated the Soldier Creek Coal Co. This company mined coal in two Utah counties, part of which California Portland Cement used in two cement plants. By 1980, in addition to its other facilities, the company had cement bulk transfer terminals in Phoenix and at Santa Fe Springs, Fremont, and Stockton in California. In 1979 Martin Marietta Corp., a major aerospace, construction materials, and chemical concern, offered to buy the Dan Murphy Foundation's holdings in California Portland Cement for about $62 million. This charitable foundation, formed by the heirs of the company, declined the offer. Its holdings in the firm then represented about 30 percent of the common stock outstanding but by 1988 had shrunk to about 14 percent.

A lawsuit in 1980 alleged that California Portland Cement and about 50 others conspired to fix cement prices and restrain competition between the beginning of 1968 and the end of 1976. The company denied any illegal activity or liability. Nevertheless, California Portland Cement paid a $6.5 million settlement for the litigation pending in a U.S. district court in Arizona and a related state court action.

California Portland Cement had record net sales of $218.5 million and record net income of $22.7 million in fiscal 1981. The following year was not as good, however, and in fiscal 1983 the company lost $1.8 million on sales reduced to $161.1 million. By then its long-term debt had climbed to $89 million, much of it to pay for a $112-million modernization of the Mojave plant.

By 1980 Conrock was southern California's largest asphalt producer as well as its leading sand and gravel miner. It operated 54 plants and 4 landfills and also hundreds of motor trucks and many miles of conveyor belt. The company, which according to one reckoning owned 6,828 acres and rented 3,176 more, had entered real-estate development through a subsidiary handling an additional 1,848 acres. Net sales came to $134.8 million and net income to $7.5 million in 1983. By this time California Portland Cement held 28 percent of its stock.

Merger and Divestments, 1984–1990

In 1984 California Portland Cement and Conrock merged, with California Portland shareholders assuming 57 percent of the combined company and Conrock shareholders the remaining 43 percent. William Jenkins, president of Conrock, became chairman and chief executive officer of the combined company, which took the name CalMat Co. The merger made CalMat the largest supplier of concrete, asphalt, and gravel in California, Nevada, and Arizona. Many observers saw the transaction as a bonanza for California Portland Cement shareholders by allowing them a stake in Conrock's real-estate holdings at far below market value. Of CalMat's $331.7 million in 1984 revenue, aggregates and ready-mixed concrete came to 48 percent, cement to 47 percent, and properties to 5 percent. The next year properties again accounted for 5 percent of revenue but 20 percent of profit.

The drop in oil prices during the early 1980s had made Statex Petroleum a losing proposition, and in 1985 CalMat sold it for $19.3 million. Soldier Creek Coal was sold the same year to a subsidiary of Sun Co. for about $22 million in cash. Also that year, CalMat sold its cogeneration and electrical generating facilities at its Colton plant for $54.6 million to Trust Co. Bank, which leased it back to CalMat for 15 years. The proceeds for these sales helped CalMat earn a record $44.1 million on record revenue of $605.9 million in 1986, and to reduce its long-term debt to $30 million.

In 1986 CalMat acquired Coast Asphalt Inc., the remaining half-interest in Industrial Asphalt, a joint-venture partnership producing asphalt paving materials. The other half-interest partner, Huntmix, Inc., had been acquired by the company between 1983 and 1985. This enabled CalMat to become the largest commercial supplier of hot-mix asphalt west of the Mississippi. Just before the end of 1986, CalMat announced the sale of Valley Reclamation Inc. to Waste Management Inc. for $61.3 million. Formerly a Conrock subsidiary, Valley Reclamation was a solid-waste company operating a 200-acre landfill in the San Fernando Valley area of Los Angeles. In 1987 CalMat sold a 100-acre parcel of land in Orange, California, for $12 million.

CalMat's fortunes continued to advance during this period despite heavy competition in the cement business from low-priced Mexican imports, which had come to account for about one-quarter of the southern California market. In 1987 it garnered net income of $78.1 million on revenues of $602 million, for a very handsome 19.3-percent return on equity. In December 1987 it agreed in principle to sell most of its developed commercial and industrial real-estate properties to Shidler Group for $112 million. One of these developments was an office and hotel complex in Mission Valley, an area near San Diego where the company owned about 100 acres of prime real estate. Although talks ended in March 1988 with no agreement reached, CalMat said it had not changed its plan to sell all of its real estate—developed and undeveloped—in Los Angeles, San Diego, and Phoenix, and to focus on its core business of mining and producing asphalt, concrete, rock, and sand. The value of the company's real estate in California was estimated at $350 million to $500 million.

New Zealand investor Ronald A. Brierley, holder of 19 percent of CalMat's shares through a Hong Kong investment firm, offered $40 a share, or nearly $1 billion, for the company in March 1988. To avert a takeover, CalMat announced that it intended to sell its cement and real-estate operations and distribute the estimated $800 million in proceeds to shareholders. Under the restructuring, CalMat would retain its concrete, asphalt, and aggregate operations, which in 1987 generated 72 percent of its total sales. In July 1988 Brierley reluctantly ended his takeover bid, agreeing to sell his 19-percent stake in CalMat to Japan's largest cement maker, Onoda Cement Co. for $41.75 a share, or $242 million. CalMat offered Onoda the option to buy in two years its California Portland Cement Co. unit, including the Mojave and Colton plants, and 13 ready-mix concrete plants in the Los Angeles area, for $310 million in stock. This deal angered some holders of CalMat stock. One indignant shareholder, economist Benjamin E. Stein, wrote in *Barron's* "It is difficult to escape the conclusion that CalMat's management sold a valuable asset at far below full value primarily to get a worrisome corporate raider and greenmailer [Brierley] off its back." The value of CalMat's stock subsequently declined from a record $46 a share.

Onoda exercised its option in 1990. In the transaction CalMat also received $68 million in cash, and Onoda's cement subsidiary assumed $18 million in CalMat debt. The cement subsidiary had accounted for about 15 percent of CalMat's $29 million in profit during the first half of 1990, but it had the company's narrowest profit margins. CalMat retained 74 ready-mix concrete plants and 37 crushed-stone plants and about 34,000 acres in real estate. It had added to its holdings in 1988 by acquiring two rock and sand production plants and four ready-mix concrete batch plants, plus certain land equipment, from Sundt Corp. of Tucson for about $19 million in 1988. In 1990 it sold its 190,000-square-foot Carroll Center industrial park in San Diego County for $15.7 million.

A Difficult Environment, 1991–1996

CalMat's asphalt operation, Industrial Asphalt, had grown from a single plant in Sun Valley, California, in 1941, to 39 plants in three states by 1992. In 1991 it produced 8.2 million tons of asphalt and accounted for $170 million in sales, about 46 percent of CalMat's total. The company's production of aggregate—sand and gravel, the basic components of concrete and asphalt—included about 2 million tons of building materials out of its San Bernardino, California, plant alone. This plant was making 18 products out of the sand and gravel, including washed plaster sand—used in roofing tile and stucco—and washed and unwashed concrete sand and large-size gravel.

In 1992 CalMat announced an agreement to acquire substantially all the assets of The Jamieson Co., a major producer of aggregates located in Pleasanton, California. CalMat paid $34 million for the production facility—which included exclusive rights to mine in excess of 100 million tons of reserves—mining equipment, and related real estate. This acquisition increased CalMat's holdings in northern California, where it was also operating a number of asphalt plants, including one located on the property being acquired. At the close of the year the company took a $9.9 million pretax, noncash charge to earnings. As a result, the firm recorded a net loss of $10.5 million for the year. Because of the Jamieson acquisition, the use of company funds to retire 8 million shares of common stock—mostly in connection with the disposition of the cement business—and accounting changes, CalMat's long-term debt now had reached $117 million, or 27 percent of the firm's total capitalization.

When California's economy went sour in the early 1990s, CalMat was hard hit with its revenues declining from $422 million in 1990 to $342 million in 1992, and not increasing greatly in the next three years. The value of the stock fell below $17 a share in 1993, 1994, 1995, and 1996. Between 1990 and early 1994 the work force was reduced by 11 percent. About the only bright spot was the properties division, which accounted for 35 percent of profits in 1992 on only 4 percent of revenues.

In the summer of 1995 unionized operating engineers initiated a strike at 33 CalMat building-materials plants in southern California, objecting to a request that they take a 25 percent pay cut. Three months later the strike had cost the company more than $2.1 million and cut its sales by about 25 percent. Also in 1995, CalMat was hurt by record rainfall and related flooding in California and lower real-estate gains. Taking a $26.5-million writeoff, CalMat ended the year with a net loss of $21.4 million on revenues of $370.3 million. In 1996 the company fared better, earning $9.3 million on $407.2 million in revenues. Its long-term debt was $98 million in mid-1996.

At the end of 1996 CalMat was operating aggregates-processing plants at 32 locations, hot-mix asphalt plants at 35 locations, and ready-mix concrete batch plants at 25 locations. It also operated 14 asphalt recycling systems and 10 landfills and had a fleet of about 375 trucks mixing concrete from aggregates, cement, water, and other materials as well as paving machines and specialty paving equipment.

CalMat also owned or leased 36,000 acres of land operated by its properties division. Reclaimed post-mining properties were typically subdivided into lots and developed by the company or sold in lot parcels to developers once necessary zoning and permits were obtained. CalMat was the master developer of Rio Valley West, the first major project started in San Diego in a decade. Construction began in 1995 on the 94.5-acre development, whose value was estimated at $175 million. Nevertheless, CalMat had decided to discontinue its business of developing industrial and office buildings as part of its 1988 restructuring. It sold 35 industrial and office buildings between 1988 and 1996 and was intending to dispose of its remaining commercial and industrial developments, except for certain industrial buildings related to its mining and production operations.

Principal Subsidiaries

CalMat Co. of Arizona; CalMat Co. of Central California; CalMat Co. of New Mexico; CalMat Land Co.; CalMat Properties Co.

Principal Divisions

Construction Materials Division; Properties Division.

Further Reading

Bradsher, Keith, "A Reluctant Brierly Will Sell Holdings in CalMat to Japanese," *Los Angeles Times,* July 21, 1988, pp. 1D–2D.

Brammer, Rhonda, "Diamond's Gems," *Barron's,* May 16, 1994, p. 18.

Campanella, Frank W., "Sunny Skies and Brisk Building Spur Consolidated Rock Results," *Barron's,* September 2, 1968, p. 20.

"Consolidated Rock Products Enjoys Right Mix for Gain in Profits," *Barron's,* January 4, 1971, pp. 23, 28.

Elliott, Suzanne, "Road to Riches May Be Paved with Asphalt," *San Bernardino County Sun,* February 3, 1993.

Gellene, Denise, "Investor Offers $998 Million to Acquire CalMat," *Los Angeles Times,* March 24, 1988, pp. 1D, 13D.

Sanchez, Jesus, "CalMat Swaps Its Cement Unit for Stock," *Los Angeles Times,* October 2, 1990, p. 8D.

Schwab, Dave, "Rio Vista West Offers Two Firsts for County," *San Diego Business Journal,* March 14, 1994, p. 1.

Stein, Benjamin J., "The CalMat Maneuver," *Barron's,* September 12, 1988, pp. 13, 37–39.

Whitehair, John, "Cal-Mat Has Concrete Plans for the Future," *San Bernardino County Sun,* September 13, 1992.

——, "CalMat: Strike Is Costly," *San Bernardino County Sun,* October 31, 1995, p. 8B.

—Robert Halasz

CALTEX

Caltex Petroleum Corporation

P.O. Box 619500
Dallas, Texas 75261-9500
U.S.A.
(972) 830-3929
Fax: (972) 830-3034

Joint Venture of Texaco, Inc. and Chevron Corporation
Incorporated: 1936
Employees: 7,300
Sales: $15 billion (1995)
SICs: 2911 Petroleum Refining

Caltex Petroleum Corporation is the world's largest and most successful joint venture in business history. The company's revenues are larger than such well-known oil firms as Unocal, Phillips, and USX-Marathon, and its assets are greater than its closest rival, the huge Royal Dutch/Shell Group. Formed by Chevron Corporation and Texaco, Inc. in 1936, the company refines, produces and markets a wide array of petroleum and convenience products. Caltex Petroleum holds equity interests in 14 fuel refineries, 17 lubricant blending plants, six grease plants, two lubricant refineries, and 526 ocean depots and terminals. In addition to its thousands of branded retail outlets and gas stations, Caltex also provides fueling services at 38 airports and 103 saltwater ports in 22 countries around the world. The company has a major presence in East Africa, South Africa, East Asia, China, the Middle East, Southeast Asia, and the South Pacific, and is the only international petroleum firm that operates in all major Asian markets. With a well-trained and highly efficient international work force of approximately 7,300, more than 98 percent of the company's employees are nationals of the countries within which the various oil refining, marketing, and producing facilities operate.

Early History

Caltex, an abbreviation for the California Texas Oil Company, was formed during the height of the Great Depression in 1936. With businesses going bankrupt throughout the United States and the petroleum drilling and refining industry in particular losing large amounts of revenue from decreasing demands for gas and oil, management at Chevron (known at the time as Standard Oil of California) and Texaco decided to combine their resources and develop their promising overseas operations. Chevron needed new markets for its recently discovered, extensive Middle Eastern oil reserves, while Texaco needed large amounts of crude oil for its burgeoning overseas refining facilities and its ever-increasing number of gas stations. The joint venture was a success from the very beginning, especially with the growing production of oil from its refineries in the Middle East and Asia.

From its inception, Caltex focused on developing overseas opportunities for oil refining and marketing its products. One of the company's most important discoveries occurred just before World War II, when engineers found the vast Duri oil field in the dense and difficult terrain of the central Sumatran rain forests. The company wasted no time in signing a contract with the Indonesian government and immediately constructed a drilling rig to extract the oil. However, before the company could begin to reap profits from its most significant discovery to date, the Japanese invaded the country and confiscated all of the Caltex drilling equipment. Unfortunately for Caltex, the Japanese conquest of a large portion of Asia resulted in a forced takeover of almost all its equipment and facilities, as these resources were needed to fuel Japan's wartime military. When the United States entered World War II after the Japanese attack on Pearl Harbor, management at Caltex were hopeful that the company would eventually reclaim its refinery and drilling operations.

After World War II ended in victory for America and its allies, Caltex management decided to reinvigorate its operations by adopting a unique strategic approach for the development of new markets. Originally an extremely bold and unprecedented alliance between two of the most successful companies in the industry, Caltex proposed to draw on the expertise and capabilities of these two leading petroleum enterprises in a way never done before. In order to restart its business after much of it was destroyed during the war, Caltex drew on the resources of Chevron and Texaco to raise capital more efficiently, apply the

---

Company Perspectives:

"We are committed to delivering superb service and top quality products, and we will rely on our tradition of innovation to do more than satisfy customers; we intend to win their loyalty. Our core beliefs of people, service and value are the foundation of a new Caltex—a service-driven, innovative marketer that consistently meets or exceeds the expectations of its retail, industrial and commercial customers. This is the spirit by which we live, work and measure our performance."

---

appropriate technology to increase the capacity of its drilling operations, and organize comprehensive support services to initiate and maintain new major projects. One of the most successful advertising campaigns in the company's history was created during this time, emphasizing Caltex's ability as a joint venture to offer its business partners and customers a range and depth of products no single firm would be able to match.

During the late 1940s, and throughout the decade of the 1950s, Caltex reaped the rewards of its new strategic approach. Focusing on emerging markets in Asia, the company began to create a reputation for itself as a creative, efficient, pragmatic and—most important—culturally sensitive international organization.

When Caltex was forced to relinquish its Duri oil field in central Sumatra during World War II, the Japanese appropriated one of the company's drilling rigs and accidentally discovered the much larger Minas oil field close by. After the war Caltex reclaimed both the Duri and Minas oil fields, and restarted its crude oil drilling, but implemented a far-reaching policy of hiring local workers to operate the rigs and supervise their output. This hiring policy, which became a company standard, had the effect of attracting individuals who would ultimately be placed in major positions of authority within Caltex. By the end of the 1950s, Caltex had played a significant part in helping Japan build its petroleum industry after the massive destruction caused by World War II, and in the same way had guided South Korea's petroleum industry after the Korean War.

Growth and Expansion during the 1960s and 1970s

With its South Korean affiliate, Caltex had already established a major presence in the country during the 1950s. In collaboration with Koa Oil Company and Nippon Oil Company from Japan, Caltex and South Korean engineers designed and constructed the largest tanker and oil holding facility in the world. By the end of the 1960s, Caltex had also assisted its affiliate in developing Korea's second refinery, located at Yocheon. At the same time, Caltex also duplicated its own joint venture structure and began to enlist and contract companies that were willing to engage in joint venture partnerships within such countries as Australia, New Zealand, and the Philippines.

With its growing presence throughout Asia, Caltex was well positioned to take advantage of one of the century's most im-

portant developments in the petroleum refining industry. During the 1960s and 1970s, as the economies became more prosperous and as the per capita income began to rise in the developing nations of Asia, oil consumption increased dramatically in the region. This typically occurred when the per capita income, adjusted for purchasing strength, reached the equivalent of US$1,000. Japan reached this milestone during the early 1950s, while South Korea and Hong Kong surpassed it during the mid-1960s. For example, most people in South Korea and China had been using either wood, dung, or charcoal for heating purposes. However, as the per capita income increased, people shifted away from these traditional sources of fuel to kerosene. The result was an explosive demand for oil, and Caltex was there to provide it.

During the same period, there was an enormous increase in motorized vehicles, particularly small automobiles, delivery trucks, and scooters. In order to meet this rising demand from motorized consumers for petroleum products in the Asia-Pacific region, Caltex initiated a full-service fueling and automotive care retail chain. Caltex service stations were opened in Hong Kong, Japan, South Korea, Australia, Singapore, and the Philippines. By the end of the 1970s, Caltex's retail chain had developed into a combination service station/convenience store concept similar to those operating in the United States.

The 1980s Bring Rewards of Strategic Planning and Hard Work

The decade of the 1980s saw the rise of Caltex to a preeminent position in the petroleum industry across the Asia-Pacific region. During the early 1980s, Caltex reached an agreement with the Chinese government to develop a network of service stations through numerous joint ventures in the Shenzhen Special Economic Zone, an area designated by the socialist leaders of the country as a focal point of foreign investment and free market economy. In Korea, the demand for oil was growing at an incredible 18 percent annually, and with equity interests in Samnam Petrochemical Company, Hoyu Tanker Company, and more that 1,500 service stations, Caltex was well poised to sell gasoline, diesel lubricants, and kerosene to consumers. In Hong Kong, Caltex was operating over 50 service stations, three marine stations, over 100 dealerships and car service centers, and an aviation refueling facility at the city's International Airport. In Singapore, the company constructed a lube oil blending plant, while also providing aviation fuel services at Changi International Airport. In Taiwan, Caltex opened a chain of retail outlets selling refined petroleum products, while in Japan the company and its affiliate Nippon Oil Company had opened a vast network of more than 6,000 service stations.

Caltex was not only interested in expanding its holdings and market share in East Asia. Management made the strategic decision to expand its activities to Africa, where joint ventures were established by the company in Egypt, Kenya and South Africa to operate oil refineries, lube oil blending plants, grease manufacturing plants, a network of service stations, and aviation services at Cairo, Nairobi, Mombasa, Johannesburg, and Cape Town airports. Caltex also arranged joint ventures in India and Pakistan, where the company operated lube oil blending plants, oil refineries, and service stations. Another region of interest encompassed the Middle East, where Caltex once again entered into various joint ventures for oil refining, lube oil and grease manufacturing, gas processing plants, and such specialty product sales as marine lubricants and asphalts.

Perhaps the most revealing story of the company's determination to succeed during this time occurred in the Philippines. When the political situation in the country grew more turbulent, and many companies began to withdraw their operations and close their facilities in the face of apparent anti-American sentiment, Caltex stood firm and weathered the storm, as did its arch-rival, the Dutch/Shell Group. This steadfastness of the two companies resulted in a total dominance of the petroleum market within the country. By the end of the decade, Caltex was operating a Philippine oil refinery, lube oil blending plant, grease manufacturing facility, aviation services at Manila International Airport, and over 700 retail outlets selling a wide variety of products that included gasoline, kerosene, diesel fuel and lubricants.

The 1990s and Beyond

Anticipating that Asia will account for approximately two-thirds of the net growth in demand for oil up to and beyond the year 2000, Caltex continued its remarkably successful expansion. In Shanghai, China, the company started a joint venture lubricants blending plant, as well as a large retail network in Guangdong Province. In 1994, Caltex opened an office in Hanoi and in Ho Chi Minh City, Vietnam, and arranged a joint venture for the nationwide distribution of its lubricants. The company ventured into Cambodia, where a network of service stations were opened in Phnom Penh, and a marine terminal opened in Sihanoukville. By the mid-1990s, Caltex had opened its first service station in Laos.

Contributing to Caltex's success in South Korea is its unique position as the only occidental company to own a portion of a refinery in the country. The Honam Oil Refinery, which has captured over 30 percent of the market for refined petroleum products, is owned jointly by Caltex and the Lucky Goldstar Group. In a stroke of fortune for Caltex, the South Korean government passed legislation prohibiting any new foreign petroleum company from entering the nation's rapidly growing, and extremely lucrative market. In Singapore, Caltex reached an agreement with the Singapore Refining Company to upgrade and expand its facilities. By the mid-1990s, Caltex had reached a production volume of 720,000 barrels of crude oil per day at the Minas oil field in Sumatra, approximately half of the total crude production of Indonesia. In Thailand, Caltex's application to build a $1.7 billion oil refinery was approved by the government and the company entered into a joint venture with the Petroleum Authority of Thailand. Named the Star Petroleum Refining Company and located in Map Ta Phut, Thailand, the new facility quickly garnered a reputation as one of the world's most technological sophisticated and efficient refineries.

In early 1994, management at Caltex, in close consultation with parent companies Texaco and Chevron, decided to invest approximately $6 billion through the year 2000 in order to upgrade and improve capacity at its Asian refineries. With six percent annual economic growth in the Asia-Pacific region, and regional demand for crude oil having increased more than 4.5 percent per year from 1988 to 1994, more than double the rate of the rest of the world, Caltex regarded its investment as a necessary step for its crude output to keep pace with the fastest-growing market for petroleum products. Accordingly, Caltex expanded its presence in Vietnam by purchasing nearly 500,000 barrels of Bach Ho oil field crude from Vietnam for use in its ever-expanding refinery in Singapore. Other major expansion moves included an agreement with the government of Oman to engage in establishing joint venture operations for the purpose of building oil refineries in India, South Korea, and Oman, and an agreement with Lebanon to expand the country's refinery in Tripoli.

In 1988 Caltex's net income, split between Texaco and Chevron, provided the parent firms with 18 percent and 13 percent, respectively, of their total earnings. By 1993, the 50/50 split had increased dramatically to 34 percent for Texaco and 28 percent for Chevron. More recently, in order to maintain its level of capital spending, Caltex has reduced its dividends by 17 percent to both Texaco and Chevron due to a slight dip in the price of oil worldwide.

Texaco and Chevron, publicly held companies, would find it difficult for any reason to implement such a drastic reduction in dividends to its shareholders, but Caltex does not have to worry about the stock market. Indeed, Texaco and Chevron appear more than willing to forgo short-term profit for long-term gain.

Further Reading

"Caltex Buys Vietnamese Oil," *Oil Daily,* March 23, 1994, p. 5.

"Caltex Is Expected to Spend $6 Billion," *Oil & Gas Journal Newsletter,* January 3, 1994.

"Caltex Petroleum Corporation," *Oil & Gas Journal,* April 4, 1994, p. 36.

"Caltex Signs Pact to Build Thailand's Fifth Refinery," *Oil & Gas Journal,* January 27, 1992, p. 40.

"Caltex to Invest $8 Billion," *Oil Daily,* September 26, 1995, p. 5.

Jones, Gregg, "Caltex Petroleum, Oman Sign Asian Oil Agreement," *Wall Street Journal,* May 16, 1993, p. B10(E).

"Lebanon and Caltex," *Oil & Gas Journal,* December 13, 1993, p. 26.

Mack, Toni, and Tanzer, Andrew, "The Jewel in the Crown," *Forbes,* September 26, 1994, pp. 76–78.

"Oman Moves to Expand Industry Operations," *Oil & Gas Journal,* May 3, 1993, p. 42.

"Three Japanese Refiners," *Oil & Gas Journal Newsletter,* November 15, 1993.

—Thomas Derdak

Caraustar Industries, Inc.

3100 Washington Street
Austell, Georgia 30001
U.S.A.
(770) 948-3101
Fax: 770-732-3401

Public Company
Incorporated: 1938 as Carolina Paper Board Corp.
Employees: 4,114
Sales: $602.69 million (1996)
Stock Exchanges: NASDAQ
SICs: 2652 Setup Paperboard Boxes; 2655 Fiber Cans
Tubes Drums; 2657 Folding Paperboard Boxes
Including Sanitary; 6719 Holding Companies, Not
Elsewhere Classified

Caraustar Industries, Inc. is a leading manufacturer of recycled paperboard and converted paperboard products with more than 70 facilities in the United States and Mexico. Caraustar's position as a diversified, low-cost producer and supplier of paperboard and paperboard products has allowed the company to capture a strong share of each of four key paperboard markets: tubes, cores, and drums; folding cartons; gypsum wallboard facing paper; and other specialty and converted paperboard products. Caraustar is the only major paperboard producer to serve each of these four markets, providing the company both stability and flexibility in a traditionally cyclical, commodity-based industry. The company also produces extruded and injection-molded plastic products to complement its paperboard product lines. Since the early 1980s, Caraustar has pursued an aggressive growth plan through acquisition and internal expansion, raising net sales (after freight costs) from $94 million in 1980 to more than $600 million in 1996. Caraustar has a nearly unbroken record of sales and income growth.

Caraustar operates 14 paperboard mills in North Carolina, South Carolina, Georgia, New Jersey, Virginia, Illinois, Ohio, Iowa, Tennessee, New York, and Pennsylvania. Caraustar's paperboard mills recycle paperstock, reducing this stock to pulp, then cleaning, refining, and processing the pulp into various grades of uncoated and clay-coated paperboard. Each of Caraustar's mills has the flexibility of producing paperboard for two or more of the company's four key markets, allowing the company to react quickly to market conditions and maintain high plant productivity rates. Approximately 33 percent of the resulting paperboard is used internally by Caraustar; the remaining 67 percent is sold to other manufacturers of paperboard and related products. External sales of paperboard typically account for 36 percent of Caraustar's annual sales.

The company and its subsidiaries operate some 40 converting facilities directly serving Caraustar's primary markets. The company's largest and oldest subsidiary, Star Paper Tube, Inc., operates 28 tube, core, and can converting plants, providing cores for the carpeting, textile, paper, plastic film, and other industries. In 1996, Caraustar produced some 268 thousand tons of tube and core products, which, together with sales of unconverted paperboard to other tube and core manufacturers, represented 36 percent of the company's net sales.

Folding carton operations, produced at ten plants in North Carolina, Ohio, and Tennessee, provided 27 percent of Caraustar's net sales in 1996. In that year, Caraustar's 13 gypsum wallboard facing paper plants shipped 263 thousand tons, capturing roughly 17 percent of the North American market, for 17 percent of the company's net sales. The company's sales of specialty paperboard products—for the bookbinding, printing, games, puzzleboard, furniture, and other industries—accounted for 14 percent of Caraustar's net sales. Caraustar operates five specialty converting plants in Georgia, North and South Carolina, and Texas. Sales of injection-molded and extruded plastics and external sales of paperstock each accounted for approximately three percent of the company's net sales in 1996.

A Recycling Pioneer in the 1930s

Caraustar was formed as the Carolina Paper Board Corporation in Charlotte, North Carolina in 1938 by Ross Puette and other investors. Puette already had more than a decade of experience in the paperboard industry, beginning his career in the 1920s at Richmond, Virginia-based Manchester Board and

Company Perspectives:

"At Caraustar we are committed to excellence and continuous improvement in every facet of our operation. Employee and Customer relationships will be built on mutual respect and concern for each other's well-being. We will conduct our business guided by high ethical standards in accordance with all laws and regulations and will constantly strive to be responsible corporate citizens in the communities in which we are located. Caraustar Industries will produce and sell products and services that will earn a level of profits that enhances shareholder value, fairly rewards our employees for their contributions, and provides the capital necessary to maintain a leadership position in the recycled paperboard and packaging industry. To achieve these results we recognize we must provide quality goods and services that are superior to competition and that consistently meet customer requirements."

Paper Co. (which became a subsidiary of Caraustar in 1994). With $25,000 in startup funds, Puette and his partners built North Carolina's first paper recycling plant, with 45 employees producing 25 tons of folding carton per day. The company's operations grew quickly: by 1940, more than 60 employees produced some 8,000 tons of paperboard, generating sales of $374,000. The choice of location—a major urban market with a ready supply of waste paper—would become a key element of the company's growth strategy.

During the 1940s, Carolina Paper Board branched out, forming affiliated companies in Charlotte and in Greenville, South Carolina and building two recycled paper processing plants to supply the company's Charlotte paperboard mill. This move toward vertical integration, which assured the company a ready supply of low-cost fiber, would also become a company hallmark. In 1947, the company added forward integration capacity, when it built a second paperboard mill in Austell, Georgia. In addition to the paperboard mill, the Austell site featured a converting facility, serving the folding carton market, and a recycled fiber processing plant, tapping the low-cost supply of waste paper in nearby Atlanta. By the end of the decade, Carolina Paper Board's two mills were producing 125 tons per day. The company's sales grew to $2.3 million on a total volume of 30,000 tons, and its payroll had swelled to 140 employees.

The first of the company's strategic acquisitions occurred in the early 1950s, when Carolina Paper Board purchased a minority interest in Star Paper Tube, which operated a tube and core converting plant in Rock Hill, South Carolina. By 1958, Carolina Paper Board had gained a majority share of Star Paper Tube and had expanded the subsidiary by building two additional tube and core converting plants, in Danville, Virginia and in Austell, Georgia, serving the textile industry. At the end of the 1950s, Carolina Paper Board's operations had grown to eight facilities, and sales had tripled to $6.4 million on more than 50,000 tons. The company was now represented in three key markets: folding carton, other specialty products, and tube and core.

Steady Growth in the 1960s and 1970s

The booming economy of the 1960s helped Carolina Paper Board increase its production more than 150 percent over the decade to an annual capacity of 128,000 tons. The company opened a third paper mill in 1964 in Greenville, South Carolina. Three years later, spurred by growth in the tube and core market, the company opened a fourth tube and core plant, which in turn prompted the opening of the company's fourth paper mill. In the mid-1960s, Carolina Paper Board also increased its folding carton capacity with the acquisition of Charlotte-based Atlantic Coast Carton Company. With 870 employees, Carolina Paper Board's sales quadrupled to $24.5 million, producing operating profits of more than $3 million. The company's push toward integration was already nearing a 30 percent integration level among its paper mills and converting plants.

The Atlantic Coast Carton acquisition marked a new era of growth strategy for the company. During the 1970s, acquisitions played a major role in Carolina Paper Board's expansion. Between 1970 and 1980, the company acquired one folding carton plant, two recycled fiber processing plants, and eight tube and core converting plants. At the same time, the company continued its internal growth, building five new tube and core converting plants, a recycled fiber processing plant, and a fifth paperboard mill. The new mill also enabled the company to move into a new paper market, the gypsum facing paper market, completing the company's target market areas. Meanwhile, the company was also expanding within the tube and core market, moving beyond its reliance on the textile industry to supply the paper, construction, metal, and film industries. The company already exhibited another ingredient to its later growth, that of achieving a reasonable balance among its target markets. Many of the company's plants were already capable of converting quickly from one market to another, helping to buffer the company during cyclical downturns in any of its core markets. As the 1970s ended, Carolina Paper Board had continued its strong growth, reaching revenues of $93.8 million and operating profits of $12.8 million. The company's 1,650 employees produced more than 264,000 tons.

Converting to Caraustar in the 1980s

Until 1980, the company had operated as six affiliated corporations, with common management and ownership. In that year, the company consolidated its operations under the holding company, Caraustar Industries, and relocated its headquarters to its 150-acre Austell site. The newly incorporated company continued the internal and external expansion set during the previous decade. Between 1981 and 1986, the company built three tube and core converting plants and acquired two folding carton plants, a plastic extrusion and injection molding plant, three tube and core converting plants, and four recycled paperboard mills. In 1986, however, the company expansion slowed after a leveraged recapitalization added some $300 million to the company's debt. In the late 1980s, Caraustar acquired only one recycled paperboard mill in Camden, New Jersey. The company also backed into another acquisition, that of Standard Gypsum Corp., a maker of gypsum wallboard, after that company was unable to pay its paperboard bill. In 1996, however, Caraustar sold 50 percent of its interest in Standard Gypsum and relinquished the directorship of that business.

Despite the slowdown in the company's growth, Caraustar managed to post a 187 percent increase in revenues during the 1980s, raising net sales to $141 million by 1990. Operating profits grew still more strongly, gaining 272 percent to reach $47.6 million. The company's 2,567 employees, meanwhile, had increased mill production to 565,000 tons.

Public in the 1990s

At the start of the 1990s, Caraustar's holdings had swelled to 44 facilities, including 11 paperboard mills located in Texas, North and South Carolina, Illinois, Ohio, New Jersey, and Tennessee. The company had grown to become one of the top ten recycling companies in the United States. The company's Star Paper Tube subsidiary had grown to become the second largest tube and core producer in the country. As the recession of the early 1990s took hold, Caraustar formulated a newly aggressive strategic plan, which called for the company to step up its vertical integration and diversification in its key market areas. Part of that plan included taking the company public, to alleviate the debt load incurred during the 1980s. The company made an initial public offering (IPO) of 11.1 million common shares in December 1992, raising some $90 million.

Part of the funds raised in the company's IPO was earmarked for stepping up the company's acquisition program. Between 1991 and early 1997, Caraustar added some 30 facilities to its recycling empire. During 1992 and 1993, the company acquired two recycled paperboard mills, Buffalo Paperboard and Manchester Board and Paper, which was renamed Richmond Paperboard Corp. Caraustar bought two tube and core converting plants in Salt Lake City and Phoenix and acquired Federal Packaging Corp., a maker of composite containers using paperboard and injection-molded plastics. The following year, the company added to its folding cartons capacity with the acquisition of Mid-Packaging Group Inc. and that company's two Tennessee-based folding carton plants. While investing in upgrades and maintenance of its existing facilities, Caraustar also built two new tube and core converting plants, in Lancaster, Pennsylvania and in Mexico City, as well as a new production facility for the company's Star-Guard product in Lancaster, South Carolina.

In 1995, the company added GAR Holdings, with two specialty products plants and a folding carton plant, and Summer Paper Tube of Kernersville, North Carolina, with two core manufacturing plants. Summer also manufactured specialty adhesives used in the tube and core and paperboard lamination production processes, helping the company further solidify its diverse operations and integration within the paperboard industry. Toward that end, also, Caraustar entered a joint venture with Tenneco Packaging Co., which involved a $114.5 million purchase of an 80 percent interest in Tenneco's clay-coated paperboard mills in Rittman, Ohio and Tama, Iowa, expanding Caraustar's capacity in that high-growth area of the paperboard industry.

By 1996, the company's revenues had more than doubled, reaching $629.67 million and generating nearly $58 million in net income. The company's flexibility and diversity enabled the company to outpace its competitors, many of which struggled through industry downturns and booming paperstock costs. Caraustar promised to continue its expansion drive. In April 1997, the company reached agreement to acquire General Packing Service, Inc. of Clifton, New Jersey, adding that company's lines of pharmaceutical, medical, and health, beauty, and personal care packaging products.

Principal Subsidiaries

ACC Services, Inc. (North Carolina); Mid Packaging Group— Alabama, Inc. (Alabama); Atlantic Coast Carton Company (North Carolina); Austell Box Board Corporation (Georgia); Buffalo Paperboard Corporation (New York); Camden Paperboard Corporation (New Jersey); Caraustar Paper Sales, Inc. (Georgia); Caraustar Paper Sales South; Caraustar Paperboard Corporation (Ohio); Carolina Paper Board Corporation (North Carolina); Carolina Paper Box Co., Inc. (North Carolina); Carolina Recycling, Inc. (North Carolina); Carotell Paper Board Corporation (South Carolina); Chattanooga Paperboard Corporation (Tennessee); Chicago Paperboard Corporation (Illinois); Cincinnati Paperboard Corporation(Ohio); Columbus Recycling, Inc. (Georgia); Federal Packaging Corporation (Delaware); Federal Transport, Inc. (Ohio); GAR Holding Company (Delaware); Macon Recycling, Inc. (Georgia); Mid-State Paper Box Company, Inc. (North Carolina); Packrite Packaging, Inc. (North Carolina); Paper Recycling, Inc. (Georgia); Paragon Plastics, Inc. (South Carolina; 80%); Quality Design Products, Inc. (Georgia); Reading Paperboard Corporation (Pennsylvania); Richmond Paperboard Corporation (Virginia); Special Packaging, Inc. (Delaware); Standard Gypsum Corporation (Texas); Star Paper Tube de Mexico, S.A. de C.V. (Mexico; 65%); Star Paper Tube, Inc. (South Carolina); Star Recycling Incorporated (Georgia); Sweetwater Paper Board Company, Inc. (Georgia); The Garber Company (Delaware); The Mid/ Packaging Group, Inc. (Tennessee).

Further Reading

Harte, Susan, "Upward Bound," *Atlanta Journal and Constitution,* May 19, 1996, p. 21G.

Jones, John A., "Caraustar Diversifies To Outperform Slow Paper Industry," *Investor's Business Daily,* October 7, 1996, p. B14.

Krantz, Matt, "How Flexibility Lets Paper Firm Beat the Cycles," *Investor's Business Daily,* November 5, 1996, p. A4.

Shaw, Monica, "Caraustar Industries: Growth Company Focuses on Diversity, Low-Cost Production," *Pulp & Paper,* January 1997, p. 40.

—M.L. Cohen

Casey's General Stores, Inc.

1 Convenience Boulevard
Ankeny, Iowa 50021
U.S.A.
(515) 965-6100
Fax: (515) 965-6160
Web site: http://www.caseys.com

Public Company
Incorporated: 1967
Employees: 8,343
Sales: $954.8 million (1996)
Stock Exchanges: NASDAQ
SICs: 5399 Miscellaneous General Merchandise Stores;
5499 Miscellaneous Food Stores; 5541 Gasoline
Service Stations

Casey's General Stores, Inc. operates convenience stores in the Midwest under the "Casey's General Store" name that sell a wide range of food, beverages, tobacco products, health and beauty aids, automotive products, gasoline, and other items. The company was the nation's sixth-largest convenience store chain in the early 1990s and, according to its co-founder and chief executive officer, the third-largest in 1996. At the end of fiscal 1996 (the year ended April 30, 1996) there were 983 Casey's stores, including 182 franchised units, in nine states. All were within a 500-mile radius of company headquarters in Ankeny, Iowa, with most in Iowa (312), Illinois (235), or Missouri (222). About 72 percent were in areas with populations under 5,000 and only 6 percent in communities of over 20,000.

The Early Years, 1967–1983

Casey's origins can be traced to Domenic Lamberti, an Italian immigrant and former coal miner who opened a coal- and ice-delivery business on the north side of Des Moines, Iowa, at Broadway and Northeast 14th streets, in 1935. His business developed into a neighborhood grocery store with gasoline outside. (It later became a Casey's.) Donald F. Lamberti, his son, began working in the store, in his words, "about

the time my chin could get above the counter." He left his accounting studies at Drake University in 1960 to take over the store when his father became ill.

In 1967 Kurvin C. Fish, a salesman who sold Lamberti his gasoline, persuaded him to buy an Ames, Iowa oil company, which owned four Square Deal service stations. Lamberti provided the capital: $40,000 down on a total cost of $200,000, plus a $40,000 equipment loan from a local bank. Fish agreed to operate the enterprise, which got its name from his first and middle initials. "We talked about calling it 'Lamberti's General Stores,'" Lamberti told a *Chicago Tribune* reporter in 1994, "but there are a lot of folks who don't like Italians. We wanted a generic name that no one would dislike."

The first Casey's convenience store was one of the four properties, a converted three-bay gasoline station in Boone, Iowa. It opened in 1968 and was, according to Lamberti, "a hit from day one." In its first year the store attained profit margins the partners had projected for the third year. "We didn't call it a convenience store early on," Lamberti later recalled to a newspaper reporter. "We called it just a general store with gasoline." Soon they opened similar stores in Creston, Waukee and Saylorville.

After Fish's refinery was taken over by Ashland Oil in 1970, financing growth became more difficult, so Lamberti and Fish took two more partners. When they needed more money to expand further, they started franchising stores. According to Fish, "After we had four or five stores, we thought if we built 15 that would be all we'd want. And then after we had 15 built, we thought, well, there are 90 counties in the state and if we put 90 stores in Iowa that would be about all we could ever hope to develop."

Casey's outlets offered products found in grocery stores, except for produce and fresh meats, and many nonfood items not found in a traditional convenience store, such as ammunition for hunters. The company's concentration on small towns gave it the advantage of little competition. Bigger convenience store chains like 7-Eleven and Circle K had abandoned these areas for more profitable major metropolitan markets. Gas stations and fast-food restaurants also were becoming scarcer in the rural Midwest, where population was stagnating or declining.

Lamberti laid great emphasis on keeping Casey's stores spotlessly clean. Speaking to a Des Moines group of financial analysts in 1985, he said, "Surveys show that customers will enter a dirty store and go straight to the item that they need and leave the store as quickly as possible. On the other hand, a customer entering a clean store is more likely to browse and purchase additional needs. Cleanliness is especially important when you're dealing with fast-food items."

Interviewed by the *Chicago Tribune* in 1994, Lamberti said, "We are comparable to the old ma and pa stores, only with a little more structure and discipline. . . . We don't handle cigarette rolling papers or risque magazines because we don't think small-town America wants us to handle those, and we don't do pinball machines or video games." (However, tobacco products, including cheap, generic cigarettes, represented an important sales segment, and almost all Casey's stores sold beer.) Almost all the stores closed at 11 P.M.—both to meet concerns for employee safety and to keep company insurance policies low. (After three employees were murdered during a late-night robbery at a Casey's in Columbia, Missouri, in 1994, the company, which said it had been averaging only seven or eight holdups a year, was prompted to alter its security procedures.)

In 1979, while businesses heavily dependent on motor traffic were reeling from the second energy crisis of the decade, Casey's made the critical choice to expand still further. "We decided to grow as long as the wheels didn't fall off the buggy," Lamberti told a *Des Moines Register* reporter in 1996. "We built a lot of stores when everybody else was sitting on their hands. Some people were closing down." In that year, Casey's nearly doubled its outlets, growing from 119 stores to 226. Net sales rose from $58.6 million in fiscal 1979 to $188.5 million in fiscal 1983, and net income from $418,000 to $1.8 million.

In 1980, Casey's established a profit-sharing and stock-ownership plan for employees who had worked at Casey's for 12 consecutive months and were at least 21 years of age. Fish sold his share of the company to the plan shortly afterward. In 1990, when this plan owned about 35 percent of the company's shares, Casey's was matching up to 2 percent of employees' salaries with stock shares.

A 55,000-square-foot distribution center was opened in Urbandale, Iowa, in 1983 to serve the chain and was furnished with a state-of-the-art computer system. The company owned its own trucks and trailers and hired its own drivers. An in-house printing and graphic-arts department was established the same year. At the end of 1983 there were 191 company-owned and 215 franchised stores in 8 states. Net sales came to $188.5 million and net income to $1.8 million. A breakdown showed that while gasoline was the chief sales item, its profit margin was far lower than that for grocery and general goods, reflecting Casey's strategy of drawing customers first to the pumps, then into the stores to buy higher-profit goods.

Casey's in the 1980s

Casey's went public in October 1983, offering about one-quarter of its outstanding shares of common stock at $15 a share. Proceeds from the offering enabled the company to fully purchase three subsidiaries engaged in the operation of its stores. Casey's also decided it would not issue any more franchises, although existing franchisees could continue building and opening new stores. Long-term debt was $12 million at the end of fiscal 1984 and represented 41 percent of total capital, but an additional stock offering in 1985 allowed the company to reduce this debt.

Gasoline sales provided about 60 percent of sales volume and 30 percent of the company's gross and net profits in fiscal 1985, when sales reached nearly $250 million and earnings $1.3 million. In 1984 Casey's began making and selling fresh carry-out pizza in a small number of its stores. By the end of 1985 pizza was available in 85 stores, and the following year the stores started selling by the slice as well. The recipe was never changed, and by the end of 1994 Casey's was, according to one reckoning, the nation's seventh-largest retailer of pizza. A company commissary began preparing sandwiches in 1986 for sale in the stores.

A typical Casey's of the mid-1980s was a white barnlike metal structure with a red roof. The newer buildings were 36 by 54 feet and included space for pizza and homemade doughnuts. Each detail of the store, including a preset layout of merchandise, refrigeration, and counters, was planned in advance, with energy efficiency a prime concern. Typically there were three gas pumps outside, with two hoses each. Start-up costs, including construction, inventory, and land, averaged $250,000, about half the price of the typical convenience store, mainly because land costs in the countryside were lower. For many years Lamberti chose the building sites personally, with the biggest considerations being the traffic count, population in a 15-block area around the site, and the need for Casey's product mix.

In 1985 Casey's began installing high-quality, noncorroding fiberglass gasoline storage tanks in all new-store constructions. Older steel tanks were replaced with new fiberglass tanks or retrofitted with fiberglass lining. By contrast, and to Casey's competitive advantage, many mom-and-pop gas stations closed because they could not afford to comply with the stricter federal and state directives that began to be imposed in this period to combat underground storage-tank leaks.

During the late 1980s Casey's line of goods included beauty aids, school supplies, housewares, pet and photo supplies, and automotive products. Videotape rentals were available in 94 percent of the company-owned stores in 1989. Introduced in the mid-1980s, Casey's own takeout fried chicken was in 36 percent of the stores in 1989, but its popularity dwindled in subsequent years.

Casey's in the 1990s

By 1990 start-up stores were costing Casey's from $350,000 to $400,000 each and were about six feet longer, providing room for an office and facilities for the handicapped. The average store did nearly $800,000 worth of business that year. Food items continued to total about one-quarter of revenue at the average store. Sandwiches and baked goods had become standard fare, although not every store had a kitchen area. About 4 million pizzas and 40 million doughnuts were being made a year, as well as about 45 million coffees in containers. Gasoline operations accounted for 45 percent of sales volume and 24 percent of gross profits, with most of the stations open 18 hours a day, seven days a week.

Fiscal 1990 ended with $500.7 million in net sales and $8.3 million in net income. The number of stores had grown to 769, of which 566 were owned by the company and 203 by franchisees. Long-term debt was $31.2 million. In that year Casey's began paying cash dividends and moved its corporate offices from leased space in West Des Moines to a 36-acre, $19.2-million complex in suburban Ankeny, where the distribution center had grown to 140,000 square feet. There was a separate vehicle maintenance center for the company's 70 trucks. The site also included a day-care center for employees' children and a full-scale company store for training purposes where new employees were brought in for two-week training periods before assignment to specific locations. "Successful business is probably 5 percent strategy and 95 percent execution," Lamberti said in 1994, "and I think that can be taught to about anyone."

In 1990 an association representing 180 Iowa fuel merchants challenged Casey's policy of drawing customers into its stores by offering gas outside at low prices. The group, in a federal class-action suit, charged Casey's with "predatory pricing for the purpose of destroying and unreasonably restricting competition in these small markets." This suit was dismissed by a district-court judge in 1994, but the dealers immediately filed an appeal. Casey's denied the accusation but did not reverse its policy of offering the lowest fuel prices in any given setting. It was restricting its gas profit margin to about 11 cents a gallon in 1996.

At the end of 1993 Casey's stock price reached an all-time high of $24.50 a share, and the company authorized a 2-for-1 stock split, the third time it had split its common stock since going public. *Forbes* ranked Casey's as the 15th most profitable company in the food-distribution category that year. It was named convenience-store chain of the year by *Convenience Store Decisions* magazine for its "well-documented ability to parlay an impressive living out of small towns that don't even get on the search routes when most other operators are looking for new corners to conquer."

Casey's growth rate slowed between 1990 and 1994. During this period it added 107 new stores, fewer than half the number it built between 1985 and 1989. "They are growing intelligently and methodically at about 20 percent growth a year," an investment analyst said in 1995. "They don't want to get into a position of overextending." Casey's nevertheless had identified 4,000 small towns within its operating area that might be sites for expansion. The Ankeny warehouse was said to be big enough to handle supplies for another 500 stores. For every store opened, Lamberti estimated in 1992 that three full-time and nine part-time jobs were created.

Casey's dedicated its 1,000th store in Altoona, Iowa, in 1996. By this time the typical Casey's cost $680,000 to open, but the price remained a bargain compared to big-city costs. Casey's was still benefiting from inexpensive, low-turnover labor and from lack of competition from supermarkets, gasoline stations, and other convenience stores in its targeted areas. Acting as its own wholesaler, the company also was able to

purchase goods at deep discounts and control product quality. The store design for the mid-1990s called for an air-conditioned 40-by-68-foot building that included 500 square feet for kitchen space. All featured the company's bright red-and-yellow pylon sign and facade. Most were open from 6 A.M. to 11 P.M.

Casey's announced record earnings for the seventh consecutive year in 1995, but the company's stock immediately fell from $22.50 to $19 a share because analysts had expected profits to be even higher. "This is the first time in probably several years where the numbers didn't meet or beat expectations," said one securities researcher. Revenues came to $954.8 million and net income to $26.8 million, with a record 65 company-owned stores opened. The company's long-term debt was $81.2 million at the end of the fiscal year.

Each Casey's typically carried more than 2,500 items in 1996. Snack centers selling sandwiches, doughnuts, fountain drinks, and other fresh-food items were in 99 percent of the stores, and pizza was available in 92 percent. Gasoline accounted for 56 percent of net sales. Wholesale revenue, from sales to franchised stores, came to 7 percent of the total. In 1996 franchisees were paying Casey's a royalty fee equal to 3 percent of gross receipts, excluding gasoline, and a royalty fee of $.018 cents per gallon of gasoline. They also paid a fee for rental of Casey's sign and facade. At the end of fiscal 1996 Casey's owned the land at 711 locations and the buildings at 738 locations. It was leasing the land at 90 locations and the buildings at 63 locations.

Principal Subsidiaries

Casey's Marketing Co.; Casey's Service Co.

Further Reading

Bouyea, Bob, "Small Towns, but Big-City Convenience," *Peoria Journal Star,* July 11, 1995, p. 1C.

Braatz, Jonathan P., "Casey's General Stores, Inc.," *Wall Street Transcript,* February 6, 1984, pp. 72697, 72700.

"Casey's General Stores, Incorporated," *Wall Street Transcript,* January 20, 1986, pp. 80550-80551.

Daughton, Andrew, "Tough Minded and Tender-Hearted," *Business Record,* November 28, 1994, p. 14.

Dryer, Steve, "Iowa Marketers Vow Continued Fight on Pricing Suit," *National Petroleum News,* January 1995, pp. 14, 20.

Gubernick, Lisa, "Small Towns, Big Money," *Forbes,* November 17, 1986, pp. 50, 52.

Kasler, Dale, "An American Success Story," *Des Moines Register,* August 11, 1996, pp. 1G-2G.

Moore, Tammy Williamson, "Convenience Still Key to Casey's Success," *Business Record,* September 21, 1992, p. 1.

Sandler, Linda, "Casey's General Stores Is Counting on Pizza to Boost Sales, but Some Predict Indigestion," *Wall Street Journal,* October 14, 1985, p. 33.

Sanger, Elizabeth, "Casey's: Retailer to Rural America," *Barron's,* October 20, 1986, p. 75.

Shaner, J. Richard, "How Small Town America Made Casey's a Big Name," *National Petroleum News,* September 1990, pp. 56–58, 60.

Smith, Wes, "Mighty Casey's," *Chicago Tribune,* February 1, 1994, pp. 1V-2V.

—Robert Halasz

Chevron Corporation

575 Market Street
San Francisco, California 94105-2856
U.S.A.
(415) 894-7700
Fax: (415) 894-8897
Web site: http://www.chevron.com

Public Company
Incorporated: 1906 as Standard Oil Company
   (California)
Employees: 35,310
Sales: $42.78 billion (1996)
Stock Exchanges: New York Midwest Pacific Vancouver
   London Zurich
SICs: 1311 Crude Petroleum & Natural Gas; 2911
   Petroleum Refining

One of the many progeny of the Standard Oil Trust, Chevron Corporation has grown from its modest California origins to become a major power in the international oil market. Its dramatic discoveries in Saudi Arabia gave Chevron a strong position in the world's largest oil region and helped fuel 20 years of record earnings in the postwar era. The rise of the Organization of Petroleum Exporting Countries (OPEC) in the early 1970s deprived Chevron of its comfortable Middle East position, causing considerable anxiety and a determined search for new domestic oil resources at a company long dependent on foreign supplies. The firm's 1984 purchase of Gulf Corporation at $13.2 billion, the largest industrial transaction to that date, more than doubled Chevron's oil and gas reserves but failed to bring its profit record back to pre-1973 levels of performance. By the mid-1990s, however, Chevron was posting strong earnings, a result of higher gasoline prices and the company's restructuring and cost-cutting efforts.

Company Origins

Chevron's oldest direct ancestor is the Pacific Coast Oil Company, founded in 1879 by Frederick Taylor and a group of investors. Several years before, Taylor, like many other Californians, had begun prospecting for oil in the rugged canyons north of Los Angeles; unlike most prospectors, Taylor found what he was looking for, and his Pico Well #4 was soon the state's most productive. Following its incorporation, Pacific Coast developed a method for refining the heavy California oil into an acceptable grade of kerosene, then the most popular lighting source, and the company's fortunes prospered. By the turn of the century Pacific had assembled a team of producing wells in the area of Newhall, California, and built a refinery at Alameda Point across the San Francisco Bay from San Francisco. It also owned both railroad tank cars and the *George Loomis,* an ocean-going tanker, to transport its crude from the field to the refinery.

One of Pacific Coast's best customers was Standard Oil Company of Iowa, a marketing subsidiary of the New Jersey-headquartered Standard Oil Trust. Iowa Standard had been active in northern California since 1885, selling both Eastern oil of Standard's own and also large quantities of kerosene purchased from Pacific Coast and the other local oil companies. The West Coast was important to Standard Oil Company of New Jersey not only as a market in itself but also as a source of crude for sale to its Asian subsidiaries. Jersey Standard thus became increasingly attracted to the area and in the late 1890s tried to buy Union Oil Company, the state leader. The attempt failed, but in 1900 Pacific Coast agreed to sell its stock to Jersey Standard for $761,000 with the understanding that Pacific Coast would produce, refine, and distribute oil for marketing and sale by Iowa Standard representatives. W.H. Tilford and H.M. Tilford, two brothers who were longtime employees of Standard Oil, assumed the leadership of Iowa Standard and Pacific Coast, respectively.

Drawing on Jersey Standard's strength, Pacific Coast immediately built the state's largest refinery at Point Richmond on San Francisco Bay and a set of pipelines to bring oil from its San Joaquin Valley wells to the refinery. Its crude production rose steeply over the next decade, yielding 2.6 million barrels a year by 1911, or 20 times the total for 1900. The bulk of Pacific Coast's holdings were in the Coalinga and Midway fields in the southern half of California, with wells rich enough to supply Iowa Standard with an increasing volume of crude but never enough to satisfy its many marketing outlets. Indeed, even in

Company Perspectives:

Chevron's goal is to exceed the performance of its strongest competitors with a total stockholder return averaging at least 15 percent a year—an aggressive target because worldwide petroleum demand is increasing only 2 percent annually. This goal demands an entrepreneurial spirit, and it signals a need for greater innovation, creativity, and flexibility.

1911 Pacific Coast was producing a mere 2.3 percent of the state's crude, forcing partner Iowa Standard to buy most of its crude from outside suppliers like Union Oil and Puente Oil.

By that date, however, Pacific Coast and Iowa Standard were no longer operating as separate companies. In 1906 Jersey Standard had brought together its two West Coast subsidiaries into a single entity called Standard Oil Company (California), generally known thereafter as Socal. Jersey Standard recognized the future importance of the West and quickly increased the new company's capital from $1 million to $25 million. Socal added a second refinery at El Segundo, near Los Angeles, and vigorously pursued the growing markets for kerosene and gasoline in both the western United States and Asia. Able to realize considerable transportation savings by using West Coast oil for the Pacific markets of its parent company, Socal was soon selling as much as 80 percent of its kerosene overseas. Socal's head chemist, Eric A. Starke, was chiefly responsible for several breakthroughs in the refining of California's heavy crude into usable kerosene, and by 1911, Socal was the state leader in kerosene production.

The early strengths of Socal lay in refining and marketing. Its large, efficient refineries used approximately 20 percent of California's entire crude production, much more than Socal's own wells could supply. To keep the refineries and pipelines full, Socal bought crude from Union Oil and in return handled a portion of the marketing and sale of Union kerosene and naphtha. In the sale of kerosene and gasoline, Socal maintained a near-total control of the market in 1906, supplying 95 percent of the kerosene and 85 percent of the gasoline and naphtha purchased in its marketing area of California, Arizona, Nevada, Oregon, Washington, Hawaii, and Alaska, although its share dipped somewhat in the next five years. When necessary, Socal used its dominant position to inhibit competition by deep price cutting. By the time of the dissolution of the Standard Oil Trust in 1911, Socal, like many of the Standard subsidiaries, had become the overwhelming leader in the refining and marketing of oil in its region while lagging somewhat in the production of crude.

From 1911 to World War II: Growth as an Independent Company

In 11 short years the strength of Standard Oil and a vigorous Western economy combined to increase Socal's net book value from a few million dollars in 1900 to $39 million. It was in 1911, however, that Jersey Standard, the holding company for Socal and the entire Standard Oil family, was ordered dissolved by the U.S. Supreme Court in order to break its monopolistic

hold on the oil industry. As one of 34 independent units carved out of the former parent company, Standard Oil Company (California) would have to do without Standard's financial backing, but the new competitor hardly faced the world unarmed. Socal kept its dominant marketing and refining position, its extensive network of critical pipelines, a modest but growing fleet of oil tankers, its many oil wells, and, most helpfully, some $14 million in retained earnings. The latter proved useful in Socal's subsequent rapid expansion, as did California's growing popularity among Americans looking for a fresh start in life. The state population shot up quickly, and most of the new residents found that they depended on the automobile—and, hence, on gasoline—to navigate the state's many highway miles.

The years leading up to World War I saw a marked increase in Socal's production of crude. From a base of about 3 percent of the state's production in the early part of the century, Socal rode a series of successful oil strikes to a remarkable 26 percent of nationwide crude production in 1919. As the national production leader, Socal found itself in a predicament that would be repeated throughout its history—an excess of crude and a shortage of outlets for it. For most of the other leading international oil companies, the situation was reversed, crude generally being in short supply in a world increasingly dependent on oil. Particularly in the aftermath of World War I—of which the British diplomat George Curzon said "the Allies floated to victory on a wave of oil"—there was much anxiety in the United States about a possible shortage of domestic crude supplies. A number of the major oil companies began exploring more vigorously around the world. Socal took its part in these efforts but with a notable lack of success—37 straight dry holes in six different countries. More internationally oriented firms like Jersey Standard and Mobil soon secured footholds in what was to become the future center of world oil production, the Middle East, while Socal, with many directors skeptical about overseas drilling, remained content with its California supplies and burgeoning retail business.

In the late 1920s Socal's posture changed. At that time Gulf Corporation was unable to interest its fellow partners in Iraq Petroleum Company in the oil rights to Bahrain, a small group of islands off the coast of Saudi Arabia. Iraq Petroleum was then the chief cartel of oil companies operating in the Middle East, and its members were restricted by the Red Line Agreement of 1928 from engaging in oil development independently of the entire group. Gulf was therefore unable to proceed with its Bahrain concession and sold its rights for $50,000 to Socal, which was prodded by Maurice Lombardi and William Berg, two members of its board of directors. This venture proved successful. In 1930 Socal geologists struck oil in Bahrain, and within a few years, the California company had joined the ranks of international marketers of oil.

Bahrain's real importance, however, lay in its proximity to the vast fields of neighboring Saudi Arabia. The richest of all oil reserves lay beneath an inhospitable desert and until the early 1930s was left alone by the oil prospectors. But at that time, encouraged by the initial successes at Bahrain, Saudi Arabia's King Ibn Saud hired a U.S. geologist to study his country's potential oil reserves. The geologist, Karl Twitchell, liked what he saw and tried on behalf of the king to sell the concession to a number of U.S. oil companies. None was interested except the now-adventurous Socal, which in 1933 won a modest bidding war and obtained drilling rights for a £5,000 annual fee and a loan of £50,000. After initial exploration revealed the fantastic extent of Arabian oil, Socal executives realized that the company would need access to markets far larger than its own meager foreign holdings, and in 1936 Socal sold 50 percent of its drilling rights in Saudi Arabia and Bahrain to the Texas Company, later Texaco, the only other major oil company not bound by the Red Line Agreement. Once the oil started flowing in 1939, King Saud was so pleased with his partners and the profits they generated for his impoverished country that he increased the size of their concession to 440,000 square miles, an area the size of Texas, Louisiana, Oklahoma, and New Mexico combined.

Postwar Expansion

Socal and the Texas Company agreed to market their products under the brand name Caltex and developed excellent representation in both Europe and the Far East, especially in Japan. The new partners realized soon after the end of World War II, however, that the Saudi oil fields were too big even for the both of them, and to raise further capital they sold 40 percent of the recently formed Arabian American Oil Company (Aramco) for $450 million, leaving the two original partners with 30 percent each. With its crude supply secure for the foreseeable future, Socal was able to market oil around the world, as well as in North America's fastest-growing demographic region, California and the Pacific Coast. As later Chairman R. Gwin Follis put it, Saudi Arabia was a "jackpot beyond belief," supplying Caltex markets overseas with unlimited amounts of low-priced, high-grade oil. By the mid-1950s Socal was getting one-third of its crude production out of Aramco and, more significantly, calculated that Saudi Arabia accounted for two-thirds of its reserve supply. Other important fields had been discovered in Sumatra and Venezuela, but Socal was particularly dependent on its Aramco concession for crude.

On the domestic scene, Socal by 1949 had grown into one of the few American companies with $1 billion in assets. No longer the number-one domestic crude producer, Socal was still among the leaders and had recently made plentiful strikes in Louisiana and Texas, as well as in its native California. In addition to its original refineries at Point Richmond and El Segundo, Socal had added new facilities in Bakersfield, California, and in Salt Lake City, Utah. Socal's marketing territory included at least some representation in 15 Western states and a recent, limited foray into the northeastern United States, mainly as an outlet for some of its cheap Middle Eastern oil. The heart of Socal territory was still west of the Rocky Mountains, where the company continued to control about 28 percent of the retail market during the postwar years, a far cry from the 90 percent it owned at the turn of the century but still easily a dominant share in the nation's leading automotive region.

In the two decades following the war the U.S. economy became completely dependent upon oil. As both a cause and an effect of this trend, the world was awash in oil. The Middle East, Latin America, and Southeast Asia all contributed mightily to a prolonged glut, which steadily lowered the price of oil in real dollars. The enormous growth in world consumption assured Socal of a progressive rise in sales and a concomitant increase in profits at an annual rate of about 5.5 percent. By

1957, for example, Socal was selling $1.7 billion worth of oil products annually and ranked as the world's seventh-largest oil concern. Its California base offered Socal a number of advantages in the prevailing buyer's market. By drawing upon its own local wells for the bulk of its U.S. sales, Socal was able to keep its transportation costs lower than most of its competitors, and California's zooming population and automobile-oriented economy afforded an ideal marketplace. As a result, Socal consistently had one of the best profit ratios among all oil companies during the 1950s and 1960s.

California crude production had begun to slow, however, and along with the rest of the world Socal grew ever more dependent on Middle Eastern oil for its overall health. The rich Bay Marchand strike off the Louisiana coast helped stem the tide temporarily. By 1961 Socal was drawing 27.9 million barrels per year from Marchand and had bought Standard Oil Company of Kentucky to market its gasoline in the southeastern United States. But the added domestic production only masked Socal's increasing reliance on Saudi Arabian oil, which by 1971 provided more than three-quarters of Socal's proven reserves. As long as the Middle Eastern countries remained cooperative, such an imbalance was not of great concern, and by vigorously selling its cheap Middle Eastern oil in Europe and Asia, Socal was able to rack up a perfect record of profit increases every year in the 1960s. By 1970, 20 percent of Socal's $4 billion in sales was generated in the Far East, with Japan again providing the lion's share of that figure. The firm's European gas stations, owned jointly with Texaco until 1967, numbered 8,000.

Challenge of OPEC beginning in the 1970s

The world oil picture had changed fundamentally by 1970, however. The 20-year oil surplus had given way in the face of rampant consumption to a general and increasing shortage, a shift soon taken advantage of by OPEC members. In 1973 and 1974 OPEC effectively took control of oil at its source and engineered a fourfold increase in the base price of oil. Socal was now able to rely on its Saudi partner for only a tiny price advantage over the general rate and it was no longer in legal control of sufficient crude to supply its worldwide or domestic demand. The sudden shift in oil politics revealed a number of Socal shortcomings. Though it had 17,000 gas stations in 39 U.S. states, Socal was not a skilled marketer either in the United States or in Europe, where its former partner, Texaco, had supplied local marketing savvy. In its home state of California, for example, Socal's market share was 16 percent and continuing to drop and Socal had missed out on both the North Sea and Alaskan oil discoveries of the late 1960s.

Socal responded to these problems by merging all of its domestic marketing into a single unit, Chevron USA, and began cutting employment, at first gradually and later more deeply. Also, Socal stepped up its domestic exploration efforts while moving into alternative sources of energy, such as shale, coal, and uranium. In 1981 the company made a $4 billion bid for AMAX Inc., a leader in coal and metal mining but had to settle for a 20 percent stake. In 1984 Standard Oil Company (California) changed its name to Chevron Corporation. Also in 1984, after a decade of sporadic attempts to lessen its dependence on the volatile Middle East, Chevron Corporation met its short-term oil needs in a more direct fashion: it bought Gulf Corporation.

The $13.2 billion purchase, at that time the largest in the history of U.S. business, more than doubled Chevron's proven reserves and created a new giant in the U.S. oil industry, with Chevron now the leading domestic retailer of gasoline and, briefly, the second-largest oil company by assets. Certain factors made the move appear ill-timed, however. Oil prices had peaked around 1980 and begun a long slide that continued until the Gulf War of 1990, which meant that Chevron had saddled itself with a $12 billion debt at a time of shrinking sales. As a result, it was not easy for Chevron to sell off assets as quickly as desired, both to reduce debt and to eliminate the many areas of overlap created by the merger. Chevron eventually rid itself of Gulf's Canadian operations and all of Gulf's gas stations in the northeastern and southeastern United States, paring 16,000 jobs in the meantime, but oil analysts pointed to such key figures as profit per employee and return of capital as evidence of Chevron's continued poor performance.

Developments in the 1990s

In the early 1990s Chevron began publicizing its environmental programs, a response in part to public pressure on all oil companies for more responsible environmental policies. From 1989 to 1993 Chevron Shipping Company had the best overall safety record among major oil companies. In 1993, while transporting nearly 625 million barrels of crude oil, Chevron Shipping spilled an amount equaling less than four barrels. During this same period, Chevron utilities supervisor Pete Duda recognized an opportunity to convert an abandoned wastewater treatment pond into a 90-acre wetland. Fresh water and new vegetation were added to the site, and by 1994 the area was attracting a variety of birds and other wildlife, as well as the attention of the National Audubon Society, *National Geographic,* and the California Department of Fish and Game. The conversion saved Chevron millions, as conventional closure of the site would have cost about $20 million.

Financially the company began the 1990s with less than glowing returns. Chevron's 1989 results were poor, and in that year's annual report, Chairman Kenneth Derr announced a program to upgrade the company's efficiency and outlined as well a five-year goal: "a return on stockholders' investment that exceeds the performance of our strongest competitors." The company also took important new initiatives. In 1993 Chevron entered into a partnership with the Republic of Kazakhstan to develop the Tengiz oil field, one of the largest ever discovered in the area.

In 1994, five years after Derr's announcement, Chevron had met its goal for stockholders, largely through restructuring and efforts to cut costs and improve efficiency. From 1989 to 1993 Chevron cut operating costs by more than $1 per barrel and the company's stock rose to a 18.9 percent return, compared with an average of 13.2 percent return for its competitors. The company celebrated this achievement by giving 42,000 of its employees a one-time bonus of 5 percent of their base pay.

After meeting its five-year goal, Chevron continued its cost-cutting and efficiency efforts. In December 1995 the company announced a restructuring of its U.S. gasoline marketing. It combined regional offices, consolidated support functions, and refocused the marketing unit toward service and sales growth. One example of the company's new efforts toward marketing

was a joint initiative with McDonald's Corp.. In April 1997, as a response to "one-stop shopping" marketing trends, Chevron and McDonald's together opened a new gas station and food facility in Lakewood, California. The two companies shared the space and customers could order food and pump gas at the same time. They could pay for the order with a Chevron card. More Chevron/McDonald's facilities were planned for California and elsewhere in the United States.

Chevron also cut its refining capacity, where margins were especially low in the early 1990s. Capacity dropped by 407,000 barrels a day from 1992 to 1995. The company helped reduce its refining capacity by selling its Port Arthur, Texas, refinery in February 1995. The company controlled 10.2 percent of U.S. refining capacity in 1992 but just 7.5 percent by 1995. These measures seemed to improve the company's fortunes, as its earnings jumped in 1996 to more than $2.6 billion, an all-time high. Stockholder return for the year was 28.5 percent. High gasoline prices also contributed to Chevron's huge profits. The company was able to take advantage of high crude prices by increasing production at their Kazakhstan and West African facilities.

Principal Subsidiaries

Chevron Canada Limited; Chevron Canada Resources; Chevron Chemical Company; Chevron Information Technology Company; Chevron International Oil Company, Inc.; Chevron Land and Development Company; Chevron Overseas Petroleum Inc.; Chevron Petroleum Technology Company; Chevron Pipe Line Company; Chevron Research and Technology Company; Chevron Shipping Company; Chevron U.S.A. Production Company; Chevron U.S.A. Products Company; Gulf Oil (Great Britain) Limited; The Pittsburg & Midway Coal Mining Co.; Warren Petroleum Company.

Further Reading

Blackwood, Francy, "Chevron Environment Effort: Think Locally, Act Globally," *San Francisco Business Times,* November 4, 1994, p. 2A.

"Chevron, Which Met Its 5 Year Goal of Achieving the Highest Total Return to Stockholders Among its Competitors," *The Oil and Gas Journal,* January 10, 1994, p. 4.

Culbertson, Katherine, "Share of U.S. Refining Capacity Controlled by Top 4 Majors Dwindles, API Study Says," *The Oil Daily,* July 31, 1996, p. 1.

Fan, Aliza, "Analysts Praise Chevron Restructuring as Bold Move to Boost Downstream," *The Oil Daily,* December 19, 1995, p. 3.

Hidy, Ralph W., and Muriel E. Hidy, *History of Standard Oil Company (New Jersey): Pioneering in Big Business, 1882–1911,* New York: Harper & Brothers, 1955.

Klaw, Spencer, "Standard of California," *Fortune,* November 1958.

Liedtke, Michael, "Gasoline Price Hikes Fatten the Profits at Chevron," *Knight-Ridder/Tribune Business News,* April 24, 1997, p. 424B0935.

Sampson, Anthony, *The Seven Sisters: The Great Oil Companies and the World They Made,* New York: The Viking Press, 1975.

Smallwood, Lola, "McDonald's, Chevron Team Up for Food & Gas Station in Lakewood, Calif.," *Knight-Ridder/Tribune Business News,* April 17, 1997, p. 414B1272.

—Jonathan Martin
—updated by Terry Bain

Christian Dior S.A.

30, Avenue Montaigne
75008 Paris
France
(33) 1 40 73 54 44
Fax: (33) 1 40 70 90 32

Public Company
Incorporated: 1946 as Christian Dior Ltd.
Employees: 1,500
Sales: FFr 1.03 billion (U.S. $177 million) (1996)
Stock Exchanges: Paris
SICs: 2844 Toilet Preparations; 2331 Women's &
    Misses' Blouses & Shirts; 5122 Drugs, Proprietaries,
    and Sundries

Celebrating its 50th anniversary in 1996, Christian Dior S.A. is one of the largest and most famous firms in the world of fashion. The company burst on the haute couture scene in the post-World War II era with a revolutionary "New Look" that took the world by storm. Though its founder and namesake only lived long enough to direct the firm's first ten years in business, subsequent decades launched the careers of such stars of the fashion firmament as Yves Saint Laurent and Pierre Cardin. Originally backed by French textile magnate Marcel Boussac, Maison Dior was acquired by financier Bernard Arnault in the 1980s, forming what *Time* magazine called "the jewel in Arnault's crown" of luxury goods companies.

Christian Dior S.A.'s couture and licensing operations generate about FFr 1.03 billion (U.S. $177 million) in retail and wholesale sales of apparel and accessories. A separate subsidiary, Christian Dior Perfumes, sells another FFr 9.3 billion (U.S. $1.6 billion) in fragrance each year. Furthermore, in the mid-1990s Dior controlled 41.8 percent of luxury goods giant LVMH Moet Hennessy Louis Vuitton through a 100 percent-owned holding company, Financier Jean Goujon. As the lead stakeholder in LVMH, Dior claimed FFr 30.8 billion (U.S. $6.3 billion) in consolidated sales. Despite the company's larger profits from LVMH and its perfume subsidiary, the focus of this essay will be on the much smaller Christian Dior Couture fashion design business. Nearly one-third of Dior Couture's sales come from licensing agreements, and of those FFr 328.4 million (U.S. $63.2 million) in licensing revenues, almost half are generated in Asia and over one-fourth are made in the United States. To emphasize quality and exclusivity over quantity, management whittled away at Dior Couture's more than 125 licensees in the mid-1990s.

A Winding Path to Fashion

The couture house is named for its founder, Christian Dior, a bon vivant born in 1905. As heir to a family fortune built on fertilizer and chemicals, Dior had little ambition to finish college, instead whiling away his twenties in Paris bars in the company of poets and artists. Dior dabbled in art, and in 1928, launched a gallery financed with a large gift from his father. But when heavy borrowing and the Great Depression combined to bankrupt the family business in the early 1930s, Dior's family was forced to sell homes, furniture, jewelry, and other heirlooms.

Dior moved in with a friend in Paris and decided to utilize his artistic talents in the fashion industry. Beginning in the mid-1930s, he designed on a freelance basis, selling drawings of hats and gowns to magazines and couture houses. He snared a full-time position with Robert Piguet's fashion design house in 1938, but was soon drafted into service for World War II. Assigned to "farm duty"—helping farmers' wives and other short-handed agriculturists tend their land—Dior was fortunate to be in unoccupied Provence when the German Army advanced in June 1940 and was subsequently discharged from the service. He returned to Paris in 1941 and found work as a design assistant with the couture house of Lucien Lélong, designing custom-made dresses, suits, and ball gowns for some of the wealthiest women in the world.

Postwar Origins of the House of Dior

In 1946, French fabric maven Marcel Boussac—then the nation's wealthiest man—offered to back Dior's launch of his own maison de couture. Though the new house of fashion became part of a vertically-integrated textile business, it was initially a vanity property for Boussac, comparable to his world-renowned stable of racehorses. Christian Dior Ltd. started out that year with 85 employees, capital of FFr 6 million, and "unlimited credit." In exchange for his creative genius, Dior negotiated a generous salary; a significant, though not controlling, stake in the firm; legal status as its leader; and one-third of pretax profits. It was quite an unusual arrangement, given Boussac's legendary—and eventually self-defeating—appetite for control. The company was a majority-owned affiliate of Boussac Saint-Freres S.A.

The designer introduced his first and most famous line—dubbed the "New Look" by Carmel Snow of *Harper's Bazaar*—in 1947. The collection was a striking refutation of the war's deprivation: whereas rationing restricted the amount of fabric used in a dress or skirt, Dior used an extravagant 20 yards of only the finest fabrics in his long, wide skirts. With help from elaborate undergarments, the dresses emphasized the feminine figure, from the tiniest of waists to peplum- or tulle-enhanced hips and tight-fitting bodices, often with deep décolletage.

The line was an immediate and nearly complete success, garnering a clientele ranging from European royalty to Hollywood starlets and generating sales of FFr 12.7 million by 1949. Dior opened a New York outlet before the year was out and established London operations in 1952. From the outset, fully half of the company's sales were made in the United States. By the end of 1953, the company had operations in Mexico, Canada, Cuba, and Italy. Women who could not afford the haute couture copied it at home. Soon enough—and to Dior's chagrin—knock-off artists did the "dirty work" for them. Eventually, the maison fought fire with fire, establishing a prêt à porter (ready to wear, abbreviated in the trade as "rtw") line of somewhat less expensive versions of the couture line. The designer stayed with the "New Look" for seven years, becoming a virtual dictator of hem lines and lengths in the process.

Diversification, Licensing Speed Growth in the late 1940s

Again backed by the Boussac fortune, Dior launched Christian Dior Perfumes Ltd. in 1948. The namesake owned one-fourth of the new venture, a childhood friend who managed France's Coty perfumery held another 35 percent, and patron Boussac owned the remaining stake. By 1950, a licensing program devised by Dior General Manager Jacques Rouët put the now-famous name on dozens of accessories, including ties, hosiery, furs, hats, gloves, handbags, jewelry, lingerie, and scarves. While denounced by Dior's colleagues in the French Chamber of Couture as a cheapening of the high-fashion industry's image, this licensing scheme would become a cornerstone of the company's long-term success and a trend that would only grow stronger in the decades to come.

By the mid-1950s, the Dior empire included eight companies, 16 affiliates, and employed 1,700 people on five continents. In 1949 alone, Christian Dior fashions constituted 75 percent of Paris fashion exports, and five percent of all French export revenues. Though Christian Dior launched several successful lines—including the "A," "Y," "Arrow," and "Magnet"—from 1954 to 1957, none would surpass the initial introduction of the

"New Look" in impact. By the time the house celebrated its tenth anniversary in 1957, it had sold 100,000 garments. Though in his early fifties, Dior was by this time preparing for his retirement, having suffered two heart attacks. A third seizure took his life in 1957, ironically while on a recuperative trip to Italy. Though his couture career spanned scarcely a decade, he had established himself as one of the modern era's best known fashion designers. Writing for *Contemporary Fashion,* Kevin Almond asserted that "By the time Dior died his name had become synonymous with taste and luxury."

New Generations of Design Leadership after Dior's Death in 1957

The founder's death left the house in chaos. Jacques Rouët considered shuttering the worldwide operations, but neither Dior's licensees nor the French fashion industry—which owed 50 percent of its export volume to the House of Dior—would consider it. Instead, Rouët—who would continue to guide the company's day-to-day operations into the 1980s—promoted 22-year-old Yves Saint Laurent, whom Dior had hired just two years previous, as lead designer. Launched in 1958, the young designer's trapeze line was successful, but his 1960 "bohemian" look met heavy criticism from the press, especially the influential fashion industry magazine *Women's Wear Daily.* When Saint Laurent was drafted into the armed service that year (he went on to found his own house in 1962), he was succeeded by Marc Bohan, another protégé of Dior hired to head the London outlet shortly before the founder's death. Bohan would go on to serve Dior until 1989, far longer than the founder. *Contemporary Fashion*'s Rebecca Arnold credited Bohan with keeping the House of Dior "at the forefront of fashion while still producing wearable, elegant clothes," and *Women's Wear Daily,* not surprisingly, claimed that he "rescued the firm."

Troubles at Dior's parent company, Boussac, would visit drastic change on the maison de couture in the 1980s. The roots of the problems reached back to the 1970s. Still owned and led by its octogenarian founder (known as "King Cotton" in his home nation), Group Boussac had by this time grown to encompass 65 textile mills and 17,000 employees. Despite its size, several imperatives of the maturing industry—consolidation, competition from imports, the shift to synthetics—had knocked Boussac from the top of France's fabric heap to a struggling number five by 1971. Reluctant to close money-losing plants and lay off workers, King Cotton did little to prevent his textile operations from suffering heavy losses in the 1970s. Money generated by his remaining one-third share of Dior helped to prop up the Boussac group for several years, and the parent company raised millions by selling its stake in Dior Perfumes. In 1981, the government-owned Institute de Development Industriel took control of the insolvent company, infusing FFr 1 billion (almost U.S. $200 million) in the company from 1982 to 1985. When Boussac finally went bankrupt, a group of investors led by Bernard Arnault acquired it for "one symbolic franc" in December 1984. The 34-year-old Arnault divested the textile group's industrial operations, focusing on its Bon Marché department store and Christian Dior.

Evolution into a Luxury Powerhouse in the 1980s

Under Arnault, Dior became the cornerstone of one of the world's largest and most important fashion companies. The new leader formed Christian Dior S.A. as a holding company for the fashion house, then used the holding company as a vehicle to purchase a controlling stake in Moet Hennessy Louis Vuitton in 1990. (His Au Bon Marché and Financiere Agache companies were also involved in the complex acquisitions.) Before long, Arnault had woven an intricate web of high-end brands, including the Christian Lacroix and Celine fashion houses; the Hubert de Givenchy fashion and fragrance operations; and the Dior fragrance business. By 1991, when Arnault sold a minority stake in Dior on the public market, LVMH had grown to become France's top luxury goods group and its second-largest publicly-traded firm.

Dubbed "king of luxury goods" by *Time,* Arnault took part in the supervision of Dior's design direction as well as its operations. Though the couture division was by this time an unprofitable operation, Arnault considered it a fundamental element of the Dior brand cachet. In 1989, he hired Italian designer Gianfranco Ferré to succeed Marc Bohan as the maison's artistic director. In keeping with his standing as the first non-Frenchman to guide the house, Ferré broke from the romantic and flirtatious traditions set by Dior and Bohan respectively, opting instead to continue in his own well-established vein with a collection described by Kevin Almond in *Contemporary Fashion* as "refined, sober and strict."

Arnault even served as managing director of Dior from the December 1990 firing of Beatrice Bongibault to September 1991, when he hired former Au Bon Marché president Philippe Vindry. Vindry's strategies included a ten percent average reduction in the retail price of Dior prêt à porter. (A wool suit still cost more than U.S. $1,500.) The change helped increase sales at Dior's headquarters store by 50 percent from 1990 to 1991. Vindry also reorganized Dior into three divisions: women's ready-to-wear (also encompassing lingerie and childrenswear), accessories and jewelry, and menswear. Management also strove to rein in internal management of the Dior brand and image by reducing licensees and franchised boutiques. Arnault and Vindry nearly halved the number of Dior licensees from 280 in 1989 to less than 150 by 1992, opting for quality and exclusivity over quantity and accessibility. By mid-decade, Christian Dior S.A. had added company-owned stores in Hong Kong, Singapore, Kuala Lumpur, Cannes, and Waikiki to its core shops in New York, Hawaii, Paris, and Geneva. This strategy held out the potential to increase direct sales and profit margins while maintaining high-profile locations. Francois Baufume, who succeeded Vindry as managing director of Dior Couture in 1993, continued to reduce licensees, which numbered around 120 by mid-decade.

Christian Dior Couture's sales increased from FFr 673 million ($129.3 million) in 1990 to just over FFr 1 billion (U.S. $177 million) in 1995, while net income grew from FFr 115 million (U.S. $22 million) to FFr 156 million (U.S. $26.9 million).

New Designer to Lead House in the Late 1990s

In 1996, Arnault "ruffled some French feathers" by appointing British designer John Galliano to succeed Gianfranco Ferré as Dior's head. Arnault noted that while he "would have preferred Frenchmen," he chose a Briton "for a very simple reason: talent has no nationality." The CEO even compared maison Dior's newest designer to the founder in a December 1996 *Women's Wear Daily* article, noting that "Galliano has a creative talent very close to that of Christian Dior. He has the same extraordinary mixture of romanticism, feminism, and modernity that symbolizes Mr. Dior. In all of his creations—his suits, his dresses—one finds similarities to the Dior style."

Further Reading

Adler, Jerry, "The Riches of Rags," *Newsweek,* December 16, 1996, p. 77.

"Boussac Bows Out," *Economist,* December 12, 1970, p. 85.

"Boussac Tries to Save His Empire," *Business Week,* July 3, 1971, p. 31.

"Boussac Unbowed," *Economist,* April 26, 1975, p. 115.

Cattani, Jane, "Dior Lives," *Harper's Bazaar,* December 1996, pp. 195–198.

Deeny, Godfrey, "Francois Baufume: Directing Dior," *Women's Wear Daily,* February 28, 1995, pp. 6–7.

——, "A New Dior Taking Shape under Vindry," *Women's Wear Daily,* October 28, 1992, pp. 1–3.

"Dior's Birthday: Let 'Em Eat Cake," *Women's Wear Daily,* March 23, 1987, pp. 1–3.

Duffy, Martha, "The Pope of Fashion," *Time,* April 21, 1997, pp. 112–113.

Jacobs, Laura, "Dior's Couture D'Etat," *Vanity Fair,* November 1996, pp. 92–97.

Kurzwell, Allen, "Dior: 40 Years of Triumph," *Harper's Bazaar,* September 1987, pp. 152–153.

Middleton, William and Kevin West, "In Arnault's Worlds, Luxury and the Future Are Keys to Empire," *Women's Wear Daily,* December 9, 1996, pp. 1–4.

Pochna, Marie-France, *Christian Dior: The Man Who Made the World Look New,* New York: Arcade Publishing, 1996.

Raper, Sarah, "Dior Holders Are Feisty at First Annual Meeting as a Public Company," *Women's Wear Daily,* June 17, 1992, p. 15.

Weisman, Katherine, "Arnault Sees Sales, Profits Growing at LVMH and Dior," *Women's Wear Daily,* May 31, 1996, pp. 2–3.

—April Dougal Gasbarre

CKE Restaurants, Inc.

1200 North Harbor Boulevard
P. O. Box 4349
Anaheim, California 92803
U.S.A.
(714) 774-5796
Fax: (714) 490-3695
Web site: http://www.ckr.com

Public Company
Incorporated: 1966 as Carl Karcher Enterprises, Inc.
Employees: 12,000
Sales: $614.08 million (1997)
Stock Exchanges: New York
SICs: 5812 Eating Places

CKE Restaurants, Inc., known as Carl Karcher Enterprises, Inc. for much of its history, is a multi-brand restaurant empire, focusing mostly on fast food, especially hamburgers. From its beginnings as a hot dog cart run by company founder Carl N. Karcher, CKE grew into a firm with more than 4,000 owned or franchised restaurants across the United States, under the flagship Carl's Jr. brand, as well as such 1990s-acquired brands as Hardee's, Taco Bueno, and Casa Bonita. As of mid-1997, CKE also owned family-dining specialist Summit Family Restaurants Inc.—which owned or franchised 117 JB's Restaurants, HomeTown Buffets, and Galaxy Diners—but planned to divest most or all of these holdings. The company also made various strategic investments in the mid-1990s in the Rally's and Checkers double drive-thru hamburger chains (which were the subject of a proposed merger as of mid-1997).

Early History

Carl N. Karcher was born in 1917 in Upper Sandusky, Ohio, the third of eight children. Karcher's great-grandfather had immigrated to the Ohio Valley from Germany in 1840, leading to a growing population of Karchers in northwest Ohio. It was the Karcher who left Ohio, however, who set Carl Karcher on the road to entrepreneurial success. Karcher had been helping on his father's farm since he quit school after the eighth grade. But when his uncle offered him a job at his Anaheim, California feed and seed store in 1937, Karcher and his brother, Ralph, set off for the West Coast.

Karcher did not remain with his uncle for long. By 1939, Karcher had secured a job as deliveryman at the Armstrong Bakery in Los Angeles and had married Margaret Heinz. On his 75-mile delivery route, Karcher noticed the growing number of hot-dog carts and stands on various Los Angeles street corners. When a customer offered him the chance to purchase one for himself, Karcher acted quickly. Over his wife's objections, he secured a $311 loan using their new 1941 Plymouth as collateral. Fifteen dollars in cash provided the rest of the $326 needed to buy the cart and put Karcher in business on July 17, 1941.

Karcher located his cart at Florence and Central in South-Central Los Angeles, across the street from a Goodyear plant busy with wartime work. First day receipts were $14.75 from the sale of hot dogs, chili dogs, tamales, and soft drinks. Karcher displayed his knack for innovation when he started to offer curbside service, enabling his customers to remain in their cars.

In May 1942, Karcher bought a second hot-dog cart—with the full support of his wife this time—which he relocated near a service station on another busy intersection. Later in the year a third was added, also near a service station. The next year Karcher added a fourth unit, which was not a cart but a stand—a small building with five stools placed around an outside counter for on-premise eating.

Though Karchers' enterprise was successful, Margaret Karcher wished to be closer to her family in Anaheim. Carl Karcher decided to expand his business; he soon found a Bob's Restaurant for sale, not far from where Margaret's family lived. Eager to move into the family restaurant sector, Karcher bought the facility's furnishings and equipment for $4,200 and signed a 12-year lease at $120 per month. The Karchers purchased a house down the street from the restaurant.

In January 1945, the newly named Carl's Drive-in Barbeque opened in Anaheim, serving a variety of sandwiches, chicken fried steak, barbecued ribs, and hamburgers. The hamburgers proved to be particularly popular and were added to the hot-dog stand menus after 15-inch grills were installed at each location in 1946. At Carl's Drive-in, Karcher installed a large neon sign with a flashing star on top to draw attention to a menu that was "out of this world." The star later evolved into the "happy star" logo that became synonymous with the Carl's Jr. chain.

Carl's Jr. Launch Highlighted 1950s

In the late 1940s and early 1950s Karcher's enterprises became increasingly sophisticated. The hot-dog carts and tiny stands evolved into larger hamburger stands with warehouse rooms to store supplies on-site, brick exteriors, and an overhang as standard features.

The 1950s were a time of increasing affluence in America and eating out became more common. At the same time the pace of life was quickening, providing the right ingredients for the explosion of what would later be called "fast food." Karcher recognized these trends and decided to create mini-versions of the full-service Carl's Drive-in Barbeque, calling the smaller spinoffs Carl's Jr. The first Carl's Jr. opened in Anaheim in 1956, followed quickly by a second in nearby Brea. Each Carl's Jr. had about a thousand square feet of space, two customer windows—one to place orders and another to pick them up—, and a small patio with redwood picnic tables for on-site eating. The Carl's Jr. menu was much more varied than the typical quick-service restaurant of the time—notably McDonald's. Carl's Jr. served hot dogs, shrimp baskets, hamburgers, tacos, and even pizza. The star logo was featured at each site, though now personified with the addition of a freckled, smiling face; this "happy star" wore booties and held a shake in one hand and a hamburger in the other. Carl Karcher asked his brother Don to manage the Carl's Jr. operations.

By the end of the 1950s, there were four Carl's Jr. restaurants in Orange County, one of which had briefly experimented with a drive-thru years before drive-thrus became standard fast-food restaurant features. Other Carl's Jr. innovations of the time were not so quickly abandoned. An inside take-out window and an enclosed patio were both quickly accepted by the public, as was the procedure of paying for one's order before receiving it—unheard of at the time but later standard practice in the industry.

Slow Growth and Miscues in the 1960s

The 1960s were a time of slow growth and missteps for the operations of Carl Karcher. Karcher owned five separate corporations when, in 1964, he hired management consultant Irving J.

Mills as a consultant. Under Mills's guidance, the five corporations were consolidated in 1966 under Carl Karcher Enterprises, Inc. The firm was divided into two branches. Don Karcher became vice-president of field operations, overseeing all restaurants, while another brother, Frank, became vice-president of services, overseeing purchasing, construction, financing, real estate, and public relations.

Mills next suggested that Karcher Enterprises needed a theme to differentiate itself within the exploding fast-food scene. Designers and architects developed a railroad-themed concept called Carl's Whistle Stop and three opened in 1966 in La Habra, Garden Grove, and Long Beach. The Whistle Stops were among the first fast-food restaurants with ordering areas that were enclosed and air-conditioned. They failed, at least in part, because they were ahead of their time. People mistook the Whistle Stops for coffee shops because the order windows were hidden inside (and because of the buildings' architecture). This confusion led Karcher to convert the Whistle Stops to Carl's Jr. restaurants, with outside walk-up windows. Ironically, within a few years enclosed, air-conditioned ordering areas became the industry norm and the converted Whistle Stop units were changed back to their original inside ordering area style.

A second failure of the mid-1960s came when the company decided to expand by purchasing three full-service, Scottish-themed coffee shops called Scot's. They were never successful, however, and were sold soon after the Whistle Stops were converted. Mills soon parted ways with the company, which proceeded to return to its roots.

Carl's Jr. Revamped in the Late 1960s

In 1968, Carl Karcher Enterprises had 25 restaurants in operation when Karcher decided to refocus on the Carl's Jr. brand. His concept of a "new" Carl's Jr. featured a more attractive exterior with used brick and a tiled roof; upgraded interiors with carpets, cushioned booths, and music; and a re-tooled ordering procedure whereby customers still ordered and paid for food at an outside walk-up window but now were served their food at tables by employees—so-called partial dining room service. Most of these changes were firsts for the fast-food industry. The most radical change, however, was a streamlining of the menu in order to offer quicker service—Karcher decided to offer only hamburgers, hot dogs, french fries, malts, and soft drinks.

Despite numerous objections raised by others at Karcher Enterprises, the first revamped Carl's Jr. opened in Fullerton in 1968 and met with immediate success. This restaurant was the first in the company to rack up $1,000 in a single day's sales. It also helped Karcher Enterprises's 1968 sales reach almost $5 million.

Other Carl's Jr. restaurants were soon converted to the new format and the company embarked on an expansion plan which enabled it to reach the 40-restaurant mark by the end of the decade. The Carl's Jr. "happy star" logo appeared in San Diego County and the San Fernando Valley for the first time. To support the expansion, advertising increased, featuring the star and the slogan "It's out of this world."

As growth increased, Karcher Enterprises became more concerned with quality control and training. The company developed its first procedures manual to ensure that customers received the same product from all Carl's Jr. restaurants and created a training department to make training more uniform.

Tremendous Expansion in the 1970s

Carl's Jr. transformed into a major regional chain during the 1970s. In that decade, Carl Karcher Enterprises grew from 40 restaurants to 289, from 300 employees to 8,500, and from $5.6 million in annual revenue to $138.6 million. Carl's Jr. and additional innovations led the way.

In 1974 Carl's Jr. successfully reintroduced the drive-thru abandoned a decade earlier. Two years later, the industry's first soup and salad bar appeared in a Carl's Jr.; this innovation was rolled out chainwide three years later. Carl's Jr. expanded outside Southern California for the first time in 1975, when seven units opened in Northern California. The following year Karcher Enterprises built a 29,000-square-foot corporate headquarters in Anaheim, then two years later added a $5-million, 145,000-square-foot commissary and warehouse adjacent to the headquarters. The company also began to manufacture most of the products it sold.

During the late 1970s several of the older Carl's Jr. units were remodeled, and some were upgraded with drive-thrus. In 1977 the 200th Carl's Jr. opened. With the chain's expansion going so well, the company decided it was time to expand outside California. After a year spent investigating possible areas, Las Vegas, Nevada, was identified as the best site for the first out-of-state unit. This was a logical choice because of the city's proximity to Southern California and because 60 percent of Las Vegas tourists came from Southern California. In June 1979 the first Carl's Jr. in Nevada opened.

Karcher Enterprises suffered one notable failure in the 1970s when it decided to start its own chain of Mexican fast-food restaurants, called Taco de Carlos. Attempting to cash in on the increasing popularity of Mexican food, the company opened the first Taco de Carlos in 1972 and had 17 of them operating by decade-end. The chain was never given the attention necessary for success and was abandoned in the early 1980s and all of the units were sold, 12 of them to Del Taco for $2.2 million.

Various Setbacks Plague Company in the 1980s

Carl's Jr. had become the largest privately held, nonfranchised restaurant chain in the United States by the 1980s. After the successes of the 1970s, management boldly set goals for the year 1990: 1,000 Carl's Jr. restaurants and $1 billion in annual revenue. Unfortunately, the company would fall far short of these figures. In 1980 Carl Karcher promoted Don Karcher to president and chief operating officer of Karcher Enterprises. Carl Karcher remained chairman and CEO.

To reach their lofty goals, the Karchers needed to accelerate Carl's Jr.'s expansion program. To help finance the expansion, they decided to take the company public, raising $13.79 million through the October 1981 initial public offering. In 1981 the 300th Carl's Jr. opened. The following year the Carl's Jr. chain

entered its third state when a Yuma, Arizona, restaurant opened in June. That same year several locations began to offer 24-hour service. In 1984, Carl's Jr. was franchised for the first time, an unusually long-delayed entry into franchising for a fast-food chain.

In the mid-1980s, Carl's Jr. ran aground from overexpansion and excessive tinkering with the menu. Earlier in the decade the chain had successfully introduced a Western Bacon Cheeseburger and a Charbroiler Chicken Sandwich. Then in an attempt to be a cross between a fast-food restaurant and a coffee shop, four charbroiler dinners were added to the menu in 1983—top sirloin steak, boneless chicken breast, rainbow trout, and ground beef steak. Each came with a choice of baked potato, fried zucchini, or wedge-cut potatoes and garlic toast. The dinners were served on platters rather than paper plates, and customers were provided with silverware, not plastic utensils. Unfortunately, the charbroiler dinners created a host of problems: the need to install dishwashers, traffic backups at the drive-thrus thanks to the length of time it took to prepare the dinners, and general customer confusion over what Carl's Jr. was. In 1985, the chain abandoned the dinners in another return to roots; restaurants signs which had read "Carl's Jr. Restaurant" were changed back to "Carl's Jr. Charbroiled Hamburgers." Prices were cut and all-you-can-drink beverage bars were added.

Compounding the company's difficulty was the chain's expansion into Texas, which began in 1984, just as the state economy was entering a prolonged depression. Texas had been chosen as the first state in a national roll-out of the Carl's Jr. brand. The three dozen units established there never came close to meeting sales expectations and by early 1987 Carl's Jr. had pulled out of the state entirely, taking a $15 million writeoff as a result and posting a loss for fiscal 1986. The company decided to limit the areas where it would build company-owned stores to California and Arizona and also converted a number of company-owned units to franchised units. Over the next few years, national expansion was placed on the back burner; instead more than 200 older Carl's Jr. restaurants were remodeled.

By 1988 the chain included 383 units and Carl Karcher Enterprises posted record earnings of $16 million. Carl Karcher credited the turnaround in part to the 1986 hiring of Raymond Perry as vice-president of operations; Perry had more than 20 years of restaurant experience, including serving as president of Straw Hat Pizza.

The Securities and Exchange Commission (SEC) filed a lawsuit against Carl Karcher in April 1988 alleging that in late 1984 he had tipped off relatives to an upcoming announcement that profits were expected to drop by half. Karcher vigorously denied the insider-trading charges, but in July 1989, he and six relatives agreed to settle the case by paying a total of $664,245, without admitting guilt. In related insider-trading cases, Al DeShano, the company's accountant, agreed to pay $24,794; and six other Karcher family members, including Don Karcher, settled with the SEC for $187,561.

As if all these problems were not enough, the Carl's Jr. chain had the added burden of a chairman and CEO who took public positions on controversial issues. Carl Karcher was a dedicated conservative Republican and had served as the party's finance chairman for Orange County, one of the most conservative counties in the country. His support for right-wing Republican John Schmitz, who had tried in the 1970s to ban homosexuals from teaching in public schools, came to the attention of gay rights groups. And Karcher's adamant opposition to abortion— a result of his devout Catholicism—led to demonstrations at Carl's Jr. restaurants organized by abortion rights groups in the late 1980s and early 1990s. In 1991 opposition from gay and abortion rights groups led students at California State University, Northridge, to narrowly vote down the establishment of a Carl's Jr. on their campus.

Meanwhile, Carl's Jr. brand expanded internationally for the first time. In 1988 a license agreement was signed with the Friendly Corporation of Osaka, Japan, to develop at least 30 Carl's Jr. restaurants in Japan by 1993. Two years later a license agreement with Malaysia-based MBf International (later known as MBf Holding Berhad) called for 16 restaurants to be built in the Pacific Rim—including Malaysia, Singapore, Hong Kong, Australia, New Zealand, Taiwan, Thailand, the Philippines, and Indonesia—over five years. In 1995 a new joint venture agreement with MBf was signed and called for 130 Carl's Jr. units to be built in a five-year span. In October 1990 Carl Karcher Enterprises signed an agreement with a third licensee, Valores Matalicos, to expand the chain into Mexico.

Management Chaos in the Early 1990s

The early 1990s were marked by turbulence in the management ranks at Carl Karcher Enterprises. Perry had been considered an heir apparent to the aging Karcher, but was abruptly dismissed from his number three position in 1991. Then Don Karcher died of cancer the following year. Carl Karcher began to lose control of the company board at the same time he was experiencing personal financial difficulties. In December 1992 Karcher attempted to simultaneously regain control and solve his money woes through a $103 million leveraged buyout of Carl Karcher Enterprises that he proposed with the Los Angeles investment firm, Freeman Spogli & Co. The deal might have earned him $43 million. The board rejected the offer, then the following month appointed Donald Doyle, former head of Kentucky Fried Chicken USA, CEO and president, with Karcher remaining chairman. In addition to the management upheaval, chainwide sales were beginning to level off thanks to fierce competition in the industry and the company posted a fiscal 1993 loss of $5.5 million, the first loss since fiscal 1986.

Karcher and Doyle clashed throughout 1993, most notably over a Karcher proposal to test dual-branded restaurants featuring both Carl's Jr. fare and that of the ailing Mexican food chain Green Burrito, run by Anaheim-based GB Foods Inc. If approved by the board, Karcher's financial problems would have reportedly been solved. In August the board rejected the proposal, which led Karcher to threaten a proxy fight to oust certain board members. In October the board voted Karcher out as chairman for interfering with long-term management strategy, replacing him with long-time board member Elizabeth A. Sanders.

Two months later Karcher was back on the board but with the more or less honorary title of chairman emeritus. To regain his seat and to solve his financial woes Karcher struck a deal with a partnership led by William P. Foley II, an entrepreneur who had built Fidelity National Title into the nation's fourth-largest title insurance company. Foley's partnership paid off Karcher's $23 million bank loan in exchange for the 3.8 million shares of company stock posted as collateral. The partnership then controlled about 25 percent of the stock, gaining Foley a seat on the board.

For the next several months Sanders and Doyle led Carl Karcher Enterprises and decided that for Carl's Jr. to better compete its traditional premium pricing strategy should be changed to one based on lower prices. When sales continued to drop during fiscal 1994, Foley stepped in to challenge Doyle's leadership. Doyle soon resigned, Foley was appointed chairman and CEO, and Foley brought in Bay Area franchisee Tom Thompson as president and COO. Also in 1994 the new board received shareholder approval for a new corporate structure, which created a new parent company called CKE Restaurants, Inc., with subsidiary Carl Karcher Enterprises, Inc. in charge of the Carl's Jr. chain.

Mid-1990s Transformation into Multi-Brand Empire

In July 1994 the CKE board reversed course and approved a test of dual Carl's Jr./Green Burrito restaurants. Then in a further twist CKE decided early in 1995 to abandon the dual branding with Green Burrito and instead develop a dual concept with its own Mexican concept called Picante Grill. GB Foods subsequently sued CKE, calling the new concept a "knock-off." Finally in June 1995 the two parties settled their differences and agreed to develop a minimum of 140 dual-branded locations. Twenty-two of them were operating in fiscal 1996 and posted sales 25 percent sales higher than when the units were simply Carl's Jr. outlets. Also in 1995 the company signed a deal with UNOCAL 76 Products Company to open Carl's Jr. restaurants within ten UNOCAL Fast Break convenience stores and gasoline stations in California. Remarkably, Foley and Thompson had turned the Carl's Jr. chain around.

The defining move toward improvement came in mid-1995 when the chain abandoned value pricing and developed a new advertising campaign which emphasized quality and quantity through the slogan "If it doesn't get all over the place, it doesn't belong in your face." According to a company annual report, ads featured "big, messy, juicy burgers dripping on a variety of targets including a basketball player's high-tops, a motorcycle cop, and an unsuspecting pigeon." Backed by the campaign, same-store sales began increasing for the first time in five years.

With Carl's Jr. on the rebound, CKE officials confidently looked outside the company for undervalued restaurant properties for acquisition or investment. In April 1996 CKE spent $4.1 million for a 15-percent stake in the struggling Rally's Hamburgers, Inc., operator of a chain of nearly 500 Rally's double drive-thrus. This stake was increased to 18 percent later in 1996 and CKE also began managing 28 Rally's in California and Arizona. The two companies also agreed not to compete against each other in the same markets—Rally's was primarily located in the southeastern United States—and Rally's borrowed Carl's Jr.'s "messy" advertising strategy to turn around its fortunes.

CKE acquired Summit Family Restaurants Inc., which operated the 104-unit JB's Restaurant chain, six Galaxy Diners, and

16 HomeTown Buffets as a franchisee. CKE quickly made Summit profitable again but just as quickly determined that it did not want to focus on family dining and so would likely divest most of these holdings and earn a profit in the process.

In October 1996 CKE bought Casa Bonita Incorporated from Unigate PLC for $42 million in cash, gaining the 107-unit Taco Bueno fast-food chain and two Casa Bonita family restaurants, which featured entertainment. The deal returned CKE not only to the Mexican food sector that the company abandoned when it gave up on Taco de Carlos but also to that nettlesome state of Texas, which was where Casa Bonita was headquartered and where it operated 67 Taco Bueno units.

Continuing a whirlwind year, in November 1996 CKE became involved with another struggling double drive-thru hamburger chain when it purchased $12.9 million of Checkers Drive-In Restaurants, Inc. senior secured debt. CKE followed up by acquiring a 10 percent stake in the 475-unit Checkers in February 1997. In April CKE helped to craft a proposed merger of Checkers and Rally's, which if consummated would combine the similar chains into a single system of nearly 1,000 units.

CKE's stock split 3-for-2 in January 1997 and the company announced an amendment to its dual-brand agreement with GB Foods whereby the original 140-unit commitment was increased to a minimum of 306 stores, with a minimum of 60 restaurants to be converted each year over a five-year span. But the company announced a real blockbuster in April 1997 when it said it would acquire Hardee's Food Systems Inc. from Imasco Ltd. of Montreal for about $327 million—the number seven burger chain buying the number four chain. Hardee's, yet another struggling burger chain, boasted 3,100 units located in 41 states and 10 foreign countries and had 1996 revenues of almost $3 billion. Its U.S. units were strongest in the Midwest and Southeast, which meshed well with Carl's Jr.'s predominance in the West. CKE planned to test dual-branded Carl's Jr./Hardee's units, with Hardee's strong breakfast lineup teaming with Carl's Jr.'s lunch and dinner sandwiches.

After a few years of Foley's leadership, CKE was barely recognizable as the same company. Fiscal 1997 revenue reached a healthy $614.1 million, while net income was a record $22.3 million. With the addition of the Hardee's brand, it was even questionable whether Carl's Jr. was still the firm's top brand. Future prospects appeared bright for this multi-brand giant, although somewhat difficult to predict given the dynamism of the mid-1990s.

Principal Subsidiaries

Boston Pacific, Inc.; Carl Karcher Enterprises, Inc.; Casa Bonita Incorporated; Hardee's Food Systems Inc.; Summit Family Restaurants Inc.; Checkers Drive-In Restaurants, Inc. (10%); Rally's Hamburgers, Inc. (18%).

Further Reading

Alva, Marilyn, "Star Man: Bill Foley Knew Nothing about Restaurants. So How Did He Work Miracles with the Ailing Carl's Jr. Chain?," *Restaurant Business,* October 10, 1996, pp. 90–93, 96, 100.

Barrett, Amy, "One Burned-Up Burger Baron: Why Carl's Jr. Founder Carl Karcher Was Ousted by His Own Board," *Business Week,* October 18, 1993, pp. 62–63.

Barrier, Michael, "Building on a Better Burger," *Nation's Business,* January 1988, pp. 63–64.

Bell, Alexa, "Carl's Quandary: Now 75, Carl Karcher Must Decide Who'll Carry the Family Torch," *Restaurant Business,* July 1, 1992, pp. 52–53, 56–57.

Carlino, Bill, "CKE Acquires Taco Bueno, Makes Push into Texas, Okla.," *Nation's Restaurant News,* September 9, 1996, p. 1.

Gomez, James M., "Carl's Jr. Founder Ousted as Chairman of Burger Chain," *Los Angeles Times,* October 2, 1993.

Hamstra, Mark, "CKE Crafts Merger of Checkers, Rally's," *Nation's Restaurant News,* April 7, 1997, pp. 1, 6.

Hamstra, Mark, and Bill Carlino, "CKE Restaurants Inc. to Acquire Hardee's, Roll Out Carl's Jr. Brand," *Nation's Restaurant News,* May 5, 1997, p. 5.

Knight, B. Carolyn, *Making It Happen: The Story of Carl Karcher Enterprises,* Anaheim, Calif.: Carl Karcher Enterprises, 1981.

——, *Never Stop Dreaming: Fifty Years of Making It Happen,* San Marcos, Calif.: Robert Erdmann Publishing, 1991.

Lubove, Seth, "Inexperience Pays: Bill Foley Didn't Know How to Run a Restaurant Chain, but He Learned Quickly How Not to Run One," *Forbes,* September 23, 1996, pp. 60–61.

Martin, Richard, "CKE Buying JB's Parent for $37M," *Nation's Restaurant News,* December 11, 1995, pp. 1, 74.

Veverka, Mark, "CKE, Grilled on McDonald's News, Is a Good Bargain Now, Experts Say," *Wall Street Journal,* March 12, 1997.

Woodyard, Chris, "The Commercial Life of Happy Star Karcher," *Los Angeles Times,* November 10, 1991.

—David E. Salamie

Columbia Sportswear Company

6600 North Baltimore
Portland, Oregon 97203
U.S.A.
(503) 286-3676
Fax: (503) 289-6602
Web site: http://www.columbia.com

Private Company
Incorporated: 1938 as Columbia Hat Company
Employees: 950
Sales: $299 million (1996)
SICs: 2329 Men/Boys' Clothing, Not Elsewhere
   Classified; 2339 Women/Misses' Outerwear, Not
   Elsewhere Classified

The largest outerwear manufacturer in the world, Columbia Sportswear Company designs, manufactures, and markets outdoor apparel and footwear, distributing its merchandise to more than 10,000 retailers in North America, South America, Europe, Asia, and Australia-New Zealand. Columbia's rise to the top began during the 1980s, when Gertrude Boyle and her son, Tim, orchestrated the remarkable growth of their family-owned business nearly 50 years after the company began doing business as Columbia Hat Company. With mother and son at the helm, Columbia's sales grew quickly after the company entered the skiwear market in 1986 with its trademarked Interchange System of layered outerwear. Building on the success achieved during the late 1980s, the company diversified during the 1990s, entering the footwear market in 1993 and the snowboard apparel market in 1994. In 1996, the company opened its flagship retail outlet in Portland, Oregon, and the following year it opened a store in Seoul, Korea.

1930s Origins

One family able to escape Nazi-controlled Germany before the start of World War II was the Lanfrom family, who fled their native country in 1937 and resettled in Portland, Oregon. The following year, the family, headed by Paul Lanfrom, purchased a small hat distributorship named Rosenfeld Hat Company and renamed it Columbia Hat Company. Such were the origins of Columbia Sportswear, a small, unknown hat company tucked away in a corner of the United States that half a century later held sway as a national leader in the sportswear market. Aside from the company's headquarters location in Portland, however, few vestiges of Columbia Sportswear's past remained during the 1990s. The transition from a small, locally oriented hat distributorship into a corporation with a global reach took decades to complete, but it began early, starting a few short years after Paul Lanfrom took control of the company.

The first of the many changes that shaped Columbia Hat Company into Columbia Sportswear occurred when Paul Lanfrom encountered problems with his vendors. The solution, as Lanfrom perceived it, was to begin manufacturing his products on his own. Though the move into manufacturing represented a signal milestone in Columbia Sportswear's development, it did not ignite the prolific growth that would later characterize the company. Rather, the company maintained a minor presence in the Portland area, operating as a small manufacturing concern capable of supporting Paul Lanfrom, his wife Marie, and their daughters in their new life in America.

A decade after Paul Lanfrom acquired Rosenfeld Hat Company, his daughter, Gertrude, married Neal Boyle, who subsequently joined the family business he would later lead. Neal Boyle's ascendancy to control over the family business occurred in 1963 when Paul Lanfrom died and Boyle became president. By the time Boyle took charge, Columbia had begun to carve a niche for itself in the hunting and fishing apparel market thanks in large part to his wife's contributions. Three years before her father died, Gertrude Boyle designed and made a fishing vest jacket on her home sewing machine that paved the way for the company's future. The bolero-style vest, which was outfitted with numerous pockets, was revolutionary in concept and moved the company headlong into the market for fishing and hunting apparel. Neal Boyle expanded his company's presence into this market once he took control. His era as company president, however, was unexpectedly brief. In 1970, at age 47, Neal Boyle died of a heart attack, leaving Columbia in the hands of his wife, Gertrude Boyle.

1970s: Mother and Son Take Charge

At the time of Neal Boyle's death, Columbia was generating $650,000 a year in sales but was teetering on the brink of insolvency. Although the company had made headway into the market for fishing and hunting apparel, profitability in this line of business had been a problem for years, leaving Gertrude Boyle in the unenviable position of inheriting a floundering business. To make matters worse, Neal Boyle had offered three family-owned homes and his life insurance policy as collateral for a Small Business Administration loan several months before his death, which exacerbated the financial pressures Gertrude Boyle inherited in 1970. Despite the bleak prospects Columbia faced and despite her lack of any managerial experience, Gertrude Boyle showed up at the company's headquarters the day after her husband's funeral ready to take charge, vowing to keep the three-decade-old family business running under her command.

In the months that followed Neal Boyle's death, Columbia's financial health went from bad to worse. Bankers were reluctant to provide credit, some stores refused to stock Columbia's merchandise, and others experienced delivery problems. By the end of Gertrude Boyle's first year of leadership, the situation was grave, prompting the mother of three to sit down and negotiate for the sale of the company her family had owned since she was a child. From across the table came an offer of $1,400, which Boyle flatly refused, reportedly telling Columbia's prospective buyer, "For a lousy $1,400, I'll run the company into the ground myself." Boyle nearly did.

Gertrude Boyle's son, Tim, who had been working part-time at the company, left his final semester at the University of Oregon to join Columbia full-time after his mother balked at what she perceived to be an insulting bid for her family's apparel manufacturing business. Two years later, mother and son could not point to anything positive. Columbia had a negative net worth of $300,000, and as Tim Boyle later remembered, both he and his mother were at fault. "We really blew it," the younger Boyle admitted to *Sporting Goods Business* 20 years later. "You name it, we did it wrong. We went in and fired everyone. We just didn't know what in the world we were doing."

Gradually, however, Columbia's anemic financial health began to improve under the determined control of Gertrude and Tim Boyle. The mother and son team were given credit after pledging Columbia's $200,000 manufacturing facility. Subsequently, they dramatically reduced the company's involvement in the wholesaling side of the apparel business, which had been stifling profits for years. Once this was done, the company was able to scrape by during the mid-1970s by targeting specialty catalog operators. In 1976, however, Tim Boyle made a decision about Columbia's future course that put an end to the years

of merely striving to eke out an existence in the sportswear apparel market. Boyle resolved to concentrate on building a brand-label presence in Columbia's markets. From 1976 forward, marketing the Columbia label represented the number one priority and, as a consequence, nearly every available dollar was earmarked for advertising.

Columbia reached the $1 million mark in sales in 1978, as the company earned a reputation in specialized circles as a hunting and fishing apparel resource. The explosive growth that would catapult the company and the Columbia label toward global prominence was still several years away, but one of the key individuals for engendering such growth joined the Portland apparel manufacturer before the 1970s came to an end. In 1979, Don Santorufo began superintending all the purchasing of materials and the manufacturing of merchandise at Columbia's manufacturing facility in Portland and then quickly expanded production by contracting out work to several independent Pacific Northwest contractors. It was a definitive move that marked the gradual decline of production activities in Portland and set the stage for years of exponential sales growth. Within ten years, all production in Portland would come to an end.

Explosive 1980s Growth

Columbia's annual sales climbed robustly as production expanded, rising from the $1 million recorded in 1978 to $12 million by 1983, when Santorufo hired Korean nationals to oversee manufacturing overseas. The decision to manufacture overseas proved to be instrumental in Columbia's resolute rise during the 1980s because offshore production enabled the company to make its apparel items at a significantly lower price. "What we did was lower the price of quality," Boyle explained years later. "There was no need for performance apparel to cost what most manufacturers were charging for it. We were able to source better-made goods off-shore and offer them to consumers at a reasonable price." Santorufo's deal with the Koreans was pivotal, but equally important was the development of what Columbia designers christened the Interchange System. Introduced the year before Columbia began manufacturing overseas, the trademarked Interchange System consisted of a lightweight shell jacket and a warm liner that zipped together, giving the wearer three jackets for different weather conditions.

Together, the decision to manufacture offshore and the development of the Interchange System provided two key ingredients for the success Columbia achieved during the late 1980s and into the 1990s. One other decisive move spurred the exponential growth to follow: in 1986 Columbia entered the skiwear market with a parka called the "Bugaboo," featuring the company's Interchange System of layered outerwear. The Bugaboo, which ranked as the greatest selling parka at its price point in the industry by the end of its debut year, put the company on the map, touching off prodigious growth that elevated Columbia into the elite of nationally recognized contenders. In the decade that followed the introduction of the Bugaboo, annual sales soared 1,600 percent as the Boyles inundated the skiwear market with their highly popular Interchange System products.

By 1989, after sales had swelled from $18 million the year before the Bugaboo entered the market to nearly $80 million two years later, Columbia's ski sales outstripped all other competitors in the United States. It was a remarkable rise underpinned by aggressive and creative advertising that transformed the Columbia name into a widely recognized apparel label. The Boyles set aside large sums of cash for advertising, spending twice as much as their nearest competitor, and starred in their own humorous advertisements. In the series of commercials, which debuted in 1983, Gertrude Boyle put her son, Tim, through a series of tests designed to illustrate the durability of Columbia's garments. The humorous advertising campaign featured Tim Boyle as the test dummy and Gertrude Boyle as "One Tough Mother" and proved to be highly effective. By the beginning of the 1990s, Columbia had eclipsed the $100 million sales mark and the Boyles were mapping ambitious plans for the future.

In 1991, Tim Boyle announced his intention to reach $1 billion in sales by the year 2000, informing a reporter from *Sporting Goods Business,* "I'm very serious about that figure. We have the management team in place and the product development to do it." To achieve this formidable objective, Boyle expanded the company's product lines during the first half of the 1990s, adding several different lines of apparel and accessories that contributed significantly to the company's revenue volume. In 1993, a line of denim apparel was introduced, featuring jeans, vests, and shirts marketed under the "Tough Mother" name. That same year, the company started a footwear division that manufactured the "Bugaboot," a rugged, outdoor shoe worn by Gertrude Boyle in advertisements featuring the tag line, "My Mother Wears Combat Boots." As the company moved into the mainstream of the apparel market with its line of denim wear, the awareness of the Columbia label grew significantly, aided by the perennially popular image of "Mother Boyle," by then in her 70s, in print and television advertisements.

1990s Diversification

In response to the growing, broad-based appeal of the Columbia label, sales surged ahead. Record sales were recorded in 1991 and again in 1992, when the one millionth Bugaboo parka was sold, making it the best-selling parka in ski apparel history. Following the introduction of Tough Mother denim wear and footwear in 1993, record sales were once again recorded, fueling confidence at the company's Portland headquarters that the strength of the Columbia label could indeed carry the outerwear manufacturer toward $1 billion in sales by the end of the decade. In 1994, when Columbia was named the official supplier to CBS Sports for the Winter Olympic Games in Lille-

hammer, Norway, the company entered the burgeoning market for snowboard apparel by introducing its Convert line of loose-fitting, insulated outerwear, which helped make 1994 a record year in sales.

By the mid-1990s, Columbia was growing by leaps and bounds, particularly overseas, where the company's revenue volume tripled between 1993 and 1995. At the end of 1995, President and Chief Executive Officer Tim Boyle made a move to steer Columbia in a new direction when he acquired retail space for the company's flagship store in Portland. The store opened the following year, showcasing the full range of Columbia apparel, footwear, and accessories. Next, Boyle sought to extend Columbia's retail presence overseas by opening a retail store in Seoul, South Korea, where 14 years earlier Santorufo had negotiated the first deal that inaugurated Columbia's offshore manufacturing.

The first Seoul store opened in 1997, with another 16 retail outlets slated for grand openings in Seoul by the end of 1997, giving Columbia a powerful new engine for sales growth as the late 1990s began and the company pursued its goal of $1 billion in sales by the decade's conclusion. Although not halfway toward its lofty sales objective by the late 1990s, the company was nevertheless performing admirably as it neared its sixtieth year of business. With Gertrude and Tim Boyle still at the helm, it was expected that Columbia would continue to flourish into its seventh decade of business.

Further Reading

Black, Jeff, "3 Hot Houses in a Cool Retail Climate," *Daily News Record,* May 28, 1990, p. 16.

Caminiti, Susan, "When Your Back Is Against the Wall," *Fortune,* March 7, 1994, p. 139.

Hill, Luana Hellmann, "Hot Flashes from a Hot Company," *Oregon Business,* October 1988, p. 34.

Marks, Anita, "Columbia Hopes Korean Climate Spells Hot Sales," *Business Journal-Portland,* May 31, 1996, p. 1.

Moffatt, Terrence, "Hail Columbia," *Sporting Goods Business,* March 1991, p. 40.

Slovak, Julianne, "Columbia Sportswear," *Fortune,* April 24, 1989, p. 188.

Spector, Robert, "Columbia Gets Street-Smart," *WWD,* March 16, 1995, p. 10.

Yang, Dori Jones, "This Grandma Wants To Keep You Warm," *Business Week,* December 5, 1994, p. 111.

—Jeffrey L. Covell

Comptoirs Modernes S.A.

1, place de Gué de Maulny
72019 Le Mans Cedex
France
(02) 43 86 28 20
Fax: (02) 43 72 32 75

Public Company
Incorporated: 1896 as l'Union Commerciale de Meaux;
   1928 as les Comptoirs Modernes
Employees: 23,088
Sales: FFr 30.2 billion (1996)
Stock Exchanges: Paris
SICs: 5411 Grocery Stores

Of the leading independent food retailers in France, Comptoirs Modernes S.A. is one of the smallest. Comptoirs Modernes' three percent market share distances it from market leaders such as Leclerc (15.3 percent), Intermarché (15.1 percent) and Carrefour (12.9 percent). But as its larger competitors have struggled through the extended French economic crisis of the 1990s, Comptoirs Modernes has been able to show impressive growth, posting a gain of nearly 12 percent on annual sales and 11 percent on net profits in 1996, reaching FFr 30.2 billion and FFr 501 million, respectively.

Long focused exclusively on the French domestic market, Comptoirs Modernes, driven in part by government restrictions on new supermarket openings, has begun to expand internationally. In 1996, the company, which had been operating supermarkets in the Catalonia region of Spain through its Comodisa subsidiary, acquired controlling interest in a partnership between Comodisa and Spain's Maxor supermarket chain. Controlling interest in a second Spanish supermarket partnership, with Supermercats Economics, expanded Comptoirs Modernes' Spanish holdings to 75 supermarkets, making the company the second-largest food retailer in the Catalonia region and Spain's 12th-largest independent food retailer. Comptoirs Modernes expected more foreign expansion to fuel company growth. Principal expansion targets include Italy, Poland, and Brazil, and potentially countries in Eastern Europe and Latin America.

In France in the 1990s, Comptoirs Modernes operated three supermarket chains, each exploiting a specific market niche. The company's flagship is its chain of Stoc supermarkets. With an average selling space of 1,244 square meters, the Stoc stores position themselves between the growing numbers of hard discounters in France and the larger hypermarket chains, which reach an average selling space of nearly 9,000 square meters. Unlike the hypermarkets, which sell everything from food to clothing to car parts and appliances, Stoc stores concentrate sales on food, primarily fresh foods, which account for nearly 44 percent of total Stoc sales. Stoc stores appeal to a largely loyal customer base with a limited but complete selection of everyday groceries. The company competed with hard discounters and traditional supermarkets alike by offering a distinct selection along three price points: generic-priced products, mid-priced products under the company's private-label Stoc brand name, and premium-priced brand name products. In 1996, the Stoc chain of 385 supermarkets, of which 29 were operated as franchises, produced nearly 73 percent of the company's total sales.

While the majority of the Stoc supermarkets remain company-owned, Comptoirs Modernes has developed a second, largely franchised chain, operating under the Comod name, of smaller supermarkets and even smaller superettes. Comod stores, which range in average size from 292 square meters for the smaller superettes to 414 square meters for the Comod supermarkets, complement the Stoc chain by targeting a separate marketing niche. Where the Stoc stores operate primarily in the commercial areas located in a city's periphery, the Comod chain operate within residential areas, using competitive pricing, emphasis on fresh foods, and proximity to draw customers and achieve market leadership in smaller areas. Managers of Comod franchises have been generally community residents with strong relationships with their customers; new Comod stores often have been conversions of Stoc and other supermarkets that do not fulfill that chain's selling area requirements. Nearly 80 percent of the 266 Comod stores were operated as franchises; of the total number of Comod stores, 93 are supermarkets serving rural areas and 173 are superettes serving more urban areas. Comod operations were concentrated almost entirely in the north and northwest of France in the 1990s.

The third branch of the Comptoirs Modernes group is The Marché Plus chain, which totaled 38 stores in 1996, and was being developed as a franchise. Marché Plus stores, with average selling space of 264 square meters, target the long-neglected urban market with a selection of fresh foods at prices comparable to supermarkets, while also offering complementary services such as dry cleaning, video rentals, ticket sales, newstands, and film processing. Another feature of the Marché Plus chain was its extended operating hours, which are seven a.m. to nine p.m. six days per week, including Sunday hours from nine a.m. to one p.m., in a country where stores traditionally close by 7:30 p.m. and remain closed on Sundays. Typical Marché Plus customers range from the young, urban shopper to older shoppers who tend to be accustomed to daily shopping in their neighborhoods.

In addition to its Stoc, Comod, and Marché Plus chains, the Comptoirs Modernes group, through its jointly owned subsidiary Sogramo, operated 16 Carrefour hypermarkets, primarily in the company's northwest base of Le Mans, with average selling space of 8,800 square meters. Carrefour was also the major shareholder in Comptoirs Modernes, with 23 percent of the company's stock and 32 percent of the voting rights. Comptoirs Modernes' 50 percent ownership of Sogramo provided the group with approximately 14 percent of the company's total sales. In Spain, the company operated 50 supermarkets under the Maxor and Maxim names through its 60 percent ownership of the Maxor partnership, and 25 supermarkets under the Supeco and Merca Plus names through its 72 percent ownership of the Supeco partnership.

The Comptoirs Modernes group operated as a decentralized organization operating through six regional operating divisions in the 1990s. Comptoirs Modernes Economiques de Normandie (CMEN) operated 181 Stoc, Comod, and Marché Plus stores in 15 departments in the Pays-de-Loire, Haute and Basse Normandie, Poitou-Charente, and Ile de France regions, with a base in Le Mans. Comptoirs Modernes-Badin-Defforey (CMBD) operated 79 Stoc stores in 14 departments in the Auvergne, Bourgogne, Franche-Compté, and Rhône-Alpes regions, with a base in Lagnieu. Comptoirs Modernes Economiques de Rennes (CMER) served 11 departments in the Bretagne, Basse-Normandie, and Pays-de-Loire regions with 182 Stoc, Comod, and Marché Plus stores. Comptoirs Modernes-Major Unidis (CMMU), formed by the merger of the two supermarket chains in 1990, served the Auvergne, Bourgogne, Centre, and Limousin regions, with 93 Stoc stores in 10 departments. Comptoirs Modernes-Union Commercial (CMUC), which celebrated its 100th anniversary in 1996, operated in the northern regions of the Ardennes, Centre, Champagne, Haute Normandie, Ile de France, Nord-Pas-de-Calais, and Picardie, with 151 Stoc, Marché Plus, and Comod stores. The operating division, Stoc Sud Est, formed in 1995, brought the company into the southern Aix-en-Provence region, with three stores operating at the end of 1996 and five new stores planned for 1997. Each operating division was led by its own president; Jean-Claude Plassart served as president and director general of the Comptoirs Modernes group in the 1990s.

Combining a Century of Growth

The first step in the development of the modern-day Comptoirs Modernes group was taken in 1896 with the formation of the Union Commerciale, based in Meaux, in the north of France. The next member of the future supermarket group, the Société Economique de Rennes, was created in 1912 in the northwest region of the country, which was followed by the creation of Etablissements Badin-Defforey in 1929. In that year, Comptoirs Modernes itself was established, in Le Mans, in order to build a network of food stores. Comptoirs Modernes opened its first self-service store in 1948, and its first supermarket, under the Suma name, in 1960. In 1965, Comptoirs Modernes went public, trading on the Paris stock exchange. Two years later, the Badin-Defforey group opened the first Stoc supermarket.

After forming the Sograma joint venture with Carrefour in 1972, which gave the hypermarket operator a 20 percent ownership in Comptoirs Modernes, the company began taking steps toward forming the modern-day organizational structure of the group. In 1977, the Société Economique de Rennes was merged into Comptoirs Modernes; this merger was followed by the mergers of Union Commerciale, in 1978, and of Badin-Defforey in 1979. In 1981, all of the supermarkets in the Comptoirs Modernes group took the Stoc name. The groups smaller, neighborhood-based stores were given the Comod name, under which Comptoirs Modernes had been operating its stores since 1978. The group's combined operations reached FFr 7.45 billion in 1981; Comptoirs Modernes itself posted FFr 2.1 billion for that year. The combined Comptoirs Modernes operations quickly proved successful; by 1984, the groups consolidated turnover neared FFr 8.5 billion, with the Comptoirs Modernes division's FFr 2.5 billion continuing to lead the group, followed by the Sograma joint venture's contribution of FFr 2.4 billion.

In the late 1980s, Comptoirs Modernes added two more divisions to its group. In 1987, the company acquired the three supermarkets and 40 corner stores of former Primisteres subsidiary Economiques de Normandie, adding that chain's FFr 250 million in sales to the group, which had topped FFr 10.1 billion by 1985 and which grew to FFr 14 billion by 1988. Following the Economiques de Normandie acquisition, Comptoirs Modernes reached an agreement with another French supermarket chain, Major Unidis, to merge the two chains. The stock-swap deal, worth FFr 1.45 billion, added Major Unidis's FFr 2.6 billion in sales and created a chain of 300 supermarkets and 1,000 smaller stores, as well as the group's 12 Carrefour hypermarkets. By 1992, the final phase of the Major Unidis merger was completed, when all of that division's Major supermarkets took on the Stoc name.

With consolidated turnover topping FFr 22.5 billion in 1992, Comptoirs Modernes was also expanding its activities. In 1988, the group had opened its first two supermarkets in Spain, under the name Merca Plus, which would grow into an 11-store chain by the mid-1990s. The company also began testing its new Marché Plus store concept in 1990, and began franchising the concept in 1993. By then the economic crisis of the early to mid-1990s had begun to take its toll on the food retailing market. Further exacerbating the difficult conditions for supermarket operators was the aggressive expansion of hard discounters, including such German chains as Aldi and Lidl, into the French market. Comptoirs Modernes and its Stoc chain fought back with its own discount pricing policy; that and the group's high quality standards helped ensure the loyalty of its customers and enabled the company to buck the downward trend in the industry. By 1994, Comptoirs Modernes posted consolidated turnover of nearly FFr 26 billion, for a net income of FFr 450million.

In 1995, the group restructured its Comod operation, converting the neighborhood stores to franchises in order to accelerate growth in the number of stores in the chain. The following year, the group, which had been criticized by stock market analysts as being too focused on the domestic market in a period of increasing globalization, returned to acquisitions for its internal expansion. In January 1996, the company reached an agreement with Spain's Maxor to merge the Comodisa subsidiary's 11 Merca Plus supermarkets with 47 Maxor and Maxim supermarkets, giving Comptoirs Modernes an enhanced presence around the Barcelona area and throughout the Catalonia region. Three months later, Comptoirs Modernes reached a merger agreement with another Spanish supermarket company, Supermercats Economics, which operated 13 supermarkets under the Supeco name in Catalonia. The two mergers gave Comptoirs Modernes controlling interest in a chain of 71 supermarkets with more than 83,000 square meters of selling space in Catalonia.

Comptoirs Modernes followed this international growth with the creation of a new domestic division, Stoc Sud Est, introducing the Stoc supermarket concept to the south of France. Based in Aix-en-Provence, the division quickly grew to three supermarkets by the end of 1996. By then, the company's turnover had risen past FFr 30 billion. As the Union Commerciale division of the group celebrated its 100th anniversary, Comptoirs Modernes began looking forward to a new period of growth. In 1997, the company announced its intention to explore expansion possibilities in Poland and Brazil, and in other Eastern European and Latin American countries. On the home front, Comptoirs Modernes revealed plans to open 17 new Stoc supermarkets, nine Comod supermarkets, two Comod superettes, and 20 new Marché Plus stores by the end of 1997.

Principal Divisions

Comptoirs Modernes Economiques de Normandie (CMEN); Comptoires Modernes-Badin-Defforey (CMBD); Comptoirs Modernes Economique de Rennes (CMER); Comptoirs Modernes-Major Unidis (CMMU); Comptoires Modernes-Union Commerciale (CMUC); Stoc Sud Est; Maxor (60%); Supermercats Supeco (70%); Sogramo Carrefour (50%).

Further Reading

"Comptoirs Modernes—L'Associé de Carrefour Sort des Frontières," *La Vie Française,* March 16, 1996.
"Comptoirs Modernes Stock to Continue with Discount Policy," *Le Figaro,* March 25, 1992. p. 43.
"Comptoirs Modernes Targets Poland and Brazil," *Les Echos,* March 13, 1997, p. 15.
"Comptoirs Modernes—Un Turbo dans la Croissance," *La Vie Française,* March 18, 1995.
Savin, Virginie, "Comptoirs Modernes—De la Croissance en Stock," *La Vie Française,* March 20, 1993.

—M.L. Cohen

Consolidated Natural Gas Company

625 Liberty Avenue
Pittsburgh, Pennsylvania 15222-3199
U.S.A.
(412) 227-1000
Fax: (412) 227-1002
Web site: http://www.cng.com

Public Company
Incorporated: 1942
Employees: 6,600
Operating Revenues: $3.79 billion (1996)
Stock Exchanges: New York
SICs: 4924 Natural Gas Distribution; 4922 Natural Gas
     Transmission; 1311 Storage Natural Gas

Consolidated Natural Gas Company (CNG) is one of the nation's few integrated natural gas systems, and one of its largest natural gas systems. CNG produces, transports, and distributes natural gas, as well as provides energy marketing services, through North America. CNG also explores and produces natural gas and oil in the United States, Mexico, and Canada, and provides energy services to international markets. The company owns the largest group of underground gas-storage fields in the nation, and is involved in subsidiary businesses including gas by-products and oil production.

CNG's varied functions are implemented through its subsidiaries. Consolidated Natural Gas Service Co. is responsible for administration and technical services. CNG Producing Co. explores and produces natural gas and oil. CNG Energy Services markets gas and is one of the ten largest independent wholesale power marketers in the United States. CNG Power Services markets electricity; CNG Research performs research; CNG Coal Co. is involved in coal mining; and CNG Transmission operates a regional interstate pipeline system serving each of the company's distribution subsidiaries.

Company Origins Under Rockefeller's Standard Oil

In the late 1870s, when the companies that later became CNG were being formed, western Pennsylvania held the same

promise of profit that the Middle East oil fields were to have 100 years later. The company was founded by the merger of five individual businesses that were formed, merged, or acquired by John D. Rockefeller as a part of his Standard Oil Company, then consolidated to form one of the largest fully integrated producers and distributors of natural gas in the United States. Based on its early history of growth through mergers and reliance on its skills in exploring and developing new gas wells and properties, CNG has been able to expand as a service and distribution company as well as a producer of natural gas.

The companies that became CNG were born of an important by-product of the Standard Oil Company's search for oil. Standard Oil's original mission was to find and develop oil in the Appalachian mountains of western Pennsylvania, and early in Standard Oil's history, Rockefeller saw that natural gas, the discovery of which goes hand-in-hand with oil, was a valuable commodity. Within the first 30 years after Standard Oil's founding in 1870, Rockefeller had formed and acquired companies that explored for gas throughout the Appalachian basin and piped it to Pittsburgh, Pennsylvania; Cleveland and Akron, Ohio; and other growing industrial centers in the region. Natural gas fueled the nascent iron, steel, rubber, and glass industries. It also provided home heating and, in the early portion of this period, municipal street lighting.

In 1911 the network of natural gas production, transmission, and distribution companies assembled by Standard Oil came under the umbrella of the Standard Oil Company (New Jersey), one of the 34 companies that resulted from the dissolution of Standard Oil that was ordered by the U.S. Supreme Court under the Sherman Antitrust Act. At that time, Standard Oil Company (New Jersey) held four of the five companies that were to form the Consolidated Natural Gas system: The Peoples Natural Gas Company, of Pittsburgh, Pennsylvania, which had been founded in 1885; The River Gas Company, of Marietta, Ohio, which had been founded in 1894; The Hope Natural Gas Company, now known as Hope Gas Inc., of Clarksburg, West Virginia, which had been founded in 1898; and The East Ohio Gas Company, of Cleveland, Ohio, also originating in 1898. Each of these companies remained in the early 1900s as operating units of CNG. They were augmented in 1930 by a pipeline that supplied nonaffiliated utilities in New York state. In 1942

Standard Oil (New Jersey) organized Consolidated Natural Gas Company as a subsidiary and transferred to CNG its natural gas gathering and transmission assets. CNG was spun off as a privately held, independent company from Standard Oil (New Jersey) in 1943 because Standard did not want to be declared a public utility holding company falling under the Public Utility Holding Company Act of 1935.

An Independent Company is Formed in the 1930s

CNG began its independent corporate history with assets of more than $211 million and with 750,000 retail customers in Ohio, western Pennsylvania, and West Virginia. In its first year as an independent company, it sold 127 billion cubic feet of gas. During World War II defense production created such a demand for natural gas that CNG contracted for the first time to purchase gas, piped from the southwestern United States, to supplement the gas it produced in the Appalachian basin.

In 1947 to cope with the postwar surge in demand, CNG made its first public stock offering, totaling $8.2 million. CNG's first debenture issue, which totaled $30 million, came in 1948. Postwar growth forced the company into occasional restrictions on gas sales, and proceeds from the equity and debt issues were used to finance the construction of additional pipelines and storage fields.

By the early 1960s CNG had extended its market saturation in northeastern Ohio from Cleveland to the Pennsylvania border with the purchase of Lake Shore Gas Company of Ashtabula, Ohio, and had reached a market share of 92 percent for space heating and 96 percent for water heating. At the same time, in pursuing additional supplies of natural gas, CNG in 1957 became one of the first companies to explore and drill in the Gulf of Mexico and was a lease owner in the gulf by 1962. With a group of partners, CNG purchased 168,000 acres of developable drilling sites in the gulf that year, and in 1966 established a full-scale exploration and production staff in New Orleans to become the operator on many of its leases. By 1972 the New Orleans office was made into a subsidiary, CNG Producing Company.

CNG formed Consolidated Natural Gas Service Company, Inc. in 1961 to centralize accounting, data processing, employee relations, marketing, and rate and tax administration functions. In 1965 CNG merged its Hope and New York State Natural Gas interstate pipeline companies to form Consolidated Gas Supply Corporation, now known as CNG Transmission Corporation. CNG Transmission Corporation continues to supply gas to CNG's six distribution companies and sells gas at wholesale to utilities throughout the northeastern United States. In 1969 CNG acquired the West Ohio Gas Company, of Lima, Ohio, along with its 50,000 customers.

Supply and Demand in the 1970s and 1980s

In the early 1970s CNG and its competitors were faced with shortages of natural gas supplied from the southwestern United States. The company established CNG Producing Company to pursue new production sources and Consolidated System LNG Company to import liquefied natural gas (LNG) from Algeria and convert the LNG back to gas.

The record cold winter of 1976–1977 led the U.S. Congress to pass the Natural Gas Policy Act of 1978. CNG, which by then had plentiful gas supplies, expected the act to encourage conservation. At the same time, the steel industry, an important GNG customer, was undergoing an historic contraction. This prompted CNG to develop nontraditional markets for gas and its other services. In 1979 CNG became the first gas utility company to sell significant amounts of gas and associated storage to neighboring pipelines and utilities, and later sold independent storage services.

CNG, like the United States in general, developed an oversupply of natural gas by the mid-1980s. That oversupply, worsened by a string of unusually warm winters, led to declining gas and oil prices, and produced a trying time for CNG. Profits remained flat or fell off while corporate revenues reached peak levels, cresting at $3.5 billion in 1984. Despite this difficulty, CNG continued its exploration and development activities, taking advantage of low costs to build reserves and to increase its drilling prospects. CNG made a major find of oil at Cottonwood Creek in Carter County, Oklahoma, in 1988. It was the second largest oil- and gas-producing well in the history of Oklahoma, with production levels of 3,700 barrels of crude oil per day and 2.9 billion cubic feet of gas per day. The company centralized all of its drilling in the Appalachian region under the CNG Development Company, a non-utility subsidiary established in 1982 and, in 1990, merged CNG Development with CNG Producing, which then oversaw all of the company's drilling programs in the Appalachian basin, in the Gulf of Mexico, and in other areas.

In 1983 CNG negotiated agreements with a group of utilities in New England, New Jersey, and the New York City metropolitan area, under which CNG would sell gas at wholesale prices to the utilities. Those negotiations produced contracts to supply 20 utilities with a total of up to 39 billion cubic feet of gas annually. Deliveries began in 1984. In 1988 CNG expanded its market again, beginning deliveries of gas under 20-year contracts to utilities in Washington, D.C., New York City, and Baltimore, Maryland.

Although CNG's year-to-year profitability was volatile, the company provided a 24 percent average annual return to investors during the 1980s, and by January 1990, had a 98 percent saturation of its traditional distribution area. At that point, it moved to expand this area by acquiring Virginia Natural Gas, Inc., of Norfolk, Virginia, from Dominion Resources Inc. for $160 million. This gave CNG access to a fast-growing and economically diversified region. It also required a 162-mile pipeline extension, construction of which began in early 1990.

CNG has always depended on the discovery and successful exploitation of supplies of natural gas. To cope with peaks and valleys in natural gas demand, CNG has developed a system of storage for the gas it produces throughout the year. Since 1937 CNG has led the United States in natural gas storage capacity. The capacity was developed through conversion of depleted Appalachian gas fields into 26 underground storage pools. CNG also has used its storage capacity as a new source of revenue. It provided 128 billion cubic feet of storage service to other companies in 1990.

Gas distribution, historically the company's core business, accounted for $102.1 million of CNG's 1990 operating income, a 16 percent decline from the previous year, due to abnormally warm weather in its service areas. The income came on sales of 125.2 billion cubic feet of gas to industrial customers and 185.9 billion cubic feet of gas to residential customers, both down slightly from 1989, while sales to commercial customers were 80.8 billion cubic feet, about the same as in 1989.

Gas transmission activities contributed $74 million to the company's operating income in 1990, compared with $64.9 million in 1989. The increase resulted from the positive impact of a rate settlement case, higher transportation rates, and higher prices for by-products and lower income taxes, all of which combined to offset reduced demand.

Exploring New Markets and Expanding Facilities in the 1990s

To enhance its position in this area of service, CNG embarked on a five-year, $900 million capital improvement program in 1990 aimed at adding transportation and storage facilities. This program was the largest single investment in the company's history and was financed partly through the company's first stock offering since the 1950s. CNG has won praise from the investment community for its conservative finances, including a generally low amount of debt.

It was in 1993, however, that the natural gas industry began a major change when the Federal Energy Regulatory Commission deregulated certain parts of the industry. This action was followed by deregulation of certain parts of the electric industry. The changes allowed markets to be opened to competition, by allowing end-users to choose their energy source according to price, while the utilities were still responsible for delivering the energy. To effectively compete in this new market, CNG Energy Services was established in 1993 to market both natural gas and electricity throughout North America.

In 1994, the company drilled two gas wells in the Gulf of Mexico, in partnership with Oryx Energy in a project known as Popeye, and added 190 billion cubic feet to its gas reserves. In 1994, a marketing agreement was formed with both Hydro-Quebec, the largest hydroelectric producer in North America, and with gas distributor Noverco, Inc., to market energy services in parts of the U.S. and Canada. In 1995, another alliance was formed with electric utility, Energy Australia, to develop cogeneration and gas projects in Asia and Australia.

In 1996, CNG International was created to look for overseas markets. Also in 1996, CNG merged two of its local natural gas utilities in Ohio, The East Ohio Gas Company and West Ohio Gas Company; and began production of oil and natural gas in its second Gulf of Mexico deepwater project, called Neptune. In 1997, CNG Energy Services agreed to built a 26-megawatt electric power plant on the Hawaiian island of Kauai. The plant, which used Advanced Cheng Cycle technology to increase power production and reduce exhaust emissions, was part of a power purchase contract signed with the utility, Kauai Electric.

It was in 1997 that states began to deregulate their gas and electric utilities, and CNG began to reap the rewards of its marketing efforts. First, the Pennsylvania Public Utility Commission authorized CNG to sell electricity directly to industrial and residential customers in a pilot program. Then, an agreement to take effect in 1998, was created with Seattle City Light to provide up to 30 megawatts of power to members of the Association of Bay Area Governments (ABAG), an agency of 104 local governments in the San Francisco Bay area.

Throughout its history, CNG has grown by providing a basic utility service to its residential, industrial, and commercial customers under the direction of its conservative management. Through considered acquisitions, measured capital expansion, and the exploration and development of oil and gas resources, the company won a high ranking in the industry. With its transmission and storage facilities expansion under way, with the wellhead price of natural gas expected to rise through the 1990s as resources become depleted, and with deregulation of gas and electricity coupled with aggressive marketing, CNG seems to be headed for increasing profits.

As chairman and chief executive officer, George A. Davidson, Jr. told stockholders at the company's annual meeting on May 20, 1997, the company is expanding its business in unregulated aspects of the energy industry, including exploration and production, wholesale energy marketing, retail natural gas marketing, and, when approved, retail electricity marketing.

Principal Subsidiaries

CNG Energy Services Corp.; CNG Producing Co.; CNG Transmission Corp.; The East Ohio Gas Co; West Ohio Gas Co.; The Peoples Natural Gas Co.; Virginia Natural Gas, Inc.; Hope Gas, Inc.; CNG Power Co.; CNG International.

Further Reading

"Cleaning Up with Natural Gas," *American Gas,* September 1996, p. 7.

Gottschalk, Arthur, "North American Energy Majors Form Marketing Alliance," *Journal of Commerce and Commercial,* November 16, 1994, p. 5B.

—Bruce Vernyi
updated by Dorothy Kroll

Cordis Corp.

P.O. Box 025700
Miami, Florida 33102-5700
U.S.A.
(305) 824-2000
Fax: (305) 842-2080

Wholly Owned Subsidary of Johnson & Johnson
Incorporated: 1957 as Medical Development Corp.
Employees: 3,370 (1994)
Sales: $443.2 million (1994)
SICs: 3841 Surgical & Medical Instruments; 3845
    Electromedical Equipment

Cordis Corp. is one of the world's leading manufacturers of cardiac angiography catheters and a growing player in the larger cardiac angioplasty market. Plagued throughout its relatively brief history by product recalls and marketing missteps, Cordis appeared to have found a profitable niche in the cardiac catheter industry in the early 1990s. Sales more than doubled during the first half of the decade, from $202.6 million in 1990 to more than $443 million in 1994, whereas net multiplied from $20.1 million to $50.2 million. Johnson & Johnson made a hostile bid for control of the fast-growing firm late in 1995 and won the takeover battle early in 1996 with a $109 per share stock swap valuing Cordis at $1.8 billion.

Postwar Origins

The medical device company was founded in Miami, Florida by Dr. William Murphy. The son of Nobel laureate Dr. William Parry Murphy, Murphy was immersed in medicine from his youngest days. A 1984 *Inc.* article by Eugene Linden noted, "So total was the medical environment of his youth that it never occurred to him not to go into medicine." The younger Murphy also realized early on that he had a particular aptitude for mechanical engineering. The self-described "tinkerer" even designed his own medical devices as a teen.

After pursuing a dual education in medicine and engineering, Murphy was involved in the creation of the first artificial kidney. He also served briefly at Miami's Dade Reagents Inc., but when that company was bought out by American Hospital Supply Corp., it became clear to the ambitious Murphy that his career at this big, relatively anonymous company was limited.

Murphy formed Medical Development Corp. in 1957. One of the first products he developed was a "lumbar puncture tray," a disposable set of needles and tools used for spinal taps. Noticing that doctors performing this procedure often used dull and sometimes burred needles, making the test difficult and often painful, Murphy developed the concept of using a disposable kit, meaning that each patient would get a sterile, sharp needle. The doctor/engineer/entrepreneur developed several elaborations on this basic concept, patented them, and licensed the core concept to Mead John & Co. He used the $300,000 in royalties that accrued over the next couple of years to finance research and development at his own company. (Ironically, the disposable procedural tray business would grow to $60 million per year by the early 1980s.)

Realizing that his strengths lay more in research and development than operational management, in 1959 Murphy induced John Sterner to serve as president of his small, but growing, company, which had moved from its original garage headquarters to a house. Sterner, a physicist, introduced Murphy to venture capitalist General Georges F. Doriot, whose American Research and Development Corp. would invest nearly a quarter of a million dollars in the start-up business.

By 1960, Murphy had changed the business's name to the more distinctive Cordis ("of the heart"), a moniker that indicated the primary focus of the company's efforts. During the decade, Cordis became involved in the relatively new field of cardiac pacemaking, which utilizes a small, usually battery-operated electronic device known in the industry as a pacer to stimulate the heartbeat with electrical charges. By the early 1970s, Cordis ranked second only to Medtronic among America's pacemaker manufacturers. Cordis introduced its first remotely programmable pacemaker in 1973 and launched improved electrodes (which make the actual connection to the heart muscle) mid-decade.

Company Perspectives:

"The combination of Cordis and Johnson & Johnson's interventional cardiology business is an important strategic step for both companies to meet the challenge of providing for customer needs in the fast changing healthcare industry."

Despite infusions of more than $500,000 in cash in its first few years, Cordis had a rocky start. Under Murphy, the company was so devoted to research and development that it would be 1980 before it achieved a positive net operating cash flow. Murphy and Sterner were forced to sell their stock to keep the firm afloat; by 1984, they held less than five percent between them.

Quality Control Crisis in the 1970s

Cordis found itself facing poor quality control, both within its own manufacturing operations and in components from an important supplier, in the mid-1970s. Flawed circuits from supplier CTS Corp. and an internal rejection rate that soared to 30 percent contributed to the U.S. Food and Drug Administration's (FDA) issue of a product advisory against Cordis in 1974. Cordis's share of the pacemaker market declined from 20 percent in 1975 to 13 percent in 1978. With sales and net plummeting, too, corporate executives were compelled to cut salaries by 20 percent across the board.

The supplier, CTS Corp., agreed to keep Cordis afloat via a $5 million injection of capital in exchange for control of nearly one-fourth of the pacemaker manufacturer's stock. For its part, Cordis promised to buy back the shares at a premium, which it was able to do in 1977. Hoping to reinvigorate the company after its near-death experience, Murphy and Sterner brought in a new president, Dr. Norman Weldon, in 1979.

Characterized by *Forbes* as "a husky Indiana farm boy turned biochemist, economist and businessman," the 40-something Weldon had served as CTS's president before moving to Cordis. For two years, Sterner, Murphy, and Weldon formed a management troika that focused on a costly restructuring of Cordis's manufacturing and marketing operations. Among other things, Weldon organized the company's first independent marketing department and boosted the sales force by 30 percent. The restructuring cost dearly. Cordis lost $8.3 million in 1981 and by that time had racked up $89 million in debt.

A Second Dilemma Mars the Early 1980s

Cordis's luck appeared to be changing in the early 1980s. Four years after a competitor launched the first lithium-powered implantable pacemaker, Cordis introduced its first lithium model in 1979. The Miami company's version featured an encapsulated battery that purported to be smaller, yet more efficient, than its predecessors. Just three years later, Cordis won FDA approval for an innovative "physiological" or "synchronous" pacemaker, which issued electric pulses only when

needed by regulating two chambers of the heart instead of one. At the same time, several competitors—including Intermedics, which had supplanted Cordis as number two in pacemakers in 1979—were reeling from a kickback scandal.

Cordis took good advantage of the situation, increasing sales by more than 75 percent, from $117.7 million in 1984 to $207 million. It also recovered from a net loss of $8.2 million to more than $10 million in profits during the period. Furthermore, it regained the number-two rank among pacemaker manufacturers.

In the meantime, however, engineers at the company had discovered two potentially devastating problems with the lithium-powered pacer. First, they learned that their method of encapsulating the battery had a high potential for corrosion and, possibly, leakage. Though not legally obligated to do so at the time, Cordis modified the battery and notified both the doctors and the FDA about the possibility that the device could become corrupted. The close monitoring of the 8,500 patients who had already received the pacers revealed a second, more serious problem; a totally unforeseen chemical reaction was sapping the power of the batteries. The FDA ordered recalls of Cordis's pacemakers in 1983 and 1985 and prohibited the company from testing and selling new products for 18 months.

Cordis's sales were more than halved from 1984's $207 million down to just $80 million in 1986. The company sold the pacemaker division, which had at one time contributed more than half its annual revenues, in 1987 and reached a $5.7 million settlement with claimants two years later. CFO Robert Strauss succeeded Weldon as president and CEO upon the latter's resignation in 1987.

Under Strauss, Cordis fell back on a secondary business interest, diagnostic cardiac catheters, in the late 1980s. These fine-gauge tubes are used in angiography, the injection of special dyes into blood vessels and the heart chambers to conduct tests for impairment of this vital muscle. By 1990, Cordis had captured 40 percent of the global angiography market, and this business segment constituted 85 percent of the company's total revenues.

Rapid Growth Marks the Early 1990s

During the first half of the 1990s, Strauss guided what investment bankers Hambrecht & Quist characterized as a "metamorphosis" from a "troubled, unfocused, regulatory-hindered Cordis [to] a streamlined one." Moreover, Strauss's reorganization planned to transform it from a firm focused almost exclusively on development of new technology to one emphasizing customers' needs. Having eradicated the company's pacemaker obligations, Strauss focused on maintaining the company's leading share in angiography catheters and diversifying into the larger and more profitable therapeutic heart catheter market. Commonly known as angioplasty, this therapy uses specialized catheters to ream out blockages in the arteries around the heart, or, in the case of balloon angioplasty, to expand the artery to allow increased blood flow.

CEO Strauss hoped to increase Cordis's share of the therapeutic catheter market from two percent in 1991 to 15 percent by mid-decade, but he faced daunting competition from well-established giants in the medical business, including market-leading Eli Lilly & Co. and Pfizer Inc. He reorganized Cordis's staff into product-oriented teams focusing on balloon catheters, interventional catheters, steerable guidewires, and diagnostics, thereby encouraging the development of a comprehensive line. He used competitive pricing and dynamic marketing to make Cordis the industry's fastest growing competitor in the early 1990s. By 1994, the company had captured ten percent of total U.S. angioplasty sales—short of Strauss's ambitious goal, but an impressive expansion nonetheless.

Perhaps more important, the company made dramatic inroads into the global heart catheter business, achieving a third-ranking 17 percent of the worldwide angioplasty market by the middle of 1994. By that time, overseas sales constituted more than 50 percent of Cordis's total annual revenues. Strauss also reduced the company's debt from $31.6 million in 1990 to a mere $1.1 million by the end of 1993. Sales increased from $202.6 million in 1990 to more than $443 million in 1994, while net income multiplied from $20.1 million to $50.2 million.

Takeover by Johnson & Johnson in 1995

Cordis's speedy growth attracted the attention of health care giant Johnson & Johnson, which initiated a highly unusual (for this industry, at least) hostile takeover of the Miami manufacturer in October 1995. Eager to create a total cardiac package of products, Johnson & Johnson offered $100 per share in cash for a company that was then trading at $81. Cordis initially resisted the assault, but in November it agreed to a stock swap valued at $1.8 billion. Cordis became a Johnson & Johnson company in February 1996. The merger combined Johnson & Johnson's cardiac stents—minuscule steel tubes that repair damaged arteries—with Cordis's balloon catheters, which were used to deliver the stents, forming a globally significant manufacturer of cardiac devices.

Principal Subsidiaries

Cordis International Corp.; Cordis Holding BV (Netherlands); Cordis Europa NV (Netherlands).

Further Reading

Abelson, Reed, "Cordis Corp.," *Fortune,* June 5, 1989, p. 176.

"Catheters Unclog Cordis' Growth," *Florida Trend,* January 1994, p. 8.

"Cordis: Building Marketing Muscle To Pump Up Strength in Biomedicine," *Business Week,* December 20, 1982, p. 63.

"Cordis Faces Import Sanctions, Begins Heart-Valve Recall," *South Florida Business Journal,* May 18, 1992, p. 7.

"Cordis Quality Starts with Suppliers," *Florida Trend,* May 1988, pp. 50–52.

"Cordis Receives Approval for New Catheter," *South Florida Business Journal,* March 19, 1990, p. 6.

Davis, Philip M., "Beware of Corporate Criminal Conduct," *Design News,* November 7, 1988, p. 214.

Engardio, Pete, "Why Cordis' Heart Wasn't in Pacemakers," *Business Week,* March 16, 1987, p. 80.

Farley, Dixie, "Firm Pleads Guilty To Selling Faulty Pacemakers," *FDA Consumer,* September 1989, pp. 38–39.

Hambrecht & Quist Incorporated, "Cordis Corporation—Company Report," *The Investext Group,* December 26, 1980.

"Johnson & Johnson Launches Hostile Bid for Miami Firm," *The Atlanta Constitution,* October 20, 1995, p. F6.

Linden, Eugene, "The Role of the Founder: Murphy's Law," *Inc.,* July 1984, pp. 90–96.

McGough, Robert, "Choppy Waters," *Forbes,* September 12, 1983, p. 183.

——, "Mr. Clean," *Forbes,* April 23, 1984, pp. 141–142.

Miller, Susan R., "Snag Slows Down Cordis Deal with Johnson & Johnson," *South Florida Business Journal,* December 29, 1995, pp. 3–4.

Nesse, Leslie Kraft, "Change in Cordis' Structure Leads to Increased Sales, Profits," *South Florida Business Journal,* June 10, 1994, pp. 8B-9B.

——, "Cordis in Licensing Agreement," *South Florida Business Journal,* June 17, 1994, pp. 3–4.

Painewebber Inc., "Cordis Corp.—Company Report," *The Investext Group,* November 25, 1994.

Paltrow, Scot J., "Cordis Stock Plunges on J&J Delay," *Los Angeles Times,* December 28, 1995, p. D2.

Petruno, Tom, "Johnson & Johnson Makes Bid for Cordis," *Los Angeles Times,* October 20, 1995, p. D2.

Raloff, J., "Keeping Pace," *Datamation,* January 1984, p. 38.

Resnick, Rosalind, "Cordis Recovers; Can It Catch Up?," *Florida Trend,* June 1991, pp. 41–43.

Waresh, Julie, "Back to the Drawing Board," *South Florida Business Journal,* August 14, 1989, pp. 1–2.

——, "Spin-offs Lift Burden from Cordis Corp.," *South Florida Business Journal,* December 12, 1988, pp. 5–6.

Westlund, Richard, "Cordis Corporation: A Wellness Program with 'Heart,' " *South Florida Business Journal,* June 9, 1995, p. 12B.

—April Dougal Gasbarre

Crowley, Milner & Company

2301 West Lafayette Boulevard
Detroit, Michigan 48216-1891
U.S.A.
(313) 962-2400
Fax: (313) 962-2529

Public Company
Incorporated: 1909
Employees: 1,300
Sales: $105.9 million (1996)
Stock Exchanges: American
SICs: 5311 Department Stores

Crowley, Milner & Company is the owner and operator of ten different specialty department stores throughout the eastern half of Michigan. The company retails moderately-priced apparel items for men, women, and children, as well as home furnishings and linens, electronics, and cosmetics. Crowley's stores carry the company's own line of products, while also supplementing that merchandise with other brand names such as Alfred Dunner, Bugle Boy, Coach, Haggar, Lee, Levi Strauss, Liz Claiborne, and London Fog. The majority of Crowley's stores are located in or near Detroit, with the remainder located in suburban Flint. The company also owns and operates numerous Steinbach Stores in the eastern United States, which were acquired in 1995.

The Early Years

Crowley, Milner and Company was created in 1909 when Joseph J. Crowley, his brothers William and Daniel, and William L. Milner joined together to save a struggling department store in Detroit called Partridge and Blackwell. Joseph Crowley had spent the previous few years working as a credit manager for Detroit wholesaler Burnham Stoepel, a job which often required that he help reorganize struggling ventures. His brothers had joined him in 1902 to form the Crowley Brothers Wholesale Dry Goods Company. Meanwhile, Milner was operating the W.L. Milner Department Store in Toledo, Ohio, a

company that was a regular customer of the Crowley Brothers' enterprise.

After leaving Burnham Stoepel to fully focus his energy on Crowley Brothers, Joseph Crowley was approached by an executive of the Central Savings Bank of Detroit about the Partridge and Blackwell opportunity. The company was a specialty retailer teetering on the edge of bankruptcy due to organizational problems that were exacerbated by the recession in 1907. Crowley agreed to take over the struggling company on the condition that his two brothers and Milner join him in the endeavor. They all agreed, and in 1909 Crowley, Milner and Company was incorporated as the successor to Partridge and Blackwell.

Crowley, Milner & Co. immediately set about the task of positioning itself as one of Detroit's highest quality retail operations. In the early 1900s, Detroit was regarded as one of the country's most beautiful and affluent cities, and Crowley, Milner & Co. catered to this image. The store was stocked with luxurious clothing and gifts, much of which was imported from Europe, as well as a fancy full-service restaurant and one of Detroit's best grocery stores. The newly-refurbished store soon enjoyed a great deal of success, which in turn helped the real estate business in the area surrounding the store. In less than ten years, the Crowley, Milner & Co. store had been expanded in size and was the largest department store in Michigan.

Unfortunately, the company's success was marred when Milner was killed in an automobile accident while traveling to his original Toledo store in 1923. Not only did the company lose its president and merchandising expert, but his 42 percent interest in the store was sold by his family. Without Milner, the store eventually came to be known as Crowley's, but the company has retained its full name to the present day. Joseph Crowley succeeded his friend and partner as the company's president, but the loss of full control of its holdings hit the company hard for many years thereafter.

Further damage was done to the company by the stock market crash in 1929, which caused a recession that was devastating to the retail industry. Sales the previous year had reached $39 million, which was the company's highest recorded annual income since its inception almost 20 years before. In 1929, however, sales plummeted to approximately $10 million. Customers simply were not buying things unless absolutely necessary, as the depression had depleted the resources of families and businesses alike. Gone were the frivolous spending frenzies of the 1910s, and Crowley, Milner & Co. struggled to stay afloat.

Post-Depression Rebuilding Efforts

It was not until 1937 that the Crowleys regained a majority control of their enterprise. Following Joseph Crowley's death, his widow repurchased the lost shares and once again gave the family a more than 50 percent interest in the company. That year, Crowley, Milner & Co. was just beginning to rebound from the worst effects of the depression, and regaining a majority control of the company's holdings was especially helpful to its recovery.

When Joseph Crowley passed away, the presidential position was filled by his son, Daniel J. Crowley, who acted in that capacity for the next 20 years. His business strength was in the field of accounting, which was helpful as the company attempted to rebuild its financial stability. Also, he was an effective manager who possessed the ability to choose a quality staff, to whom he delegated a good deal of the company's operations.

One of Crowley's new staff members who took on an integral role in the redevelopment of the company's business was J.D. Runkle. After spending a short time as a college instructor in the field of business administration, Runkle came to Crowley, Milner & Co. as its general manager. He held weekly meetings for the company's management team, utilizing chalk and a blackboard to preach the importance of store policies, procedures, and goals. The company's employees came to refer to him affectionately as "The Professor," and his efforts combined with the direction provided by Daniel Crowley to lift the company back to its standing before the depression had hit.

Runkle was a no-nonsense manager who demanded only the best from his staff. In fact, the company's present-day mission statement, which emphasizes the refusal to "accept anything less than first-rate performance," was derived directly from his influence. Much of the company's success throughout the years of World War II, which involved the rationing of materials and control of pricing, can be attributed to the firm management provided by Runkle and Crowley. Following the war, the company continued to prosper under their direction until the mid-1950s. When Crowley left the company, Runkle succeeded him as president.

Retail Expansion: The 1950s Through 1980s

The 1950s marked a period of rapid expansion in Detroit, both in the population and in the infrastructure. Expressways were constructed to connect the city with the surrounding towns, and suburban Detroit was born. As access between the suburbs and the city improved, downtown retailers began to open satellite branches in nearby communities. Runkle saw the growth potential that new branch stores would offer Crowley, Milner & Co., and began planning for expansion. He retired in 1954, though, and the introduction of branch stores was actually completed by his successor, James H. Chamberlain.

In late 1959, the first new store was opened in West Dearborn, Michigan. The store was a 100,000 square foot unit comprising three stories and was located in a shopping center called Westborn. The store was almost immediately successful, and soon thereafter another unit was opened at the site of another major center of activity in Detroit. This store was one-third the size of the second, but nonetheless, its retail success soon paralleled that of the other two.

Entering the 1960s, Crowley, Milner & Co. decided to try its hand at operating stores located in two of the many new indoor shopping malls that were popping up throughout suburban Detroit. New locations at Livonia Mall and Macomb Mall opened on the same day in late 1964, both of which were the largest enclosed shopping facilities in the country at the time. The Crowley's stores were the largest stores featured in each of the malls, and both became prosperous and helped the company gain greater recognition and exposure throughout eastern Michigan.

Chamberlain died of a heart attack soon after the mall locations were opened, and his presidency was followed by that of Robert E. Winkel. When Winkel inherited the company, it was composed of five stores throughout metro Detroit, which were soon joined by three more when Crowley, Milner & Co. purchased units from Demery's Inc. in 1972. Shortly thereafter, another Crowley's unit was constructed in a shopping mall in Sterling Heights, Michigan, and was opened in late 1975.

All of the company's branch locations continued to experience great success, but the original store downtown began to suffer as Detroit did the same. Over the years, that store's sales figures had been declining, and actually reached the lowest point in the company's history in 1976. The following year, the store was closed and the building was demolished. One chapter in the company's history was closed, while many others were just being opened.

By 1980, two more Crowley's stores were opened in regional shopping malls in the Detroit metro area. Although both stores achieved substantial success, the location at Arborland Mall was closed three years later because its developers had decided to turn it into an off-price shopping center. Crowley's had traditionally been an upscale marketer of high-quality items, and the company decided that the mall's change in focus did not match the image that Crowley's wanted to maintain.

In 1984, after having led the company to heightened success for 20 years, Winkel retired from his post and was followed by Robert B. Carlson. Carlson immediately initiated the addition of a tenth store in Southfield in 1985, and then two more in Burton and in Westland a year later. Also in 1986, a unit was opened near Flint, Michigan. This move drew some concern and criticism from analysts, who believed that Crowley's may have been extending itself beyond its true sphere of influence in the Detroit area. While the Flint unit was marginally less successful than its Detroit siblings, it achieved decent sales and within five years was doing quite well.

In the end of the 1980s, Crowley, Milner & Co. underwent two significant changes. First, its second branch store—and one of its most successful—was closed in 1987. The unit's lease had run out, and the property owner wanted to segment the building and bring in new businesses. Crowley's was invited back, but was offered only a portion of the space it had once inhabited. Management felt that downsizing that store location would not benefit the company, and rejected the new lease offer. The following year, Carlson was promoted to the newly-created post of chairman of the board, and the company appointed Andrew J. Soffel to serve as president. Previously, Soffel had been acting as vice-president and chief operating officer.

The 1990s and Beyond

At the turn of the decade, Crowley, Milner & Co.'s sales declined slightly. The company began making moves to recapture its customer base and raise its yearly revenue to the level that had been achieved in the past. First came the introduction of a prototype men's clothing store in Farmington, Michigan. Sales there were strong, and the company discussed plans to introduce more similar stores in the future. Also, Crowley's instituted a "Frequent Buyer" program at all of its stores, as a method of getting customers to come back again and again. The program kept track of each customer's monthly purchase amounts, and then the stores issued gift certificates based on each person's sales figures.

Initially, the Frequent Buyers program was a huge hit with customers. By mid-1992, there were approximately 55,000 participants and new members were being added at a rate of about 3,000 each month. Unfortunately, however, the company's yearly sales figures continued to drop, with the 1992 figures almost $10 million less than those of 1991. Crowley, Milner & Co. began aggressively searching for a merger partner that was large enough to help the company expand. It was management's opinion that long-term growth for the Crowley's chain would come through acquisition of some type, with the most likely scenario being an acquisition by another party.

Near the end of 1992, the company tried to expand its reach to Lansing, Michigan's capital city, opening a specialty store for women there that was similar to the men's store in Farmington. The store was unsuccessful, however, either due to its location or to its design. Some felt that the Farmington store, which carried only men's items, had been successful because men appreciated a store in which they could quickly and easily locate the merchandise they sought. Women, on the other hand, typically liked a department store which had merchandise for everyone under one roof. Some speculated that the women's-only Crowley's in Lansing may have suffered for that reason,

while others once again cited the difficulty in expanding to a locale which was unfamiliar with the Crowley's name.

In January 1993, Soffel retired from the company and was followed by Dennis Callahan, who came to Crowley, Milner & Co. with over two decades of experience in retail. One of his first tasks was to sign a revolving loan agreement with Schottenstein Stores Corp., which provided Crowley, Milner & Co. with money to resume payments to its creditors. The company then implemented a new workforce management computer software system, as a means of saving money on the tasks of tracking employees' work time and attendance. The program was called Smart Scheduler. Another change that came in 1993 was the close of the Westland store, which had been struggling. The Frequent Buyers program was cut at the end of the year.

In 1994, sales began to increase once again, and the company announced its first profitable quarter in almost five years. Callahan continued to rebuild the company's financial stability, through such moves as the acceptance of a new working capital loan agreement with Congress Financial Corporation, which replaced the previous agreement with Schottenstein Stores Corp. Also initiated was a two-for-one split of the company's common stock that spring.

Sales in 1995 rose to $109.9 million, and the company made moves to purchase department stores previously owned and operated by Steinbach Stores, Inc. of Columbus, Ohio. Steinbach's stores were spread throughout the northeastern United States, in New York, Connecticut, Vermont, New Jersey, and New Hampshire. Entering the end of the decade, it was clear that Crowley, Milner & Co. was committed to rebuilding what had once been a great dynasty in the Detroit area. The company was actively seeking out new endeavors throughout eastern Michigan—and with the Steinbach acquisition, throughout the eastern United States—that would help increase profits and aid in expansion. These continued efforts would undoubtedly position the company for future growth and success, as long as the retail environment remained strong.

Principal Subsidiaries

Steinbach Stores, Inc.

Further Reading

Crowley, Milner & Co. Corporate History, Detroit: Crowley, Milner & Co., 1997.
"Crowley's Will Add Store at Tel-Twelve," *Crain's Detroit Business,* April 30, 1990, p. 2.
Crump, Constance, "Crowley's Goals: Black Ink, Merger Partner," *Crain's Detroit Business,* June 15, 1992, p. 3.
——, "Improvement In Sight?: Crowley Execs Say Focused Strategy Will Restore Profits," *Crain's Detroit Business,* February 25, 1991, p. 1.
"Interfacing With the Time Clock System," *Chain Store Age Executive,* November 1993, p. 61.
Wilson, Melinda, "Out-Of-Towners Increase Stake in Crowley's," *Crain's Detroit Business,* March 19, 1990, p. 1.

—Laura E. Whiteley

Cubic Corporation

9333 Balboa Avenue
P.O. Box 85587
San Diego, California 92186
U.S.A.
(619) 277-6780
Fax: (619) 505-1523

Public Company
Incorporated: 1951 as Cubic Corporation
Employees: 3,300
Sales: $407.6 million (1996)
Stock Exchanges: American
SICs: 3663 Radio & T.V. Communications Equipment;
   3581 Automatic Vending Machines; 3827 Optical
   Instruments & Lenses

A leader in its two diverse businesses, Cubic Corporation is the parent company of two major business segments: Cubic Automatic Revenue Collection Group and Cubic Defense Group. Cubic began as a small electronics enterprise housed in a garage before developing into a sophisticated manufacturer of defense electronics systems. From there, the company moved into the freight and passenger elevator business by acquiring U.S. Elevator Corporation in 1969 and into the production of automatic fare collections systems three years later. Cubic exited the elevator manufacturing business in 1993, leaving it with its defense electronics and automatic fare collection businesses as the primary money earners for the company. During the late 1990s, Cubic's defense electronics subsidiary manufactured a wide range of instrumented training systems for the U.S. Army, Air Force, and Navy. The company's automatic fare collection subsidiaries designed and manufactured systems for mass transit projects throughout the world. A smaller component of the company's operations was its industrial operations segment, comprising Consolidated Converting Co., a corrugated-paper converting company, and businesses that manufactured emergency highway call boxes and optical tooling instruments.

1950s Origins

Cubic was founded in 1951 by Walter J. Zable, a retired professional football player and professional engineer. The company founded by Zable would later rise to prominence in three distinct business areas, evolving into a leading manufacturer of defense electronics systems, electronic freight and passenger elevators, and automatic fare collection equipment for mass transit systems, but in 1951 Zable's business interests were less ambitious and not nearly as wide-ranging. Zable started Cubic in a garage, where he assembled digital voltmeters. Quickly, however, Zable's business took the steps toward progress that led to the sophisticated and multifaceted Cubic Corporation of the 1990s.

In a decade's time, Cubic's business evolved remarkably. From its unpretentious beginnings in Zable's garage, the company quickly matured; it was engineering the downrange tracking system for the Mercury space program ten years later. This was an enormous leap for the company to make, placing it in a business arena that would serve as the chief revenue-generating engine for decades to come. Cubic, in the years ahead, would be known primarily for its talents in the defense electronics systems industry, but Zable was not content with his achievements during his inaugural decade of business. A little more than a decade after securing a contract to supply downrange tracking systems for the Mercury space program, Zable steered Cubic in other directions, acquiring two companies that provided entry into two different business areas.

Diversification Begins in the 1960s

As his military equipment business was growing during the 1960s, Zable looked to broaden Cubic's business interests and establish a presence in a market not subjected to the unpredictable forces directing national defense spending. Accordingly, in 1969 Zable acquired U.S. Elevator Corporation, then a $2-million-in-sales maker of freight and passenger elevators. Zable, through acquisitions and internal development, shaped U.S. Elevator into an industry leader, making it the first elevator company in the United States to manufacture programmable computerized controls in its passenger elevators.

As Cubic was developing a solid presence in the elevator market and attending to its mainstay defense electronics business, another opportunity for the growing company was emerging. During the 1960s, metropolitan mass transit systems were becoming the rage of the decade, attracting federal spending and some of the largest corporations, who were intent on grabbing a piece of the burgeoning business. Litton Industries was an early competitor in the business, followed by the arrival of Control Data, General Electric, and IBM, all in pursuit of the vast sums to be spent on subway and rail transit systems. Before long, however, the well-financed contenders for the mass transit market became disenchanted with the business, opting to abandon their involvement when their growth projections did not immediately materialize. For Zable, the flight of the large corporations represented an opportunity with two benefits. By entering into the mass transit market, he could further lessen Cubic's dependence on military spending and jump into a business that could garner the company appreciable market share. Zable demonstrated his commitment with the 1972 purchase of Los Angeles-based Western Data Products, Inc., a floundering maker of rail transit fare collections systems that was staffed by former Litton Industries engineers.

The decision to buy Western Data Products added the third leg that would support Cubic in the decades ahead. The company was heavily involved in supplying military training systems to the armed forces, was a manufacturer of freight and passenger elevators, and by 1972 was a manufacturer of the machines that opened gates when coins were dropped into a box or encoded cards were inserted into a slot. In this new business, Zable would enjoy as much success as he was registering in the production of elevators, shrewdly shaping his automatic fare collection business into the nation's largest competitor as larger contenders looked elsewhere for profitable ventures. One of those companies to turn away from the mass transit business was IBM, and Zable took advantage of the behemoth corporation's decision to cut short its plans by acquiring IBM's fare collection technology and engineering drawing at bargain basement prices. This transaction, which the business press hailed as a shrewd move on Zable's part, further enriched Cubic's capabilities in the automatic fare collection business and set the stage for a number of lucrative contracts that would be awarded to the company.

Filing a void made vacant by the large corporations, Cubic was able to win the contract to complete the second phase of San Francisco's BART mass transit system, a project IBM had declined to finish. Other large-scale projects followed, as Zable outmaneuvered rivals. Cubic was awarded the final $53 million contract for Washington, D.C.'s Metro mass transit system in 1975 and three years later won the contract to supply Atlanta, Georgia's rapid rail system. It was an encouraging start for the new business, adding volume and stability to Cubic's annual revenue and profit totals. Soon, the company would stand as the only major domestic manufacturer of automatic fare collection equipment and hold sway over a market worth hundreds of millions of dollars. Elsewhere in Cubic's operations, business was advancing admirably; the company's elevator business was solidly positioned in its markets and defense electronics systems continued to underpin operating profits and sales. The 1970s had proven to be a decade of achievement for Cubic, but the progress did not segue into commensurate success during the 1980s. The difficulties began with the company's flourishing automatic fare collection business.

1980s Downturn

Large-scale contracts had been awarded to Cubic's automatic fare collection group—marketing masterstrokes, to be sure—but in the engineering side of the business Cubic recorded several distressing failures. Fare cards jammed in the gates at Washington, D.C.'s Metro system and vending machines broke down at an alarming rate. The problems with Cubic's equipment prompted Washington, D.C.'s Metro Board chairman to denounce the company's equipment as a "$50 million disaster" and led local officials to push for scrapping Cubic's fare collection system altogether. Cubic eventually spent $10 million to improve the operating efficiency of its equipment in Washington, but the company's problems did not end there. Similar ire was raised in Atlanta, where Cubic's fare collection gates failed at least once in less than 1,000 transactions, far more frequently than the failure rate specified in the contract of no more than one failure in every 34,000 transactions.

The rampant equipment failure in major metropolitan markets exposed Cubic to a spate of bad press, coverage that helped to give room and business to competing firms, particularly foreign manufacturers of automatic fare collection equipment. The debacle with the contracts in Washington and Atlanta set a bad tone for Cubic's performance during the 1980s, as sales and profit growth nearly came to a halt. By 1987, the prognostications were bleak. During the previous five years sales had increased only 15 percent, while profits during the same period stagnated. The biggest plunge occurred in 1986 when profits plummeted from $14.7 million to a paltry $1.1 million, as the company suffered from dismal performances by each of its three major business segments. Cubic's electronic defense systems subsidiary, which was focused mainly on producing flight training and simulation gear, fell victim to costly software changes on B1-B bomber and AWACS simulators. The adjustments nearly erased all of the subsidiary's operation profits for the year. Cubic's electronic freight and passenger elevator business, which was conducted through the company's U.S. Elevator subsidiary, lost half of its projected earnings to escalating insurance and construction costs. Last, the company's automatic fare collection business, which had been on the mend since the early problems in Washington and Atlanta, suffered from new product development costs, rounding out the wide-ranging problems that afflicted Cubic during the year.

In the wake of Cubic's less-than-spectacular 1986, speculation abounded concerning the company's future. Some Wall Street analysts were recommending that Zable break up the company into separate businesses to arrest the enterprise's financial slide. Zable, on the other hand, had other ideas. He resolved to rebuild the company, and he began making sweeping changes. Zable terminated those responsible for the software mishap and restructured the $150-million-in-sales defense electronic subsidiary. Shortly thereafter, in August 1987, Cubic was awarded a $100 million contract for five new combat jet training systems for the Navy, the type seen in the film "Top Gun," designed to plot and track up to 36 aircraft in mock aerial dogfights. To cure U.S. Elevator's ills, Zable moved 65 percent of the subsidiary's production south to Mexicali, Mexico and acquired New York City-based Central Elevator Co., a deal that extended Cubic's presence into the Northeast (the nation's largest elevator market) and strengthened the maintenance side of the subsidiary's business. The company's automatic fare collection business was invigorated by placing a greater emphasis on retrofitting existing fare collection systems, which helped compensate for the dwindling number of new mass transit systems being built. Zable also steered the company into other markets for automatic fare collection systems, such as the August 1987 purchase of New York-based Automatic Toll Systems, a leading, $20-million-in-sales manufacturer of toll road automatic coin collection equipment.

Sales and net income rose strongly after the changes, reaching record highs of $349 million in sales and $21 million in net income by the end of the 1980s. With its early problems in the fare collection business long put to rest, Cubic entered the 1990s as a vibrant company poised for growth. To Zable's chagrin, however, the nation's economy during the early years of the decade did not provide a fertile climate for businesses to grow. Recessive economic conditions during the early 1990s stifled financial growth for a wide spectrum of businesses, Cubic included. To make matters worse, defense spending was on the decline during the early 1990s and the elevator industry was suffering from overcapacity, developments that had a decided influence on Cubic's bottom line. Sales dropped from $352.7 million in 1990 to $307.7 million in 1991 and net income plunged from more than $23 million to $14 million; the one bright spot for the company was the progress made by its revenue collection group.

Comprising eight companies, Cubic's revenue collection group represented the only company in the world capable of designing, building, installing, and maintaining automatic fare collection systems covering all phases of computerized revenue collection. Not surprisingly, this dominant position had enabled Cubic to expand its business overseas during the latter half of the 1980s, and as the 1990s began the automatic revenue collection group was grabbing the lion's share of the worldwide market for automatic fare collection systems. In 1991, as its two other business segments were struggling, Cubic secured several new contracts both at home and abroad, including one in New York for the city's subways and buses and another for CitiRail in New South Wales, Sydney, Australia. Cubic's automatic revenue collection group also was awarded a contract for a statewide toll system in Florida and a contract for 523 new fare card machines for Washington's Metro subway system, evidence of the new confidence in Cubic's technological abilities. In addition to these contracts, Cubic also received follow-up orders from several large international clients, including Singapore-based Mass Rapid Transit Corp., Hong Kong Mass Transit Railway Corp., and the London Underground.

Despite the steady flow of work directed toward its revenue collection group, Cubic, as a whole, did not break free from its downward financial spiral until 1994, a recovery made after the company sold its U.S. Elevator subsidiary for $40 million in 1993. The divestiture, which ended nearly a quarter of a century of elevator production, left Cubic with two major business segments: its defense electronics systems subsidiary and its automatic revenue collection group. Sales in 1994 reached $260 million, then recorded two substantial leaps, swelling to $370 million in 1995 and $407 million in 1996.

Entering the late 1990s, Cubic could draw on the promise of several developments in 1996 to fuel confidence for the future. During the year, the company eliminated the losses recorded by the toll road component of its fare collection business by selling the business it had acquired nine years earlier. Cubic registered a profit on the deal and moved forward with two other deals that pointed toward further growth for its revenue collection business. In September, Cubic acquired complete ownership of a joint venture company it had co-owned previously, called Westinghouse Cubic Ltd. The decision to acquire full control of Westinghouse was indicative of Cubic's goal to win the contract for the privatization of the ticketing and fare collection for London Transport, including the London Underground and London-area buses. The following month, October 1996, Cubic was awarded a $27.9 million contract to design and install automatic fare collection equipment in Shanghai, China. It was the second time China had accepted bids for new fare collection systems, and Cubic had won the first contract, a project in Guangzhou, China. On the heels of these two moves, Cubic prepared for the beginning of the 21st century and the completion of its first half century of business, its prospects for future growth as strong as its leading market positions in defense electronic systems and automatic fare collection systems.

Principal Subsidiaries

Consolidated Conversion Co.; Cubic Applications, Inc.; New York Revenue Automation, Inc.; Southern Cubic Pty. Ltd.; Cubic Communications, Inc.; Cubic Defense Systems, Inc.; Westinghouse Cubic Ltd.; Cubic Worldwide Technical Services.

Principal Operating Units

Cubic Automatic Revenue Collection Group; Cubic Defense Group.

Further Reading

Beauchamp, Marc, "How Walter Zable Missed His Wake-Up Call," *Forbes,* December 28, 1987, p. 72.
Byrne, John A., "Fare Feud," *Forbes,* September 26, 1983, p. 68.
Jaffe, Thomas, "Will Lightening Strike?," *Forbes,* February 11, 1985, p. 180.
Lappen, Alyssa A., "Trouble in Defense," *Forbes,* October 3, 1988, p. 8.
Rowe, Bruce, "Tweed Hoists U.S. Elevator to Top Rung at Cubic Corp.," *San Diego Business Journal,* November 2, 1987, p. 12.

—Jeffrey L. Covell

Cyrk Inc.

3 Pond Road
Gloucester, Massachusetts 01930-1886
U.S.A.
(508) 283-5800
Fax: (508) 281-8062

Public Company
Incorporated: 1976
Employees: 600
Sales: $250.9 million (1996)
Stock Exchanges: NASDAQ
SICs: 2389 Apparel and Accessories, Not Elsewhere
    Classified

Cyrk Inc. is the leading company in the American promotional products market. Headquartered in Gloucester, Massachusetts, the company provides apparel, accessories, and promotional products and services to corporations around the world. Cyrk's most important customer during the early 1990s was Philip Morris, which Cyrk provided with products for the Marlboro Adventure Team promotion. Consumers traded "miles," earned by purchasing cigarettes, for sports bags, jackets, caps, and other items. Besides its complete range of promotional products, the company is acknowledged within the promotional industry as the most successful provider of consumer loyalty programs, and is the only firm to offer fully-integrated and comprehensive marketing services. One of Cyrk's most successful diversifications came when management initially decided to design and manufacture private label sports clothing for companies, such as Timberland and Reebok, and then thought it even more lucrative to manufacture its own line of clothing. With over 600 employees worldwide, the company has offices in Boston, New York, London, Hong Kong, Taiwan, and Seoul, South Korea, with more offices being contemplated. All this activity has resulted in a dramatic increase in net sales; from $135.8 million in 1995 to $250.9 million in 1996, a hefty jump of $115.1 million, or 85 percent. Yet even such an impressive success story has not prevented Cyrk from forging greater

possibilities for the future. In the spring of 1997, Cyrk signed an agreement to merge with Simon Marketing, Inc., a privately-held global promotion agency based in Los Angeles, California.

Early History

Cyrk Inc. was founded in 1976 by Gregory P. Shlopek, a marine biology professor teaching at a small community college in Philadelphia, Pennsylvania. While reading the financial section of the paper one day, Shlopek was reportedly impressed with an article that described the print-screen industry as fairly recession-proof. Having had an interest in graphic design since he was a teenager, Shlopek decided to leave his position at the community college and try his hand at becoming an entrepreneur. Off he went to Cape Ann, Massachusetts, a resort area that his family had visited for years, and there he established a screen-printing firm. Shlopak decided to name his company Cyrk, which means circus in Polish. The name was short, like "Nike" or "Fila," and it was clever enough, he thought, to attract large firms to a small silk-screen company.

Shlopek and his company had come along at the right time. In the mid-1970s, as the American way of dressing became more and more casual, not only teenagers but young adults and senior citizens began wearing T-shirts. T-shirts that identified one's affiliation with a college, team, or even city grew in popularity. When people starting wearing T-shirts with bright graphics and names on them, such as T-shirts with multi-colored lettering, sales skyrocketed upward. Cyrk was soon selling T-shirts to small local businesses and gift shops in the Cape Ann resort area, and then to a wider scope of customers up and down the Massachusetts seaboard.

Growth and Diversification in the 1980s

For ten years, Shlopek worked diligently with a small number of employees in his silk-screen shop to provide customers with T-shirts. Sales increased rapidly at first, then leveled off to a comfortable but unspectacular period of growth. Yet Shlopek was quite satisfied with the earnings his company was making and saw no need to alter the strategy he started out with. Suddenly, during the late 1980s, however, a recession hit the retail industry, and sales of Cyrk T-shirts fell drastically. Not sure of what to do, Shlopek decided to hire new personnel that would help his company make the turnaround that was necessary.

When Shlopek hired Patrick D. Brady as chief operating officer, he had been working as director of the mergers and acquisitions group in the investment banking department of BNY Associates, Inc., a subsidiary of the Bank of New York Company, Inc. Brady, with his vast experience in the financial sector, quickly recognized that Cyrk had to diversify if the company was to survive. Accordingly, Brady convinced Shlopek to shift the focus of his company from producing T-shirts to promotional programming. Brady's idea was that all retailers felt threatened by the growing competition in a very tough market, and companies would listen to a firm who provided them with a way to increase their visibility and also build customer loyalty. Soon Cyrk was putting a great deal of effort into designing and developing promotional programs for consumer products.

Brady's argument was based on hard data. Marketing analysts had discovered that there was a major increase in the use of premiums, namely, products received in exchange of purchase, by companies throughout the United States to build brand loyalty. According to information compiled by Promo Magazine, a trade publication based in Connecticut, in just one year American companies had earmarked over $60 billion for consumer promotions, and nearly $20 billion of that amount was set aside for premium incentives.

Cyrk began working with Fila, Reebok, and Timberland, assisting them with promotional campaigns that included custom-designed sports apparel and accessories. The company's first major promotional contract other than sports clothing and accessories, however, involved the design and development of a fully-integrated line of products for Mars Inc., such as a plastic dispensing machine for M&M's candy, T-shirts, lunchboxes, and other items for Snickers, Twix, and Skittles brand lines. Cyrk was now doing much more than merely supplying the products for another company's promotional campaign. Cyrk was handling every aspect of a promotional program, from the initial concept to the actual fulfillment. The company started its own concept and design team, including in-house designers whose specialty was in the fields of apparel, graphic, product, and accessories design and development. Along with the most modern facilities for screenprinting and embroidery located at their headquarters in Massachusetts, the company also implemented a fully integrated management and fulfillment service,

created its own global distribution network, and began to offer a comprehensive range of integrated marketing services.

By the end of the 1980s, Cyrk had created a new type of business in the United States. To further their success, and to expand their horizons, Cyrk management decided to form a partnership with an Asian trading company, Li & Fung. The arrangement gave Cyrk access to Li & Fung's manufacturing contacts throughout Asia, and significantly helped Cyrk to broaden its product line while lowering its costs at the same time.

Strategic Change and Development in the Early 1990s

Cyrk, of course, was not immune to the variations of the marketplace. When purchase orders for plastic dispensers began to decrease among retailers, Mars Inc. decided to reduce its business with Cyrk. Sales to Mars steadily declined from $24.1 million to $13 million in two years. Fortunately for Cyrk, Philip Morris picked up where Mars left off. Sales to Philip Morris catapulted from $10.5 million in 1992 to an astronomical $128.9 million in 1993.

The first promotional campaign Cyrk designed and developed for Philip Morris was the Marlboro Adventure Team promotion, where customers would trade in their "miles," having earned them by purchasing so many cigarettes, and in turn receive such items as caps, T-shirts, sports bags, and jackets with the Marlboro logo on them. One of the most successful promotional campaigns in history, Cyrk's role in the overall design and development of the program helped Philip Morris build an unparalleled type of brand loyalty to Marlboro cigarettes. By the end of 1994, Cyrk reported that 89 percent of its sales were accounted for by the Marlboro Adventure Team promotion.

When Philip Morris decided to switch the focus of its promotional campaign from the Adventure Team to the "Marlboro Country Store," Cyrk was at the forefront of companies that provided the giant tobacco firm with both products and services. The Marlboro Country Store promotion suited up smokers in barn jackets, boots, and blankets, which Cyrk had designed to recreate the aura and feeling of the Old West and its wide open plains. Yet the new promotion was not nearly as large as the first one, and industry analysts on Wall Street began to wonder whether or not Cyrk would be able to maintain its growth rate. The company had gone public in 1993, and based on its growth record seemed to offer one of the most promising stocks on the exchange. Nevertheless, with such a heavy reliance on one single customer, Cyrk began to worry analysts, especially during a time when the cigarette industry was coming under attack by anti-smoking consumer groups across the country.

Aware of its precarious position, Cyrk management initiated a strategy to develop a more diverse customer list. One of the first new clients included Fidelity Investments, the financial services firm specializing in mutual funds. Cyrk reached an agreement with Fidelity to design and develop a promotional campaign involving the sale of golf shirts, jackets, desk clocks, and various other products. Within a short time, Fidelity saw the assets within its mutual funds increase dramatically. Another major client contracted during this time was Gillette, manufacturer of shaving products for both men and women. Cyrk not only provided ties and warm-up suits as promotional items, but helped convince Gillette management that it would be in their best interest to sponsor the World Cup soccer match. Once again, Cyrk's strategy helped another company to increase its profile and thereby its revenues. In addition to Fidelity Investments and Gillette, Cyrk reached agreements with growing companies such as Showbiz Pizza Time Inc. and the Firestone-Bridgestone Tire Company.

The Mid-1990s and Beyond

By 1995, Cyrk had succeeded in its quest to build a new client list. The company's heavy dependency on Philip Morris began to decline, and sales to that firm went from a high of 89 percent of total revenues in 1994 to 57 percent of total revenues by 1995. One of Cyrk's most important new clients was the Pepsi-Cola Company. The company's business with Pepsi, involving the ''Pepsi Stuff'' promotion, was based on the purchase orders placed by Pepsi over the period of time that the promotion was ongoing. Traditionally, Cyrk never reached any written agreement with a client that committed the company to reach a certain level of purchases. Rather the level of purchases depended on a variety of factors, including consumer redemption rates and the duration of the promotion. Thus Cyrk's total sales volume was difficult to predict and varied significantly not only from year to year but from quarter to quarter.

All this changed, however, with the ''Pepsi Stuff'' promotion. For the first time in its history Cyrk signed a written agreement with a major company. Cyrk's agreement with Pepsi regarding the ''Pepsi Stuff'' promotion involved an exclusive role for the firm to design, develop, and produce all the promotional merchandise (wristwatches, posters, beach towels, and other items) and clothing for the duration of the campaign. In addition, the signed contract included a statement that provided for the negotiation of gross margins at different volume levels. The initial ''Pepsi Stuff'' promotional campaign expired in October 1996, and Cyrk entered into another written agreement with Pepsi to provide similar promotion products and services during 1997. The influence of the Pepsi account on Cyrk's business cannot be underestimated. While 1996 sales to Pepsi accounted for 38 percent of its net sales, Cyrk was able to further reduce its reliance on Philip Morris, who accounted for 30 percent of the company's net sales.

In March of 1997, Cyrk acquired Tonkin, Inc., a privately-held company based in Woodinville, Washington, that specialized in custom promotional programs and licensed promotional products. Revenues for the company amounted to only $41 million during fiscal 1996, but Tonkin had worked with some of America's largest companies, including Caterpillar, Peterbilt, Consolidated Freightways, Kenworth, Fluke, John Deere, Volvo, Emery Worldwide, Conway Transportation, Weyer-

haeuser, Mercury, and Freightliner to provide them with new logos and trademarks. In fact, Cyrk purchased Tonkin because the latter had developed one of the most successful corporate logo programs in the United States.

Continuing with its strategic acquisition and expansion policy, Cyrk decided to merge with Simon Marketing, Inc. in May 1997. Simon Marketing, a privately-run global promotion agency operating out of Los Angeles, California, was one of the premier providers of marketing programs and promotional products to such clients as MacDonald's, Chevron, and Blockbuster Entertainment. It was Simon Marketing that helped MacDonald's develop its Happy Meals and Monopoly promotions. Perhaps the most important aspect of the merger was that Cyrk would benefit from Simon Marketing's international experience in Europe and Asia. Cyrk's expertise with loyalty and brand-building promotions, and Simon's experience in leveraging sports and entertainment properties, along with a highly successful history in youth market promotions, would provide clients with one of the most sophisticated line of promotion services and products within the industry.

Having broadened its client base, and having allied itself with two of the most successful companies in the promotional service and products industry, Cyrk would likely continue as a leader. And with clients such as Pepsi-Cola, Philip Morris, MasterCard, Timberland, Fila, Tommy Hilfiger, F.A.O. Schwarz, and M&M Mars, the future looked even better than the past.

Principal Subsidiaries

Tonkin, Inc.

Further Reading

Bond, Cathy, ''Relationships Designed to Last,'' *Marketing,* April 4, 1996, p. IX.
Clift, Vicki, ''Small Firms Benefit from a Promotional Partner,'' *Marketing News,* September 23, 1996, p. 25.
Ebenkamp, Becky, ''No Instant Wins,'' *Brandweek,* March 17, 1997, p. 46.
Freeman, Laurie, ''Premium Giveaway Products Pass Cost-Benefit Analyses,'' *Advertising Age,* March 17, 1997, p. S4.
Howard, Lemier, ''News You Can Use: Incentive Marketing Isn't about T-Shirts and Coffee Mugs Anymore. It's about Information,'' *Working Women,* March 1997, p. 56.
Hwang, Suein L., ''All Aboard for Marlboro Country . . . Someday,'' *The Wall Street Journal,* November 7, 1996, p. B1(E).
Matthews, Virginia, ''Loyal to What End?'', *Marketing,* August 29, 1996, p. 34.
Smith, Steve, ''Nearing Zero,'' *Brandweek,* March 17, 1997, p. 44.
Steinberg, Howard, ''The Fourth 'P' Should Head the Queue!,'' *Brandweek,* March 17, 1997, p. 33.

—Thomas Derdak

D'Agostino Supermarkets Inc.

1385 Boston Post Road
Larchmont, New York 10538-3904
U.S.A.
(914) 833-4000
Fax: (914) 833-4060

Private Company
Founded: 1939
Employees: 2,000 (est.)
Sales: $220 million (1995 est.)
SICs: 5411 Grocery Stores; 5812 Eating Places

D'Agostino Supermarkets Inc. is a privately owned supermarket chain in New York City and suburban Westchester County, New York. Most of the 26 units in 1996 were in Manhattan. Geared to the middle- to upper-class shopper, D'Agostino's has long been well regarded for quality meat and fish and fresh produce.

D'Agostino's to 1980

The founders of D'Agostino Supermarkets, Pasquale and Nicholas D'Agostino, were born in Italy and came to the United States in 1924 with their parents, settling in New York City, where they helped their father with his fruit and vegetable pushcart. Already in their teens, they received their American education on the streets rather than in school. In 1932 they opened a small dry goods and grocery store on Manhattan's Upper East Side. Even in the depths of the Depression, this was a neighborhood able and willing to pay for quality goods.

In 1939 the D'Agostino brothers moved their store from Lexington Avenue and 83rd Street to Third Avenue and 77th Street, taking advantage of more space to add a meat operation and calling their store the Yorkville Food Market. Trained as a butcher, Nicholas D'Agostino went every morning to the city's main meat market to find the best beef, veal, and lamb available, but he and his brother kept their prices competitive with those of their rivals. At a time when many shoppers had to visit one store

for meat, another for milk, and yet another for produce, the D'Agostinos' food mart was one of the first to put meat, dairy products, baked goods, dry goods, and produce under one roof.

Business boomed after World War II, and a second store was opened farther downtown, at 20th Street near the East River. The brothers shared all responsibilities, although Pasquale's title was president and Nicholas held the title of vice-president. By 1960, the year Pasquale died, there were seven or eight D'Agostino stores, all of them on Manhattan's East Side. Capitalizing on its reputation for quality meat, D'Agostino's ran highly successful advertisements in the 1960s that declared, "Please don't kiss the butcher." Nicholas D'Agostino turned over day-to-day operations of the business in 1964 to his two sons, Stephen and Nicholas, Jr. Stephen was named president and chief executive officer in 1972.

D'Agostino's spread to Manhattan's West Side in the 1970s and issued extra-large, white plastic "D'Ag Bags" that publicized the store's name. Fashion models were especially fond of them for their size, and they used the bags to carry extra shoes, clothes, and makeup, thereby giving the supermarket chain a cachet. The company's singing commercial, with the theme line, "Mr. D'Agostino, Please Move Closer to Me," reverberated on radio in this period.

D'Agostino's in the 1980s

By the 1980s D'Agostino's, still a private company with all of the stock owned by Nicholas and his two sons but now based in the Westchester County suburb of New Rochelle, was one of the most profitable in the metropolitan area. There were 17 stores in 1981, with annual sales totaling an estimated $70 million to $100 million. Fifteen were in Manhattan, one in Brooklyn, and one, known as Foodtown, in the suburban community of Cross River. Interviewed by the *New York Times* in 1981, Stephen D'Agostino said, "Our plan is to develop our present core as a primary goal, filling in on the island of Manhattan." To squeeze the maximum selling space from its small outlets (averaging only 7,000 square feet), the company was building shelves nearly to the ceiling and installing triple-deck cases inside meat freezers. Stephen D'Agostino resigned as chief executive officer of the firm in 1982, yielding the post to his brother, although he remained as chairman until 1986.

Under the direction of Nicholas, Jr., D'Agostino's expansion continued during the 1980s, albeit at a more conservative pace. The eighteenth store opened in Manhattan's Chelsea neighborhood in 1982, the nineteenth opened in the Westchester County community of Bedford in 1986, and the twentieth, also in Westchester, opened in 1987. Like the city stores, the suburban ones were serving the upper end of the supermarket trade. The suburban stores were much larger, however, 20,000 to 30,000 square feet, allowing larger perishables sections and service counters. By the end of 1988 the chain had grown to 24 stores—20 in Manhattan—and an estimated $200 million in sales.

Special Features, 1986–1990

One of these new outlets was a prototype East Side specialty-oriented store called Fresh Market. Although decorated with the usual D'Agostino black, red, and green colors, little of the interior of the small (5,000-square-foot) unit resembled the chain's customary stores. Fruits and vegetables were displayed in their original crates and cases, and there were few staple grocery items like canned goods and cereals. The back was reserved for a bakery and a butcher counter selling fresh chickens and homemade sausage. Nicholas D'Agostino was hopeful that Fresh Market would provide the type of services to which residents were accustomed formerly in delicatessens, which had all but disappeared from the city. "We don't want to be all things to all people," he told a *Crain's New York Business* interviewer. "The middle-to-upper-income consumer is our customer."

During this period D'Agostino's also introduced President's Choice, a new line of upscale private-label products. Unlike most private-label groceries, which sold at a discount, President's Choice, distributed through a Canadian firm, Loblaw Cos., generally consisted of gourmet items not available at other grocery stores. The first heavily advertised President's Choice product, its Decadent Chocolate Chip cookie, sold 4,500 cases in six weeks (albeit at an introductory discount), compared with 3,000 cases of the leading national brand for the entire year. D'Agostino's also issued an in-store circular with features about various President's Choice products and other private-label items.

For the nondecadent health-conscious and environmentally sensitive shopper, D'Agostino's began offering a wide variety of new items. Among the perishable products introduced in a "Good For You, New York" weekly circular in 1990 were organic produce, deli selections low in fat and cholesterol, "light" selections from the dairy case, and preservative-free lasagna and carrot cake. There was also a chicken raised on a pesticide-free diet. All of these items were under the D'Agostino private label.

In 1986 D'Agostino's introduced Tele-A-Dag, a telephone delivery service offering goods available through a rented warehouse in the Bronx. This warehouse had a meat, fish, produce, delicatessen, and dairy operation, and a full line of about 2,000 grocery items. The phone service attracted interest among the

elderly, working people, and mothers with young children. (It was dropped in 1990, however, because of high costs and traffic and parking problems in New York City; one employee had to bring the order to the shopper's door while a second one drove the truck around the block because of the scarcity of parking.) In 1991 D'Agostino's became the first supermarket in the New York area to accept bank debit (ATM) cards for payments at its checkout counters. It had been taking credit cards since 1987.

D'Agostino's also was counting on customer service to distinguish itself from its rivals. A comprehensive system was tabulating information on every employee to match personal background, needs, education, and ambition with the company's requirements. Unlike other chains, it began hiring its own delivery people in 1986, rather than continuing to rely on an outside service, and it offered them benefits to motivate better service. Finding its employees' skills to be subpar, in 1990 the company introduced a "Career in Focus" program, with two company-paid 13-week sessions of three-hour Friday afternoon classes, held at a neighborhood college.

D'Agostino in the 1990s

In 1992 D'Agostino's opened its first pharmacy department in a store at Amsterdam Avenue and 59th Street in Manhattan, near Roosevelt Hospital. During the same year all of its 26 stores introduced frozen organic produce, wrapped in polybags, for the organic produce sections it introduced in 1991. The line of goods included blueberries, raspberries, strawberries, peas, green beans, corn, and a mixed-vegetable item called Gardener's Blend.

In addition to customers preoccupied with healthy eating, D'Agostino's was targeting Manhattan's large Hispanic population in the 1990s. "About a year ago we introduced a Spanish produce section in stores where we knew there was a Hispanic community," the company's public-relations director told *Supermarket News* in 1993. "We then rolled it out to some other stores and found there was a marketplace for Hispanic produce no matter where the store was located.... We think this is because in New York City people are just interested in the cuisine of a lot of different areas."

Private labels were still working for D'Agostino's in the early 1990s, when they were said to constitute between 15 to 20 percent of sales. In 1993 the company was selling more than 200 President's Choice products and 15 premium perishable products under its own name, including juices as well as chicken. D'Agostino's had most recently added an ice cream under its own name that competed directly with Haagen-Dazs but sold for around 30 cents less per quart. In addition it was maintaining its long-standing Foodtown line of value products.

D'Agostino's got into the coffee-bar business in 1996 by opening its first two D'Ag Coffee Works in Manhattan, one in a Greenwich Village store, the other next to the store at Ninth Avenue and 57th Street. The latter was the prototype, offering several rare estate-grown coffees along with prepackaged sandwiches, salads, and sushi as well as tea. "Our research tells us the coffee-bar market in New York is only one-third saturated," said Walter D'Agostino, vice-president for merchandising.

In 1996 D'Agostino's had 26 stores and annual sales estimated at between $200 million and $220 million. These stores ranged in size from 4,000 to 30,000 square feet. Company headquarters were moved in 1993 from New Rochelle to nearby Larchmont, where Greenwich Associates, a real estate company owned by the D'Agostino family, purchased a 16,000-square-foot building, leasing much of it to D'Agostino's.

Further Reading

Barmash, Isadore, ''D'Agostino Aims for Top Recognition,'' *New York Times,* June 23, 1981, p. D6.

''Downsized D'Ags Offsets Rent,'' *Chain Store Age Executive,* February 1989, pp. 20, 26.

Duff, Mike, ''Nick D'Agostino Is Doing the Shopping for His Customers,'' *Supermarket Business,* February 1989, pp. 15, 93.

Greenhouse, Steven, ''Nicholas D'Agostino Sr., 86, Founder of Grocery Chain,'' *New York Times,* June 25, 1996, p. B9.

Hammel, Frank, ''Case Study: D'Agostino's 'Careers in Focus,' '' *Supermarket Business,* November 1990, p. 28.

Klepacki, Laura, ''D'Agostino Introduces Frozen Organic Produce,'' *Supermarket News,* March 30, 1992, p. 15.

Rigg, Cynthia, ''D'Agostino's Fresh Approach,'' *Crain's New York Business,* January 2, 1989, pp. 1, 28.

——, ''Stores Put Stock in Private Labels,'' *Crain's New York Business,* November 22, 1993, pp. 3, 39.

Turcsin, Richard, ''A Latino Accent,'' *Supermarket News,* January 25, 1993, pp. 15–16.

Williams, Mina, ''D'Agostino Introduces Store Branded Chicken,'' *Supermarket News,* March 5, 1990, p. 24.

—Robert Halasz

𝔇𝔞𝔦𝔩𝔶 𝔐𝔞𝔦𝔩

Daily Mail and General Trust plc

Northcliffe House
2 Derry Street
London W8 5TT
England
(011) 171 938 6000
Fax: (011) 171 938 4626

Public Company
Incorporated: 1896
Employees: 10,500
Revenues: £100.6 million (1996)
Stock Exchanges: London
SICs: 6719 Holding Companies, Not Elsewhere
  Classified

The Daily Mail and General Trust plc is one of the largest media holding companies in the world. With its main office in London, England, the company owns and operates five main groups, including Associated Newspapers, Northcliffe Newspapers, Euromoney Publications, Harmsworth Publishing, and Harmsworth Media. Associated Newspapers publishes the *Daily Mail,* the *Mail on Sunday,* and the *Evening Standard.* Northcliffe Newspapers, one of the largest regional newspaper publishers in Britain, prints 17 daily titles from 25 centers throughout the United Kingdom. Euromoney Publications is one of the leading international business-to-business publishers, with titles in law and tax, energy and transport, and international finance. Harmsworth Publishing is primarily responsible for the company's informational and educational publishing activities, while Harmsworth Media supervises the company's nonpublishing media activities, including network television, cable television, and commercial radio.

Early History

The founder of the *Daily Mail,* Alfred Harmsworth, was born in 1866, near the beginning of what was later to be called the Golden Age of British journalism. Harmsworth's interest in publishing was encouraged by his father, who purchased a printing set for the young boy's seventh birthday. Although young Harms-

worth was a sports enthusiast and—as most young men of his upbringing and generation—interested in a great many pursuits, he nonetheless remained enthralled with the world of publishing and during his school years was editor of a weekly magazine in which he wrote a column called ''Answers to Correspondents.''

After Harmsworth graduated with a university degree, he decided to become a newspaper publisher but in a decidedly different way from all others. There were numerous halfpenny papers published throughout Britain during the latter half of the 19th century, but most of them were printed on cheap paper and written in a dull and wordy manner. Remote from the people, these ''halfpenny's,'' as they were called, did not provide much information for a public that was growing more and more literate and hungry for knowledge about the momentous events happening around the world. With a clear vision and untold amounts of energy, Harmsworth formed a partnership with his brother Harold, later the first Viscount Rothermere, and began working on a bold and radical newspaper, the *Daily Mail.*

On a spring morning in early May of 1896, Harmsworth shut himself up in his office at 2 Carmelite Street and worked nonstop for the next two days and two nights to write, edit, and produce the first paper in Britain that brought essential information into the homes of working-class people on a day-to-day basis. The initial circulation of the *Daily Mail* was estimated at 100,000, but by the time the news vendors had sold the final copy of Harmsworth's publication, the *Daily Mail* had sold out at 397,215 copies. From the very first page, the reading public was enthralled with the *Daily Mail.* One of the most popular and radical innovations of the new upstart paper was the inclusion of a daily women's page, which not surprisingly attracted intense derision from other newspapers and journals that regarded female readers as beneath journalistic consideration.

Harmsworth is widely regarded as one of the progenitors of modern journalism. He had an uncanny instinct for what was important news and an ability to see the potential in a story even before the events fully unraveled. Harmsworth also displayed an intuitive gift for anticipating public opinion and, in many instances, knew what the public wanted to read in his newspaper. One of the best examples of Harmsworth's talent is illustrated by his persistence in bringing the truth about the Boer War to the people of Britain.

By the beginning of the Boer War in the late 1890s, circulation of the *Daily Mail* had risen to over one million, higher than any other newspaper in the western world. Harmsworth sent a team of journalists, including Edgar Wallace and George Warrington Steevens, to cover the events and battles between the British soldiers and the Dutch Afrikaners in South Africa. Dispatches from the first female war correspondent, Lady Sarah Wilson, the aunt of Winston Churchill, from the besieged town of Mafeking, brought to the reading public the plight of the British soldier when facing almost insurmountable odds. Yet the British government insisted that all dispatches from South Africa undergo censorship due to the harmful effect military losses might have on public support for the war. In short, Harmsworth was adamant that the truth of what was happening in the Boer War should not be hidden or repressed simply because it was unpleasant.

The British government, forced to listen to the mounting outcry of public opinion, finally relented and agreed to allow one newspaper the right to print uncensored news from the battlefront. After a hotly contested and bitter fight with other newspapers, the *Daily Mail* finally won the right to print uncensored news from South Africa. Much to the dismay of the government, the *Daily Mail* published reports which His Majesty's government had been denying for many months. In 1902, at the conclusion of the hostilities between the British and the Afrikaners, the *Daily Mail* published the terms of the peace treaty as a world exclusive, even before the announcement was made by the British government. From that point onward, the *Daily Mail*'s reputation for exclusive and reliable news, and its championing the cause of the ordinary citizen, was unquestioned throughout the United Kingdom.

The Early 20th Century and World War I

From the first day of publication, Harmsworth's *Daily Mail* was at the forefront of advocating technological advances in the British newspaper industry. Taking advantage of the advances in worldwide communications, the *Mail* established direct telegraphic contact between its London and New York offices within the first year of operation. From 1905 onward, the paper was printed in Paris so that the *Daily Mail* could be on Continental breakfast tables ten hours earlier than other British papers which had to be transported across the English Channel. In addition, the offices of the *Daily Mail* were the first in Britain to install equipment that enabled its staff to develop pictures.

Even more important, the *Daily Mail* was a strong advocate of technological advances in society at large. The *Daily Mail* took up such unpopular causes as the utility of the motor car, the installation of telephones in police stations, and the supply of fire brigades with modern emergency and rescue equipment. One of the most significant and far-reaching causes undertaken by the *Daily Mail* was its support of the infant technology of aviation. To encourage technological advances in flight, the *Daily Mail* was one of the first newspapers to offer a £10,000 prize to a person who could fly from London to Manchester in one day. Ridiculed by rival newspapers and scorned by high society, most of the landmarks and records set in early British aviation history were a direct response to challenges of the *Daily Mail*. In 1909, the first Englishman to fly across the English Channel claimed a *Daily Mail* prize as a reward. In 1910, the *Daily Mail* sponsored the first airship crossing of the English Channel in order to emphasize the importance of air power in any future conflict with a Continental power such as Germany.

The Growth of Influence—From World War I to the 1950s

During the years immediately before World War I, Harmsworth began to use the *Daily Mail* in order to warn the British public about the growing militarization of Germany and the threat she posed to peace in Europe. Campaigning vigorously to change the Seas Laws, which would seriously hamper the effectiveness of British seapower during wartime, Harmsworth and the *Daily Mail* were not only dismissed but roundly portrayed as engaging in "warmongering." When Harmsworth's predictions came true in August 1914, however, the *Daily Mail* decided to devote itself to making the public aware of the common soldier's trials and tribulations on the front lines.

By 1915, the *Daily Mail* was reporting that British soldiers were being butchered by the thousands on the front lines in France, and that one of the reasons for the appalling attrition rate was that the soldiers were supplied with inferior weapons and inadequate ammunition. The "Shell Crisis," as it came to be called, gave rise to an intense confrontation between the Asquith government and the British national press. Harmsworth was hanged in effigy in front of the *Daily Mail* offices, and copies of the paper were burned by a crowd at the London Stock Exchange. Not the least, circulation declined a million copies in one day. Yet Harmsworth held his ground, and, by the time all of the facts were made public, the Asquith government was forced to resign. David Lloyd George formed a national coalition government and successfully prosecuted the war until its conclusion. Harmsworth and the *Daily Mail* had extended their influence to the halls of Parliament.

When Harmsworth died in 1922, at the height of his prestige, influence, and fame, he was already dubbed Lord Northcliffe by the King of England. As tributes poured in from around the world, Harmsworth was remembered for his innovative approach to publishing, including the establishment of a paper-making facility in Newfoundland and the retraining of London's hansom cab drivers so they could adapt to driving motor vehicles. Upon Harmsworth's death, his brother Harold, known as Lord Rothermere, took effective control of all the operations of the *Daily Mail*.

Lord Rothermere continued in the tradition of his brother during the 1930s in trying to warn the British public about the danger of Adolf Hitler's rise to power. As the *Daily Mail* began to champion Winston Churchill as the one to lead Britain's government in the possible event of a Second World War, the newspaper began to increase its circulation dramatically. When war was declared in September 1939, the *Daily Mail* strongly supported British military aviation and the creation of the Bristol Blenheim, then the most powerful bomber ever made. The bomber played a significant role in the Battle of Britain and the fight against Germany's Luftwaffe and was the first bomber to sink both German and Japanese submarines.

When World War II ended in 1945, the *Daily Mail*'s circulation continued to rise. Having garnered a sterling reputation for reporting reliable and trustworthy information during both world wars, the *Daily Mail* renewed its commitment to portraying momentous events with a journalistic flair. One of the newspaper's great foreign correspondents, Noel Barber, became renowned for his elegant anecdotal reports on such topics as the Soviet invasion of Hungary in 1956, where he held a women who died in his arms facing Russian tanks; his visit to the South Pole, where he was the first Englishman to make the trip since Captain Scott; and his coverage of Sir Edmund Hillary's trek up the Himalayas. Throughout the 1950s and 1960s, the *Daily Mail* set a standard and defined a style of reporting that legions of young reporters around the world tried to emulate.

Expansion and Consolidation

Over the years, the *Daily Mail* and its subsidiary, Associated Newspapers, had grown dramatically. The purchase and sale of numerous London and regional publications marked the growth of the company from its inception in 1896. In order to centralize operations and standardize publishing procedures, the company decided to relaunch itself as a compact newspaper in 1971. Under the editorship of Sir David English, who later became the chairman of the company's Associated Newspapers subsidiary, the revised *Daily Mail* garnered more awards than any other newspaper.

One of these awards came in 1983, when the *Daily Mail* received one of the special British Press Awards for a "relentless campaign against the malignant practices of the Unification Church." The *Daily Mail* assumed the responsibility of exposing the brainwashing techniques of the Moonies under the headline: "The Church Breaks Up Families." As a result of its reporting, the Moonies brought a libel suit against the *Daily Mail,* ultimately leading to the longest libel action in British legal history. In the end, the *Daily Mail* was vindicated and, as a consequence of the evidence made public at the trial, the Moonies' activities were reviewed by the British government and severely curtailed.

In 1988, the company left its headquarters at Carmelite House on Fleet Street, the traditional site of British publishing companies for hundreds of years, and relocated to new quarters at Northcliffe House in Kensington, West London. As the newspaper offices moved to Kensington, the printing works moved eight miles away to a 12-acre parcel of land at Rotherhithe in London's Docklands. This state-of-the-art printing and distribution facility completed the company's modernization program. The distance that separates the editorial, advertising, printing, and distribution offices are linked together by a highly sophisticated electronic communications systems known as one of the most advanced and also one of the best in the world.

The 1990s and Beyond

Under the leadership of the present Viscount Rothermere, the great-nephew of the founder, the company has expanded its activities into educational publishing, financial publishing, radio and television. In fact, the age of electronic media has completely changed the face of the British publishing industry. Since its formation in 1969, the company's Euromoney

Publications has become one of the leaders in providing electronic business information through its development of various databases, and its website on the Internet. Harmsworth Publishing, the company's information publisher, has created College-View, an innovative software program in which colleges market themselves to students at over 4,000 high schools in the United States. In association with this program, two new CD-Rom titles were released, one providing information on careers and the other dealing with scholarships. Perhaps most important is the company's rapid expansion into the television and radio industries. The company owns Channel One, a cable television channel specializing in City news and features, the Arts Channel, a music and arts programming channel, and British Pathe, Britain's leading news film archives from 1896 to 1970. The company's radio holdings include a controlling interest in the Broadcast Media Group, an Australian radio firm that operates 12 regional radio stations in southern Australia, a controlling interest in Klassiska Hits, a radio station in Stockholm, Sweden, and Classic FM, the national classical music station of Britain.

The average daily circulation of the *Daily Mail* surpassed two million in its centenary year, while the regional publications throughout Britain, under the auspices of Associated Newspapers, continued to grow dramatically. In spite of its success in traditional print journalism, the *Daily Mail* is committed to expanding its activities in the electronic media field, where Viscount Rothermere believes the future of the industry lies.

Principal Subsidiaries

Daily Mail and General Investments plc; Daily Mail and General Holdings Ltd.; Daily Mail and General Funding (UK) Ltd.; Associated Newspapers Holdings Ltd.; Associated Newspapers Ltd.; Northcliffe Newspapers Group Ltd.; Euromoney Publications plc (73%); Bouverie Investments Ltd.; Continental Daily Mail S.A.; Carmelite House Ltd.; Harmsworth Media Ltd.; Harmsworth Publishing Ltd.; John M. Newton & Sons Ltd.; Kisalfold Deposit Ltd. Partnership; Pressprint Kft.; Associated Newspapers North America Inc.; Daily Mail & General Finance b.v.

Further Reading

Carlisle, Cristina, "The Media Business: What They're Buying in Nine Countries," *New York Times,* May 27, 1996, p. 32(L).

"Daily Mail & General Trust," *Wall Street Journal,* March 14, 1996, p. C22(E).

"Daily Mail Gets Stake in British TV Operation," *New York Times,* April 23, 1996, p. D6(L).

Edmondson, Gail, "Waltz of the Media Giants," *Business Week,* September 12, 1994, p. 52.

"The Expanding Entertainment Universe," *Business Week,* August 14, 1995, p. 114.

Farrell, Christopher, "Media Control Is Narrowing: Should We Worry?" *Business Week,* August 14, 1995, p. 37.

"Multimedia's No-Man's Land," *The Economist,* July 22, 1995, p. 57.

"Pre-Tax Profit Increases 7% as Sales, Ad Revenues Rise," *Wall Street Journal,* June 14, 1996, p. A7D(E).

Pruzan, Todd, "Global Media: Distribution Slows, but Rates Climb," *Advertising Age,* January 16, 1995, p. 119.

—Thomas Derdak

Dixons Group plc

29 Farm Street
London W1X 7RD
United Kingdom
(071) 499 3494
Fax: (071) 629 1402
Web site: http://www.dixons.co.uk

Public Company
Incorporated: 1937 as Dixon Studios Ltd.
Employees: 15,849
Sales: £1.9 billion (US $2.9 billion)
Stock Exchanges: London Tokyo
SICs: 5734 Computer & Software Stores; 5722
     Household Appliance Stores; 5946 Camera &
     Photographic Supply Stores; 7384 Photofinishing
     Laboratories; 6552 Subdividers & Developers, Not
     Elsewhere Classified

With nearly one-fifth of Britain's consumer electronics market, Dixons Group plc ranks among the world leaders in that retail segment. The family of specialty retailers includes 350 Dixons consumer electronics stores, 378 Currys appliance superstores, 26 PC World computer stores, 48 The Link communication equipment stores, and 247 Mastercare service centers. The driving force behind the company's expansion from one small portrait studio was the man who continued to head it in the mid-1990s, Stanley Kalms. Dixons' chairman achieved this stunning growth by entering two fast-growing markets at an early stage in their development: photographic goods in the 1950s and consumer electronics in the 1970s. In both cases, Dixons helped to build these markets in the United Kingdom and grew with them. Also credited with bringing the superstore concept to Britain, Kalms was knighted for ''services to electrical retailing'' in 1996.

Having made an ill-timed entry into the U.S. retail electronics market in the late 1980s, Dixons regrouped in the early 1990s. After the group recovered from after-tax losses in the fiscal years spanning 1992–1993 and 1993–1994, Chairman Kalms declared himself ''very bullish'' on Dixons' future in a 1995 *Management Today* article.

Founded in the 1930s

The retail powerhouse's origins can be traced to the 1930s, when Charles Kalms, a Jewish immigrant from Eastern Europe, founded a portrait photography studio in London. In 1937 he and a friend decided to set up a photographic studio at Southend-on-Sea, not far from London. They incorporated the business as Dixon Studios Ltd., choosing the name Dixon out of a telephone directory in preference to their own. Kalms's friend gave up his share in the business within two years, and Kalms took full control, while continuing to run another business at the same time.

During World War II, when so many men and women were separated from their families, there was a great demand for portrait photographs, and the business flourished. By the end of the war the company had expanded to a chain of seven studios in the London area. After 1945, however, the market contracted as fast as it had grown, and Dixon was reduced to a single studio in the North London suburb of Edgware.

Postwar Expansion into Retailing

In an effort to boost sales, Charles Kalms began to sell cameras and other photographic equipment, and the studio gradually turned into a shop. This changeover gathered pace when Charles Kalms's son Stanley joined the business in 1948. Although only 17, he proved to be a natural salesman with remarkable ambitions. A onetime colleague recalled that Stanley Kalms sold some cameras with great success even before he had discovered how to load the film. The retail side of the business grew quickly, and father and son agreed to concentrate on developing it. By 1953 the company was able to start opening branches again, this time under the name Dixon Camera Centres.

In those early postwar years, few people in Britain could afford to spend much on their hobbies, but interest in photography grew fast. Dixon met this situation by selling new and used goods at attractive prices and by offering credit terms. At an early stage it started advertising, at first in photographic magazines and local papers, then in national newspapers. In this way it built up a large mail order business as well as retail sales. By 1958 it had 60,000 mail order customers, and the shop business had grown to six branches. In that year Dixon moved its head office to larger premises, still in Edgware. The company then employed almost 100 people.

The company showed unusual enterprise in buying as well as selling. In the 1950s the photographic market in the United Kingdom was dominated by British, American, and German manufacturers, and the law at that time allowed manufacturers to dictate the prices at which their products were retailed. This did not suit Dixon's competitive style, and Stanley Kalms began to look elsewhere for manufacturers who would supply him directly at low prices. He began regular buying trips to the Far East and by hard bargaining and bulk buying was able to import goods at prices that enabled Dixon to offer unbeatable value to its customers. In Japan he found manufacturers willing to supply products made to Dixon's specifications. At that time Japanese goods were not highly regarded in Europe, so Dixon marketed the goods under the German-sounding name of Prinz.

Dramatic Growth in the 1950s Culminates in 1962 IPO

By the end of the 1950s incomes in Britain were rising sharply, and the market for photographic goods doubled in value between 1958 and 1963. Camera design was improving, color film prices were falling, and a craze for home-movie kits—camera, projector, and screen—swelled demand. Dixon, having established a reputation for good value and quality, was one of the chief beneficiaries. Its profits rocketed from £6,800 in 1958 to £160,000 in 1962, and in that year the company went public under the new name of Dixons Photographic Ltd. The Kalms family retained voting control, with more than three-quarters of the shares in their hands at this time, but the shares released to the market proved highly popular.

At the time of the stock offering Dixons had only 16 shops, five of them in London, and with the help of the offering it acquired more. Two chains of camera shops, Ascotts, with 13 stores, and Bennetts, Dixons' largest specialty competitor, with 29 branches, were bought in the next two years. Dixons also opened more shops from scratch, including one on a prime site near Marble Arch, London. By the end of 1964 the company had 70 shops and by 1969 it had more than 100.

Growth in profits was more erratic. Retail sales were depressed in some years by government action to restrict credit,

and some of the company's expansionary moves lost money in the short term. In 1967 a large color film processing plant at Stevenage was purchased, the most up-to-date one in Europe at the time; it operated at a loss for a while before making a profit. Dixons also began to manufacture photographic accessories and display material and made substantial losses on this business before abandoning it in 1970.

Increase in Profitability in the 1970s

The key to Dixons' next leap in profits, in the early 1970s, was its move into electronics retailing. This began very cautiously in 1967, when some audio and hi-fidelity units were put on sale in six branches as an experiment. They sold well and were soon introduced into all branches. By 1970 Dixons had introduced its own Prinzsound brand. The next year, television sets were sold experimentally in 25 stores. They, too, were a great success, partly because the recent arrival of color television had created a large television replacement market. After that, Dixons introduced a host of new products in quick succession, including electronic calculators, radio/cassette recorders, music centers, and digital clock/radios. To make room for all these new products, the company had to enlarge its stores. In two consecutive years its total selling space was increased by 30 percent or more.

The effect of these developments on profits was dramatic. From £226,000 in 1970—a bad year—profits soared to £828,000 in 1971, £2.3 million in 1972, and £4.9 million in 1973. The company had established itself in a new market with tremendous growth potential, and its reputation with the investing public, who by this time held the majority of its shares, stood high.

In fact, its next few years proved to be an unhappy period. This was partly because the economic climate changed for the worse in 1974, but chiefly because the company tried to buy its way into other new markets with less positive results.

Forays into Overseas Markets in the 1970s

Dixons started to expand abroad in the early 1970s, at first with success. Through small marketing companies in Sweden and Switzerland, it found valuable new outlets for its own brand of products throughout Europe. In 1972 it bought a large Dutch photographic and optical retail business, G.H. Rinck NV, a company with nearly 60 stores in the Netherlands, compared with Dixons' 150 stores in the United Kingdom at that time. As in Britain, Dixons opened more branches and introduced more products, but the Dutch business never approached the U.K. stores in profitability and for two consecutive years incurred losses.

This experience deterred Dixons from further expansion overseas for some years. Instead, it embarked in 1976 on a new form of expansion in the United Kingdom. With the hope of achieving a large increase in outlets for its goods at one stroke, it bought Weston Pharmaceuticals, a chain of 200 drugstores, for £11 million, together with a wholesale business supplying independent druggists. The idea was to widen Weston's range to include Dixons products, in the same way that Boots, originally a pharmaceutical company, had so successfully broadened its range to include other consumer goods. "Boots must be our model," said Peter Kalms in the *Investors Chronicle* of January 30, 1976 soon after the takeover.

These hopes were never realized. It became apparent within a short time that Weston had serious problems within its existing business and that any major expansion was out of the question. Its profits declined, then turned to losses. Dixons wrestled with Weston's financial problems for four years in an effort to turn it around, but in 1980 decided to recoup what it could of its investment by selling all the drugstores. The wholesale business was kept for some years longer, but seldom produced a substantial profit.

Meanwhile, the struggle to save Weston's retail business had left Dixons with a shortage of working capital, and this had led the company to sell G.H. Rinck in 1978. Thus by 1980 two major investments had come to nothing, and the company's reputation as a growth stock was tarnished. The recession of 1981–1982 delayed Dixons' recovery, with the result that its profits, after discounting inflation, showed no real growth for six years.

Re-Emphasis on Electronics Business in the 1980s

Dixons' main electronics retailing business, however, continued to expand throughout this period. By 1982 the company had raised the number of its stores to 260 and increased their average size. New electronic products were introduced as they were manufactured, including home computers, video recorders, and digital watches. By competitive pricing policies, Dixons won a sizable share of all these new markets. It launched a new house brand, this time with a Japanese name, Saisho. The photographic side of the business also continued to grow; its processing capacity was increased, and a property development unit was established successfully.

All of these investments paid off handsomely once Weston's problems had been left behind and the recession ended. In 1984 Dixons' profits jumped by 46 percent. On the strength of this fresh spurt of growth, the company made its biggest-ever takeover in December of that year. This time it chose a British company with a business closely complementary to its own. Currys Group PLC (Currys) was a chain of 570 shops, selling refrigerators, freezers, washing machines, and electronics, including a television rental business. Although it owned twice as many shops as Dixons, Currys' turnover was no greater, and its recent performance had been less dynamic. Nevertheless, it was a very sound business with a good name, and Dixons had to pay £248 million for it. Kalms would later reflect that it was "one of the deals of the century."

Currys was a much older business than Dixons. It began in Leicester in 1888 as a bicycle shop and, in the cycling boom of the 1890s, manufactured and sold bicycles. When its founder, Henry Curry, retired in 1910, his sons carried on the business—a partnership formed in 1897 as H Curry & Sons—and expanded it greatly. It ceased to manufacture, but developed into a nationwide chain of shops selling cycles, radios, baby carriages, toys, and sporting goods, and became a public company in 1927. The second and third generations of the Curry family continued to manage it, however, until the Dixons takeover. By

that time the company had ceased to deal in cycles and sporting goods, but had become one of the leading retailers of domestic electric appliances of all kinds. The acquisition included Currys' Mastercare service division and the Bridgers chain of discount electronics and appliance stores.

The merger of Dixons and Currys, under the name of Dixons Group, put the company into the top echelon of British retailers. Even after selling the television rental shops, the new company had more than 800 stores in the United Kingdom and its staff had grown to 11,000. Currys retained its separate identity within the company, but its business methods were brought more into line with Dixons'. In the boom conditions of the mid-1980s, the combination brought further large increases in profits.

Flurry of Acquisitions in the Late 1980s

Stanley Kalms, however, was not content even with this empire. In 1986 he launched a bid for Woolworth Holdings, the British branch of Woolworth. The U.S. parent had sold its 52 percent controlling stake in this to a consortium of British investors in 1982, and Woolworth Holdings was still struggling to raise its profits after a long period of stagnation. Kalms believed that Dixons could do the job better, as well as obtain new outlets for its own merchandise. In the end, Dixons' £1.8 billion bid was turned down by the institutional investors who controlled most of Woolworth Holdings' shares.

Thwarted in this plan, Dixons looked around for other investment opportunities. In 1986 it acquired the 340-shop Supersnaps chain, the leading U.K. specialist in retail film processing. Then, in 1987, it made two major acquisitions in the United States, the Silo and Tipton electrical and appliance retailing chains. Silo Inc., with 119 stores and 2,000 employees, was the third largest electrical retailer in the United States and was strong in the East and Midwest. Tipton Centers Inc. was based in St. Louis and had 24 other stores.

With these acquisitions Dixons controlled more than 1,300 stores worldwide, with 3.5 million square feet of selling space. By 1991 it doubled the number of its U.S. outlets, gaining a presence on the West Coast as well, and the worldwide store total had risen to nearly 1,450.

But size did not necessarily equate with success. Dixons' pretax profits peaked at £103 million in 1988, and when recession softened the consumer electronics market, profits started to decline. As a result, Dixons found itself at the receiving end of a takeover bid in 1989. The bidder was none other than Woolworth, by then renamed Kingfisher, a company that had made a strong recovery since its 1986 financial difficulties. Dixons was saved from this threat by the Monopolies and Mergers Commission, which ruled that Dixons and Kingfisher as a unit would have an excessive share of the electrical goods market. Kalms later estimated that the two companies wasted £40 million in fees on the bid and counter bid.

The 1990s and Beyond

The Silo acquisition proved, as one analyst put it, "disastrous," racking up millions in losses under Dixons' management. In 1993, the U.K. parent sold the chain to America's

Fretter Inc. in exchange for a 30 percent stake in the acquiring company. Dixons also divested its Supersnaps subsidiary to Britain's Sketchley plc during this period.

Hoping that it had stanched the flow of red ink, Dixons refocused on the domestic market, acquiring Vision Technology Group Ltd. (VST) in 1993. VST had been formed just two years prior via the amalgamation of several mail order computer companies in 1991. The merged firms opened their first retail outlet, PC World Superstore, that same year, offering computers, peripherals, software, and accessories. Following the acquisition, Dixons divested VST's mail order operation and concentrated on a dramatic expansion of the four-store chain. By the end of 1996, there were 25 PC World outlets throughout the United Kingdom. Dixons also hatched a new member of the retail family in 1994, launching The Link stores, specializing in retail communications services and products. By the end of 1995, this new chain boasted 48 outlets throughout the United Kingdom.

After four decades at the helm, a sexagenarian Stanley Kalms began to relinquish many of the day-to-day operations of his retail empire to a new CEO, John Clare, in the late 1980s and early 1990s. Remaining as chairman, Kalms continued to oversee strategy. Although earnings remained fairly flat at £1.9 billion in the early 1990s, pretax profit rose from £76.7 million in fiscal 1992–1993 to a record £135.2 million in fiscal 1994–1995.

Principal Subsidiaries

Dixons Stores Group Limited; Mastercare Limited; Dixons Commercial Properties International Limited.

Principal Divisions

Dixons; Currys; PC World; The Link; Mastercare.

Further Reading

Cope, Nigel, "The Vogue for Looking Good," *Management Today,* October 1993, pp. 68–71.

Davidson, Andrew, "Stanley Kalms," *Management Today,* January 1995, pp. 38–41.

"Dixons a Powerhouse in U.K. & U.S.," *Discount Store News,* May 6, 1991, p. 96.

Fallon, James, "Dixons Fights Takeover Bid: Silo Pretax Net Dives 86.4 Percent," *HFD-The Weekly Home Furnishings Newspaper,* January 29, 1990, pp. 105–106.

Hisey, Pete, "Silo Decides Its Future Is Better with Fretter," *Discount Store News,* October 4, 1993, pp. 1–2.

"Silo's $326 Million Loss Drags Dixons Down," *Television Digest,* July 13, 1992, pp. 13–14.

—John Swan
updated by April Dougal Gasbarre

Dominion Homes, Inc.

5501 Frantz Road
Dublin, Ohio 43017-0766
U.S.A.
(614) 761-6000
Fax: (614) 761-6899

Public Company
Incorporated: 1952 as Borror Construction Co.
Employees: 328
Sales: $175.5 million (1996)
Stock Exchanges: NASDAQ
SICs: 1521 Single-Family Housing Construction; 8712 Architectural Services; 5039 Construction Materials, Not Elsewhere Classified; 5023 Home Furnishings

Headquartered in a suburb of Columbus, Ohio, Dominion Homes, Inc. (known as Borror Corporation until May 1997) is one of the metropolitan area's largest builders of single-family homes. *Builder* magazine listed it 53rd among the nation's top home builders in its 1996 ranking. Borror's more than 20 percent share of the Columbus area's housing construction market ranked second only to M/I Schottenstein Homes Inc.'s estimated 25 percent stake. The dominance of these two companies has helped to make the 40-community metropolitan region one of the nation's most highly consolidated markets. Analyst Ken Danter told *The Columbus Dispatch* that the competitive structure of the city's home construction market was unique, noting, ''I don't know of another market where two builders combine for [nearly] 50 percent of the market.''

Family owned until its 1994 initial public offering, the residential construction company built and sold nearly 1,200 homes in 1996. Founder Donald Borror and his three children continued to control about two-thirds of the company's stock into the late 1990s. A brisk residential construction market saw Borror's closing rate increase from 708 in 1992 to 1,138 in 1994, but rising interest rates and intense local competition helped push the firm into a $3.5 million loss in 1995. Borror's 1996 net recovered to a near-record $4 million in 1996. The company planned a major image shift in 1997, moving to phase out the Borror Corporation name in favor of Dominion Homes, the designation of its most popular line of custom-built homes.

In 1996, Borror offered three classes of homes and more than 30 floor plans within its Dominion line. Entry-level Century homes priced from $95,000 to $130,000 made up 60 percent of sales. Move-up homes in the Celebrity class were priced from $125,000 to $180,000 and made up about 30 percent of sales. Tradition homes priced at $180,000 and above constituted about ten percent of sales. Borror's average sale price stood at $144,900 in 1996, up from $140,000 in 1994.

Postwar Origins

The company was founded in 1952 by Donald A. Borror. Son of an electrician, Borror was then working for a local building materials company and studying law at Ohio State University. The first house he built was apparently his own, but it was not long before he was putting up five homes per year. By the early 1960s, the Borror Construction Co. had branched out into multifamily developments and even some commercial construction. Its building interests would remain focused on the apartment market throughout the 1960s and 1970s.

Borror pursued dual careers in the 1970s. His namesake company dabbled in everything from apartments and condominiums to advertising, a lumberyard, and West Virginia coal mining. Then, in 1971, Borror was appointed president of Beasley Investments, the real estate division of Beasley Industries, Inc. Named for Fred R. Beasley, the parent company's interests included remanufacturing of automotive and heavy equipment parts for the Ford Motor Co.; car dealerships; gas, oil, and coal production; warehousing; and home-building. Donald Borror became the head of this $20 million, public company following the death of the founder in the late 1970s. Not surprisingly, the new leader brought Beasley's construction interests to the fore, concentrating less and less on its other businesses as the years went by. Beasley Homes focused on the entry-level home and condominium market, while the separately held Borror Co. continued to pursue multifamily projects.

1980s Bring Shift in Emphasis

In 1984, Borror acquired a controlling stake in Beasley, took it private, and merged it with his own interests to create Borror Corp. Donald's son, Doug, joined the family business as general manager of multifamily housing in 1979, having earned a degree in history from Ohio State University just two years before. As Donald Borror told *Business First-Columbus*'s Melissa Widner in 1986, his son focused squarely on expansion. "The real impetus [for growth] came when Doug joined the company. He's the one that juiced us up." The younger Borror spurred an increase in the multifamily segment from $600,000 revenues in 1980 to $20 million in 1985. He advanced to executive vice-president of the parent company in 1985 and ascended to the presidency two years later.

In the meantime, Borror also expanded its single-family residential group under the Beasley Homes division. Early in the decade, the subsidiary established Dominion Homes to build single-family homes in Raleigh, North Carolina. By mid-decade, Beasley also was generating annual revenues of $20 million.

Borror's generational leadership shift was reflected in a multifaceted corporate transition in the late 1980s. During this period, the company gradually sold off its non-real estate interests, choosing a single industry focus over the counter-cyclical benefits of diversification. The corporation also abandoned its geographic expansion into east coast markets in favor of a concentration on the fast-growing local market. At the same time, taxation and demographic issues fueled a shift in emphasis from the rather limited multifamily segment of the building industry to the larger, faster-growing single-family home segment. As the baby boomer generation moved into the prime earnings age bracket, demand for larger, so-called "move-up" homes grew substantially. In line with this trend, the company phased out the Beasley line of affordable housing by 1989 in favor of entry-level residences under the Dominion Homes trademark.

Rising interest rates, a scarcity of prime lots, and a tight lending market helped force Borror to form an allegiance with key competitor M/I Schottenstein Homes Inc. in the late 1980s. While remaining independent of one another, the two companies would continue to cooperate where feasible in the years to come.

The 1990s and Beyond

Despite industrywide challenges, Borror managed to more than double its sales from an estimated $37 million in 1987 to $93.8 million by 1992, as closings on houses increased from 452 in 1989 to more than 700 in 1992. Douglas Borror advanced to chief executive officer of the company in the latter year. Under his leadership, the firm placed a strong emphasis on customization. In 1992, the company set up a decorating shop so that customers could choose carpeting, cabinetry, flooring, and other finishing touches. Later in the decade, the company began to offer homes especially designed and equipped for persons with disabilities. The company also made home-office and cable wiring standard equipment in all new construction.

As it had in the past, demography continued to drive Borror's strategy in the 1990s. With the baby boomer generation moving into "empty nest" stage, Borror re-entered the condominium market in 1993, after a seven-year absence.

Although 1994 was the nationwide single-family housing industry's best year since 1986, rising interest rates, which increased by 2.5 points over the course of the year, and intense competition helped to burst Borror's bubble in 1994. Sales increased nearly 73 percent from $93.8 million in 1992 to $161.9 million in 1994, but the builder's net slid almost 63 percent, from a high of $5.4 million in 1993 to less than $2 million in 1994. Regional competition was so hot that Ryland Homes, the country's third largest home builder, announced that it would begin to phase out its Columbus operations. Borror's stock declined more than 57 percent over the year, from its initial public offering of $11.50 to $5 at December 1994. Although these were admittedly steep declines, some analysts gave the company credit for sacrificing profits to maintain its market share.

The local situation worsened in 1995, when rising costs and competitive discounting continued to batter Borror's bottom line. Although the builder's revenues rose ten percent to $178.1 million, it recorded a net loss of nearly $3.5 million on the year. Not surprisingly, the company's stock price slid as well, declining to a low of $3 during the year. In an effort to return to productivity, Borror reduced its inventories of land and speculative (not under contract) housing, and embarked on a cost-cutting program. A key element of the corporation's efficiency efforts was its adoption of a single corporate identity, Dominion Homes. The image shift allowed it to concentrate marketing, advertising, personnel, and purchasing on a single brand identity rather than diffusing these efforts. Aided by the single-family housing industry's best year in a decade, Borror's net recovered to $4 million in 1996 on record unit sales of more than 1,300 homes and condos.

Prospects for the future remained mixed, however. U.S. Housing Markets, a trade analysis group, cited projections that new household formations would increase over the waning years of the decade in its forecast of "a period of relative prosperity for the home-building industry." But Standard & Poor's predicted that rising interest rates would drive down nationwide housing starts by more than eight percent in 1997. The Ohio Company, a "market maker" in Borror's stock, noted that cost controls and debt reduction boded well for the company's performance in 1997.

Further Reading

Blackford, Darris, "Building on Local Success Is Key to Borror's Strategy," *The Columbus Dispatch,* May 3, 1995, pp. 1G, 2G.

Blundo, Joe, "Home Builder Plans To Close Up Shop," *The Columbus Dispatch,* December 21, 1995, p. 1F.

——, "Model Suited to Disabled," *The Columbus Dispatch,* August 27, 1994, p. 5C.

"Borror Corporation: Company Report by The Ohio Company," The Investext Group, October 15, 1996.

Lilly, Stephen, "Home Market Moderates as Interest Rates Increase," *Business First-Columbus,* October 10, 1994, p. 27.

——, "Tighter Credit Hammers Market for Real Estate," *Business First-Columbus,* October 15, 1990, pp. 1, 40.

Mollard, Beth, "Dicey Market Spurs Builders To Join Forces," *Business First-Columbus,* September 19, 1988, pp. 1, 39.

Otolenghi-Barga, Carol, "Growing Dad's Company," *Business First-Columbus,* February 13, 1995, pp. 29–30.

Porter, Phil, "Borror Corp. Sells Final Piece of Beasley Empire," *The Columbus Dispatch,* August 2, 1993, p. 1C.

Shook, Carrie, "Interest Rates Drive Down Home Builder Stocks," *Business First-Columbus,* January 16, 1995, p. 6.

Standard & Poor's Industry Surveys, New York: Standard and Poor's Corporation, October 31, 1996.

U.S. Housing Markets, "U.S. Home Builders Match Production to Household Growth; Period of Steady Construction Seen for Next Five Years," http://www.housingUSA.com/ushm/pr/hhpr0196.html.

——, "Weather Cools 4th Quarter Housing Construction, But Records Fall," http://www.housingUSA.com/ushm/pr/flash496pr.html.

Widner, Melissa, "The Book of Borror," *Business First-Columbus,* January 27, 1986, pp. 3S, 6S.

Wolf, Barnet D., "Rising to the Top: Borror Customizes Empire To Keep Up with Consumer Demands," *The Columbus Dispatch,* August 16, 1993, pp. 1S, 2S.

—April Dougal Gasbarre

Dow Jones & Company, Inc.

World Financial Center
200 Liberty Street
New York, New York 10281
U.S.A.
(212) 416-2000
Fax: (212) 416-4348
Web site: http://www.dowjones.com

Public Company
Incorporated: 1930
Employees: 11,800
Sales: $2.48 billion (1996)
Stock Exchanges: New York
SICs: 2711 Newspaper Publishing & Printing; 2721
    Periodicals Publishing & Printing; 7375 Information
    Retrieval Services; 7383 News Syndicates

Dow Jones & Company, Inc., is best known for publishing *The Wall Street Journal* in its U.S., Asian, and European versions and for the worldwide stock market intelligence it provides. Like much of the business-journalism industry, Dow Jones has diversified from print to on-line newspapers and information retrieval. The company's three main product divisions are information services, business publications, and community newspapers. While business information and journalism have been the core of Dow Jones in the past, electronic publishing that packages a range of financial information services and community newspaper segments are its future.

Company Origins

The popular reputation of Dow Jones & Company as one of the leading publishers of business news, information services, and community newspapers came nearly a generation after the founding fathers, Charles Henry Dow and Edward Jones, came to New York City from Rhode Island in 1879 with a liking for journalism and an ear for financial gossip. In their own day the two men were not especially well known outside trade circles.

Dow had worked for a number of newspapers before moving to New York City, where he teamed up with Edward Jones and Charles Bergstresser to found Dow, Jones & Company in 1882. In 1885 Dow became a member of the New York Stock Exchange, where he formulated what would be called the Dow theory of stock market movements. He launched *The Wall Street Journal* in the summer of 1889 with Jones, a fellow journalist. Knowledge of the very earliest years of the company is sketchy.

Dow is said to have traded only infrequently on the exchange and to have taken his seat as a favor to a friend in immigration difficulties. Yet Dow's membership put him in a good position to observe the exchange and to overhear tips. Dow apparently wrote most of the copy for the early issues of *The Journal,* working only part-time at the newspaper, while Edward Jones edited the news-bulletin service and acted as managing editor. Reporters Thomas Woodlock and Charles M. Bergstresser covered Wall Street. Many of Dow's early articles were editorials, and information gleaned by Jones in the hotel bars formed the core of the news service.

Dow and Jones joined in a news-exchange agreement with Clarence Barron, the proprietor of the Boston News Bureau. Barron had begun to publish a financial newspaper in Boston two years before *The Wall Street Journal* was founded, and the two offices, *The Journal*'s in New York and Barron's in Boston, reinforced one another's coverage, with the aggressive Barron expanding into Philadelphia with his *Financial Journal* in 1896.

Edward Jones left *The Journal* in January 1899. The family relationship between Dow and his cousin by marriage, Charles Bergstresser, who was also a partner in the firm, might have precipitated Jones's departure. Jones continued to live a good life on Wall Street, and his eulogy of Dow three years later was respectful and even loving, calling his former partner a "tower of strength" and one of "the most honest exponents" of financial journalism.

In 1900 the stockholders of Dow Jones, members of the Dow and Bergstresser families, and a few company employees received $7,500 each in addition to $1.20 a share in annual dividends. In March 1902 Clarence Barron purchased Dow,

Jones & Company—including the news agencies in Boston and New York and *The Wall Street Journal*—for $130,000. Dow and Bergstresser resigned their directorships. There was no public announcement, only the appearance of names for the first time on *The Journal*'s masthead. Although Barron had bought the company, he listed Dow, Bergstresser, Woodlock, and J.W. Barney, not himself. In December of the same year, Charles Dow died of a heart attack at age 51 in his Brooklyn home.

In 1905 Charles Otis was elected president, and F.A. Russell was named to the board of directors. Both Jessie Barron, Barron's wife, and Sereno Pratt were reelected directors of the company, and John Lane and Hugh Bancroft were added to the board.

Bancroft and the Barrons's daughter, Jane, married in 1907, and when Clarence Barron became ill, his son-in-law assumed increasing responsibilities in the New York offices. By 1911 the elder Barron's health had improved, but newspaper circulation, advertising, and profits were down, which precipitated a bitter quarrel between Barron and Charles Otis. Barron also fought with Bancroft and soon drove out president Otis and director Sereno Pratt. On March 12, 1912, he reinstated himself in their places.

When Clarence Barron stormed into the editorial office of *The Journal* in March 1912 following his election to the presidency, the staff was terrified. Though lore has it that Barron harassed some employees into quitting, he is said to never have fired a man. A flamboyant, eccentric, and corpulent figure, Barron's genius for journalism, according to his contemporaries, along with his tough mindedness, drove the ensuing prosperity of the publication.

The Great Depression and the Wartime Years

In 1921 Barron hired Kenneth Craven (Casey) Hogate, a second-generation newspaperman. Later in 1921 Clarence Barron died, leaving an estate of $1.5 million to his daughter Jane Bancroft, who in 1918, at her mother's death, had inherited the majority shares. Hugh Bancroft was elected president and Casey Hogate vice-president. Bancroft and Hogate managed a steadily prospering company until the stock market crash of 1929, when the paper began to sustain severe losses in circulation and advertising.

By 1932 the company had dropped the comma in its name. Despite the Great Depression, on June 27, 1932, Dow Jones & Company published an 80-page edition of the paper celebrating

its 50th anniversary and its new building on Broad Street. Although Hugh Bancroft's name continued to be listed as president, Casey Hogate was chiefly responsible for running the company in the Depression era, as Bancroft's health deteriorated.

In 1938 Richard Whitney—former president of the New York Stock Exchange, whose name was synonymous with the careless profiteering accused of causing the stock market crash—provided *The Journal* with a significant scoop when he telephoned the newsroom and confessed fraud before turning himself in to authorities. In the post-crash years, *Journal* editorials defended the financial community and free enterprise and supported the formation of the Securities and Exchange Commission and regulatory legislation while condemning Whitney's behavior and Wall Street fraud. Hogate, meanwhile, struggled with a low in circulation in 1938 of 28,000.

About this time, with Barney Kilgore as president and William Kerby and Buren McCormack as directors in the company, Hogate took a risk with *The Journal* in order to revive the paper. He moved from strictly financial reports to include general news as well. Though Hogate fell into ill health, his formula worked, and his policy was carried out by the others. Kilgore, meantime, made the decision to produce the Monday morning paper on Sunday instead of Saturday so that the news would be fresh.

Throughout the war years *The Journal* became increasingly news oriented, as political and economic news became inextricably mixed with the fate of the markets. Although at the beginning the editorials were staunchly antiwar, even isolationist, the editorial policy became supportive in due course. After the armistice the trend toward news orientation, developed during the war years, remained with the paper.

Developments in the '50s, '60s, and '70s

On December 21, 1949, Jane Bancroft, the last of the original Barron family, died in Boston. Throughout her life Jane Bancroft had been involved deeply in the growth of the paper, and her last acts had been to create an employee profit-sharing pension plan and to approve the postwar reorganization of Dow Jones.

Bancroft's daughter, Jane Cook, assumed her mother's place on the board, and before the end of 1949 treasurer William Kerby drafted the new Dow Jones management chart, with Kilgore as president and chief executive officer. At this time the company portfolio included the Dow Jones News Service (in the United States and Canada); a commodity news service; *The Journal,* with editions in New York, Dallas, and San Francisco; and *Barron's,* a weekly periodical that continued to struggle with lagging circulation until 1955, when editor Robert Bleiberg turned the situation around. In the 1950s *The Journal*'s layout was modernized, using more two-column heads and readers' letters, cartoons, and drawings. In 1953 new equipment was used to set stock and bond quotations, which made it possible eventually to publish simultaneous editions of the newspaper, with identical news content and typographical quality, anywhere in the United States.

The Journal's long-standing conservative editorial stance was disrupted when it supported the U.S. Supreme Court's decision in Brown vs. Board of Education, the historic civil rights case of 1954. Kilgore stayed at the helm of *The Journal* through John F. Kennedy's presidency, and the paper's editorial policies continued to take on issues of widespread social consequence. *The Journal* reporters, too, became increasingly well known to political leaders. Notoriety was good for business. In 1961 circulation came close to 800,000, with total advertising revenues of $47.7 million. The estimated value of Dow Jones stock was $235 million.

Technology moved the paper forward into the information services industry. By the 1960s facsimile pages of newspapers could be transmitted by coaxial cables and microwave transmitters. By the end of 1964 Dow Jones reported news-ticker clients in 676 U.S. cities and 48 of the 50 states. This business provided the company with the highest revenue after *The Journal*. With the advice of professional portfolio managers, the company began to move further into allied industries, venturing, for example, into textbooks with its purchase of Richard D. Irwin Inc. in 1975.

The change of leadership traditionally had been smooth at the company helm, and so it was when Kilgore handed over the reins to William Kerby in March 1966. Under the new management Vermont Royster directed editorial policy, and executive editor Warren Phillips headed news operations. Within two years the newspaper operation produced 94 percent of Dow Jones's profits, and it reached 1.5 million readers by 1978, when Warren Phillips became chairman, president, and chief executive officer. Dow Jones's operation of the *National Observer* never took off, and it ceased publication in 1977, when losses totaled $16.2 million after 15 years of existence. Its purchase of *Book Digest* magazine proved to be disappointing. In 1980 the company was reorganized along product lines into seven divisions under Phillips. While the main product lines had remained steady for nearly a century, revenue potential favored electronic publishing and information services, not the slow-growth textbook and community newspaper segments.

Transition to Electronic Publishing in the 1980s

After being the company's most lucrative business for a century, *The Journal* began to lose strength during the late 1980s, and electronic publishing became Dow Jones's primary growth sector. *The Journal*'s circulation fell from its 1983 high of 2.11 million to 1.95 million in 1989, a decrease of 7.5 percent. In March 1989 advertising revenues were down for the 19th straight month. For the first quarter of 1989, operating income of business publications fell 33 percent, and profits were down 13 percent in its community newspaper chain. The company had been through difficult times before, but the volatility of the world political and financial scene was changing the financial journalism business. The marketplace was placing increasing emphasis on user-friendly, computerized, fast-news delivery. Phillips, observers said, needed to bring *The Journal* in line with the "real time" requirements of fast-breaking financial news.

The October 1987 stock market crash also had a negative impact on *The Journal*'s financial advertisement revenue. Phillips countered flat revenues by revamping the look of *The Journal*, expanding it from two to three sections. But all at Dow Jones was not bad. In 1989 *American Demographics*, owned by the company, reported a 10 percent growth in revenues and

circulation. The European and Asian editions of *The Wall Street Journal* reported modest growth in circulation, *Barron's* reported steady circulation, and the *Far Eastern Economic Review* and *National Business Employment Weekly* were holding their own. Dow Jones also acquired Telerate, a real-time quote service, and sold its textbook division, Richard D. Irwin, for $135 million. The start-up of Telerate's foreign-exchange trading service accounted for some of Dow Jones's downturn in earnings in 1989 and 1990. In 1997 the company sold *American Demographics* and its associated publications to Cowles Media.

Dow Jones News/Retrieval, a market leader in on-line data bases, was one of several businesses the company brought together to form the Information Group, which grew to 835 employees and $177 million in revenues by 1989. The Information Group had developed an innovative on-line searching system that made Dow Jones's electronic database more accessible than those of its closest competitors. The major problem with the electronic publishing business had been executives' reluctance to learn computer access codes in order to gain information. Dow Jones's system delivered the information to subscribers automatically. The Dow Jones system ranked and weighed articles by the number of times the user's access term occurred, delivering a text search with more specific targeting capability rather than a lengthy list of peripherally related articles.

Another information service owned by the company was the Dow Jones News Service, called the Broadtape, which supplied information to brokerages, banks, investment houses, and corporations. *Professional Investor Report* was started in 1987 as a companion product to the Broadtape, focusing on daily trading activity, and it became profitable in its second full year of operation, with a reported 29 percent growth in subscribers. The Dow Jones News Service changed its name to Dow Jones Newswires in 1996. Other company services included Dow-Vision, launched in 1990 as a customized newswire merging information from several data bases; and DowPhone, a subscription-based telephone information service for investors, providing stock quotes, news reports, and investment analysis. JournalPhone was a 900-number (pay per call) installation derivative of DowPhone offering business and financial news updates. Dow Jones Voice Information Network was the satellite delivery system that provided customized news and information to about 75 voice-service providers.

Changes in the 1990s

During this transition to electronic publishing, Phillips retired from his company positions, first as chief executive officer in January 1991 and then as chairman the following July. Peter R. Kann—a 25-year veteran of the newspaper whom Phillips appointed publisher of *The Journal*, as well as president and chief operating officer of Dow Jones & Company—became the new chairman and chief executive officer.

By 1990, with a multiplicity of news-service products and its acquisition of Telerate, Dow Jones had positioned itself in the global financial market to expand into intercultural databases. Telerate's foreign exchange operation was the highest risk, most intensely competitive of such ventures. There were about a dozen other Telerate products, including SportsTicker, a sports news service. In 1994 Dow Jones sold an 80 percent share of its successful SportsTicker enterprise to the sports network ESPN. But Dow Jones & Company faced many other challenges during the early and mid-1990s, not the least of which was relatively stagnant growth in its *Wall Street Journal* subscriber base. New ventures, moreover, met with mixed success. In 1993 the company, in alliance with the Hearst group, launched the successful magazine *Smart Money*. In 1994 Dow Jones and American City Business Journals launched *BIZ*, a monthly magazine for small business. *BIZ* was discontinued in 1995.

Hoping to strengthen its television presence, Dow Jones launched Asia Business News (ABN) in November 1993 and European Business News (EBN) in February 1995. In partnership with ITT Corp., Dow Jones announced plans in 1996 to purchase the New York television station WNYC from New York City for $207 million. With the acquisition complete, the partnership launched a combination business and sports channel, named WBIS+, in January 1997. Later that year Dow Jones and ITT agreed to sell WBIS+ to Paxson Communications for $257.5 million.

In 1996, despite heavy criticism, Dow Jones promised to spend $650 million on its lagging Telerate service. Dow Jones's first major move to invigorate its market share was to rename the service Dow Jones Markets. Kenneth L. Burenga, company and *Wall Street Journal* president, was appointed chief executive officer of Dow Jones Markets.

The press, market analysts, and even investors were critical of such a large reinvestment in the information delivery service, which had been quickly losing market share to competitors. Though the policy of the Bancroft family had long been that of noninterference with Dow Jones operations, partly to protect the editorial integrity of its news publications, a few of the younger generation of Barron heirs, including the executive director William Cox III, began to ask questions and make demands of their investments. Cox later resigned.

Despite rumors that Dow Jones could be subject to takeover, the vote-controlling segment of family ownership (the family owned 30 percent of total shares and 70 percent of vote-controlling shares) stood behind the management's $650 million decision. Though the company's earnings would slip because of the reinvestment, Dow Jones was committed to its on-line market, hoping that long-term earnings potential would outlive any short-term squabbles among investors. To shore up this potential, Dow Jones formed an alliance with Microsoft to upgrade the PC software for Dow Jones Markets.

Subscriber base for *The Wall Street Journal* had been stagnant throughout much of the 1990s, but ad lineage had increased overall. Still, high newsprint prices cut into profits for the paper until 1996, when advertising lineage increased 13.9 percent, circulation increased slightly, and newsprint prices leveled off. Perhaps more significantly for Dow Jones was the early success of *Wall Street Journal Interactive*, the internet

edition of the venerable paper. The interactive edition was launched in April 1996, and with over 70,000 subscribers by early 1997, it was the largest paid publication on the internet (where consumers were accustomed to accessing information for free).

The Wall Street Journal, however, suffered a setback in 1997, when a federal jury in Houston found the paper guilty of libel and ordered them to pay $223 million in damages to MMAR Group Inc., a failed investment company. The suit was filed shortly after MMAR folded. MMAR claimed that *The Journal* had committed libel while describing MMAR's difficulties with a major client. But *The Journal* did not agree. "We were chronicling the difficulties of this company," said managing editor Paul Steiger. "We did not cause them."

In the late 1990s, despite criticism that it had stagnated somewhat and was no longer capable of making good, quick decisions in the modern marketplace, Dow Jones was a profitable company that had expanded impressively into electronic publishing. It remained, moreover, a respected source of business information and traditional journalism, areas that had established its core business identity from the days of Dow, Jones, and Bergstresser.

Principal Subsidiaries

Dow Jones Markets; Dow Jones Newswires; Barron's; Ottaway Newspapers, Inc.

Further Reading

Bernicker, Mark, "ESPN Buys 80% of SportsTicker," *Broadcasting & Cable,* November 14, 1994, p. 47.

Brown, Rich, "Countdown to WBIS Debut; Just What the Focus of New Dow Jones ITT Station Will Be Remains Unclear," *Broadcasting & Cable,* August 5, 1996, p. 62.

Carvell, Tim, "Family Disunion at Dow Jones: The Owners Are Restless," *Fortune,* February 17, 1997, p. 25.

Chakravarty, Subatra N., "Fortune's Wheel," *Fortune,* February 10, 1997, p. 16.

Cohen, Jodi B., "Online Early and Still Going," *Editor & Publisher,* November 16, 1996, p. 26.

Hackney, Holt, "Dow Jones: More Than the Journal," *Financial World,* July 4, 1995, p. 22.

King, Angela G., "Dow Jones Financial News Service Decision Draws Controversy," *Knight-Ridder/Tribune Business News,* February 26, 1997, p. 226B1059.

King, Angela G., "Dow Jones to Pump $650 Million into Troubled Telerate Service," *Knight-Ridder/Tribune Business News,* January 21, 1997, p. 121B1060.

"More Bad News for Dow Jones," *Time,* March 31, 1997, p. 64.

Saloman Jr., R. S., "The Outdated Dow Jones," *Forbes,* April 7, 1997, p. 132.

—Claire Badaracco
updated by Terry Bain

The Dun & Bradstreet Corporation

One Diamond Hill Road
Murray Hill, New Jersey 07974
U.S.A.
(908) 665-5000
Fax: (908) 665-5524
Web site: http://www.dnb.com

Public Company
Incorporated: 1933 as R.G. Dun-Bradstreet Corporation
Employees: 16,000
Sales: $2.1 billion (1996)
Stock Exchanges: New York London Tokyo Geneva
    Zurich Basel
SICs: 2741 Miscellaneous Publishing; 6289 Services for
    Security Exchanges, Not Elsewhere Classified; 7323
    Credit Reporting Services; 8741 Management Services

The Dun & Bradstreet Corporation is in the information business. Among its vast array of products are Yellow Pages advertising, the Moody's manuals for investors, and business to business credit information. Begun as a credit-reporting service a century and a half ago, Dun & Bradstreet is still a leader in that field. In addition, the company supplies information-dissemination technology, commercial credit reports, analytical risk-assessment services, and small-business pension plans.

Company Origins

Dun & Bradstreet traces its origin to Lewis Tappan, who in 1841 left Arthur Tappan & Company (a New York silk trading firm that he ran with his elder brother) to found a credit information bureau called the Mercantile Agency. Tappan had long been aware of the need for better credit reporting. As the borders of the United States expanded westward, traders were moving beyond the easy view of the East Coast merchants and bankers who kept them supplied and capitalized. Information on the creditworthiness of these far-flung businesses was collected by individual trading houses and banks in a scattershot fashion,

and Tappan saw that centralizing the process of collecting information would result in greater efficiency. Accordingly, he took out an advertisement in the *New York Commercial Advertiser* on July 20, 1841, and opened shop 11 days later on the corner of Hanover and Exchange streets in Manhattan.

The Mercantile Agency operated by gathering information through a network of correspondents and selling it to subscribers. The agents were attorneys, cashiers of banks, merchants, and other competent persons—anyone who might have an impartial familiarity with local merchants through business or civic affairs. Over the years people as famous as U.S. presidents Abraham Lincoln, Ulysses S. Grant, Grover Cleveland, and William McKinley, as well as presidential candidate Wendell Willkie, would serve as agents for the company that Tappan founded.

The Mercantile Agency opened branch offices in Boston in 1843 and Philadelphia in 1845. In 1846 Benjamin Douglass, a young New York businessman with connections in the Southern cotton trade, joined the firm. When Lewis Tappan retired in 1849, Douglass and Tappan's brother, Arthur, ran it as partners until 1854, when the elder Tappan sold out to Douglass. Then, in 1859, Douglass sold out to Robert Graham Dun, who immediately changed the firm's name to R.G. Dun & Company. That year the company published its first reference book of credit information, the *Dun Book*.

As the nation grew and commerce boomed in the decades following the Civil War, Dun had to keep up with it by establishing new branch offices. The firm expanded into the South, west to California, and north into Canada. An office in San Francisco opened in 1869. In 1891 there were 126 Dun branch offices. Robert Dun Douglass, who was Benjamin Douglass's son and Robert Graham Dun's nephew, became general manager of the firm in 1896. After his uncle died in 1900, the company operated as a common-law trust with Douglass in charge as executive trustee. He retired as general manager in 1909 and was succeeded by Archibald Ferguson.

R.G. Dun also began to expand overseas at about this time. The firm opened its first office in London in 1857, and added five more foreign offices—in Glasgow, Paris, Melbourne, Mexico City, and Hamburg—by the turn of the century. From 1901 to 1928 R.G. Dun opened 41 overseas branches, scattered across Europe, South Africa, and Latin America.

Growth and Acquisitions: 1930s to 1980s

In 1931 R.G. Dun acquired National Credit Office (NCO), a credit-reporting service. The firm then reorganized into a holding company called R.G. Dun Corporation, which assumed control of the assets of both NCO and the original R.G. Dun & Company. NCO president and former owner Arthur Dare Whiteside became president of the new entity.

In 1933, at the nadir of the Great Depression, R.G. Dun merged with one of its main competitors, the Bradstreet Company. Since the two companies overlapped each other in many activities and resources, an amalgamation at that time made sense. Bradstreet was founded in Cincinnati, Ohio, in 1849 by John Bradstreet, a lawyer and merchant whose ancestors included Simon Bradstreet, a colonial governor of Massachusetts, and the prominent colonial American poet Ann Bradstreet. A large file of credit information had come into John Bradstreet's possession as he was overseeing the liquidation of an estate, and he decided to enter the same business in which Lewis Tappan had pioneered eight years earlier. In 1855 Bradstreet packed up and moved to New York, where he challenged the Mercantile Agency directly. Two years later the firm started publishing a semiannual reference book that offered more extensive coverage than the early *Dun Book.*

John Bradstreet died in 1863 and was succeeded by his son, Henry, who ran the firm until it incorporated in 1876 under the name the Bradstreet Company. A group headed by Charles F. Clark then ran the company until 1904, when Clark died and was succeeded by Henry Dunn. Dunn retired in 1927 and gave way to Clark's son, Charles M. Clark. The younger Clark was still chief executive when Bradstreet merged with Dun in 1933. The new company changed its name to R.G. Dun-Bradstreet Corporation and then to Dun & Bradstreet, Inc., in 1939.

Business remained slow for Dun & Bradstreet through the 1930s and during World War II and then picked up again after the war ended. In 1942 the company acquired Credit Clearing House, a credit-reporting agency that specialized in the clothing industry. In 1962 Arthur Dare Whiteside retired and was succeeded by J. Wilson Newman, who headed Dun & Bradstreet as president until 1960 and then as chairman and chief executive until 1968. Under Newman, Dun & Bradstreet embarked on a course of expansion and technological improvement. In 1958

the company began operating its own private wire network, which linked 79 of its major offices. This allowed credit information to be handled more expeditiously.

In 1961 Dun & Bradstreet acquired the Reuben H. Donnelley Corporation. Donnelley, best known for publishing the Yellow Pages telephone directories, was founded in Chicago in 1874 and also published trade magazines. The next year Dun & Bradstreet acquired Official Airline Guides and added it to the Donnelley division. The company also acquired Moody's Investors Service, which provided financial data for investors on publicly owned corporations through its series of Moody's manuals.

In 1966 Dun & Bradstreet acquired Fantus Company, which specialized in area development surveys. In 1968 it bought book publisher Thomas Y. Crowell. When Newman retired that year, he was succeeded by former University of Delaware president John Perkins, who served as chairman for one year.

In 1971 Dun & Bradstreet acquired Corinthian Broadcasting, which owned five CBS television affiliates and publisher Funk & Wagnalls. In 1973 the company changed its name to the Dun & Bradstreet Companies Inc. It had acquired some 40 businesses since J. Wilson Newman inaugurated this expansion in 1960 and had seen its annual sales rise from $81 million in 1960 to $450 million in 1973. In 1973 the Dun & Bradstreet Corporation was formed to become the parent company.

In 1978 Dun & Bradstreet acquired Technical Publishing, a trade and professional magazine publisher. The next year it acquired National CSS, an information-processing technology company. In 1983 it diversified into computer software when it acquired McCormack & Dodge, which published systems software for mainframe computers. The next year it cut back a bit on diversification when it spun off Funk & Wagnalls and sold most of its Corinthian Broadcasting television assets to A.H. Belo. The company, however, acquired Datastream, a British business information company, and the market research firm A.C. Nielsen. Nielsen, famous for its television rating service, was founded in Chicago in 1923 by Arthur C. Nielsen Sr. Harrington Drake, chief executive officer of Dun and Bradstreet, was a longtime friend of the Nielsen family, and the two companies had been discussing a merger on and off since 1969.

Divestiture and Acquisitions during the 1990s

Dun & Bradstreet continued restructuring itself—through divestiture and acquisitions—from the late 1980s and into the 1990s. It sold Official Airline Guides to Propwix, an affiliate of British Maxwell Communications, in 1988 and Zytron, Petroleum Information, and Neodata in 1990. Also in 1990 the company announced its intention to sell two divisions of Dun & Bradstreet Software: Datastream International, Ltd., and Information Associates, Inc. The company sold Donnelley Marketing, the IMS communications unit, and Carol Write Sales in 1991.

By 1993, however, Dun & Bradstreet began shifting gears and entering a phase of acquisitions. Through the various divisions of Dun & Bradstreet, the company focused on acquiring smaller, primarily information-based companies. For example, it acquired a majority interest in Gartner Group Inc., an international market research firm, on April 8, 1993. Dun & Bradstreet

Information Services acquired Solidited, a Swedish company that provided commercial-credit information for Scandinavian businesses, on May 12, 1993. Also in 1993 the company formed HealthCare Information Inc. to conduct research in the health care industry, and on February 17, 1994, HealthCare Information acquired Lexecon Health Service Inc.

Acquisitions continued in 1994. A.C. Nielsen acquired two companies: IPSA S.A. (Argentina) and Survey Research Group, Hong Kong. IMS America acquired Emron Inc. and Amfac Chemdata (Australia), and Dun and Bradstreet Information Services purchased Orefro L'Informazione (Italy), S&W (France), and Novinform A.G. (Switzerland) and formed an alliance with Tokyo Shoko Research (Japan). The Dun & Bradstreet Corporation acquired Pilot software, an on-line software company. Also in 1994 Dun & Bradstreet announced that it would be getting out of the magazine-publishing business and in the process ceasing publication of *D & B Reports*.

On January 9, 1996, Dun & Bradstreet announced plans to divide itself into three new publicly traded corporations: Cognizant Corporation, which consisted of IMS International, the Gartner Group, Nielsen Media Research, Pilot Software, and Erisco; the Dun & Bradstreet Corporation, made up of Dun & Bradstreet Information Services, Moody's Investors Service, and Reuben H. Donnelly; and A.C. Nielsen. The Cognizant Corporation was created to focus on such high-growth business segments as health care and media markets. The Dun & Bradstreet Corporation was to continue its historically successful financial information services. A.C. Nielsen was to focus on marketing research in the consumer packaged-goods industry, where it was already the global leader. As part of the reorganization, several Dun & Bradstreet divisions, including Dun & Bradstreet Software Services, Inc. and American Credit Indemnity, were scheduled to be sold.

In 1997 Dun & Bradstreet announced the release of two coding systems designed to simplify the process of making purchases on the internet. The first was the Data Universal Numbering System (DUNS), which employed nine-digit company identification tags. Until then the DUNS system had been used only internally by Dun & Bradstreet. The second release was an internet database of the Standard Products and Service Code (SPSC). This database provided 11-digit codes that identified product types. With the help of the codes, internet users could more easily find companies that provided particular products or services. Although the internet was a new medium for Dun & Bradstreet, its internet products were in line with its traditional mission of providing information and information services.

Principal Subsidiaries

Dun & Bradstreet, Inc.; Moody's Investors Service, Inc.; Reuben H. Donnelley Corporation.

Further Reading

Abrahams, Paul, "Dun & Bradstreet Opts for Divorce," *The Financial Times,* November 1, 1996, p. 26.

Bowen, Ted Smalley, "Dun & Bradstreet Agrees to Acquire Pilot Software," *PC Week,* July 25, 1994, pp. 105–106.

Byrne, John A., "Why D&B is Glued to the Ticker: Wall Street Greets a Breakup Plan with Deafening Silence," *Business Week,* February 19, 1996, pp. 58–59.

Doescher, William F., "A Final Word," *D & B Reports,* March-April 1994, pp. 6–7.

Dun & Bradstreet: A Chronology of Progress, New York: Dun and Bradstreet, Inc., 1974.

Dun & Bradstreet: The Story of an Idea, New York: Dun and Bradstreet, Inc., 1966.

King, Julia, "D&B Software Users Cheer Sell-Off Plan," *Computerworld,* January 15, 1996, p. 4.

Moeller, Michael and Jim Kerstetter, "E-Commerce Grows Up with Aid of D&B, Actra," *PC Week,* March 10, 1997, pp. 1–2.

Pine, Michael, "Dun's Do-Over: Two of Dun & Bradstreet's Three Parts Are Worth More Than the Whole," *Financial World,* July 8, 1996, pp. 44–45.

—Claire Badaracco and Douglas Sun
—updated by Terry Bain

El Chico Restaurants, Inc.

12200 Stemmons, Suite 100
Dallas, Texas 75234
U.S.A.
(972) 241-5500
Fax: (972) 888-8198

Public Company
Incorporated: 1957
Employees: 3,600
Sales: $104.4 million (1996)
Stock Exchanges: NASDAQ
SICs: 5812 Eating Places; 6794 Patent Owners & Lessors

One of the largest Mexican dinner house chains in the United States, El Chico Restaurants, Inc. operates El Chico restaurants throughout the southwestern and southern United States. During the late 1990s, there were approximately 100 units composing the chain. In addition to the company's El Chico units, it also operated a small number of more upscale restaurants under the Cantina Laredo, Cactus, and Casa Rosa banners.

1920s Origins

The history of El Chico restaurants began when the matriarch of the family-operated restaurant empire first cooked for the public. In 1926, Adelaide Cuellar set up a tamale stand at the Kaufman County fair, unwittingly starting a family-operated business that would endure for the remainder of the century. Adelaide Cuellar's first unpretentious steps into the business of selling Mexican food to the public were followed up by her five sons—Willie, Mack, Alfred, Gilbert, and Frank—who began the transformation of the family's tamale stand into a family dynasty by opening an El Chico restaurant in Dallas and incorporating the business in 1940. From this official starting point, the Cuellar-owned and -operated business grew briskly under the stewardship of the five Cuellar brothers.

By the 1960s, the Cuellar brothers had distinguished themselves admirably, particularly Gilbert Cuellar, who had taken charge of the family enterprise. El Chico restaurants flourished during the 1960s, developing into the largest Mexican dinner house chain in the United States and becoming recognizable enough in the corporate world to successfully complete a public offering of stock in 1968. Following the initial public offering, El Chico began offering franchises. "Everybody was franchising so we thought we would too," recalled Gilbert Cuellar, as El Chico quickly attracted individuals interested in operating their own El Chico restaurants. Over the course of four years, Gilbert Cuellar granted 22 franchises, but the move into franchising proved to be an imprudent one, creating a collection of restaurant units that demonstrated poor profitability. Franchising was discontinued in 1972, ending as an entirely unsuccessful venture. "It turned out to be the worst thing we ever did," Cuellar later remarked, "because at the time we weren't equipped to maintain standards." For Cuellar and the rest of his family, however, the worst was yet to come. As lucrative as the 1960s were for El Chico, the 1970s would be equally as disastrous.

1970s Downturn and New Ownership

El Chico entered the 1970s as a pioneer in its industry niche, having tapped a passion for Tex-Mex food strong enough to support a chain of restaurants. The company's role as elder statesman in its industry, however, began to work against it during the 1970s. The Cuellar family had been involved in the restaurant business for nearly four decades. Over the years they maintained a tight grip of control over their enterprise and admitted few non-family members into the company's executive ranks. Few changes were made in the operation of the chain as a result, and the restaurants began to show their age, causing profits and sales to wilt as the El Chico concept grew stale. The affect of the anemic financial performance was sufficient to halt unit expansion entirely by the end of the decade, but before the company completely bottomed out it was acquired by a much larger suitor, thereby ending the lengthy ownership of the Cuellar family.

In 1977, Campbell Taggart, Inc. acquired El Chico, paying more than $20 million for the 79-unit chain. A billion-dollar-in-sales baked goods manufacturer, Campbell Taggart had no prior experience in the restaurant business, but its success as a baked

Company Perspectives:

*"El Chico is committed to provide uncompromising person-
alized service to each guest through superior operational
execution, resulting in increased sales and profits."*

goods manufacturer had necessitated the move into a new
business area. The company had reached its enormous size by
swallowing up competing baked goods companies, eventually
gaining such dominance in its markets that the federal government began to take notice. Campbell Taggart held considerable
sway, reaching 98 percent of all American households with its
baked goods and exerting enough dominance that the Federal
Trade Commission had prohibited the company from completing any more baking acquisitions in the future. Consequently,
the company was on the prowl for acquisitions in other business
areas, and El Chico was selected.

Campbell Taggart executives were not drawn to El Chico
because of its mainstay restaurant chain. Instead, the company
was primarily after the frozen and canned Mexican food business that was part of El Chico. El Chico's frozen and canned
food business, which accounted for one-third of the company's
revenue volume, was performing well, unlike the company's
restaurants, and represented a complementary addition to
Campbell Taggart's pervasive presence in grocery stores and
supermarkets. Campbell Taggart's plans for El Chico's canned
and frozen food business, did not keep it from fostering interest
in the El Chico restaurants. Ambitious plans were developed,
plans that in five years would transform El Chico restaurants
from a regional chain into a national chain, but the plans proved
to be too ambitious and the already floundering restaurant
business deteriorated further.

Campbell Taggart had no experience in the restaurant business before the company acquired El Chico, and after the
acquisition, it made no attempt to hire anyone with the requisite
expertise. Consequently, the combination of aggressive expansion and unqualified management made for a bad mix. In a
17-month span, 20 new El Chico restaurants were opened—the
greatest expansion spree in El Chico's history—but the new
units performed poorly. In their zeal to establish new restaurants, Campbell Taggart executives did not pay proper attention
to site selection and situated new restaurants too far away from
the chain's central commissary in Dallas, which made supplying the new units a costly endeavor. Further, the chain's standards loosened and customer satisfaction dropped, leading to
the inevitable result of declining sales and profits. Already
reeling before being acquired by Campbell Taggart, the El
Chico chain was in serious trouble after three years of imprudent management. By 1980, the restaurant division was a
bothersome drain on profits and desperately in need of sweeping changes.

The inexperience of Campbell Taggart management caused
its most decisive blow after El Chico's financial condition
turned grave. Struggling to revive profits, Campbell Taggart
executives attempted to squeeze greater profits out of the chain

by cutting costs, which lowered the quality of food and service
throughout the chain. In reference to this period in Campbell
Taggart's ownership, a Cuellar family member later remarked
to *Restaurant Business,* "Campbell Taggart was a fine company
with good intentions, but as a manufacturing giant the company's focus was on cost control and management efficiencies,
which unfortunately isn't compatible with operating a chain of
restaurants." Exasperated and struggling to find a solution,
Campbell Taggart executives did what critics had contended the
company should have done in 1977, and hired an executive with
restaurant experience.

Richard Rivera, a senior executive at Steak & Ale, was hired
in November 1980 to lead the charge toward profitability for the
crippled El Chico chain, the first time an experienced restaurant
manager had presided over the chain since Gilbert Cuellar.
Rivera's mood was decidedly upbeat as he assumed control and
assessed the condition of the 40-year old restaurant chain. "The
concept was sound, it always had been," Rivera informed a
Restaurant Business reporter. "All El Chico needed was some
money put into it and some house cleaning done. The company
had a long-standing reputation of being a good value, and I
knew if we could just get operations back up to speed the rest
would take care of itself." Rivera quickly went to work
rebuilding El Chico's image, intent on recultivating customer
loyalty. In the remodeling program that ensued El Chico units
were refurbished at a cost of between $40,000 and $50,000 per
restaurant. Manager training was stressed, employee uniforms
were changed, and the menus, signage, and the El Chico logo
were redesigned.

1982 Divestiture by Campbell Taggart

Gradually, the restaurant chain began to show small signs of
recovery under Rivera's stewardship, but before the full effect
of his changes could be realized, developments beyond Rivera's
control called a halt to the progress. In November 1982—two
years to the month after Rivera's arrival—Campbell Taggart
agreed to be acquired by brewing giant Anheuser-Busch, a
merger that marked the end of El Chico's ownership by Campbell Taggart. For the $570 million merger to occur, the El Chico
restaurant division had to be sold to comply with federal and
state laws prohibiting a brewing company from operating under
a retail license. The frozen and canned food business and the
commissary in Dallas could still remain under Campbell Taggart's control, but the restaurants had to go. Rivera, who felt El
Chico's full recovery was imminent, wanted to continue his
healing work after the Campbell Taggart/Anheuser-Busch
merger and attempted a leveraged buyout of the El Chico
restaurant chain. Rivera failed, but other interested parties were
waiting in the wings. W.R. Grace made an offer for the restaurant division, followed by Pillsbury and General Mills, but these
industry behemoths were outbid by a familiar figure in El
Chico's history: Gilbert Cuellar.

Cuellar, 73 years old at the time, offered $12.6 million for
the business his family had founded, by far exceeding the
amount of all other offers, including the bids submitted by
multi-million-dollar conglomerates. Rivera, who had done
much in a short time to get the El Chico chain pointed in the
right direction, offered his explanation: "Gilbert was in a
unique position. The company had begun turning around, but on

paper it still wasn't profitable. Anyone else who bid on El Chico offered quite a bit less because they weren't involved all along and really couldn't get a handle on the company's true value. Gilbert knew El Chico's potential worth, and knew he could organize a management team to keep the company on track.'' Cuellar made the purchase with the help of a guaranteed personal loan and resumed Cuellar family control over the enterprise, enlisting the help of his son, Gilbert Cuellar, Jr.

Father and son took charge of El Chico following Campbell Taggart's troubled five-year ownership and served together for less than four years. In July 1986, Gilbert Cuellar, Sr. died, leaving his son in control of the nearly half-century old Cuellar business. Under the combined tutelage of the Cuellars several new dining concepts were developed that would consume the company's efforts for the ensuing decade. The oldest of these new concepts was Cactus, a theme restaurant developed under Campbell Taggart's control and slated for expansion under Cuellar management. Featuring mesquite-grilled, half-pound hamburgers and finger foods in a club atmosphere, the three Cactus restaurants in Dallas, Oklahoma City, and Fort Worth depended heavily on liquor sales, generating 45 percent of total sales from alcohol compared to 16 percent generated by El Chico units. Of the three new concepts born in the 1980s, Cactus presented the only genuine opportunity for expansion during the 1980s, at least in the minds of management midway through the decade. Looking ahead, Cuellar, Jr. hoped to open three to four new Cactus units per year, each modeled after a 6,000-square-foot, 220-seat prototype. The other two concepts, Casa Rosa and Cantina Laredo, were related more closely to El Chico restaurants than Cactus. Casa Rosa, which had been opened by Cuellar, Jr. prior to his father's reacquisition of El Chico, operated as an upscale Mexican dinner house in a Dallas suburb and was more expensively appointed than El Chico units. Cantina Laredo, which debuted in late 1984, featured home-style Mexican cuisine using ingredients indigenous to the rural areas of Mexico. Its menu items were spicier than the traditional Tex-Mex fare offered by El Chico and were targeted at both Mexicans and more adventurous Americans. One Cantina Laredo was in operation in Forth Worth, with only limited expansion potential for the future.

Gilbert Cuellar, Jr. pinned considerable hope on the development of new restaurant concepts as a substantial engine for growth during his years of leadership. The El Chico chain, meanwhile, did not regain the strength lost during the 1970s. After its divestiture by Campbell Taggart, the chain was beginning to make encouraging strides but competition was fierce, one of the major differences contrasting El Chico's heyday and the 1980s. The industry niche El Chico had helped to create during the 1940s was heavily populated by the 1980s, its ranks swelled by the broad-based appeal of Tex-Mex and traditional Mexican cuisine. Profitability problems continued to hound the El Chico chain as the decade progressed, leading to a number of restaurant closings during the late 1980s. Despite the anemic performance of some units, El Chico still ranked as a formidable force in its markets, serving nearly 16 million people in an 11-state territory. By 1987, the company's long-held presence in the southwestern and southern regions of the United States was staked out by more than 100 restaurants that generated more than $100 million in revenue each year. Gilbert Cuellar, Jr., El Chico's president, chief executive officer, and chairman,

occupied himself with the development of other restaurant concepts, however. His plans would manifest themselves in a grand fashion as the 1990s began.

1990s Management Shakeup

By early 1991, the number of El Chico restaurants had been whittled to 89, but the biggest news of the year was not the declining number of El Chico units. Instead, the focus was on the other concepts under development by El Chico Corp., the composition of which had been in flux since the mid-1980s. Two of the concepts had endured from the early 1980s, Casa Rosa and Cantina Laredo, and had been joined by Cuellar's Cafe and Lupita's, along with a new concept, scheduled for debut in mid-1991, called Texana Grill. To underscore the importance of these new dining concepts, the company targeted its Cantina Laredo formula as the growth vehicle for the company's future, a designation that for decades had only applied to the El Chico chain, and then management made a startling change. In early 1991, El Chico Corp. changed its name to Southwest Cafes Inc., further committing itself to the strategy embraced by Gilbert Cuellar, Jr. of emphasizing more upscale, higher-ticket dining concepts. Paul Vinyard, a company senior executive, explained the name change, providing a clear idea of where the Cuellar enterprise was headed in the future. ''We did it to reflect that the company is different from what people perceive it to be. We're a lot more than El Chico now.''

Slightly more than a year after the name change, Southwest Cafes' board of directors convened and resolved to fire Gilbert Cuellar, Jr. as chief executive officer. Cuellar's strategy, which had been in effect since the mid-1980s, had shaped the company into a different type of restaurant competitor, a type the board of directors had decided not to become. Instead, the board of directors voted to refocus resources and attention on the company's largest dining concept, the El Chico chain, and deemphasize the company's forays into new, more upscale dining concepts. Referring to Gilbert Cuellar, Jr.'s removal, one industry analyst offered his opinion, ''My impression is that Cuellar liked looking for other concepts. The obvious conclusion is that it cost him his job.''

In the wake of Gilbert Cuellar, Jr.'s dismissal, the search was on for a replacement, as the company once again canvassed for a leader to invigorate the El Chico chain. Several weeks after the power struggle that ended with Cuellar's removal, J. Michael Jenkins was hired as chief executive officer and chairman by the board of directors. Jenkins, who himself had recently been ousted as chief executive officer of Metromedia Steakhouses Inc., confidently declared on his arrival, ''My career is about turnaround and growth,'' and proceeded to demonstrate the validity of his boast.

When he joined the recently rechristened El Chico Restaurants Inc., Jenkins inherited 84 El Chico restaurants. Jenkins added to this total steadily, as he tinkered with designs for the El Chico restaurant of the future. One year after his arrival, Jenkins came out with a smaller restaurant prototype located in Tyler, Texas, that measured 4,900 square feet, compared to 5,700 square feet for the average El Chico unit, but seated the same number of patrons (roughly 190). After the Tyler restaurant opened another similarly sized unit was under construction in

Jackson, Tennessee, with agreements or letters of intent for five other sites in Texas, Tennessee, and Oklahoma.

Jenkins and his management team did not settle on the Tyler prototype as the model for expansion, however. Company executives continued to alter designs and layouts. In 1996, at which time the El Chico chain once again had been built up to 100 units, management believed it had found the answer with a new prototype in Richardson, Texas. The new version was slightly larger than the 1993 prototype, measuring roughly 5,500 square feet, and featured a larger central bar area that offered full-service. The exterior was different from older units as well, sporting a cantina-style facade rimmed in neon. Further changes were found on the menu, which included several new fat-free selections such as Toblano Chicken Salad, UnLite Chicken Fajitas, and Santa Fe Chicken Burrito. With this new unit, Jenkins and his senior executives prepared to move forward with expansion, hoping to bolster sales and profits with newer restaurants as the 21st century drew near. "The newer stores have a lot more appeal," the company's chief financial officer explained, "and we think we've hit the formula that we've been searching for."

Principal Subsidiaries

Pronto Design and Supply, Inc.

Further Reading

"After Writedowns in 1996 El Chico Lists $3.06 Million Loss," *Nation's Restaurant News,* February 24, 1997, p. 12.

Dawson, Barbara Magan, "Poco Prices and Mucho Menu Choices Drive Traffic Jump," *Restaurants & Institutions,* July 24, 1991, p. 111.

Kelly, Frank, "El Chico Looks to History for Future Market Success," *Dallas-Fort Worth Business Journal,* February 9, 1987, p. 8.

Nichols, Don, "Shakeup at Southwest Cafes: El Chico Prevails," *Restaurant Business,* March 1, 1992, p. 28.

Raffio, Ralph, "El Chico's Turnaround Strategy," *Restaurant Business,* January 1, 1985, pp. 97–108.

Ruggless, Ron, "El Chico Flying High as New Unit Prototype Lifts Off in Texas," *Nation's Restaurant News,* July 29, 1996, p. 7.

——, "El Chico Launches Smaller, More Flexible Prototype," *Nation's Restaurant News,* March 15, 1993, p. 47.

——, "El Chico Plotting Strategy to Reverse Sales Declines," *Nation's Restaurant News,* May 13, 1996, p. 3.

Scarpa, James, "El Chico Corrals New Chairman; Jenkins Replaces Cuellar at Southwest Cafes," *Restaurant Business,* March 20, 1992, p. 22.

Van Warner, Rick, "El Chico Scrapping to Reduce Losses," *Nation's Restaurant News,* March 21, 1988, p. 106.

Woodard, Tracey, "El Chico Revamps: Tex-Mex Chain, Image, Repositions Cantina Loredo Concept," *Nation's Restaurant News,* January 21, 1991, p. 3.

—Jeffrey L. Covell

Enron Corporation

1400 Smith Street
Houston, Texas 77002-7369
U.S.A.
(713) 853-6161
Fax: (713) 853-6790
Web site: http://www.enron.com

Public Company
Incorporated: 1930 as Northern Natural Gas Company
Employees: 6,700
Sales: $13.28 billion (1996)
Stock Exchanges: New York Boston Chicago Pacific
    Cincinnati Philadelphia
SICs: 4922 Pipelines, Natural Gas; 5172 Gases; 1311
    Natural Gas Production; 1321 Crude Petroleum
    Products; 2911 Natural Gas Liquids; 4613 Petroleum
    Refining

Enron Corporation is one of the largest integrated natural gas and electricity companies in the world. It markets natural gas liquids worldwide and operates one of the largest natural gas transmission systems in the world, totaling more than 36,000 miles. It is also one of the largest independent developers and producers of electricity in the world, serving both industrial and emerging markets. Enron is also a major supplier of solar and wind renewable energy worldwide, manages the largest portfolio of natural gas-related risk management contracts in the world, and is one of the world's biggest independent oil and gas exploration companies. In North America, Enron is the second biggest buyer and seller of natural gas and the largest nonregulated marketer of electricity. Enron's stated goals are to become the largest retailer of electricity and natural gas in the United States and the largest provider of both in Europe.

Company Origins

Enron began as Northern Natural Gas Company, organized in Omaha, Nebraska, in 1930 by three other companies. North American Light & Power Company and United Light & Rail-

ways Company each held a 35 percent stake in the new enterprise, while Lone Star Gas Corporation owned the remaining 30 percent. The company's founding came just a few months after the stock market crash of 1929, an inauspicious time to launch a new venture. Several aspects of the Great Depression actually worked in Northern's favor, however. Consumers initially were not enthusiastic about natural gas as a heating fuel, but its low cost led to its acceptance during tough economic times. High unemployment brought the new company a ready supply of cheap labor to build its pipeline system. In addition, the 24-inch steel pipe, which could transport six times the amount of gas carried by 12-inch cast iron pipe, had just been developed. Northern grew rapidly in the 1930s, doubling its system capacity within two years of its incorporation and bringing the first natural gas supply to the state of Minnesota.

Public Offering in the 1940s

In the 1940s there were changes in Northern's regulation and ownership. The Federal Power Commission, created as a result of the Natural Gas Act of 1938, regulated the natural gas industry's rates and expansion. In 1941 United Light & Railways sold its share of Northern to the public, and in 1942 Lone Star Gas distributed its holdings to its stockholders. North American Light & Power would hold on to its stake until 1947, when it sold its shares to underwriters who then offered the stock to the public. Northern was listed on the New York Stock Exchange that year.

In 1944 Northern acquired the gas-gathering and transmission lines of Argus Natural Gas Company. The following year, the Argus properties were consolidated into Peoples Natural Gas Company, a subsidiary of Northern. In 1952 Peoples was dissolved as a subsidiary, its operations henceforth becoming a division of the parent company. Also in 1952, the company set up another subsidiary, Northern Natural Gas Producing Company, to operate its gas leases and wells. Another subsidiary, Northern Plains Natural Gas Company, was established in 1954 and eventually would bring Canadian gas reserves to the continental United States.

Through its Peoples division, the parent company acquired a natural gas system in Dubuque, Iowa, from North Central Public

---

Company Perspectives:

Enron's mission is "to become the most innovative integrated natural gas company in North America. After recognizing early on that the natural gas pipeline business was the backbone of the corporation, we concentrated on growing our existing businesses—our exploration and production, gas liquids and cogeneration operations—which best complemented and are complemented by our pipeline activities."

Service Company in 1957. In 1964 Council Bluffs Gas Company of Iowa was acquired and merged into the Peoples division. Northern created two more subsidiaries in 1960: Northern Gas Products Company, now Enron Gas Processing Company, for the purpose of building and operating a natural gas extraction plant in Bushton, Kansas; and Northern Propane Gas Company, for retail sales of propane. Northern Natural Gas Producing Company was sold to Mobil Corporation in 1964, but the parent company continued expanding on other fronts. In 1966 it formed Hydrocarbon Transportation Inc., now Enron Liquids Pipeline Company, to own and operate a pipeline system carrying liquid fuels. Eventually, this system would bring natural gas liquids from plants in the Midwest and Rocky Mountains to upper-Midwest markets, with connections for eastern markets as well.

Growth through Acquisitions

Northern made several acquisitions in 1967: Protane Corporation, a distributor of propane gas in the eastern United States and the Caribbean; Mineral Industries Inc., a marketer of automobile antifreeze; National Poly Products Inc.; and Viking Plastics of Minnesota. Also in 1967, Northern created Northern Petrochemical Company to manufacture and market industrial and consumer chemical products. The petrochemical company acquired Monsanto Corporation's polyethylene marketing business in 1969.

Northern continued expanding during the 1970s. In February 1970 it acquired Plateau Natural Gas Company, which became part of the Peoples division. In 1971 it bought Olin Corporation's antifreeze production and marketing business. It set up UPG Inc., now Enron Oil Trading & Transportation, in 1973 to transport and market the fuels produced by Northern Gas Products. UPG eventually would handle oil and liquid gas products for other companies as well.

In 1976 Northern formed Northern Arctic Gas Company, a partner in the proposed Alaskan arctic gas pipeline, and Northern Liquid Fuels International Ltd., a supply and marketing company. Northern Border Pipeline Company, a partnership of four energy companies with Northern Plains Natural Gas as managing partner, began construction of the eastern segment of the Alaskan pipeline in 1980. This segment, stretching from Ventura, Iowa, to Monchy, Saskatchewan, was completed in 1982. About that time, it became apparent that transporting Alaskan gas to the lower 48 states would be prohibitively expensive. Nevertheless, the pipeline provided an important link between Canadian gas reserves and the continental United States. Northern changed its name to InterNorth, Inc. in 1980. That same year, while attempting to grow through acquisitions,

InterNorth became involved in a takeover battle with Cooper Industries Inc. to acquire Crouse-Hinds Company, an electrical-products manufacturer. Cooper rescued Crouse-Hinds from InterNorth's hostile bid and bought Crouse-Hinds in January 1981. The takeover fight brought a flurry of lawsuits between InterNorth and Cooper. The suits were dropped after the acquisition was finalized.

While InterNorth grew through acquisitions, it also expanded from within. In 1980 it set up Northern Overthrust Pipeline Company and Northern Trailblazer Pipeline Company to participate in the Trailblazer pipeline, which runs from southeastern Nebraska to western Wyoming. Also that year, it created two exploration and production companies, Nortex Gas & Oil Company and Consolidex Gas and Oil Limited. The latter company was a Canadian operation. In 1981 InterNorth set up Northern Engineering International Company to provide professional engineering services. In 1982 it formed Northern Intrastate Pipeline Company and Northern Coal Pipeline Company as well as InterNorth International Inc., now Enron International, to oversee non–U.S. operations.

InterNorth significantly expanded its oil and gas exploration and production activity in 1983 with the purchase of Belco Petroleum Corporation for about $770 million. Belco quadrupled InterNorth's gas reserves and added greatly to its crude oil reserves. Exploration efforts focused on the United States, Canada, and Peru.

Other acquisitions of the early 1980s included the fuel trading companies P & O Falco Inc. and P & O Falco Ltd.; their operations joined with UPG—renamed UPG Falco—in 1984; and Chemplex Company, a polyethylene and adhesive manufacturer, also acquired in 1984. InterNorth had sold Northern Propane Gas in 1983.

InterNorth made an acquisition of enormous proportions in 1985, when it bid to purchase Houston Natural Gas Corporation for about $2.26 billion. The offer was received enthusiastically, and the merger created the largest gas pipeline system in the United States—about 37,000 miles at the time. Houston Natural Gas brought pipelines from the Southeast and Southwest to join with InterNorth's substantial system in the Great Plains area. Valero Energy Corporation of San Antonio, Texas, sued to block the merger. InterNorth had entered into joint ventures with Valero early in 1985 to transport and sell gas to industrial users in Texas and Louisiana. Because these ventures competed with Houston Natural Gas, InterNorth withdrew from them when it agreed to the merger. Valero alleged that InterNorth had breached its fiduciary obligations, but the Valero lawsuit failed to stop the acquisition.

Although still officially named InterNorth, the merged company initially was known as HNG/InterNorth, with dual headquarters in Omaha, Nebraska, and Houston, Texas. In 1986 the company's name was changed to Enron Corp., and headquarters were consolidated in Houston. After some shuffling in top management, Kenneth L. Lay, HNG's chairman, emerged as chairman of the combined company. HNG/InterNorth began divesting itself of businesses that did not fit in with its long-term goals. The $400 million in assets sold off in 1985 included the Peoples division, which sold for $250 million. Also in 1985, Peru's government nationalized Enron's assets there, and Enron began negotiating for payment, taking a $218 million charge against earnings in the meantime. In 1986 Enron's chemical subsidiary was sold for $603 million. Also in 1986, Enron sold 50 percent of its interest in Citrus Corporation to Sonat Inc. for $360 million but continued to operate Citrus's pipeline system, Florida Gas Transmission Company. Citrus originally was part of Houston Natural Gas.

In 1987 Enron centralized its gas pipeline operations under Enron Gas Pipeline Operating Company. Also that year, Enron Oil & Gas Company, with responsibility for exploration and production, was formed out of previous InterNorth and HNG operations, including Nortex Oil & Gas, Belco Petroleum, HNG Oil Company, and Florida Petroleum Company. In 1989 Enron Corp. sold 16 percent of Enron Oil & Gas's common stock to the public for about $200 million. That year Enron received $162 million from its insurers for the Peruvian operations, and it continued to negotiate with the government for additional compensation.

Enron made significant moves into electrical power, in both independent production and cogeneration facilities, in the late 1980s. Cogeneration plants produce electricity and thermal energy from one source. It added major cogeneration units in Texas and New Jersey in 1988; in 1989 it signed a 15-year contract to supply natural gas to a cogeneration plant on Long Island. Also in 1989, Enron reached an agreement with Coastal Corporation that allowed Enron to increase the natural gas production from its Big Piney field in Wyoming; under the accord, Coastal agreed to extend a pipeline to the field, since the line already going to it could not handle increased volume. The same year, Enron and El Paso Natural Gas Company received regulatory approval for a joint venture, Mojave Pipeline Company. The pipeline transports natural gas for use in oil drilling.

The 1990s and Beyond

In the early 1990s, Enron appeared to be reaping the benefits of the InterNorth-Houston Natural Gas merger. Its revenues, at $16.3 billion in 1985, fell to less than $10 billion in each of the next four years but recovered to $13.1 billion in 1990. Low natural gas prices had been a major cause of the decline. Enron, however, had been able to increase its market share, from 14 percent in 1985 to 18 percent in 1990, with help from efficiencies that resulted from the integration of the two predecessor companies' operations. Enron also showed significant growth in its liquid fuels business as well as in oil and gas exploration.

Beginning with the 1990s, Enron's stated philosophy was to, "get in early, push to open markets, position ourselves to compete, compete hard when the opening comes." This philosophy was translated into two major sectors: international markets and the newly deregulated gas and electricity markets in the United States.

Beginning in 1991, Enron built its first overseas power plant in Teesside, England, which became the largest gas-fired cogeneration plant in the world with 1,875 megawatts. Subsequently, Enron built power plants in industrial and developing nations all over the world: in Italy, Turkey, Argentina, China, India, Brazil, Guatemala, Bolivia, Colombia, the Dominican Republic, the Philippines, and others. By 1996, earnings from these projects accounted for 25 percent of total company earnings before interest and taxes.

Enron expects that further overseas growth will come from the privatization of government-owned companies in the fields of energy, transportation, and telecommunications. In 1997, Enron became the first company to develop a privately-owned independent power plant in Poland when a subsidiary, Elektrocieplownia Nowa Sarzyna Sp., signed a 20-year power purchase contract with the Polish Power Grid Company. The contract called for Enron to build a 116 megawatt, natural gas-fired combined heat and power plant in Nowa Sarzyna.

In North America, the states were given the power to deregulate gas and electric utilities in 1994, which meant that residential customers could choose utilities in the same way that they chose their phone carriers. In 1996, Enron agreed to acquire the utility, Portland General, whose transmission lines would give the company access to California's $20-billion market, as well as access to 650,000 customers in Oregon.

In 1997, Enron Energy Services began to supply natural gas to residential customers in Toledo, Ohio, and contracted to sell wind power to Iowa residents. Through a subsidiary, Zond Corporation, the company contracted with MidAmerican Energy Company of Houston to supply 112.5 megawatts of wind-generated electricity to about 50,000 homes, the largest single purchase contract in the history of wind energy. Zond was to build the facility in northwestern Iowa, using about 150 of its Z-750 kilowatt series wind turbines, the biggest made in the United States.

Interest in industrial customers also continued, and in 1997, Enron Capital & Trade Resources contracted with Amtrak to buy electric energy at reduced rates. Amtrak functions as a wholesale purchaser of electric power, using it for its own system and reselling it to commuter lines. Amtrak planned to use the electric energy to run nearly 600 of its own trains daily in the Northeast Corridor and another 100 commuter trains on the Keystone line between Philadelphia and Harrisburg. Savings to the electric-powered trains were estimated to be as much as $40 million per year.

Principal Subsidiaries

Enron Gas Pipeline Group; Enron Capital & Trade Resources; Enron International; Enron Oil & Gas Company; Enron Renewable Energy Corp.

Principal Operating Units

Enron Ventures Corp.; Enron Energy Services; Enron Oil and Gas India.

Further Reading

"Enron Chief Criticises U.S. Congress and World Bank," *International Trade Finance,* October 11, 1996, p. 8.
"Enron Joins West Coast Team," *ENR,* February 17, 1997, p. 12.
Kemezis, Paul, "Why Enron Paid a Premium for Portland General," *Electrical World,* September 1996, pp. 57–58.
"O'Reilly, Brian, "The Secrets of America's Most Admired Corporations," *Fortune,* March 3, 1997, pp. 60–64.
"Power Players," *Fortune,* August 5, 1996, p. 94.

—Trudy Ring
—updated by Dorothy Kroll

Escalade, Incorporated

817 Maxwell Avenue
Evansville, Indiana 47717
U.S.A.
(812) 467-1200
Fax: (812) 425-1425
Web site: http://www.escaladesports.com

Public Company
Incorporated: 1922 as The Williams Manufacturing
   Company
Employees: 700 (est.)
Sales: $93.2 million (1996)
Stock Exchanges: NASDAQ
SICs: 3949 Sporting & Athletic Goods, Not Elsewhere
   Classified; 3579 Office Machines, Not Elsewhere
   Classified

The largest manufacturer of table-tennis tables and pool tables in the world, Escalade, Incorporated manufactures and sells a variety of recreational merchandise, as well as office and graphic arts products through its subsidiary, Martin-Yale Industries, Inc. Along with table-tennis equipment and billiards equipment, Escalade's chief products during the late 1990s included basketball backboards, goals, and telescopic poles, darts and dart cabinets, and home fitness machines, weight benches, cast iron weight sets, steppers, and other home fitness accessories. The company's involvement in the sporting goods industry began in 1927 with the founding of Indian Archery and Toy Corp., a manufacturer of archery equipment, badminton sets, and darts. Diversification decades later brought Escalade into new business lines. The company began producing table-tennis tables in the 1960s, pool tables in the 1970s, and basketball equipment in the 1980s. In 1989, Escalade entered the home fitness market through the acquisition of Marcy Fitness Products, Inc., a California manufacturer of home fitness and exercise equipment. During the late 1990s, the company derived roughly 80 percent of its total sales from sporting goods. The balance was realized through its Martin-Yale subsidiary, which manufactured paper trimmers, paper folding machines, paper drills, collators, letter openers, paper shredders, and other related products. Manufacturing facilities for the company's products were located in Evansville, Indiana, Wabash, Indiana, Compton, California, and Tijuana, Mexico.

Early History

Escalade's corporate roots trace the development of several different companies, the oldest of which was The Williams Manufacturing Company, an Ohio-based manufacturer and retailer of footwear and hobby and craft products founded in 1922. Although the Williams business began operating first, the driving force behind the creation of Escalade was another company, a sporting goods manufacturer situated in Evansville, Indiana. Founded in 1927, Indian Archery and Toy Corp. operated as a small but thriving enterprise for nearly four decades before coming under the control of management that steered it toward diversification and more prolific growth. It was the influence of this new management team—led by Robert Griffin, Escalade's chief executive officer during the 1990s—that shaped Escalade into a global leader.

During the decades bridging Indian Archery and Toy's inception and the beginning of the company's transformation into Escalade, a legacy of modest success was established in Evansville. The company was founded by a former Ohio resident named H. M. Brading, who enlisted the financial support of three Evansville car dealers to start his small business. Initially, Indian Archery and Toy sold "bat-minton" sets, darts, dart games, and stilts through catalogs, with Brading and one other employee, who occupied a small upstairs room in an Evansville building, composing the company's payroll. By Indian Archery and Toy's second year of business, remarkable progress had been made. In 1928, there were 22 employees assembling bow and arrow sets by hand and shipping them as far away as Switzerland, Denmark, Australia, New Zealand, and China. Still in its infancy, Indian Archery and Toy appeared on the verge of explosive growth, but forces outside the company's control conspired to stifle such growth as quickly as it had developed.

The stock market crash of 1929 signalled the beginning of a decade-long economic depression that stunted Indian Archery and Toy's growth. The company struggled throughout much of the 1930s, its business severely crimped by the reluctance of many consumers to spend their dwindling dollars on recreational products. By the end of the decade, however, the economic climate began to improve and Indian Archery and Toy could once again look toward expansion. Larger offices were occupied by 1937, when fiberglass bows were introduced and the company began manufacturing its own targets, as the Evansville enterprise regained some of the luster lost during the Great Depression.

Post–World War II Transformation

Once back on track, Indian Archery and Toy experienced years of steady growth, with annual sales eclipsing half a million dollars by the end of the 1950s. After more than a quarter century of business, the company was a modestly-sized but well-recognized competitor in the sporting goods industry and about to enter a decade of definitive change. The 1960s would prove to be a signal decade in Indian Archery and Toy's development, a decade during which the company began to assume the characteristics that would define it during the 1990s. Some of the changes were superficial, such as the two name changes effected during the 1960s, but other events represented milestones in the company's history, marking Indian Archery and Toy's development into a diversified sporting goods manufacturer.

The decade began with a name change, effected in 1961 when Indian Archery and Toy Corp. shortened its name to Indian Archery Corp., one year before the company's 35th year of business. During the company's anniversary year, when sales reached $800,000, new management took the helm, led by Robert Griffin who would spearhead Indian Archery's transformation into Escalade. Griffin had arrived in Indiana two years earlier, deciding after completing his college education that he would work with an Evansville native named Robert Orr in the metal fabrication business. Orr, who would later be elected governor of Indiana, Griffin, and two other partners, Jim McNeely and Joseph Derr, acquired Indian Archery in the fall of 1962 and immediately began experimenting with new products that would extend the company's presence into new markets. As Griffin later related about the mindset of the new leadership, "We felt that the opportunity was there, and our vision was to build on it," but determination did not translate into instant success for the new owners. Their early efforts—manufacturing skateboards and plastic skis—failed, as did their venture into the production of hand-pulled golf carts, entered into by the 1966 acquisition of Chicago-based Kunkel Industries, a golf-cart manufacturer. Griffin and his associates were forced out of the golf-cart market because of stiff competition,

but the manufacturing operations gained through the Kunkel acquisition steered the company toward a lucrative path. Despite the dubious start, Griffin, Orr, McNeely and Derr were headed in the right direction

The same year the Kunkel acquisition was completed, Indian Archery Corp. changed its name to Indian Industries, Inc. to better reflect the company's involvement in different business lines. One of these different business lines, and the chief benefit of the Kunkel acquisition, was Indian Industries involvement in the table-tennis market. While Indian Industries was attempting to make a name for itself in the golf-cart business, Sears, Roebuck & Co. approached the Evansville manufacturer about making table-tennis tables. With his golf-cart business floundering but with the metal-working operations still under his ownership, Griffin confided later, "We decided to go for it [the Sears offer] because we were already set up for tubular metal working and stamping. So we started from scratch and that worked for us." The deal marked the beginning of a lasting relationship with Sears and the first significant achievement realized by Indian Industries' new owners.

Once the company entered the table-tennis manufacturing business, it quickly sought to increase its presence in the market, as it embarked on a development program that would eventually make it the largest table-tennis manufacturer in the world. Toward this end, Indian Industries entered a joint venture project called Cal-Dana to manufacture table-tennis tables in California and Indiana, which was merged into the company in 1970, and acquired the trademark "Ping Pong" from Parker Bros. Shortly after these deals were completed, the paths of Indian Industries and The Williams Manufacturing Company joined together. The result was Escalade, Incorporated.

1970s Birth of Escalade

The flurry of corporate transactions that engendered Escalade began in 1972 when Williams, the footwear manufacturer based in Ohio, merged with Illinois-based Martin-Yale Industries, Inc., a manufacturer of office and graphic arts products, and crafts and toys. The following year, Williams acquired Indian Industries and Harvard Table Tennis, Inc., a Massachusetts-based manufacturer of table-tennis accessories, creating a diversified manufacturer involved in the production of footwear, recreational products, office products, graphic arts products, and hobby and craft items. At roughly the same time that this multifaceted manufacturer was created through merger and acquisition, Williams executives resolved to rename the new enterprise and hired a New York consultant to do the job. The consultant suggested "Escalade," which was subsequently adopted as the new corporate title for the combined entities of Williams, Indian Industries, Martin-Yale, and Harvard Table Tennis.

Although Williams had orchestrated the deals that brought Escalade together, the heart of the new company was Indian Industries, from which Escalade's management and mainstay business was drawn. Griffin and his partners took control of Escalade, intent on building the company into a sporting goods powerhouse. To make room for a broader presence in the sporting goods industry, Griffin and his associates stripped Escalade of assets deemed unrelated to the company's future. Along these lines, Griffin discontinued Williams's footwear operations in 1976 and sold Martin-Yale's product line of crafts and hobby merchandise in 1979, retaining only one of Martin-Yale's original products, a paper trimmer. Around the paper trimmer, Griffin rebuilt Martin-Yale into an office and graphic arts operator, while efforts elsewhere were aimed toward increasing Escalade's involvement in the sporting goods market.

A new product line was added to Escalade's business in 1977 when the company began manufacturing pool tables. It was a significant addition, representing the first step toward becoming the largest pool-table manufacturer in the world. As Escalade's pool-table manufacturing activities quickly accelerated, the company completed an acquisition that strengthened its table-tennis business, its burgeoning pool-table business, and extended the geographic reach of its manufacturing operations. In 1980, Escalade acquired the Crown Recreation (West) division of Ideal Toy Company, which manufactured table-tennis tables and pool tables in Compton, California. Three years later, when billiards accessories were added to Escalade's merchandise mix, the acquired company was consolidated with Harvard Table Tennis, Inc., creating Harvard Sports, Inc.

As the Harvard Sports subsidiary was being reorganized, Escalade added another product line to its business when it began manufacturing basketball backboards, goals, and poles in 1982. Next on the acquisitive front, the company strengthened the graphic arts business of Martin-Yale by acquiring the graphic arts assets belonging to Geiss America, Inc. in 1986. Following this acquisition, Escalade purchased the business machine division of Swingline, Inc. in 1988, thereby bolstering the revenue-generating capability of Martin-Yale. As the 1980s drew to a close, Escalade made one other addition to its sporting goods business by acquiring a 55 percent interest in Marcy Fitness Products, Inc., a California manufacturer of such home exercise equipment as home gyms, barbells, weight benches, and recumbent bicycles.

While the company added to its magnitude through acquisitions during the 1980s, it also struck an important licensing deal that added a well-recognized brand name to the company-owned "Indian" and "Harvard" brands. In 1985, Escalade reached an agreement with Evenflo Companies, Inc. for the exclusive right to use the "Spalding" trademark on sporting goods products manufactured and distributed in the United States. From 1985 forward, Escalade used the Spalding name on its line of basketball backboards, goals, and poles, indoor darts, table tennis sets, and pool accessories. As the 1990s

began another important licensing agreement was reached when Escalade gained the exclusive right to manufacture and distribute table-tennis equipment in the United States and Canada under the brand name "STIGA."

Propelled by the strength of the Indian, Harvard, Spalding, and STIGA brand names, sales eclipsed $80 million by the beginning of the 1990s. Early in the decade, the remaining 45 percent interest in Marcy Fitness Products was acquired, adding a new wholly owned subsidiary to Escalade's collection of companies. As the 1990s progressed, Escalade increased its manufacturing capabilities and endeavored to increase its business overseas, where the company had been operating since the late 1920s. In 1990, a new manufacturing and office facility was built in Wabash, Indiana, one year after production had begun in Tijuana, Mexico. In 1992, as part of the effort to expand business abroad, the company established Escalade International Limited, which comprised a sales office and warehouse in Swansea, Wales.

By the mid-1990s, Escalade's annual sales had eclipsed $90 million. Although the company ranked as the largest table-tennis and pool table manufacturer in the world, its preeminence did not make the company immune to the affects of the stiff competition mounted by its smaller competitors and the cyclical nature of the sporting goods business. Profits dipped and rose during the first half of the decade, prompting management to dedicate its efforts during the second half of the 1990s toward shoring up the company's position. In pursuit of this goal, Escalade executives were placing a premium on removing unnecessary costs, improving the quality of products, and introducing new products as the 21st century approached.

Principal Subsidiaries

Martin-Yale Industries, Inc.; Indian Industries, Inc.; Harvard Sports, Inc.; Escalade International Ltd. (United Kingdom); Sweden Table Tennis AB (37.5%)

Further Reading

Saenz, Lisa, "Are You Ready for Archery?" *Shooting Industry,* February 1992, p. 20.
Wiesjahn, Lisa, "On Target: Indian Industries and Parent Company Escalade Take Aim at the Sports-Equipment Market," *Indiana Business Journal,* July 1994, pp. 8–12.

—Jeffrey L. Covell

Evans & Sutherland Computer Corporation

600 Komas Drive
Salt Lake City, Utah 84108
U.S.A.
(801) 588-1000
Fax: (801) 588-4510
Web site: http://www.es.com

Public Company
Incorporated: 1968
Employees: 784
Sales: $131 million (1996)
Stock Exchanges: NASDAQ
SICs: 3571 Electronic Computers; 3577 Computer
    Peripheral Equipment; 7372 Prepackaged Computer
    Software

Evans & Sutherland Computer Corporation is an industry leader in computer graphics, especially in providing realistic simulators to train military and commercial pilots. E&S provides the majority of worldwide civilian pilot simulators and NASA and all branches of the U.S. military use its products. In the 1990s more foreign nations began using E&S simulators for military training. Avionics display systems for cockpit training are other E&S products. According to independent authorities, Evans & Sutherland ranked in 1996 as one of the nation's most competitive firms in the aerospace industry. The firm also provides graphics accelerator technology for some leading workstation and personal computer manufacturers, such as Digital Equipment Corporation, IBM, Sun Microsystems, Mitsubishi, and Hewlett-Packard. Many professionals, including scientists, architects, engineers, and historians, use Evans & Sutherland products to digitally create and manipulate images.

Evans & Sutherland has also used its technology for entertainment and education. It is the world leader in creating and producing computerized planetarium projection systems. Its virtual reality products, such as its trademarked Virtual Glider simulator, are targeted to the general consumer market. The firm also produces virtual studios for customers in the television,

video, and film industries. Although E&S continues to produce expensive technology for large corporate and government customers, it also has taken advantage of the fact that smaller firms and even consumers have access to increasingly powerful computers. Thus Evans & Sutherland in the last few years has diversified and expanded its goals to give new customers access to its advanced graphics technology. The applications seem limited only by human imagination.

Founders and Company Origins

E&S began with the collaboration of two men, David C. Evans and Ivan E. Sutherland. Evans was born in 1924 in Salt Lake City, where in 1953 he received his Ph.D in physics from the University of Utah. From 1953 to 1962, Evans was director of engineering in Bendix Corporation's computer division. In 1962 he started a visiting professorship at the University of California at Berkeley. In those early years Evans became more and more interested in using computers for more than just number crunching. Since humans use sight as a primary means of interacting with the world, Evans became focused on using computers to produce visual images for a wide range of applications. When in 1966 he returned to Salt Lake City to start the University of Utah's computer science department, he continued his interest in computer graphics and was on the lookout for others with similar interests.

Ivan Sutherland at the same time was working in the field of computer graphics. In 1960, as part of his Ph.D. dissertation at the Massachusetts Institute of Technology, he produced a movie called *Sketchpad: A Man-Machine Graphical Communication System*, which for the first time portrayed three-dimensional objects on a two-dimensional computer screen.

In 1967 Sutherland and Evans talked about collaborating in the relatively new field of computer graphics. Sutherland, then a Harvard professor, told Evans he could get him a position at Harvard, while Evans made a similar proposal for Sutherland to come to the University of Utah. In the end, Evans decided he definitely could not leave Utah, partly because of his devout faith as a member of the Latter Day Saint church headquartered in Salt Lake City. So Sutherland decided to join Evans at the University of Utah.

About the same time, the University of Utah computer science department began receiving $5 million from the Defense Department's ARPA (Advanced Research Projects Agency) to develop a flight simulator. However, both Evans and Sutherland felt that their common goals concerning the development of graphics as a means to create computer simulations would require the creation of a private company.

In 1968 the two founders created Evans & Sutherland on a financial shoestring. They and some employees and family friends contributed what they could. Venrock, a group of investors associated with the famous Rockefeller family, also provided crucial funds for the firm incorporated on May 10, 1968 in Utah.

At its base in an old Army barracks at the University of Utah, E&S produced in 1969 its first product, LDS (Line Drawing System) 1. Although E&S sold only three or four of this new and expensive technology, the firm later used LDS 1 in its first simulator.

By 1972 the firm had developed LDS 2 and other new products but had not generated any profits. At the same time it recruited three key engineers from General Electric. Rod Rougelot, Bob Schumacker, and Ed Wild had approached GE about using computers for pilot training, but GE was not interested at the time. GE's loss eventually proved to be a huge gain for E&S.

Writing in the firm's 1990 newsletter, secretary/treasurer Dick Leahy described what had happened as Christmas approached in 1972: ''The company had around $700 left in the bank, had used up its lines of credit, and was running on personal loans taken out on the founders' homes.'' Just in time, an overseas investment firm sent a check for $500,000 to save the struggling company.

Expansion in the 1970s

With the aid of the three former GE engineers, Evans & Sutherland entered what would become one of its key markets. In 1973 the company began a joint project with RSL (Rediffusion Simulation Limited) of Great Britain, in which E&S would make NOVOVIEW visual simulators for commercial airlines, and RSL would market those items. The Dutch airline KLM bought the first NOVOVIEW system.

NOVOVIEW products brought E&S its first profits in 1974 and continued success as the decade progressed. The flight simulator business boomed following the Arab oil embargo of 1974, which made fuel and thus live pilot training much more expensive. By 1977, the SP1, NOVOVIEW's successor, was certified by the Federal Aviation Administration and brought in more sales to E&S than all its other simulators combined. In 1978 the SP2 became a full color product and in 1980 the FAA certified the SP3 for meeting its requirements for a daylight training system.

At the same time, E&S was developing its CT (continuous tone) line of high-performance image generators. In 1972 the company sold a CT1 system to Case Western Reserve University, and in 1975, a CT2 was shipped to CAORF, a maritime facility for training and research. E&S also contracted with NASA in 1976 for a CT3 and with Lufthansa for a CT4 in 1977.

The CT systems to that point were specialized products for single customers and therefore not very marketable. But then engineer Bob Schumacker designed the CT5 which increased the system's capability about 1,000 percent. That gained the firm a contract with the Naval Training Equipment Center. Delivered in 1981, the CT5 was so powerful it could serve many customers without individual changes.

In the 1970s David Evans led the E&S effort to produce graphics systems for the CAD/CAM (computer-aided design/computer-aided manufacturing) market. The company created the picture system family, starting with PS1 in 1973 and culminating in the PS 300 in 1981. One key advantage of the more advanced PS systems was decreasing reliance on one host computer; for the first time several designers could work simultaneously.

With this variety of products, E&S expanded it workforce in the 1970s and early 1980s. The firm employed 88 persons in 1973 and 144 in 1975. During the company's early years as a private firm, it was backed by eastern companies, including Venrock, the Venture Capital Investment Company of the Rockefeller family, GCA Corporation, the Endowment Management and Research Corporation, and Hambrecht & Quist investment bankers. E&S continued to grow after it became a public firm in 1978. By 1983, 779 individuals worked for E&S.

Realizing they could not run such a growing firm and fulfill their faculty responsibilities, both Evans and Sutherland had resigned from the University of Utah by 1974. And in 1974, Sutherland decided to resign as the vice-president and chief scientist of the firm he helped start. However, he continued his role as a company director into the 1990s.

Boom Times in the 1980s

Although E&S had started creating products for military flight simulators in the mid-1970s, that aspect of its business rapidly expanded in the 1980s, in part because of the growth of the military under President Ronald Reagan.

In his firm's 1990 newsletter, founder David Evans pointed out key challenges in approaching military markets: ''There's a lot of ritual, a lot of regulation, a lot of standards that are required of military contractors in terms of documentation, the security of. . .information, and the nature of contracts. The typical military contractor is not a risk taker. Your typical military contractor does research and development paid for by the government and produces intellectual property they don't own. E&S has always developed products at its own expense and offered those products for sale. That's part of our. . .culture.''

Military requirements, tremendous growth, and more competitors influenced E&S to become more structured in the 1980s. By 1986 E&S employed 1,072 persons. More firms entered the simulator market after the 1986 federal deregulation of civilian airlines. So E&S in June 1986 created three formal company divisions.

The Simulation Division was headed by Rod Rougelot, and Gary Meredith led the Interactive Systems Division. Previously both divisions had operated as informal working groups. E&S also created the Computer Division from a new group of European employees. Unlike the other two divisions based in Salt Lake City, the Computer Division was based in Mountain View, California.

Shortly after this reorganization, E&S also renegotiated its contract with RSL regarding marketing tactics. E&S now began its own marketing efforts to the United States military, which RSL had been cautious about approaching. Since E&S products had been marketed under the name RSL, many in the military were not aware of E&S's contributions until the late 1980s.

At the same time, E&S improved its product lines for both the military and civilian markets. It began creating simulators to train entire crews, not just the pilot or main operator. In 1988 E&S also renamed the CT and SP product lines to use the ESIG (Evans & Sutherland Image Generator) prefix.

In the 1980s Evans & Sutherland entered into several joint agreements to share technology and in some cases acquired related firms. For example, it invested in VLSI Technology Inc. in 1980 to gain access to that company's computer modeling tools, which enabled E&S to develop its Shadowfax circuit chips. Shadowfax enabled E&S to display nonvertical and non-horizontal lines in a smooth and continuous manner, instead of the jagged stair-step lines previously used.

In 1987 the firm acquired Tripos Associates, a St. Louis based firm which in 1979 had pioneered the field of Molecular Information Analysis Systems. That important new technology for the scientific community enabled researchers to see and manipulate either two or three-dimensional images of simple or complex molecules.

In 1988 E&S and Digital Equipment Corporation (DEC) announced the availability of the VAXstation 8000, a color workstation featuring DEC's VAX computer and a very fast graphics system produced by E&S. Both corporations marketed the jointly produced item.

E&S also diversified in the 1980s by beginning to use its technology for entertainment and education. For example, the 1982 movie *Tron,* a science-fiction tale of human entities living inside a computer at the microchip level, employed some E&S products to create its special effects.

In the 1980s the company cooperated with Salt Lake City's Hansen Planetarium to create Digistar, a computerized projection system which could do much more than the old mechanically based methods of projecting stars onto the dome of a planetarium. E&S sold a couple Digistar systems in the 1980s, but the market for this technology was quite limited.

To finance such expanding operations, E&S in 1987 offered investors convertible debentures worth $56 million. Then it started constructing its new Building 600 at the University of Utah Research Park and planning for another building to house the Simulation Division's dome projection system.

Not all E&S ventures succeeded in the 1980s. One dead end was its supercomputer project. In April 1988 the firm announced it would develop and market the world's first general supercomputer and in 1989 it introduced the ES-1 supercomputer. However, about 70 other firms also were exploring new technology sponsored by the Department of Defense's ARPA and based at Carnegie-Mellon University. By 1989 commercial versions were available from not only E&S, but also three other companies. All these supercomputer projects featured parallel processing, in which several microchips were linked together for advanced computing power. Due to technical problems and severe competition, in late 1989 Evans & Sutherland decided to end its supercomputer project and use its funds for other purposes.

In 1989, after being diagnosed with a neurological condition, David Evans retired from his position as president and CEO, while remaining company chairman. The offices of president and CEO were turned over to Rodney Rougelot, who would then work with Stewart Carrell, who became chairman of the board in 1991.

Challenges in the 1990s

With the end of the Cold War and the dissolution of the Soviet Union, the U.S. military closed many bases and in other ways decreased its forces. At the same time, total U.S. aerospace sales dropped dramatically from almost $140 billion in 1991 to about $108 billion in 1995.

Like other military contractors, Evans & Sutherland during this period significantly reduced its workforce. In 1991, 50 employees lost their jobs. In January 1994 E&S announced that 170 workers would lose their positions, and the following January the firm reduced its numbers by another 200. By 1997 it had downsized to only about 800 employees, several hundred less than the boom times of the 1980s.

At the same time, E&S experienced declining finances. Compared to 1988 and 1989 when the company had net earnings of $1.88 million and $1 million, in 1994 it had a net loss of $3.7 million. Due to Evans & Sutherland's declining revenues and profits and several other difficulties, Moody's Investors Service in March 1994 reduced the Utah firm's convertible subordinated debentures rating from B1 to B2.

However, Evans & Sutherland made several positive moves in the midst of these trying times. In November 1993, E&S and Iwerks Entertainment introduced their jointly produced "Virtual Adventure," a location based system used at theme parks. Whether traveling through space or through an underwater scene, individuals enjoyed themselves without the risk of real dangers. By 1997, E&S had sold 22 of its Virtual Glider systems to customers in several American cities, London, Hong Kong, and Canada. These products represented the company's diversification into the rapidly growing consumer market for entertainment and education, a small but expanding part of the firm's business in the 1990s.

International sales also increased significantly for Evans & Sutherland in the 1990s. For example, in April 1991 E&S sold a newly introduced ESIG-2000 image generator to Germany's Krupp Atlas Elektronik. By 1993 Krupp was using that E&S

technology in simulators to train operators of Britain's main Challenger battle tank. In 1994, E&S opened an office in Beijing.

To expand into such foreign markets, E&S took advantage of the language abilities and cultural sensitivities learned by employees who had served foreign missions for the LDS church. The bottom line: by 1996 almost half of Evans & Sutherland's annual revenues were from international sales.

Since 1973, E&S and Rediffusion jointly had sold over 400 simulator systems to civil airlines worldwide. But since Rediffusion, renamed Thomson Training and Simulation, began offering its own image generators, E&S in 1994 ended their contract and began marketing its own systems directly to civil aviation customers.

The company in 1994 also spun off its Tripos, Inc. subsidiary to become an independent public company. E&S shareholders each received one share of Tripos common stock for every three shares of E&S common stock they owned.

The following year, 1995, the corporation sold two of its CAD/CAM products called CDRS (Conceptual Design and Rendering System) and 3D Paint. Those systems had been developed in the late 1980s and early 1990s to help designers of automobiles and other products become more efficient. Evans & Sutherland had contracted with Ford, Chrysler, Fiat, Hyundai, and other companies for these products.

In December 1994, upon the retirement of Rougelot, James R. Oyler became the company's new president and CEO. There were some indications by the mid-1990s that managerial and technological changes at E&S were good for the company. After a 14-month study of the American aerospace industry, *Aviation Week & Space Technology,* in its June 3, 1996 issue, ranked E&S second in the total company index of competitiveness and first in the total multi-industry company index of competitiveness. The magazine cited Evans & Sutherland as a good example of smaller firms which generally had done better than those with over $500 million in annual sales. The company attributed its success to significantly slashing operating expenses and increasing research and development spending.

In the E&S 1996 annual report, Oyler noted that other signs were very positive. For example, in August 1996 the firm announced that the U.S. Air Force had awarded it a contract to provide upgrades on training systems for KC-135 and KC-10 pilots. The firm estimated that this contract, the largest in its history, could generate about $70 million in revenues over the next five years. Moreover, Oyler stated that "only company in the world supplying a complete range of graphics systems priced from $2,000 to $2 million." To implement that goal, in late 1996 the company initiated a new strategy called Universal 3D to make its graphics technology available to customers using widely available Windows NT workstations and personal computers.

In 1996, E&S sold a subsidiary called Portable Graphics Inc., an Austin, Texas, based firm acquired just two years earlier. It also completed its purchase of Terabit Computer Specialty Company, Inc., a firm which provided cockpit instruments and other displays for airplane simulators. E&S organized its new Display Systems division using these new resources.

To market its trademarked REALimage technology which produced 3D graphics for personal computers, Evans & Sutherland organized in 1996 its new Desktop Graphics division or business unit. E&S and Mitsubishi had formed a nonexclusive partnership to create REALimage.

Also that year, David Evans and Ivan Sutherland received a major honor for their contributions to the computer industry. They won the Price Waterhouse Information Technology Leadership Award for Lifetime Achievement at the annual Computer World Smithsonian Awards ceremony. That recognition for past work and the fact that for two years (1995 and 1996) the firm had continual growth in operating profits and annual revenues proved to the company's leadership that it had completed its turnaround from the struggles of the early 1990s and had created a strong basis for future growth.

In cooperation with Salt Lake City's Bonneville International, E&S in January 1997 formed Digital Studios to real time virtual sets for television, film, and video producers. That year, Evans & Sutherland's leadership seemed quite upbeat about the firm's future prospects in the rapidly changing high tech field. President/CEO Oyler said in the February 2, 1997, issue of Salt Lake City's *Deseret News,* "What excites me is the chance to develop at the high end and migrate down to the desktop. There really is no other company in the world doing that. Our belief is that we're only at the beginning of this. We're at the edge of doing things that have been too expensive [for the consumer or small firm] to do in the past."

Principal Divisions

Government Simulation; Commercial Simulation; Displays; Digital Studio; Desktop Graphics; Entertainment and Education

Further Reading

Brennan, Laura, "Color Workstation Offers High Speed, Exceptional Clarity," *PC Week,* February 9, 1988, p. 23.

Carricaburu, Lisa, "A Whole New Mind-Set," *Deseret News,* January 21, 1997, p. D1.

Cortez, Marjorie, "Evans & Sutherland Lays Off 170 Workers in Restructuring Move," *Deseret News* (Web Edition), January 13, 1994.

Davidson, Lee, "Evans, Sutherland Win Life Achievement Awards," *Deseret News* (Web Edition), June 3, 1996.

"Evans & Sutherland Computer Corporation Completes Spin-off of Tripos," company press release, June 1, 1994.

"Evans & Sutherland Enters Visual System Business for Civil Aviation Training," company press release, July 7, 1994.

Evans & Sutherland News, special issue, "E&S Since 1968: The Early Years, Getting Established, Maintaining Industry Leadership," 1990.

"Evans & Sutherland Gets $3.4 Million in [CDRS] Contracts," *Deseret News* (Web Edition), January 17, 1991.

"Evans & Sutherland Lays Off 50 Workers," *Deseret News* (Web Edition), May 8, 1991.

Evans, David C., papers, Ms 625, Manuscripts Division, Special Collections, University of Utah Marriott Library, Salt Lake City [a huge collection with items up to 1987].

"Index of Competitiveness," *Aviation Week & Space Technology,* June 3, 1996, pp. 42–49.

Knudson, Max B., "Evans & Sutherland Branching into the Entertainment Business," *Deseret News* (Web Edition), September 22, 1993.

Knudson, Max B., "E&S Cuts 200 From Work Force," *Deseret News* (Web Edition), January 13, 1995.

McWilliams, Gary, "Parallel Processing Finds a Champion in Carnegie Project," *Datamation,* February 15, 1988, p. 19.

Rapaport, Richard, "Mormon Conquest," *Forbes ASAP* [a special technology supplement], December 7, 1992, pp. 76–81, 84–88, 91.

Rashid, Richard, "A Catalyst for Open Systems," *Datamation,* May 15, 1989, pp. 32.

Rivlin, Robert, "Filming by Computer," *Technology Illustrated,* February 1983, pp. 26, 28–30.

Siegel, Lee, "The Reality Factory," *Salt Lake Tribune,* April 17, 1994, pp. A1, A3.

"A Virtual Vision: Evans & Sutherland Using its Technology to Conquer New Worlds," *Deseret News* (Web Edition), February 2, 1997.

Wysocki, Bernard Jr., "Global View Part of Faith and Business," *Deseret News* (Web Edition), March 29, 1996.

—David M. Walden

Fansteel

Fansteel Inc.

One Tantalum Place
North Chicago, Illinois 60064
U.S.A.
(847) 689-4900
Fax: (847) 689-4555

Public Company
Incorporated: 1914 as Pfanstiehl Company
Employees: 850
Sales: $120.83 million (1996)
Stock Exchanges: New York
SICs: 3339 Primary Nonferrous Metals, Not Elsewhere
Classified; 3443 Fabricated Plate Work—Boiler
Shops; 3541 Machine Tools—Metal Cutting Types;
3728 Aircraft Parts and Equipment, Not Elsewhere
Classified

Fansteel Inc. is a manufacturer of specialty-metals products, including cutting and milling tools, toolholding devices, coal-mining tools and accessories, construction tools, wear-resistant parts, powdered-metal components, sand-mold castings, investment castings, forgings, and special wire forms. These products are divided by Fansteel into two business lines—industrial tools and metal fabrications—and are used in metalworking; the automobile, aircraft, aerospace, and weapons industries; coal mining; gas and oil drilling; and agricultural machinery and electrical equipment industries. Interturbine Fansteel, Fansteel's joint-venture company with Interturbine Holland, manufactures, repairs, and markets parts for jet engines in Europe, the Middle East, and the Far East. The company, whose headquarters are in North Chicago, Illinois, operates from nine manufacturing facilities located in various parts of the United States. It calls itself an "industrial company serving industry."

The Early Years: Pfanstiehl Electrical Laboratories

The development of Fansteel Inc., founded in 1917 by Carl A. Pfanstiehl, parallels the growth of American industry and technology from World War I to the present. Born in 1888 in Columbia, Missouri, Pfanstiehl was raised and educated in Highland Park, Illinois. While still in high school, he exhibited an interest in science and technology. He was responsible for building the first X-ray machine in the area and was frequently called on to perform X rays at surrounding hospitals. At age 16 he attended the Armour Institute of Technology, where he met his future partner, James M. Troxel. Together, with an initial capital stock of $10,000, they launched the Pfanstiehl Electrical Laboratories in January 1907. During this same period Pfanstiehl had also developed a unique induction coil and was selling the coils for medical use. Troxel believed that the emerging automobile industry could use Pfanstiehl's coils for the construction of ignitions.

The early years were less than a stunning financial success. According to Robert Aitcheson, an early bookkeeper for the company (and later a Fansteel president), the company in the beginning "was just a little business and in five years they were in trouble with practically all of their accounts receivable in hock." Still, the company had a good reputation in the automotive field, and until World War I it produced various parts for that industry, including magnetos, master vibrators, starter coils, and transformer coils. It also manufactured an electric household iron, one of the company's few attempts to enter the consumer market.

Especially important to the company was its development of automotive contact discs, made with tungsten, at the time a new metal. Introduced just before the war, these Pfanstiehl contacts soon became common in automotive ignition systems. They also helped boost profits from $49,152 in 1914 to $361,909 in 1917. During this period, in 1914, the company was incorporated as the Pfanstiehl Company of Delaware with an initial $150,000 of preferred stock and $150,000 of common stock.

After the war, because of the anti-German sentiment in the United States, the company's name was changed to Fansteel Products Company, Inc. The new name was a simple Anglicizing of the Dutch spelling. Thus, although the company was in the metal-fabricating business, the name reflected only by chance the metals it developed for industrial use.

Production during World War I

During World War I Pfanstiehl spent much of his time in the laboratory. He patented a method of welding steels of different "analyses," and he also received a patent for a tungsten target for X-ray tubes.

During the war years the company profitably produced tungsten for use in electrical contact points and was operating at high capacity. Much of the company's production, in fact, was in the manufacture of tungsten spark gaps for wireless apparatus and special strip contacts of tungsten for signaling equipment used during the war. It was also producing the metal cerium, as well as a cerium-iron alloy, which were used to make miners' lamps and munitions.

For its Tungsten products Fansteel initially purchased tungsten rods, but difficulties with the purchased metal led the company to produce its own. It was to help him with this job that Pfanstiehl decided to contact Dr. Clarence Balke, a University of Illinois chemistry professor who was conducting research on rare metals, including tantalum (a metal that would become important to the growth of Fansteel). In 1916 Balke became the research director at Fansteel.

Pfanstiehl also worked on the development of specialty chemicals needed for medical treatments during the war. Rare sugars and amino acids that had been supplied by Germany before the war were in short supply. To tackle this problem, Pfanstiehl established the Specialty Chemicals Company, which was located in the basement of his home. From 1919 until his death in 1942, he devoted himself to this laboratory, leaving the management of Fansteel in the hands of others. He developed a tooth paste, a pen nib, a new dental drill, and an improved phonograph needle. He had 135 patents issued in his name in areas as diverse as metallurgy, chemistry, and electronics.

From the 1920s through World War II

For years Fansteel conducted research on tantalum, the rare metal in which Clarence Balke had focused much of his energy as a professor. One commercial result was the company's Balkite Tantalum Rectifier, or radio, which in the early 1920s became hugely popular, though demand for the product would not last long. In 1923 Fansteel was manufacturing rectifiers and "B" power units in the millions and establishing distribution outlets throughout the country. From 1923 to 1924 sales of the rectifier jumped from $73,263 to $918,237. Fansteel sponsored the first New York Symphony Orchestra broadcast over radio. By 1926 sales at Fansteel had nearly reached the $5 million mark, most of it coming from radio and railway use of rectifiers. But in 1927 the rectifier was replaced by the AC (alternating current) tube, and Fansteel found itself in a downhill slide. It had tried not to be dependent on the automobile industry after World War I, and now it had become too dependent on the radio industry. The company, however, retained sustaining products in rectifiers for railway signals, telegraph and telephone uses, and fire and burglar alarm systems. Tungsten and molybdenum production for radio tubes also helped production at Fansteel during the late 1920s.

The collapse of the radio market left the company with a $322,828 net loss in 1928, and the stock market crash of 1929 and the subsequent Depression pushed Fansteel to a more desperate position. Research at this time, however, had continued on shortwave and ultra-high frequency tubes, which would become important products for Fansteel during World War II. Moreover, in 1930 Fansteel began to market carbide tools and dies that the company had developed from tantalum and tungsten carbides. Perhaps the most important development during the 1930s was the company's redefinition of itself—"an industrial company serving industry." Metallurgy was the business Fansteel knew best, and in 1935 it changed its name to Fansteel Metallurgical Corporation.

One way Fansteel was to serve industry was finding industrial outlets for the metal tantalum. In the early 1930s the company produced it for VASCO, an alloys steel company, which was later merged into a subsidiary of Fansteel. Fansteel's tantalum capacitors, developed in 1930, seemed destined to grow with the electronics industry. Throughout the 1930s tantalum production continued to help Fansteel grow, helping the company move from a $218,900 net loss in 1932 to a profit of $35,409 in 1933. By 1942 the company had installed more than 70 tantalum units for the absorption of hydrochloric acid in plants across the United States, Canada, South America, Australia, and India. Besides its use in acid plants, tantalum products for medical and surgical uses became an important part of Fansteel production. Many skull and nerve injuries were repaired during World War II using tantalum implants and tantalum wire for sutures. During the 1930s Fansteel produced a metal alloy that was used in the manufacture of tools in hundreds of metal-cutting operations.

Also notable during this period was a sit-down strike staged by employees in 1937. The strike led to the dismissal of 37 employees after they had caused considerable damage to the physical plant. Most of the employees, however, were forgiven and rehired.

The short supply of weapons and metals at the beginning of World War II proved to be a boon for Fansteel, and by 1943 it was able to list 135 uses and applications for its metals and products. It was involved in fabricating tantalum and other specialty metals, electrical contacts, cutting tools, powder metallurgy products, rectifiers, acid-plant chemical equipment, arresters, and surgical products. As a result, Fansteel experienced exceptional growth—216 percent in 1941, 354 percent in 1942, and 701 percent in 1943. Because of the labor shortage during the war, Fansteel had to mechanize more of its equipment, a development that also added to its financial growth. Fansteel was one of many companies that received the Award for Chemical Engineering Achievement from the U.S. government for work on the atomic bomb.

Although Fansteel benefited from the war, it still faced the challenge of finding peacetime uses for many of its products. One area that seemed poised for Fansteel's products was the rapidly growing aerospace industry. Peacetime uses for the company's wartime discoveries would also be found in the areas of electronics, radar, television, plastics, and the X-ray. In 1946 Fansteel had an operating loss of $438,000. In 1947, when it posted a net profit of $61,000, the company was able to buy on extremely favorable terms a tantalum plant the government had constructed during the war. In the aftermath of World War II,

Fansteel had solid productive capacity, but again it needed to redefine its markets.

Postwar Growth

As the economy recovered after World War II, Fansteel began to benefit from the high demand of products that used its metals and metal parts. Among these products were automobiles, airplanes, electronic equipment, home appliances, and business machines. Its acid-proof process equipment produced drugs, dyes, petrochemicals, plastics, and food products. Its carbide tools were used in the mining, construction, and machining industries.

As Fansteel recovered with the postwar boom, so, too, did it find itself with increased competition. In the early 1950s Fansteel was the only company producing tantalum. By 1960 it had nine competitors. As a result, by the early 1960s the company's sales of tantalum were not producing profits, and in 1965, Fansteel sold all its inventory and production equipment in this area. The company recognized that it had come to the end of an era and needed a new strategy for growth.

During the 1960s Fansteel tried to reshape itself through acquisitions. In 1961 it purchased the Wesson Tool Company, which gave the company four new plants. These plants produced cutting tools that Fansteel was able to add to its existing product line. In 1963 Fansteel agreed to acquire the metals division of the Stauffer Chemical Company, providing Fansteel with four electron-beam vacuum furnaces. Between 1963 and 1968 the company made 15 acquisitions, in the process significantly increasing its sales. Its 1966 sales were $53,745,550. In general, the company hoped not only to manufacture rare metals but to use these metals to produce finished parts for industry. On May 1, 1968, it adopted a new name, Fansteel Inc.

During the 1970s Fansteel continued to reshape itself. Most importantly, it diversified its product lines, producing such items as artificial limbs, golf club heads, surgical instruments, and insulation and structural products for the building industry. In addition, the company continued to produce some of its traditional products—such as a wide range of electrical contacts from tungsten—as well as parts for the aerospace industry. Tantalum was also a source of revenue for the company through the 1970s. Along with these changes came increased sales, from $90 million in 1973 to $104 million in 1976, the year when Fansteel was acquired by H.K. Porter Company, Inc., of Pittsburgh, Pennsylvania. H.K. Porter would own Fansteel for just seven years, and in 1983, it distributed all its Fansteel shares to its shareholders, thus restoring Fansteel as an independent company.

Declining Sales and Recovery: The 1980s and 1990s

For Fansteel the 1980s were years of mixed fortune. The company began the decade with its purchase in 1980 of Pasco Gear & Machine, Inc., for $5 million. In 1984 and 1985 it made two purchases—Hydro Carbide Corp. and Custom Technologies Corp., respectively. Hydro Carbide was a producer of high-quality tungsten carbide products, such as saw blades, dies, and oil-well drilling nozzles. Custom Technologies specialized in large aluminum and magnesium sand castings used in missile systems, helicopters, and gas turbine engines. Also in 1985 the company divested itself of the Advance Casting plant and Federal Stampings Inc.

During the 1980s net sales for Fansteel at first appeared promising but then entered a period of instability. Sales of $153 million in 1983 bumped up to $180 million in 1984 and $208 million in 1985. But sales of $210 million in 1986 would be a high point. The following year sales dipped $33 million, in part because a sharp decline in orders from companies manufacturing space systems, aircraft, and weapons systems.

It was this decline in military-related orders, combined with the recession of the late 1980s, that proved disastrous for the company. Under the guidance of Keith R. Garrity, Fansteel's chief executive officer (formerly president of H.K. Porter), sales began to totter then plummet. Sales of $168 million in 1989 fell to $134 million in 1991 and $127 million in 1992. In the following year the bottom seemed to fall out, and the company managed sales of only $89 million.

Some of this fall in sales can be attributed to divestment of the company's metal products business in 1989. This segment had been faring poorly for some time, and the proceeds from its sale went to retire completely the company's term debt. In the 1991 annual report, moreover, Fansteel conceded that its losses were also the result of "costs to remediate certain environmental problems related to operations previously discontinued." Even during the worst of Fansteel's troubles, however, the company was essentially sound, especially because it remained "unencumbered by any significant amount of debt."

Fansteel began to dig its way back up in the mid-1990s, and, with the help of a capital-spending program, it started to reduce its dependence on military markets and to position itself to serve commercial ones. The company also made its manufacturing facilities more efficient and improved its marketing strategies. No doubt an improved economy helped as well, as sales, still at $89 million in 1994, jumped to $102 million in 1995 and $120 million in 1996. Sadly, in 1995, at the age of 63, Keith Garrity died. By the following year William D. Jarosz had become the company's chairman, president, and chief executive officer.

Principal Subsidiaries

American Sintered Technologies; Custom Technologies Corporation; Fansteel Holdings Incorporated; Fansteel Sales Corporation, Inc. (Barbados).

Further Reading

Leach, Mark, "Metal Fabricating Industry," *Value Line Investment Survey,* January 3, 1997, p. 578.

Petry, Corinna C., "Fansteel Profits Rise 28% on Higher Sales," *American Metal Market,* February 5, 1997, p. 3.

Tennyson, Jon R., *$2500 and a Dream: The Fansteel Story,* Chicago: Fansteel Inc., 1982.

—Vita Richman

Fletcher Challenge Ltd.

Fletcher Challenge House
810 Great South Road
Penrose
Auckland
New Zealand
(9) 525-9000
Fax: (9) 525-0559
Web site: http://www.fcl.co.nz

Public Company
Incorporated: 1981
Employees: 23,000
Sales: NZ $9.14 billion (US $6.27 billion) (1996)
Stock Exchanges: Auckland Perth Sydney London
    Toronto Montreal Vancouver Frankfurt New York
SICs: 0831 Forest Nurseries & Forest Products; 1382 Oil
    & Gas Field Exploration Services; 2411 Logging
    Camps & Logging Contractors; 2421 Sawmills &
    Planing Mills, General; 2611 Pulp Mills; 2621 Paper
    Mills; 6719 Offices of Holding Companies, Not
    Elsewhere Classified

Fletcher Challenge Ltd., New Zealand's largest group of companies, specializes in transforming resources into value-added products that are marketed both domestically and around the globe. The company was formed on January 1, 1981, by the merger of Challenge Corporation Ltd., Fletcher Holdings Ltd., and Tasman Pulp and Paper Company Ltd. In March 1996 Fletcher Challenge was reorganized into a group consisting of four separate publicly traded companies. Fletcher Challenge Building is a leader in New Zealand in building materials, notably concrete, steel, plasterboard, lumber, wood fiber-based panel products, and aluminum extrusion. It is also involved in residential and commercial construction. Fletcher Challenge Energy maintains petroleum exploration, production, and distribution operations in New Zealand and Canada and has utilities operations in New Zealand. Fletcher Challenge Forests is a world leader in solid wood plantation forestry and manages plantation forests in New Zealand, Chile, and Argentina. Fletcher Challenge Paper is a leading maker of communications papers and specialty pulp.

Challenge Corporation Ltd.

The origins of Fletcher Challenge Ltd. can be traced to the 19th century. Its history began when John T. Wright and Robert M. Robertson set up a business partnership called Wright, Robertson & Company as a merchant, stock and station agent, and woolbroker in Dunedin in 1861. Four years later John Stephenson joined the partnership and in 1868, when Robertson retired, the business was renamed Wright Stephenson & Company. It was floated as a public company in 1906 and opened its first overseas branch in London that year. An office was opened in Wellington in 1908. By 1916 the company was already expanding rapidly when it took over W. & G. Turnbull & Company of Wellington and W. Gunson & Company of Auckland. Many more mergers and acquisitions followed and the company continued to grow. In 1920 Wright Stephenson & Company became one of the first companies in New Zealand to diversify into fertilizers, and shortly afterward it further expanded its range with the establishment of a bloodstock and studstock department.

In 1927 the company began to expand out of the stock and station business. It started to trade in motor cars and subsequently added the retailing of electrical appliances, land development, and department stores to its range of activities. In 1962 it acquired Morrison Industries Ltd., marking the company's first major involvement in manufacturing motor mawers and bicycles.

Wright Stevenson opened its first office in Australia in 1938 and expanded during the next 30 years, with branches being opened all over New Zealand. In 1972 Wright Stephenson merged with the National Mortgage Agency of New Zealand Ltd. National Mortgage, too, had grown through acquisition since its beginnings in the mid-19th century. The takeover brought Wright Stephenson an increased range of activities, including extensive fishing and meat exporting operations.

Company Perspectives:

"Fletcher Challenge is a New Zealand headquartered corporation devoted to creating superior shareholder value by taking resources to customers better in pulp and paper, energy and building industries. Fletcher Challenge strives for excellence in everything it does through industry leadership in fulfillment of customer needs and dynamic utilization of human skills and financial and material resources. Fletcher Challenge operates with integrity and a people oriented management style which stresses openness, communication, commitment, innovation and co-ordinated decentralization of authority, responsibility and accountability."

With this merger a new name was sought that would be synonymous with both the united and diversified character of the company. The name chosen was Challenge Corporation Ltd. The company's chairman between 1970 and 1981 was Ronald Trotter. By 1980 Challenge Corporation had assets of NZ $7.6 billion.

Fletcher Holdings Ltd.

Fletcher Holdings Ltd. began when James Fletcher, a carpenter and joiner by trade, emigrated from Scotland to New Zealand in 1908. Recalling this period, James Fletcher wrote, "I arrived in Dunedin on a Tuesday. Conditions in the building trade in 1908 were bad, and starting on the morning I arrived, I canvassed practically every job in the city, including house building and alterations, without success. I got a job on Friday evening with a firm called Crawford and Watson, the first firm I had called on the Tuesday. Watson was rather amused at my persistence in coming back a second time within a matter of three days, but he gave me the job."

Within a year Fletcher and another immigrant, Bert Morris, set up as builders and won their first contract—to build a house. On completion they were paid £375, of which just NZ $3.6 was profit. Four years later Morris sold his share of the partnership to Fletcher for £500. Fletcher's brother, William, arrived from Scotland to join him and the company became Fletcher Brothers Ltd. By 1919 two more Fletcher brothers, John and Andrew, had joined the company. Its name was changed to the Fletcher Construction Company Ltd. and the headquarters moved to Wellington. Over the next ten years Fletcher Construction continued to expand. To service its building growth the company acquired several joinery factories, quarries, and brickyards, and also set up its own steel fabricating yard.

By the 1930s the effects of the worldwide depression began to be felt in New Zealand, and Fletcher Construction's work slowed down for the first time. Undaunted, James Fletcher toured the country, encouraging the building of large-scale projects. He argued that building when costs were low made economic sense, helped the economy, and also boosted morale. Although the company's rate of expansion declined, it won tenders, or bids, for several important contracts, including the National Art Gallery, the Post Office in Dunedin, and the

railway station in Wellington, the latter being then the largest individual building contract ever awarded in New Zealand.

In 1937 the New Zealand government launched its public housing scheme. Fletcher Construction had the foresight to consult architects and draw up specifications in advance of tenders being invited, thus enabling the company to respond extremely rapidly to the government's plans. Fletcher was awarded contracts for houses in Wellington and Auckland. Within two years it was a major builder for the government and had regained its former impetus. With the outbreak of World War II in 1939, Fletcher Construction realized that a regular supply of essential materials from overseas was likely to be placed in jeopardy. To counter this shortage, the company set up enterprises in sawn timber, plywood, and door manufacturing.

Further expansion continued, and in 1940, the company went public with the formation of Fletcher Holdings Ltd. James Fletcher, who served in the honorary post of commissioner of defense construction and later as the first commissioner of works, received a knighthood in 1946. His son, James C. Fletcher, was appointed managing director of the company in 1942 at the age of 28. Under the guidance of James C. Fletcher the company began to expand its horizons. Fletcher traveled widely and recognized the value of new methods. An early example was his bringing two leading U.S. construction companies into a partnership with Fletcher, to undertake the expansion of Auckland's wharves. James C. Fletcher is also remembered as a pioneer of welfare schemes for his employees. Among other benefits he introduced the first wholly subsidized superannuation scheme for construction workers and a medical scheme for employees before general medical insurance had been introduced.

After the war the Fletcher group continued to acquire established companies in the construction industry. It also diversified into new industries such as readymix concrete, long-run roofing (the production of preformed roof trusses that needed no additional carpentry on installation), and galvanizing. The company had a major influence on the New Zealand steel industry through the development of Pacific Steel Ltd. and New Zealand Wire Ltd., and it also diversified into merchant banking and financial services.

Tasman Pulp and Paper Company Ltd.

In 1951 the New Zealand government showed an interest in using the country's natural resources to establish a paper, pulp, and newsprint industry. Fletcher Holdings offered to build a pulp and newsprint mill if the government provided the infrastructure that such a large-scale project needed. The result was the Tasman Pulp and Paper Company, which was formed the following year with shares held by the government, Fletcher Trust and Investment Ltd., and the public. By 1955 the pulp mill and the newsprint machine were brought into production and the sawmill came on line in 1956. From the beginning the company had targeted the export market, and so Tasman Pulp and Paper (Sales) Ltd. was established in Australia. By 1962 Tasman Pulp and Paper had commissioned a second newsprint machine and in 1970 there was further expansion of the pulp mill with the aim of producing enough pulp for a third machine plus a surplus for sales elsewhere. In 1975, under an arrangement made with the Union Steam Ship Company, Tasman Pulp and Paper had sole operation of two ships to transport its products to South Island and to Australia. The government sold its shares in the company in 1979. By 1980 Fletcher Holdings owned 56.46 percent and Challenge Corporation owned 28.23 percent of Tasman Pulp and Paper.

Fletcher Challenge Forms in 1981

James C. Fletcher received a knighthood for services to industry in 1980. Following the formation of Fletcher Challenge Ltd. in 1981, he was appointed president of the new company and Sir Ronald Trotter of Challenge Corporation was appointed chairman. Since its inception, Fletcher Challenge has grown from being an exclusively New Zealand-based company to an industrial group with its headquarters in New Zealand. It was assisted in this expansion by the relaxation of New Zealand's capital laws in the early 1980s, which encouraged overseas investment.

The company's international expansion started in Canada with the acquisition of Crown Forest Industries in British Columbia in 1983. The main activities of this company were pulp and paper, wood products, packaging, and merchandising. By 1987 Fletcher Challenge acquired a majority share of British Columbia Forest Products Ltd., one of Canada's largest producers of forest products. In the following year these two companies were combined to form Fletcher Challenge Canada Ltd. Fletcher Challenge also acquired pulp and paper interests in South America and Australia. In 1989 the company was adversely affected by a huge fall in pulp and paper earnings as a result of lower newsprint prices and a strong Canadian dollar. The company was able to overcome these setbacks, however, owing to strong performances from its other operations.

Fletcher Challenge extended its construction business into the United States by acquiring companies in Seattle, Washington; Los Angeles; and in Hawaii in the latter half of the 1980s. The company became a leading building contractor in the United States as well as in southeast Asia and the South Pacific.

Fletcher Challenge also expanded its activities in New Zealand. In 1988 it bought the Petroleum Company of New Zealand (Petrocorp) from the government and thus became the country's largest oil, gas, and petrochemicals company. It has built on this diversification into energy by making a considerable investment in further oil and gas exploration. Also in New Zealand, Fletcher Challenge bought the Rural Bank from the government in 1989, which consolidated its leading position in the provision of finance and services to New Zealand's large agricultural community.

In 1990 Fletcher Challenge made its first big move into the European market with the takeover of the British fine-paper manufacturer, UK Paper. The company aimed to expand production and increase exports to continental Europe. UK Paper also would be used as a convenient base for acquiring similar interests in Europe. UK Paper had been bought out by its management in 1986 and consequently had a tradition of strong employee involvement. Fletcher Challenge, which was virtually unknown to the British work force, took steps to get to know its new employees. Garry Mace, chief executive of the forest industries division, spent two weeks visiting all of the U.K.

manufacturing sites and ensured that every employee was given an opportunity to attend one of the many seminars that he ran to explain the objectives of the Fletcher Challenge organization.

In 1991 the chief executive of Fletcher Challenge Ltd. was Hugh Fletcher, grandson of the founder of the Fletcher group. Fletcher joined the company in 1969 at the age of 22 and attained the chief executive position in October 1987. He had been at the forefront of Fletcher Challenge's expansionist activities.

Hugh Fletcher quickly gained a reputation as a dealmaker. In October 1990 he acquired the New Zealand gas production interests of British Petroleum in the Maui Field. Production from the Maui Field was equivalent to 30 million barrels of oil a year, or more than half of New Zealand's total demand at the time. It was anticipated that production will continue until at least the year 2020. The timing of the deal was extremely fortunate for Fletcher Challenge as it was negotiated three months before the Persian Gulf crisis, when oil prices were relatively low. As a result of this acquisition, Fletcher Challenge dominated the New Zealand oil and gas sector.

Interviewed in the *Financial Times* on October 31, 1990, Hugh Fletcher likened his aspirations for the company's expansion to "the Hannibal instinct to go over the next mountain range," and it was clear that Fletcher Challenge's strategy for the 1990s was to continue to expand worldwide. At the same time, the company was prepared to sell off any subsidiaries that would not play a part in international expansion. Consequently, Fletcher Challenge sold its Fletcher Fishing subsidiary to Carter Holt Harvey of New Zealand. Fletcher Fishing, a profitable company with export markets in the United States, Japan, and France, held 18 percent of the New Zealand fish quota, but Fletcher Challenge was unable to acquire any compatible overseas companies with which to merge Fletcher Fishing.

Divestment Plan Launched in 1992

By 1992, however, the continuing burden of a high debt load—the result of the numerous acquisitions of previous years—proved to be too much of a drag on company earnings and its stock. Although Fletcher Challenge's debt-to-equity ratio had fallen from 194 percent in June 1990 to 134 percent in June 1992, it was still considered much too high and contributed to a fiscal 1992 after-tax loss of NZ $157.5 million and to a drop in Fletcher Challenge stock from NZ $3.53 on June 30, 1992 to NZ $2.33 on August 14—a fall of more than one-third in just six weeks.

The company responded in August 1992 by announcing a divestment plan through which it hoped to shed up to NZ $2.6 billion (US $1.3 billion) in assets and thereby reduce the debt-to-equity ratio to 100 percent by the end of 1993. These goals were soon met. In 1992 Fletcher Challenge sold Crown Packaging, which had been part of Crown Forest Industries; one-third of Natural Gas Corp., New Zealand's monopoly natural gas distributor, to the public; and Rural Bank, acquired only three years earlier, to National Bank of New Zealand. The following year the company sold Wrightson Limited, the leading rural servicing company in New Zealand, and agreed to merge its methanol subsidiary, Fletcher Challenge Methanol, into Methanex Corp. of Canada. In the latter deal Fletcher Challenge ended up with a 47 percent stake in the newly bolstered Methanex and NZ $480 million (US $250 million) in cash.

At the conclusion of the asset sales Fletcher Challenge had essentially reduced itself to four main areas of operation: plantation forestry, pulp and paper manufacturing, energy, and building materials and construction. Along with what it called its newfound ''focused diversity,'' Fletcher Challenge was also able by fiscal 1995 to reduce its debt-to-equity ratio to 35 percent. The company returned to profitability in fiscal 1993 and posted healthy earnings of NZ $464 million by fiscal 1995.

With its financial health improving, the mid-1990s saw Fletcher Challenge expand internationally, with Asia its main destination, a logical choice for a company with a strong position in New Zealand and Australia. In 1995 Fletcher Challenge took a 20 percent stake in a US $300 million project to construct a newsprint plant in fast-growing Malaysia. Other Asian investments were made in China and India.

Restructuring in the Mid-1990s

The mid-1990s were also highlighted by significant structural changes. In late 1993 Fletcher Challenge floated its forestry division into a separate publicly traded company, Fletcher Challenge Forests, still under the control of Fletcher Challenge. Then in March 1996 Fletcher Challenge codified its four-division structure when it split its main stock into three more separate publicly traded companies, all remaining part of Fletcher Challenge: Fletcher Challenge Paper, Fletcher Challenge Energy, and Fletcher Challenge Building. The company stated that these moves would enable investors to target their stock purchases more precisely, and they were made in response to another drop in Fletcher Challenge's main stock (which ceased trading following the 1996 split).

Later that year, in July, Fletcher Challenge Building began a major restructuring when it decided to scale back considerably its construction activities outside New Zealand (its building materials manufacturing operations were not affected by this downsizing). As a result, three U.S. operations were sold, offices in Kuala Lumpur and Jakarta were closed, and operations in Western and South Australia were divested.

Meanwhile, in August 1996 Fletcher Challenge Forests was part of a consortium that purchased Forestry Corporation of New Zealand from the New Zealand government for NZ $2.026 billion (US $1.395 billion), forming the CNI (Central North Island) Forest Partnership. The partnership, which gained cutting rights to 188,000 hectares (464,000 acres) of mainly pine plantation forests via the purchase, consisted of Fletcher Challenge Forests, with a 37.5 percent stake; Citifor, a subsidiary of the China International Trust and Investment Corporation, also with 37.5 percent; and Brierly Investment Limited, with 25 percent. Fletcher Challenge Forests was to manage the entire estate, which was adjacent to its own 117,000 hectares (289,000 acres) of plantation in the Central North Island.

Fletcher Challenge's history is rife with strategic shifts, but it seemed no period could compete with the enormous changes of the early and mid-1990s. The year 1997 was also destined to be significant since Hugh Fletcher announced early in 1997 that he intended to retire later in the year, after serving as a company

executive for 20 years. By this time, however, the company appeared to be content to fine-tune its four-division structure and, perhaps, finally enter a more stable period in its history.

Principal Subsidiaries

Fletcher Challenge Industries Overseas Limited; Fletcher Challenge Industries Limited; Fletcher Challenge Finance Limited; Fletcher Challenge Acceptances Australia Pty. Limited; Fletcher Challenge Discounts (Australia) Pty. Limited; Fletcher Challenge Industries Australia Limited; Fletcher Challenge Capital Canada Inc.; Fletcher Challenge Finance Canada Inc.; Fletcher Challenge Industries Canada Inc.; Fletcher Challenge Finance Netherlands B.V.; Fletcher Challenge Finance UK Limited; Fletcher Challenge Forest Industries Plc (U.K.); Fletcher Challenge Finance USA Inc.; Fletcher Challenge Industries USA Limited; Tasman Pulp and Paper Company Limited; Tasman Asia Shipping Company Limited (70%); Endeavor Papers Pty. Limited (Australia; 80%); PISA - Papel de Imprensa S.A. (Brazil; 51%); Fletcher Challenge Canada Limited (51%); Papeles Bio Bio S.A. (Chile; 51%); Tasman Asia B.V. (Netherlands; 70%); Guppy Paper Limited (U.K.); UK Paper Plc; Blandin Paper Company (U.S.A.; 51%); Fletcher Merchants Limited; Fletcher Building Products Limited; Scott Panel & Hardware Limited; Plyco Doors Limited; Winstone Wallboards Limited; Fletcher Homes Limited; Duroid Limited; Residential Mortgages Limited; Fletcher Wood Panels Limited; Challenge Properties Limited; The Golden Bay Cement Company Limited; Firth Industries Limited; Winstone Aggregates Limited; Firth Certified Concrete Limited; Fletcher Construction New Zealand and South Pacific Limited; The Fletcher Construction Company Limited; Fletcher Challenge Steel Limited; Fletcher Aluminum Limited; Fletcher Challenge Forests (Manufacturing) Limited; Hikurangi Forest Farms Limited; Tarawera Forests Limited; Tasman Forestry (Nelson) Limited; Fletcher Challenge Forests Limited; TFL Gisborne Limited; Fletcher Construction Company North America (U.S.A.); Fletcher Challenge Industries Finance USA Limited; Petrocorp Exploration Limited; Petrocorp Offshore (No.7) Ltd.; Kapuni Gas Contracts Limited; Fletcher Challenge Petroleum Investments Ltd.; Fletcher Challenge Petroleum Limited; Fletcher Challenge Petroleum Marketing Ltd.; Southern Petroleum No Liability; Power Supply Corporation Ltd.; Fletcher Challenge Utilities Investments Ltd.; Fletcher Challenge Petroleum Borneo Ltd. (Brunei); Fletcher Challenge Petroleum Inc.; Petrocorp Exploration Indonesia Ltd.; Fletcher Challenge Petroleum U.S.A. Corp.

Principal Divisions

Fletcher Challenge Paper; Fletcher Challenge Energy; Fletcher Challenge Building; Fletcher Challenge Forests.

Further Reading

Baldo, Anthony, ''A Challenge Down Under: Acquisitions Have Made New Zealand's Fletcher Challenge a Global Force,'' *Financial World,* February 20, 1990, p. 60.

Bywater, Marion, ''Company Profile: Fletcher Challenge Surfs the Pacific Rim,'' *Paper & Packaging Analyst,* February 1997, p. 35.

Du Bois, Peter C., ''A Kiwi Tree Saga,'' *Barron's,* December 6, 1993, p. 60.

Hargreaves, Deborah, ''Fletcher Challenge Extends Its Global Reach,'' *Financial Times,* November 3, 1995, p. 24.

James, Colin, ''A Challenge Confronted: New Zealand's Fletcher Nears Asset-Sales Goal,'' *Far Eastern Economic Review,* February 18, 1993, p. 56.

——, ''Dinosaur No More: New Zealand's Fletcher Challenge Side-steps Asia in Its Growth,'' *Far Eastern Economic Review,* September 29, 1988, p. 116.

——, ''Divided We Stand: New Zealand's Fletcher Challenge Splits Its Stock,'' *Far Eastern Economic Review,* April 18, 1996, p. 80.

——, ''Slimmer Yet: New Zealand's Fletcher Challenge To Shed Assets,'' *Far Eastern Economic Review*, September 3, 1992, pp. 50, 52–53.

Norman, James R., ''Head Up Down Under,'' *Forbes,* December 10, 1990, pp. 80–83.

—Susanna Wilson
—updated by David E. Salamie

Flying J Inc.

9900 S. 50 W.
Brigham City, Utah 84302
U.S.A.
(801) 734-6400
Fax: (801) 734-6556

Private Company
Incorporated: 1968
Employees: 8,000
Sales: $1.6 billion (1996)
SICs: 5172 Petroleum Products, Not Elsewhere
      Classified; 5541 Gasoline Service Stations; 2911
      Petroleum Refining

Flying J Inc. owns and operates the United States' largest chain of truck stops. Its fast-growing, national chain of 96 Flying J travel plazas not only sells more diesel fuel than any other chain, but has also set a new standard for roadside accommodation for the trucking industry. Flying J is also one of the country's largest independent, vertically integrated petroleum fuel corporations, with its own oil and gas exploration company, petroleum refinery, and truck, barge, and pipeline distribution system. Together, this private company's operations produced an estimated $1.6 billion in sales in 1996. Day-to-day operations are led by President Phil Adams. Founder Jay Call remains as company chairman, and the Call family continues to own more than 75 percent of the company.

Flying J has pioneered a novel concept in the truck stop industry: that truckers deserve clean, friendly, comfortable facilities with a range of amenities, from hotel and motel accommodations, to restaurants, to computer access, well-stocked convenience stores, and even bars with nightly music. The company's innovative service has all but defined a new category of roadside accommodation, the travel plaza, helping to distinguish the chain from the traditional truck stop's more rough-and-ready image. A new full-service Flying J typically occupies some 20 to 25 acres, costs from $5 to $7 million to build, and features up to 12 diesel fuel islands and parking spaces for 50 trucks or more. Beyond truckers' amenities, the chain also seeks to attract the "four-wheel" and recreational vehicle market, and it includes propane hookups as well as fast food restaurants and the company's own Country Market family restaurants. But the chain continues to emphasize the trucker. Each Flying J, which ranges up to 20,000 square feet or more, features a truckers-only section, with a barber shop, telephone booths, television lounge, arcade game room, laundry facilities, and showers. The plaza's convenience store, which serves to separate the trucker's area from the restaurant and the rest of the driving public, is also highly geared toward truckers' needs, stocking as much as $250,000 or more in inventory ranging from lug nuts to underwear to hiking boots, as well as an extensive array of electronic goods that can draw power from a dashboard cigarette lighter.

In addition to the chain's Flying J Inn motels, the company has also linked with the growing Crystal Inn hotel chain, formed by Flying J founder and chairman Jay Call and his daughter Crystal. A Crystal Inn features an "all-suite" concept of 100 rooms catering to the business traveler. The Crystal Inns operate independently from Flying J, but the two chains are closely linked, with many Crystal Inns slated to be built on land owned by Flying J and adjacent to its travel plazas. The management company of Crystal Inn, MacCall Management, has also been contracted to operate the Flying J economy motels. Rounding out Flying J's services offerings, the company has also instituted its own line of truckers' credit, contracting with national fleet operators.

Pioneering the Travel Plaza in the 1980s

O. Jay Call, a native of Idaho, came to Willard, Utah in the mid-1960s to run a gas station he had bought from his family. Call's father had owned a gas station in Idaho; his relatives also owned the successful Maverik chain of convenience stores and service stations, founded in 1930. Call set out to build a chain of his own. By 1968, Call owned four gas stations; in that year, Call organized his company as "Flying J," named for his love of flying. By the late 1970s, Call had recognized an opening in the market for a different kind of truck stop. The typical truck stop of the day could be classified as somewhat squalid, rough-

and-ready places offering few amenities. The truck stop industry itself was highly fragmented. Call took a tip from the booming fast food industry and its growing chains of restaurants offering consistency, quality, and cleanliness, as well as low prices. In 1979, Call debuted the Flying J "travel plaza," in West Haven, Utah, adding amenities such as a restaurant, motel, shower stations, and fuel islands for both cars and trucks. An early hallmark of the Flying J concept was its emphasis on cleanliness. Another was its low fuel prices, with which it lured customers.

In 1980, Flying J took a step to ensure its ability to keep its fuel prices low. The company moved into integrated operations, buying refinery and gas processing assets from Inter-City Gas Ltd., based in Canada. The $31 million purchase gave Flying J refineries and gas processing plants in Cut Bank, Montana and Williston, North Dakota, as well as a number of retail gasoline and propane outlets in Montana, Oregon, Washington, and North Dakota. The sale also gave Flying J its own exploration operation, based in Williston. The company's refinery operations concentrated on blending, upgrading, and distributing petroleum fuels, rather than refining crude oil. The following year, the company was awarded a $4.9 million contract from the Defense Logistics Agency for gasoline and other petroleum products. But the company's emphasis remained on its own chain of service stations and its drive toward vertical integration.

By the mid-1980s, Flying J had expanded its operations through much of the northwest. With 35 Flying J gasoline and truck stops and convenience stores, the company was achieving annual sales of some $240 million and a spot on *Forbes's* list of the largest private companies in the United States. In 1986, Flying J made its next major move, more than tripling its annual sales with the $70 million purchase of the U.S. refining and retail operations from Canada's Husky Oil Ltd. The purchase included a 35,000 barrel-per-day refinery in Cheyenne, Wyoming; a pipeline stretching from Wyoming to Nebraska; and a refinery in Salt Lake City, Utah with a capacity of 14,000 barrels per day, as well as a closed refinery, capable of 15,000 barrels per day, in Cody, Wyoming. The purchase also gave Flying J some 550 retail outlets and 40 gasoline stations and truck stops under the Husky brand name. The acquisition made Flying J the largest independent oil company in the northwest.

With the acquisition, Call set out to build Flying J into a national chain, starting with 50 Flying Js, including 15 former Husky stations to be converted to the Flying J concept. Call envisioned a chain of at least 300 Flying Js; once again turning to the fast food industry, Call's original plan was to build a franchise concept for the truck stop industry. As he told *National Petroleum News*, "We're putting together an extremely sophisticated franchise program for the truckstop industry, including credit systems, cash transfer systems, and marketing programs." Although the company continued to lease its Husky stores to existing dealers, the Husky name would be phased out through the rest of the decade, allowing Husky Oil Ltd. to retain exclusive control of the brand. Dealers participating in the franchise program would have their truck stop remodeled and converted to the Flying J concept.

That concept was itself undergoing an expansion, as Flying J unveiled its "next generation" travel plaza concept of ex-

panded facilities, heightening the company's emphasis on its food, lodging, and convenience amenities. As Adams, then executive vice-president, told *National Petroleum News*, "We're more in the hospitality business, not necessarily the oil business." The franchise program attracted the interest of Phoenix-based Franchise Finance Corp. of America, an investment syndicator that had built up a portfolio of more than 1,000 fast food and other real estate franchises since the early 1980s. In 1987, Franchise Finance Corp. raised $52 million to acquire 11 Flying J travel plazas, while beginning a $1 billion plan to build its Flying J franchise holdings to as many as 250 by the mid-1990s.

Leading the Industry in the 1990s

The Flying J franchise network proved to be short-lived, however. By the early 1990s, the company had moved to maintain full ownership of the Flying J chain. With the truck stop industry remaining highly fragmented (there were an estimated 3,000 truck stop companies at the beginning of the 1990s), the time was right for consolidation, with Flying J leading the way. Aiding the company was a rising trend in the trucking industry itself, as more and more husband-wife driving teams began to take to the road. And while some in the industry regretted the slow passing of the traditional image of the rough-hewn truck stop, Flying J's travel plaza concept, with amenities including restaurants, lodging, barber shops and hairdressers, television lounges and other comforts for the truck driver, coupled with its insistence on cleanliness, quality, consistency, and low fuel prices, proved attractive not only to the trucking industry, but to the automobile and recreational vehicle traveler as well.

By 1993, Flying J operated 63 travel plazas and, coupled with its refinery operations, was generating between $800 and $900 million per year. By then, Call had stepped down from the day-to-day running of the company. Call remained chairman of the company, and his family continued to hold a majority of the private company's shares. But, telling the *Salt Lake Tribune*, "I'm not an operator. I've done it, but I don't want to any more," Call had moved on to new projects, including developing a 1,500-acre cattle ranch in Montana. Call, together with his son and daughter, was also developing another side business, forming Call's Investment to build a new chain of all-suites hotels. Dubbed the Crystal Inn after Call's daughter, the hotels would feature indoor pools, jacuzzis and workout areas, as well as a kitchen to serve breakfast. The first Crystal Inn opened in Salt Lake City. By 1995, Call had stepped aside from that project as well, allowing daughter Crystal and her husband to operate and expand the new hotel chain, which would remain closely linked with the family's Flying J chain.

Meanwhile, Flying J, now under the leadership of Adams, stepped up its expansion. By 1995, the company was operating nearly 90 travel centers, while continuing to upgrade its amenities offerings. In that year, the company introduced a new restaurant concept to its travel centers, opening the family-style Country Market Restaurant and Buffet, offering 24-hour, buffet-style service with seating for up to 150 people. Meanwhile, the company turned over management of its Flying J motels to Crystal Inn, while making plans to add the all-suites hotel concept to some of its sites as well. With the state-of-the-art Flying Js costing up to $10 million to build, Flying J, which had been serving the freeway and interstate market, began developing a smaller-scale concept for the secondary roadways. The company also expanded its oil well operations with the acquisition of Cenex Inc.'s oil and gas production operations. The acquisition more than doubled Flying J's production to 6,000 barrels per day.

By 1996, the chain had grown to 96 Flying Js, with the company announcing plans to add 15 to 20 travel centers per year toward the end of the century. Flying J, which had already grown to become the country's largest diesel fuel retailer, had by then climbed to number 152 on *Forbes's* list of the largest private companies in the United States, with sales topping $1.3 billion in 1995. The company, which had begun marketing to national trucking fleets in the early 1990s, was also getting into the credit business, promoting its own fuel transaction card, a position that led to a conflict with Comdata, one of the leading credit transaction processors for the trucking industry. When Comdata and Flying J began negotiating to renew their contract, Comdata pressured Flying J to stop promoting its own card. Flying J refused, announcing that its travel centers would no longer accept Comdata's Comcheck card, and began encouraging customers to switch to its own or other third party cards; the break was complete when Comdata announced that it would no longer process transactions made at Flying J travel centers. With Comdata remaining a major supplier of credit transactions to the nation's trucking industry, the effect of the break on Flying J remained to be seen. Nonetheless, Adams told *The Tennessean,* "We're comfortable about life without Comdata." Indeed, Flying J's reputation among its customers in both the trucking industry and the general motoring public appeared solid. Estimates of the company's sales for 1996 were at $1.6 billion.

Principal Subsidiaries

Big West Oil Co.

Further Reading

Carey, Bill, "Comdata Ends Relationship with Flying J Truck Stops," *The Tennessean,* June 3, 1996, p. 1E.

Green, Steve, "Low Gas Prices, Hot Meals, Quality Facilities Mean Brigham City's Flying J Is Flying High," *Salt Lake Tribune,* November 3, 1996, p. E1.

"Husky Acquisition Makes Flying J Biggest Independent in Mountain West," *National Petroleum News,* February 1986, p. 35.

Keahey, John, "Inn Idea Is Crystal Clear," *Salt Lake Tribune,* December 24, 1995, p. F1.

Smith, Gordon, "Space-Age Truck Stop Is Roadside Oasis," *San Diego Union-Tribune,* July 21, 1994, p. A1.

Timmons, Tony, "Truck Stops Convert To 'Travel Plazas'," *Las Vegas Business Press,* February 10, 1997, p. 3.

—M.L. Cohen

Forest Oil Corporation

1600 Broadway, Suite 2200
Denver, Colorado 80202-4722
U.S.A.
(303) 812-1400
Fax: (303) 812-1602

Public Company
Incorporated: 1916
Employees: 250
Sales: $317.5 million (1996)
Stock Exchanges: NASDAQ
SICs: 1311 Crude Petroleum and Natural Gas

A producer of oil and natural gas in the United States, Forest Oil Corporation is credited with developing and implementing the secondary recovery of oil technique (''waterflooding'') in the early 1900s, a revolutionary occurrence in the oil and gas industry at that time. The company acquires, explores, and develops reserve properties throughout the world, with concentrations in the United States and the Gulf of Mexico. Through the acquisition of new reserves and the increased production capacities of existing ones, Forest Oil produces approximately 1.5 billion barrels of oil and 40 billion cubic feet of natural gas each year. The company also actively pursues new reserves.

The Early Years, 1916–1939

Forest Dale Dorn and Clayton Glenville Dorn created Forest Oil Corporation in 1916 as an oil field waterflooding company in northern Pennsylvania. The company's roots can be traced to an oil field in Bradford, Pennsylvania, that was discovered in 1871. By 1916, oil production at the Bradford site had declined to just under 40 barrels a day, and the reserve was considered by many to be dry. On this ''dry'' site, Forest Dale Dorn tried out a new waterflooding technique to initiate secondary recovery of oil. The process involved the injection of fluid into the oil reservoir to create energy to produce additional oil. The success of Dorn's technique prompted him to create his own wa-

terflooding company with his father and partner, Clayton Glenville Dorn.

Within 5 years, Forest Oil was widely recognized throughout the oil and gas industry as not only the innovator of waterflooding, but the authority and leader in secondary oil recovery systems. The company was quickly contracted by other companies to recover oil through waterflooding techniques at drilling sites around Pennsylvania that were either in the process of being depleted or completely exhausted. Forest Oil's ideas were soon being applied throughout the industry, and were aiding in the extension of oil wells' lives by as much as ten years, in some cases.

Meanwhile, Forest Oil continued drilling wells at the Bradford site. In the late 1920s and early 1930s, the company drilled over 1,000 wells per year, and production increased from the 1916 low of under 40 barrels per day to over 9,300 barrels per day in 1939. Soon thereafter, the reserve at the Bradford site was finally exhausted, and Forest Oil moved on to new properties in Illinois and Oklahoma.

Postwar Diversification

After contributing resources to the World War II effort, Forest Oil changed its emphasis. The company began to focus more on its own exploration endeavors as well as on secondary recovery techniques. To these ends came further geographic expansion into Texas, New Mexico, Louisiana, and several areas in the Rocky Mountains. Then came the decision to seek out not only the properties that were well-suited for implementation of secondary recovery techniques, but also properties that would yield oil and gas on their own. It was at this time that Forest Oil developed three guiding principles that would lead the company for years to come: (1) to explore only in areas of high potential, (2) to employ only the most-qualified personnel, and (3) to seek out and enter ventures and partnerships with others. Forest Oil began to deal more in the area of natural gas as well as in oil.

Forest Oil's expansion and diversification following the war enabled it to join the major oil and gas companies when the industry moved its operations offshore in the early 1950s.

Company Perspectives:

"Management's role in achieving success is to provide a work environment and performance incentives that will attract and retain superior talent. Success in the oil and gas business requires determination, innovative thinking, proper application of technology and the relentless pursuit of the highest standards of performance."

Forest Oil entered into its first offshore lease agreement in 1952, and was one of the first and only independent companies to drill offshore in the Gulf of Mexico.

Within five years, Forest Oil was comprised of operations in 15 states and four countries on three different continents, and its international holdings were increasing. The company successfully produced oil in the United States, Canada, Colombia, and Cyprus. These foreign ventures, as well as others, continued to prosper for the next decade. In 1969, Forest Oil had grown to be large enough that the company issued its first public offering of stock in the beginning of that year.

A Strong Reputation in the 1970s and 1980s

Entering the 1970s, very few undeveloped areas existed in the United States any more. Companies began to battle for the exploration areas that required deep drilling, and Forest Oil proved that it was up to the task. It set up operations in the Deep Delaware Basin, which meant drilling wells at depths of more than 20,000 feet. The company soon built a solid reputation as a producer who could drill in deep and expensive territory with success, and continued its tradition of using its innovations to overcome technological problems in the industry.

The company's expensive exploration and problem-solving ventures were funded by the high gas and oil prices from which the industry benefitted in the early 1970s. In 1974, Forest Oil sold the bulk of its oil properties to Sun Oil for over $114 million. The company then shifted the majority of its focus to the exploration for natural gas reserves, in the belief that natural gas would be the fuel of the future.

In the early 1980s, Forest Oil's annual revenues continued to climb. Throughout the middle of the decade, however, the prices for natural energy such as oil and gas began to decline. Take-or-pay contracts, which had been popular in the past, soon became undesirable for buyers and Forest Oil was quickly subject to a lower earnings potential. As an independent, the small company had traditionally reinvested a good portion of its earnings into exploration and the development of new reserves. But as its cash flow decreased, so did its ability to explore.

The company braced itself to weather the economic storm by continuing its exploration operations at a slightly less aggressive level, while also beginning to focus more of its money on the acquisition of other small oil and gas companies at a time when price tags were reasonable. In 1987 and 1988, Forest Oil discovered two large reserves at its exploratory wells in the Gulf of Mexico, and scheduled production to begin in the early

1990s. In 1989, Forest's revenues reached $131.6 million, but the company suffered a loss of $15 million for the year.

The 1990s and Beyond

In early 1990, as Forest Oil made plans to begin production at its new reserves in the Gulf, the company earned approximately $58 million in a secondary offering of its stock. Furthermore, a corporate restructuring was planned to save the company approximately $10 million per year. The restructuring included the consolidation of management's operations to its Denver, Colorado, office, which subsequently led to the closing of its offices in Midland, Texas. It retained its office locations in Denver; Lafayette, Louisiana; Bradford, Pennsylvania; and Canada. In addition, the company had also reduced its staff by about 60 people since 1989.

By 1991, Forest Oil faced the lowest natural gas prices (adjusted for inflation) that it had seen in 15 years. This was problematic for the company, given that natural gas accounted for approximately 80 percent of the company's production output; crude oil was the source of Forest's remaining 20 percent of production. Once again, the company reduced its staff, this time by about 80 people. Forest Oil also explored new ways for the company to cut costs in order to stay afloat during the economic downturn. To these ends, Forest Oil entered into an almost-$48 million deal with Enron Corporation, owner of the largest pipeline system in the United States, in exchange for interest in its reserves and properties.

By early 1992, Forest Oil's corporate management believed that the industry had cycled to its lowest point, and that it would begin to rebound soon. Management remained optimistic, as was noted in the company's 1991 annual report, which stated: "Those independent producers who are able to expand quality reserve bases through exploration or acquisition at competitive prices in the face of this hostile industry environment will be positioned to reap the benefits as the cycle again turns upwards." Regarding acquisitions, Forest Oil did well during that time period, purchasing Harbert Energy Corp. and Transco Exploration in 1992, as well as the working rights to property owned by both Amoco and ORYX.

Two years later, Forest Oil continued to expand its reach. The company acquired a 50 percent interest in Eugene Island Block 235, and an almost-67 percent interest in Ship Shoal Block 275. Sales for the year signified an upward trend; they topped off at $115.9 million—the highest yearly revenues since the 1991 low of $69.9 million. In 1995, the company sealed a deal involving earnings from stock with the Anschultz Corporation for $45 million, and purchased a controlling interest in Saxon Petroleum, Inc. Activity in 1996 followed suit, as Forest Oil acquired ATCOR Resources, Ltd. and made a limited partnership with Delaware called JEDI.

Entering the end of the century, Forest Oil's operational emphasis lay in acquiring additional reserves in the United States and increasing production from its existing production fields. Two 1996 acquisitions, Canadian Forest Oil Ltd. and ProMark, immediately yielded positive results for the company, helping Forest achieve 1996 sales of $317.5 million. Also contributing to that almost 400 percent increase in revenue for the year was the solid performance of the company's reserves in the Gulf of Mexico, which were churning out over 40 million cubic feet of gas per day. With an improving financial situation and the apparent upswing of the oil and gas industry, Forest Oil seemed poised for future success as it neared the end of the decade.

Principal Subsidiaries

Canadian Forest Oil Ltd.; Forest Pipeline Co.; Forest I Development Co.; Producers Marketing Ltd.

Further Reading

Dowling, Mark, "Forest Prunes Operations as It Bids to Buy Big Houston Firm," *Denver Business Journal,* November 9, 1990, p. 7.
——, "Local Gas Companies Forced to Cut Payroll by Declining Prices," *Denver Business Journal,* July 19, 1991, p. 1.
"Forest Oil Corp.," *Denver Business Journal,* July 31, 1989, p. 30.
Forest Oil Corp. Corporate History, Denver: Forest Oil Corp., 1992.
McNamara, Victoria, "Gas Firms Sign New Long-term Contracts to Control Prices," *Houston Business Journal,* June 10, 1991, p. 12.

—Laura E. Whiteley

Framatome SA

Tour Framatome
92084 Paris La Défense
France
33 (1) 47 96 14 14
Fax: 33 (1) 47 96 30 31
Web site: http://www.framatech.com

Public Subsidiary of Acatel Alsthom
Incorporated: 1958 as Société Franco-Américaine de
    Constructions Atomiques (FRAMATOME)
Employees: 20,000
Sales: FFr 17.9 billion (1995)
Stock Exchanges: Paris
SICs: 3443 Fabricated Plate Work, Boiler Shops; 8711
    Engineering Services; 3679 Electronic Components,
    Not Elsewhere Classified; 6719 Holding Companies,
    Not Elsewhere Classified

Framatome SA is a diversified, international manufacturing company and also the world leader in nuclear power generation. There are 64 nuclear power plants operating Framatome-built reactors worldwide, and another six reactors under construction in France and the People's Republic of China, representing a total energy output capacity of more than 58,000 megawatts. Beyond designing and constructing nuclear power islands, the company provides a full spectrum of nuclear power services, including maintenance, inspection, and upgrading services for utilities operating its own and third party nuclear plants; manufacture of nuclear components for power plant construction and maintenance; and the design, fabrication, marketing, and sale of nuclear fuel assemblies.

Although nuclear power continues to represent approximately two-thirds of Framatome's annual sales, the company has responded to the worldwide slowdown in the nuclear power market (in the United States, for example, no new nuclear power plants have been constructed since 1980) by diversifying into other areas of manufacturing. Chief among these, produc-ing nearly one-fourth of the company's annual sales, is the connectors business, operated through Framatome's wholly owned Framatome Connectors International subsidiary. Connectors refer to the wide variety of interconnection techniques and devices used to transmit electrical energy or electronic and optical signals between and among equipment and electronic circuits. Framatome supplies connectors to the automotive, electronics, aerospace, telecommunications, computer and computer network, and other industries. Framatome is the leading European supplier and third largest worldwide in the design, manufacturing, marketing, and sale of connectors.

The next major area of Framatome diversification is mechanical engineering. Framatome and its subsidiaries design, manufacture, and install equipment and machinery for a range of industries and applications. The mechanical engineering division's products include heavy components for nuclear steam supply systems, reactor coolant systems, control rod drive mechanisms, closure heads, and other electromechanical components for the nuclear power industry. Beyond nuclear power, Framatome supplies turbines and compressors, large-capacity heat exchangers, electric generators and motors, twin-screw extruders, tunneling machines, large astronomical telescopes, and other machinery and equipment on the leading edge of technology.

An attempted merger with GEC-Alsthom, a joint venture operation between Britain's GEC and longtime Framatome rival Alcatel-Alsthom, the former French electric monopoly, was successfully scuttled in April 1997. Framatome, which posted revenues of FFr 17 billion in 1995, remains 51 percent owned by the French government.

Building the Nuclear Society in the 1950s

When the world turned toward peacetime use of the newly emerging nuclear technology after the Second World War, France, with limited natural fuel resources of its own, determined to develop its own nuclear reactor program as a means for preserving its independence. By 1955, the country, in a joint effort with England, had debuted a reactor technology that could rival that developed by Westinghouse in the United

States. Although there were as many as 12 competing technologies, an atomic summit among European countries confirmed the French-English GCR (gas-cooled reactor) and the American PWR (pressurized water reactor) as the two most viable technologies. Both types of reactors were already in operation. But GCR offered the French the independence they sought, as that technology made use of natural uranium, rather than the enriched uranium of the American system. The process of enriching uranium for use in nuclear reactors was too expensive for the postwar European economy. While the Americans offered to supply enriched uranium for European reactor use, the French government, jealous of its independence, appeared to lean toward authorizing GCR as the "national" nuclear reactor technology. Spurring this preference was the crisis in the Suez of 1956, an event that helped expose the French dependence on foreign-supplied fuel resources. The first three reactors built in France were of the GCR type.

In Belgium, however, PWR reactors were preferred. In the late 1950s, the Belgians sought bids for building their first full-scale nuclear reactor, eventually called Chooz 1, to be built in the Ardennes region near the French-Belgian border. Although the French government, through the CEA (the French atomic energy commission), favored the GCR technology, a group of French engineers saw an opportunity to pursue the PWR technology and to compete for the Belgian reactor contract. In 1958, several companies of French industrial giant the Schneider Group joined with Empain, Merlin Gérin, and the American Westinghouse to license Westinghouse's PWR technology and develop a bid for Chooz 1. Called Franco-Américaine de Constructions Atomiques, the new company flew in the face of the rising anti-Americanism of the rebuilding French society. The original mission of the company, which consisted of four engineers, one each from each of the parent companies, was to act as a nuclear engineering firm and to develop a nuclear power plant that was to be identical to Westinghouse's existing product specifications. The first European plant of Westinghouse design was by then already under construction in Italy.

Meanwhile, the EDF (the French government-owned electric utility), in opposition to the CEA, maintained an interest in PWR technology. The Chooz contract offered the EDF, which joined with the Belgian electric utilities to call for the Chooz bids, the opportunity to explore PWR without offending the French national pride in its homegrown GCR technology. By the beginning of 1960, only two bids remained in contention; in the middle of the year, Framatome received informal permission to begin the design work on the Chooz reactor. A formal contract was signed in September 1961 for Framatome to deliver a turnkey system, that is, not only the reactor, but an entire, ready-to-use system of piping, cabling, supports, and other auxiliary systems, propelling Framatome from a nuclear engineering firm to an industrial contractor.

Through the 1960s, Framatome worked very much as a Westinghouse protégé, and development of the Chooz plant was restricted to Westinghouse requirements. The Chooz 1 reactor went critical in October 1966 and was attached to the French electric system in April of the following year. Several months later, a deformation in the reactor core's internal thermal shield, which had begun to break apart, caused the reactor to be shut down. The unprecedented nature of the repair work that needed to be performed, however, placed Westinghouse and Framatome on equal footing. This development was seen as an integral part in the creation of a true French nuclear technology. From this point, Framatome, aided by the French nuclear and electric agencies, began to "franconize" the Westinghouse technology. Chooz 1 went back on line after two years of repair work and continued to operate without incident until 1993, when it was shut down.

In the meantime, the French government appeared to have decided on GCR as the national nuclear technology. Much of the Framatome team returned to their parent companies. A break for the company came in 1966, with a report from leading members of both the EDF and the CEA recommending that France continue to pursue an interest in PWR technology. Then, in 1969, Framatome won its second nuclear plant contract, again from a French-Belgian cooperative agreement, to build the Tihange 1 plant in Belgium. Tihange not only breathed new life into Framatome, it also allowed the company to begin diverging from Westinghouse specifications with its own improvements on the design. By 1969, the company received a new boost: the French military had successfully built a uranium enriching plant, freeing the light water reactor technology from dependence on U.S. or Soviet Union supplies of the material. GCR faded from the French focus. But two competing light water reactor technologies remained—PWR, used by Framatome, and BWR (boiling water reactor), developed by General Electric and promoted by the CGE in France.

The two technologies went head to head for a contract to build the first Fessenheim plant. CGE had yet to build a light water reactor, while Framatome had not only Chooz, but Tihange, under its belt. In a meeting with CGE, Framatome's chief executive, Maurice Aragou, warned of the high cost associated with building the Chooz reactor. CGE took his advice to heart and submitted a bid of 360 million francs for the Fessenheim reactor. Framatome, however, was able to base its bid on its costs of building Tihange (at the same time the company was able to extrapolate the cost of building a *series* of reactors) and brought in a bid of only 242 million francs. Framatome won not only the Fessenheim 1 contract, but an option to build Fessenheim 2 as well. The following year, Framatome repeated its success, winning the contracts for two new French reactors, Bugey 1 and 2, as well as the options to build Bugey 3 and 4. Nonetheless, the French government pursued a course of encouraging the development of both light water reactor technologies.

Benefiting from the Oil Crisis of 1973

The French economy boomed during the 1960s, and with it, the national energy demand soared. Petroleum and coal continued to be the focus of the country's energy supply, despite the French dependence on foreign suppliers; 76 percent of the country's oil, gas, and coal supplies were imported. The oil crisis of 1973, however, forced France to revise its energy policy entirely. Weeks after the OPEC decision to raise the price of oil, the French government directed the EDF to step up its nuclear plant construction, with a goal to achieving a 50 percent domestic supply of the country's energy needs. EDF, in turn, adopted a policy of ordering plants on a standardized, series-built, multiyear contract basis, and not one by one as had been the previous policy. Framatome won the first of these contracts, for 16 plants, in 1974. But the company's future was not fully assured until the following year, when the EDF finally abandoned its policy of encouraging competing nuclear reactor technologies. On August 4, 1975, the nod went to PWR and Framatome.

In 1976, Framatome was awarded the second multiyear contract, this time for ten reactors; this was soon followed by a third contract for eight reactors, which was later extended to include 12 more reactors. In that year, also, Framatome began accepting its first foreign orders. By the end of the decade, the company had become the leader in the worldwide nuclear power plant industry. Many, including parent Westinghouse, expressed doubts that the company could meet the challenge ahead of it. But Framatome rose to the occasion. At the beginning of the decade, Framatome numbered only some 200 employees, including only 25 engineers. By 1975, the company's payroll had swelled to 2,000. By 1981, Framatome employed some 5,000; the following year, its engineering staff alone numbered 5,000 employees.

The nuclear power industry hit a bump in 1979 with the accident at Three Mile Island. With U.S. nuclear plant construction already slowing down under the Carter administration, new construction orders ground to a halt. Elsewhere in the world, orders for nuclear power plants were being put on hold. But the French nuclear power policy remained intact, allowing Framatome to continue to thrive. Meanwhile, the company was also gaining its independence from its parents. In 1982, its license contract with Westinghouse expired, allowing Framatome to develop its own in-house specifications for the first time. Then, another Framatome parent, the industrial manufacturing giant Creusot-Loire, went bankrupt. As its largest creditor, Framatome took over much of its former parent's operations, including the mechanical engineering and metalworking businesses of Creusot-Loire and its subsidiaries. A reorganization of Framatome's shareholder base followed, with archrival CGE (which was shortly to become known as Alcatel-Alsthom when it was privatized as a public company) taking a major stake in the company.

Diversifying for Survival in the 1980s

Meanwhile, the global nuclear power plant market was reaching saturation. By the early 1990s, new plant construction orders were expected to dwindle to a handful, and the market's return to health was not expected until the year 2010 at the earliest. In response, Framatome, under leadership since 1985 of Jean-Claude Leny, who had served as a managing director for the company since the early 1970s, set out to diversify its operations to survive. The first steps toward this diversification had occurred in the 1980s, particularly with the move into mechanical engineering with the Creusot-Loire acquisition. The company had also taken steps toward vertical integration in the nuclear power industry, including supplies and maintenance operations for its own and third party reactors.

But Framatome was determined to look beyond the nuclear energy market for its survival during the industry's coming lean years. In 1988, Framatome saw its chance. When former parent Schneider attempted a takeover of Télémécanique, a French specialist in industrial control components and automated systems, that company approached Framatome as a white knight. Framatome placed a counter bid for the company and reached an agreement to acquire Télémécanique. At the last moment, however, one of Framatome's shareholders, CGE, blocked the acquisition. Télémécanique went to Schneider, and Framatome was forced to look elsewhere for its diversification effort.

The company had already taken a step in its eventual direction in 1987 when it had acquired a stake in the connectors business of Souriau. After the failure of its Télémécanique bid, Framatome decided to place its diversification strategy fully into the connectors industry. The company acquired full control of Souriau, as well as two other French connectors companies, Burndy and Jupiter, and in 1989 formed its Framatome Connectors International (FCI) subsidiary. FCI continued to expand into the 1990s, acquiring Schmid in 1991, and Daut + Rietz and Connectors Pontarlier in 1993, as well as taking control of Burndy Japan and OEN Connectors in 1992. By the mid-1990s, FCI had grown to become the largest European connectors supplier and the third largest in the world. The move was not without its difficulties; the prolonged European recession of the 1990s caused a drop in the connectors market overall. Nevertheless, the boom in the computer, networking, and telecommunications industries in the mid-1990s would help FCI overcome the difficulties of its early years.

Meanwhile, Leny and Framatome had already found their revenge on CGE, now known as Alcatel-Alsthom and shortly to become aligned with the British GEC. Knowing that Alcatel-Alsthom and Siemens were bitter competitors, Framatome entered negotiations with Germany's Siemens to form Nuclear Power International in 1989 to develop the next generation nuclear reactor technology. The alliance not only placed Framatome in direct competition with the British-French alliance, it also placed the company in opposition with its largest shareholder—Alcatel-Alsthom held 44 percent of Framatome.

Alcatel-Alsthom struck back the following year, when it received authorization from the French government to increase its position in Framatome to 52 percent; however, Alcatel-Alsthom was forced to back down, selling eight percent of its Framatome stock to Credit Lyonnaise, the CEA, and to Framatome management. Alcatel-Alsthom's next attempt against Framatome came in 1994, when the French government, under Eduouard Balladur, decided to privatize Framatome and give the government's controlling share of the company to Alcatel-Alsthom. This action fell through, but two years later, Alcatel-Alsthom, through its GEC-Alsthom alliance, struck again, proposing a fusion of Framatome with GEC-Alsthom. The merger nearly went through, but foundered as both the French government and GEC-Alsthom insisted on retaining 51 percent of the merged corporation. Leny retired as Framatome's chief executive in December 1996. He was replaced by Dominique Vignon as chairman and CEO. A future union between Framatome and Alcatel-Alsthom remained a possibility.

Meanwhile, contracts to build nuclear power plants in China helped spike Framatome's revenues to nearly FFr 20 billion in 1994. With no new reactor contracts on the table in 1995, however, sales slipped back to FFr 17.9 billion. The company's corporate share of net income had also slipped, from FFr 863 million in 1993 to FFr 663 million in 1995. The revitalization of the French economy, and the worldwide boom in the international connectors market, as Framatome entered the remaining years of the 20th century appeared to confirm the company's diversification for survival strategy. Framatome appeared healthy and able to maintain its nuclear power leadership position in preparation for the next wave of reactor construction expected in the early years of the next century.

Principal Subsidiaries

Nuclear: Cerca SA (France; 51%); Framex SA (France); Nuclear Power International (France; 50%); Fbfc International SA (Belgium; 51%); Framex South Africa (South Africa); Framatome USA, Inc. (U.S.); B&W Nuclear Technologies, Inc. (U.S.). Industrial Equipment: Atea SA (France); Athen SA (France); Clextral SA (France); Proser SA. Connectors: Framatome Connectors International FCI SA (France); Framatome Connectors USA (U.S.).

Further Reading

Framatome Corporate Communications, and Le Seac'h, Michel, *Framatome: An Industrial and Business Success Story,* Paris: Albin Michel Communications and Framatome, 1995.

Gallois, Dominique, "Jean-Claude Leny, le Nucleocrate Obrageux," *Le Monde,* December 3, 1996, p. 14.

Gallois, Dominique, and Martine Orange, "Le Gouvernement Est Favorable au Rapprochement de Framatome avec Alcatel-Alsthom," *Le Monde,* April 12, 1997.

Gonnot, Francois Michel, "Framatome: Union Libre ou Mariage Forcé?," *Le Monde,* January 21, 1997.

"Trente-huit Ans d'Affrontements," *Le Monde,* September 2, 1996.

—M.L. Cohen

Gallaher Limited

Members Hill
Brooklands Road
Weybridge, Surrey
KT13 OQU
United Kingdom
(44-1932) 85-9777
Fax: (44-1932) 84-9119

Public Company
Incorporated: 1896
Employees: 3,700
Sales: $4.3 billion (1996 est.)
Stock Exchanges: New York London
SICs: 2111 Cigarettes; 2121 Cigars; 2131 Chewing and
    Smoking Tobacco; 2085 Distilled and Blended
    Liquors

Gallaher Limited is an international company whose interests include tobacco, distilled spirits, optical services and products, retail distribution, and housewares. Its employees are spread throughout the world, with the majority located in the company's headquarters country of the United Kingdom. Until 1997, Gallaher was a wholly-owned subsidiary of American Brands, Inc., of Old Greenwich, Connecticut, in the United States. Following the divestiture, American Brands then changed its name to Fortune Brands, Inc. That company is itself a diversified group of companies, with core businesses in tobacco, distilled spirits, life insurance, office products, hardware, and home improvement products.

The Early Years

Gallaher was founded by Tom Gallaher, who in 1857 started his own business in Londonderry, making and selling pipe tobaccos. Within sixteen years, he had prospered enough to move to larger premises in Belfast. Toward the end of the 1870s, Tom Gallaher crossed the Atlantic for the first time in order to personally supervise the buying of his company's tobacco leaves. He visited Kentucky, North Carolina, Virginia, and Missouri, and following his first trip the expedition became an annual event. Gallaher rose to become a notable figure in trade on both sides of the Atlantic.

During the first half of the 19th century, the pipe had gradually given way in popularity to the cigar. The military was largely credited with this shift, as British soldiers returning from the Crimea campaign of 1854–1856 introduced an item they had adopted from their French and Turkish allies—the cigarette. Smoking fashions in Britain underwent a change that Gallaher was astute enough to exploit. Soon other tobacco manufacturers also began to cater to this change in tastes. By 1888, he was producing flake tobaccos and cigarettes, which, included in the full range of Gallaher products, were displayed at the Irish exhibition in London during that same year. The expedition also saw the opening of Gallaher's first London premises, just inside the famous "square mile" of the City, at 60 Holborn Viaduct.

The first London factory was opened the following year at Clerkenwell Road to increase production, and in 1896 the Belfast factory moved into larger quarters. That same year, the company was incorporated as Gallaher Limited. An important development two years later was the discovery of a yellow and white burley leaf. Gallaher started to use it immediately, and in 1908 completed a transaction important to the history of the industry by purchasing the entire Irish tobacco crop.

The social history of smoking in the late Victorian and Edwardian ages was marked by the triumph of the cigarette. To that point in time, tobacco manufacturers had employed manual labor to make cigarettes as required, but soon cigarette-making machinery sped up production and thus, satisfied the rising demand. It became acceptable for women to smoke, and new types of cigarettes were created to serve that market as well. By the outbreak of World War I in 1914, the cigarette had established its dominance over all other forms of smoking; it was considered vital to the welfare and morale of the armed forces and a valuable means of exchange.

Production increased hugely, and Tom Gallaher was the master of a thriving business when he died in 1927 at the age of 87. He had maintained an active interest in the company until the time of his death, and had achieved great civic respectability as a governor of the Royal Victoria Hospital in Belfast. He was also credited with being the first person in the tobacco industry to introduce a 47-hour working week and annual paid holiday.

The Mid-1900s: Gallaher's Expansion Efforts

Smoking, and cigarette smoking in particular, enjoyed a continuous popularity throughout the 1930s and 1940s. The anxieties of World War II were a further stimulus to tobacco consumption. In the 1950s, however, evidence was produced that not only linked smoking to lung cancer and heart disease, but also suggested that long-term cigarette smokers might be more susceptible to lung cancer than pipe or cigar users, or nonsmokers. These findings seemed to do no harm to Gallaher Limited, however, which was looking to expand in 1955 and succeeded in acquiring the U.K. and Irish interests of the prestigious Benson & Hedges company.

Benson & Hedges had enjoyed parallel development and success to Gallaher Limited, though in a more elevated style. Richard Benson and William Hedges began their business in 1873. Benson & Hedges notably departed from the custom of dispensing tobacco by weight. Their tobacco was prepared as a blend or mixture, and packed in a sealed tin. This assured the customer that his goods would reach him in the freshest possible condition, and also had experienced no tampering. The business also benefited from the patronage of the *bon vivant* Prince of Wales, later King Edward VII, who asked Benson & Hedges to prepare and make into cigarettes a parcel of Egyptian tobacco leaf that he had acquired. They did this, and adapted the style to market "Cairo Citadel," one of the first Egyptian-type cigarettes to be made in Britain.

When smoking became popular with women during Edward's reign, Benson & Hedges produced variations of the cigarette designed to appeal to women, tipped with rose leaves or violets for example, or on a miniature scale. Increasing demand led to the establishment of a separate factory, although their original shop remained at its location on Old Bond Street. During World War II, the shop was bombed and practically destroyed, but was rebuilt with the return of peace. When Benson & Hedges joined Gallaher, it brought not only its best-selling cigarettes, but also its Royal Warrant, which was first bestowed by Queen Victoria "to purvey cigarettes and cigars for use in her household," and later renewed by subsequent monarchs.

In 1962, Gallaher acquired J. Wix and Sons Ltd. of London, the makers of Kensitas, a well-known cigarette. The company's vendor was The American Tobacco Company, which made the transaction in exchange for a stake in Gallaher's stock. By 1968, American Tobacco had increased its holdings in Gallaher shares to 67 percent. American Tobacco had been a relative failure in its native tobacco market, but was now using a steady cash flow wisely to buy and diversify. In 1969, in recognition of its changing profile, it was renamed American Brands, Inc.

The 1970s and 1980s as an American Brands Subsidiary

Meanwhile, Gallaher itself began to broaden its scope. An interesting and substantial acquisition in 1970 was the Dollond & Aitchison Group, whose main specialty was the supply of optical services and advice, spectacles, contact lenses, and accessories. Dollond & Aitchison possessed an extensive branch network throughout the United Kingdom. Also acquired was a small ophthalmic instruments manufacturing and distributing operation, called Keeler Limited.

Gallaher continued this diversification phase by making its first foray into retail distribution. In 1971 it established the Marshell Group, a retail franchise operation that sold mainly tobacco products and confectionery through concessions within major retail stores across the United Kingdom. Within 20 years the concessions numbered around 635, and the company also had over 50 of its own retail outlets.

Two similar acquisitions followed in 1973. The TM Group, previously called Mayfair, was a company operating vending machines that dispensed cigarettes, drinks, and snacks in licensed and industrial catering outlets. Perhaps TM's best known manifestation in the United Kingdom was the ubiquitous Vendepac machine. Another purchase was that of Forbuoys plc, a chain of shops selling tobacco, confectionery, newspapers, and magazines, again with branches throughout the United Kingdom.

Using its standing as a subsidiary of a giant conglomerate, Gallaher was able to continue its expansion and diversification without severely troubling its balance sheet. Dollond & Aitchison's overseas expansion began in 1974 with the acquisition of the Italian company Salmoiraghi Vigano, which added the retailing of optical and medical instruments to the group's interests. The following year, American Brands finally controlled 100 percent of Gallaher's shares. It was arranged that the chairman and chief executive of Gallaher Limited would sit on the board of American Brands, while American Brands would have non-executive directors on the Gallaher board.

Gallaher continued to make acquisitions. In 1984, it purchased Prestige Group plc. Under the "Prestige" brand name, the company produced stainless steel cookware, pressure cookers, bake ware, and kitchen tools and accessories. Under another brand name, Ewbank, it also marketed carpet sweepers. Established in 1937, Prestige was the leading non-electrical housewares manufacturer in the United Kingdom. Following the Prestige acquisition in 1984, Dollond & Aitchison opened the first fast-service optical department store in Europe at Yardley near Birmingham, England. Further stores called "Eyeland Express" have followed since then.

In 1988, along with other companies in Northern Ireland, Gallaher was approached by the former Fair Employment Agency for Northern Ireland, which sought cooperation in a study to ascertain to what degree equality of opportunity was being afforded to Protestants and Roman Catholics. The agency had been advised of Gallaher's long-standing interest in the question, and the report concluded: "The efforts made by the company and the local Trade Union officials to introduce locally meaningful equal opportunity measures are positive and encouraging and the Agency is satisfied that the action taken is indicative of real commitment to provide equality of opportunity.''

The following year, the section of Gallaher's business represented by Dollond & Aitchison suffered a setback when the British government abolished free vision tests for the majority of people, and spectacles and contact lenses for retail became liable for value-added tax. In fact, this severely affected the entire industry in the United Kingdom, but Gallaher remained confident, and continued as planned with the expansion of the Eyeland Express chain. Within two years, Dollond & Aitchison had virtually completed a major restructuring of its retail and service facilities. It became the largest optical group in Europe, with more than 500 outlets in the United Kingdom alone and strong and profitable overseas business.

The 1990s and Beyond

Gallaher Limited began the 1990s with a strategy based on diversification. Further strategic development of the Gallaher's non-tobacco interests continued with the acquisition of Whyte & Mackay Distillers Ltd., in February 1990. The company, as well as its three Scottish distilleries, was headquartered in Glasgow. One of those distilleries was a bottling company, William Muir (Bond 9) Limited, based in Leith, near Edinburgh. Its products were the blended whiskeys Whyte & Mackay Special Reserve and The Claymore, as well as the single malts The Dalmore, Tomintoul-Glenlivet and Old Fettercairn. In April 1990, Whyte & Mackay reinforced its branded business and acquired the worldwide trademark rights to Vladivar vodka, the United Kingdom's second-largest vodka brand. Other than scotch whisky, vodka was the most popular distilled spirit in the United Kingdom.

Meanwhile, the tobacco business, managed by Gallaher Tobacco, remained a strong performer. In the declining U.K. cigarette market, Gallaher had increased its volume of sales and was making the three leading brands: Benson and Hedges Special Filter, Silk Cut, and Berkeley Superkings. Gallaher also manufactured the leading U.K. pipe tobacco, the leading cigar, and the second largest brand of hand-rolling tobacco in the United Kingdom. Gallaher International, the export arm, was also undergoing increased development in the early-1990s, and was well placed to take advantage of the trend toward low-tar cigarettes, pushing for markets in France, Spain, and Greece.

Since its inception, Gallaher had maintained considerable holdings in Northern Ireland, and by the 1990s was one of the largest manufacturing employers there. Operations included a warehouse complex for tobacco leaf at Connswater, East Belfast, and a sales distribution center on the outskirts of the city. Production took place at Lisnafillan, near Ballymena, County Antrim, in a modern factory complex handling cigarettes, pipe tobacco, and handrolling tobacco. Also at Lisnafillan was the company's research and development division, which was a particularly vital establishment to Gallaher's drive to keep its position as market leader in low-tar cigarettes.

Gallaher also continued to operate in the Republic of Ireland, where it was the second largest tobacco company. Cigarettes, pipe tobacco, and hand-rolling tobacco were manufactured in a factory just outside Dublin. On the British mainland, three top-selling cigarette brands and a wide range of smaller brands were made at the famous Senior Service factory at Hyde, east of Manchester, and cigars were produced at Cardiff and Port Talbot in South Wales.

In the mid-1990s, Gallaher continued to increase recognition of its name in its home market, through various types of sponsorship. Although it had withdrawn patronage of the Silk Cut Tennis Championship in 1990, the Benson & Hedges Cup at Lord's remained an important sponsorship. This cricket competition was vital to the Test and County Cricket Board during those years, as the sponsorship arrangement guaranteed the organization £3 million over a five year period. Other sponsorships within the Benson & Hedges portfolio were the International Open Golf Championship at St. Mellion, Cornwall; the Masters Snooker Tournament at Wembley; the Silk Cut Showjumping Derby; and the Silk Cut Nautical Awards. In Northern Ireland, small business development was encouraged by the Gallaher Business Challenge Award Scheme, and the company was also the major private sponsor of the Ulster Orchestra.

As Gallaher entered the last few years of the century, the strength of its tobacco industry holdings was tested when the European Community (EC) banned all advertising of tobacco products on U.K. television. At the time the ban was instituted, Gallaher owned the United Kingdom's biggest cigar brand, Hamlet, but was fighting for continued market share dominance with Imperial's Castella brand. During the weeks preceding the ban, Gallaher ran most of its old and new advertisements on U.K. television in a last-ditch effort to maintain its edge. For years, the Hamlet television advertisements had been wildly popular with the U.K. public, and had won 15 Lion awards at the International Advertising Film Festival at Cannes. Gallaher also produced a 30-minute video showcase of the best of the Hamlet advertisements over the years, which was then sold to the public to keep the spirit of the 27-year Hamlet campaign alive.

Within a year of the tobacco advertising ban, Gallaher introduced a new entry in the budget-priced sector of the cigarette market. The brand Mayfair was introduced, and joined Gallaher's Berkeley Superkings brand, which was currently the best selling brand in the budget-priced market. Mayfair was immediately given a poster advertisement campaign, which focused mainly on the low price of the product. Furthermore, Gallaher attempted to appeal to potential customers by lowering the cost of Mayfair by the same amount that the government had just added as duty to the cost of the cigarettes. Soon thereafter, Gallaher also introduced its Eclipse brand, which was classified as a ''super luxury length'' product and joined other cigarettes at the opposite end of the spectrum from Mayfair. At that time, Gallaher was producing the top three cigarette brands in the United Kingdom.

Gallaher continued to reap success, even despite criticisms and raised eyebrows from industry analysts regarding marketing and pricing decisions made by the company. By 1996, Gallaher had grown to account for more than 50 percent of American Brands' yearly sales figures. The following year, American Brands made the decision to spin off Gallaher to become its own free-standing entity. Prior to the spin-off, Gallaher had helped American Brands achieve $6.9 million in 1996 tobacco sales alone. Following the divestiture, American Brands changed its name to Fortune Brands, Inc. The new name more accurately reflected that corporation's holdings, as ironically "American" Brands had been responsible for numerous international holdings for years, including Gallaher. As the end of the decade ushered in the 21st century, Gallaher's ability to stand on its own and enjoy future profitability and growth would be decided.

Principal Subsidiaries

Benson & Hedges, Ltd.; Cope Brothers & Co. Ltd.; Cope & Lloyd (Overseas) Ltd.; John Cotton Ltd.; J.R. Freeman & Son Ltd.; Gallaher International Ltd.; Gallaher Tobacco Ltd.; Gallaher Tobacco (UK) Ltd.; Old Holborn Ltd.; Senior Service Tobacco Ltd.; Silk Cut Ltd.; Sobranie Ltd.; Sullivan Powell & Co. Ltd.; Benson & Hedges (Dublin) Ltd.; Gallaher (Dublin) Ltd.; Silk Cut (Dublin) Ltd.; Gallaher Canarias SA (Spain); Gallaher España SA (Spain); Silk Cut France SARL; Silk Cut Hellas Epe. (Greece); Dollond & Aitchison Group plc; Dollond & Aitchison Ltd.; Theodore Hamblin Ltd.; First Sight; Keeler Ltd.; Filotecnica Salmoiraghi SpA (Italy, 99.9%); Istituto Ottico Vigano SpA (Italy); General Optica SA (Spain, 92.5%); Donal MacNally Opticians Ltd. (80%); Forbuoys plc; NSS Newsagents plc; TM Group plc; Hargreaves Vending Ltd.; UBM Wittenborg Ltd.; Marshell Group Ltd.; The Prestige Group plc; Prestige Group UK plc; Bonny Products Ltd.; Prestige Medical Ltd.; Prestige Industrial Ltd.; Prestige Group (Australia) Pty. Ltd.; Prestige Housewares (NZ) Pty. Ltd. (New Zealand); Prestige Benelux SA (Belgium); Prestige France SA (France): Prestige Haushaltswaren GmbH (Germany); Prestige Italiana SpA; Fabricados Inoxidables SA (Spain); The Galleon Insurance Co. Ltd.; The Schooner Insurance Co. Ltd.; Whyte & Mackay Distillers Ltd.; Dalmore Distillers Ltd.; Fettercairn Distillery Ltd.; The Tomintoul-Glenlivet Distillery Ltd.; William Muir (Bond 9) Ltd.; The Scotch Whiskey Heritage Centre Ltd. (54.9%).

Further Reading

Bowes, Elena, "Hamlet Cigars Skirt TV Ban," *Advertising Age,* July 1, 1991, p. 28.

Johnson, Mike, "Gallaher Bids to Make it Third Largest Whisky," *Marketing,* August 8, 1991, p. 3.

——, "Gallaher's Shock Price Cut on Mayfair," *Marketing,* May 28, 1992, p. 3.

——, "Last Big Puff for Cigars as EC Snuffs Out Use of TV," *Marketing,* September 12, 1991, p. 8.

Meller, Paul, "Gallaher Brand Bumps up Budget Sector," *Marketing,* February 20, 1992, p. 4.

——, "Gallaher Cost Freeze Heightens Price War," *Marketing,* March 19, 1992, p. 7.

——, "Hamlet Enters Post-TV Era," *Marketing,* April 2, 1992, p. 14.

——, "Silk Cut Lowers Kingsize Tar Levels," *Marketing,* April 2, 1992, p. 8.

—Paul Stevens
—updated by Laura E. Whiteley

GEHL

Gehl Company

143 Water Street
West Bend, Wisconsin 53095-0179
U.S.A.
(414) 334-9461
Fax: (414) 334-1565

Public Company
Incorporated: 1904 as Gehl Brothers Manufacturing
    Company
Employees: 842
Sales: $159.6 million (1996)
Stock Exchange: NASDAQ
SICs: 3523 Farm Machinery and Equipment; 3531
    Construction Machinery

The Gehl Company is one of the oldest manufacturing firms in the midwestern United States. The company makes a wide range of construction equipment, including such products as skid loaders, rough-terrain telescopic forklifts, and paving equipment distributed through independent dealers for the construction industry. In addition, Gehl Company manufactures agricultural equipment used in day-to-day livestock farming and is widely recognized as the leader in the non-tractor manufacturing industry, with a comprehensive product line of hay-makers, forage harvesters, feed makers, manure handlers, and materials handlers. The company has been on the cutting edge of recent technological developments in the construction and agricultural equipment industry, and has introduced highly innovative and durable machinery, including the 35 Series Skid Loaders, the 1300 Series Scavenger Manure Spreader, and the 2345 and 2365 Disc Mower Conditioner models, both with 12-foot wide swing frame disc mowers. Headquartered in West Bend, Wisconsin, the company has distributed its products overseas to Latin America, Asia, and Europe for nearly 50 years.

Early History

The roots of Gehl Company go back to 1859, when Louis Lucas opened an iron foundry in central Wisconsin. Lucas established his business in order to manufacture plows and cultivators, and for the repair of farm implements. As more and more immigrants from Europe swept into the Midwest, settled down, and started farms of their own, they came to rely heavily on the services provided by men like Lucas.

By 1880, Lucas was joined by M. Silberzahn, a German immigrant with experience as a blacksmith. The two partners soon came up with one of the most important innovations in agricultural machinery during the late 19th century, the *Hexelbank,* a feed cutter which replaced the need to chop livestock feed by hand, usually with a beet knife. The popularity of the hand-cranked *Hexelbank* grew so rapidly that is was soon used not only for sugar beet crops but for other root crops as well.

In 1902, John W. Gehl acquired part interest in the firm of Lucas and Silberzahn. One year later Gehl, who had been raised on a homestead in central Wisconsin, asked his brothers Mike, Henry, and Nick to join him and purchase all the assets of Lucas and Silberzahn. By 1904, the Gehl Brothers Manufacturing Company was producing a wide range of basic farm tools and, of course, the extremely lucrative *Hexelbank.* During the next two years, the company prospered and the four brothers began to consider the manufacture of more innovative farm equipment.

Unfortunately, in 1906 the company plant and its entire inventory was destroyed in a fire. But the Gehl brothers were undaunted, and rebuilt the company factory through the sale of stock, and by reaching deep into their own pockets. Two years later, the Gehl brothers introduced a larger feed cutter, an elevator, and began producing stone and wood-stave silos. Two additional innovations during this time included an advanced-design, engine powered recutter for malt grain, corn cobs and stalks, and a new silo filler, which quickly developed into the standard for the farm equipment industry.

As Gehl Company continued to grow during the early part of the 20th century, the firm developed a reputation as one of the most innovative and reliable farm equipment operations in the Midwest. By the 1920s, the company was one of the undisputed leaders in the region. With the growth of the dairy industry during the decade, farmers were looking for a more convenient way to grind homegrown grains. The company responded to this need by developing the Gehl hammer mill, which would dominate the market for the next 30 years. At the same time, in addition to the stationary hammer mill, the company developed a portable truck-mounted mill. One of the most common sights during the late 1920s throughout central Wisconsin was the portable truck-mounted mill, stationed in the back of a Chevy truck, traveling from farm to farm grinding feed. In 1927, Gehl initiated the manufacture of manure spreaders, which rapidly become one of the company's most popular products. The Gehl manure spreader was developed with a number of new features, including an auto-style steering mechanism rather than the normally-produced wagon style. The new style of steering allowed the operator to position the spreader much more precisely under a manure carrier or in a small space such as a barnyard, and also made it more convenient and easier to steer through the narrow gates and lanes so common to farmland terrain.

The Great Depression and World War II

Gehl Company weathered the volatile economic climate of the Great Depression as well as, and perhaps better, than any other firm in the United States. When Franklin Delano Roosevelt issued his Bank Holiday proclamation after his inauguration in 1933, the country was beset with bankruptcies, foreclosures, and lack of public confidence in the banking system. Yet farm foreclosures didn't seem to be as common in Wisconsin as in other parts of the country, like the Plains states, and farmers continued to order and purchase new farm equipment from Gehl. The company was able to retain most of its employees, albeit on a somewhat reduced work week.

As the country began to recover from the Depression, Gehl Company benefitted from the economic activity. During the late 1930s, there was a dramatic expansion of dairy herds and farm feedlots which continued into the early 1940s. With America's entry into World War II on December 8, 1941, the day after the Japanese surprise attack on the U.S. Naval Base at Pearl Harbor, a farm labor shortage began to hold back any further expansion of dairy herds and farm feedlots. One of the most obvious needs, therefore, was a labor-saving method of putting up hay and putting corn into a silo. In order to respond to the requests of the U.S. government for labor-saving farm machinery, not to mention the needs of farmers throughout the Midwest, the Gehl Company designed and developed a silo filler that was placed on wheels and pulled across the fields with a wagon-box behind it. This innovative corn chopper was welcomed by farmers everywhere in the United States, since it was far easier and less time-consuming to unload chopper corn into a blower than it was to throw corn stalk bundles with a pitchfork into a silo filler. It was also just as easy and convenient to make hay with a Gehl chopper.

A man pulling a Gehl chopper and wagon into a field of hay could blow two acres of hay into a wagon in no time at all.

One of the most important changes that occurred within the Gehl Company during the late 1930s and early 1940s was the change in management and leadership at the firm. As the original Gehl brothers grew older and either retired or passed away, each of them was replaced by a second-generation Gehl family member. By the mid-1940s, the second generation of four Gehl brothers was supervising the operations of the company. Mark Gehl supervised engineering and manufacturing, Al Gehl was head of all the company's business and financial affairs, Carl Gehl was responsible for developing the firm's export market, while at the same time supervising the personnel, labor relations and legal affairs departments, and Dick Gehl assumed the responsibility for selling and marketing all the Gehl products. Interestingly, the four Gehl brothers managed the company as a committee by mutual consent, and without any formal titles.

The Postwar Era and Agricultural Changes

By the end of World War II, Gehl Company was ready for the expansion that came with America's role as the "breadbasket" of the world. Although there wasn't much technological innovation and change during the immediate postwar years, the four Gehl brothers had positioned themselves carefully to take advantage of the agricultural changes that were on the horizon. By the early 1950s, however, the farmland of the American Midwest and Plains states began to experience dramatic and far-reaching changes. Due to the American public's demand for more livestock and dairy produce, livestock numbers began to rapidly increase, along with the size of the average farm. This expansion of farming activities led to the need for labor-saving machinery, and resulted in such items as the homemade, rear-loading forage box as inadequate to meet the task at hand.

Gehl invented a front-unloading forage box that placed chopped forage into a blower which then enabled a farmer to put forage into a 100-foot silo more quickly than any homemade box could unload it. The high capacity blowers and innovative unloading boxes soon became standards in the farm machinery industry. At the same time, Gehl introduced a self-propelled forage harvester. The first such machine in the industry, the harvester was powered by a Continental engine that soon set new records in chopping capacity. The self-propelled harvester also became one of the most popular products of the company, and could be seen filling the large silos on farms throughout the Midwest and Plains states.

In addition to the design and development of new farm machinery, such as the self-propelled forage harvester and the front unloading forage box, the company was instrumental in developing better ensiled ear corn. Working closely with major universities in the Midwest and drawing on the company's long experience with recutters, Gehl came up with a faster, more convenient, and economical way to ensile high-moisture ear corn. By designing and manufacturing a silo-based recutter that could process just over 400 bushels of ear corn an hour, the cut feed when mixed with alfalfa haylage could supply enough food for thousands of dairy herd cows. The collaboration between Gehl Company and research facilities in the Midwest provided the firm with a growing reputation as one of the most innovative and experienced farm machinery manufacturers in the United States.

Growth and Expansion During 1960s, 1970s and 1980s

In 1960, Gehl manufactured what has been regarded as the very first efficient green chop machine. Replacing the traditional hammer-type flail shredder, the more efficient curved flail knives machine, with a 72-inch cut and a blower, provided farmers with a reliable machine they could use day after day. In fact, the design of this model was so good that it was still in use during the mid-1980s. In 1968, the company introduced newly designed cylinder-cut forage harvesters. This model quickly led Gehl to manufacture the largest capacity choppers ever designed. During the same year, the company also introduced the pull-type mower conditioner. Especially designed and introduced for farmers who refused to invest in a self-propelled machine, the pull-type mower provided the best alternative method to cut alfalfa.

In 1970, Gehl Company management decided to enter the construction machinery industry and introduced its very own skid steer loader. The Gehl loader had unique controls that enabled the driver to control all the machine's functions with his hands and, as a result, became very popular within the construction industry. By 1973, the company had created a marketing subsidiary in West Germany, Gehl Gmbh, to sell its skid loaders in Europe, the Middle East, and Africa markets. Gehl also designed another first within the construction machinery industry—a totally hydraulic grinding mixer.

The decade of the 1980s was the best ever for the company. Gehl experienced explosive growth in all of its construction and agricultural equipment product lines. Six years of increasing sales and expansion-oriented acquisitions policies pushed revenues up by 220 percent; net sales skyrocketed from $38.5 million in 1985 to $174.9 million by 1990. The company owned four manufacturing facilities, located in West Bend, Wisconsin; Lebanon, Pennsylvania; Madison, South Dakota; and Yankton, South Dakota. With its marketing subsidiary in West Germany, Gehl Company was planning a strategic move into worldwide markets for construction and agricultural equipment. And management, more confident than ever, was ready to assume its place along side of the industry giants—Case, Deere, and Caterpillar.

The 1990s and Beyond

During the early 1990s, however, everything began to change. A slower economy and higher interest rates placed Gehl, still in its expansionist mode, in trouble. By 1992, management was forced to scale back its strategic acquisitions policy and re-evaluate its future policies. A new management team, more conservative and more than willing to eliminate unprofitable product lines, was brought in to reorganize and revitalize the company. Although sales had fallen to $153.5 million in 1995, the company's products began to sell more briskly in 1996.

The company continued to emphasize its construction equipment product line, with newly designed skid loaders, rough terrain telescopic forklifts, Power Box asphalt pavers, and an improved line of material handlers. At the same time, Gehl relied heavily on its agricultural equipment product line, which included machinery for hay making, forage harvesting, feed making, manure handling and materials handling. Many of the company's agricultural products, such as the disc mower conditioner and its line of forage harvesters, have become standard equipment in the industry.

After its expansion and acquisition activities during the 1980s, Gehl Company rediscovered its niche. The company concentrated on designing and manufacturing high-quality, dependable, and economical construction and agricultural equipment for discerning customers. Perhaps one reason behind this resurgence was that the new management team formed during the early 1990s included William D. Gehl, one of the descendants of the founders, as president and chief executive officer.

Principal Subsidiaries

Gehl GmbH; Gehl International

Further Reading

Henke, Russ, "Agdraulics Goes Galactic: 21st Century Ag Equipment Technology Is Ready for Takeoff," *Diesel Progress Engines & Drives,* April 1996, p. 50.
Lacina, Jeff, "Chopping Stalks at Harvest," *Successful Farming,* October 1994, p. 40.
——, "Planter Tag Alongs," *Successful Farming,* April 1995, p. 46.
——, "Production," *Successful Farming,* October 1995, p. 29.
Mercer, Mike, "Gehl Company Gets Back to its Niche," *Diesel Progress Engines & Drives,* August 1996, pp. 20–24.
Osenga, Mike, "Market Forces Continue to Drive Agricultural Equipment Towards Greater Use of Hydraulics," *Diesel Progress Engines & Drives,* April 1996, p. 66.
Smith, Rod, "Gehl Reports Success Reducing Dealer Inventories," *Feedstuffs,* November 21, 1994, p. 7.
Three Generations: 1859–1984, 125 Years Of Good Ideas, West Bend, Wis.: Gehl Co., 1984.

—Thomas Derdak

INDUSTRIES, INC.

Giant Industries, Inc.

23733 Scottsdale Road
Scottsdale, Arizona 85255
U.S.A.
(602) 585-8888
Fax: (602) 585-8893

Public Company
Incorporated: 1969
Employees: 1,386
Sales: $499 million (1996)
Stock Exchanges: New York
SICs: 2911 Petroleum Refining; 5541 Gasoline Service
Stations

Giant Industries, Inc. is one of the fastest growing independent petroleum companies located in the southwestern portion of the United States. Operating in the Four Corners area, where Utah, Colorado, New Mexico, and Arizona converge, the company is involved in a wide range of refining and marketing activities, including two oil refineries at Gallup, New Mexico and Bloomfield, New Mexico; a crude oil gathering operation with approximately 340 miles of pipeline; a transportation company with 90 trucks that carry crude and finished petroleum products to its own service stations in the Four Corners area; 56 retail convenience stores/service stations in Arizona, Colorado, and New Mexico; and one of the most impressive, state-of-the-art Travel Centers located near Gallup, New Mexico. Headquartered in Scottsdale, Arizona, the company prides itself on being one of the leading minority employers in the Southwest, with more than 400 Native Americans working in various capacities throughout its facilities in the Four Corners region.

Early History

The founder of Giant Industries, Inc. has become one of the living legends in the Southwest. James E. Acridge started his rise to prominence in 1961 when, at the tender age of 21, he leased a small gasoline station in Glendale, Arizona from Richfield Oil (later to change its name to Atlantic Richfield). Four

years later, the ambitious young man leased another station in the southern part of Phoenix, Arizona. This time he operated it under his own sign, Giant, while still holding onto his first station in Glendale. The new station was a much larger, three-island, nine-pump gas station, supplied by Shell Oil Company. Within one year, Acridge had his new Giant gas station pumping more than 60,000 gallons per month. When the owner of the property on which his Giant station was situated demanded 1.5 cents per gallon instead of a flat rent fee, Acridge moved into another station where he put up his Giant shingle and was soon pumping 50,000 gallons per month.

It was not until 1968, however, that Acridge jumped into the big league of gas station operators. He purchased a small two-island station, an old Signal Oil gas station in Phoenix, and put up the first self-serve sign in the region. Almost overnight the volume jumped to 150,000 gallons per month. The next step was a natural one. Acridge purchased a plot of land near Mesa, Arizona, borrowed $30,000 from a bank to begin operations, leased all the necessary equipment, and built his own multipump gas station. This station was pumping 150,000 gallons of gas by its third month in operation. Acridge incorporated his company in 1969, and from that time on he was the undisputed king of self-serve gas stations in Arizona.

Expansion and Growth in the 1970s

Fully aware that he was 15 years ahead of the market, Acridge built his second self-serve unit in 1970. The design of this unit was the forerunner of all subsequent self-serve gas stations. Under the world's largest gas station canopy up to that time, Acridge wanted to make it a pleasant experience for his customers to pump gas, so he piped in soft, soothing music under the canopies, constructed high retaining walls so that people would not be embarrassed if their friends saw them at a self-service station, and provided ample space between all the gas pumps for customers to pump their own gas without any significant delay. Within a short time, the two self-serve stations were pumping between 250,000 and 300,000 gallons of gas per month. By 1973, Giant Industries had expanded to include 12 self-serve gas stations and was pumping more than one million gallons of gasoline per month.

Acridge was confident that the full service gas stations were not able to compete with his innovative units. Soon major oil companies began to court the rapidly growing company, and Acridge decided to switch from his traditional independent supply sources to Phillips Petroleum. But almost as soon as the ink had dried on the contract, Phillips informed Acridge that the company was pulling out of the Phoenix market and cutting off Giant's supply of gasoline. When Acridge discovered that most independents like Giant had been cut off by the larger oil companies, he went into federal court and procured an injunction requiring Phillips to continue supplying his company. After a meeting of more than 60 independents in Phoenix, the group devised a strategy to lobby Washington and the Federal Energy Office to enact new rules that would allow for a more equitable sharing of oil supplies. Before the regulation went into effect, however, Giant was forced to close all but four of its gas stations.

When the oil embargo by OPEC exacerbated an already existing supply crisis, Acridge decided to enter into the refinery business to ensure a steady supply for his own stations. He purchased a small gas processing facility located in Carthage, Texas, had it completely dismantled, and transported the entire plant to Farmington, New Mexico, where it was reassembled and put in working order. As the worry about supply subsided, Acridge focused on reopening his closed units and constructing new ones. As his operation grew, he also decided to develop tie-in businesses that augmented his self-serve stations. His first idea involved what he called a "C-Store," a huge store situated in back of his gas stations that sold a large line of groceries, including such items as sporting goods and automotive parts, and included an on-site dry cleaners. The customers did not come, sales were almost nonexistent, and Acridge was forced to close the stores within a few months. Other misguided tie-in developments included a tire business and a fast food restaurant called "Fast Eddie's."

One of the tie-in businesses that did work was a scaled-down version of the C-Store concept, which Acridge named Giant's "Goodies C-Store." Designed as a small kiosk of approximately 1,000 square feet, situated in the middle of a gas station between the pump islands, it allowed customers to pay at a window for their gas or to enter the store and purchase an item. The stores carried about 400 to 450 products, mostly such things as cigarettes, beer, soft drinks, pre-made sandwiches, snacks, candies, and picnic-type supplies. The per-store average sales figure quickly climbed to $10,000 per month, and some were even averaging sales as high as $25,000 per month. With this income, Acridge was able to reopen most of his stores that were forced to close during the early 1970s. By the end of 1979,

Giant was operating 23 gas stations and pumping more than four million gallons of gasoline per month.

Consolidation and Profitability During the 1980s

The 1980s were years of dramatic change for the company. In 1981, the major oil companies initiated a strategic campaign to squeeze out the independent gas station entrepreneurs like Acridge and re-establish themselves in markets from which they had long been absent. During the middle and late 1970s, independents had captured 55 percent of the gas station market in Phoenix. But after companies like Shell and Texaco increased their presence, most independents were soon pushed out of the market. Giant, however, was one of the few that remained, and at some cost. Acridge was forced to scale back his operations dramatically, and he closed all of his stations in the Phoenix metropolitan area. Branching out into smaller towns, Giant found a more stable, and lucrative, market.

In 1982, Giant acquired the Ciniza refinery from Shell, a more sophisticated and modern facility, and closed down the refinery it had built in Farmington, New Mexico. Acridge decided to close the New Mexico refining operation since the regional demand for residual fuel began to subside. At Ciniza, Giant added a $12 million, state-of-the-art 5,000 b/d isomerization unit to enhance the facility's ability to produce unleaded gasoline. By the mid-1980s, Ciniza was producing approximately 25,000 barrels per day and supplying motor fuels to more than 100 different customers throughout Arizona and New Mexico. Almost 25 percent of the company's annual production was sold through its own retail outlets, service stations, and two super retail centers.

Heartened by the success of his Goodies C-Stores during the early and mid-1980s, Acridge decided to open what has become known as a "highway extravaganza," an enormous combination truck stop/gas station/retail store close to the Ciniza refinery, about 20 miles west of Gallup, New Mexico. Opened in 1988 and covering about 35 acres of property, the Travel Center complex included a Truck Center; a fueling center for truckers with its own C-Store; a travelers' fueling center for passenger cars and recreational vehicles, separate from the Truck Center; and a 29,000-square-foot shopping mall with six retail stores, a restaurant, and a movie theatre.

The first and, many truckers say, still the only one of its kind, the Travel Center went against one of the principles upon which Acridge built his independent business. The Truck Center itself had 18 fully attended pumping islands that provided diesel fuel—at self-serve prices, of course. The decision to have attendants was based on the fact that Giant had to get certain information from truckers who paid their fuel bills with credit cards or vouchers. The Truck Center also included a service center, where truckers could have repairs done by a staff of certified mechanics and service technicians. Oil changes, grease jobs, and tire replacements were the most common types of maintenance required by truckers, and Giant began to garner a reputation for its efficiency and competence. In addition, the service center had the only truck wash between Barstow, California and Oklahoma City, Oklahoma and, as word of the facilities at the Travel Center spread, truckers would sometimes drive 350 miles out of their way just to get their rig washed.

Although tourists and local customers were always welcomed at the Travel Center, it was the intention of Acridge to cater to and treat the truckers as if they were royalty. Truckers were spending an average of between $100 to $150 on fuel alone, not to mention all the other purchases they made at the retail stores and restaurant. So Acridge arranged for a van to carry truckers back and forth from their rigs in the vast parking lot of the Travel Center, built 26 shower stalls of hotel-like quality for truckers who wanted to clean up between rides, installed laundry facilities, and a shoe shine. Perhaps most important of all, a trucker could order a 16-ounce t-bone steak for $10.95, have it cooked to order, and call home from the telephone situated on his table. As business boomed and more truckers began to arrive at the Travel Center, Acridge expanded his operation to include more retail stores and a new restaurant whose staff included a head chef trained at the highly respected Culinary Institute of America.

The 1990s and Beyond

During the early 1990s, Giant Industries continued its rapid growth. In 1993, the Travel Center alone reported that it pumped more than 20 million gallons of fuel. Over the years, the company had built up its transportation operation to include a fleet of 90 trucks that carried crude and finished petroleum products not only to its own facilities but a growing number of customers in the Four Corners region. At the same time, Acridge made an investment in acquiring a crude oil gathering operation located in San Juan County that included approximately 340 miles of pipeline.

By 1996, Giant Industries was one of the most successful petroleum products companies in the southwestern part of the United States. Having found its niche in the Four Corners area, the company increased its revenues from $301 million in 1992 to $499 million by the end of fiscal 1996. Giant Industries purchased its second refinery in 1996, located in Bloomfield, New Mexico, from the Gary-Williams Energy Corporation. This acquisition helped the company to consolidate some of its refining operations, lower transportation costs, and improve production. With the Ciniza and Bloomfield refineries working at full capacity, the company increased the number of barrels sold per day from 27,000 to 39,000 in less than one year. Because of the growing demand for more of its products, Giant has decided to initiate a capital project that will increase the number of barrels produced per day at both the Ciniza and Bloomfield refineries.

Also during 1996, Giant made a major purchase involving Diamond Shamrock, Inc. For $5.4 million the company acquired seven gasoline stations operated by Shamrock in northwestern New Mexico. This acquisition brought the total number of Giant-run gas stations to 56, largest of all the independents in the Four Corners region. The company also built two new combination service stations/convenience stores in Albuquerque, New Mexico and Sedona, Arizona and initiated a major campaign to remodel 28 of its existing service stations/convenient stores.

Having built an extensive network of service stations and convenience stores from one small gas station, Jim Acridge succeeded in an area of the United States where most independents have failed. Not intimidated by the major oil companies, Acridge's confidence and determination have resulted in a firm that provides high-quality products and enviable customer service to travelers in the southwestern United States. Of all the compliments Acridge has received about his company, none is more satisfying than to hear truckers advising other truckers to go to a Giant station.

Further Reading

Barrett, William P., ''The Mother of All Truck Stops,'' *Forbes,* April 12, 1993, pp. 116–118.

Byrne, Harlan S., ''Giant Industries,'' *Barrons,* May 13, 1991, pp. 31–32.

Emond, Mark, ''Giant Industries Expands in Far Southwest,'' *National Petroleum News,* October 1995, p. 28.

''Giant Buys Seven Stations,'' *The Oil Daily,* June 3, 1996, p. SW2.

''Giant's Profits Grow with Refining Sector,'' *The Oil Daily,* May 14, 1996, p. 4.

Kovski, Alan, ''Plant Purchases Help Giant Increase Profits,'' *The Oil Daily,* March 5, 1996, p. 3.

''Mapco, Giant Industries Beat Segment Trend,'' *The Oil Daily,* October 31, 1996, p. 2.

Reid, Marvin, ''Flying High in Tough But Tempting Phoenix,'' *National Petroleum News,* September 1980, pp. 60–66.

Victoria, Frank, ''How Giant's 'Travel Center' Shatters Old Truck Stop Image,'' *National Petroleum News,* March 1988, pp. 32–38.

—Thomas Derdak

Graco Inc.

4050 Olson Memorial Highway
Minneapolis, Minnesota 55422
U.S.A.
(612) 623-6000
Fax: (612) 623-6777

Public Company
Incorporated: 1926 as Gray Company, Inc.
Employees: 1,997
Sales: $391.8 million (1996)
Stock Exchanges: New York
SICs: 3561 Pumps and Pumping Equipment; 3586
Measuring and Dispensing Pumps; 3594 Fluid Power
Pumps and Motors

Graco Inc. is a world leader in fluid-handling systems and components. The company designs and manufacturers products which move, measure, control, dispense, and apply a wide range of fluids and viscous materials for over 40 different industries, ranging from shipbuilding and aerospace to construction contracting and fast-lube outlets. According to Harlan S. Byrne in a February 1997 *Barron's* article, ''Graco is one of those companies, nearly invisible to investors, that makes a steady living by supplying humdrum products—in its case, application systems for paint, sealants, adhesives and lubricants.'' Low-profile Graco Inc. serves such industry giants as Nissan and Pennzoil while quietly holding a number one position in a majority of its markets.

First Products: 1920s and 1930s

Graco traces its history to Gray Company, Inc., which was founded in 1926 by Leil and Russell Gray to manufacture and sell the air-powered grease gun the brothers had developed for use in automobile maintenance. The men, who worked in a downtown Minneapolis garage, found hand-operated grease guns cumbersome to operate, especially in the winter months when lubricants were more difficult to move. After field tests showed their invention was easier to handle and more effective than the hand-operated devises, the brothers hired three employ-

ees and began manufacturing ''Graco'' air-powered grease guns. First year sales were about $35,000.

Within two years of founding, the men added other products to the Graco line, such as an air-powered pumping unit which moved automotive fluids directly from shipping containers through a flexible hose to the service area. The company also began a nation-wide marketing program directed primarily to car dealers and service station owners.

Sales had reached $65,000 by 1931. The company continued to grow even during the Depression years, and in 1938, the business moved into a new plant, where Russell Gray further expanded the product line. Leil Gray, as company president, accelerated marketing and sales efforts; a branch office opened in New York, and salesmen carried Graco products in trailers bearing the company insignia. Sales topped $1 million in 1941.

Postwar Change of Focus and Rapid Growth

During World War II, Gray Company designed mobile lubrication equipment for use on the battlefield, while a tire retreading system helped extend limited resources at home. After the war the company turned its attention to industrial uses of the pumping technology it had been developing over the years. Spraying units, finishing equipment, and dispensing systems were designed for uses ranging from spreading adhesives to handling food.

By the mid-1950s, the 400-employee company had revenues in excess of $5 million. Driven by the needs of its customers, Gray Company continued play the role of innovator. The company was the first to use hydraulics for cleaning, and the first to develop cold airless atomization (a process which used pressure to separate liquid into fine particles) for spray painting and coating. The company also began to design automated systems for manufacturing plants and implement plans for international operations.

Airless-spray technology propelled the company's growth in the 1960s. In 1965, Gray Company developed an electrically-powered airless-spray system which freed painting contractors from bulky compressors. The company also introduced equip-

Company Perspectives:

"Graco's mission is to serve its customers, employees, shareholders and communities by generating sustained profitable growth. Our goal is to be the world's leading supplier of fluid handling equipment and systems in the markets we serve."

ment which permitted hot airless pumping, proportionate mixing, and automatically controlled dispensing of fluids.

In 1962, Leil Gray's son-in-law, David A. Koch was named president, succeeding Harry A. Murphy, who had served in the position since 1958. In the early years of his tenure, Koch guided the company through a plant modernization program and an important period of growth. In 1969, Gray Company, Inc. was taken public and changed its name to Graco Inc. Sales for the year were $33 million up from about $12 million when Koch assumed company leadership.

International expansion moved forward with the purchase of majority interest in a French automobile servicing equipment and products manufacturer and with the establishment of a Canadian sales subsidiary. Domestically, Graco purchased Chicago-based H.G. Fischer & Co., a finishing and electrostatics business. Sales topped $50 million in 1971. The company experienced an annual growth rate of 17 percent in sales and about 20 percent in net earnings over the ten-year period from 1963 to 1973.

A Decade of Change: 1970s

Graco's rapid growth faltered in 1974. Financial analyst Ken Johnson, in a 1975 *Corporate Report* article, suggested that Graco was surprised by a weakening market which had been disguised by customer purchases made in response to rapidly rising raw material prices. Net sales for 1974 rose only 6.3 percent, and net earnings fell 50 percent. The slide continued in 1975 with a significant drop in revenues.

Nevertheless, Graco rebounded in 1976. Pumps and spray-painting equipment for the construction and decorating trades led the recovery. Graco sales more than doubled over four years, and earnings reached a high of $10 million or $4.45 per share in 1979. Concern regarding future growth prompted the company to develop technology acquired earlier in the decade.

Electrostatic painting, which required less paint and reduced emissions, had become a preferred finishing method in increasingly cost-conscious, competitive, and environmentally-concerned times. A heavy investment in the technology paid off: Graco developed a successful new line of sophisticated products and positioned itself as an electrostatic equipment supplier for automobile makers.

Robotics Venture

In 1981, the company established a joint-venture, Graco Robotics, Inc. (GRI), with Edon Finishing Systems of Troy, Michigan, in order to develop a robotics paint-finishing system.

According to Eben Shapiro, in a June 1987 *Minneapolis/St. Paul City Business* article, Graco saw robotics as "a logical and necessary extension of its finishing business."

In 1982, Graco sales and earnings were hit by a combination of poor market and economic conditions, but the company continued to pump research and development dollars into the slowly progressing robotics venture and even increased its ownership from 51 to 80 percent. GRI sold its first robots in 1983 and became profitable in 1984. With 1985 sales around $20 million, GRI contributed about ten percent of total Graco sales.

David Koch stepped down as president of Graco in 1985. Walter Weyler, a vice-president with General Electric Co., succeeded him. Quoted in an April 1985 Minneapolis *Star Tribune* article, Koch remarked that he intended to focus on the strategic direction of the company as it made the transition from an emphasis on components to high-tech systems.

Activity continued in other businesses segments. In 1984, Graco discontinued a consumer painting business started in the late 1970s. The purchase of Lockwood Technology, Inc. (LTI), a supplier of chemical bonding and sealing equipment, broadened the fluid handling group that same year. The company acquired 100 percent ownership of former Japanese joint venture in 1985, thus expanding its international operations in the Far East.

By 1986, GRI had become a major supplier of paint-spraying robots, and its customers included Chrysler, Ford, Fiat, Ferrari, Volvo, and Rolls-Royce. Moreover, Japanese auto makers purchased robotics paint sprayers for plants located in the United States. GRI was one of only a few U.S. robot makers that had been able to maintain profitability.

A Changing Marketplace: The 1990s

However, demand for finishing equipment fell off as U.S. auto makers completed installation of the new generation of paint sprayers in the late 1980s; and profits on foreign sales of large automated systems were low due to customizing costs. Graco's 1988 domestic sales were flat, while a 31.7 percent increase in international sales was attributable to its traditional products, such as portable airless-spray painters.

International sales slowed in 1990, but increased U.S. sales in architectural coating and cleaning equipment helped Graco achieve both record sales and earnings for the year; net revenues were $321.3 million, and net earnings were $17.7 million. Continuing recession in the United States and poor economic conditions in several European countries resulted in decreased earnings in 1991, which fell by nearly 50 percent. The company also reported losses associated with the divestment of its robotics division; pressure from larger competitors had prompted the sale.

The company initiated a year-long strategic review in 1992, while it refined various aspects of its businesses. As a result, Graco exited the packaging and converting aspect of the adhesive equipment market with the sale of LTI and a related joint-venture, two Detroit-area operations were consolidated in the building that was constructed for Graco Robotics, and a new spray-gun manufacturing plant was planned.

Weyler resigned his positions as president and chief operating officer in January 1993. Koch—who was the major company shareholder as well as CEO and chairman—commented at the time that he and Weyler had important differences regarding the future direction of the company. "The sudden resignation of a president is enough to throw most public companies into a tailspin," wrote Scott Carlson, in the *St. Paul Pioneer Press* in March 1993. But with Koch once again at the helm, Wall Street was not fazed; Graco had a solid reputation as a well-run company, with little long-term debt, no across-the-board competition, and the ability to meet the challenges of changing internal and external conditions.

New Leadership for the Future

George Aristides, a 20-year Graco veteran, was promoted to president and chief operating officer in June 1993. Aristides had served as vice-president of manufacturing operations since 1985 and led the $20 million, five-year conversion of Graco's two sprawling Minneapolis plants to a cellular operation with work groups producing components or products from start to finish.

Also in 1993, Graco became the first company in its industry to become ISO 9000-registered at all its major sites. ISO 9000, which set business practice standards, was adopted by the International Organization for Standardization in 1987. Forty percent of Graco's 1992 sales had been in the international marketplace where certification was increasingly expected. More American companies, such as Sherwin-Williams, one of Graco's largest customers for pumps and paint spraying equipment, were also asking their vendors to be certified.

Ongoing recessions in Europe and Japan, both important overseas markets, had forced Graco to downsize operations in those regions. In 1994, Graco restructured its operations in the Pacific and in Europe. In order to boost product development, the company pumped in $23.1 million in capital expenditures into engineering and manufacturing capabilities in 1994 and added another $19.8 million in 1995. Late in 1995 plans for a $17 million distribution and manufacturing center were announced.

After 33 years as CEO, David Koch stepped down from the post in January 1996. Koch was succeeded by Aristides, while maintaining his position as chairman. Net earnings grew by 31 percent to $36.2 million in 1996 on little change in revenue, which was up just one percent to $391.8 million. But profits were slim on foreign sales which contributed nearly one-third of total volume.

Harlan S. Byrne, in a February 1997 *Barron's* article, credited Aristides with shaking up "the once sleepy organization." Product development spending was increased by nearly 50 percent from 1992 to 1996. Graco introduced 130 new items in 1996 and expected to increase that number to 160 in 1997. Products introduced in the previous three years generated 21 percent of 1996 worldwide sales. Selling, general, and administrative expenses were cut from 40 to 31 percent of revenues from 1992 to 1996.

Byrne regarded Graco's gains in earnings under Aristides as dramatic. Net earnings, before special items, had more than tripled since 1992. Nevertheless, he noted that "Aristides won't be happy until annual revenues rise, on average, at a double-digit clip." Graco predicted future growth in sales and profitability would be driven by increased global industrialization, changes in materials, improved manufacturing processes, and the use of applied technologies all of which would necessitate new fluid handling products and systems solutions.

Principal Subsidiaries

Graco K.K. (Asia Pacific).

Principal Divisions

Automotive and Industrial Equipment; Lubrication Equipment; Contractor Equipment.

Further Reading

Byrne, Harlan S., "Revitalized," *Barron's,* February 3, 1997, p. 22.

Carlson, Scott, "Restructuring Graco," *St. Paul Pioneer Press Dispatch,* March 1, 1993.

"Corporate Capsule: Graco Inc.," *Minneapolis/St. Paul CityBusiness* July 15, 1991 and April 23, 1993.

"David Koch Ending His 33-Year Tenure as CEO at Graco," *Star Tribune* (Minneapolis), December 16, 1995, p. 2D.

Ewen, Beth, "Graco Reports Earnings Downturn Due to Lower Profit Margins," *Minneapolis/St. Paul City Business,* August 7–20, 1989, p. 16.

"Fast-Forward on the Paint-Spray Line," *Financial World,* October 31–November 13, 1984, p. 70–71.

Feyder, Susan, " 'Stick-To-Itiveness' Pays Off for Graco," *Star Tribune* (Minneapolis), May 5, 1986, p. 1M.

Fredrickson, Tom, "Aristides Primes the Pump at Graco," *Minneapolis/St. Paul City Business,* November 12–19, 1993, p. 1.

——, "Woes Across the Water," *Minneapolis/St. Paul CityBusiness,* May 27–June 2, 1994, p. 1.

"Graco Hires GE Official as President," *Star Tribune* (Minneapolis), April 12, 1985.

Johnson, Ken, "Graco at the Gap," *Corporate Report Minnesota,* June 1975, p. 35–36.

——, "Graco at the Ready," *Corporate Report Minnesota,* September 1981.

Kearney, Robert P., "A Pumped Up Graco," *Corporate Report Minnesota,* April 1986, p. 45+.

Maturi, Richard J., "The Age of Robots," *Barron's,* August 18, 1986, p. 36.

Peterson, Susan E., "Graco Reports Record Sales and Earnings for Last Year," *Star Tribune* (Minneapolis), February 15, 1991, p. 2D; "Walter Weyler Resigns from Graco Because of 'Differences' with CEO," *Star Tribune* (Minneapolis), January 16, 1993, p. 1D; "Graco Names Aristides President, COO," *Star Tribune* (Minneapolis), June 25, 1993, p. 3D; "Aggressive Graco Pumps Up the Volume," *Star Tribune* (Minneapolis), May 17, 1993, p. 1D; "Global Competition Spurs ISO 9000," *Star Tribune* (Minneapolis), November 22, 1993, p. 1D.

Randle, Wilma, "Dollar's Strength Hit Graco in '84," *St. Paul Pioneer Press Dispatch,* May 8, 1985.

Shapiro, Eben, "Graco Robots Wow Even the Japanese," *Minneapolis/St. Paul City Business,* June 3, 1987, p. 1.

—Kathleen Peippo

The Great Universal Stores plc

Universal House
Devonshire Street
Manchester M60 1XA
United Kingdom
+44 (161) 273-8282
Fax: +44 (161) 277-4881
Web site: http://www.gus.co.uk

Public Company
Incorporated: 1917 as Universal Stores (Manchester)
   Ltd.
Employees: 33,150
Sales: £2.8 billion (US$4.2 billion) (1996)
Stock Exchanges: London
SICs: 5961 Catalog and Mail-Order Houses; 6282
   Investment Advice; 5651 Family Clothing Stores;
   6510 Real Estate Operators and Lessors

The Great Universal Stores plc (GUS) is the leading mail-order company in the United Kingdom with the mail-order brand Kays and a 40 percent share of the market. It is one of the two largest operators in this field outside the United States, the other being Otto Versand of Germany. In addition to its mail-order core, the group derives around one-third of its profits from real property and financial services. Property assets exceed £1 billion and yield substantial rentals. GUS is Europe's largest non-bank provider of consumer and industrial finance, mainly through its Whiteaway Laidlaw and General Guarantee subsidiaries. Retail clothing, represented by the upscale Burberry's Ltd. and Scotch House Ltd., is a relatively small, yet important part of the company. There is a continuing small interest in manufacturing, especially clothing, bedding, and printing. Overseas interests, including mail-order and conventional retailing, contribute around 28 percent of total revenues. GUS maintains a low level of debt, large cash reserves, and a strong balance sheet. Annual pre-tax profits rose for 48 consecutive years from 1948 through 1996, suffering a decline in fiscal 1997. The Wolfson family, which has maintained a significant stake in the company throughout that entire period, continued to lead the company through the mid-1990s.

Turn of the Century Origins

The company's history began in Manchester in 1900. Three brothers, George, Jack, and Abraham Rose, started a general dealing and merchanting business. By 1917, when Universal Stores was registered as a limited, or incorporated, company, it supplied a wide range of consumer goods. Increased success accompanied a move into mail order in the 1920s. The Roses, who had previously relied on newspaper advertising of single items, began to draw up catalogs instead. Early versions were small in format but bulky, containing about 100 pages, with one product illustrated on each page. Agents were recruited to promote sales via the catalog and were allowed discounts on their own purchases. Customers paid by installment, usually over a period of up to 20 weeks. Sometimes the credit club method was employed, by which members paid a weekly sum and drew lots to determine the order in which they would receive their chosen goods. The catalog, the commissioned agent, and installment credit have remained the characteristic institutions of mail-order operations. Another form of direct selling by credit had been established earlier. This was the tallyman—or salesman collector—system, which was later used by some GUS subsidiaries. The salesman made regular home visits to collect installments and deliver goods.

Universal Stores grew rapidly toward the end of the 1920s. Profits averaged £244,000 over the three years 1929 to 1931, reaching a peak of £411,000 in 1931. The company added the word "Great" to its title in 1930, and successfully went public in 1931. A combination of falling demand—induced by the Great Depression—and poor stock control reduced profits by half in 1932 and resulted in a small loss in 1933. The Roses, who had benefited considerably from the public issue, felt obliged to pay nearly £100,000 out of their own pockets in order to maintain the dividend at its previously anticipated level. Several members resigned from the board in late 1932, and three new directors, including Sir Philip Nash as chairman, were appointed to represent the interests of the U.K. securities firm Cazenove's clients. The most significant change precipitated by this crisis was the appointment of a new joint managing director, Isaac Wolfson, along with George Rose, who resigned two years later. Under Wolfson's leadership, GUS was to make the lengthy transition from the unpromising circumstances of 1932 to its present financial strength.

Wolfson's Career at GUS Begins in 1930s

Wolfson was born in Glasgow in the late 1890s, starting his career as a salesman for his father's modest furniture business. Moving to London in 1920, he traded on his own account, selling such items as clocks and mirrors and also building up an informal private banking practice. By 1932 Wolfson had become merchandise controller of GUS, having first met and impressed George Rose at a trade exhibition in Manchester. Wolfson specified that not all his time would be devoted to his employer, and his remuneration consisted at least in part of an option to buy GUS shares from the Roses. The option was exercised when the share price fell heavily in 1932, with the assistance of both his father-in-law, Ralph Specterman, and of his stockbroker friend, Sir Archibald Mitchelson, who later succeeded Nash as chairman of the company. Though Wolfson would not advance to chairman until after World War II, he has been credited with transforming the company over the course of his half-century career. A 1994 profile of GUS in *Management Today* characterized Wolfson as ''the secretive financial wizard who turned GUS from a small trading operation in Manchester into one of Europe's three largest mail order companies.''

GUS soon recovered. Despite high unemployment, the majority of working-class consumers enjoyed rising real incomes, and the company had prospects of increased sales once the internal problems were under control. By 1934 the new 150-page catalog claimed to be the largest of any mail-order house in Europe. A few years later GUS took over the similar business of its Manchester neighbor Samuel Driver. However, acquisitions were not confined to mail order. A Wembley-based furniture concern, with large factory and warehouse capacity, had already been added to the company. Midland and Hackney, a recent amalgamation of two of the oldest established installment-purchase furniture businesses in the country, joined GUS in 1934. A feature of this firm that made it an attractive proposition was its substantial debts in installment purchases. Collection of outstanding debt and mortgaging of properties—wholly owned properties were mortgaged, then rented back—could unlock valuable cash resources. In 1938 Alexander Sloan of Glasgow, with 20 shops and a tallyman—an installment selling business—and two other similar Scottish concerns, were brought into the group. These 1930s acquisitions were on a cash basis and were financed by a combination of retained profit and debenture issues. Altogether, more than £2 million was raised in this way in 1936 and 1938. Expansion into the retail trade in the prewar years was not very successful in the short run, however. Profits fell in 1935, and thereafter grew more slowly than assets until after the outbreak of World War II.

Acquisitions Pace Post World War II Growth

GUS's profits were maintained during the war. By the late 1940s it had emerged as the owner of a large chain of furniture shops, while the mail-order base had been strengthened further by the purchase of Kays of Worcester in 1943. Jays and Campbells, with nearly 200 furniture outlets, was bought in 1943 for £1.2 million, after the previous owners had run into trouble with wartime price control legislation. In 1945 the British and Colonial Furniture Company sold a controlling interest to GUS for around £1 million. This included some 75 Cavendish and Woodhouse stores in the United Kingdom and a larger number in Canada. Another important furniture business, Smarts, was taken over in 1949, again for about £1 million. Jackson's followed soon after. By fiscal 1953–1954 furniture sales, mainly by installment buying, accounted for about a third of the company's expanded profits of some £15 million.

The major acquisitions of the 1940s owed much to three major factors. One was that wartime trading restrictions, regulating allocation and use of raw materials, plus controls on capital and on profit margins in distribution, were a less severe constraint for GUS—which was accustomed to working on lower margins—than for retail concerns with weaker and more traditional management. Another was that Wolfson was sufficiently confident and farsighted to anticipate a postwar housing boom and a strong demand for furniture on credit. A final consideration was that after the war many retailers continued to hold properties at prewar valuations. Current values understated the potential for a buyer aware of the possibilities of property sales, or mortgage-and-lease-back deals with insurance companies. Property revaluation strengthened the balance sheet of the buyer and lifted the price of its shares.

In the postwar years GUS and Wolfson, who had become chairman in 1945 on the death of Mitchelson, quickly gained a higher public profile. The new leader's growing reputation rested on the rapid growth of the firm and especially on his success as a practitioner of the takeover bid. Some of the techniques employed in the acquisitions of the 1950s were already familiar—notably the targeting of companies with undervalued properties, and the sale, with or without lease-back, of selected properties. A major new element was the creation of new, mostly nonvoting, shares, of which GUS issued more than five million in a new ''A'' class via a stock split in 1952. Eventually the ''A'' shares vastly outnumbered the ordinary, allowing the Wolfson family, to maintain control with a minority of the total stock. For the larger takeovers of the 1950s GUS offered a combination of cash and ''A'' shares. Bids on this basis were frequently acceptable and recipients, like the directors of the women's clothing group Morrison's in 1957, announced their willingness to hold GUS ''A'' shares as a long-term investment. Similar offers succeeded in some cases where the bid was resisted or contested, as in 1954 with Jones and Higgins, the drapers and house furnishers. Probably the most publicized disputed takeover was for control of Hope Brothers in late 1957, for which Debenhams was also competing. As GUS grew and flourished, the ''A'' shares were a highly marketable security. As the *Economist* observed, on July 26, 1958, their holders were generally ''content with bigger dividends, scrip issues and high market values.''

In 1955 the family created a trust, the Wolfson Foundation, to hold its shares. The entity grew to become one of the U.K.'s largest philanthropies, with major beneficiaries including Oxford, Cambridge, and University College. The positive press arising from these donations were perceived as a foil to the veil of secrecy that surrounded GUS. For though the firm was more profitable and paid higher dividends than most of its peers, its stock price lagged behind many competitors' throughout the 1950s and 1960s. Analysts blamed the lower valuation on the Wolfsons' tight-fisted voting control and the dearth of public communication.

Acquisitions promoted the company's growth in the 1950s, and at times did so at a hectic pace. During fiscal 1953–1954, 350 retail outlets were added to the existing 870. In the fiscal year 1957–1958, the contribution of new subsidiaries exceeded the total increase in profits. Takeovers preserved the record of unbroken profit growth. Expansion of this kind resulted in diversification of trading interests. By the early 1960s the established base in mail order and furniture had been broadened not only by large investments in drapery and men's and women's clothing, but also by stakes in footwear, hotels, electrical goods, builder's merchants, food retailing, and a travel agency. Two of the less predictable of these purchases were perhaps most significant for the future of GUS. The arrival in the group of Burberry's in 1956 signaled a move into more specialized and upmarket areas of the clothing trade, and the absorption in 1957 of Whiteaway Laidlaw, an export drapery and finance company, pointed in some new directions. By the beginning of the 1960s the board had indicated its awareness of reduced opportunities for growth by takeover, and of the need for expansion within the existing structure.

Pace of Geographic Expansion Quickens in 1960s and 1970s

Since the 1960s the company has experienced major acquisitions, more disposals, and increasing concentration on a reduced number of principal sectors. However, the high degree of diversification was a factor in spreading risk and in enabling the group to avoid any setback to the growth of profits. The chairman complained in 1974 of 18 changes in hire-purchase—or installment buying—regulations over the previous 19 years. A further contribution toward smoothing the retail cycle came from GUS's own accounting practice, by which revenue from hire-purchase sales was not credited to profit until after the final installment was paid. Thus, when such sales were rising, debt provision rose faster than profit, but when they were falling, profits were boosted by sales made before the downturn. An additional factor in the stability of GUS's profit growth was the rising share from overseas, which reduced dependence on the performance of the U.K. economy. Until the early 1960s there were only modest earnings abroad, mainly from stores in the United Kingdom, Commonwealth markets of Canada and South Africa. Then entry into both the United States and continental Europe helped to lift the overseas contribution of total profits to around ten percent by the end of the 1960s and to 12.5 percent ten years later.

Much of GUS's postwar growth had been in the sector in which it achieved early market leadership—mail order. Even here, some expansion has been bought by absorbing smaller competitors, although the last occasion was the acquisition of John Myers in 1981. A proposed deal with Empire Stores was blocked on antimonopoly grounds in 1982. By then GUS held a position of strength in a market that had expanded since the war to a point where mail order represented perhaps eight percent of nonfood retail sales in the late 1970s. Before the war, mail order

had been popular mainly in northern England and Scotland, in rural areas, and among low-income groups. Since the early 1950s it has expanded both geographically and socially. The fastest phase of growth occurred in the late 1950s and 1960s before alternative sources of credit became more readily available in shops. The worst setback to the mail-order market was felt in the early 1980s, when recession and unemployment had a negative impact on installment buying. Some of GUS's techniques were unchanged—for example, the reliance on commissioned agents. The major catalogs were transformed into color-printed, 1,000-page, 26,000-item publications. Computerized stock control was introduced, along with automated storage buildings. The stock itself was to a large extent designed and manufactured to the company's own specifications. Deliveries were handled increasingly by GUS's own national distribution network, which included the White Arrow fleet.

Apart from its home-shopping division, GUS was also expanding vigorously in the 1970s and 1980s in property and finance and was disposing of its less successful retail interests. Two important milestones were passed in 1977, when turnover first reached £1 billion and profits £100 million. A new orientation towards property became apparent in the growing tendency to retain the owned property and longer leaseholds when a subsidiary was sold, as in the cases of the Paige clothing shops and Times Furnishing in 1986. By then, the company had long since discarded the image it had sported during earlier phases of growth. Its shares had once been regarded as volatile and speculative, and concern was sometimes expressed about the size of borrowings. More recently, criticism had come from a different angle. The group made appearances on lists of British firms with "cash mountains." Some well-known GUS characteristics did not change at all—the relatively conservative accounting policies and the ungenerous rationing of public information about its activities. Shareholders had to wait a long time for full lists of subsidiaries and even longer for breakdowns of turnover or profit by sector.

Late 1980s, Early 1990s Bring Management Shifts

Sir Isaac Wolfson, made a baronet in 1962 for his charitable activities, stepped down as co-chairman in 1986 in favor of his son Leonard, Lord Wolfson of Marylebone, who had become joint managing director in 1963 and later co-chairman. In contrast with his acquiring father, Lord Wolfson was credited with a shrewd program of strategic divestment, shedding over 2,000 shops via the sale of such chains as Waring & Gillow, the Houndsditch Warehouse, and Times Furnishing. The new leader kept the units' real properties, renting them back to their new owners in a move that essentially transferred these businesses into GUS's real estate management division.

Some industry analysts observed that competition within GUS's core mail order business was heating up in the mid-1990s. The U.K. mail order market's share of nonfood retail sales shrunk from six percent in 1980 to little more than three percent in 1994, and challenges from French and German catalog powerhouses began to encroach on GUS's home turf. Nonetheless, the British firm maintained a 40 percent share of the nation's catalog sales and, more importantly, earned more than two-thirds of the industry's profits.

GUS surprised many observers in 1995, when it extended voting rights to all shareholders and appointed four non-executive directors. One of the new board members, Lord (David) Wolfson of Sunningdale, a cousin of Leonard's, had served the company as chairman of the Home Shopping Division from 1973 to 1978, but was believed to have had a disagreement with Leonard that precipitated his departure. The "family reunion" sparked speculation with regard to the line of succession, and indeed, the 69-year-old Leonard relinquished the day-to-day responsibilities of the chairmanship to David in the summer of 1996. Leonard was given the title of Honorary President.

David Wolfson tapped some of GUS's long dormant financial resources. He set the ball rolling in February 1997 through a deal with British Land that took advantage of the retail conglomerate's £900 million real estate portfolio. The new leader quickly parlayed that nest egg into back-to-back investments in GUS's financial and information services operations. In 1996 the company made its first major acquisition in more than three decades, the £1 billion (US$1.7 billion) purchase of Experian Corp. (better known as TRW Inc.), a U.S. credit reporting group. Experian was merged with GUS's existing CCN Group and its headquarters was moved to Nottingham. A second acquisition in this segment, that of Direct Marketing Technology Inc., followed in April 1997. The moves, which bolstered CCN's ranking in the U.S. credit bureau industry, signaled the British company's global aspirations. Though bold, David Wolfson's moves had a major drawback; the company announced in December 1996 that its nearly 50-year string of uninterrupted profit increases had come to an end. Whether the newest Wolfson to lead Great Universal Stores had launched on his own earnings trend remained to be seen.

Principal Subsidiaries

G.U.S. Home Shopping Limited; Burberry's Limited; The Scotch House Limited; G.U.S. Canada Inc.; CCN Experian Limited; All Counties Insurance Company Limited; Whiteaway Laidlaw Bank Limited; G.U.S. Property Management Limited.

Further Reading

Aris, Stephen, *The Jews in Business,* London: Jonathan Cape, 1970.

Buckingham, Lisa, "GUS Catalogues £1bn Deal," *The Guardian,* November 15, 1996, p. 19.

Bull, George, and Anthony Vice, *Bid for Power,* London: Elek Books, 1958.

Cowe, Roger, "Grandpa GUS is Strong But Old-Fashioned," *The Guardian,* July 21, 1989, p. 18.

——, "Agents Go the Way of Cold War Warriors," *The Guardian,* December 6, 1996, p. 26.

Fickenscher, Lisa, "Experian and British Credit Firm Merged in Push for Global Scope," *American Banker,* November 15, 1996, pp. 1–2.

"GUS: The Olde Curiosity Shoppe," *The Guardian,* July 19, 1991, p. 13.

Laurance, Ben, "GUS Shares Soar on Founder's Death," *The Guardian,* June 22, 1991, p. 10.

Newman, Aubrey, "A Wealth of Generosity," *The Guardian,* June 22, 1991, p. 21.

Springett, Pauline, "GUS Frees Pounds 900m Asset," *The Guardian,* February 17, 1997, p. 15.

Woolcock, Keith, "The Great Universal Mystery," *Management Today,* November 1994, pp. 48–52.

—Gerald W. Crompton
—updated by April D. Gasbarre

The Greenbrier Companies

1 Centerpointe Drive
Lake Oswego, Oregon 97035
U.S.A.
(503) 684-7000
Fax: (503) 684-7553

Public Company
Incorporated: 1981
Employees: 2,803
Sales: $530.0 million (1996)
Stock Exchanges: New York
SICs: 3743 Railroad Equipment; 7359 Equipment Rental
  & Leasing, Not Elsewhere Classified; 6719 Holding
  Companies, Not Elsewhere Classified

The Greenbrier Companies is the largest manufacturer of railroad freight cars in North America through its Gunderson, Inc. and TrentonWorks Limited subsidiaries. Gunderson also refurbishes railroad cars and builds ocean-going barges and other heavy marine equipment, while a third subsidiary, Greenbrier Leasing Corporation, owns or manages more than 45,000 rail cars and provides logistical services, including fleet management, warehousing, and new vehicle transport using the Gunderson Autostack system.

The Greenbrier Companies is based in Lake Oswego, a suburb of Portland, Oregon. The Gunderson manufacturing site outside Portland on the Willamette River includes the largest side-launch marine facility on the West Coast. In addition, Gunderson Rail Services, a division of Gunderson, Inc., refurbishes rail cars at facilities in Cleburne, Texas; Springfield, Oregon; Pine Bluff, Arkansas; and Tacoma, Washington. TrentonWorks Limited, in Nova Scotia, Canada, includes the largest forge in Canada, capable of making steel forgings up to 100 tons each.

Origins of Greenbrier Companies

Alan James and William A. Furman, two former executives of the TransPacific Financial Corporation, a Northwest-based finance and heavy equipment company, created the Greenbrier Companies as a holding company in 1981. James and Furman had started their own company when they purchased the lease-underwriting division of their former employer in 1974. Through their company, James and Furman had managed the Greenbrier Leasing Corporation for its owner, Commercial Metals Company, since 1979.

The Greenbrier Leasing Corporation was formed in 1970 as a joint venture between the M.D. Friedman Company in Huntington, West Virginia, and the Commercial Metals Company in Dallas, Texas, to acquire and manage a fleet of flatbed railroad cars. In 1979, Commercial Metals bought out M.D. Friedman and hired the newly formed James-Furman and Company to manage the leasing operation. When Commercial Metals decided to sell its leasing operation in 1981, James and Furman purchased it through The Greenbrier Companies. They moved the business from Dallas to Portland, Oregon, soon afterwards.

Gunderson, Inc. Acquired in 1985

In 1985, The Greenbrier Companies purchased the Portland-based Marine and Rail Car Division of the FMC Corporation, restoring the name Gunderson, Inc. Gunderson was a venerable company founded in 1919 as the Wire Wheel Sales and Service Co. by Chester E. Gunderson. He was joined four years later by his brother, Alvin E. Gunderson, and they incorporated in 1921. The original business sold and repaired both wood-spoked and wire wheels.

In the early 1930s, the Gundersons began selling engine parts and by 1935 were also repairing trailer brakes. Two years later, the Gundersons were manufacturing trailers for hauling logs, dry cargo and petroleum products. The company also made Superior School Bus bodies, hearses, and vans. The Gundersons spun off the manufacturing side of the business in 1938, calling it Gunderson Brothers, Inc. They also added underground and above-ground storage tanks to the product line, and purchased the Mogul Transportation Co., which included a small fleet of tanker trucks and trailers. In 1939, Gunderson Brothers introduced one of the first trailers designed for hauling automobiles.

During World War II, the Gundersons manufactured a variety of marine equipment for the U.S. military, including assault landing craft. After the war, the renamed Gunderson Brothers Engineering Corp. continued manufacturing tugboats and cargo lighters for the military and commercial fishing vessels. The company also began manufacturing equipment for sawmills and became a general steel fabricator, erecting buildings and bridges in the Portland area.

From 1946 to 1950, the Gundersons experimented with a variety of innovative products, introducing an aluminum ironing board, cartop carriers, motorized rototillers, and a collapsible, plywood boat. But the company's primary business had become heavy steel construction; their projects included the Oregonian, Flintcote, and Federal Reserve buildings in Portland. During the 1950s, the company also continued building barges, tugboats, and other marine vessels, including more military landing craft during the Korean War.

In 1958, the Gundersons built their first railroad-car underframe for the Pacific Fruit Co. Two years later, the company delivered 200 coal cars to the Union Pacific Railroad. Rail cars quickly became a significant part of the company's business although it continued building bridges, barges, and other marine equipment, including the Floating Laboratory Inverted Platform for the Scripps Institute of Oceanography in 1962 and an experimental, hydrofoil ship hull for The Boeing Co. in 1967. In 1969, Gunderson Brothers produced more than 2,300 railroad cars, along with railroad-car barges for the Pacific Inland Navigation Co. and Crowley Launch and Tug Co. By 1995, Gunderson had built more than 85,000 railway cars.

In 1970, Gunderson Brothers Engineering became Gunderson, Inc., and produced the first 100-ton, all-steel covered hopper cars for the newly merged Burlington Northern Railroad. Throughout the 1970s and into the mid-1980s, Gunderson continued making railroad cars and barges. It also manufactured several oil tankers for Chevron, the first ships built in Portland since World War II. The first of the oil tankers, the 650-foot Oregon, was launched in 1974 and christened by the wife of Oregon's governor.

Al Gunderson died in 1971 and the company was sold two years later to the FMC Corporation. Chester Gunderson was then in ill health and died in 1974. FMC expanded Gunderson's rail-car operations and, in 1978, built the 580-foot, triple-deck La Reina, then the largest roll-on, roll-off railroad barge in the world. Under FMC, Gunderson also unveiled a prototype, intermodal freight car built for the Itel Corporation, a cargo barge built for the Zidell Exploration Co. that could be converted to a petroleum tanker, and an ice-breaker barge, also built for Zidell. The Greenbrier Companies purchased the rail car and marine division from FMC in 1985, during a restructuring of the chemical and heavy-equipment manufacturing conglomerate.

In 1985, the renamed Gunderson, Inc. introduced the Twin-Stack, an innovative railroad container car that had been developed as a prototype by FMC. The Twin-Stack, a system for transporting automobiles in standard intermodal trailer containers, quickly became the mainstay of Gunderson manufacturing. From an initial order of 500 in 1985, Twin-Stack production rose to nearly 3,000 in 1990.

Greenbrier Goes Public in 1994

With a surge in railway freight, sales at The Greenbrier Companies more than doubled between 1989 and 1993, from $113.6 million to $264.3 million. Profits increased nearly five-fold, from $1.76 million to $8.2 million. In 1994, The Greenbrier Companies decided to go public. James, then chairman, and Furman, then chief executive, retained 65 percent ownership of the company.

In 1995, The Greenbrier Companies acquired a majority interest in the Trenton Works, a railroad-car manufacturing facility in Nova Scotia, Canada. The purchase nearly doubled the company's rail-car manufacturing capacity to more than 5,000 a year.

Like Gunderson, the renamed TrentonWorks Limited was a company with a storied history. In 1872, two blacksmiths, Graham Fraser and Forrest MacKay, formed the Hope Iron Works in Trenton to make anchors and iron fittings for sailing ships. In 1878, they changed the name to the Nova Scotia Forge Company.

The Nova Scotia Steel Company, the first steel-making plant in Canada, was established in Trenton in 1882 specifically to supply Nova Scotia Forge. In 1895, the two companies, along with the New Glasgow Iron, Coal and Railway Co., which was then mining iron ore at Wabana, Newfoundland, merged under the name Nova Scotia Steel. In 1890, Nova Scotia Steel merged with Sidney Mines to become the Nova Scotia Steel and Coal Company.

Steel making ended abruptly in 1904 because of the poor quality of iron ore available locally, but two rolling mills were added to the company in 1910, and Nova Scotia Steel and Coal began manufacturing heavy forgings. In 1912, the company formed the Eastern Car Company at a site adjacent to the forge to manufacture railroad cars. The Dominion Steel Corporation also established a cast-iron railway wheel foundry on the same site, adding a bolt and rivet factory in 1913.

In 1921, as the era of rapid rail expansion came to an end, the Nova Scotia Steel and Coal Company merged with Dominion Steel to become the British Empire Steel Corporation, which was then acquired by Dominion Steel and Coal Corporation, Ltd., in 1928.

A.V. Roe Canada Ltd. acquired controlling interest in Dominion Steel and Coal in 1957, and sold the Trenton Works to Sidbec, a Quebec government corporation. A management group, Hawker Industries Ltd., later acquired the Trenton Works from Quebec, and was itself acquired by Hawker Siddeley Canada. Hawker Siddeley sold the Trenton Works to

Lavalin Industries, then part of the Lavalin Group, in 1988. Lavalin spun off the railroad-car manufacturing facility in 1991, which operated independently as Trenton Works, Inc. until it was purchased by The Greenbrier Companies.

Transportation Logistics in the 1990s

In 1995, Gunderson launched its first barges built since the company was acquired by the Greenbrier Companies. The two 296-foot, ocean-going hydraulic-dump barges, built for The Dutra Companies of San Rafael, California, were designed for hauling waste out to sea.

A year later, The Greenbrier Companies began providing logistical support for companies that were shipping products by rail, including warehousing and vehicle transportation. To gain a toehold in the expanding transportation-services market, The Greenbrier Companies acquired Interamerican Logistics, Inc., Ontario, Canada, and Superior Transportation System, Lake Oswego, Oregon, merging them with the Autostack Corporation to form Greenbrier Logistics Inc.

Despite consolidations in the rail industry in the late 1990s, including the proposed merger of the CSX Corporation and Conrail, Inc., the outlook for continued growth at The Greenbrier Companies remained strong. Only about ten percent of Greenbrier Companies's freight cars were sold or leased to Class I railroad companies, and Greenbrier Companies expected an increase in orders from short-line railroads spun off in the mergers. In addition, railroad freight was increasing significantly as more shippers turned to intermodal transport. Industry analysts also predicted a healthy future for logistics companies as railroads began outsourcing more of their needs, including the repairing and refurbishing of railway cars, which continued to be a significant share of Greenbrier Companies's business.

The Greenbrier Companies did receive a setback in 1996 when year-long negotiations with Conrail Inc. to manufacture and repair freight cars in Pennsylvania collapsed, apparently because neither company could guarantee enough business to make the joint venture viable.

Principal Subsidiaries

Gunderson, Inc.; TrentonWorks Ltd.; Greenbrier Capital Corporation; Greenbriar Logistics Inc.; Greenbrier Leasing Corporation.

Further Reading

Gonzales, Gloria, "Greenbrier Expands Role in Logistics," *Oregonian,* March 13, p. 16B.
"Greenbrier Cos. Purchasing Canadian Rail Car Maker," *Business Journal* (Portland, Oregon), December 2, 1994, p. 4.
Mahar, Ted, "Gunderson, Inc. Launches Huge Barge into Willamette," *Oregonian,* July 16, 1996, p. 6C.

—Dean Boyer

Grupo Financiero Serfin, S.A.

Prol. Paseo de la Reforma 500
01219 Mexico City, D.F.
Mexico
(525) 257-8000
Fax: (212) 421-5128 (New York office)
Web site: http://www.infosel.com.mx/serfin

Public Company
Incorporated: 1864 as Banco de Londres, Mexico y
    Sudamerica
Employees: 19,164
Sales: 59.26 billion pesos ($8.7 billion, 1995)
Stock Exchanges: New York Mexico City
SICs: 4225 General Warehousing & Storage; 6021
    National Commercial Banks; 6162 Mortgage Bankers
    & Loan Correspondents; 6163 Loan Brokers; 6211
    Security Brokers, Dealers & Flotation Companies;
    6311 Life Insurance; 6321 Accident & Health
    Insurance; 6331 Fire, Marine & Casualty Insurance;
    6712 Offices of Bank Holding Companies

Grupo Financiero Serfin, S.A. is the holding company for Banca Serfin, Mexico's third largest bank. Dating back to 1864, it has the longest pedigree of any Mexican bank. Banca Serfin provides commercial banking services to individuals and businesses. The Serfin financial group contains other subsidiaries providing such financial services as investment banking, factoring, lease financing, warehousing, and insurance.

European Control, 1864–1936

Two Englishmen, William Newbold and Robert Geddes, founded the Banco de Londres, Mexico y Sudamerica in Mexico City in 1864, acting for the Bank of Mexico Ltd., an English company. It was the first branch of a foreign bank in Mexico and the first Mexican bank to issue checks and notes. The bank opened agencies in ten Mexican cities and also in Cuba, Peru, and British Columbia. Although installed under the regime of Emperor Maximilian, one of the bank's first transactions was a remittance of 3,000 pesos from London for the account of Benito Juarez, the ousted Mexican president leading the fight against French occupation. When Juarez returned to the capital in 1867 Banco de Londres enjoyed his full confidence.

Except for insignificant Chihuahua banks, Banco de Londres was the only banking institution in Mexico until the 1880s, yet it struggled with serious difficulties. Founded in 1884 by the merger of two banks, the rival Banco Nacional Mexicano enjoyed greater privileges; its notes were the only ones accepted in government offices, and it served as the government depository for money, securities, and metals. In 1886 Banco Nacional had almost nine times the assets of Banco de Londres, which that year bought the concession of the failing Banco Comercial.

The bank's name was shortened by eliminating "Sudamerica" in 1889 to reflect its reduced scope of operations. In 1897 it won the right to establish banks of emission in the states and territories. By 1901 it had narrowed the Banco Nacional's lead in assets to about five to two. Banco de Londres came under French control in 1904, with Banque de Paris et des Pays Bas and the Société Financière pour l'Industrie au Mexique (an investment company representing Mexican industrialists and a consortium of Swiss banks as well as the Banque de Paris) holding 62 percent of the shares.

The revolution against the rule of Porfirio Diaz that began in 1910 presented great difficulties for Banco de Londres. It had loaned money to the insurgent Francisco Madero shortly before he crossed into the country from Texas, yet its branches in territory captured by the rebels were subject to looting and even destruction. Order was restored after Madero assumed the presidency, but in 1913 the bank was forced to make loans to Victoriano Huerta, who captured and executed Madero. After the forces of Venustiano Carranza defeated those of Huerta, Mexican banks had to accept their paper as legal tender in payment of debts. Banco de Londres partially retrieved the situation by purchasing valuable real estate and buildings with its depreciated currency.

By 1916 paper currency had become worthless. The government canceled the emission privileges of the banks and expropriated the precious metals in their vaults. Under Carranza's successor Banco de Londres recovered its privileges but not its treasure. Aside from a claim of 29 million pesos against the federal government, it had little in the way of assets. The government agreed to pay 21.8 million pesos in 1925, but in that year the creation of Mexico's central bank, Banco de Mexico, ended Banco de Londres's privilege of issuing currency. Nevertheless, the bank found another field of operations in 1928 by installing Mexico's first trust department.

In Private Mexican Hands, 1934–1982

The onset of the world depression of the 1930s forced Banque de Paris to reduce its capital in Banco de Londres from 21.5 million to five million pesos in 1934. Both Banco de Mexico and Mexican private banks intervened to keep Banco de Londres solvent, with a group of Mexican businesses assuming the majority of the shares. The biggest block of shares (28 percent in 1941) was taken by the Compania General de Aceptaciones, created in 1936 as an arm of the Garza Sada family. This family controlled the Monterrey Group, Mexico's most powerful industrial combine, and Compania General de Aceptaciones facilitated the transfer of funds between different firms of the group. Banco de Londres participated in the creation of the Sociedad Financiera Mexicana (Sofimex) in 1937, another powerful investment bank and holding company that in turn took shares in the bank.

The Garza Sada family and other interests also formed, in 1939, a holding company, Union Financiera, through which they exercised control over three other institutions established within the next two years: Monterrey, Compania de Seguros sobre la Vida, an insurance company covering accident, illness, and property damage as well as life that subsequently became Seguros Monterrey; Banco Capitalizador de Monterrey, a capitalization bank; and Credito Provincial Hipotecario, a mortgage bank. These would later be merged into the future Banca Serfin, as would such subsequent creations as Fianzas Monterrey.

Banco de Londres grew by acquisition during the 1950s and 1960s, absorbing Banco del Norte in 1951, five banks in 1956, Banco de Mexicali in 1958, Banco del Norte de Mexico in 1962, and Banco Industrial de Monterrey in 1963. Its book value rose from 39.9 million pesos ($8.3 million) in 1940 to 9.28 billion pesos ($742.3 million) in 1975, its profits increased from 566,716 pesos ($117,594) to 28.5 million pesos ($2.3 million), and its number of branches grew from two to 194. It obtained its first computer in 1967, began issuing life insurance in 1969, and joined other banks in creating Mexico's first credit card.

Compania General de Aceptaciones (later Financiera Aceptaciones) also thrived, its book value growing from 15 million pesos ($2.2 million) in 1946 to 15.4 billion ($1.2 billion) in 1975. Its share of all financial investments in Mexico grew from less than three percent in 1946 to 14 percent in 1960 before falling to ten percent in 1975. In 1969 it was extending credit to 745 Mexican enterprises.

The shareholders in the various firms and institutions that held majority control of Banco de Londres in the late 1950s constituted a coalition of different investment groups with some interlocking interests. At this point no one group controlled the bank, but subsequently the Garza Sada interests became dominant. After the division of the Monterrey Group in 1974 into four giant holding companies the children of Eugenio Garza Sada inherited the largest block of stock in Valores Industriales S.A. (Visa) and also came to control Banco de Londres.

Banca Serfin was created in 1977 by the merger of Banco de Londres and Financiera Aceptaciones, Serfin being short for *servicios financieros integrados* (integrated financial services). The new institution combined the function of a bank of deposit, savings bank, investment bank, mortgage bank, and trust company. Banca Serfin also acquired 13 Mexico City branches of Banco Azteca. It took third place among banks in 1978, with assets of 61.2 billion pesos ($2.7 billion), or ten percent of the nation's total, and 335.2 billion pesos ($5.9 billion) in 1982, also ten percent of the total. Banca Serfin opened a Los Angeles branch in 1978, a London branch and New York City agency in 1980, 16 regional computer centers in 1981, and a Bahamas branch in 1982. Visa held 77 percent of Banca Serfin in 1980.

Government Control, 1982–1992

Following four years of unprecedented prosperity as a result of greatly increased income from oil exports, Mexico suffered its worst economic crisis within memory in 1982. After large amounts of private capital left the country President Jose Lopez Portillo nationalized the nation's private banks, accusing a group of wealthy Mexicans, encouraged by the banks, of draining the country's wealth by investing it abroad. The main business of the nationalized banks became financing government borrowing.

Lopez Portillo's successor, Miguel de la Madrid, embarked almost immediately, after assuming the presidency in late 1982, on a drive to win back business confidence through partial privatization of the banks. In 1984 the government sold off bank holdings in 339 companies, including financial services companies, allowing bank shareholders to purchase them with indemnity bonds issued in compensation for the takeover. Financial services companies quickly became the core of a de facto parallel banking system, holding nearly a quarter of national savings. In 1987 one-third of the shares of the three major banks were sold at discount prices to bank executives and employees and lists of politically well-connected clients and subsequently were traded publicly on the Bolsa de Valores Mexicanos, Mexico's stock exchange.

The reprivatization of Banca Serfin was completed in 1992, when the Mexican government sold 51 percent of its remaining two-thirds stake for about $940 million to an investor group headed by Adrian Sada Gonzalez. With his brother Federico, Adrian Sada Gonzalez (a great-grandson of family patriarch Francisco Sada, Isaac Garza's brother-in-law) was running Vitro S.A., the world's third largest producer of glass containers. Banca Serfin had about $22 billion in assets at the end of 1991 and earned about $125 million in profits that year.

Problems of the 1990s

The new management changed the company name to Grupo Financiero Serfin and moved its headquarters from Mexico City to Monterrey. It overextended itself by making a number of loans that could not be repaid when the peso went into free fall in late 1994, touching off another national economic crisis. In June 1995 the Mexican government agreed to assume 4.3 billion pesos ($750 million) in Banca Serfin's problem loans in return for a commitment from Grupo Financiero Serfin's existing shareholders to inject 2.17 billion pesos ($350 million) of fresh capital into the bank. Serfin's nonperforming loans had reached 11.3 billion pesos ($1.8 billion), or 12 percent of its total loan portfolio, in March. This rescue scheme was regarded as the only way of keeping the bank afloat. The U.S. firm General Electric Capital Corp. acquired 13 percent of Grupo Financiero Serfin in exchange for its previous investment in Serfin's leasing, factoring, and warehousing subsidiaries.

Adolfo Lagos Espinosa, a seasoned bank officer who became chief executive officer of Grupo Financiero Serfin in March 1996, returned corporate headquarters to Mexico City. During the next six months he replaced half of the group's top managers and laid off nearly ten percent of its 18,000 employees. Although 45 percent of Banca Serfin's loan portfolio was now regarded as uncollectible, he ended all rollovers and set aside reserves to fully cover bad loans. In May Lagos Espinosa negotiated a second, $2.6 billion government purchase of the company's bad loans and by September had raised 61 percent of the $1.3 billion it pledged to pay the government as part of the deal. Some of the money came from J.P. Morgan & Co., which was searching for an investor to buy 20 percent of the Serfin group.

In 1995 Grupo Financiero Serfin had total revenues of 59.26 billion pesos ($8.7 billion) and a net loss of 3.1 billion pesos ($455 million). Grupo Financiero Serfin had about 640 offices in Mexico and offices in eight foreign countries. Banca Serfin alone was operating 509 branches, 33 convenience-banking units, and 18 Serfin financial centers throughout Mexico. The bank had deposits of 77.2 billion pesos (about $10.2 billion), or 13 percent of the Mexican total, at the end of 1995. Banca Serfin introduced its own credit cards in 1994. The group's investment banking arm, Operadora de Bolsa Serfin, ranked first in Mexico at the end of 1994 in money-market, equity, and fixed-income trading. It was operating four equity and six fixed-income mutual funds, while Banca Serfin offered one equity and five fixed-income funds through its branches.

Still suffering the effects of bad loans, Grupo Financiero Serfin was in the red by nearly seven billion pesos ($915 million) in 1996. Banca Serfin created allowances for loan losses of 8.34 billion ($1.09 billion) during the year and reported a net loss of 7.45 billion pesos ($974 million) for the year. In December 1996 the financial group sold its Afianzadora Insurgentes Serfin surety-bond subsidiary, which it had purchased in 1993, to USF&G for $65 million.

Principal Subsidiaries

Almacenadora Serfin, S.A. de C.V.; Arrendedora Serfin, S.A. de C.V.; Banca Serfin, S.A.; Factoraje Serfin, S.A. de C.V.; Operadora de Bolsa Serfin, S.A. de C.V.; Serfin Casa de Cambio, S.A. de C.V.; Seguros Serfin, S.A.; Servicios Corporativos Serfin, S.A. de C.V.

Further Reading

Crawford, Leslie, ''Rescue Package for Banca Serfin,'' *Financial Times,* June 14, 1995, p. 31.

Gardner, David, ''Pricing and Politics Spice Mexican Sell-Off,'' *Financial Times,* April 24, 1987, p. 35.

Hamilton, Nora, *The Limits of State Autonomy: Post-Revolutionary Mexico,* Princeton, NJ: Princeton University Press, especially pp. 286–336.

McCaleb, Walter Flovius, *Present and Past Banking in Mexico,* New York: Harper, 1920.

Moreno Hernandez, Wolfrano, *El Grupo Financiero Visa-Serfin,* Unpublished thesis, Mexico City: Universidad Autonoma Metropolitana, 1986.

Smith, Geri, ''Mexican Banks Pull Out of a Dive,'' *Business Week,* September 2, 1996, p. 56.

Solis, Dianna, ''Mexico Sells 51% Stake in Banca Serfin to Investor Group for About $940 Million,'' *Wall Street Journal,* January 27, 1992, p. 6.

''Un banco en la historia de Mexico,'' *Historia ilustrada,* October 1980, pp. 44–48.

—Robert Halasz

Grupo Industrial Bimbo

Etienne Cabet 1000
Colonia Santa Fe Zedec
Delegacion Alvaro Obregon
01210 Mexico City, D.F.
Mexico
(525) 229-6600
Fax: (525) 229-6640

Public Company
Founded: 1965
Employees: 44,087
Sales: 10.16 billion pesos ($1.49 billion, 1995)
Stock Exchanges: Mexico City
SICs: 2024 Ice Cream & Frozen Desserts; 2033 Canned Fruits, Vegetables, Preserves, Jams & Jellies; 2034 Dried & Dehydrated Fruits, Vegetables & Soup Mixes; 2041 Flour & Other Grain Mill Products; 2051 Bread, Cake & Related Products; 2066 Chocolate & Cocoa Products; 2086 Salted & Roasted Nuts & Seeds; 2096 Potato Chips, Corn Chips & Similar Snacks; 2099 Food Preparations, Not Elsewhere Classified; 5149 Groceries & Related Products, Not Elsewhere Classified

Mexico's biggest baker and food company, Grupo Industrial Bimbo, is a Mexican multinational conglomerate that derives about two-thirds to four-fifths of its revenue from bakery products, of which it had 94 by 1992. It controls 85 to 95 percent of the commercial bread market in Mexico. Bimbo also produces a variety of other baked goods and has broadened its base to include salted snacks, tortillas, and deli and frozen foods. The company's scope of operations has expanded to take in the United States and Latin American countries as distant as Chile and Argentina. Bimbo, which means "child" in Italian, is the name for the company's cartoon-character mascot, a little white bear, and is almost synonymous with bread in Mexico. The company's products are oriented toward families with children.

Bimbo Before the 1970s

The founder of Grupo Industrial Bimbo, Lorenzo Servitje Sendra, was born in Mexico City in 1918, the son of immigrants from Spain's Catalonian region. When his father died in 1936 he had to abandon his studies and become patron of "El Molino," his father's cake shop. In 1938 he opened his own bakery with his cousin, Jaime Jorba, and Jose T. Mata. Seven years later he started Panificadora Bimbo with Jorba, Jose Torrallardona and Alfonso Velasco, his brother Roberto, and his uncle Jaime Sendra.

The entrepreneurs began with 38 or 39 employees, five vehicles, and four types of bread. At the prompting of Velasco, the technical director, they adopted as their symbol the Bimbo little white bear to stand for the whiteness of their bread. For the first decade the bakery operated exclusively in Mexico City. In 1956 or 1957 the company opened its first Productos Marinela plant to make cakes and pastries and also began operations in Guadalajara. It founded Bimbo, subsequently Spain's largest baker, in 1965 and later operated it as a joint venture with Dallas-based Campbell Taggart, Inc. for several years before selling it to this firm.

Bimbo's first northern Mexico plant opened in 1960, in Monterrey. The company began operations in the northeast, at Hermosillo, in 1966, and in the Gulf of Mexico region, at Veracruz, in 1970. A second Mexico City plant opened in 1972. The company added to its line by introducing a division for sweets and chocolates in 1971.

Expansion in the 1970s and 1980s

The growth of Bimbo continued unabated through the 1970s and early 1980s. New Bimbo plants opened at Guanajuato in 1977, Villahermosa in 1978, Mazatlan in 1981, and Chihuahua and Toluca in 1982. Other divisions opened plants at Queretaro in 1978, Gomez Palacio in 1982, and Mexico City in 1983 and 1985. By 1988 Bimbo had three more factories in operation. It entered the U.S. market in 1984 by shipping cake products with a long shelf life under the Suandy label. Soon after it purchased the Wonder bread operation in Mexico from its American owner and thereby entered the milling business for the first time.

In 1988 Bimbo was producing bread and sponge cake under the names Bimbo, Sunbeam, Suandy, and Tia Rosa; cakes and cookies under the name Miranela; sweets and chocolates under the Ricolino name; snacks under the Barcel name; and jams under the name Carmel. The company also was producing machines for the food industry and employing more than 25,000 people. It opened the first of its overseas Bimbo operations in Guatemala in 1989 by purchasing a small bakery outside Guatemala City. About this time the company built a $14 million factory to make hamburger buns for McDonald's Corp.

By not going into debt Bimbo emerged from the 1982 Mexican economic crisis without major problems. Nevertheless, it avoided further expansion until 1987, when it began work on a $25 million Toluca plant to produce its Tia Rosa line. At this time the firm also had joint ventures with the U.S. subsidiary of the French firm SIAS to produce food preservatives and with Celanese to make wrapping material. It also began selling bread in Los Angeles and Houston in 1987.

Bimbo in the 1990s

Profiled by the *Wall Street Journal* in 1991, Grupo Industrial Bimbo was described as a pillar of conservatism with no corporate offices and no annual report but unlimited ambitions. In that year it was completing a four-year, $400 million investment program, opening plants in ten cities and upgrading those in five others. A flour mill built that year was described by the company's Swiss technical advisers as the most advanced on the continent. Most of these projects were funded internally, without taking on debt. One of the company's most potent assets was its distribution system, consisting in Mexico of 11,000 delivery trucks making 75 to 80 percent of its sales to 200,000 mom-and-pop stores.

In 1993 Grupo Industrial Bimbo (formed in 1966) was divided into eight divisions, each a subsidiary. Bimbo itself, the bread division, had 16 plants. Despite its predominance in the Mexican bread market, Bimbo was hardly a staple of the Mexican diet. Only about 20 percent of Mexican families were buying commercial bread, considered something of a luxury, regularly—and "regularly" was defined to mean as little as two loaves a month. Instead, most Mexicans consumed either tortillas or rolls called *bolillos* produced by thousands of small bakeries.

The Marinela division was producing and distributing cookies, pastries, and baked snacks under the brand names Marinela, Tia Rosa, Skandia, and Lara from six Mexican plants. It ranked second in this field to Gamesa with a market share of 20 percent. Lara also was producing and distributing salads and pastas. The Wonder division was established after Bimbo acquired the Mexican subsidiary of Continental Baking Co., producer of Wonder bread, in 1986. In addition to this product, the Wonder division was making a Party line of lower-end cookies and snack cakes and a Suandy line of pastries, pound cakes, and coffee cakes. It also had a line of products under the Trigoro name.

Ricolino, with three plants, was producing and distributing sweets, chocolates, and chewing gum to more than 240,000 customers. It had the exclusive right to distribute Wrigley's chewing gum in Mexico. Barcel was making and distributing

snacks under the names Barcel and Chip's. These were potato chips, corn products, dried fruit, and seeds. This division's products were being made in three plants. Alpre was a new division producing and distributing three main products: Paty-Lu (baked goods and confections), Lonchibon (prepared foods), and Milpa Real (corn tortillas).

Altex was Bimbo's service agency, acquiring the raw materials, machinery, other equipment, supplies, and services the company needed to assure uniform quality. It consisted of 11 subsidiaries. Among its holdings were mills in Mexico City, Toluca, and Veracruz providing about half the parent corporation's flour needs. It also had agreements for joint venture manufacturing operations and transfer of technology with several baking equipment manufacturers in the United States and Europe.

The International division became increasingly important. In Guatemala Bimbo's subsidiary was producing bread, doughnuts, cakes, cookies, pastries, processed fruits, and tortillas under several names, including Bimbo, Marinela, and Ricolino. In Chile a subsidiary made bread, rolls, small cakes, and snack salads under the brand names Ideal, Cena, and Barcel. A Venezuelan subsidiary produced small cakes, sweet breads, cookies, and Twinkies under the brand names Marinela, Taoro, and Twinkies. In El Salvador a subsidiary produced bread and small cakes under the Bimbo, Marinela, and Ricolino names. Bimbo later established operations in Costa Rica and in 1994 was building a $30 million plant in Argentina to produce bread, rolls, and cakes.

Bimbo also was exporting goods to many U.S. cities in the early 1990s, including New York, Los Angeles, Chicago, Houston, Dallas, San Antonio, and Miami. Under a joint venture with Sara Lee Corp., it was distributing Sara Lee products in refrigerated trucks to stores in Mexico. Bimar Foods Inc., the Texas-based Bimbo subsidiary through which this joint venture was established, also entered the U.S. tortilla market by acquiring six plants and building a new one in Houston. By the end of 1994 Bimbo was exporting 23 different products and operating 100 routes in California alone.

Bimbo found that the market for its mass-produced, packaged tortillas under the Tia Rosa label was much larger in the United States than in Mexico, where small shops licensed and subsidized by the government remained dominant, selling fresh tortillas. In 1994 Bimbo and a competitor, Grupo Industrial Maseca S.A. (Gruma), combined sold more than $400 million worth of packaged corn and flour tortilla in the United States—quadruple their tortilla sales in Mexico, even though Mexicans were eating ten times as many tortillas per capita as Americans.

In 1996 Bimbo made its first venture into bread baking in the United States by acquiring Pacific Pride Bakeries, the San Diego area's largest independent baking company. That year Bimbo received $130 million in financing from the International Finance Corp., representing seven institutions. In 1997 the company began construction of its first Mexican plant to produce flour and corn tortillas, at Atitalaquia, Hidalgo.

Bimbo entered the ice cream field at the end of 1993 by acquiring a 40 percent stake in Grupo Quan, the leader in Mexico and Central America in the production and distribution of ice cream and popsicles. Grupo Quan and Bimbo formed a joint venture with Unilever for this purpose in 1997.

Bimbo survived the peso crisis of 1994 and its aftermath without falling into the red, although net income fell in 1994 and 1995, especially in terms of the dollar equivalent. In 1995 the company earned 265 million pesos ($39 million) on net sales of 10.16 billion pesos ($1.49 billion). Of its sales that year, Mexico accounted for 89 percent, Central and South America accounted for nine percent, and the United States accounted for two percent. The company's long-term debt was 443.5 million pesos ($65.2 million). At the end of the year Bimbo owned 47 processing plants in 14 Mexican cities and was operating processing plants in seven other countries.

During 1995–1996 Bimbo adopted a ten-point program to reorganize its operations. One of these steps was a simplification of its distribution routes. Traditionally, Bimbo owed much of its success to a superior distribution system that delivered fresh products to the consumer. For example, bread delivered to retailers on Monday and not sold by the end of Wednesday was returned to the distributor. This system was recalculated by Bimbo on a refined just-in-time basis. Bimbo also made available to some of its distributors a computerized system to help them manage their operations in a more efficient manner.

Lorenzo Servitje Sendra was chairman of Grupo Industrial Bimbo and Roberto Servitje Sendra was president and chief executive officer in the early 1990s. Lorenzo retired in 1994. His son Daniel was president of Marinela and overseer of the group's Latin American operations at this time, while Roberto's son Roberto Servitje Achutegui was president of Altex and chairman of several companies partially or wholly owned by Bimbo. Grupo Industrial Bimbo went public in 1980. According to a 1989 account, its major stockholders were the Servitje family (41 percent), Mata family (25 percent), Sendra family (13 percent), and the Banco Nacional de Mexico (Banamex). About ten percent of the stock was owned by an employee trust in 1991.

Principal Subsidiaries

Organizacion Altex; Organizacion Barcel; Organizacion Bimbo; Organizacion Internacional; Organizacion Marinela; Organizacion Ricolino; Organizacion Wonder-Suandy.

Further Reading

"Bimbo Acquires Pacific Pride in California," *Milling & Baking News,* April 2, 1996, pp. 1, 9.
"Bimbo Diversifies, Expands as Reforms Continue in Mexico," *Milling & Baking News,* November 3, 1992, pp. 1, 23, 26–27.
Canal, Maria Josefa, "Bimbo: 10 en uno," *Expansion,* June 19, 1996, pp. 48, 51.
Magana Godinez, Monica, and Mariscal Servitje, Pilar, "Base y susteno de la empresa Grupo Industrial Bimbo," Unpublished thesis, Instituto Tecnologico Autonomo de Mexico, 1993.
Malovany, Dan, "Bimbo Barges Beyond the Borders," *Bakery Production and Marketing,* September 1994, pp. 106–107, 110, 112, 114, 116.
——, "On the Road to Economic Revolution," *Bakery Production and Marketing,* April 1992, pp. 112–113, 116, 118, 120, 122–124, 126.
Mayoral Jimenez, Isabel, "Se alian Bimbo, Unilever, y Quan para venta de helados," *El Financiero,* January 31, 1997, p. 17.
Mejia Prieto, Jorge, *Mexicanos que escalaron el exito,* Mexico City: Editorial Diana, 1988, pp. 81–88.
Millman, Joel, "Mexican Tortilla Firms Stage U.S. Bake-Off," *Wall Street Journal,* May 10, 1996, p. A6.
Moffett, Matt, "Mexico's Biggest Bread Maker Sees Opportunity in Free Trade," *Wall Street Journal,* October 3, 1991, p. A10.

—Robert Halasz

Haggar Corporation

6113 Lemmon Avenue
Dallas, Texas 75209
U.S.A.
(214) 352-8481
Fax: (214) 956-4367

Public Company
Incorporated: 1926
Employees: 6,000
Sales: $437.9 million (1996)
Stock Exchanges: NASDAQ
SICs: 2325 Men's/Boys' Trousers & Slacks; 2311 Men's/
Boys' Suits & Coats; 2321 Men's/Boys' Shirts; 6719
Holding Companies, Not Elsewhere Classified

When it comes to casually dressy clothing for men, few companies are in the same league as Haggar Corporation. Haggar is the leading maker of dress pants, sport coats, and custom-fit suits (suits consisting of separately sized slacks and matching jackets), and the second-place producer of men's casual pants. Although the company's industry ranking is important, its historic role is even more significant. "Slacks" did not exist until Haggar introduced them in the 1940s. Since that time, Haggar has expanded its line to include shorts, wrinkle-free cotton shirts, and pants, including occasional forays into women's clothing. The company's goods were sold through about 7,000 stores nationwide, and the Haggar brand accounted for 80 percent of its sales in the 1990s. The items were sold through major department stores as well as in the approximately 35 Haggar outlet stores. Haggar also sold a lower priced line called Reed St. James through mass market retailers, and manufactured private label clothing for department stores and others. Haggar has managed to maintain a dominant position in the menswear industry through several generational shifts in stylistic tastes, material preferences, and technology.

J. M. Haggar, a 34-year-old Lebanese immigrant, started Haggar in 1926. Born in 1892, Haggar sailed from his homeland to Mexico at the age of 13. He moved to the United States a few years later, settling first in Texas, moving on to New Orleans, and finally reaching St. Louis, Missouri. His first jobs were menial ones, such as dishwasher and window washer, but over the years his skill with people landed him inevitably in sales. After stints in the oil and cotton businesses, where his prowess as a salesman became legendary, by 1921 Haggar found himself selling overalls in Texas, Louisiana, and New Mexico for a company based in Missouri. While working at that job, Haggar concluded that selling many items at a single, stable price would bring more profit than selling a lot of different grades of merchandise each of which yielded a different and constantly shifting profit margin.

No Depression at Haggar

By 1926, Haggar had saved enough money to launch his own enterprise. He set up shop in Dallas, and began to make and sell high-quality, low-cost pants for working men. Within three years, his Dallas Pant Manufacturing Company had 250 employees and occupied 6,000 square feet of space on two floors of the Santa Fe Building in Dallas. The company managed not only to survive, but to thrive during the Great Depression. In 1933 Haggar staged a "Prosperity Picnic/Parade" in downtown Dallas to demonstrate that his company was still hiring, and that good times were bound to return. By 1936 the company had opened a facility in Greenville, Texas, its first outside of Dallas.

Haggar's son, E.R. (Ed) Haggar, joined the company in the 1930s. Until the late 1930s, Haggar products were sold to chain stores and other accounts with no brand name attached to them. Under E.R. Haggar's direction, the company introduced brand names. In 1938, Haggar began its first national advertising campaign and began the creation of a national sales organization in order to raise customer awareness of the Haggar name, as well as its trademark Mustang brand.

Haggar's second son, J.M. (Joe Jr.) Haggar, Jr., began to play a major role in company operations in the 1940s. During that decade, Haggar, with the assistance of the Tracey Locke Advertising Agency—a forerunner of advertising giant DDB Needham—coined the term "slacks." The idea behind slacks was that they were to be worn during the slack time away from

Company Perspectives:

"We continue to provide quality men's apparel at afford-able prices through our three sales divisions. Haggar brands are represented in major department stores. Our Horizon Group markets the Reed St. James and other prod-ucts to the mass merchant retailers, and our Specialty La-bels division provides men's wear under department store and other private labels. We continue to expand our market presence through our new Haggar retail outlet stores; through international agreements; and through licensing arrangements to extend the Haggar and Reed St. James brands across product and geographic boundaries. We dili-gently look for ways to become more productive, to reduce costs, and to better serve our customers. Each decade in our history has brought the challenge to work smarter, faster, and better without sacrificing the quality for which we have become known. And each decade we have met that challenge to thrive, to grow, and to remain a market leader in our business. This is what we believe Haggar has in store."

work. Slacks quickly became an accepted part of the American male wardrobe vocabulary.

Around the same time, the Haggar name was becoming increasingly familiar across America through relentless adver-tising. The company became the first pants manufacturer to advertise in the trade journals, beginning with *Daily News Record* and *Men's Wear Daily*. With the success of those early ads, the company gradually expanded its advertising budget. Its ads soon appeared in such big-name magazines as *Life, Col-lier's,* and *Esquire.* Haggar's *Life* ad featured a gimmick called the "Haggar Harmony Chart." The chart showed men how to "mix and match" in order to triple their wardrobe with the purchase of a few pairs of Haggar slacks. The charts were also made available through retailers and by mail-order from the company. The chart eventually disappeared, but by that time the idea of mixing and matching had sunk into the heads of previ-ously fashion-shy American men. Several other now-common merchandising tactics can be credited to Haggar during this period, including two-pairs-at-a-reduced-price offers and pre-packaged, precuffed, ready-to-wear slacks.

Haggar regularly placed ads in at least a dozen major maga-zines by 1950, and its distribution system grew accordingly. By 1954 there were 32 Haggar sales representatives roaming the country, more than double the number during World War II. As the "slacks" concept continued to gain momentum, Haggar latched onto the idea of well-known sports figures as the ideal pitchmen for their products. Advertising heavily in such publi-cations as *Sport* and *Sports Illustrated,* the company began to associate its name with dashing sports heroes like Mickey Mantle, Bobby Lane, and Arnold Palmer.

1950s: The Television Age

One of Haggar's product innovations of the 1950s was "for-ever-prest," one of the first lines of pants made from wrinkle-

resistant material. Meanwhile, television was emerging as an important new way to advertise, and Haggar became one of the first clothing manufacturers to take advantage of this new me-dium. One of Haggar's early television spots showed a pair of Haggar "forever-prest" slacks being crumpled up and run over by a steamroller. They were then picked up, shaken out, and shown to be wrinkle-free. The ad was so successful that the Gimbels department store in New York sold out of the slacks less than 24 hours after its initial airing in that city. As with its early magazine ads, the success of Haggar's first television commercials led to a full-blown commitment to television ad-vertising. The company became a sponsor of such shows as *Sugarfoot, Bronco, Twelve O'Clock High,* and *Naked City.*

As television expanded its coverage of sports in the 1960s, Haggar found a new male-dominated outlet for its advertising. The company became a sponsor of ABC's *Wide World of Sports* in 1963, and a few years later it became a major advertiser during NFL football game broadcasts. Haggar also advertised during other televised sporting events, including baseball, bas-ketball, hockey, and tennis, as their television coverage grew.

In addition to advertising, Haggar meanwhile continued to innovate in other areas as well. New products such as the "Imperials" line of dress slacks created new market niches in the gaps between "casual" and "dress" clothing. Haggar also introduced the "Haggar hanger," a special hanger that stream-lined the distribution process by allowing the company to ship pants already on hangers, ready to be put on racks by retailers. Among other innovations were Haggar's precuffed pants that didn't need to be tailored.

In the late 1960s, Haggar popularized polyester-and-wool permanent press pants. By the beginning of the 1970s, Haggar controlled the biggest chunk of the men's dress slacks market, with a 20 percent share, and the Haggar brand name was the one recognized most for dress pants among American men. So omnipresent was the Haggar label in American retail outlets that the company's unofficial slogan was "We cover the asses of the masses."

In the 1970s, Haggar introduced leisure tops to go with its slacks. By the company's 50th birthday in 1976, it increased its sales of slacks during a year in which sales for the industry had experienced substantial dropoff. As in previous decades, new styles and products were added on a regular basis. A line of slacks called 640 was introduced in 1972, and in 1976, a contemporary line of slacks and tops called The Gallery, featuring a trimmer, updated fit and made of slick 1970s fabrics, was launched. A young men's line called Body Work was also added. The 1970s also brought the addition of Haggar sport coats and vests, and by the middle of the decade a customer fond of Haggar merchandise could pretty much clothe himself entirely in Haggar goods re-gardless of the occasion. By the end of the 1970s, the aging J.M. Haggar, while still retaining a powerful voice in company affairs, had handed over most of the duties of operating the company to sons Ed, who served as president, and Joe Jr., executive vice president. By this time their were 16 plants manufacturing Hag-gar clothing, located across Texas and Oklahoma.

In 1983, Haggar launched the Reed St. James brand, a clothing line specifically conceived to be sold through discount retailers. The development of the Reed St. James brand solved the problem of how to tap into the lucrative discount store market without cannibalizing the company's department store sales. By creating a quality brand that could compete favorably with cheap imports, Haggar was able to gain a strong foothold in discount stores. The idea was so good that within a few years Haggar was licensing the Reed St. James name to several other men's wear manufacturers, including Levi Strauss and Jockey. By 1986 the line was generating sales of $50 million for Haggar. Other 1980s breakthroughs for Haggar included the first use of both bar codes and Quick Response electronic data interchange technology among apparel manufacturers.

In 1986 competitor Levi Strauss caught Haggar off-guard when it introduced its Dockers line of all-cotton pants. Dockers did what Haggar had made its reputation by doing; it found a space between casual and dressy that was not yet occupied. Since the tastes of American men had taken a turn toward the casual, Dockers took a sizable bite out of the market for Haggar's slightly dressier slacks. Haggar responded with its own line of all-cotton pants, but the company did not initially focus its marketing attention on this line. In 1990, Haggar's sales dropped six percent to $292 million, its first backslide in many years.

Cotton is King in the 1990s

In 1990 Joseph Haggar III—known inside the company as Joe Three—took over company leadership from his father Joe Jr. Under Joe Three, Haggar unveiled a new line of wrinkle-free cotton pants, and spent $20 million advertising it. In 1992, after operating as a family business for its first 65 years of existence, Haggar went public, offering its stock on the NASDAQ exchange. By 1993, Haggar's wrinkle-free line had seized the momentum from Dockers in the race for king of the all-cotton's, and the company's position as a prime mover in casual pants— tough competition from Levi Strauss notwithstanding—was once again secure. Led by this new line, Haggar's sales rebounded to $380 million.

In 1994 Haggar introduced shirts made out of its fabulously successful wrinkle-free cotton material. The company also launched a line of casual/office clothing called the City Casuals Collection. Revenue reached $491 million that year. Disaster struck in 1995, as the roof on the company's main distribution center collapsed, interfering with Haggar's ability to keep stores supplied with its merchandise. As the company recovered from this mishap and worked out the bugs at its new Customer Service Center, Haggar recorded a net loss, the third in its history, in 1996.

In 1997 Haggar invented Cotton Flex, an all-cotton fabric with advanced stretch and memory capabilities, to compete against Levi Strauss. Officials at Haggar expected the company's new line of pants using Cotton Flex—dubbed the Black Label collection—to become dominant as everyday pants, taking over the wardrobe spot occupied by basic cotton twills. If they predicted accurately, Haggar may remain the leader among pants manufacturers for the time being.

Principal Subsidiaries

Haggar Clothing Co.; Haggar Direct, Inc.; Haggar UK.

Principal Divisions

Horizon Group; Specialty Labels.

Further Reading

Forest, Stephanie Anderson, ''Pumping No-Iron Slacks,'' *Business Week*, February 7, 1994, pp. 30–31.
Haggar, Joe M., Jr., ''Our Game Plan to Beat the Competition,'' *Venture*, October 1987, p. 126.
J.M. & Haggar Company: The First Fifty Years, Dallas: Haggar Company, 1976.
Palmeri, Christopher, ''Joe Three Fights Back,'' *Forbes*, November 22, 1993, pp. 46–47.
Romero, Elena, ''Haggar Ups Ante in Wrinkle-resistant Game,'' *Daily News Record*, May 30, 1997.
Sloan, Pat, ''Haggar Targets Women; Dumps TV, Men's Titles,'' *Advertising Age*, January 27, 1997, p. 3.
Spiegel, Joy G., ''J.M. and His Haggar Slacks,'' *Dallas Magazine*, November 1975.
——, *That Haggar Man*, New York: Random House, 1978.
Stern, Aimée, ''Success Has Seventeen Fathers,'' *Dun's Business Month*, August 1986, pp. 54–55.
Verespej, Michael A., ''Creativity and Technology,'' *Industry Week*, April 6, 1987, pp. 55–56.

—Robert R. Jacobson

Harland and Wolff Holdings plc

Queens Island
Belfast BT3 9DU
Ireland
+44 (1232) 458456
Fax: +44 (1232) 458515

Private Company
Incorporated: 1861 as Edward James Harland &
  Company
Employees: 1,426 (1995)
Sales: £118.1 million
SICs: 3730 Ship and Boat Building and Repairing

Best known as the company that built the *Titanic,* Harland and Wolff Holdings plc has for more than 150 years built some of the largest and grandest vessels to ply the world's waterways. Over the course of its history, the company has built merchant ships and luxury liners, warships and fighter planes, oil tankers and bulk cargo vessels. Privately held from its foundation in the mid-19th century until the mid-1920s, the firm suffered several ''near-death experiences'' in the 20th century before being nationalized by the British government in 1975. Under threat of closure in 1989, Harland and Wolff's managers and employees joined forces with Norwegian ship owner Fred Olsen to buy the company in 1989. Though losses continued into the mid-1990s, the company, under the majority ownership and direction of Olsen, made a £3 million pretax profit in 1996.

Foundation in Mid-19th Century Belfast

The company is named for Edward J. Harland and Gustav W. Wolff, who founded the storied yard in 1858. Son of a doctor and inventor, Harland was educated at Edinburgh Academy and started a five-year apprenticeship in engineering in 1846 at the age of 14. Upon completing his indenture, he worked for several shipyards, rising quickly from draftsman to yard manager. After just four years managing the Robert Hickson & Company shipyard, he purchased the company for £5,000 and renamed it Edward James Harland & Company. The

27-year-old hired his personal assistant (the nephew of a family friend) as head draftsman. The yard was located on Queen's Island, a manmade plot in the middle of Belfast's River Lagan. Harland invited Wolff into the partnership in 1861 and the company name reflected that change by 1867.

Personal connections brought in the shipbuilder's earliest contracts, but Harland's own technical innovations led to rapid expansion in the late 19th century. The yard's ''coffin-style'' cargo ships featured a square bottom and patented iron deck. To take advantage of burgeoning inter-oceanic trade and a tidal wave of immigration between Europe and America, Harland and Wolff formed a joint venture in transatlantic shipping in 1869. For its 25 percent stake, H&W built a steady stream of vessels for the Oceanic Steam Navigation Company's passenger and cargo lines. With accommodations patterned after the finest hotels in Europe, the passenger ships were some of the largest and most luxurious vessels ever built. The partnership made for highly profitable and reliable work for H&W.

In 1875, Harland and Wolff invited several key managers to enter into their partnership. At the time of the company's reincorporation that year, it had grown from one shipbuilding berth to six and its work force had expanded from 48 to more than 1,000. Though the firm endured a difficult period of successive losses in the late 1870s, the owners' investments in steel making equipment and other plant upgrades prepared the shipyard well for an upturn in the 1880s. The business became so profitable that its founders gradually retired to political careers and withdrew their investment.

Leadership of the shipyard fell to William J. Pirrie, who had started out as an apprentice at H&W in 1868 and was among those invited to become a partner in the company in 1875. During his first decade at the helm, Pirrie catapulted H&W to the pinnacle of worldwide shipbuilding by devoting the yard to total excellence in plant and process with little regard for expense. Costs mattered little because the new leader negotiated commission contracts with longtime customers, who agreed to pay the shipyard a given percentage over its costs. The program was, in the words of company historians Michael Moss and John Hume, an ''almost unbelievable success'': profits nearly tripled from £32,000 in 1885 to more than £91,000 in 1899.

Company Perspectives:

"For a company such as Harland and Wolff, which relies entirely on customers from beyond Northern Ireland for its very existence, our future success will also depend on factors beyond our immediate control. We are prepared to seek to bring real, lasting employment opportunities to Northern Ireland and, in so doing, further advance the political impetus for a lasting peace."

Despite devastating fires, political disruptions, and strikes, Pirrie—who formally advanced to chairman after Edward Harland died in 1895—had by the turn of the century made H&W the world's leading shipbuilder.

Pirrie Guides First Quarter of 20th Century

As chairman and later principal shareholder of H&W, Pirrie earned a reputation for making the best of difficult situations. The new century greeted him with a particularly troublesome dilemma. U.S. steel and railway mogul J.P. Morgan was in the midst of forming an international transportation cartel to monopolize shipping and railway transport. By 1901, Morgan had purchased one of H&W's key commission customers, Atlantic Transport Company. Realizing the looming threat to his very successful strategy and seeing few alternatives, Pirrie opened secret negotiations with Morgan. By spring 1902, Pirrie had convinced four European shipping lines to create an intricate affiliation known as the International Mercantile Marine (IMM). In exchange for its $3.25 million (£615,000) investment in IMM, Harland and Wolff gained the exclusive contract to build the ships for member companies.

In 1907 J. Bruce Ismay, chairman of both IMM and one of its affiliates, the White Star Line, ordered three "super liners" from Harland and Wolff. Appropriately named *Olympic, Titanic,* and *Gigantic,* these passenger ships were intended to help White Star compete more effectively with the Cunard Line. The most infamous of these was the *Titanic,* a sumptuously appointed gargantuan with a length of nearly one-sixth of a mile. The "unsinkable" liner set out on its maiden voyage on April 2, 1912. Twelve days into the trip, the vessel struck an iceberg, tearing a 300-foot hole down one side. More than 1,500 of the *Titanic's* 2,206 passengers, among them Pirrie's nephew and H&W's Managing Director Thomas Andrews, died when the ship sank early on the morning of April 15. It would go down as the worst disaster in maritime history. Ironically, the 703 survivors were rescued by a Cunard liner, the *Carpathia.* An inquiry into the tragedy by the British government absolved Harland and Wolff of all blame.

During World War I, H&W converted cargo ships to "dummy battleships" and troop transport vessels, reconditioned submarines, and built monitor ships. The company even diversified into aircraft manufacture in 1917. Pirrie's personal contribution to the war effort included service as the nation's Controller General of Merchant Shipbuilding.

IMM had proven a disastrous failure and was in receivership by 1915. H&W sold its interest in the combine—and with it the commission system—that year, and by the war's end was gearing up to build replacements for the many vessels destroyed during the hostilities. The company also expanded into construction of oil tankers during this period. Orders slowed in the 1920s, but Pirrie masked the shipyard's mounting losses with intricate financial accounting. The chairman had, in fact, used these techniques with success for many years, taking loss-making projects to gain or maintain more profitable business and buttressing the firm with debt in the meantime. Growing ever more dictatorial, the septuagenarian hid H&W's mounting liabilities from his management team, instead announcing growing profits nearly every year.

When Pirrie died in June 1924, he left no successor. More significant, he left a labyrinthine accounting system that masked £613,500 in bank debt at the end of the year. He was succeeded by Baron Kylsant, chairman of the Royal Mail Group, which, unbeknownst even to Pirrie's wife, had owned a controlling interest in Harland and Wolff for five years.

World War II Pulls Company Out of Insolvency

In an effort to raise capital Kylsant took the company public with an initial offering of £4 million. But with poor operating results predominating the British shipbuilding industry, only 12 percent of the shares were sold. Kylsant reduced the work force from 40,548 in 1925 to barely more than 21,000 by 1930 and pushed through salary and wage cuts, but shaving expenses at a company accustomed to making the best ships at any cost proved difficult. Inexplicably, Kylsant continued to build ships at losses sometimes totaling ten percent of the cost. Net profit declined from a dubiously figured £410,000 in 1924 to a loss of £158,000 in 1927, recovering somewhat to a profit of £106,000 by 1930. Bank debt grew to more than £2 million during the period, and government loans outstanding totaled an additional £1.2 million. The spiraling global depression only exacerbated H&W's existing problems.

Kylsant resigned in 1930 (he would later serve a year in jail for "issuing a false prospectus") and Frederick Rebbeck was appointed chairman. With orders dropping to one in 1931, the new chairman slashed the work force down to barely 7,000 in 1932, cutting the wages and salaries of those who remained. For its part, the government agreed to postpone collection on its debt. Nevertheless, by the end of 1932 H&W's assets of £4.2 million were far outstripped by its £7.7 million in debt. With unemployment in Northern Ireland exceeding 25 percent, the company diversified into manufacture of diesel locomotives, seaplanes, and airplanes mid-decade in an effort to keep plant and people occupied. Although H&W continued to launch more tonnage than any shipyard in the United Kingdom, it was merely the top of a sorry heap.

Even though the shipyard made small profits in 1935 and 1936, in 1937 its creditors at the Midland Bank and the Bank of Ireland joined forces with government representatives to enforce a drastic refinancing. Shareholders' equity was slashed from £12.1 million to less than £1.8 million, and a new share issue placed majority ownership with the banks and the government. Representatives of both those groups took positions as trustees of the company and set out to return H&W to profitability and to reduce its mountainous debt, but with little new work to be found, it was a daunting proposition. They liquidated more than £1.1 million in assets and investments in 1938, but the company's liabilities remained high, at more than £7.7 million.

Beginning in the late summer of 1938, rearmament for World War II rescued Harland and Wolff from its creditors, who sold their stake in the firm to a newly formed holding company. The shipbuilder added nearly 8,200 employees from 1938 to 1939 to accommodate a deluge of orders for lookout towers and bomb shelters. At the peak of the war, H&W employed more than 51,000 in the manufacture of gunmounts, aircraft, munitions, and tanks as well as aircraft carriers and warships. A sesquicentennial history of the corporation noted that "the company had fully justified the efforts to save it." Perhaps more significant for the continued existence of H&W, the company emerged from the Second World War free of bank debt. After-tax profits had mounted steadily from £394,000 in 1939 to more than £546,000 in 1945.

Fleeting Prosperity in Postwar Era

Alhough the company continued to function into the latter years of the 20th century, the late 1940s and early 1950s were, in many respects, a last hurrah for Harland and Wolff. The firm rebuilt war-damaged plants to state-of-the-art specifications, and it could rest easy in the knowledge that it could expect little competition from global rivals in Japan and Germany—for the time being, at least. A postwar boom in liner retrofits as well as new merchant ships helped boost after-tax profits to more than £619,000 by 1949. The company also diversified into oil tankers and whalers during this period.

But while after-tax profits rose to more than £1.1 million in the mid-1950s, this financial success masked a shift in the worldwide shipbuilding industry that would prove devastating. Under pressure from low-cost producers in Japan, Sweden, Germany, and Korea, the United Kingdom's stake in the world market for merchant ships eroded rapidly in the 1950s and 1960s, declining from more than 40 percent to about six percent by 1970. As one of the industry's least efficient producers, H&W lost a significant amount of business. Between 1953 and 1962, the company built only 25 big ships. Its balance sheet evinced the damage; profits slid to less than £150,000 in 1961.

After three largely harrowing decades of leading H&W, Francis Rebbeck retired in 1962. He was succeeded as chairman by J.S. Baille and as managing director by his son, Dr. Denis Rebbeck. The new management team worked quickly to reduce overheads by shutting down its in-house foundry and most of its shipbuilding berths, reducing the work force (in part by instituting a mandatory retirement age of 65) to barely 9,000 in 1968, and even shuttering entire shipyards.

Plants that remained in operation effected several milestones during this otherwise trying period. In 1967, H&W launched the United Kingdom's first very large crude carrier (VLCC), which also took the title of Europe's largest-ever vessel. The company's woodworking department, which had until 1965 made interiors for passenger ships, was converted to the manufacture

of prefabricated housing. The division made nearly 700 homes before closing in 1969.

But in spite of these efforts, annual losses began to mount in the mid-1960s, totaling a cumulative £16.5 million from 1964 to 1970. In fact, 1963's meager profit of £145,000 would be the company's last year in the black for more than a decade.

A 20-Year Fight for Survival

From the mid-1960s through the late 1980s, Harland and Wolff endured virtually in spite of itself, incurring mounting losses and colossal debt. Several factors seemed to conspire against the company: high internal costs, civil unrest, a lack of skilled labor, a "revolving door" in the chief executive office, and cutthroat competition. From 1965 to 1985, ten chairmen would attempt to steer the company through these treacherous waters.

In 1966, J.S. Baille resigned and was briefly succeeded by Denis Rebbeck, who would serve as a managing director through the end of the decade. In exchange for a £1.5 million guaranteed loan that year, the government effectively assumed control of the company, appointing John S. Mallabar as chairman and financial controller. Mallabar oversaw the construction of a "super dock" to accommodate continued production of VLCCs, improved the company's accounting methods, and prepared H&W for a specialization in large tankers and bulk carriers. Pronouncing that he had "disposed of the matters which called for his personal attention," Mallabar resigned the chairmanship in 1970. J.R. Edwards advanced to the helm for a brief period before resigning that December. Managing Director Alan Watt assumed the role of interim chairman until 1971, when the government brought in Iver Hoppe, a Dane, to replace Watt in both roles.

In the meantime, the ascent of the Conservative party brought something of a change in attitude toward H&W. The Heath administration announced that it was "not the Government's intention to continue to support British shipbuilding" and branded the company a "lame duck." Paradoxically, the government was also fully aware that closure of one of Belfast's most important employers could prove disastrous during this period of intense rioting, strikes, and violence known as the "troubles." Although successive administrations would attempt to limit H&W's losses, the shipbuilder recorded only one year of profitability from 1971 to 1985.

Ironically, H&W was regarded by many in the industry as the best equipped shipbuilding yard in the world, but high wages and low worker productivity hamstrung its potential for profitability. Having appointed key leaders since the late 1960s and granted the company millions in debt, the British government purchased a controlling stake in the company in 1971. Complete government ownership was effected in 1975, with the stated objective of protecting the already heavy investment of public funds from takeover by a private company.

But nationalization did nothing to improve Harland and Wolff's bottom line. Hoppe was forced to resign when the shipbuilder's net worth reached a negative £32 million in 1974. A painfully typical government-sponsored bureaucracy consumed more than a year reviewing outside applications for a successor before promoting Production Manager Ronald Punt to managing director. At the same time, the administration pursued the paradoxical policy of seeking to increase productivity through investment in plant while boosting employment by 4,000. Despite these initiatives, H&W's work force had declined from more than 9,000 in 1971 to 5,100 in 1985. Ironically, throughout this period, the firm continued to build record-breaking vessels, accounting for nearly one-third of total U.K. output.

Parker Leads Privatization in the Late 1980s

After Punt retired in 1982, the government appointed John Parker to the chief executive office. The new leader guided a diversification into a broader variety of defense, cargo, and petroleum ships. One of the company's most exciting new developments was the launch of a line of Single Oil Well Production System (SWOPS) ships. These vessels not only processed oil en route from oil fields to their destination, but also used the gas byproduct of the processing to fuel the ship's own engines. A company history dubbed it "the world's most sophisticated merchant ship." Furthermore, H&W delivered Europe's largest bulk carrier, the *British Steel,* in 1984. Parker also reduced the shipbuilder's work force to less than 4,000 by the end of 1988. Despite its diminished roster, H&W remained Northern Ireland's second largest industrial employer.

Still, the company's annual losses continued to grow, reaching a colossal £75 million in fiscal 1986–1987. Having poured more than £1 billion into the company from 1966 to 1988, the government announced its intention to sell the firm. In 1989, a consortium led by John Parker and Norwegian ship owner Fred Olsen and including management and employees purchased Harland and Wolff. The government retained £400 million in existing debt and started the new owners off with nearly £160 million in new loans. Fred Olsen's shipping companies purchased a majority £12 million stake in the reorganized firm, and the remainder was owned by management, employees, and outside investors. Olsen also supported his new affiliate with an order for $150 million in new oil tankers.

H&W was reorganized as a holding company with subsidiaries organized by function. In the early 1990s, the firm manufactured oil rigs and tankers as well as marine furnishings and paint, operated repair and design subsidiaries, and participated in the management of residential and commercial redevelopment of Queen's Island properties. By 1991, H&W showed signs that its efforts to improve productivity and reduce costs had begun to pay off, when it received its first order from outside the Olsen group. Under the guidance of Chief Executive Per Nielsen by 1996, revenues mounted to £118.1 million and the company reported what must have been its first profit in years, if not decades, a pretax surplus of £3 million. While clearly proud of this achievement, Olsen and Nielsen noted that "the level of profitability is still not satisfactory when compared to our turnover."

Principal Subsidiaries

Harland and Wolff Shipbuilding and Heavy Industries Limited; Harland and Wolff Protective Coatings Limited; Harland and Wolff Outfit Service Limited; Harland and Wolff Ship Repair and Marine Services Limited; Harland and Wolff Technical Services Limited; Harland Ocean Transport Limited; Harland Wolff Properties Limited; Harland and Wolff Employee Market Making Trust; Harland and Wolff Employee Pension Trustee Limited.

Further Reading

Pierson, J. Gordon, *Great Ship Builders; or the Rise of Harland and Wolff,* A.H. Stockwell Lt.: London, 1935.
McCaughan, Michael, *Steel Ships and Iron Men: Shipbuilding in Belfast 1894–1912,* Belfast: Friar's Bush Press, 1989.
Moss, Michael S., and Hume, John R., *Shipbuilders to the World: 125 Years of Harland and Wolff, Belfast 1861–1986,* Belfast: Blackstaff Press, 1986.
Porter, Janet, "Management, Employees To Buy N. Ireland Yard," *The Journal of Commerce,* March 23, 1989, p. 3B.
Ryle, Margaret, "Harland and Wolff Looks Offshore," *Motor Ship,* June 1996, pp. S21–S23.
Selwitz, Robert, "Diversification Keeps Harland and Wolff Alive," *Journal of Commerce & Commercial,* May 26, 1987, pp. 3B-8B.
"Sinking Ships," *The Economist,* March 26, 1988, p. 54.
"A Slow Death," *The Economist,* November 26, 1988, p. 63.

—April Dougal Gasbarre

The Hearst Corporation

The Hearst Corporation

959 Eighth Avenue
New York, New York 10019
U.S.A.
(212) 649-2000
Fax: (212) 765-3528
Web site: http://www.hearstcorp.com

Private Company
Incorporated: 1943
Employees: 14,000
Sales: $2.51 billion (1995)
SICs: 2711 Newspaper Publishing & Printing; 2721
Magazine Publishing Only, Not Printed Onsite; 2731
Books Publishing Only; 4832 Radio Broadcasting
Stations; 4833 Television Broadcasting Stations; 7383
News Feature Syndicate

The Hearst Corporation is one of the largest diversified communications companies in the world. It has interests in print, broadcasting, and the news media, including newspapers, magazines, book and business publishing, television and radio broadcasting, cable network programming, newspaper features distribution, television production and distribution, and electronic publishing. Hearst Magazines is the largest publisher of monthly magazines in the world, with distribution in more than 100 countries. A subsidiary, the National Magazine Company Limited, is one of the leading magazine publishers in the United Kingdom. Hearst Newspapers publishes 12 daily and seven weekly newspapers in the United States. Its division, Associated Publishing Company, which was acquired in 1993, publishes yellow-page telephone directories listing information for West Texas communities.

Hearst Broadcasting is one of the largest independently owned broadcasting groups in the nation; it includes nine television stations and six radio stations. Hearst Broadcasting Productions is a television and corporate video production unit. This unit is also a partner with Continental Cablevision in New England Cable News, a 24-hour all-news network. Hearst En-

tertainment and Syndication includes the company's cable network partnerships with ABC, NBC, and ESPN; television programming and distribution activities; and the King Features group of syndication companies, which is the world's largest distributor of editorial features, comic strips, and panels to newspapers.

Hearst Books/Business Publishing includes William Morrow & Company, which publishes hardcover books, and Avon Books, which publishes paperbacks. This unit also publishes business publications and database catalogs. Hearst New Media & Technology, created in 1993, works with all other company divisions to adapt editorial and programming content to new media technologies. This division also has an interest in Netscape Communications, the software provider on the Internet.

Founder William Randolph Hearst

The shape and history of the company's early years were intertwined with the history and designs of its founder, William Randolph Hearst. A man who inherited enormous wealth, Hearst was also a person of enormous ambition and activity, whose initial interest in journalism in an era when the newspaper business could hardly be separated from the political arena led to a consuming passion for political office that was destined to end in frustration.

The company that became a behemoth in communications started out as payment for a gambling debt, when William Randolph Hearst's father, George Hearst, a self-made millionaire who had earned his fortune in mining and ranching, took possession of the *San Francisco Examiner* in 1880 after its owner had lost a wager with him. Seven years later, William Randolph Hearst, recently expelled from Harvard College for an elaborate prank, took over the paper he desired to run.

Newspapers in that day were, for the most part, organs of propaganda for individual politicians and political parties. Indeed, Hearst's father had accepted the paper only for the purpose of enhancing his own political career. William Randolph Hearst had big plans in mind for the money-losing four-page daily paper. Taking Joseph Pulitzer's *New York World* as his model, he began by sinking large sums into the latest printing technology and changing the paper's appearance to make it more compelling. In addition, he hired new staff members—bagging such luminaries as Ambrose Bierce—and charged them with the aggressive pursuit of stories that would improve the paper's circulation. The first big coup came with the *Examiner's* sensational coverage of a big hotel fire, just one month after Hearst took over. Slowly the paper's fortunes improved, helped along by a large dose of self-promotion. Hearst was soon referring to his paper as "A GREAT PAPER."

Hearst employees were diligent in their pursuit of shocking and titillating material to draw in more readers. In the absence of genuinely sensational news, they did not hesitate to manufacture newsworthy events, or simply to make things up. Much of the manufactured news was billed as crusading exposure of social ills, as when a woman reporter feigned illness to expose the condition of the city's ambulance corps and hospital, or when one intrepid Hearst journalist threw himself into San Francisco Bay from a ferry to test rescue procedures. Both of these stories did in fact result in improvements in the city agencies involved. In his first year, Hearst launched more than a dozen crusades, taking on such established powers as the city's political machine and the Southern Pacific Railroad. All of this activity, along with Hearst features such as the publication of the scores of popular songs on Sunday and the introduction of a column devoted to union activities, added up to a new kind of journalism and contributed to a slowly growing circulation. Advertising revenues remained low, however, and Hearst's paper continued to consume large sums of his father's money until 1890, when it first went into the black.

By 1895 the *Examiner* was thriving, both in terms of circulation and revenue, and Hearst was ready for a new challenge. He found it in New York, taking over a decrepit daily paper, the *New York Journal.* He began by sending for the best of his San Francisco staff, dropping the price of the New York paper to 1¢, and increasing its size. Hearst was going after his old ideal, Pulitzer's *World,* and his most successful tactic was the wholesale raiding of Pulitzer's staff. Waving enormous salaries, he lured some of his rival's best staff away, including the creator of the popular comic "The Yellow Kid," which would inspire the phrase "yellow journalism," used to describe the sensational and irresponsible coverage that Hearst and his rivals pioneered.

In the ensuing contest between the two papers, the techniques that Hearst's organization had first polished in San Francisco—sensationalism and crusading campaigns on behalf of the ordinary person—were taken to new heights. In addition, the paper became inextricably involved with political parties, power, and disputes, becoming heavily identified with presidential candidate William Jennings Bryan and the Democratic Party. Since all the other large newspapers backed William McKinley, the *Journal* rapidly became the leading Democratic newspaper in the country.

Perhaps the ultimate manufactured news event was the one that started the Spanish-American War. From the start, Hearst's paper had strongly supported Cuban independence from Spain. When the American battleship *Maine* mysteriously blew up in Havana harbor in February 1898, Hearst and his employees printed two weeks' worth of fraudulent material blaming Spain for the attack. This coverage, which Hearst orchestrated but in which he was not alone, resulted in increased circulation for the paper—and in war.

With the dawning of the new century, Hearst's fledgling network of newspapers continued to expand. Attempting to bolster support for Bryan's 1900 presidential bid, Hearst founded the *Chicago American,* whose first issue rolled off the presses on July 4, 1900. Bryan lost once again to McKinley. Hearst's overwhelming identification in the public's mind with opposition to the president became a grave liability after McKinley was assassinated in September 1901. Some groups boycotted and banned Hearst papers. Nevertheless, his New York paper, the *Journal,* claimed the greatest number of paid subscribers in the world by the end of the year. When Hearst was elected to Congress the following year, his papers became his personal forum for conducting political activity. In 1904 the *Boston American* was added to the fold. Two years later, the 1906 San Francisco earthquake dealt a major blow to the flagship of the Hearst organization, reducing the physical plant of the *Examiner* to a ruin. Despite the devastation, the three San Francisco papers produced a joint issue on the first day after the quake and, shortly thereafter, the *Examiner* was back on its feet.

The Hearst organization branched out into magazines in 1903, with the founding of *Motor* magazine, a venture inspired by *The Car,* a British publication Hearst had come across on his honeymoon. Two years later, he bought *Cosmopolitan,* a magazine of fiction and nonfiction. Filled with the work of some of the best writers of the day, its circulation soon doubled. Hearst's most important magazine acquisition was *Good Housekeeping* in 1911. This purchase also included the laboratory facilities that would develop into the Good Housekeeping Institute and the Good Housekeeping Seal, heavily promoted under the new owners.

Hearst papers took a vigorous anti-British and isolationist stance in the era leading up to the United States's entry into World War I, bannering slogans like "America First" and "No Entangling Alliances" in fierce opposition to the policies of President Woodrow Wilson. When the United States declared war in April 1917, Hearst's opposition to the U.S. effort to aid the Allies and perceived pro-German sentiment, resulted in lower circulation for his newspapers in many cities. Throughout this era, William Randolph Hearst continued his political activities in pursuit of the presidency, and Hearst papers were instruments in his crusade.

Nevertheless, throughout the second decade of the century, Hearst enterprises grew at a prodigious pace. By 1920 the print operations numbered 13 newspapers and seven magazines, including the profitable *American Weekly* newspaper insert and the British *Nash's.* As offshoots of the newspapers, the organization also owned a money-losing newswire, the International

News Service, which had emerged from World War I with its credibility badly damaged, and the King Features Syndicate, which sold the work of Hearst writers and artists to other papers.

In addition, Hearst had entered the film industry in 1913, when the first newsreel—footage of Woodrow Wilson's inauguration—was shown in movie theaters. This showing led to the establishment of the Hearst-Selig News Pictorial in 1914, which pioneered film journalism throughout the 1920s, evolving into Hearst Metrotone News with the arrival of sound in 1929. For entertainment, Hearst produced in partnership with Pathé Fréres such long-running serials as *The Perils of Pauline.* Intent both on promoting the career of his mistress, Marion Davies, and becoming a movie mogul himself, William Randolph Hearst formed Cosmopolitan Productions and in 1919 built a studio in Harlem where movies could be filmed. Hearst papers duly praised the resulting products. In time, the studio moved to Hollywood where it joined with other studios, producing musical extravaganzas like *Broadway Melody,* and other films.

As William Randolph Hearst continued to seek political office in the 1920s, Hearst operations continued to grow. Papers were acquired or founded at a brisk pace, including three in 1921, six in 1922, one in 1923, and three in 1924. On the international front, Hearst expanded its magazine holdings in Britain to include *Good Housekeeping, Connoisseur,* and *Harper's Bazaar.* By the early 1930s the tally of Hearst papers was up to 28 and the magazines numbered 13. Along with his other ventures, this necessarily gave Hearst great influence in public affairs. His influence was enhanced by the Hearst company's entry into the fledgling radio industry in 1928 with the purchase of WISN in Milwaukee, Wisconsin. By the mid-1930s it owned ten radio stations. In 1934, the Hearst organization was restructured to give Hearst editorial control while trusted subordinates handled day-to-day business matters. By the following year Hearst had become implacable in his opposition to the policies of Franklin Delano Roosevelt whom he had initially helped to win the Democratic nomination in 1932. In the 1936 campaign Hearst papers supported Roosevelt's opponent Alf Landon. Throughout the 1930s, Hearst papers were unstinting in their opposition to socialism and communism. This fact, combined with Hearst's love for Germany, where he traveled often, and his growing conservatism, often led his opponents to charge him with fascism.

Repercussions of the Great Depression

Throughout the years of financial turmoil and decline that began with the stock market crash in 1929, Hearst, who was accustomed to wealth of unimaginable proportions, had not significantly altered his activities. He continued to spend lavishly on art and on the construction and upkeep of his several estates. In addition, the company had used several bond issues to raise capital, resulting in debts that reached $137 million. In 1937 under pressure from the shareholders, and various banks and newsprint companies to whom Hearst owed money, the company tried to float another set of debentures, but was prevented from doing so by the Securities and Exchange Commission. The crash had come. Faced with the virtual bankruptcy of his vast empire, Hearst, now nearly 75 years old, turned over complete financial control of his holdings to a lawyer approved by his creditors, who quickly began to restructure drastically the Hearst organization. Six money-losing newspapers and seven radio stations were sold,

a magazine was scrapped, and Hearst's New York flagship paper, the *New York American,* was merged with its evening counterpart. A Conservation Committee was formed to sell off assets, including two-thirds of Hearst's art collection.

Four years later, in 1941, the Hearst organization was still fighting for fiscal survival. By that time there were 94 Hearst entities with complex financial ties. With the entry of the United States into World War II, Hearst papers (reduced to a total of 18) dropped their isolationist stance and wholeheartedly supported the war effort. It was the war, opposed so staunchly by Hearst editorialists, that helped the company to regain its financial health, as the war sent circulation and advertising revenues rising.

At the end of 1943 the trustee and the Conservation Committee appointed in 1937 were succeeded by a voting trust that included two of Hearst's five sons. The trust continued to sell off property, including two-thirds of Hearst's vast San Simeon estate, and to rearrange assets, in 1943 consolidating everything within The Hearst Corporation holding company. By the end of the war in 1945, the company was on more solid financial ground once again. Three years later, the company entered a new field in communications when WBAL-TV in Baltimore, Maryland, began to broadcast.

New Leadership in the Postwar Period

By 1947 William Randolph Hearst, elderly and suffering from heart problems, had little involvement in company operations. On August 14, 1951, Hearst died, ending an era in U.S. journalism. His will stipulated that his $57 million estate be divided for tax purposes into a charitable trust and a restructured corporation. Hearst left the 100 shares of voting stock that controlled the company in the hands of a board made up of five family members and six company executives, insuring that those outside the family would have control of the corporation. One of the executives, Richard Berlin, took over as chief executive officer at Hearst's death, after 32 years with the company.

During Berlin's tenure, the company saw the collapse of its first base of operations, its newspapers, and expanded its holdings in other fields of the communications industry, such as magazines and television. The advent of television ended newspaper journalism as William Randolph Hearst had known it. No longer did the papers provide the public's primary source of news. This change in social habits resulted in a vast shake-out in the newspaper industry, in which afternoon papers in particular were hard hit, the Hearst publications included. The first paper to go was the *Chicago American,* a long-time money-loser, which was sold to its competitor, the *Tribune,* in 1956. Two years later, the Hearst newswire, International News Service, and its affiliated photo service were sold to rival United Press. Under Berlin's direction the company shed papers in San Francisco, Pittsburgh, Detroit, Boston, Los Angeles, and Milwaukee in quick succession. In 1963 Hearst sold its money-losing morning tabloid the *New York Mirror,* which had the second largest circulation in the United States. The cruelest blow came in 1966, when Hearst's flagship *Journal-American* folded in New York.

In contrast, Hearst expanded its magazine operations throughout this period, concentrating on special interest publications rather than broad, general interest titles. In 1953 the company purchased *Sports Afield* and five years later added another men's magazine, *Popular Mechanics.* Shortly thereafter, a Spanish edition of the magazine was granted the first license for a Hearst magazine foreign edition. Eventually, the company would successfully license nearly 60 foreign editions of its publications. In 1959 the company branched out into book publishing when it purchased Avon Publications, Inc., which produced paperbacks. In addition to new acquisitions, old publications underwent renovations, enabling them to contribute strong performances to the magazine group. *Cosmopolitan,* for instance, retooled in 1965 from a general interest magazine of fiction and nonfiction to the interests of working women and became a huge money-maker. In 1966 another venerable Hearst magazine, *Good Housekeeping,* became the leader in its field.

At his retirement in 1973, Berlin left Hearst debt-free and rich in capital, yet far poorer in publications and importance than it had once been. The following year the company was again restructured when it used the cash built up during Berlin's tenure to buy back the stock held by Hearst charitable foundations, which had been established at Hearst's death to avoid inheritance taxes. The Hearst family regained control of the company's assets, now privately owned, and the chain of command within the company was simplified. Throughout the second half of the 1970s under the leadership of John R. Miller, Hearst experienced a huge growth in profits, as properties that had been allowed to lie dormant began to produce. For instance, the company tapped the reserve of goodwill built up in the names *House Beautiful* and *Good Housekeeping* when it successfully spun off *Colonial Homes* and *Country Living* from the older publications.

New Ventures in the 1980s and 1990

In 1979 Hearst again began to expand its newspaper holdings by buying five daily papers in mid-sized cities in Michigan, Texas, and Illinois. In the early 1980s acquisitions continued until the newspaper group was 15 strong, with publications in Houston, Seattle, Los Angeles, and San Francisco, as well as other, smaller cities.

By the start of the 1980s, the Hearst magazine division was the largest U.S. producer of monthly magazines. It continued to perform well throughout the 1980s, adding *Redbook, Esquire,* a U.S. version of the British *Connoisseur,* and other titles. The Hearst magazine distribution network, which already included three subscriber services, purchased a fourth, Communications Data Services, Inc., in 1982.

During the 1980s the company's scope shifted beyond print to encompass the whole spectrum of communications enterprises. Television and radio stations were acquired; and partnerships were formed to create the Arts & Entertainment Network (A&E) and LIFETIME, a network devoted to programming for women. In late 1990 the company bought a 20 percent interest in the sports network ESPN.

In 1995, A&E launched The History Channel, devoted to historical programming and viewed by more than 37 million households in the United States. Also that year, Hearst partnered New Century Network, a national network of local online newspaper services, with eight other newspaper publishers; the company ceased, however, its CD-Rom operations that were

part of Hearst New Media & Technology. In 1997, A&E teamed up with Groupe AB of France to launch La Chaine Histoire, to offer French viewers French and international history programming drawn from the History Channel International's program catalogue.

More joint ventures allowed Hearst to enter and expand into new markets. In 1997, the company announced that *SmartMoney,* its print magazine dealing with personal business and partnered with Dow Jones & Company, would have a new Web edition, called SmartMoney Interactive. The edition, paid by subscriptions, would have daily news coverage and features not provided in the print version. In 1997, Hearst opened another web site, HomeArts, which used some Hearst magazines as sources for lifestyle and home services marketing on the internet.

Print was still very much a main focus for Hearst, however. In 1997, the publisher signed up Dan Rather to write a once-a-week column dealing with national and international news, to be syndicated internationally by King Features. Another print effort was a joint venture with ESPN, which involved taking its content to create a new sports magazine to be called *ESPN Magazine* for a 1998 debut.

Broadcasting, too, remained a vital part of the company. In 1997, Hearst announced plans to merge its broadcasting division with Argyle Television Inc. of San Antonio. The new division, to be called Hearst-Argyle Television Inc., would be one of the largest independent television groups of network-affiliated stations in the nation.

The Hearst Corporation had thus evolved from a newspaper chain known for sensationalism and irresponsible journalism, and dominated by the will of one man, to a vast and highly profitable enterprise encompassing a broad range of communications fields. As it entered the 21st century, the company appeared to be firmly positioned to use its resources for further growth.

Principal Subsidiaries

The National Magazine Company Limited.

Principal Operating Units

Hearst Magazines; Hearst Newspapers; Hearst Broadcasting; Hearst Entertainment & Syndication; Hearst Books/Business Publishing; Hearst New Media & Technology; Hearst Real Estate.

Further Reading

Chaney, Lindsay, and Cieply, Michael, *The Hearsts: Family and Empire—The Later Years,* New York: Simon & Schuster, 1981.
Lundberg, Ferdinand, *Imperial Hearst: A Social Biography,* New York: Equinox Cooperative Press, 1936.
O'Donnell, James F., *100 Years of Making Communications History: The Story of the Hearst Corporation,* New York: Hearst Professional Magazines, Inc., 1987.
Swanberg, W.A., *Citizen Hearst: A Biography of William Randolph Hearst,* New York: Charles Scribner's Sons, 1961.

—Elizabeth Rourke
—updated by Dorothy Kroll

HILTON

Hilton Hotels Corporation

9336 Civic Center Drive
Beverly Hills, California 90209
U.S.A.
(310) 278-4321
Fax: (310) 205-4611
Web site: http://www.hilton.com

Public Company
Incorporated: 1946
Employees: 48,000
Sales: $3.9 billion (1996)
Stock Exchanges: New York Pacific
SICs: 7011 Hotels & Motels; 7999 Amusement and
  Recreation, Not Elsewhere Classified; 5812 Eating
  Places; 6794 Patent Owners & Lessors

Known as "the granddaddy of the hospitality industry," Hilton Hotels Corporation is best known for its 240 hotels and almost 100,000 rooms. Its 1996 acquisition of Bally Entertainment Corp., however, made gambling the company's largest business interest, with that segment's 17 casinos contributing about 60 percent of revenues.

Though publicly traded, the chain was for most of its history led by members of the Hilton family from 1919, when founder Conrad Hilton bought his first hotel. By the late 1940s, Hilton owned a worldwide chain of premium hotels. In the 1960s, Hilton sold its international operations and concentrated on management contracts and franchising. The company created innovative joint-venture arrangements that became standard industry practice. It then entered what would become a prime source of revenue for the company: casino-hotels. Hilton expanded into gaming in 1971; by 1989, gaming provided 44 percent of the company's income. In 1996, Barron Hilton relinquished day-to-day management of the chain to Stephen F. Bollenbach. Asserting that "Big companies do big things," Bollenbach revitalized the company with bold actions. His merger with Bally made Hilton the world's largest gaming

company, and a 1997 bid to acquire ITT Corp. proposed to form the biggest hotel chain in the world.

Early 20th-Century Origins

Conrad Nicholson Hilton was born in San Antonio, New Mexico, the second of eight children. Before he was 18, Conrad had worked as a trader, a clerk, a bellboy, and a pianist. By age 25 he had also worked in politics and banking. In 1919, following the death of his father, Hilton left the army and went to Texas. He had intended to take advantage of the oil boom by buying a small bank. Instead, he found bank prices prohibitive and hotels so overbooked he could not find a place to sleep. When one owner in Cisco, Texas, complained he would like to sell his property in order to take advantage of the oil boom, Hilton struck a deal. Hilton pulled together an investment group and the funds were transferred within a week. The Mobley, in Cisco, became Hilton's first hotel.

The hotel was booked solid, and Conrad and his partner, L. M. Drown, rented their own beds and slept on chairs in the office. They also converted much of the hotel's public space into additional guest quarters. Making use of wasted space became a hallmark of the Hilton chain. With the Mobley running smoothly, Hilton bought two more Texas properties in 1920; the Melba, in Fort Worth, and the Waldorf in Dallas—named after the prized New York hotel. In 1925 Conrad Hilton built the first hotel to carry his name, in Dallas.

With expansions well underway, Hilton consolidated his properties into Hilton Hotels, Incorporated, in 1929, when the stock market crashed. The El Paso Hilton was completed in November 1930 and opened with a fanfare. A year later, Hilton owned eight hotels and was more than half a million dollars in debt when a young bellboy slipped him $300—his life savings—so Hilton could feed himself and his family.

Depression-Era Wrangling over Corporate Ownership

In 1931 the Moody family of Galveston, Texas, from whom Hilton had borrowed, took possession of his hotels when he defaulted on a $300,000 loan. The Moodys then hired Hilton to manage their own and his hotels, now known as the National

205

Company Perspectives:

"Hilton Hotels Corporation is the world's leading lodging and casino gaming company. Among our 240 hotels are some of the most well-known properties to be found anywhere, including the Waldorf-Astoria, Hilton Hawaiian Village and Palmer House Hilton. Our hotels offer guests and customers the finest accommodations and amenities for business or leisure. As the world's largest gaming company, our 17 hotel casinos and riverboat casinos provide the excitement of gaming entertainment in such major destinations as Las Vegas, Atlantic City and Australia. For more than 75 years, the Hilton brand name has been synonymous with excellence in the hospitality industry."

Hotel Company. Nine months later, in 1932, Hilton and the Moodys decided to part. The separation, however, was in no way peaceful. The Moody family and Hilton sued and countersued each other regarding the terms of their agreement for separation, which Hilton claimed allotted him one-third of the hotels and one-third of the stock if the arrangement failed to prove satisfactory. In 1933, while Hilton continued to battle the Moodys in court, the Moodys defaulted on the loan for the El Paso Hilton, and Conrad Hilton managed to raise the necessary $30,000 to buy back that hotel. In 1934 Hilton settled with the Moodys, who lent him $95,000 and returned the Lubbock, Dallas, and Plainview hotels. According to Conrad Hilton, while Depression-era hotel owners saved less than one hotel out of five, Hilton emerged with five of his eight hotels, and he met his debts by the summer of 1937.

In 1938, Hilton bought his first hotel outside of Texas, the Sir Francis Drake in San Francisco. He sold it two years later at a $500,000 profit to raise capital to purchase the Stevens in Chicago, then the largest hotel in the world.

Although U.S. entry into World War II spawned caution, Hilton acquired three new properties, one in Los Angeles and two in New York. Thus, in 1942, his name stretched from coast to coast. The New York properties included the Roosevelt and the Plaza. Hilton claimed he was practicing for New York's Waldorf-Astoria, a picture of which he had clipped from a magazine and carried with him since the hotel opened in 1931.

Postwar Expansion

In 1945, Hilton traveled to Chicago to complete the purchase of the Stevens, which he had initiated in 1940, and ended up acquiring the Palmer House as well. In May 1946, Hilton Hotels Corporation was formed. It made history the next year as the first hotel company to have its stock listed on the New York Stock Exchange. Conrad N. Hilton was president and the largest stockholder.

Despite its reputation, the Waldorf-Astoria was not a profitable hotel. While negotiations to lease that hotel were taking place, Hilton worried his board members with his interest in international hotels in a postwar climate uncertain for interna-

tional business. Nevertheless, Conrad Hilton pursued the venture that would become the Caribe Hilton in San Juan, Puerto Rico. An agreement was made to form a wholly owned subsidiary—Hilton Hotels International—for which Hilton formed a separate board. In 1949 Conrad Hilton bought the lease on the Waldorf-Astoria. The Waldorf made a $1 million profit in its first year under Hilton management. The first European Hilton was opened in Madrid in 1953.

The largest hotel merger in the industry took place in 1954 when Hilton Hotels purchased the Statler Hotel Company for $111 million. The Statler chain consisted of eight hotels, with two more under construction. Statler was noted for its fine properties and solid reputation. The chain was about to be sold to a New York realty firm when Hilton made a plea to Statler's widow. She agreed to sell to Hilton, in order to keep the hotels in "the hands of hotel people." Earnings per share nearly doubled between 1953 and 1955, largely as a result of this acquisition. In 1955, another overseas Hilton was opened, in Turkey, and the Continental Hilton of Mexico City opened the following year. In 1964 Hilton International was spun off and became a public company with Conrad Hilton as its president. Hilton was made chairman of the board of Hilton Hotels that same year.

Second Generation of Management Guides Development of Casino-Hotels

The late 1960s saw significant changes, beginning with the 1965 formation of Statler Hilton Inns, a corporate franchising subsidiary, and a change of presidents. In 1966 Hilton's son, William Barron Hilton—known as Barron—assumed the presidency. Barron Hilton's conservative fiscal strategies set a decidedly different course for the company his father had built. The following year, Barron Hilton persuaded his father, as the largest shareholder of Hilton International, to swap his stake in the overseas operation for shares of Trans World Airlines (TWA). Hilton remained chairman of Hilton International. The expectation had been that TWA stock would rise, but its value halved over the next 18 months. Meanwhile, foreign travel boomed, and Hilton lost the rights to his name overseas.

In 1970, Barron Hilton engineered the $112 million purchase that would generate the largest percentage of the company's revenues within a decade: two casino-hotels in Las Vegas, Nevada. While Conrad Hilton had dabbled in gaming via a Puerto Rican casino in the late 1940s, the acquisition of the Las Vegas Hilton and the Flamingo Hilton marked the launch of a consistent strategy. This move paid for itself, particularly during the late 1970s and early 1980s, when the occupancy rate at both hotels remained steady in contrast to industrywide trends.

Barron Hilton then concentrated on franchising the Hilton name and managing other hotels. In 1973, the company launched a computerized hotel reservation dubbed "HILTRON." The system served not only the Hilton chain but was also employed by other chains in the industry, providing yet another source of revenue. In 1975 Hilton sold a 50 percent interest in six major hotels to Prudential Life Insurance Company of America for $85 million. Hilton continued to manage the properties in exchange for a percentage of room revenues and gross profits. This was one of the first management lease-back deals in the industry. Joint-venture arrangements later became standard industry practice.

In 1977 the purchase of the Waldorf-Astoria's building and land was finalized for $35 million. The decade closed with the death of Conrad N. Hilton in 1979, at age 91. Barron Hilton became chairman of the board. During the 1980s Hilton continued to make its money primarily though casino gambling, leasing and management, and franchise fees. These were sound measures during recession years: while revenues for owned hotels increased an average of four percent in 1980 and 1981, management contract fees increased by six percent in 1980 and 14 percent in 1981. Overall earnings for Hilton increased by six percent during these years, and the company grew rich in liquid assets. It put this capital to use in hotel improvements and in 1981, the $34.4 million purchase of another casino-hotel in Nevada, the Sahara Reno. Barron Hilton maintained a no-partnership policy for the company's casino-hotels. Although the hotels suffered from the loss of convention bookings during the recession, an addition to the Las Vegas Hilton in 1982 made it the largest hotel in the world, and further convention facilities were added in 1985.

Having sold the international rights to the Hilton name, the corporation resumed international growth in 1982 under a new subsidiary, Conrad International Hotels. Construction began on a casino-hotel in Australia the following year. Over the course of the next decade, this division established hotels (many of them joint ventures) in Turkey, Egypt, Hong Kong, Uruguay and New Zealand.

By 1985 gaming was providing 40 percent of the company's operating income, and earnings had increased 20 percent annually since Hilton's entry into that industry. In 1985, however, after spending $320 million to build a casino in Atlantic City, New Jersey, Hilton was denied a license to operate. The New Jersey Casino Control Commission's primary objection was Hilton Hotel's longstanding relationship with Chicago labor attorney Sidney Korshak, who had been linked with organized crime figures and who the *New York Times* in 1976 had labeled "a behind-the-scenes fixer." Hilton severed its ties with Korshak, who had acted as a labor consultant for the company, and the gaming commission granted a new hearing. In April 1985, before the rehearing took place, however, the hotel-casino was sold to Donald Trump at cost.

While Hilton focused on the casino-hotels, Marriott and Hyatt were expanding in the luxury-hotels market. To keep pace with its competitors, Hilton pledged $1.4 billion to renovate older properties during the late 1980s. Barron Hilton also concentrated on solving the problem of his father's will.

Dispute over Founder's Will Spans 1980s

When Conrad Hilton died, he had bequeathed the bulk of his holding—a 27 percent block of Hilton shares—to the Conrad N. Hilton Foundation. This foundation, incorporated in 1950, gives aid to Roman Catholic nuns. This provision left Barron Hilton with 3.6 percent of Hilton Hotels, but he claimed to have exercised an option on the foundation's shares immediately, buying their portion at the market rate of $24. Ownership of the stock was contested for the next decade. At issue was the interpretation of an option Conrad Hilton had allotted Barron Hilton in his will: Barron Hilton claimed the will allowed him to buy the entire stock from the foundation at the 1979 price. The estate's executor, who was Conrad's personal attorney, claimed the will intended that Barron Hilton be entitled to no more than seven percent of the shares. Meanwhile, Hilton and ex-wife Zsa Zsa Gabor's daughter also contested the will. The attorney general's office of California joined the case, arguing that the foundation was entitled to the shares at market value, or $225 million, in 1985. To complicate the issue further, Golden Nugget casino's chairman Steve Wynn attempted to buy the disputed shares in 1985 at their current market price—$72 a share—in order to launch a takeover of Hilton.

A November 1988 settlement gave Barron Hilton four million of the disputed shares, a stake valued at $204 million. The foundation kept 3.5 million shares, worth $178 million at the time, and six million shares, a $306 million stake, went into a trust with Barron Hilton serving as executor. Perhaps most significant, the agreement gave the CEO the trust's voting privileges, for a total voting presence of 25 percent. In addition, Hilton was to receive 60 percent of the trust's share dividends until 2008, after which they would revert to the foundation.

The chain closed the decade enjoying a 70 percent occupancy rate in its newly rejuvenated domestic hotels, greater international expansion, and properties totaling an estimated $4 billion to $6 billion. In May 1989, Chairman Barron Hilton solicited bids for the chain. By December 1989, however, the company had not received a satisfactory bid, and Hilton decided not to sell.

The 1990s and Beyond

After three decades of leadership, Barron Hilton relinquished the chief executive office of the corporation in 1996. While his final years at the helm were criticized as indecisive and overly conservative, the fact remained that its revenues increased from less than $1 billion in 1989 to $1.6 billion in 1995. Net income increased at an average annual rate of 19.6 percent, from $84.3 million in 1991 to $172.8 million in 1995.

In 1996 53-year-old Stephen F. Bollenbach became the first non-Hilton to guide the company. He came to the job with incontrovertible credentials, having engineered both a debt restructuring for the Trump empire and Walt Disney's $19 billion acquisition of Capital Cities/ABC. A spate of high-profile deals quickly ensued. Within five months, the new CEO had merged Hilton with Bally Entertainment Corp. via a stock swap valued at $2 billion. In one move, the deal created the world's largest gaming concern and made casino gambling Hilton's largest business. However, in the interest of equilibrium, Bollenbach also executed several key moves to expand the hotel chain. First, he repurchased the Prudential Insurance Company's stake in six Hiltons for $433 million. He also pledged to increase via franchising Hilton's budget Garden Inns chain by 50,000 rooms over the remaining years of the decade.

Before 1996 had ended, Bollenbach had also pulled off a reunification of the global Hilton presence. By the mid-1990s, ownership of Hilton International (and the overseas rights to the

Hilton name) had passed to London's Ladbroke Group plc. Hilton purchased a three percent stake in Ladbroke and in return the British concern agreed to invest in future Hilton enterprises. The two companies planned to create cooperative marketing programs (including honoring each other's frequent stay plans) and develop new hotels together.

On January 27, 1997, Hilton bid $55 per share for New York–based ITT Corp., aiming primarily to acquire its ITT Sheraton subsidiary's 415 hotels and 14 casinos. If completed, the merger would create the world's biggest hostelry.

Principal Subsidiaries

Destination Resorts, Inc.; Hapeville Investors, Inc.; Hilton Employee Relief Fund; Hilton Equipment Corp.; Hilton Gaming Corp.; Hilton Hawaii Corp.; Hilton Hotels Partners I, Inc.; Hilton Hotels Partners II, Inc.; Hilton Hotels U.S.A., Inc.; Hilton Inns, Inc.; Hilton Insurance Corp.; Hilton Pennsylvania Hotel Corp.; Hilton Recreation, Inc.; Hilton Resorts Corp.; Hilton San Diego Corp.; Hilton Suites, Inc.; Hilton Systems, Inc.; Hilton Washington Corp.; Kenner Investors, Inc.; Beverly Hilton Corp.; Hotel Waldorf-Astoria Corp.; New Yorker Hotel Corp.; Palmer House Hilton Hotel Co.; Attiki Casinos, Hsa (Greece) (50%); Compass Computer Services, Inc. (50%); Earlsfort Centre Hotel Proprietors Ltd. (Ireland) (14.7%); Greenroll Ltd. (Hong Kong) (30%); Hilton Service Corp.

(51%); International Company for Touristic Investments, Sae (Egypt) (20%); Jupiters Management Ltd. (Australia) (66.6%); Jupiters Ltd. (Australia) (19.9%); Windsor Casino, Ltd. (Canada) (33.3%); Yeditepe Beynelmilel Otelcilik Turizm Ve Ticaret Anonim (Turkey) (25%); Hilton Beverage Corp.; New Orleans Hilton Beverage Corp.

Further Reading

Gibbs, Melanie F., "Hilton Hotels Corp.: The Sleeping Giant Wakes," *National Real Estate Investor,* February 1997, pp. 40–41.

Goldgaber, Arthur, "Honeymoon Hotelier: Hilton's Stock Quickly Doubled after Stephen Bollenbach Took Over as CEO," *Financial World,* January 21, 1997, pp. 34–37.

Hilton, Conrad N., *Be My Guest,* New York: Prentice-Hall Press, 1957.

Lee, Daniel R., "How They Started: The Growth of Four Hotel Giants," *Cornell Hotel & Restaurant Administration Quarterly,* May 1985, pp. 22–32.

Liou, Su-Lan Bethany, *Hilton Hotels Corporation: A Strategic Analysis,* n.p., 1993.

Moore, Thomas, "Barron Hilton Fights for Hilton Hotels," *Fortune,* May 27, 1985.

Wrubel, Robert, "Rumors at The Inn: The Wall Street Sharks Are Circling Hilton Hotels, Eager to Break Up the Family Dynasty," *Financial World,* April 4, 1989, pp. 32–33.

—Carol I. Keeley
—updated by April Dougal Gasbarre

Holophane Corporation

250 East Broad Street, Suite 1400
Columbus, Ohio 43215
U.S.A.
(614) 224-3134
Fax: 614-341-2142

Public Company
Incorporated: 1989
Employees: 1,612
Sales: $190.9 million (1996)
Stock Exchanges: NASDAQ
SICs: 3646 Commercial Lighting Fixtures

Holophane Corporation is a leading global manufacturer of highly engineered lighting fixtures for industrial, commercial, and outdoor applications, and its products are used as new or retrofit fixtures in factories, offices, schools, stores, sports arenas, warehouses, power plants, highways, and correctional facilities around the world. In 1996 it was the sixth largest producer of commercial lighting fixtures in the United States. Holophane occupies the premium-quality, low-unit-sales niche of the commercial lighting fixture industry, where it operates in all but the residential and automotive segments. In the industrial lighting sector, Holophane makes light fixtures for large indoor spaces with high ceilings as well as facilities that contain large pieces of equipment or require lighting at different heights. It also manufactures fixtures for specialized environments, such as explosion- or hazard-resistant lighting. In the outdoor lighting segment it manufactures large-area lighting for highway interchanges, tunnels, and other outdoor areas such as advertising billboards, highway signs, and building facades. It also manufactures architectural specialty lighting for downtown renovations and housing developments. In the field of commercial/institutional lighting Holophane manufactures designer fixtures for restaurants and bars as well as so-called upright fixtures for offices in which the light is reflected up at the ceiling as well as downward. Holophane also manufactures specialty high-performance fluorescent fixtures, emergency lighting equipment, glass refractors for street lighting fixtures, and injection-molded plastic and glass lenses for use in fluorescent fixtures.

Holophane is a vertically integrated manufacturer: it operates in virtually all stages of the raw-materials-to-finished-product process and produces its own glass, processes its own aluminum, and fabricates its own electrical components. Its Mexican facility, for example, performs sand casting and aluminum foundry operations for making light poles; its Springfield, Ohio facility performs sand- and die-cast production; its Newark, Ohio facility makes molds, produces glass, and performs plastic injection molding and special engineering; its Pataskala plant produces ballasts (the voltage-producing or current-stabilizing device housed in the light) and assembles electronic components and emergency products; and its Utica, Ohio facility fabricates sheet metal parts and poles and performs assembly and product painting.

Holophane employs a 185-strong in-house sales staff to sharpen its marketing efforts, which are focused on the lighting project's design stage. By marketing directly to architectural, engineering, and electrical contracting firms and distributors Holophane improves its chances of having its fixtures incorporated into the final building design. Among the many institutions that have installed Holophane products are the California school system, Sam Goody music stores, Office Depot, London's Underground subway, Coors Brewery, San Francisco's Embarcadero city center, the Chicago Park system, the Titleist golf products company, the *Daily Mail* newspaper of London, and Coca-Cola. Among its historical milestones are the original illumination for the crown of the Statue of Liberty and a new lighting system for both houses of Congress as well as London's Westminster Abbey.

Bright Idea: 1895–1920

In the late 19th century, two Parisian factory workers, a Frenchman named Andre Blondell and a Turk named Mr. Psaroudaki, came upon the idea of enhancing the illuminating effects of gas lights by enclosing them in crystal glass globes. After refining their idea and detailing its design on paper in 1895 they were awarded France's patent number 563836 and formed a new firm, Holophane Company of France (from the Greek words Holos and Phanein, meaning "to appear wholly or completely luminous"). With their invention of a method for intensifying the illumination of artificial light sources, the science of prismatic refraction was born and with it a new industry. In 1896, a British firm licensed Blondell and Psaroudaki's patent and began manufacturing products incorporating the new technology under the name Holophane Ltd. Two years later, an American named Otis A. Mygatt purchased Blondell and Psaroudaki's patent rights from Holophane Ltd. and founded the Holophane Company of the United States in New York City.

In search of an appropriate location to house his new plant, Mygatt turned to his associate August Heisey, who allowed him to use the Heisey Glasswork Company's facility in Newark, Ohio, which by 1902 was up and running (and still used by Holophane in 1997). Mygatt's timing could not have been better. U.S. industry was growing by leaps and bounds and the availability of strong and efficient factory lights made night shifts possible and enabled workers to fabricate precise parts requiring brightly lit conditions more easily. Gone were the days when factory roofs had to be installed with skylights to illuminate the manufacturing floor and night-shift workers had to squint through the light cast by bare incandescent lamps. Holophane's prismatic glass reflectors not only solved the problem of poor illumination, they also did not wear out and required no maintenance.

In 1906 Mygatt's Holophane sponsored a meeting of U.S. lighting industry leaders at Holophane's New York office. In the course of the conference he established the Illuminating Engineering Society to promote the advancement of the field of scientific lighting, a role it continued to play in the 1990s. Over the next several years, Holophane invented the first method for measuring light intensity and light distribution. With this data the company began publishing the photometric performance of its products, enabling customers to determine precisely the amount of lighting they would need for every corner of their factories, offices, roadways, and outdoor areas. Lighting design had become a science.

Holophane's technical breakthroughs in prismatic refractors, reflectors, and lenses or globes improved American business's ability to control light. Light refractors were soon in use in gas street lights, and light reflectors were incorporated into many interior gas lights. When electric light began to replace gas light, Holophane's products proved just as useful in enhancing the illumination of electric light, and the nation's two largest producers of light bulbs—General Electric and Westinghouse—were soon promoting the use of Holophane's refractors and reflectors on the corrugated sleeves that contained their lamps. By 1910, Holophane also had introduced a method for measuring glare and had established optimal lighting patterns for roadways that were soon included in the Illuminating Engineering Society's standard industry lighting code. As a result of its development of glare measuring methods, Holophane's new-

est light refractors could disperse glare-free light over sharply defined areas. Holophane also began manufacturing refractor products to conform to its new road-lighting standards. Its early formulation of the principles of effective road lighting, including the appropriate positioning of lights at intervals along streets and highways, was still in use in the 1990s.

High Bays, NBC, and the Infrared Signal Lamp: 1920–1945

During the next several decades Holophane's growth continued to parallel that of U.S. industry as a whole. Manufacturing technology grew in sophistication, and higher wattage incandescent lamps were continually introduced. Holophane responded by designing and marketing ever larger prismatic reflectors for factory light fixtures. In the 1920s it also introduced "high-bay" lighting, which enabled large factories to be effectively illuminated for the first time. Moreover, by overcoming the problem of heat buildup, which had stood in the way of the widespread adoption of recessed lighting, Holophane became a leading manufacturer of recessed lighting products for offices, stores, and schools, a niche that would eventually become its largest and most profitable segment.

In 1932 the company took a decisive step forward when it designed special lighting equipment for NBC's Radio City studios in New York City. This was the first practical application of recessed incandescent "luminaires" (or light fixtures) using flat lenses. The result was the first truly recessed ceiling light system, in which no part of the lighting system protruded from the ceiling. Holophane was soon installing the lighting systems for other parts of the NBC network and, later, for CBS as well. Another major product breakthrough was the development of the first light reflector for use with mercury vapor lamps, which by the mid-1930s had become a practical light source for American industry.

America's entrance in the Second World War once again required Holophane to apply its technological resourcefulness to a new social need. Holophane's lights were used in countless airfields, hangars, and armaments factories throughout the war, and 50 years later some of the airfield runway lights it installed were still in use. Perhaps its most important contribution, however, was the infrared signaling lamp. German and Japanese submarines wreaked havoc among Allied fleets in part by honing in on the light of the signaling lamps used to exchange maneuvering information. To enable its fleets to slip through the seas undetected, the Allies needed a way for ships to signal each other without alerting enemy subs of their presence. Holophane answered by developing a signal lens that used invisible infrared radiation, or heat, rather than light. The innovation proved so successful that Holophane's invention remained a closely held secret of the U.S. Navy for many years. For its war contributions, Holophane was awarded two Army-Navy "E" awards for excellence, a commendation enjoyed by fewer than one percent of U.S. defense companies during World War II.

The Postwar Years: 1946–1971

In the decades after World War II, Holophane unleashed a stream of new lighting technologies that helped to transform the American factory and workplace. Over the next four decades it would establish the Light and Vision Conference Center for professionals and students interested in scientific light control and would introduce a system of "high-mast" lighting for highway throughways and interchanges that would improve illumination while reducing the number of light poles needed to light a road. It also developed new luminaires for high-intensity discharge (HID) lamps that allowed these traditionally outdoor lights to be introduced inside factories. Later improvements softened the intensity of the HID lamp's light, reduced the amount of sound it emitted, and minimized the heat it gave off, enabling Holophane eventually to introduce high-intensity discharge luminaires in offices and stores. Moreover, Holophane's Refractive Grid lens represented a significant improvement over cone prism lenses in reducing glare while increasing the amount of useful light emitted.

In the 1950s fluorescent lamp technology continued to improve, and during the decade Holophane introduced such innovations as the first recessed fluorescent fixture lens (offering enhanced glare-control features); the so-called cone prism lens that proved so successful it was still in production in the 1990s; and the first surface-mounted fluorescent wraparound luminaire, which combined very wide light distribution with excellent glare control and superior "cutoff" (the fixture's ability to keep light from shining above the fixture). With Holophane's development of the first luminaire ballast with a built-in heat-dissipating heat sink, lighting fixtures could run cooler for longer periods of time.

Holophane also suffered setbacks. In November 1956 the U.S. Supreme Court ruled that Holophane had violated U.S. antitrust law by agreeing with Holophane Ltd. of the United Kingdom and La Societe Anonyme Francaise Holophane of France to divide up the world's commercial lighting fixtures industries among themselves, each staying clear of the others' territories. The Court also ruled that the three Holophanes had agreed to pass new product discoveries along to each other and had secretly promised not to attempt to get patent or trademark protection in the others' territories. The U.S. Holophane countered that the anti-compete agreement had been inherited from the British firm Holophane Ltd. when the former had been purchased from the latter by its American owners at the turn of the century. It had not created the arrangement, it argued, so it should not be held accountable for it. The Supreme Court disagreed and ordered the U.S. Holophane to begin competing in its competitors' foreign markets and, if necessary, to change some of its overseas trademarks. Meanwhile, the company's net income, which had peaked at $1.7 million in 1957, began to slide, tripping to $1.3 million in 1958 and then lifting slightly to $1.5 million in 1959. Holophane's president, Charles Franck, lay the blame at the feet of its Canadian subsidiary, which had suffered because of a general economic slump in that country. When a shareholder at the October 1958 stockholder's meeting suggested that perhaps Holophane should split its stock price to make it cheaper, thereby encouraging public buying and media coverage, Franck snapped, "We don't want any gambling. We don't want people just buying and selling this stock; we like the privacy of our business. I can tell you the suggestion [to split the stock] is a waste of time. Management is against it." In June 1961, Franck was replaced at Holophane's helm by Clarence C. Keller, and Holophane's fortunes began to improve. From a level of $1.8 million in 1961–1962, net income rose to $2.1 million in 1963, $2.3 million in 1964, and then $2.9 million in 1965. In September 1965, Holophane returned to its roots by

acquiring, for $650,000, Holophane Ltd., the same company from which Holophane had sprung more than a half century before. It also drew on its heat-sinking technology to introduce the first integrally ballasted HID luminaire for indoor applications. HID represented a new source of light from fluorescent methods and Holophane quickly embraced it. The innovation meant significantly diminished installation costs for customers, and it shortly became standard equipment in almost all indoor and outdoor luminaires.

Holophane's net income rose to a historical high of $3.3 million in 1966–1967, only to fade to about $3 million in 1967–1968. "July and August [1967] weren't good months for us," Keller explained, "But ... we would expect that fiscal 1968 will be better than fiscal 1967." It was, and Holophane's net income rebounded to $3.1 million in 1968–1969. In October 1967, Keller disclosed his vision of Holophane's future to the New York Society of Security Analysts: "We are continuously exploring possibilities for acquiring organizations which might enable us to enter lighting fields in which we aren't heavily engaged," such as, he elaborated, the lighting of stadiums, tennis courts, and other recreational facilities, and architectural lighting, as for residences and hotel lobbies. A just completed plant expansion program had also given Holophane room to grow its business by 50 percent. As a result, Keller continued, "Our concern for the foreseeable future will be to develop sales rather than production facilities." By the end of September 1970, Holophane's sales had grown from $8 million the year before to $9.5 million. Keller described the gain as only "modest," however, because labor and materials costs and a general reduction in spending by government and industry were eating into Holophane's profit margin.

Johns-Manville's Lighting Division: 1971–1989

In April 1971 the building products giant Johns-Manville Corporation offered to buy Holophane in a stock swap that when approved by Holophane's board of directors resulted in a transaction valued at more than $60 million. While Holophane's board mulled the Manville offer, it snapped up the Strong Electric Corporation from Singer Co. in May. Within a week, the Manville deal was done, and after years as a publicly traded company Holophane officially became the Holophane Lighting Division of Johns-Manville.

Under Manville's umbrella, Holophane continued to innovate in the lighting fixtures business and experienced virtually uninterrupted growth. In the early 1970s it developed its first practical "High Mast" roadway lighting system for large highway interchanges, a niche in which it would become the world leader. The technology used a combination of reflectors and refractors to allow the greatest possible spacing thus far between roadway light poles and featured a device for conveniently raising and lowering the fixture for easy street-level maintenance. High Mast products were soon appearing in parking lots, container yards, rail yards, sea ports, and truck stops. In the 1980s Holophane also began using HID luminaires with "upright" and "sidelight" components. This allowed the ceiling itself to be used as a lighting element, improving illumination and visibility. After several years of research and development, in 1986 Holophane introduced its GranVille series of decorative lighting fixtures for design-sensitive projects like the renovation of Fisherman's Wharf in San Francisco. In November 1988 Manville, on the verge of bankruptcy because of asbestos-related lawsuits, announced that it was selling Holophane along with its sealing components business. In May 1989, Holophane's management and a group of financial advisers formed the Holophane Corporation to acquire the assets and capital stock of Manville's Holophane division for more than $100 million.

The DallePezze Years: 1989–1997

On July 1, 1989, Holophane became an independent company again for the first time in almost two decades, and by October John DallePezze, a former executive with N. L. Industries, was named Holophane's new president and CEO. DallePezze led Holophane to some of its best years ever, with record sales driven by a continuing stream of new product introductions. For example, Holophane updated its HID luminaire product line by introducing fixtures with as much as 60 percent upright, reflecting the trend toward brighter ceilings in the office construction industry. Known as PrismGlo, this series of fixtures was used in retail, textile, industrial, and other applications, most notably the cavernous parking garage of the O'Hare International Airport in Chicago.

Holophane's sales were given a big boost in 1992 when Congress passed the Federal Energy Act, which called for the abandonment of certain types of fluorescent lamps. In the long run the act improved sales of Holophane's line of HID fixtures and by 1993 Holophane's U.S. sales were up 13 percent over 1992. In 1993 Holophane also brought its new $4.5 million glass furnace on line, completed shipments of light fixtures for the retrofitting of the 182-mile London Underground subway, and introduced its Computer-Aided Lighting Analysis (CALA) software so sales reps could calculate accurate light levels for customers' sites. By reinvesting three to 3.5 percent of sales annually into new product development, well above the industry average, Holophane introduced four to five new products or enhancements of existing lines each year, and by 1995 products introduced since 1990 represented 25 to 30 percent of net sales. The new lines ranged from Prismalume and Paradome store lighting fixtures to the Holophane decorative Classics series, Big Eye emergency lighting fixtures, and Predator floodlights. But the largest product introduction in company history occurred in January 1996 when Holophane unveiled PoleStar, a family of outdoor architectural lighting fixtures designed for everything from parking lots and roadways to public common areas and bike paths. Aided by the discontinuation of its Canadian operations and the acquisition of Antique Street Lamps of Texas, a producer of decorative and historically styled light poles and fixtures, Holophane's net income rose to $151 million in 1994. In 1995, Holophane announced its plans to capitalize on the influx of highway funding made possible by the Intermodal Surface Transportation Efficiency Act. Throughout the year Holophane consolidated its Ohio operations and continued lowering its corporate debt. In the spring Holophane sent representatives on a China trade mission with the governor of Ohio and 14 other companies. Between 1996 and 1997 company officials made at least five more Asian sales trips, selling products from every corner of its product line. With Asian sales expected to exceed $1 million, Holophane planned new trade missions to Korea, Taiwan, and Australia. To solidify its international gains, Holophane also formed Holophane International Corporation, a foreign sales company; Holophane Lighting GmbH of Germany; and Holophane Australia Corporation Pty. Ltd. Holophane's biggest coup was domestic, however, when it won a contract with the city of Atlanta to install the lighting for 26 miles of the roadway leading to the Olympic Games.

Despite the jolt of income and publicity bestowed by the Olympics project, bad winter weather slowed U.S. construction activity in the first quarter of 1996, and Holophane was forced to lay off workers and watch as its earnings dropped 48 percent. In September it nevertheless made its second purchase of a Texas-based lighting firm by acquiring MetalOptics Inc., a producer of high-efficiency fluorescent lights, for $6.1 million. Through 1996 Holophane had enjoyed growth for 25 of the past 27 years and was sustaining an industry-leading ten percent annual growth rate.

Principal Subsidiaries

Holophane Canada, Inc.; Luxfab Limited (United Kingdom); Holophane Lichttechnik (Germany); Holophane Europe Limited (United Kingdom); Antique Street Lamps, Inc.; Castlight (Mexico); Holophane International, Inc. (Barbados); Holophane Australia Corporation Pty. Limited; Unique Lighting Solutions Pty. Limited (Australia); The Austphane Trust (Australia).

Further Reading

"Bedrock Principles: Let the Market Swing and Sway," *Barron's,* April 28, 1997.
Benedetti, Jef, "Holophane Increases Income in Third Quarter," *Daily Reporter* (Columbus), October 18, 1996.
——, "Holophane Sheds Light on Plans," *Daily Reporter* (Columbus), May 12, 1995.
Hill, Miriam, "Holophane Sees Bright Future," *Cleveland Plain Dealer,* February 16, 1997, p. 2H.
"Holophane Acquires Singer Unit," *Wall Street Journal,* May 19, 1971.
"Holophane Acquires Specialty Lighting Fixture Maker," *Daily Reporter* (Columbus), September 5, 1996.
"Holophane Approves Buyback," *Wall Street Journal,* February 25, 1994.
"Holophane Co. Net Rose in 1st Quarter; 2-for-1 Split Voted by Holders," *Wall Street Journal,* September 22, 1965.
"Holophane Expects Net in Year to End June 30 Equal or Above Fiscal 58," *Wall Street Journal,* October 17, 1958, p. 14.
"Holophane Files Suit Against Glendon Industries," *Business Wire,* April 8, 1997.
"Holophane Says Sales, Earnings Fell 10% to 15% in First Fiscal Quarter," *Wall Street Journal,* October 6, 1967, p. 21.
"Holophane Sues Over Patent Issue," *Daily Reporter* (Columbus), April 12, 1996.
"Johns-Manville Raises Its Offer To Merge with Holophane Co.," *Wall Street Journal,* May 24, 1971.
"Johns-Manville Set To Negotiate To Buy Holophane," *Wall Street Journal,* April 30, 1971, p. 8.
Preston, Candace L., "China Trade," *Business First* (Columbus), March 10, 1997.

—Paul S. Bodine

In-N-Out Burger

4199 Campus Drive, 9th Floor
Irvine, California 92715
U.S.A.
(714) 509-6200
Fax: (714) 854-3675

Private Company
Employees: 3,700
Sales: $120 million (1994)
SICs: 5812 Eating Places

In-N-Out Burger, a California Corporation, is a leading fast-food retail chain with more than 120 locations in California and Nevada. Known for its made-to-order hamburgers, fresh ingredients, and efficient service, it has maintained the same basic menu and a simple, customer-friendly philosophy since its founding in 1948. In-N-Out Burger is a private, family-run, nonfranchised company.

Dawn of the Drive-Thru: The Early Years

In-N-Out Burger started in the Los Angeles suburb of Baldwin Park, California, in 1948. Harry Snyder developed the idea of a drive-thru hamburger restaurant where customers would be able to order their food via a two-way speaker unit. This was a rather novel idea, as most hamburger stands of the post-World War II era employed carhops to serve food to customers seated in their cars. And so Harry Snyder and his wife, Esther, opened what is said to be California's first drive-thru restaurant. The menu was limited to burgers, french fries, soft drinks, and milk shakes. The Snyders' priorities were simple: serve customers high-quality, fresh food with efficient, friendly service in a clean and tidy environment. This business philosophy and the original menu have remained largely unchanged throughout the years.

It was very important to the Snyders to maintain control of each location in order to continue achieving the high standards they had set as In-N-Out Burger's norm. Thus, Harry and Esther Snyder did not rush to open further outlets. In fact, three years passed before they added a second In-N-Out Burger location. This new outlet was in the San Gabriel Valley east of Los Angeles in the town of Covina. As Californians became progressively car dependent and fast-food drive-thrus grew in popularity, the Snyders gradually added more outlets, some with double-lane drive-thrus to accommodate more customers. The Snyders' two sons, Rich and Guy, began working at In-N-Out Burger at an early age. They were expected to work in the restaurants and learn the business from the ground up.

Harry Snyder oversaw In-N-Out Burger until 1976, when he passed away from cancer. By then In-N-Out Burger had grown to 18 drive-thrus, all in Los Angeles County. Though only 24 years old, Rich Snyder assumed the role of president. His older brother, Guy, became vice-president, and Esther continued to work in the accounting department.

Corporate Strategy

Though Rich Snyder had plans for In-N-Out Burger's expansion and growth, one thing he would not change after taking over as president was the menu, which included the following items: Double-Double (a double cheeseburger); cheeseburger; hamburger; french fries; milk shakes in vanilla, chocolate, or strawberry; milk; coffee; pink lemonade; iced tea; and various sodas. The only addition to the original menu was a lemon-lime soda. A nonmenu item that eventually gained word-of-mouth popularity in southern California was the Animal—a Double-Double with grilled onions and extra sauce (all In-N-Out burgers came with a special sauce somewhat similar to Thousand Island dressing)—voted ''Best Off-the-Menu Special'' in the 1996 *Buzz Magazine* restaurant awards.

Refusing to change the menu was unusual for a fast-food chain, but adding other items, the Snyders feared, would affect the quality of the food and the service. By keeping the menu short, In-N-Out Burger could maintain control and guarantee high-caliber food. In the July 24, 1989, issue of *Forbes,* Rich Snyder stated, ''It's hard enough to sell burgers, fries and drinks right. And when you start adding things, it gets worse.''

Rich Snyder remained true to his parents' goal of serving only the freshest foods available. None of the ingredients were frozen, and no microwaves were used. All orders were made to

---

Company Perspectives:

In-N-Out Burger exists for the purpose of: 1. providing the freshest, highest-quality foods and services for a profit and a spotless, sparkling environment whereby the customer is our most important asset; 2. providing a team-oriented atmosphere whereby goal-setting and communications exist and providing excellent training and development for all of our associates; 3. assisting all communities in our marketplace to become stronger, safer, and better places to live.

---

order, contributing to what some in the food industry considered a long wait for a fast-food hamburger. The milk shakes were made with real ice cream, and the burgers were 100 percent beef. The beef was ground and formed into patties by In-N-Out workers at the Baldwin Park facility. The lettuce was broken into leaves by hand, and the buns were baked fresh using an old-fashioned sponge dough that took six to eight hours to rise. The potatoes for the french fries were shipped in burlap sacks to the outlets, where associates cut them by hand. In-N-Out has used southern California-grown Kennebec potatoes, which are said to be ideal for frying. The french fries have always been fried in cholesterol-free vegetable oil.

Rich Snyder also maintained his family's opposition to franchising. While McDonald's, which began the same year as In-N-Out, decided to franchise in 1954, the Snyders, though inundated with franchise inquiries, remained firm. They thought franchising would cause them to lose control of In-N-Out Burger and the business philosophy they had worked so hard to achieve and maintain. As Rich Snyder commented about franchising in *Forbes:* "My feeling is I would be prostituting my parents by doing that. There is money to be made by doing those things, but you lose something, and I don't want to lose what I was raised with all my life." Fast growth was not one of the Snyders' goals, but they did have plans for In-N-Out Burger's expansion.

The Snyders were also committed to viewing employees as if they were family members. Employees, called associates, were treated with respect. Pay was a step above that at other fast-food restaurants. In 1989 part-time associates earned $6 per hour, well above the minimum wage of $4.25. Managers made an average of $63,000 annually. The combination of intensive training and good wages parlayed the associates into capable and friendly workers. At In-N-Out the customer did not receive a pile of change but had the change counted back out loud. Because the Snyders demonstrated their appreciation of the associates, employee loyalty has been high at In-N-Out Burger. Some associates have been with the company for more than 20 years, and many have worked their way up from entry-level to managerial positions.

Growth in the 1980s

Soon after taking the reins at In-N-Out Burger, Rich Snyder founded a commissary at the In-N-Out Burger headquarters in Baldwin Park. The establishment of this commissary, where In-N-Out Burger could receive, store, and ship equipment and food supplies to its outlets, gave In-N-Out Burger quality control

over all In-N-Out ingredients. The commissary was a busy location: hamburger patties were formed, potatoes were checked for blemishes and quality, equipment was maintained, and supplies were received and distributed to In-N-Out locations. Rich Snyder also established the In-N-Out University in 1983. The university, a training school for new managers, reinforced In-N-Out Burger's business tenets and standards and ensured uniformity of management techniques and methods.

The number of outlets continued to grow steadily under Rich Snyder's guidance. Expansion, however, was still a slow process, which can be partly attributed to the difficulties involved in securing building permits. Because In-N-Out Burger's food was cooked to order, the average wait at a drive-thru was approximately 12 minutes, significantly longer than at other fast-food drive-thrus. This long wait occasionally resulted in traffic jams along busy urban streets, which caused city officials to delay building permits for In-N-Out Burger.

In-N-Out Burger changed tactics in the late 1980s and chose to open fewer double-lane drive-thrus and more restaurants with one drive-thru lane plus indoor and outdoor seating for patrons. The Snyders felt this change would accommodate larger crowds and better serve the customer, which was still one of their top priorities. Another change was their decision to lease property rather than to purchase it. Until 1989 In-N-Out Burger purchased most of their property. This meant seeking lower-priced locations, which were usually in outlying, suburban areas. Leasing property allowed In-N-Out to venture into more metropolitan areas with high property values, such as Santa Monica and West Los Angeles.

During Harry Snyder's leadership, expansion was limited to the Los Angeles County area. Rich Snyder decided to take In-N-Out Burger south of Los Angeles County to the growing counties of Orange, Riverside, and San Bernardino. Most of the outlets were strategically located near freeway or highway off-ramps in highly visible locations to cater to the car-reliant customer.

Rich Snyder also expanded the company's nonfood items. At In-N-Out customers could purchase not only a juicy burger but also t-shirts, bumper stickers, and caps. Because of the success of the t-shirts, Rich Snyder in 1989 began a mail-order catalog, which eventually also included pins, key chains, mugs, and golf balls. Most of the t-shirts were emblazoned with artists' renderings of vintage cars parked outside In-N-Out Burger drive-thrus, arousing the nostalgic spirit that pervaded In-N-Out.

In-N-Out Burger became active in donating funds to the prevention of child abuse in 1986. The In-N-Out Burger Foundation was established, and every April In-N-Out sponsored a company-wide fund-raising campaign. Canisters were placed in all In-N-Out outlets. In-N-Out matched three dollars for every dollar given up to $100,000. In-N-Out Burger also hosted a Children's Benefit Golf Tournament every spring. The money raised from this event was added to funds collected from the stores. All funds were then donated to various organizations throughout California with the intent to help abused and neglected children.

Corporate Changes in the Early 1990s

By the time Rich Snyder readied In-N-Out Burger to venture out of the Los Angeles area and into San Diego County in 1990, he had brought the number of locations up to 55. The first San Diego location was in Lemon Grove, south of the city of San Diego. The second unit, planned for northern San Diego County, was in Vista.

As In-N-Out Burger outlets were spreading outside Los Angeles County, Rich Snyder decided to relocate the corporate headquarters and the In-N-Out University from Baldwin Park to Irvine, California, a city 45 miles south in Orange County. The move, which took place in 1994, affected most of In-N-Out Burger's 200 corporate employees. The commissary, including the maintenance, meat plant, and warehouse employees, would remain in Baldwin Park. Irvine was home to the corporate offices of many other food-service giants, including Taco Bell, Red Robin, and El Torito. Another factor that might have been involved in selecting Irvine was that Rich Snyder resided in Newport Beach, located less than ten miles from Irvine.

On December 14, 1993, just months away from moving the corporate headquarters to Irvine, Rich Snyder was killed in a commuter plane crash. Snyder was on board an executive jet when it crash-landed at Irvine's John Wayne Airport. Snyder, Philip R. West (a childhood friend of Snyder's who was In-N-Out Burger's chief operating officer and executive vice-president), Jack Sims (another friend), and two pilots were killed. They were returning from a one-day trip to scout possible In-N-Out locations in southern California and also to attend the opening of a Fresno store. Snyder and West had a personal agreement not to fly on the same plane together but apparently had broken the policy for this flight. It is believed that Rich's mother, Esther, had also been aboard the plane, but she chose to deplane at an earlier stop.

Rich Snyder was 41 years old at the time of his death. He had been married for the first time just a year before and had a daughter. During his tenure as president, he had increased the number of In-N-Out Burger units from 18 to 93. A born-again Christian, philanthropist, and conservative Republican supporter, he began each company meeting with the Pledge of Allegiance. Rich Snyder led In-N-Out Burger to tremendous growth while maintaining the simple philosophy his parents adopted in 1948.

Growth from the Mid-1990s

As a result of Rich Snyder's untimely death, Esther Snyder assumed the role of president and continued to work in the corporate offices. Rich's brother, Guy Snyder, who had been an executive vice-president but had not been actively participating in daily management duties at the time of Rich's death, was named chairman of the board. Rich Snyder's widow was appointed to the board of directors.

In April 1994 the corporate headquarters relocated to Irvine, California, as planned. Expansion continued under Guy Snyder's direction, with new In-N-Out Burger outlets opening in northern California and Las Vegas, Nevada, as well as in towns with existing In-N-Out outlets. In-N-Out offered rentable cookout trailers for special occasions or corporate functions. Despite this growth, Guy Snyder did not stray from his family's business outlook and continued to promote simplicity, efficiency, and fresh, cooked-to-order food.

By the late 1990s, with more than 120 outlets in California and Nevada, In-N-Out Burger showed no signs of slowing down, and as the number of their restaurants grew, so did their popularity. In-N-Out Burger was the winner, for example, in the quick-service burger division in the 1997 *Restaurants & Institutions* annual poll. In-N-Out beat Wendy's, which had won the category for the previous eight years. According to the February 1, 1997, issue of *Restaurants & Institutions,* the criteria upon which the restaurants were judged included quality of food, menu variety, service, atmosphere, value, cleanliness, and convenience. In-N-Out Burger ranked first in four (quality of food, service, value, and cleanliness) of the seven categories. It was quite a coup for the family-owned chain, as this was the first year In-N-Out Burger was eligible to compete in the survey. In-N-Out Burger scored highly in the customer-loyalty category as well, with many respondents ranking it highest in overall satisfaction.

Within its base of southern California, In-N-Out was also maintaining a popular, almost cultlike following. In *Pasadena Weekly*'s "Best of 1996" readers' poll, In-N-Out Burger won the categories "Best Fast Food" and "Best Burger." And according to the July 24, 1989, issue of *Forbes,* In-N-Out Burger's following included movie stars and corporate executives. Bob Hope, David Letterman, Farrah Fawcett, and Ryan O'Neal were among some of In-N-Out's more famous patrons.

Further Reading

Martin, Richard, "In-N-Out Burger Pulls Away from Drive-thru-Only Focus," *Nation's Restaurant News,* June 19, 1989, pp. 3–4.

——, "Top In-N-Out Burger Execs Killed in Calif. Plane Crash," *Nation's Restaurant News,* January 3, 1994, pp. 1–2.

Paris, Ellen, "Where Bob Hope Buys His Burgers," *Forbes,* July 24, 1989, pp. 46–48.

Puzo, Daniel P., "America's Favorite Chains," *Restaurants & Institutions,* February 1, 1997, pp. 26–34.

Wright, Nils J., "In-N-Out Burger Wants into Sacramento Area," *The Business Journal Serving Greater Sacramento,* July 18, 1994, p. 1.

—Mariko Fujinaka

Inland Steel Industries

Inland Steel Industries, Inc.

30 West Monroe Street
Chicago, Illinois 60603
U.S.A.
(312) 346-0300
Fax: (312) 899-3197
Web site: http://www.inland.com

Public Company
Incorporated; 1893 as Inland Steel Company
Employees: 10,200
Sales: $4.58 billion (1996)
Stock Exchanges: New York
SICs: 3312 Blast Furnaces and Steel Mills; 5051 Plate,
Sheet and Strip, Except Coated Products; 3399 Bars,
Iron: Made in Steel Mills; 1011 Primary Finished or
Semifinished Shapes; 4432 Metals Service Centers
and Offices

Inland Steel Industries, Inc. is a materials management, logistics, and technical services company that provides value-added steel products and materials-related services to manufacturers in the automotive, appliance, furniture, equipment, electric motor and a variety of other industries. As a holding company, it has three operating units which are wholly-owned subsidiaries. Inland Steel Co. is the sixth largest steel producer in the nation; Inland International Inc., sells, trades and distributes steel and other industrial materials globally; and Inland Materials Distribution Group, which is the largest metals distributor in the United States and operates some 50 steel service centers nationwide. In addition, Inland has an interest in Ryerson Tull, Inc., the largest North American metals and industrial plastics service center operator, and partnerships overseas with such nations as Mexico, China, and India, which enable Inland to provide steel products to industrial users.

Inland Steel has long been one of the most innovative and technologically advanced major U.S. steel companies, as well as one of the most successful of the major independents in the steel industry. In fact, the company has a reputation as a top performer in both prosperous and lean periods for steel producers. In the early 1980s, when a poor economy coupled with the rising tide of imports and a depressed international steel market took its toll on the whole of the industry, Inland remained a leader in modernization and in utilizing technology. By relying on continued new developments in steel production, Inland was restored to profitability by the early 1990s.

Nineteenth-Century Founding

Inland had its beginnings in the depression of 1893. It was in that year that the Chicago Steel Works, a manufacturer of farm equipment, along with many other companies, went out of business. A group that included a foreman from the defunct company made an attempt to form a new company to begin producing steel on a site that Chicago Steel Works had acquired, in the village of Chicago Heights, Illinois. The necessary capital to finance the venture, however, could not be found, until the group enlisted Joseph Block, a Cincinnati, Ohio, iron merchant, who was in Chicago to visit the World's Fair. He brought his son Phillip D. Block into the venture.

After incorporating as Inland Steel Company in October 1893 and purchasing the idle machinery of Chicago Steel Works, Inland was ready to begin production in early 1894. By the end of the year, another of Joseph Block's sons, L.E. Block, had joined the company. In the next few years, the business grew steadily, with production centered on agricultural implements. Sales were boosted by a new product, the side rails for bed frames.

In 1897 sales topped $350,000, and the company, which had been sinking much of its profits into improving machinery at the mill, purchased the East Chicago Iron and Forge Company and renamed it Inland Iron and Forge. The new addition was operated by L.E. Block and produced equipment for the railroad industry. The plant was sold in 1901 for ten times its original purchase price of $50,000.

By the end of the 19th century Inland was doing well, and sales were growing steadily. In 1901 it found itself in a position to accept an offer by a real estate developer promising 50 acres of land to any firm that would spend at least $1 million to build a steel plant on the site. The patch of land was beside Lake Michigan, which could provide water needed for operating a mill and a waterway for transporting material. The land was also near several major railroad lines. In 1902, when the first phase of construction of the new Indiana Harbor, Indiana, plant was completed, Inland had a steel ingot capacity of 60,000 tons. Due to a general recession, Inland lost $127,000 in 1903–1904. Due to debt and the recession, from 1901 until 1906 the company did not pay dividends. By 1905, however, the plant got its first big order, for 30,000 tons of steel channels and plates.

In 1906, to meet the growing demand for steel, Inland added its fifth open hearth furnace and constructed the first blast furnace in northern Indiana. By purchasing the lease on an iron mine in Minnesota, Inland ensured itself of a source of iron ore to feed its furnaces that allowed it to reduce costs and significantly increase steel production. Production was increased further as Inland added more open hearth furnaces and sheet mills. In 1911 the Inland Steamship Company was formed to transport ore from Inland's growing mining concerns in Minnesota to the Indiana Harbor mill. A year later, Inland was manufacturing spikes and rivets for the railroad industry.

Innovations and Expansion in the Early 20th Century

By 1914, when Joseph Block died, Inland had a steel ingot capacity of 600,000 tons. Capacity reached one million tons by 1917, and to accommodate the world market's growing demand for steel, Inland completed construction of a second plant at Indiana Harbor that year. Demand for steel increased during World War I, and following the war, between 1923 and 1926, all of the mills and machinery at the new plant were completely electrified, which provided the efficient production. When the war ended, the railroad industry became Inland's top customer, replacing agriculture. When Phillip D. Block became president of Inland in 1919, Inland started to improve working conditions and to provide benefits for its employees. It was one of the first companies in the steel industry to introduce an eight-hour workday. The measure was soon abandoned, however, when the rest of the industry did not follow suit. In 1920 Inland was the first steel company to adopt a pension plan for its employees.

In the early 1920s Inland began to make steel rails in its 32-inch roughing and 28-inch finishing mills that previously had been used only for rolling structural shapes. This was an innovation in the steel industry, and within a short time rolling and finishing rails was Inland's most successful operation in terms of both sales and earnings. At the same time, the company

spent $1 million to build a structural steel finishing mill. During this period, Inland continued to modernize and expand. Millions of dollars were spent to improve quality and efficiency as demand for steel rose and sales skyrocketed.

The early 1920s were not only a time of great prosperity for the steel industry, they were also a period of upheaval. The second great wave of mergers and attempted mergers in the steel industry since the turn of the century began in 1921. As it had been in the early 1900s, Inland was again the object of schemes designed to merge smaller independent companies into one huge corporation. A plan initiated in 1921 envisioned the consolidation of seven large steel companies—Inland, Republic Steel Corporation, Brier Hill, Lackawanna, Midvale Steel and Ordnance, Youngstown, and Steel and Tube Company of America. Rumors of the proposed plan circulated in the press in late 1921 and early 1922, but in May 1922 Lackawanna withdrew from the plan. Negotiations continued between Republic, Inland, and Midvale. After the Federal Trade Commission (FTC) issued a complaint in August 1922, however, executives of the three companies announced that financing would be difficult while the legal issues raised by the FTC complaint were being resolved. The plan was dropped.

Sales at Inland increased, and while the company continued to spend on expansion, it became the number one U.S. steel company in rate of return on fixed assets in the period from 1926 to 1930. In 1928 Inland was able to acquire a limestone quarry on the upper peninsula of Michigan, and formed Inland Lime and Stone Company. Inland acquired another source of raw materials by purchasing 15 acres of land in Kentucky holding high-grade coking coal.

Inland's expansion continued through the late 1920s and did not stop even when the Great Depression hit in 1929. Between 1929 and 1932 Inland spent $30 million on expansion. In 1932, the only Depression year in which Inland was not in the black, the company unveiled the widest continuous hot-strip mill in the United States. At a cost of $15 million, the mill was 76 inches wide and would later be used to roll sheet for the auto industry and for the navy during World War II. While 1932 was a financially dismal year for Inland, operating at only 25 percent of capacity, that figure was one-third higher than that for the balance of the industry. During the period from 1931 to 1935, Inland's operating profit in terms of fixed assets was 6.1 percent, the highest in the industry.

At the time that Inland built the new mill, competition in the steel industry was intense, and Inland was forced to compete with companies like United States Steel, among others, that had their own warehouse operations through which to market its products. To remain competitive with its rivals, Inland chose to go into the steel warehouse business and in 1935 acquired Joseph T. Ryerson and Son Inc., a steel-warehousing and -fabricating chain. Ryerson provided an outlet through which Inland's customers could buy steel and have it custom processed. In 1936 Inland acquired Milcor Steel Company of Milwaukee, Wisconsin, which made a wide variety of steel products and had plants and warehouses in seven cities. Milcor provided Inland with a market for the products of its sheet-rolling mills.

War and Labor Unrest in the 1940s

When World War II began, Inland, still under the direction of Chairman Phillip D. Block, immediately began a program of expansion to provide added capacity by building new blast furnaces and coke ovens to provide steel for bombs, shells, tanks, ships, and planes. By 1944 Inland had become completely integrated. The company controlled its own sources of raw materials including coal, ore, and limestone. With a total ingot capacity of 3.4 million tons by 1944, Inland's sales in the years between 1940 and 1950 ranged from $200 million to $400 million per year.

In the 1940s prosperity was tempered somewhat by a series of labor disputes in which the United Steel Workers of America (USWA) sought higher wages and certain benefits for its members. Although labor and industry had agreed to a no-strike, no-lockout pledge during the early 1940s, steel workers across the country went on strike to demand a $1 a day wage increase in March 1942. The effects of the strike on war production were not significant, and Inland and the USWA signed a contract covering working conditions for the company's 14,000 employees at both Indiana Harbor and Chicago Heights.

A much more serious strike, involving 750,000 steel workers, took place in 1946 and virtually crippled the steel industry as production fell to its lowest level in half a century. The strike lasted 26 days and affected 11,000 employees at Inland's Indiana Harbor and Chicago Heights plants. Only after Inland and the other companies involved agreed to a wage raise of 18.5¢ per hour did the strike end. Inland was then able to continue to produce the steel required by the huge postwar demand for consumer products. The steel Inland produced then went primarily to the automobile and home-appliance industries. After the war, Inland continued to expand its facilities for sheet and strip and also acquired more property from which to mine raw materials, in Minnesota, Michigan, and Kentucky. In 1945 Phillip D. Block resigned as chairman after serving for more than 22 years. He was replaced by his brother, L.E. Block, who served until 1951.

The Postwar Period

During the early 1950s expansion slowed at Inland. From 1952 to 1955 steel production capacity increased by 700,000 tons. This was half the amount needed to close the gap between Chicago area demand and capacity. In the years between 1947 and 1958 Inland's capital expenditures of $121 million were the most modest among the major steel companies. Expansion, however, picked up during the steel boom of 1956, when Inland began a new program in which the company spent $360 million to modernize its plants, to acquire new mining properties, and to build a steel building to serve as its new headquarters in downtown Chicago. The stainless steel for the curtain walls of the 19-story building had to be purchased from another steel company because Inland was still producing carbon steel almost exclusively.

Although the early 1950s were relatively unremarkable for Inland in terms of production and growth, they marked the beginning of a decade that was to include two bitter and costly disputes between the steel workers and the industry. The first

conflict began in November 1951 when the USWA notified the industry that it wanted to bargain for a wage increase. In December, after no agreement was reached, union president Phillip Murray called for a strike. Almost immediately, President Harry S Truman referred the case to the Wage Stabilization Board. The board held hearings and made a recommendation that the union accepted but that was rejected by the industry. In April 1952 the board tried unsuccessfully to avert a strike. A few days later, on the eve of a strike, President Truman issued an order for the nation's steel mills to be seized by the government to keep them open and avert a strike. The industry was outraged by the president's order and Inland's president, Clarence B. Randall, was chosen to give the industry's viewpoint in an address that was broadcast on nationwide radio and television. Randall called the president's order an ''evil deed'' that he had no legal right to issue. The U.S. Supreme Court agreed that the move was not legal and in June 1952 ordered that the mills be returned to their owners. Within a few hours, 600,000 workers walked off their jobs to begin a strike that would affect 95 percent of the nation's steel mills and would last for 55 days.

Randall became chairman of Inland in 1953. After a few years of calm, the industry and the USWA became involved in another dispute that was to prove the longest and most costly in the industry's history. The dispute began in May 1959 when the industry called for a wage freeze. When negotiations stalled in July 500,000 steel workers went on strike. In October, President Dwight D. Eisenhower applied for an 80-day injunction under the Taft-Hartley Act, ordering the workers back to the plants while negotiations continued. The Supreme Court upheld the injunction, and the plants reopened in November. In January 1960 the USWA won an agreement that gave it a substantial wage increase. The agreement brought to an end the 116-day strike that had shut down the steel industry and forced the closing of automobile plants because of a shortage of steel.

The 1960s: New Facilities and Processes

As the 1960s began, the steel industry planned record production to fill consumer orders and replenish inventories left depleted by the strike. Inland's steel shipments in the years 1961 to 1965 averaged 4.1 million tons per year, compared to 3.6 million tons per year in the previous five years. To keep up with new production demands, Inland embarked on a new expansion program in 1962. The plan included a new 80-inch continuous hot strip mill as well as Inland's first oxygen steel-making shop. The new shop meant a shift away from the open hearth steelmaking process. It had a capacity to produce more than two million tons per year and enabled Inland to close down its oldest open hearth furnace plant, which had been operating for 60 years, since 1902.

The expansion plan was completed in 1966 and helped Inland to lower costs, improve product quality, and increase capacity. An important milestone for Inland was the completion in 1967 of its new research facilities in East Chicago, Indiana, where company scientists could investigate new processes in steel metallurgy and production. The large amount of capital that Inland invested in expansion in the mid-1960s, along with stronger competition, had the effect of lowering earnings by 25 percent in the period from 1964 to 1967. Joseph L. Block, who succeeded Randall as chairman in 1959, believed that the expansion was important for the future, as Inland faced stiff competition for its midwestern market.

When Joseph L. Block retired in 1967, he had earned a reputation as a maverick in the steel industry. In 1962, when the steel industry had clashed with President John F. Kennedy over a proposed rise in steel prices, Block broke with industry ranks and insisted that the time was not right for a steel price hike. In 1966, however, Block took the lead in raising prices with the largest increase since 1963. Block was well known, as reported in *Time* magazine, November 3, 1967, for strengthening "Inland's reputation as a civic-minded company" by among other things supporting a fair-employment law in Illinois as well as a redevelopment project for East Chicago.

New Leadership for the 1970s

Block was replaced as chairman by his cousin Phillip D. Block, Jr. Under the new chairman, Inland was able to maintain its share of the midwestern market and also achieved the highest profit-to-sales ratio among the big-eight steel makers. In the late 1960s, as competition increased from foreign imports and markets eroded, Inland began a diversification program. The first step was into the housing market with the acquisition of Scholz Homes Inc. and later the formation of Inland Steel Urban Development Corporation. By 1974 diversification had led Inland into areas such as steel building products, powdered metals, and reinforced plastics.

The steel business started off slowly in the 1970s for the whole industry. Profits were down, and Inland's net profit declined from $81.7 million in 1968 to $46.7 million in 1970. By 1974, however, things had turned around, and the steel industry experienced one of the biggest booms in its history. After a tight period in the previous two years, demand for steel increased dramatically in 1974, and Inland's sales climbed to $2.5 billion. With demand showing no evidence of slowing, Inland, under Chairman Frederick G. Jaicks, who had replaced Phillip D. Block Jr. in 1971, made plans for a $2 billion expansion, which it planned to finance from strong earnings and outside financing. Inland, however, along with the rest of the industry was hurt by the recession of 1975, and by 1977 the industry, plagued by overcapacity, faced another downturn, as imports flooded the market at prices domestic companies were unable to match. Inland's earnings slumped as costs went up and demand dropped, forcing the company to hold up the first phase of its expansion plan.

Business turned around for Inland in 1978, a record year for the company, in which it was able to capture 6.5 percent of the domestic steel market. The company produced 8.6 million tons of steel and generated profits of $158.3 million on $3.25 billion in sales. By the early 1980s, however, the steel industry was in trouble again. A combination of factors, including the high level of imports, decreased demand, and an oversupply of steel drove down prices at the same time that costs such as labor and energy were on their way up. These factors, combined with high investment expenses as well as depressed midwestern industries—autos, farming, construction, and appliances—caused Inland's profits to drop 64 percent from their 1978 peak to $57.3 million in 1981.

Inland suffered four straight years of losses totaling $456 million in 1982 through 1985. The company was forced to shut down some of its steel mills and to lay off some workers. Yet Inland continued to develop new products and improve production efficiency. The company had success with lightweight, high-strength, and corrosion-resistant steel for the auto, farm, and construction industries; and in 1981 it was able to push its market share to a record 6.7 percent.

Recovering from Industry Downturns

In order to survive in a depressed industry, Inland—under Chairman Frank Luerssen, who took over in 1983—cut costs by shutting down unprofitable operations and divesting itself of certain assets. Inland began to sell various subsidiaries, including companies that had supplied it with raw materials. In addition, seven major operations at the Indiana Harbor works were shut down. Steel making capacity was reduced by 30 percent. While producing less steel, Inland began to shift its efforts into more profitable areas such as its highly successful steel-distribution operations which it sought to expand by acquiring J.M. Tull Metals Company, a large metal-products maker, processor, and distributor, in 1986.

In May 1986 Inland made a move to separate its waning steel manufacturing operations from its profitable steel distribution sector by reorganizing as Inland Steel Industries, Inc., a holding company for Inland Steel Company, and Inland Steel Services, Inland's service-center operations. Inland executives hoped that the reorganization would facilitate diversification and joint ventures.

Shortly thereafter, Inland formed a partnership with a Japanese firm, Nippon Steel Corporation. The partnership, known as I/N Tek, was created to construct a continuous cold rolling facility near New Carlisle, Indiana. The I/N Tek facility was the only U.S. continuous cold rolling mill. By combining five basic operations that were usually done separately, the facility was able to complete in less than an hour a process that had taken as many as 12 days. The cold rolled steel produced by the plant was used for, among other applications, autos and appliances. Another joint venture with Nippon Steel, I/N Kote, was started in 1989 to construct and operate two steel-galvanizing lines adjacent to the I/N Tek facility. The project was to be used in combination with I/N Tek to galvanize the cold rolled steel.

With profits having declined 54 percent in 1989 and losses of $21 million for 1990, Inland expected its continued expansion and modernization through projects such an I/N Tek and I/N Kote to result eventually in profits nearly double the then-record $262 million earned in 1988. Such a turnaround would ensure that Inland would remain an industry leader in growth and technology, while once again becoming a top industry performer.

The 1990s and Beyond

By 1994, the steel industry began to recover. The overall economy had picked up and there was an increased demand for cars—good news for Inland, which was a leading supplier of steel to such auto makers as Honda, Toyota, Ford, General Motors, and Chrysler. Also, the dollar remained inexpensive so that foreign competitors with their cheaper currencies didn't have the advantage of asking lower prices, and difficulties with labor unions were resolved.

As a result of these combined factors, in 1994 Inland enjoyed its first profit since 1989. Other moves by the company also ensured greater revenues and profits. Inland closed some units that were unprofitable; sold off businesses that were outside its core steel business; and began the search for emerging markets overseas to compensate for slower growth in the domestic market. A separate operating unit, the company's third, was created. Called Inland International, the unit sold and distributed products to industrial customers all over the world.

One market was Mexico, where the company formed a joint venture in 1994 with Altos Hornos de Mexico S.A., to be called Ryerson de Mexico. In 1995, a joint venture was created with China's Baoshan Iron and Steel, called Ryerson de China; and another to deal with exports was formed in Hong Kong with two partners: South African Macsteel and Canada's Federal Industries. In 1996, a partnership was formed in India between Inland Steel Industries and Tata Iron and Steel Co. of Numbai, called Tata-Ryerson, which provided industrial materials management services to Indian customers.

Inland had focused on serving high-end customers with high quality steel bars and other products. However, some quality problems resulted in the loss of some customers and the company returned to the commodity steel markets.

As the 1990s drew to a close, steel prices remained strong and demand for steel had remained constant. Moreover, the steel industry was experimenting with the development of alternative irons and new ways to fire up furnaces for ironmaking, such as using pulverized-coal injection (PCI). The next century thus seemed an exciting time for the steel industry, and for innovative Inland Steel, in particular.

Principal Subsidiaries

Inland Steel Co.; Inland International Inc.; Ryerson Tull, Inc. (87%).

Principal Divisions

Inland Steel Bar Company; Inland Steel Flat Products Company; I/N Tek (60%); I/N Kote (50%); I.M.F. Steel International, Ltd. (Hong Kong; 50%); Inland Industries de Mexico SA de CV; Inland International Trading, Inc.

Further Reading

Gilbert, R., and W. Korda, *The Story of Inland Steel,* Chicago: Inland Steel Company, 1974.
"Help Thy Customer, Help Thyself," *Forbes,* December 18, 1995, pp. 196–197.
"New Lease on Life," *Forbes,* May 9, 1994, pp. 82–87.
"Picking Nickels Off the Floor," *Forbes,* October 26, 1992, pp. 106–108.

—Patricia Leichenko
—updated by Dorothy Kroll

International Speedway Corporation

P.O. Box 2801
Daytona Beach, Florida 32120-2801
U.S.A.
(904) 254-2700
Fax: (904) 254-6712

Public Company
Incorporated: 1953
Employees: 4,000
Sales: $96 million (1996)
Stock Exchanges: NASDAQ
SICs: 7948 Racing Including Track Operations

International Speedway Corporation is one of the largest and most prestigious promoters of car and motorcycle racing in the United States. Three of the company's properties are the premiere speedways of America, including Daytona International Speedway, location of the Daytona 500, the most popular stock car race in the world; Darlington Raceway, located in South Carolina, site of the first stock car superspeedway; and Talladega Superspeedway, situated in Alabama and widely regarded as the most competitive of all the stock car tracks in the United States. Other company operations include the Tucson Raceway in Arizona and the Watkins Glen International Road Course in New York, where management controls a 50 percent interest. Although International Speedway Corporation is best known for its management of Daytona, Darlington, and Talladega raceways, the company also promotes a number of annual racing events across the United States, such as the Winston Cup Races and the Busch Grand National Races, the most high-profile sports car endurance race in the country. Attracted to the growth of motor racing as a major spectator sport, blue-chip companies like Pepsi, Anheuser-Busch, Sears, Gatorade, Ford, Chevrolet, and Goodyear Tire have expanded their participation in and sponsorship of races promoted by International Speedway Corporation.

Early History

The history of racing and the legendary names of automotive competition in the Daytona Beach area of the state of Florida can be traced back to 1903. Legend has it that racing on the beach started when two gentlemen entered into a friendly wager as to which one of them had the most reliable and fastest "horseless carriage." That one wager, and resulting race, gave rise to what soon became known as the "Birthplace of Speed." Within a very short time, the wagers between gentlemen stopped but the competition to settle who had the fastest automobile continued. As word of the competition grew, and more people began to visit Daytona Beach just to view the automotive races, even the nascent film industry took an interest. The 1905 silent movie, "Automobile Races at Ormond, Florida," provided the first glimmerings of an allure that would attract people for years to come. Suddenly, throngs of people came to watch the speed trials for the ever-improving motorized road vehicles. One of the most famous of all the speed trials during these early years involved Ransom E. Olds, the creator of what was later known as the "Oldsmobile" and the first man to engage in a race on Daytona Beach in a timed run.

During the years leading up to World War I, Daytona Beach attracted competitors from around the world to test the speed of their automobiles. In fact, most of the land speed records set during the early part of the 20th century were accomplished by drivers at Daytona Beach. Although the advent of World War I and America's involvement in the European conflict slowed the development of Daytona Beach as the gathering place for land speed trials, nonetheless, the attraction to the Florida location experienced an immediate resurgence following the end of the war in November of 1918.

Through the 1920s, and even during the height of the Great Depression, Daytona Beach attracted drivers who competed in speed time trials. As the Daytona Beach races grew in reputation and prominence, drivers from as far away as Britain, France, Italy, Hungary, Germany, and Spain become regular competitors. Major H.O.D. Segrave of Great Britain was the first man to exceed 200 mph on the beach. Frank Lockhart from the United States died on the same stretch of beach while attempting to establish a new speed record. As the motor car developed in both power and speed, however, the organizers of the Daytona Beach speed trials soon recognized that racing cars were outgrowing the facilities available at the beach. As a result of these developments, it was decided that the speed trials should be relocated to the Bonneville Salt Flats in the state of Utah. The last (and one of the legendary) land speeds trials on Daytona Beach was held in March of 1935, when Sir Malcolm Campbell in his famous Bluebird V set the best speed ever recorded on the beach at 276 mph.

Having already firmly established an international reputation as the "Birthplace of Speed" in the automotive racing industry, the organizers of the original Daytona Beach speed trials began looking for something new to continue the area's famous legacy. They found it in stock car racing. Although not a brand new sport, the organizing committee initiated a decidedly innovative approach. Regularly scheduled stock car races would be held on a course that combined a portion of Daytona Beach with a portion of a public road. The original course of 3.2 miles incorporated a north turn immediately south of the center of the city of Daytona. Running approximately 1.5 miles on the beach and then turning 1.5 miles onto a paved public highway, the two sections of the course were connected by banked sand turns. The inaugural race on March 8, 1936 signaled the start of a new era in the history of racing at Daytona Beach. Most of the initial competitors were from the United States, but as the reputation of the race grew, drivers from around the world began to flock to the beach once again. Not satisfied with sitting on their laurels, the organizers decided to take the next step and on January 24, 1937 inaugurated the Daytona 200 motorcycle race, the first of its kind in racing history.

World War II and the Postwar Years

Because of the reconfiguration of most American industrial factories in the name of national defense, racing at Daytona Beach was suspended for the duration of World War II. Most of the organizers closely associated with the racing at Daytona Beach were either serving in the Armed Forces or working in various industrial capacities for the American war effort. When the war ended in the summer of 1945, the organizers banded together once again to restart the racing tradition at Daytona Beach.

One of the most important influences on the postwar era of racing at Daytona was a man named Bill France. France, a mechanic from a local shop in Daytona, had entered the first stock car race in March of 1935. Although he had finished fifth in the race, he developed a lifelong enthusiasm for the sport of racing. During the war, France worked as a welder and mechanic building submarine chasers at the Daytona Beach Boat

Works. But when the war ended, he once again took his place among the competitors at Daytona Beach.

After the 1946 racing season had come to an end, France decided to retire from competitive racing and devote his energies to promoting stock car and motorcycle racing on the beach. A tireless and enthusiastic man, in 1947 France initiated the organizational meetings for what was to become NASCAR, the National Association for Stock Car Auto Racing. NASCAR was established in 1948, and France and NASCAR became the driving force behind Daytona Beach racing.

One of the most important actions taken by France and NASCAR during the years after World War II was the promotion of a new design for the beach/road course in Daytona. The racing circuit was moved down to the south end of the beach, near Ponce Inlet, primarily because of the growth in Daytona. The newly designed course measured 2.2 miles for stock cars and 4.1 miles for motorcycles. Yet France soon realized that the continued and rapid growth in both Daytona's population and the racing crowds signaled the end of racing on the beach. Consequently, in April of 1953, France decided to form his own corporation, Bill France Racing, and begin planning the construction of a permanent speedway facility in Daytona.

By 1955, France's dream of a modern speedway facility in Daytona began to take shape when he entered into negotiations with the Daytona Beach Racing and Recreational Facilities Authority to construct and operate a $2.5 million motorsports arena. After private funding had been arranged for building the facility, the most up-to-date engineering and construction methods were used to follow the blueprint for a 2.5-mile tri-oval circuit that incorporated 31-degree banking in both its east and west turns.

In November of 1957, the Daytona Beach Racing and Recreational Facilities Authority signed an agreement with France and his Daytona International Speedway Corporation to lease the property indefinitely. One year later, the beach/road course was used the final time for auto racing.

With much fanfare and publicity, the Daytona International Speedway hosted its inaugural race on February 22, 1959. The first Daytona 500 fielded an array of 59 cars and posted a sweepstakes award totaling $67,760. More than 41,000 people were in attendance to watch the first race of the Daytona 500. As history would have it, they were not disappointed. The finish of the race was too close to call, yet Johnny Beauchamp was declared the "unofficial winner" and basked in the adulation of Victory Lane. Unfortunately for Beauchamp, the final results were determined three days later by a clip of newsreel that provided conclusive evidence that Lee Petty had won the close race in his Oldsmobile. The first of many close stock car races that enhanced the reputation of Daytona International Speedway, it was followed by another dramatic finish on July 4th when Fireball Roberts won the first Firecracker 250 stock car race in a modified Pontiac.

The Growth of Racing from the 1960s through the 1980s

During the next three decades, many new races were added to the schedule of Daytona International Speedway. The last motorcycle race on Daytona Beach was held in 1960; one year later it was moved to the Speedway, with Roger Reiman winning the first Daytona 200 on a Harley-Davidson. In 1962, Dan Gurney won the first Daytona Continental Sports Car Race in a Lotus Ford. Other races established during these years included the Pepsi 400; the Daytona Speedweeks, a 16-day preliminary set of races that initiates the major league racing season; the Rolex 24 at Daytona; the Exxon World SportsCar Championship and Supreme GT Series; the Busch Clash and Daytona ARCA 200; the ARCA Bondo/Mar-Hyde Supercar Series; the Gatorade 125-Mile Qualifying Races for the NASCAR Winston Cup, which determines the entrants for the Daytona 500; the Discount Auto Parts 200; the Firebird International Race of Champions; and the Daytona 300 NASCAR Busch Race.

By the early 1980s, Daytona International Speedway had become so famous that the running of the 25th anniversary of the Daytona 500 was a major international sports event. Drivers from more than 20 countries competed for the honor of driving in Victory Lane, which was won by Cale Yarborough in his Super-Pontiac. In 1984, President Ronald Reagan was the Grand Marshal for the NASCAR Winston Cup Race, won by Richard Petty. During these years, corporate sponsorship of racing at Daytona increased dramatically. Racing became known as one of the few sports where commercialism was not only accepted but expected. As a result, major corporations such as Ford, Chevrolet, Gatorade, DuPont, Goodyear, Anheuser-Busch, STP, and Western Auto signed on to sponsor major races at Daytona Speedway, which had the effect of significantly offsetting costs associated with those races.

The 1990s and Beyond

Having changed its name from the Daytona International Speedway to International Speedway Corporation, the firm, which was first headed by Bill French and then by his son, began to expand its holdings in the early 1990s. Talladega Superspeedway in Alabama, Darlington Raceway in South Carolina, and Tucson Raceway in Arizona were purchased by International Speedway Corporation. In addition, management decided to acquire a 50 percent interest in Watkins Glen International Road Course in New York. The company also purchased a 12 percent interest in Penske Motorsports, Inc., the owner and operator of Michigan International Speedway and Nazareth Speedway in Pennsylvania. In 1996, the company initiated construction of a new, state-of-the-art California Speedway, located near Los Angeles.

During the 1990s, International Speedway Corporation expanded into areas other than speedway operation and management and racing promotion. American Service Corporation was formed by International Speedway Corporation to operate the food, beverage, and souvenir concession stands at the Daytona, Talladega, and Darlington speedways. Also responsible for providing catering services to corporate customers in suites at these facilities, in 1995 Americrown expanded its services to other unaffiliated sporting events, such as the LPGA championships. International Speedway Corporation added a radio station to its holdings, MRN Radio Network, to produce and syndicate races promoted by the company. Finally, in July of 1996, the company opened Daytona USA, a motorsports museum and theme park complex that includes such attractions as interactive media, racing exhibits, theaters, and a racing museum.

One of the fastest growing spectator sports in the United States is stock car racing, and International Speedway Corporation is at the forefront of its development and promotion. More than 70 stock car, sports car, truck, and motorcycle races are held annually at the company's properties, and nearly 80 percent of its income is derived from NASCAR sanctioned races at Daytona, Talladega, and Darlington. With increased revenues every year during the 1990s, International Speedway Corporation has a clear road ahead for ever-larger profits.

Principal Subsidiaries

Americrown Service Corporation; MRN Radio Network; Daytona USA; Daytona International Speedway, Inc.; Darlington Speedway, Inc.; Talladega Speedway, Inc.; Watkins Glen Speedway, Inc.; Tucson Raceway Park, Inc.; Daytona Properties, Inc.

Further Reading

Cohen, Adam, "Blowing the Wheels Off Bubba," *Time,* February 26, 1996, pp. 56–57.
"From the Green to the Pits," *Forbes,* July 4, 1994, p. 20.
Mitchell, Mary A., "Racing Museum Revs Up," *Travel Weekly,* July 11, 1996, p. F3.
——, "Winter Business Picks Up Speed," *Travel Weekly*, March 21, 1994, p. F26.
Powell, Tom, "NASCAR Touring Show To Make Debut in August," *Amusement Business,* May 23, 1994, p. 15.
Rouch, Chris, "Red Necks, White Socks, and Blue Chip Sponsors," *Business Week,* August 15, 1994, p. 74.
Sullivan, Lee, "Brickyard Brickbats," *Forbes,* April 11, 1994, p. 20.
Waddell, Ray, "Interactive Motorsports Attraction Daytona USA To Open Summer '96," *Amusement Business,* September 4, 1995, p. 34.
——, "New Daytona USA Tops Projections," *Amusement Business,* August 5, 1996, p. 43.

—Thomas Derdak

Jefferson Smurfit Group plc

Beech Hill
Clonskeagh
Dublin 4
Ireland
(01) 269 6622
Fax: (01) 269 4481
Web site: http://www.smurfit.ie/welcome.htm

Public Company
Incorporated: 1934 as James Magee & Sons Ltd.
Employees: 43,000
Sales: IR £3.03 billion (US $4.86 billion) (1995)
Stock Exchanges: Dublin London New York
SICs: 2421 Sawmills & Planing Mills, General; 2493
    Reconstituted Wood Products; 2621 Paper Mills; 2631
    Paperboard Mills; 2653 Corrugated & Solid Fiber
    Boxes; 2655 Fiber Cans, Tubes, Drums & Similar
    Products; 2657 Folding Paperboard Boxes, Including
    Sanitary; 2671 Coated & Laminated Paper & Plastic
    Film; 5093 Scrap & Waste Materials; 6719 Offices of
    Holding Companies, Not Elsewhere Classified

The Jefferson Smurfit Group plc is the world's leading paper-based packaging group, having expanded from its origins in the Irish packaging industry. In addition to packaging, the group also has significant operations in paper bags and recycled newsprint. Jefferson Smurfit and its associated companies—which include the U.S.-based Jefferson Smurfit Corporation, 46 percent of which is held by the group—have a total of 400 facilities operating in more than 20 countries. About 60 percent of group sales are generated in Continental Europe, 21 percent in Ireland and the United Kingdom, 14 percent in Latin America, and seven percent in the United States. The Jefferson Smurfit Group is the fourth largest company based in Ireland.

Early History

The history of the company began with a young man from England making good in Ireland. Jefferson Smurfit, the son of a shipyard worker, was born in Sunderland, in northeast England, in 1909. His father died when he was ten years old. He became an apprentice salesman in a large department store at 14; he once said that life had made him into a little old man by that age.

In 1926 he accepted his uncle's offer of work in the tailoring business in St. Helens, Lancashire. Eight years later he moved to Belfast and opened his own tailoring business, James Magee & Sons Ltd., after marrying a local woman. The priest who conducted his wedding introduced him to the box-making business in Dublin. The priest had become involved with a factory there through one of his parishioners. The priest noticed Smurfit's keen business sense and asked the young man to act as an advisor. Smurfit saw the potential of the business and turned his attention to learning more about the technology of box-making. Meanwhile the tailoring business was expanding rapidly, and soon Smurfit owned four shops. He acquired full control of the Dublin box-making factory in 1938 and poured more of his energies into that business, giving up his tailor's shops and moving permanently to Dublin.

After 1939, when World War II broke out in Europe, the materials for box-making became much harder to find. Smurfit was able to keep his business going because he adapted the technology and his products to meet the demands of wartime. An example of this adaptation was the production of thick paper with straw in it for use in Irish schools. Because of the scarcity of paper and packaging during the war, Smurfit was able to capitalize on the overwhelming demand. The company concentrated on corrugated box production and had two paper-making machines working at full capacity. He had good relations with the trade unions and was proud that there were no strikes. By 1950, his Dublin factory was five times its initial size and producing eight times the original turnover. His sons, Michael and Jefferson Jr., were brought into the business at this date; accordingly, the company was renamed Jefferson Smurfit & Sons Ltd.

Michael, the eldest of Jefferson Smurfit's four sons, started on the factory floor, as Jefferson Jr. did later. Their father insisted that they join the appropriate union. Both went on to specialize, Jefferson Jr. in sales, Michael in company administration. Michael then took the opportunity to continue studying management techniques in Canada and the United States. After completing his training he ran a corrugated box factory with another brother, Alan, in his father's hometown, St. Helen's, returning to his father's company in 1966 as joint managing director with Jefferson Jr.

Rapid Expansion through Acquisitions in the 1960s and 1970s

The 1960s were a period of considerable expansion for the company. In 1964 Jefferson Smurfit & Sons Ltd. became a public company quoted on the Dublin Stock Exchange. Smurfit acquired Temple Press Ltd., a manufacturer of cartons and boxes, in 1968, and then took its first steps outside its original area of business when, in 1969, it acquired Browne & Nolan Ltd., a printing, packaging, publishing, and educational supply company. The parent company was now large enough to be quoted on the International Stock Exchange in London. Jefferson Sr. realized that his son Michael should be given more incentive to stay with the company and not become a potential rival. In 1969 he was appointed deputy chairman just as the company began to look seriously at acquisitions beyond the United Kingdom. In 1970 the company doubled its size with the purchase of the Hely Group of companies, which were involved in radio and television distribution, educational and office supplies, and packaging. Two years later the continuing expansion of the Smurfit businesses was symbolized in a change of name, to Jefferson Smurfit Group Ltd. Michael Smurfit brought the corrugated box factory in St. Helen's into the new group. The group concentrated a great deal of effort on its overseas expansion plans. It acquired the British carton making and printing company W. J. Noble and Sons in 1972. A year later its purchase of the print and packaging division of the U.K. firm Tremletts Ltd. brought plants in the United Kingdom and in Nigeria into the group. But the American market proved to be the most lucrative of its overseas ventures. Its 40 percent investment in the paper and plastic manufacturing firm Time Industries of Chicago, in 1974, gave it a foothold in the United States. It increased this initial investment to 100 percent in 1977.

Jefferson Smurfit Sr. died in 1977, at the age of 68. Michael succeeded him as chairman and Jefferson Jr. took over as deputy chairman. Their younger brothers moved up too, Alan to head United Kingdom sales and Dermot Smurfit to become managing director of the paper and board division. Their father left them a company that was beginning to diversify and internationalize itself in earnest yet continuing to lay stress on its base in Jefferson Sr.'s adopted homeland.

In 1968 Jefferson Sr. had seen the acquisition of Temple Press as an act of faith in the future of the Irish economy. The new chairman did not abandon this faith. The group carried on investing in Ireland, by acquiring, for example, Irish Paper Sacks Ltd.; Goulding Industries Ltd., maker of plastic film and sacks; and half the equity of the Eagle Printing Company Ltd. The more companies Jefferson Smurfit acquired, the more raw materials it needed. It decided to sell 49 percent of its corrugated box interests in Ireland and the United Kingdom to the Swedish paper company Svenska Cellulosa Aktiebolaget in return for a guaranteed supply of kraftliner. The sale also provided cash for further expansion abroad. Jefferson Smurfit acquired 51 percent of the Australian company Mistral Plastics Pty Ltd. in 1978. In 1979, it paid US $13 million for a 27 percent share of the Alton Box Board Company. At the time this was the largest investment by an Irish company in the American economy. It increased to 51 percent five months later.

U.S. Investments Highlight 1980s Acquisitions

The Jefferson Smurfit Group established itself as a major supplier of print and packaging in the United States in the 1980s. In Ireland it bought a small stake in the Woodfab group, the largest user of native timber and a significant presence in the Irish forestry sector. But Smurfit saw its greatest potential in the American market, where there have never been tight restrictions on foreign ownership or investment. Smurfit's method, a relatively cautious one, was to purchase a minority holding of an American company, observe its profits rising, and then move to 100 percent ownership. Thus the 27 percent holding in the Alton Box Board Company, acquired in 1979, formed the bridgehead for complete acquisition in 1981. And, in a variation on the same technique, in 1982 Smurfit formed a 50-50 joint venture to take over the packaging and graphic arts divisions of Diamond International, then bought out the partner's shares to gain full control in 1983.

Clearly, the group's long-term strategy of becoming an international competitor was coming closer to realization and Michael Smurfit was earning his reputation as a canny businessman. In 1983 shares in the American wing of the group, the Jefferson Smurfit Corporation, were floated on the market, generating US $46 million for further investment. The group then decided to expand into a new area of business, setting up a joint venture with Banque Paribas, known as Smurfit Paribas Bank Ltd. Jefferson Smurfit Jr. left the group in 1984, because of ill health, and his two younger brothers were appointed joint deputy chairmen. The following year, the fiftieth since the company's founding, was marked by re-registration as a public limited company. After achieving considerable success in its purchases of packaging companies, Smurfit acquired the Publishers Paper Company, based in Oregon, in 1986. This company supplied newsprint to such well-known papers as the *Los Angeles Times*. It was renamed Smurfit Newsprint Corporation and continued to supply several newspapers. The same year, in its largest deal yet, Smurfit set up a joint venture with Morgan Stanley Leveraged Equity Fund to pay Mobil US $1.2 billion for its subsidiary, Container Corporation of America (CCA), which produced paperboard and packaging, and in 1987 it purchased outright the manufacturing operations of CCA on the European continent and in Venezuela. The group thus more than doubled the value of its American holdings and moved into manufacturing in mainland Europe for the first time.

The second half of 1987 was a difficult time for the Smurfit family. First, Jefferson Smurfit Jr. died at the age of 50. He had contributed a great deal to the group's expansion through his expertise in sales and marketing. Then, like many other companies, Smurfit lost an enormous amount of value in the stock market crash in October. The value of its shares fell by more than half, but since demand for paper products remained steady it was just a question of riding out the storm.

In 1988, Dublin marked its millennium as a city, and Jefferson Smurfit Group, with its strong ties to the Irish capital, played a part in the celebrations by donating the Anna Livia Fountain in memory of Jefferson Smurfit Sr. Anna Livia, symbolizing the River Liffey flowing through the city to the sea, is a leading character in James Joyce's novel *Finnegan's Wake.* The group also contributed to the restoration of the Mansion House, the residence of the lord mayor of Dublin, and sponsored a Millennium Science Scholarship, to be awarded to a doctoral student specializing in high technology. Other Smurfit activities in 1988 included the establishment of Smurfit Natural Resources to continue its own private afforestation program in Ireland and the purchase of the Spanish packaging firm Industrial Cartonera, as well as 30 percent of Papelera Navarra, also based in Spain. Adding to these a 35 percent stake in Inpacsa, in 1989, gave the group interests in four paper mills, eight corrugated box plants, and 20 percent of the paper and packaging market in Spain.

In 1989 the group's publishing division grew with the launch of a new weekly newspaper, the *Irish Voice,* in the United States, where it also had an interest in the magazine *Irish America.* The *Irish Post* in the United Kingdom increased its circulation and Smurfit Print in Ireland produced more computer manuals. In America, an industrial dispute at Smurfit Newsprint Corporation lasted more than seven months and cost the company about US $25 million in profits. The group was also affected by lengthy strikes in the packaging industry in Italy. Latin American operations were slowly expanding. Smurfit Carton de Colombia and Smurfit de Venezuela put much effort into researching and developing the genetic enhancement of eucalyptus trees. Researchers believed that eucalyptus trees could be harvested in five years rather than the normal eight years. This was done by clonal reproduction, producing the fastest growing commercial trees in the world, from which a good quality uniform pulp can be manufactured. The Colombian company also produced writing paper, using a mix of different species of hardwood found in the tropical forests. By 1989, Smurfit Latin America had substantially more than 20 percent of the paper and board market in Venezuela and Colombia. The Latin American companies in the group provided opportunities for further education to their employees. In Colombia, for example, the company offered training in farm and forest tending as well as elementary schooling for children in the country areas near Smurfit timberland.

In 1989 the group made heavy use of junk bonds to restructure its American operations, which had accounted for about 65 percent of its profits in 1988. A 50-50 joint venture between the Smurfit group and the Morgan Stanley Leveraged Equity Fund created a new private holding company, SIBV/MS Holdings, for most of the group's subsidiaries in the United States. The reorganization generated US $1.25 billion and boosted the value of the group's shares by 50 percent. The group next decided to continue to expand north of the U.S. border, and it purchased 30 percent of PCL Industries Ltd., a Canadian company specializing in the conversion of plastics, with its own interests in the United States. The group also formed a partnership with the Canadian firm Tembec, Inc. to build a bleached lightweight coated mill in Quebec. Meanwhile, Smurfit International, the European division of the group, added to its operations the German company C.D. Haupt, a major paper-recycling mill, placing Smurfit in a strong position to profit from new opportunities in reunited Germany and in Eastern Europe. More Italian firms such as Ondulato Imolese, an integrated corrugated manufacturer, and Euronda, producer of corrugated cases and sheets, also joined the group.

By 1990 the Jefferson Smurfit Group had established itself as the largest gatherer and consumer of waste paper in the world, and it completed the purchase of Golden State Newsprint Co. Inc., which was renamed Smurfit Newsprint Corporation of California, and Pacific Recycling Co. Inc. As environmental awareness became commercially viable the group began to build up its recycling division by acquiring several existing units and announcing its intention to invest in a newsprint production unit, using scrap paper, in New York State.

In the United States, as in Latin America, Smurfit tried to involve itself within the community. It provided special programs for its employees, such as training at the Smurfit Technical Institute, and sponsored young children in Fernandina Beach's Literacy Program. In Ireland, too, some of the Irish universities were endowed with chairs and financial support for academic projects, of which the leading example is the Michael Smurfit School of Business at University College, Dublin.

By the beginning of the 1990s the Smurfit Group was producing a diversity of goods, from presentation boxes for Waterford crystal to takeout pizza boxes, and it continued to diversify further. It formed Nokia Smurfit Ltd. in a joint venture with Nokia Consumer Electronics, which distributes television, video recorders, and satellite equipment in Ireland and is a division of the Finnish company Oy Nokia Ab. It bought back its 49 percent interest in Smurfit Corrugated Ireland from Svenska Cellulosa and bought another 24.5 percent of U.K. Corrugated, boosting its ownership to 50 percent. One of its subsidiaries in the United Kingdom bought Texboard, a manufacturer of paper tubes. The group aimed to extend its already diversified board manufacturing and conversion business. It also purchased another U.K. firm, Townsend Hook, a leading producer of corrugated paper cases and coated papers, which gave Smurfit more than 20 percent of the corrugated case industry in Britain.

In 1991 Jefferson Smurfit added to its recycling business with the acquisition of several French companies, such as Centre de Dechets Industriels Group (CDI), the second largest waste paper company in France, and the Compagnie Generale de Cartons Ondules, an integrated mill and converting operation. In addition, it bought the Lestrem Group, which specialized in manufacturing solid board, accounting for about 20 percent of the market in France. It also set up a new subsidiary, Smurfit France.

The Smurfit Group carried diversification still further by deciding to invest in the leisure business in Ireland. Its activity in this area included the RiverView Racquet and Fitness Club, Waterford Castle Golf and Country Club, and the new development of the Kildare Hotel and Country Club.

Major Mid-1990s Acquisitions in Europe

In the mid-1990s Jefferson Smurfit turned to Continental Europe for acquisitions, beginning with France. In a deal that doubled the company's European operations, Jefferson Smurfit in late 1994 purchased the paper and packaging unit, Cellulose du Pin, of France's Compagnie de Saint-Gobain for IR £684 million (US $1.04 billion). Cellulose du Pin brought with it operations in France, Italy, Spain, and Belgium and manufactured recycled paper, corrugated boxes, coated woodfree paper, and paper bags. Following the acquisition, Jefferson Smurfit assumed the top position in the European corrugated industry.

To held fund the purchase, the company turned to its U.S. operation, taking it public once again, with Jefferson Smurfit Corporation reemerging as a public company. About IR £155 million (US $248 million) was raised through the offering, after which the Jefferson Smurfit Group retained a 46.5 percent stake in Jefferson Smurfit Corporation.

Additional European acquisitions quickly followed that of Cellulose du Pin. In May 1995 Jefferson Smurfit paid FrF 452 million for Les Papeteries du Limousin of France, an independent corrugated packaging firm with capacity of 220,000 metric tons of recycled containerboard. The purchase enabled Jefferson Smurfit to cancel plans to build a new mill in France. The following month saw the company make its first move into Scandinavia, with the IR £68 million (US $109 million) purchase of a 29 percent stake in Munksjö, a Swedish producer of bleached pulp, specialty papers, and board. Also acquired in 1995 was a 27.5 percent stake in Austria-based Nettingsdorfer, a producer of paper and board, with interests in corrugated container operations.

These 1995 moves, coupled with the 1994 acquisition of Cellulose du Pin, meant that Jefferson Smurfit had quadrupled its Continental European operations in less than two years. Further, Continental Europe had become the Jefferson Smurfit Group region generating the most revenue, surpassing the Ireland/United Kingdom region for the first time.

Always looking for new opportunities, Jefferson Smurfit made a few inroads into Asia in 1995. In May Jefferson Smurfit Corporation formed a joint venture in China, which soon thereafter bought a controlling interest in a linerboard mill near Shanghai. In December the Jefferson Smurfit Group formed a joint venture, called Smurfit Toyo, with the New Toyo Group of Singapore. Smurfit Toyo planned initially to manufacture folding cartons in Singapore, Hong Kong, and China. Jefferson Smurfit's approach to Asia was clearly a cautious one, though the company had a long-term goal of being an important player in the region.

Although Jefferson Smurfit's financial results fluctuated some in the mid-1990s thanks in part to the cyclical nature of the paper industry, the group's position was generally considered strong because of its geographic diversity and highly integrated operations (which tended to mitigate the effects of the industry's ups and downs). With its successful acquisition track record and the likelihood of more deals in the coming years, Jefferson Smurfit faced a bright future of continued growth.

Principal Subsidiaries

Cartón de Colombia, S.A. (67%); C.D. Haupt Papier-und Pappenfabrik GmbH & Co., K.G. (Germany); Inversiones Isica, C.A. (Venezuela); Jefferson Smurfit Italia, S.r.l. (Italy); Smurfit Capital Funding plc; Smurfit Cartón y Papel de Mexico, S.A. de C.V.; Smurfit España, S.A. (Spain); Smurfit International B.V. (Netherlands); Smurfit International France S.A.; Smurfit Investments U.K. Limited; Smurfit Ireland Limited; Smurfit Mercurius Verpakking B.V. (Netherlands); Smurfit Packaging Corporation (U.S.A.).

Further Reading

Brown, John Murray, ''High Prices and French Input Boost Smurfit,'' *Financial Times,* August 24, 1995, p. 20.

Byrne, Harlan S., ''Jefferson Smurfit Corp.: The Paperboard Producer Plans More Acquisitions,'' *Barron's,* March 27, 1989, p. 39.

——, ''Paper De-Cycler,'' *Barron's,* August 7, 1995, p. 21.

Cordell, Valerie, *The First Fifty Years,* Dublin: Jefferson Smurfit Group, 1984.

DeKing, Noel, ''Smurfit Moves to the Top through Acquisitions, Skilled Management,'' *Pulp & Paper,* December 1988, p. 110.

Du Bois, Peter C., ''Irish Alchemy: The Acquisitive Smurfit Group Turns Paper into Sizzling Profits,'' *Barron's,* August 28, 1995, pp. MW7–MW8.

Hargreaves, Deborah, ''US Flotation Boosts Jefferson Smurfit,'' *Financial Times,* September 29, 1994, p. 22.

Hollinger, Peggy, and Buchan, David, ''Smurfit To Double European Operations,'' *Financial Times,* August 3, 1994, p. 17.

Klebnikow, Paul, ''Who Needs Trees?: There's Always the Sunday New York Times,'' *Forbes,* June 26, 1989, pp. 108, 110, 114.

Loeffelholz, Suzanne, ''Equity Is Blood: Why Michael Smurfit's Bedroom Walls Are Lined with Spreadsheets,'' *Financial World,* April 3, 1990, pp. 96, 98.

—Monique Lamontagne
updated by David E. Salamie

Just For Feet, Inc.

153 Cahaba Valley Parkway North
Pelham, Alabama 35124
U.S.A.
(205) 403-8000
Fax: (205) 403-8200
Web site: http://www.feet.com

Public Company
Incorporated: 1977
Employees: 344
Sales: $256.40 million (1996)
Stock Exchanges: NASDAQ
SICs: 5661 Shoe Stores

Just For Feet, Inc. is an athletic shoe retailer with 60 stores in 16 states. Just For Feet superstores carry a broad range of brand-name athletic and outdoor footwear as well as a selection of sports related attire. The company is a "category killer," carrying 4,500 styles of athletic shoes compared to the 400 styles stocked by most of Just For Feet's competitors. The company's superstores include not only a wide selection of merchandise but also provide such entertainment features as basketball courts, video screens and snack bars. The management of Just For Feet is very tightly controlled by founder and CEO Harold Ruttenberg who has overseen the rapid expansion of the shoe store chain since the first Just For Feet superstore was opened in 1988.

Company Origins in the 1970s

Just For Feet founder, Harold Ruttenberg, began his career as an independent businessman in his native South Africa in the 1960s by hawking brand-name blue jeans to retailers from the trunk of his car. Eventually Ruttenberg built up enough capital to start a retail venture of his own and by the mid 70s his chain of menswear stores had made him one of South Africa's wealthiest entrepreneurs. From the vantage of the 70s, the political and economic future of South Africa looked bleak and Ruttenberg decided to move his family and business to the United States.

South African emigration laws, however, prohibited citizens from exporting all but a small fraction of their wealth and Ruttenberg was left with only $30,000 to start his new business in the United States. After shopping around for affordable locations, in 1977 Ruttenberg finally settled on a mall in Birmingham, Alabama, as the site for a youth oriented sportswear store called Hang Ten Sports World.

Ruttenberg sank all his remaining capital into the new venture and plowed all profits back into buying more stock. The first few years were rough going for Ruttenberg who had to adjust his business approach to the buying habits and laid back attitude of the American South. "I was used to doing a lot of business with Northerners, New Yorkers in particular," Ruttenberg said in a profile in *Success*. "But this was a very slow-moving environment. Even to this day I'm not always well understood by Southerners. I'm very vocal—I say it the way it is. But they're much more diplomatic, and you never know where you stand with them." In spite of a slow start, Ruttenberg's unique personal style and distinctive South African accent began to make its mark amongst the local sports oriented youth and after a few years he was able to open a second outlet. Ironically it was the very success of Hang Ten Sports that would create the biggest problem for Ruttenberg. Like most mall owners, Ruttenberg's landlord based rents on a percentage of profits. As the sports store became more and more successful Ruttenberg was faced with spiralling, and to his mind unfair, rent increases. "The developer was getting rich off me," Ruttenberg complained in an interview with *Chain Store Age*, "and I was fed up with it. I just wasn't enjoying myself anymore." Unable to arrange better terms, in 1986 Ruttenberg liquidated his inventory and closed the store.

Ruttenberg, constitutionally unable to remain idle for long, began to search for a new retail enterprise. Unlike his first foray into the American business world, Ruttenberg now had considerable capital to work with but he felt that he had to come up with a truly innovative concept to avoid the dependence on mall space that had soured his previous venture. He purchased the real estate to build a freestanding store and then spent months brainstorming with his son, Don, to come up with a strategy to lure customers away from the mall. One of his first decisions was to concentrate on athletic footwear instead of a whole line of sportswear. The high priced brand name athletic shoe market was coming into its own in the mid-80s and full price sales of these shoes was guaranteed to generate healthy profit margins. The challenge for retailers like Ruttenberg, however, was to avoid the deep discounting of merchandise that consumers had begun to expect in large retail environments. Ruttenberg decided that he could stick to full price merchandising if he could generate the kind of excitement about his store that brand name manufacturers were creating around their athletic shoes. High profile advertising and promotion had been fundamental to the development of the athletic shoe phenomenon and Ruttenberg was quick to adopt these methods in drawing customers to his new retail concept. The grand opening of the first Just For Feet store in 1988 was accompanied by a media blitz, in-store contests and the endorsement by professional athletes that had become the hallmark of the athletic shoe industry. The 15,000 square foot store featured a restaurant, nursery, video wall, glass-walled basketball court and a lot of neon. The store was an overnight success and Ruttenberg was soon able to open a second Just For Feet outlet in Birmingham.

The Development of the Superstore Concept in the 1980s

Ruttenberg was convinced that in the social climate of the 80s the busy consumer would be drawn to a store where the shopping experience provided entertainment as well as merchandise. Just For Feet stores were designed to create a carnival atmosphere. ''The bottom line is that people have a good time and enjoy themselves,'' Ruttenberg told *Chain Store Age*. ''That's what keeps them coming back.'' The Ruttenbergs introduced countless gimmicks to promote the ''store as entertainment'' concept that was fundamental to Just For Feet's success. Many, such as a nursery and drive-through window, were quickly dropped but certain features became an essential part of all Just For Feet outlets. Among these were a half-court basketball court, a snack bar and a video wall featuring sports videos. A sign at the front door read: ''This establishment does allow you to eat, drink, breathe, spend money and have a good time in our store.''

While the role of entertainment in the success of Just For Feet was heavily touted in the media and in company literature, merchandising techniques were also critical to the company's growth. Just For Feet relied on the sale of full priced brand name athletic shoes, and its promotion of these brands was therefore crucial. One of the important innovations introduced

by Ruttenberg was a vendor oriented store layout. Just For Feet was one of the first big-box retailers to exploit this store-within-a-store concept. Each major brand was given its own distinct space where the entire range of the manufacturer's line, as well as brand logos and promotions, could be displayed. The layout encouraged a close relationship between the store and its vendors who were willing to offer financial and technical support of the display area. As a concession to consumers who might be intimidated by the choice of brands, Just For Feet also offered the ''Great Wall'' of shoes where a selection of merchandise was organized by functional category. In addition, each Just For Feet store included a separate discount area called the ''Combat Zone'' where sale or closeout items could be featured.

An important part of Ruttenberg's concept for Just For Feet was the combining of a full service sales approach with the selection usually associated with self service merchandising. Although Just For Feet typically carried about 4,000 different styles of athletic and outdoor shoes, as compared to the average mall store's 600, customers could count on a full service sales staff to assist them. Stock was not set out on the sales floor but was stored in the back room as in a traditional shoe store. This high service strategy would help to convert casual shoppers, attracted by the entertainment atmosphere of the stores, into hard sales.

Expansion in the Late 1980s and 1990s

The instant success of the first Just For Feet store surprised even Ruttenberg himself. His initial objective of $2 million in sales in the first year was surpassed within a few months of the store's opening and Ruttenberg realized that his gamble had paid off. After opening another outlet in Birmingham, Ruttenberg decided that by franchising his concept he could expand without the large outlay of capital required by the superstore format. Three franchises were sold with the license to operate stores outside Alabama.

Ruttenberg's first chance for a major expansion of Just For Feet came in 1992 when he was offered a site at Caesar's Palace in Las Vegas. ''It was a huge risk,'' Ruttenberg told *Success*. ''But Las Vegas always fascinated me. It has the most expensive real estate in America, but when I saw the plans, I knew it was for me.'' The Las Vegas store was designed to be a flagship for the company. The two storey showplace included the Just For Feet trademark basketball court and video wall as well as a laser show and sculpture gallery of famous sports personalities. Just For Feet management was soon able to boast that their Las Vegas store was ''the highest-volume store of its kind in the world.''

By the end of 1992, sales from the three Just For Feet company owned stores as well as fees from the three franchises totalled $17 million. Ruttenberg decided that in order to maintain control of the Just For Feet concept, further expansion should be undertaken directly by the company instead of through franchising. Ruttenberg opened two more Just For Feet stores, in Nashville and Kansas City, Missouri and then, in March 1994, he took the company public to raise capital for further expansion.

With the cash from the public offering, Just For Feet was able to accelerate its rate of expansion. By the end of 1994 the company had opened ten new stores, five more than was anticipated in the IPO statement. The following year saw the addition of 12 more outlets, again surpassing management projections. At first, Ruttenberg confined the expansion of Just For Feet to southern states. "We tend to do the best where the sun shines," Ruttenberg told *Success* magazine. "When it gets cold, people wear shoes other than athletic shoes, but down here just about everybody wears them all the time." With stores in Florida, Georgia, Alabama, Tennessee, Texas, Arizona, Nevada, Kansas and Missouri, by 1996 Just For Feet had a presence in most southern urban markets. In keeping with his policy of retaining tight control over the growth of his company, Ruttenberg also moved to buy back the three Just For Feet franchises. Two of the franchisees were willing to sell but the company was unable to come to terms with the Ohio based franchisee, which continued to open new outlets into the mid 90s.

Just For Feet's public offering was an immediate success. Annual sales doubled from $23 million in 1993 to $56 million in 1994 and then soared to $120 million in 1995. Just For Feet stock became the darling of Wall Street. Shares that had sold at the IPO price of $6.22 more than quadrupled in two years, reaching a high of $37 in the last quarter of fiscal 1995. A damper was placed on the popular stock in the summer of 1995 when analysts from Duff and Phelps Equity Research Co. issued a report claiming that Just For Feet management was boosting reports of profits by using "aggressive accounting policies." The controversy surrounded the company's practice of spreading preopening costs over a twelve month period instead of recording the expenses, and the consequent reduction in income, as the stores opened. Analysts estimated that this unusual treatment of store opening costs was inflating Just For Feet's profits by as much as 10 cents a share. Although Ruttenberg vehemently denied the irregularity of his accounting methods, in 1997 the company adopted the more conservative practice of immediately expensing costs upon the store opening.

The rapid expansion of Just For Feet continued through 1996 with the opening of 23 new stores. Most of these outlets were located in the southern states where Just For Feet had built its success but the chain also began to expand into northern markets with stores in Minnesota, New Jersey and New York. Leading the push into the north was a planned 25,000 square foot flagship store to be located on 42nd Street in Manhattan.

Just For Feet made a strategic entry into the smaller store segment of the athletic shoe market in 1997 with the purchase of the Athletic Attic and Imperial Sports store chains. Athletic Attic, a privately owned athletic footwear retailer based in Gainseville, Florida, operated 30 company owned and 48 franchised stores across the country. Imperial Sports, a Michigan-based company, owned 56 stores in Michigan, Illinois, Indiana and Ohio. These two acquisitions allowed Just For Feet to target the smaller store, mall-based market that Ruttenberg had abandoned when he developed the superstore format. By entering this market through acquisitions rather than through internal growth, Ruttenberg was able to maintain the company's focus on its core superstore business.

Through the mid-90s Just For Feet continued to surpass projections for sales growth. The rapid expansion of the company caused total sales to more than double from $120 million in fiscal 1995 to $256 million in 1996. More significantly, comparable store sales were up by 16 percent and net income rose from $10 million to $16 million during the same period. As Just For Feet moved into the late 90s, management began the process of transforming the company from an innovative newcomer to an established retailer. Experienced adminstrators were hired and a training system, dubbed "Just For Feet University," was set up to train new employees in Just For Feet corporate culture. Some analysts speculated that the attraction of the carnival atmosphere of Just For Feet stores might wane, but felt that, if Ruttenberg could maintain his innovative entrepreneurial attitude, Just For Feet would find new ways to attract customers and continue to grow.

Further Reading

Brooks, Rick, "Just For Feet Doesn't Toe the Line on Accounting, Two Analysts Say," *Wall Street Journal,* August 30, 1995, p. 2.

Emert, Carol, "Just For Feet IPO for Expansion," *Footwear News,* February 7, 1994, p. 20.

Feldman, Amy, "Trouble Afoot," *Forbes,* November 6, 1995, p. 364.

Godsey, Kristin Dunlap, "Hit the Ground Running," *Success,* December 1996, pp. 37–41.

"JFF Plans Expansion," *Footwear News,* February 13, 1995, p. 9.

"Just For Feet Slates First Manhattan Store in '97," *Footwear News,* July 29, 1996, p. 7.

McEvoy, Christopher, "Nine Feet . . . and Counting," *Sporting Goods Business,* August 1993, p. 90–91.

"Stand by your Brand," *Sporting Goods Business,* February 1996, p. 92.

"Stepping Forward: Retail Entrepreneur of the Year," *Chain Store Age,* December 1996, pp.68–69.

—Hilary Gopnik

Justin Industries, Inc.

2821 West Seventh Street
P.O. Box 425
Fort Worth, Texas 76101
U.S.A.
(817) 336-5125
Fax: (817) 390-2477
Web site: http://www.justinind.com

Public Company
Founded: 1879
Employees: 4,481
Sales: $447.8 (1996)
Stock Exchanges: NASDAQ
SICs: 3251 Brick & Structural Clay Tile; 3271 Concrete
    Block & Brick; 3143 Men's Footwear Except
    Athletic; 2731 Book Publishing

Justin Industries, Inc. combines two very disparate businesses—boots and building materials—to form a uniquely successful corporation. While outsiders struggle to perceive the synergies between boots and bricks, Chairman and Chief Executive Officer John Justin Jr. drew parallels between them in a 1981 interview with *Forbes* reporter Anne Bagamery: "Why, just take a look at them. They're both made of natural materials and they both protect you—that puts them practically in the same family." Dan McGraw of *U.S. News & World Report* averred that wily CEO's "very name is an icon of Western heritage," while analyst David Leibowitz called his company "a perennial standout and the quintessential Lone Star firm." Over the course of his more than 45 years at the helm, the CEO—an octogenarian in 1997—increased annual sales from less than $1 million to nearly $450 million.

Widely known as the "Standard of the West," the company's high-quality boots have been worn by the likes of Lyndon Johnson and Michael Jackson, not to mention tens of thousands of cowboys. Its line includes the venerable Justin brand, produced since frontier times; Nocona boots, also made

by the Justin family since the turn of the century; pricey Tony Lama boots; and Chippewa work and hiking boots. Even into the 1990s, it did not seem to matter that, in the words of John Justin Jr., "God ain't making any more cowboys," there were enough cowboy wannabes in the world to justify the company's production of 6,500 pairs of boots *every day*.

Justin Industries' building materials segment was led by the Acme Brick Company subsidiary. As one of the nation's largest brick manufacturers, Acme churns out more than 750 million face bricks each year, accounting for an estimated ten percent of the domestic industry's output. Other subsidiaries manufacture concrete building materials as well as ceramic and marble tile. The company also owns Northland Publishing, which "specializes in Western and Southwestern Americana, art, history, and Native American culture."

Origins in Frontier Texas

The business was founded and named for H.J. Justin, who as a teenager moved from Indiana to Spanish Fort, Texas in the 1870s. Spanish Fort was located on what would become the West's famous Chisholm Trail and was, therefore, a stop for cowboys driving cattle to market. In 1879, Justin borrowed $35 from the local barber (for whom he had been doing odd jobs) and started a boot repair business in service to the nomadic cowboys. His "on-the-job training" soon led to full-fledged bootmaking. The business grew rapidly in concert with Justin's skill and renown for quality. He moved the operation to Nocona, Texas to be near the railroad station built there in the late 19th century.

Second Generation Diversifies in Early 20th Century

When the founder died in 1908, sons John, Earl, and Samuel took charge and renamed the company H.J. Justin & Sons. A second and final move, to Fort Worth, Texas in 1925, split the business in two. H.J.'s daughter, Enid Justin, remained in Nocona as leader of Nocona Boot Co., while her brothers continued on as Justin Boot & Shoe Co. (The two businesses were reunited in 1981, when Justin acquired Nocona.)

231

Company Perspectives:

Justin Industries is a unique combination of businesses, a combination that provides stability, flexibility, and unusual opportunities to serve not only one of the fastest-growing regions in the country, but also growing markets nationally and throughout the world. With emphasis on the quality of our people, our products, and our service, and with the determination to expand the markets for our superior products, we at Justin Industries are proud of our past and prepared for the future.

Believing that the urbanization of the West would bring the demise of the cowboy—and with him his particular footwear—Justin's second generation managers began to deemphasize bootmaking in favor of city-style shoes in the 1930s and 1940s. By the postwar era, John Justin was ready to abandon the boot trade, according to a 1981 *Forbes* article. In fact, he discouraged his son and namesake from joining the family business. Little did he know that his own son would take the company to heights heretofore unimagined.

Third Generation Sets the Stage for a Postwar Rejuvenation

Given his father's attitude about the future of the footwear company, it is not surprising to find that John Justin Jr. took a circuitous route to the family firm. Born in 1917, he studied in Washington, D.C. and Oklahoma during the Great Depression, eventually returning to Fort Worth and Texas Christian University. When he was not studying, the restless young man crafted belts from scraps of leather. Demand for his hand-made, fire-branded belts grew such that the young Justin could not concentrate on his school work. In 1938, at the age of 21, he left school and worked briefly at the family business. Later that year, he borrowed $1,000 to launch the Justin-Barton Belt Co. with partner W.D. Barton.

Military service during World War II interrupted Justin's career again, but upon his return he was able to buy out his partner's stake in the company and rename it for himself. By 1949, Justin had accumulated enough money—and moxie—to acquire a controlling stake in the struggling family business. Convinced that cowboy boots were not a product for the past, the 33-year-old designed and launched a new model called the "roper." It featured a rounded toe that made it easier for rodeo competitors and performers to dismount from their horses. The new style appealed not only to rodeo riders and ranchers, but also to what would come to be called "urban cowboys." John Justin Jr. was appointed president in 1951.

Justin set out to bolster both quality and service, both of which would become company hallmarks. He established close communication with retailers, who assured him that the market for western-style boots was far from dead. Attention to customer service would lead Justin to maintain rather large inventories. Although costly, this enabled the company to fill orders

in a timely fashion. Furthermore, it was a strategy that would also apply to Justin's future business interests.

Diversification into Brickmaking in the Late 1960s

The new CEO was not content to remain in boots alone. In 1968, he guided Justin's merger with Acme Brick Company to form First Worth Corporation. The Justin Boot Co. must have remained privately held throughout most of its first hundred years in operation; an October 1981 *Forbes* article noted that the Acme union was made "to protect the family business from estate taxes." Based in Bennett, Texas, Acme also boasted a history that dated back to the 19th century. These two disparate businesses complemented each other surprisingly well, for when one was in decline, the other was usually on the rise. This countercyclicality made for steady, and sometimes rambunctious, growth. Within a couple of years of the merger, John Justin Jr. had advanced to the miniconglomerate's chief executive office. In 1972, the enterprise was renamed Justin Industries, Inc.

Despite dire predictions that less expensive aluminum and wood sidings would supplant brick, especially in residential construction, Acme Brick grew rapidly in the 1970s. Sales more than doubled from 1975 to 1979 alone, totaling $184.5 million in the latter year. Shareholders made out handsomely as well; the stock increased from a low of $2.50 in 1975 to a high of nearly $22 in 1979. By 1980, Acme's 19 plants in six southwestern states manufactured nearly 50 percent of the region's face brick, giving it a ten percent stake nationwide.

Growth Slows Dramatically in the 1980s

Justin's bipolar formula for success did not add up nearly as well in the early 1980s, however. In 1982, brickmaking profits were not sufficient to offset an operating loss of $8.9 million in the footwear division, resulting in the company's first-ever overall loss, a $6.3 million shortfall. But the 1980s were actually hardest on the brick business. In the last half of the decade, Acme's sales declined by more than ten percent to less than $114 million in 1989. Moreover, brick price reductions ate away at this segment's operating margins.

As it turned out, 1982's bootmaking lapse preceded a much-needed housecleaning. With costs in line, Justin sought to broaden its shoe business mid-decade, acquiring Chippewa Shoe, a manufacturer of sport and work boots. The "new" subsidiary (Chippewa was 83 years old at the time of the purchase) increased Justin's potential footwear market fourfold from the ten-million-unit cowboy boot segment. Justin also acquired the Larry Mahan line of boots from Hyer Boot and added its first line of children's boots, dubbed "Justin Junior Ropers," during this period. Boot sales increased from $103.9 million in 1985 to $142.1 million in 1989 to surpass the brick business, which had dominated Justin's balance sheet for nearly 20 years.

Though its growth rate had slowed substantially from that of the 1970s, Justin's overall revenues increased by 50 percent over the course of the 1980s, from $184 million in 1979 to nearly $278 million in 1989. Return on sales declined substantially, however, from six percent in 1978 (or more than $10 million) to barely more than two percent in 1989, for a net of $7.2 million.

Early 1990s Bring Tandem Growth

Justin's two main businesses grew in tandem in the early 1990s, as the southwestern United States enjoyed a housing boom, country-western music and fashion grew ever more mainstream, and the company's Chippewa work boots became the footwear of choice for many fans of Seattle-style ''grunge'' music. Footwear sales burgeoned nearly 63 percent from $181.4 million in 1990 to $295.2 million in 1993, and brick revenues increased more than 50 percent from $118.9 million to $179.7 million over the same term.

But the early 1990s were not without conflict, specifically the threat of a hostile takeover. The dilemma actually began in 1989, when Barry Rosenstein and Perry Sutherland formed JTN Acquisition Corp. and purchased six percent of Justin's outstanding shares. Both of the 30-something investors had trained at the knee of Asher Edelman, an early 1980s takeover maven. Justin's stock was then trading at $10, a 20 percent discount on its book value, which the raiders perceived as a juicy bargain. By the fall of 1990, they had doubled their stake in the company and secured $112 million in junk bond financing to back an $18 per share buyout offer.

Believing that the raiders planned to auction off his family's boot business and merge the remaining building materials interests with the Sutherland family's Sutherland Lumber Co., John Justin Jr. staunchly opposed the takeover. In keeping with the dual nature of his business, the chairman and CEO pursued a two-fold defense. He personally owned about 20 percent of the company's outstanding stock and solicited the solidarity of shareholding employees, relatives, insiders, and friends in the impending battle for control. At the same time, Justin cannily pursued the acquisition of a troubled competitor, Tony Lama Company Inc. The fall 1990 purchase cost the company $18 million in cash and, more important, required the assumption of $35 million in debt. Like a stinkbug to a hungry bird, Justin suddenly did not seem so appetizing to JTN—or its bankers. To add insult to injury, though Justin's stock was trading at about $14, only ten percent of the company's shareholders voted with the raiders in favor of the $18 per share tender offer that fall. Thoroughly repulsed, Rosenstein and Sutherland withdrew their bid in March 1991.

Boosted by record unit sales and a strategic acquisition, sales in Justin's building materials segment continued to grow through the mid-1990s. Its sale of more than 750 million bricks in 1996 established a new company record and pushed divisional revenues to more than $260 million that year. The addition of American Tile Supply Company, a 1994 acquisition, also benefited this segment of Justin's business. Footwear sales, however, did not fare nearly as well, declining from a historic high of $295.2 million in 1993 to $186.5 million in 1996. Net, too, declined mid-decade, from a high of $37.1 million in 1993 to 23.3 million in 1996. In its January 1997 evaluation of the company, *Value Line* forecast that Justin's building materials

segment would continue to grow and that its footwear sales would continue to shrink.

Principal Subsidiaries

Acme Brick Company; Featherlite Building Product Corporation; American Tile Supply Company; Tradewinds Technologies, Inc.; Justin Boot Company; Tony Lama Company; Nocona Boot Company; Chippewa Shoe Company; Northland Publishing.

Further Reading

Bagamery, Anne, ''You Can't Just Go with the Flow,'' *Forbes,* October 26, 1981, pp. 59–61.

Button, Graham, ''These Boots Are Made for Performing,'' *Forbes,* May 25, 1992, p. 16.

Farman, Irvin, *Standard of the West: The Justin Story,* Fort Worth, TX: Texas Christian University Press, 1996.

Gabel, Roxanne, ''Cowboy and Culture,'' *The Cattleman,* December 1990, pp. 90, 112–126.

Genusa, Angela, ''Master: John Justin Created a Boot-Making Empire,'' *Dallas Business Journal,* June 24, 1994, p. C4.

Goodman, Susan E., ''Justin Boot,'' *Footwear News,* November 26, 1984, p. 2.

Gordon, Mitchell, ''Back in Style: Western Boots Step High Again, and So Does Justin,'' *Barron's,* March 12, 1984, pp. 64–65.

——, ''Profits to Boot,'' *Barron's,* June 3, 1985, pp. 56–58.

Jacobs, Rick, ''Fate of Justin Takeover Fight Rests in Shareholders' Hands,'' *Dallas Business Journal,* October 5, 1990, p. 11.

Jaffe, Thomas, ''Justin Time?,'' *Forbes,* January 8, 1990, p. 341.

''JTN Withdraws Bid for Justin,'' *Footwear News,* March 4, 1991, p. 32.

Justin Industries, *From the Frontier to the Future with Justin Industries: 100 Years,* Fort Worth, TX: Justin Industries, 1979.

——, ''Justin's History,'' http:www.justinind.com/histmain.html.

Leibowitz, David S., ''Bear Market Beauties,'' *Financial World,* January 8, 1991, p. 69.

——, ''Of Cowboy Boots and Partnerships,'' *Financial World,* August 9, 1988, p. 105.

McGraw, Dan, ''The Hard Sole of Texas,'' *U.S. News & World Report,* May 9, 1994, p. 56.

Mehlman, William, ''Justin Industries Viewed as Promising Recovery Bet,'' *The Insider's Chronicle,* February 14, 1983, pp. 1–4.

Pattie, Jane, *Justin Boot: Standard of the West,* Fort Worth, TX: Justin Industries, 1979.

Rieger, Nancy, ''Justin Gets Takeover Bid of 'Friendly' $18.50/ Share,'' *Footwear News,* March 12, 1990, p. 39.

Seckler, Valerie, ''Justin Sees Sales Tripling,'' *Footwear News,* July 29, 1981, pp. 11–12.

Smith, Frank, ''Justin Industries Digs in To Fight Hostile Takeover Attempt,'' *Dallas Business Journal,* June 5, 1990, p. 5.

Verespej, Michael A., ''John Justin's Ride To Success,'' *Industry Week,* January 20, 1986, p. 56.

Weisman, Katherine, ''How To Skin Dealsters,'' *Forbes,* June 24, 1991, pp. 76–78.

Wessling, Jack, ''Justin Buys Tony Lama; Qtr. Shoe Net Holds Up,'' *Footwear News,* October 22, p. 4.

——, ''Justin Rejects 2d Buyout Offer,'' *Footwear News,* September 24, 1990, pp. 2–3.

—April Dougal Gasbarre

Karstadt Aktiengesellschaft

Theodor-Althoff-Strasse 2
Postfach 10 21 64
4300 Essen 1
Federal Republic of Germany
+49 (201) 7271
Fax: +49 (201) 727 4791

Public Company
Incorporated: 1920 as Rudolph Karstadt AG
Employees: 105,129
Sales: DM26.9 billion (1996)
Stock Exchanges: Berlin Bremen Düsseldorf Frankfurt
    Hamburg Hanover Munich Stuttgart
SICs: 5311 Department Stores; 5961 Catalog & Mail-
    Order Houses; 4724 Travel Agencies; 4725 Tour
    Operators; 5411 Grocery Stores

Karstadt Aktiengesellschaft is Germany's largest publicly traded retailer, with 569 stores in Germany covering 2.5 million square meters of sales area. Its 1994 merger with Hertie Waren & Kaufhaus GmbH ranked it among Europe's largest retailers. Karstadt is principally known for its department and specialty stores, and this sector accounted for 68 percent of its annual sales in 1995. Specialty outlets include three home furnishings stores, 19 sporting goods outlets, 12 carpet centers, and several other focused retail shops. Yet Karstadt, through its subsidiaries Neckermann Versand AG and NUR Touristic GmbH, is also active in the mail-order and travel businesses, which accounted for 17 percent and 15 percent of 1995 sales, respectively.

The company originated in northern Germany in the late 19th century; its development since then has been determined largely by changes both in the economic climate and in attitudes toward retailing in Germany. Phases of expansion and diversification have alternated with periods of crisis, cutbacks, or consolidation. Major shareholders in the group are Commerzbank and Deutsche Bank, holding 10 percent each.

Mid-19th Century Origins

Rudolph Karstadt, founder of the company and a pioneer of department store retailing in Germany, was born near Lübeck on February 16, 1856. He completed his commercial apprenticeship in Rostock and then worked in his father's textile shop in Schwerin. Rudolph soon became impatient with the business customs of the time, whereby customers generally bought items on credit, forcing merchants to set prices high as protection against nonpayment and hindering flexibility in terms of stock changes. He saw the secrets of successful retailing as low prices, cash payment, and rapid stock turnover—a revolutionary concept that caused some disagreements within the family. Finally in 1881 Rudolph's father lent him 3,000 marks to put his ideas into practice. On May 14, 1881, Rudolph, with his brother Ernst and sister Sophie, opened a shop, Rudolph Karstadt—selling dress materials and ready-to-wear clothes—in the harbor town of Wismar. Newspaper advertisements excited local interest and ensured large crowds on the opening day. Despite the low prices, however, customers were unused to the idea of immediate payment, and monthly sales in the first year were modest. Rudolph Karstadt's brother and sister withdrew from the business at this stage, leaving him as the sole owner.

Karstadt stuck to his convictions and was soon proved right—in the second year of business monthly sales rose to 20,000 marks, and in 1884 another shop was opened in Lübeck, with a range of goods extending to household items, leather goods, and toys. Further branches were opened in Neumünster in 1888 and in Braunschweig in 1890. The business grew rapidly: the balance sheet total in 1882 was 49,000 marks, which rose to 613,000 marks in 1890, and to 1.8 million marks in 1894. Rudolph Karstadt's conception of the modern department store was perfectly in tune with the times: the increasing economic power of the middle and working classes meant that consumer goods were demanded in ever larger quantities. In founding his business, Karstadt was also in line with a broader European trend: department stores had already been successfully established in France—notably with Bon Marché, Magasins du Louvre, Samaritaine, Printemps, and Galeries Lafayette—and in England, with Whiteleys, Harrods, and Selfridges.

Turn-of-the-Century Expansion

A new branch was opened in Kiel in 1893, and Karstadt, who had previously moved from Lübeck to Berlin, now moved from the capital to this rapidly growing town, a focus of imperial military expansionism. During the 1890s and the first decade of the 20th century the business continued to expand at a considerable rate: new branches were opened, established branches were extended, and in 1900 Rudolph Karstadt took over 13 stores owned by his brother Ernst, who had gotten into financial difficulties. By 1906, the 25th anniversary of the company, Rudolph Karstadt owned 24 department stores in northern Germany. In 1912 a prestigious new store was opened in Hamburg, with 10,000 square meters of sales area and a turnover of nearly seven million marks in the first year, and in 1913 Rudolph Karstadt reestablished the headquarters of the company in that city.

While Karstadt was establishing his chain of stores in northern Germany, a business run by Theodor Althoff in the western part of Germany was following a very similar course. Althoff, born in 1858, had taken over a millinery and linen shop from his mother in 1885 and had soon succeeded in expanding the business considerably, following principles similar to those espoused by Karstadt—cash payment and low prices. In 1904 Althoff opened his first department store, in Dortmund, with a sales area of 5,000 square meters, and in 1910, the 25th anniversary of the business, the enterprise consisted of 11 stores in all. The year 1912 saw the establishment of Althoff's largest store yet, in Essen, with 10,000 square meters of selling space and 53 departments.

Interwar Merger of Karstadt and Althoff

World War I put an end to the years of prosperity and expansion for both Karstadt and Althoff. People hoarded their money, and goods became increasingly scarce. The similarity of the two businesses and the need to concentrate resources during this crisis brought the two department store pioneers together for the first time in 1917. In 1919 the firms agreed on a common purchasing arrangement. In 1920 Rudolph Karstadt KG was converted into an Aktiengesellschaft—joint stock company—with founding capital of 40 million marks, based in Hamburg. Theodor Althoff was chairman of the supervisory board. A complete merger of Karstadt AG and Theodor Althoff KG followed in May of the same year, and the share capital was raised to 80 million marks; at this time Karstadt had 31 stores and Althoff 13.

The decade which followed the merger was one of rapid expansion, funded by numerous capital-raising measures. The company opened new branches and extended existing ones, as well as acquiring a number of manufacturing businesses in the furniture, textiles, and grocery sectors. EPA Einheitspreis AG, a subsidiary enterprise started by Theodor Althoff's son Heinrich, was established in 1926 following the American model of five-and-dime stores, with goods sold at four prices: 10, 25, 50, and 100 pfennigs. This business was tremendously successful, with 52 branches in Germany and a turnover of about 100 million Reichsmarks (RM) in 1932. In 1927 Karstadt acquired the 19 stores owned by M.J. Emden Söhne KG, and in 1929 a new store was opened in Berlin, one of the largest and most modern in Europe at the time, with a sales area of 37,000 square meters. Another 15 stores were added by the merger with Lindemann & Co. KG in the same year. By the time of the company's 50th anniversary, in 1931, Rudolph Karstadt AG and its subsidiaries had 89 branches and about 30,000 employees—compared with 11,500 in 1924—and a turnover of around RM200 million.

Great Depression Threatens Retailer's Survival

This phase of growth—conceived and carried through, it appears, on the initiative of Hermann Schöndorff, a dominant member of the company's management board at the time—reached its climax with the construction of an impressive new headquarters in Berlin, covering 70,000 square meters. Employees in the former headquarters in Hamburg were transported to Berlin in a specially commissioned train on January 1, 1932. The plans for expansion ended in crisis, however. The national and international economic difficulties of the early 1930s, combined with debts incurred during the previous decade, brought the company into severe financial trouble. In 1931 only five of Karstadt's stores were showing any profit. Theodor Althoff died in August 1931, when the business he had helped to found was approaching collapse. In April 1933 a consortium of banks assisted in drawing up a program of reorganization in order to ensure the company's survival. All the production subsidiaries were to be divested, share capital was to be reduced from RM80 million to RM7.6 million, the branch network was to be reduced, and EPA Einheitspreis was to be sold. The newly built headquarters was sold in 1934, and the company's administration moved into smaller premises in Berlin.

The restructuring effected a recovery in financial terms. Karstadt then, however, had to contend with difficulties arising from the National Socialists' (Nazi) campaign against department stores, involving boycotts and restrictive legislation, as some department stores had Jewish owners and were seen as representing a threat to the specialty German retail tradition. Despite these obstacles the company reached an economic high point before World War II: in 1939 it had 67 branches, a total sales area approaching 260,000 square meters, and a work force of 21,000. Annual sales rose from RM190 million in 1933 to RM300 million in 1939.

Wartime Difficulties Yield to Postwar Growth

Business conditions during and immediately after World War II became increasingly primitive, determined by rationing and the scarcity of goods, by changes of staff as women replaced the men who were called for military service, and—especially in the later years—by the damage to or destruction of stores by Allied bombing. In 1944 Rudolph Karstadt died at the age of 88. The end of the war saw the expropriation of 22 stores in the Soviet occupation zones and the destruction of more than 30 of the 45 branches in the western zones.

The currency reform of 1948 marked the beginning of West Germany's economic recovery. In this year Karstadt had 6,700 employees, 55,000 square meters of sales area, and an annual turnover of DM172 million. During the years that followed, rising incomes and consumer confidence fueled the reestablishment and renewed growth of Karstadt's retail business. In 1952 Karstadt reacquired 75 percent of the former EPA Einheitspreis AG, now called Kepa Kaufhaus GmbH (Kepa); the remaining 25 percent was acquired in 1958. In 1956, the year of the company's 75th anniversary, the turnover of Rudolph Karstadt AG exceeded DM1 billion for the first time. By this stage Karstadt had 49 branches and Kepa 51, with a total sales area of 222,000 square meters and 31,000 employees. The company name was changed to Karstadt AG in 1963, and a new administrative headquarters was opened in Essen in 1969.

Diversification in 1970s

The 1970s saw another important phase of expansion for the group, accompanied, as in the 1920s, by a diversification of interests. A travel company, TransEuropa Reisen GmbH, was jointly founded by Karstadt and mail-order company Quelle Gustav Schickedanz KG in 1971. The following year the company was renamed KS-Touristik-Beteiligungs GmbH. KS-Touristik itself held 25 percent of Touristik-Union International GmbH KG. In 1976 Karstadt agreed to buy a stake in the mail-order company Neckermann Versand, which was experiencing financial difficulties. As Neckermann itself had a travel subsidiary, the Federal Monopolies Commission required Karstadt to sell its share in KS-Touristik. In 1977 Karstadt raised its share in Neckermann to a controlling 51.2 percent. Neckermann was converted to a joint-stock company in the same year.

As well as moving into the mail-order and travel businesses, Karstadt diversified its retailing interests during this decade. The group's first furniture and home decoration store was opened in Munich in 1972. By 1980 the group had nine such furniture outlets. Seven self-service department stores began operation with the foundation of Karstadt SB Warenhaus GmbH, a subsidiary of Kepa, in 1974. The first specialized sports equipment store was opened in 1976: nine of these outlets were in operation in 1980. Further specialty outlets for fashion, music, books, and leisure activities were opened between 1977 and 1980.

The second half of the decade also saw the rationalization of Karstadt's retailing businesses. In 1977 it was decided that the concept behind the Kepa outlets would not be successful in the long run, and 25 of Kepa's outlets were reintegrated into the Karstadt chain; the remaining 42 branches were sold or leased. The self-service department stores—by then numbering 18—were also brought into the main Karstadt network. Between 1977 and 1979, 17 of Neckermann's stores were turned into Karstadt outlets and 17 new Karstadt stores were established.

Pursuit of Productivity in the 1980s

By 1981, Karstadt's department store business had 155 branches and 71,000 employees, and accounted for 77 percent of turnover. Neckermann Versand AG, the mail-order subsidiary, had a work force of 6,600 and accounted for 13 percent of the group's annual sales. NUR Touristic GmbH, Neckermann's travel subsidiary, had 1,500 employees and a 10 percent share of sales. The restructuring at the end of the 1970s indicated a shift in strategy from expansion in store numbers to increasing the productivity of each store. This policy was pursued through the 1980s. Karstadt, in 1991, had 155 stores—the same number

as in 1981. However, sales area during the decade increased from 1.3 million square meters to 1.4 million square meters. Work force numbers have tended to decline—from 79,500 in 1981 to 71,000 in 1990. Annual turnover was DM12.7 billion in 1981; after a decline in the first half of the 1980s, this had risen to DM16.8 billion in 1990.

Facing increasing competition from self-service and out-of-town stores, Karstadt's strategy in the 1980s was to maintain its traditional emphasis on department stores carrying a full range of goods in town centers. In the late 1980s, however, the company implemented a refurbishment and realignment program by which individual stores have been modernized and adapted to the nature of their localities. Furthermore, a distribution center was established at Unna, near Dortmund. The project was started in 1987 and was fully operational for the first time in 1990, costing DM210 million. This center replaced regional warehouses and has enabled Karstadt AG to make efficiency and cost improvements in the area of logistics, the distribution of goods between warehouses and stores. Diversification, which was at the core of Karstadt's development in the 1970s, was not part of the company's strategy during the 1980s. Although the company retained specialty outlets for sports equipment and furniture, accounting for about nine percent of annual turnover, all other ventures into specialty areas, except Runners Point, had ceased operations by 1987.

In 1981 Karstadt raised its stake in Neckermann Versand AG to more than 94 percent, and in 1984 the group acquired all remaining shares in this subsidiary. Both Neckermann Versand AG and its travel subsidiary NUR Touristic GmbH continued to take losses during the first half of the 1980s, returning profits only since 1986 and 1987 respectively. Improvements at Neckermann were due largely to its abandonment of specialty catalogs, returning to one main catalog targeting families in the medium- to lower-income groups. Staff reductions also played a part. Neckermann, which produced around three million catalogs each season, was by the end of the decade the third-largest mail-order company in Germany, behind Otto and Quelle, and had subsidiaries in the Netherlands, Belgium, France, and joint ventures in Greece and Poland. NUR Touristic, which has subsidiaries in the Netherlands and Belgium, also reduced its work force, from 1,445 in 1981 to 937 in 1989. Despite these improvements at Neckermann and NUR, the problems were not entirely eradicated: while both businesses showed increases in turnover, their profits declined in the waning years of the decade.

The 1990s and Beyond

The reunification of Germany, along with tax reforms that increased consumer spending power, brought Karstadt and its subsidiaries a significant boost in sales in the early 1990s. Department stores along the border with the former German Democratic Republic benefitted from visiting customers from the new federal states, while the mail-order business was able to penetrate into the eastern territories and take advantage of the rise in consumer demand without having to establish retail outlets. Karstadt had believed its coverage of western Germany to have reached saturation point, but the new Länder, or federal regions, presented the group with an opportunity for further expansion. In 1990 a cooperation agreement was reached with the Centrum department stores in eastern Germany; in March 1991 Karstadt acquired seven of these stores—in Dresden, Görlitz, Halle, Hoyerswerda, Leipzig-Lindenau, and Magdeburg—as well as leasing two former Magnet stores in Brandenburg and Wismar. Conversion of these stores to western standards required considerable investment. Neckermann and NUR also developed mail-order and tourism infrastructures in the East.

Further consolidation of Germany's retailers came in 1994, when Karstadt merged with Hertie Waren & Kaufhaus GmbH. The DM1.5 billion deal added Hertie's 300 department and specialty stores with US$4.2 billion in sales to form what *Daily News Record*'s James Fallon called "the richest retailing group in Europe."

Karstadt showed off its "cyber-savvy" with the launch of "My-World," Europe's largest online shopping site, in October 1996. The electronic mall offered over 150,000 items and generated an average of $20,000 in sales every day. However, while the chain continued to seek new ways to present its wares to the buying public, it did not neglect the old ways. That same year, Karstadt staged a grand reopening of its Berlin outlet, Kaufhaus des Westens. Known in the vernacular as KaDeWe ("ka-day-vay"), the store had first been built in 1907 and had long been sequestered in East Germany by the Cold War–era Berlin Wall. A renovation and expansion made it the largest department store on the European continent, with 60,000 square meters of selling space.

Karstadt was among the retailers who helped to slowly erode Germany's "blue laws" in the early 1990s. Won by the nation's powerful unions, these laws prohibited work on Sundays (known as "Feiertag" or "free day") and ended the workday at 6:30 p.m. weekdays and 2 p.m. on Saturdays. As the retail environment in the nation worsened, store operators were able to convince local and, in November 1996, the national government to ease restrictions on store hours. The national reform did not allow Sunday hours but did allow the extension of the weekday to 8 p.m. and Saturday hours to 4 p.m. Karstadt took advantage of the new selling time, but like many of its competitors did not see an immediate payoff.

In fact, while Karstadt's sales rose more than 60 percent in the early 1990s, from DM16.77 billion to DM26.98 billion, its net income declined from DM227.8 million in 1990 to a low of DM41.9 million in 1994 before recovering somewhat to DM109 million in 1995.

Principal Subsidiaries

Neckermann Versand AG; NUR Touristic GmbH; Kepa Kaufhaus GmbH; Runners Point Warenhandelsgesellschaft mbH; Versandhaus Walz GmbH; Neckermann Postorders B.V. (Netherlands); Neckermann Postorders N.V. (Belgium); Neckermann Sarl (France); Neckermann Vliegreizen Nederland B.V. (Netherlands); Neckermann Reizen België N.V. (Belgium).

Further Reading

Cole, Deborah, "Berlin Reopens Beloved Symbol of Consumer Freedom," *Reuters Business Report,* September 24, 1996.

Doran, Patricia, "Konig Karstadt," *Sporting Goods Business,* August 1994, p. 56.

Fallon, James, "Confirm Karstadt to Acquire Hertie Department Stores; Deal Worth $1.6 Billion," *Daily News Record,* November 16, 1993, p. 10.

Gilardi, John, "German Retail Unions Stage More Strike Actions," *Reuters,* May 30, 1995.

Karstadt Magazin: Jubiläumsausgabe, 1881–1981, Essen: Karstadt AG, 1981.

"A Little Online Shopping but with a European Flair," *PCWeek,* January 20, 1997, p. 115.

Miller, Marjorie, "Unions Seeing Red as German Blue Laws Ease," *Los Angeles Times,* October 29, 1994, p. 2A.

Spahr, Wolfgang, "Merger Causes Alarm in Germany; Retailers Told to Sell Some Music Outlets," *Billboard,* March 19, 1994, pp. 49, 50.

"West German Shops; Geschlossen," *The Economist,* March 1, 1986, pp. 67–68.

Whitney, Craig R. "Comfortable Germans, Slow to Change (Especially if It Means More Work)," *New York Times,* January 16, 1995, p. 6A.

—Susan Mackervoy
—updated by April Dougal Gasbarre

Kobe Steel, Ltd.

Tekko Building
8-2, Marunouchi 1-chome
Chiyoda-ku, Tokyo 100
Japan
(03) 3218-7111
Fax: (03) 3218-6330
Web site: http://www.kobelco.co.jp

Public Company
Incorporated: 1911 as Kobe Steel Works, Ltd.
Employees: 15,652
Sales: ¥1.53 trillion (1996)
Stock Exchanges: Tokyo
SICs: 3369 Nonferrous Foundries, Not Elsewhere
　　Classified; 3548 Welding & Soldering Equipment;
　　6719 Holding Companies, Not Elsewhere Classified

Kobe Steel, Ltd., is Japan's 5th-largest and the world's 15th-largest steelmaker. The company markets a wide variety of iron and steel products and is the Japanese leader in welding rods and titanium products. It is a strong competitor in rolled aluminum and copper. Kobe Steel has consistently shown a progressive edge. The company entered specialty steel markets early in its development and was one of the first steelmakers to diversify into related markets such as machinery and plant engineering. Kobe has also shown a keen interest in developing foreign markets; it established offices in New York and Düsseldorf as early as 1960.

Kobe has focused on higher value-added steel products and has expanded into such high-technology industries as computer components and bioengineering. Kobe leads its Japanese competitors in establishing U.S. subsidiaries and joint ventures. In 1989 it incorporated Kobe Steel Co. to administer more efficiently its growing number of U.S. enterprises. Lower demand for steel products, as well as cheaper production costs from competitors in developing countries like Brazil and Korea, have threatened steelmakers in Japan. Kobe seeks to diversify further

into related fields where the company's existing expertise can be applied.

Company Origins

Kobe Steel was established as the Kobe Steel Works (Kobe Seikosho) in 1905 by the Japanese trading firm Suzuki and Company. In 1911 the company was incorporated as Kobe Steel Works, Ltd., with capital of ¥1.4 million. Kobe Steel Works grew over the next 15 years as Japan's main industry, textiles, was replaced by heavier manufacturing. Although Kobe was relatively small among Japanese steelmakers, the company successfully carved a niche in the growing markets. Four new plants were added between 1917 and 1921. Capital had increased to ¥20 million.

The Great Depression struck Japan in the late 1920s, causing Kobe Steel Works to experience some difficult times. In 1928 ¥10 million was written off against accumulated losses, and then another ¥10 million in capital was raised to reduce debt. These measures helped the company survive the crisis. A year later Kobe established a shipbuilding subsidiary, Harima Zosenjo, Limited.

The 1930s brought substantial changes to Japan's government and industry. A militant group of nationalists dominated Japanese politics, and the country geared up for war. In 1931 Japan invaded Manchuria in the first of its military adventures. By 1937 the country was embroiled in an all-out war with China. The Japanese government encouraged rapid development of heavy industry and began to coordinate distribution of raw materials. Kobe Steel Works's production capabilities expanded over the next few years. Eight new plants opened, and two were acquired from other companies between 1937 and the end of the war in 1945. Although World War II had stimulated Japanese heavy industrial development, it also left the nation considerably weakened.

Postwar Rebuilding

After the war Allied forces wrote a new constitution for Japan. The old family-run *zaibatsu,* or trusts, were broken up, and Japanese industry began to rebuild. In 1949 Kobe Steel

238

Company Perspectives:

"Societies throughout the world are confronted every day with a number of escalating problems regarding the compatibility of continued economic growth and the need to preserve the natural environment. Accordingly, businesses must take on added responsibilities to promote industrial and other development that is in harmony with the natural environment and to reduce the negative impact of such development. Kobe Steel, Ltd., a diverse and technologically advanced corporation, is well positioned to meet the challenges posed by the new era. Our goal is to produce a stream of high-quality products that accurately meet customer needs while, at the same time, improve the compatibility of our products and operations with the environment."

Works was restructured. Its Moji and Chofu plants were spun off into a separate company, Shinko Kinzoku Kogyo Ltd., while its Toba, Yamada, Matsuzaka, and Tokyo plants formed yet another company, Shinko Electric Company, Ltd. The remaining nine plants continued to operate as Kobe Steel Works, Ltd.

During the 1950s Japanese industry pursued rebuilding at a furious pace. The Japanese government instituted two five-year plans aimed at boosting steel production levels. Like other Japanese steelmakers, Kobe Steel Works embarked on a program of expanded production. Kobe supplied materials to Japan's peacetime industries, which was producing television sets, refrigerators, and washing machines for eager consumers. A new plant was brought on line in 1951, while another was acquired from the Japanese Ministry of Finance in 1953. Several of Kobe's divisions were turned into subsidiaries to foster their own growth. In 1954 the Amagasaki plant became the Shinko Wire Company, Ltd., and the enameled products department became the Shinko Pfaudler Company, Ltd., then called Shinko Pantec Company Limited. In 1957 the construction department became Shinko Koji K.K. In 1959 the steel works in the Nadahama area of the city of Kobe was upgraded and named the Kobe works, making the company a fully integrated steel manufacturer. By that year Kobe Steel Works had capital of ¥12 billion.

The high cost of raw materials, which to a great degree had to be imported to Japan, forced Kobe—along with other Japanese steel producers—to find new ways to streamline production costs. Japanese steelmakers developed techniques to reduce the amount of coke used in production, thereby diminishing the impact of high-priced imported coal. Emphasis was also placed on exporting steel to balance the cost of importing raw materials. Relatively low labor costs, new plants, and the technological superiority dictated by necessity catapulted Japan's steel industry to the top of the world steel manufacturing league. By 1960 Japan had pushed past the United Kingdom and France to become the fourth-largest producer of steel in the world behind the United States, the Soviet Union, and West Germany. In 1964 Japanese steel production surpassed that of West Germany.

Kobe Steel Works found a unique position among Japanese steelmakers. In 1961 it was the sixth-largest steel manufacturer in Japan. Yet Kobe was the only one of the leading eight manufacturers that did not supply steel in sheets or plate, instead focusing on steel pipes and tubing, wire rods, and specialty steels. In addition, Kobe's steel bars gained an uncommon reputation for quality over the years.

The engineering division of Kobe Steel Works, first licensed in 1950, was thriving. Kobe received its first order to build a complete plant in 1958. The ¥19 billion fertilizer plant in Bangladesh was the first of dozens of plants that the engineering division would build. Kobe's machinery operations also expanded in the 1950s and 1960s. Machinery production began in the late 1930s, when a demand for cutting tools and welding supplies combined with Kobe's steel stockpile to create a natural diversification.

Export Growth: 1960s and 1970s

In 1960 Kobe Steel Works, Ltd., opened liaison offices in New York and Düsseldorf to help coordinate the company's sales efforts overseas. Japanese steelmakers had the most up-to-date manufacturing facilities, low labor costs, and a desire to increase exports. China and Australia proved to be good markets for Japanese steel, but the United States became the biggest importer of steel from Japan, actually accounting for one-third of the country's steel exports. By the mid-1960s U.S. steel manufacturers began to charge Japanese exporters with dumping—selling below cost to gain market share. These charges persisted for years, but no antidumping legislation was introduced because evidence that Japanese domestic prices were higher and that U.S. producers were injured by the low-priced imports was difficult to substantiate. U.S. construction contractors and other manufacturers, meanwhile, enjoyed high-quality Japanese steel at relatively low prices.

Three new plants were opened between 1961 and 1962 and an older plant was closed. In 1965 Kobe Steel Works, Ltd., merged with the Amagasaki Steel Company, Ltd., bringing three more plants into the Kobe family. One of these, the Sakai plant, was sold to Nisshin Steel a year later. Between 1966 and 1970 five more plants, including a steel-plate facility, were brought on line. By the 1970s Kobe Steel operated some of the most efficient steelmaking factories in the world.

In 1968 the two largest Japanese steelmakers, Yawata Iron & Steel and Fuji Iron & Steel, combined to form Nippon Steel, making it the largest Japanese steel manufacturer. Kobe Steel Works was then the fifth-largest producer in the country, and competition for Japanese automobile and appliance makers' accounts remained fierce, keeping the price of domestic steel low in Japan.

The oil crisis of 1973 caused a worldwide recession that severely affected heavy manufacturing. Kobe Steel streamlined its iron and steel division and expanded its machinery division. The engineering division received two large orders for plants in 1974, cushioning the impact of the recession. Kobe's engineering division played a crucial role throughout the later 1970s and the 1980s. Basic steel production was not ignored, however; in 1975 the new Fukuchiyama plant was opened.

Kobe Steel continued to fare well with exports. Liaison offices were opened in Singapore and Los Angeles in 1976, in

Sharjah in 1977, and in London in 1978. The company's success in the United States continued to disturb U.S. manufacturers, and charges of unfair trade practices increased. In October 1977 Kobe Steel Works and the four other top Japanese steel manufacturers were accused of dumping carbon steel plate at a loss of up to $50 per ton—32 percent below fair value. The Treasury Department investigated and found dumping margins of 5.4 percent to 18.5 percent. In January 1978 it was established that Kobe was selling steel at about 13.9 percent below fair value. The worst offender, Sumitomo Metal Industries, was found to be dumping carbon steel at 18.5 percent below fair value. At these percentages actual damage to U.S. producers was not clearly evident.

Continued protests from U.S. manufacturers led to the institution of a trigger price system for steel imports. If a foreign company attempted to sell below a stipulated trigger price, an investigation could begin automatically without the formality of a suit being filed by a U.S. company. Companies caught dumping would have to pay penalties. The system resulted in the voluntary reduction of exports of certain steel products by Japanese companies.

Challenges in the 1980s

By the late 1970s it was clear that global production capacity for steel was much greater than anticipated demand; the steel industry was maturing. At the same time, developing countries like Korea were producing more and more steel with the most modern plants and lower labor costs than in Japan, putting pressure on Japanese steel manufacturers, much as U.S. and European manufacturers had been pressured by the Japanese 15 years earlier. Kobe Steel Works, while maintaining its efforts in machinery and engineering, reduced its emphasis on basic steel products and began to focus on higher value-added steel products.

Kobe began to streamline its facilities and increase spending on energy-saving equipment in 1980. The appreciation of the yen against the dollar in the mid-1980s had a serious effect on revenues. Kobe Steel showed a net loss of $36.7 million in 1984. Five steel plants were closed between 1984 and 1987. In December 1986 Kobe announced plans to reduce its labor force by 6,000 workers—21 percent of its entire staff—over a three-year period. The measures were considered drastic in a country that traditionally guaranteed workers employment until retirement.

At the same time that Kobe Steel was encountering flattening demand for basic steel products, it was preparing for the future by expanding into new but related fields. In 1981 the company became the largest shareholder in a Wisconsin-based construction equipment manufacturer, the Harnischfeger Corporation. In 1983 Kobe took over the U.S. engineering company Midrex Corporation and its Japanese affiliate, Yutani Heavy Industries, Ltd. In 1987 Kobe began construction on a metal powders plant in the United States. Steel powders had growing use in the automotive industry. In 1988 Kobe Precision Incorporated began producing aluminum substrates for magnetic computer discs. Kobe Copper Products, a U.S. subsidiary, made copper tubing for cooling systems, and in 1989 Stewart Bolling Company, a U.S. rubber and plastics firm, was acquired.

In the late 1980s Kobe Steel entered a number of joint ventures with U.S. firms. In 1989 USX, the largest U.S. steelmaker, formed a 50-50 partnership with Kobe to produce steel bars for Japanese automakers, who were now locating their plants inside the United States. In 1990 a major joint venture with Texas Instruments was undertaken to produce application-specific integrated circuits. Later in 1990 the Aluminum Company of America entered a 50-50 joint venture with Kobe to produce aluminum can stock in Japan.

In spite of difficult times in basic products during the mid-1980s, research and development in new areas remained a priority. In 1985 Kobe opened a Biotechnology Research Laboratory in the city of Kobe. In 1987 the first phase of another major research facility, the Seishin Laboratories in Kobe, was completed. In 1988 the Kobe Steel Europe Research Laboratory in Surrey, England, was opened. In 1989 the Kobe Steel Research Laboratories USA-Electronics Materials Center was opened in Research Triangle Park, North Carolina, and an Applied Electronics Center was opened in 1990 in Palo Alto, California. The Palo Alto facility was soon expanded to include artificial intelligence research.

Kobe's overseas expansion had reached fever pitch in the 1980s. A new office was opened in Mexico City in 1981, and the New York City and Los Angeles offices were incorporated as Kobe Steel America Inc., later combined to form Kobe Steel USA. An office was opened in Melbourne in 1983. In 1984 the London office became the subsidiary Kobe Steel Europe, Ltd., and the Sharjah office was moved to Bahrain and incorporated as Gulf Engineering Company Ltd., later renamed Kobelco Middle East.

In 1988 Kobe Steel America was reorganized into a holding company, Kobe Steel USA Inc., to manage Kobe's growing number of diversified U.S. holdings, which now numbered 15 companies. By placing the company's U.S. subsidiaries under one corporate roof, a quicker response to changing market conditions was made possible. Kobe was the first Japanese steelmaker to reorganize itself in this way.

Kobe entered markets previously considered impenetrable. A liaison office was established in Beijing in 1986 and in Moscow in 1989. In 1990 the Singapore office was incorporated as Kobe Steel Asia Pte Ltd. Also in 1990 Kobe Steel Australia Pty. Ltd., based in Sydney, absorbed the Melbourne office. By the early 1990s, under President Sokichi Kametaka, Kobe Steel was well diversified both geographically and by industry and ready for growth in new areas.

Diversification and Expansion during the 1990s

Throughout the early 1990s Kobe Steel formed many new ventures in conjunction with Aluminum Company of America (Alcoa). In January 1991 they created KSL Alcoa Aluminum Company, Ltd., to produce and market aluminum can stock. The following December they formed Alcoa Kobe Tube Specialties Ltd. for the manufacture of drawn aluminum tubes. In June 1992 they created Kobe Alcoa Transportation Products Ltd. and Kobe Alcoa Transportation Products Inc. to produce and market transportation-industry aluminum sheet products in Japan and the United States, respectively. They established

KAAL in July 1993 to manufacture aluminum can stock in Japan.

Kobe Steel also formed a joint venture company with Texas Instruments. The new company, called KTI Semiconductor, Ltd., was formed in May 1990 to manufacture semiconductor products in Japan. By 1994 KTI had one facility in operation to build 4-megabit and 16-megabit DRAM (dynamic random access memory) chips and another facility planned to manufacture 64-megabit DRAM chips.

On April 1, 1995, Kobelco America Inc. (KAI) and Kobelco Construction Machinery (U.S.A.) Inc. (KCM), two of Kobe Steel's construction subsidiaries based in the United States, merged to form Kobelco America Inc. The reorganization was intended to integrate the company's U.S. functions—research and development, engineering, manufacturing, sales, marketing, and product support—in order to better service the North American and world markets. KCM produced engineering and construction machinery in Calhoun, Georgia, and KAI, based in Houston, Texas, was involved in sales, marketing, and product support for construction machinery. All 220 employees were retained in the merger, and the new company's headquarters were established in Calhoun. Kobelco America Inc. was created with an 82.3 percent ownership by the Kobe Steel Group and a 17.7 percent ownership by the Nissho Iwai Group.

In 1995 Kobe Steel suffered a loss of more than ¥100 billion in the Great Hanshin Earthquake. The company set its sights on completely recovering from the loss within two years, and most of its goals were, in fact, met by the beginning of 1997.

Also in 1995 Kobe Steel began its venture into the electricity business. With deregulation of Japan's electric power industry, Kobe Steel revised the company's articles of incorporation to include "supply of electricity" as one of its products. Supplying electricity was one way Kobe Steel was attempting to adjust to changing market conditions. Its sales in Japan were being reduced by cheap imports, and the growing economic strength of China and Southeast Asia had led to stiff competition in its overseas markets.

Principal Subsidiaries

Shinko Kenzai, Ltd.; Nippon Koshuha Steel Co., Ltd.; Sun Aluminium Industries, Ltd.; Shinko Electric Co., Ltd.; Shinko Pantec Co., Ltd.; NABCO Ltd.; Kobelco Construction Machinery Co., Ltd.; Shinsho Corporation; Yutani Heavy Industries, Ltd.; KTI Semiconductor, Ltd.; Shinko Lease Co., Ltd.; Kobelco Construction Machinery Co., Ltd.; Kobelco Research Institute Inc.; Kobelco Systems Corporation; Kobelco Telecommunications Technology Co., Ltd.; LED Corporation (80 %); Yutani Heavy Industries, Ltd. (99.1 %); Kobe Development Corporation (U.S.A.); Kobe Precision, Inc. (U.S.A.); Kobe Steel International Inc. (U.S.A.); Kobe Steel USA Holdings Inc.; Kobe Steel USA Inc.; Kobelco Compressors (America) Inc. (U.S.A., 90%); Kobelco Construction Machinery, Inc. (U.S.A.); Kobelco Metal Powder of America, Inc. (U.S.A., 70%); Kobelco Stewart Bolling, Inc. (U.S.A.); Kobelco Welding of America Inc. (U.S.A.); Midrex Corporation (U.S.A.); Kobe Steel Europe, Ltd. (U.K.); Kobelco Middle East (Bahrain); Midrex International B.V.; Earth Development Pte. Ltd. (Singapore); Kobe Copper Sdn. Bhd. (Malaysia, 70%); Kobe International Co., Pte. Ltd. (Singapore); Kobe Precision Parts (Malaysia) Sdn. Bhd.; Kobe Steel Asia Pte Ltd. (Singapore); Kobe Steel Australia Pty. Ltd.

Further Reading

"Anatomy of an Oriental Giant," *Steel,* December 24, 1962.

Furukawa, Tsukasa, "Japan's Electric Power Attracts Kobe Steel, Others," *American Metal Martet,* March 22, 1996, p. 3.

Furukawa, Tsukasa, "Kobe Combines US Subsidiaries," *American Metal Market,* April 17, 1995, p. 3.

Furukawa, Tsukasa, "Kobe Steel Diversifies into Electronics," *American Metal Market,* December 26, 1994, p. 3.

"Kobe Steel Controls 15 U.S. Firms," *Purchasing,* December 15, 1988.

"Little Industry, Big War," *Fortune,* April 1944.

Petry, Corinna C., "New Kobe President Looks to Future Plans," *American Metal Market,* March 18, 1996, p. 3.

Yoder, Stephen Kreider, "Japan's Smokestack Industries Pin Hope on Research," *The Wall Street Journal,* March 25, 1987.

—Thomas M. Tucker
—updated by Terry Bain

L. Luria & Son, Inc.

5770 Miami Lakes Drive
Miami Lakes, Florida 33014-2418
U.S.A.
(305) 557-9000
Fax: (305) 557-6133

Public Company
Incorporated: 1898
Employees: 1,258
Sales: $173.3 million (1997)
Stock Exchanges: New York
SICs: 5399 Miscellaneous General Merchandise Stores

L. Luria & Son, Inc. is a century-old, Florida-based retailer of jewelry, gifts, housewares, and electronics. Jewelry sales account for 44 percent of Luria's sales; tabletop items, giftware, clocks, and the like account for 38 percent; and consumer electronics, including cameras and home office equipment, and housewares, including luggage and furnishings, make up the rest. In its early history, Luria functioned as a general merchandise wholesaler and a catalog showroom chain. After undergoing a conversion from catalog showrooms to customer self-serve operations and closing several of its less productive stores, the Luria's chain consists of 28 large superstores throughout Florida. The company's central distribution facility is located at its Miami Lakes headquarters. Although Luria is publicly traded, majority interest in the company is owned by Ocean Reef Management, an investment company controlled by brothers Rachmil and Ilia Lekach.

In many ways, the history of Luria mirrors the classic story of immigrant success in twentieth century America. Company founder Lazer Luria began the company humbly in 1898, hawking silver on the streets of the Lower East Side of Manhattan. Ten years later, his son, Philip Luria, opened the company's first permanently-situated store, a small wholesale shop on Broadway. After Philip Luria died in 1911, his son, Joseph Luria, managed the flourishing wholesale business over the next few decades. In addition to silver, the company started dealing in radios, toasters, and other household items. The Luria family business quickly became a major supplier to retail outlets as discount stores and department stores proliferated.

The 1940s–1960s: Southward Expansion

By the 1940s, the company had expanded southward, opening outposts in Atlanta, Georgia, and Miami, Florida. Around this time, Leonard Luria, Joseph's son, began to share responsibility for running the business. Although the South later proved to be the company's destiny, the move seemed imprudent initially. Because Luria's shipping facilities were slow and out-of-date, the cost advantages of wholesaling were eventually lost to the retailers, who could move more quickly. With profit margins eroding rapidly, the company was forced to shut down its Atlanta operation in the 1950s.

A much bigger blow came in 1960, when years of heavy losses forced the closure of Luria's flagship New York operations. The Miami location had became the sole area of operation. By the middle of the 1960s, Leonard Luria, now in charge of the company, saw that the old-style of wholesaling was going the way of the dinosaurs. Tired of the problems associated with collecting from the stores he supplied, as well as the stiff competition from new wholesalers, he decided to refocus the company on jewelry retailing. His decision saved the family business.

In 1964 Luria converted part of the Miami wholesale outfit into a retail operation, from which he sold jewelry in addition to the wares he was already peddling. In order to more effectively deal in diamonds and other precious stones, he bolstered his knowledge with courses in gemology. In 1967 Luria prepared and distributed a modest retail catalog, the company's first. It was as a catalog showroom that Luria's made its name over the next decade.

The Boom of the 1970s

During the 1970s, overall catalog sales in the United States swelled from $1 billion to $7 billion. At the same time, growth of the Florida population was exploding. The combination of those two factors contributed to big growth for Luria. In 1970, the company's last year as a wholesaler, Luria's sales were $2 million. Ten years later, the company had annual revenue of $76 million. The appeal of catalog showrooms came from the convenience of ready merchandise they offered to customers combined with the low overhead costs for the company because they operated like a warehouse. At a time when catalog showrooms seemed to be popping up on every square inch of available real estate, Luria managed to distinguish itself by emphasizing high-priced gold and diamond jewelry and—perhaps with a nod to company founder Lazer Luria—silver. The company also carried standard showroom fare such as cameras, housewares, and electronics, though it tended to avoid items like sporting goods and toys, which yielded lower profit margins.

By 1976 Luria operated eight catalog showrooms across Florida. By this time, jewelry and silver accounted for about 40 percent of the company's sales. Competition soon became stiff; over the next couple of years two of the bigger catalog showroom outfits, Best Products and Service Merchandise, began to hone in on Luria's Florida territory. To fend off its competitors, Luria needed to initiate its own expansion. The needed capital came from a public offering of stock in 1978, which raised money but left the Luria family holding the majority of the stock.

In spite of fierce competition in the Florida's catalog showroom business, Luria managed to more than hold its own over the next several years. Between 1978 and 1982 the number of Luria outlets grew from eight to 21, and company sales were hovering around the $100 million mark. Luria continued to distinguish itself from the competition by keeping its focus on higher-end goods like jewelry. The company also advertised aggressively on television, radio, and in print. Another area in which Luria sought to distance itself from its competitors was in service. While sales personnel at other showrooms were few and far between, Luria sought to make itself more like a department store, so that a customer needing sales help could find assistance quickly. By 1983, with sales at its 26 Florida outlets totaling well over $100 million, the company continued to outperform the competition.

Competition from Mass Merchandisers in the 1980s

During the mid-1980s, the catalog showroom industry hit hard times, as competition stiffened not just from within the industry, but from aggressive pricing on the part of department stores, mass merchants, warehouse clubs, and other retailers. But while the top three showroom chains—Best Products, Consumers Distributing, and Service Merchandise—all showed declines in earnings in 1985, Luria managed to increase its profits 24 percent to $6.8 million, on sales of $145 million, a 17 percent increase from the previous year. Part of Luria's success had to do with the company's eight percent operating margin, the highest in the industry.

By the end of 1986 Luria operated 37 stores. The company continued to thrive in the face of tough times throughout the industry. The key lay in Luria's ability to maintain focus on jewelry, which accounted for over 40 percent of sales. Electronics, at 21 percent, and housewares, at 17 percent, made up most of the remainder. After years of steady, if not spectacular expansion, the company began to slow, but not stop, the rate at

which it was opening new stores during the mid-1980s. Luria also began to build up its ranks of middle managers. It also revamped its store design, making them a tad more upscale in order to emphasize even further the upper-end items it offered.

Luria began opening a chain of jewelry stores in malls, under the name Luria's Fine Jewelry, in the late 1980s. By this time sales, still largely generated by its catalog showrooms—which were mostly located in strip malls in major cities—were exceeding $200 million a year. As other showrooms continued to struggle and fail in droves, Luria completed a three-year program, with the assistance of an outside consulting firm, aimed at keeping the company on track for further growth. Costs were cut, unprofitable product categories were discontinued, and technology was updated, including the addition of point-of-service terminals, a new financial reporting system, and a new jewelry inventory system.

Luria unveiled its new showroom prototype in 1988. The new showrooms were designed to generate $6 to $12 million in sales per store, compared to the $4 million level used in the past. By this time, the company had 43 showrooms, still all located in Florida. Meanwhile the company shortened its catalog and shifted the saved money into promotion, and its advertising efforts were veering away from television, more toward newspapers and direct mail.

New Directions for the 1990s

Even in 1990 when the company was a 52-store empire, Luria was very much a family business. Though traded on the New York Stock Exchange, the company's top executive picture looked more like a family photo. Peter Luria, company president and chief operating officer, represented the fifth Luria generation to run the company. His father, Leonard, remained chairman of the board, chief executive officer, and treasurer. Other family members involved included vice-president of real estate Henry Luria, Peter's brother; and Peter's sister, general counsel Nancy Luria Cohen.

As the 1990s began, the share of Luria's revenue generated by jewelry sales fell below 40 percent for the first time as the company expanded its focus on housewares, such as the 20 different coffee-makers the stores carried. Nevertheless, the company continued to emphasize items for the middle- to upper-class customer, and customer service remained a higher priority than it was for other companies in the showroom business.

Mother Nature gave Luria an opportunity to completely shift gears once again in 1992. When Hurricane Andrew demolished three Luria stores, the company decided not to simply rebuild them as they were. Instead, the company used the unexpected devastation to usher in yet another new store prototype. Rather than veering toward the department store model, as did the previous design, the new store prototype more resembled a mass merchandise superstore. The new design inaugurated the company's shift from traditional catalog house to what it now called a "specialty discount store." While Luria previously had more sales help in each store than most of its competitors, it would now be largely self-serve. In fact, shopping carts were present for the first time in company history. While jewelry and electronics continued to be heavily represented on Luria's shelves, there were now many more less expensive housewares and even some toys.

Luria added two superstores in 1994, bringing the total number of superstores to nine (out of 50 total outlets). The new concept continued to evolve, featuring ''department store merchandise in a specialty environment,'' with the emphasis on value for name brand items. Despite the initial promise of the new mass merchandise format, Luria's sales fell flat as the 1990s continued. With sales slumping badly in 1996, the 73-year-old Leonard Luria decided to retire, and the Luria family sold its 25 percent controlling interest in the company to Ocean Reef Management, a company formed by brothers Ilia and Rachmil Lekach.

The Lekach brothers, Russian immigrants who had arrived in the United States in 1970 after spending 14 years in South America, were, along with a brother-in-law Simon Falic, the principal stockholders and high-ranking officers in two perfume enterprises—Perfumania Inc. and Parlux Fragrances. The acquisition of Luria gave the Lekachs access to a strong network of new outlets for the perfumes made and distributed by Parlux, which included such well-known brands as Perry Ellis and Fred Hayman Beverly Hills.

Under the Lekach brothers, Luria's stores underwent yet another transformation. Perfume and cosmetics counters were added, and the conversion of the entire chain into jewelry, gift, and houseware superstores was completed. In January of 1997, the company closed and liquidated 17 of its worst-performing stores, leaving a core of 28 stores in place. Further cost-cutting measures followed, including staff reductions and supplier contract renegotiations. Luria also raised cash by selling its corporate headquarters/warehouse facility. For fiscal 1997, a year of tumultuous change, the company lost nearly $21 million on sales of $173 million. Luria approached its 100th birthday in leaner—and, the Lekachs hope, meaner—form. Luria's performance during the earliest part of its second century of operation will answer one intriguing question: Did the magic that fueled the company's series of successful redesigns leave along with the Luria family's financial interest, or did it stick around with the family's name?

Further Reading

Byrne, Harlan, ''Showroom Operator Sees Promise in New Jewelry Chain,'' *Barron's,* February 20, 1989, p. 36.

Gordon, Mitchell, ''Sunny Showrooms,'' *Barron's,* September 22, 1986, p. 49

Greenwald, Judy, ''The Personal Touch,'' *Barron's,* August 9, 1982, p. 46.

Hisey, Pete, ''Luria Make Offer for Best Products,'' *Discount Store News,* September 16, 1996, p. 8.

——, ''Rainbow after the Storm: Luria Reinvents Itself,'' *Discount Store News,* January 4, 1993, p. 7.

Hunter-Gadsen, Leslie, ''Luria's Place in the Sun,'' *HFD,* July 23, 1990, p. 57.

''L. Luria & Son: A Cataloger Whose Profits Match Its Classy Image,'' *Business Week,* July 11, 1983, p. 98.

''L. Luria & Son: Hitting Its Stride Again,'' *Chain Store Age,* January 1988, p. 138.

Matas, Alina and DuPont, David K., ''New Owner of L. Luria & Son Makes Bid for Jan Bell Marketing,'' *Miami Herald,* October 23, 1996.

Poppe, David, ''A Scent of Trouble,'' *Florida Trend,* October 1996, p. 68.

''A Switch in Time,'' *Financial World,* May 15, 1981, pp. 65–66.

—Robert R. Jacobson

Layne Christensen Company

1900 Shawnee Mission Parkway
Mission Woods, Kansas 66205
U.S.A.
(913) 362-0510
Fax: (913) 362-0133

Wholly Owned Subsidiary of The Marley Company
Incorporated: 1882 as Layne & Sons
Sales: $222 million (1997)
Employees: 1,261
Stock Exchanges: NASDAQ
SICs: 1381 Drilling Oil & Gas Wells

Layne Christensen Company is the leading water well drilling, well repair and maintenance, mineral exploration, and environmental drilling firm in the United States. The company has four core business areas: water supply services, in which the company provides site selection, drilling and well development, pump installation, and well rehabilitation services to customers around the world; mineral exploration services, such as drilling technologies for mineral exploration that have made Layne Christensen into one of the international leaders in diamond bit technology for drilling and coring; geotechnical construction services, including innovative methods for jet grouting, ground freezing, and dewatering applications used in major construction projects by municipalities and government agencies around the world; and environmental services, where Layne Christensen provides state-of-the-art techniques for assessing and monitoring water quality, filtration and treatment, and groundwater recovery system maintenance. In 1996, Layne, Inc. merged with Christensen Boyles Corporation, one of the most promising firms with operations in mineral exploration services, geotechnical services, environmental services to form Layne Christensen Company.

Early History

Layne, Inc. was founded by Mahlon Layne in 1882 in Shawnee, Kansas. Like many during this time, Layne had traveled from the East Coast to the western plains in order to own and farm his own homestead. Initially stopping in St. Louis, the ambitious

pioneer journeyed via covered wagon with his wife and children on to Kansas to take advantage of the wide open spaces of the American plains. Having settled on a piece of land near Shawnee, Kansas, the young man began plowing wheat in his expansive fields. Soon, however, he discovered that the soil was dryer in Kansas than he had anticipated, and more water was required to make his land a profitable, let alone a living, venture. So Layne began to experiment with different types of water well drilling equipment and methods. Before long, the success of his own homestead attracted the notice of other men throughout the area.

Most of the homesteaders wanted Layne to visit their land and suggest methods for drilling water, and thereby irrigate their farm more effectively. As Layne began to experiment with various methods of well-water drilling, and showed how successful he was at it, the people whom he had helped encouraged him to establish his own company. In 1882, Layne decided to open his own business, and within a short period of time had contracted most of the homesteaders around Shawnee Mission, Kansas. As his business grew, he brought his sons into the management and supervision of the company's operations and renamed his firm Layne & Sons.

By the end of the 19th century and well into the 20th, Layne & Sons had established a reputation for reliable and inexpensive water drilling. As farms grew, however, along with the expansion of municipalities and transformation of the rural landscape by the slow encroachment of small, independently-owned manufacturing firm, a concern amount of water contamination began to surface. Cholera had been one of the most dreaded diseases of the 19th century, and it was well known that good sanitation measures significantly reduced the threat of contamination. Industrial and municipal waste compounded the water sanitation problem. Layne & Sons, now managed by the second generation of Laynes, was contracted by small municipalities throughout Kansas to advise them on the best and most cost-effective method to ensure a clean and safe water supply.

The Great Depression, World War II, and the Postwar Era

When the Great Depression swept across the United States after the stock market crash in October 1929, every business in the country was affected, including Layne & Sons. Although the company was forced to reduce its workforce, which had steadily grown since the early 1920s, Layne & Sons was able to remain free of debt and escape bankruptcy. People still needed water drilling services for their farms in Kansas, and rural municipalities that had contracted the company years earlier remained loyal customers during the difficult years of the early and mid-1930s.

As the economic climate began to improve during the late 1930s, and then expand with the advent of America's entry into World War II, Layne & Sons was asked to develop new and more innovative water drilling devices for farms to increase their produce in spite of labor shortages. Soon the government was contracting Layne & Sons for their water drilling services throughout the Plains states. It was during World War II and the immediate postwar era that Layne & Sons began to transform itself from a local or statewide water drilling services company to a regional firm. As this expansion took place, revenues also increased. Nearly 200 employees were working for the company when America became known as the ''Breadbasket'' to the world during the late 1940s and early 1950s.

As the company expanded during these years, it began to increase the kinds of services provided to customers. Layne & Sons had always engaged in such activities as site selection, pump installation, and well design, but now the company began to hire geologists and hydrologists who would analyze geological data and recommend the best placement of each well and the most suitable well type for that location. Sophisticated instrumentation began to characterize the company's water drilling services and led to an even more enhanced reputation for reliability and efficiency. Throughout the 1950s, the company contracted more and more municipalities within the Plains states, resulting in greater revenue.

Continued Growth and Expansion

During the 1960s and 1970s, company management saw significant opportunities in the increasing awareness and public concern over groundwater contamination. Taking advantage of the federal regulations passed by Congress to investigate, monitor, and correct contaminated sites and municipal aquifers, the company concentrated on providing services to federal and state agencies within the United States, as well as corporate clients, who were concerned about meeting the regulations on groundwater contamination. Access to clean and safe groundwater become more of a concern than any other issue, and the company provided extensive consulting services to assess the harmful effects of population movements and expansion, deteriorating water quality, and the limited availability of surface water.

The expansion of the company's activities consequently led to its higher profile, and a change of name to Layne-Western Company, Inc. to reflect its growth in the western portion of the United States. Not surprisingly, such a well-run and successful company garnered the attention of interested buyers. In 1968, the company was purchased by Marley Holdings, L.P., a limited partnership of individuals interested in the development of Layne-Western.

Operating as a wholly-owned subsidiary, Layne-Western was spurred on by its new owners to engage in an aggressive acquisitions policy. One of Layne-Western's most important acquisition included the during the 1970s was that of The Singer Company, a prominent well drilling and pump installation and repair business with a presence throughout the western United States. This strategic acquisition immediately added 17 locations to the company's operations. In addition, Layne-Western made smaller strategic acquisitions to expand into new geographical areas or new services. By the end of the 1970s, the company had acquired five more companies, and was not finished.

During the 1980s, Layne-Western continued to expand its operations. The company contracted more municipalities, industrial companies, agribusinesses and a smaller number of residential users. The largest contracts during this time involved the municipalities of Houston, Los Angeles, and Las Vegas, with growing populations and limited access to surface water. Layne-Western's water well drilling services became highly sought after by such municipalities due to drought and the ever-increasing need for surface water. To ensure quality service to its clients, the company continued its strategic acquisition policy by adding five more companies to its operations.

The 1990s and Beyond

In 1992 Layne changed its name from Layne-Western Company back to Layne, Inc., to reflect its broadened scope of national and international operations. At this time, the company had four core business areas, including water well drilling, which provided 31.7 percent of the firm's revenues; well and pump repair and maintenance, which accounted for 28.3 percent of revenues; environmental drilling, accounting for 22.7 percent of revenues; and mineral exploration and drilling services, which totaled 17.3 percent of company revenues.

During the early 1990s, part of Layne's strategy involved developing, designing, and installing high production municipal and industrial water wells. Requiring greater technical ability and more sophisticated drilling equipment than the capabilities of most other drilling contractors at the time, Layne began to make significant strides toward capturing a large share of the municipal and industrial markets in this area. By the end of 1992, the company reported that 56 percent of its well water drilling revenues came from municipalities and that 29 percent came from industrial manufacturers. Municipalities included regional water utilities, local water districts, cities, counties and various other local and regional government agencies responsible for providing water supplies to commercial and residential customers.

In 1992, Layne was contracted to provide water well drilling services by some of the most prestigious municipalities and industrial manufacturers in the country, such as the City of Memphis, the City of Los Angeles, Alcoa Company of America, and the Georgia Pacific Company. Interestingly, Layne's aggressive recruitment of municipal and industrial clients was so successful that even with such prominent customers not one of them accounted for more than ten percent of the firm's total revenues during the early 1990s.

Having over the years provided drilling services for geological assessment, specifically for mineral and mining exploration, for gold and copper producers within the continental United States, the company shifted its emphasis to foreign markets as these producers expanded their search for economically minable orebodies. Layne commenced its mineral and mining exploration drilling services in Mexico in 1991. Since that time, the company's international projects in the mineral exploration industry have grown dramatically. Just as important, however, is the fact that the firm's operations in the Latin American mineral industry opened up opportunities for groundwater drilling and pump repair and well rehabilitation. Layne's expanding activities were so successful in Mexico that by 1995 the company had opened a 22,000 square foot office facility in Hermosillo, and in 1996 opened an even larger office facility in Toluca, both of which functioned as water drilling and well rehabilitation service centers.

Additional water and mineral exploration projects have been undertaken around the globe. The company opened an office in Thailand in 1995, and in 1996 acquired Georesources, a Thai-based water drilling company. At approximately the same time, Layne opened a newly-constructed facility in Bangkok to manufacture drill rods for customers operating within the mineral exploration industry in Asia. The company's Canadian subsidiary, Elgin Exploration, began working near one of the world's largest kimberlite diamond mines located in the Northwest Territories, and other similar water well drilling and mineral exploration activities were begun in Bolivia, Argentina, and Peru. Perhaps one of the most important of these projects, however, was located in Chile. Along with its South American partner, Geotec Boyles Brothers, S.A., Layne initiated a $6 million water project. Drilling 13 wells ranging from 700 to 950 feet, a specially built pump rig needed to be transported from the United States to Chile in order to finish the project.

In 1996, Layne merged with the Christensen Boyles Corporation to become Layne Christensen Company. Christensen Boyles had been one of the most successful firms in the same core business areas as Layne, so the managements of both companies saw added value to the formation of one firm. Upon the conclusion of the agreement, Layne consolidated all of its mineral products manufacturing operations into the Christensen Boyles facility at Salt Lake City, Utah, while Christensen Boyles consolidated its geotechnical construction and environmental business into Layne facilities and operations.

One reason for the merger was to increase the opportunities in the international arena, where Christensen Boyles' Latin American partners and affiliates immediately enhanced Layne's ongoing operations. Joint projects were soon initiated in Bolivia, Argentina, and Chile, with plans to expand operations in Brazil. The merger with Christensen Boyles transformed the mineral-related business of Layne into its second largest product line, with revenues increasing by an astronomical 163 percent, and placed the new company into the position of soon becoming one of the world's largest providers of mineral drilling products and services.

As the century drew to a close, Layne Christensen Company intended to expand its groundwater drilling services in the United States, expanding its mineral drilling exploration business throughout Latin America so that its name would become as prominent as in the United States. Moreover, the company hoped to develop its geotechnical services into a major force within the geotechnical construction industry. With the combined management and financial resources resulting from the merger, Layne Christensen would likely have no problem at all with its ambitious strategic plans.

Principal Subsidiaries

Georesources, Inc.; Elgin Exploration, Inc.; Dunbar-Stark Drillings, Inc.; Jim Cole Enterprises, Inc.; Becker Drill, Inc.; Envirodrill Services, Inc.; Stanley Mining Services, Ltd.

Further Reading

Angelo, William, "Process Sets Two Cleanup Milestones," *Engineering News Review,* February 12, 1996, p. 42.

Brown, Richard A., and Johnson, Paul C., "How to Solve Some of Groundwater's Trickiest Problems," *Engineering News Review,* June 6, 1994, p. E57.

"Layne Christensen Offers to Buy Australian Company," *The New York Times,* April 9, 1997, p. D4.

Okun, Daniel A., "What the World Needs Now: Reliable Water for Cities," *Engineering News Review,* April 15, 1996, pp. 22–24.

"Owner Up the Creek Over Tainting of Aquifer," *Engineering News Review,* November 21, 1994, p. 72.

"Primary Treatment," *Public Works,* April 15, 1994, p. D27.

"Raw Water Preparation," *Public Works,* April 15, 1994, p. C10.

Rubin, Debra K., "Firms Predict a Bleak 1996," *Engineering News Review,* March 25, 1996, p. 28.

—Thomas Derdak

Lesco Inc.

20005 Lake Road
Rocky River, Ohio 44116
U.S.A.
(216) 333-9250
Fax: (216) 333-7789

Public Company
Founded: 1962 as the Lakeshore Equipment & Supply
    Company
Sales: $241.7 million (1995)
Employees: 1,008 (1995)
Stock Exchanges: NASDAQ
SICs: 2874 Phosphatic Fertilizers; 3524 Lawn & Garden
    Equipment

Known throughout the $4-billion green industry for its turf control products, fertilizer, and grass seed, Lesco Inc. is the largest manufacturer and distributor of turf care products and equipment in the United States. Preeminent in serving commercial clients with extensive turf areas, including the more than 41,000 golf courses in its care, Lesco also manages the lawn care needs of landscapers, lawn maintenance companies, municipalities, and industrial parks with a vertically integrated line of products. Its innovative marketing system includes Lesco Superstores, Service Centers, and Stores-on-Wheels—a fleet of tractor trailers that delivers goods directly to many of Lesco's over 90,000 customers. Sales representatives, trade shows, direct mail and selected merchandise at Home Depots help to maintain a broad customer base and to attract new clients.

A Local Greens-Keeper, 1962 to 1969

Lesco Inc. began business as the Lakeshore Equipment & Supply Company in 1962. Located on the shores of Lake Erie outside Cleveland, Lakeshore was founded by James I. Fitzgibbon and Robert F. Burkhardt to service the lawn care needs of local golf courses and cemeteries. With just five employees, Lakeshore opened its first sales office and began promoting its products at competitive prices. The company's first full-time salesperson, Tom Gartner, promoted the company by attending a local trade show. This marked the beginning of a trend, as attending and exhibiting at trade shows and seminars became a company hallmark and major venue of Lakeshore's sales and merchandising.

Before the end of Lakeshore's first year the company had expanded into irrigation products and was soon earning a reputation in the area as a dependable, one-stop turf care supplier. The company also started publication of a newsletter in 1965 (later known as the *Lesco News*) and had branched out to cover local, regional, and national trade shows.

Rapid Growth in the 1970s

The 1970s were a decade of immense growth for Lakeshore, both inside and out. After distributing other suppliers' golf course–related products the company began making its own under the private label of "Lesco," a shortened version of Lakeshore Supply & Equipment Company. In 1974 the company hit a major milestone by formulating its first proprietary fertilizer at a facility in Wellington, Ohio. Although few could foresee it at the time, the company's brand name later became synonymous with dozens of high quality, high performance fertilizer blends.

To augment the company's burgeoning sales, Fitzgibbon initiated a new program of marketing and distribution in 1976 by stocking a tractor trailer with goods and sending it directly to nearby clients. Response to the loaded truck was positive and the Stores-on-Wheels program began in earnest, calling on clients every couple of weeks. The fleet trucks were filled with fertilizers, pesticides, grass seed, and a wide range of hand tools and equipment for area greens-keepers. For customers, the convenience of immediate access to supplies, many formulated to each location's specifications, often eliminated the need for large on-site storage facilities; for Lakeshore, it meant a continuous flow of goods and increased visibility.

The Stores-on-Wheels concept worked, especially in Florida's year-round warm climate, and slowly expanded within the region. Another milestone was reached in 1978 with the opening of a manufacturing plant dedicated to formulating sulphur-coated urea. The first commercial facility of its kind in the United States, Lakeshore was betting heavily on the specialized fertilizer to revolutionize the industry. The next year, 1979, the company had a 100-plus work force, up from 40 employees earlier in the decade, with annual revenue of $13.2 million.

Lakeshore's sulphur-coated urea fertilizers were both a breakthrough and a rarity in the United States and beyond. By spraying granular urea (a soluble nitrogenous compound) first with sulphur and secondly with a polymer, nutrients were sealed in for a slower dissemination over time than traditional fertilizing products. With gradual release, clients needed fewer applications and reduced the possibility of overfertilization.

Rebirth and Growth, the 1980s

The dawn of the 1980s brought much in the way of dollars and diversification for Lakeshore. In 1980 the company relocated to its fourth headquarters, a nest of operations in Rocky River that continued the house the company administration into the mid-1990s. The year closed with sales of over $21 million, more than 60 percent higher than 1979's figure. The trend continued (as it did for the next 16 years) in 1981 and 1982 with revenue hitting $28.4 million and $32.2 million respectively.

While Lakeshore's sulphur-coated urea blends had quickly become a signature product, they represented only one facet of the company's research and development. After using a wide range of machinery designed and built by other companies, Lakeshore's first piece of lawn care equipment—a rotary spreader—debuted in 1982. By the time the Lesco Spreader made an impression on the green industry, Lakeshore was already designing additional turf care equipment and tools. With repeated success of its proprietary products, however, Lakeshore Equipment & Supply faced a new dilemma. The once-tiny company, which had begun with a handful of employees 22 years ago, now had a work force of over 200 and annual sales topping $39 million. To capitalize on the growing recognition of its product line and to simplify corporate paperwork, the Lakeshore Equipment & Supply Company officially changed its name to Lesco, Inc. in February of 1984. Soon after, the rechristened company went public on NASDAQ with 690,000 shares selling for $11–13 each. Lesco finished the year with $45 million in sales, about 15 percent higher than 1983's year-end figure of $39.1 million.

In 1985 Lesco achieved two firsts—receiving its first patent for the Jet-Action Deflector (part of a spreader to distribute fertilizer or seed) and the building of its first Service Center

supply store in Plantation, Florida (near Ft. Lauderdale). A second Service Center followed in Boca Raton, then another in Rocky River catering to landscapers, lawn care and maintenance contractors, and do-it-yourselfers. This latest merchandising concept measured approximately 5,000 square feet, was filled with a variety of bulk turf care products and equipment, and offered a drive-through purchasing window for added speed and convenience. Additional Service Centers were opened in Orlando, Florida, and Carrollton, Texas. Sales for 1985 topped $53.3 million and leapt to $69.3 million in 1986—helped by the introduction of two exclusive grass seeds (a Kentucky bluegrass and Cimarron, a tall fescue), the Lesco 300 Greensmower, and an expanded Stores-on-Wheels fleet, now servicing 31 states.

Lesco celebrated 25 years of business in 1987, with more than 500 employees, 700 proprietary products (making up 80 percent of its sales), more than 25,000 customers, nearly $89 million in sales, and the notice of *Forbes* magazine (which ranked Lesco #66 among the Best Small Companies in America). By the following year about two dozen Service Centers dotted the country, and the company passed the $100-million mark in sales ($100.3 million with income of $1 million)—nearly double its figure of just five years earlier.

A New Era, the 1990s

By the end of 1990 Lesco's sales had risen to $117.5 million and income nearly tripled from the previous year to reach $3 million. Lesco's equipment line now encompassed several mowing machines, other specialized equipment, and replacement parts for its ever-growing list of golf course customers, the majority of which were located in the South and along the Northeast shorelines. When new models were introduced, Lesco took the products directly to clients, giving greenskeepers the opportunity to "test-drive" mowers and related equipment. Additionally, the Stores-on-Wheels fleet continued to crisscross the country carrying upwards of 700 different products, while another two dozen Service Centers had opened their doors.

In 1991 Lesco's sales climbed to $131.4 million with net income of about $2.5 million, despite some tense weeks in the first quarter due to raw material price fluctuations and the company's expansion. By the following year, sales grew to $145.7 million, and income hit almost $3.6 million. Despite occasional dips in income Lesco's sales continued to be strong and garnered the company further national attention. Its brands, both in consumables and hard goods, were increasingly recognized. Consumable goods numbered not only its mainstay—fertilizers (both granular and specially formulated liquids using sulfur-coated urea)—but turf control products (herbicides, insecticides, and fungicides) and a burgeoning line of grass seed.

In hard goods, Lesco carried a myriad of equipment, including standard lawn and turf care machinery (riding and walk-behind mowers, fertilizer and seed spreaders, sprayers, dethatchers, and aerators), accessories (aftermarket parts for all of the above), irrigation systems (above- and below-ground), hand tools (tree pruners, shovels, rakes) and protective gear (gloves, goggles and masks), as well as golf course odds and ends (flagpoles, putting green cups, ball washers, tee markers, sand trap rakes, and more). For the majority of its customers,

Lesco had indeed reached its goal of decades earlier—to become a one-stop shop—supplying competitively priced products in a variety of modes.

In 1993 the company's exposure increased dramatically through an agreement with Home Depot to carry Lesco merchandise in 103 of its stores. Through this deal Lesco reached thousands of additional retail customers, primarily residential homeowners, and had the opportunity to fill the lawn care needs of this vast market segment. Service Center sales continued to grow with 103 facilities in operation. By July, the company's shareholders enjoyed a three-for-two stock split. By the end of the year Lesco had income of just over $4.7 million on sales of $166.2 million. Consumable goods made up $124.3 million or nearly 75 percent of total sales, with hard goods/equipment sales holding up the remaining 25 percent or $41.8 million.

Though 1994 proved another banner year for Lesco, it was marred by the passing of James I. Fitzgibbon in October after a lengthy illness. To insure the company's smooth passage, Fitzgibbon had selected William A. Foley to take over the reins as chairman, CEO and president. The company he founded with Burkhardt (who was retired but still worked with Lesco as a consultant), however, continued to boom beyond his or anyone's initial expectations. Analysts had estimated total 1994 sales to jump by 20 percent to between $192 and $205 million, with a 40 percent rise in income due in part to the company's Home Depot deal and Service Center expansion. With over 120 Service Centers throughout the Midwest, Northeast, and South, and plans for another 18 before the end of 1994, the Service Centers were Lesco's fastest growing segment. The company's fleet of Stores-on-Wheels, which numbered 59 in May, also helped propel sales for a year-end total of $204.5 million—for a 23.1 percent volume increase. Income was $6.9 million and consumables again dominated equipment by 75.5 to 24.5 percent respectively, or sales of $154.4 million versus $50.1 million.

As projected, Lesco had 138 Service Centers operating in the United States by early 1995 with plans for an additional 35 (for 173 total) in 34 states by year's end. Same-store sales rose 16.7 percent as stores matured and the Stores-on-Wheels fleet grew to 65, providing goods to more than 7,000 golf courses. Though expanding more slowly than the Service Centers, Stores-on-Wheels' segment sales increased 13.2 percent from 1994 and 15.1 percent over 1993.

Big news came in December when Lesco announced plans for a northeastern expansion through the purchase of Pro-Lawn, a division of Agway, one of the biggest regional agricultural cooperatives in the United States. With estimated sales for fiscal 1995 of $30 million, Pro-Lawn was the Northeast's largest turf products supplier. Lesco finished the year with sales of $241.6 million, yet income was down from the previous year's 86 cents a share to 59 cents because of delayed shipments and further urea price fluctuations. Urea prices had begun to rise in the last quarter of 1994 (by 30 percent) and continued to climb in 1995, forcing Lesco to raise prices, though this was too late to affect profit margins for the year (which fell by 4.4 percent in fertiliz-

ing products), taking overall margins down from 1994's 34.6 percent to 33.6 percent in 1995.

In January of 1996 Lesco completed its Pro-Lawn acquisition for $11.2 million in cash, taking over the company's inventories, certain fixed assets, licenses, trademarks, and key personnel. First quarter sales reflected the purchase at $53.5 million (up 13.3 percent from 1995's $47.2 million), rebounding from the last quarter of 1995. For the remainder of 1996, Lesco planned to open 20 Service Centers and add three Stores-on-Wheels trucks. In March of 1996 the company introduced its first Lesco Superstore. Located in Pinehurst, North Carolina, the store was the latest offering from its marketing and distribution think tank. Lesco also increased sales through home office staff (who fielded 1,000 calls a day), regional sales reps, telemarketing, mail order catalogs, and more frequent appearances at regional and national trade shows.

Lesco's seed, harvested from over 16,500 acres of land in the Pacific Northwest, Canada, Florida and Georgia, continued to gain popularity with 28 proprietary blends and 21 standard mixtures. To ensure quality and effectiveness, the company maintained agreements with several universities to test fertilizers, turf control products, and grass seed varieties. Nearly half of the nation's major golf courses, including many of the Top 10, have used Lesco's products (fertilizers, herbicides, grass seed, equipment and supplies) for decades. With more Lesco Superstores on the drawing board, along with increased exposure through Service Centers, Stores-on-Wheels, and Home Depot, Lesco was poised to assert itself further into the turf care marketplace and garner sales in the neighborhood of $290 million for 1996. Based on past experience, Lesco demonstrated more than enough staying power to substantially increase sales and income in 1997 and beyond.

Principal Operating Units

Lesco Service Centers; Lesco Stores-on-Wheels; Lesco Superstores.

Further Reading

Cerankosky, C. E., "Lesco Inc.," *Hancock Institutional Equity Services,* October 26, 1995, pp. 1–2.

"Company Expects 1994 Sales to Increase More Than 15%," *Wall Street Journal,* March 3, 1994, p. A5.

"Higher Costs, Weather Hurt Second-Quarter Performance," *Wall Street Journal,* June 16, 1995, p. A5.

Labate, John, "Companies to Watch: Lesco," *Fortune,* May 2, 1994, p. 79.

"Pact Is Signed to Acquire Agway's Pro-Lawn Unit," *Wall Street Journal,* December 27, 1995, p. 12.

Slawson, S. E., "Lesco Inc.," *Merrill Lynch Capital Markets,* August 1, 1995, pp. 1–3.

Winter, Ralph E., "Lesco Sees 20% Growth in Sales, Net for 1994 as Lawn Care Market Grows," *Wall Street Journal,* December 5, 1994, p. A9I.

—Taryn Benbow-Pfalzgraf

Improving Healthcare and Chemistry

Mallinckrodt Group Inc.

7733 Forsyth Boulevard
St. Louis, Missouri 63105-1820
U.S.A.
(314) 854-5200
Fax: (314) 854-5381

Public Company
Incorporated: 1882 as Mallinckrodt Chemical Works
Employees: 10,400
Sales: $2.21 billion (1996)
Stock Exchanges: New York
SICs: 2819 Industrial Inorganic Chemicals; 2834
    Pharmaceutical Preparations; 3841 Surgical and
    Medical Instruments; 3845 Electromedical Apparatus

Mallinckrodt Group Inc. is a global developer and producer of specialty chemicals and human health care products. Many of its products, such as barium sulfate (for X-ray diagnosis) and narcotic analgesics (such as codeine), have been market leaders. The company distributes its products throughout the world.

The Mallinckrodt Group is organized into two separate companies: Mallinckrodt Medical Inc. and Mallinckrodt Specialty Chemicals Company. A majority of its revenues are from its human health care products, which include, among other things, imaging agents, critical care products, and pharmaceuticals. Mallinckrodt has plants in North and South America, Europe, and the South Pacific.

Company Origins

The company can be traced back to Emil Mallinckrodt and his cousin Julius, who both left Germany for the United States in 1831 to seek opportunities in the New World. Emil settled in St. Louis, Missouri, where he became a successful farmer specializing in apple orchards and vineyards. One of his sons, Edward, who was interested in the applied uses of chemistry for farming, went to Germany with his brother Otto in 1864 to study chemistry. When the brothers returned to the United States, they started G. Mallinckrodt & Company, Manufactur-

ing Chemists, with their eldest brother, Gustav, as a partner. Founded in 1867, the business began with $10,000 capital.

Most of the major pharmaceutical companies at the time were located in the East. The Mallinckrodt brothers would have to compete with such firms as E.R. Squibb and Sons, Charles Pfizer and Company, Powers-Weightman and Company, and Rosengarten and Sons. Edward later recalled, ''We realized from the start that we would have to make it to the interest of the buyer to place his order with us by supplying goods of the highest quality.'' Working in their favor was the fact that St. Louis was fast becoming a major commercial center because of the railroad and the development of the Mississippi River. As the only chemical manufacturing company west of Philadelphia, Mallinckrodt was able to capture much of the newly emerging western markets.

The brothers manufactured chemicals and administered the business in several small buildings located on the family farm. Office management and sales were Gustav's job, while Otto was in charge of the laboratory and purchases. Edward supervised the factory. Some of the staple chemical products they produced were aqua ammonia, spirits of nitrous ether, and acetic and carbolic acids. They later began to make chloroform and burnt alum, which is used in baking powder. The hallmark of their products was the fineness of their chemicals, which were easily soluble and did not cake like some of the other powders on the market at the time. Mallinckrodt soon became identified as quality producers whose goods, unlike other producers, could withstand the scrutiny for adulteration.

Growth from the 1870s until World War I

By 1877 the company had grown from the three brothers to a work force of 40 people, and in 1882 it was incorporated as Mallinckrodt Chemical Works. Edward's bothers, Otto and Gustav, both died untimely during this period, leaving Edward in charge of the operations. One of Edward's successful innovations was the introduction of anhydrous ammonia used in the production of ice. His investment in the refrigeration industry paid off. By 1890 Mallinckrodt Chemical Works became one of the chief producers of anhydrous ammonia.

Edward had other important successes. During the 1880s he succeeded in making his company a chief supplier of chemicals used in the manufacture of photographic plates. In the 1890s Mallinckrodt entered the expanding business of narcotic analgesics, which was being spurred by German chemical companies. While he was building his business, Edward participated in St. Louis's business and civic development. He purchased real estate in the city's downtown business district and was a board member of the St. Louis Trust Company, which was active in the construction of the Memphis and Southeastern railroads. He was also active in promoting higher education, contributing to the medical departments of Washington University and Harvard University, where his son Edward, Jr., had graduated in 1901.

Edward, Jr. had an intent interest in chemical research. One of his earliest projects with the company was to develop methods for the preservation and purification of ether used for anesthesia. By 1914 he had designed a way to stabilize and protect ether from impurities by using various types of bottles and canisters. An associate of his, Henry Farr, joined the company in 1906. In 1913 Farr led the way in the development of barium sulfate for X-ray diagnosis.

At the beginning of World War I the American chemical industry was dependent on Germany for supplying the chemicals it needed. Thus, the U.S. embargo of 1914 against German goods initially hampered production for companies like Mallinckrodt.

When the United States entered the war in 1917, the demand for certain products, such as aspirin and phenobarbital, led to the passage of legislation allowing American chemical companies to manufacture these products. This legislation ignored international proprietary laws binding American companies from producing them. During this time American companies also expanded their research and development of products, an activity formerly monopolized by the German chemical industry.

Mallinckrodt, like other American chemical companies, eventually benefited from this period of turmoil. One of its major products was phenobarbital, which was used as a substitute for German coal-tar sedatives.

Developments between the Wars

In the 1920s Mallinckrodt turned out many compounds that were requested by the Washington University School of Medicine research departments. One of the most important of these compounds was Iodeikon, an X-ray contrast medium for visualizing the gall bladder. This product enhanced the company's reputation in the field of diagnostics, especially in the area of contrast media.

In 1928 Edward, Jr., took over the company on the death of his father, Edward Mallinckrodt, Sr. While the father represented the business-minded expansionism of the past, the son was more concerned with improving the quality of the company's products, manufacturing techniques, and relations with their employees.

During the Great Depression the company displayed unusual commitment to its employees. Instead of laying off workers, Mallinckrodt put employees to work at various jobs that would keep them busy. For example, they maintained the grounds of the factories and offices, fixed equipment, painted fences, and cleaned yards. In 1938 a cafeteria with picnic benches was installed on-site. During this period many service businesses grew up around the plant to provide employees with convenient shopping for their daily needs.

During the 1930s major changes taking place in the pharmaceutical industry began to challenge the existence of Mallinckrodt. Pharmacists, rather than buying and mixing bulk chemicals for their own formulations, were increasingly using wholesale drug companies like McKesson and Robbins to provide them with ready-made prescriptions and tablets. Sulfa drugs were in demand, and the new range of vitamins and other specialty drugs required the company to consider new strategies for survival.

In 1936, as a way of adjusting to the changes taking place at the neighborhood pharmacy, Mallinckrodt launched a campaign called the Prescription Department Promotion Plan. This plan gave pharmacists advice on how to advertise and increase prescription revenues. It helped the public understand what to look for when they visited their druggist and disseminated bulletins to promote information that could help pharmacists stay in business.

Also helping Mallinckrodt during the 1930s was its production of medicinal narcotics. The company's entrance into medicinal narcotics, a source of continuous and steady revenue for the company over the years, began in 1898 with its production of morphine and codeine. Research and production of narcotic drugs was later hampered in the first two decades of the 20th century by both national and international legislation designed to curtail the nonmedical traffic of narcotic drugs. These laws would create occasional shortages of opium supplies. The restrictions put on opium import made it difficult to analyze the quality of the plants that were being used for morphine production.

By the 1930s codeine, another derivative from opium, had gained popularity. It was considered less addictive than morphine. Thus, morphine sales began to decline, while codeine sales increased. Mallinckrodt became the pacemaker in refining and improving the codeine product in the 1930s. During World War II the government relied on Mallinckrodt's narcotic production capability to supply the needs of the war effort. The company found it difficult, however, to fulfill its war contracts while still serving its regular customer base because the government wanted its narcotic analgesics to be produced separately.

Although there were major problems with opium supplies after World War II, Mallinckrodt continued to be a major player in the production and research of narcotic analgesics. By the early 1990s Mallinckrodt remained a chief producer of bulk medicinal narcotics, selling more than 20 high-value products to manufacturers of prescription pharmaceuticals.

Wartime Refining of Uranium Ore

In 1942 Mallinckrodt was invited by two scientists from the University of Chicago to prepare refined uranium for secret work on a war project. Edward, Jr., eagerly accepted the job. After 90 days, even before the government project was signed, he produced 60 tons of high-level refined uranium ore. This material was used on December 2, 1942, in the first self-sustaining nuclear chain reaction, which took place beneath the west stands of the University of Chicago's Stagg Athletic Field. Mallinckrodt became the sole supplier for these experiments, known as the Manhattan project, well into 1943, and the company continued during and after the war to be a leader in the field of uranium ore refining.

In 1955 construction began on a materials plant at Weldon Springs, Missouri. It was backed with a $70 million investment by the U.S. government for the manufacturing of various types of uranium ore products. Weldon became an official site licensed by the government, and by 1957 the Weldon Springs facility was processing between 60 and 70 tons of raw materials a day. Another plant was soon opened in Hematite, Missouri, for commercial atomic power plants and atomic-powered sea vessels.

While production hummed in the 1950s for the company's atomic and traditional products, Mallinckrodt began to restructure its stock issuance program. In 1954 Class A stock was sold to the public and Class B, which held voting privileges, was owned by the Mallinckrodt family. Then, in 1956, company officers relocated sales offices to New York City, where they tried to control the production and sales of the St. Louis establishments. During this time several new projects were attempted without success, and it became apparent that the process of transformation in the next few decades would not be an easy one.

The Thayer Period, 1960–1981

In 1941 Harold E. Thayer became coordinator of the U.S. government's War Production Board. It was in this position that his attention turned toward Mallinckrodt for their processing of uranium for the Manhattan Project. He soon became an employee of Mallinckrodt, first as a plant manager and then as a project manager for all the company's uranium work at Weldon Springs. He was made a company vice-president in 1950 and ten years later became president. When Edward Mallinckrodt, Jr., stepped down as chairman in 1965, Thayer became chief executive officer and chairman of the board.

As president in 1960, Thayer saw his job as coaxing and pulling the company into the present. He maintained that if Mallinckrodt was to survive intact, it would have to transform itself from a small, family-run business to a professional and profitable modern corporation. Decentralization was the first order of business. Thayer created three new business units: medicinal, industrial chemicals, and nuclear. Employee involvement was another change he initiated. He believed that those who were close to the workplace could "make mincemeat" of any problem. Then he set up a formal operating committee to facilitate corporate decision making. In 1960 the company's sales were about $35 million. Thayer issued the slogan "70 by 70," meaning $70 million in sales by 1970. With the introduction of new management policies and the acquisition of new companies, that goal was reached before 1970.

After the death of Edward Mallinckrodt, Jr., in 1967, the Class B family stock was not passed to his surviving son, George, who preferred to follow a career in science rather than business. The stock went instead to a Mallinckrodt management team to be held in trust for fifteen years. These stock holdings infused much new capital into the growth plans during the Thayer management period.

Changes in the 1980s and 1990s

Raymond Bentle, a senior financial analyst at Mallinckrodt, was appointed president in 1978 and succeeded Harold Thayer as chief executive officer in 1981. Not long afterward, on Janu-

ary 18, 1982, the stock previously owned by Edward, Jr., but held in trust by a company management group (representing about 20 percent of the company's stock) was transferred to Harvard and Washington universities, a move that reflected the company's continued commitment to research and development. Meanwhile, other companies were trying to corner larger shares of Mallinckrodt's stock for a takeover, but, according to Bentle, "none of these companies represented the type of owner that had the quality and integrity that we desired."

While Thayer, from backstage, was advising independence from takeovers, Harvard University, the major trustee of the shares of Edward, Jr., was encouraging outside bidders. When a company executive chided Harvard for working against its benefactor's interests, he was told that "fifteen years is long enough for any man to reach from the grave."

Avon Products won Bentle's interest, and a deal for $711.5 million was struck, with Harvard and Washington universities receiving $125 million in gifts. In 1982, the year of the Avon purchase, Mallinckrodt had reached $494 million in sales, the highest it had ever achieved in its long history.

The Avon relationship lasted for only four years. "Avon thought we were a health care company," explained Mack G. Nichols, the head of Mallinckrodt's specialty chemicals division under Avon. "So for three years we pretended we were." Avon sold Mallinckrodt in 1986 to International Minerals and Chemical Corporation.

Although owned by International Minerals and Chemical Corporation, Mallinckrodt remained an independently run company, and its shares were traded on the New York stock exchange. Then, in 1989, it was decentralized into two smaller companies—Mallinckrodt Specialty Chemicals Company, headed by Mack Nichols, and Mallinckrodt Medical Inc., headed by Roy Holman—which were placed under the umbrella organization Mallinckrodt Group Inc. It was in this arrangement that Mallinckrodt stabilized, though in 1997 Mallinckrodt divested its veterinary division and its interest in Tastemaster, a worldwide flavors business with which it had entered into a 50–50 joint venture in 1992.

Principal Divisions

Mallinckrodt Baker; Mallinckrodt Catalysts and Chemical Additives; Mallinckrodt Critical Care; Mallinckrodt Medical Imaging; Mallinckrodt Nuclear Medicine; Mallinckrodt Pharmaceutical Chemicals; Mallinckrodt Pharmaceutical Specialties.

Further Reading

D'Amico, Esther, "Reorganizing Diversification," *Chemical Week,* February 28, 1996, pp. 32–33.
Mallinckrodt 125th Year Anniversary (corporate history), St. Louis, Missouri: Mallinckrodt Group Inc., 1992.
Plishner, Emily S., "No Pet Rocks Here: Mallinckrodt's Board Doesn't Win Plaudits by Sitting on Its Behind," *Financial World,* February 26, 1996, pp. 40–42.
Smith, Rod, "Mallinckrodt's 'Steady Steps' Lead to Transformation," *Feedstuffs,* October 14, 1996, p. 8.

—Jordan P. Richman

MasTec, Inc.

3155 Northwest 77th Avenue
Suite 110
Miami, Florida 33122-1205
U.S.A.
(305) 599-1800
Fax: (305) 406-1908
Web site: http://www.mastec.com

Public Company
Incorporated: 1994 as MasTec, Inc.
Employees: 7,000
Sales: $472.8 million (1996)
Stock Exchanges: New York
SICs: 1623 Water, Sewer and Utility Lines; 8741
    Construction Management; 8742 Telecommunications
    Engineering Consulting Services

MasTec, Inc., a diversified holding company, is one of the world's leading independent contractors specializing in the construction of telecommunications infrastructure. The company was founded in 1994 by the merger of publicly traded Burnup & Sims, Inc. and the privately owned Church and Tower Group, two established names in the U.S. telecommunications-construction services industry based in Florida. The principal business of the company and its family of subsidiaries consists of the design, installation, and maintenance of the outside physical plants for telephone and cable television (CATV) communications systems, public utilities, and the traffic-control and highway-safety industry. Additionally, MasTec builds coaxial fiber-optic cable networks and wireless-antenna networks. Inside buildings, the company installs and maintains telecommunications equipment and communications networks. MasTec's customers include operators of telecommunications, CATV and wireless-communication companies, as well as banks, brokerage firms, institutions of higher learning, medical facilities, multiple-product industries, and government agencies. From 1994 to 1996 MasTec revenues increased 325 percent, growing from $111.29 million to $472.8 million. A substantial part of

the company's domestic revenues derives from services to BellSouth Communications and international revenues come primarily from Telefonica de España.

The Forerunners: 1929–1994

In 1929 two unemployed carpenters—Russell Burnup and Riley V. Sims—founded Burnup & Sims to provide design, construction, and maintenance services to the telephone and utilities industries. During the years of the Great Depression, the two industrious men established an office in West Palm Beach, Florida, and by 1936 had a small fleet of trucks and staff. Burnup & Sims' first telecommunications projects occurred the following year at Cape Canaveral, where it was responsible for burying 85 miles of cable.

The company contributed to national defense during World War II by building airfields and telephone systems. After the war, Burnup & Sims became involved in the laying of underwater cable from Florida to Puerto Rico, and from there to Barbados, for such companies as AT&T and General Telephone. Projects then took on a greater geographical scope, as Burnup & Sims established underground telecommunications systems and built radio towers in Costa Rica, Barbados, Trinidad-Tobago, and Venezuela.

In 1968 Burnup & Sims went public, and the shares sold helped raised capital for new, more ambitious projects. The company is remembered for constructing the first fiber-optic link between Chicago and Washington, D.C. and, according to historian George P. Oslin in *The History of Telecommunications,* for doing ''a large and very profitable business installing cables for Cable TV.'' In fact, by 1982, Burnup & Sims ''had installed a fifth of the 500,000 miles of TV cables in use.'' The company also operated a number of telecommunications subsidiaries as well as Floyd Theaters, Inc., a movie picture chain; Lectro Products, Inc., a CATV power-protection company; and Southeastern Printing, Inc., a printing business.

By the end of the decade, however, unsettled economic conditions, changes in utility spending, and aggressive competition for contracts brought tough years for Burnup & Sims. Moreover, budgetary constrictions led certain telecommunications companies to postpone payments and to cut expenditures for plant construction and maintenance. By the end of fiscal 1993 Burnup & Sims' losses amounted to $9.31 million, and senior management was seeking a buyer for the company.

Church & Tower of Florida, Inc. (CTF) was incorporated in 1968 as a privately owned company to construct and service telephone networks in Puerto Rico and Miami. However, the company had quickly overextended itself in Puerto Rico and could not build the telephone-infrastructure networks needed in Miami. When Miami-based CTF experienced financial difficulties, the company's owner asked his friend, Cuban immigrant Jorge L. Mas Canosa, to help save the business. In exchange for half ownership of CTF, Mas Canosa began to manage the company in 1969.

Seeking to improve the business, Mas Canosa himself climbed down into ditches, manholes, and trenches to observe the workers' construction methods. He sought advice from telephone company and government inspectors and studied books about the most efficient and newest construction methods. As a result, he led the company into a fast-track, cost-effective construction program that won recognition for consistent professionalism, commitment to excellence, and cost-effective methods. BellSouth Telecommunications, Inc. awarded CTF a long-term contract for projects in the greater Miami and Fort Lauderdale areas. By 1971 Mas Canosa had turned the failing company around, borrowed $50,000, and bought the remaining shares of the firm.

Jorge Mas, Mas Canosa's eldest son, began working at CTF in 1980 and became company president in 1984. At this time the development of new technologies and the removal of legal and regulatory barriers were laying the foundation for corporate alliances among the nation's largest telephone, CATV, computer, entertainment, and publishing businesses. Telephone companies were planning to invest billions of dollars to install fiber-optic systems to bring the new technologies to homes and businesses. A rapid increase in Florida's population was placing the existing telecommunications infrastructure under tremendous strain.

In 1990 Jorge Mas established a new subsidiary, Church & Tower, Inc. (CT), to engage in selected construction projects in the public and private sectors. For some time the Mas family had been thinking about taking the company public, but 1992 Hurricane Andrew's passage over southern Florida delayed the

plans. The CTF Group, owner of a long-term maintenance contract with BellSouth, was responsible for reconstructing the damaged telecommunication infrastructure of Miami. In the wake of the hurricane, the senior managements of Burnup & Sims and of the CTF Group realized their mutual interests. Employees from both companies began talking to each other; top management met and struck a deal.

The Defining Year: Founding of MasTec, Inc.

On March 11, 1994—in a reverse acquisition—the privately owned Church & Tower Group acquired 65 percent of the outstanding common stock of publicly traded Burnup & Sims, Inc. The name of Burnup & Sims was changed to MasTec, Inc., the Church & Tower Group became a wholly owned subsidiary, and the senior management of the CTF Group took over leadership of the new entity; Jorge L. Mas Canosa became MasTec's chairman and Jorge Mas was named president and chief executive officer. Mastec was now a regarded as a "minority business enterprise," publicly traded on NASDAQ under the symbol MASX.

At this time MasTec was one of the nation's leading companies of its kind and the fifth-largest Hispanic-owned public company. To express their entrepreneurial spirit as concisely as possible, MasTec's management adopted the former Burnup & Sims slogan "Opening the Lines of Communication" and added their own vision of the future: "Throughout the World."

Following the acquisition, one of President Jorge Mas' first moves was to express the company's philosophy of leadership in word and deed. In an introduction to the company's 1994 annual report, he asserted that "MasTec's improving performance and future capabilities are in large part due to the commitment of its 2,400 employee-owners. . .who work hard, work smart and complete their jobs on time and on budget." In April 1994 he had already set up this success-driven philosophy by distributing five shares of MasTec stock to each employee and encouraging all to invest in their company's benefits program.

Realizing that the telecommunications industry was fragmented and operated mainly by family-owned businesses, Mas-Tec initiated a program for acquiring profitable, market-dominant companies in high-growth metropolitan areas nationwide. MasTec launched this acquisition program with the purchase of Designed Traffic Installation, Inc., an installer of traffic control systems in southern Florida; and Buchanan Contracting Company, Inc. the holder of two master contracts with BellSouth in Memphis, Tennessee, and Montgomery, Alabama. Furthermore, BellSouth awarded MasTec contracts for telephone networks in Nashville and Franklin, Tennessee, as well as for networks in four of North Carolina's fastest-growing cities.

From the beginning and throughout MasTec's evolution as a provider of telecommunications services, long-term (master) contracts, such as those with BellSouth, and short-term contracts with alternate-access providers—such as MCI Telecommunications Corp. and US West Communications Services, Inc.—were the backbone of the company's business operations. The deregulation process had enabled alternate-access providers to enter the territory of the regional Bell operating companies, to build networks and sell services to high-volume users, such as those clustered in downtown office buildings and commerce parks. Several MasTec subsidiaries provided fast-track construction services to these competitive-access companies.

Another item on MasTec's business agenda for growth was to increase the Latin American presence it had acquired from the merger. By the mid-1990s many international telecommunication companies had been lured to South America by its improving economy and the privatization of telecommunications, including CATV services. These companies, however, had neither the personnel nor the in-country resources to implement system upgrades of the aging infrastructure for telecommunications. They needed the services of independent contractors who could apply cost-effective methods to the upgrade and construction of these infrastructures. According to its 1994 annual report, President Jorge Mas believed that MasTec had "the cultural ties, management expertise and existing regional operations to serve these needs."

Consequently, the company's international subsidiaries secured contracts for upgrading telephone networks in Guayaquil, Ecuador; for building 35,000 telephone lines in San Salvador, El Salvador; and for constructing fiber-optic facilities in Caracas, Venezuela. Furthermore, Video Cable Comunicación, S.A. awarded a design-build contract to MasTec Argentina, S.A. for upgrading its CATV system in Buenos Aires from 30 channels to 100. This is believed to have been the first contract of its kind in Latin America. At year-end 1994 MasTec had met the challenges of establishing itself as a new company; it reported a net profit of $7.5 million on revenue of $111.29 million.

1995 Consolidation: Divestitures and Acquisitions

Ready to seize opportunities created by unprecedented changes occurring in the telecommunications industry, MasTec decided to divest itself of some subsidiaries—part of the Burnup & Sims acquisition—that were not related to its core operations: Floyd Theaters, Inc., Lectro Products, and Southeastern Printing, Inc. The proceeds from the sale of these operations was used to reduce debt and finance the acquisition of other companies related to MasTec's core business.

MasTec then acquired Utility Line Maintenance, Inc., a company engaged in clearing right-of-ways for utilities in southeastern United States. Church & Tower Fiber Tel, Inc. expanded its business to include installation of "smart highway" systems, that is, electronic systems that control highway messaging and traffic signalization. The acquisition of Tri-Duct Corporation brought two more BellSouth master contracts in Huntsville and Decatur, Alabama, thereby complementing existing contracts in Montgomery, as well as in Memphis. Consolidating administrative functions in these adjacent geographic areas reduced the company's operating expenses and enhanced service capability in the region. MasTec won new contracts to install telecommunications networks in the Dallas/Fort Worth area; to manage construction for Metro Dade Water & Sewer Authority's Pump Station Program; to install part of MediaOne, Inc.'s new CATV network in metropolitan Atlanta; and to develop and maintain infrastructure telephone services in eastern Colorado for US West.

To continue expanding into foreign countries, MasTec had to compete with large international companies having significantly greater experience and resources. The company acquired a 36 percent equity interest in Supercanal, S.A., a CATV operator in Argentina, and equity interests ranging from 14 percent to 35 percent in four other companies. The company also won a contract from The Virgin Islands Telephone Co. to restore damaged telephone facilities on the island of St. Thomas, U.S. Virgin Islands; and a contract from Tomen Corp., a leading Japanese telecommunications company, for the construction of 35,000 telephone lines in Manila.

By the end of 1995 the company had combined the strengths of its subsidiaries and organized its operations into three principal business segments: telecommunications and related construction services, CATV infrastructure construction and maintenance, and general construction services. Due primarily to acquisitions made in 1994 and expansion into new contract areas, in 1995 MasTec's total revenues increased by approximately $63 million, or 57 percent, from $111.29 million in 1994 to $174.58 million in 1995. Providing telecommunication-construction services to regional Bell operating companies, especially to BellSouth, accounted for a majority of the company's growth.

Toward the 21st Century

As MasTec entered the second half of the 1990s, the telecommunications industry continued to undergo fundamental changes. The U.S. Telecommunications Act of 1996, agreements among countries in the European Union and continuing privatization and regulatory initiatives in Latin America were removing barriers to competition. Furthermore, the U.S. government auctioned off radio-frequency bandwidth for the creation of personal communications systems (PCS), which are pure digital networks superior to the traditional analog-cellular systems. Customers' growing demand for enhanced, integrated voice, video and data telecommunications emphasized the limitations of traditional networks and increased the need for the installation of PCS networks.

MasTec competed in the new markets created by these worldwide developments by concentrating on additional relevant acquisitions and expansion of its core telecommunications services through contracts for: 1. upgrading existing networks to broadband technology, such as fiber optic cable; 2. becoming a major infrastructure-construction provider to large telecommunications companies who needed to reduce construction costs by outsourcing their outside-plant work to independent contractors; 3. constructing infrastructures for new service providers entering previously monopolistic markets; and 4. performing inside-wiring services to install intra-company communications networks having the greater bandwidth capacity required for the powerful multimedia computers being brought into businesses.

In a major acquisition, MasTec bought Sintel, S.A., the engineering and installation unit of Telefónica de España, S.A., Spain's national telephone company. Sintel was the leading builder of telecommunications infrastructures in Spain and had operations in Argentina, Chile, Peru, and Venezuela. Although Sintel's revenues, like those of the former Burnup & Sims, were spiraling downward at the time of its acquisition, the purchase actually merged the strengths of both the American and the Spanish company: it more than doubled the size of MasTec, gave it access to Sintel's established operations in Spain, opened the door to competitive opportunities in other European countries and created the possibility of Sintel's expanding in, and beyond, its existing markets in Latin America.

Among other acquisitions that reinforced MasTec's internal growth and geographic diversification were the following: the purchase of Harrison Wright Company, Inc., a telecommunications contractor with operations and BellSouth master contracts principally in Georgia and the Carolinas; and the acquisition of Shanco Corporation and Kennedy Cable Construction, Inc., CATV contractors providing services to six southeastern states as well as to New Jersey and New York. MasTec's subsidiaries installed a 370-mile fiber loop for Telergy, Inc. in upstate New York and completed a fiber loop for MCI Metro in Raleigh, North Carolina.

The limitations of analog networks were propelling the upgrading and installation of the more efficient digital networks. For instance, in a report titled *North American Premises Wiring System Markets,* the market-research firm of Frost & Sullivan Inc. noted that revenue for the premise-wiring industry in 1996 totalled $2.3 billion and could reach $4.38 billion by the year 2003. MasTec increased its penetration into this premise-wiring market (the installation of coaxial and optical-fiber cables inside offices) by combining two of its subsidiaries, Carolina Com-Tec and Burnup & Sims Communications Services, to form a new company: MasTec ComTec. This subsidiary brought single-project, turn-key and maintenance solutions to the communications problems of Fortune 500 corporations, government agencies, colleges, universities, and medical institutions. As a certified installer of wiring systems for most of the major manufacturers of network components, MasTec ComTec installed both local-area networks (LANs) and wide-area networks (WANs). The company was hired to fast-track construction of the enormous fiber-and-copper infrastructure of telecommunications equipment for the 1996 Olympic Village; to build LANs and WANs for the nationwide offices of a major stock-brokerage firm; and to install and maintain a bank holding company's consolidated voice, data, and video network.

Another subsidiary, MasTec Technologies, Inc. was established in 1996 to provide fast-track, turn-key construction management services of wireless networks. In little more than a year the company installed over 130 PCS tower-and-antenna sites for PCS companies, thereby establishing state-of-the-art wireless networks in southern Florida, Tampa, Orlando, and Phoenix.

By year-end 1996 MasTec's revenue had increased 171 percent, from $174.58 million in 1995 to $472.8 million in 1996. Earnings per share had increased from $0.50 in 1995 to $1.20 in 1996. In January 1997 MasTec announced a three-for-two stock split and on February 14 of that year began trading its common stock on the New York Stock Exchange. President Jorge Mas, in a company news bulletin released after the New York listing, declared that ''MasTec's joining the world's premier exchange is a tribute to the dedication and hard work of its 7,000 employees worldwide. The fact that a company formed by Cuban exiles is able to trade among the Fortune 500 companies is living proof that the American dream is very much alive.'' MasTec celebrated by offering its employees a new stock-purchase program that enabled them to buy stock at a 15 percent discount.

As the 21st Century drew near, MasTec was the nation's leading telecommunications company for infrastructure construction and a major supplier of premise-wiring services to Fortune 500 companies. In short, MasTec was a world leader for the design, construction, and maintenance of leading-edge telecommunications networks and hoped to remain in that position as by ''Opening the Lines of Communication Throughout the World.''

Principal Subsidiaries

B&D Contractors of Shelby, Inc.; Burnup & Sims of Texas, Inc.; Burnup & Sims Telcom of Florida, Inc.; Church & Tower, Inc.; Church & Tower Fiber Tel, Inc.; Church & Tower of TN, Inc.; Designed Traffic Installation, Inc.; Harrison-Wright Company, Inc.; Kennedy Cable Construction Co., Inc.; MasTec ComTec of the Carolinas, Inc.; MasTec ComTec of California, Inc.; MasTec International, Inc.; MasTec Technologies, Inc.; R.D. Moody & Associates, Inc.; R.D. Moody & Associates, Inc. of Virginia; Shanco Corporation, Inc.; Sintel, S.A. (Spain); Utility Line Maintenance, Inc.

Further Reading

Bussey, Jane, ''Mas,'' *The Miami Herald,* September 2, 1996, pp. 17–21.
Frost & Sullivan, Inc., *North American Premises Wiring System Markets,* Report No. 2762, Mountain View, Calif.: Frost & Sullivan, 1997, 430 pp.
Lunan, Charles, ''MasTec Buys Firm in Spain,'' *Sun-Sentinel,* April 2, 1996, p. D2.
Oslin, George P., *The Story of Telecommunications,* Macon, Georgia: Mercer University Press, 1992, 507 pp.

—Gloria A. Lemieux

Max & Erma's Restaurants Inc.

4849 Evanswood Drive
Columbus, Ohio 43229
U.S.A.
(614) 431-5800
Fax: (614) 431-4100

Public Company
Incorporated: 1972
Employees: 3,221
Sales: $79.9 million (1996)
Stock Exchanges: NASDAQ
SICs: 5812 Eating Places

Headquartered in Columbus, Ohio, Max & Erma's Restaurants Inc. is a 41-unit chain of eponymous eateries located in major metropolises in Illinois, Indiana, Kentucky, Michigan, North Carolina, Ohio, and Pennsylvania. Most units are company-owned. The company operates within the $40-billion "casual dining" segment of the restaurant industry, a niche distinguished as full service in a relaxed setting with a menu that includes alcoholic beverages. Key competitors include segment leader Red Lobster as well as T.G.I. Friday's, Applebee's, Olive Garden, and Chili's Grill & Bar. While the chain's core concept has long been a hit, Max & Erma's early history was marred by unprofitability and a lack of direction. That changed with the 1986 ouster of founder and CEO Barry Zacks. Under more conservative management, the chain's revenues increased from $15.5 million in 1987 to $79.9 million in 1996, while net earnings grew from $303,000 to $2.2 million.

Founded in the 1970s

The chain was founded by Barry Zacks, a graduate of Cornell who returned to his hometown of Columbus to take a position at his family's footwear company, R.G. Barry Corp. However, footwear didn't hold the intrepid entrepreneur's interest for long. In 1972, the 36-year-old purchased a local bar and restaurant from longtime owners Max and Erma Visconik.

Located in Columbus's historic German Village, the building had been constructed in 1889 by the Franklin Brewing Company. Known during Prohibition as Kaiser's Cafe, the pub had stayed afloat selling "near beer" and groceries.

Zacks's revamp of the business targeted the mid-priced segment of the dine-out market with a particular emphasis on singles. He cultivated a fun atmosphere with a now-ubiquitous decor that has been characterized as the "garage-sale look," featuring moosehead trophies, nostalgic photos, and memorabilia as well as plenty of brass and tiffany-style stained glass. Promotions were usually adult-oriented and sometimes raunchy. The "So Happy It's Thursday" (S-H-I-T) events of the early 1980s, for example, lampooned competitor T.G.I. Friday's salute to the beginning of the weekend. Telephones at each table encouraged patrons to flirt with one another. Max & Erma's also earned a reputation for gigantic servings, a distinction founded on its signature Garbage Burger. This hand-pattied, ten-ounce behemoth with "the works" has been credited as the original gourmet hamburger. Zacks has also been cited as the progenitor of the salad bar and potato skins appetizer. With an average tab of less than $10 and a strong emphasis on bar beverages, Max & Erma's earned a reputation as a gathering place for singles.

New Management in the 1980s

The concept was a hit. By the time the chain went public in 1982, it boasted ten locations in Ohio, Michigan, Indiana, Kansas, Kentucky, and Pennsylvania, and annual revenues of over $12.5 million. However, this growth had masked a number of problems, not least of which was a lack of profitability. In a lengthy 1990 critique of the chain for *Restaurant Business*, Ralph Raffio asserted that the company had "not once [turned] a profit in its first 15 years of existence." (It had in fact recorded a $185,000 surplus in 1982, which had been accounted for as a 44-week year.) Raffio blamed flighty management and ill-conceived programs. "Like the time the dinner house chain's new drive-thru window had to be promptly shuttered because a well-done burger took 13 minutes to cook. Never mind that within two weeks of installing the drive-thru, a customer actually ran out of gas waiting for his order.''

Critics—among them members of Max & Erma's own board of directors and executive team—cited poor site selection and an out-of-control menu as key obstacles to profitability. Some thought Barry Zacks's choices for new locations were too dependent on price instead of market and demographic characteristics. The company often entered new markets via the purchase of failed restaurants and converted them to the Max & Erma's theme, resulting in a hodgepodge of dissimilar storefronts, sometimes in less-than-ideal locations. Zacks would later acknowledge that this was a core shortcoming, telling *Business First-Columbus*'s Ann Hollifield that ''The one thing I learned from Max & Erma's is the most important thing is location, location, location, and the fourth one is location. I made those mistakes with Max & Erma's, and I don't want to make them again.''

Notwithstanding award-winning menus, a slavish attention to food trends saw the chain adding 20 to 30 new items to the menu each year, giving it a 30-plus page menu by the mid-1980s. The eclectic lineup expanded from all-American burgers and appetizers to include everything from a raw bar to homemade pasta, a variety of ethnic dishes, and exotic sauces. Furthermore, each restaurant tailored its offerings to local tastes, making chainwide procurement next to impossible.

Most of the blame for these difficulties was placed squarely on the shoulders of Barry Zacks. Raffio boiled the chain's difficulties down to a single factor: the founder's ''rambunctiousness.'' In July 1986, CFO William Niegsch told *Nation's Restaurant News* that ''This company is a textbook case of being started by an entrepreneur . . . and now it's time for more professional management.'' It was one of the most discreet criticisms made of Zacks during this period.

Zacks stepped down that year and was replaced by Todd Barnum, who with three other top executives purchased the founder's remaining 20-plus percent stake in the chain. Zacks went from Chairman and CEO to ''Founder and Independent Businessman'' in the 1986 annual report, and remained on board for awhile as a consultant. (He died from cancer four years later at the age of 54.) Barnum had been with the eatery since its inception, advancing to president in 1974. He expressed his confidence in the company's continuing viability in Raffio's 1990 article, asserting that ''No matter how terrible things got financially for us, there were still a lot of people having a great time at our restaurants. The restaurant concept itself was never the problem. Executing it was.''

Achieving Profitability in the Late 1980s

Team Barnum proved that theory by turning a $300,000 profit in its first full year at the helm. The new CEO used a variety of fairly simple strategies to achieve this heretofore rare outcome, focusing on the menu, marketing, operations, and remodeling. By eliminating low-sale, high-labor dishes, the company simplified its menu from 36 pages to six. It also shrank some of its ''enormous portions,'' offering the six-ounce Erma burger as an alternative to the Garbage Burger, for example. The company hired a marketing executive to manage promotional campaigns via outdoor, events, direct mail, and television. Market research helped the chain trace key demographic trends. For example, as Max & Erma's core baby-boomer clientele aged, married, and had children, the chain's emphasis shifted from singles to a more family-oriented clientele. A $2-million remodeling program updated equipment as well as decor.

These efforts began to bear fruit within months. Sales increased from $16.5 million in 1986 to a record $24.3 million in 1989, while net income increased from a deficit of $318 million to a record $1.2 million. The turnaround won praise from the likes of the *Wall Street Journal* and *Business Week,* and this positive press helped the relatively small company become one of the restaurant industry's most-watched growth stocks. Having stabilized the chain's finances, Barnum embarked on what he called a ''modest, controlled expansion,'' concentrating primarily on existing markets.

1990s Bring Growth, Competition

The company adhered to that reasonable plan, adding only two units by the end of 1989 for a total of 13 locations, but enthusiasm took hold in 1990, when the chain added five new restaurants. Although it tested franchising, CFO Niegsch noted in a 1993 *Nation's Restaurant News* article that the executives were ''indifferent to franchising,'' eschewing the cost savings for ''tight control.'' This growth spurt proved poorly-timed, however, with a national recession bruising the results of even the heretofore recession resistant casual theme segment of the restaurant industry. With net income declining to less than $500,000 in 1991, Max & Erma's reined in growth to just one unit per year in 1991 and 1992. Net recovered to $1.1 million in the latter year, by which time the company had 20 locations clustered in the Midwest.

Max & Erma's pursued healthier expansion in the mid-1990s, increasing revenues and profits to record levels in 1996. The chain achieved this feat through continued reductions in operating costs, a strategic menu revamp, and the introduction of a new restaurant prototype. In 1993, the company abandoned its traditional site selection strategy, which still focused on acquiring existing restaurant buildings and refurbishing them as Max & Erma's. Instead, the chain developed a stand-alone model that would provide a distinctive atmosphere and lower start-up costs. Participation in ''restaurant parks'' also proved a viable growth vehicle in some markets. These retail developments, often in suburban areas, combined several different (though mostly casual) restaurants in one destination.

In an effort to increase individual checks from less than $10, the company introduced new, slightly more expensive menu items and began to push its long-neglected bar offerings. Sales grew from $43.5 million in 1993 to $79.9 million in 1996 while net increased from $1.4 million to $2.2 million, capping five consecutive years of growth in both categories. From a well-established presence in Ohio, Michigan, Kentucky and Pennsylvania, the company established itself in major markets of Illinois and North Carolina. By the end of 1996, the company had 40 units throughout the Midwest.

Still led by Todd Barnum in 1997, Max & Erma's planned to open seven to nine new units each year in the late 1990s. New markets in the South, where balmier weather would allow the restaurants to make good use of their patio tables, were targeted, with units planned for Atlanta, Georgia, and Greenville, South Carolina. However, as Carol Casper of *Restaurant Business* warned, casual-themed restaurants faced the prospect of becoming "victims of their own success," as "hundreds of imitators and innovators flooded the market." Max & Erma's hoped to differentiate itself from its competitors via an easily recognizable (and consistent) facade, a continuously evolving, value-oriented menu, a highly-trained service staff, and a fun, yet family-oriented atmosphere.

Further Reading

Benson, Betsy, "Max & Erma's Adds Area Sites," *Pittsburgh Business Times,* August 28, 1989, pp. 1–2.

Bradford, J. C. & Co., "Max & Erma's, Inc.—Company Report," The Investext Group, December 16, 1993.

——, "Max & Erma's Restaurants, Inc.—Company Report," The Investext Group, September 1996.

Casper, Carol, "Small Is Beautiful: Max & Erma's Acts Like an Independent," *Restaurant Business,* September 1, 1996, pp. 98–99.

——, "Staying Power," *Restaurant Business,* September 1996, pp. 81–105.

"Casual-Themers Not So 'Recession-Proof' After All," *Nation's Restaurant News,* April 8, 1991, p. 14.

Farkas, David, "Disciplining the Menu: How a Process Helped Max & Erma's into the Black," *Restaurant Hospitality,* August 1990, p. 132.

Festa, Gail, "On a Diet," *Restaurant Hospitality,* April 1988, pp. 120–26.

Gindin, Rona, "Market Segment Report: Casual Theme," *Restaurant Business,* November 20, 1992, pp. 169–82.

"Godfather's, Max & Erma's Write Fun into Job Description," *Restaurants & Institutions,* August 21, 1989, p. 34.

Harton, Tom, "Max & Erma's Agrees to Move into Castleton's Defunct Diner," *Indianapolis Business Journal,* January 8, 1990, p. 4.

Hollifield, Ann, "Max & Erma's Founder Launching a New Business," *Business First-Columbus,* December 29, 1986, p. 8.

Kapner, Suzanne, "Max & Erma's Retools Menus, Adopts New Strategy to Boost Profits," *Nation's Restaurant News,* May 20, 1996, p. 7.

Keegan, Peter O., "Max & Erma's Philosophy Lets Employee Individuality Shine," *Nation's Restaurant News,* June 25, 1990, pp. 3–4.

"Max and Erma's Cuts Overhead Costs, Boosts Growth and Profits," *Nation's Restaurant News,* June 8, 1987, p. 54.

"Max & Erma's Profits Off in 3rd; Outlook Up," *Nation's Restaurant News,* September 25, 1995, p. 10.

"Max and Erma's Promotes S-H-I-T," *Restaurant Business,* January 1, 1983, pp. 162–63.

Nash, Bob, "Max & Erma's Bounces Back by Correcting Early Mistakes," *Business First-Columbus,* March 4, 1985, p. 12.

Prewitt, Milford, "Itty-Bitty Max & Erma's Gets Big-Time Press Attention," *Nation's Restaurant News,* January 22, 1990, p. 14.

——, " 'Restaurant Park' Latest Blueprint for Clustering," *Nation's Restaurant News,* December 20, 1993, p. 3.

Raffio, Ralph, "Can Max & Erma's Rebuild?" *Restaurant Business,* June 10, 1990, pp. 127–33.

Riell, Howard, "Dollar Signs for Regional Players," *Restaurant Hospitality,* July 1992, pp. 66–68.

"Scuttling a Trusty Formula Can Help Revive Growth," *Wall Street Journal,* November 27, 1990, p. B2.

"South Fits Max & Erma's Goals," *Columbus Dispatch,* March 16, 1996, p. B1.

Walkup, Carolyn, "Max & Erma's Discovers Success in Slow Growth; Chain Achieves Turnaround with Steady Approach," *Nation's Restaurant News,* March 22, 1993, p. 16.

——, "Max and Erma's Founder Zacks Dies after Cancer Bout," *Nation's Restaurant News,* August 20, 1990, p. 3.

——, "Max & Erma's Zacks Drops Management Role," *Nation's Restaurant News,* July 7, 1986, pp. 1–2.

—April Dougal Gasbarre

The May Department Stores Company

611 Olive Street
St. Louis, Missouri 63101-1799
U.S.A.
(314) 342-6300
Fax: (314) 342-4461
Web site: http://www.maycompany.com

Public Company
Incorporated: 1910
Employees: 130,000
Sales: $11.7 billion (1996)
Stock Exchanges: New York
SICs: 5311 Department Stores; 5661 Shoe Stores

The May Department Stores Company is the second-leading upscale department store chain operator in the United States. The St. Louis-based company operates ten department store chains, composed of approximately 370 stores throughout over 30 states, under the well-known names of Lord & Taylor, Robinson's-May, Kaufmann's, Foley's, Filene's, Hecht's, Meier & Frank, Strawbridge's, L.S. Ayres, and Famous-Barr.

The Early Years

The beginnings of The May Department Stores Company can be traced to 1877, when company founder David May opened his first store in the mining town of Leadville, Colorado, at the age of 29. An immigrant from Germany, May had settled in Indiana during his teen years, where he earned his living as a salesman in a small men's clothing store. Diligence and marketing flair won him a quarter-interest in the business, but ill health forced him to sell his stake and seek a drier, healthier climate in the West, where he tried prospecting. Inexperience brought swift failure, though, and thus he returned to the field he knew and opened a men's clothing store with two partners.

The firm of May, Holcomb & Dean supplied the miners with red woolen underwear and copper-riveted overalls. The store was an instant success, but a real estate disagreement dissolved the partnership, leaving May alone to put up a building on newly purchased ground. This second venture was called The Great Western Auction House & Clothing Store, an enterprise that was soon large enough to welcome a partner, Moses Shoenberg, whose family owned the local opera house. By 1883, the new partnership was flourishing, for the town's population had become sophisticated enough to demand clothing for many purposes. May and Shoenberg kept pace with the demand, ensuring success with aggressive advertising methods and conservative fiscal management.

Before long, The Great Western Auction House & Clothing Store was financially able to expand its merchandise to include women's apparel, after testing the market with a huge stock of expensive dresses bought from an overstocked Chicago store. Two years later, despite a post-boom depression that would doom Leadville's prosperity by the end of the decade, May bought out Shoenberg's interest in the store in 1885. He went on to add a branch store in Aspen, Colorado, and then another called the Manhattan Clothing Company in Glenwood Springs, Colorado.

Corporate strategy was already firmly established by this time. Print advertising that trumpeted genuine bargain prices lured an ever-escalating, middle-class clientele, while frequent sales kept the merchandise moving. Fast stock turnover kept the customers in the height of fashion. Energy and swift management decisions were David May's trademarks. A frequently-quoted story tells that he paid $31,000 for the stock of a bankrupt clothing store he spied during an 1888 visit to Denver, Colorado. By the end of the day, he had installed a brass band out front to help sell out the existing stock. It only took him one week to clear the inventory, remodel the store, and establish the property anew as The May Shoe & Clothing Company.

May's expansion efforts continued through the 1890s. First came the 1892 purchase of the Famous Department Store in St. Louis, Missouri, for which he and three Shoenberg brothers-in-law paid $150,000. Six years later, spreading his interests to Cleveland, Ohio, he spent $300,000 to buy the aging Hull & Dutton store, renaming it May Company. In order to more easily manage his many holdings spread across the country, in

Company Perspectives:

"May is committed to treating the customer right through enhanced floor-level execution. We strive to keep our stores well staffed with friendly sales associates who are trained and sensitive to the needs of our customers."

1905 May moved the company headquarters to St. Louis, Missouri, where it remained into the 1990s.

Expansion Throughout the Early 1900s

In 1911, one year after The May Department Stores Company was incorporated in New York, it was listed on the New York Stock Exchange. May used proceeds to purchase a second St. Louis chain, the William Barr Dry Goods Company. To consolidate the firm's Missouri holdings, he merged the two St. Louis chains, forming the Famous-Barr Company. In spite of the large investment this move demanded, sales for the year reached $14.8 million, with net profits of $1.5 million.

By 1917 David May was ready to hand the company presidency over to his son, Morton. He named himself as the company's chairman of the board, but did not reduce his active interest in business affairs; in 1923, at the age of 75, he bought a Los Angeles department store, A. Hamburger & Sons, for $4.2 million cash. He then personally supervised its renovation and its energetic promotion. Renamed The May Company, the store opened new avenues in California and helped to produce 1926 sales figures that surpassed the $100 million mark for the first time in the company's history. It was a final triumph for David May, who died in 1927 at the age of 79.

That same year, the company acquired Bernheimer-Leader Stores, Inc., of Baltimore, Maryland. At a price of $2.3 million, the new acquisition was also renamed The May Company, and by newly established company policy, was the last acquisition for some time to follow. Top priorities then became consolidation, improvement in performance, and store remodeling. Systematic modernization plans to update delivery systems and to provide customer parking began in 1928, and were completed in 1932.

May's sales reached $106.7 million in 1929. During the bleak years that followed, the company maintained its stability with strict financial planning and a greater focus on inventory. Buyers had always maintained large stocks of merchandise, regardless of the external economic climate. This practice now proved to be profitable, for higher purchase costs were not a problem; the company simply added the old and the new prices of an item, averaged the two, and held one of its famous sales. Large inventories thus became an asset, leaving the stores unaffected by the Depression-era foundering of distressed suppliers.

A distinct advantage to the company lay in the wide geographical spread of May's subsidiaries. Each store had its own buying department, allowing it to cater to its individual needs. Since the Depression's depth likewise varied from area to area, buyers could gauge their stock requirements with accuracy. Additional centralized buying facilities, however, allowed buy-

ers to take advantage of mass-purchasing practices to keep their costs down. Careful planning paid off—although sales dipped to $72.5 million by 1932, they slowly recovered, rising to $89.2 million by the end of 1935.

Post-Depression Diversification

By 1939 the company was ready to expand once again. Foreshadowing a 1940s trend toward suburban shopping centers, May opened a Wilshire Boulevard branch of its Los Angeles store, stocking it with merchandise for the upper-income customer. Then in 1946, May organized a merger with Kaufmann Department Stores, Inc., of Pittsburgh. With a history stretching back to 1871, Kaufmann's was western Pennsylvania's largest department store, and had cordially shared several May buying offices for many years. Together, the two operations were large enough to produce combined 1945 sales of $246.4 million. Kaufmann's brought to the partnership a higher-income clientele, seven new units, and its own brand of paint, linens, and toiletries. In 1948 there was another important acquisition: the Strouss-Hirshberg Company of Youngstown, Ohio. This gave the company stores in Youngstown and Warren, Ohio, and New Castle, Pennsylvania.

The company founder's formula of aggressive promotion, competitive pricing, and wide selection gave the company dominance in five of the eight cities that were now home to May stores. Liberal salaries and incentive plans ensured staff loyalty, as exemplified by several department store heads who had been with the company for numerous years. The different elements made a successful mix, resulting in 1949 sales that reached $392.9 million, despite population shifts to the suburbs, competition from discount houses, and increases in customer spending for food and gasoline.

In 1951, Morton D. May succeeded his father as company president, and Morton J. May moved on to the company chairmanship, just as his own father had done previously. Continuing in his father's expansion and consolidation footsteps, the younger May held the reins of 25 stores by the end of 1953; the lineup now consisted of ten large downtown stores, five large branch stores, and ten smaller branch stores. Sales for that year topped off at $447.5 million, and the company could well afford the $10 million it spent over the 1954–1955 period to remodel, modernize, and enlarge suburban stores. Additional potential for suburban expansion spurred construction of the firm's first shopping plaza, The Center of Sheffield. Covering 55 acres near Lorain, Ohio, the development contained about 40 retail stores as well as parking for 3,000 cars. It proved so popular that another center was constructed in Los Angeles within the next two years.

Other new ventures in the 1950s included the 1957 purchase of Denver's Daniels & Fischer Stores Company, which was subsequently merged with existing Denver operations and renamed May D&F. Hecht Company of Washington, D.C. was also acquired in 1959, with branch operations in Baltimore. Though start-up costs and refurbishing usually curbed earnings in an acquisition's first year, Hecht's merger did not affect profits. May finished the decade with record sales reaching $645.1 million.

The 1960s and Beyond:
Social and Demographic Influences

As the 1960s began, demographic research, used to track present and future buying patterns, showed two new trends. On one hand, there was a shift to discount merchandising, bringing the company into competition with drugstores, supermarkets, and discount houses. On the other hand, the more expensive end of the spectrum was now showing an increased emphasis on fashion in clothes, linens, and other May staples. To move inexpensive staples more efficiently, the company increased automation in most units. At the specialty merchandise end, the company upgraded its merchandise to include even more exclusive brands.

Two important acquisitions were negotiated in 1965, both of which were finalized the following year. One was a merger with Meier & Frank Co., Inc., of Portland, Oregon. Another acquisition, G. Fox & Company, brought May into Hartford, Connecticut. Both of these mergers were scrutinized by the Federal Trade Commission (FTC), whose restrictive powers were broadened early in 1966. As both transactions had been initiated before the new restrictions came into force, both acquisitions were allowed, although the company had to agree to make no further acquisitions for ten years, unless specifically permitted by the FTC.

When Morton D. May became chairman of the board in 1967, to be succeeded as president by Stanley J. Goodman, a disturbing new trend appeared: the vigorous acquisitions program and its concomitant store renovations and expansions began to eat into profits. Downtown stores were waning in popularity, and customer demand at the new suburban branches was not yet enough to compensate. Labor costs also rose significantly. Year-end figures told their own story; in 1966 total sales reached $869.1 million, yielding a profit of $45.9 million, while 1967 total sales reached $979 million but brought a profit of just $38.4 million. The following year, although total sales passed the $1 billion mark for the first time, profit sank to $36.2 million.

Nevertheless, plans involving the discount end of the market continued. In 1968 the company hired John F. Geisse, an experienced discount merchandiser, to head its new discount subsidiary; he soon became a vice-president. The new enterprise, called Venture, started in St. Louis in 1970. Achieving quick success, it burgeoned to a 12-unit chain by 1972. Three years later there were 20 stores, serving a population of over eleven million.

In 1975 the Venture subsidiary contributed an estimated 9 percent of May's $1.75 billion in sales. Focusing on the Midwest market, the company had eight Chicago-area Venture stores, a number too small to give the advantages of increased productivity or warehousing and distribution savings. To remedy this problem, in 1978 the subsidiary purchased 19 Turn-Style stores with a combined annual sales figure of about $180 million from Jewel Companies. The units were then redesigned and restocked, at a cost of $27 million. Further expansion had to be temporarily shelved, however, because existing distribution and inventory monitoring systems were unable to cope with the sudden increase in the Chicago-area activities.

Catalog shopping, accommodating the ever-swelling numbers of working women, was another new enterprise of the 1970s. In a 50–50 partnership with Canadian Consumers Distributing Company, Ltd., May opened 18 catalog showrooms in the mid-1970s, planning an eventual 150 more. Unlike other catalog stores that offered merchandise that was dispatched from separate warehouses, these supplied catalog-ordered items from storage facilities on the premises. Although hopeful that the new enterprise would at least break even by the end of 1976, this was not the case, and May sold its 70 U.S. showrooms to Consumers Distributing Company (CDC) in 1978.

In November 1979 the company bought Volume Shoe Corporation for about $150 million in stock. A Topeka, Kansas, family-owned chain of more than 800 self-service stores, Volume was then enjoying annual sales totaling more than $200 million. The following year, a recession combined with negative effects of start-up costs for an enlarged shoe distribution center, and cut deeply into profits. Between 1979 and 1983, however, the chain showed the biggest earnings increase of any May Department Store Division. Moving purposefully toward its goal of establishing a "Payless Shoe Outlet" chain nationally, Volume purchased 83 stores from HRT Industries as well as 38 from Craddock-Terry Shoe, and was eyeing possibilities in east coast cities.

At the same time, a new May president, David Farrell, instituted a program of refurbishments to renovate some of the company's more outdated units and rejuvenate their image as trendy fashion outlets. The company spent $117 million on the Famous-Barr chain alone, although other stores were also remodeled. Farrell also instituted stringent cost-cutting means, which included the installation of new telephone and energy-management systems for all 138 department stores. Merchandise was upgraded to tempt the upscale customer, for the company was competing against specialty stores whose fashion reputations were already established.

Maintaining Market Share in the 1980s

A significant threat to market share appeared in the mid-1980s, in the form of warehouse stores and off-price outlets. Offering brand-name merchandise at discount prices, they forced retailers to rethink their customary strategy. May's answer, to fulfill its requirements of upgrading merchandise at one end of their market niche and meeting the off-price challenge at the other, was the 1986 acquisition of Associated Dry Goods (ADG), at a cost of $2.5 billion. This steep purchase price brought the company the quality Lord & Taylor chain, J.W. Robinson department stores, L.S. Ayres units, Caldor discount operations, and Loehmann's off-price apparel shops. As was the case with the other May subsidiaries, each chain continued to operate independently.

In 1987 May formed a 50-50 partnership with PruSimon, called May Centers Associates (MCA). May transferred its shopping center operations to MCA. Two partners owned PruSimon: Melvin Simon & Associates, Inc., of Indianapolis, Indiana, and the New York-based Prudential Insurance Company of America. PruSimon paid $550 million in cash for its share of the partnership. May's chief benefit was to disengage from management functions unrelated to the stores, which increased in number once again with the $1.5 billion acquisition of Filene's of Boston and Foley's of Houston in 1988.

After spending two years acquiring a huge chunk of the upscale department store market, the company then decided to narrow its retailing focus, and made moves to discontinue its discount operations. Loehmann's was sold in 1988, two years after it was acquired. Offered next were Venture and the Caldor chain that had been part of the ADG acquisition. Unfortunately, there were a large number of retail operations for sale at the end of the 1980s, and the company was unable to reach its asking price of almost $600 million for Caldor. Therefore, it sold this unit to an investor group, which formed a company called Odyssey Partners L.P., to buy an 80 percent share. In 1990 Venture was spun off to shareholders in a tax-free distribution. That same year, May acquired Thalhimers, a 26-store group based in Richmond, Virginia, which helped May's sales surpass $10 billion.

The 1990s and Beyond

In the early 1990s, The May Department Stores Company continued to expand its reach through the acquisition of stores around the country, consolidating them into one of May's own companies, depending on the geographic region in which they were situated. Thalhimers was consolidated with Hecht's, and Rochester, New York-based Sibley's was consolidated with Famous-Barr. Furthermore, in 1993 Los Angeles' May Company and Robinson's were combined to form Robinson's-May, which remained one of the area's premiere upscale department stores into the late 1990s.

Many critics began to wonder whether May's quick takeovers would backfire. Because the company was purchasing stores with names that were already established and then changing each store into one of its own, the possibility existed that customers would become confused and once-prosperous stores would lose business. Fortunately for May, however, this did not seem to be the case, and the company continued to post record earnings throughout the acquisition phase. Furthermore, the company actually saved itself money by controlling its marketing expenses; rather than spend money to promote many different individual stores from city to city, the company instead was able to advertise regionally once new stores were transformed into one of May's namesakes.

The aggressive acquisition and transformation practice continued throughout the mid-1990s. Engulfed by the rapidly expanding May holdings were ten Hess's in Pennsylvania and New York in 1994, and 16 Wanamaker and Woodward &

Lothrop stores in Philadelphia and Washington, D.C. in 1995. All in all, throughout 1995 the May Company either acquired or opened a total of 37 new department stores. It also acquired two large discount shoe store chains, Kobacker Company and The Shoe Works, in Columbus, Ohio. Together, these two chains numbered 550 stores.

The company followed their impressive expansion efforts with another key acquisition of 13 Strawbridge & Clothier stores in Philadelphia in 1996. The stores continued to be operated under the name Strawbridge's, and May opened another 15 throughout the year. May also decided to spin off its Payless ShoeSource holdings to the public in mid-1996, listing the newly-freestanding company on the New York Stock Exchange in May of that year. May achieved sales of $11.7 billion for the year.

Entering the end of the century, May stores continued to face keen competition. But the company thrived on the strength of its stellar reputation and its on ongoing efforts to upgrade products and maintain its position as marketer of high-visibility brands. With plans to build on these strengths with innovative merchandising ideas, while maintaining a focus on expansion throughout the country, May was positioning itself for continued success and growth in the late 1990s.

Principal Subsidiaries

May Capital, Inc.; May Centers Associates Corporation; May Funding, Inc.; May Merchandising Company; May Department Stores International; May Design and Construction Company.

Principal Operating Units

Lord & Taylor; Hecht's; Strawbridge's; Foley's; Robinson's-May; Kaufmann's; Filene's; Famous-Barr; L. S. Ayres; Meier & Frank.

Further Reading

"ADG Acquisition Turns May into Super Power," *Chain Store Age Executive,* September 1986.
"A Discounter Bids for Power in Chicago," *Business Week,* August 28, 1978.
"May Department Stores," *Barron's,* March 29, 1954.
"May Stores: Watch Them Grow," *Fortune,* December 1948.
"Retailers Discover Their Real Estate Riches," *Business Week,* January 19, 1981.

—Gillian Wolf
—updated by Laura E. Whiteley

The Mead Corporation

Courthouse Plaza Northeast
Dayton, Ohio 45463
U.S.A.
(513) 495-6323
Fax: (513) 495-3869
Web site: http://www.mead.com

Public Company
Incorporated: 1930
Employees: 21,600
Sales: $4.71 billion (1996)
Stock Exchanges: New York Midwest Pacific
SICs: 2411 Logging Camps & Logging Contractors; 2421
    Sawmills & Planing Mills, General; 2426 Hardwood
    Dimension & Flooring Mills; 2611 Pulp Mills; 2621
    Paper Mills; 2631 Paperboard Mills; 2653 Corrugated
    & Solid Fiber Boxes; 2657 Folding Paperboard
    Boxes, Including Sanitary; 2741 Miscellaneous
    Publishing; 2761 Manifold Business Forms; 2782
    Blankbooks, Loose Leaf Binders & Devices; 2861
    Gum & Wood Chemicals; 2893 Printing Ink; 3861
    Photographic Equipment & Supplies; 3955 Carbon
    Paper & Inked Ribbons; 5111 Printing & Writing
    Paper; 5113 Industrial & Personal Service Paper;
    5199 Nondurable Goods, Not Elsewhere Classified

The Mead Corporation is one of the world's largest manufacturers of paper (producing more than 1.7 million tons each year) pulp, and lumber. Each year Mead produces more than 1.5 million tons of paperboard and the company is an industry leader in coated paperboard, containerboard, and multiple packaging. Mead also distributes paper and packaging and is a leading maker and distributor of school supplies in the United States and Canada.

Early History, 1846–1910

The Mead Corporation began as Ellis, Chafflin & Company. Founded in 1846 by Colonel Daniel Mead and his partners, the company produced book and other printing papers at a mill in Dayton, Ohio. In 1856 Mead bought out his original partners with a friend from Philadelphia, Pennsylvania, forming Weston and Mead. This company became Mead and Weston in 1860, then Mead and Nixon in 1866. In 1873 Daniel Mead spearheaded a reorganization of the firm as the Mead & Nixon Paper Company, and in 1881 Mead bought out Nixon, establishing the Mead Paper Company in 1882. He immediately upgraded the Dayton mill and in 1890 purchased a facility in nearby Chillicothe, Ohio. During the first decade of its existence, Mead Paper Company averaged annual profits of $22,000, peaking at nearly $50,000 in 1891, the year of Mead's death.

In the years after Mead's death, the management of the company passed to his sons, Charles and Harry, who became president and vice-president, respectively. Despite the fact that Mead had left a thriving business, Mead Paper soon fell on hard times, owing largely to personal overdrafts by family members amounting to more than $200,000, as well as to the substantial salaries drawn by Harry and Charles Mead and Charles's travel expense and cash accounts, which in 1900 amounted to $13,800. Combined losses for 1901 and 1902 added up to more than $36,000, and banks began calling in the company's loans. By 1904 the Teutonia National Bank instituted a suit that resulted in trusteeship of the company by bankers in Dayton, Chillicothe, and Cincinnati, Ohio.

As Mead Paper Company teetered on the brink of total collapse in 1905, the banker-trustees turned to George Mead, Harry Mead's independent and business-minded son, requesting that he take over the helm at Mead. George, then about to leave his post at the General Artificial Silk Company in Philadelphia, accepted the opportunity to rejuvenate the family company. He reorganized it as the Mead Pulp and Paper Company and was appointed vice-president and general manager. George Mead's business philosophy would influence the company substantially during his 43-year tenure.

Mead Pulp and Paper made its first public stock offering in 1906. A year later operations were consolidated at the Chillicothe mill, costing the company more than $32,000. The economic recession of 1907 and the tremendous cost of moving almost destroyed Mead once again, but the sale of the Dayton property saved the company. Finally, in 1908, the company

---

Company Perspectives:

Mead's Vision is "to become recognized by the results we achieve for customers, shareowners and employees. To act in ways consistent with a set of shared values: honesty, integrity and candor; customer focus; individual participation; results driven; a learning organization. To use a common set of tools to achieve results: total customer satisfaction, total productivity improvement, and commitment to high performance. Mead's Mission: To become number one in customer satisfaction in the markets we choose to serve."

---

made profits of almost $25,000, and it continued to operate in the black until the Great Depression.

Growth via Acquisitions, 1910s through 1940s

During the 1910s, Mead expanded through acquisition and began to maximize machine output by restricting its product lines. In 1916 Mead purchased a share in the Kingsport Pulp Corporation of Kingsport, Tennessee, and in 1917 it acquired full control of the Peerless Paper Company of Dayton. George Mead had been reducing the number of different types of paper made at Mead since his entry in 1905, when the company produced 15 different grades of paper. Seeing that profits would be maximized if each machine could concentrate on producing one type of paper rather than continually changing production methods for different papers, Mead specialized his mills as far as possible.

Toward this end, in 1917 Mead secured a five-year contract to produce magazine paper for Crowell Publishing Company. The magazine paper called for 75 percent of the Chillicothe mill's production. Consequently, Crowell remained Mead's principal customer throughout the decade. In 1918 the Management Engineering and Development Company was established in Dayton as a separate firm to supervise engineering of new Mead plants and to market Mead's engineering services to other paper companies. In 1921 the Mead Sales Company was established as a separate corporation to sell white paper produced by Mead mills and other U.S. and Canadian mills.

In 1920 Mead bought out the other owners of Kingsport Pulp. The plant began white paper production in 1923 and became a central Mead factory. Mead began to diversify its product lines in the 1920s as it started to manufacture paperboard. By 1925 Mead research led to the discovery of the semichemical pulping process by which wood chips from which tannin had been extracted could be converted into paperboard. Mead expanded the paperboard business in the late 1920s with the purchase of mills throughout Appalachia that produced corrugating medium from wood waste. In 1927 The Mead Paperboard Corporation was founded as a holding company for the paperboard operations, including the Sylvia Paperboard Company, The Harriman Company, The Southern Extract Company, and the Chillicothe Company.

The Mead Corporation was incorporated on February 17, 1930, and George Mead was appointed president. The company subsumed the operations of the Mead Pulp and Paper Company, The Mead Paperboard Corporation, and the Management Engineering and Development Company, although the separate legal existence of these organizations continued for some years. At that time, the company had 1,000 employees and plants in four states. In 1935 Mead's common and preferred stock were listed on the New York Stock Exchange.

During the 1930s Mead made substantial acquisitions that diversified its lines. Although concentration on a few types of paper was necessary when the company was small, Mead had grown large enough to produce a number of grades of papers profitably. Mead's own major mills had attempted to sell business, envelope, and writing papers, but they had no luck. Two major purchases were Dill & Collins in 1932 and Geo. W. Wheelwright Company in 1934. Each of these companies had established names and well-developed distribution systems. This allowed Mead to market effectively large quantities of specialty papers produced at Chillicothe as well as smaller quantities produced in the acquired mills.

In 1938 Mead entered two joint ventures in an effort to reduce its dependence on imported pulp and to enter the kraft linerboard business. With Scott Paper Company, it formed the Brunswick Pulp & Paper Company at Brunswick, Georgia to supply both parent companies. In addition, with the holding company of the Alfred du Pont estate, Almours Security Company, it built a huge pulping plant in Port St. Joe, Florida. By 1937 the Brunswick mill was producing 150 tons of pulp per day. Soon the Port St. Joe facility was yielding 300 tons of pulp and 300 tons of linerboard daily. It was widely regarded as the leading linerboard mill in the country and by 1940 was making $1 million a year before taxes. Relations with the Almours Security Company deteriorated, however, and Mead sold its share of the operation. Mead intended to launch another linerboard mill immediately, but World War II halted this plan.

In 1942 George Mead became chairman of the board and Sydney Fergusen, who had been with the company since the 1910s, became the corporation's president. In the same year, Mead purchased a small white-paper mill from the Escanaba Paper Company in Michigan's upper peninsula. Eventually the Escanaba mill would become one of Mead's largest operations. Two other acquisitions were made, in 1943, that of the Manistique Pulp and Paper Company, of Manistique, Michigan and, in 1946, that of the Columbia Paper Company in Bristol, Virginia. The Manistique plant was sold in the early 1950s, and the Virginia company was consolidated with the Wheelwright plant in 1946. Other plants bought to meet postwar demand were subsequently sold.

Although Mead had continued production at a breakneck pace to meet domestic and overseas container and paper requirements, wartime price and profit controls, as well as raw material shortages, stunted the company's growth. In 1945 Mead's assets had risen only $2.1 million from a prewar figure of $37 million.

Immediately following the war, however, Mead was back on course. Its well-defined postwar plan allotted $23 million for plant expansion. In the brown paper division, plans were readily revived to build a kraft linerboard plant to replace the Port St. Joe operation. Mead firmly entrenched itself in paperboard-making through its joint projects with Inland Container Corporation. The companies first collaborated in 1946 to found the Macon Kraft Company to build and operate a paperboard mill in Macon, Georgia. This was followed by successive joint mills built in Rome, Georgia in 1951 and Phenix City, Alabama in 1966.

Diversification Beyond Paper Products in the 1950s

Mead saw a rapid succession of presidents after Fergusen, who in 1948 became chairman of the board and handed the presidency on to Charles R. Van de Carr, Jr. In 1952 Howard E. Whittaker became president, and five years later he was replaced by Donald R. Morris. The year 1955 marked the beginning of a new period of growth for Mead, as the company diversified beyond its traditional paper products. A 1957 acquisition, the Atlanta Paper Company, led Mead into the packaging business and was the forerunner of Mead's packaging division, which invented the familiar paper six-pack carrier for bottled beverages and became the largest supplier of paperboard beverage packaging in the world. The specialty paper division, which produced papers for filters and insulation, was started with the purchase of Hurlburt Paper Company of South Lee, Massachusetts in 1957.

Mead entered the container business in 1955 and 1956 with the acquisition of Jackson Box Company of Cincinnati, Ohio. This firm became the nucleus of Mead's containerboard division. In 1960 Mead's rapid expansion in paperboard manufacture prompted the Federal Trade Commission (FTC) to file a complaint against Mead, alleging that Mead's growth since 1956 was anticompetitive. Mead and the FTC settled in 1965 when Mead signed a consent decree, agreeing to sell off seven of its plants over five years and place a ten-year moratorium on paperboard acquisitions.

Mead began its wholesale distribution network with the acquisition of Cleveland Paper Company in 1957. Mead's aggressive expansion of its wholesale force provoked a 1968 suit by the Justice Department. The suit claimed that Mead's acquisition between 1957 and 1964 of six paper wholesalers with 38 outlets caused an unlawful concentration in the paper industry. Mead agreed in 1970 to sell off within two years 22 of the outlets operated by Chatfield & Woods Company, acquired in 1961, and Cleveland Paper Company.

Acquired Businesses Unrelated to Papermaking in 1960s

With the retirement of Chairman Howard E. Whitaker and President George H. Pringle in 1968, the new president, James W. McSwiney, began to acquire businesses that were unrelated to papermaking. During the 1950s, and with the 1968 allocation of $50 million for the expansion of the Escanaba mill, Mead had spent in excess of $400 million on maintaining and improving its papermaking facilities. Then its business emphasis in paper products shifted from production to marketing. The paper markets, however, were fairly mature, and growth had to be sought elsewhere. Mead's management anticipated a boom in family spending and homebuilding and bought companies that would benefit from such a boom. Mead's acquisition of an educational products supplier in 1966 was followed in 1968 by the purchase

of Woodward Corporation, a maker of pipe and pipe fittings, castings, and chemicals and of Data Corporation, which produced computer software. In 1969 Mead bought a furniture maker.

1970s Recession Leads to Divestments

These purchases did not shield Mead from an economic recession in the early 1970s. In 1971 the Escanaba mill was operating at a loss despite a $15 million investment in upgrading the plant. Another $45 million investment went into the plant the following year, but profitability continued to elude the operation. As a result of its flagging profits, Mead began to sell off some of the acquisitions it had made only a few years earlier.

Mead managers sold more than $80 million of interests in low-growth markets between 1973 and 1976. For example, lower-grade tablet paper and low-volume colored envelope interests were eliminated. Mead sold off facilities such as the corrugated-shipping-container plant it had built at a cost of $3.5 million in Edison, New Jersey in 1967, but which had never made a profit. Mead's corrugated-paper business was concentrated in Stevenson, Alabama in 1975. Mead also directed its attention to potential growth in paper; for example, the company responded to an anticipated hike in mail rates by investing $60 million in a computer-controlled paper machine to make lightweight paper.

Mead retained substantially diverse operations, including furniture factories, foundries, and Alabama coal mines. Despite these far-flung interests, in 1974, about 24 percent of Mead's pretax earnings came from paper, 35 percent from paperboard, and 5 percent from wholesaling. Metal products contributed 11 percent and furniture five percent, while about 20 percent was derived from sundry jointly owned forest products operations. Mead lost an estimated $85 million in sales owing to strikes at several pulp and paper mills. By 1975, however, sales and profits were on the upturn.

In 1977 the consolidation of the box-making business became problematic as two small Pennsylvania paper-box makers, Franklin Container Corporation, of Philadelphia, and Tim-Bar Corporation, filed a $1.2 billion antitrust suit against Mead and eight other box makers. The suit charged the defendants with price fixing and with attempting to push smaller makers out of the market by buying independent box makers and opening operations where they would compete with smaller businesses. The suit was one of the largest price fixing lawsuits in U.S. legal history. Mead was found not guilty in a 1979 criminal trial, but a jury found the company guilty in a civil class-action suit of 1980. The other defendants had settled out of court prior to the civil suit, and Mead was left with a potential liability of $750 million. Finally, Mead also settled out of court in 1982 for $45 million, considerably less than it might have had to pay in court, but still five times more than any of the other defendants paid.

1980s Highlighted by the Increasing Success of Mead Data Central

In 1979 Mead ranked fourth among forest products companies and hit its all-time earnings peak of $5.19 a share while fending off an unwanted takeover by Occidental Petroleum

Corporation. By the early 1980s, earnings began to fall from their 1979 peak of $141 million to a loss of $86 million in 1982—Mead's first loss since 1938. Among the factors responsible were a drastic decrease in demand for lumber products and the costly settlement of the box suit. In addition, Mead's $1.5 billion five-year expansion plan begun in 1978 may have equipped it to benefit from the next paper market boom, but it also left the company in 1983 with a debt amounting to more than half of its total capitalization. Mead whittled away at the sum by selling several noncore businesses. By 1984 debt was down to 42 percent of capital, still a dangerously high level but better than in the previous year.

Business improved in 1984, as Mead's electronic information-retrieval services became profitable. Mead Data Central Inc. (MDC), the subsidiary whose primary product was LEXIS, a service that made case law and statutes available through online computer searches, had been growing at a rate of 43 percent a year. Unveiled in 1973, LEXIS took in about 75 percent of the computerized legal research market by the late 1980s. The system's success was enough to spark its own court battle with West Publishing Company, which claimed that MDC intended to infringe on its copyrights by distributing its information with West's pagination. Mead in turn filed its own antitrust suit against West. The case was settled in 1988 with a licensing agreement permitting MDC to offer West-copyrighted material via the LEXIS service.

By 1988 MDC boasted 200,000 subscribers, who bought $300 million worth of information. In 1988 LEXIS was responsible for MDC's 33 percent growth. LEXIS accounted for an estimated $215 million of MDC's $307.6 million revenues. MDC's other products included NEXIS, which distributed newspaper and magazine reprints. MDC also carried other services, such as LEXPAT, which distributed patent information, and LEXIS Financial Information Service, which provided stock information. Micromedex, a subsidiary acquired in 1988, provided information about poison and emergency medicine on compact disc.

In 1988, to enhance the scope of its service to attorneys, paralegals, and the court, MDC purchased The Michie Company, a legal publisher based in Charlottesville, Virginia, publishing statutes from 24 states in printed form. MDC made these statutes searchable electronically through the LEXIS service and developed compact disc products combining case law and statutes.

In addition to the promising enterprises at MDC, in 1988 Mead unveiled Cycolor, a new paper for color photocopying. The specially coated paper contained a chemical that, like an instant film, performs the reproduction internally, eliminating the complex machinery formerly needed to create color photocopies. Mead contracted several Japanese companies to manufacture copiers compatible with the paper. By 1990, two Japanese companies were marketing copiers using Cycolor. Development of this product was costly, and it diminished Mead's earnings from 1986 to 1990. After losing almost $200 million developing the special paper, Mead closed its Cycolor division in December 1990.

While developing these nonpaper interests, Mead also undertook some rationalization of its traditional sectors. Most important was the restructuring of its paperboard operations to focus on the production of coated board. Mead dissolved its partnerships with Temple-Inland in the Georgia Kraft Company, sold six of its container plants, and doubled its coated board capacity. The Macon mill was sold in 1987 to Pratt Holding, Ltd., an Australian firm; Temple-Inland took control of the Rome, Georgia plant; and in 1988 Mead took full control of the Phenix City coated board mill. In 1991, Mead completed a $580 million expansion of this mill, which added 370,000 tons of coated board annually. Mead also sold its share of the Brunswick pulp and paper mill in August of 1988 and sold its recycled products business to Rock-Tenn Company in 1988.

Steven Mason Leads 1990s Turnaround

These rationalization moves were important, but Mead's revenues were flat from 1988 through 1992 and net earnings fell from a record $352.7 million in 1988 to $38.5 million in 1990, $6.9 million in 1991, and $71.6 million in 1992. After ten years as chairman and CEO, Burnell Roberts retired in 1992 and was replaced by Steven Mason, who had been president and vice-chairman. A third-generation Mead employee with 35 years at the company, Mason moved quickly and boldly to turn Mead around.

In mid-1992 Mason announced the start of a three-year performance-improvement plan that aimed to increase both productivity and customer satisfaction. As part of the plan, Mead laid off about 1,000 employees, setting up a $95 million special reserve for such expenses as severance pay, retraining, relocation, counseling, and outplacement. Another component of the plan called for overall productivity increases of three percent per year, which would lead to annual savings of about $60 million. By year-end 1996 Mead had successfully hit this target, as it had achieved an overall productivity gain of 12 percent since 1992. During this same period Mead's customer satisfaction rankings markedly improved; in 1992 less than half of the company's business units were ranked first in customer satisfaction compared with Mead competition, but by 1996 three-quarters were ranked first.

Equal in significance to the performance-improvement plan was Mason's decision to refocus Mead on core value-added forest products. In addition to selling its imaging and re-insurance businesses, Mead reduced its uncoated paper operations through the 1995 sale of the loss-making Kingsport, Tennessee uncoated paper mill. The largest divestment, however, came in December 1994 when the company sold Mead Data Central to Anglo-Dutch publishing giant Reed Elsevier for $1.5 billion, taking Mead out of the electronic publishing business. Following these moves, Mead had three core areas of operation: paper (primarily coated paper, a sector with more growth potential than uncoated paper), packaging and paperboard, and distribution and school/office supplies.

Much of the $1 billion after-tax proceeds from the MDC sale was used to pay down debt and make stock repurchases. Overall, from 1992 to 1996 Mead was able to reduce its debt-to-capital ratio from 47 percent to 36 percent. Meanwhile, company shareholders were kept happy through repurchases of 8.7 million shares valued at $459 million.

To shore up its core areas, Mead spent heavily to upgrade and add machinery to its mills and also made one strategic acquisition. The Escanaba and Chillicothe coated paper mills were the recipients of large capital investment programs, with $200 million spent in 1994 and 1995. In November 1996 Mead increased its coated paper capacity by 600,000 tons a year with the $640 million purchase of a coated paper mill located in Rumford, Maine from Boise Cascade. The mill also brought with it 667,000 acres of woodlands, which increased Mead's timber holdings to 2.1 million acres in eight states, a 65 percent increase over 1992 holdings.

Mead's paperboard capacity was also increased through the 1996 completion of a 225,000 ton-per-year, $176 million corrugating medium machine at the Stevenson mill. That same year the company announced a second phase to the capital upgrades at this mill, whereby the new machine's output would increase to 390,000 tons annually when virgin pulp-making capability, a wood fuel boiler, and additional dryers were added by 1999. The second phase was expected to cost an additional $224 million.

Following record-breaking revenues of $5.18 billion and robust net earnings of $350 million in 1995—a year with market conditions favorable to paper companies—Mead celebrated its 150th anniversary in 1996 with solid revenues ($4.71 billion) and earnings ($195.3 million). Mason's various initiatives as chairman and CEO clearly had born fruit. The company's future also seemed bright, as the April 1996 appointment of Jerome F. Tatar—a 23-year Mead veteran and former president (over an eight-year period) of Mead's Fine Paper Division—as president and chief operating officer (and expected Mason successor) pointed to the likelihood that Mead would continue on a steady course into the early 21st century.

Principal Subsidiaries

Escanaba Paper Co.; Forest Kraft Company; LCC Holding Company; M-B Pulp Company; Mead Coated Board Intl., Inc.; Mead European Holdings, Inc.; Mead Export, Inc.; Mead Foreign Holdings, Inc.; Mead International Holdings, Inc.; Mead Packaging International, Inc.; Mead Panelboard, Inc.; Mead Realty Group, Inc.; Mead Reco, Inc.; Mead SA, Inc.; Mead Supplyco, Inc.; Mead Timber Co.; Pulp Asia Limited; Zephyer Properties, Inc.; Mead Packaging Proprietary Ltd. (Australia); Bermead Insurance Company Ltd. (Bermuda); Mead Packaging (Canada) Ltd.; Mead Holdings S.A. (France); Mead-Emballage S.A. (France; 99.53%); Mead Europe Engineering, S.A.R.L. (France); Mead Reassurance S.A. (France); Mead Packaging Europe, s.a.r.l. (France); Mead Verpackung G.m.b.H. (Germany); Aviocart S.p.A. (Italy); Mead Packaging Korea, Inc.; Productros para Escuela y Oficina, S.A. de C.V. (Mexico); Mead Holdings B.V. (Netherlands); Mead Coated Board Europe B.V. (Netherlands); Mead Verpakking B.V. (Netherlands); Mead Packboard B.V. (Netherlands); Mead Sistemas Embalaje S.A. (Spain); Mead Management Services S.A. (Switzerland); Mead Packaging Ltd. (U.K.).

Principal Divisions

Fine Paper Division; Gilbert Paper; Mead Coated Board Division; Mead Containerboard; Mead Packaging; Mead Publishing Paper; Mead Pulp Sales, Inc.; Mead School & Office Products; Mead Specialty Paper; Zellerbach Division.

Further Reading

Carr, William H. A., *Up Another Notch: Institution Building at Mead*, New York: McGraw-Hill, 1989.

David, Gregory E., ''A Machine Called Chief: How Modest Steve Mason Saved Mead from Mediocrity,'' *Financial World*, March 14, 1995, pp. 42–43.

Fischl, Jennifer, ''Mead and Boise: The Long and the Short,'' *Financial World*, November 18, 1996, p. 24.

Hodgson, Richard S., ed., *In Quiet Ways: George H. Mead, The Man and the Company*, Dayton, Ohio: The Mead Corporation, 1970.

Jaffe, Thomas, ''Paper Values,'' *Forbes*, August 20, 1990, p. 124.

Livingston, Sandra, ''Mead Corp.: Attention to Detail Boosts Productivity,'' (Cleveland) *Plain Dealer*, June 26, 1996.

''Mead Corporation History,'' Dayton, Ohio: Mead corporate typescript, 1990.

Narisetti, Raju, ''Mead Corp. Decides To Go Back to Its Roots, Literally: Company Bets Future on Forest Products, Not Electronic Data Services,'' *Wall Street Journal*, May 27, 1994, p. B4.

——, ''Mead To Buy Coated-Paper Mill, Woods from Boise Cascade for $650 Million,'' *Wall Street Journal*, October 1, 1996, p. A4.

Young, Jim, ''Mead: Performance Improvement Program on Track,'' *Pulp and Paper*, June 1994, pp. 30–31.

—Elaine Belsito
updated by David E. Salamie

Mercantile Stores Company, Inc.

9450 Seward Road
Fairfield, Ohio 45014
U.S.A.
(513) 881-8000
Fax: (513) 881-8689
Web site: http://www.mercstores.com

Public Company
Incorporated: 1914 as Mercantile Stores Corporation
Employees: 34,276
Sales: $2.94 billion
Stock Exchanges: New York
SICs: 5311 Department Stores

Mercantile Stores Company, Inc., a traditional department store retailer, operates over 100 primarily fashion apparel stores and 15 home fashion stores, most of which are mall-based, in 17 states. The stores operate under 13 names, with regional store groups: Bacons, McAlpin's, Lion, and Root's (Mercantile East); Gayfers and J.B. White (Mercantile Southeast); Castner Knott (Mercantile Central); Gayfers and Maison Blanche (Mercantile South); and The Jones Store Company, Joslins, Hennessy's, de Lendrecie's, and Glass Block (Mercantile West). The stores are found in over 50 markets and in most cases hold the dominant general merchandise retailer position. The typical Mercantile department store measures about 170,000 square feet and offers apparel, cosmetics, accessories, and home fashions designed to appeal to the middle to upper-middle income consumer. Mercantile also has a partnership interest in five operating shopping centers; it operates a full-line department store in each and a home fashion unit in two.

Company Origins

The company got its start in 1914 in the wake of the failure of a chain of dry goods stores, H.B. Claflin Company. One of Claflin's largest creditors was the Milliken family, which owned a textiles firm in the South. Claflin's assets were divided into two groups, and the group of less valuable stores was taken over by a committee of creditors that included the Millikens.

This new entity, named Mercantile Stores Corporation, assumed ownership of 22 stores on December 14, 1914. Although the company established headquarters in New York City, its stores were located from Washington state to New York and Pennsylvania, as far north as Canada and as far south as Alabama. In its early years, the main preoccupation of the company's leaders was to overcome the Claflin company's heritage of debt and stay in business, so that creditors could receive a portion of what they were owed. At the end of 1917, eight months after the United States entered World War I, the company found itself unable to sell enough assets to pay off the $33 million in notes it had issued three years earlier to old creditors, and the notes were extended two years.

As this new deadline drew near, however, the uncertainty of the postwar U.S. economy, with large-scale unemployment and a spiraling cost of living, made it less likely that the company would be able to meet it obligations. Mercantile's leaders again decided to start anew, and the company was reorganized at the start of 1919 under a new name, Mercantile Stores Company. The old company's outstanding notes were replaced with newly issued stocks and bonds. Mercantile Stores Company was incorporated in Delaware, under the state's favorable corporate statutes, and a new president, Alexander New, was elected shortly thereafter. New, the son of a dry-goods merchant, brought legal training and a life-long familiarity with retailing to his position.

As the United States entered the turbulent postwar years of the 1920s, Mercantile Stores set about solidifying its shaky financial position. Although the company issued additional stock, both common and preferred, Mercantile Stores continued to struggle. As a later company president commented in *Barron's*, December 28, 1987, the individual stores "were then mostly third and fourth rate." In 1925 Mercantile Stores's many diverse parts were linked more closely when the company discontinued its practice of allowing each store to purchase wholesale goods separately. Instead, the company centralized its purchasing by taking over a New York dry-goods buying office in 1925.

Depression Setbacks

By 1929 the company had experienced some modest growth, as its assets increased 25 percent from the start of the decade. Late that year, however, the stock market crash of October 29 plunged the country into the Great Depression. Mercantile Stores, entirely dependent upon strong consumer spending, found itself in a perilous position as bank failures, widespread unemployment, and wage cuts reduced the buying power of most U.S. consumers. In 1930 the company was set further adrift when its president for the last decade, Alexander New, resigned due to ill health and died shortly thereafter. For the next several years, Mercantile Stores was led by an executive committee of four vice-presidents, with a member of the Milliken family as the fifth member and chairman of the committee.

Under this joint management, the company retrenched. Stores losing in money were sold, and only those properties turning a profit were buttressed by further investment. At one point, fearing the spread of rumors that would set off a frenzy of stock selling and ruin the company's worth, Mercantile Stores's chief executive bypassed the telephone in favor of traveling personally to each store in the chain to tell the manager to sell everything, so that desperately needed cash could be raised to pay off debts. With these measures, the company narrowly staved off collapse, but this close call helped to instill cautious and conservative business principles in the company's leaders.

Resurgence in the 1930s under Firm Leadership

In 1934, after the resignation of one short-term president, Mercantile Stores emerged from its leaderless limbo: Francis G. Kingsley, who would become a close associate of the Milliken family, assumed the company's top spot. Under Kingsley the company further centralized its operations in New York. Since ready-to-wear clothing purchased off the rack was rapidly replacing clothing made at home, Mercantile also began to devote more of its energy to marketing fashionable clothes. The company farmed out its purchasing in other areas, but kept decisions about coats, dresses, and other manufactured clothing in-house, under a top Mercantile buyer, Rosalie Lavain. By the end of the decade, Mercantile Stores had brought all its purchasing under its own roof to ensure greater control of the merchandise sent to its stores.

In 1941 Kingsley was elevated to chairman, and Harold Jockers, who would also develop close ties to the Millikens, became the fourth president of Mercantile Stores. At the end of that year, the United States entered into World War II, after the bombing of Pearl Harbor. The war brought further changes in U.S. society and consumer needs. As men entered the armed forces, women entered the work force in large numbers for the first time and found themselves with increased spending power. The company, whose fashionable goods were sold primarily to women customers, profited from this development, despite the difficulty of obtaining merchandise during times of wartime shortage. By 1945, at the war's end, Mercantile's profits had nearly tripled their 1941 level.

Postwar Consumer Demands and Expansion

In the second half of the 1940s, the U.S. economy enjoyed a postwar boom, and Mercantile Stores grew along with the vast overall demand for consumer goods. The company began a strong expansion. It acquired additional stores—Duluth Glass Block Store Company, in Minnesota, in 1944, and J.B. White & Company, of Greenville, South Carolina, the following year. In 1946 the company's stock was listed on the New York Stock Exchange for the first time, and expansion continued. Stores in Colorado, North Dakota, and Alabama were soon added to the fold.

In addition to expanding the number of stores it owned, the company also began to change its focus within each separate market. Realizing that the greatest population growth in the postwar years would take place not in the inner city, where previous waves of immigrants from abroad had concentrated large numbers of people, but on the outskirts of urban areas, where internal migration of young city dwellers filled vast new suburban housing tracts, Mercantile Stores began to open branch versions of its downtown stores on the outskirts of metropolitan areas to reach this new breed of customer. The company sought to tap into the vast demand for home furnishings and appliances to fill the new homes of the baby-boom generation.

Throughout the late 1940s and early 1950s, the company continued its strong trend toward centralizing operations for all of its stores to maximize efficiency. Under Kingsley and Jockers, Mercantile Stores embarked on a strategy to compete with the largest national retailing chains, such as Sears, on an equal footing by keeping costs and therefore, prices, down. The resulting policy of maintaining a small profit margin through conservative business practices was based on the company's large degree of centralization for economies of scale and strict limitations on operating expenses. In addition, the introduction of merchandise sold under its own labels allowed Mercantile Stores to market high-quality goods without incurring the expenses of buying through an intermediary. By the end of 1955, these policies started to pay off, enabling Mercantile Stores to solidify its strong position in the postwar department store industry, and sales had more than doubled from their level of ten years earlier. In the second half of the 1950s, sales continued to rise, reaching $170 million by the end of 1960.

The presidency of Mercantile Stores was taken over by F.K. Bradley in 1960, and the company continued on its postwar path of steady expansion into the suburbs. This effort was headed by the Mercantile Stores Real Estate Division, which grew eventually to encompass all aspects of store construction, from property acquisition to architectural design to interior decoration.

Emphasis on Clothing in the 1960s

In addition, the company began to shift its emphasis in marketing away from appliances, a growth area of the 1950s, to clothing and accessories. To do this more effectively and to garner the business of a more affluent clientele, Mercantile Stores began to supplement its own private-label merchandise with the brand name wares of other manufacturers and to feature products imported from other countries.

In 1964 the company presidency passed to R. Nelson Shaw. By the mid-1960s, its annual sales were nearing $200 million, as Mercantile Stores continued its efforts to maintain its market share by staying abreast of latest fashions. In 1965, for instance, the Mercantile Stores Wig Division was inaugurated, as a result of a fad for hairpieces, and soon shops to make and style wigs of imported human hair and other materials had been set up in all major stores throughout the company's chain.

During the late 1960s and the 1970s, Mercantile continued its steady growth. The number of restaurants within its stores was increased, and its successful beauty salon sideline, which was begun before World War II, was expanded to include freestanding stores. The installation of electronic cash registers in many stores enabled Mercantile Stores to fine-tune inventory control, and plans were made to expand this capability.

In 1974 the chain's 72 stores were generating more than $500 million in sales, although profits had gone flat because of the poor economy. Nevertheless, the company continued its plans to build new stores, primarily in suburban locations, and to renovate its older facilities. Mercantile's fortunes overall picked up in the years following 1974, and demand for apparel and the company's growth continued throughout the late 1970s.

By the early 1980s, the chain encompassed 84 stores, and sales had reached $1.4 billion, despite a recession of the U.S. economy. Mercantile Stores had a year of flat revenues in 1980, but overall they continued to do well, placing its emphasis on flexibility in the mix of products it sold.

Renovating Existing Stores in 1980s

The late 1980s were a period of consolidation in the department store business, as healthy chains borrowed heavily to finance large mergers and takeovers, and venerable names closed their doors forever. The large-scale discounting and heavy advertising undertaken by competitors softened profits for the company, and Mercantile concentrated on enlarging and renovating existing stores rather than on purchasing or opening new ones. The company continued to de-emphasize goods such as housewares, in favor of higher-profit items like fashionable clothing and accessories, and also phased out less profitable downtown stores for newer, suburban mall stores. Sales and profits in the late 1980s, dampened by in-store construction, fell flat. In 1987 Mercantile sold its Canadian operations.

Relocation of Headquarters

In 1990 the company began relocating its headquarters from New York City to a suburb of Cincinnati, and undertook a program of brisk expansion, laying plans to open two or three new stores a year for five years in hopes of reversing its sluggish sales growth, which resulted in lowered earnings for 1990. The move cut costs and centralized operations, with everything in one location, from visual merchandising to product development and advertising. In addition, the company made plans to finally implement advanced computerized inventory control procedures under a system called Quick Response.

In 1992 Mercantile acquired Maison Blanche, Inc. and consolidated operations from some existing company divisions. Two other important events occurred that year. David L. Nichols, a longtime company veteran, was promoted to chair and CEO. He previously served as executive vice-president, chief financial officer, and treasurer. Under Nichols's direction Mercantile completed its move to new corporate offices and there established Mercantile Stores University, a 30,000-square-foot facility for training managers, merchandisers, and other personnel in the subjects of finance, leadership, business ethics, negotiations, international trade, teamwork, and other subjects. The

school included ten classrooms, a 180-seat auditorium, a library, and six-acre outdoor educational area.

Mercantile reported financial success in 1995 with revenues of $2.9 billion, up from $2.8 billion in 1994. Also in 1995 Mercantile debuted its first free-standing home store in Cincinnati and announced plans to open more. These Signatures Home Stores were promoted as a "seamless home stores," which sought to transcend traditional boundaries in displaying home furnishings. Quoted in a May 1996 article in *HFN—Home Furnishings Network,* home furnishings manager Robert Christnacht commented, "We don't have all leather together, we don't have all the recliners together; we don't have all the chairs together; we don't have all the lamps together; it's all lifestyle."

Mercantile opened five new stores in 1996. Mercantile's revenues in 1996 increased 2.9 percent to about $3 billion. In the first nine months of the year, the company showed a 4.4 percent increase in net income for the year as profit per share went up to $3.50. However, the fourth quarter rendered less than satisfactory results. Chairman David Nichols attributed this lackluster performance to a comparatively short Christmas selling period. Nevertheless, Mercantile retained market share during this difficult season for all retailers.

Looking to the next century, Mercantile set up "brand teams," with an eye on increasing its private label merchandise business by 50 percent. The plan, key to Nichols's strategy, would broaden the Mercantile's customer base considerably. Another challenge was growing the business in non-real-estate ways. Mercantile planned on opening a few stores a year, but much of the future lay in innovative marketing.

In the early 1990s rumors had spread that Mercantile was ripe for takeover by industry giants May Department Stores or Dillard Department Stores. The company denied any possibility of merger, however, and by mid-1996 the media was reporting that Mercantile was on solid ground and an able regional competitor. Industry observers suspected that any big changes in Mercantile's future most likely would depend on the wishes of the Milliken family, the textile dynasty that controlled the department stores with a 40 percent stake. But as the century drew to a close, the Millikens were affording Mercantile a great deal of autonomy and were apparently happy with the company's performance; Mercantile was referred to in a 1996 *Cincinnati Enquirer* article as a "jewel" among small retailers.

Principal Subsidiaries

Hennessy Company; Duluth Glass Block Store Company; DeLendrecie Company; J.B. White & Company; The McAlpin Company; The Joslin Dry Goods Company, Inc.; Castner-Knott Dry Goods Company; The Jones Store Company; C.J. Gayfer & Company, Inc.; J. Bacon & Sons; Root Dry Goods Company, Inc.; The Lion Dry Goods Company; Maison Blanche, Inc.; Jones Store Company Hairstyling School.

Further Reading

Byrne, Harlan S., "Mercantile Stores Co.: It Survives In a Battered Industry, Resumes Expansion," *Barron's,* June 11, 1990.
Cochran, Thomas N., "Merchandising Genius: In Good Times or Bad, Mercantile Stores Prosper," *Barron's,* December 28, 1987.

Erlick, June Carolyn, ''Mercantile Goes Seamless,'' *HFN—Home Furnishings Network,* May 13, 1996, pp. 1, 83.

Grossman, Karen Alberg, ''Psyched in Cincinnati: Mercantile Emerges as a Power to Contend With,'' *MR—The Magazine of Menswear Retailing,* June 1994, pp. 69–71.

Henterly, Meghan, ''Mercantile Jewel among Retailers,'' *The Cincinnati Enquirer,* August 11, 1996, pp. H1–H2.

Kincaid, Valerie, ''Mercantile in Midst of Biggest Expansion,'' *Cincinnati Business Courier,* October 14–20, 1996, p. 27.

Marcial, Gene G., ''A Red-Tag Special at Mercantile Stores?,'' *Business Week,* September 19, 1994.

''Presidential Perspectives: Mercantile Stores Company's David Nichols,'' *Visual Merchandising & Store Design,* January 1993, pp. 40–48.

—Elizabeth Rourke
—updated by Catherine Hamrick

Mohawk Industries, Inc.

P.O. Box 12069
160 South Industrial Boulevard
Calhoun, Georgia 30703
U.S.A.
(706) 629-7721
Fax: (706) 625-5271
Web site: http//www.mohawkind.com

Public Company
Incorporated: 1902 as Shuttleworth Brothers Company
Employees: 11,450
Sales: $1.8 billion (1996)
Stock Exchanges: NASDAQ
SICs: 2273 Carpets & Rugs; 6719 Holding Companies,
Not Elsewhere Classified

With three of the industry's most recognized brands—Karastan, Mohawk, and Bigelow—Mohawk Industries, Inc. ranks second among America's largest carpet and rug makers. As one of the U.S. carpet industry's oldest players, the company's history echoes that of the trade, from its foundation in 19th century New England to its move to Georgia in the 1980s. A period of intense growth through acquisition sextupled Mohawk's sales from $280 million in 1991 to nearly $1.8 billion by 1996. In 1995, it held 17 percent of the $9.8 billion wholesale carpet and rug market, compared to leader Shaw Industries' 26 percent share. Mohawk's acquisition spree gave it a family of more than a dozen brands and made it the nation's largest manufacturer of machine-made rugs, a key segment of the maturing, consolidating market. By the mid-1990s, the company had a presence in virtually every segment of the industry, from mass-produced area rugs sold at promotional prices to custom-made wool carpets.

19th Century Origins

The company was founded in 1878 by four brothers in the Shuttleworth family. That year, the family shipped 14 used Wilton looms from Great Britain to Amsterdam, New York and launched their own carpet mill. At the time, New England, with its corresponding emphasis on textile mills, was the carpet capital of the nation. For most of its history, Mohawk and its competitors wove floor coverings from wool, a naturally water-repellent and insulating fiber. In fact, little about the industry changed from the time of the invention of the power loom in the mid-19th century until after World War II. Even with mechanization, carpetmaking was a highly labor-intensive prospect using massive, complicated machinery. Manufacturers' dependence on unpredictable wool production added another variable to the equation, making for steep fluctuations in expenses. For most families, carpeting was an expensive luxury, so costly that per household shipments peaked at four square yards in 1899 and did not exceed that mark until the mid-1960s.

The Shuttleworth family business was not incorporated until after the turn of the century. A generational shift in leadership probably precipitated the 1902 incorporation as Shuttleworth Brothers Company. The firm's reputation grew substantially after 1908, when it introduced the Karnak carpet pattern. This new style was so popular that a company history noted: "Weavers worked four and five years without changing either the color or the pattern on their looms."

Three generations of Shuttleworths dominated the carpet mill's first century in business. In 1920, they guided the first of what would become many mergers and acquisitions. That year, the family combined its firm with carpetmakers McCleary, Wallin and Crouse to form a leading force in the then-fragmented industry. Renamed Mohawk Carpet Mills, Inc., the company was America's only weaver with a full line of domestic carpets, encompassing the Wilton, Axminster, Velvet, and Chenille weaves. Mohawk did not rest on its laurels, creating the industry's first textured design, Shuttlepoint; the first sculptured weave, Raleigh; and Woven Interlock, "the first successful application of the knitting principle to the manufacture of carpet."

Postwar Era Brings Rapid Change

Several trends converged in the 1950s to reshape the carpet industry drastically. Wartime restrictions on the use of wool fueled research into alternative fibers, especially petrochemical-based synthetics like nylon and, later, acrylics. These man-made

Company Perspectives:

"The key to growth is not only to establish effective strategies, but also to follow through on them. By taking sound strategic action, we have created opportunity—opportunity to grow."

materials were much cheaper to produce and the supply was much more consistent than that of wool. At the same time, a revolution in the main weaving methods was under way. The new technique found its origins in Dalton, Georgia, which boasted a thriving cottage industry in tufted coverlets. In the late 1940s, housewives there had built up something of a tourist-trap industry in tufted bedspreads. Machines were soon developed to tuft carpets by the same process—inserting loops of fiber into a jute backing. These broadlooms could manufacture carpet many times faster than previous methods. Faster manufacturing methods, combined with the new materials developed in the ensuing decades, made the now-familiar tufted carpets inexpensive and popular. By 1968, tufted carpeting accounted for 90 percent of all carpet sales.

In 1956, Mohawk merged with Alexander Smith, Inc. to form Mohasco Industries. Though the acquisition made Mohasco the world's largest carpet company, it proved to be poorly timed. The troubled Alexander Smith brought with it a high level of debt and a large inventory of outdated carpeting at a time when competition from imports was gaining steam. Tariff relaxations during the 1950s increased importers' share of the U.S. industry from two percent to 25 percent by the end of the decade. At the same time, Mohasco was compelled by industry imperatives to consolidate its mills in the south. Notwithstanding these problems, Mohasco President Herbert L. Shuttleworth II, the third and last of the family to lead the business, was able to stabilize the business enough to purchase high-ranking Firth Carpet in 1962.

Diversification into Furniture in the 1960s

Dreaming of "a home furnishings empire," Shuttleworth turned his attention to the furniture industry in 1963, acquiring nine furniture makers by 1970. Two years later, Mohasco ranked number two in the overall home furnishings market and second only to Bassett in furniture; carpet contributed only about one-fourth of sales. *Forbes* dubbed the company the "GM [General Motors] of the living room."

But Shuttleworth did not forsake the core carpet business. He launched a joint venture carpet plant in Belgium as well as subsidiaries in West Germany and Mexico in the 1960s and invested more than $100 million in production capacity from 1963 to 1973. Baby boomers, who had by this time had grown to marrying and house-buying age, fueled the rapid expansion of the carpet industry in the late 1960s and early 1970s. Carpet volume increased from 138 million square yards in 1955 to 430 million square yards in 1965, surpassing one billion square yards in 1973. In the early 1970s, Mohasco's sculptured, brightly colored "Canyon Paradise" carpet, in classic 1970s color schemes like orange and gold, became the carpet indus-

try's "all-time best-seller." But when tastes changed and more muted colors came into style, Mohasco failed to pick up on the trend. *Forbes* compared the mill to "those clothing companies that were caught with warehouses of polyester leisure suits."

When combined with a mid-decade recession and price controls, Mohasco's lack of fashion savvy proved to be a major misstep; by 1975, Burlington Industries had surpassed it in carpet production. Perhaps more telling, its earnings were declining precipitously. Furthermore, carpet industry shipments peaked in 1979 over the one billion square yard mark, then entered a steep and ongoing decline. In the wake of this decline was a mature industry burdened with overcapacity and facing ferocious competition.

Reorganization in the 1980s Leads to LBO

In 1980, Mohasco hired David Kolb, an attorney who had served as comptroller and director of the nylon carpet fibers division at Allied Fibers, as CEO. Kolb was charged with turning the then unprofitable company around. The new chief undertook a five-year modernization program that encompassed plant and systems modernizations, cost reductions, and development of new managers. He even moved the company's headquarters from Amsterdam, New York to Atlanta, Georgia, to be nearer to what had become the "carpet capitol of the world," Dalton, Georgia. He also shifted the company to higher margin products and increased direct distribution to retailers (thereby cutting out the middleman). Having achieved his profit goals, Kolb took the carpet division private via a $120 million leveraged buyout in 1988.

Public Stock Offering Launches Acquisition Binge in the Early 1990s

Mergers and acquisitions reduced the number of carpet producers from more than 300 in 1980 to 100 by the mid-1990s, with vertically integrated—and, in Mohawk's case, well-diversified—"mega-mills" emerging at the top of the heap.

Kolb used the $38 million proceeds of Mohawk's 1992 public stock offering to reduce the company's LBO debt in preparation for a rapid-fire series of acquisitions funded in part by new debt. Four key acquisitions from 1992 to 1994 catapulted Mohawk from eleventh in the industry to number two, increased its sales from less than $300 million to nearly $1.5 billion, and multiplied its market share from less than four percent to 17 percent. In addition, Mohawk's growth rate ranked it second among the Fortune 500's fastest growing companies in 1993.

The first purchase came in October 1992. Although larger than Mohawk, Horizon Industries was vulnerable because of back-to-back losses in the early 1990s. It nearly doubled revenues. Less than eight months later, Kolb engineered the acquisition of American Rug Craftsmen (ARC), a ten-year-old manufacturer of area rugs. ARC made Mohawk the nation's leading producer of mass-market rugs. Hoping to capitalize on fragmentation within the area rug segment, the new parent boosted ARC's manufacturing and distribution capacity. Under the care of its doting new parent, ARC's sales burgeoned from $50 million in 1993 to $150 million in 1996.

The August 1993 purchase of Karastan Bigelow from Field-crest Cannon added two of the industry's best known and most valuable brands. In fact, Bigelow was named for Erastus B. Bigelow, the 19th century ''Father of the Modern Carpet Industry,'' so named for his invention of the power loom. The addition of Karastan Bigelow pushed Mohawk past competitor Beaulieu of America to become the United States' second largest carpet company.

But Mohawk's most important acquisition was yet to come. In 1994, the carpetmaker merged with highly profitable and privately held Aladdin Mills Inc. via a $430 million ''pooling-of-interests.'' Mohawk paid a premium price for Aladdin, but felt justified by the target's comparatively high profitability. Aladdin's compound sales growth had averaged 20 percent from 1988 to 1993, and after the merger, the ''subsidiary'' contributed 40 percent of sales and 50 percent of net income. Because Aladdin was more profitable than Mohawk, the privately held company's owners, the Lorberbaum family, ended up with a controlling 39 percent stake in Mohawk.

In 1995, Jeffrey Lorberbaum, son of Aladdin founder Alan Lorberbaum, was appointed president and chief operating officer. Lorberbaum was charged with boosting profitability. He planned to ''rationalize'' the corporation's manufacturing capacity along product lines, closing several mills over the ensuing years and consolidating their operations at the most efficient plants. He also expected to expand Aladdin's existing warehousing and distribution system to service all of Mohawk's operations. A more dynamic marketing program emphasized the strength of the company's core brands.

Whether Mohawk would follow carpeting giant Shaw's lead and begin acquiring retail carpet outlets to further integrate its operations remained to be seen in the mid-1990s. At that point, Mohawk was still concentrating on consolidating and rationalizing its family of companies and brands. Ongoing industry-wide difficulties included declining wholesale prices and rising raw material costs. Mohawk's high debt load, the legacy of the acquisition spree, did not help matters. Debt service ran at $40 million in 1995, cutting a large chunk of cash flow.

Nevertheless, Mohawk continued to eye acquisition candidates mid-decade. In 1995, it purchased Galaxy Carpet Mills Inc. for $43.3 million. The new subsidiary added $200 million in sales of higher-margin residential carpets. And in 1996, Mohawk purchased Diamond Rug & Carpet Mills, a bankrupt manufacturer of inexpensive cut pile polypropylene rugs. These two additions exemplified Mohawk's continuing quest to add capacity in all price and quality ranges, from mass to class. That year, the company proudly trumpeted its highest-ever sales and earnings, at nearly $1.8 billion and $49 million, respectively.

Principal Subsidiaries

Mohawk Carpet Corp.; Horizon Europe, Inc.; Rainbow International, Inc.; Mohawk Marketing, Inc.; Aladdin Manufacturing Corp.; Mohawk Mills, Inc.; Horizon & Owens Properties (50%); Delaware Valley Wool Scouring, Inc.; Galaxy Carpet Mills, Inc.

Further Reading

''Acquisition Adds Luster to Outlook of Mohasco,'' *Barron's,* January 21, 1963, p. 21.

Allison, David, ''Mohawk Weaves a Carpet Giant: Atlanta Company Threads Acquisitions into a Growing Business,'' *Atlanta Business Chronicle,* April 9, 1993, pp. 1B.

''Clean Sweep at Mohasco,'' *Forbes,* December 15, 1958, pp. 27–28.

Elliott, J. Richard Jr., ''Carpet Magic,'' *Barron's,* March 16, 1959, pp. 3, 15–16.

Feldman, Andy, ''A Slippery Rug,'' *Forbes,* May 22, 1995, pp. 68–69.

''From Rugs to Riches,'' *Forbes,* March 15, 1973, p. 31.

''GM of the Living Room?,'' *Forbes,* February 15, 1966, p. 38.

Greene, Joan, ''Wall-to-Wall; Carpet Makers Are Piling Up Handsome Gains,'' *Barron's,* February 16, 1976, pp. 11, 53–54.

Hussey, Allan F., ''Mohasco—It's Spinning Bright Earnings Pattern,'' *Barron's,* May 24, 1976, pp. 34, 36.

Joyce, Amy, ''American Rug Craftsmen's Plans,'' *HFD-The Weekly Home Furnishings Newspaper,* March 22, 1993, p. 30.

Kolb, David L., ''The Metamorphosis of Mohawk from LBO to Big Acquirer,'' *Mergers & Acquisitions,* Nov–Dec 1994, pp. 47–50.

McCurry, John, ''Mohawk Signs Letter of Intent To Buy Assets of Diamond Rug,'' *Textile World,* November 1996, p. 26.

''Mohasco Industries Benefits from Stake in Home Furnishings,'' *Financial World,* November 17, 1971, p. 18.

''Mohawk Buys Aladdin Mills,'' *Textile World,* January 1994, p. 23.

''Mohawk in Deal for Karastan-Bigelow,'' *Textile World,* August 1993, p. 23.

''Mohawk To Buy Galaxy Carpet for $42.4 M,'' *HFD-The Weekly Home Furnishings Newspaper,* December 19, 1994, p. 24.

Montero, Santiago, and Naughton, Julie, ''Walking Away with the Rug Business: Karastan Bigelow Buy Gives Mohawk Industries Commanding Market Share,'' *HFD-The Weekly Home Furnishings Newspaper,* July 12, 1993, p. 16–17.

Naughton, Julie, ''Mohawk Acquires American Rug Craftsmen,'' *HFD-The Weekly Home Furnishings Newspaper,* May 17, 1993, p. 26.

——, ''Mohawk Continues Buying Spree,'' *HFD-The Weekly Home Furnishings Newspaper,* July 26, 1993, p. 24.

——, ''Mohawk To Shut Tufting Mill in S.C., Ga., Yarn Spinning Unit,'' *HFN-The Weekly Newspaper for the Home Furnishing Network,* May 8, 1995, p. 19.

——, ''Mohawk's Tribe Increases,'' *HFD-The Weekly Home Furnishings Newspaper,* June 21, 1993, p. 20.

''New Lines Furnish Lift to Mohasco Industries,'' *Barron's,* December 27, 1965, p. 18.

''No Turn in Sight for Carpet Makers,'' *Financial World,* March 26, 1958, pp. 11, 27.

Pacey, Margaret D., ''Flying Carpets,'' *Barron's,* December 16, 1963, pp. 11, 20, 22–23, 25, 32.

''Prosperous Carpet Makers,'' *Financial World,* May 15, 1968, pp. 10, 22.

''Roll Out the Carpets!,'' *Forbes,* March 15, 1964, p. 42.

Saltzman, Cynthia, ''Make Mine Beige,'' *Forbes,* May 28, 1979.

Schonbak, Judith, ''New Horizons for Mohawk Industries,'' *Business Atlanta,* October 1992, p. 10.

Wyman, Lissa, ''American Rug: The Big Payoff,'' *HFN-The Weekly Newspaper for the Home Furnishing Network,* May 13, 1966, pp. 13–14.

—April Dougal Gasbarre

Myers Industries, Inc.

1293 S. Main Street
Akron, Ohio 44301
U.S.A.
(330) 253-5592
Fax: (330) 253-6568
Web site: http://www.amex.com/weblink/mye/
    index.htm

Public Company
Incorporated: 1955
Employees: 1,800
Sales: $320.9 million (1996)
Stock Exchanges: American
SICs: 5014 Tires & Tubes; 3089 Plastics Products, Not
    Elsewhere Classified; 2542 Partitions/Fixtures, Except
    Wood; 3052 Rubber & Plastics Hose & Belting

By many accounts, Myers Industries, Inc. is the largest wholesale distributor of tire servicing equipment and supplies in the world, with outlets throughout the United States and in Canada. At the core of the company's distribution operation is its Myers Tire Supply subsidiary, which boasted more than 40 branch warehouses nationwide and 11 international depots in 1996. But the distribution segment is no longer Myers's largest business interest. Beginning in the late 1980s, more than half of its revenues were generated via the manufacture of plastic and metal storage systems and rubber automotive parts. The manufacturing division included subsidiaries Akro-Mills Inc., Ameri-Kart Corp., Buckhorn, Patch Rubber Co., and Plastic Parts, Inc. International sales contributed less than ten percent of revenues in the mid-1990s. Co-founder Louis Myers continued to serve as chairman into the mid-1990s, and his son Stephen was president and CEO in 1996. In addition to their managerial roles, the founding family continued to hold about a 25 percent stake in the firm, a factor that was considered influential in the company's maintenance of steady growth and profitability in spite of the cyclical nature of its chief markets.

Myers's performance, if not its products and services, earned it increasing attention from stock pickers in the late 1980s and early 1990s. Cash dividends, though described as "miserly," were paid every year from 1972 through the mid-1990s and increased each year from 1976 onward. Each year since 1983 saw a stock dividend or split. This predictable performance record caused *Financial World's* David S. Leibowitz to nominate Myers "most boring company in the country" in a 1992 review of dull but prosperous firms. In 1993, analysts with Smith Barney Shearson described it as "a tightly managed company with a focus on disciplined, long-term growth."

Depression-Era Roots

The company was founded in 1933 by Meyer Myers and his younger brother Louis, who scraped together $620 to start a tire repair and retreading business in Akron, Ohio, which was by then well established as the "Rubber Capitol of the World." Both brothers had experience in the field; Louis worked with an area tire patch company, and Meyer had his own used tire store. There must have been quite a few people who were repairing and retreading tires in lieu of purchasing new ones, for within six years, Myers Tire Supply had generated enough business to support a third brother, Isidore.

The family business specialized in supplying equipment and supplies to tire service shops. Products included patches; steel curling rims; wheel-balancing, alignment, and tire-valve hardware; servicing tools and accessories like jacks, hand tools, air compressors, tire changers, tire display and storage units, and tire vulcanizing machines used in retreading. In the ensuing decades, this core interest expanded into a full-scale, nationwide distribution operation offering, as the corporate slogan stated, "Everything for the Tire Dealer." Its catalog, launched in 1937, soon became known as the "bible" of the retreading industry.

Meyer ran the business alone during World War II, while Louis served in the Pacific theater as—what else?—an Army captain in charge of tire retreading and distribution. Meanwhile, Isidore served in the Army on the Continent.

Company Perspectives:

"Myers Industries, Inc. is a diversified manufacturer of polymer and metal products for industrial, commercial, and consumer markets, and a nationwide wholesale distributor of tools, equipment, and supplies used in tire servicing and automotive underbody repair. Myers Industries has been traded publicly since 1971 and is listed on the American Stock Exchange under the symbol MYE."

Postwar Expansion

Myers diversified into the manufacture of rubber and plastic products via the 1947 creation of Akro-Mills Inc. and Patch Rubber Co. These two companies formed the core of the company's manufacturing operations and established its bipolar nature. Founded in Akron and moved to North Carolina in 1978, Patch would grow to become one of the country's biggest producers of tire repair kits. It manufactured adhesives, cleaners, pre-cured treads, cord stocks, and repair patches. Akro-Mills started out as a mail order company under the direction of Isidore. It began manufacturing its own products in 1964 and would later expand overseas.

The expansion into manufacturing would prove fortuitous. In a 1986 interview with *Barron's* Mitchell Gordon, Chairman Louis Myers noted that the cycles of the distribution and manufacturing interests usually offset each other, thereby resulting in steady growth. "We've no explanation for it, but we seem to have been blessed—for the last 30 years or so, anyway—by the fact that when one has gone down, the other has gone up."

In the postwar era, the tire supply business was growing as well, helped along by interstate highway projects and burgeoning auto production. The growing family firm incorporated in 1955. By 1970, the company had 14 locations throughout the United States. Myers entered the Canadian market with the creation of a branch warehouse in London, Ontario in 1953 and established a full-fledged international division in 1959. In the ensuing decades, the company established warehouses throughout Canada and in Central and South America.

Myers acquired Cleveland's James C. Heintz Company, a high-ranking manufacturer of molds, presses, rims, and parts for tire and retread makers, in 1968. In 1969, Myers acquired Elrick Industries, Inc., a manufacturer of curing rims and tire-changing stands headquartered in Oakland, California. That same year brought a name change, to Myers Industries, Inc., in acknowledgment of the expansion of the parent company's manufacturing interests. Co-founder Meyer Myers retired from the company in 1969, and partner Isidore divested his stake to pursue real estate development in California.

The U.S. advent of radial tires—which were invented in France in the 1930s but not widely accepted in America until the late 1960s—proved particularly positive for Myers. Radials could accommodate two or more retreads, as opposed to their bias-belted forebears, which could only take one. The new tires'

high sticker price (two to three times that of bias-belted tires) provided another incentive for budget-conscious consumers and commercial fleet operators to take advantage of the opportunity to save money by retreading. In response to this demand, Myers Tire Supply added 12 branches in major metropolitan areas from 1970 to 1980.

The company made its initial public offering in 1971, when the Myers family sold a minority stake in the firm to the public. Annual revenues increased from $31.6 million in 1973 to $65.5 million in 1979, and net income grew from $1.4 million to $3.3 million. Myers Industries was listed on the American Stock Exchange in 1983.

Second Generation of Management Ascends in the 1980s

Having logged more than a dozen years of experience at the family firm, Stephen L. Myers, son of Louis Myers, advanced to president and CEO in 1980. The thirty-something executive guided the company's 1987 acquisition of Buckhorn, Inc., an Ohio-based manufacturer of multi-use plastic containers. The $40 million purchase ($22 million cash and the assumption of $18 million in debt) increased Myers's overall sales volume by nearly 47 percent from 1986 to 1987, making manufacturing account for more than 50 percent of revenues in the process.

The acquisition proved to be well timed. Buckhorn's sales benefited from two key trends in the late 1980s and early 1990s: environmentalism and just-in-time inventory control. As David Prizinsky of *Crain's Cleveland Business* pointed out in 1988, just-in-time meant "smaller but more frequent shipments of parts, which will generate more demand for Buckhorn's products." Burgeoning efforts to curb waste, both solid and operational, encouraged companies in a wide variety of industries to implement reusable containers. Buckhorn worked with its customers to design containers for particular applications. In the late 1980s, for example, the company developed bulk cranberry containers for Ocean Spray that enabled the fruit company to switch from truck transport, which often marred the cranberry bogs, to helicopter airlifts of fruit. By the early 1990s, Buckhorn's reusable plastic containers were used to distribute food, apparel, electronics, automotive components, health and beauty aids, and hardware, as well as for in-plant material handling and agricultural applications. Its line includes tote boxes, bins, tubs, straight-walled boxes, and a line of modular cabinets. They are sold direct and via independent dealers and product representatives.

Buckhorn also manufactured consumer lawn and garden supplies, including tool boxes, storage containers, and planters. These were distributed throughout the United States via mass merchandisers, department stores, hardware chains, warehouse outlets, and specialty shops.

Acquisitions in both the manufacturing and distribution segments (the company added 11 Myers Tire Supply branches over the course of the 1980s for a net total of 37 by 1990) helped boost revenues from $67.5 million in 1980 to $194.8 million by 1989, and net income increased from $3.4 million to $9.6 million.

Growth Continues in the Early 1990s

Acquisitions in both of Myers's business segments supplemented growth in the 1990s. In 1992, the company acquired Alpha Technical Systems (renamed Myers Systems), an Ohio-based manufacturer of material handling systems like conveyors and hoists. Ameri-Kart Corp., a producer of municipal, industrial, and commercial waste handling and collection products, was acquired in 1995. By 1996, Myers Tire Supply had 42 domestic branch outlets. Myers's revenues increased from $195.6 million in 1991 to nearly $321 million in 1996. Profit kept pace, growing from $10.5 million to more than $21 million during the period.

Plans for the future included a continuing focus on the keys to Myers's past success: heavy reinvestment in production capacity and diversification via acquisition, maintenance of a low level of debt, steady geographic expansion (with a particular focus on Asia and the Pacific Rim in the 1990s), and continued dividend increases. The company planned annual investments of $15 to $20 million in increased manufacturing capacity, efficiency programs, and product development in each of the years from 1995 to the end of the century.

Principal Subsidiaries

Ameri-Kart Corp.; Buckhorn, Inc.; Eastern Tire Equipment & Supplies Limited (Canada); Elrick Industries, Inc.; The James C. Heintz Company; MICO, Inc.; Midland Tire Supply, Inc.; Myers International, Inc.; Myers Systems, Inc.; Myers Tire Supply (Canada) Limited; Myers Tire Supply (Chicago), Inc.; Myers Tire Supply (New York), Inc.; Myers Tire Supply (Nevada), Inc.; Myers Tire Supply (Virginia), Inc.; Patch Rubber Company; Plastic Parts, Inc.

Further Reading

Byrne, Harlan S., "Myers Industries Inc.," *Barron's,* February 19, 1990, pp. 40–41.

Ellis, Junius, "Hit This Bull's-Eye for Investing Profits," *Money,* July 1993, pp. 100–106.

"Everything for the Tire Dealer," *Tire Review,* April 1993, p. 28.

Gordon, Mitchell, "Doubly Blessed; Myers Industries Prospers on Two Fronts," *Barron's,* October 6, 1986, pp. 50–52.

——, "On the Road Again: Myers Industries Rolls Back from a Slump That Defied History," *Barron's,* October 3, 1983, pp. 62–63.

——, "Smooth Ride; Few Potholes Jar Earnings Record of Myers, Tire-Repair Servicer," *Barron's,* November 12, 1984, pp. 80–82.

"In High Gear," *Barron's,* June 8, 1981, p. 52.

Leibowitz, David S., "Dull, Dull, Dull," *Financial World,* June 13, 1989, p. 104.

——, "It's Time To Go Bottom Fishing," *Financial World,* January 26, 1988, p. 66.

——, "Let's Hear It for Boring," *Financial World,* November 24, 1992, p. 84.

Marcial, Gene G., "These Two Just Look Humdrum," *Business Week,* July 31, 1995, p. 71.

"Mighty Myers: Tire Equipment Firm Should Enjoy Up Year Even If Detroit Doesn't," *Barron's,* January 29, 1979, p. 35.

"Myers Industries," *Rubber World,* October 1992, pp. 8–9.

"Myers Tire Supply," *Modern Tire Dealer,* September 1994, p. 89.

Prizinsky, David, "Growing Myers Industries Profits on Acquisition Road," *Crain's Cleveland Business,* August 29, 1988, p. 16.

——, "Myers Industries: Success Based on Investment, Diversification, Management Autonomy," *Crain's Cleveland Business,* May 24, 1993, p. S14.

Sheets, Ken, "When Boring Stocks Are Beautiful," *Kiplinger's Personal Finance Magazine,* February 1995, pp. 81–83.

—April Dougal Gasbarre

National Public Radio

635 Massachusetts Avenue NW
Washington, D.C. 20001-3753
U.S.A.
(202) 414-2000
Fax: (204) 414-3329
Web site: http://www.npr.org

Private Nonprofit Corporation
Incorporated: 1970
Employees: 459
Operating Revenues: $55 million (1994)
SICs: 4832 Radio Broadcasting Stations

National Public Radio is the world's first noncommercial, satellite-delivered radio system. As an organization consisting of member radio stations, NPR serves over 17 million Americans each week through over 555 public radio stations in the United States and Guam by distributing cultural and news programming, providing training and promotional services, and representing public radio interests before the Federal Communications Commission (FCC) and Congress.

Public Broadcasting Emerges

Public broadcasting got its first boost with the FCC's decision in the 1940s to reserve a segment of the FM radio spectrum for educational stations. While various noncommercial educational stations had already developed throughout the country in the 1920s, many at America's universities, their financial well-being and integrity was threatened first by the Great Depression and later by commercial pressures. The first nonprofit community group to establish a public FM radio station was the Pacifica Foundation, which established a public station in Berkeley, California, in 1949.

Prompted largely by severe criticism of the quality of television programming, President Lyndon B. Johnson and Congress passed the Public Broadcasting Act in 1967, which sought provide the nation with noncommercial radio programming of an educational nature. Soon thereafter, the Corporation for Public Broadcasting (CPB) was formed as a government-sponsored corporation that derived its funding through the U.S. Department of Housing, Education, and Welfare.

NPR is Formed in 1970

In helping the many small educational radio and tv stations develop professional standards, CPB promptly formed two organizations: The Public Broadcasting Service (PBS) produced and distributed television programming, while National Public Radio (NPR) did the same for radio. The funds derived from Congress were allocated by CPB to PBS, NPR, and creative outsiders who helped introduce and implement new programs. NPR's original mission was to serve as a leader in national news gathering and production as well as to provide a national interconnection between local noncommercial radio stations. Incorporated on February 26, 1970, NPR soon boasted over 90 charter member stations.

NPR's first programming foray consisted of live coverage of the Senate Vietnam hearings, which first aired in April 1971. This was quickly followed by the debut of a daily news program called "All Things Considered," which would steadily grow in listenership and eventually enjoy tremendous success in providing listeners with weekday drive-time news and information. In fact, in 1973, "All Things Considered" garnered its first Peabody Award for NPR, which then built on the success of this program by extending it to weekends with *Weekend All Things Considered* in 1974, mornings with *Morning Edition* in 1979, and *Weekend Edition* and *Weekend Edition Sunday* in 1985 and 1987, respectively. Thus, an NPR news presence seven days a week was ensured. Over the years, NPR news programs provided member stations with live coverage of the Watergate hearings in 1973, as well as extensive reporting on presidential and Congressional elections and Supreme Court nominating procedures, including the Senate hearings on Judge Clarence Thomas in the early 1990s.

During its first five years in existence, NPR focused on production and distribution for its member stations. Public radio further benefitted when, following NPR's merger with the Association of Public Radio Stations in 1977, NPR began providing member stations with training programs, management, and lobbying activities in Washington, D.C. NPR developed the first nationwide, satellite-delivered radio distribution network in 1979. This enabled smaller stations in rural areas to receive programming as easily as their city counterparts. It also provided NPR with a larger audience.

Funding: A Perennial Issue

From their inception, NPR and public broadcasting in general were plagued by internal and external funding pressures. In the early 1970s, President Nixon, Vice-President Agnew, and their administration expressed disapproval of programming they regarded as politically controversial and biased. In 1973, Nixon vetoed a planned endowment to the CPB and encouraged member stations to become more autonomous, believing that local stations would naturally become more conservative in their programming.

While CPB struggled with budget cuts and bureaucracy, eased somewhat during the Carter administration but reinstated during the Reagan presidency, NPR faced severe financial problems, ending 1983 somewhere between $7 and $9 million in debt. Moreover, NPR's CEO resigned during this time under allegations of mismanaging funds, and congress began pressuring NPR to stabilize its financial situation. In addition to staff layoffs and cutbacks on programming, NPR sought a loan from CPB in order to retire its debt and restructure its financial backing.

By July 1983, the situation was indeed bleak; NPR was advanced $500,000 by CPB so that the former could meet its payroll. Further loans followed, with the proviso that ownership of NPR's equipment be shifted to a group of independent trustees to prevent seizure of the equipment by creditors. NPR also agreed to cut costs, raise the fees it charged member stations, and work to increase its contributions from listeners. The restructuring also involved a change in operating arrangements with NPR's member stations. Specifically, NPR sought money from the public and private sectors, while its member stations received CPB funds directly.

The 1990s and Beyond

In 1995, a member radio station receiving all of NPR's programming paid 10.2 percent of its revenues to NPR, according to Marc Gunther of the *New York Times*. This meant that when key stations had unsuccessful fundraising drives, or when Congress voted to cut the annual budged for public broadcasting, NPR also suffered.

Such a scenario came to pass in 1995, when, in its zeal to reduce the federal budget deficit, Congress agreed to reduce public broadcasting dollars from $285 million to $275 million in 1996 and to $260 million in 1997. As a result, NPR's new CEO Delano Lewis was forced to eliminate 20 positions and drop several programs including a minority-oriented news program *Horizons* and other cultural programs.

Delano Lewis was hired as NPR's president and CEO in 1994. As the former head of Chesapeake & Potomac Telephone with 20 years experience in that industry, Lewis had no previous experience in broadcasting. His corporate experience however, was viewed as crucial to NPR's success in a competitive broadcast environment. In addition, Lewis had also served as a lawyer under Robert Kennedy's Justice Department, which led to positions with the Equal Employment Opportunity Commission, the Peace Corps, former Senator Edward Brooke, and Congressman Walter Fauntroy. Such Capitol Hill contacts could only help an organization which depended on congressional goodwill. Finally, Lewis was the first African-American executive at NPR and was expected to lead the organization in more cultural programming and broaden its appeal to a wider range of listeners. As of the late 1990s, however, Lewis's primary achievement was to keep NPR solvent. He helped do this by expanding NPR's reach into different markets and by pursuing corporate and foundation support to bolster dwindling public dollars.

Some forays into new markets had already been initiated, since, in October 1993, NPR began broadcasting for six-hours each day in Europe via satellite. Later that year, NPR partnered with CPB and Public Radio International in a venture known as "America One," which extended NPR's broadcasts in Europe to 24 hours a day via direct-to-home satellite.

In addition to expanding its markets, NPR under Lewis pursued corporate and foundation dollars with increased vigor. This took several forms, including "enhanced underwriting." In the early years of public broadcasting, public broadcasters were forbidden by law from accepting commercials; as commercial pressures mounted, the FCC has relaxed rules regarding what public stations can broadcast. Kathy Scott, an NPR spokesperson, told David Barboza in the *New York Times* in 1995 that the organization's goal was to become more self-sufficient and that its new guidelines were changed "with an eye toward not passing up opportunities." While NPR did not interrupt programming, permit "calls to action" or comparative or qualitative language, it relaxed its policies regarding the inclusion of phone numbers in underwriter acknowledgements and broadcasting slogans. It also accepted grants earmarked for coverage of particular issues. For example, in 1994, the General Motors automaking subsidiary Saturn began sponsorship of *Car Talk,* an NPR call-in program on cars and car repair. In the late 1990s, concepts like "brand leveraging" were also being reviewed along with revenue generation in the form of a record label called "NPR Classics," a music-ordering service, and individual station fundraising initiatives.

Keeping abreast of technology, the NPR web site at http://www.npr.org was established in 1994 and beginning in 1995 pioneered the use of technology known as audio streaming or RealAudio to allow users to hear prerecorded audio files of NPR programs. In 1996, NPR began 24-hour service for the Armed Forces Radio and Television Service offering programs to military radio stations abroad. At that time, NPR broadcasted in over 140 countries around the world.

Lewis also worked to rid NPR of some negative publicity surrounding several discrimination lawsuits, hearkening back to the mid-1970s, when CPB was criticized for not hiring enough minorities to meet the requirements of civil rights legislation. A number of these lawsuits, alleging sexual discrimination against women, were settled out of court. In 1997, an African-American Muslim reporter based in Cairo filed a lawsuit alleging race and religious discrimination. After an April 1997 article summarizing the charges in *Time,* CEO Delano Lewis responded with a letter, quoting staff percentages of 29.2 percent minorities and 48 percent women and noting both minority and female representation in senior management positions. Said Lewis, "the advancement of minorities and women is an ongoing commitment, and our record compares favorably with that of other broadcasters. I have made it my objective to ensure that our employees are treated with dignity and respect."

From its inception, NPR has become famous for the high sound quality of its programs and its engaging radio personalities. Professionals such as *Morning Edition's* host Bob Edwards, interviewer Terry Gross of the program *Fresh Air,* former *All Things Considered* host Susan Stamberg, reporter Nina Totenberg, and many others have received several awards for their work with NPR. NPR is also known for its "quirky" features such as Stamberg's perennial Thanksgiving presentation of her mother-in-law's cranberry relish recipe and David Sedaris's retelling of his stint as a Christmas elf at Macy's. Moreover, NPR has cultivated the distinctive sound of its broadcasts in such features as *Radio Expeditions,* which takes listeners on "audio journeys" to remote areas and includes wildlife recordings.

By the late 1990s, about 60 percent of NPR's operating income was derived from member stations' dues and fees, two to three percent from CPB and other governmental sources, with the remaining funding coming from corporate and foundation contributions. Funding concerns continued to vex NPR and public broadcasting in general. Ironically, contrary to its original purpose of serving as an outlet for alternative programming that could not survive commercially, NPR has needed to become more commercial in order to continue to provide that programming. Liberty Media, a subsidiary of Tele-Communications Inc. (TCI), which already had a two-thirds interest in public television's Macneill/Lehrer Productions in 1996, expressed serious interest in similar funding of public radio programming in exchange for "content." Such offers have led to questions regarding the amount of control corporate sponsors would have on editorial and news coverage, as well as concerns over a possible backlash from listeners in the form of reduced donations.

In the convergence of electronic media (cable, computer, radio, television), public radio has also been looked to as a possible starting point for the National Information Infrastructure (NII), due to its existing network, listener base (according to Mitch Ratcliffe in *Digital Media,* 85 percent of U.S. homes can receive public radio), and proven abilities in community-building. While the NII could certainly prove to be a boost for NPR, many industry observers regarded this as unlikely scenario, due to the probable involvement of media conglomerates with more dollars and power than public radio. Given the competitive media climate of the late 1990s, however, it is certain that NPR will need to continue to search for options in its never-ending battle for funding.

Further Reading

Auderheide, Pat, "Will Public Broadcasting Survive?," *The Progressive,* March 20, 1995, p. 19–21.

Barboza, David, "The 'Enhanced Underwriting' of Public Broadcasting is Taking a More Commercial Flair," *New York Times,* December 27, 1995, p. D2.

De Witt, Karen, "New Chief Wants to Widen NPR's Financial Base," *New York Times,* March 28, 1994, p. D6.

Duhart, Bill, "First Black Director Increases NPR Base," *The Philadelphia Tribune,* April 19, 1994.

Gleick, Elizabeth, "Static on Public Radio: Seven Discrimination Cases in Two Years Have Taken Their Toll on NPR's Warm-and-Fuzzy Image," *Time,* April 7, 1997, p. 55.

Gunther, Marc, "At NPR, All Things Reconsidered," *New York Times,* August 13, 1995, p. H1.

Husseini, Sam, "The Broken Promise of Public Radio," *The Humanist,* September/October, 1994, p. 26–29.

Lewis, Delano, "Letters: NPR's Record on Employment," *Time,* April 28, 1997, p. 8.

Ratcliffe, Mitch, "Public Radio on the Digital Edge," *Digital Edge,* May 16, 1994, p. 3.

Speer, Tibbett L., "Public Radio: Marketing Without Commercials," *American Demographics,* September 1, 1996, p. 62.

Tolan, Sandy, "Must NPR Sell Itself," *New York Times,* July 16, 1996, p. A17.

—Karen Troshynski-Thomas

The New York Times Company

229 West 43rd Street
New York, New York 10036
U.S.A.
(212) 556-1234
Fax: (212) 556-4011
Web site: http://www.nytimes.com

Public Company
Incorporated: 1851 as Raymond, Jones & Company
Employees: 12,300
Sales: $2.61 billion (1996)
Stock Exchanges: American
SICs: 2711 Newspaper Publishing & Printing; 2721
    Magazine Publishing Only, Not Printed Onsite; 4832
    Radio Broadcasting Stations; 4833 Television
    Broadcasting Stations; 7383 News Feature Syndicate

The New York Times Company (NYTC) is a diversified media company including newspapers, magazines, television and radio stations, electronic information services, and electronic publishing. The company publishes two major daily newspapers, *The New York Times* and *The Boston Globe,* 21 regional newspapers, and nine magazines, and it has a 50 percent interest in the *International Herald Tribune.* The company operates eight network-affiliated television stations and two New York City radio stations. The Times Syndicate sells columns, magazine and book excerpts, and feature packages to more than 2,000 newspapers and other media to clients in more than 50 countries. It is the largest syndicate in the world specializing in text, photos, graphics, and other noncartoon features. The company also owns two newspaper distributors and has interests in one newsprint mill and one supercalendered paper mill.

19th Century Founding

The principal founders of *The New York Times* were Henry Jarvis Raymond, a sometime politician, reporter, and editor who learned his trade working for Horace Greeley on the *New York Tribune,* and George Jones, an Albany, New York, banker who had also once worked for Greeley as a business manager on the *Tribune.* Raymond proposed a newspaper that would present the news in a conservative and objective fashion, in contrast to the yellow journalism of the day, which emphasized crime, scandal, and radical politics. They raised $70,000 to establish Raymond, Jones & Company, largely by selling stock to wealthy upstate New York investors, and set up their editorial offices in a dilapidated six-story brownstone on Nassau Street in downtown New York City. The first issue of *The New York Daily Times* (the word "Daily" was dropped from the title in 1857) was dated September 18, 1851, and it announced an editorial policy that would emphasize accurate reporting and moderation of opinion and expression.

Jones handled the company's business affairs, and Raymond, as editor, provided journalistic leadership. Under their management, helped by booming population growth in New York City, the *Times* grew rapidly, reaching 10,000 circulation within ten days and 24,000 by the end of its first year. In 1858 the paper moved into a new five-story building containing the most modern printing equipment. As the *Times* prospered, Raymond established and continually encouraged the high standards of journalism that prevail to this day. It also became a newspaper of record. For example, it carried the entire text of Lincoln's "Gettysburg Address" on the front page on November 20, 1863. Among other journalistic successes, the *Times* provided outstanding coverage of the U.S. Civil War, with Raymond himself reporting on the Battle of Bull Run.

Raymond was active in Republican politics throughout the war. He was present at the creation of the party in Pittsburgh in 1856 and wrote its first statement of principles. He wrote most of the party platform in 1864. Between political activity and journalism, Raymond was chronically overworked for years, and his health suffered. On June 19, 1869, at the age of 49, he died. George Jones assumed the editorial leadership of the *Times.*

By the time of Raymond's death, each of the 100 shares of stock in the company had increased in value from the original $1,000 to about $11,000, with 34 shares held by Raymond and 30 by Jones. In 1871 after a series of *Times* articles on the misdeeds of corrupt New York City politicians headed by William Marcy (Boss) Tweed, an attempt was made by Tweed interests to buy Raymond's 34 shares from his widow. Jones

quickly arranged to have the shares purchased by one of his
associates, thus establishing his control of the newspaper. In
1884 Jones chose to oppose the nomination by the Republican
Party of James G. Blaine for president, thus losing the much-
needed support of Republican readers and advertisers. The
paper's profits fell steadily until Jones's death in 1891. His heirs
had little aptitude for the newspaper business, and the panic and
depression of 1893 brought the *Times* close to failure.

In 1893 the *Times's* editor-in-chief, Charles Ransom Miller,
bought control of the paper from Jones's heirs with $1 million
raised from Wall Street interests. Miller, a fine editor, had no
business aptitude and was unable to maintain the newspaper's
capital requirements. Staff reductions and declining journalistic
quality brought the *Times* to its historic low point, and by 1896
it was on the verge of bankruptcy and dissolution. During this
critical year salvation came in a dramatic fashion. A group of
Wall Street investors in what was then called the New York
Times Publishing Company arranged to save the firm—and
their investments—by placing it in receivership and recapi-
talizing it as a new company, The New York Times Company.
The new capitalization was 10,000 shares with 2,000 being paid
out in exchange for the original *Times* stock. A large stock
position with contractual assurance of eventual majority stock
ownership was purchased with borrowed money by a then-
little-known but respected newspaper editor and publisher from
Chattanooga, Tennessee, Adolph Simon Ochs.

Ochs, the son of German immigrants, had received little
formal schooling, but had learned the newspaper business from
the ground up as newsboy, printer's devil, journeyman printer,
business manager, and reporter. He was hard-working and ambitious. In 1878, at the age of 20, he borrowed $250 to buy the
controlling interest in a failing Tennessee newspaper, the *Chattanooga Times,* thus beginning his career as a newspaper publisher
before he was old enough to vote. He promoted high standards of
journalism in the Chattanooga paper and soon brought it back to
financial health. In 1896, looking for new challenges, he heard
about *The New York Times's* troubles. Ochs offered to take over
as publisher in return for a contract that would give him a
majority of the paper's stock if he succeeded in making it
profitable for three consecutive years. One of his early acts after
becoming publisher of the *Times* on August 18, 1896 was to add
the slogan, ''All the News That's Fit To Print,'' thus serving
notice that the *Times* would continue to avoid sensationalism and
follow high editorial standards.

Adolph Ochs Arrives at the Turn of the Century

Ochs's first two years with the *Times* were a continual struggle to carry on operations and improve the paper with inadequate
capital. The expenses of covering the Spanish-American War in
1898 came close to ruining the paper, which sold then for 3¢ a
copy. Some *Times* executives advised raising the price, but Ochs
made the brilliant and daring decision to reduce the price to 1¢.
Within a year paid circulation trebled from 26,000 to 76,000.
Advertising linage increased by nearly 40 percent, and the paper
was profitable. Despite subsequent price increases, this was the
beginning of a long upward trend in circulation and profitability.
On August 14, 1900, Ochs received the NYTC stock certificates
that established his control over the paper and the company, a
controlling interest that was still held by his descendants in 1991.

The *Times's* success under Ochs was due to much more than
price cutting. He improved financial and Wall Street coverage,
added a Sunday magazine supplement, and a Saturday book review section, which was later moved to Sunday. With a brilliant
managing editor, Carr Van Anda, the *Times* carried out numerous
journalistic coups. It scooped the world on the Japanese-Russian
naval battle in 1904 by sending the first wireless dispatches from
a war area. It again scooped the world on the *Titanic* shipwreck in
1912 and outdid all competition in reporting the events of World
War I. The paper warned of the excesses of the 1920s, but was
well equipped financially to survive the Great Depression thanks
to Ochs's conservative policy of plowing back into the paper a
major portion of its profits.

Under Ochs, the NYTC followed a general policy of avoiding diversification, although Ochs himself continued as the
personal owner and publisher of the *Chattanooga Times* and
had a private investment in a Philadelphia paper between 1901
and 1913. In 1926, however, the NYTC did take part ownership,
along with Kimberly & Clark Company, in a Canadian paper
mill, the Spruce Falls Power and Paper Company, to assure its
supplies of newsprint.

The *Times* did relatively well during the Great Depression,
with daily circulation holding in the 450,000 to 500,000 range.
Ochs's health declined during the early 1930s, and he died on
April 8, 1935. On May 7, 1935, the company's directors elected
as president and publisher Ochs's son-in-law, Arthur Hays
Sulzberger, who had married Ochs's daughter Iphigene in 1917
and subsequently worked his way up through the executive
ranks of the newspaper.

New Leadership in the Postwar Period

Under Sulzberger the *Times* improved steadily in news coverage, financial strength, and technical progress. In a diversification
move in 1944 the NYTC purchased New York City radio stations
WQXR and WQXR-FM. Sulzberger opposed without success the
unionization of *Times* employees. The company's first published
financial statement in 1958 showed 60 consecutive years of increasing profits. In 1957 a recapitalization split the common stock
into A and B common stock, with the B shares, mostly held by the
Ochs trust, having voting control over the company. Sulzberger's
health began to fail in the late 1950s. He retired in 1961. His
successor as president and publisher was his son-in-law, Orvil E.
Dryfoos. Dryfoos died in 1963. On June 20, 1963, he was succeeded in turn as president and publisher by Arthur Hays

Sulzberger's son, Arthur Ochs Sulzberger, who continued in 1991 to lead the NYTC as chairman and chief executive officer.

Although Sulzberger made some administrative changes and broadened the scope of the *Times* news coverage, the company continued to earn a relatively low profit margin on revenues, partly because of his policy of spending freely for thorough reporting, even to the extent of throwing out advertisements to make room for news. A second bitter strike against the paper in 1965 unsettled the management, and a decision was made to undertake a significant program of diversification. In 1967 the company's book and educational division was enlarged, and in 1968 the *Times* purchased a 51 percent interest in Arno Press. In 1969 the A common stock was given the vote for three members of the nine-member board. This action together with a public offering qualified the A stock for listing on the American Stock Exchange. The B stock, which controlled the company, continued to be held mostly by the Ochs family trust. In 1971 the NYTC paid Cowles Communications Company 2.6 million shares of class A stock to purchase substantial newspaper, magazine, television, and book properties, including *Family Circle* and other magazines; a Florida newspaper chain; a Memphis, Tennessee, TV station; and a textbook publisher.

During the 1970s the newspaper's profit margins continued to be under pressure because of competition, especially in New York City suburban areas. The former Cowles properties helped buoy earnings despite the 1976 sale of some medical magazines acquired from Cowles. In 1980 the NYTC paid about $100 million for a southern New Jersey cable television operation, its largest acquisition since the Cowles deal. In 1984 the book publishing operation was sold to Random House, but in 1985 the NYTC, flush with record profits, spent about $400 million on the purchase of five regional newspapers and two TV stations. In 1986 yet another recapitalization converted every ten shares of B stock into nine shares of A and one share of B, with the B stock still controlling the company. Since more than 80 percent of the B stock was held by the Ochs trust, this move gave the trustees more liquidity without sacrificing control of the company. The years 1989 and 1990 continued to be profitable. In 1989 the NYTC, admitting it was not making progress with cable, sold all of its cable TV properties to a consortium of Pennsylvania cable companies for $420 million. Also in 1989 the company acquired *McCall's* magazine, which, together with the acquisitions in 1988 of *Golf World* and *Sailing World,* substantially strengthened the NYTC's magazine group. The company's large new automated printing and distribution facility in Edison, New Jersey, which had been under construction for several years, was scheduled to become operational in late 1990.

The 1990s

Throughout the 1990s, the company would buy and sell properties in the areas of print, cable broadcasting, and electronic media because the decline in newspaper readership in the United States was continuing. In 1993, NYTC bought Affiliated Publications, which owned *The Boston Globe* and specialty magazines published by its division, BPI Communications. In 1994, the company sold its one-third interest in BPI, as well as sold a group of women's magazines, including *Family Circle* and *McCall's,* to Germany's Bertelsmann AG. Also in 1994, NYTC began construction on a state-of-the-art printing plant that would allow adding more color to newspapers and allow for later deadlines.

In 1995, the purchase of a majority interest in Video News International, a video news-gathering company, was made. A return to cable was made when the company bought a minority stake in the cable arts network, Ovation, and launched two cable news channels in Arkansas. Also in 1995, the company entered cyberspace in two ways. One was by joining with eight other newspaper companies in an online news service, New Century Network. The other was creating The New York Times Electronic Media Company as a wholly owned subsidiary that would develop new products and distribution channels for the *Times,* such as on the Web, America Online (AOL), and The New York Times Index.

Two years later in 1997, a new, expanded version of the AOL site debuted with a new design, improved navigation and functionality, new content areas, and expanded advertising opportunities, such as allowing advertisers to target ads to readers of particular sections. The new content, available only to AOL members who made the Times site one of the service's most popular since its debut in 1994, included People in the News area, enhancements to Science Times, live crosswords and news chats, a weekly news quiz, a Topic of the Day message board for discussions based on Page One articles, monthly Times Looks Back retrospectives, free access to Times Crossword Puzzles and the Bridge and Chess columns, a themed monthly crossword puzzle, and The New York Times Magazine.

The New York Times Syndicate launched a weekly column written by the Duchess of York in 1997. The Duchess, who was the former Sarah Ferguson and former wife of Prince Andrew, the second son of England's Queen Elizabeth, wrote about current events and social issues that interested her.

The New York Times Company has come a long way from the small brownstone on Nassau Street where Henry Raymond published the first issue of *The New York Times* in 1851. Company success has resulted not only from strong business leadership during much of its history but also from a series of capable publishers, editors, and reporters who built and continue to operate one of the world's great newspapers, in print and online.

Principal Subsidiaries

The New York Times Syndication Sales Corp.; The New York Times Electronic Media Company; NYT Business Information Services.

Principal Operating Units

The New York Times New Service; The New York Times Index.

Further Reading

Berger, Meyer, *The Story of the New York Times, 1851–1951,* New York: Simon and Schuster, 1951.
Goulden, Joseph C., *Fit to Print,* Secaucus, NJ: Lyle Stuart Inc., 1988.
Salisbury, Harrison E., *Without Fear or Favor,* New York: Times Books, 1980.
Talese, Gay, *The Kingdom and the Power,* New York: World Publishing Company, 1969.

—Bernard A. Block
—updated by Dorothy Kroll

O'Charley's Inc.

3038 Sidco Drive
Nashville, Tennessee 37204
U.S.A.
(615) 256-8500
Fax: (615) 256-8443

Public Company
Incorporated: 1984
Employees: 3,500
Sales: $164.5 million (1996)
Stock Exchanges: NASDAQ
SICs: 5812 Eating Places; 6794 Patent Owners & Lessors

A major regional restaurant chain in the southeastern United States, O'Charley's Inc. operates a chain of casual-theme dinner houses that feature aged prime rib, chicken, seafood, pasta, and homemade soups. The chain was developed by David K. Wachtel, who purchased one existing O'Charley's restaurant in 1984 and quickly built it into a regional chain. During the late 1990s, the O'Charley's chain included more than 70 restaurants clustered in the Southeast.

Origins

Two distinct eras described O'Charley's first three decades of existence. One was a period of little change and the other was a period of constant change and ambitious growth that transformed a solitary restaurant into a chain of restaurants generating nearly $200 million a year in sales. Not surprisingly, the two contrasting eras were led by different individuals pursuing different objectives. First came Charlie Watkins, the founder of O'Charley's, who opened the company's first restaurant in 1969. Watkins ran his lone O'Charley's for the next 15 years. Watkins sold his restaurant in 1984, marking the beginning of O'Charley's era of steady expansion and the arrival of the company's second leader.

Watkins sold his restaurant to David K. Wachtel, whose professional life had been spent in the restaurant business. For 23 years Wachtel had worked for Shoney's, a Nashville, Ten-

nessee-based family dinner house chain. Wachtel eventually became president and chief executive officer of the restaurant company, resigning his twin posts in 1982. Two years later, he struck the deal with Watkins and gained control of the solitary O'Charley's restaurant; he had in mind, however, plans different from operating a single restaurant. Wachtel was intent on developing O'Charley's into a restaurant chain and, in less than three years, he accomplished much toward expanding the dining concept that he had acquired. In mid-1987, the twelfth O'Charley's opened in Lexington, Kentucky, occupying a site formerly used by the Bennigan's chain of restaurants. While the Lexington grand opening was under way, Wachtel was working on plans to convert two more Bennigan's units into O'Charley's by the end of the year—one in Huntsville, Alabama and the other in the company's headquarters city of Nashville.

Quickly, Wachtel had developed one restaurant into a small regional chain that operated as a casual-theme dining concept featuring fresh fish, cut and aged meats, hamburgers, and fresh-baked products. Although expansion had been rapid, it had not been wide-ranging. Of the 12, 180-seat O'Charley's units in operation during the summer of 1987, all were located within 200 miles of each other. It was a strategy Wachtel planned to follow in future expansion. ''We'll concentrate on our current O'Charley's cities in the Southeast,'' he informed a reporter from *Nation's Restaurant News,* ''which should keep us busy for three years but will interfere with my golf game.'' Wachtel's hours away from the restaurant business were a precious few, indeed, leaving little time for recreational pursuits. In addition to opening his twelfth O'Charley's and planning the establishment of two others, he also opened his first Trapper's restaurant in Nashville in 1987, a ''red-meat-and-alcohol'' concept that he planned to expand in the southeastern United States. Wachtel's involvement with business ventures aside from O'Charley's would eventually lure him away from leading the company, but during the immediate years ahead he spearheaded the expansion of his flowering O'Charley's chain.

1990 Public Offering

From the end of 1987 to the beginning of the 1990s, 13 new O'Charley's restaurants were opened, with expansion expected to pick up pace following the company's July 1990 initial public

286

offering of shares. The conversion to public ownership represented the second tool used by Wachtel to speed expansion. The first had been establishing a franchising program, which had engendered eight franchised restaurants by the time of the July public offering, but the timing of the stock sale reduced its effectiveness as a means for expansion. The timing could not have been worse. O'Charley's made its debut in the public spotlight just before tensions in the Persian Gulf flared and the United States implemented Operation Desert Storm. Many of the company's 27 restaurants at the time were situated near military bases with populations drained by the transfer of troops to the Middle East, and patronage at the company's restaurants declined as a result. Further, a national economic recession also was under way, exacerbating the effects of O'Charley's ill-timed initial public offering.

In the wake of O'Charley's July 1990 offering, per restaurant sales and profits plunged, falling to among the lowest in the restaurant industry nationwide. At the same time, investors decided to risk their dollars elsewhere, and O'Charley's stock price fell to roughly two-thirds of its initial value. Changes were clearly needed, as the company took faltering steps under the eye of public scrutiny and into the new decade. Wachtel and other company executives assessed their position, looking at O'Charley's operations and the demands of its customers. In early 1991, management made the moves it hoped would restore vitality to the ailing chain.

What management found were problems associated with the restaurants' menus, which, as one industry observer noted, were beginning to resemble tomes the size of *War and Peace.* O'Charley's was not alone in this practice—it was an industry-wide phenomenon—but the company's commonality with its competition did not lessen the effects of its burdensome menus. As part of the effort to find a solution to O'Charley's difficulties in late 1990, Wachtel hired Charles F. McWhorter Jr. as senior vice-president and chief operating officer to help improve service and bolster customer traffic. A long-time employee of the Ryan's and Quincy's steak-house chains, McWhorter noted that O'Charley's lengthy menu "was hard to execute 100 percent all the time; we were trying to be all things to all people." The solution was a smaller menu, which the company began testing in February 1991 in Knoxville, Tennessee and in Biloxi, Mississippi. The scaled-down menu was then refined and tested at a restaurant in Atlanta in preparation for chainwide distribution, which occurred in mid-1991.

The smaller menus offered roughly half of the entrees listed in the larger menus. "We looked at what was selling and what wasn't," McWhorter explained, "and dropped all the marginal items." Dropped from the old menu were four appetizers, five hamburger and sandwich selections, four steak and rib entrees, and items from the soup and salad listings, leaving O'Charley's with a pared-down menu that enabled quicker service and heightened food quality because kitchen staff had less menu selections with which to contend. "With the smaller menu we can do more things from scratch, and it frees up more time to do different things," McWhorter explained, declaring the switch to a more concise menu a success. Further adjustments were made in 1991, including a reduction in prices for dinner entrees to lunchtime prices and the addition of an Express lunch menu featuring 13 entrees priced under $6 that were guaranteed to be on the diner's table in less than ten minutes.

While these changes were being made and company officials waited to gauge their success in sparking customer traffic, sales, and profits, expansion of the O'Charley's concept continued. Five new restaurants were opened in 1990 and another five debuted in 1991, entrenching the company's presence in Atlanta; Jackson and Memphis, Tennessee; and Brandon, Florida. By mid-1992, O'Charley's was a 37-unit chain with restaurants clustered in eight states, having blanketed the southeastern United States in less than a decade. Three more restaurants were slated for openings by the end of 1992 and another five units were scheduled to be developed in 1993, as Wachtel steadily added more links to his fast-growing chain. Part of the renewed optimism regarding the company's expansion plans was attributable to the first financial results recorded after the menu and pricing changes were made in 1991. For the first fiscal quarter of 1992, O'Charley's reported a 30 percent jump in sales and a more encouraging 37 percent gain in profits, convincing management that the switch to a smaller menu had been the right move.

On the heels of the welcomed financial news, Wachtel led O'Charley's in a new direction that promised to strengthen the company's financial clout. In June 1992, O'Charley's signed a letter of intent to form a partnership to purchase Logan's Roadhouse Restaurant, a casual steak-house restaurant with a grill in public view, concrete floors, muraled walls, and buckets of peanuts in a "honky-tonk" atmosphere. Under the terms of the deal, the partnership called for the establishment of a minimum of five additional Logan's Roadhouse restaurants during the ensuing five years, with the second unit targeted for its grand opening in Nashville in August 1992. O'Charley's became a 20 percent owner in the partnership with the remaining 80 percent belonging to a small group of investors that included Wachtel and McWhorter.

Slightly less than a year after Wachtel signed the Logan's Roadhouse agreement, he began to fade from the foreground at O'Charley's. In May 1993, Wachtel relinquished day-to-day control as president and chief executive officer to devote more time to other business projects, but continued to serve as chairman of O'Charley's. In his place, Gregory L. Burns was named president and selected to the additional post of chief financial officer, while McWhorter climbed the corporate rungs to the chief executive position. Although the orchestrator of O'Charley's resolute expansion for the previous nine years had stepped aside, the pace of expansion did not slacken in his absence. Five new O'Charley's were opened in 1993, giving O'Charley's a total of 45 restaurants. By the end of the year, future expansion seemed destined to be brisk.

In December 1993, Burns and McWhorter announced the formulation of a growth strategy designed to carry the 45-unit chain into the ranks of the country's largest regional dinner-house chains. "Over the past two years, we strengthened many of our internal programs and execution," Burns explained before vowing, "We plan to aggressively grow this company." According to the projections of the five-year plan, the company would lift its restaurant count to 100 units by 1998, a goal that would require it to exceed the expansion rate of the previous years. The company also announced plans to open a minimum of two Logan's Roadhouse units to add to the three restaurants already in operation.

Mid-1990s Lawsuit

Heading into 1994, the company planned to open at least eight new O'Charley's restaurants, situating the new units primarily in southeastern markets such as Cookeville, Tennessee; Louisville and Paducah, Kentucky; and Palm Harbor, Florida. It was a year expected to be filled with news of new restaurant openings, but as the calendar flipped to 1994 other headlines grabbed the attention of both those inside and outside the company. In February 1994, Wachtel resigned as chairman of O'Charley's, citing his "pressing commitments" with other business interests, the most notable of which was the 300-unit Western Sizzlin' budget steak-house chain he had acquired in 1993. Wachtel's full departure from O'Charley's made room for advancement for Burns and McWhorter. Burns was named chief executive and co-chairman and McWhorter was tapped as president and co-chairman. One month after Wachtel's resignation, the company received devastating news when it was announced that four former O'Charley's employees had filed a federal lawsuit charging the restaurant chain with racial discrimination practices against African Americans in the company's hiring, assignment, and promotion procedures. Burns flatly denied the charges, saying the lawsuit was "without merit and the company intends to defend it vigorously."

Brighter news for O'Charley's management arrived in 1995 when the company's involvement in the Logan's Roadhouse partnership turned into a source of cash to fund expansion during the year. The partnership completed an initial public offering in July 1995, netting O'Charley's $11 million, or more than half of the money needed to open the 11 new restaurants scheduled for grand openings in 1995. Meanwhile, to Burns's and McWhorter's consternation, the attorneys for the plaintiffs in the racial discrimination lawsuit were seeking to win class-action status, which threatened to broaden the scope and deepen the damage of the lawsuit. The attorneys were successful in winning class-action status.

With the specter of the lawsuit casting a dark cloud over corporate headquarters in Nashville, senior executives moved forward with their expansion plans, striving to open between 12 and 14 new O'Charley's restaurants in 1996. By July 1996, there were 60 O'Charley's restaurants in operation and a new concept as well. The company opened a more upscale restaurant called Rhea Station Grille in historic downtown Nashville that featured herb-encrusted salmon, lemon artichoke chicken, and pasta and fresh fish in a setting decidedly unlike O'Charley's. Inside, piano entertainment was offered, as well as a room for private parties able to accommodate as many as 100 people. The Rhea Station Grille restaurant basked in the limelight for barely more than a month, its

debut occurring weeks before O'Charley's agreed to settle the racial discrimination lawsuit it had been facing since 1994. In agreeing to settle the suit, and pay what eventually would amount to $6.2 million, Burns was adamant in his denial that there was any truth supporting the charges, declaring, "We agreed to this settlement because of the significant distraction the lawsuit has had on management and the uncertainty it has caused in the marketplace." One month after the settlement was announced, another management shakeup occurred when McWhorter resigned as president after his six-year tenure at the company. His departure left Burns in full power, occupying the posts of chief executive officer, president, and chairman of the board.

The settlement of the lawsuit struck a decisive blow to O'Charley's profit total for 1996. After recording $10.6 million in profits for 1995, which had been inflated by the money gained through the sale of its stake in Logan's Roadhouse, O'Charley's registered a $1.15 million loss for 1996 on an 11 percent gain in sales to $164.5 million. The lawsuit was behind it, however, as it entered 1997, freeing the company to concentrate on expansion. Twelve new O'Charley's were added during the disruptive 1996 year, and in the first two months of 1997 four more restaurants were added to the chain. With 72 restaurants in operation in early 1997, Burns was anticipating adding between 12 and 14 more restaurants by the end of the year, as O'Charley's moved toward its thirtieth anniversary year and prepared for the new century ahead.

Further Reading

Carlino, Bill, "O'Charley's Charts Growth Plan," *Nation's Restaurant News*, December 13, 1993, p. 3.

"Former O'Charley's Employees Claim Race Discrimination," *Nation's Restaurant News*, March 7, 1994, p. 2.

Frydman, Ken, "Wachtel Rolls 12th O'Charley's," *Nation's Restaurant News*, July 13, 1987, p. 2.

Howard, Theresa, "O'Charley's Reaps Pay-Off from Service, Value Focus," *Nation's Restaurant News*, June 8, 1992, p. 14.

Keegan, Peter O., "O'Charley's Trims Menu, Cuts Prices, Adds Express Lunch," *Nation's Restaurant News*, June 10, 1991, p. 4.

"Lawsuit, Writedowns Result in Year-End Loss at O'Charley's," *Nation's Restaurant News*, March 3, 1997, p. 12.

"O'Charley's Beats Bad Weather," *Nation's Restaurant News*, May 24, 1993, p. 27.

"O'Charley's Debuts Rhea Station Grille," *Nation's Restaurant News*, July 29, 1996, p. 66.

"O'Charley's Inc. Agrees To Settle Class-Action Suit," *Nation's Restaurant News*, August 5, 1996, p. 156.

"O'Charley's Inks Deal with Logan's," *Nation's Restaurant News*, June 15, 1992, p. 14.

"O'Charley's Names Burns Prexy, Chairman," *Nation's Restaurant News*, September 23, 1996, p. 132.

"O'Charley's Prexy McWhorter Exits after 6-Year Stint," *Nation's Restaurant News*, September 16, 1996, p. 68.

"O'Charley's To Develop Logan's Roadhouse," *Nation's Restaurant News*, July 20, 1992, p. 18.

Papiernik, Richard L., "Partnership Payout Finances O'Charley's Unit Expansion," *Nation's Restaurant News*, September 11, 1995, p. 3.

Pollack, Neal, "Chains Promote Diverse Menus and Family Dining," *Restaurants & Institutions*, July 24, 1991, p. 99.

"Wachtel Resigns as O'Charley's Chair," *Nation's Restaurant News*, February 21, 1994, p. 2.

—Jeffrey L. Covell

Patterson Dental Co.

1031 Mendota Heights Road
St. Paul, Minnesota 55120
U.S.A.
(612) 686-1600
Fax: (612) 686-9331
Web site: http://www.pdental.com

Public Company
Incorporated: 1925 as Patterson (M.F.) Dental Supply
    Co. of Delaware
Employees: 2,500
Sales: $581.9 million (1996)
Stock Exchanges: NASDAQ
SICs: 5047 Medical, Dental & Hospital Equipment &
    Supplies; 5112 Stationery & Office Supplies

Patterson Dental Co. was, in the mid-1990s, the largest distributor of dental products in North America, with a share of about 20 percent of the annual $2.5 billion dental distribution market in the United States and Canada. In 1996 it was supplying a full line of more than 70,000 dental supplies and equipment to dentists, dental laboratories, and institutions in the United States and Canada, including its own private label line of dental supplies, consisting of about 1,500 items. Patterson Dental also was offering related services, including the installation, maintenance, repair, and financing of dental equipment. The company more than doubled its revenues between fiscal 1991 and 1995 (the years ending April 30). It was the most profitable of 194 companies listed on the NASDAQ stock exchange during this period, with a five-year average return on equity of 81 percent. In 1996 it ventured into a new market by acquiring a producer and marketer of stationery and office supply products to health care providers.

Patterson Dental to 1985

The company was established in 1877, when Myron F. and John G. Patterson bought a Milwaukee drugstore, driving up sales volume by offering customers free swigs from a keg of bourbon. It was incorporated in Delaware in 1925 as Patterson (M.F.) Dental Supply Co. of Delaware. In the 1950s it was distributing dental supplies and equipment west of the Mississippi River. Net sales grew from $12.8 million in 1954 to $15.7 million in 1958, and net profit grew from $349,000 to $541,000 in this period. In 1959 the head office was in St. Paul, and the company, in addition to office buildings in St. Paul and Minneapolis, owned buildings occupied by six branches. Its eight subsidiaries included M.F. Patterson Dental Supply Co. of Minnesota and M.F. Patterson Dental Supply Co. of Wisconsin. W.O. Patterson was the president.

Owners and directors of Patterson Dental owned 16 percent of the company, with another 42 percent of the shares held in trust, when the company went public by offering a small block of shares for $10.50 a share in 1959. Also in that year, the company acquired California Dental Supply Co. for $2 million. Net sales grew slowly, from $18.4 million in 1959 to $19.6 million in 1963, and net income of $453,000 in 1963 failed to reach the 1959 peak of $556,000.

By this time high-speed drills and improved devices for cleaning teeth and performing other dental functions had done much to reduce the pain and discomfort suffered by patients and had also provided an important sales stimulant for manufacturers of dental equipment. Of about 200 companies making and distributing dental equipment in 1962, Patterson Dental was among only a handful that were publicly owned. In 1964 it was acquired by another public dental supply firm, Ritter Co., in an exchange of stock valued at about $11.8 million. The transaction gave Ritter a retail operation for the first time, since it had been selling its products through independent dealers.

This merger was formally enacted in 1965 despite a request by the U.S. Department of Justice for delay on the ground that it might raise some questions under federal antitrust laws. In 1970 a federal district court found that the acquisition ''might substantially lessen competition in the dental-equipment market'' and, therefore, that it violated the Clayton Antitrust Act. Sybron Corp.—the name Ritter had taken in 1968—was ordered in 1971 to divest itself of Patterson Dental within three years.

Company Perspectives:

"The mission of Patterson Dental Company is to remain the leader in the dental marketplace by assessing, meeting and exceeding customer needs which provide tangible value for the customer and profitable growth opportunities for the company while providing personal and professional growth opportunities for our employees."

Sybron sold Patterson Dental to Doric Corp., a conglomerate, in 1972 for $20 million in cash. That year Patterson Dental, which was made a Doric subsidiary, had pretax earnings of $1.6 million on sales of $22.9 million, of which equipment accounted for about 41 percent and supplies and other for the remainder. The dental equipment it was distributing and selling included dental chairs, X-ray machines, sterilizers, lighting, cabinets, and power supplies. Dental supplies sold by the company included artificial teeth, gold, filing materials, instruments, and anesthetics. Its own subsidiary, Dental Capital Corp., was financing customer purchases. At this time Patterson Dental had its headquarters and a central warehousing facility for special products in Bloomington, Minnesota. There were 39 distribution outlets in 17 states in the western United States.

Patterson Dental's sales grew to $40.7 million in 1974, and its pretax earnings rose to $3 million that year. Doric was sold in 1975 to Esmark Inc., a conglomerate holding company, and Patterson Dental became a unit of Estech, Inc., a subsidiary of Esmark. In 1976 Patterson Dental expanded its distribution through the acquisition of certain assets of the Dental Products Division of Litton Industrial Products, Inc. By 1980 Patterson Dental believed itself to be the second largest distributor of dental equipment and supplies in the United States. Soon after that the unit was transferred to Estronicks, Inc., another Esmark subsidiary.

Private Company, 1985–1992

The Beatrice Cos., Inc. acquired Esmark in 1984. In May 1985 PDA Inc., a holding company formed by Patterson Dental's management and certain investors, purchased the company from a subsidiary of Beatrice in a leveraged buyout. Peter L. Frechette, president since 1982, continued as chief executive officer of the private company, which had 1,280 employees and sales of $168 million in 1985. "We bought the company with a fairly simple strategy," Frechette later told a Minnesota reporter. "Buy it at the right price [$50 million] and have a financing portfolio in place which would allow us to pay off the debt right away and give us time to put our distribution strategy in place. We didn't buy this company to make money. ... Making money is more a byproduct of doing something else."

Following the acquisition, management implemented strategies to increase profitability by improving efficiency and the quality and breadth of customer service. One means of doing this was a computerized order-processing network. The company also improved its inventory tracking and other management-information systems, introduced centralized purchasing,

and reduced the number of distribution locations in the United States from 56 to 11. It also induced revenue growth by internal expansion and strategic acquisitions, including the 1987 acquisition of D.L. Saslow Co., the third largest distributor of dental products in the United States, for $12 million, and the purchase of smaller firms in 1990. During fiscal 1986 the company had an operating loss of $12,000 on net sales of $165.8 million, but its fortunes improved rapidly thereafter. In fiscal 1990 it earned $6 million in net income on net sales of $220.6 million.

Public Enterprise Again, 1992–1996

Patterson Dental Co. was incorporated in Minnesota in 1992 through the merger of PDA and Patterson-Minnesota. Shortly thereafter it went public, offering three million shares of common stock at $16 a share, the proceeds enabling the company to retire a long-term debt of $19.2 million as well as to clear its balance sheet and store funds for future acquisitions. Following the completion of the offering, prior stockholders retained 79 percent of the shares, with an employee stock ownership plan holding 18 percent of the shares and Frechette and Ronald Ezerski, vice-president of finance, each holding 14.5 percent.

By this time the company was distributing dental supplies and equipment throughout the United States, with a full line of more than 50,000 products, including 1,400 private label products sold under the Patterson name. It also was offering customers a full range of related services, including dental equipment installation, maintenance, and repair, and dental office design. Net income in fiscal 1992, when the company had 79 sales offices in 43 states, was $8.5 million on $277.1 million in revenues.

Patterson Dental proved to be a hit with investors, its stock rising as high as $25.50 a share before 1992 ended. It rewarded them with rosy results for fiscal 1993: $12.8 million in net income of $342.8 million in net sales. In October 1993 the company swallowed the Canadian subsidiary of HealthCo International, Inc., purchasing it from a U.S. bankruptcy trustee for $13.5 million. Prior to HealthCo's bankruptcy, it had been the leading distributor of dental supplies in the United States, a position Patterson Dental now enjoyed. The company hired 73 of Healthco's sales representatives. It also was expanding its electronic order system, in part by the installation, beginning in 1987, of a computer in any dental office. Some 3,000 were already in place, with 100 being added each month.

Patterson Dental's sales and income grew vigorously in fiscal 1994, reaching $466.9 million and $19.3 million, respectively. Some 12.3 percent of its revenue growth was attributed to the U.S. Healthco salespeople it hired and 8.5 percent to the acquisition of the Healthco Canadian subsidiary. The company's stock advanced to a high of $46.50 a share before a three-for-two split at midyear. Investment analysts were bullish on Patterson Dental's business sector, forecasting that, along with greater wealth, aging baby boomers would have more dental care needs. One analyst predicted, "The first generation able to hold on to their teeth for life will be willing to pursue aggressive treatment to keep them in good condition." With dental spending only 4.7 percent of the total $943 billion health care bill in the United States, this item was not seen as a prime target for cost cutting by the federal government.

Patterson Dental ended fiscal 1995 with handsome growth in net sales to $532.6 million and net income to $24.2 million. Sales had now nearly quadrupled and earnings had risen more than sevenfold since the 1985 management-led leveraged buyout. The stock, in October 1995, had almost tripled in value since the 1992 public offering. The following month Patterson Dental agreed to acquire Omaha-based Barber Dental Supply Inc., which had annual sales of about $5 million.

During fiscal 1996 Patterson Dental posted new records, although it was growing at a slower rate. It ended the fiscal year with net sales of $581.9 million and net income of $28.7 million. The company's stock advanced to nearly $37 a share in 1996. In August of that year it acquired Deluxe Corp.'s Colwell division, a national direct supplier of stationery and office products to dental, medical, and allied health providers. Colwell had sales of about $55 million in 1995.

1996 and Beyond

At the end of fiscal 1996 Patterson's full line of products included supplies such as X-ray film and solutions, impression and restorative materials, hand instruments and handpieces, dental chairs, dental handpiece control units, diagnostic equipment, sterilizers, dental lights, and compressors. Its full range of related services included dental equipment installation, maintenance, and repair, dental office design, and equipment financing. Supplies came to 60 percent of net sales and equipment amounted to 29 percent, with other sales accounting for the remaining 11 percent. Patterson Dental was processing an average of more than 8,000 customer orders each business day and estimated that 97 percent of the consumable goods orders were being shipped complete within 24 hours.

In addition to its computerized remote-order entry (REMO) systems permitting customers to place orders directly to the company around the clock through a personal computer, Patterson Dental was offering "use installed" customers PDXpress, a computerized order-entry system introduced in 1991 utilizing a hand-held bar-code scanner to eliminate handwritten order forms. More than 5,500 of its customers were utilizing either REMO or PDXpress to order dental supplies. During the fiscal year the company also originated more than $42 million of equipment finance contracts.

Patterson Dental maintained 90 sales offices at the end of fiscal 1996 and had a staff of more than 750 direct-sales representatives and equipment specialists. There were nine distribution centers. In 1994 corporate headquarters were moved from leased space in Bloomington to a two-story, 52,100-square-foot acquired building on a 12-acre site in Mendota Heights, south of St. Paul. Managers and directors held 26 percent of the company's stock and an employee stock ownership plan accounted for 18 percent in 1995. The company's long-term debt was $3.2 million at the end of fiscal 1996.

Principal Subsidiaries

Direct Dental Supply Co.; Patterson Dental Canada, Inc.; Patterson Dental Supply, Inc.

Further Reading

Brammer, Rhonda, "Prudent Bear," *Barron's,* July 29, 1996, p. 19.

"Doric Agrees To Buy Sybron Dental Unit for $20 Million Cash," *Wall Street Journal,* March 10, 1972, p. 6.

"The Graying of America," *Money,* May 1994, pp. 63–64.

Nissen, Todd, "Amid Weak IPO Market, Patterson Dental Is Biting," *Minneapolis-St Paul CityBusiness,* September 4, 1992, p. 2.

"Patterson Dental," *Barron's,* January 31, 1994, pp. 49–50.

"Patterson Dental Company Reports Third Quarter Results," *PR Newswire,* February 17, 1997, p. 217CLM021.

"Recovery for Dental Equipments," *Financial World,* August 15, 1962, p. 13.

Reingold, Jennifer, "Patterson Dental," *Financial World,* October 24, 1995, p. 24.

"Ritter, M.F. Patterson Merge Despite Request of Justice Unit To Wait," *Wall Street Journal,* April 28, 1965, p. 19.

"Ritter Plans To Acquire Retail Dental Concern for $11.8 Million Stock," *Wall Street Journal,* December 9, 1964, p. 12.

Solberg, Clara, "Patterson Dental Set To Cut Teeth on Bigger HQ," *Minneapolis-St Paul CityBusiness,* September 9, 1994, p. 2.

"Sybron Says U.S. Court Orders It To Rid Itself of Patterson Dental Co.," *Wall Street Journal,* August 26, 1971, p. 26.

Weinberger, Betsy, "Managers of a Languishing Big-Company Division Have Remade Patterson Dental into the Largest Independent Distributor of Its Kind in the Country—Patterson's," *Corporate Report Minnesota,* November 1993, p. 40+.

—Robert Halasz

Penske Corporation

13400 Outer Drive West
Detroit, Michigan 48239
U.S.A.
(313) 592-5000
Fax: (313) 592-5256
Web site: http://www.penske.com/

Private Company
Incorporated: 1969
Employees: 25,000
Sales: $4 billion (1996)
SICs: 7513 Truck Rental & Leasing Without Drivers;
7948 Racing Including Track Operations; 5511 New
& Used Car Dealers

Ranked among America's 50 largest private companies, Penske Corporation is a transportation services firm with major interests in truck leasing, diesel engine manufacture, auto racing, and retail automobile sales. Founded by former Indianapolis 500 racer Roger Penske, the company has revenues approaching $5 billion. Principal owner and CEO Penske has earned a reputation for building contenders on and off the racetrack with the simple business philosophy: ''Effort Equals Results.'' His company's stunning turnaround of ailing businesses like General Motors' Detroit Diesel and Hertz's Truck Leasing is at least as impressive as his racing team's record ten Indianapolis 500 wins and nine national IndyCar championships.

The corporation operates in three distinct groups: transportation services, retail/service automotive, and performance automotive. The $1.8 billion (revenues) transportation services group includes the nation's second largest full service truck leasing and renting business, Penske Truck Leasing Co., L.P., and the diesel engine manufacturing company Detroit Diesel Corporation. The retail automotive group includes six California car dealerships that collectively sell more than 35,000 Cadillacs, Chevrolets, Hondas, Lexuses, and Toyotas a year. The automotive performance group is built upon the highly successful Penske racing team and also runs the Michigan International

Speedway and the Pennsylvania International Raceway. Penske took this division, including its Competition Tire businesses and racetracks, public as Penske Motorsports Inc. in 1996. The Penske group's 1995 acquisition of more than 850 Kmart Auto Centers added service to its roster and made it the nation's largest independent tire dealer.

Origins in Founder's Successful Racing Career

Roger Penske attended his first Indianapolis 500 race at age 14, and he bought his first car with money from a paper route. Although he was ''addicted to racing,'' Penske was also pragmatic; after earning a degree in business administration from Pennsylvania's Lehigh University in 1959, he went to work at the Aluminum Company of America (Alcoa) as a sales representative. But the world of work did not keep him from the racetrack.

In the early 1960s, while still a sales representative for Alcoa, Roger Penske became one of the most successful race car drivers around, competing in sports car, endurance, and Formula One races on weekends. His first win came in 1959, and over the next few years the accolades poured in. In 1962 Penske was voted Sports Car Driver of the Year by *Sports Illustrated, The New York Times,* and *The Los Angeles Times.* Having won five races in 1964, he left Alcoa for a job as general manager of the McKean Chevrolet dealership in Philadelphia. Having won the NASCAR Grand National in 1965, Penske retired from racing and bought the dealership. He returned to the sport in 1966 as the owner of Team Penske. The racing organization would go on to become the most successful in history.

Diversifications Contribute to Growth in the 1960s and 1970s

In the middle and late 1960s, Roger Penske's Chevy dealership prospered such that it generated capital for acquisitions, including a pair of specialty tire distributorships, Competition Tire East and Competition Tire West, and a small truck leasing operation. The truck leasing business soon enjoyed spectacular growth as private fleet owners discovered the benefits of leasing versus buying their trucks—purchasing, fuel supply, scheduled maintenance, and repair were left in the hands of the lessor, allowing the fleet operator to focus on the distribution and routing of their products. By 1969 Penske Leasing had 33 locations in the northeastern United States. The Penske Corporation was set up that year as a holding company for Roger Penske's automotive-related enterprises.

By 1971 Roger Penske had auto dealerships in Philadelphia and Allentown, Pennsylvania, and in Detroit. His nearly legendary attention to detail set the pace at the dealerships. Sales climbed, helping to fuel expansion into other ventures.

Started as a business, Team Penske in many ways revolutionized motor sports. J. Douglas Johnson of the *Indiana Business Magazine* credited Roger Penske with bringing ''orderliness and professionalism to auto racing.'' One of Penske's racing competitors conceded to *Forbes,* May 28, 1979, ''He markets his car and sets up sponsorship programs more effectively than anyone else.'' Moreover, the exposure on televised broadcasts of major racing events, including the Indianapolis 500, provided enormous value when compared with the cost of a 30-second commercial spot, benefiting Penske's other businesses immeasurably.

Renowned drivers like Mark Donohue, Mario Andretti, Bobby Unser, and Tom Sneva in the 1970s; Danny Sullivan, Rick Mears, and Al Unser Sr. in the 1980s; and Emerson Fittipaldi and Paul Tracy in the 1990s helped make Team Penske the most successful organization in the history of racing, winning more than 80 IndyCar races, among them a record nine Indianapolis 500 titles by 1994 and eight IndyCar National Championships. Penske's winning image was clearly valuable to the corporation's nonracing businesses—buying a new car from auto racing's most successful team seems just a little flashier than buying it from an average dealer.

Accelerated Growth Via Acquisition and Turnaround in the 1980s

Although Penske's businesses enjoyed satisfactory growth throughout the 1970s, its expansion accelerated in the 1980s. Sales were $254 million in 1981, but by 1988 sales had topped $2 billion. The first business segment to swell was truck leasing. The unit had enjoyed excellent growth throughout the 1970s, but in 1982, Penske entered a joint venture with the ailing giant Hertz Truck Leasing. The Hertz unit had lost $40 million in 1981, and the company considered unloading it altogether. Roger Penske was invited to tour Hertz's operations, and soon he agreed to merge Penske Leasing with Hertz's truck operations. Penske trimmed 500 jobs and 30 locations from Hertz. After one year, the new Hertz-Penske Leasing made $1.2 million. Penske's initial stake in the company was 35 percent. By 1986 the share was upped to 50 percent, and Hertz-Penske acquired the heavy-duty truck leasing business of another major company, Leaseway Transportation, for $94 million. The company grew to become the second largest truck leasing company in the United States behind Ryder System, Inc., although a distant second, as Ryder's sales quadrupled those of Hertz-Penske.

In June 1988 Penske Corporation bought Hertz's half of Hertz-Penske Leasing. Two months later, in August, Penske Corporation's truck leasing operations merged with General Electric Credit Corporation's Gelco Truck Services. The resulting company was a limited partnership named Penske Truck Leasing Co., L.P., with a Penske Corporation subsidiary as the general partner, responsible for operation of the firm. Penske initially owned 69 percent of the partnership and GE purchased another three percent in January 1989. The joint venture operated 400 locations and leased a fleet of more than 65,000 vehicles, but remained second to Ryder System in market share in the early 1990s.

Penske Corporation's retail automotive group also made large acquisitions in the 1980s. In 1985 the nation's largest Toyota dealership, Longo Toyota of suburban Los Angeles, came up for sale. Founded by Dominic Longo in 1967, the dealership had been the number one Toyota dealership in the United States since 1969. After Dominic Longo died in 1985, Penske agreed to buy it.

In 1988, Longo Toyota moved into a brand new facility in El Monte, California. The new facility covered 23 acres, employed more than 360 people, and boasted 104 service bays and 54 body shop stalls. Penske's continued emphasis on service was crucial to Longo's exceptional rate of repeat and referral business. The dealership carefully targeted its market. For example, it employed special teams of salespeople who were fluent, collectively, in Mandarin and Cantonese Chinese, Japanese, Korean, Vietnamese, and Thai, as well as Spanish and English, making it easy and comfortable for L.A. residents originating from the Pacific Rim to do business at Longo. Roger Penske's son Greg serves as general manager of the dealership. In 1989 Penske started Longo Lexus; for both 1990 and 1991 this dealership was the Lexus retail sales leader in the United States.

Late 1980s Acquisition Brings Challenges, Growth

In December 1987 Penske Corporation made its biggest acquisition ever and plunged into the large-scale manufacturing sector at the same time with the purchase of 60 percent of General Motors' $900-million-in-sales Detroit Diesel Allison division. Penske was approached in late 1987 by GM's investment banking firm, Salomon Brothers, with the possibility of a deal. General Motors hoped an entrepreneurial infusion could save the troubled engine-maker. Detroit Diesel's North American market share had declined from 33 percent in 1979 to three percent, and it had lost a total of $600 million in the previous five years. Problems with labor relations, product design, performance, and consumer service were the root of the trouble. GM lost its diesel customers to Cummins and Caterpillar, and despite sinking $100 million into an upgraded plant during the 1980s the automotive giant seemed incapable of turning the unit around by itself.

Penske Corporation's experience with fleet truck purchasing and its earlier operation of Detroit Diesel Allison distributorships in the East made the company an excellent choice as a partner. Roger Penske's $300 million infusion bought him 60 percent of the company and control of operations. He quickly began streamlining the new Detroit Diesel Corporation. The operating budget was slashed by more than $70 million by cutting jobs, consolidating facilities, and cutting unnecessary computer costs.

GM's poor management of the unit throughout the 1980s and uncertainty about the immediate future had depressed the morale of Detroit Diesel workers. Roger Penske set out to convince his new employees that their company would be competitive once again. In August 1988, several months after he began running Detroit Diesel, Roger Penske invited his 3,000 Detroit Diesel employees to the Michigan International Speedway for the Marlboro 500. After watching Team Penske drivers Rick Mears win the pole position, Al Unser Sr. in the Detroit Diesel-sponsored car lead for a time, and Danny Sullivan win the race, the Detroit Diesel employees were elated. But free race tickets were not Penske's only labor relations tool. He also made a point of scheduling regular meetings with union officials and members alike, thereby fostering a spirit of unanimity among the workers.

Revitalizing Detroit Diesel's work force was a key to improving the company's fortunes. Also essential was bringing a better product to market. General Motors had invested a good deal of research and development into a new engine—the Series 60. The six-cylinder, four-stroke diesel featured integral electronic controls, improved fuel efficiency, and durability, and was relatively low-cost. The new engine was well received in the marketplace, helping Detroit Diesel turn a profit.

In September 1988 Penske Transportation bought the diesel electronic unit injector line from GM's Rochester Products Division. Penske's transportation services group also expanded Detroit Diesel's product range through an operating agreement with Perkins Engines, a British subsidiary of the Canadian machinery maker Varity, formerly Massey-Ferguson, to market Detroit Diesel engines overseas and to provide smaller diesel engines for Penske to sell in North America. The arrangement gave Detroit Diesel a wide range of diesel engines, from five horsepower to 2,000 horsepower.

Penske's leaner Detroit Diesel began to win back market share by offering its customers significant savings. Confident of the subsidiary's future, Penske upped its stake to 100 percent in 1994. By that time, Detroit Diesel's share had rebounded to more than one-fourth of the heavy-duty North American market.

The 1990s and Beyond

In 1995, Penske acquired 860 Kmart Auto Centers for $112 million and renamed them Penske Auto Center Inc. The purchase allowed Penske Corp. to surpass Discount Tire Co. and become the nation's largest independent tire dealer. Under Kmart, the operation had lost $19 million on sales of $360 million in 1994. Roger Penske Jr., CEO of the new division, expected to double the business by 1999. The acquisition helped

increase corporate revenues from around $3 billion in 1994 to an estimated $4 billion in 1996.

Roger Penske took his Pennsylvania, California, and Michigan racetracks, as well as the corporation's two Competition Tire businesses, public as Penske Motorsports, Inc. in 1996. Early the following year, Penske Motorsports moved to acquire a controlling interest in the North Carolina Motor Speedway, Inc. In 1996, the spin-off earned $10.9 million on revenues of $55.2 million.

Although it is clear that Roger Penske Sr. has come a long way from his first win on a motor speedway, he likens business to racing, noting, "If you want to get ahead, you have to make things happen. If you rest on your laurels for five minutes, there's always someone ready to pass you." As the champion driver and CEO neared his 60s, he appeared to be far from ready to "rest on his laurels."

Principal Subsidiaries

Detroit Diesel Corporation; Penske Truck Leasing Co.; Diesel Technology Co.; Longo Toyota; Longo Lexus; Penske Honda; Penske Racing; Penske Cars, Ltd.

Further Reading

DeLorenzo, Matt, "Roger Penske: Multi-Talented Entrepreneur Just Keeps on Growing," *Automotive News,* January 18, 1988.

Finch, Peter, "Roger Penske: Running on 16 Cylinders," *Business Week,* June 1, 1987.

Frame, Phil, "Penske, GM Drift Apart After 20 Years," *Automotive News,* June 20, 1994, pp. 3–4.

Johnson, J. Douglas, "Driven," *Indiana Business Magazine,* May 1994, pp. 8–11.

Lowell, Jon, "Roger Roars Ahead: Penske Fires Up GM's Dying Diesels; Profits Replace Problems," *Ward's Auto World,* November 1988.

Moses, Sam, "His Time is Money," *Sports Illustrated,* November 21, 1988.

"Penske To Acquire Kmart Auto Service," *Discount Store News,* October 16, 1995, pp. 7–8.

Sedgwick, David, "Leuliete's Job at Penske: Expand World Business," *Automotive News,* November 11, 1996, pp. 1–2.

Ulrich, Robert J., and David Drushal, "Penske Races to the Top," *Modern Tire Dealer,* July 1996, pp. 16–21.

Vroom at the Top, (film) New York: Association Films, 1976.

Woodruff, David, "Talk about Life in the Fast Lane," *Business Week,* October 17, 1994, p. 155–158.

—Thomas M. Tucker
—updated by April Dougal Gasbarre

Petroleos Mexicanos

Avenida Marina Nacional 329
Col. Huasteca
C.P. 11320
Mexico, DF
Mexico
(5) 531-6061
Fax: (5) 726-1381

State-Owned Company
Incorporated: 1938
Employees: 108,000
Sales: $25.167 billion (1995)
SICs: 2869 Industrial Organic Chemicals, Not Elsewhere
   Classified; 2911 Petroleum Refining

Petroleos Mexicanos (Pemex) is Mexico's largest enterprise in terms of total sales, total assets, personnel employed, and tax payments. By the early 1990s it was the fourth-largest crude-oil producer behind Saudi Arabian Oil Co., National Iranian Oil Co., and Chinese National Petroleum Co. In 1995 it averaged 2.7 million barrels of crude oil production a day, increasing to 2.9 million barrels a day in March 1997. In addition to crude oil, Pemex produces natural gas, petrochemicals, gasoline, and diesel fuels.

Company Origins

Oil has been known in Mexico since ancient times, and Mexico was one of the earliest oil- and gas-producing countries in the Western Hemisphere. The first significant commercial exploitation was started by Edward L. Doheny in 1901 at Ebano, in the eastern part of the state of San Luis Potosi. Until 1938, when Pemex was founded, production was largely controlled by American and British interests, including Royal Dutch/Shell, Exxon, the Pearson family, Sinclair, and Gulf Oil. Production increased considerably during World War I, reaching a peak of 530,000 barrels per day. In 1921 Mexico was the second-largest oil producer in the world after the United States. It was responsible for about a quarter of the world's oil supply.

The seeds for the creation of a national oil company in Mexico can be traced back to the 1910 revolution. In order to ensure adequate supplies of fuel for its locomotives, the National Railways of Mexico created a petroleum division to exploit the hydrocarbons found on its lands in the rich Ebano and Panuco oil fields. Soon afterward it became apparent that the government itself, in order to meet its oil demand, would have to develop the oil fields found on its federal lands (not including the land belonging to the railway company). At the end of December 1925, the Control de Administración del Petróleo Nacional (Control of the Management of National Petroleum) was set up in order to concentrate into one entity the government's participation in the development of its reserves. This government entity competed directly with private capital in the production and refining of crude oil but at the same time regulated the domestic price of petroleum products. In December 1933 a Congressional decree established Petróleos de México S.A. (Petromex)—a publicly traded company in which only Mexican nationals could purchase equity—with the purpose of supplying the fuel requirements of the National Railways in particular and the domestic market with petroleum products in general. It was also given the responsibility of regulating the domestic petroleum markets and training Mexican personnel in all aspects of the industry. Petromex lasted only until September 1934, when it was dissolved owing to a lack of interest on the part of the investing public, and the assets and shares of the company were transferred to the Control de Administración del Petróleo Nacional. In November 1936 a law was passed that expropriated for the state all assets considered to be of public utility, including oil and natural gas, and in January 1937 the state-owned Administración General del Petróleo Nacional was created to explore and develop the national reserves that were assigned to it.

As a result of long-existing conflict between the oil workers' union and the companies, which at one stage threatened to bring the oil industry to a standstill, President Lázaro Cárdenas nationalized the oil industry on March 18, 1938. A number of reasons were given for this drastic measure, among which the most important were the following: the foreign-owned companies had adopted inadequate conservation measures for existing reserves; there was a lack of interest on the part of the companies in exploring for new reserves; and the companies had used unfair labor practices.

On March 19, 1938, the day after expropriation, the Consejo Administrativo del Petróleo (Petroleum Administrative Council) was established, with nine government members, to administer the assets it had taken over. In June the administration of the country's oil and gas industry was split between two government agencies: Petróleos Mexicanos, or Pemex, which took over the properties and functions assigned to the Petroleum Administrative Council, and the newly created Distribuidora de Petróleos Mexicanos, which distributed and marketed petroleum products. By August 1940, however, it became obvious that this delegation of responsibilities was not working because of conflict between the two agencies, and so it was decided that all matters related to hydrocarbons should become the sole responsibility of Pemex. The Administración del Petróleo Nacional and the Distribuidora de Petróleos Mexicanos were abolished.

With the creation of Pemex, Mexico faced an economic boycott instigated by the governments of the expropriated companies, which included an economic blockade to prevent the company from selling its oil in world markets; a ban on selling raw materials, replacement parts, and equipment needed by Pemex; pressure on shipping lines to refuse transportation of Mexican oil; legal action to embargo the oil that Pemex managed to export through other countries; and a massive withdrawal of bank deposits held in Mexico by foreign companies. After long and strenuous negotiations, the Mexican government finally agreed to indemnify the foreign oil companies for US$114 million, with the first payment beginning in 1940 and the last one in 1962.

Pemex's original brief from the Mexican government was to supply the Mexican market with oil, gas, and petrochemical products at the lowest possible cost. The mandate was not profit motivated, and there was a strong desire on the part of the government to improve the living standards of its employees.

Growth of Pemex: 1940 to the 1980s

Since 1940 Pemex's board of directors, headed by the secretary of patrimony and industrial development, has been filled with five other government representatives—the secretary of finance, the secretary of commerce, the deputy secretary of patrimony and industrial development, the director general of the Federal Electricity Commission, and the director general of the Nacional Financiera, a financial institution—as well as five union representatives. The executive officers of the company are headed by a director general and seven subdirectors in charge of production, refining, finance, sales, exploration, personnel administration, and project administration.

About 72 percent of Mexico's surface area of 2.5 million square kilometers is covered by sedimentary basins—potentially oil-producing areas—and only about 10 percent of this area has been explored. The proved hydrocarbon reserves are located mainly in the Chicontepec basin in the northern part of the state of Veracruz, the Tabasco-Chiapas Mesozoic area in the continental shelf of the Gulf of Campeche, and the Sabinas basin in the states of Coahuila and Nuevo Leon.

In 1938 Pemex inherited total reserves of 1.276 billion barrels of what is termed oil equivalent (boe)—including oil and gas—from the expropriated oil companies. This number increased steadily to reach 5.568 billion boe in 1960, undergoing a spectacular rise in the 1980s to 60.126 billion boe in 1980. At the end of 1990 it stood at 64.96 billion boe.

After the first commercial exploitation of the country's reserves at Ebano, production was concentrated in the zone of Tuxpan in the northern part of the state of Veracruz, where the famous Golden Lane complex, dating from the first two decades of the 20th century, was located and where the productivity of the wells was legendary. Between 1910 and 1937 the Potrero del Llano well produced 117.3 million barrels of crude oil, and the Cerro Azul well produced an average of 261,400 barrels per day of crude in the early stages.

At the time of nationalization, Pemex's production averaged 104,110 barrels per day of crude oil and liquid natural gas (LNG), increasing to just over 197,260 barrels per day in 1950 and undergoing a spectacular rise in the 1980s to an average of 2.54 million barrels per day of crude oil and LNG. After leaping into the forefront of world crude oil production a decade earlier, Pemex in 1989 reached its production plateau of 2.5 million barrels per day of crude and almost 400,000 barrels per day of LNG. In 1989 more than two-thirds of Pemex's crude output was heavy Maya crude from the offshore Gulf of Campeche, while the lighter Olmeca and Isthmus blends came from onshore areas where reserves were declining.

Most of Pemex's gas production was associated with crude oil production, although there were also natural gas fields independent of oil fields. Gas production at the time of nationalization was 600 million cubic meters per annum, and in 1990 stood at around 36 billion cubic meters. Pemex's oil fields was able to produce much higher ratios of gas per barrel of oil than was previously estimated.

In 1976 Pemex launched an ambitious program for gas treatment plants to enable the company to handle the large amounts of gas produced from its oil fields. Most of the gas was processed by Pemex's petrochemical complexes in southern and central Mexico, and a proportion of it was fed into Mexico's gas system. The gas was transported through Pemex's 12,788-kilometer network of gas pipelines.

Until 1971 Mexico was self-sufficient in crude oil and natural gas, as well as being a net exporter of refined products. In the early 1970s, in order to meet its domestic consumption requirements, Pemex became a net importer, importing 64,600 barrels per day of crude oil in 1973. As a result, there was a radical adjustment of Pemex's role, which up until then had been to provide energy to the ever-increasing domestic market at low prices. When the country's balance of payments was adversely affected in 1974, Pemex was forced to double the prices of its products to reduce demand, and a decision was taken to allow the company to invest more money in exploration and development in order to reestablish itself as a major oil exporter. Pemex was called on by the government to export oil, gas, and petrochemical products and to become the cornerstone of Mexican industrial development. The 1974–1976 development plan, costing $3 billion, was the largest in Mexico's history and called for $240 million to be spent on geological and seismic studies and $728 million to be invested in drilling development and exploration wells. This plan was followed by an even bigger one in 1977, when Pemex approved an ambitious $15.5 billion development program with the aim of increasing by 1982 the company's production in the following areas: crude oil to 2.2 million barrels per day; gas to 113.3 million cubic meters per day; crude oil exports to 1.1 million barrels per day; refining capacity to 1.7 million barrels per day; and petrochemical output to 15.5 million tons per annum. Almost half the budget would be spent on the drilling of 2,152 development wells, and $1.2 billion would be spent on drilling 1,324 exploration wells. The plan called for the surveying of 1.2 million square kilometers of prospective oil-bearing areas.

The exploration and development effort led to a spectacular increase in reserves and production in the 1980s. With increased production, Pemex also boosted it exports, which in 1989 were just under 1.3 million barrels per day. In 1976 the Mexican government established a ceiling on exports of 1.35 million barrels per day to keep its prices high in world markets. Pemex had three main export markets, with the United States being by far its largest customer, taking 57 percent of its exports in 1989. It was followed by Spain with 15 percent and Japan with 13 percent.

During the 1980s Pemex's crude oil reserves remained remarkably static despite a significant reduction in the number of exploration wells drilled during the period—from 305 in 1983 to 123 in 1989—because of the country's austerity program, which involved a reduction in government expenditure. Domestic demand was heavily geared toward transport fuel, such as gasoline and fuel oil, which accounted for 32 percent and 33 percent, respectively, out of the total consumption of petroleum products in 1989 of 1.3 million barrels per day.

In 1977 Pemex embarked on an expansion program intended to triple its petrochemical output by 1982. It aimed to be self-sufficient in basic petrochemicals by 1979 and subsequently to develop large volumes of feedstocks—raw or partially processed products destined for further processing—for export. This policy was successful, with basic petrochemicals production increasing from 1.931 million imperial tons in 1980 to 16.9 million tons in 1989. Private capital was allowed to account for up to 40 percent of total issued capital in the petrochemical industry mainly because of Pemex's lack of technological expertise. In 1989 petrochemicals exports climbed by 50 percent to US$110.4 million, while imports declined to US$21.7 million. Export earnings from petrochemicals represented only 1.4 percent of Pemex's total export earnings, but their growth helped to offset the company's deteriorating trade in refined products, which accounted for 6 percent of Pemex's gross exports. Pemex operated a shipping fleet that grew from 6,438 dead-weight tons in 1938 to 618,780 dead-weight tons in 1988.

Although not as dependent as Venezuela on oil, this commodity in the early 1990s accounted for 70 percent of Mexico's foreign exchange and provided around 45 percent of government tax receipts. Crude oil exports also enabled the country to keep up with the repayment of its $103 billion foreign debt. As a decentralized public agency of the Mexican government, Pemex paid 18 percent tax on total revenues from oil and gas, 13 percent on total revenues from petrochemicals, and a 50 percent corporation tax.

Privatization in the 1990s

In June 1990 the international marketing division of Pemex was split off from the main organization. This division, Petróleos Mexicanos Internacional Comercio Internacional, was responsible for the marketing of crude oil, refined products, and petrochemicals. In 1992 Pemex itself was split into four operating divisions, one each for exploration, refining, gas, and chemicals.

In October 1995 Pemex announced that it would begin denationalization of its petrochemical division. Pemex was prepared to offer 10 petrochemical complexes, consisting of 61 plants, as possibilities for privatization. The plan received heavy criticism in Mexico, however, especially from Sindicato de Trabajadores Petroleros, the oil workers' union. Carlos Romero Deschamps, head of the union, said, "We cannot permit the crisis that we face to destroy the solidity of Pemex, which is a fundamental pillar of Mexican development."

Though Pemex had cut its staff almost in half in the years between 1989 and 1995, the company still employed 108,000 people. Even the American oil producer Exxon, which had approximately five times Pemex's revenues in 1995, had fewer employees. Much of the criticism, then, could be attributed to fear that more efficient, private companies would eliminate employees. Opposition to privatization had the law on its side, as Mexico's constitution forbid anyone but the state to invest in oil development.

Pemex has taken steps to work around the constitutional restrictions—for example, entering joint ventures with Amoco Corp. and Mobil Corp., both of which opened stores in Mexico to sell Mexican fuel. Still, much of Mexico saw the petroleum industry as belonging to Mexico and the Mexican people. As a compromise, the Mexican government agreed in March 1996 to limit foreign participation in the sale of its petrochemical complexes to 49 percent. This was intended to guarantee participation of local companies in the privatization.

Meanwhile, Pemex continued to suffer environmental and safety setbacks. In April 1992 a Pemex depot leaked fuel into the Guadalajara sewer system, resulting in an explosion that killed more than 200 people. In November 1996 Pemex workers were repairing a valve at a storage facility when it caught fire. The resulting explosion and fire killed 4 people and injured 19, and eventually more than 5,000 people were evacuated from their homes. In May 1997 an explosion at a Pemex gasoline storage plant in northern Mexico killed 2 people and injured 3.

Responding to safety difficulties, Adrian Lajous, Pemex general director, said, "It is likely that we are not clearly in line with standards that prevail in other countries around the world."

At the Cosoleacaque petrochemical facility near Coatzacoalcos, more than one million cubic meters of wastewater was dumped into the Coatzacoalcos River each day in 1996. Cosoleacaque was to be the first plant to privatize, though analysts said it would be one of the toughest to sell, partly because its antiquated facilities would make it difficult to compete in a market made more competitive by NAFTA (North American Free Trade Agreement). Some environmentalists had hoped that the sale of this facility and others would initiate environmental cleanup of the sites by the new owners. Others feared that Pemex was simply dumping an environmental hazard before it became too much of a problem.

In February 1997 Pemex petrochemical workers signed wage accords and agreements that recognized the breakup and privatization of the state petrochemical assets. The contracts were signed with four new petrochemical companies— Petroquimica Camargo, Petroquimica Cosoleacaque, Petroquimica Escolin, and Petroquimica Tula. This was just the first step in selling the 49 percent stake in Pemex petrochemical interests, and Mexican labor made it clear that privatization would not be an easy or speedy process. Even so, the need to improve efficiency and safety conditions at Pemex was creating strong pressure for increased privatization.

Principal Subsidiaries

Tetraetilo de Mexico S.A.; Compañía Mexicana de Exploraciones S.A. (COMESA); Instalaciones Inmobiliarias para Industria S.A. de C.V.; Compañía Operadora de Estaciones de Servicio S.A. de C.V.; Distribuidora de Gas Natural del Estado de Mexico S.A. de C.V.; Distribuidiora de Gas de Queretaro S.A.; Cloro de Tehuantepec S.A. de C.V.; Empresas del Grupo PMI; Respol, S.A.

Further Reading

Baker, George, *Mexico's Petroleum Sector: Performance and Prospects,* Tulsa, Okla.: PennWell Publishing Co., 1984.

Bermudez, Antonio J., *The Mexican National Petroleum Industry: A Case Study in Nationalization,* Stanford, Calif.: Stanford University Press, 1963.

Mack, Toni and Joel Millman, "Petroleum Machismo," *Forbes,* April 10, 1995, p. 46.

Philip, George, *Oil and Politics in Latin America,* Cambridge: Cambridge University Press, 1982.

Randall, Laura, *The Political Economy of Mexican Oil,* New York: Praeger, 1989.

Richards, Don, "Ammonia Complex to Start Pemex Privatization Push," *Chemical Marketing Reporter,* October 2, 1995, p. 7.

Sepulveda, Isidro, "Pemex in a Dependent Society," *US-Mexican Energy Relationships,* by Jerry R. Ladman, et. al., Lexington, Mass.: Lexington Books, 1981.

Sissel, Kara, "Ownership Restrictions Drive Mexican-Multinational Linkups," *Chemical Week,* March 27, 1996, p. 8.

Szekely, Gabriel, *La economía política del petróleo en México, 1976–1982,* El Colegio de México, 1983

Thurston, Charles W., "Mexican Slowdown," *Chemical Marketing Reporter,* September 4, 1995, p. SR10.

"Troubled Waters: Mexico's Economy," *The Economist,* October 19, 1996, p. 77.

Williams, Edward J., *The Rebirth of the Mexican Petroleum Industry,* Lexington, Mass.: Lexington Books, 1979.

"Workers Sign-On to Sell-Off," *The Oil Daily,* February 28, 1997, p. 5.

—Brian S. McBeth
—updated by Terry Bain

Piccadilly Cafeterias, Inc.

3232 Sherwood Forest Boulevard
P.O. Box 2467
Baton Rouge, Louisiana 70821
U.S.A.
(504) 293-9440
Fax: (504) 296-8370
Web site: http//www.piccadilly.com

Public Company
Incorporated: 1944
Employees: 8,500
Sales: $300.6 million
Stock Exchanges: New York
SICs: 5812 Eating Places

Piccadilly Cafeterias, Inc. operates 130 cafeterias in 17 states, mostly in the southern and central regions of the United States, with the majority of units in the Gulf Coast states of Florida (22), Alabama (six), Louisiana (28), and Texas (17). The company planned to open two more cafeterias by June 30, of 1997, but the new openings were to offset the closing of two unprofitable units. The company also manages eight Ralph & Kacoo's seafood restaurants, operating in Louisiana, Mississippi, Alabama, and Texas. Most of the cafeteria units are located in suburban malls or strip centers, but some are located in separate, free-standing buildings. All of the units are company owned or leased under long-term arrangements.

The standard Piccadilly Cafeteria seats between 250 and 450 lunch or dinner patrons. It features a wide range of foods at moderate prices and traditional cafeteria-style service. All of the food is prepared from standard recipes used at all locations, with only seasonal variations in the menu offerings and some adjustments to reflect taste preferences of customers in disparate geographical locations. The Ralph & Kacoo's restaurants are full-service establishments specializing in Cajun seafood. They accommodate between 250 and 600 patrons.

Wartime Beginnings

Piccadilly Cafeterias, Inc. was founded during World War II, by Tandy Hannibal Hamilton, who had already been working in the cafeteria business for 21 years when he traveled to Louisiana to consider purchasing the small Piccadilly Cafeteria located on Third Street in downtown Baton Rouge. At the time, Hamilton was living in Kansas City, where he was serving as general manager of The Forum, a Midwestern cafeteria chain. After forming a family partnership with his wife, Tela, his daughter, Julia, and his son-in-law, William A. Richards, Hamilton bought the Piccadilly from the original owner, Thomas J. Costas, for $65,000. Hamilton and Costas closed the sale on February 1, 1944.

H. L. "Tandy" Hamilton was born in the Indian Territories of Oklahoma in 1897, son to a former federal marshal who had served Judge Isaac Parker, a "famous hanging judge" in Fort Smith, Arkansas, and his father's second wife. He was just eight when an outlaw fatally shot his father in the back at a baseball game. Although his mother remarried, the family was poor, and Tandy and his brothers had to help make ends meet by picking cotton. In his early teens, Tandy worked with his half-brother, Doug, rounding up cattle strays near McAlester, Oklahoma, and then drifted some as a hobo before taking various restaurant jobs in Wichita, Kansas. By the time he joined the Army in 1918, Tandy had served a full apprenticeship as a chef, and he got further training under European chefs while on his duty tour in France. After the war, Tandy returned to Oklahoma, where he met his future wife, Tela Meier, a court clerk in Shawnee. After they married, the couple moved to Wichita Falls, Texas, where Hamilton secured a job as *sous* chef in the deluxe Kemp Hotel. Because of the oil boom and the scarcity of inexpensive housing, the Hamiltons had to live in a tent city set up for oil-field transients near downtown Wichita Falls. Their daughter, Julia, was born there.

In 1923, the Hamiltons moved to Kansas City, where The Forum Cafeterias chain had its central office. At the time, The Forum operated 15 units in Midwestern states. The operation intrigued Hamilton, and he sought and secured a chef's position through the company's president, C. M. Hayman. Within just a

Company Perspectives:

"It's the food. No, it's the people. It's the food and *the people. At a time when people are eating out and taking out more and more, Piccadilly has all the ingredients for success. The flexibility of our menu, our years of cooking experience, our face-to-face contact with our customers— all have prepared us to respond quickly to customer preferences. A reputation for excellent food. The counsel of experienced employees. A growing customer base. It's an enviable combination."*

couple of years, Tandy advanced into management, moving from one operation to another, until, in 1934, he became the chain's general manager and settled in Kansas City. He spent the next ten years learning the cafeteria business inside and out. By 1941, partly because nepotism in The Forum organization limited his prospects for further promotion, he had also decided that he wanted to begin his own cafeteria chain. The first step in his dream of owning and operating a 40-unit cafeteria chain was taken when he purchased the Piccadilly from Costas in 1944.

Hamilton began building the business immediately, despite the wartime difficulties imposed by food rationing and equipment shortages. He contacted several friends and associates, some still in the service, encouraging them to join the operation. He also opened a small cafe just across Third Street from the Piccadilly, naming it Tandy's Eat Shop. He opened the cafe to provide temporary employment for those he was hiring as future chefs and managers as his Piccadilly chain expanded, and the establishment was sold off soon after the chain's expansion got under way.

Hamilton and his family partners set up business headquarters in the limited office space on the second floor, above the Third Street cafeteria. Tandy put together a small but dedicated staff whose primary function was to facilitate his expansion plans. H.J. DeBlanc and Allen Dyer were his key headquarters personnel.

As a way of accommodating the planned growth, Hamilton chartered individual corporations for funding the start-up of new units in the Piccadilly chain. He believed that key personnel should invest in the business, so he sold part interest in each of the five corporations he created for the company's expansion. In the basic plan, Tandy and his wife owned 25 percent, his daughter Julia and her husband Bill Richards owned 25 percent, and the remainder was sold to employees selected to participate in ownership. Upon occasion, Hamilton lent the purchase money to his associates, convinced that they would have no problem in repaying the loan from their corporate earnings.

The first corporate group put the second Piccadilly Cafeteria into operation in Beaumont, Texas, in October of 1946, under the management of Frank Emmer, who would later become Piccadilly's first district manager. The next year, a Memphis corporation was chartered to open a new unit in that city. It started up in 1948, under the management of Meredith Curtis,

assisted by Phil Listen, an old Navy friend of Bill Richards. In that same year, Hamilton organized a third corporation to start up a fourth Piccadilly, in Waco, Texas. It opened its doors in January, 1949, under the management of Jim Sorrells. Dick Quick, another of Richards's service friends, became Sorrells's assistant.

To ensure quality control, Tandy Hamilton insisted on consistency throughout the burgeoning chain of cafeterias. He personally developed and field-tested most of the recipes used in each of the Piccadilly locales, but he also encouraged chain managers to submit their own recipes for his approval. Any such approved recipe would then be used at each establishment. Hamilton was also a great proponent of efficiency, partly because he was determined to keep his prices fair, the quality of the food high, and the portions generous. To that end, he and his staff worked out a fairly rigorous and complicated system of purchasing and kitchen control designed to avoid food waste and other unnecessary expenses.

Systemization in the 1950s

By the 1950s, Hamilton and his son-in-law, Richards, had instituted "standard recipe costing," involving an exact determination of cost per serving for each of the chain's standard recipes, with some allowance for food cost variations at the individual cafeterias. By the end of the decade, they had issued various company manuals to ensure uniform practices in such diverse policies as meat cutting procedures and purchasing and pricing specifications. They also encouraged individual managers to make suggestions for cutting or controlling costs, incorporating some of these into standard, chainwide policies.

Expansion accelerated in the 1950s, and then boomed in the next three decades. By the end of 1959, 11 units were operating in three states: Louisiana, Texas, and Tennessee. After 1956, thanks to the great success of a unit located in the Gulfgate Shopping Center in Houston, the company elected to locate new cafeterias in the proliferating suburban malls located in or near larger southern and southwestern cities. It proved to be a wise move, for, from 1960 through 1969, Piccadilly was able to add 25 units, operating in a range that then extended from Jacksonville, Florida to Phoenix, Arizona. That growth and obvious success prompted J. C. Penney, in 1969, to offer $30 million for the whole 36-unit chain. While rejecting the offer, the Piccadilly front office began to reappraise its self-image as a family business. A new sense of being a large and valuable corporate entity would force policy and organizational changes during the 1970s.

New Leadership in the 1970s

In 1971, Hamilton met his personal goal of developing a 40-unit cafeteria chain, when, on November 27, the 40th Piccadilly Cafeteria opened its doors at the South DeKalb Mall in Decatur, Georgia. In the same year, at age 75, Tandy Hamilton assumed the title of chairman of the board and, although he remained active until his death in 1981, he turned the day-to-day operations over to Bill Richards, his successor as president. Hamilton served largely in an advisory capacity, giving Richards free rein.

In 1974, three years before Richards's death in a bicycling accident, Piccadilly moved its central operations into its current corporate headquarters, a 45,000-square-foot building on Sherwood Forest Boulevard in Baton Rouge. In addition to an office complex, the new center housed a test kitchen and an archive for its collection of more than 1,000 current Piccadilly recipes. Piccadilly also maintained a 26,500-square-foot storage facility or commissary in Baton Rouge. Much of the seafood bought in season for off-season use in both cafeterias and restaurants was stored there, in a $2.5 million inventory. It allowed even the more remote cafeterias to serve some dishes at standard prices, even when the food was either not available from wholesalers or was too inflated in cost.

Corporate restructuring was completed in 1979, when Piccadilly went public. It made its first stocking offering on January 30, 1979. Until then, the Piccadilly chain had operated under the auspices of two partnerships and five corporations, the last of which, the Louisiana Corporation, was chartered in 1965. Employee participation in ownership had worked well, but toward the end of the 1970s, stock transfers made through inheritance to outside owners was pushing the legal limit for private corporations. In addition, the complex corporate structure had become unwieldy, and consolidation into a single corporate entity helped streamline operations. The move forced a new employee incentive plan, however, and in 1981 a bonus plan went into effect that within a year doubled the pay of unit managers and associate managers.

Phenomenal growth in the Piccadilly chain continued through the 1980s. At the time of Hamilton's death in 1981, the 40 units of his original dream had doubled to 80. By 1984, all cafeterias and restaurants had also been newly constructed or remodeled. Further, the company reopened the door to partial employee ownership in 1987, when it adopted a stock purchase plan allowing employees to buy up to 1,500 shares of common stock annually. In December of 1988, Piccadilly purchased six Ralph and Kacoo's restaurants, some properties, and all shares of the common stock of Cajun Bayou Distributors and Management, Inc., for barely more than $38 million.

But there were also problems. In 1986, in a move to cut costs, Piccadilly began reducing the quality of its foods. In protest, James W. Bennett, the financial officer, resigned and sold off his Piccadilly stock. The recipe skimping at first paid off. Between 1987 and 1989, profits increased 24 percent, but, noticing the decline in quality, long-standing customers began staying away, and their boycott was soon reflected in declining earnings. In the fall of 1991, Piccadilly suffered its first quarterly loss in its 48-year history. In 1992, with the approval of the board of directors, Julia Hamilton induced Bennett to return to Piccadilly as CEO.

Retooling for the 1990s

Bennett's strategy was to return to the old Hamilton recipes to restore quality. He attempted to offset rising food and utility costs by improving the efficiency of the units in other ways. For example, by changing some of the flatware in use, Piccadilly was able to increase the hourly number of customers it could pass down its cafeteria line from 260 to 400. Bennett also began an aggressive remodeling campaign to refurbish about 25 cafe-

terias a year at a half-million dollar cost per unit. Customer counts immediately started up again, and so did profits. In fiscal 1993, the company turned a $4.8 million profit on gross sales of $271 million. But the rise was short-lived, and in 1994 Bennett resigned when further implementation of his five-year, $65 million makeover plan was blocked by his board of directors.

Prompted by reported efforts of Luby Cafeterias, Inc. to buy the Piccadilly chain and his personal belief that he could lead the business out of it stagnant condition, Bennett then led a consortium of investors in an attempt to negotiate a friendly buyout. He was convinced that his group could return the business to its former glory and bring its stock value up from $8 to $13 per share. The board of directors under Chairman Paul Murrill, and the new CEO, Ronald A. LaBorde, refused to consider any of the offers.

LaBorde inherited major problems. Despite Bennett's 1993 success, over four years, from 1990 to 1994, Piccadilly sales had dropped 11 percent and profits had declined sharply to an average of barely more than $2.75 million per year, down 69 percent from the previous four years. In contrast, in the same period, Luby's sales grew by 25 percent to $390.6 million, and its profits increased 22 percent to $39.3 million. Piccadilly was simply no longer an attractive business for investors. Its market value had dropped from about $227 million in 1986 to $86 million in 1995, and its stock showed no signs of breaking out of its doldrums. The chain's problems seemed to have stemmed from investing too much money in the purchase of the Ralph & Kacoo's restaurants and overestimating potential earnings from their operation. In addition, a rapid changeover in top management led to too many policy changes, including the termination of Bennett's remodeling plan upon his resignation. Also blamed were Piccadilly's "tired assets" and underchallenged employees.

In an effort to turn things around, LaBorde took some aggressive steps to reduce costs through improved efficiency. He cut some jobs and improved purchasing through a more centralized system. Piccadilly also downsized its prototype cafeteria from 10,000 square feet to 6,000 square feet, a move designed to allow the company to develop new market options. On October 1, 1996, the company also raised its prices to offset the rising cost of food and the impact of the minimum wage increase. The meal costs to patron remained low, however, with a check average of between $5 and $6 at the cafeterias and $15 to $17 at the Ralph & Kacoo's restaurants. Some improvement in the company's earnings followed. Its end-of-year earnings for 1996 rose 22 percent over the same period of the prior year, though its net sales increased only one percent.

As LaBorde and the Piccadilly directors see it, tapping new markets seems to offer the best hope for future growth in sales and profits. In the mid-1990s, Piccadilly developed plans for a new type of unit, the Piccadilly Express, offering a takeout and pickup service located within retail stores. In May 1997, it announced a joint venture with Associated Grocers, Inc., a distributor of foods to 230 retail food stores. The two companies planned to place Piccadilly Express units in Associated member supermarkets in Louisiana, east Texas, and Mississippi. Each of the mini-cafeterias is to feature hot entrees prepared on the site, providing costumers with convenient meals to take out or eat during a shopping break. The first of the units was scheduled to open in the Hi Nabor Supermarket in Baton Rouge. Piccadilly's directors and upper management believe that this fast-food marketing strategy and other streamlining policies will get the company moving again.

Further Reading

Alexander, Kelly King, "Facing a Full Plate," *Greater Baton Rouge Business Report,* April 7, 1992, p. 34.

Bennett, Fran, *Tandy: T. H. Hamilton and the Founding of Piccadilly Cafeterias,* Baton Rouge, La.: Piccadilly Cafeterias, 1995.

Hayes, Jack, "Piccadilly's Bennett Exits Chairman, Chief Exec Post," *Nation's Restaurant News,* October 10, 1994, p. 3.

Law, Dennis, "This Is a Cafeteria?," *Restaurants and Institutions,* February 1, 1994, p. 22.

Mukul, Verma, "Piccadilly Rejects Offers To Buy Cafeteria Chain," *Greater Baton Rouge Business Report,* November 14, 1995, p. 16.

Nao, Philippe, "Too Many Cooks?," *Forbes,* February 13, 1995, p. 19.

Ruggless, Ron, "Cafeterias Struggle as Market Dwindles," *Nation's Restaurant News,* September 18, 1995.

Spence, Holly, "Hearty and Healthy," *Restaurants and Institutions,* July 15, 1995, pp. 142–144.

Stern, William M., "Lumpy Mashed Potatoes, Yuck," *Forbes,* March 28, 1994, pp. 63, 66.

Walkup, Carolyn, "Piccadilly Banks on Deluxe Unit To Step Up Traffic," *Nation's Restaurant News,* February 21, 1994, p. 7.

—John W. Fiero

Pillowtex Corporation

4111 Mint Way
Dallas, Texas 75237-1605
U.S.A.
(214) 333-3225
Fax: (214) 330-6016
Web site: http://www.pillowtex.com

Public Company
Incorporated: 1954
Employees: 4,250
Sales: $490.7 million (1996)
Stock Exchanges: New York
SIC: 2392 Housefurnishings, Not Elsewhere Classified;
    2221 Broadwoven Fabric Mills-Manmade

With nearly half a billion dollars in sales in 1996, Dallas-based Pillowtex Corporation is a leading manufacturer and distributor of what it calls "top-of-the-bed textile products." That year, the company ranked number one in bed (or sleep) pillows, with more than 50 percent of the U.S. market. It also led the down comforter and blanket markets and ranked among the top five producers of mattress pads and throw blankets. These top stakes in key segments of the home textiles market helped position Pillowtex fourth in the overall industry, according to a survey published in the January 13, 1997 edition of *Home Textiles Today.*

Diversifications through more than a dozen acquisitions over its nearly five decades in business had kept Pillowtex in the bedroom, but expanded its product offerings from basics to more fashion-oriented goods. By the mid-1990s, it made everything from basics like pillow protectors and comforter covers to decorative throw blankets and pillows as well as coordinated pillow shams, dust ruffles, and window treatments. Its products were sold under such well-known licensed brands as Ralph Lauren Home Collection, Fieldcrest Cannon, Royal Velvet, Disney, and even the U.S. Postal Service. They were distributed primarily through department stores and mass merchandisers. Known by some competitors as "the mill of pillows," its Dallas facilities

included what was arguably North America's biggest feather and down processing plant. Following a 1993 initial public offering, the firm accelerated its long-held strategy of growth through acquisition. While its shares were publicly traded, company insiders continued to control a majority stake through early 1997.

Postwar Origins

Pillowtex was founded in 1954 by John H. Silverthorne to manufacture bed pillows in Dallas. The company soon began acquiring manufacturing plants in Atlanta, Chicago, Connecticut, and Los Angeles, forming the basis of what would become a "hub and spoke" manufacturing and distribution network, one of the most sophisticated systems in the industry. Sales mounted slowly, but steadily, from 1958 on, reaching $4 million by 1965 and $7.5 million in the early 1970s.

Notwithstanding its relatively modest growth in the early years, Pillowtex developed a reputation as a potent competitor. According to a 1990 article in trade journal *HFD-The Weekly Home Furnishings Newspaper,* one customer went so far as to nickname it "the gorilla." Rivals had no choice but to concede the company's preeminence in pillows. One unidentified competitor told *HFD's* Sharyn Bernard, "They're an excellent company. . . . Everyone thinks of Pillowtex [when they want bed pillows]." The firm also garnered a reputation for having a creative sales force and for establishing, rather than following, product trends.

John Silverthorne would continue to own and operate Pillowtex throughout much of its first four decades in business. In 1973, the founder established a long-range succession scheme by promoting Charles "Chuck" Hansen, Jr. to president. Hansen had joined the company in 1965 at the age of 25 and quickly advanced from the ranks of sales representatives to the executive offices. Although he had not originally expected to make a lifetime career at Pillowtex, he told the *Dallas Business Journal's* Sean Wood that he hoped to make it "the largest and most profitable maker and seller of pillows, comforters and bed pads."

Hansen and Silverthorne believed that the best way to achieve that goal was to "buy" market share. The company

---

Company Perspectives:

"We are committed to being a market leader in home textiles and providing a superior return on the investment of our shareholders. We will strive to achieve unparalleled customer satisfaction by assessing, understanding and fulfilling the needs and desires of our customers, and providing the best marketing and merchandising support in the industry. We will provide the highest quality and most competitive products available. We will seek to achieve measurable annual improvements in operating productivity and cost control. We will grow revenues through customer-focused product development, expanding distribution of current products and acquisitions. We will maintain a stimulating work environment that offers opportunities for challenging professional growth, and retains and motivates our employees. We will actively seek to enhance the quality of life in those communities in which we have operations and offices. We will adhere to the highest ethical business practices."

---

averaged one acquisition about every four years from 1970 to 1981, adding Perl Pillow, Synthetic Pillows, Inc., and Globe Feather & Down during the period. By 1982, organic growth and acquisitions had boosted the pillow company's sales to about $56 million and made it the leader of the industry.

Diversification into Other "Top-of-the-Bed" Goods in the 1980s

Having achieved dominance in its core business, Pillowtex sought growth through other avenues in the 1980s. Acquisitions throughout the decade both supplemented Pillowtex's pillowmaking operations and added mattress pads to the product line. The company purchased two mattress pad companies—Los Angeles-based Bedcovers, Inc. and Acme Quilting Co., Inc., America's oldest mattress pad producer—in 1983 alone. The Acme purchase also gave Pillowtex the capacity to manufacture comforters, throw pillows, moving van pads, and such decorative goods as dust ruffles and pillow shams.

Hansen noted that these additions not only boosted Pillowtex's sales volume, but also helped to shield it from downturns in individual categories. A desire to gain manufacturing and marketing synergies was another motivation behind the acquisition strategy.

Pillowtex grew so fast in the late 1980s that one competitor filed suit against it, charging that the company had violated antitrust laws and was becoming a monopoly. The lawsuit arose from Pillowtex's 1987 acquisition of Sumergrade Corporation, a North Carolina manufacturer. The $9.3 million purchase of this bankrupt business made Pillowtex the nation's leading producer of down comforters and boosted its capacity in decorative throw pillows, a fast-growing, high margin segment. (The Texas company would further augment its decorative pillow business with the 1991 acquisition of Nettle Creek Corporation.) Sumergrade also gave its new parent a valuable Ralph Lauren Home Furnishings license and enhanced its presence on

the East Coast. The antitrust suit was unsuccessful, and Pillowtex's growth continued unabated.

Some competitors speculated that Pillowtex's rapid expansion would be its downfall, making it a slow-moving giant. The company combated that tendency with a quick response (QR) program that incorporated electronic data interchange (EDI). QR coordinated information shared by the merchandiser and the manufacturer such that when a sales clerk scanned the inventory number of a given product, the network automatically reordered the item from Pillowtex. The system reduced paperwork and lead time, thereby cutting costs for both parties and creating a "just-in-time-like" operation. By the mid-1990s, all but about ten percent of the company's customers placed their orders through EDI, leading analysts with Wheat, First Securities to call Pillowtex "one of the most technologically integrated and advanced" of pillow and blanket manufacturers.

Rapid Growth Marks the Early 1990s

Chuck Hansen advanced to chief executive officer and chairman when the founder died of cancer in December 1992. The new leader quickly prepared Pillowtex for an initial public offering (IPO) in 1993. The floatation offered about one-third of the company's equity to the public, while Hansen and Silverthorne's widow, Mary R. Silverthorne, split most of the remaining interest. This arrangement permitted the company to raise funds for both the Silverthorne estate and Pillowtex's growth, while maintaining control among corporate insiders.

Pillowtex moved boldly into the blanket segment in the ensuing 30 months, using part of the $53 million proceeds of the IPO to bankroll the acquisition of three blanket companies and two pillow/comforter manufacturers. The growth-hungry firm bought two old-line blanket manufacturers, Tennessee Woolen Mills, Inc. and Manetta Mills, Inc., in 1993 at a total cost of $20.9 million in cash. A year later, Pillowtex shelled out a whopping $112 million ($101 million cash and $11 million debt) for Beacon Manufacturing Company, then the largest player in the blanket segment.

Other acquisitions diversified Pillowtex internationally. Torfeaco Industries Limited, a well-established producer of pillows, mattress pads, and decorative bedding, came on board in 1993. In 1994, the growing firm paid $3.6 million for Imperial Feather Company, a pillow and comforter manufacturer. With overseas sales totaling about ten percent of total revenues in 1995, Pillowtex laid plans to launch production and distribution operations in Europe and South America.

Pillowtex's pro forma sales nearly doubled in the early 1990s, from $259 million in 1991 to $474.9 million in 1995. Operating income increased from $19.1 million to $36.5 million during the same period, due in part to rising productivity. The company's selling, general, and administrative expenses (already ranked among the industry's lowest) declined from nearly 13 percent of sales in 1991 to nine percent of sales by 1995. Nevertheless, net income declined from $13.2 million to a low of $7.7 million in 1994. The decreases in bottom-line profitability were attributed to debt service from Pillowtex's mid-decade acquisition spree, rising raw materials costs, and difficulties in reconciling its new affiliates. The decline in net earnings pushed

Pillowtex's stock, which had risen from an introductory price of $14 per share in 1993 to a high of more than $21 early in 1994, down to less than $9 by the end of the year.

The company tried to alleviate some of its raw materials problems with the $6 million acquisition of Newton Yarn Mills, a North Carolina cotton yarn spinning factory, from Dixie Yarns Inc. in 1995. In addition, a savvy acquisition in 1996 gave Pillowtex Fieldcrest Cannon's $71 million blanket and throw business at a cost of $30 million.

Pillowtex's revenues rose to $490.7 million in 1996, and its net climbed to more than $14 million. Though in 1995 Hansen had told the *Dallas Business Journal's* Wayne Carter, ''We don't control the stock price; I just try to run the company,'' by the end of 1996 he took a more considered approach to share-holders' concerns, noting in that year's annual report that ''the heart of Pillowtex's mission is the commitment to provide a superior investment return to our shareholders.'' Buoyed in part by the late 1995 institution of a dividend, the stock rose from less than $12 to $18 over the course of 1996.

The Mid-1990s and Beyond

A major management shift that started in 1995 reflected Pillowtex's transition from an ''entrepreneurial'' firm into a diversified corporation and telegraphed possible management succession scenarios. That year, the company reorganized into two operating segments, the Pillowtex division, in charge of pillows, mattress pads, and comforters, and the Beacon division, manufacturing woven blankets. This transitional phase soon yielded to a second shuffling. In 1997, the company reorganized along functional lines, appointing former Chief Financial Officer and Executive Vice-President Jeffrey Cordes as president and chief operating officer, former Pillowtex division President Christopher Baker as president of the manufacturing division, and hiring Kevin Finlay away from Fieldcrest Cannon Inc. to serve as president of the sales and marketing division.

Wheat, First Securities' late 1996 analysis of Pillowtex fore-cast earnings growth of 22 percent in 1997, as efficiencies from its earlier acquisitions began to take effect and the company paid down substantial amounts of debt. In 1995, CEO Hansen told *Dallas Business Journal's* Wayne Carter, ''We're not obsessed with the need to grow. We're obsessed with being the most profitable.'' Nonetheless, he affirmed that the company would continue to pursue growth through acquisition in the waning years of the 20th century, noting in Pillowtex's 1996 annual report the firm's ''next major milestone: $1 billion in annual sales.''

Pillowtex intended to achieve that goal through internal development as well as its ongoing acquisition strategy. Or-ganic growth strategies included a plan to leverage brand eq-uity, especially among its own labels like Health Horizons antibacterial pillows and mattress pads, to boost sales in the late 1990s. The company also boldly mounted a challenge to Sun-beam's utter domination of the electric blanket category in early 1997, hoping to capture 20 percent of this $150 million market. Acquisitions were sure to remain focused on textiles for the bedroom.

Principal Subsidiaries

Beacon Manufacturing Company; Tennessee Woolen Mills, Inc.; Manetta Home Fashions, Inc.; Torfeaco Industries Limited (Canada).

Principal Divisions

Manufacturing Division; Sales & Marketing Division.

Further Reading

Bernard, Sharyn K., ''Pillowtex Prestige: 36-Year-Old Company Builds Strength through Diversification,'' *HFD-The Weekly Home Furnishings Newspaper,* December 3, 1990, pp. 40–41.

Carter, Wayne, ''Pillowtex Straightens Out Lumps,'' *Dallas Business Journal,* September 22, 1995, pp. 8, 22.

Eckhouse, Kim, ''Brands Boom in Basics: Adding Names to Pillows and Pads,'' *HFN-The Weekly Newspaper for the Home Furnishing Network,* April 21, 1997, pp. 27–28.

Frinton, Sandra, ''At Home in Bed; Pillowtex's Growth Stays Close to Basics,'' *HFN-The Weekly Newspaper for the Home Furnishing Network,* September 11, 1995, pp. 23–24.

——, ''Buy, Pay, Diversify: Companies Map Out '96 Strategies,'' *HFN-The Weekly Newspaper for the Home Furnishing Network,* December 11, 1995, pp. 21–22.

——, ''Health Push in Pillows and Pads,'' *HFN-The Weekly Newspa-per for the Home Furnishing Network,* April 22, 1996, pp. 35–36.

——, ''Pillowtex '95 Results Up,'' *HFN-The Weekly Newspaper for the Home Furnishing Network,* February 19, 1996, p. 32.

Hitchcock, Nancy A., ''Business Strategy Speeds Flow of Goods and Data,'' *Modern Materials Handling,* March 1993, pp. 54D5–54D7.

''Home Textiles Today Top 15,'' *Home Textiles Today,* January 13, 1977, pp. 6–9.

Johnson, Sarah, ''Finlay to Pillowtex,'' *HFN-The Weekly Newspaper for the Home Furnishing Network,* March 10, 1997, pp. 27–28.

Kinter, Kim, and Schwartz, Donna Boyle, ''Pillowtex Aims To Ex-pand,'' *HFD-The Weekly Home Furnishings Newspaper,* February 2, 1987, pp. 29–30.

Palmeri, Christopher, ''Southern Comfort,'' *Forbes,* April 25, 1994, p. 191.

Rush, Amy Joyce, and Johnson, Sarah, ''Pillowtex Going Electric in Blankets,'' *HFN-The Weekly Newspaper for the Home Furnishing Network,* February 17, 1997, p. 4.

Schwartz, Donna Boyle, ''User-Friendly Basic Bedding: Technical Jar-gon Yields to Lifestyle Marketing,'' *HFN-The Weekly Newspaper for the Home Furnishing Network,* October 21, 1996, pp. 41–42.

Slott, Mira, ''Sumergrade Acquisition Brings Pillowtex Decorative Pillow Gains,'' *HFD-The Weekly Home Furnishings Newspaper,* January 18, 1988, pp. 43–44.

Troy, Colleen, and Schwartz, Donna Boyle, ''Purofied Antitrust Suit Fails,'' *HFD-The Weekly Home Furnishings Newspaper,* July 13, 1987, pp. 59–60.

Wattman, Karla, ''Duties, China Quota Roil Industry,'' *HFD-The Weekly Home Furnishings Newspaper,* May 2, 1994, pp. 40–41.

——, ''In the Public Eye: Cash Infusion Puts Pillowtex into High Growth Mode,'' *HFD-The Weekly Home Furnishings Newspaper,* April 26, 1993, pp. 33–34.

——, ''Pillowtex Gains Northern Exposure,'' *HFD-The Weekly Home Furnishings Newspaper,* November 15, 1993, p. 48.

Wood, Sean, ''Pillowtex Tries To Keep from Getting Comfortable,'' *Dallas Business Journal,* June 25, 1993, p. S23.

—April Dougal Gasbarre

❦ PRINTEMPS

Pinault-Printemps-Redoute S.A.

18, Place Henri-Bergson
75008 Paris
Cedex 09
France
(33) 1 42 82 62 42
Fax: (33) 1 42 82 62 78
Web site: http://www.redoute.fr

Public Company
Incorporated: 1972 as Au Printemps S.A.
Employees: 59,299
Sales: FFr 77.79 billion (US $15.36 million) (1995)
Stock Exchanges: Paris
SICs: 5961 Catalog & Mail-Order Houses; 5310
    Department Stores; 5411 Grocery Stores

Pinault-Printemps-Redoute S.A. ranks among France's most diversified retailers. The conglomerate was formed in the early 1990s, when investor Francois Pinault's Groupe Pinault acquired a controlling stake in Au Printemps SA. In 1994, he directed Printemps's purchase of the remaining shares of La Redoute S.A. that it did not already own and merged the three businesses as Pinault-Printemps-Redoute S.A. In the mid-1990s, its retail operations included 57 Printemps department stores; La Redoute, the world's fourth largest catalog business; the Prisunic chain of nearly 190 variety stores; more than 170 Conforama furniture outlets; and 50 Fnac book and music stores. Its Printemps chain is one of the few department stores to achieve international expansion. By the mid-1990s, it had affiliates (mostly franchised stores) in Portugal, Turkey, Korea, Thailand, China, Taiwan, and in at least two dozen other nations around the world. In addition to its retail interests, the firm owns a financial services company, wholesales electrical equipment and building materials, and has significant holdings in West Africa.

Mid-19th Century Origins

In 1865, 31-year-old Jules Jaluzot, who had been a department head at Bon Marché, France's oldest department store,

opened Au Printemps, a small store on the corner of boulevard Haussmann and rue du Havre in Paris. The store consisted of a basement for stock, a ground floor, and the mezzanine of a residential building, some 200 square meters in all. Au Printemps was a rapid success and Jaluzot purchased the upper floors of the building. By 1870 the staff had grown from 30 to 250. The acquisition of adjacent buildings followed, and the store soon occupied a whole block on boulevard Haussmann, between rue du Havre and rue Caumartin. As its reputation grew, Jaluzot began mail-order operations in France and other European countries, with catalogs in different languages.

In 1881 a fire destroyed two-thirds of the somewhat ramshackle store, which by then employed more than 700 people. Jaluzot decided to rebuild immediately, turning the business into a *société en commandite par actions*—limited partnership—called Jaluzot & Cie. This form of company was common in France at the time, consisting of a managing partner (or partners) and shareholders who played no part in the management of the business. The managing partner, appointed for life, named his co-partners and successors and was guaranteed a fixed percentage of the profits—in this case, 18 percent. He was also entirely responsible for any debts incurred by the company. Jules Jaluzot provided about 35 percent of the capital of the new company, and the shareholders provided the rest. In 1882 the new department store was opened. It occupied a ground area of 2,900 square meters and had six floors, occupying the entire area between rue de Provence and rue Caumartin. Further commercial success followed, but Jaluzot, a Member of Parliament for his native Nièvre and a prominent figure in Paris society, became involved in financial speculation of various sorts. In 1905 he speculated in sugar, using his own money and also in the name of and with capital from Au Printemps (Printemps), but this venture failed and he had to resign. His initials, JJ, can still be seen in the ceramic tiles on the facade of his 1882 store. His place as managing partner was taken by Gustave Laguionie, who had worked alongside Jaluzot at Au Printemps from 1867 to 1882, before leaving to become director of a wholesale business in piece goods. In 1907 Laguionie, then age 64, named his 23-year-old son Pierre as joint managing partner, and in the same year the foundation stone was laid for an adjacent store between rue Caumartin and rue Charras. The new building was opened in 1910. It was larger than the first store, occupying six floors, with a ground floor of 5,000 square meters.

Company Perspectives:

"Pinault-Printemps-Redoute is a multi-purpose distribution group split into four operating divisions—Retail, Wholesale, Financial Services and International Trade. It is now one of the leading quoted companies in France. The group's strength lies in its diversified structure, a precious source of resilience to the vicissitudes of economic cycles. The twin offensives on which current efforts are being focused across the group involve the pro-active development of core businesses alongside lasting improvements to profitability. A five-part agenda has been drawn up for implementation groupwide—galvanize human resources; improve sales margins; increase productivity; bolster the marketing drive and seek new outlets in France and abroad."

Modern Management Strategies Adopted in Early 20th Century

Gustave Laguionie died in 1920, leaving the business under the control of his son Pierre, alongside Alcide Poulet, named partner in 1920. In 1921 there was another disaster when the 1910 store partially burned down; rebuilding began immediately and the store was reopened in 1924. Adjacent buildings were acquired in rue du Havre and used for mail-order operations (then about 20 percent of total sales) and small stores were purchased in Le Havre, Rouen, and Lille in 1928 and 1929. Furthermore, some independent retailers became affiliated with Printemps for the purchase of merchandise. More important were the changes in management methods. Between 1926 and 1930 a number of innovations were introduced. Advertising and sales promotion formed an integral part of the selling activities of the firm, which adopted a strict budget. A house magazine was started in addition to training and research departments. In 1929 the functions of buying and selling were separated instead of being the responsibility of a single department head, and a separate buying company, the Société Parisienne d'Achats en Commun (SAPAC), was founded. In 1930 a system of budgetary control was introduced, by which each major activity had a planned budget of expenditure and results. In 1928 Pierre Laguionie became a founding member of the International Association of Department Stores, a society for management research.

The year 1931 saw Printemps involved in an entirely new form of retailing, the limited-price variety store. In that year the first Prisunic store opened in Paris, operated by Prisunic SA, a wholly controlled subsidiary. A central buying company, SAPAC-Prisunic, was created in 1932, and by 1935 there were eight Prisunic stores in operation, four in Paris and four in the provinces, with another 30 stores operated by retailers affiliated with SAPAC. In 1932 one of the first groups to become a Prisunic affiliate was Maus Frères of Geneva, which opened Prisunic stores in eastern France with French associates, including Pierre Lévy, the textile manufacturer. In 1936, however, a law was passed forbidding companies to open more one-price stores. This virtually brought to an end the expansion of Prisunic through new stores, but progress was made with affiliated stores, as in most cases these were establishments that did not necessarily carry the Prisunic name.

Wartime Difficulties Yield to Postwar Growth

At the outbreak of World War II the Printemps group consisted of the Paris store and seven stores elsewhere in France, plus 20 stores affiliated with the SAPAC buying organization. The Prisunic division had ten stores of its own and 60 affiliated stores, which employed about 5,500 workers. The group was still a limited partnership, and after the death of Alcide Poulet in 1928, Pierre Laguionie appointed his two brothers-in-law, Georges Marindaz (who died in 1931) and Charles Vignéras, as co-partners. Both were married to daughters of Gustave Laguionie.

The war, the German occupation, and the postwar shortages of merchandise meant a period of survival rather than of growth. But with the economic recovery starting in the early 1950s expansion again gathered pace, in two overlapping phases. The first was vigorous growth of the Prisunic variety store chain from 1950 to 1965. The number of Prisunic stores owned by the group rose from 13 in 1950 to more than 80 in 1965, and in the same period the number of affiliated stores rose from 80 to more than 230. Affiliated stores were a very effective way of earning commission on sales and increasing the purchasing power of the central buying organization with virtually no investment in land, buildings, or stock. Furthermore, it was no secret that, for the Printemps group, the Prisunic operation was extremely profitable and provided capital for the subsequent growth of the department store division.

Starting in 1954, the buildings of the Paris department store were completely transformed. Although the facades were untouched, the interiors were changed beyond recognition. All nonselling activities were transferred to the outskirts of the city, the enormous lightwells were filled in to provide selling space, the buildings on the north side of rue du Havre became the large Brummell menswear and sporting goods store, new banks of escalators were installed, and in 1963 two additional sales floors were built on top of the 1882 building. Selling space in these units was increased from 32,000 square meters in 1950 to 45,000 in 1970. Apart from the main store, heavy investments were made in rebuilding, enlarging, and modernizing seven provincial stores between 1956 and 1964. In the latter years a completely new store was built in Paris at the Nation, and in 1969 the Printemps opened its first store in the Parly-2 regional shopping center near Paris.

Corporate Reorganization in the 1970s

The various activities of the group during these years were handled mostly by separate limited partnerships, which by the early 1970s numbered more than 120, including 50 separate Prisunic companies. This structure was adopted partly because the managing partners did not want to risk their personal wealth in other activities but also because of the effects of the La Patente tax, which, until it was reformed, increased in proportion to the number of people employed by each company. The slowing of Prisunic's profitable expansion from 1965 onward and the heavy capital expenditure by the department store division, which did not lead to immediate returns, led shareholders and the managing partners to realize that the limited partnership system was no longer an effective way of running a diversified business employing more than 13,000 people. Furthermore, Pierre Laguionie was by this time 87 years old and wanted to retire from active management. In 1971 the managing partners, Pierre Laguionie and his nephew Jean Vignéras, son of Charles Vignéras, who had died in 1970, agreed with the shareholders to consolidated the partnerships into a limited company, or *société anonyme*.

The process was not a simple one. Capital had to be found for the managing partners, and some interested parties were more concerned with the group's real estate value than its commercial activities. Eventually an agreement was reached with the Swiss retail group, Maus-Nordmann of Geneva. Maus-Nordmann, a private family company, operated a chain of more than 60 department stores in Switzerland and owned a store chain, P.A. Bergner, in the United States. They were also familiar with the French retail industry since they had important shareholdings in the department store groups Nouvelles Galeries Réunies (SFNGR) and Bazar de l'Hotel de Ville (BHV). Perhaps most important, the Maus group had become an affiliate of Prisunic as early as 1932. By 1970 its company, Société Alsacienne de Magasins SA (SAMAG), had 45 affiliated Prisunic stores in eastern France. In a series of complicated transactions that involved the transfer of the assets of SAMAG to Printemps, the withdrawal of Maus-Nordmann from its holdings in SFNGR and BHV, and the compensation of the managing partners, a new company—Au Printemps S.A.—came into being in 1972. The Maus-Nordmann group owned 34 percent of the share capital, a figure that increased to 42.7 percent 20 years later, while the next largest shareholder held six percent. Pierre Laguionie was made honorary president, and Jean Vignéras continued for a while as president director general. But Laguionie died in 1978 and Vignéras withdrew in the same year, thus ending some 70 years of control and management by the Laguionie family.

The first five years of the new company were not easy. The French economy was in recession following the oil crisis, the profits of the company fell, and the new management was faced with commitments that had been entered into by the previous management, such as opening new stores in shopping centers in the Paris area. These included stores in Vélizy, opened in 1972; Créteil, opened in 1974; and Galaxie in Paris, opened in 1976. These new stores were not very profitable. Eventually the Créteil store was closed, and a contract to open a store in the Défense shopping center was canceled.

The Prisunic variety store division, though profitable, was no longer expanding. Competition from hypermarkets—combined grocery and general merchandise stores—and specialty shops had reduced the general appeal of variety stores, and emphasis was placed on the development of supermarkets and increasing food sales in the downtown locations of most of the stores. As a result of the stagnation of the variety stores, an attempt was made to develop the Escale chain of hypermarkets. The first of these opened in 1969, and by 1972 there were five in operation. Printemps realized that it did not have the expertise to start up a new hypermarket chain, and by 1976 its Escale stores had been transferred to the established Euromarché group of hypermarkets, with Printemps acquiring a 26 percent share in Euromarché SA.

New Management, New Direction
Beginning in the Late 1970s

The years from 1977, however, were to see the beginning of a transformation in the activities of the Printemps group that

was possibly more important than the opening of the Prisunic variety stores in the 1930s. Responsible for this change were Jean-Jacques Delort, who was appointed managing director in 1978 and had joined the group 18 months earlier, and his president, Bertrand Maus. Commercial strategy consisted of four main policies. First was the recognition that well-managed department stores and variety stores could, provided with the necessary investments, continue to be profitable. These methods of retailing, however, did not constitute important areas of expansion and growth. Second, commercial activities in the food sector offered growth prospects, particularly in more modern forms such as supermarkets, hypermarkets, and affiliated food stores. Third, specialty stores and home shopping, including mail order and shopping by telephone, were growing retail sectors. Fourth, when opportunities occurred or could be created, the export of know-how and merchandise was to be pursued vigorously. These policies dominated the activities of Printemps beginning in 1978.

No great change took place in the number of owned department and variety stores. Some smaller stores were closed, a few new stores were acquired or built, and investments continued to be made in existing stores. In the case of Prisunic, emphasis continued to be placed on increasing food sales and by 1980 food accounted for 58 percent of Prisunic's total sales. At the same time the concept of exporting department and variety store expertise and merchandise gathered strength. In 1979 an important agreement was made with Japan's Daiei retailing group to open Printemps department stores in Japan. Printemps provided the expertise and Daiei the building, so Printemps's capital investment was negligible. Daiei opened several such stores in Japan and similar agreements were made in other countries, including Portugal. By the early 1980s there were 11 stores outside France carrying the Printemps name, and a larger number affiliated with Printemps for supplies of merchandise. Prisunic followed a similar policy, and soon there were Prisunic or Escale—large supermarket—stores in French territories overseas and in Greece and Portugal. Specialty nonfood retailing was developed in the menswear market. In 1974 the Printemps group had opened a specialty menswear store called Brummell in Toulouse. But perhaps the most important step forward took place in 1980 when Printemps bought a 40 percent share in Magasins Armand Thiéry et Sigrand (ATS), an existing menswear chain. This shareholding was increased to 80 percent in 1981 and 87.4 percent by the early 1980s.

In 1984 an entirely different type of move was made with the purchase of 51 percent of Disco SA, a food wholesaling group, and 99 percent of a related company called Discol SA. In association with seven other wholesalers, Disco, the second largest food wholesaler in France, supplies more than 1,500 affiliated food retailers. Discol acts as a food wholesaler to restaurants, schools, and hospitals, and is France's second largest firm in this sector. Together Disco and Discol own and operate 18 food distribution centers and their associated firms have a further 38. These acquisitions, along with the significant food sales of Prisunic stores, afforded Printemps a strong presence in France's food industry.

Acquisition of La Redoute in the Late 1980s

Printemps's most dramatic acquisition took place in 1987–1988, when first 15 percent, then 20 percent, then 32 percent, and finally, on an agreed bid, 54.7 percent of the shares of La Redoute S.A., the largest mail-order company in France, passed to its control. Founded in 1831, La Redoute owned not only two smaller mail-order firms in France, Vert Baudet and Maison de Valérie, but also controlled Vestro, the second largest mail-order company in Italy, and the Prénatal chain of stores, which boasted more than 325 branches in Italy, Spain, Austria, Germany, and Portugal. Since Printemps took control, mail-order selling has been developed in the Benelux countries and Portugal and an agreement has been made with Sears Canada. La Redoute's 25 percent share of Empire Stores, the fifth largest mail-order firm in the United Kingdom, was increased in 1991 to virtually complete control at 98.9 percent.

In the hypermarket retail sector, the Printemps group had acquired a 25 percent interest in the Euromarché hypermarket company in 1975. Through crossholdings in Viniprix SA, this share rose to 43.5 percent by 1986. The profits of Euromarché fell, however, in 1987 and 1988, and in 1989 the firm incurred a heavy loss, with only a marginal improvement in 1990. Unable to control the management of Euromarché, Printemps disposed of its share in 1991, selling it at a profit to the hypermarket group Carrefour.

Another, but less important, change occurred in 1991 when the Printemps group sold the Disco food wholesale company. In effect, however, this made little difference to the commitment of the Printemps group to food wholesaling. While giving up the day-to-day operation of wholesale depots, Printemps, through its Prisunic buying organization, remained the chief source of supply for the 1,775 franchised retailers of Disco.

The 1990s and Beyond

In December 1992, Francois Pinault's Groupe Pinault, which had itself only just gone public in 1988, acquired a controlling (two-thirds) stake in Printemps. Since the 1960s, Pinault had expanded his business from a small timber company into a Ffr 40 billion conglomerate with interests in distribution and retailing. The companies merged as Pinault-Printemps-Redoute S.A. in 1994 after Printemps acquired the 46 percent of Redoute it did not already own. Over the first half of the 1990s, the conglomerate's sales increased from Ffr 31.3 billion (US $5.6 billion) in 1991 to Ffr 77.8 billion (US $15.4 billion) in 1995.

Having guided a successful reorganization of France's Le Bon Marché, Philippe Vendry returned to Printemps in 1995 to guide a revitalization of the chain. Vendry had advanced to the post of managing director of Printemps during his 22-year career at the chain before leaving in 1987 to serve as president of Le Bon Marché. According to Katherine Weisman of *WWD* magazine, he earned a reputation as "France's Dr. Retail" in the intervening years. His multifaceted prescription for Printemps included limiting its merchandise to five key categories: women's apparel, men's apparel, home furnishings, cosmetics, and leisure goods. Store remodelings reorganized goods into product "universes," as contrasted with traditional "bazaar-style" displays. Vendry also hoped to improve customer service, which he himself admitted was "lousy." Strategies to improve back-office operations included development of computer automation, centralization of purchasing, and market research. Whether these changes would improve Printemps's sagging operations [the chain suffered a Ffr 34 million (US$6.7 million) loss in 1995] remained to be seen.

Despite Printemps's poor showing, the group as a whole achieved a Ffr 1.5 billion net income, nearly triple the pro forma profit of Ffr .5 billion of 1993. Management feels that the company's broad diversification protects it from negative economic forces and positions it well to take advantage of upturns.

Principal Subsidiaries

France Printemps; Prisunic; Conforama; Groupe la Redoute; Fnac; Finaref; Groupe Rexel; Pinault Distribution; CFAO.

Further Reading

Aktar, Alev, "Printemps To Expand Self-Service Concept," *WWD,* August 4, 1995, p. 5.

"Au Printemps Profits in '91 Boosted by Sale of Hypermarket Stake," *WWD,* March 30, 1992, p. 15.

Carracalla, Jean-Paul, *Le Roman du Printemps, Histoire d'un Grand Magasin,* Paris: Denoël, 1989.

D'Aulnay, Sophie, "French Facelifts: Department Stores Say It's Time To Compete on a New, Focused Level," *Daily News Record,* October 30, 1995, p. 7.

Dumas, Solange, *Cent ans de Jeunesse,* Paris: Printania, 1965.

Mac Orlan, Pierre, *Le Printemps,* Paris: Ed. Gallimard, 1930.

"Printemps, in Denver, Shuts Doors," *Daily News Record,* April 6, 1989, p. 3.

Raper, Sarah, "Pinault Buys 40.56 Percent of Au Printemps Group," *WWD,* November 26, 1991, p. 10.

Rives, Marcel, *Traité d'Economie Commercial,* Paris: Presses Universitaires de France, 1958.

"Share and Share Unlike," *The Economist,* December 21, 1991, pp. 94–95.

Tahmincioglu, Eve, "Printemps' U.S. Future Rocky," *Footwear News,* April 3, 1989, p. 12.

Weisman, Katherine, "Bourse Probing Redoute, Pinault-Printemps Merger," *WWD,* March 28, 1994, p. 15.

——, "Printemps' Stock Price Still on Rise After Buying Conforama," *WWD,* April 27, 1992, p. 2.

——, "Putting Printemps into Gear," *WWD,* May 18, 1995, p. 14.

—James B. Jefferys
updated by April Dougal Gasbarre

Pioneer-Standard Electronics Inc.

4800 East 131st Street
Cleveland, Ohio 44105
U.S.A.
(216) 587-3600
Web site: http://www.pios.com

Public Company
Incorporated: 1963
Employees: 2,052
Sales: $1.5 billion (1996 est.)
Stock Exchanges: NASDAQ
SICs: 5065, Electronic Parts & Equipment, Not
Elsewhere Classified; 5045 Computers, Peripherals, &
Software; 7629 Electrical Repair Shops, Not
Elsewhere Classified

In 1996 Pioneer-Standard Electronics, Inc. was the sixth largest firm among the 1,500 companies in the $19 billion North American industrial electronics distribution industry. As a middleman in the industrial/commercial segment of the U.S. electronics business, Pioneer-Standard sells more than 135,000 products from more than 100 manufacturers. Its 24,000 customers range from original equipment manufacturers (OEMS) and resellers to research laboratories, government agencies, and end users divided into such major "vertical market segments" as industrial controls, computer, data and telecommunications, medical, financial, and retail. Among the leading U.S. manufacturers whose products it distributes are Digital Equipment Corp. (DEC), Intel, IBM, Cisco Systems Inc., Microsoft, and Oracle. In 1996, DEC and Intel were its two largest suppliers, accounting for 45 percent of its sales volume.

The three main categories on Pioneer-Standard's product "line card" were computer products (40 percent of its 1996 sales), semiconductors (including microprocessors; 38 percent), and passive and electromechanical electronic components (20 percent). Its computer products include disk drives, display terminals, printers, modems, minicomputers, networking products, and PCs; its semiconductor line includes analog and digital

integrated circuits, memory devices, microprocessors, and programmable logic devices; and its electronic components include capacitors, resistors, potentiometers, connectors, and switches. In addition to its traditional distribution business, Pioneer-Standard is a purveyor of a wide range of value-added services including device programming, just-in-time product kitting and turnkey manufacturing, systems integration, enterprise network services, power systems integration, automated inventory replenishment, financial services, and Internet services such as design, connection, and World Wide Web home page design. In 1996 Pioneer-Standard maintained 53 distribution operations across the United States and Canada.

"Vacuum Tubes by the Pound": 1921–1963

The U.S. electronic components distribution business was born in the 1920s in Courtland Street in lower Manhattan, a location that came to be known as Radio Row because of its profusion of radio parts stores. Before the commercial battery-operated radio was developed, ham radios ruled the industry, and in 1921 Charles Avnet, the founder of the firm that would lead the industry 70 years later, opened one of the first electronics distributorships for ham radio replacement parts, passive components, and connectors on Radio Row—only to see it fall victim to the Depression in 1931. In the 1930s Avnet tested the waters again with a car radio kit and antenna manufacturing business, which succumbed to competition and went bankrupt as well. Small radio and electrical goods stores were springing up across the country, however, in major U.S. port cities like Boston, Philadelphia, and Chicago. In 1922, for example, industry pioneer Charles Kierulff (later part of the Arrow Electronics empire) opened his own radio parts store in Los Angeles, and in 1928 Allied Radio, a mail order radio parts store, opened in Chicago.

By 1932 the radio parts distribution industry had reached Ohio, where a small distributorship named Standard Radio Supply—Pioneer-Standard's first incarnation—opened for business in Dayton. Around the same time an entrepreneur named Murray Goldberg founded Arrow Radio on New York's Radio Row to sell used radio equipment, marking the birth of the firm—Arrow Electronics—that together with Avnet would

Company Perspectives:

"We will be the preferred strategic link between our suppliers and customers. We will serve today's needs for electronic components, systems, and services—and tomorrow's needs for technology. We will be among the top independent distributors. We will provide our investors with attractive financial growth and our employees with an equal opportunity for personal and professional growth. We take pride in our culture, dedicated to: integrity, flexibility, fairness, growth, quality, success in all regards. We are committed to doing what we say we will do!"

dominate the industry in the 1990s. For all this entrepreneurial fervor, however, it was only with the explosion in manufacturing brought on by World War II that the U.S. electronics industry really came into its own. Simple ham radio parts suddenly became high-priority defense products, and for security reasons the federal government banned the manufacturing of radio sets for home or hobbyist use. With their traditional customers now off limits, radio part resellers and distributors like Standard Radio turned to the U.S. military and the war industry for sustenance. Charles Avnet, for example, made his third and finally successful attempt at business success at the height of the war by buying surplus electrical and electronic parts and selling them to the government. After the war, the private radio and electronic parts market was flooded by government war surplus parts, and the electronics distribution industry flourished. Among the many distributors who began in the postwar electronics boom were two new Cleveland firms, Premier Industrial Corporation and Pioneer-Standard's other forerunner, Pioneer Electronics Supply, both of which opened in 1946.

In 1947 the invention of the solid-state transistor rendered the vacuum tube obsolete, and during the 1950s the emergence of the television provided a new outlet for industry sales. In 1953, Wyle Electronics was formed in California, and a year later Marshall Industries began business in the same state. Charles Avnet's distributorship incorporated as Avnet Electronics Supply Co. in 1955 and saw its sales climb above the $1 million mark for the first time. By the mid-1950s, some electronic parts distributors were selling parts for televisions, car radios, and sound systems, primarily to the consumer market, and in the late 1950s the growing U.S. space industry provided another lucrative new market. A growing number of OEMs began to join the consumer market as buyers of industry products, and industry firms began selling power electronics products and high-current devices for heavy equipment in addition to TV and radio components. To lessen its dependence on the military market, the electronic components industry increasingly began to sell its products directly to distributors like Avnet, Pioneer, and Standard, who for their part began to develop new methods to protect their prices and inventories from the competition and demand swings of the electronics market.

Pioneer-Standard Electronics: 1963–1971

As the semiconductor industry began to grow in importance in the 1960s, electronics distributor Hamilton Electro (later acquired by Avnet) popularized the "broad-line" approach to distributing by carrying a range of electronics products from a variety of manufacturers rather than a limited line of select goods. It thus created the industry niche that Pioneer-Standard would later exploit on its path to industry leadership. By 1963 the electronic parts distribution business had grown into a roughly $500 million industry, and Cleveland's Pioneer Electronics Supply merged with Dayton's Standard Radio Supply to form Pioneer-Standard Electronics, incorporated in Ohio. Three years later in 1966, Pioneer-Standard purchased 50 percent of Frontier Electronics (itself founded in 1964) of Gaithersburg, Maryland, and rechristened it Pioneer-Washington and then later Pioneer/Technologies Group. By the mid-1960s, Pioneer's sales of electronic components and audio equipment stood at $5 to $9 million. In 1966 Preston (Pete) Heller Jr., the CEO who would preside over Pioneer-Standard's growth into an industry giant, joined the firm as an executive vice-president of the Pioneer Division after a career with Crane Packing Company, Inland Steel, and Arthur Young & Company. Throughout the 1960s the leading firms in the electronics distribution industry grew by acquisition. In addition to Pioneer-Standard's purchase of Frontier, Avnet acquired Time Electronics, for example, and an investment group bought up Arrow Electronics. In its 1969 annual report Arrow's management sketched the future of the electronics distribution industry: it would soon be dominated by "those few substantial distribution companies with the financial resources, the professional management, and the modern control systems necessary to participate in the industry's current consolidation phase."

Pioneer Goes Public: 1971–1982

In 1969 Pete Heller was named Pioneer's president and director, and James L. Bayman (later Heller's successor as CEO) joined the firm as the general manager of its Dayton branch after several years in management positions in the electronics industry. Despite the national recession of 1970–1971, several electronics distribution firms broke the $100 million sales level in the early 1970s, and by 1971 total industry sales were closing in on $1 billion. The industry solidified its place in the electronics industry food chain by developing product return privileges and further price protection guarantees. With sales at roughly $13 million, in June 1970 Pioneer-Standard registered an initial public offering (IPO) of company stock with the Securities and Exchange Commission. The $2.47 million in common stock sold quickly in January 1971, and Pioneer-Standard joined 14 other electronics distributors in the publicly owned arena (by the mid-1990s, only nine—Pioneer-Standard, Arrow, Avnet, Bell Industries, Jaco Electronics, Marshall Industries, Milgray Electronics, Sterling Electronics, and Wyle Electronics—remained).

Although Wall Street ignored the electronics distribution industry in the early 1970s, under Heller's command Pioneer-Standard raised its net income from $949,000 in 1973 to $2.33 million in 1975 and investors were soon watching its stock price with anticipation. Between 1975 and 1980 the electronics distribution industry as a whole grew at an annual pace of 17 percent as distributors grabbed a larger share of the electronics parts market and the largest firms grew even larger. As the growth of the computer industry began to spark investors' interest in electronics distributors in the late 1970s, industry earnings began to climb, carrying stock prices with them. Pioneer-Standard topped the $36 million mark in sales in 1976, and in 1977 sales broke past the $46 million mark. By 1980, the stocks of many distributors were selling at four to five times their 1971 prices, and Pioneer-Standard's net income had reached $3.95 million.

The onset of the recession of the early 1980s interrupted Pioneer's ascent, however, and in mid-1980 Heller was forced to admit to securities analysts that "if business remains flat and expenses remain frozen, profits will be under great pressure. . . . We're no different from any other concern in the industry." Unless the industry could cut costs or raise prices, he warned, its sales would have to grow at a 20 percent clip to match 1979 profit levels. As Wall Street saw stocks fall 24 percent between 1981 and 1982, distributors' stocks performed even worse. Many industry firms reported losses, and stock price declines of 50 percent were not unusual.

The Computer Revolution: 1982–1989

In 1982 IBM introduced personal computers with greater computing power than any that had previously been marketed to American business. Almost immediately, sales of computer electronics were accounting for nearly 20 percent of the distribution industry's sales. With businesses and consumers buying PCs to power spreadsheet, word processing, and video game applications, the computer segment of the electronic distribution market was enjoying an annual growth rate of almost 100 percent, and price/performance ratios for industrial electronics began to improve by leaps and bounds every year. To capitalize on the trend, in late 1982 Heller engineered a $50 million credit agreement with four Ohio banks that enabled Pioneer-Standard to purchase the electronics distribution division of the Harvey Group of New York, pay down its existing debts, and cover its existing capital requirements. By early 1983, the electronics distribution industry had recovered from its recession and enjoyed an 18-month expansion in which sales grew at a 30 percent annual clip. Heller was named Pioneer-Standard's chairman and CEO in 1983, and by March 1984 the company's net income had recovered from its prerecession level, and then some, to $4.1 million.

The early 1980s were a period of heavy capital spending in the U.S. semiconductor industry, and Pioneer-Standard stock began to be touted as a way for investors to "play" the semiconductor industry without investing directly in the major semiconductor makers like AMD, Intel, and National Semiconductor. By 1984 Pioneer had established a distributor relationship with computer product maker Symbios Logic Inc. of Colorado; Peter Heller's future successor, James Bayman, had been promoted to president and chief operating officer; and the company's net income was climbing toward $3.67 million. The company established its System Integration Value-Added Center (SIVAC), a customer support/cost-control consulting service, in 1985 and in 1986 founded its End-User sales group to provide greater focus to its sales efforts. In 1989 Pioneer-Standard acquired California-based distributor Compumech

Technologies and its net income broke past the $6.7 million mark on sales of more than $250 million.

"The Keys to the Kingdom": 1990–1997

For all Pioneer-Standard's steady expansion, however, by the late 1980s it had become apparent to many companies in the distribution industry that growth alone was no longer enough. Despite increasing industry sales, electronic components were becoming cheaper and cheaper to make, and distribution industry profit margins were declining. Firms like Pioneer-Standard were forced to scratch for improved cost savings and offer value-added services to maintain their profits and market share. In a crowded industry of 1,000 or more players, companies had to find new ways to distinguish themselves from their competitors.

For Pioneer-Standard's James Bayman offering value-added services in addition to distribution became "the keys to the kingdom" of bigger profits and stronger market share. In fact, when it had begun offering systems integration services to customers in the mid-1970s, Pioneer-Standard had already began transforming itself from a plain-vanilla parts distributor to a value-added firm. By the late 1980s, however, there was no turning back. Electronics industry suppliers were reducing the number of distributors with which they worked and expecting more from the ones they kept. (Intel, for example—one of Pioneer's two largest suppliers—was among the first electronics manufacturers to insist that its distributors understand and technically support the products they sold.)

By 1990, Pioneer-Standard was not only supplying bowling automation system components for supplier AMF, for example, it was participating in their manufacture as well. "They [AMF] get the order," Bayman told *Barron's* magazine, "We configure it. We load the software, and ship it directly to the bowling alley, where it's installed by AMF service people." Similarly, in 1990 Pioneer-Standard opened "demonstration centers" in five U.S. cities, where its sales staff showed small- and medium-sized software companies how to adapt their products for use with DEC's computers. By 1997, Pioneer-Standard would be offering everything from product evaluation, demand generation services, warehousing, and package labeling to technology "migration" consulting and upgrading services and Internet and firewall design and connection services. Moreover, in addition to its army of increasingly technically trained sales people Pioneer-Standard added 150 "field application engineers" (FAEs) to support its sales force. The image of the electronics distributor as a mere "parts" supplier with only a big warehouse and a team of salesmen was giving way to automated warehouses, bar-coding of product shipments, overnight product delivery, and stock-tracking software and electronic data interchange systems for accurate, real-time sales and inventory information. By 1996, Pioneer-Standard could claim the highest FAE-to-salesperson ratios in the industry.

Pioneer-Standard opened its Central Distribution Center in Cleveland in 1990 and acquired the LCS computer systems division of the U.K. firm Lex Service plc the same year. By 1991 Pioneer's vow to become "a solutions company" seemed to be coming true, and its share of the North American electronic distribution market rose from 5.5 percent in 1990 to 5.8 percent. Following further expansion to the West Coast, Pioneer's sales surged to $552 million in 1992, representing 6.6 percent of the total North American electronics distribution market. In 1993 Pioneer acquired Siemens Components Inc.'s Hamilton/Hall-Mark distribution franchise and won a crucial vote of confidence for its campaign (called "FutureStart") to become a quality-driven distributor when the International Standards Organization certified Pioneer as compliant with its ISO-9002 international quality standards program.

In 1994 Pioneer entered the international distribution market for the first time by acquiring Zentronics, one of Canada's largest industrial electronics and computer products distributors, from United Westburne Inc. for $10 to $12 million. While its share of Pioneer/Technologies was enabling it to make further inroads into the California distribution market, Pioneer signed a distribution agreement with California-based integrated circuit maker Atmel and won service awards from 15 of its suppliers and customers. Fueled by strong demand for microprocessors, Pioneer's sales broke the billion-dollar mark in 1994, and its share of the North American distribution market rose again, to 7.3 percent. By 1995, Pioneer could boast that its stock had risen 17.4 percent a year since its IPO in 1971 and that it did more business in a single day than it had in all of 1969.

In April 1995, James Bayman succeeded Pete Heller as Pioneer's CEO and announced his intention to continue Heller's expansion and value-added services strategies: "Our strategy is to grow internally and pursue acquisitions domestically and overseas in Europe and the Pacific Rim. . . . We [electronic distributors] are no longer just logistics managers. We are information managers. . . . We can't just sell a product, we have to show our client how to use it to become more competitive." In November Pioneer-Standard's long anticipated acquisition of the remaining 50 percent of Pioneer/Technologies was finalized, and in a deal estimated at about $50 million Pioneer/Technologies officially became Pioneer-Standard of Maryland. "With our buying technologies," Bayman quipped, "we finally put to bed the longest-running rumor in the industry, a rumor 20 years running." In one fell swoop Pioneer-Standard had become the third largest electronics distributor in North America, absorbing Pioneer/Technologies' 11 branch operations in the northwestern and southeastern United States and expanding its line card of products to one of the industry's most extensive. Rumors immediately began circulating that Pioneer-Standard would soon merge with another major distributor to gain ground on Arrow Electronics and Avnet—or even attempt to merge with one of those two industry leaders itself. "As usual, there is no basis for any of the rumors," Bayman asserted, while admitting coyly, "We are very interested in expanding."

The unprecedented growth of the distribution industry in 1991–1995 tailed off in 1996, and Pioneer lost its rank as the third largest North American distributor. Nevertheless, in 1996 it announced distribution agreements with RadiSys Corporation, Cisco Systems, Micron Technology, AccelGraphics Inc., Tadpole Technology, Network General, Murata Electronics, Symbios Logic, Lucent Technologies, Actel Corporation, and Cipher Systems. It also entered into an increasingly typical "remarketing" agreement with IBM, in which Pioneer-Standard would not only distribute Big Blue's computer systems but would support them by providing value-added resellers (VARs) with an umbrella of services such as sales and technical ser-

vices, direct marketing services, product evaluation, financial services, and business planning. With semiconductors representing an ever larger segment of the distribution market, in 1996 Pioneer-Standard also relocated its semiconductor marketing operations to California's Silicon Valley, the heart of the U.S. high-tech industry.

Between 1991 and 1996, the industrial electronics distribution industry had grown from $9 billion to more than $20 billion, a 300 percent increase over its volume in 1986. Despite the cost of its acquisition of Pioneer/Technologies and a slowdown in industry sales, Pioneer-Standard's sales topped $1.5 billion in 1996, and in 1997 it announced new distribution agreements with U.S. Robotics, Celestica Inc., and Fairchild Semiconductor. Its implementation of Total Quality Management (TQM) principles had lifted its quality control score to the "world-class" level, and the American Society for Quality Control was citing the company's quality program as a "textbook example of comprehensive planning activity, followed by rigorous implementation, producing results." The year 1996 was the tenth consecutive year of record sales for Pioneer-Standard; since its 1971 IPO its sales had increased every year but one. Despite the soft market of the mid-1990s some stock analysts were predicting that Pioneer-Standard's earnings would grow 22 percent in 1998 and another 15 percent in 1999.

Principal Subsidiaries

Pioneer-Standard of Maryland, Inc.; Pioneer-Standard Canada Inc.

Further Reading

Baird, Kristen, "Setting New Standards at Pioneer-Standard," *Crain's Cleveland Business,* July 24, 1995, p. 3.

Bounds, Wendy, "Pioneer-Standard Acquires Remainder of Pioneer Technologies for $50 Million," *Wall Street Journal,* December 1, 1995.

"Cipher Systems and Pioneer-Standard Canada Form Strategic Alliance," *PR Newswire,* December 5, 1996.

Cohodas, Marilyn, "Siemens Teams with Pioneer," *Electronic Business Buyer,* November 1993, p. 22.

Harrison, Kimberly P., "Pioneer-Standard Electronics, Inc.," *Crain's Cleveland Business,* May 23, 1994, p. S-15.

"How They Rank," *Electronic News,* December 2, 1996.

Levine, Bernard, "Pioneer-Standard Buys Remainder of Tech Affiliate," *Electronic News,* December 4, 1995.

McCausland, Richard, Untitled, *Electronic News,* July 26, 1993, p. 18.

"Pioneer Announces New Franchise Agreement with Celestica, Inc.," *PR Newswire,* March 3, 1997.

"Pioneer Milestones" (company historical chronology), Cleveland, OH: Pioneer-Standard Electronics, 1996.

"Pioneer Projects Lower Results," *Electronic News,* September 16, 1996.

"Pioneer-Standard and Actel Corporation's Distribution Agreement Is Extended To Cover All Pioneer Locations in North America," *PR Newswire,* December 13, 1996.

"Pioneer-Standard and Lucent Technologies Distribution Agreement Is Extended To Cover Canada," *PR Newswire,* October 22, 1996.

"Pioneer-Standard Announces Asset-Liability Transaction," *PR Newswire,* December 28, 1990.

"Pioneer-Standard Electronics," *Wall Street Journal,* March 3, 1994.

"Pioneer-Standard Electronics Achieves IBM's First RS/6000 Authorized Assembler Certification," *PR Newswire,* December 20, 1996.

"Pioneer-Standard Electronics Achieves UTEC Quality Certification," *PR Newswire,* February 3, 1997.

"Pioneer-Standard Electronics Inc.," *Wall Street Journal,* January 14, 1993.

"Pioneer-Standard Electronics Inc.: Who's News," *Wall Street Journal,* April 30, 1997.

"Pioneer-Standard Names Arthur Rhein President, Operations Chief," *Dow Jones Newswires,* April 29, 1997.

"Pioneer-Standard Says Bookings Are Declining," *Wall Street Journal,* May 30, 1980.

"Pioneer-Standard's Centers," *Wall Street Journal,* January 24, 1991.

"Pioneer-Standard Sees 'Above Average' Rise in Fiscal 1977 Results," *Wall Street Journal,* May 21, 1976.

"Pioneer-Standard Stocks Sold," *Wall Street Journal,* January 8, 1971.

"Pioneer-Standard To Buy Some Assets of Harvey Unit," *Wall Street Journal,* November 2, 1982.

Ruston, Richard E., and Bussey, John, "Semiconductor Issues Have Soared as Outlook for Prices, Orders Growth Is Seen Brightening," *Wall Street Journal,* August 27, 1984.

Savitz, Eric J., "More Than Their Name Implies: Electronic Distributors Widen Horizons," *Barron's,* June 25, 1990, p. 15.

"U.S. Robotics and Pioneer Team Up To Provide Customers New X2 Technology," *PR Newswire,* March 31, 1997.

—Paul S. Bodine

Pitney Bowes, Inc.

One Elmcroft Road
Stamford, Connecticut 06926-0700
U.S.A.
(203) 356-5000
Fax: (203) 351-6835
Web site: http://www.pitneybowes.com

Public Company
Incorporated: 1920 as Pitney-Bowes Postage Meter
   Company
Employees: 28,700
Sales: $3.86 billion (1996)
Stock Exchanges: New York
SICs: 3579 Office Machines, Not Elsewhere Classified; 3861
   Photographic Equipment and Supplies; 3661 Telephone
   & Telegraph Apparatus; 3669 Communications Equip-
   ment Not Elsewhere Classified; 6159 Miscellaneous
   Business Credit Institutions; 7389 Business Services,
   Not Elsewhere Classified; 3578 Calculating &
   Accounting Equipment; 8741 Management Services

Pitney Bowes, Inc. (PB) is the world's largest manufacturer and supplier of postage meters and mailing equipment. The company originally built its reputation on its postage meter invention and other paper-mail processing products, but has recently been expanding its scope to keep up with the onset of the electronic information age. With respect to product development, PB's main areas of focus now lies in traditional paper mailing systems, facsimile systems, copier systems, and computer software solutions. The company also provides business support services and financial services to customers worldwide. PB remains the world's leader in the production and leasing of postal meters, which are used by postal services in countries around the world.

The Early Years

Pitney Bowes' beginnings can be traced to the year 1902, when Arthur Pitney patented his newly-created postage-stamp-

ing machine. He then spent the next 12 years fine-tuning it and attempting to gain acceptance and financial backing for the product from the postal service. Pitney's machine offered a solution for the U.S. Post Office, which was confronted with the impracticality of the adhesive postage stamp in the face of the increasing volume of mail. The postage-stamping machine would stamp the mail at its source, while also keeping track of the amount of postage used. This method helped save labor and also decreased costs for both the postal service and the businesses using the machine. Although achieving impressive results when tested by the post office in Pitney's hometown of Chicago in 1914, ultimate approval of the machine did not come until after World War I.

Meanwhile, in New York, Walter Bowes' Universal Stamping Machine Company was doing brisk business with the U.S. Postal Service, providing stamp-cancelling machines on a rental basis. Bowes also had some international success, selling his machines in Germany, England, and Canada. In 1917 Bowes moved his operations to Stamford, Connecticut, a location which evolved into the company headquarters for years to come. Although Bowes' machine was profitable, he worried that Pitney's similar invention would render it obsolete. Thus, in April 1920, the two men decided to pool their resources.

The merger of Pitney's American Postage Meter Company and Bowes's Universal Stamping Machine Company created the Pitney-Bowes Postage Meter Company. The day after the merger officially took effect, Pitney and Bowes succeeded in pushing legislation through Congress to allow all classes of mail to be posted by meters instead of stamps, and the Pitney-Bowes postage meter was licensed for use throughout the postal system.

By 1922, PB had branch offices in 12 cities and 404 postage meters in operation. In the same year, Bowes's previous international experience paid off and PB's postage meter was approved for use in England and Canada. PB experienced early growing pains, however. As the meter gained exposure in the early 1920s, demand for the machines began to outpace the company's ability to manufacture, distribute, and service them. Also, it was felt in many quarters that PB enjoyed a government-created monopoly. Thus, in its first decade of existence, PB's scope of operations was limited by government regula-

Company Perspectives:

"The number of ways to communicate has increased dramatically, adding digital and electronic options to mail, overnight packages, photocopies and facsimile documents. Pitney Bowes is keeping pace with these innovations. We do this by adding value to every message we touch, measured in terms of reduced cost and increased reliability, security, privacy, convenience, effectiveness and impact."

tion—lobbied for by PB's competition—restricting PB from reaping the advantages of its technologically superior product.

Expansion Efforts in the Early and Mid-1900s

In 1924, Arthur Pitney retired from the company after a dispute with Bowes and started a company of his own, manufacturing postage-permit machines to compete with PB's meters. Even without Pitney, the company name remained Pitney-Bowes, due to the recognition factor the name had earned throughout those first four years. After the co-founder's departure, however, uncertainty reigned at PB, and Walter Wheeler II, Bowes' stepson, was promoted from New York branch manager to general manager in Stamford in an attempt to utilize new leadership and find new direction.

PB's share of the market was still uncertain because of the postal service's equivocation on postal regulations. Permit mail required counting to assess fees, while metered mail did not; but the postal service, wary of establishing a monopoly for PB, required all mail to be counted. Although PB's future hung by a thread during the early and mid-1920s, by 1927 the company had 2,849 meters in operation and branches in 20 cities. Finally, after a congressional hearing at which Arthur Pitney testified by letter against preferential treatment for the system he invented, a bill to impose uniform regulations on permit and metered mail was killed in the Senate. The postal service was free to exercise its preference for the more efficient, reliable, and safe postage meter. From that point on, first-class mail was posted only by meter or adhesive stamp.

Pitney-Bowes began to grow and diversify, producing machines for stamping, counting, canceling, and metering mail. PB's 1929 profit of $300,000 represented a 100 percent increase over that of the previous year. The company expanded abroad as well, establishing cross-licensing and patent-sharing agreements with similar firms in Great Britain and Germany. Throughout the 1930s, government restrictions on the metered-mail business eroded, and Pitney-Bowes's field of operations grew wider. By the end of 1933 there were 9,620 PB postage meters in service.

The Great Depression meant retrenchment at Pitney-Bowes, as it did in most sectors of the economy. PB was fortunate to be in a growth industry and did not face critical financial difficulties, but its profits shrunk considerably during these years. The company was forced to cut wages by ten percent and also suspended stockholder dividends. The union movement re-

ceived a boost during the Depression, but found little support at PB, which had provided benefits to its employees for years. PB emerged from the Depression earlier and healthier than most firms, partly due to the nature of its product, and partly due to the leadership of Walter Wheeler. He became the company president in 1938.

Pitney-Bowes's success in the industry and the further relaxation of postal service restrictions on metered mail stimulated competition in the production of postage meters. Many small firms sought a share of the market, as did some heavy hitters like IBM and NCR. Nonetheless, PB consistently kept ahead of its competition. Its development of the omni-denomination meter in 1940 was a breakthrough in the industry. Not only was PB prospering, with over 27,000 meters in service in 1939, but the U.S. Postal Service had a $2 million dollar budget surplus in fiscal 1939, largely due to the efficiency of the metered-mail system.

Like most other large manufacturers, PB converted its plant to defense production during World War II. PB's wartime priorities, as established by Walter Wheeler, were maximum production of war goods, maintenance of meters in operation to handle American mail, and planning for postwar manufacture of new products. The production of postage meters was completely halted during the war. Instead, PB manufactured replacement parts for guns, aircraft, and radios, and was a four-time recipient of the army-navy "E" Award, given for excellence in wartime production.

Post-World War II Diversification

In 1945, anticipating the broadening of its product base, Pitney-Bowes Postage Meter Company shortened its name to Pitney-Bowes, Inc. By the end of 1947, the number of PB postage meters in service had more than doubled to over 60,000 in less than ten years. PB expanded and modernized its plant and office space in Stamford to accommodate projected growth. Two years later, PB introduced a desktop postage meter, which brought small business customers within its reach. Further diversification continued with the acquisition of the Tickometer Company, whose namesake product counted paper items such as labels and tickets. PB simplified the Tickometer machine's design and promoted its use for many new purposes. For the most part, though, PB limited its diversification to fields related to those functions performed in mail rooms.

Throughout the 1940s and 1950s, Wheeler worked hard to maintain good labor-management relations and progressive incentive, benefit, and profit-sharing plans. This was reflected in a high rate of productivity at PB, and in the decision of the majority of workers not to seek union representation. The wisdom of this strategy was demonstrated by PB's continual outperformance of its competition during those years.

By 1957, however, due to the virtual disappearance of domestic competition, PB was faced with government antitrust action. The company cooperated fully with investigators. Wheeler even went so far as to prepare a 12-volume history of Pitney-Bowes and submit it to the Department of Justice. Wheeler maintained, as he always had, that it was PB's productivity, efficiency, and personnel relations that made it difficult for other companies to compete, not anti-competitive practices. PB eventually agreed to sign a consent decree that required the company to license its patents to any manufacturer who wished to compete, at no charge.

In 1960, when Walter H. Wheeler retired as president and chief operating officer, PB had 281,100 postage meters in service and metered mail accounted for 43 percent of U.S. postage. PB's gross income was over $57 million. Furthermore, products other than postage meters accounted for 20 percent of the company's gross income, a result of PB's increasing diversification measures.

Entering the 1960s, diversification became an even more important facet of PB's strategy. Because PB no longer had a monopoly in the postage-meter market, diversification into new product areas was necessary for company growth. In 1967, the company established a copier-product division whose first product was a tabletop office copier. Although PB was a latecomer to a market already dominated by Xerox, its copiers had two advantages: they were reasonably priced, and included excellent service packages. Service had long been a hallmark of PB's operations because the U.S. Post Office never allowed PB to sell its meters, only lease them. PB was responsible for the day-to-day operations of every meter it leased, so a large service fleet was already in place. This service team made expansion into other markets much more manageable.

The following year, PB acquired Monarch Marking Systems, which soon grew into the largest U.S. supplier of price-marking, merchandise-identification, and inventory-control equipment and supplies. By the end of the decade, PB's sales of postage meters, while still growing, accounted for only just over 50 percent of its total sales. Pitney Bowes dropped the hyphen from its name in 1970.

The 1970s and 1980s

In the early 1970s, PB began to experience financial losses that stemmed from a joint venture with Alpex Computer Corporation to manufacture point-of-sale terminal systems. PB was forced to write off its 64 percent investment in the venture, at a loss of $42 million. More modest losses from this venture continued to mount for several years, due to disputes with the Internal Revenue Service over allowable write-offs and an $11 million lawsuit filed by Alpex.

By the late 1970s, however, PB was back on track. The company established leasing companies in the United States and in the United Kingdom in 1977 to support marketing efforts for its business products. This was a record year for the company, with both postage meters and price-marking systems posting record sales. In 1979 PB made a major acquisition, adding the Dictaphone Corporation and its subsidiaries Data Documents and Grayarc to the company, for a $124 million price tag. The purchase made PB the worldwide leader in sales of voice-processing and dictation equipment, while still enjoying a 90 percent controlling share of the postage-meter market.

In the early 1980s, PB made moves to solidify its standing as the country's leader in the mail-room and office equipment market. It first filled a gap in its copier line in 1981 by arranging a marketing agreement with the Ricoh Company of Japan to make its tabletop model available in the United States. This increased the number of copier models marketed by PB to eight. PB also received a $111 million contract from the post office to help further automate the handling of mail by developing computers to "read" envelopes and parcels. PB then entered the facsimile-machine market in 1982, and soon became the leader in new placements of facsimile equipment. The company became one of the top suppliers of fax machines to large and medium-sized businesses in the United States, and began seeking new international markets by the late 1980s.

Keeping in line with company policy to compete mainly in markets in which it was guaranteed a prominent share, in 1987 about 80 percent of the company's sales were in industry segments that PB led. The Data Documents subsidiary, however, deviated from this standard, and was sold in 1988. The company also laid off 1,500 workers and underwent a costly retooling in 1989, and began to push more sophisticated mailing systems, like its Star system, which picked the most efficient carrier method for each package. PB also got a boost from the U. S. Post Office, which began pushing big mailers to use bar-code envelopes.

The 1990s and Beyond

Entering the final decade of the century, PB saw its sales surpass the $3 billion mark for the first time in company history, topping off at $3.2 billion in fiscal 1990. Furthermore, the company's extensive sales force had earned PB a 45 percent share of the market for fax machines in corporate America. Following the course charted by that success, the company continued to penetrate the domestic market for business machines with the introduction of another line of copiers in 1991. This line of machines, the 9000 series, was targeted mainly at large businesses. 1991 also saw the introduction of computerized software programs focusing on automated freight management, address and mail list management, and medical records transcription.

The 1990s ushered in the "information age," which included an increase in communications by electronic means, in the form of both facsimile and electronic mail. PB attempted to keep pace with the world's new communication needs, shifting its operations from a mechanical base to that of computerization and software solutions. In order to ease the transition, the company instituted a program of self-directed work teams on both the production floor and in the management ranks. PB also trained its management and sales teams to become proficient in the use of computers. The changes helped to integrate the ideas and actions of everyone in the company, while also technologically enabling PB to more easily expand its scope in line with technological advances.

Meanwhile, PB worked to maintain its standing as the country's leading producer of mail room equipment. In fact, its work in that area was honored in 1993, when the company was featured in the National Postal Museum in Washington, D.C., a recognition of numerous PB innovations throughout history. The company also continued to expand worldwide, nailing down deals with three other countries in 1994. PB introduced its popular Paragon mailing system in Germany, while it also began to aid China and Mexico in the modernization and automation of their postal systems.

The following year, PB sold its Dictaphone subsidiary to an affiliate of Stonington Partners, a New York investment group, for $450 million. The company also divested its Monarch Marking Systems subsidiary, selling it for $127 million. More sales and service offices were opened in Europe, and product development efforts utilizing new technology continued. An important introduction in late 1995 was a computerized mail tracking and accounting system called PostPerfect.

Nearing the end of the century, PB was manufacturing and distributing its products worldwide. After building its reputation on the success of the postage meter nearly 80 years earlier, PB had diversified to include traditional paper mailing systems, facsimile systems, copier systems, and computer software solutions, while also providing business support services and financial services to customers. The company's commitment to growth—through expansion, diversification, and research and development efforts—was apparent as PB tackled new technological advances and entrances into foreign markets with ease. The company's secure market positions and strong management should provide a solid base for continued expansion and diversification in the years to come.

Principal Subsidiaries

Adrema Leasing Corporation; Adrema Maschinen und Auto-Leasing GmbH (Germany); Adrema Mobilien Leasing GmbH (Germany); Andeen Enterprises, Inc. (Panama); Artec International Corporation; Atlantic Mortgage & Investment Corporation; B. Williams Holding Corp.; Cascade Microfilm Systems, Inc.; Chas. P. Young Health Fitness & Management, Inc.; Colonial Pacific Leasing Corporation; Datarite Systems Ltd. (U.K.); Dodwell Pitney Bowes K.K. (Japan); ECL Finance Company, N.V. (Netherlands); Elmcroft Road Realty Corporation; Financial Structures Limited (Bermuda); FSL Valuation Services, Inc.; Harlow Aircraft Inc.; Informatech; La Agricultora Ecuatoriana S.A. (Ecuador); Norlin Australia Investment Pty. Ltd. (Australia); Norlin Industries Limited (Canada); Norlin Music (U.K.) Ltd. (England); PB Forms, Inc. (Nebraska); PB Funding Corporation (Delaware); PB Global Holdings, Inc.; PB Leasing Corporation; PB Leasing International Corporation; PB CFSC I, Inc. (Virgin Islands); PBL Holdings, Inc.; PB Nikko FSC Ltd. (Bermuda); PB Nihon FSC Ltd. (Bermuda); Pitney Bowes AG (Switzerland); Pitney Bowes Australia Pty. Limited (Australia); Pitney Bowes Aus-

tria Ges.m.b.H. (Austria); Pitney Bowes Canada Holding Ltd. (Canada); Pitney Bowes Credit Australia Limited; Pitney Bowes Credit Corporation; Pitney Bowes Data Systems, Ltd. (U.K.); Pitney Bowes de Mexico, S.A. de C.V.; Pitney Bowes Deutschland GmbH (Germany); Pitney Bowes Espana, S.A. (Spain); Pitney Bowes Finance, S.A. (France); Pitney Bowes Finans Norway AS (Norway); Pitney Bowes Finance plc (U.K.); Pitney Bowes Finance Ireland Limited; Pitney Bowes France S.A.; Pitney Bowes Holdings Ltd. (U.K.); Pitney Bowes Holding SNC (France); Pitney Bowes Insurance Agency, Inc. (Connecticut); Pitney Bowes International Holdings, Inc.; Pitney Bowes Italia S.r.l. (Italy); Pitney Bowes (Ireland) Limited (Ireland); Pitney Bowes Leasing Ltd. (Canada); Pitney Bowes Macau Limited (Macau); Pitney Bowes Management Services, Inc.; Pitney Bowes Management Services Canada, Inc. (Canada); Pitney Bowes Management Services Limited (U.K.) Pitney Bowes Oy (Finland); Pitney Bowes Limited (U.K.); Pitney Bowes Properties, Inc.; Pitney Bowes Real Estate Financing Corporation; Pitney Bowes Servicios, S.A. de C.V. (Mexico); Pitney Bowes Shelton Realty, Inc.; Pitney Bowes Svenska Aktiebolag (Sweden); Pitney Bowes World Trade Corporation (FSC) (Virgin Islands); RE Properties Management Corporation; Remington Customer Finance Pty. Limited (Australia); Remington (PNG) Pty. Limited (Papau New Guinea); Remington Pty. (Australia); ROM Holdings Pty. Limited (Australia); ROM Securities Pty. Limited (Australia); Sales and Service Training Center, Inc, (Georgia); TECO/Pitney Bowes Co., Ltd. (Taiwan) (50%); Time-Sensitive Delivery Guide, Inc.; Towers FSC, Ltd. (Bermuda); Universal Postal Frankers Ltd. (U.K.); Walnut Street Corp.; 1136 Corporation; 75 V Corp.

Further Reading

Babyak, Richard J., ''Low-Cost, High-Tech,'' *Appliance Manufacturer,* March 1994, p. 36.

Cahn, William, *The Pitney-Bowes Story,* New York: Harper and Brothers, 1961.

Day, Charles R., Jr., ''Faceless But Fantastic,'' *Industry Week,* November 15, 1993, p. 7.

Hitchcock, Nancy A., ''Can Self-Managed Teams Boost Your Bottom Line?: How Pitney Bowes Establishes Self-Directed Work Teams,'' *Modern Materials Handling,* February 1993, p. 58.

Paley, Norton, ''Fancy Footwork,'' *Sales & Marketing Management,* July 1994, p. 41.

Taylor, Thayer C., ''Does This Compute?'' *Sales & Marketing Management,* September 1994, p. 115.

—Robin Carre
—updated by Laura E. Whiteley

IIIIIPITTSTON

The Pittston Company

1000 Virginia Center Parkway
P.O. Box 4229
Glen Allen, VA 23058-4229
U.S.A.
(804) 553-3600
Fax: (203) 553-3750

Public Company
Incorporated: 1930
Employees: 27,000
Sales: $3.1 billion (1996)
Stock Exchanges: New York
SICs: 4512 Air Transportation Scheduled; 1222
   Bituminous Coal Underground; 7381 Detective Guard
   & Armored Car Services; 6719 Holding Companies

The Pittston Company is a diversified corporation with operations in coal mining, air-freight delivery, and security services. It began as a coal company in northeastern Pennsylvania and expanded to include holdings in Virginia, West Virginia, and Kentucky. Pittston's coal division specializes in providing low-sulfur coal to domestic utility companies and metallurgical coal (suitable for fueling smelters and other metallurgical equipment) to both domestic and overseas steel producers. Since World War II Pittston has diversified its interests. It moved into security transportation with the acquisition of Brink's, Incorporated, and developed oil retailing operations through its subsidiary Metropolitan Petroleum Corporation. During the oil crisis of the 1970s, Pittston increased its coal production to meet the demand for alternative fuels, but it faced serious setbacks when falling oil prices and labor disputes hurt its production in the 1980s. By 1991 Pittston had started to recoup these losses, thanks to a 1990 labor settlement and to its growing security and air-freight operations.

The Early Years

The seeds of the Pittston Company were planted in the 19th century, when the U.S. coal-mining and railroad industries developed alongside each other. In 1838 the Pennsylvania Coal Company was organized in Pittston, Pennsylvania, to mine coal for Eastern markets. This company produced anthracite, or hard, coal and built a 46-mile railroad to transport it from Scranton, Pennsylvania, to the Hudson River. The Erie Railroad bought the Pennsylvania Coal Company in 1901, making it a subsidiary of its own mining and railroad operations. Fifteen years later an even larger company, the Alleghany Corporation, acquired the Erie Railroad. The Alleghany Corporation served as a holding company for a variety of businesses owned by the Van Sweringen brothers of Cleveland, Ohio, and their associates. It continued to operate the Erie Railroad and Pennsylvania Coal Company as parts of its railroad empire.

The Alleghany Corporation created the Pittston Company in January 1930. Competition in the hard-coal industry had intensified in the late 1920s, and antitrust laws prevented the Erie Railroad from entering new markets. To solve this problem, Alleghany organized Pittston and offered its stock at $20 per share to Erie Railroad stockholders. Alleghany retained a controlling interest in Pittston, and the Van Sweringens continued to run Pittston. Pittston then leased mines from the Erie Railroad and sold its coal through its own wholesale and retail subsidiaries. At the time of its founding, Pittston also acquired United States Distributing Corporation. United States Distributing was a holding company that owned United States Trucking Corporation; Independent Warehouses, Inc.; Pattison & Bowns, Inc., a wholesale coal distributor; and a Wyoming mining company.

Although it began as part of a large railroad empire, Pittston experienced hard times in its early years. The Great Depression slowed the nation's coal consumption, and Pittston had to borrow between $1 million and $2 million annually from its sister companies just to stay afloat. In 1935 J.P. Morgan & Co. stopped backing the Van Sweringens, and the Alleghany empire crumbled. Two years later investors Robert R. Young and Allan P. Kirby took over the remaining pieces of the Alleghany Corporation, including Pittston.

Pittston's fortunes began to turn around when Young and Kirby convinced J.P. Routh to become the Pittston Company's president. When Routh took over in 1939, Pittston's stock was down to 12.5cn per share, and the company owed the Erie

---

Company Perspectives:

"The success of both the Services and Minerals groups of the Pittston Company has been derived in two ways. First, by our insistence on providing the highest-quality customer service and products possible. And second, from our extensive, successful experience in cost containment and productivity improvement in the midst of changing market conditions."

Railroad $10 million. Routh, who had owned his own wholesale coal business, established a plan for servicing Pittston's debt and began looking for ways to expand its business. He turned his attention to the growing bituminous, or soft, coal market. In 1944 he brought Pittston its first bituminous reserves with the purchase of 60 percent of Clinchfield Coal Corporation. Clinchfield Coal had been formed in 1906 when Ledyard Blair, Thomas Fortune Ryan, and George L. Carter merged together several smaller coal companies. Clinchfield Coal owned 300,000 acres of coal reserves in southwestern Virginia, and this acquisition permanently shifted Pittston's coal operations from Pennsylvania to Appalachia. Over the next four years Pittston invested heavily in Clinchfield Coal. In 1945 Pittston and Clinchfield Coal jointly acquired 67 percent of the Davis Coal & Coke Company. Seven years later Davis Coal & Coke was merged into Clinchfield Coal. In 1947 Pittston acquired Lillybrook Coal Company to increase its coal reserves. It also extensively drilled the Clinchfield properties for natural gas. In 1956 Pittston purchased the remaining 40 percent of Clinchfield Coal, making this highly profitable company a wholly owned subsidiary.

Postwar Developments

Under Routh's direction Pittston developed interests in oil marketing. In 1951 it acquired the Metropolitan Petroleum Corporation, a wholesale and retail oil distributor in New York City. Pittston expanded Metropolitan's geographical range by purchasing terminal facilities in Philadelphia, Boston, and Chicago. Its share of the fuel-oils business in the northeast rose considerably, and by 1954 fuel oil accounted for 38 percent of Pittston's net income. Metropolitan's expansion continued during the 1960s with the acquisition in 1963 and 1964 of two Boston fuel operations—Burton-Furber Company and Crystal Oil Company. It also entered the petrochemicals market by forming Metropolitan Petroleum Chemicals Company in 1965.

Pittston diversified beyond energy markets by developing trucking and warehousing operations under its United States Distributing Corporation subsidiary. This holding company's most important component was United States Trucking Corporation (USTC), which had been formed in 1919 by the merger of 26 trucking companies. USTC operated in five areas—armored-car services, truck rental, general rigging, baggage transfer, and general trucking. It handled newsprint deliveries for New York's and New Jersey's major newspapers, as well as the rigging work for Western Electric Company in New York City. Western Electric's rigging work included using pulley systems to move unwieldy switchboard equipment into skyscrapers. In 1954 Pittston acquired USTC's most prominent

competitor, Motor Haulage Company, and merged its operations. In that same year, Pittston's trucking and warehousing operations accounted for 43 percent of its net income, surpassing both its coal and oil divisions. When Alleghany, Pittston's parent company, purchased the New York Central Railroad in 1954, antitrust concerns were raised about this new acquisition and Pittston's transportation operations in general. Alleghany solved this problem by divesting itself of its remaining 50 percent interest in Pittston, leaving it a fully independent company.

Pittston's most important diversification soon followed with the purchase of an interest in Brink's, Inc., a Chicago-based security transportation company. Brink's had been founded as a delivery company in 1859 and began making payroll deliveries in 1891. From there it had grown into the world's largest armored-car company, providing services to private businesses, banks, the Federal Reserve, and U.S. government mints. Pittston's interest in Brink's began in 1956, when it bought 22 percent of its stock. Pittston then applied to the Interstate Commerce Commission (ICC) for approval to purchase a majority share in Brink's. In 1958 the ICC approved Pittston's proposal, but the Justice Department objected on grounds that it could violate antitrust laws. A year later Pittston increased its interest in Brink's to 90 percent, but it ran into antitrust difficulty again when it proposed merging the operations of Brink's and United States Trucking. Pittston finally completed its purchase of Brink's in 1962 and made it a wholly owned subsidiary distinct from United States Trucking. During the early 1960s, under Pittston's direction, Brink's expanded its business to include coast-to-coast air-courier service and established subsidiaries in France, Brazil, and Israel.

Pittston's rapid diversification after World War II culminated in a corporate reorganization in 1960. Chairman and President Routh divided Pittston into three operating divisions—coal, oil, and transportation and warehousing—each of which contributed about one-third of Pittston's profits. In 1960 coal accounted for 36 percent of net income, oil for 31 percent, and transportation and warehousing for 33 percent. Pittston had achieved financial stability through diversification.

Despite this diversification, Pittston did not neglect its coal division. In the early 1950s the conversion of the railroads to diesel fuel and the use in many homes and factories of oil energies lessened the demand for coal. In light of these trends Pittston decided to focus its production on specific coal markets. Its reserves in Appalachia were rich in metallurgical coal, necessary in the manufacturing of steel. Over the next 20 years Pittston became the largest U.S. exporter of this type of coal, feeding the booming steel industry in such recovering postwar economies as Japan's. Pittston also turned its attention to the production of steam coal—coal best suited for producing steam—for electric utilities, such as the American Electric Power Company, which signed a long-term agreement with Clinchfield Coal in 1959. Adding substantially to Pittston's reserves in the 1960s were several acquisitions, including the Kentland-Elkhorn Coal Corporation and the Jewell Ridge Coal Corporation in 1966, the Sewell Coal Company in 1967, and the Eastern Coal Corporation in 1969. Through these efforts the coal division experienced a resurgence, and by 1971 it was contributing more than 55 percent of the company's net income.

Challenges during the 1970s and 1980s

The energy crisis of the 1970s dramatically increased the world's demand for coal, and Pittston shifted its resources to take advantage of this change. Under the leadership of its chairman, Nicholas T. Camicia, elected in 1969, Pittston spent heavily in its coal division, opening new mines and modernizing its production. The company adapted to changes in environmental laws by increasing its output of low-sulfur coal, which burns much more cleanly than other types. Pittston supplied compliance coal—so called because it helped utilities comply with environmental laws—to such utility companies as the Tennessee Valley Authority, which agreed to a ten-year contract with Pittston in 1978. The energy crisis and the OPEC oil embargo squeezed Pittston's other divisions, but by 1976 the company's coal operations had expanded enough to bring in 91 percent of the company's profits. This boom period, however, was not without its difficulties.

In February 1972 disaster struck the Buffalo Mining Company, a Pittston subsidiary in Logan County, West Virginia. A coal-waste refuse pile that the company had been using to dam a stream near its plant collapsed, flooding 16 communities and killing more than 125 people. Chairman Camicia appeared before a Senate hearing investigating the disaster in May 1972, and survivors filed a $65 million lawsuit against Pittston for psychological damages. In a landmark settlement Pittston agreed to pay $13.5 million to about 625 residents suffering from ''survivor's syndrome'' in the Buffalo Creek Valley. Pittston faced further legal action brought by the state of West Virginia, with whom it settled in 1977 for $4 million. Labor disputes and a slumping world steel industry in the late 1970s subsequently hit Pittston hard. A United Mine Workers Union (UMW) strike from December 1977 to March 1978, the longest in UMW history up to that time, severely curtailed production. This decline was worsened by a railway-workers strike from July to October 1978 that disrupted Pittston's deliveries to its buyers. Pittston's profits fell from a high of $200 million in 1975 to $25.2 million in 1978.

Pittston's other divisions fared as poorly as its coal sector in the late 1970s. The oil crisis left Metropolitan Petroleum dependent on its suppliers and facing much higher costs. It tried to develop its own oil-refining capacity, but a proposed refinery in Eastport, Maine, was unable to overcome opposition from environmental groups and was never built. In 1980, still without refining capacity, Metropolitan changed its name to Pittston Petroleum in an effort to improve name recognition and sales. Brink's faced difficulty in the 1970s as well because of rising costs and increasing competition. In 1976 a federal grand jury began investigating possible antitrust violations in the armored-car business. A year later Brink's paid $5.9 million to settle some of the resulting antitrust charges. Brink's settled the last of the antitrust indictments handed down by the 1976 grand jury in 1980, when it paid $2.7 million to 12 Federal Reserve banks. Also in 1980 Pittston decided to merge its trucking and warehousing operations under one structure. All its United States Distributing group companies thus became subsidiaries of Brink's.

Pittston's performance continued to decline in the 1980s, resulting in four annual net losses between 1982 and 1987. A continued decline in foreign demand for metallurgical coal pro-

duced a $17.3 million loss in Pittston's coal operations in 1982. By 1987 Pittston was closing and writing off many of the mines it had opened during the expansive years of the early 1970s. In an attempt to recover these losses, Pittston devoted more resources to developing its low-sulfur coal sales, establishing the Pyxis Resources Company to market this product in 1986. The world oil glut of the early 1980s decreased Pittston Petroleum's profits by 48 percent in 1981. Two years later Pittston decided to get out of the oil business and sold Pittston Petroleum to Ultramar American Limited for $100 million.

Of Pittston's three divisions only Brink's managed to sustain expansion in the 1980s. After several years of declining profitability, Brink's sold off its warehousing interests in 1984 and diversified into home-security services. Pittston established a Brink's Home Security subsidiary and began test marketing home-alarm and medical-monitoring systems. Through gradual expansion into new regional markets, Brink's Home Security became a successful venture and a national leader in this industry.

In 1982 Pittston undertook its first major diversification in 25 years with the acquisition of Burlington Northern Air Freight for $177 million. Pittston entered the air-freight business during a highly competitive period, hoping to carve out a place for itself in the overnight-express market. It invested heavily in building a hub for Burlington in Fort Wayne, Indiana, and then renamed the company Burlington Air Express to emphasize its overnight services. Despite these efforts Burlington's initial performance was disappointing, posting a $19 million loss in 1987. Nevertheless, Pittston, led by chairman, president, and chief executive officer Paul W. Douglas beginning in 1984, remained committed to developing its air-freight business. In 1987 it bought WTC Airlines, Inc., a group of companies specializing in air freight for the fashion industry, to expand Burlington's capacity and business. Soon thereafter Burlington began to turn around, experiencing net gains in 1988 and 1989 and accounting for 51 percent of Pittston's total revenues.

By the end of 1988 Pittston appeared to be on the road to recovery. It posted a $48.6 million gain, as compared to a $133 million net loss a year earlier. A prolonged labor dispute with the UMW, however, brought more hard times. In 1988 the Bituminous Coal Operators' Association (BCOA), an industry trade group, had negotiated a new contract with the UMW in which the UMW promised to continue production in the coal industry without a strike. But Douglas, Pittston's chairman, decided to drop out of the BCOA and refused to offer the BCOA contract to Pittston employees. (Pittston dropped out of the BCOA because the BCOA represented domestic steam coal producers, and Pittston was primarily in the export metallurgical coal market. Owing to low-cost competition from South Africa, South America, and Australia, Pittston's exports were facing severe pricing and volume pressures, while domestic steam markets were stable.) Instead, Pittston sought reductions in its miners' health benefits and tighter control over their work schedules in exchange for job security. Angry miners walked out on April 5, 1989, and sympathy strikes by other UMW members quickly followed. By July 1989 30,000 miners were participating in wildcat strikes across the nation in support of 1,800 Pittston workers. The strike, marked by hostility on both sides, continued through the end of 1989 and cost Pittston's coal division $27 million that year. Pittston and the UMW finally reached a settlement on January 1, 1990, with both sides making concessions. Workers won back their health benefits, while the company got its desired changes in work rules. Pittston miners ratified the contract the next month, ending one of the most costly and violent strikes in UMW history.

Despite the losses incurred during the strike, Pittston emerged in a stable position. Its Brink's subsidiary, buoyed by the strong performance of its home-security operations, had been operating with consistent profitability. While Burlington Air Express's profits had yet to match expectations in 1990, its air-freight business continued to climb as an important part of Pittston's overall revenues. The company's coal division remained a question. Its performance depended on its ability to reduce the ill will in its labor relations and on the world's volatile energy markets.

Growth during the 1990s

In 1993 Pittston began using a separate class of common stock known as Tracking stock (or targeted or letter stock), which "tracked" the performance of the company's individual businesses. Pittston Common Stock was split into two parts: Pittston Services Group Common Stock and Pittston Minerals Group Common Stock. At the same time, for each share of Pittston stock, shareholders also received a tax-free distribution of one-fifth of a Pittston Minerals Group. By the end of 1993, as a result of the conversion to Tracking stock, the market value of the Pittston Company's common stocks had more than doubled.

The company further divided its services stock (which held Brink's, Brink's Home Security, and Burlington Air Express) in 1995 by separating the Services Group into two new common stocks—the Pittston Brink's Group and the Pittston Burlington Group. In the transition Pittston Services Group shares became Pittston Brink's Group Common Stock, and one-half share of Pittston Burlington Group Common Stock was distributed tax-free for every share owned of Pittston Services stock. Many investors were attracted to tracking stocks because they were able to invest in one type of stock, such as Pittston Burlington Group, without worrying about a downturn in another portion of the Pittston business, such as the Pittston Minerals Group.

Profits for Burlington Air Express improved during the years 1993–1997 thanks to an overall upturn in the economy, to rapid growth in the worldwide air-freight markets, and to traditional domestic commercial airlines shrinking their heavy freight capacity. The importance of international freight was emphasized in 1997, when two-thirds of Burlington's revenue came from shipments either traveling to or arriving from other countries.

The 1990s were also good years for Brink's, Incorporated. When it increased its profits in 1996, it marked its 13th consecutive year of increasing profitability. Brink's also continued its worldwide expansion in the 1990s, and by 1996 it had operations in more than 50 countries. That year Brink's Home Security had its ninth year in a row of record profits. With a customer base of 447,000, the home security segment generated operating profits in 1996 of $44.9 million, 14 percent higher than in 1995.

Profits for the Pittston Minerals Group, however, continued to be sluggish in the 1990s. In 1996 profits were down to $15 million compared with $16 million the year before. Though its gold operations in Australia set records with more than 90,000 ounces produced in 1996, and the Silver Swan nickel mines showed all the signs of being a promising venture for the company, the huge costs associated with idle mining properties, as well as low coal prices, hampered the Minerals Group bottom line.

In September 1996 Pittston moved its headquarters from Stamford, Connecticut, to Glen Allen, Virginia. With this move the company hoped to be better able to lure top executives, an important factor in maintaining its growth into the 21st century.

Principal Subsidiaries

Pittston Coal Group, Inc.; Brink's, Incorporated; Brink's Home Security, Inc.; Burlington Air Express, Inc.

Further Reading

Dinnen, S.P., "Burlington Air Express Buys Assets of Roadway Global," *Knight-Ridder/Tribune Business News,* November 20, 1995, p. 11200113.
Mitchell, Russell, and Hazel Bradford, "Paul Douglas Has His Guard Up at Pittston," *Business Week,* June 27, 1988.
Page, Paul, "Burlington Air Profit Up, More Gains Seen in 1994," *Knight-Ridder/Tribune Business News,* May 1, 1994, p. 05010286.
"Pittston: Counting on 'Clean' Coal to Reverse the Tumble in Profits," *Business Week,* September 8, 1980.
Routh, Joseph P., *The Pittston Company: A Bright Future in Energy!* New York: The Newcomen Society in North America, 1956.
Scott, Gray, "Burlington Air Express Challenges FedEx with New Flights," *Knight-Ridder/Tribune Business News,* May 27, 1997, p. 527B0965.
Slack, Charles, "Pittston, a Fortune 500 Firm, Now Calls Richmond, Va., Home," *Knight-Ridder/Tribune Business News,* February 11, 1997, p. 211B0981.

—Timothy J. Shannon
updated by Terry Bain

Proffitt's, Inc.

115 North Calderwood
P.O. Box 9388
Alcoa, Tennessee 37701
U.S.A.
(423) 983-7000
Fax: (423) 982-0690
Web site: http://www.proffitts.com

Public Company
Incorporated: 1919
Employees: 17,000 full-time
Sales: $1.89 billion (1997)
Stock Exchanges: NASDAQ
SICs: 5311 Department Stores

Under the dynamic leadership of R. Brad Martin, Proffitt's, Inc. grew from five stores in eastern Tennessee in 1984 to a 175-store chain in 24 states in early 1997, with annual revenues of nearly $2 billion. Proffitt's primarily offered moderate- to better-brand-name fashion apparel, accessories, cosmetics, and decorative home furnishings. Most of its stores were in shopping malls in the Southeast and Midwest. Each of its five divisions had its own merchandising, marketing, and store-operations team.

Under the Proffitt Family, 1919–1984

Proffitt's was founded in 1919 by David W. Proffitt. It was a department store in Maryville, Tennessee (near Knoxville) selling everything from clothing and bedding to furniture and farm implements. Evidently no place for sophisticates, it attracted customers to anniversary sales during the 1920s and 1930s by hurling live poultry from its second floor windows. Another Proffitt's was later opened in Athens, Tennessee. D.W.'s son Harwell took charge of Proffitt's in 1958. He closed the Maryville store in 1962, moving to a strip shopping center his family had developed a mile away in suburban Alcoa. "My father thought that was awful," he told a (Norfolk) *Virginian-*

Pilot reporter in 1993. "Then, after we doubled our sales, he thought it was just great."

Proffitt's opened a store in Knoxville's first mall in 1972 and a store in Oak Ridge two years later. In 1984, when a fifth store opened in another Knoxville mall, D.W.'s heirs, including another son and daughter, began looking for a buyer who would keep the family on as managers. They found their man in Brad Martin, who, at the age of 21, became in 1972 the youngest state legislator in Tennessee history. While serving in the state assembly for ten years he earned two degrees, pieced together deals to build shopping centers in three states, and became a venture capitalist. Martin and his partners bought Proffitt's in October 1984 for $14 million. At this time the company had annual sales of about $40 million.

First Expansion Moves, 1987–1993

After Martin pulled out of a planned race for governor in 1986, he began to take a more active role in his investment. He succeeded Harwell Proffitt as chairman of the company in 1987 and Harwell's son, Fred, as chief executive officer in 1989. Proffitt's went public in 1987, offering 28 percent of its common stock at $8 a share. The company had record net sales of $43.5 million and net income of $1.4 million in fiscal 1987 (the year ended January 31, 1987) but also had a long-term debt of $18.4 million.

The $8 million or so raised by public subscription enabled Proffitt's to buy the Loveman's, Inc. five-unit chain, based in nearby Chattanooga, in 1988 for $9.3 million in cash and notes. Proffitt's thereby doubled in size overnight but also assumed Loveman's considerable debt, weakening earnings in 1989 and 1990. During 1990 Proffitt's also opened stores in Chattanooga and Asheville, North Carolina, but closed an unprofitable store in Chattanooga.

By selling more stock at $12 a share in 1992, Martin raised an added $29 million. He then bought eight stores from Hess Department Stores Inc.—seven in eastern Tennessee and the eighth in Bristol, Virginia. In April 1993 Proffitt's bought eight more stores from Hess—five in the Hampton Roads area of Virginia, two in Kentucky, and one in Georgia—for $7.4 million, selling more stock to finance the purchase and to pay for store renovations. Two months later Proffitt's bought two more Hess stores in Richmond, Virginia, for about $1.6 million.

This acquisition proved to be one of Martin's few mistakes because Hess's unprofitable stores cut into company income. Revenues rose from $128 million in fiscal 1993 to $201 million in fiscal 1994, but net income dropped from $6.7 million to $5.7 million. In December 1996 Dillard Department Stores agreed to buy the Hampton Roads and Richmond stores for an undisclosed sum, and Proffitt's took a $2 million aftertax charge on the sale.

McRae's Acquisition, 1994

Martin's next move was bolder. In March 1994 he purchased McRae's, Inc., a retailer about twice Proffitt's size, for $176 million in cash and $32 million in notes. Founded in 1902 by Samuel P. McRae in Jackson, Mississippi as a dry goods store, McRae's was a privately held chain with 28 stores (compared with Proffitt's 25) in Mississippi, Alabama, Louisiana, and Florida with $419 million in sales in 1993. It was strong in home furnishings, men's apparel, and cosmetics. Thirteen of its 14 Alabama stores had been purchased from Pizitz, Inc. in 1987. In acquiring McRae's, Proffitt's assumed about $109 million in long-term debt and other financing and also paid $18 million to purchase four regional mall stores owned by McRae family partnerships. The McRae's stores retained their name and operated as a subsidiary.

Despite the high price Proffitt's paid, investor reaction was favorable. McRae's was regarded as one of the most successful family-owned businesses in the United States, its sales having grown from only $1 million in 1955 to $10 million in 1970. Just months before the sale, Richard McRae, Jr., president and chief executive officer, told *Daily News Record,* "Our debt-to-equity ratio is the lowest it's been since the early 1970s, yet all of our growth has been from internal financing. We are sound. No one has ever lost a dollar by selling McRae's. . . . In fact, we have a higher Dun & Bradstreet rating than any of our competitors."

Younkers Acquisition, 1996

With the acquisition of McRae's, Proffitt's revenues swelled to $617 million in fiscal 1995, and its net income grew to $16.1 million. In April 1995 Proffitt's acquired a majority interest in Parks-Belk Co., owner and operator of four Tennessee department stores. But this transaction paled in relation to Proffitt's

purchase, in February 1996, of Younkers, Inc., a midwest 53-store chain with annual sales slightly larger than Proffitt's own.

Based in Des Moines, Iowa, Younkers had a history even longer than Proffitt's or McRae's, dating back to 1856. Acquired by Equitable of Iowa in 1979, it became an independent company again in 1992 but soon found itself the object of a takeover bid by Carson, Pirie Scott & Co. Younkers' management turned down Carson's offer of about $163 million for the company but succumbed to Proffitt's bid of $216 million. Like McRae's, Younkers continued to operate under its own name as both a division and a subsidiary of Proffitt's. Counting Younkers, Proffitt's revenues for fiscal 1996 surpassed $1.3 billion. Younkers was described by Martin as a "fashion-driven" business. Proffitt's converted its shoe departments from leased to inhouse, and Martin said there were opportunities for the chain to grow in cosmetics and accessories.

Parisian Acquisition, 1996

Hardly had Martin completed the Younkers acquisition when he purchased Parisian, Inc., a 38-store chain in the Southeast and Midwest with annual sales of $675 million, for $110 million in cash, $100 million in stock, and assumption of $243 million in debt. Well regarded for quality and customer service, Parisian began as a Birmingham, Alabama fabric store in 1887. It was acquired by the Hess and Hollner families in 1920. Until 1963 Parisian was a single store, but over the next 14 years it built a network of a half-dozen stores, all in Alabama.

Parisian sold stock to the public for the first time in 1983. It was acquired in a leveraged buyout by Australia-based Hooker Corp. in 1988, but after Hooker filed for bankruptcy the following year, Birmingham's Hess and Abroms families bought it back, with investment from Lehman Merchant Bank Partners. The new owners opened stores in Atlanta, Indianapolis, Cincinnati, suburban Detroit, Nashville, and Orlando. Because of the large debts inherited from Hooker and disappointing 1994 results, Standard & Poor's placed $125 million in notes issued by the company on its CreditWatch. The company lost $5.5 million in 1994 but returned to profitability the next year, earning $8.8 million.

Like Younkers and McRae's, Parisian became a division and subsidiary of Proffitt's, but its corporate offices were moved to Jackson. Martin indicated that Parisian would be the company's upscale division and that home furnishings might be added to what had been almost purely an apparel chain. Interviewed by *WWD* in 1997, he said, "We see it as the premier specialty store, with many resources that aren't in traditional department stores." Parisian President and Chief Executive Officer Donald Hess remained president and joined Proffitt's board of directors.

Herberger's Acquisition in 1996–1997

Proffitt's topped off 1996 by agreeing, in November, to acquire G.R. Herberger's for $153 million. Based in St. Cloud, Minnesota, Herberger's was a chain of 40 department stores in ten midwest and western states that became Proffitt's fifth division. Strong in women's, children's, and moderately priced men's apparel, Herberger's was scheduled to develop lines in shoes and cosmetics. Martin indicated that it would focus on branded businesses, adding name brands such as Nautica, Ralph Lauren, and Tommy Hilfiger.

Founded in 1927, the chain was sold by the Herberger family in 1972, a year in which it consisted of 11 department stores and six fabric stores with $17 million in sales. In subsequent years it made a transition from downtown locations to anchor tenant in regional malls. In 1993, when the company had sales of $265 million and income of $5.5 million, it was about 55 percent owned by an employee stock option plan. About 450 employees, including officers and directors, owned the rest of the stock. Herberger's had revenues of $327 million in 1995. The acquisition was ratified as Proffitt's ended its 1997 fiscal year in early February 1997.

Status in 1997 and Future Plans

Because of its acquisitions Proffitt's in fiscal 1996 more than doubled its revenues. The company lost $6.4 million after special charges of $31.4 million, including merger, restructuring, and integration costs of $20.8 million. During fiscal 1997 Proffitt's had net income of $37.4 million on sales of $1.89 billion. Its long-term debt was $510.8 million in November 1996.

As fiscal 1997 ended on February 3 of the calendar year, Proffitt's had 19 stores in its Proffitt's division (12 in Tennessee), 29 in the McRae's division (14 in Alabama and 12 in Mississippi), 48 in the Younkers division (18 in Iowa and 17 in Wisconsin), 40 in the Parisian division (15 in Alabama), and 39 in the Herberger's division (14 in Minnesota). A Proffitt's Merchandising Group had recently been formed to coordinate merchandising planning and execution, as well as visual, marketing, and advertising activities between the merchandising divisions. Certain departments in Proffitt's stores were being leased to independent companies and included fine jewelry, beauty salon, and maternity departments. During fiscal 1997 women's apparel was the leading sales category in all five Proffitt's divisions. Men's apparel ranked second in all but the Proffitt's division, where it trailed cosmetics. The other categories, in order of overall sales, were home furnishings, cosmetics, children's apparel, accessories, shoes, and lingerie.

The distribution facility serving the Proffitt's division was located in the metropolitan Knoxville area. McRae's distribution center was in Jackson, Parisian's was in Birmingham, and Herberger's was in St. Cloud. Younkers was being served by two facilities: Ankeny, Iowa, for its southern stores and Green Bay, Wisconsin, for its northern stores.

Interviewed for *Chain Store Age* in 1996, Martin indicated that he had his mind on further growth. "We will look for acquisitions," he said. "Between 1997 and 1999 we will add 15 to 20 stores, with some new-unit construction and the acquisi-

tion of some buildings that fit better in our corporate family than in another corporate family." In a 1997 *DNR* interview Martin said the major factor in considering an acquisition target was "great real estate." He projected 16 to 24 company new stores by 2000, with an increase in private-brand sales from about six to 12 percent of the total by 2000. These brands would include RBM, a men's furnishings line bearing the owner's initials.

Principal Subsidiaries

G.R. Herberger's, Inc.; McRae's, Inc.; McRae's of Alabama, Inc.; McRae's Stores Partnership, G.P.; Parisian, Inc.; Proffitt's Credit Corporation; Younkers Credit Corporation.

Principal Divisions

Herberger's; McRae's; Parisian; Proffitt's; Proffitt's Merchandising Group; Younkers.

Further Reading

"Accord Is Signed To Acquire Herberger's for $153 Million," *Wall Street Journal,* November 11, 1996, p. B4.

Barr, Elizabeth, "Proffitt's Signs Agreement To Buy Loveman's," *Daily News Record,* March 10, 1988, p. 11.

Diel, Stan, "Chain Buys Parisian," *Birmingham News,* July 9, 1996, pp. 1A–2A.

Dinsmore, Christopher, "Brad Martin: Pushing Proffitt's to the Max," *Virginian-Pilot,* June 13, 1993, Bus. Sec.

Hazel, Debra, "Man with a Mission," *Chain Store Age,* August 1996, pp. 41–43.

Hierlmaier, Christine, "Herberger's Legacy Lives, Thanks to CEO," *St. Cloud Times,* January 30, 1997, p. C6 and continuation.

Lawson, Skippy, "Keeping It Friendly," *Women's Wear Daily,* March 26, 1991, pp. 6–7.

Lee, Georgia, "Dillard's To Acquire 7 Proffitt's," *WWD,* December 16, 1996, pp. 2–3.

——, "Proffitt's Power Play," *WWD,* February 3, 1997, pp. 8–9.

Lloyd, Brenda, "McRae's Plans To Acquire Pizitz," *Daily News Record,* December 11, 1986, p. 2.

Palmieri, Jean E., "Men's Wear a Bigger Part of McRae's Overall Sales," *DNR,* September 15, 1993, p. 3.

——, "Proffitt's Takes Unorthodox Road to Bigger Profits," *DNR,* February 17, 1997, pp. 24, 26, 48–50.

"Proffitt's To Acquire 8 Units in Tenn., Va. from Hess's," *WWD,* October 27, 1992, p. 12.

Strom, Stephanie, "Proffitt's Department Stores To Buy McRae's Retail Chain," *New York Times,* March 4, 1994, p. D4.

Underwood, Jerry, " 'Class Retailer' Built on 'Good Name, Reputation,' " *Birmingham News,* July 9, 1996, pp. 1A–2A.

Wieffering, Eric J., "The Wealthiest Minnesotans," *Corporate Report Minnesota,* August 1994, p. 34 and continuation.

Williams, Roy, "Parisian Looks on Bright Side," *Birmingham News,* January 22, 1995, p. D1.

Zissu, Alexandra, "Proffitt's Sees Payoff on Money Spent," *WWD,* February 19, 1997, p. 30.

—Robert Halasz

Groupe Promodès S.A.

123, rue Jules Guesde
92309 Levallois Perret Cedex
France
(01) 47 15 67 51
Fax: (01) 61 63 88
Web site: http://www.promodes.fr

Public Company
Incorporated: 1957
Employees: 55,012
Sales: Ffr 103.54 billion (1996)
Stock Exchanges: Paris
SICs: 5400 Food Stores; 5411 Grocery Stores

With 11 percent of the French market, Groupe Promodès S.A. ranks among the top three food distributors in its home country. Stores in the Promodès network are grouped into five business segments—hypermarkets, supermarkets, discount supermarkets, convenience stores, and institutional food services—each exploiting a specific market niche. In each segment, stores are either owned outright by Promodès or affiliated with the company through franchised partnerships. Built by a succession of acquisitions, the company's foreign growth has largely fit a pattern of regional, rather than national expansion. In general, the company enters a region—whether through an acquisition or through a partnership—only when it can achieve a dominant presence. In this way, the company promotes not only synergies among its store concepts but also economies of scale in purchasing. And, with 1996 net sales of more than Ffr 103 billion, generated through more than 4,000 stores targeting five distinct marketing segments in 11 countries, Promodès is well on its way to achieving its long-treasured goal of being one of the top three food distributors in Europe.

The bulk of Promodès' activity is directed toward southern European and nearby countries. France—where legislation passed in the 1990s severely restricted new store openings—remained the company's largest revenue source, with Spain and Italy the next largest sources of revenue. The company opened operations in Greece, Portugal, and Turkey, and more recently in Belgium. In late 1996, Promodès all but exited Germany after unsuccessfully competing with that country's own supermarket heavyweights. Unlike competitors such as Carrefour, Promodès has pursued a limited global expansion, preferring to stick close to its European base. However, Promodès has entered partnerships and opened stores in Morocco, Dubai, Taiwan, and Argentina.

Promodès' flagship and chief revenue generator is its chain of Continent (called Continente in Spain and Portugal) hypermarkets. The first of the Promodès concepts to be exported, the Continent format features selling areas of a minimum of 6,000 square meters, ranging to 12,000 square meters or more. While the hypermarket itself sells merchandise apart from food—spanning categories from books and compact discs to bicycles, major appliances, and televisions, to gardening, furniture, and toys—many Continent stores also function as anchors to Promodès-owned shopping malls, in which selling space is rented at a discount price to other merchants complementing Continent sales. The Continent chain also features its own Continent private label for foods and other products. After the divestiture of 36 German hypermarkets to that country's Spar Handels group in 1996, the Continent chain counted more than 160 hypermarkets owned and operated by Promodès and its franchise partners.

While Continent fills the hypermarket niche, Promodès' Champion stores operate within the more traditional supermarket concept. Approaching 550 units, all but approximately 65 of which are franchised, the Champion network operates three basic supermarket formats, depending on location. The smallest format, designed for urban selling areas, is limited to 1,200 square meters, while the mid-sized Champions, which operate in urban peripheries and rural areas, reach 1,800 square meters. These two formats form the bulk of the Champion chain. The third format, introduced in 1995 and dubbed Hyper Champion, features floor space ranging between 2,500 square meters and 3,500 square meters and operates as a bridge between the supermarket and hypermarket concepts. Until the mid-1990s, the Champion chain remained entirely based in France; with the introduction of legislation barring new supermarket construction, Promodès has begun exporting the Champion concept, principally to Greece, Portugal, and Belgium. Champion stores, as well as Continent stores operating within France, are supplied by Promodès' Logidis distribution network.

Company Perspectives:

"On each of Promodès' markets, and in each of its business segments, the mission of its 55,000 employees is to meet customer requirements with professionalism and to offer them quality products at the best possible price."

The third segment in the Promodès Group is its chain of Dia discount supermarkets. Featuring limited assortments, the more than 2,000-store chain ranged from 250 square meters to 650 square meters in selling space and operated primarily within city centers. The chain originated in 1979 in Spain, where it has achieved dominance in that country's discount market. The chain's multitude of food products were displayed warehouse-style on pallettes. Approximately 50 percent of these products were sold under the Dia private label; stores were supplied through a European-wide network of 12 warehouses providing integrated organization, purchasing, and logistics. After more than a decade of operation in the Spanish market, Dia began to enter the French, Italian, Portuguese, and Greek markets.

Rounding out Promodès' retail operations is its convenience store segment. This segment, restructured in the mid-1990s, featured three distinct store concepts. Shopi, with some 800 stores located primarily in rural and suburban locations, featured a sales area ranging from 450 to 600 square meters and locations offering close proximity to its customers. The smaller 8 à Huit stores offered, as their name implies, extended opening hours, as well as a range of services and an 1,800-product assortment, including national and private label brands. The third convenience store concept, the 75-year-old Codec, purchased by Promodès in the early 1990s, specifically targeted high-end consumers with quality products, including fine wines, champagne, exotic fruit, coffee, tea, and other specialty products. At an average size of 500 square meters, Codecs were typically located in urban city centers, suburbs, and resort areas. Promodès supplied its convenience store network with its "Grand Jury" private label products.

The fifth segment of the Promodès group was its institutional food service operations. Promocash, one of the oldest divisions of the company, operated as a cash-and-carry chain and provided nearly 10,000 products, including wines, seafood, fruits and vegetables, and meats to the institutional food service and restaurant industries. The 126 units in the France-based Promocash chain featured selling space of 2,500 to 3,500 square meters. An affiliated chain of nearly 50 Puntocash stores offered similar services in Spain. A third unit, Prodirest, operated 47 product distribution warehouses targeting institutional food services including hospitals, schools, military installations, and other businesses, as well as caterers, cafeterias, and hotel chains.

Building a Supermarket Giant

Promodès was formed in 1957 by combining the food distribution interests of five founding families, with the Halley family assuming the company's leadership. Originally focused on wholesale food distribution, a position reinforced by the creation of the company's Promocash subsidiary in 1965,

Promodès shifted towards the retail food market when Paul-Louis Halley replaced his father as head of the company in 1971. Paul-Louis Halley remained in command of the company in 1997, and the Halley family controlled about 40 percent of the company and 51 percent of the company's voting rights. Members of four other founding families controlled an additional 15 percent of the company's stock.

With two marketing concepts, the Champion supermarkets and the Continent hypermarket, Promodès remained an entirely French-based concern in the 1970s, a time of crushing competition among food retailers in France. The proliferation of supermarkets and hypermarkets neared saturation of the market, and these stores faced the rise of new co-op store chains, including eventual French market leaders Leclerc and Intermarché. In the mid-1970s, faced with the difficulties of expanding within Promodès domestic market, the younger Halley began transforming Promodès into a major international food distributor. The first steps into the foreign market were taken in Spain and Germany with the introduction of the company's Continent hypermarket concept. Rather than going in alone, Promodès established a network of partnerships in each country, achieving economies of scale and greater purchasing power, while drawing on their partner's knowledge of these countries' markets. Wholesale distribution, however, remained the chief revenue generator for the company. Yet, by the end of the decade, the company's hypermarket and supermarket activities had grown to represent nearly 40 percent of Promodès' annual sales.

Within five years, that balance would shift in favor of retail sales as Halley led Promodès on an aggressive expansion program. In Spain, the company established its new Dia network, with the first store opening in Madrid in 1979. The Dia concept of limited assortment discount stores, which adopted a warehouse-style shopping concept, with food displayed simply on palettes, remained largely focused on Spain for the next decade. But Halley had his eye on an even larger market: the United States. In 1979, Promodès made a bid to buy Chattanooga-based Red Food Stores, Inc. for $23 million. By 1980, the acquisition was completed, for a total of $36 million. The Red Food purchase gave Promodès a chain of 23 supermarkets centered primarily in southern Tennessee, but with stores in Georgia and Alabama as well. In order to finance Promodès' expansion, which would invest more than Ffr 2 billion between 1979 and 1984, the company went public in 1979.

Promodès' international expansion came at just the right time. By 1982, the international recession had caught up to the French market, leading to a devaluation of the French franc. Most of the major supermarket chains experienced tighter profit margins as sales volumes slumped across the country. Adding to the gloomy retail climate were a series of price control restrictions, which saw the major independent chains lose still more market share to the rising co-op chains. Promodès' international investments, however, helped buffer the company from the domestic crisis. The domestic recession caused sagging profits among its French holdings, which by then numbered 40 Champion supermarkets and 23 Continent hypermarkets, as well as the company's wholesale operations. But the company's Spanish holdings, which by then included eight Continente hypermarkets, and U.S. holdings were performing well. In 1983, Promodès moved to expand further in the United States, acquiring the 40-store chain of Houchens supermarkets, based in Bowling Green, Kentucky, for $25 million. That acquisition raised the company's total U.S. annual sales volume to $600 million, representing 12 percent of Promodès consolidated 1983 sales of Ffr 19.8 billion. Despite the difficult economic climate, Promodès posted a profit of Ffr 203 million for the year.

Refocused Expansion in the 1990s

While continuing to develop its French and Spanish markets, Promodès began eyeing further expansion in the United States, setting up a wholesale distribution arm in New York to import French food products, signing up with Bloomingdale's to provide gourmet products and Giant Food Stores to provide basic products. But the company's focus remained on expanding within the retail sector, and in particular by importing the superstore concept to the U.S. market. With plans to invest $100 million over three years, Promodès moved into the Chicago market, opening a series of warehouse stores under the Cub Food franchise name. Promodès' Chicago foray would not last long however. Unable to build sufficient market share against established leaders Dominick's and Jewel, the company would exit the Chicago area by the beginning of the 1990s.

Meanwhile, Promodès prepared to launch a fresh expansion program in the European market. In 1987, the company returned to the stock market, selling shares worth Ffr 600 million to help it finance a two-year, Ffr 2 billion investment drive. Plans called for the opening of ten hypermarkets, 100 Dia stores, and four new U.S. warehouse stores. At the same time, the company prepared to enter new markets in Portugal, Italy, and Greece. Next, in 1990, the company went on an acquisition binge, buying up, among others, the Plaza hypermarket chain in Germany, part of the Codec retail group in France, and the 900-store chain of Alf stores in Spain—activity which helped make Promodès the fastest-growing French food distributor. By that year the company was operating nearly 3,000 stores in six European countries and the United States, with consolidated sales of $11.6 billion.

The company still hoped to make its mark in the United States, announcing a new $100 million investment program for the Red Food Store chain. But Promodès' U.S. holdings grew slowly, reaching $650 million by the beginning of the new decade. While other French and European-based supermarketers were attempting to introduce the hypermarket concept to an American consumer base uncomfortable with the idea of buying their food and refrigerators in the same store, Promodès rejected that approach in favor of a more limited 'superstore' approach offering, a 50/50 mix of food and general merchandise. That concept, too, proved a hard sell with American shoppers. While the Red Food stores remained profitable, that chain's sales amounted to only four percent of the parent company's total sales. Promodès, involved in a fresh expansion drive in its European base, found itself unable to achieve its expansion goals in the United States. In 1994, the company sold off its Red Food holdings to Netherlands-based Ahold for $120 million.

In Europe, the company made plans to position itself among the top three European food distributors by the end of the century. The 1993 acquisition of the Ffr 2.6-billion Discol wholesale food chain, a subsidiary of France's Pinault-Printemps retail group, placed Promodès firmly in the lead in France's wholesale food

distribution industry. The company's retail arm was also growing rapidly, particularly with the expansion of the Dia chain into the French, Italian, Greek, and other markets during the first half of the decade. By 1994, the company's Continent chain totaled 170 stores across Europe, while in France, the Champion chain of supermarkets numbered more than 450. Promodès also began eyeing new markets in Turkey and Taiwan.

Despite a new economic crisis in Europe in the first half of the 1990s, Promodès grew rapidly and profitably. In 1994, the company topped Ffr 1 billion in profits for the first time in its history, on net sales of nearly Ffr 95 billion. The following year, the company's net sales topped Ffr 100 billion. The company's German holdings were struggling, however, posting losses of DM 43 million by 1995. The purchase of the Plaza hypermarket chain, which adopted the Continent name, had been made during the euphoria of Germany's reunification. But the costs of the reunification led to a slump in that country's economy. Unable to achieve any significant market share—and thus more favorable purchasing terms—against its larger German competitors, Promodès sold off its German subsidiary's 36 hypermarkets to Spar Handels in September 1996.

The company remained dedicated to its foreign expansion, however, introducing the Continent name to Belgium, as well as to Morocco and Dubai. Within France itself, meanwhile, Halley began hinting at a possible merger between Promodès and another of the country's major retailers, Casino. With consolidated net sales rising to Ffr 103.5 billion in 1996, Promodès remained in position to reach its year 2000 goal as a top-three European food distributor.

Principal Operating Units

Continent and Continente (hypermarkets); Champion (supermarkets); Dia (discount supermarkets); Shopi, 8 à Huit, Cedec (convenience stores); Promocash, Prodirest (institutional food service).

Further Reading

"Accent on Quality at Promodès," *Financial Times,* March 7, 1997, p. 30.

Betts, Paul, "French Retailer Shops Abroad," *Financial Times,* November 10, 1984, p. 5.

Dowdell, Stephen, "Promodès Tries American Approach," *Supermarket News,* January 28, 1991, p. 1.

Fallon, James, "Growth Goals Aired in European Forum," *Supermarket News,* October 21, 1991, p. 49.

Jack, Andrew, "Promodès Considers French Tie-up," *Financial Times,* October 5, 1996, p. 11.

Marguerite, Catherine, "Interview de Paul-Louis Halley," *La Vie Française,* March 4, 1995.

"Promodès—La Marche Forcée," *La Vie Française,* May 21, 1994.

"Promodès Reste Fidèle au Service de Proximité," *Le Monde,* May 16, 1995.

Savin, Virginie, "Promodès—Á la Fête," *La Vie Française,* July 24, 1993.

Silbert, Nathalie, "Le Distributeur Améliore Son Score Malgré la Conjoncture," *La Vie Française,* March 20, 1993.

Weisman, Katherine, "Europe Prime Target for Promodès," *Supermarket News,* May 29, 1995, p. 10.

—M.L. Cohen

Publicis S.A.

133, avenue des Champs-Elysées
75008 Paris
France
1-44-43-37-00
Fax: 1-44-43-75-60
Web site: http://www.publicis.fr

Public Company
Incorporated: 1926
Employees: 7,000+
Sales: FFr21.9 billion
Stock Exchanges: Paris
SICs: 7311 Advertising Agencies

Publicis S.A. is the largest advertising agency in France, the largest advertising network in Europe, the number one agency in North America, and one of the top seven advertising agencies worldwide. Initiated in 1926 by the founder of modern French advertising, Marcel Bleustein-Blanchet, Publicis has developed a network of subsidiary and affiliated agencies in more than 60 countries, with annual billings of more than US$7.5 billion. Present in the United States since the 1950s through its Publicis-Bloom subsidiary, Publicis's major growth beyond Europe has occurred especially in the mid-1990s, with acquisitions of shares in major agencies in Latin America, Asia, and Canada. About 59 percent of the company's revenues are generated in Europe, excluding France; French billings account for 35 percent of the company's revenues, while the United States, which itself represents more than half of the world's advertising revenues, accounts for approximately six percent of Publicis revenues.

Publicis's principal activities—advertising and media buying—are organized under two major divisions. Publicis Communications is the umbrella for the company's advertising activities, both in France and abroad. Publicis Conseil provides the basis for the group's French business, through some 40 agencies in 20 cities, including FCA/B.M.Z., Publicis Direct, Publicis Design, Mundocom, and Loeb et Associés. The company's European activities are guided by Publicis Europe, formerly known as Publicis-FCB Europe, and includes subsidiary agencies and offices in every country in Western and Eastern Europe and Russia. Also grouped under Publicis Communications are Publicis-Bloom, the company's U.S. wing; Publicis Centre Média, and Publicis Consultants. In Latin America, the company is represented through a 51 percent ownership position in Mexico's Paulino Romero y Asociados and a 60 percent share of Brazil's Norton Publicidade, both leading agencies in their respective countries and both acquired in 1996. Publicis's Asian expansion, begun during 1997, includes a 60 percent share of Eureka Advertising, the largest independent advertising agency in Singapore, and a 30 percent interest in Basic Advertising, the second largest advertising agency in the Philippines. In 1996, Publicis also acquired 60 percent of Canada's seventh largest advertising agency, BCP, which has been renamed Publicis-BCP.

Publicis's second major division is its Medias and Media Sales division. Within this group are three main subsidiaries: Medias et Régies Europe; Régie 1; and Métrobus. These subsidiaries provide press media sales and services, financial services, radio airtime buying, and billboard services throughout France and in Europe.

Beyond advertising, Publicis is also engaged in retailing, through its world-renowned Drugstores on the Champs-Elysées and in Matignon, both in Paris (a third Drugstore, on Saint-Germain, also in Paris, was sold in 1996 to Giorgio Armani). The company's data processing subsidiary, S.G.I.P., provides multimedia solutions for the French Minitel system, the Internet, and CD-ROM and diskette-based products. In 1995, Publicis launched Publicis AdNet, an intranet system that allows Publicis advertisers and agencies to communicate in real-time throughout the world.

Publicis's founder, Marcel Bleustein-Blanchet remained active as the company's chairman until his death at the age of 89 in 1996. Since the 1970s, however, the company has been led by Maurice Levy. The Bleustein-Blanchet family continues to hold more than 65 percent of the company's stock, which trades on the Paris Stock Exchange. In 1997, on consolidated revenues of FFr21.9 billion, the company posted net earnings of FFr1.7 billion.

Company Perspectives:

"Our Idea of Advertising: We feel that advertising is primarily all about ideas. Ideas that are meaningful, new, justified, long-lasting, forceful, disturbing, positive, seductive, convincing, funny, touching. Fresh new ideas that shake up old habits. Ideas that help the consumer appreciate the brand and the products, and get to know more about the manufacturers. Ideas that lead to other ideas: that urge one to try the product, compare it, buy it. Ideas that linger for a long while, much like a melody, or a poem. Ideas that are eager, likeable and simple like everyday life. Because we must never forget that advertising was born in the marketplace and all stores carry its message. We have graduated from the University of the Street, our science and our art is knowing the consumers, speaking their language and of course, seducing them. We have a passionate need to convince. But it is not that simple to be simple. There is nothing more precious and fragile than an idea. And for a great idea we are ready to give it our all."

The Father of French Advertising

Marcel Bleustein founded Publicis (a combination of the French word for advertising, 'publicité,' and the sound of the French 'six' to denote the year of the company's formation) in Paris in 1926. Bleustein was then 20 years old. His family had emigrated to France from the Russian-Polish border and built a successful furniture business following the First World War; Bleustein was also related to the Lévitan brothers furniture empire (three of Bleustein's sisters married Lévitans). At the age of 14, Bleustein dropped out of school to work in the family's business, before completing his compulsory military service at age 18. Returning from the army, however, Bleustein decided to leave the furniture business and enter advertising, setting up France's fourth advertising agency.

"My son is leaving me to go and sell hot air," was Bleustein's father's reaction. Indeed, by the 1920s, advertisers had earned the disdain of French consumers, with ads that displayed little regard for the truth. Nevertheless, Bleustein's father gave his blessing, if only so that his son would not reproach him later. With only 40,000 francs in savings, Bleustein set up shop in a small office above a delicatessen on the Rue Montmartre, and set out to change the nature of French advertising. After studying the market, Bleustein drafted two edicts: the product must be entirely visible; and the product must not be tampered with, but shown as is. Bleustein began to search for clients, literally going from door to door.

Finding clients, however, proved difficult, as potential clients shared consumers' distaste for advertising. Bleustein's first break came through his family. His mother, who was active in many charities, prevailed upon a friend, the owner of the Comptoir Cardinet, who reluctantly agreed to allow Bleustein to draft an advertisement. Bleustein chose two products, a silver set and a clock, and asked his illustrator, Aristide Perré to illustrate them exactly as they were and in detail. Within two days after the advertisement appeared, Comptoir Cardinet sold 15 sets of silver and 12 clocks.

Next, Bleustein lined up Brunswick furriers (for whom he created the famous slogan: "the furrier that creates a furor") and brother-in-law Wolf Lévitan and the family's Lévitan furniture stores (slogan: "Lévitan furniture is guaranteed to last," a promise few French furniture manufacturers could make in the postwar years). Publicis's first large advertising budget followed by the end of the decade. The owners of André Shoes, a chain of some 100 shoe stores, were equally wary of the need for advertising, but Bleustein managed to persuade them, and won a 600,000 franc full-service budget—and created another famous French advertising slogan: "Andre, le chausser sachant chausser" ("the shoe store that knows how to shoe you").

Bleustein's agency took off. By the age of 23, he was already a millionaire, and by the beginning of the new decade, he had taken the French advertising industry into a new era. Bleustein had traveled to the United States in 1929, where he discovered radio advertising. Returning to France, Bleustein made an arrangement to advertise Brunswick's furs on Radio Eiffel Tower. Brunswick was skeptical; but the radio ads proved immediately successful. Publicis was also gaining momentum. After winning the André contract and a contract with Sools, the largest hatter in Paris, Bleustein began eyeing the national market. He bought a plane—he already had a pilot's license— and began flying across France to sign up advertising contracts with radio stations in other cities. In exchange for exclusive rights to a station's advertising time, he offered a fixed yearly revenue. Twenty of the country's 29 public and private radio stations signed on, and Publicis soon became one of the largest agencies in the country, signing on such major clients as Max Factor, Procter & Gamble's Monsavon, Renault, and others.

In 1934, the government banned advertising from its public radio stations, leaving Publicis with only 11 private stations. These stations quickly demanded a larger share of Publicis's profits—with Radio Lyon, led by M. Pierre Laval, later the premier of Vichy France, among them. After meeting with Laval, Bleustein decided to buy his own station, rather than bow to the private stations' demands. Publicis paid 3.5 million francs for Radio-L.L., located in a Parisian suburb, changed its name to Radio Cité, in homage to Radio City Music Hall in New York, and promptly created a new sensation. Among Radio Cité's innovations was the institution of regular news broadcasts, in a deal with *L'Intransigeant* newspaper, which supplied the news staff in exchange for 25 percent of Radio Cité. Radio Cité would become a Parisian institution in the years leading up to the war and would be responsible for launching the careers of such noted French stars as Edith Piaf and Yves Montand.

Rebuilding after World War II

The outbreak of the Second World War put an end to Publicis's success. Bleustein flew in the French air force, then returned to Paris after France's defeat. He was soon forced to abandon Publicis and Radio Cité, after the German occupation of France and Vichy's France's promulgation of laws barring Jewish ownership of radio stations and other media outlets.

Bleustein joined the resistance, helping to smuggle British pilots back to London. However, when word came that he was wanted by the Gestapo, Bleustein—using the *nom de guerre* Blanchet—was forced to leave France. He spent three months in prison in Spain, then was allowed to leave for London, where he joined De Gaulle and flew as an assistant pilot on U.S. Air Force reconnaissance and bombing runs.

When Bleustein returned to Paris on the day of that city's liberation, Publicis had been destroyed by the Germans and Radio Cité had been taken over by the new French government, which banned the formation of private French radio stations. Bleustein, who added Blanchet to his surname, was forced to rebuild his business from scratch. In 1946, he won the advertising franchise for the newly created *France-Soir* newspaper, and formed Régie-Presse to operate his media-buying business. Soon after, Bleustein-Blanchet was able to resurrect his agency, as his former clients, also rebuilding their businesses, began to return to Publicis. With advertising banned from radio, Publicis began placing its clients' ads on billboards, buses, subway stations, and in the cinema.

Publicis again rose to the top of the French advertising industry. By the late 1950s, the company was posting yearly billings of more than US$15 million per year. Its clients included 50 top French companies, and the French market for such international clients as Shell, General Motors, Dunlop, Colgate-Palmolive, Nestlé, and Singer Sewing Machines. At the same time, Publicis had helped to organize the French advertising industry trade association, which effectively ensured that companies could only use French agencies for the French ad market. Publicis continued its history of innovation as well. In 1954, the company conducted France's first pubic opinion poll (Bleustein-Blanchet had met George Gallup on a trip to the United States in 1938). In 1957, Publicis made its first international moves, opening an office in New York (primarily to serve the company's French clients) and forming alliances with agencies in other European countries.

Since his youth, Bleustein-Blanchet's dream had been to own a building at the top of the Champs-Elysées. In the 1958 that dream was realized when Publicis bought and moved into the former Astor Hotel (and later General Eisenhower's Paris headquarters) opposite the Arc de Triomphe. In that building, Bleustein-Blanchet introduced another of his American discoveries—the Publicis Drugstore, which quickly became a popular Parisian fixture. The following year, Bleustein-Blanchet, critical of the typical secrecy of French businesses, introduced the concept of institutional advertising, in which a company spoke about its business and manufacturing techniques, rather than its products.

During the 1960s, Publicis established a firm reputation as the most modern of French advertising agencies, particularly with its ad campaign for a pantyhose maker, which was one of the first advertisements to use a symbolic emblem, rather than the product itself, to promote the product. In the late 1960s, Publicis introduced advertising to television. The company also moved into crisis communication, successfully helping French glassmaker Saint-Gobain to defend itself from France's first hostile takeover in 1968.

Starting Again in the 1970s

Publicis's Champs-Elysées headquarters—and all of its records—burned in 1972, and the company was forced to rebuild yet again. Publicis built a new headquarters on the same location; but by then, the company, which had gone public in 1970, was itself evolving. Bleustein-Blanchet named his successor, Maurice Levy, who effectively took over the agency's day-to-day operations, leaving Bleustein-Blanchet as chairman. During the 1970s, Publicis began to expand its international operations, acquiring Intermarco, which had been formed as the in-house advertising arm of Philips Electronics, and Farner, a leading agency for the Swiss and German markets. The combined Intermarco-Farner subsidiary brought Publicis representation into more than fifteen European countries, including, with the acquisition of McCormick Agency, the United Kingdom. Publicis also opened a full-service Intermarco agency in New York. Meanwhile, Publicis was also branching out into the nascent data processing and graphics industry, establishing its S.G.I.P. subsidiary in 1973.

By the 1980s, Publicis had grown to become a worldwide leader in the advertising industry. In 1988, the company grew even stronger, signing an alliance agreement with Chicago-based Foote, Cone & Belding that gave Publicis a 20 percent ownership of FCB and its dominance of the North and Latin American markets. FCB, in turn, received 49 percent of Publicis's European network, which was renamed Publicis-FCB. During the first half of the 1990s, Publicis, through Publicis-FCB, continued to solidify its dominance of the European market, acquiring, among other, the Dutch agency Overad, and moving into the newly opened Eastern European market with agreements with Hungary's Hungexpo, Czechoslovakia's Mertis, and Poland's Estra. From 1988 to 1996, the company shifted its revenues from 69 percent billed in France to more than 65 percent billed beyond the French border.

The international recession of the 1990s helped dampen Publicis's revenue growth. Despite a series of acquisitions, including the Feldman, Calleux et Associés (FCA) network in 1993, Publicis's revenues remained largely flat during the first half of the decade, hovering around FFr20 billion, while net income saw steady declines, from FFr318 million in 1990 to a low of FFr220 million in 1994. Nevertheless, Publicis remained among the healthiest of advertising agencies, with zero long-term and medium-term debt. The agency also scored a major coup when it was awarded the international advertising account for Coca Cola's Diet Coke and Coca Cola Light products. The following year, the agency also won the British Airways account through its alliance with the New Saatchi Agency formed by former Saatchi & Saatchi founder Maurice Saatchi.

The Publicis-FCB alliance ground to a halt in 1995, when FCB changed its name to True North and announced its intention to create its own network of agencies. Publicis demanded to be released from the alliance, and in 1996, the two agencies reached agreement to separate. In 1997, the separation was finalized, with Publicis taking 100 percent ownership of the former Publicis-FCB European network, renamed Publicis Europe. Publicis was also freed to enter True North's Latin American and Asian territories, as well as to consolidate its position in North America. The agency moved quickly, purchasing interests in agencies in Singapore, the Philippines, Brazil, Mexico, and Canada. Marcel Bleustein-Blanchet, the father of French advertising, died in April 1996 at the age of 89.

Principal Divisions

Publicis Communications (Publicis Conseil; Publicis Europe; Publicis Centre Media; Publicis Consultants; Publicis Bloom); Media and Media Sales (Régie 1; Métrobus; Publex; Giraudy; Médiavision; Régie T); Diversified Businesses (S.C.I de Etoile; S.G.I.P.; Publicis Drugstores; GPS).

Further Reading

Bleustein-Blanchet, Marcel, *The Rage to Persuade,* New York: Chelsea House, 1982.

Bozonnet, Jean Jacques, "Publicis Regie Son Conflit avec L'Americain True North," *Le Monde,* February 21, 1997.

Doyere, Josee, and Labe, Yves Marie, "La Mort du Dernier Empereur de la Publicité," *Le Monde,* April 13, 1996.

"France's Marcel Bleustein-Blanchet: The Ad Man Who Built 'Publicis,' " *Printer's Ink,* August 7, 1958, p. 46.

Labe, Yves Marie, "Numero Un Européen, Publicis S'Implante au Mexique et au Bresil," *Le Monde,* August 20, 1996.

Negreanu, Gerard, "Le Point Bas Est Atteint," *La Vie Française,* March 19, 1994.

——, and Savin, Virginie, "Publicis—Maurice Levy," *La Vie Française,* December 4, 1993.

Subramanian, Dilip, "A Eulogy for France's Advertising Patriarch," *Marketing (Canada),* May 6, 1996, p. 5.

—M. L. Cohen

QUAD/GRAPHICS

Quad/Graphics, Inc.

W224 N3322 Duplainville Road
Pewaukee, Wisconsin 53072-4195
U.S.A.
(414) 246-9200
Web site: http://www.qg.com

Private Company
Incorporated: 1971
Employees: 9,500
Sales: $1 billion plus (1996)
SICs: 2752, Commercial Lithographic & Offset Printing;
2754, Commercial Gravure Printing

Quad/Graphics, Inc. is the largest privately owned printing company in the western hemisphere and the fifth largest printer in the United States behind R. R. Donnelly, Quebecor, World Color Press, and Banta Corporation. Among catalog printers, Quad/Graphics ranked second nationally in 1996 and among magazine printers it ranked fourth. With more than 900 customers, Quad/Graphics prints such major U.S. magazines as *Time, Newsweek, U.S. News & World Report, People, Black Enterprise, Journal of the American Medical Association,* and *Popular Science* as well as catalogs for such mail order companies as L. L. Bean and Lands' End. It also prints books, newspaper inserts, newsstand cookbooks, direct mail materials, and fine art posters. In 1996, 46 percent of its work consisted of catalog printing, another 40 percent consisted of publication printing (such as magazines), and 14 percent consisted of other materials.

Besides its printing operations, Quad/Graphics offers a full gamut of press printing services from electronic and conventional imaging services, computer disk file conversion, typesetting and graphic design, copywriting and editing, art direction and artboard preparation, and printing production management. Other prepress services include studio photography, desktop publishing services, film stripping and final preparation, digitized data archiving, platemaking, gravure cylinder preparation, direct digital cylinder engraving, and direct-to-plate imaging.

Through such divisions as Duplainville Transport and Quad/ Direct, Quad/Graphics offers such postprinting services as publication binding, distribution and transportation of finished pieces to newsstands and postal center, and direct mail publication mailing and mailing list services. In 1996 Quad/Graphics maintained 16 production facilities in Wisconsin, New York, and Georgia; 15 sales offices across the United States; and international facilities in the Netherlands, Japan, Singapore, Argentina, and Brazil.

''There Has To Be a Better Way'': 1906–1971

The origins of the Quad/Graphics printing empire stretch back to the arrival of the Quadracci family in the United States from Italy in 1906. Settling in southeastern Wisconsin, the Quadraccis ran a grocery store in Racine until, in 1930, 16-year-old Harry R. Quadracci founded the Standard Printing Company behind the store, first as a hobby and then, as the Great Depression worsened, as a source of extra income for the family. In 1934, Quadracci sold his press and print shop assets to another printer, William A. Krueger, with whom he founded W. A. Krueger Co. of Milwaukee, Wisconsin. Over the years the small two-man shop became one of the largest publicly held regional printing companies in the United States (by the mid-1990s it was part of the printing firm Ringier America, which was itself purchased by World Color Press in 1996).

Quadracci's son Larry cut his entrepreneurial teeth early on by starting ''Quad Photo,'' a photography service for his family's church, at age 14, and later, while in college, a canteen. After graduating from Columbia Law School, he joined the Krueger firm as a lawyer in 1962 and then worked his way up to vice-president and general manager by 1965. In 1970, following a bitter three-month strike, Krueger's management acceded to the demands of its unionized work force, which left Larry Quadracci, who had been the company's lead negotiator with the workers, disenchanted with the company's adversarial relationship with its employees. Before the year was out Krueger and Quadracci had parted company.

After Quadracci's plans to buy an existing company collapsed, in 1971 he formed a limited partnership tax shelter

Company Perspectives:

"Ink is in our veins; ink is in our blood. It is our heritage, our mission and our business to be the very best at putting ink on paper. By making intelligent use of intelligent systems, we offer our best to our clients, whether we are printing on a press or putting virtual ink on the web of cyberspace. . . . Where do we go from here? We'll tell you when we get there."

named Press Associates and joined with 11 other entrepreneurs to raise $250,000, which he used to obtain a $650,000 loan to buy a Baker-Perkins color printing press. He then leased the machine back to his newly formed company, which he christened Quad/Graphics, and took out a $35,000 second mortgage on his home, tapped the savings of some of his associates, and sold a 30 percent stake in his new company to raise more capital. With the new capital he bought an abandoned millwork factory in rural Pewaukee, Wisconsin, which became Quad/Graphics' first plant and headquarters.

The Lean Years: 1971–1979

In the midst of a national recession, Quadracci convinced key production personnel from Krueger to join him at Quad/Graphics, and in 1972 he brought his father aboard as chairman of the board. Although he had originally planned to print newspaper inserts, Quadracci discovered to his chagrin that he had overestimated the insert market and he turned to magazine and catalog work instead. He managed to pay back his investors' initial outlay within two years, but Quad/Graphics struggled to stay afloat throughout the 1970s. Quadracci himself embarked on coast-to-coast sales trips to drum up business and, by accepting work that other printers would not do, Quad/Graphics gradually built up a network of customers, including *Investor* magazine of Wisconsin (its first customer) and similar small four-color magazines like *Fishing Facts* as well as catalogs/inserts for Mail Inc. Desperate for work to keep the company afloat, Quadracci also began printing adult men's magazines, which grew to account for nearly a third of Quad/Graphics' business in the early 1970s. Quadracci defended the practice by adopting the "airport rule," in which any magazine that was displayed in airport newsstands was deemed mainstream enough to justify Quad/Graphics' presstime. (By 1997 the company had ceased printing *Penthouse* and other men's titles but still counted *Playboy* and a small number of more explicit magazines among its customers.)

The years 1972 through 1976 were particularly difficult for Quad/Graphics. Surviving such catastrophes as press breakdowns and expensive press rebuilds, however, by 1973 sales had climbed to $2.8 million and the work force had grown to 25. Quadracci founded Duplainville Transport (named after the street on which the company plant was located) in 1973 to provide distribution services and in the same year began adding new presses to his plant. In 1974 he added a saddle stitcher to enhance his production capabilities; hired his first customer service rep; and adopted a three-day, 12-hour-shift work week

so his presses could run around the clock, seven days a week. In 1974 he implemented an employee stock ownership plan (ESOP), which over the years began to buy back the warrants his early incarnation, Press Associates, had issued to the company's original investors. (By 1997, Quad/Graphics' ESOP was the second largest shareholder of company stock after Quadracci himself.)

Despite the company's continuing struggle to keep the presses running, Quadracci optimistically began investing in new plants and equipment to the tune of seven times his annual cash flow. In 1975, he opened sales offices in New York and Los Angeles, began performing his own platemaking in 1976, and raised employment to more than 100 the same year. The year 1976 was also the first in which Quadracci began requiring his delivery fleet to locate cargo to haul during their empty return trips. When his drivers asked him what kinds of loads they should haul, Quadracci replied, "How should I know?" The incident exemplified a key Quadracci management principle that came to be known as "Management by Walking Away" and established Quadracci's budding reputation as a guru of modern management techniques. Quadracci was soon espousing such principles as "Respondepity" (the ability to respond to clients' needs before they are even aware of them), "Active risk taking" (in which mistakes are not only tolerated but celebrated because they lead to innovation), and "Hunchmanship" (in which rigid corporate planning is replaced by bold, on-the-fly decision making).

With no major customers to stake its future on, however, Quad/Graphics' prospects were still in doubt. In 1976, Quadracci fired his sales staff and flew to New York to market personally Quad/Graphics' services to the big U.S. magazine publishers. He brought potential customers back to Pewaukee to show off his state-of-the-art machinery and used smoke-and-mirrors tactics to convince visitors that his often idle plant was running at full capacity. Quadracci's hands-on approach worked, and in 1977 *Newsweek* agreed to give Quad/Graphics a try when its regular printer was unable to complete a press run. Quadracci made sure the magazine was printed perfectly, and by October 1978 Quad/Graphics was also binding a portion of each week's *Newsweek* as it came off the presses. By giving Quad/Graphics the opportunity to demonstrate that it was a quality *weekly* printer and by supplying it with a steady stream of work *Newsweek* seemed to secure Quad/Graphics' future. "From there on," the company's vice-president of finishing operations later said, "I felt we were going to make it." For the next decade Quad/Graphics' annual growth rate would climb as high as 40 percent—versus the industry's average growth rate of ten percent—and year after year Quad/Graphics was named *Newsweek's* "Printer of the Year."

Quadracci celebrated the company's success by buying its fifth printing press in 1978 and in 1979 established the Quad/Tech division to manufacture computer-based press and bindery controls for the printing industry. Enterprise Graphics (later renamed Quad/Imaging) was also established to provide prepress services. With *Newsweek* now on board, Quad/Graphics' reputation spread quickly through the close community of the U.S. publishing industry.

"Theory Q": 1980–1989

Quadracci's disenchantment with the hostility between labor and management during his years at W. A. Krueger as well as his reliance on his employees' team work and inventiveness during Quad/Graphics' early years produced an egalitarian, nonhierarchical corporate culture that came to be known as "Theory Q." Newly hired employees were often only high school graduates but though they started at low hourly rates ($7.50 in 1996) they could advance more quickly than in union print shops. Quadracci fostered a family atmosphere in which there were no time clocks, any employee could E-mail Quadracci at any time and get an answer within a day, and Quadracci himself was visible to most workers through a glass-enclosed office situated next to the press floor in the heart of the plant. The company's "family feeling" also had a literal side: by 1996, 58 percent of Quad/Graphic employees could claim some familial relation to another employee.

A key component of Quadracci's business philosophy was that work should be fun. Company holiday parties revolved around song-and-dance revues featuring "The World Famous Singing Vice-Presidents" and such themes as "The H.M.S. Printafore." Quadracci had tons of sand shipped in for a Christmas party with a beach theme, he was known to appear at corporate parties riding an elephant or dressed as a drum major or a clown, and the company maintained a 40-acre nature preserve replete with baseball diamonds, volleyball and basketball courts, and an archery range.

Quad/Graphics' Pewaukee facility came to be known as "Quad/World," a self-contained corporate community in which by the 1990s employees worked a three-day, 36-hour work week, received free health care and on-site child care, and owned shares in the company's current profits and future growth. The Quad/Education division (formed in 1983) offered employees technical, leadership, and personal development classes; Quad/Cuisine operated cafeterias and sold take-home food; Quad/Med Clinic (opened in 1991) and Quad/Care provided the company's in-house medical services and child care centers, respectively; Quad/Temps offered a part-time, on-call employee pool; Quad/Travel (formed in 1990) booked employees' business and personal trips; and Quad/Pop provided employees and visitors with a bottomless supply of free popcorn.

Beneath the carnival touches, however, lay a thorough commitment to maintaining Quad/Graphics' leadership in the printing industry. By keeping his firm private and building it through bank credit rather than public stock offerings, Quadracci kept Quad/Graphics free from the threat of acquisition, enabling him to focus corporate capital on upgrading plant and equipment—a necessity in an industry in which new technology became obsolete almost overnight. Quadracci saw that four-color offset lithography, for example, was replacing the traditional one- or two-color letterpress (which used cast metal plates to apply ink directly to the paper), offering substantial improvements in printing speed and quality. As Quadracci later explained, "We thought we had as much chance as the established companies to get business if we had the latest technology. We didn't have old presses to phase out and write off." By 1985, Quad/Graphics had grown big enough and established a strong enough credit rating to be able to turn to the private placement market for

capital. By selling subordinated notes to General Electric's Pension Trust it now had a semipermanent source for financing equipment purchases and building expansions. As a result, the average age of its presses was only five to six years, compared to the ten-year average for the printing industry as a whole.

Moreover, by eschewing such standard corporate practices as establishing budgets and long-term planning, Quadracci kept Quad/Graphics nimble, able to shift resources quickly to exploit new printing industry trends. "No planning allowed" was Quadracci's rule: "If you start planning, you blind yourself to opportunity." Quadracci's prescient understanding of the growing importance of the computer in the printing industry convinced him that the traditional budgeting and forecasting process would soon be rendered obsolete by the up-to-the-minute status reports made possible by computer technology.

In the early 1980s, Quad/Graphics held its first CAMP/Quad (for Catalog And Magazine Production) to educate clients in the latest printing technologies, and by the mid-1990s CAMP/Quad had trained more than 3,000 industry professionals. In 1982, Quadracci broke ground on a new plant in Sussex, Wisconsin, to augment the now crowded Pewaukee plant and founded Quad/Graphics' ink manufacturing division (Chemical Research/Technology) and Quad/Tech, its division for designilng and manufacturing microprocessor-based press and bindery controls for the printing industry. In 1983 *American Printer* magazine named Quad/Graphics to its Top 100-Plus Printers list, and in 1984 the company was named as one of the "100 Best Companies To Work for in America" in a popular book of the same name. In 1985 Quad/Graphics opened a new plant in Saratoga Springs, New York, and a year later—with sales topping $154 million—it unveiled its first gravure press in its Lomira, Wisconsin plant (purchased in 1984) and brought its first multimailer machine on line.

When it began printing *People* magazine in 1987, Quad/Graphics had become the world's largest printer of newsweekly magazines, with more than 3,100 employees and sales of $226 million. In 1988, it launched Quad/Tech Europe and broke ground on its High Tech Centre in Sussex. In 1989 Quadracci acquired W. R. Bean & Son of Thomaston, Georgia, established CB Graphics (now Quad/Sheetfed), and began offering customers in-house mailing list management services initially under the name of Quad/List Management, then later Quad/Data Services. Despite a national recession, layoffs, and the threat of bankruptcy if it failed to find a buyer for its lagging Quad/Marketing subsidiary (it eventually did), by the late 1980s company sales were surpassing $375 million and employment had topped the 4,500 mark. Within a year *Lithoweek* magazine was posing the rhetorical question, "Quad/Graphics: The Best Printer in the World or What?"

Growth in the 1990s

Quadracci's pursuit of business growth and cutting-edge printing technology continued in the 1990s. In 1990, Quad/Graphics established its Quad/Photo division, which began providing digital photography services in 1994; in the early 1990s the company became one of the first U.S. printers to use Heidelberg Harris press technology; and in 1993 it became the first North American printer to acquire a high-speed Ferag drum stitcher. By 1991, Quad/Graphics had become the ninth largest printer in the United States and was operating 43 web offset presses, five gravure presses, 38 saddle stitchers, and 11 perfect binders. By 1996 Quad/Graphics was operating no fewer than 70 presses in eight locations.

The company also continued to expand geographically. In 1993 it broke ground for its Automated Storage and Retrieval System facility in Sussex; began construction of a new plant in The Rock, Georgia, in 1994; and the same year purchased a vacant manufacturing facility in West Allis, Wisconsin, to expand further its production capacity. In 1995 it broke ground on another new plant in Martinsburg, West Virginia (opened in 1997); purchased a vacated printing plant in New Berlin, Wisconsin; and broke ground for an employee housing project near its Lomira plant. In 1996 it also announced its first joint venture with an international printer by buying a substantial portion of Anselmo L. Morvillo S.A. of Argentina, reflecting Quadracci's strategy to build a global network of locally managed printing firms that were jointly owned by Quad/Graphics and its local partners. In 1997 it followed this with an agreement to print catalogs through Brazilian printer Plural Editora e Grafica and pursued ventures with printing firms in China and India. In early 1997 Quadracci announced the ninth expansion project for its Sussex, Wisconsin, headquarters facility and a $50 million expansion for its Saratoga Springs, New York, plant so that Time Inc. could print more of its weekly magazines with Quad/Graphics.

By 1993 Quad/Graphics was printing more than 400 publications and catalogs (100 million magazines a month) and sales had spiraled to more than $703 million, representing ten straight years of double-digit growth. By this time, all Quad/Graphics management as well as entry-level pressmen were sporting identical blue shirts with Quad/Graphics logos on their arms in an effort to instill a team atomosphere. In May 1994, the company established a company record when it stitched more than 912,000 copies of *Newsweek* in a single day. In 1996 it complemented its magazine/catalog niche by adding hardcover book binding to its capabilities and in November of that year it began printing its first multicolor hardcover and softcover books.

Quadracci's "stay nimble" management strategy, meanwhile, was permitting the company to ride the revolutionary changes afoot in the application of computerized and digital technologies to the printing process. By the early 1990s off-the-shelf software packages were enabling anyone with a computer to do many of the prepress functions traditionally performed by specialized typesetting and printing firms. By 1997, for exam-

ple, more than half the companies in the U.S. printing industry either owned or used computerized prepress, color scanner, and image-setting technology, and the majority of U.S. printers had some customers who were now delivering their printing jobs to the printer stored on computer disks. The days of creating film prior to printing appeared to be numbered. Quad/Graphics had anticipated the rapid growth in this so-called computer-to-plate technology as early as 1990 when it bought Orbis Graphic Arts facility in Anaheim, California, later renamed Anaheim Imaging. By 1994, Quad/Graphics' Quad/Imaging division had performed its first live direct-digital-to-plate run, and in 1994–95 Quad/Imaging satellites were operating in Boston, Minneapolis, and New York. Sales broke the billion dollar mark in 1995, and in 1996–1997 Quad/Graphics launched a World Wide Web site, printed *Sports Illustrated*'s daily Olympic Games magazine, upgraded its printing facilities to take on tabloid newspaper and magazine printing, and entered the fulfillment business through its Quad/Data Services division.

Principal Subsidiaries

Chemical Research/Technology; Duplainville Transport; Quad/Creative, Inc.; Quad/Med, Inc.; Quad/Tech; Quad/Tech Europe.

Further Reading

Barnes, Brooks, "Quad Sets $50 Million Expansion," *Milwaukee Journal Sentinel,* May 16, 1997.
Berman, Phyllis, "Harry's a Great Storyteller," *Forbes,* February 27, 1995.
Caruso, Gary, "Sports Business: Daily Grind," *Atlanta Business Chronicle,* July 15, 1996.
"Changing Business as Usual," *Working Woman,* November 1993.
Hendrickson, David, "There's No Place Like Quad," *Wisconsin Magazine,* March 22, 1992.
Ink on Paper, Quad/Graphics Corporate Viewbook, Pewaukee, WI: Quad/Graphics, 1996.
Levering, Robert, and Moskowitz, Milton, *The 100 Best Companies To Work for in America*, New York: Currency Doubleday, 1993.
"Quad/Graphics: Business as Social Experiment," *Business Ethics,* May/June 1993.
Quad/Views, Special Edition 1996: 25th Anniversary, Pewaukee, WI: Quad/Graphics, 1996.
Resnick, Brahm, "Quad's New Plant Produces First Book," *Milwaukee Journal Sentinel,* November 22, 1996.
Sink, Lisa, "Quad/Graphics Gets OK To Expand Headquarters," *Milwaukee Journal Sentinel,* February 24, 1997.
Waldman, Barry, "Printers Feel Impact of Computer Technology," *Capital District Business Review,* January 20, 1997.

—Paul S. Bodine

Quaker Fabric Corp.

941 Grinnell Street
Fall River, Massachusetts 02721
U.S.A.
(508) 678-1951
Fax: (508) 678-5979

Public Company
Incorporated: 1941 as Vertipile, Inc.
Employees: 1,647
Sales: $198.9 million (1996)
Stock Exchanges: NASDAQ
SICs: 2221 Broadwoven Fabric Mills, Manmade Fiber &
    Silk; 2299 Textile Goods, Not Elsewhere Classified

Quaker Fabric Corp. and its subsidiaries design, manufacture, and distribute woven upholstery fabrics to the residential furniture industry and specialty yarns to the upholstery and apparel industries in the United States and certain foreign countries. By upscaling its products and installing new machinery, this Massachusetts-based company prospered in the early 1990s although nearly every other textile and apparel operation seemed to have closed or left the state. In 1994 it was the second-largest U.S. manufacturer of jacquard upholstery fabrics and the fifth-largest upholstery-fabric supplier overall.

Vertipile before 1980

Quaker Fabric began as Vertipile, Inc., a company founded by Clive E. Hockmeyer in 1939 and incorporated in New York in 1941. In 1971, the year the company went public, it was leasing six buildings in Lowell, Massachusetts, for the manufacture of loose flock and flock-coated materials, used mainly in the apparel, home furnishings, and packaging industries to imitate the feel and appearance of velvet, suede, and velveteen. Net sales increased from $3.5 million in fiscal 1968 (the year ended February 29, 1968) to $4.8 million in fiscal 1971, and net income from $80,198 to $250,971. In 1971 Vertipile offered 300,000 shares of common stock to the public at $10 a share. Upon completion of the offering the founder's sons Langdon, who was president, chairman, and chief executive officer of the

firm, and Eastham, executive vice-president and secretary, owned about 63 percent of the stock.

At this time Vertipile was unique in the flocking industry for manufacturing its own loose flock and flock-coated goods for direct sales as well as commission work for clients. Flock consists of short strands of synthetic or natural textile fibers of various diameters and lengths; coating is a process by which loose flock is fixed to a backing, or substrate. Most of the company's flock was made at this time from rayon tow, although it also was turning out nylon, polyester, and cotton flock and producing random-cut fibers for making suede flock-coated goods. Its operation also handled woven and nonwoven textiles, plastic films and sheetings, vinyl foams, and most substrates. The company had more than $2 million invested in buildings, processing equipment, and testing facilities.

Vertipile moved in 1972 from Lowell to a new plant and corporate quarters on a 12-acre site in Leominster, Massachusetts. A seven-year bank loan the same year enabled the company to acquire Claremont Flock Corp., a subsidiary of Applied Synthetics Corp., for $3.2 million in cash and notes. Based in Claremont, New Hampshire, Claremont was cutting and dying textile fibers.

Vertipile's sales and income advanced rapidly in the late 1970s, reaching $22 million and $1.8 million, respectively, in fiscal 1980. By this time the company was reducing its dependence on the apparel industry by increasing its emphasis on other sectors of the product line, including not only upholstery and home furnishings but also lining for radio, camera, and eyeglass cases. Vertipile's own loose flock, accounting for 41 percent of sales in fiscal 1979, was used in flock printing on wallpaper, curtains, greeting cards, and women's apparel as well as in its production of flock-coated materials. In December 1978 Eastham Hockmeyer resigned as an officer and director and completed selling his shares in the company, for the most part to the employee stock-ownership fund and the company itself.

Vertipile-Quaker Fabrics Merger
and Aftermath, 1984–1989

In 1984 Vertipile acquired Quaker Fabric Corp., a much larger concern with four manufacturing plants in Fall River,

Massachusetts, making it one of the top three upholstery fabric mills in the country. Quaker Fabric's product line consisted of a variety of upholstered fabrics: flat and jacquard woven fabrics; printed, tufted, and woven velvets; and knitted fabrics. It also operated a converting division, and as such was a substantial purchaser of Vertipile's flock-coated fabrics for finishing as part of the Quaker line. The company had been incorporated in 1945 as General Textile Mills and had changed its name to Quaker Fabric at the end of 1979, following a merger with a sales company that operated as a wholly owned subsidiary of Providence Pile Fabric. Quaker Fabric had sales of $104 million and net income of about $1.5 million in 1983, compared to $24.3 million and $578,000 for Vertipile in fiscal 1984.

In order to purchase Quaker Fabric, which became a subsidiary, Vertipile paid $8 million in cash, 300,000 new common shares, and a $1.5-million, 12-percent subordinated note, borrowing $8.5 million from a bank. Quaker Fabric refinanced $15.5 million of its existing bank debt. Alan E. Symonds, president and principal shareholder of Quaker Fabric, emerged with 14 percent of the stock and became president and chief executive officer in 1985. When Langdon Hockmeyer died later that year, Symonds also became chairman of the firm. He purchased 305,000 shares of common stock from Hockmeyer's estate in December 1986, raising his stake in the company to about 34 percent.

The enhanced Vertipile did poorly in its first year, losing $1.8 million on sales of $104.3 million in fiscal 1985. Management said that Vertipile had lost much of its flock-fabric business to Quaker's own converting operation. The company made a profit in subsequent years. During this period its chief product was mid-priced, high-volume upholstery fabrics sold to furniture manufacturers, although it also was selling some fabrics for other home-furnishing applications, such as curtains. Vertipile changed its name to Quaker Fabric Corp. in 1987.

Following the merger, Quaker Fabric took steps to sell its tufted, velvet, and flock operations and concentrate on textured jacquard and dobbie upholstery fabrics. In March 1988 the company sold its flock and tufted upholstery-fabric product lines, including all its knitted fabrics (comprising about 25 percent of total sales), plus substantially all related equipment and inventory, to Culp Inc. for about $5.6 million. In December of that year it sold the Claremont operation to a group of employees for $2.1 million. The Leominster plant was sold in 1989 for $3.3 million. This left Quaker Fabric in the business of making jacquard woven fabrics—the most complex form of fabric sold—having eliminated dobbie weaving entirely.

Merger with Nortex and Aftermath, 1989–1993

During fiscal 1988 Quaker Fabric had net income of $1.9 million on net sales of $105.6 million, but in fiscal 1989 it lost $7.3 million on sales of $83.1 million, which amounted to a $7.3-million drop in sales even taking into consideration businesses that the company had sold. In July 1989 the company agreed to be acquired by Unione Manifatture, S.p.A., a Milan-based holding company, for $20.5 million. Two months later Nortex International, a novelty-yarn manufacturer, took a minority stake in Quaker Fabric, which merged with Nortex. A

Nortex partner, Larry Liebenow, became president of the combined privately held company.

By this time Quaker Fabric had the second-largest jacquard-weaving capacity in the United States. In contrast to the original jacquard method for weaving, by which a card with punch holes steered the loom, the weaving patterns for Quaker Fabric's looms were governed by computers. Nevertheless, the equipment was out of date, and the company's new owners spent $25 million to buy new looms that moved four times faster than the old ones. The consequent savings in labor costs made Quaker more competitive with Southern factories and East Asian operations. However, management decided it could not compete in the high-volume, low-cost trade and shifted its output to a dramatically expanded product line turned out in small, customized lots. The addition of Nortex made Quaker Fabric's Fall River operation the most vertically integrated in the industry, shortening lead times and affording the company flexibility in styling. Liebenow claimed in 1991 that Quaker Fabric was the largest chenille manufacturer in the world and the lowest-cost producer.

Quaker Fabric's revenues climbed to $98.4 million in 1991, $123.4 million in 1992, and $147.9 million in 1993. Net income rose from $1.6 million to $4.1 million before dropping to $2.8 million in 1993 because of an extraordinary $2.55-million charge for doubtful accounts stretching back to 1991. By mid-1993 the company had a product line of nearly 1,500 different upholstery fabrics, all for use in the furniture industry. Export business, accounting for less than two percent (excluding Canada) of sales in fiscal 1989, had grown to 16 percent of the total, of which more than half was going to Mexico, where the company had established a warehouse. Ninety percent of the company's products were being sold to furniture manufacturers in 1994, and nearly two-thirds of revenue were coming from the higher end of the marketplace, compared to only 14 percent in 1990. Quaker Fabric was also selling specialty yarns to apparel and upholstery manufacturers, accounting for six percent of overall sales.

Public Company Again, 1993–1997

Quaker Fabrics repurchased its debt and equity securities from Unione Manifatture in 1993 for $32.5 million. It became a public company again in November of that year, when it sold 2.3 million shares of stock at $12 a share. By 1994 it was the fifth-largest overall upholstery fabric supplier in the United States, selling to more than 600 furniture manufacturers. Its sales grew to a record $180.8 million in 1994 and its net income to a record $9.5 million.

By contrast, 1995 results were disappointing, with net sales falling to $173.5 million and net income to $5.5 million. Liebenow attributed the drop to an erratic market, raw-material costs, and a fall in the volume of the company's higher-margin products. He also noted a drop in export revenue of 30 percent, primarily due to a reduction in demand in Canada and Mexico. In March 1996 the company brought in a new vice-president of marketing and appointed a new vice-president of styling and design.

Quaker Fabric increased its net sales to $198.9 million in 1996 and its net income to $8.6 million. Middle-to-better-end fabric sales accounted for 69 percent of the total. Fabric sales accounted for 86 percent of the revenue total and yarn sales for 13 percent. International fabric sales increased to 18 percent of the total. In March 1997 the company consummated a public offering of 3.4 million shares of its common stock at $13.50 per share. Its long-term debt was $47.2 million at the end of 1995.

In 1996 Quaker Fabric was a full-service supplier of jacquard and plain woven upholstery fabric to the furniture market, with a product line of more than 3,000 fabric patterns. It was selling its upholstery fabrics to more than 600 domestic furniture manufacturers as well as distributing its fabrics internationally. The average gross sales price per yard was $4.05, but prices ranged from $2.50 to $18 per yard. The company's staff of professional designers and designer technicians was creating the majority of the designs on which the company's fabric patterns were based. While most were sold under the Quaker label, in October 1996 the company began marketing a select group of its middle-to-better-end fabrics under its Whitaker label.

Quaker Fabric's specialty yarns included its proprietary, abrasion-resistant Ankyra chenille yarns and were being used in its own upholstery fabrics as well as being sold to outside customers, generally under the Nortex Yarns name. The company's product offerings were noted for their wide use of chenille yarns, which have a soft, velvet-like feel. Ankyra-based chenille fabrics were developed by the company for abrasion resistance in order to compete effectively with flocks, velvets, and tufted fabrics.

Quaker Fabric was manufacturing all of its products in its four plants in Fall River, Massachusetts, where it also maintained corporate headquarters and a warehouse. The company had more than one million square feet of manufacturing space and had invested more than $51 million in new manufacturing equipment since 1991. All of the looms were equipped with jacquard heads, required to produce the complex designs referred to in the industry as ''jacquards,'' including a broad

assortment of striped, plaid, and plain fabrics. Quaker Fabric also maintained distribution centers in Los Angeles; Tupelo, Mississippi; High Point, North Carolina; and Mexico City.

The company, Fall River's largest manufacturer, was operating three shifts, six days a week, in 1994. About 70 percent of its employees were first- or second-generation Portuguese, and 15 to 20 percent of them spoke little or no English. As a result, its personnel staff and most of its supervisors were bilingual. All company signs and written communications were in both English and Portuguese.

Further Reading

DeMaio, Don, ''Textile Mill Weaves Fabric of Success in Fall River,'' *Providence Business News,* May 2, 1994, p. 6.

''Flockers Are on the Move Again,'' *Textile World,* June 1970, pp. 94–97.

Green, John H., ''Quaker Feels Its Oats,'' *HFD,* September 2, 1991, pp. 31, 36.

——, ''Vertipile to Acquire Quaker,'' *HFD,* February 20, 1984, pp. 1, 23.

Hyten, Todd, ''Poor 1995 Sales Figures Prompt Quaker Shake-Up,'' *Boston Business Journal,* March 29, 1996, p. 6.

Kalogeridis, Carla, ''Liebenow Reveals Key to Quaker Comeback,'' *Textile World,* September 1990, p. 35.

McCurry, John W., ''Quaker Takes Quick Path to Profitability,'' *Textile World,* December 1994, pp. 34–38.

Rush, Amy Joyce, ''Quaker: Broadening Its Appeal,'' *HFN,* January 9, 1995, p. 30.

Smith, Lyn, ''How Computers Are Changing the Textile Industry,'' *Business Digest of Southeastern Massachusetts,* November 1989, p. 17.

Tooher, Nora Lockwood, ''Italian Firm Buys Quaker Fabric,'' *Providence Journal-Bulletin,* July 15, 1989, p. 11.

Zitner, Aaron, ''Looming Large,'' *Boston Globe,* December 7, 1993, pp. 39, 46.

—Robert Halasz

Rare Hospitality International Inc.

8215 Roswell Road
Building 200
Atlanta, Georgia 30350
U.S.A.
(770) 399-9595
Fax: (770) 399-7796

Public Company
Incorporated: 1981 as Contemporary Restaurant
    Concepts Inc.
Employees: 6,321
Revenues: $218.7 million
Stock Exchanges: NASDAQ
SICs: 5812 Eating Places

With over 100 company-owned and franchised restaurants throughout the Eastern and Midwestern United States, RARE Hospitality International Inc. has a fast-growing presence in the steakhouse segment of the dining industry. This relative newcomer to the market—at scarcely 15 years in business, compared to such 1960s-era chains as Ponderosa and Bonanza—RARE's irreverent style of "cowboy cuisine" shook up the segment. By 1996, the company's core chain of LongHorn Steakhouses numbered 81 units. Following its initial public offering in 1992, the company acquired the Bugaboo Creek Steak House chain and its smaller The Capital Grille group of pricey eateries. Founder George W. McKerrow, Jr. continued to serve the company as chairman through the mid-1990s.

Early 1980s Origins

George McKerrow had nearly a decade in food service under his belt when he made his first stab at restaurant ownership in the 1970s. A 1972 graduate of Ohio State University's political science program, he had worked in a Cleveland pancake house as a teen and was tending bar at Columbus's Smuggler's Inn when he bought his first restaurant, a West Virginia supper club, in 1973 at the age of 22. McKerrow quickly sold the eatery, however, and went to work for the Victoria Station chain of restaurants in 1974. He relocated to Atlanta to take a management position with the chain in 1976, and had advanced to a regional manager prior to leaving the enterprise in 1978.

With support from a partner who lined up $100,000 in startup capital, McKerrow bought a shuttered adult bookstore on Atlanta's Peachtree Road in 1981 and started renovations that would eventually transform the location into a "traditional Texas roadhouse." The 30-year-old supported himself with a bartending stint by night and directed construction at the restaurant by day.

McKerrow suffered a serious setback when his financial backing—and his partner—disappeared in March 1981. Repairs and renovations came to a halt for two months while McKerrow sought new financing. He found it close to home; his father and another investor came through with enough funds to resurrect the project. They created a parent company, Contemporary Restaurant Concepts Inc. (CRC), resumed construction, and launched the first LongHorn Steaks Restaurant & Saloon that August. Not content to be a silent partner, George McKerrow, Sr. soon joined the company as chairman.

In a 1991 interview for the *Atlanta Business Chronicle,* McKerrow recounted the early months, noting that he served as "cook, waiter, busboy and bartend." But it wasn't as if he was especially harried; at the time, the restaurant was only serving about 18 tables per day, divided among lunch and dinner shifts. Within just three months, the struggling business required another $30,000 capital injection.

The establishment got its big break when a January 1982 snowstorm stranded hundreds of commuters on Peachtree Road. McKerrow saw an opportunity and didn't hesitate to grab it, hosting an impromptu $1 drink special. The promotion brought in $700 and, more importantly, introduced hundreds of customers to the steak joint.

Core Concept Establishes "Cowboy Cuisine" Segment in the 1980s

The budding restaurateur aimed to serve "the best steaks and the coldest beer in town," in a deliberately rustic if not "dumpy" decor. The ambiance has since been compared by one industry observer to a "honky-tonk Texas roadhouse filled with stuffed jackalopes, armadillos and rusty license plates." A country-western radio jingle summed-up the atmosphere: "Talkin' 'bout LongHorn/And their pan-fried steaks/Come on and eat one/No matter what it takes/They got big bowls of peanuts, Texas taters and ice cold brew/And some animal heads on the walls staring back at you." Large portions and moderate prices completed the casual ambiance.

Though the decor was originally intended to set a casual mood, it took on a strategic element as the restaurant evolved into a chain. Low-cost furnishings allowed the restaurateur to purchase high quality beef, which was cut by hand by the manager of each restaurant, without handing the entire cost on to customers. McKerrow also limited expenses by restricting the dinner menu to seven cuts of steak, one potato, and a salad, adding only a salmon entree and some desserts in 1989. This limited menu allowed for a bare-bones kitchen with just one grill and two fryers. As he told *Nation's Restaurant News* in July 1989, "Too many choices only confuse the customer and paralyze the kitchen."

McKerrow opened his second location, this one in suburban Atlanta, in 1983. By the end of the decade, CRC had 15 restaurants and had expanded from its geographic base in Atlanta into North Carolina. The company also had its own meat processing subsidiary, Superior Meats. Growth accelerated in the ensuing years, as the company more than doubled the number of restaurants and increased revenues from less than $25 million in 1988 to $39 million in 1991.

Transition to ''Big-League Restaurant Corporation'' in Early 1990s

By 1992, CRC had 32 restaurants in the southeastern United States and three Skeeter's Mesquite Grilles (described as "slightly more upscale" in a 1989 *Nation's Restaurant News* article) in the Atlanta metropolitan area. Along with dozens of Georgia-based companies, the chain went public that March with a two million share offering constituting about 38 percent of the company at $16 per share, applying part of the proceeds to reducing its "minimal" debt. The remaining 62 percent stake was divided among McKerrow, his father, CFO Ronald San Martin, and Vice-President of Operations Joseph Norman. Buoyed by investor interest in the specialty steakhouse segment, the stock jumped 50 percent in the first day of trading and stood pat at about $25 per share through the end of 1992.

It seemed at first that the renamed LongHorn Steaks Inc. would live up to all the hoopla surrounding its initial public offering; its sales rose by more than one-fourth to $50 million by the end of the year, and net income more than doubled, reaching $3.4 million. Egged on by eager Wall Street analysts, McKerrow dove into an ambitious expansion program, launching 24 new locations in just over 18 months. As McKerrow later acknowledged to Bill Carlino of *Nation's Restaurant News,* "We were a little too aggressive with some of our new restaurant openings, and it hurt us." Some new units were only doing half the volume of LongHorn's existing restaurants. Internal problems included hasty management training, inadequate introductory marketing, and inappropriate site selection. External influences included rising beef prices, which ate into profit margins. The chain was also buffeted by ever-intensifying competition in the steakhouse segment, with rivals ranging from high-end players like Ruth's Chris to budget chains like Ryan's, Ponderosa, and Bonanza. Direct competitors in the steak theme subset included Outback Steakhouses and Lone Star Steakhouse & Saloon. In June 1993, when the company announced that the second quarter's earnings would not meet projections, its stock plummeted to $11.

Same-store sales declined by four percent in 1993 and profits remained flat at $3.4 million despite an increase in revenues to $70 million that year. With quarterly unit profit margins eroding from nearly 20 percent in early 1993 to less than 12 percent in the fall of 1994, and the stock price declining to single-digits, McKerrow made a gutsy, selfless decision. That February, he assumed the position of chairman to make room for a new president and chief executive officer; someone who, as *Georgia Trend'*s Lindsey Kelly put it, would help the chain "complete its transformation from an entrepreneurial, seat-of-the-pants kind of outfit to a big-league restaurant corporation." The man he chose, Richard "Dick" Rivera had been called an icon in the restaurant industry by *ADWEEK's* Julie Soble. One of the few Hispanics to penetrate the upper echelons of management in the business, Rivera made a name for himself when he guided TGI Friday's early 1990s turnaround. In five years as that chain's CEO, he not only nearly doubled annual sales and number of restaurants, but also achieved record profits every year.

Reforms Bring Stability and Renewed Growth in the 1990s

Rivera's reforms at LongHorn included a moderate but chainwide renovation program, menu additions, and a reduction in the rate of unit growth. Atmosphere changes amounted to a subtle homogenization, changing from rustic dark paneling to brightly-lit beige walls, reducing the amount of taxidermy, and taking down the racy posters featured in restrooms. The menu was expanded to appeal to a broader range of customers—particularly families—adding chicken, pork, seafood, and barbecue entrees; appetizers; salads; and a wider variety of side dishes. Management reigned in new restaurant openings to less than ten in 1994 and would eventually close several underperforming locations and terminate its meat cutting and distribution business. Rivera also fortified the marketing department and hired a new advertising agency to manage the company's growing national presence.

Sales advanced from $115 million in 1994 to $156.4 million in 1995, and net income multiplied from $1.5 million to $6.6 million in the same period. Wall Street acknowledged the changes, boosting the share price to a high of over $18 by the end of 1995.

With its finances stabilized, LongHorn moved into the hotly-contested northeastern U.S. market via the 1996 purchase of Bugaboo Creek Steak House Inc. The stock swap, valued at $53.2 million, added the namesake 14-unit chain as well as a subsidiary of three high-end Capital Grille restaurants. Named for an actual region of Canada, Bugaboo Creek featured a family-oriented "mountain-lodge-theme," while The Capital Grille's Providence, Boston, and Washington D.C. locations were bedecked with African mahogany paneling and other fine furnishings. An early 1997 name change rechristened the parent company RARE Hospitality International Inc. to reflect its broadened array of restaurants and menus. Some analysts believed that the alteration also telegraphed the multinational ambitions of this growing business.

Principal Divisions

RARE Hospitality; LongHorn Steakhouse; Bugaboo Creek Steak House; The Capital Grille.

Further Reading

Allen, Robin Lee, "LongHorn Steaks Hooks Bugaboo in $53.2M Deal," *Nation's Restaurant News,* July 8, 1996, pp. 1–2.

Anthony, Margaret, "Those Two Guys That Sing," *Atlanta Business Chronicle,* February 5, 1993, pp. 3A, 4A.

Aven, Paula, "Wall Street Burns Steak House Stocks," *Denver Business Journal,* November 15, 1996, pp. 3A–4A.

Brammer, Rhonda, "What's the Beef?," *Barron's,* January 2, 1995, pp. 23–24.

Carlino, Bill, "LongHorn Rides Again, Stresses Internal Focus," *Nation's Restaurant News,* August 2, 1993, pp. 8–10.

——, "LongHorn Steaks Grabs the Billboard by the Horns," *Nation's Restaurant News,* August 27, 1990, p. 12.

——, "LongHorn Steers New Ads Toward Traditional Route," *Nation's Restaurant News,* June 13, 1994, p. 12.

——, "Shareholder Files LongHorn Suit, Says Company Inflated its Finances," *Nation's Restaurant News,* February 28, 1994, p. 3.

——, "TGI Friday's CEO Rivera Exits to Lead LongHorn," *Nation's Restaurant News,* January 17, 1994, pp. 1–2.

Curtis, Susan K. "LongHorn May Hit the Trail Outside U.S.," *Atlanta Business Chronicle,* June 30, 1995, pp. 3A, 4A.

Feuerstein, Adam, "He's Hooked on Steaks," *Atlanta Business Chronicle,* August 19, 1991, pp. 3A–4A.

Garrett, Echo Montgomery, "Rare Sticks to Southeast and Three Brands," *Atlanta Business Chronicle,* January 24, 1997, p. 17B.

Hayes, Jack, "Casual Steak Houses Lasso Value-Minded Customers," *Nation's Restaurant News,* January 28, 1991, pp. 32–33.

——, "LongHorn's Sizzling Nationwide," *Nation's Restaurant News,* July 31, 1989, p. F18.

Kelly, Lindsey, "Can Rivera Put the Sizzle Back in LongHorn?" *Georgia Trend,* June 1994, pp. 77–78.

Norvell, Scott, "Trading Saddles," *Restaurant Business,* May 1, 1994, pp. 58–62.

Papoiernik, Richard L., "LongHorn: Stampeding on the Fast Track to a Turnaround," *Nation's Restaurant News,* December 11, 1995, pp. 11–12.

——, "LongHorn Steaks Shows 1st Signs of Turnaround," *Nation's Restaurant News,* May 15, 1995, p. 4.

Ruggless, Ron, "Richard Rivera: Chairman, Chief Executive, LongHorn Steaks Inc., Atlanta," *Nation's Restaurant News,* January 1995, pp. 173–174.

Schonback, Judith, "Bully for LongHorn Steaks," *Business Atlanta,* June 1992, p. 8.

Soble, Julie, "LongHorn's Wild Ride," *ADWEEK Eastern Edition,* November 4, 1996, pp. 54–58.

"Turnaround Expert Rivera to Dissect Change at MUFSO," *Nation's Restaurant News,* May 30, 1994, pp. 1–2.

Walkup, Carolyn, "LongHorn Steaks Files for IPO," *Nation's Restaurant News,* March 2, 1992, pp. 14–15.

—April Dougal Gasbarre

**Reliance Steel
& Aluminum Co.**

Reliance Steel & Aluminum Co.

2550 East 25th Street
Los Angeles, California
U.S.A.
(213) 582-2272
Fax: (213) 582-2801

Public Company
Incorporated: 1939 as Reliance Steel Products Co.
Employees: 1,400
Sales: $654 million (1996)
Stock Exchanges: New York
SICs: 5051 Metals Service Centers

The Reliance Steel & Aluminum Co. is the second-largest West Coast-based metals processing and distribution company in the United States. In 1997, the company operated more than three dozen metals service centers in 14 states, more than half of them in California. The company buys steel and nonferrous metals in bulk from primary producers and cuts it to size for smaller buyers. According to the 1996 annual report, Reliance regularly distributed more than 20,000 metal products to 30,000 customers in various industries.

In an industry dominated by small, family-owned businesses, Reliance grew from a single metals-processing center in Los Angeles into a major corporation by acquiring more than three dozen competitors during its nearly 60-year history. In an interview with an industry publication in 1992, Joe D. Crider, then president and chief operating officer, explained, "You can pay the bill [for higher market share] through price cutting, or through paying goodwill to buy a competitor. In cutting prices, you often trash the marketplace. So over time, the latter route is usually the less expensive, as long as you buy at a reasonable price."

Growth through Acquisition, 1939–1987

Reliance Steel & Aluminum Co. was founded in Los Angeles in 1939 by Thomas J. Neilan. Originally named Reliance

Steel Products Co., the business made and sold steel reinforcing bars (rebar) for the construction industry. In 1944, the name was shortened to Reliance Steel Co.

In 1948, Reliance Steel also began manufacturing products of aluminum and magnesium. As William T. Gimbel, Neilan's nephew who joined the company as a trainee in 1947, later told *Metal Service News,* "We started out (in 1939) with the dirty, old, down-in-the-gutter carbon steel, but that became a world commodity. So we decided that we wanted to upgrade into something that had a little bit more pizzazz, and we picked aluminum and magnesium."

Gimbel, who started as a warehouse man, succeeded Neilan as president of the company in 1957, a year after the company name was changed to Reliance Steel & Aluminum. Under Gimbel Reliance began its long-running territorial expansion, naming a resident sales agent in Phoenix in 1958. Two years later, Reliance acquired a small Phoenix-based competitor, the Effron Steel Co. With the purchase of another competitor, the Westates Steel Co., in Santa Clara, Reliance Steel expanded into Northern California in 1961.

In 1963, Reliance continued its growth through acquisition by purchasing the Drake Steel Supply Co., which operated metals service centers in Fresno and San Diego, California. With the purchase, Reliance also acquired the services of Joe D. Crider, who had joined Drake in 1949 as a billing clerk and worked his way up to Fresno sales manager. After several years as manager of Reliance Steel's Los Angeles division, Crider was named executive vice-president in 1975, teaming up with Gimbel to form what *Metal Service News* would later call "perhaps the best known management team in the service center industry."

In 1966, Reliance extended its reach into Texas by acquiring metals service centers in Dallas and San Antonio from Delta Metals, Inc. Two years later, the company bought out another Los Angeles competitor, the Catalina Steel Co., its fifth acquisition in 10 years. By then, Reliance Steel had also established SupraCote, a coil-coating division, in Cucamonga, California. It became a separate subsidiary in 1973, and was sold to a management group in 1980.

Reliance Steel acquired Southern Equipment & Supply Co., San Diego's oldest metals service center, in 1972, and immediately launched a $1.8 million project to double the size of the San Diego facility. Two years later, the rapidly growing company announced a $4 million expansion in Los Angeles.

Reliance Steel also wanted to strengthen its position in Texas, and after attempting to acquire a Houston business, temporarily abandoned its acquisition philosophy and opened a new metals service center in the port city in 1975. Gimbel told *Metal Service News,* "we had spent probably two years trying to buy out somebody, but at the time there was a big boom there, and everyone felt the streets of Houston were paved with gold. We just could never make a deal to buy someone. So we started our own company." Reliance closed the Houston center in 1984 due to a slump in the oil industry.

Reliance also ventured into the Eastern United States for the first time in 1975 when it acquired the Purchased Steel Products Co., in Atlanta. The move never panned out, however, and Reliance sold the center in 1987. Gimbel told *Metal Center News,* "We learned a lesson in Atlanta. If we're going to go further east, that probably means the Chicago area. And you don't move into Chicago on a shoestring."

Specialty Metals Since the Late 1970s

After more than three decades of operating full-service metals service centers, Reliance opened its first "specialty store" in 1976, forming the Tube Service Co., in Santa Fe Springs, California. The subsidiary specialized in tubular products. A second Tube Service Co. opened three years later in Milpitas, California. In 1977, Reliance also acquired Bralco Metals, in Pico Rivera, California, which specialized in brass, aluminum, and copper. To manage its aluminum, magnesium, and stainless steel products, Reliance created a nonferrous metals division, Reliance Metalcenter, in 1980.

In 1980, Reliance also acquired Foucar, Ray & Simon, a specialty tube distributor in Hayward, California, with a branch in Portland, Oregon. The Hayward center was eventually merged into the Reliance center in Santa Clara. The Portland operation foundered and then closed in 1984. Gimbel told *Metal Service News* the acquisition had been a mistake. "Foucar was probably the second oldest service center in California, with a good reputation. They'd done well over the years, but I guess they'd gotten rigor mortis. We thought that we could change all that. We tried and tried to change it, and it didn't work. So we had to admit defeat and close up the place."

The setback, however, did not slow the company's aggressive growth. In 1981, Reliance purchased the Cd'A Service Center in Salt Lake City, Utah, from Spokane-based Cd'A Steel Service Center. The company then acquired Circle Metals in Carson, California, in 1983, and Tricon Steel & Aluminum in Fremont, California, and Arnold Engineering Co. in Fullerton, California, in 1984. Arnold Engineering Co. was renamed Arnold Technologies, Inc. and relocated to Anaheim. In the mid-1980s, Reliance gobbled up assets of the Ducommun Metals Co. in Phoenix and Los Angeles, the Lafayette Metal Service Corp. in Long Beach, California, and the assets of the Livermore, California, metals service center from Capitol Metals Co.

The company also acquired the Valex Corp. in Ventura, California, which made stainless steel components for electronic and pharmaceutical applications, the Dallas/Forth Worth Russell Steel Division of the Van Pelt Corp., and the Morris Steel & Aluminum Co. in Albuquerque, New Mexico. In 1988, Reliance also acquired the Los Angeles Sheet & Steel Division from Earle M. Jorgensen Co.

The acquisitions certainly fueled growth. By 1988, the company's 50th year, sales topped $350 million. But the company continued to expand. Over the next two years, Reliance acquired the Albuquerque, New Mexico, assets of the Smith Pipe & Steel Co. and the Los Angeles and Phoenix operations of Lusk Metals. Other acquisitions in the 1990s included Affiliated Metals, an aluminum and stainless steel specialty center in Salt Lake City, Utah, and the Wichita, Kansas, operations of National Steel Service Center Inc., which stocked aluminum plate, sheet, and coil for the aerospace industry. The National Steel acquisition marked Reliance Steel's first foray into the Midwest.

Going Public in 1994

In 1994, after 55 years as a closely held company, Reliance issued its first public stock. At the time, Reliance Steel had about 180 stockholders, most of them company employees or relatives of founder Thomas J. Neilan. The company had previously considered, and rejected, going public several times. In 1984, Gimbel told *Metal Service News,* "We'd go and talk to the brokers, but, unfortunately, anything with the name steel in it didn't get them very excited." In its prospectus, Reliance also signaled its intention to continue growth through acquisitions: "Traditionally, metals service centers have been small, family-owned businesses that lack the diversity of experience and successful operating techniques of Reliance and thus have and may in the future become candidates for acquisition or consolidation."

A year later, Reliance acquired a 50 percent interest in American Steel, L.L.C. for $19 million, its largest purchase to date. That was followed in 1996 with the acquisition of VMI Corporation, an 11-year-old nonferrous metals service center in Albuquerque, New Mexico, and CCC Steel, Inc., which operated carbon-steel service centers in Los Angeles and Salt Lake City. Reliance also announced the acquisition of the Siskin Steel & Supply Company, Inc., with metals service centers in Chattanooga and Nashville, Tennessee, Spartanburg, South Carolina, and Birmingham, Alabama. Reliance Steel paid $71 million for the 47-year-old company, which had revenues of $151 million and would operate as a wholly owned subsidiary. David H. Hannah, then president, called the acquisition "an integral part of our strategy to become a national company with operations extending beyond the Western half of the United States."

In 1997, Reliance reported net income of $29.8 million on record sales of $654 million. It was the sixth consecutive year of record financial results. The company also acquired Amalco Metals, Inc., a metals service center company in Union City, California, that specialized in processing and distributing aluminum plate and sheet, and AMI Metals, Inc., a Brentwood, Tennessee, company that specialized in processing and distributing aluminum plate, sheet and bar products for the aerospace industry. AMI operated service centers in Fontana, California; Wichita, Kansas; Brentwood, Tennessee; Fort Worth, Texas; Kent, Washington; and Swedesboro, New Jersey.

Crider, who became chairman, succeeding Gimbel, who remained on the board of directors as chairman emeritus, said in interviews that he expected Reliance Steel to continue growing through acquisitions. Industry analysts expected Reliance to focus its expansion on the strengthening Midwestern market.

Principal Subsidiaries

Reliance Steel Division; Bralco Metals Division; MetalCenter, Inc.; Tube Service Co.; Affiliated Metals; Eureka Metals, Inc.; Siskin Steel & Supply Company, Inc.; CCC Steel, Inc.; American Steel, L.L.C. (50%); Valex Corp.

Further Reading

Berry, Charles, "The Art of the Deal: Growth by Acquisition," *Metal Center News,* December 1992.
——, "Reliance Takes the Road Less Traveled," *Metal Center News,* December 1992.
Cole, Benjamin Mark, "Reliance Steel Plans $51.7 Million IPO; Plans Listing on Big Board," *Los Angeles Business Journal,* October 3, 1994.
——, "Man of Steel (Aluminum, Brass Too)," *Los Angeles Business Journal,* June 17, 1996, p. 17.
Joch, Alan, "Tube Service Co.: A Generalist's Specialist," *Metal Center News,* December 1984.
——, "When Entrepreneurs Manage Entrepreneurs," *Metal Center News,* December 1984.
MacKey, William, "Flatrolled Vendor to the High-Tech Market," *Metal Center News,* December 1984.
"Reliance MetalCenters: A History of Innovation," *Metal Center News,* December 1984.

—Dean Boyer

Reynolds Metals Company

6601 West Broad Street
Richmond, Virginia 23261
U.S.A.
(804) 281-2000
Fax: (804) 281-3695
Web site: http://www.rmc.com

Public Company
Incorporated: 1928
Employees: 29,000
Sales: $7.01 billion (1996)
Stock Exchanges: New York Chicago
SICs: 3411 Aluminum Cans; 3353 Beverage Cans Metal,
    Except Beer; 3497 Beer Cans, Metal; 3354 Food
    Containers, Metal; 3355 Foil, Aluminum; 3334 Flat
    Rolled Shapes, Aluminum

Reynolds Metals Company is the world's third largest aluminum and packaging company. As a fully integrated manufactuer, distributor, and marketer of primary and value-added fabricated aluminum products, the company operates 100 manufacturing facilities in 24 nations. Reynolds also produces plastic products which are primarily used in its packaging and consumer products businesses. Other end-uses for Reynolds products are aluminum beverage cans, flexible and foodservice packaging, consumer home food managment, transportation, building, and construction. In addition, the company has a metal supply system with operations in bauxite mining, alumina refining, and primary and reclaimed aluminum production. As a leader in consumer aluminum recycling, Reynolds distributes aluminum and stainless steel mill products through a nationwide network of metal service centers.

Reynolds began as a supplier of foil for cigarette packaging. The company was founded by R.S. Reynolds, a former law student and nephew of R.J. Reynolds, one of the first U.S. tobacco barons. After spending several years in the tobacco business working for his uncle, R.S. Reynolds borrowed $100,000 and in 1919 he purchased a small, one-story building in Louisville, Kentucky, and founded the United States Foil Company (U.S. Foil). The increased demand for foil was the result of the ever-increasing public appetite for cigarettes, the demand for which was so great that it created constant shortages of foil used for packaging.

U.S. Foil's entrance into the market generated a price war with other foil manufacturers, who hoped that by cutting prices they could drive the fledgling company out of business. Their plan did not work. At the time, most foil was manufactured in tall, multi-storied buildings. The material was moved manually from one floor to another before the finished product was ready for shipment. All the lifting and transferring of raw materials was a costly and inefficient way to manufacture foil. The newly purchased Reynolds plant in Kentucky, however, was all on one floor, at ground level. The production equipment was, therefore, installed in long rows, which eliminated the need for the expensive transporting of the product. The resulting lower manufacturing costs allowed the company to undersell its competitors by several cents per pound, ensuring the company's share of the growing market. During the 1920s most foil for packaging was made of lead and tin alloys. R.S. Reynolds recognized the advantages of using lighter-weight, less-expensive aluminum foil. In 1928, after buying back the stock he had sold to R.J. Reynolds to start U.S. Foil, R.S. Reynolds built the company's first aluminum foil plant and rolling mill in Louisville, and the Reynolds Metals Company was formed.

The Great Depression did not affect the growth of the newly formed company. In fact, the company recorded annual sales of $13 million in 1930 and moved its corporate headquarters to New York City. In 1935 Reynolds developed a method of printing on aluminum foil, employing the rotogravure process, which enabled the company to expand quickly into other aluminum foil packaging markets. The following year, Reynolds ventured outside the United States for the first time by opening a foil production plant in Havana.

In 1938 R.S. Reynolds decided to move the company's headquarters south again. Taking his son, Richard S. Reynolds, Jr., with him as assistant to the president, the company settled in Richmond, Virginia. Reynolds, Jr. had previously founded a stock-brokerage firm that would later become Reynolds Securities, which eventually merged with Dean Witter.

In 1937, in Europe to search for new sources of raw materials, Reynolds, Sr. observed that German production capacities for aluminum were more than two times that of the combined production capabilities of the United States, England, and France. Reynolds deduced that Germany was preparing for war, with a massive production effort in aluminum sheet used to build military airplanes. After his return to the United States, taking his cue from what he observed in Germany, Reynolds set about to increase dramatically his own production capacity. The company borrowed $15 million and began construction on its first smelting facility, located at Sheffield, Alabama. The company also acquired a bauxite mining operation in Arkansas to help feed the smelters. Reynolds's World War II production was extensive. By the end of World War II, Reynolds had increased the company's production capacity to more than 450 million pounds. Impressive as the wartime figures were, they were dwarfed by postwar demand for aluminum.

With the end of World War II, the company focused its direction on consumer goods and construction. Reynolds developed aluminum siding for the booming postwar housing market. In 1946, the company leased, then purchased six government-owned production plants, and by doing so doubled its production capacity. Reynolds Wrap, the company's well-known household aluminum foil, was introduced in 1947.

R.S. Reynolds, Jr. was named the company's new president in 1948. His three brothers, David, William G., and J. Louis, also assumed much of the responsibility for running the business, concentrating primarily on a program of rapid overseas expansion. Reynolds expanded its holdings worldwide, and in 1953 the company organized Reynolds International, Inc. in an effort to consolidate and further expand foreign operations. Reynolds closed the 1950s with a move to a new, modern corporate headquarters in suburban Richmond, Virginia.

During the 1960s the company continued to grow and introduce new all-aluminum products for home and industry. Included were the first aluminum drill pipe in 1960 and the first aluminum beverage can in 1963, both successful. An attempt to increase production capacities by 20 percent cost Reynolds an estimated $650 million in the mid-1960s. Plagued by cost overruns and delays, by the time the project was finished demand for aluminum had leveled off. Reynolds's leadership came under criticism from the financial community, particularly for what was perceived as the Reynolds family having too much control over the company. The company began a reorganization during the late 1960s, and separate operating divisions were

formed, each of which was responsible for its own profit performance. R.S. Reynolds, Jr. brought in a financial consulting firm to streamline operations. Control of the company was still held by the Reynolds family. In 1976 David P. Reynolds was its chairman; J. Louis and William G. Reynolds were board members; a cousin, A.D. Reynolds was a vice-president; and William G. Reynolds, Jr. was the company's treasurer.

In 1973 a Reynolds unit pleaded guilty to charges of importing ores from Rhodesia, in violation of U.S. government sanctions against the country at the time. In 1975 the company's assets in Guyana were nationalized and Reynolds was forced to settle for a $10 million payment for its Guyanese holdings. In 1980, 51 percent of its Jamaican assets and operations and all of its Jamaican land holdings were sold to the Jamaican government. The company continued to offer new products to the marketplace. In 1970 the first all-aluminum automobile engine block was introduced. All-aluminum car bumpers were in use in 1973. The beverage can with the stay-on, pull-top tab was well received in 1975.

Reynolds has been involved in an impressive recycling effort since 1968. It has received a great deal of praise for its recycling philosophy. As of 1980, the company was recycling almost half the number of cans it produced. In 1981, the company expanded its recycling capacity with two more facilities. In 1990 Reynolds recycled 438 million pounds of consumer-generated aluminum scrap, paying out $123 million to the recycling public. The company recycles more cans than it produces. In addition to its environmental advantages, recycled aluminum requires only five percent of the energy that would be used to produce aluminum from virgin materials.

Like most U.S. industrial giants, Reynolds lost sales in the recession of the early 1980s. Reynolds looked into new products and areas of manufacturing to redeploy its assets, seeking businesses that would provide higher profits and faster growth than those of aluminum. In the early 1980s, David Reynolds and William Bourke, a former Ford Motor Company vice president and now Reynolds's chairman and CEO, realized that Reynolds's upstream costs—for mining, smelting, and refining—were cutting into downstream profits on finished goods, like aluminum foil and cans. Reynolds then embarked on a capital-improvements program that involved the expenditure of billions of dollars and the shutting down of some of the company's less-profitable operations. By 1988 Reynolds had cut the number of employees by one-third and reduced by almost 25 percent its production costs, reversing the drain on company profits.

Reynolds fortunes were greatly improved by the discovery of gold at one of the company's bauxite properties in Australia in 1986. The company's entrance into the gold market, an unexpected upsurge in aluminum prices in the late 1980s, the company's continued commitment to the modernization of its production facilities, and the expansion of its consumer products division made Reynolds a solid, profitable enterprise with the ability to weather the cyclical nature of the aluminum business.

Under the leadership of chairman and CEO Bourke the company moved into the 1990s with its focus on consumer products and on gold. By using its well-established marketing, sales, and distribution organizations, Reynolds was able to add new products without increasing employment. Late in the 1980s the company introduced a line of colored plastic wraps and resealable plastic bags. In May 1988 Reynolds acquired Presto Products, Inc., a $200-million-a-year producer of plastic bags. Presto produced a full range of plastic bags and wraps for both indoor and outdoor use, including freezer, sandwich, and food storage bags, along with a line of moist paper tissues and cotton swabs. In line with its commitment to recycling, Reynolds set a long-term goal of recycling more plastics each year than it produces.

As Reynolds Metals entered the 1990s, the company was in the best financial condition in its history. Modernization of its plants continued with the construction of a new 120-metric-ton-per-year facility at the company's Baie Comeau, Quebec, smelter, along with expansion and modernization of other company plants in Western Australia, Texas, and Louisiana. Reynolds invested more than $400 million in Alabama to ensure its position as a world-class producer of aluminum-can stock and can-end stock. In addition to its capital investment program, the company expanded its research-and-development efforts. The company has developed new process technologies in aluminum-lithium casting, electromagnetic casting, and various techniques in automation. In 1991 new products included a light-weight, stronger composite architectural panel metal for the construction industry.

With the demand for lighter, more fuel-efficient automobiles, the use of aluminum in U.S. cars was expected to rise during the 1990s. Reynolds's research had helped develop technology for the manufacture of aluminum automobile drive shafts and radiators. In 1989 the company acquired an interest in the Fata European Group in Italy, a company with strong ties to and business experience in Eastern Bloc countries. Fata, Reynolds, and a group of Soviet organizations began constructing a $200 million aluminum-foil plant in Siberia in the 1990s.

In 1992, Reynolds sold its wire and cable operations, as well as its 84 percent interest in Eskimo Pie. The company also announced that employment would once again be reduced by 12 percent to cut costs. In 1993 Reynolds underwent a restructuring that included reducing alumina production and aluminum production by 21 percent, and sold its aluminum reclamation plant in Benton Harbor, Michigan.

In 1994, Reynolds purchased the aluminum and stainless steel products distribution business of Prime Metals. The company also sold its 40 percent interest in Australia's Boddington Gold Mine, but was to exit the gold business altogether the next year. In 1994, a pact to scale back production in the next two years among the chief aluminum-producing nations helped Reynolds to achieve strong sales. However, decline for beer beverage cans was continuing, and another can-making plant

was closed in Fulton, New York. One market that did show promise, though, was bridge deck replacement, and in 1996 Reynolds renovated the Corbin suspension bridge in Huntingdon County, Pennsylvania. The 320-foot bridge built in the 1930s was refitted with 22 aluminum deck panels.

In 1996, another can-making plant was closed in Houston, Texas, but the modernization of a plant in Torrance, California, neared completion with the number of manufacturing lines reduced from six to three. Many of the other modernized plants were making cans with smaller, lighter ends which reduces the amount of metal needed for a 12-ounce can by three percent.

Even with smaller cans, recycling them and other aluminum products was achieving record levels. Reynolds recycled 584 million pounds of aluminum, including more than 11 billion aluminum beverage cans, and nearly 228 million pounds of non-can aluminum scrap in 1996 alone. Furthermore, the company noted that as more and more aluminum is used in automobiles, appliances, building products, packaging items, foil and foil products, and other household goods, there will be more metals entering the recycling stream.

Disappointing sales in 1996, due to low aluminum prices and lower demand for some of its products, led to yet another company restructuring. Effective April 1, 1997, the company was organized into six global units, down from its former 20 operating units, that would focus on the most profitable aluminum markets around the world. The new units were packaging and consumer products, construction and distribution, transportation, metals and carbon products, bauxite and alumina, and cans. The year also saw a milestone for Reynolds Wrap Aluminum Foil, which celebrated its 50th year. In tribute, Reynolds donated $1 million to Meals on Wheels.

Principal Subsidiaries

Reynolds Metals Development Company; Southern Reclamation Company; Reynolds Consumer Products, Inc.; Reynolds International Inc.

Principal Operating Units

Packaging and Consumer Products; Construction and Distribution; Transportation; Metals and Carbon Products; Bauxite and Alumina; Cans.

Further Reading

Mehegan, Sean, ''Betty & Pat: Beyond Ads,'' *Brandweek,* January 20, 1997, pp. 18–19.

—William R. Grossman
—updated by Dorothy Kroll

RIO TINTO

Rio Tinto plc

6 St. James's Square
London SW1Y 4LD
England
+44-171-930-2399
Fax: +44-171-930-3249

Public Company
Incorporated: 1962
Employees: 44,499
Sales: $8.40 billion
Stock Exchanges: London New York Paris Frankfurt
    Amsterdam Brussels Zürich Australia
SICs: 1021 Copper and Mining and Preparation; 1479
    Bauxite Mining; 1499 Tin Mining; 1041 Gold Ore
    Mining; 1044 Silver Ore Processing; 1241 Coal
    Mining Services

*When the London-based RTZ Corporation plc and its Australian subsidiary CRA Limited completed a dual-listed companies merger in December 1995, the largest mining company in the world was created, RTZ-CRA Group. Combined revenues for the next year were $8.4 billion, double the $4.22 billion in sales reported by RTZ alone for 1995. As a result of the unique merger, both companies maintained separate identities and stock market listings.

An estimated 79 percent of company assets are in Australia, New Zealand, and North America, with the rest divided among Africa, Asia, and Europe. The company owns mines worldwide, for coal and such metals as copper and gold, and the industrial minerals borax, silica and talc. In addition to being one of the largest producers of copper and coal in the United States, the company's boron mine in the Mojave Desert produces 50 percent of the world's borax. Among Rio Tinto's international mine holdings are Kennecott in Utah which mines copper, coal, and gold; U.S. Borax which mines borates and silica; Palabora

in South Africa which mines copper; Corumba in Brazil which mines iron and manganese; Escondida in Chile which mines copper; and Freeport-McMoRan Copper & Gold in Irian Jaya, Indonesia.

Throughout its long history, the company has successfully confronted recessions, political turbulence, oversupplies and low prices, labor disputes, and environmental and human rights issues, because of its diversity and disparity. If one mineral in one part of the world is priced lower because of over production from competitors, for example, another mineral in another part of the world will be prospering because of positive market conditions.

It had been the policy of the RTZ Group, since its formation in 1962 through the merger of the Rio Tinto Company (RTC) and the Consolidated Zinc Corporation (CZ), to invest only in first-class mining properties with large reserves and low production costs. Both the RTC and CZ were formed during the years between 1870 and 1914, when London rose to prominence as the hub of international mining and metallurgical activities. The number of overseas metal mining and processing companies listed on the London Stock Exchange climbed from 39 in 1875 to 913 in 1913, with the long-term capital employed in the industry rising at an average annual rate of more than eight percent over the same period. In the City of London, for every prospective mine or group of mines, a new operating company would be created. A syndicate composed of city interests—specialist company promoters, bankers, stockbrokers, merchants, mining engineers, and others—would purchase a concession from a foreign vendor or exploration company, and a mining company would be formed to purchase the concession from the syndicate. Syndicates usually profited from the sale of the concession, and from securing contracts for financial or other services.

Rio Tinto's Origins

When launched in 1873, the RTC was by far the biggest international mining venture ever brought to market, and it remained the flagship of the British-owned sector of the international industry until well into the 20th century. The Rio Tinto

*Rio Tinto plc was known until mid-1997 as the RTZ-CRA Group.

mines, in the province of Huelva in southern Spain, had produced large quantities of copper, on and off, since before Roman times, most recently under the ownership of the government of Spain. In 1872, following a series of financial losses, the mines were offered for sale at a price equivalent to several million pounds sterling. The Spanish government was in a financial crisis and did not have the cash or the expertise needed to exploit the large reserves of cupreous pyrites known to exist at Rio Tinto. Substantial investments were needed to introduce opencast mining, and to build workshops, tramways, crushing and metallurgical plants, a railway from the mines to the seaport of Huelva, a shipping pier, and the many other works necessary to operate on a large scale.

The availability of the mines was brought to the attention of Matheson & Company, the London-based agent for the Far Eastern merchants Jardine Matheson, by Heinrich Doetsch of Sundheim & Doetsch, a general merchant of Huelva. Doetsch had the foresight to see that if the Rio Tinto mines were developed to their full potential, his business eventually stood to gain from a large increase in trade. A syndicate to purchase the Rio Tinto concession was organized by Hugh Matheson, senior partner in Matheson & Company, in London. The mines were purchased by the syndicate for £3.7 million, over a period of nine years, and immediately sold to the RTC. The new company was floated on the London Stock Exchange with an issued share capital of £2 million and debentures valued at £600,000. Hugh Matheson was appointed as first chairman of the RTC with Heinrich Doetsch as his deputy.

Matheson remained chairman of the RTC for a quarter of a century until his death in 1898. Matheson was a shrewd dealer in commodities, an outstanding entrepreneur with an ability to think on a scale that few could match, and a natural leader who could win the support needed to build very large enterprises in distant lands. The formation, survival, and ultimate prosperity of the RTC was the crowning achievement of his life. Matheson held together the original German and British banking, trading, and engineering consortium formed to launch the RTC in the crisis that followed the issue of its prospectus. The claims made in this document, especially the report of the mining engineer David Forbes, were vigorously denounced by the Tharsis Company, a Scottish-based firm set up in 1866 to work a group of mines not far distant from those at Rio Tinto. It was alleged that Matheson and his associates had falsely inflated potential revenues and grossly underestimated development and operating costs. The new company, it was said, could never earn a positive

rate of return on the huge capital it was seeking to raise from investors. Matheson launched a massive press campaign, an early example of skillful public relations, and he won the day.

The Tharsis assault, however, did do some damage, and this was further compounded by a three-year price war between the two companies. The pyrites mined in southern Spain and in Portugal were first burned to drive off the sulfur content. The sulfurous gases were used to make sulfuric acid, one of the fundamental products of the chemicals industry. The burnt ore from the chemical works was then treated to remove the copper and other valuable metals it contained. The iron cinders that remained were sent to iron works for smelting. During these difficult years, revenues were low and development costs were running at more than £100,000 per month. The purchase agreement with the Spanish government was renegotiated on more favorable terms, the company was financially restructured, and additional funds were raised through the issue of mortgage bonds. Eventually, in 1876, a favorable price-fixing and market-sharing agreement was made with Tharsis, and the prospects for both companies began to improve.

The RTC was the major beneficiary of the 1876 agreement. Under this, the company gained control of the lucrative and rapidly expanding German market for pyrites, and within a matter of years it had become the dominant firm—with a 50 percent market share—in an oligopolistic world industry, with some degree of control over prices. At the same time, more of the product of the mines was treated locally to recover the copper contained therein. By the end of the 1880s, Rio Tinto was the leading producer of copper in the world. The company had smelters in Spain and a smelter and refinery in south Wales. In 1887, when the French entrepreneur Hyacinthe Secrétan attempted to corner the world copper market to raise prices, RTC at first reaped the benefits of its participation in the scheme, whereby Secrétan undertook to buy all its copper at fixed prices, and was not severely affected when Secrétan's scheme backfired in 1889, resulting in a spectacular collapse in the copper market. The strong market position of the company—by 1887 it was responsible for eight percent of the total world copper supply—was reflected from the 1880s onwards in high profits. The larger part was returned to shareholders as dividends.

New Technology at the Turn of the Century

Hugh Matheson laid the foundations for the subsequent prosperity of the RTC, which rose to a high level under the leadership of Sir Charles Fielding. In his first ten years as chairman, 1898 to 1908, the company paid an average annual dividend of 41 percent on a share capital of £3.5 million. Fielding built solidly on the achievements of the Matheson era, assuming personal responsibility for the introduction of a range of new technologies such as pyritic smelting. He also streamlined management, accounting, and decision-making practices, and, at a time of strong market growth, these innovations helped elevate the company to a higher level of profitability. The Spanish government, under pressure from nationalists of all descriptions, tried to lay claim to a larger share of company revenues, but these efforts were generally thwarted; nor did the laborers of the mining district have much success in raising the level of wages paid by Rio Tinto. The company showed scant regard for the argument that it could afford to pay much more than it did, pointing out that it already paid more in cash and kind than most other large employers in Spain. The real wages per head of the 15,000 workers employed by the RTC in Spain in 1913 were actually less than those paid to 10,000 workers employed 20 years earlier. Low-cost housing; discretionary pensions; and company stores, schools, taverns, and other recreational facilities began to cause resentment—as substitutes for higher wages—among the workers and their families.

Strikes of varying length and bitterness became commonplace at Rio Tinto following the outbreak of World War I, exacerbated by ever-rising prices and declining real wages. A violent and acrimonious nine-month strike in 1920 ended with the unions exhausted and the company resented in many sections of Spanish society, across the political spectrum. From this time onward, the fate of the RTC in Spain was bound up with the turbulent course of national politics. There was a period of relative stability between 1923 and 1929 under the dictatorship of Miguel Primo de Rivera, and the company was fortunate to escape lightly when it was discovered to have been evading export taxes through under-recording of the copper content of minerals shipped from Huelva. After Primo de Rivera left office, however, there followed a long period of disruption and uncertainty that lasted until the mines were sold to Spanish interests in 1954. As left- and right-wing political factions vied for power between 1929 and 1936, the RTC came to be seen as an economic Rock of Gibraltar that must concede more in the interests of Spain. Damaging labor laws and taxation policies were introduced at the very time when the company was suffering from depressed trading conditions around the world, and when the copper content of the ores mined at Rio Tinto was plummeting. The decision was made by the third chairman of the company, Sir Auckland Geddes, who served from 1925 to 1947, to invest only as much money in Spain as was needed to sustain the operation

The 1936–1939 Spanish civil war brought further problems. From an early date, the Rio Tinto mines were occupied by the Insurgent forces led by General Francisco Franco. The mineral wealth of the district was seen by Franco as a means of procuring arms from the Axis powers, and within months the RTC found itself caught up in a complex web of diplomatic intrigue involving London, Berlin, Rome, and the Franco regime. Control over the company's Spanish assets had been lost, and was never effectively regained. During World War II and the period of reconstruction which followed, the RTC had little control over production, prices, or the numbers of workers employed in Spain. The company was held in check by restrictive laws and regulations, causing the real value of its assets to fall with the passage of each frustrating year. It was with great relief that the RTC managed to sell its Spanish operations in 1954. After many years of negotiations, involving Franco himself, the business was sold to a newly formed Spanish company in exchange for a one-third interest in the enterprise plus £7.7 million in seven annual installments.

Global Expansion

Auckland Geddes involved the company in ventures in other parts of the world and brought to the RTC a new style of business leadership. Unlike previous chairmen, he eschewed close involvement in day-to-day administrative matters in favor of major questions of policy and organization. He delegated responsibilities to full-time directors recruited from outside the business, and he initiated a search for major new investment opportunities in mining and related fields. Exploration subsidiaries were formed and research stations opened. A large minority shareholding in the Davison Chemical Corporation, a leading United States artificial-fertilizer manufacturer, was purchased. Together with Davison, the RTC set up a series of subsidiaries throughout Europe to manufacture and market the versatile chemical absorbent, silica gel. Substantial minority shareholdings were also acquired in several other companies devoted to exploration and the development of new products.

By far the most significant of the new departures inspired by Geddes was the involvement of the RTC in the development of the Northern Rhodesian (now Zambian) copperbelt. The opportunity to secure a stake in the field came early in 1929 when U.S. interests attempted to take over the promising N'Changa deposits. Along with Sir Ernest Oppenheimer and other members of the British-cum-South African business community, Geddes judged this move to be detrimental to British business interests, and led the resistance to it. By the time the struggle was over, the RTC had acquired sizable copperbelt holdings and valuable information which suggested that the deposits were amongst the richest and most extensive ever discovered. Further shares were purchased in major copperbelt development companies in the months following the N'Changa struggle, and by 1930 the RTC had become a major economic force in Northern Rhodesia. In that year Geddes and Sir Ernest Oppenheimer, whose Anglo American Corporation was the leading company in copperbelt finance, forced through the merger of three of the biggest development companies to form the Rhokana Corporation. Geddes was appointed chairman of the new company. Under his leadership Rhokana emerged during the next 17 years as one of the largest and lowest-cost copper companies in the world.

Not all of Geddes's business initiatives were so successful. The RTC's venture into chemicals proved in the end to be a financial disaster, and the firm's exploration activities never yielded anything of worth. Failure in these fields was largely a consequence of the world economic depression but in part such losses were due to ill-informed and hasty judgments on the part of the RTC board. The returns on the Northern Rhodesian investments, however, more than compensated for these setbacks, enabling the firm to survive the protracted decline of its Spanish business, and laying the foundations for its emergence as a modern multinational enterprise.

The Postwar Period

The regeneration of the RTC after World War II was, to a great extent, the work of two men, Mark Turner and Val Duncan, who formed one of the most creative business partnerships of modern times. Turner, the elder of the two and an investment banker by training, was appointed acting managing director of the company in 1948 on a part-time basis. He was charged with finding a full-time replacement, and for the position he groomed Duncan, a younger lawyer he had met during the war. Duncan was appointed managing director of the RTC in January 1951, allowing Turner, who remained a leading member of the RTC board and Duncan's closest colleague, to devote more of his time to the banking business of Robert Benson, Lonsdale—later Kleinwort Benson. Together, Duncan and Turner persuaded their colleagues and leading shareholders that Rio Tinto should aim to become a growth-oriented, broadly based natural resource company with operations concentrated in politically stable parts of the world, especially the Commonwealth countries. In the late 1940s and early 1950s, interests in a range of potential mines were secured, from tin and wolfram in Portugal to diamonds in South Africa and copper in Uganda. Between 1952 and 1954, a network of amply funded exploration subsidiaries was established to search for mineral deposits that might be exploited on a large scale in Canada, Africa, and Australia.

The sale of the Spanish mines in 1954 released further human and financial resources for the task of rebuilding and reorienting the RTC. An intense period of exploration followed, which sent Duncan and other executives to all parts of the world to supervise exploration agreements and consider the mine-development deals put to the company from time to time. The first tangible result of this activity came in 1955 with the purchase of a majority interest in the Algom group of uranium mines in the Elliot Lake district of Canada. The authorized capital of the RTC was raised from £8 million to £12 million to accommodate the purchase, and a loan of US$200 million was raised against various supply contracts to fund the development of seven major mines. The company's position in the uranium industry was consolidated by the simultaneous acquisition of a controlling interest in the Mary Kathleen mine in Australia. By the end of the 1950s Rio Tinto was responsible for the production of 15 percent of the world's uranium oxide, and along the way the company had gained control over two highly promising mineral prospects: the vast Hammersley iron ore deposits in Western Australia and the Palabora copper deposit in South Africa.

Merging Rio Tinto and Consolidated Zinc

By the early 1960s Duncan was confident enough to take the decisive step toward realizing his vision of the RTC as a first-rank multinational enterprise. Merging was the obvious means of speeding the process of building up the organization, and he found an ideal prospective partner in the London-based Consolidated Zinc Corporation. This company had steadily expanded its activities since 1905 when it was launched to recover the large quantities of zinc remaining in the tailings dumps of the legendary silver-lead mines at Broken Hill in New South Wales, Australia. CZ's operations were still concentrated in Australia, but had been progressively extended to include a wide range of mining and metallurgical activities. The compatibility of CZ and the RTC was both strategic and structural. Strategically, the leading directors of CZ wished to attain major-company status through geographic diversification and the development of important new prospects, particularly the vast Weipa bauxite deposits of northern Queensland. Structurally, the company was about the same size as the RTC with net profits running at a little over £1 million per annum, and its major interests were in complementary rather then competing areas. The merger would, at a stroke, produce a large and broadly-based organization with financial and technological resources to undertake a range of promising new ventures. In July 1962 the two companies came together to form RTZ. Duncan was appointed managing direc-

tor of the new concern, and in 1963, on the retirement of A.M. Baer, he became chairman and chief executive of RTZ—positions which he retained until his death in December 1975.

Under Duncan's leadership, RTZ rapidly rose to prominence in the natural resource industries of the world. In partnership with Kaiser Aluminum, the firm established an integrated aluminum business in Australasia, Comalco Limited. The Hammersley iron and Palabora copper projects were brought to fruition. Extensive exploration was continued, eventually yielding large-scale mines in Papua New Guinea (Bougainville Copper), Canada (Lornex Copper), and Namibia (Rössing Uranium). Meanwhile, the scale and the scope of the business was further expanded through the purchase of going concerns: Atlas Steels (high-grade specialty steels) in Canada, Borax Holdings (industrial raw materials) in the United States, and Capper Pass (tin refiners) and Pillar Holdings (aluminum fabricators) in the United Kingdom. By the early 1970s RTZ had achieved the geographically and geologically diverse pattern of operations long pursued by Val Duncan.

Duncan made an important contribution to advancing the fortunes of the enterprise. He was the principal architect of the strategy of promoting growth through involvement in a stream of large-scale, capital-intensive natural resource projects. Potential financial limits to growth were overcome through the funding of massive projects with a high ratio of loan capital to equity. Multi-million dollar loans were raised by Duncan and his team throughout the world through the device of offering long-term supply contracts as collateral. Potential organizational and managerial limits to growth were overcome by the progressive devolution of responsibilities to a series of nationally based companies, each charged with the goal of involving RTZ in substantial new projects. By the early 1970s RTZ had emerged as a loosely knit family of companies with the activities of the parent concern limited to the provision of group services, the controlling of major strategic and financial decisions, and the appointment of top personnel.

The strategy, organization, and policies devised by Val Duncan remained in place in the 1980s. Duncan was succeeded as chief executive by Mark Turner. He continued in office until his death in December 1980. Turner saw no need to change course, nor did Anthony Tuke who replaced him, nor has Alistair Frame or Derek Birkin, the latest in the long line of distinguished chairmen which began with Hugh Matheson. The essential integrity of RTZ has been maintained while growth has continued. New mines and smelters have been brought on stream, and new processing facilities have been developed. Some businesses have been bought; others have been sold. The biggest boost to the enterprise came in 1989 with the acquisition of BP Minerals for £2.6 billion. This deal brought to RTZ one of the greatest names in world mining, the Kennecott Corporation, and a portfolio of assets in 15 countries, including the world's largest opencast copper mine and the world's largest producer of titanium dioxide feedstock. RTZ immediately became one of the world's largest producers of gold outside South Africa. The shares of world output accounted for by the much-enlarged company in 1989 were 55 percent of borates, 30 percent of titanium dioxide feedstock, 13 percent of zircon, 15 percent of industrial diamonds, 14 percent of vermiculite, eight percent of talc, and five percent or more of uranium, copper, and molybdenum. RTZ also ranked amongst the world's largest producers of tin, bauxite, silver, iron ore, gold, lead, and zinc.

In the mid-1990s, the company's exploration of mines around the world continued, with projects for gold in Papua New Guinea, prospecting in northern Norway's Finnmark region, and expanded coalmining by buying U.S. operators Nerco and Cordero Mining. In 1997, copper and gold exploration looked promising at Famatina in northwestern Argentina.

In March 1997, RTZ-CRA announced a management restructuring into six new global product businesses, with three to be based in London and three in Australia. Copper, gold and other minerals, and industrial minerals, were now based in London. In Australia, aluminum was headquartered in Brisbane, energy in Melbourne, and iron ore in Perth. The businesses would be supported by the worldwide technology and exploration groups which remained headquartered in London. In June 1997, the name was changed to Rio Tinto plc.

As the 1990s drew to a close, Rio Tinto was looking at a strong world economy that would demand primary raw materials, such as copper, gold, and coal. Prices were holding, as well, but competition might be a concern from such emerging markets as Russia and China. With its long view in production and project development, many new projects, open management style, and responsiveness to opportunity, Rio Tinto was expected to remain the world's top global mining company.

Principal Subsidiaries

Kennecott Corp. (U.S.); Nerco, Inc. (U.S.); Cordero Mining Co. (U.S.); U.S. Borax Inc. (U.S.); Rio Tinto Zimbabwe Ltd. (Zimbabwe; 56.04%); QIT-Fer et Titane Inc. (Canada); Coal & Allied Industries (Australia; 71.46%); Comalco Ltd. (Australia; 50%); Dampier Salt Ltd. (Australia; 67.4%); Hamersley Iron Pty. Ltd. (Australia; 64.94%); Queensland Coal Pty. Ltd. (Australia); Rio Paracatu Mineracao S.A. (Brazil; 51%); Novacoal Australia Pty. Ltd.; Angelesey Aluminium Ltd. (U.K.; 51%); Talc de Luzenac S.A. (France; 99.75%); P.T. Kelian Equatorial Mining (Indonesia; 90%); Rossing Uranium Ltd. (Namibia; 68.58%); New Zealand Aluminium Smelters Ltd. (79.36%); Bougainville Copper Ltd. (Papua New Guinea; 53.58%); Palabora Mining Co. Ltd. (South Africa; 64.9%).

Principal Operating Units

Minera Escondida (Chile); Argyle Diamonds (Australia); Talc de Luzenac (France).

Further Reading

Avery, David, *Not on Queen Victoria's Birthday: The Story of The Rio Tinto Mines,* London: Collins, 1974.

Harvey, Charles E., *The Rio Tinto Company: An Economic History of A Leading International Mining Concern 1873–1954,* St. Ives: Alison Hodge (Publishers), 1981.

Lucas, Alastair, "How CRA and RTZ went Dutch," *Corporate Finance,* December 1996, pp. 18–20.

"Northern Gems," *Maclean's,* March 4, 1996, pp. 54–55.

"When Will the Rio Carnival End," *The Economist,* July 29, 1995, pp. 46–47.

—Charles Edward Harvey
—updated by Dorothy Kroll

Rite Aid Corporation

30 Hunter Lane
Camp Hill, Pennsylvania 17011
U.S.A.
(717) 761-2633
Fax: (717) 975-5871
Web site: http://www.RiteAid.com

Public Company
Incorporated: 1968
Employees: 73,000
Sales: $6.97 billion
Stock Exchanges: New York Pacific
SICs: 5912 Drug Stores and Proprietary Stores; 8741
    Management Services

Rite Aid Corporation, one of the largest retail drugstore chains in the United States, operates over 3,600 drugstores in 27 eastern and western states, and the District of Columbia. Rite Aid's newer stores average just under 11,000 square feet and offer a professional pharmacy service, a full selection of health and personal care products, and over 1,200 Rite Aid brand products. The company also operates Eagle Managed Care Corp., a wholly-owned subsidiary that markets prescription plans and sells other managed health-care services to large employers and government-sponsored employee benefits programs.

Company Origins

Although Rite Aid was not formally incorporated until 1968, it got its start a few years earlier through Rack Rite Distributors, developed by Alex Grass, Rite Aid's founder and later chairman and chief executive officer. In 1962 U.S. federal legislation repealed the fair trade laws that fixed minimum retail prices on most products, opening up the door to discount stores, price wars, and vigorous competition. Quick to take advantage of the situation, Rite Aid opened its first discount drugstore in 1962 in Scranton, Pennsylvania. Called the Thrif D Discount Center, this was the forerunner of the modern Rite Aid drugstores.

By Christmas 1962 Thrif D was taking in $25,000 each week. It tripled its first-year projected sales of $250,000, pulling in $750,000. While the company continued to develop Rack Rite distributors, Thrif D's sales results proved that discount drugstores were truly profitable. In 1963 Rite Aid opened five more drugstores, extending its market area to New York.

By 1964 Rite Aid's market territory included New Jersey and Virginia. Its store count doubled, bringing the total to 12. The number of employees had grown to 200. Expansion did not stop there; in 1965 Rite Aid penetrated Connecticut, and its store count rose to 25.

In 1966 Rite Aid continued to expand. Its number of stores reached 36. The growth of both the retail chain and the "rack-jobbing" portion of the business, Rack Rite Distributors, generated the need for more space, so Rite Aid began to construct a new corporate headquarters and distribution center. It also opened the first Rite Aid pharmacy in one of its drugstores in New Rochelle, New York. The following year Rite Aid introduced 70 of its own private-label products. The results of the Rite Aid pharmacy's first year were so positive that the company planned to continue installing pharmacies throughout its drugstore chain.

Acquisitions and Change in the Late 1960s and 1970s

The following years brought many changes and firsts for the company. Rite Aid made its first acquisition when it bought the Philadelphia-centered 11-store Martin's chain. Its store count rose to 60, and its market share began to grow in Baltimore, Maryland; Newark, New Jersey; and Rochester and Buffalo, New York. Also, Rite Aid made its first public stock offering, issuing 350,000 shares at $25 per share, as well as formally changing its name to Rite Aid Corporation.

In 1969 Rite Aid acquired the 47-store Daw Drug Co. of Rochester, New York, bringing Rite Aid's store count to 117. The company also acquired Blue Ridge Nursing Homes along with Immuno Serums, Inc., and Sero-Genics, Inc., incorporating them into the company's medical services division. Offering more than 260 of its own private label products also contributed to Rite Aid's growth. The company increased its mechanical efficiency, installing material-handling equipment, such as conveyers, in its drug warehouse. It hooked up a telephone-order transmission system between the warehouse and drugstores to move orders swiftly. In addition, Rite Aid installed electronic data-processing equipment to produce price tags. That year expansion was so visible that Rite Aid declared a two-for-one stock split.

On January 20, 1970, Rite Aid was admitted to the New York Stock Exchange and began trading on the big board at $25 per share with 2.8 million shares outstanding. Although the U.S. economy moved into a recession, Rite Aid was among the discount stores that flourished. Also in 1970 Rite Aid acquired the 16-store Fountain Chain in Clarksburg, Virginia. By that time the company offered more than 300 of its own products bearing the Rite Aid logo, prompting the addition of 100,000 square feet to its main distribution center in Shiremanstown, Pennsylvania. In November 1971 Rite Aid sold 250,000 new shares of common stock to the public.

In 1971 the company acquired Sera-Tec Biologicals, Inc., of New Jersey, which was combined with the company's prior acquisitions of Immuno Serums and Sero-Genics to comprise the company's medical services division. Rite Aid also purchased a 50 percent equity in Superdrug Stores Ltd., of the United Kingdom. During this period of rapid growth, Rite Aid pharmacies were filling more than five million prescriptions a year. To consolidate management and increase efficiency of the rapidly growing number of stores, Rite Aid separated its market area into five divisions and 20 supervisory districts.

In 1972 Rite Aid focused on internal efficiency in preparation for additional expansion. Also in 1972, Sera-Tec Biologicals, Biogenics, Inc., and Immuno Blood Services, Inc., were merged to form what would become known in the early 1990s as Sera-Tec. When 1972's Hurricane Agnes wrought severe damage on the company's stores in Wilkes-Barre, Pennsylvania, and Elmira, New York, it also damaged the phone and water service at corporate headquarters. Teams worked around the clock to make the necessary repairs, and stores were reopened fairly rapidly. In fact, Rite Aid handled the disaster so impressively that it still was able to report filling more than 6.25 million prescriptions that year.

In 1973, despite the Middle East oil embargo and ensuing recession, Rite Aid again began making acquisitions. It acquired the 49-store Thomas Holmes Corp. chain and the 50-store Warner chain, both in greater Philadelphia. The company also set about creating distribution centers that could handle the rapidly multiplying number of Rite Aid stores. It expanded its Shiremanstown distribution center by 71,000 square feet, enabling the facility to supply up to 500 stores. The company also built an automated distribution center in Rome, New York, to handle the growing northeastern market. Rite Aid's accounting and data processing departments moved to a separate building in Shiremanstown, which became the hub of the Rite Aid complex.

Further activity during this time included reducing its holdings in Superdrug PLC, the successor to Superdrug Stores, Ltd., to 42.5 percent, selling a 7.5 percent interest. The number of private label products that appeared bearing the Rite Aid logo climbed to 700. In addition, Rite Aid became one of the first drugstore chains in the United States to implement a senior citizen discount cardholder program.

By 1974 the Rome distribution center was supplying 131 Rite Aid stores. Rite Aid also created a fifth Sera-Tec center in Pittsburgh, just as the Dow Jones Industrial Average was falling to 663—the lowest since 1970—and worldwide inflation set in. Over the next year Rite Aid focused on internal organization and increased its security department in an effort to reduce shoplifting.

By 1976 Rite Aid resumed acquisitions, purchasing the 52-store Keystone Centers, Inc. of Pennsylvania and New Jersey. The following year, it to acquired 99 more stores by buying the Read's Inc. drug chain in Baltimore. This purchase led to Rite Aid's garnering the largest market share in Baltimore. In 1977 Rite Aid's private label products, with almost 900 different items, accounted for nine percent of its retail sales.

Although the value of the dollar plunged in 1978, Rite Aid's momentum did not. Rite Aid acquired 11 stores from Red Shield in Pittsburgh and the four-store Quality Drugs chain of greater Philadelphia. By focusing on providing value in the most efficient manner possible, Rite Aid gained substantial market share in the major metropolitan markets of Buffalo, Rochester, and Syracuse, New York; Charleston, South Carolina; Baltimore; and Philadelphia. The company also added 11,500 square feet to its executive space in Shiremanstown, where it bought a 79,000-square-foot building to house the growing finance, advertising, store engineering, and construction departments. Then, focusing on its central businesses, Rite Aid sold the Blue Ridge Nursing Homes in Camp Hill and in Harrisburg, Pennsylvania, for an after-tax profit of $1.8 million.

In 1979 Rite Aid acquired six U-Save stores in North Carolina and eastern Tennessee, as well as nine Shop Rite stores in the Hudson Valley. It redesigned its company logo and updated its store interiors, using mirrored canopies and bright colors throughout, while streamlining checkout counters in the process. In order to save time and money on West Virginia store openings and transportation costs among 140 of its existing stores, Rite Aid started up a 210,000-square-foot distribution center in Nitro, West Virginia. Moreover, the company set ambitious goals, such as increasing store count by ten percent every year and continuing to open higher-margin pharmacies throughout its drugstore chain.

New Strategies in the 1980s

In 1980 Rite Aid adopted some new tactics in its growth plan. Its board of directors agreed tentatively to buy back as many as one million shares of Rite Aid common stock. These shares would be retained as treasury shares to provide liquid assets that could be quickly translated into cash for acquisitions, funds for the employees' stock option plan, or any other corporate purposes. That year Rite Aid acquired the six-store Schuman Drug of Landsdale, Pennsylvania, and the four-store Lane drugstores in Youngstown, Ohio, establishing a new prescription division for Ohio and western Pennsylvania. To expedite the processing of third-party claims, Rite Aid installed a scanning system in its data processing department. The company opened a 43,000-square foot addition to its finance and accounting building. Also in 1980 Rite Aid became one of the nation's largest suppliers of plasma with the opening of its ninth plasmapheresis center.

By 1981 Rite Aid had become the third-largest retail drug chain. It acquired the 31-store South Carolina division of Fays Drug and made its third stock split since its initial public offering in 1968, issuing additional common stock contingent on the four-for-three stock split. The company also set up a new division to handle its business in West Virginia and western Pennsylvania.

In 1982 Rite Aid became the largest U.S. drug chain as measured by the number of stores and market share in New York, Pennsylvania, New Jersey, Maryland, and West Virginia. Rite Aid continued to expand its market area westward, acquiring the four-store Cochran Drugs in Columbus, Ohio; the 16-store Lomark Discount Drug Stores Inc., in Cincinnati, Ohio; and the 26-store Mann Drugs of High Point, North Carolina. In addition to these drugstores, Rite Aid acquired the fifth-largest toy store in the nation, the 128-store Circus World Toy Stores, Inc. Rite Aid also expanded its Nitro, West Virginia, distribution center. The company now had total distribution capacity for 1,200 stores, which was essential and timely; Rite Aid opened its 1,000th store in Durham, North Carolina.

Rite Aid's sales exceeded $1 billion in 1983. It was listed among *Forbes* magazine's top 500 companies in both sales volume and number of employees. It issued a three-for-two stock split, its fourth stock split since it became listed and its second in two years. The value of Rite Aid's holdings in Superdrug PLC increased when that company went public and began trading its shares on the London Stock Exchange—at which point Rite Aid sold one-third of its interest in Superdrug, bringing its holdings down to 28.2 percent of the company's outstanding shares. Partially because of this, Rite Aid was able to offer a new employee stock purchase plan; to acquire the four-store Beagle chain in West Virginia and Ohio; to open its first Heaven novelty shop; and to integrate a point-of-purchase and pharmacy computer system. All of this helped to establish Rite Aid as the largest drugstore chain in the Northeast.

Expansion beyond Core Business

By 1984 Rite Aid started expanding beyond its core business. It bought American Discount Auto Parts (ADAP), a 32-store chain based in Avon, Massachusetts. It also purchased Encore Books, Inc., a 19-store deep discount bookstore chain in Philadelphia. In addition to these departures from the company's core business, Rite Aid acquired the three-store Nifty Norm's, Inc. of Philadelphia, the 24-store Muir Drug, the six-store Herrlich Drugstores, the five-store Remes Drug Stores, the 13-store Lippert Pharmacies, three State Vitamin stores of Michigan, and the three-store Jay's Drugstores in western New York. In 1984 Rite Aid also spun off its subsidiary wholesale and grocery division, Super Rite, as an autonomous public company, selling a partial interest in its holdings for $22 million.

In 1985 Rite Aid focused less on acquisitions than on internally generated growth. While Rite Aid that year acquired four Midland Valley Drug stores in Midland, Michigan, and eight State Vitamin discount stores in Lansing, Michigan, it opened five stores of its own, moving into the deep discount drug market with the company's Drug Palace. Rite Aid further penetrated new markets by opening video rental departments in more that 160 of its drugstores. It also installed point-of-pur-

chase scanning registers and more computerized pharmacy equipment. The newly spun-off Super Rite took its first step into retail grocery with its purchase of the 47-store Food-A-Rama supermarket chain in Baltimore and Washington, D.C. Rite Aid's subsidiary, Sera-Tec, opened two new plasma centers, bringing the count to 11. That year, Rite Aid sold Circus World Toy Stores, Inc., for $35 million cash and 185,000 common shares. In addition, Rite Aid bought 1.1 million shares of its own common stock at $19 per share.

Rite Aid did not experience major expansion in 1986. It acquired only two Revco stores in Buffalo and opened six more Drug Palaces, bringing its deep discount drugstore total to 11. The year was nevertheless notable in that two of Rite Aid's corporate officers received prestigious positions. Preston Robert Tisch of Rite Aid's board of directors was appointed Postmaster General of the United States, and company President Alex Grass was named chairman of the board and president of the National Association of Chain Drug Stores.

In 1987 Rite Aid acquired the nine-store Harris Drug in Charleston, South Carolina; 113 SupeRx stores in Florida, Georgia, and Alabama; a 200,000 square-foot distribution center in Florida from the Kroger Co.; and 94 Gray Drug Fair, Inc., stores in Florida and Maryland, from the Sherwin-Williams Company. These acquisitions substantially expanded Rite Aid's southern market area. Because of the success of its pilot video departments in 1986, Rite Aid added 429 more video departments to its drugstores in 1987, bringing the total to 971. Rite Aid also continued to install pharmacy and point-of-purchase automated systems throughout the chain. That year *Dun's Business Month* ranked Rite Aid 25th among all publicly traded companies for consistent dividend advances. In 1987 Rite Aid was the largest employer in the retail drug industry.

The following year Rite Aid purchased from Sherwin-Williams the balance of Gray Drug Fair, consisting of 356 stores in Delaware, District of Columbia, Indiana, Maryland, New York, Ohio, Virginia, West Virginia, North Carolina, and Pennsylvania. This purchase brought Rite Aid's store count to more than 2,100 and greatly expanded the company's market penetration in these states. That year, in Winnsboro, South Carolina, Rite Aid opened its fifth distribution center. This 265,000 square-foot distribution center enabled Rite Aid to supply up to 450 more stores in the Southeast. In April 1988 Rite Aid acquired the Begley Company, consisting of 39 drugstores in Kentucky and 140 dry cleaners in ten states.

In 1989 the company continued to expand and enhance the technology available to its stores. Moreover, Rite Aid finalized a deal with Super Rite Foods Holding Corporation in March 1989 to sell its 46 percent interest in Super Rite Foods, Inc. Rite Aid also acquired 99 People's Drug Stores and 18 Lane Drug units. In September of that year, it disposed of its 46.8 percent equity in Super Rite Foods for $18.37 million, with a positive cash flow in excess of $40 million. That same year showed record sales for Rite Aid; its revenues of $2.87 billion for this 53-week fiscal year represented a 15.4 percent increase from the previous 52-week fiscal year. Company earnings, however, continued to absorb the cost of the enormous acquisitions the company made in 1987.

The company in 1990 continued to focus on the integration of both its past and present acquisitions. Rite Aid added 1,754 store computer systems, and it enhanced 2,279 pharmacy terminals. The pharmacy terminals enabled drug interaction analysis and cumulative tax information, all of which resulted in speedier prescription service. Prescription sales for 1990 advanced 17.8 percent from the previous year, and then represented a full 43 percent of store revenues. Rite Aid's computerization also propelled the company toward greater efficiency, enabling it to cut back on unnecessary corporate staffing in spite of the fact that the company's store count had continued to grow.

From 1987 to 1991, Rite Aid acquired more than 800 drugstores and opened 276 new stores, closing only 103 units. Within this period, Rite Aid's store count grew by nearly 60 percent. In 1991 Rite Aid added 68 stores and bought prescription records from 65 drugstores in Washington, D.C.

While some organizations viewed the recession of the early 1990s as a bleak period, Alex and Martin Grass, the father-and-son team then running Rite Aid, said it was a good time to buy, according to a January 13, 1992, *Business Week* article. The recession brought opportunities to acquire vulnerable companies, and Rite Aid bid for the bankrupt Revco D.S. chain in early 1992. Although the deal later fell through, Rite Aid had demonstrated its ability to move decisively and quickly. Significant acquisitions included 34 Whelby Super Drug Stores in Maine and New Hampshire in 1993; 72 La Verdiere Enterprises, Inc. drugstores and 16 Revco drugstores in 1994; and all Perry drugstores in 1995.

Beginning in 1994 Rite Aid opened 50 state-of-the-art drugstores in New York City, boosting the total to 67 within the city. Rite Aid planned to bring more stores into all of New York's boroughs later in the decade. In fiscal 1994 Rite Aid acquired Pharmacy Car, Inc. and Intell Rx Inc., a drug review company with proprietary software that reviewed physicians prescription patterns. From these two purchases emerged the subsidiary Eagle Managed Care Corp.

Martin Grass succeeded his father, Alex Grass, as Rite Aid's chairman and CEO in 1995. At the same time, the company shed four unrelated businesses in order to focus on its pharmaceutical operations: Encore Books, Concord Custom Cleaners, Sera-Tech Biologicals, and ADAP, the auto parts dealer. By mid-year Rite Aid appeared well positioned. Market value, once $1.3 billion in 1993, reached about $2.5 billion. Rite Aid set out to open, renovate, or expand 1,000 more stores over a three-year period.

In 1996 Rite Aid continued to restructure its business to operate larger, higher volume, and more profitable drugstores. In June the company purchased Taylor Drugs, a chain of 34 stores operating in Louisville, Kentucky. Rite Aid, already the largest drugstore operator in the state, entered Louisville with a major share of the market.

In November 1996 the company entered into a joint venture to provide mail order pharmacy services with Smith Kline Beecham's Diversified Pharmaceutical Services, a leading pharmacy benefit manager. This move was seen as another channel of distribution to offer prescriptions to select managed care customers.

Another attempt was made by the company in 1996 to its rival, Revco, but when the Federal Trade Commission rejected the plan, Rite Aid moved on to other prospects. December marked the largest acquisition in Rite Aid history—a merger with Thrifty PayLess, Inc., which had sales of $4.4 billion in 1,007 stores in the western United States. It was the largest chain drugstore operator in California, Oregon, Washington, and Idaho.

In 1997 Rite Aid integrated this West Coast operation into the chain, installing new computer hardware in all Thrifty PayLess stores. Rite Aid operated more than 3,600 stores, with revenues for fiscal 1998 expected to exceed $11 billion. In addition, in 1997 Rite Aid opened 369 new, 10,500 square foot prototype stores, which seemed to pay off. These new stores generated more than $3 million compared with the $2 million average of older, smaller stores, thanks to added space and innovative design.

Looking toward the year 2000, Rite Aid planned to seek opportunities to expand through mergers and acquisitions—but with a disciplined strategy. Not all drugstore chains fit the company's strategic plan, according to company executives. A primary goal was to achieve dominance in the markets Rite Aid served and in the new markets it chose to enter. The Thrifty PayLess addition was seen as a great opportunity to enhance earnings at a faster rate.

Improving return on assets was key. One goal was to achieve better working capital utilization over the next two years. To achieve a fast growth rate, Rite Aid planned on relocating or enlarging about 250 stores annually, expanding square footage on the East Coast by seven to eight percent per year. Technology was set to be another player in driving down costs along with productivity improvements.

Principal Subsidiaries

Eagle Managed Care Corp.; GDF, Inc.; Gray Drug Fair, Inc.; Keystone Centers, Inc.

Further Reading

"Bar Codes and RFDC Fill the Information Gap at Rite Aid," *Modern Materials Handling,* October 1993.
"Eagle Managed Care: A Wrong Way and a Rite Way," *Drug Topics,* September 5, 1994.
Gerber, Cheryl, "High Tech Pain Killer," *Forbes ASAP,* December 4, 1995, pp. 108–110.
"Lost in Space," *Financial World,* November 21, 1995, pp. 46–47.
"Groomed for Success," *Chain Store Age Executive,* April 1995, pp. 25–28.
"Rite Aid Sees a Future in Capitated Managed Care," *Drug Topics,* November 1993, p. 52.
"Rite Aid's Softer Side," *Chain Store Age Executive,* April 1995, p. 28.
Weber, Joseph, et. al., "Seizing the Dark Day," *Business Week,* January 13, 1992, pp. 26–28.

—Maya Sahafi
—updated by Catherine Hamrick

The Rival Company

800 E. 101st Terrace
Kansas City, Missouri 64131
U.S.A.
(816) 943-4100
Fax: (816) 943-4123

Public Company
Incorporated: 1932
Employees: 3,000
Sales: $313.86 million (1996)
Stock Exchanges: NASDAQ
SICs: 3634 Electric Housewares & Fans; 3561 Pumps & Pumping Equipment; 6719 Holding Company

The Rival Company is a leading manufacturer and marketer of small household and personal care appliances, as well as commercial and industrial fans and ventilation equipment. The company also manufactures a line of sump, well, and utility pumps. Rival became a household word in the early 1970s with the introduction of the Rival Crock Pot, a slow cooker that literally changed the way dinners were made for many people. Other items manufactured include can openers, meat slicers, grinders, toasters, ice cream makers, space heaters, ceiling fans, shower head massagers, humidifiers, air purifiers, and more. Rival products are sold under many brand names, including Rival, Rival Select, Simer, Pollenex, Patton, Fasco, Bionaire, and White Mountain.

The Founding in 1932

Rival was founded by Henry J. Talge in 1932. Talge was born in Russia in 1892 and moved to the Kansas City area in 1925, following sales jobs in Chicago, Detroit, New York, and St. Joseph, Missouri. Then called Rival Manufacturing Co. (a name carried through the early 1990s), the firm started as a specialty die cast operation. With eight employees, Talge set up his first factory at the former Hempey-Cooper building at the corner of Archibald and Pennsylvania in the Westport district of Kansas City.

Rival's first product was a manual citrus juicer, called the Juice-O-Mat. The "O-Mat" tag later become a trademark on many new product names, including the Can-O-Mat (can opener), Broil-O-Mat (broiler), and Ice-O-Mat (ice crusher). Talge saw a need for many products to make cooking and other food preparation procedures faster and easier.

The War Years

Like hundreds of manufacturers across the country, World War II completely halted production of all Rival products, and 100 percent of factory operations were switched to producing wartime products for three years. Rival began producing various tools for the aviation industry, but later switched to armaments. The company started making 13-pound practice aerial bomb castings for the U.S. Navy. Soon they were manufacturing 40,000 to 45,000 castings per month, and, during the war, made about 1.5 million for the Navy.

The company also produced 20mm shell fuses and 5-inch rocket heads. In the spring of 1942, Rival accepted a challenge to produce a special type of switch for the Navy. Each switch was made up of about 500 parts, each part small and precisely machined. Rival was proud of the fact that its rejection rate was extremely low, and, even for a period after the war, Rival continued to make three styles of the switch for the Navy.

Wartime production boosted employment to 350 at Rival's several factories in the Kansas City area. The Army-Navy "E" flag was displayed at these plants.

Postwar Growth

With World War II over, Rival re-introduced its various "O-Mat" products to a booming market. By 1945, Talge's son, Foster L. Talge, was general manager of the company at the young age of 34, and within four years he was president of the firm. Foster Talge expanded the product line, offering three types of wall can openers, five types of juicers, seven types of broilers, and two styles of ice crushers. Talge made an effort to hire former servicemen and started an apprentice program modeled after the Pratt and Whitney method.

In 1948, the company made its first major acquisition, purchasing Waverly Products, Inc., makers of the "Steam-O-Matic" irons. Waverly was in receivership at the time, but its irons were nonetheless extremely popular, with an estimated two million in use. Within a year, Rival had moved the manufacturing from Sandusky, Ohio, to Kansas City, leased a two-story manufacturing facility, and hired an additional 150 workers. The company had been producing 1,000 irons a day, but Talge ordered that boosted to 2,500 to meet demand.

By the end of the 1940s, total employment at Rival had reached 750, and the company continued to introduce new products, including a knife sharpener, called the "Knife-O-Mat." The Juice-O-Mat, developed 17 years prior, was still a major seller, with an estimated six million in use. Henry and Foster Talge both played a major role in designing and testing new products. Distribution was worldwide by this time.

1950s Bring Expansion, Innovations

The 1950s was a time of continued growth for the firm. In 1950, Rival of Canada began as an assembly operation in Montreal. In 1956, the company made another major acquisition, buying the National Slicing Machine Company, in White Plains, New York. Meat slicing and grinding became a major part of the product line offered by the company. A year later, Rival introduced the first electric can opener.

In the mid-1950s, the company opened a new manufacturing factory at 35th and Bennington in Kansas City on an 11-acre tract. That move allowed for future expansion, as well as consolidation of various warehouses, sales, and general offices scattered throughout the city. Within ten years, the company expanded the facility to about one-quarter million square feet under one roof, as the firm continued to introduce new products. Its product line now included the Shred-O-Mat, Steam-O-Mat, and Grind-O-Mat.

One of Rival's hallmarks was the vast majority of parts production done in-house, rather than being farmed out to smaller companies or to overseas operations. Rival's die casting operations included stamping, welding, screw machining, and polishing. The company received raw materials, including ingots of aluminum and zinc, as well as various sizes of steel, brass, copper, and bronze, and formed its products under one roof. All of the plating was done at the manufacturing facility, too. It was a triple-plating process, which called for the heated casting to be plated with copper, then nickel, then finally chromium. It was the largest plating operation in the Kansas City area.

The company also developed an electrostatic painting operation, which resulted in a more uniform and faster enameling of the products. The castings were electrically charged and put on a revolving disc while being coated with a thin layer of paint containing an opposite electrical charge. This created a fine paint mist that was attracted to the casting.

Talge Era Ends in the 1960s

In 1963, Henry and Foster Talge sold the company to Stern Bros. Investment Bank for $6.3 million. Foster remained with the company for a few years. By this time, sales had reached $12 million annually. Stern Bros. took the company public the next year. By 1967, Isidore H. (I.H.) Miller was president and another major plant expansion was in the works, this time totaling 115,000 square feet. Rival also had a 96,000-square-foot production facility in Sedalia, Missouri, about 80 miles east of Kansas

City. The company also acquired the Titan Manufacturing Company in Buffalo, New York, makers of portable electric heaters. Production was moved to Sweet Springs, Missouri, as the company began to open plants in smaller cities in Missouri, where labor costs were not as high and where union activity was less of a factor. Sales reached $21 million for fiscal 1966.

Innovations continued, as in 1968, the company introduced the first "Click N' Clean" feature on its can openers, a removable cutting assembly designed for easy cleaning.

Introduction of the Crock Pot in 1971

Nearly every company seems to have one or two major milestones in its history; for Rival, that undoubtedly would be the introduction of the Crock Pot in 1971. The Crock Pot redefined how many Americans cooked their meals, and at the height of its phenomenal growth, the company reported receiving letters claiming saved marriages, meals salvaged, and inspirations of poetry—all due to this revolutionary method of cooking.

The origins of the Crock Pot were very much unheralded. Rival purchased Naxon Utilities Corp., a Chicago-based maker of sun lamps and portable laundry equipment in 1970. Naxon also had a product called the Bean Pot, a slow-cooking pot that could prepare a bean meal without anyone attending to it. Miller said the Bean Pot was almost an afterthought during the negotiations. "No one paid any attention to it," he told the *Kansas City Times.* "We almost forgot about it."

After the acquisition, Miller asked Rival's home economist to experiment with the product. She developed an entire recipe book of dishes, with and without beans, that could be used to produce gourmet meals. The cooker's casing was redesigned to give it a dressy look, and it was renamed the Crock Pot. The Crock Pot made its debut at the National Housewares Show in Chicago in 1971, and it retailed for about $25.00.

Sales skyrocketed in the first few years. The Crock Pot posted sales of $2 million in its first year, leaping to $10 million in 1972, doubling to $23 million in the next year, totaling $57 million in 1974, and topping at $93 million in 1975. Like any buying craze that takes over the country, sellouts were common at retail stores. One retailer planned a major promotion of the Crock Pot, but canceled all advertising after its employees bought every Crock Pot prior to the store's opening.

The Crock Pot Roller Coaster

It has been said, "What goes up, must come down." But for Rival, the Crock Pot's descent was more like a plummet. Any item that goes from $2 million to $93 million in sales in a mere four years requires major retooling, and Rival turned to a Japanese manufacturer to help produce Crock Pots under the Rival label. Soon the foreign market was flooded with Crock Pot clones, however, and sales suffered dramatically.

In 1976 sales fell to $78 million and, a year later, sunk to $32 million. "We were living in anxiety on the way up and on the way down," Miller told the *Kansas City Times.* "We never knew how low sales would go." Two plants had to be closed, and the firm cut back on its import orders. The only consolation for Rival was that its competitors were also suffering from slack orders, and many went out of business. At its heyday, there were

40 manufacturers of the slow cooker. By the early 1980s, Miller said there was no import competition and only a handful of domestic manufacturers. Yet, when the roller coaster ride was over, the Crock Pot still emerged as Rival's leading sales product, responsible for about one-third of the company's sales. It surpassed the can opener, which had been the leading product.

Rival's total sales reached $126 million in 1975, the peak year for the Crock Pot, and fell to $73 million only three years later. But the company remained profitable throughout and, guided by Miller's austere financial controls, did not undergo the growth pains most companies experience with such huge sales. "We didn't allow the kind of expansion we thought we would regret at a later point," Miller said. "That allowed us to handle the downturn in an orderly fashion."

By the mid-1970s, Rival had six manufacturing facilities, all in Missouri except for a pottery plant in Jackson, Mississippi, which manufactured stoneware for the Crock Pot. The company continued to move all its manufacturing out of Kansas City to other towns and, in 1976, transferred the last of 80 die cast operators to Sedalia. This left only 50 workers in the shipping and receiving area in Kansas City and about 200 corporate employees at the company's headquarters.

Company Goes Private in 1986

With the Crock Pot frenzy over, the company began to build sales during the 1980s. It introduced different styles of the Crock Pot and, in 1987, brought out the Potpourri Crock, which allowed users to heat spices while using the cooker to produce various aromas. It also reintroduced a deep fryer, an item it had not produced in 20 years, as well as air fresheners, a convection oven, and new types of can openers.

In 1986, the company went private. The New York investment firm of Gibbons, Green, van Amerongen arranged for the company to borrow money to buy back all of its stock. This leveraged buyout lasted only six years, as by 1992, the firm again became a publicly traded company. During its years as a private firm, Rival introduced the electric Crock Grill, the Rival Cookie Factory, and bought the Richmond Cedar Works, one of its principal competitors in the ice cream freezer market.

Period of Acquisitions in the 1990s

The 1990s was an era of acquisitions for Rival, as well as a time of diversification. For more than six decades a manufacturer of kitchen and household items, the company began to expand into the industrial and commercial sector. These acquisitions came under the direction of Thomas K. Manning, who was appointed CEO in 1989 after 16 years with the firm.

In 1992, the company acquired the Simer Pump Company from the Marley Co. Simer was a leading manufacturer in sump, well, and utility pumps for the "Do It Yourself" market. The $9.5 million purchase could not have been better timed, as the summer of 1993 brought heavy rains and flooding throughout the Midwest, and Simer pumps were heavily in demand for the draining of flooded basements.

Next on the acquisition list was Chicago-based Pollenex Corp., maker of air cleaners, hand-held massagers, and shower heads. The purchase price was reported at $18 million. Rival also expanded its overseas presence by entering a joint distributing agreement with Kenwood Appliance Limited, a firm based in England. Under the agreement, Rival created a line called Rival Select, which included the top line of its products, and Kenwood did likewise. These products were then marketed to more upscale retailers.

In 1994, the company added White Mountain Freezers to its product chain. The ice cream freezers made by this 150-year-old company complimented Rival's line of ice cream makers. These various acquisitions helped open channels to the hardware/home center stores and other department stores.

The company's biggest acquisitions, however, were yet to come. During a 12-month period in 1995–1996, the company made three large purchases with combined sales of $140 million. First, Rival acquired Patton Electric Company, Inc., based in New Haven, Indiana. The firm made space heaters and fans sold in the retail and industrial markets. Shortly after that, Rival purchased Fasco Consumer Products, manufacturers of heating, ventilating, and other products for the industrial and retail markets. Later, Rival bought Bionaire, Inc., a Canadian corporation that manufactured and distributed high quality portable air purifiers and humidifiers.

The many acquisitions of the 1990s were reflected in the company's strong growth in revenues. In 1992, the firm reported sales at $163.5 million. In 1994, sales increased to $229.23 million, and in 1996, grew to $313.86 million. The company reported to shareholders that fiscal 1997 sales would be at about the $400 million level. It offered more than 275 varieties of products that heat, cool, cook, steam, sharpen, clean, purify, toast, dry, slice, crush, and whip. Rival remained a leader in slow cookers (Crock Pot), meat slicers, heaters, and can openers.

Rival's move toward diversification has opened up new distribution channels in the United States and abroad. Although the firm has gone through the difficulty of integrating all of its acquisitions into a common system, the company expects to see the dividends pay off in the long run. It is clearly trying to position itself so that it no longer has to rely on any single class of the retail market for its financial strength.

Principal Subsidiaries

RC Acquisitions, Inc.

Further Reading

"Big Rival Plant Unit," *Kansas City Star,* September 8, 1963.

Hendricks, Mike, "KC Is Home to the Crock Pot King," *Kansas City Star,* September 24, 1991, p. E64.

"Highlight of Company History," The Rival Co., 1996.

Johnson, Roxane, "Rival Rides Herd on Crock Pot Craze," *Kansas City Times,* November 9, 1981, p. D1.

"Major Addition for Rival Mfg. Co.," *Kansas City Star,* January 29, 1967.

Reeves, Gregory S., "Henry J. Talge, 98, Philanthropist and Businessman, Dies," *Kansas City Star,* August 21, 1990, p. A1.

"Rival Manufacturing Co.," *Kansas City Star,* December 23, 1945.

"Rival Manufacturing Co.," *Kansas City Times,* September 3, 1948.

"Rival Manufacturing Iron Unit," *Kansas City Star,* January 30, 1949.

Rosenberg, Martin, "Shrewd Acquisitions Help Make Crock Pot Company Hot," *Kansas City Star,* September 27, 1994, p. E13.

—Gordon L. Heft

Furniture • Appliances • Electronics

Roberds Inc.

1100 East Central Avenue
Dayton, Ohio 45449-1888
U.S.A.
(513) 859-5127
Fax: (513) 859-8125

Public Company
Incorporated: 1971
Employees: 1,700
Sales: $342.1 million (1996)
Stock Exchanges: NASDAQ
SICs: 5712 Furniture Stores; 5719 Miscellaneous Home
 Furnishings Stores; 5731 Radio, Television &
 Electronics Stores; 5722 Household Appliance Stores;
 5713 Floor Covering Stores; 6141 Personal Credit
 Institutions

Characterized as "one of the most successful retailers of appliances in the Dayton area" by the *Dayton Daily News,* Roberds Inc. has used innovative merchandising to carve out profitable niches in its chosen markets. It is ranked among the nation's top 25 furniture sellers. Although it had six stores near its suburban Dayton headquarters, most of the company's stores were located in the Atlanta, Georgia area. Another eight units covered the region of Tampa, Florida.

Following its initial public offering in 1993, the chain adopted a new "megastore" merchandising concept known as Roberds Grand. It used this new model to break into the Cincinnati, Ohio market in 1996 and planned another opening in Columbus, Ohio for 1997. Roberds faced stiff competition from a number of national and local retail powerhouses in the mid-1990s, and its declining stock price reflected these uncertain market conditions. After established sales and earnings records in 1995, the company suffered a net loss in 1996.

Rescued from Bankruptcy in 1971

The Roberds story might have ended in bankruptcy in 1971 were it not for Kenneth Fletcher. Born and raised in Depression-era Texas, where he picked cotton and pumped gas to help support his family, Fletcher's biography reads like "a classic rags to riches tale," in the words of Terrence Johnson of the *Dayton Daily News.* Fletcher worked his way through East Texas State University. Upon his graduation in 1955, he got into the retail appliance business by selling Frigidaire refrigerators. A quick succession of promotions brought him to Dayton.

Fletcher quit Frigidaire at the age of 39 to form a partnership with local realtor Donald C. Wright and two minor investors, Howard Smith and Howard Robbins. Although Wright and Smith would go on to play hands-on roles as executives and directors of Roberds (Robbins eventually divested his stake), it was Fletcher who assumed the leading role. Together, they acquired the bankrupt Roberds furniture chain in West Carrollton, Ohio (a southwest suburb of Dayton) and set out to make it profitable. As president of the firm, Fletcher put in 12- to 14-hour days. His hard work paid off almost immediately; the store's sales jumped from $1 million in 1971 to $8.5 million in 1976.

Fletcher has been characterized as an aggressive, fearless, and hard-nosed businessman, but he is also modest. In a 1988 article for the *Dayton Daily News,* reporter Terrence L. Johnson quoted the retailer as saying, "You don't have to be overly intelligent. You have to put out effort in business." He would later attribute the chain's growth to nothing more complicated than "good deals" and "good service," but there was more to the formula than that.

The Roberds strategy was to offer a broad array of brand-name merchandise in a relatively large-format store. The company used consumer electronics (known as "brown goods" in industry parlance) and major appliances (known as "white goods") as something of a "loss leader." Low margin goods like ranges, dishwashers, washers and dryers, televisions, and stereos helped increase store traffic and generate economies of scale. But the real profits came from furniture and bedding, which generated about 50 percent of sales and more than 60 percent of operating income. Roberds's 60,000-square-foot store encouraged customers to browse through all of these products.

Company Perspectives:

"Roberds is a leading home furnishings retailer specializing in furniture, bedding, major appliances and consumer electronics products. Growing steadily from one store beginning in 1971, Roberds at December 31, 1995, operated 23 stores in Dayton, Ohio, Atlanta, Georgia, and Tampa, Florida. This growth has been sustained by our approach to satisfying customers: we combine high quality merchandise with outstanding customer service and guaranteed lowest prices. Our plans for the future involve continuing to set ourselves apart from our competition through strategic merchandising, pricing, and customer service. Our stores are spacious, modern facilities designed to create an open, pleasant shopping environment for our customers. We are known for our broad selection of name brands and our distinctive product mix. Our well trained professionals sales team provides friendly, knowledgeable service to our customers. We offer in-home delivery seven days a week with next-day delivery on big screen televisions, refrigerators, and bedding. Roberds's 1,700 employees share in our ongoing commitment to the customer and our mission to be the dominant home furnishings retailer in each of our markets and product categories."

Brief Diversification in the 1980s

Fletcher attempted to apply his turnaround strategy to a local apparel retailer, Metropolitan Clothing Co., in 1982. The partnership with former Elder-Beerman executive Richard Karp, however, was short-lived. Even injections of $750,000 cash from Fletcher and $3 million in bank loans could not turn the enterprise around. It lost money nearly every year it was under the Roberds umbrella and was liquidated in 1985.

Geographic Expansion in the Mid-1980s

Having established its second furniture/appliance store in Norcross, Georgia, outside Atlanta, in 1979, Roberds embarked on a period of intense growth in the mid-1980s. The company launched a Piqua, Ohio location in 1983 and established its second and third Georgia stores in 1984 and 1985. Roberds also penetrated the Tampa, Florida market in 1985 with the acquisition of Alpert's Furniture Store from General Cinema Co. The following year saw the addition of two more Florida stores via acquisition. Roberds built stores in Georgia in 1987 and 1989 and entered Indiana with a unit in Richmond in the intervening year. After adding three stores in 1990—one in Georgia and two in Florida—the company took a three-year hiatus from expansion. Sales had increased from less than $10 million in 1976 to $162.5 million in 1990. Net income neared $3 million.

At first glance, the chain's pattern of growth appears rather haphazard, jumping from Ohio, to Georgia, then Florida, and back again. But further examination reveals a pattern: through the mid-1990s, all Roberds stores were located along Interstate 75 within a 75-mile radius of a city having a population of more than one million. Roberds's suburban locations were key to its

strategy. Overhead and competition was generally lower in these areas, yet their placement near major highways made them easily accessible to customers as well as delivery trucks.

IPO, New Strategy Mark the 1990s

Roberds underwent something of a retrenchment in the early 1990s. It did not open any new outlets in 1991 and 1992, instead concentrating on increasing same-store sales and net income in the face of recession and intensifying competition. Rivals included national chains like Loew's Companies, Circuit City, and Best Buy Co., Inc., as well as regional opponents like Columbus's Sun Television and Appliances and REX Stores Corp. Despite its comparatively small size, Roberds felt it had an important advantage over its competitors; while they all concentrated on appliances and electronics, Roberds could afford to shave its profit margins on these brown and white goods and make up the difference via furniture and bedding sales. In fact, Roberds's sales increased by nearly 18 percent from 1990 to 1992, and net income more than doubled from $3 million to $7.4 million.

The company joined a veritable stampede of privately held firms to the public markets with an initial offering (IPO) of 2.7 million shares at $13 each (about a 46 percent stake) in November 1993. After expenses, the IPO raised about $30 million, which was applied to a chainwide renovation and expansion. Selling space was reorganized from brand-oriented "galleries" into product showcases by dismantling walls and partitions in favor of an "open store" format. This new display strategy featured groupings by type, for example, dining room sets or bedroom suites, as well as by function. For example, a home office grouping would combine a desk, office chair, and storage units with a multimedia computer package. A home theater grouping might showcase a big screen television, VCR, and stereo with a storage cabinet, sofa, recliner, and occasional tables. Roberds could then offer package deals including all components of the grouping or sell the individual pieces.

Proceeds of the IPO also enabled Roberds to resume expansion. The company added one store in Florida in 1993, three in Georgia in 1994, and four more (one each in Ohio and Florida and two more in Georgia) in 1995. But even before this growth spurt ended, the company had developed a new expansion strategy, one that would allow it to, as CEO Fletcher told the press, "leapfrog the competition."

Roberds adopted the "megastore" model in the mid-1990s, using it to establish a foothold in the Cincinnati market in 1996. Dubbed "Roberds Grand," the near-six-acre store was located in Springdale, a northwest suburb of the Ohio River city, and cost $10 million. Local ads noted that it was "bigger than a breadbox/bigger than Riverfront Stadium/bigger than Union Terminal." James McConville upped the ante by calling it a "gigastore" in his 1995 coverage for the trade journal *HFD*. Patterned after a Las Vegas casino, the behemoth featured a canopied circle drive out front, scads of red carpeting, and classically styled statuary and columns. Roberds reasoned that it could use one mammoth outlet to effect a strong presence, generate consumer excitement, broaden its price points at the high and low ends, economize on overhead, penetrate new markets, and do all this at a more rapid pace than it could with its traditional multistore expansion strategy. The company had plans to open a second "gigastore" in another new market, Columbus, in 1997. In 1996, Roberds launched a new, 480,000-square-foot warehouse east of Dayton to serve its three key Ohio markets.

In the wake of this rapid expansion, Roberds's sales increased by more than 55 percent, from $191.7 million in 1992 to $301.3 million in 1995, but its net income increased by only 7.5 percent, from $7.4 million to $8 million during the same period. The chain slid into the red in 1996, recording losses in the first half of the year. An $885,000 profit in the third quarter amounted to less than half of the previous year's net for the period and was not enough to offset the first half's shortfall.

The company blamed its 1996 losses on heavy competition, lackluster consumer spending, an unseasonably mild summer, and even the Olympics, but other factors also played a role. In June 1996, Roberds paid an undisclosed amount to settle a wrongful termination suit brought by an employee that also charged that his wife had been sexually harassed by another employee of the company. In the fourth quarter of that year, Roberds set aside $2.6 million to cover a workers' compensation judgment against it. Although the company was appealing its case to the Ohio Supreme Court early in 1997, that contingency fund contributed to its $830,760 loss in the fourth quarter of 1996. Roberds ended 1996 with a $910,000 net loss on sales of $342.1 million.

Not surprisingly, Roberds's stock price faltered in the wake of its poor showing, declining from an issued price of $13 in 1993 to just $7 in early 1997. The decline triggered yet another lawsuit. In December 1996, Roberds agreed to pay $1.6 million to settle a shareholder suit first brought in 1994 and elevated to class action status in October 1996. Shareholders who had charged that Roberds's forward-looking projections were deceptively rosy found that subsequent company reports laid out a litany of unforeseen events that could influence actual performance, including everything from "general economic conditions" to "Acts of God."

CEO Fletcher, who at more than 65 years of age continued to own about one-fourth of Roberds into 1997, must have hoped that his megastores would bring his company megaprofits in the waning years of the 1990s. Given his reputation as a tenacious competitor, he was not likely to retire until the chain had returned to healthy profitability.

Principal Subsidiaries

Roberd Insurance, Inc.

Further Reading

Bohman, Jim, "Roberds Chain Still Turning Up Volume," *Dayton Daily News,* June 13, 1988, pp. 1S, 2S.
——, "Tune in to Bouts: TV, Appliance Retailers To Battle for Lowest Prices," *Dayton Daily News,* June 6, 1994, pp. 1G, 3G.
Boyle, Bob, "Roberds Opens the View in Its Stores," *HFD-The Weekly Home Furnishings Newspaper,* June 13, 1994, p. 73.
Dillon, Jim, "Roberds Resolves To Compete with Vigor," *Dayton Daily News,* November 18, 1994, p. 7B.
Greenberg, Manning, "At Home with Multimedia Computing," *HFD-The Weekly Home Furnishings Newspaper,* November 15, 1993, pp. S6–S7.
——, "Showtime: Merchandising Home Theater," *HFD-The Weekly Home Furnishings Newspaper,* July 26, 1993, pp. 49–50.
Johnson, Terrence L., "Rags to Roberds: Hard-Nosed Stance Pays Off in Big Way for Company CEO," *Dayton Daily News,* October 31, 1993, pp. 1F, 2F.
"Judgment Lands Roberds in Red," *Computer Retail Week,* March 3, 1997, p. 3.
McConville, James A., "Roberds Assesses Strategy: Several New Units or Single Gigastore," *HFN-The Weekly Newspaper for the Home Furnishings Network,* February 6, 1995, p. 56.
Monk, Dan, "Roberds Touts Store Size in Ads," *Cincinnati Business Courier,* June 24, 1996, pp. 1–2.
Olenick, Doug, "A Store Beyond Super," *HFN-The Weekly Newspaper for the Home Furnishings Network,* May 15, 1995, p. 57.
"Outlet Store Opens; Roberds' New Clearance Center Discounts Dented and Discontinued Goods," *Dayton Daily News,* September 7, 1996, p. 4B.
Richter, Allan, "Chain Bets on a New 'Casino'; Roberds Grand Offers Furniture, Function and Fun," *HFN-The Weekly Newspaper for the Home Furnishings Network,* July 8, 1996, pp. 1–2.
"Roberds Lawsuit Over Shares Is Settled," *Dayton Daily News,* December 4, 1996, p. 7B.
Smith, Katherine Snow, "Furniture Retailer Makes Big Moves," *Tampa Bay Business Journal,* August 26, 1994, pp. 1–3.
"2 Chains Plan Expansions," *Television Digest,* November 8, 1993, p. 14.

—April Dougal Gasbarre

Robertson-Ceco Corporation

5000 Executive Parkway
Suite 425
San Ramon, California 94583
U.S.A.
(510) 358-0330
Fax: (510) 244-6780

Public Company
Incorporated: 1990
Employees: 1,400
Sales: $255.9 million (1996)
Stock Exchanges: New York
SICs: 3442 Metal Doors, Sash & Trim; 3444 Sheet Metal
   Work

Robertson-Ceco Corporation, through its subsidiaries, is a leading manufacturer of pre-engineered metal buildings, marketed chiefly within North America. All other operations, such as manufacturing of wall, roof, and floor building components, were discontinued during the 1990s. The company was formed in 1990 by the merger of H.H. Robertson, Inc. and Ceco Industries, Inc., a merger that followed several years of losses and attempted buyouts and involuntary takeovers. Turmoil continued through the early years of the new company, as reflected by repeated headquarters relocations within seven years—from Pittsburgh to Boston to San Ramon, California—and accompanying changes of management and employees. In the late 1990s the company was focusing on restoring profitability by cutting costs and concentrating on its core metal building operations.

Origins of the Company

The Robertson-Ceco Corporation was born in 1990 from the merger of two large building materials and construction companies, H. H. Robertson, Inc. of Pittsburgh, and Ceco Industries, Inc., of Oakbrook Terrace, Illinois. Both of these companies had had troubled histories during the 1980s, with buyout and hostile takeover attempts vying for management attention along with everyday business operations.

Ceco Industries had endured the death of its founder, C. Louis Mayer, after which a group led by senior management of the company, including Chairman Erwin Schulze and some of the founder's family members, offered to buy the company from other shareholders in 1986, with plans to take the company private. However, the buyout initially failed because the stock prices mysteriously began to rise, causing speculation that there might be another bid in the works. A special committee of the board of directors then refused the offer made by the original group, but no offer from another party ever materialized. Eventually a price was agreed on with the original group and the company went private. However, Ceco also incurred $80 million in debt along with the privatization, a major burden even though profits remained healthy.

H.H. Robertson had an even more colorful time just prior to the merger. Beginning in 1983, Canadian corporate raider Samuel Belzberg began a campaign to take over the Pittsburgh company, but he underestimated the resistance he would encounter from the existing management and other shareholders. Robertson appointed a new president and CEO, James L. Davis, who hoped to increase profits by moving from expensive office projects to lower-cost construction projects. A successful antitrust suit also was launched against Belzberg in an attempt to stop a takeover. As Davis and Belzberg carried on their struggle, the company began to flounder. It tried to boost sales by making low bids on projects, and losses piled up. Robertson incurred losses of over $30 million in 1985 and, by 1986, its financial condition was so shaky that it could not obtain the construction bonding insurance necessary for bidding on projects.

Under pressure from the board, Davis opted for early retirement in 1986 and was replaced by Jack Hatcher, who immediately began to cut unprofitable operations and reduce overall operating costs. The company continued to operate at a loss until 1989, its first profitable period in six years. Along the way other crises arose, including a patent infringement suit and a strike. Belzberg's company, First City Financial Corporation Ltd. of Vancouver, British Columbia, had become Robertson's largest shareholder, and it initiated discussions of a merger with Ceco.

The transition was anything but smooth; a dissident shareholder group at Robertson bitterly opposed the terms of the merger, but the opposition largely dissipated after the death of the leader of the dissident group, Anthony Pedone, in mid-1990. Bolstered by a $40 million investment from Frontera SA, a Swiss investment company, Robertson and Ceco merged into Robertson-Ceco Corporation in 1990. Ceco chairman Schulze retired and served as a consultant; Robertson chairman Hatcher was chosen to head the new company, which would have headquarters in Robertson's home city of Pittsburgh. Robertson agreed to assume Ceco's debt, now grown to $85 million.

Restructuring and Management Changes Begin

Unfortunately, the merger did not have the anticipated results. A national recession within the construction industry led to major losses for the new company. It also remained laden with debt and was still engaged in a hodge-podge of business activities carried over from the time of the merger, even though some no longer were profitable. Its major business segments consisted of a Metal Buildings Group, which manufactured, sold, and installed pre-engineered commercial and industrial metal buildings throughout North America; a Building Products Group, which manufactured, sold, and installed non-residential building components (wall, roof, and floor systems), operating on a worldwide basis; a Door Products Group, which manufactured and distributed metal, wood, and fiberglass doors and frames for commercial and industrial use and operated throughout the United States; and a Concrete Construction Group, which provided subcontracted services for forming reinforced concrete structures, also operating throughout the United States.

Within a year after the merger, Robertson-Ceco stock values had plunged, and losses of almost $125 million were recorded in 1991. Robertson-Ceco entered into a $135 million agreement with a Canadian company, United Dominion Industries, to sell its operations that manufactured wall products, industrial cladding and accessories, and similar products. Hatcher, while remaining chairman of the board of directors, resigned as president and CEO and was replaced by John O'Malley, a Massachusetts executive with international management consulting experience. O'Malley immediately announced a move of corporate headquarters to Boston, along with a downsizing of management and staff, consolidation of operations, and closing of some of the company's manufacturing facilities.

In early 1992, the company sold some of its domestic building products operations and its South African building products subsidiary. After the company defaulted on its loan payments in mid-1992, a major debt restructuring was announced under which debt holders would be given a 90 percent share of the company. Suddenly a new face appeared: investment banker Andrew Sage II, a former president of investment firm Lehman Brothers, bought up over one-third of Robertson-Ceco's common stock in late 1992. Sage, noted for his involvement in major corporate turnarounds, was in a prime position to force a major restructuring of Robertson-Ceco.

Rapid Divestitures and More Management Changes

With the involvement of Sage as a major shareholder, more changes at Robertson-Ceco began. A total management changeover occurred once again, with Sage becoming chairman in July 1993, temporary president (November 1992–July 1993) and tem-

porary CEO (November 1992–December 1993), Michael E. Heisley becoming CEO and vice-chairman in December 1993, and E.A. Roskovensky becoming president and chief operating officer in November 1994. Building products operations in Great Britain were sold in 1993, and late the following year, the company sold its Cupples Products Division, which manufactured curtainwall systems, to a newly formed company owned by its board of directors. Management also decided to dispose of its remaining European building product operations (located in Holland, Spain, and Norway), which were gradually sold off during the next two years. Other cost-cutting measures continued, such as downsizing the corporate office, redistributing manufacturing operations, and reducing work force levels.

In 1995 another business operation, the Ceco Concrete Division, was sold for $14.5 million to Pettibone Corporation, a newly-formed company controlled by CEO Heisley. Building products operations in Australia, Asia, and Canada also were discontinued. These divestitures marked the company's complete exit from the building products business, and operations were then focused on the remaining metal buildings operations.

This restructuring had an immediate positive impact on Robertson-Ceco's financial condition. Revenues rose from $251.58 million in 1994 to $265 million in 1995. A net loss of $21.76 million in 1994 fell to a net loss of $3.54 million in 1995.

1990s Operations and Future Outlook

As of 1996 Robertson-Ceco concentrated its efforts solely on the metal buildings business, which had remained successful. This operation consisted of three pre-engineered metal building companies: Ceco Building Systems; Star Building Systems; and H.H. Robertson Building Systems (Canada). Although sales of metal buildings traditionally had been aimed at the one-story small/medium building market, Robertson-Ceco was expanding into larger and multistory buildings, with custom design possibilities.

These metal building systems were manufactured at five plants within the United States (two in Iowa, and one each in California, Mississippi, and North Carolina), plus one plant in Ontario, Canada. Sales were made primarily through builder/dealer networks in the United States and Canada. Some sales were made to the Asian market, through local unaffiliated dealers and by sales staff employed by the company itself. The principal materials used in manufacturing these buildings were hot and cold rolled steel products, and the buildings had three components: primary structural steel; secondary structural steel; and cladding.

In mid-1996 Robertson-Ceco moved its corporate headquarters once again, this time from Boston to San Ramon, California. According to the company's 1996 annual report, the move was undertaken in order to incur lower occupancy costs. However, the move also initiated a major personnel housecleaning. Key management figures remained (Sage, Heisley, and Roskovensky), but most of the existing corporate staff chose not to move cross-country. An almost completely new staff, described by the report as bringing an "operationally oriented viewpoint" to the company, was in place by early 1997, with the most notable executive addition being that of Ronald D. Stevens as chief financial officer and executive vice-president following the move to California.

Along with the relocation, Robertson-Ceco's management renegotiated a new credit agreement under which it financed a loan of $20 million and had access to a revolving loan of another $25 million. The agreement enabled Robertson-Ceco to repay an outstanding $5 million note and to redeem other notes. It also would significantly lower financing costs for 1997 and the years beyond, hopefully allowing the company to get out from under the burden of carryover debt that had plagued it since its first days when the debt of Ceco Industries was assumed. One advantage of the remaining carryover losses was that Robertson-Ceco most likely would not incur any federal income tax liability for several years.

In the 1996 annual report, Chairman Sage and CEO Heisley strongly emphasized their commitment to focusing on the metal buildings business and on cost reduction in all operations. Specific strategies mentioned were improving plant efficiency, undertaking additional administrative streamlining, and enhancing the company's computer systems.

In the mid-1990s, it appeared that the management's approach might be working. Boosted by a $31 million tax credit in 1996, Robertson-Ceco finally experienced an encouraging year. While its 1996 revenues of almost $256 million were slightly lower than the $265 million of 1995, they were a huge improvement over the $187.5 million of 1992. Perhaps more importantly, Robertson-Ceco reported net income of $51.3 million in 1996, rather than the losses of several previous years (a bleak $71 million net loss in 1992, $21 million in 1993, $21.76 million in 1994, and $3.54 million in 1995).

Early 1997 brought more good news for the company. Its income in the first quarter of the year increased 54 percent over the same quarter in 1996, from $3.3 million to $5.1 million (although a substantial portion of this increase could be attributed to the redemption of some company debt under its new credit agreement). In a corporate press release dated April 24, 1997, President and Chief Operating Officer E.A. Roskovensky attributed the increase to "the strong demand in the metal buildings market and to the aggressive cost cutting actions taken over the past few years." He also mentioned the benefits of the debt refinancing, which lowered interest expense by $500,000 million in the first quarter of 1997 alone. A further encouraging sign was the size of the current backlog plus the level of new orders. Roskovensky did add a cautionary note, saying that the company's performance for the remainder of the year (and presumably for future years as well) would be "heavily influenced by general economic activity and the trend in interest rates."

Robertson-Ceco should continue to be strongly influenced by the executive officers and directors serving in 1997, who collectively controlled almost two-thirds of the common stock shares. CEO Heisley alone held almost 56 percent, enough to forestall any future takeover attempts.

Principal Subsidiaries

Ceco Dallas Company; Ceco Houston Company; Ceco San Antonio Company; M C Durham Company; M C Windsor Company; Meyerland Company; Robertson-Ceco Industries, Inc.; Star Construction Company; Star Building Systems, Inc.; H.H. Robertson, Inc. (Canada).

Further Reading

"The Belzbergs Start a Fight," *Business Week,* April 29, 1985.
"Ceco Bid to Go Private Falls Apart," *Crain's Chicago Business,* May 26, 1986, p. 82.
"Ceco Industries Gets Buyout Offer," *New York Times,* April 16, 1986, p. 4.
"Chief Retiring at Robertson," *New York Times,* September 22, 1986, p. D8.
Cotter, Wes, "Robertson Chief Climbs Aboard in Midst of Reorganization," *Pittsburgh Business Times,* December 9, 1991, p. 6.
"H.H. Robertson Stock Declines at News of Pedone Death," *Metalworking News,* August 27, 1990, p. 27.
"It'll Be Robertson-Ceco Following Acquisition," *Chicago Tribune,* July 27, 1990, p. 3.
Miles, Gregory L., "This Time the Belzbergs Picked a Lemon," *Business Week,* April 11, 1988, p. 96.
O'Connor, Matt, "Ceco Industries Buyout Offer is Pulled Back," *Chicago Tribune,* May 24, 1986, p. 7.
Olson, Thomas, "Turnaround Pro Buys Up Rob-Ceco," *Pittsburgh Business Times,* October 19, 1992, p. 1.
"Robertson-Ceco Closes Sale of Its Ceco Concrete Division," *Business Wire,* March 3, 1995.
"Robertson-Ceco Corp.; Robertson-Ceco Consented to Provide Its Debt Holders With a 90% Stake in the Firm," *Wall Street Journal* (Eastern ed.), August 3, 1992, p. B3.
"Robertson-Ceco Leaving Pittsburgh; Headed for Boston," *Pittsburgh Press,* February 29, 1992, p. A6.
"Robertson, Ceco Merge," *Pittsburgh Business Times,* June 4, 1990, p. 18.
"Robertson-Ceco Reports 54% Increase in Pre-Tax Earnings," *Business Wire,* April 24, 1997.
"Robertson-Ceco Reports Fourth Quarter Results of Operations," *Business Wire,* February 14, 1997.
Rossi, Cathy, "$40 Million Swiss Capital Spurs Robertson, Ceco Merger," *Metalworking News,* May 28, 1990, p. 4.
Rothman, Matt, et al., "How H.H. Robertson Is Fending Off the Belzbergs," *Business Week,* May 6, 1985, p. 77.
"Sharp Rise for Ceco's Stock; Action Follows Board Approval of Going Private," *Chicago Tribune,* September 3, 1986, p. 3.
Zapf, Karen, "Robertson-Ceco's Stock Continues Dip After 10 Years of Turmoil and Trouble," *Pittsburgh Business Times,* January 6, 1992, p. 16.

—Geraldina Azzata

Rothmans UK Holdings Limited

15 Hill Street
London W1X 7FB
England
(071) 491-4366
Fax: (071) 493-8404

Wholly Owned Subsidiary of Compagnie Financier Richemont AG
Incorporated: 1903 as Carreras, Limited
Employees: 29,600
Sales: £2.4 billion (1996 est.)
SICs: 2111 Cigarettes; 2121 Cigars

Although it holds only about two percent of the global cigarette market, Rothmans UK Holdings Limited ranks among the world's top four tobacco companies. In spite of high taxes, grave health concerns linked to tobacco use, and strict limits on advertising its products, Rothmans continued to achieve profitable growth in the early 1990s by targeting overseas growth, especially in Asia and Eastern Europe.

Rothmans International was established in 1972 under the direction of Dr. Anton Rupert, a South African who headed the Rembrandt Group, one of South Africa's largest enterprises, with interests in mining, textiles, and brewing as well as tobacco. Rembrandt (now Compagnie Financier Richemont AG) expanded its activities outside South Africa by buying into Rothmans Limited in 1954 and Carreras in 1958. It was Rupert's philosophy to allow these companies to operate independently, but with the companies beginning to duplicate resources and compete against each other, the formation of Rothmans International seemed preferable.

This organizational scheme held until 1993, when a group restructuring separated the company into Vendome, in charge of the luxury brands, and Rothmans International plc, the tobacco interests. In 1995, the Richemont Group acquired all of Rothmans' outstanding shares, making it a wholly owned subsidiary.

Origins in the 19th-Century

By 1972 Rothmans Limited had been in existence, in one form or another, for more than 80 years. Its founder, Louis Rothman, was born into the tobacco industry. His family owned a large tobacco factory in the Ukraine, and he became an apprentice there. He emigrated to London in 1887, at the age of 18, and easily found work in the British tobacco industry. At that time there was a demand for handmade cigarettes using the blends of Balkan, Crimean, Turkish, and Oriental tobaccos which Rothman had learned how to make during his apprenticeship.

In 1890, he opened his own business, a small kiosk on Fleet Street, selling to the reporters and printers of the area by day and making his cigarettes by night. He also built his reputation by supplying to wealthy businessmen and aristocrats. This enabled him to open two more shops, but it was not until 1900 that he had a proper showroom on Pall Mall, from which he launched his Pall Mall brand of cigarettes.

The success of Rothman's Pall Mall, Royal Favourites, and other brands in the United Kingdom allowed him to extend the business into overseas markets. By 1902 he was exporting to South Africa, the Netherlands, India, and Australia. In 1903 his company was incorporated under the name of Rothmans of Pall Mall in order to distinguish it from his brother Marx's tobacco business. In 1906 Louis created the menthol cigarette, by inserting menthol crystals into the ends of the cigarettes. He also developed a better filter for his Russian cigarettes, known as the "Barber's Neck," which did not leave loose pieces of tobacco touching the lips as earlier filters had. By 1905 Rothmans of Pall Mall was supplying tobacco products to the British royal family and extended its services to the royal family of Spain in 1910. When Louis went on to open a new store in Regent Street, his brother Marx joined the business, but by 1913 the partnership broke up, with Marx controlling the Regent Street operations and Louis the Pall Mall business. Later that year, Louis acquired a new factory in London and entered into partnership with his friend Markus Weinberg as the Yenidje Tobacco Company Limited.

Shift to Mass Production during World War I

The early stages of World War I were difficult for the new company. The markets for special blends of Turkish tobacco and handmade cigarettes were in decline, while demand for the cheaper, mass-produced Virginia brands and cigarettes was increasing. Weinberg did not agree with Louis Rothman's proposal to move into this market and the business folded in 1916, after a court case which ended with Louis reviving Rothmans of Pall Mall. Like other tobacco companies, Rothmans contributed to the war effort by supplying duty-free cigarettes to British troops. Louis also concentrated on reorganizing his factory to incorporate new methods of producing Virginia cigarettes.

After the war, in 1919, Louis Rothman brought his son Sidney into the business as an apprentice. Sidney became a partner in 1923, initially concentrating on expanding the company's advertising. The company had advertised in tobacco journals since 1908 but now began to use the national newspapers and leading periodicals. By 1921 such new Rothmans brands as the Marksman and Rhodesian Virginia were reaching a large market through the Rothman Diary Service, which offered customers lower prices for large orders. The use of Rhodesian tobacco was a reflection of a change in government policy. In response to the growing popularity of American tobacco, the British government was trying to encourage the import of tobacco from such Commonwealth states as Rhodesia and Nyasaland, India, and Canada by cutting the tariff on unmanufactured tobacco from these countries. The opening of six more shops in the heart of London between 1923 and 1926 indicates Rothmans's increasing commercial impact. In 1926, a new subsidiary, Rothmans (India) Limited, was established in Bombay. Louis Rothman died in 1926, at the age of 57, but his company's record of success continued under his son's management.

The company opened new premises in Liverpool in 1927. It was the first of many shops to open outside London. Meanwhile its mail order service was doing well, and in 1928 it introduced a new scheme of coupons for the Rothmans Direct Supply Association, which supplied many items, ranging from gardening tools to furniture, at discount prices, including a service inscribing customers' initials in gold leaf. Many manufacturers were reducing their prices at this time, forcing Rothmans to follow suit. Although the company experienced heavy competition at home, its exports were increasing with sales to China, South America, and particularly the territories of the British Empire. In 1929 Rothmans Limited, a public company, was formed, with Sidney Rothman as its first chairman and managing director. With the capital from the new shareholders, shops were established in Glasgow, Manchester, and Bristol, selling the new brands of cigarettes White Horse and Dance Time, as well as Louis D'or and Tuya tobaccos. Throughout the 1930s the company continued to develop new methods of filtration for cigarettes.

Rothmans was persuaded to drop its coupon scheme in 1933, with compensation from one of the larger tobacco companies, as restrictive practices were introduced by the Tobacco Trade Association of which Rothmans was not a member. However, expansion continued. By 1935 Rothmans had additional branches in Hull, Manchester, Birmingham, and Cambridge. Overseas, it had an office in Cuba and had established a factory in Ceylon (now Sri Lanka), though this closed after only two years because of a shortage of staff. The introduction of the famous Consulate Menthol Filter-Tipped Virginia brand secured the company's reputation, while the acquisition of Martins of Piccadilly and its associates, in 1937, secured its supplies

of leaf tobacco for the duration of the international crisis of the late 1930s and World War II which followed it. During the war Rothmans supplied parcels to British troops and prisoners of war. Its tins became famous for their adaptation to various uses, for example as material for wireless sets in the prison-camps.

Postwar Merger with Rembrandt Group, Carreras

After the war Rothmans Limited made the important decision to look overseas for funds to finance expansion. It had started discussions with the newly founded Rembrandt Tobacco Company, part of Dr. Anton Rupert's Rembrandt Group, on making Rothmans cigarettes in South Africa, and production began in 1951. The decision to associate with this South African company significantly changed Rothmans's position within the tobacco industry: by 1954 Rembrandt was in effective control.

Rothmans's association with Carreras, a significantly older company, began four years later. Don Jose Carreras-y-Ferrer, its founder, came from a family of tobacco producers in Spain whose business dated back to the 18th century. He traveled to London in 1843 seeking political asylum and soon gained a reputation as a maker of fine cigars, which were just starting to become popular. His son Don Jose Joaquin concentrated on blending tobacco and snuff and opened a shop off Leicester Square in 1852. By 1874, Carreras was producing a thousand brands of tobacco products.

The company remained a family business until it was taken over by W. J. Yapp in 1894. Yapp had been involved in the shoe leather industry but saw the economic potential of tobacco. Like Louis Rothman he saw the importance of marketing and achieved great success with the Carreras pipe tobacco Craven Mixture. In 1897 he managed to get the novelist and playwright J. M. Barrie to endorse the product. Barrie confirmed that the fictional Arcadia Mixture featured in his book *My Lady Nicotine* was in fact Craven Mixture. Carreras continued to use the endorsement for another 40 years. Yapp ran the company until 1903 when Bernhard Baron joined as director of what now became a public company. Baron had come from the United States with his cigarette-making machine looking for a company to use it. He had been turned down by the larger companies but Carreras offered him his opportunity in 1904 by setting up Carreras and Marcianus Limited, an associated company concentrating on the production of machine-made cigarettes. Baron and his family gained a controlling interest in Carreras, which introduced new brands such as Black Cat, Carreras Ovals, and Seven Up. In 1904 Carreras was the first tobacco firm to introduce coupons for customers to redeem for gifts, in the packets of the new Black Cat cigarettes. This innovation was such a success that new premises were needed to cope with the demand. Many other companies, including Rothmans, took up the idea. In 1909, the Baron automatic pipe filler cartridges brought Carreras new custom among pipe smokers.

During World War I, Carreras supplied cigarettes to the troops but, unlike Rothmans, it added to the containers such items as French dictionaries and grammar books. In 1921 Carreras produced the first machine-made cork tip cigarette, Craven A. The demand for cigarettes grew, and a new factory was needed. The Arcadia Works, which opened in 1928 in London, was unique in its design and organization. It was the first cigarette factory in Britain to have air conditioning, a dust extraction plant, and a welfare service for its workers.

In 1931 Carreras introduced Clubs, a smaller than standard cigarette sold with redeemable coupons for gifts, which was such a success that 14 factories were needed to meet demand. The "coupons war" which followed led some of the tobacco companies to approach the government and seek to have the coupons banned as detrimental to the public interest. An official report issued in 1933 concluded that there was no real problem, since cigarettes with coupons accounted for only one percent of total retail sales. The coupon war came to an end when the major tobacco companies formed the Tobacco Trade Association: Carreras was a founding member.

During World War II, the allocation of leaf tobacco to the various companies was rationed by the government. Some of the small companies felt that the system favored the majors, but Carreras enjoyed good relations with such large companies as Imperial and Gallaher. Tobacco consumption increased sharply during the war, and with import restrictions maintained until the early 1950s it became difficult for the industry to meet the demands of consumers. In 1953 Carreras acquired Murray, Sons & Company of Belfast, which still manufactures today. Carreras also moved to a new plant in Essex at that time. The new plant overstretched the resources of the company, and in 1958 the Baron family sold its shares to the Rembrandt Tobacco Corporation (S.A.) Limited, which merged the company with Rothmans to create Carreras Rothmans Limited. By the 1960s the tobacco companies were spending heavily on television commercials, but in 1965 commercials for cigarettes were banned, though commercials for cigars continued until December 1991. Carreras Rothmans and its rivals reverted to using coupon schemes and began to sponsor sports events and the arts.

Creation of Rothmans International in 1972

The Third World offered new markets and resources, and in 1966 Carreras Rothmans was one of the first tobacco companies to operate in Brazil, though its venture there was subsequently sold. The beginning of the 1970s saw a series of takeovers in the tobacco industry, to which Rembrandt responded with the creation of Rothmans International in 1972, bringing together Carreras Rothmans of the United Kingdom, Martin Brinkmann of West Germany, the Belgian company Tabacofina, and Turmac of the Netherlands. Anton Rupert controlled Rothmans International through his Luxembourg-based company, the Rupert Foundation, which in turn controlled Rothmans Tobacco (Holdings), the owner of 44 percent of the equity and 50 percent of the votes and convertible stock at that time.

Rothmans International began to diversify away from tobacco products in 1978 when it acquired Rothmans of Pall Mall Canada with its holdings in the Carling O'Keefe brewery. In 1967 Carreras acquired 51 percent of Alfred Dunhill Limited, a rival tobacco firm that was well established in the Netherlands, Denmark, Switzerland, Germany, and France. Alfred Dunhill Limited later widened its range to include toiletries, men's wear, and other luxury items.

By the mid-1970s, cigarette sales were dropping as the issue of smokers' health came to the fore. Less than half of the world's cigarette market was controlled by half a dozen multinationals, including Rothmans International. Markets in the United States and Europe were saturated, and it was the markets of the Third World in which Rothmans now sought to build its presence, discussing the formation of a joint venture with the American firm R.J. Reynolds, the world's third largest cigarette producer. Rothmans by this time was an attractive associate for any large company, holding more than 40 percent of the markets in Ireland, the Netherlands, and Belgium, 18 percent in West Germany, 13 percent in the United Kingdom, 75 percent in New Zealand, 36 percent in Australia, and 26 percent in Canada. R.J. Reynolds, makers of such brands as Camel and Winston, saw great potential in the proposal, but it was abandoned when Rupert decided to sell 25 percent of the company to Reynolds's main competitor, Philip Morris, noted for its Marlboro cigarettes, and the second largest tobacco company in the world.

In 1983 Rothmans acquired an interest in Cartier Monde, which specializes in jewelry, watches, and other luxury accessories. In the United Kingdom, Carreras Rothmans Limited changed its operating name to Rothmans (UK) Limited in 1984, then to Rothmans International Tobacco (UK) Limited in 1986. In 1987 Rothmans decided to sell its 50 percent share in the Carling O'Keefe brewery in Canada, which was not meeting expectations. In 1988 the Rembrandt Group decided to restructure its international activities with the formation of a new holding company based in Switzerland, Compagnie Financier Richemont (CFR), which has only 39 shareholders. Rembrandt wanted to separate its international operations and its South African activities to concentrate on developing its interests in Europe during the development of the single European market. This reorganization meant that Richemont held 33 percent of Rothmans International plc. This rose to 63.2 percent in 1990 when Richemont bought back Philip Morris's shares. Rothmans International then acquired the Dutch company Theodorus Niemeyer, makers of fine cut and pipe tobaccos such as Samson and Sail, increased its holding in Dunhill to 56.9 percent, and in 1991 signed an agreement with the China Tobacco Corporation to produce Rothmans and Dunhill brands in China.

Group Restructuring in 1993

Richemont restructured its holdings again in 1993, separating its luxury brands from its tobacco interests via an exchange of shares. The decoupling, which created Vendome to manage the luxury brands and Rothmans International plc to control the tobacco interests, marked a major shift in the group's marketing strategy. *Marketing* magazine noted that Richemont's "exploitation of the links between tobacco brands and luxury goods was the foundation of its success" in the 1980s. However, health concerns regarding tobacco began to tarnish the image of the stylish smoker in the early 1990s, and marketers for both groups of products began to favor the demerger.

Despite the many negative factors Rothmans faced—high taxes, heavy competition, negative press, a shrinking market, and strict limits on advertising—the company found ways to maintain growth and profitability in the early to mid-1990s. For example, British legislation banned targeting minors, using humor, and "suggesting that [smoking is] healthy, attractive, safe, relaxing, or a key to social or sexual success." Rothmans battled domestic difficulties with the introduction of Royals as a budget brand offering packs of 25 cigarettes and Black Cat cheap smokes in 1991. Rothmans also continued to pursue its longstanding overseas strategy, focusing on countries like India and the nations of the former Soviet Union, where smoking remained prevalent, especially among adult men.

As a wholly owned subsidiary of Richemont beginning in 1995, Rothmans stopped releasing company-specific public relations information. Nevertheless, it could be surmised that the company's strengths in its home market, early and vigorous pursuit of international growth, and emphasis on targeted marketing, will help it survive the rigors of the tobacco industry in the 1990s.

Principal Subsidiaries

Tabacofina-Vander Elst N.V. (Belgium); Tobacco Exporters International Limited (United Kingdom); Martin Brinkmann AG (Germany); Turmac Tobacco Company B.V. (Netherlands); Murray, Sons and Company Limited (United Kingdom).

Further Reading

Corina, Maurice, *Trust in Tobacco,* London: Michael Joseph, 1975.
Fallon, James, "Dunhill, Cartier Merger Okayed; Will Create $1.5B Luxury Group," *Daily News Record,* September 8, 1993, p. 14.
Finger, William, ed., *The Tobacco Industry in Transition,* Lexington, Mass.: Lexington Books, 1981.
Hall, Malcolm Macalister, "The Big Cigarette Scramble," *World Press Review,* April 1993, p. 38.
Kinkead, Gwen, "The Shy King of Snob Smokes," *Fortune,* August 10, 1981, pp. 194–200.
Malik, O. P., "The World's Tobacco Marketers Think 20 Million Indians Can't Be Wrong: Cigarette Merchants Are Set to Invade the Subcontinent," *Brandweek,* October 9, 1995, pp. 46–47.
Marsh, Harriet, "Tobacco Companies Cram in Pre-Ban Ads," *Marketing,* February 1, 1996, p. 8.
Meller, Peter, "Rothmans—Leader of the Budget Pack?" *Marketing,* February 4, 1993, pp. 22–23.
——, "Rothmans Looks for Luck with Economy Black Cat," *Marketing,* January 24, 1991, p. 17.
——, "Rothmans Undercuts Rivals," *Marketing,* November 28, 1991, p. 4.
O'Connor, John J., "PM-Rothmans Tie Stuns RJR," *Advertising Age,* April 27, 1981, pp. 1–2.
Rothmans Company History, London: Rothmans International plc, 1986.
Taylor, Peter, *Smoke Ring,* London: Bodley Head, 1984.

—Monique Lamontagne
—updated by April Dougal Gasbarre

Safelite Glass Corp.

P.O. Box 2000
Columbus, Ohio 43216
U.S.A.
(614) 842-3000
Fax: (614) 842-3395
Web site: http://www.safelite.com

Private Company
Founded: 1947 as Service Auto Glass
Employees: 4,000
Sales: $438.3 million (1996 est.)
SICs: 3211 Flat Glass; 7536 Automotive Glass
   Replacement Shops

With an estimated 14 percent share of the $2.4 billion market for replacement automotive windows, Safelite Glass Corp. and its employees have aptly been dubbed "Wizards of Windshields." Safelite boasts nearly 500 company-owned stores across the country, two manufacturing plants, and a fleet of 1,000 "Glassmobile" vans for at-home service. Having endured several changes in corporate ownership over the course of its 50 years in business, the company was acquired by the Boston-based investment banking firm of Thomas H. Lee Co. late in 1996. The new owners have hinted that an initial public offering could come in the not-too-distant future.

Postwar Origins

The firm was founded as Service Auto Glass in 1947 in Wichita, Kansas, by the appropriately-named Bud Glassman and his partner, Art Lankin. The duo did not limit themselves to replacement service for long. While not a primary focus of the business, the company started manufacturing laminated glass block for architectural applications and laminated flat glass for windshields in 1951 and continued to manufacture glass block for more than 40 years. Also in 1951, the firm adopted the Safelite name. The "safe" in Safelite refers to laminated glass, which incorporates a layer of plastic film between two sheets of glass. The plastic prevents shards of glass from flying free in case of impact. "Lite" is an automotive term for the windows in a car.

The proliferation of automobiles—and auto accidents—in the postwar era led inexorably to an increased need for windshield replacements. Safelight added a second installation center in 1964 and a windshield production plant three years later. The company's vertical integration into manufacturing not only cut costs but also helped it ensure quality control.

Throughout its first two decades in business, Safelite's growth was apparently limited to the greater Wichita area, but its 1968 acquisition by Royal Industries, Inc. launched a period of rapid expansion. Royal had been incorporated in 1949 as a defense contractor known as Century Engineers. The firm took the Royal moniker after merging with Royal Jet Inc. in 1957. Safelite was one of over 30 acquisitions made by Royal from 1969 to 1972. This three-year flurry of activity transformed Royal into an $80 million manufacturer and distributor of original and aftermarket automotive parts and accessories, nuclear and aerospace materials, and a diverse array of industrial and consumer goods made from rubber. Under its new parent, Safelite soon became the biggest component of Royal's automotive segment. It established three new warehouses in 1971 (for a total of nine warehouses) and acquired 18 separate retail glass outlets in Dallas, Tulsa, and Oklahoma City. The company built a second windshield manufacturing plant in Enfield, North Carolina, on the East Coast in 1969 and acquired a Denver glass factory, Pennco Enterprises, Inc., in 1972. Royal augmented Safelite's capacity to produce tempered safety glass in 1973 and doubled production capacity at its original factory a year later. Having the support of a much larger corporation also allowed Safelite to boost its advertising budget in the early 1970s as well.

Acquisition Opens New Chapter in 1976

Royal was itself acquired by Lear Siegler Inc. (later renamed Lear Seating Corporation), a $700 million conglomerate, in 1976. Now best-known for its automotive seats, Lear Siegler was then a widely diversified manufacturer with interests in everything from electronics to plastics. The acquisition was part of a reorganization that turned the parent into a $1 billion

---

Company Perspectives:

"Our Mission: Become the dominant, low-cost manufacturer, distributor and installer of quality replacement auto glass and related services in the U.S.A. Our Values: 1. Our customers come first. 2. Associates are our most valuable resource. 3. We constantly improve. 4. Every associate is empowered. 5. We recognize and reward results. 6. We win through teamwork. 7. Our business relationships reflect mutual respect, trust and integrity."

---

company by the end of the decade. Under Lear, Safelite consolidated its Colorado and Kansas lamination operations at a new facility in Wichita in 1978. Safelite thrived during the 1980s: by the latter years of the decade, it had manufacturing facilities in Wichita, Salt Lake City, and Enfield, North Carolina; 45 warehouses nationwide; 550 retail shops across the country (this was later reduced to 495); 4,000 employees; and an estimated $400 million in annual sales.

Third Acquisition Marks Late 1980s

After nearly two decades as a subsidiary of public companies, Safelite was taken private as part of Forstmann, Little & Co.'s $2.1 billion leveraged buy out of Lear Siegler Inc. in 1987. Determined to capitalize on its investment, the new parent quickly spun off several of Lear's operations. Safelite was one of the few components the investment bank kept for any length of time.

In 1989, the investment bankers hired Robert Morosky, former vice-chairman and chief financial officer of The Limited, Inc., as chairman and CEO of the windshield company. Over the course of his brief tenure, Morosky focused on marketing and unit growth, establishing a goal of 1,500 stores and $1 billion in sales. Although Safelite only had one Columbus outlet, Morosky also moved his new employer's headquarters to Columbus, Ohio (where he not coincidentally maintained a home), in 1990. The new leader also oversaw the company's implementation of the SAFENET intranet. This accounting and management system linked virtually all aspects of the business and would form the backbone of Safelite's next key growth program.

New Management and Marketing Strategy for the 1990s

In 1991, Forstmann, Little elected to shift Safelite's target market, and with it the company's management roster. Morosky advanced to the part-time position of chairman emeritus, and the parent company installed Garen K. Staglin as chairman and CEO. Staglin's previous experience as chairman of ADP Inc.'s Automotive Services Group shed light on his plan for Safelite. The executive had helped turn ADP into North America's top provider of automotive services to the insurance industry.

Noting that administrative costs to insurers for replacing automotive glass were inordinately high in proportion to the

work done—sometimes amounting to $100 on a $300 repair job—Safelite proposed to process the individual claims as well as service them. The windshield company added an automated claims processing system to its existing SAFENET network and sold 21 of America's top 30 insurance companies—among them Aetna, Safeco, Travelers and State Farm—on its "Total Claims Solution" (now known as the "Total Customer Solution"). By linking its computer network with those of major auto insurers via electronic data interchange, Safelite was able to take on the windshield claims processing functions normally performed within the insurance company. Employees at Safelite's new National Referral Phone Centers registered claims, assessed coverage, and scheduled repairs at one of the company's retail outlets. This "one-stop service" often proved more convenient to insurance customers as well as to insurers. Staglin told the *Columbus Dispatch* that "Our goal is to be a business partner with our insurance companies, a claims processor instead of (only) a window replacer." Launched in 1991, the program reduced participating insurance companies' processing costs from as high as $100 per windshield claim to as little as $.25 per claim. Needless to say, the marketing program also benefitted Safelite's bottom line; its market share grew by one-fifth, its inventory decreased by $23 million, and its net income (while rarely specified by this privately-held firm) was said to have increased fourfold.

Staglin also increased customer service, implementing two distinctive types of mobile service. Specially-equipped vans dubbed "Glassmobiles" provided at-home windshield repair and replacement at no additional cost. A Catastrophe Action Team (CAT) comprising about 100 members and their equipment, stood at the ready to provide emergency repairs and replacements in tandem with insurers. The CAT performed an estimated 4,000 windshield installations in the wake of 1992's Hurricane Andrew. Safelite added another innovation to its roster in 1995. Its proprietary windshield duplicating device could measure the profile of a windshield and reproduce it without removing it from the vehicle. This technique added custom design to Safelite's existing roster of more than 900 windshield styles.

Staglin oversaw the implementation of a new compensation plan based on an old idea—piecework—for hourly employees. Wary of the potential pitfalls, including deflated employee morale and declining output, the company installed a computerized system to monitor inventory and installation rates. Beginning in 1994, the firm phased in a changeover from the hourly pay rate to a piece rate. In order to satisfy its unionized employees (about 10 percent of the total work force), Safelite offered a guaranteed minimum wage of $11 per hour or $20 per unit installed over a given minimum. The system ensured quality by keeping track of who did what job: if an auto came back because of an installation defect, the worker who installed it had to redo the work without pay. The program received wide press coverage and praise. It increased average productivity per worker by 20 percent, hiked per employee earnings by 10 percent, and boosted overall output by 36 percent—a rate *Business Week*'s Gene Koretz called "eye-popping" in a February 1997 article. Furthermore, absenteeism, turnover, and paid sick leave declined dramatically, and Safelite's already-high rate of customer satisfaction rose five percentage points to 95 percent.

New Ownership for the Late 1990s

In 1996, Boston's Thomas H. Lee Co. acquired Safelite from Forstmann, Little for an undisclosed sum. Having made headlines—not to mention a $900 million profit—on the sale of Snapple Beverage Co. to Quaker Oats Co. in 1995, Lee possessed ready cash for the purchase. Although Lee told the *Columbus Dispatch* that "We have no plans to change anything," in 1996, executives hinted that the new owner might take Safelite public.

Further Reading

Amatos, Christopher A., "Safelite Shatters Old Ways of Doing Business," *Columbus Dispatch,* September 27, 1993, pp. 1S, 2S.

Ball, Brian R., "Hot Rumor Has Safelite Moving," *Business First-Columbus,* October 2, 1989, p. 3.

Francis, David R., "Incentive Pay Boosts Output on Shop Floor," *Christian Science Monitor,* December 23, 1996, p. 1.

Gilbert, Evelyn, "Windshield Repair Plan Gets You on the Road," *National Underwriter Property & Casualty-Risk & Benefits Management,* October 5, 1992, pp. 15–16.

Gordon, Mitchell, "Wide Product Mix Enhances Results at Royal Industries," *Barron's,* February 21, 1972, pp. 27, 29.

"Industry Interview: New Rules and New Tools," *US Glass Metal and Glazing,* February 28, 1994, p. 51.

Koretz, Gene, "Economic Trends: Truly Tying Pay to Performance," *Business Week,* February 17, 1997, p. 25.

"Lear Siegler Solves Its Identity Problem," *Financial World,* April 15, 1979, pp. 21–22.

Leitzke, Ron, "Wizards of Windshields," *Columbus Dispatch,* October 27, 1992, p. 1F.

Loftus, Geoffrey, "Ultimate Pay for Performance," *Across the Board,* January 1997, pp. 9–10.

"Paid by the Widget, and Proud," *New York Times,* June 1, 1996, p. 3.

Porter, Phil, "Morosky Turns over Reins as Safelite Chief," *Columbus Dispatch,* August 26, 1991, p. 2E.

Sheban, Jeffrey, "Boston Firm Buys Safelite," *Columbus Dispatch,* November 13, 1996, p. 1B.

—April Dougal Gasbarre

Delivering More Than Power.™

Salt River Project

SRP Corporate Offices
1521 North Project Drive
Tempe, Arizona 85281-1206
U.S.A.
(602) 236-5900
Fax: (602) 236-5240
Web site: http://www.srp.gov

Private Company (Salt River Valley Water Users'
  Association)
Incorporated: 1903 as Salt River Valley Water Users'
  Association
Employees: 4,261
Total Assets: $5.6 billion (1996)
SICs: 4911 Electric Service; 4941 Water Supply

The Salt River Project (SRP) calls itself a "major multipurpose reclamation project serving electric customers and water shareholders in the Phoenix area." More simply, it can be described as a water and electric utility. It consists of two organizations: the Salt River Project Agricultural Improvement and Power District, a political subdivision of the state of Arizona, providing electricity to the Phoenix area; and the Salt River Valley Water Users' Association, a private, nonprofit corporation, which stores and delivers water in a 240,000-acre service area in central Arizona. In 1996 SRP supplied 625,000 electric customers in the Phoenix area from its combined facilities, which included six hydroelectric plants and several smaller facilities on various canals throughout the area.

The Salt River Valley until 1900

The Salt River Valley, a half million acres of semidesert land, is located in Central Arizona. Around 200 B.C. the Hohokam built an elaborate system of canals to irrigate their corn and cotton fields from the waters of the valley's Salt and Verde rivers. Their efforts, however, were stymied by either periods of drought, which dried out the rivers, or times when heavy rains flooded their canals and washed away their desert homes. The Hohokam, along with other native Americans of the Southwest, vanished before the arrival of Columbus and left only vestiges of their culture, which was based on their canal-building technology. Their system of canals, however, was virtually the same system that the Salt River Project later developed in the region.

The first European settlements in the Salt River Valley began in the 1860s. In 1868 the first canal was built and was called the Salt River Canal. The site of this canal was in what is now the downtown area of Phoenix. By the spring of 1868 irrigation from this canal produced the first successful crops in the valley. As more settlers moved to the valley, more canals were built.

By 1888 more than 100,000 acres were being farmed. Problems with water rights, however, soon followed in the wake of this canal-building activity. Some canals were washed away by heavy rains since there were no storage sheds for excess water, and litigation took place over disputed water rights. Sometimes these disputes led to armed conflict. By the turn of the century, many began to leave the valley because of the water problems.

To stem the tide of people leaving and to resolve the issues raised by conflicts over water rights, a committee was formed at the turn of the century to report to the citizens of Phoenix on the feasibility of a reservoir for the rivers feeding the valley. They suggested that the reservoir be placed where Tonto Creek flowed into the Salt River (about 80 miles from Phoenix). Their recommendations required the raising of $2 million to $5 million in capital, but since Arizona was still a territory, it was not entitled to assume such a large debt from the United States government, and there were no private companies ready to offer the money.

The Formation of SRP: 1903 to 1917

In order to meet the rising demand for water development in the West, President Theodore Roosevelt enacted a Federal Reclamation Program on June 17, 1902. Under the act, money was raised by the sale of western lands and then loaned to a territory to help build a reservoir. The money would then be repaid by the revenues from the water and from power provided by the projects. Before the money was loaned, it was stipulated that all disputes would be resolved by a 25-man committee. Judge Joseph H. Kibbey led the way to the formation of the Salt River Valley Water User's Association—incorporated under the laws of the Arizona territory on February 7, 1903—and to building a dam that was first called the Tonto Reservoir and then the Theodore Roosevelt Dam (1961), which was completed and dedicated on March 18, 1911. The members of the association were area farmers.

All members of the association had equal rights to the water from the dam, and the costs of construction were also equally divided among the members. Assessments were equally divided regardless of the use or nonuse of the water. The Roosevelt Dam fed the system of canals that had been developed beginning with the Arizona Canal in 1883 and culminating with the development of the Western Canal in 1912 and 1913. Over the years improvements to the canal system were undertaken.

On June 25, 1904, the Salt River Project was recognized by the Department of Interior as the first reclamation project of the 1902 reclamation act. An agreement was signed with the association for a dam to be built at the mouth of Tonto Creek on the Salt River for an estimated cost of $2,700,000, which amounted to $15 an acre on the 180,000 acres that were covered at that time by the project.

In this early period of development, the landowners thought mainly of the need for water, but the U.S. Reclamation Service as early as 1902 realized the need for electric power as well. It recommended the construction of a 20-mile power canal installed with 300-kilowatt hydro generators. After it was constructed, most of the power from the generators was initially used for a cement mill built near the dam.

In 1917 the operation of the water system, called the Salt River Project, was turned over to the Water Users' Association. At the time the project consisted of the Roosevelt Dam, the Granite Reef Diversion Dam, irrigations canals, laterals, and ditches. One of the association's first steps was to obtain a hydroelectric generating plant in the eastern part of the Salt River Valley region. This unit helped the association pump more water and sell electrical power, in the process increasing its revenues.

Rapid Growth in the 1920s and 1930s

There was a greater need for both water and electricity as the valley's population increased and as the area's major businesses—copper, cattle, citrus, and cotton—began to grow. SRP responded to those needs. During the 1920s the company built a number of new dams. Mormon Flat Dam was built between 1923 and 1925. It was located downstream of Roosevelt Dam and formed Canyon Lake, where a generating station was installed. In 1924 the Horse Mesa Dam was built between the two existing dams. It formed Apache Lake. This third dam supplied power for copper mining operations in Miami and Globe, Arizona.

Stewart Mountain Dam was built between 1928 and 1930 to increase water storage capacity and improve electrical power generation. While the problem of sufficient water for agricultural uses was relieved during this period, the 1929 stock market crash and the banking crisis in 1933 caused a sharp drop in crop prices. After several difficult years, the farmers who made up the Water Users' Association were able to convince the federal government in 1935 to construct a dam to store the flood waters of the Verde River; by 1939 the project, Bartlett Dam, was completed. Although the federal government built the dam, SRP ultimately paid 80 percent of the total cost.

Financing for the next project, the Horseshoe Dam, was provided by the copper mining company Phelps Dodge. As an amenity for its role in building Horseshoe Dam, Phelps Dodge earned water credit to use in its Morenci mining operation. Horseshoe Dam was completed in 1946. Phelps Dodge later also financed the building of the Show Low Dam and the Blue Ridge Dam. Similarly, spillway gates built in 1949 resulted in a water credit arrangement with the city of Phoenix, which paid for the gates. These financial arrangements with industry and government enabled SRP to grow and serve its users.

In 1937, in order to provide electric power to thousands of customers, the Salt River Project Agricultural Improvement and Power District was formed as a political subdivision of the state of Arizona. The establishment of the district helped valley farmers after the Depression meet their financial obligations because they were then eligible through the district to refinance outstanding bonds at lower rates with tax-exempt, municipal bonds. That year the association transferred its rights, title, and interest in the Salt River Project to the district. The legal relationship between the two organizations would be redefined in 1949, when the district assumed responsibility for the construction, operation, and maintenance of both the electric and irrigation systems. The district then appointed the association to operate and maintain the project's irrigation and water supply. The Salt River Project thus became "one organization with two compatible business units."

Postwar Developments

The population in the Salt River Valley began to grow rapidly after the Second World War, and water distribution patterns began to change from agricultural uses to urban ones. Moreover, after the war the area experienced a drought that drained its stored water supply. Expecting that 90 percent of the valley would become urbanized by the year 2000, SRP sought new ways to manage water storage. One step was the development of underground water sources, which SRP began in 1948. In 1952 SRP entered into an agreement with the city of Phoenix to supply the city with its domestic water needs. The surrounding cities of Tempe, Glendale, Mesa, Scottsdale, Chandler, Peoria, and Gilbert entered into similar domestic supply contracts with SRP.

While SRP supplied only 12,400 customers with electricity in 1947, by 1988 there would be about a half million users. During the early 1940s SRP gained additional electric capacity by completing transmission lines from Parker Dam on the Colorado River to Phoenix. In 1952 the Kyrene Generating Station was built south of Tempe; it had a capacity to produce 300,000 kilowatts of electricity. In 1957 the Agua Fria Generating Station was built west of Glendale, and by 1984 it would generate nearly 600,000 kilowatts. These two stations met the needs of the eastern and western parts of the valley.

Population growth eventually made it necessary for SRP to look for sources outside the state for electricity. In 1961 it signed an agreement with the Colorado-Ute Electric Association to buy power from a generating station to be built in Hayden, Colorado. Power from this source began in 1965. SRP also entered into a partnership with five Southwest utilities to construct a generating station at Farmington, New Mexico, and participated in a consortium that developed the Mohave Generating Station, located in southern Nevada along the Colorado River across from Bullhead City. For the Navajo Generating Station in northern Arizona, built by a consortium in the early 1970s, SRP served as the project manager. In 1979 and 1980 SRP built four generating units at the Santan Generating Station near Gilbert in the southeastern section of the valley. It also opened two units at St. Johns during the same period.

Population pressures made it necessary to modernize the canal system. A program begun in 1950 and completed in 1974 allowed remote operation and monitoring of the canal gates and automatic gauging of water levels anywhere on the canals. In order to supplement its water sources in Arizona, SRP participated in the Central Arizona Project to deliver water from the Colorado River to the valley.

As population growth continued to accelerate in Phoenix and in the surrounding cities during the 1980s, SRP contributed to the Electric Power Research Institute (EPRI) to investigate ways to improve the production, transmission, distribution, and use of electric power. This institute, with 498 utility members nationwide, enabled members like SRP to benefit by sharing the costs of research that were beyond the means of individual local governments.

Besides its cooperation with other utilities in the United States, SRP, through its Office of International Affairs (established in 1984), held seminars and workshops for water officials from foreign countries. In 1982 it helped the Egyptian government rehabilitate their irrigation system. SRP also had an employee exchange program that was rated the top program in 1983 by the United States Agency for International Development.

The 1990s: The Roosevelt Dam Upgrade and Community Involvement

SRP was not given a specific role for flood control when it was established. Its water storage dams did not contain the structures needed for flood control and were able to release only small amounts of water from their bases. In order for large amounts of water to be released in a water storage dam, the spillways at the top of the dam had to be full. Even with these limitations, the dams of SRP helped curtail some major floods by carefully using the dams' runoff capabilities. In a project started in 1988 and completed in 1996, Roosevelt Dam was upgraded to store 1.6 million acre feet of water—enough to provide water for one million more residents in the Phoenix metropolitan area—and the new construction added to this early structure dedicated flood-control and dam-safety space. In addition, by this time SRP was receiving power from the Palo Verde Nuclear Generating Station, of which it shared ownership with several other utilities, including Arizona Public Service, which was another major Arizona electric utility.

SRP in the 1990s was also involved in community service, including a program to help combat hunger in the valley. Along with other organizations, SRP sponsored the Arizona Family Holiday Food Drive in 1995 and helped collect more than twice the goal it had established for the drive. Through its employee volunteer program, SRP participated in water-quality education for students, cooperated with several government agencies to help protect wildlife and the environment, initiated an exchange program for valley residents to change from gas lawn mowers to electric ones, and helped the arts by supporting local cultural organizations.

Principal Subsidiaries

Papago Park Center, Inc.

Further Reading

Ceniceros, Roberto, "Salt River Project Reviewing Risks as Utility Readies for Deregulation," *Business Insurance,* April 14, 1997, p. 128.

Estes, Mark, "Adversaries Find Common Ground," *Workforce,* March 1997, p. 97.

Loge, Peter, "PacificCorp Challenges APS, SRP," *The Business Journal* (Phoenix), March 10, 1995, p. 19.

"SRP Tapped as a Top Workplace," *Business Journal,* September 20, 1992, p. 2.

A Valley Reborn: The Story of the Salt River Project, Phoenix, Arizona: Salt River Project, n.d.

—Jordan P. Richman

Santa Fe Gaming Corporation

4949 N. Rancho Drive
Las Vegas, Nevada 89130
U.S.A.
(702) 658-4300
Fax: (702) 658-4304

Public Company
Incorporated: 1983 as Public/Hacienda Resorts, Inc.
Employees: 1,211
Sales: $148.4 million (1996)
Stock Exchanges: American
SICs: 7011 Hotels, Motels; 6719 Holding Companies,
    Not Elsewhere Classified

Through its chairman and CEO, Paul W. Lowden, Santa Fe Gaming Corporation holds a more than 20-year stake in Las Vegas casino history. Formerly known as Sahara Gaming Corporation, Santa Fe owned and operated the famous Sahara and Hacienda casino hotels. Santa Fe sold those properties in 1995 to former Circus Circus leader William Bennett, but the company remains active in Nevada's casino industry as owner and operator of the Santa Fe Casino Hotel, located in northwest Las Vegas, and the Pioneer Hotel and Gambling Hall, located in nearby Laughlin, Nevada. Santa Fe also owns extensive real estate parcels in Henderson, Nevada and on Las Vegas Boulevard South.

The Santa Fe Casino Hotel, which opened in 1991, features a 200-room hotel, a 65,000-square-foot casino, a 60-lane bowling center, a National Hockey League regulation-sized ice skating arena, three themed restaurants, and a bingo parlor on its 40-acre site. Located some nine miles north of the main Las Vegas casino strip, the Santa Fe and its southwestern theme cater primarily to Las Vegas residents. The company also owns a 22-acre parcel of land adjacent to the casino. The Pioneer Hotel and Gambling Hall, opened in 1982 and acquired by the company in 1988, sits on 12 acres of land with 770 feet of frontage along the Colorado River. Built in classical western style, the Pioneer's four buildings house a 21,500-square-foot casino and 417 motel rooms. The Pioneer's clientele comes largely from Laughlin-area residents and drive-in visitors from Southern California and Arizona.

Santa Fe's property holdings include 39 acres in Henderson, Nevada, 27 acres on the Las Vegas Strip, and 40 acres on Las Vegas Boulevard, approximately eight miles south of the Strip. The company is developing plans to build a casino hotel and entertainment complex on the Henderson site. The Las Vegas Boulevard site was acquired with the intention of relocating the company's Camperland recreational vehicle facility, which the company formerly operated adjacent to the Hacienda. In addition to these holdings, the company has interests in two aborted casino showboat projects outside of Nevada, in Parkville, Missouri, near Kansas City, and in Biloxi, Mississippi. More than 60 percent of Santa Fe's revenues are generated through its casino operations. In 1996, revenues were $148.4 million. Including a $40.8 million gain from the sale of the Sahara, Santa Fe posted net earnings of $16.2 million in 1996.

Rooted in 1950s Vegas

Both the Sahara Hotel & Casino and the Hacienda Resort Hotel and Casino were rooted in the early development of the Las Vegas casino industry in the 1950s. The Sahara, built for $5.5 million by the Del Webb Corporation, was founded by Milton Prell, a Los Angeles jewelry magnate, on the site of the former Club Bingo in 1952. The first high-rise casino in Vegas, and the fifth constructed since Bugsy Siegel's Flamingo (which was also built by Del Webb), the Sahara, and its trademark 100-foot freestanding neon sign, was also the largest at the time—until the Sands opened two weeks later. The following year, the "Jewel of the Desert," as Prell dubbed the hotel, made the first of many expansions, adding 200 rooms to its hotel. In 1961, Prell sold the Sahara to the Del Webb Corporation, although he continued to run its operations until 1964. Del Webb immediately invested some $12 million in renovations. In 1966, the Sahara added a $50 million, 14-story, 200-room tower, making it the city's tallest building. Two years later, the Sahara built again, adding a 400-room, 24-story skyscraper, expanding its casino, and extending its operations into Vegas's growing convention industry by building a 44,000-square-foot convention center. Del Webb, which had grown to become one of the industry's largest casino operators, continued to manage the Sahara through the 1970s. But when Del Webb ran into financial problems in the late 1970s and early 1980s, it sold the Sahara to Paul Lowden for $50 million in 1982.

Lowden, by then, already owned the Hacienda. That hotel, situated at the far southern end of Las Vegas Boulevard from the Sahara, was built in 1956 for $6 million as part of a California-based chain of low-rise motels owned by Judy and Warren ''Doc'' Bayley. Problems with the Gaming Control Board delayed the Hacienda's casino licensing, but by 1957 the hotel's casino was up and running. Situated far from the main strip, the Hacienda catered especially to families, locals, and ''lowrollers,'' eventually earning the hotel the nickname of ''Hayseed Heaven.'' Nonetheless, the Hacienda—which was imploded on New Year's Eve 1996, an event that was broadcast to a national television audience—was long a popular fixture on the strip and was also the first Vegas hotel to operate an airplane shuttle service, building a fleet of more than 30 airplanes serving a number of major cities. When the Federal Aviation Administration decreed the fleet an airline, that service was discontinued. Doc Bayley died in 1964; Judy Bayley continued to run the hotel casino until her death in 1971. Lowden purchased 15 percent of the Hacienda the following year and became its entertainment director. In 1977, Lowden took full possession of the Hacienda for $20 million.

Becoming a Vegas Mogul in the 1970s

Lowden was a teenager when, with $7,500 in savings, he journeyed to Nevada in 1961. He joined a band playing in a Reno casino, then moved to Las Vegas, where he worked through the decade as a keyboardist, accompanying, among others, singer Ann-Margaret. By 1970, Lowden had become the musical director of the Flamingo. But Lowden had already set his ambitions higher.

With no formal business training, Lowden began investing in the stock market. These investments proved successful enough that, in 1972, Lowden and a group of partners raised $250,000—half of which came from the Valley Bank of Nevada—to buy 15 percent of the Hacienda. One of Lowden's partners brought in Allen Glick, a land developer from San Diego, to purchase majority control of the Hacienda. Lowden became the hotel casino's entertainment director. Under Lowden, the Hacienda launched its famous ''topless'' ice skating revues, which ran in various incarnations until 1993. Lowden expanded his casino holdings in 1975, putting up $500,000 for a share of the Tropicana. By then, a fresh scandal was brewing along the Vegas Strip.

In mid-1976, Lowden walked away from his Tropicana investment, discouraged by Mafia figure Joseph Agosto's control over the hotel casino's operation. Lowden first asked the Tropicana's majority owners to buy out his investment; when they declined, Lowden simply walked away rather than jeopardize his casino owner's license through the Tropicana's Mafia association. Lowden did not begin to regain his investment until 1979, after Agosto had pleaded guilty to skimming charges and the Tropicana's owners were forced out by the state.

Meanwhile, a similar scandal was brewing at the Hacienda. Glick, who at age 29 controlled two other casino hotels, the Stardust and the Fremont, making him Las Vegas's second largest casino operator, had come under a separate skimming investigation. Glick would later admit that he had been working as a Mafia front. In 1977, facing these charges and financial problems, Glick agreed to sell the Hacienda to Lowden. Paying $21 million, raised through Valley Bank and the First American National Bank of Nashville, Tennessee, Lowden bought out Glick and the other minority owners and took full control of the Hacienda.

Lowden immediately ran into difficulties. The Gaming Control Board, concerned by Lowden's past association with Glick, recommended against allowing Lowden's purchase of the Hacienda. But the Nevada Gaming Commission overturned the recommendation and cleared Lowden of any connection with Glick, giving Lowden a new license to operate the Hacienda. Lowden was joined by William Raggio as corporate counsel, who served at the time as Republican majority leader in the Nevada state senate, and who later joined Lowden's company as a director and officer. One year after buying the Hacienda, Lowden began looking to expand his casino holdings by buying Glick's two remaining casino properties. But the mortgages to the Stardust and Fremont were held by the reputedly mob-tied Teamsters Central States Pension Fund. Because of this connection, Lowden's investment banker refused to handle the financing for the deal, and Lowden backed off on the purchase.

Building Sahara Gaming in the 1980s

Instead, Lowden concentrated on expanding the Hacienda. In 1980, he spent $30 million on a facelift and expansion of the property, revamping the hotel in the style of Old World Spain and adding a convention center and an 11-story, 300-room tower. The Hacienda proved profitable, as did the institution of a side business, that of selling timeshares in the Hacienda hotel rooms—a first in Vegas. By 1982, Lowden had built up a $25 million timeshare portfolio in that and another hotel in Hawaii. The timeshares mortgages gave Lowden valuable collateral for additional financing and Lowden began looking for a new casino purchase.

The Del Webb Corporation, which had been suffering losses since the late 1970s, put the Sahara on the block in 1982. Leveraging his assets, Lowden put together $50 million to purchase the famed casino. The following year, the Sahara and Hacienda went public, incorporating as Public/Hacienda Resorts, Inc. With the proceeds from the public offering, the company expanded the Hacienda again, adding 400 rooms and more than doubling the size of its casino, hotel, rooms, and restaurants. Next, the company acquired an additional 22 acres behind the Sahara for the hotel's future expansion plans. In the meantime, the highly leveraged company, burdened by interest payments on more than $30 million in debt, was bleeding. Losses began in 1982 and continued into the next year, when the company lost $2.6 million on $92.6 million in revenues. The following year, with revenues of $94 million, the company lost nearly $2 million. It was not until 1986 that the new corporation, by then renamed Sahara Resorts, recorded its first profit, of $411,500 on $101 million in revenues. Meanwhile, the Sahara, which had not had any large renovations in nearly 20 years, was beginning to show its age.

Lowden hit on an idea to provide financing not only for a Sahara expansion, but also to help the company reduce its debt.

In 1987, he formed publicly traded Sahara Casino Partners L.P., a master limited partnership (MLP), which sold 6.2 million units at $9 per share. A first for Las Vegas, the MLP offering was immediately successful (in fact, it was oversubscribed) and generated $63 million for Sahara Resorts, enabling the company to pay down its debt and to finance a new expansion of the Sahara. Sahara Resorts retained 63 percent of Sahara Casino Partners. Under terms of the MLP, which was executed shortly before federal tax restrictions were created to eliminate tax advantages from non-real estate partnerships, Sahara Resorts agreed to a five-year subordination of its own profit distributions until minimum distributions were made to public investors. These investors, in turn, would take no ownership position in the casinos.

After paying off the $30 million Sahara mortgage, Lowden, whose interest in Sahara Resorts remained at 73 percent, began work on the casino hotel's most ambitious renovation and expansion. In 1988, the Sahara added a third tower, this time reaching 26 stories and adding 575 rooms, bringing the Sahara's total to 1,500 rooms. Two years later, Lowden performed a still more ambitious expansion, adding a new 600-room tower to the Sahara and a 400-room tower to the Hacienda, while doubling the Hacienda's casino area, bringing that hotel's total rooms to 1,200 and its gambling space to nearly 40,000 square feet. By then, however, Lowden had already moved to expand his casino holdings.

The Way to Santa Fe in the 1990s

Las Vegas's 1980 gambling boom had spread beyond the city into other areas of the state, and in 1988, Lowden moved to capitalize on the growing casino demand by purchasing the Pioneer Hotel and Casino in Laughlin, Nevada. The 400-room hotel and casino, situated on 12 acres fronting the Colorado River, had been constructed in 1982. The Laughlin area catered to customers different from those at the Las Vegas casinos, drawing in primarily local residents and the drive-in gambling crowd from Southern California and Arizona. After paying $112.5 million for the Pioneer, Lowden raised $116 million to fund the 1990 expansions of the Sahara and Hacienda as well as to build an entirely new hotel casino and entertainment complex, the Santa Fe.

The Santa Fe took Lowden away from the Strip and into the fast-growing northwestern residential area of Las Vegas. The Santa Fe, built at a cost of $60 million, exploited a niche different from that of the company's Strip hotels. Instead of gambling tourists, the Santa Fe, with only 200 rooms, marketed to local residents, and featured a 60-lane, state-of-the-art bowling center, a swimming pool, and a National Hockey League regulation-sized public ice skating arena, with 3,000 seats for spectators, in addition to its casino facilities. The Santa Fe, which featured a Southwestern theme, opened in late 1990. Operating without competition for most of the first half of the 1990s, the Santa Fe proved immediately profitable.

Lowden's activity was taking its toll on the company's profits, however. By 1991, the company's debt had soared to $310 million, generating interest payments of some $33 million per year. Despite revenues that reached $179.5 million in 1991 and neared $220 million in 1992, Sahara had returned to the red, posting losses of $9 million and $6.5 million for those years,

respectively. These losses would continue through 1995, reaching $15 million in 1994 and $22 million in 1995.

Adding to the company's troubles were its ill-fated attempts to expand its operations beyond Nevada. Gambling fever had been spreading throughout the country in the first years of the 1990s, with more and more states legalizing gambling and a new trend, riverboat casinos, filling the docks of more and more river communities. Sahara's first target was Parkville, Missouri, located near Kansas City. In 1993, the company, now renamed Sahara Gaming Corp. after merging the Sahara Resorts and Sahara Casino Partners operations, purchased the Spirit of America riverboat casino complex for $7.8 million and paid to have it towed to Parkville. That community, meanwhile, was engaged in a drawn-out battle over whether to allow casino operations, a process that required three elections and would not be decided until November 1994. By the time Sahara received the go-ahead for its casino, the Parkville operation was losing money, to the tune of $50 million. A second investment outside of Nevada, into the Treasure Bay riverboat complex near Biloxi, Mississippi, also ground to a halt, costing the company a $12.6 million writeoff charge. By then, too, the Hacienda was faltering, draining the company's revenues. The Laughlin market was also leveling off; meanwhile, the Santa Fe was forced to greet new competition in its area.

In 1995, Lowden retrenched his operations. His first step was to sell off the Hacienda for $80 million to former Circus Circus chairman and CEO William Bennett. By June of 1995, Lowden and Bennett had struck a new deal. Bennett bought the Sahara for $193 million; under terms of the deal, Lowden took possession of an undeveloped, 27-acre parcel on the Vegas Strip. By the time Bennett imploded the Hacienda on New Year's Eve 1996, to make room for an $800 million hotel-casino megacomplex, Lowden had renamed his company to reflect its new focus. The stripped-down company, now named Santa Fe Gaming Corporation, completed its first year of operations with revenues of $148.4 million. A $40 million gain from the Sahara sale helped the company achieve its first profitable year of the decade.

Principal Operating Units

Santa Fe Hotel and Casino; Pioneer Hotel and Casino.

Further Reading

Cook, James, "Heads I Win, Tails I Also Win," *Forbes,* July 6, 1992, p. 51.

Delugach, Al, "Casino Owner Beats the Odds," *Los Angeles Times,* March 13, 1988, Sec. 4, p. 1.

McKee, Jamie, "Analysts: Hacienda Sale a Good First Step for Sahara Gaming," *Las Vegas Business,* February 27, 1995, p. 1.

Moore, Thomas, "When Will Green Valley See Gamblers' Green?" *Las Vegas Business Press,* March 27, 1995, p. 3.

Morrison, Jane Ann, "Implosion Bittersweet for Those Close to Hacienda," *Las Vegas Review-Journal,* January 1, 1997, p. 3A.

Morrissey, John, "Sahara Resorts Markets Unique MLP Offering," *Las Vegas Business Press,* July 1, 1987, p. 12.

Post, Theresa, "Sahara Partners To Expand Hotel Operation in Vegas," *Travel Weekly,* August 16, 1990, p. 20.

—M.L. Cohen

Schnitzer Steel Industries, Inc.

3200 Northwest Yeon Avenue
Portland, Oregon 97296-0047
U.S.A.
(503) 224-9900
Fax: (503) 323-2804

Public Company
Incorporated: 1946
Employees: 1,059
Sales: $339.3 million (1996)
Stock Exchanges: NASDAQ
SICs: 3312 Blast Furnaces & Steel Mills

Schnitzer Steel Industries, Inc., operates one of the largest scrap metal recycling businesses in the United States, with processing facilities in Oregon, California, and Washington. Through its Cascade Steel Rolling Mills subsidiary in McMinnville, Oregon, Schnitzer Steel also produces finished products from scrap steel. In 1997, Schnitzer Steel completed the acquisition of Proler International Corp., a major Dallas-based recycler and exporter of scrap metal to foreign markets.

Through joint ventures, Schnitzer Steel also operates 16 self-service auto parts yards in California, Texas, and Nevada, using the unsold car bodies to supply its mill works. Two other joint ventures recover scrap from asbestos removal and old railroad cars. These joint ventures provided the company with 100,000 tons of scrap metal in 1996.

Schnitzer Steel's primary competitors for scrap are LMC Metals, a California-based division of Simsmetal USA Corporation, and the David J. Joseph Company, the largest scrap broker in the country. It competes with the Birmingham Steel Corporation in Seattle, Washington; NUCOR Corporation in Plymouth, Utah; Tamco in Los Angeles; North Star Steel Company in Kingman, Arizona; and Chaparral Steel Company in Midlothian, Texas, in the sale of rebar and other finished products from its Cascade Steel mini-mill.

Schnitzer Steel, which went public in 1993, was part of the Schnitzer family business empire that included the Lasco Shipping Co., the Schnitzer Investment Corporation, and extensive real estate holdings in the Portland, Oregon area. In 1987, *Forbes* magazine estimated the Schnitzer fortune at $300 million, making the Schnitzers then the wealthiest family in Oregon. Led by the late Harold and Arlene Schnitzer, for whom the Arlene Schnitzer Concert Hall was named, the family also contributed to Portland charitable and civic affairs.

Early History

In 1906, a Polish immigrant, Sam Schnitzer, then 26, began collecting scrap metal in Portland, Oregon. Six years later, he and H.J. Wolfe formed the Alaska Junk Co. and Schnitzer & Wolfe Machinery Co. In the 1940s, Schnitzer started Oregon Steel Mills and Industrial Air Products. The Schnitzer family bought out the Wolfe family in the 1950s, and those related businesses eventually became Schnitzer Industries. At the dedication of a new corporate headquarters building in 1962, Portland newspaper columnist Gerry Pratt described Schnitzer, who died in 1952, as "a brilliant immigrant who began with a sack on his back, a horse and wagon, and whose portrait hangs in the board room of the fine Schnitzer Building."

Despite their success, the family always acknowledged the company's roots. Dr. Leonard Schnitzer, then head of the Woodbury Co., the industrial supply and equipment division of Schnitzer Industries, told Pratt, "Father had a sack on his back. He was junking. There's no doubt about that."

Leonard Schnitzer also noted, "We have been fighting competition for years and the weapons the competitors like to use the most is, 'These guys are junkmen. Why do you want to buy steel from junkmen? Why liquid air from junkmen? Why industrial supplies and machinery from junkmen?' The people who built this business are the customers who got what they paid for and paid for what they got; who knew that when we said something, we would do something."

It was shortly after World War II that the patriarch Schnitzer turned the businesses over to his sons. In addition to Leonard at the Woodbury Co., Manuel Schnitzer, the oldest brother, who had joined his father's junk business in 1928, headed up the Alaska Steel Co., which then handled plumbing supplies and heavy machinery. Morris Schnitzer, who had gone to work for his father in 1932 scrapping old railroad trestles, was president of Schnitzer Steel Products Co., already one of the biggest scrap metal companies on the West Coast with annual revenues of $10 million. Gilbert Schnitzer was president of Industrial Air Products, which manufactured industrial air, medical gases, and welding equipment. A fifth brother, Harold, quit the business in 1950.

The family also managed the Island Equipment Co. on Guam, Schnitzer Steel in Eugene, Oregon, Schnitzer Industries in Europe, Dorenbecher Properties in Portland, and a Japanese trading company in Tokyo. Said Pratt, quoting an unnamed competitor, ''They got so many corporations going, they got to call a board meeting to see what they still operate.'' Leonard Schnitzer became chief executive officer at Schnitzer Steel in 1973 and was named chairman in 1991.

Current Structure

The company's present day organization began developing in the early 1980s, when Schnitzer Steel acquired Cascade Steel Rolling Mills, Inc., in the Portland suburb of McMinnville, which produces steel reinforcing bar (rebar), fence posts, and grape stakes. Cascade Steel, founded in 1968, also included distribution centers in Los Angeles and Union City, California.

Cascade Steel opened a new mill in 1991 that was designed specifically to recycle shredded cars, home appliances, and machine-shop debris, and made Schnitzer the largest steel recycler on the West Coast. Commenting on the mill's computerized controls, Mort Michelson, then Cascade Steel plant manager, told *The Oregonian,* ''Old time mills didn't come close to our efficiency. There used to be a lot of guesswork involved—the color of the molten steel, the amount of time in the furnace. If you made your chemistry, great. If you didn't, you just threw the steel away or used it in some no-grade product.''

In 1989, Schnitzer also sold Metra Steel, its distribution division, to Joseph T. Ryerson & Son, Inc., a Chicago subsidiary of Inland Steel Industries, Inc., to focus on recycling.

After more than 80 years as a privately owned business, Schnitzer Steel Industries announced in 1993 that the business would issue an initial public offering of 2.75 million shares of Class A common stock to retire more than $42 million in debt.

Less than two years earlier, Leonard Schnitzer had told the industry magazine *Recycling Today* that the family was committed to keeping the company private. But there was speculation by *The Oregonian* that the ultimate decision to go public was the first step in restructuring the ownership ''of (the Schnitzers') vast empire to avoid disruption as one generation supplants another.'' The newspaper noted, ''The surviving sons of founder Sam Schnitzer, though still involved in business, are past retirement age. And members of the following generation of Schnitzers are increasingly less involved in company affairs.''

Even with the public offering, however, the Schnitzer family remained firmly in charge, controlling 95 percent of the voting shares of stock. In 1997, several key executive positions also continued to be held by family members, including Leonard Schnitzer, chairman; Robert Philips, Leonard Schnitzer's son-in-law, president; Kenneth Novack, Gilbert Schnitzer's son-in-law, executive vice-president and president of Schnitzer Investment Corp.; Gary Schnitzer, Gilbert Schnitzer's son, executive vice-president; and Dori Schnitzer, daughter of Morris Schnitzer, secretary.

Expansion in the 1990s

Late in 1993, the newly public Schnitzer Steel also acquired Sessler Inc., a Eugene-based competitor in recycling scrap metal. The $5 million purchase united the families of two old-time scrap dealers, Sam Schnitzer and Milt Sessler, who started the original Sessler Inc. in Klamath Falls, Oregon, in 1932. Sessler sold the company in 1960, but his son, Ray Sessler, later started another business with the same name in Eugene. Over the next two years, Schnitzer Steel spent $2 million to upgrade Sessler operations and double the amount of scrap metal the plant could process to 90,000 tons of steel annually.

Schnitzer Steel expanded again in 1994, this time acquiring Manufacturing Management Inc., the largest scrap metal recycler in Washington with deep-water facilities at Tacoma, for $66 million. The acquisition boosted the amount of scrap metal processed by Schnitzer Steel from one million to 1.5 million tons annually. Schnitzer later sold a nonferrous processing center that Manufacturing Management had operated in Portland. Schnitzer Steel also began a $42 million expansion at its Cascade Steel Rolling Mill to increase its capacity for finished products by 60 percent. The *Portland Business Journal* noted that the acquisitions were ''an indication of the aggressiveness of the younger generation of the Schnitzer clan. The conservative and low-profile generation that succeeded founder Sam Schnitzer has been replaced by a more aggressive crop of business people.'' That year, the company reported record revenues of $261.7 million.

In 1996, Schnitzer Steel launched efforts to acquire Proler International Corporation, a scrap metal dealer about twice its size in Houston, Texas. Proler, founded by Israel Proler, a Russian immigrant, went public in 1971. It ran into financial trouble in the early 1990s, losing more than $9 million in 1993 and again in 1995. The losses stemmed, in part, from efforts to build a high-tech plant in Coolidge, Arizona, to recycle copper from old computers.

Schnitzer Steel originally offered $35 million for the company, but was forced to up the price to $42.3 million when the Hugo Neu Corporation, a New Jersey-based scrap metal recycler, made a counteroffer. Hugo Neu operated three deep-water export facilities in a joint venture with Proler and, during a bidding war for the company, filed a lawsuit to stop the release of confidential information. A spokesman for Hugo Neu told *The Oregonian,* ''We are concerned that our partnership arrangement with Proler for over 30 years has been abrogated. We are very disturbed this happened.'' Hugo Neu also criticized Schnitzer Steel's management style and asked for $50 million in damages.

Hugo Neu eventually withdrew the lawsuit after negotiating a confidentiality agreement with Proler and Schnitzer Steel.

Hugo Neu also expressed its willingness to continue the joint ventures, which included export facilities in Everett, Massachusetts; Jersey City, New Jersey; and Los Angeles, after the purchase was completed in 1997.

The acquisition gave Schnitzer Steel, which had focused primarily on the domestic market, annual exports of 2.1 million tons—an estimated one-third of the export market for processed scrap steel in an industry of predominantly small, family-owned businesses. Robert Philip, then president of Schnitzer Steel, told *Purchasing* magazine, ''This combination of our talents and operations will benefit not only both of the companies, but the scrap industry as well.''

In its 1996 annual report, Schnitzer Steel said its business strategy was to continue expanding its scrap operations through acquisitions and joint ventures and increase finished steel production and broaden its product mix. Philip told *Recycling Today* in 1994, ''There aren't too many companies that are fully integrated from cradle to grave, so to speak.'' Characterizing Schnitzer Steel as a true recycler, he noted, ''We start with (scrap) automobiles at one end of the pipeline and steel rebar, flat bar and structural steel come out the other.''

The company also noted that only about five percent of all raw steel in the United States came from recycled scrap metal in the 1950s. But in the late 1990s, that had increased to 40 percent.

Developing nations without scrap metal supplies of their own, especially Pacific Rim countries, were also eager to purchase processed scrap. Schnitzer Steel, which had scrap customers in China, India, Japan, Korea, Taiwan, and Thailand, believed its West Coast base, with deep-water export facilities at Tacoma, Portland, and Los Angeles, gave it a competitive advantage in this market.

Net income for the company more than doubled from $10.7 million in 1994, on sales of $261.7 million, to $22.2 million, on sales of $330.7 million. Although sales increased to $339.3 million in 1996, net income dipped slightly to $20.8 million. The company pointed to economic slowdowns abroad and a surplus of steel in the United States, which drove down market price for processed scrap.

Principal Subsidiaries

Cascade Steel Rolling Mills, Inc.; Manufacturing Management, Inc.; Sessler, Inc.; Proler International Corp.

Further Reading

Blackmun, Maya, ''Schnitzer Steel Industries To Go Public,'' *The Oregonian,* September 30, 1993, p. E16.

Bruening, John C., ''Building on a Scrap Foundation,'' *Recycling Today,* November 16, 1992.

Buri, Sherri, ''Testing Their Mettle: Schnitzer Steel Goes After the Growing Scrap Market,'' *The Register-Guard,* March 12, 1996, p. 1B.

Foyston, John B., ''McMinnville: It's Now a Steel Town,'' *The Oregonian,* November 14, 1991, p. 1.

Hamburg, Ken, ''Schnitzer Acquires Scrap Metal Recycler,'' *The Oregonian,* December 2, 1993, p. D18.

Leeson, Fred, ''Schnitzer Seals Deal To Acquire Proler,'' *The Oregonian,* December 3, 1996, p. C1.

Mayes, Steve, ''Schnitzer Steel: Testing Their Metal,'' *The Oregonian,* October 15, 1993, p. D1.

Pratt, Gerry, ''Peddler Operation Grows into Millions,'' *The Oregonian,* October 13, 1962, p. III-9.

—Dean Boyer

Schwinn Cycle and Fitness L.P.

1690 38th Street
Boulder, Colorado 80301-2602
U.S.A.
(303) 939-0100

Wholly Owned Subsidiary of Scott Sports Group Inc.
Incorporated: 1895 as Arnold, Schwinn and Company
Employees: 180
Sales: $250 million (1995 est.)
SICs: 3751 Motorcycles, Bicycles & Parts; 3949 Sporting
& Athletic Goods, Not Elsewhere Classified

For most of its century-long history Schwinn Cycle and Fitness L.P. has been a leading manufacturer of bicycles and bicycle accessories. Founded at the beginning of the biking craze in the 1890s, Schwinn became the most recognized name in the U.S. industry and maintained at least a 25 percent market share for decades. Schwinn dominated the U.S. bicycle market until the 1980s, when the company failed to follow the trend toward more highly engineered, lightweight bikes in the growing adult market and failed to take the new interest in mountain biking seriously. After filing for Chapter 11 bankruptcy in 1992, the company was bought by the Scott Sports Group, who brought back most of the glory of the tarnished but venerable name.

Early History

Ignaz Schwinn, an immigrant from Germany, joined the biking craze sweeping the nation by founding a bicycle manufactory in Chicago in 1895. Although bicycling was a relatively new sport, the company Schwinn founded with his partner, Adolph Arnold, was by no means a solitary venture; Chicago was home to approximately 90 other bicycle companies at the time. Arnold, Schwinn & Company proved to be the only enduring one, however.

That first year Schwinn introduced the World Roadster and manufactured about 25,000 cycles. The company grew steadily in its first decade, moving from rented facilities downtown to a larger space on Chicago's northwest side in 1900. The next year, the company relocated yet again, to a building on North Kostner Avenue that housed both the corporate headquarters and manufacturing. Schwinn made its first acquisition in 1899 (and slightly thinned the ranks of the Chicago bicycle army) when it bought competitor March-Davis Bicycle Company.

Over the next several decades, Schwinn remained a family-run business. That stability did not translate into stagnation, however. The company incorporated numerous functional advancements into its models. Such innovations as balloon tires, coaster brakes, forewheel expander brakes, and handlebar-mounted gear changers were introduced by Schwinn. Some famous bicycle designs by Schwinn include the early Aerocycle, Cycleplane, and Autocycle. The Paramount line was introduced in 1938 and the Sting-Ray in 1963.

Schwinn held 25 percent of the market by the 1950s, a distinction it maintained through the 1970s. These years as the top bicycle manufacturer in the United States represented a high point for Schwinn. With phenomenal name recognition and consumer loyalty, Schwinn dominated the market.

Slipping Market Share in the 1980s

By the time the fourth generation of Schwinns were running the company, however, Schwinn was sliding from its top position. Several factors contributed to the company's troubles. In an effort to cut costs, Schwinn moved production to Mississippi, Hungary, Taiwan, and mainland China. These mostly overseas suppliers had problems delivering their products on time, and those products they did deliver were generally of a lower quality than customers had come to expect from Schwinn. Unable to keep up with its commitments to dealers, Schwinn lost floor space to competitors. In the mass merchandise market, which represented 70 percent of all bikes sold, competitors Huffy Bicycles Co. and Murray Inc. began to take over market share.

A more fundamental problem prevented Schwinn from recovering from its supplier problem: The company had grown complacent and arrogant, certain that it could rest on its laurels. Tom Stendahl, Scott Sports Group's chief executive, told *Business Week* in 1993, "When they were asked who were their competition, they said, 'We don't have competition. We're Schwinn.'" Because of this attitude the company did not follow several trends that would prove to be enduring and profitable, allowing other companies to push it aside. Caught up in its traditional market of children's bikes, Schwinn did not take notice that adults were buying bicycles for themselves in greater numbers or that buyers desired lighter weight bikes. By the time sales of adult bikes reached 50 percent of the market in the mid-1980s, Schwinn had lost the chance of transferring its impressive name recognition to this new area. Not having invested research and development into high-tech bikes, Schwinn was perceived as "merely" a children's bike manufacturer, not a company adults trusted for their more sophisticated needs.

The company also failed to enter the new BMX (sporting) bike market and the burgeoning mountain bike market. Schwinn dismissed mountain biking as a fad and lost its chance to secure that market to several new companies in the 1980s: Trek Bicycle Corp. of Waterloo, Iowa; Giant Bicycle Inc. in Rancho Dominguez, California; and Specialized Bicycle Components Inc. in Morgan Hill, California. By 1991 these three companies made up one-third of all bicycles sold through independent dealers, the primary venue for Schwinn bikes.

By the late 1980s these problems had translated into serious losses. Bike sales fell from one million in 1987 to 500,000 in 1991 and to approximately 275,000 in 1993. By 1992 Schwinn held only about five percent of the U.S. bicycle market and had lost $50 million in the previous three years, including a $25 million loss in 1992 alone. Having lost the confidence of its dealers, fallen behind in research and development, and given up market share to new companies with aggressive distribution, the company filed Chapter 11 bankruptcy on October 7, 1992. At the time, Schwinn's debts totaled $82 million.

Turnaround in the 1990s

Despite the company's serious problems, it held some appeal to those wishing to salvage it. Schwinn's name recognition remained high in the U.S. sporting goods market, and its dealer network was extensive, comprising 1,800 dealers throughout the nation. Reversing the family's policy of not bringing in outside investors, Edward Schwinn Jr., the last Schwinn to run the company, sold the company in January 1993 to Scott Sports Group Inc. Scott USA, the world's foremost ski accessory manufacturer, already had a successful bicycle business, Scott Holdings, which was the number two seller of Asian-made bikes in Europe. Scott USA hoped the acquisition of Schwinn would be a good way to expand its bicycle business to the United States. Scott, with the investor group Zell/Chilmark Fund LP, formed Scott Sports Group and acquired Schwinn for $43.75 million.

Scott Sports Group focused on turning the company around. It immediately invested another $7 million and trimmed the work force from 400 to 180. Schwinn then set about redesigning every single bike in its 48-model line. Correcting the company's stodgy image to reflect its new direction was also a priority. As part of that effort, Scott Sports Group moved Schwinn to Boulder, Colorado, a town where mountain biking is commonplace and many of the world's top racers come to train. "We

decided to move to Boulder because we thought it was a way to change the whole appearance of Schwinn," Tom Stendahl, president of Scott Sports Group told the *Boulder County Business Report*. Stendahl and approximately 50 employees moved to Boulder. In another attempt to change the company's image, the advertising budget was doubled to around $10 million. The company then leapt feet first into the trend toward irreverent advertising with its first ad in the bike magazines since the buyout: "Schwinns are red, Schwinns are blue. Schwinns are light and agile too. Cars suck. The end."

Ensuring the company's new direction required other drastic action. Charles Ferries, chairman of Scott Sports Group, fired top management and promoted the second tier. The new management's first task was regaining the confidence of its dealers and recapturing lost floor space. The new president of Schwinn, Ralph Murray, told *Boulder County Business Report* in 1993, "This dealer network has been punished by Schwinn's failure to supply. The arrogance of the old management was enormous; they just thought that people depended on them. We're trying to regain their confidence right now by front-loading the system with inventory so we can perform up to their expectations." Management also traveled across the country, meeting personally with 800 of the company's 1,400 dealers. The message they brought could be summed up in the company's new slogan: "Established 1895. Re-established 1994."

The new owners' efforts saw some immediate results. The company returned to profitability in 1993, although sales were lower than the $150 million in 1992. But all of these changes did not come without some snags. Early in 1994 two top executives who had been with the company before the buyout chose to leave the company. Ken Lesniak, Schwinn's national sales manager, and Byron Smith, vice-president of marketing and sales, resigned in January 1994. Their departure left a void in upper management that the company tried to downplay. However, John Graves, the top Schwinn retailer in 1991, said to the *Denver Business Journal*, "It's going to be a nightmare. The only guy there with a brain at all is Ralph Murray, but he can't do it by himself. . . . It's still a good enough line that I will wait, but they don't get the priority they used to get at the store."

New Products Drive Recovery in the 1990s

Schwinn's fitness division made a significant contribution to the recovery of the company. Schwinn had entered the fitness equipment market in the 1960s with its introduction of the Airdyne stationary bike. By 1994, Schwinn was making 20 fitness products for a number of uses. Its value segment line, priced at $300 to $1,500, included the Easy Tread, a non-motorized treadmill; an Airdyne; the Recumbent, a seated bike; and the Stepper, a step machine with adjustable shock absorber resistance. Schwinn also produced two other higher-priced lines: the Home Trainer line, which included products for home and institutional use, and a commercial-institutional line, which featured a stair stepper and several weight-stack machines. Fitness equipment accounted for $29 million, or 30 percent, of total sales in 1994.

The fitness division's real contribution came in 1995, however, with the start of a new fitness craze: spinning. Highly popular at health clubs, spinning took the form of instructor-led classes set to music that imitated a bike ride, with riders turning a tension knob on an ultra-sturdy Schwinn exercise bike to simulate going up a hill. The bike, the Spinner, was created through collaboration with cross-country racer Johnny Goldberg. Goldberg had modified a Schwinn DX900 stationary bike in the mid-1980s to use in training for the Ride Across America, but kept breaking parts because of the intense use to which he put it. Kevin Lamar, dismayed at the number of replacement parts for which Goldberg was asking, went out to meet him and a partnership developed between Goldberg's company, Mad Dog Athletics, and Schwinn. The agreement stipulated that Schwinn control the manufacture of the bikes and Mad Dog Athletics develop the programming—the various techniques that help riders get the most efficient workout. Schwinn agreed not to sell the bikes without Mad Dog's programming and to pay an annual royalty fee on the concept and trademarked name. After a $1 million investment, Schwinn began selling the stationary bikes for $650 apiece or leasing it to fitness centers with two days of training for instructors. By February 1996 Schwinn was taking orders from two to three fitness centers a day. This product alone had helped raise fitness equipment to 35 percent of Schwinn sales, or $40 million.

"The key to getting Schwinn back was the product redesign," Chuck Ferries told the *Boulder Daily Camera* in May 1995. "Schwinn was not making a top-quality mountain bike. We wanted to drive the company through product." Schwinn's new American-made, top-of-the-line mountain bike, the Homegrown, retailed at $1,750. The company still had its image to overcome, however. Bicycle salesman Rob Kramer told the *Boulder Daily Camera,* "Most of the people are lured in by Trek or Raleigh, and it usually takes a comparison with Schwinn and a test ride. That's when it changes their mind." In 1995 Schwinn further committed to mountain bikes by acquiring Durango, Colorado-based Yeti Cycles Inc., a maker of high-end mountain bike frames. The ten-year-old company produced bikes in the $2000 to $6000 range for downhill racers and serious enthusiasts, a market separate from that for Schwinn's Homegrown. Yeti was lured to the merger by the financial boost it would provide, whereas Schwinn gained a respected name in a niche market. The company's bike lines would remain separate, and Yeti would keep its name and continue to control the direction and image of the company. "We're responsible for our own direction," said Brett Hahn, the general manager of Yeti, to the *Boulder Daily Camera* in 1995. "Schwinn has no desire to blend images." The acquisition also gave Schwinn a manufacturer near its headquarters, which the company hoped would improve its research and development by allowing the company to build and test prototypes in Durango.

100 in 1995 and Still Going

Schwinn celebrated its 100th anniversary in 1995 by introducing a new line of bikes, sending dealers various small gifts, and putting on a show in Las Vegas called the "SchwinnDig," with 100 cycling Elvis Presley imitators. The company also offered a limited edition of the classic Black Phantom bicycle for $5,000, some of which sold to celebrities like Jerry Seinfeld and Hugh Hefner. The real celebration, however, was for Schwinn's reentry into the mainstream of the bicycle market; in 1995 the company was selling high-performance off-road bikes, knobby-tired cruisers, and BMX children's bikes. Fitness equipment accounted for 25 percent of sales that year and parts and accessories accounted for another ten percent.

By 1996 Schwinn had climbed to second in the industry for product shipment, behind Trek. In an effort to get to the number one position, Schwinn announced in April 1997 that it was looking for a new strategic or financial partner or would be willing to sell the company or certain divisions to gain the financial backing it needed to move ahead. "I don't think we're comfortable being number two in the marketplace," said Gregg Bagni, vice-president for marketing at Schwinn, "I don't think we will be satisfied until we're number one. To get to that next level, strategic or financial partners are important for us right now." Scott Sports Group enlisted the help of Smith Barney Inc., a securities firm, in their search for a buyer.

Further Reading

Atchison, Sandra D., "Pump, Pump, Pump at Schwinn," *Business Week,* August 23, 1993, p. 79.

Gits, Vicky, "In Gear," *Boulder Daily Camera,* October 12, 1993, pp. 1D, 14D.

Gonzalez, Erika, "Schwinn Acquires Durango Bike Maker," *Boulder Daily Camera,* October 31, 1995.

Holzemer, Elizabeth, "Schwinn Pushes into Market for Home Fitness Products," *Boulder Daily Camera,* October 18, 1994, pp. 12–13B.

Miller, Mike, "End to Cycle of Complacency," *Rocky Mountain News,* December 29, 1996.

Parker, Penny, "The New Spin on Schwinn," *The Denver Post,* February 5, 1996, pp. 1C, 6C.

Schulaka, Carly, "Schwinn Seeks Partner or Purchaser," *Boulder Daily Camera,* April 17, 1997.

Shilling, Halle, "Spin City," *Boulder Planet,* February 12, 1997, pp. 1B–2B.

Snel, Alan, "Schwinn Back from the Brink at the 100-Year Mark," *Boulder Daily Camera,* April 30, 1995, p. 3B.

Wells, Garrison, "Schwinn Cycling Loses Two Top Sales Executives," *The Denver Business Journal,* February 4, 1994, p. 5A.

Wolf, Chris, "New Hometown, New Image as Schwinn Changes Gears," *Boulder County Business Report,* November 1993.

—Susan Windisch Brown

The Score Board, Inc.

1951 Old Cuthbert Road
Cherry Hill, New Jersey 08034
U.S.A.
(609) 354-9000
Fax: (609) 354-8402

Public Company
Incorporated: 1986
Employees: 187
Sales: $75 million (1996)
Stock Exchanges: NASDAQ
SICs: 5945 Hobby, Toy & Game Shops; 5947 Gift,
Novelty & Souvenir Shops; 6794 Patent Owners &
Lessors; 8742 Management Consulting Services; 2750
Commercial Printing, Not Elsewhere Classified; 3949
Sporting & Athletic Goods, Not Elsewhere Classified;
5941 Sporting Goods & Bicycle Shops

The largest distributor of sports memorabilia in the United States, The Score Board, Inc. markets sports and entertainment memorabilia through retail stores, mail-order catalogs, and on cable television. Score Board began as a distributor of baseball trading cards before branching out into other sports and into the market for entertainment memorabilia. During the late 1990s, the company owned licensing agreements to market *Star Trek* and *Star Wars* memorabilia, as well as contracts with numerous famous athletes for the provision of autographed memorabilia. Sales of memorabilia accounted for roughly one quarter of the company's total sales during the late 1990s with the balance derived from the manufacture and sale of sports related trading cards.

Origins

When seven-year-old Ken Goldin began collecting baseball trading cards in 1972, the seeds were planted for a company that would become one of the phenomenal stock market success stories of all time. Goldin's interest in baseball cards as a child sparked commensurate interest in his father, Paul Goldin, who orchestrated the development of Score Board into a national leader and created a pioneer company in a burgeoning industry. Before father and son launched into business together, however, their shared interest in baseball cards represented more of a hobby than a business, albeit a hobby pursued with considerable zeal. Ken and Paul Goldin were ardent collectors and sellers, enriching their collection and pocketbooks by travelling to trade shows and purchasing and selling cards through advertisements. By age 11, Ken Goldin undoubtedly ranked as the biggest money-earner among pre-teens in his neighborhood, frequently earning $1,000 a week by selling baseball cards.

As the Goldins delved deeper and deeper into baseball card trading, their hobby gradually evolved into a business. By 1980, father and son had spent nearly $200,000 amassing an inventory of five million cards, a prodigious collection that placed them among the ranks of the nation's most serious collectors. In the decade ahead, the number of serious collectors like the Goldins would grow exponentially as the value of famous players' cards increased robustly. During the 1980s, the sport-related trading card market grew by leaps and bounds, with the value of renowned players' rookie cards increasing 40 percent per year and the number of baseball card stores increasing from 500 at the beginning of the decade to 14,000 by the decade's conclusion.

The proliferation of these stores provided fertile ground for the type of business Paul Goldin envisioned, and their propagation was occasioned by two signal developments. In 1979, the first price guide for baseball cards was published, giving collectors for the first time the common means to determine what their collections were worth. Two years later another key development facilitated the emergence of a booming industry when the major baseball card manufacturer Topps Chewing Gum Inc. lost an antitrust suit, which provided room for additional card manufacturers such as Fleer Corp. and Donruss Leaf Inc.

More competition and the ability to assay card worth set the stage for prolific growth, but it was not until midway through the 1980s that Paul Goldin tapped into the market as a full-fledged entrepreneur. During the first half of the decade, father and son conducted their baseball trading activities much as they had done during the 1970s; they sold their cards at weekend sport-card shows and through mail order catalogs. By 1985, however, Paul Goldin began to realize the opportunity presented by the slew of new baseball card stores opening across the country. At the time, Goldin was serving as president of a medical equipment company (Creative Medical Systems Inc.), which he had helped get off the ground, while also teaching at Drexel University in Philadelphia as an associate professor of statistical economics.

Nevertheless, Goldin's hectic professional life did not preclude him from starting another business. Goldin and an associate named Arthur Sherman, who was employed as the senior vice-president of marketing for Trenton, New Jersey-based Magic Marker Industries, began discussing the possibility of turning a baseball card hobby into a business and developed a specific strategy. "There was room in the [baseball trading card] business, I figured," Goldin later told *Nation's Business,* "for someone who could supply dealers with large quantities of the best players."

1987 Public Stock Offering

Goldin and Sherman resolved to buy baseball cards in bulk from the major card producers, cull the star players out of the sets to sell them to the increasing number of card stores, and repackage the remaining cards for sale to retail stores. In November 1986, the two partners got underway, with Goldin devoting 20 percent of his time to the newly created Score Board as chairman, Sherman assuming the duties of president and chief operating officer, and Ken Goldin, by then 21 years old, beginning as merchandise manager. Much of the first year was spent organizing and equipping the company with a sufficient inventory to successfully compete as a merchandiser and wholesaler of baseball trading cards.

In August 1987, after an adequate inventory had been established, the company converted to public ownership, becoming the first company of its kind to do so, and raised $2.43 million through an initial public offering of 77 million shares of stock at 3.5 cents each. What began as a risky "penny stock" quickly developed into a lucrative investment for those who picked up the stock at its debut, because Goldin's strategy worked wonders. Score Board flourished during its inaugural decade, developing into an industry powerhouse without rival.

By the end of Score Board's first year, sales amounted to $780,692, from which the company recorded a net loss of $352,782. The year-end figures were deceptive, however, because the company was not operational until its fourth fiscal quarter, when it generated more than $600,000 and registered $42,000 in profit. From this starting point, Score Board's financial totals marched strongly upward, propelled by the insatiable demand for baseball trading cards. By the summer of 1988, after recording $1.4 million in sales and $217,000 in net income during the first fiscal quarter, Score Board's inventory was valued at $1.5 million, its breadth and depth built up by weekend trips to card shows across the nation.

From these moveable feasts of sports memorabilia, the company's purchasing agent procured older cards and other sport-related treasures, such as Pete Rose's 1978 jersey, bats used by Babe Ruth and Ty Cobb, and a 1914 Athletics vs. Braves World Series program. For the new cards, Score Board acquired substantial quantities from the three major card manufacturers, Topps Chewing Gum Inc., Donruss Leaf Inc., and The Fleer

Corp., and a Texas-based company named Score. These cards were then repackaged by the company's 20 part-time workers—high school students mainly—who sorted the cards into sets for sale through mail order and at retail outlets.

The response to Score Board's approach was immediate and widespread, as the $1.4 million in sales for the first quarter of 1988 testified. However, Goldin was not satisfied and moved quickly into other business areas before pausing to celebrate Score Board's encouraging debut. While Ken Goldin was dividing his time between his father's company and completing his business degree studies at Drexel University at night, his father diversified into markets related to merchandising sports memorabilia. In January 1988—five months after Score Board's initial public offering—Goldin reached an agreement with the National Collegiate Athletic Association (NCAA) Final Four Foundation to produce a limited-edition set of five lithographs depicting the 50th anniversary of the annual college basketball tournament.

Goldin also launched a publication division that published "The Score Board Book of Baseball Cards," "The Baseball Engagement Book," and a National Football League "Football Date Book." Complementing the product line was a videotape distribution business, featuring such titles as "The 500 Home Run Club," and the merchandising of sundry sport-related novelties, including towels, aprons, and ceramic collectibles. Midway through the year, Goldin was preparing to widen Score Board's scope further by adding a board game manufacturing subsidiary through the acquisition of Atlanta-based Gametime Ltd. and its baseball trivia board game. On all fronts, the company was moving forward, securing an intractable hold on various sports memorabilia markets before serious competition could muster a response.

Goldin did not hold back in 1989, opting instead to continue increasing Score Board's exposure and presence in various sports memorabilia niches. Sales for the year reached $20 million, thanks in large part to the debut of the company's merchandise on cable television's Home Shopping Network. In front of millions of viewers, sports celebrities such as Hank Aaron chatted with a host, who in turn sold Score Board's sports memorabilia. The contribution to Score Board's financial status was immediate and large; by the end of 1989 roughly half of the company's entire revenue volume was derived from sales made on the Home Shopping Network.

Another key development during the year was the decision to sign agreements with sports stars to autograph sports equipment and novelties for sale to the public. Million dollar deals were signed with revered athletes such as Nolan Ryan, Mickey Mantle, and Roger Clemens, who agreed to sign their name to merchandise in return for payment. Dozens of athletes were signed to multi-year deals, providing a powerful revenue-generating engine to the quickly blossoming Score Board.

1990s Diversification

Sales climbed to $32 million by the end of 1990, making Score Board the largest national distributor of sports cards and autographed memorabilia in the country. During the early 1990s, Goldin's efforts to diversify Score Board's business made for an increasingly well-rounded company, particularly his move into manufacturing. During its first years of business, Score Board profited as a merchandiser of other companies' memorabilia, but by the beginning of the 1990s the company also began to merchandise memorabilia manufactured by itself, including trading cards through a licensing agreement with the Worldwide Wrestling Federation, board games through a licensing agreement with major league baseball, and memorabilia bearing the autographs of star athletes.

Goldin's most ambitious move during the early 1990s, however, had nothing to do with sports. In pursuit of business that could maintain Score Board's prolific pace of growth, Goldin entered into the market for entertainment related memorabilia and created a wholly owned subsidiary named Catch a Star to facilitate the company's entry into the entertainment memorabilia market.

As the company's entertainment memorabilia business was taking shape, aided by memorabilia distribution contracts with Elvis Presley Enterprises and Paramount Pictures, progress continued to be made with Score Board's mainstay sports memorabilia business. Early in 1991 the company purchased Best Cards Co. and its license to manufacture and sell minor league baseball cards. Later in the year two other pivotal deals were made: In September, National Football League Properties granted Score Board a three-year license to produce and market trivia board games featuring National Football League players, and in October the company announced it had developed a basketball memorabilia program that included contracts with basketball stars Julius Erving, Kareem Abdul Jabbar, Patrick Ewing, and Dominique Wilkins.

The consistent development of new memorabilia-related business pushed sales in 1991 up to $46.5 million and lifted profits to $4.8 million, as the more than four million serious collectors in the United States continued to pay dearly for sports cards, signed memorabilia, and entertainment related merchandise. Annual sales leaped to $75 million in 1992 and the company recorded a 687 percent gain in stock performance, the second-best on the NASDAQ exchange for the year. For those investors who purchased Score Board stock at its debut of 3.5 cents per share there were bountiful yields to be realized. Score Board's stock was trading at roughly $45 per share by 1992, a prodigious climb that continued to move upward despite the sluggish economy prevailing during the recessive early 1990s. By 1993, the company's foray into entertainment memorabilia had been strengthened considerably by the addition of licenses to sell collectibles based on the films *Star Trek, Star Wars, Gone with the Wind,* and *The Wizard of Oz,* as well as certain rights to market memorabilia connected to singer/songwriters Elvis Presley and John Lennon.

The push was on to expand memorabilia lines in 1994, as the company strove to maintain the animated growth that had described its first half decade of business. During the year, an agreement was signed with Matsushita's MCA subsidiary Winterland Productions, the country's leading music merchandiser. Under the terms of the agreement, Score Board developed memorabilia based on Winterland artists, the ranks of which included recording artist Madonna. The company also began marketing prepaid, theme-based telephone cards in 1994, but

the most overshadowing development during the year was the death in May of Paul Goldin.

Retooling for the 1990s and Beyond

Goldin's son Ken assumed the responsibilities of Score Board's chief executive office. Upon taking command of a business his father had built into a $100 million company, Ken Goldin, then 29 years old, declared to *Forbes* magazine, "I'm not interested in any business that isn't profitable," words Goldin would quickly have to act upon. Competition had become intense in the baseball trading card market, leading to an oversupply of cards on the market. The surfeit of cards was exacerbated by strikes in two major league sports, the combined effect of which stripped the company's stock of much of its value. Goldin was forced to restructure Score Board in 1995 as a result, making good on his words to eschew any business deemed unprofitable. As part of the restructuring program, Goldin spun off Score Board's California Gold plaque and framing operations and laid off eight percent of the company's workforce.

After cresting at $108 million in 1994, sales shrank to $72 million in 1995 before recording a marginal gain to $75 million in 1996, the same total generated in 1993. The company's net income dipped into the red as well, but as management was taking steps to strengthen the company's position for the late 1990s it was hoped the setback during the mid-1990s was only a temporary one. As a foundation for future growth, Score Board continued to hold valuable contracts with numerous sports celebrities and maintain a broad presence in sports and entertainment memorabilia markets, factors the company's management hoped would hold Score Board in good stead as the 21st century neared.

Principal Subsidiaries

Catch-A-Star.

Further Reading

George, John, "Score Board Expanding Via Showbiz Memorabilia," *Philadelphia Business Journal,* December 2, 1991, p. S8B.

Joyce, Marilyn, "Consumer Spending is Sluggish? Someone's Buying Sports Cards," *Philadelphia Business Journal,* May 31, 1993, p. 8B.

Khalaf, Roula, "The DiMaggio Debacle," *Forbes,* August 16, 1993, p. 64.

Lefton, Terry, "Can Score Board Score as a Corporate Sports Marketer? The King of Memorabilia Forays into Merchandising," *Brandweek,* June 13, 1994, p. 34.

Leibowitz, David S., "Investing in a Second Childhood," *Financial World,* July 6, 1993, p. 70.

Macnow, Glen, "Thanks to This Form, Some Ballplayers Get Sore Arms from Swinging Pens, Not Bats," *Nation's Business,* April 1991, p. 10.

McKee, William, "It's a Clan in Phillies Land That Values Bobby Bonilla," *Philadelphia Business Journal,* August 22, 1988, p. 1.

Meece, Mickey, "MBNA to Offer Sports Collectibles Mastercard," *American Banker,* November 15, 1993, p. 15.

Meeks, Fleming, "Mound Merchant," *Forbes,* April 13, 1992, p. 20.

"Score Board," *Fortune,* October 22, 1990, p. 110.

Steinbreder, John, "The Goldins Rule," *Sports Illustrated,* November 1, 1993, p. 7B.

—Jeffrey L. Covell

ScottishPower

ScottishPower plc

1 Atlantic Quay
Glasgow G2 8SP
Scotland
011 0141 248 8200
Fax: 011 0141 248 8300

Public Company
Incorporated: 1989
Employees: 15,242
Sales: £2.27 billion (1996)
Stock Exchanges: London
SICs: 4900 Electric, Gas & Sanitary Services

ScottishPower plc is one of the leading and fastest growing utility companies in the United Kingdom, with more than five million customers in England, Wales, and Scotland. The company operates generating plants, sells electricity and gas, supplies advanced telecommunications and online information services, provides water and water waste services, operates electrical retail shops and superstores throughout the United Kingdom, and provides engineering and scientific consultancy services to various individuals, governmental, and corporate groups. One of the largest utility companies in the country, ScottishPower has three primary subsidiaries in three distinct geographical regions, including Manweb, which sells electricity to customers in Merseyside, Cheshire, and North Wales; Southern Water, which provides water and waste water services to customers in Kent, Sussex, Hampshire, and the Isle of Wight, along with designing and installing waste water treatment plants; and ScottishTelecom, which provides mobile telephone and online information services to many of Scotland's largest corporations.

Early History

ScottishPower was formed in 1989 because of the reorganization of the Scottish electricity industry. The company is the direct successor to all of the nonnuclear operations and activities of the South of Scotland Electricity Board (SSEB). The South of Scotland Electricity Board had been founded in 1955 by the legislation of the Electricity Reorganization Act of 1954, which had merged the two previous Boards that provided electricity to customers in the area after nationalization of the industry in 1948.

Prior to the formation of ScottishPower, the Scottish electrical industry consisted of the South of Scotland Electricity Board and the North of Scotland Hydro-Electric Board (NSHEB). Both of these Boards, or companies, were operating as vertically integrated monopolies, engaged in such activities as the generation, transmission, distribution, and supply of electrical energy. During this time, all of the expenditures associated with generating and transmitting electricity were shared, and each company's requirements were met according to the determination of the respective Boards.

When the British government decided to reorganize the Scottish electrical industry, it summarily rejected the proposal that a single company cover all of the electrical requirements of Scotland. Consequently, when both ScottishPower and Hydro Electric went public in 1991, the British government made the determination that it was best for each of the companies to operate as vertically integrated electrical utility firms, which was in keeping with the tradition established in their earlier history.

One of the most interesting features of the Scottish electrical industry is its large surplus of generating capacity. When the reorganization of the industry took place in Scotland, it was expected that ScottishPower and Hydro Electric would use some of this surplus capacity for export to England and Wales. A large part of the surplus was initially derived from Scotland's nuclear power plants, which existed in a much higher proportion than in any other country in Europe, except for France and Belgium. In fact, at the time of the reorganization, the Scottish nuclear power plants were capable of meeting half of the demand for electricity in the country. Once again, it was determined by the British government that ScottishPower should supervise and operate 74.9 percent of the commercial business of Scottish Nuclear, Ltd., while Hydro Electric took a 25.1 percent interest in the operations of the company.

ScottishPower inherited the entire region previously run by the South of Scotland Electricity Board, an area of 22,950 km that covered the part of Scotland south between the estuaries of the River Tay and River Clyde and encompassed a large area of Northumberland. This land included a significant portion of Scotland's industrial base and was characterized by densely populated urban areas, but also extended to the more rural regions of the Borders and Galloway. The initial customer base was approximately 1.7 million people.

Growth and Expansion

Although its main role has always been to supply electricity to the southern part of Scotland, ScottishPower has been in the electrical retail business from its inception. Inheriting 73 retail stores from the South of Scotland Electricity Board, the company sold such items as radios, alarm clocks, and a host of other electrical products, much like the other utility companies across the United Kingdom. When most of the regional electrical companies in England, Wales, and Scotland, including its northern neighbor Hydro Electric, decided to divest all retailing operations, however, management at ScottishPower made the commitment to retain and even expand its network of retail stores, but only on the condition of increasing profitability.

One of the reasons management decided not to abandon retailing operations was that customers who paid their electricity bills in the stores would have been extremely upset. Many people in southern Scotland had grown accustomed to paying their bills while visiting the company's retail stores, and management was well aware of the fact. Consequently, to strengthen its market position, in 1992 ScottishPower acquired a total of 17 units from Rumbelows chain of electrical retail stores owned by Thorn EMI and eight superstores from Atlantis Group, and soon thereafter purchased 50 superstores from the Clydesdale Group, another electrical product retailer with stores in Northern England and the Midlands. Having lost £5 million on sales of £32 million in 1990, ScottishPower Retailing Division reported an operating profit of £10 million on sales of £200 million by the end of 1994.

In 1993, ScottishPower was granted a license to enter into the public telecommunications industry, and it immediately installed fibre-optic links within its already existing network of communications between Glasgow and Edinburgh. Carried along its own high-voltage power lines, ScottishPower was soon able to provide extremely high-quality telecommunications services such as the fast transfer of voices, data, and

pictures to Scotland's major businesses, including a number of companies in the insurance and banking industries, not to mention engineering firms and universities. Christened "ScottishTelecom," it was one of the fastest growing segments of ScottishPower's business.

Although ScottishPower operated six power generating plants composed of coal, gas, and hydro power, including Longannet at Kincardine on Forth, Cockenzie, Methil, Cruachan, Stonebyres and Bonnington, and Galloway Hydro Scheme, the company was not averse to engaging in more experimental forms of generating energy. In the early 1990s, ScottishPower constructed its first wind farm, located at Penrhyddlan and Llidartywaun in Wales, a unique joint venture between ScottishPower, SeaWest of California, and the Toman Corporation of Japan. The largest such wind farm in Europe, it has a generating capacity of 31 MW. Not long afterward, the company established new wind farms in Northern Ireland, Lanarkshire, Cornwall, and Lancashire. By the mid-1990s, ScottishPower had become the largest wind farm operator in the United Kingdom.

Strategic Acquisitions

As opportunities for more customers and increased sales for electricity became limited in Scotland, management at ScottishPower embarked on a strategic acquisitions policy that extended the company's operations into other areas of the United Kingdom. The initial acquisition was Manweb plc, a regional electrical company that provided service to more than 1.3 million commercial, industrial, and residential customers in Merseyside, Cheshire, and rural North Wales. Purchased at a price of £1.1 billion, the transaction was a milestone since it was the first merger between two electricity companies in the United Kingdom.

The merger was an efficient move by ScottishPower, since common functions between Manweb and its parent firm were easily integrated, resulting in lower costs to customers and, at the same time, enabling Manweb to focus on developing its electricity distribution and supply network. With a ScottishPower investment of £300 million to improve and enhance Manweb's power system, the new acquisition was able to limit its supply interruptions significantly, reroute electricity supplies to alternative circuits when necessary, and provide better service to sparsely populated countryside in western England and northern Wales. Manweb was also at the forefront of innovations within the electricity industry. The company developed a "live line" technique, by which repairmen are able to carry out maintenance and repairs on overhead distribution lines without needing to interrupt the supply of electricity to customers in the local area. In one of the most original developments in which Manweb was involved, the company conducted experiments with "trenchless technology," which allowed the laying of cable without having to excavate pavements and streets.

In August of 1996, ScottishPower acquired Southern Water plc, a water supply and waste water services company with barely less than two million customers in Kent, Sussex, Hampshire, and the Isle of Wight, for £1.67 billion. Supplying approximately 644 million liters of drinking water per day, through an extensive system of pipes that total 13,000 kilometers, and treating more than 1,300 liters of sewerage per day, at the time of the acquisition Southern Water was one of the leaders in the water supply and waste water treatment industry. Over the years, Southern Water had garnered a stellar reputation in the United Kingdom. The company had dramatically improved the quality of drinking water to the geographical region it served and had successfully cleaned up the pollution along an extensive part of the coastline in southern Britain. Southern Water had also cleaned up the rivers within its operating region so that 94 percent of them support healthy fish stock and allow for natural breeding.

Under ScottishPower leadership, Southern Water invested £18 million to build a pipeline to transport water from the River Medway in Kent to Bewl Reservoir on the Kent/Sussex boundary. Since very dry summers bordering on drought had plagued that part of Britain during the mid-1990s, ScottishPower and Southern Water were committed to enhancing the region's water resource management. New and improved waste water treatment plants were also planned by Southern Water, to be built during the late 1990s to comply with the European Union's Urban Wastewater Directive. Perhaps the most important and far-reaching effect of ScottishPower's acquisition of Southern Water was the decrease in prices for all customers in the new subsidiary's region. Consumer prices would be reduced one percent in 1997 and two percent in 1998 and 1999.

Looking Toward the Future

One of the fastest growing segments of ScottishPower's business is the consultancy services it provides to an ever-increasing list of customers that include, among others, British Petroleum, British Steel, Motorola, and the British Energy Group. The company's consultancy services encompass a wide variety of activities, such as the design and construction of power plant buildings, the development of control systems and monitoring devices, the hands-on installation and maintenance of boilers, turbines, and other large power plant equipment, the analysis of plant components and water samples, and assistance with environmental management. The design, construction, and project management of new power stations, like Scotland's

nuclear generating stations at Hunterston and Torness, are two examples of the company's consultancy activities in the mid-1990s.

In addition, ScottishPower formed a contracting services business, which carries out a full range of electrical contracting services in the areas of security systems, large scale power plant installations, high and low voltage installations, installing electric heating systems, testing and maintaining electrical systems, and facilities management. In the mid-1990s, clients included hospitals, universities, prisons, supermarket chains, and a host of blue-chip corporations such as NEC, Motorola, Coca Cola, and Vauxhall.

Through its strategic acquisitions, astute management of a growing retail operation, cultivation of new service-oriented consulting businesses, and provision of reliable and inexpensive electricity to its customers, ScottishPower has earned the reputation as one of the best utility companies in the world.

Principal Subsidiaries

Manweb plc; Southern Water plc; ScottishTelecom plc.

Further Reading

Buxton, James, "Joint Power Plan Set Up by London Underground," *Financial Times London,* October 11, 1990, p. 8.
"Scottish Telecoms Move," *Times London,* November 23, 1994, p. 26.
"ScottishPower," *Financial Times London,* April 11, 1995, p. 23.
"ScottishPower," *Times London,* March 5, 1994, p. 27.
"ScottishPower Buys," *Times London,* March 5, 1994, p. 26.
Smith, Michael, "Ambitions Lie South," *Financial Times London,* November 14, 1995, p. III.
——, "On-Shore Gas To Fuel Power Station," *Financial Times London,* April 14, 1993, p. 10.
"The Song of the Border Reivers," *Financial Times London,* May 9, 1991, p. 20.
"Telecoms Rival in Pipeline," *Times London,* December 1, 1992, p. 23.
"Wired for Success," *Financial Times London,* June 28, 1995, p. 20.

—Thomas Derdak

The Selmer Company, Inc.

600 Industrial Parkway
Elkhart, Indiana 46516
U.S.A.
(219) 522-1675
Fax: (219) 522-0334
Web site: http://www.selmer.com

Public Company
Founded: 1902
Employees: 1,000
Sales: $189.8 million (1995)
Stock Exchanges: New York
SICs: 3931 Musical Instruments

Founded early in the 20th century to import and distribute European-made clarinets, The Selmer Company, Inc. has expanded via acquisition to become America's largest manufacturer of musical instruments. It claims a 42 percent share of the U.S. professional band instrument market and 25 percent of beginner instrument sales. The company's woodwind, brass, percussion, and stringed instruments are largely hand-crafted at plants in Indiana, North Carolina, Ohio and Illinois, and sold via more than 1,600 independent dealers. Over three-fourths of the music mammoth's unit sales are made to student musicians, but professional and advanced instruments generate 47 percent of revenues. The company hoped to increase its penetration of international markets—which contributed less than 20 percent of total revenues in 1995—in the mid- to late-1990s.

Selmer and many of its subsidiaries have an interesting trait in common: virtually all were founded in the United States by immigrants. Selmer itself became an acquisition target in the last half of the century, changing ownership four times from 1969 to 1993. Acquired via leveraged buy out by the Los Angeles-based Kirkland Messina, Inc. investment company in the latter year, Selmer became a subsidiary of a newly-formed holding company, Steinway Musical Instruments, Inc., following the investment firm's acquisition of piano-maker Steinway in 1996. The new owners took their company public that year

with the sale of a minority stake to raise over $60 million in debt reduction funds.

Roots in France

The company traces its name and history to France, where fourth-generation musician Henri Selmer founded an instrument shop in the early 19th century. Trained as a clarinetist at the Paris Conservatory, Henri started out making reeds and mouthpieces as well as repairing clarinets, eventually manufacturing models of his own design. By 1920, Henri had diversified into the manufacture of double reed instruments, including oboes and bassoons. Meanwhile his brother Alexandre, also educated at the Paris Conservatory, had moved to the United States, where he played clarinet with orchestras in New York, Boston and Cincinnati. In 1902 Alexandre began selling his brother's clarinets in New York, where the award-winning instruments caught on quickly among professional musicians.

With business on both sides of the Atlantic growing fast, Alexandre sought to return to his homeland. He sold the rights to distribute Selmer instruments in the United States to an employee, George Bundy, in 1918. Although the two businesses would develop separately over the course of the 20th century, the American firm would continue to distribute instruments manufactured by its French sister company through the 1990s. Bundy maintained his leadership of the company until his death in 1951. The remainder of this essay will focus on his U.S.-based enterprise.

Like his predecessors in France, George Bundy began to diversify into other wind instruments just a few years after Alexandre Selmer's departure. Bundy hired flute designer George W. Haynes in 1920 and brought German flute designer Kurt Gemeinhardt on board later in the decade. Bundy launched Selmer's first saxophone in 1921 and was soon "out-saxing" the instrument's inventor, Adolphe Sax. Selmer purchased the innovator's business in 1928, thereby adding trombones and trumpets to Selmer's repertoire as well as augmenting its saxophone business.

While Selmer maintained a strong presence in the market for professional instruments, it also developed an emphasis on student musicians and music education programs. This strategy forged a strong link between Selmer's prosperity and general demographic trends. The instrument-maker's sales rose and fell in concert with the birth rate, albeit with a 10- to 11-year lag. Most student instruments are purchased when children are entering middle school band programs.

Inspired perhaps by wartime shortages and consequent increases in raw materials prices, Selmer drew on some of the new materials and manufacturing methods developed during World War II to develop what the company characterizes as "one of the first commercially successful molded clarinets—the Bundy Resonite model 1400." The new instrument offered student clarinetists quality and durability at a comparatively low price. By 1978, the company had sold over one million Resonites.

Growth through Acquisition Intensifies in the 1960s

Selmer quickened its pace of growth through acquisition to capitalize on the postwar era's baby boomers, who began to reach prime music education years in the 1960s. Like the parent company, many of these new subsidiaries enjoyed interesting histories of their own.

Selmer's first major purchase, the Vincent Bach Corporation, came in 1961. This manufacturer of brass instruments was founded in 1918 by a Viennese immigrant born Vincent Schrotenbach. Schrotenbach had earned a degree in engineering in Germany, but decided to pursue a career in entertainment. After playing the trumpet in Europe, he abbreviated his name and moved to New York City during World War I. From 1914 to 1918, he advanced from the vaudeville circuit to first chair at the Metropolitan Opera House and the Boston Symphony.

Company legend has it that Bach was on tour when a Pittsburgh repairman rendered his mouthpiece unusable. The mouthpiece is a small, but vital part of many brass instruments whose shape can be changed to suit different styles of music. Orchestral players, for example, often select a broader and deeper mouthpiece than their counterparts in jazz and dance bands. Bach had a tough time finding a spare. His misfortune not only revealed a market niche, but also gave the musician an opportunity to dust off his "engineer's cap." Upon his return to New York, Bach started repairing and manufacturing mouthpieces himself, while continuing to supplement his income by performing. It was not long before word of his mouthpieces got around musicians' circles, and soon the parts were so prized that they commanded prices of over 30 times those of competitors. Bach started making trumpets in 1924 and added trombones to his line in 1928. At the age of 71, Bach sold his company to Selmer. Production was moved from New York to Elkhart four years later.

Two years after moving the Bach operations from New York to Elkhart, Selmer acquired the Buescher Band Instrument Company. Brilhard mouthpieces were added in 1966 followed closely by Lesher double reed instruments in 1967.

Changes in Corporate Ownership Mark the 1970s, 1980s

Selmer was itself acquired by Magnavox Co. in 1969, launching a long and sometimes difficult period of corporate change. In the late 1970s, Magnavox sold Selmer to North American Philips Corporation. In addition to these corporate machinations, Selmer also struggled to meet industrywide challenges. Writing for *Forbes* magazine in 1983, Laura Saunders cited demographics as a key factor in the musical instrument industry's problems, noting that the birth rate declined by nearly one-third from 1965 to 1975. The resulting decline in school-age children decimated the industry's core market. At the same time, high interest rates and rising raw materials costs accelerated the decline of the market. Competition, both from other leisure and entertainment categories and from foreign manufacturers, whittled away at domestic producers' sales and profitability.

Selmer's own opportunistic acquisitions continued, albeit at a slower pace, during this period. The company acquired Cleveland-based Glaesel String Instrument Service, an assembler and distributor of student violins, in 1978. Selmer also diversified into an entirely different area of the stringed instrument category, electric guitars and amplifiers, during the 1970s, but divested these holdings in 1980 to concentrate on the more classical instruments.

Selmer added a rhythm section to its group with the 1981 acquisition of the Ludwig Drum Company. Founded by German immigrant brothers William and Theo Ludwig in 1910, the firm started out manufacturing an improved bass drum pedal. After years of experimentation, the company expanded into the manufacture of timpani drums—a specialty of William's—in 1916. The Ludwigs sold their firm to Elkhart's C.G. Conn Company during the Great Depression, but William bought it back (along with its sister subsidiary, Leedy Manufacturing Company) in 1955. Ludwig added the Musser Marimba Company's xylophones, chimes, bells, and other mallet instruments to its offerings in 1966.

In 1988, Selmer again changed hands, this time to a New York-based realty firm, Integrated Resources Inc. Unfortunately, the new parent sought bankruptcy protection within a year of the acquisition. Integrated's insolvency didn't reflect well on Selmer, whose sales slid seven percent, from $86 million in 1989 to $80 million in 1990.

Early 1990s Bring New Ownership and Corporate Structure

After years of corporate limbo, the bankruptcy court in charge of Integrated's case put Selmer on the auction block in

1993. That is when two Los Angeles-based financiers named Kyle Kirkland and Dana Messina put together a financing package and acquired the company in a $95 million leveraged buy out. The new owners left Selmer's management team, including president and chief executive officer Thomas Burzycki, in place, and maintained its operations in the Midwest.

Under new corporate ownership Selmer bounced back slowly in the recessionary market of the early 1990s, with sales recovering to $85.9 million by 1992 and net income amounting to $2.3 million. Notwithstanding its high debt load, which *Forbes*'s Bruce Upjohn estimated at $160 million in 1995, Selmer continued to add musical instrument manufacturers to its "band" in the 1990s. The 1995 acquisition of Chicago-based William Lewis & Son, a 121-year-old violin concern, helped push sales to $189.3 million that year.

Selmer (or more correctly, its parent, the Kirkland Messina, Inc. investment firm) completed its largest acquisition to date in 1996, when it purchased Steinway Musical Instruments from another group of investors for $101.5 million. Selmer had attempted a diversification into piano manufacture decades before with the purchase of Jesse French Co. in the 1940s, but shuttered the operation in 1954.

Soon after the Steinway acquisition, Kirkland and Messina created a new holding company, Steinway Musical Instruments, Inc., with Selmer and Steinway as distinct subsidiaries. Kirkland serves the new entity as chairman, while Messina acts as CEO. In their mid-30s, both were the youngest members of the board of directors.

With over $230 million in combined sales, the new company was the largest player in its industry. In 1996, the investment firm took Selmer Musical Instruments public with an offering of about 16 percent of its equity on the New York Stock Exchange.

The more than $60 million they expected to raise would be used to reduce a heavy load of LBO debt.

According to the company's August 1996 prospectus, management hoped to increase Selmer's production capacity to meet rising demand; continue its acquisition strategy; increase overseas sales, especially in Europe; and increase efficiency.

Principal Subsidiaries

Vincent Bach International, Ltd. (United Kingdom).

Principal Divisions

Selmer Division; Ludwig/Musser Division; Glaesel/William Lewis Division.

Further Reading

Anslinger, Patricia L., and Copeland, Thomas E., "Growth through Acquisitions: A Fresh Look," *Harvard Business Review*, January-February 1996, pp. 126–35.

Cook, Daniel D., "The Beat Slackens for a Mature Industry," *Industry Week*, May 14, 1979, pp. 144–50.

Halbfinger, David M., "Steinway Is Sold to Big Producer of Instruments," *Newsday*, April 19, 1995, p. A41.

Koprowski, Gene, "Selmer Places Percussion Unit on Sales Block; Wants Focus Shifted to Other Instruments," *Metalworking News*, April 17, 1989, pp. 5–6.

Musical Instrument Makers Face Three Challenges," *Industry Week*, September 20, 1976, p. 130.

Saunders, Laura, "Mood Indigo," *Forbes*, August 29, 1983, pp. 50–52.

Selmer: Great Names in Music, Elkhart, Ind.: The Selmer Company, Inc., 1996.

Upjohn, Bruce, "The Sweet Sound of Leverage," *Forbes*, November 20, 1995, pp. 47–48.

—April Dougal Gasbarre

Service Merchandise Company, Inc.

7100 Service Merchandise Drive
Brentwood, Tennessee 37027
U.S.A.
(615) 660-6000
Fax: (615) 660-4321
Web site: http://www.servicemerchandise.com

Public Company
Incorporated: 1970
Employees: 28,000
Sales: $3.95 billion
Stock Exchanges: New York
SICs: 5399 Catalog Showrooms; 5944 Jewelry, Precious
Stones, and Precious Metals; 5961 Catalog and Mail
Order Houses

Service Merchandise Company, Inc. is one of the largest general merchandise chains in the United States. It operates over 400 stores in 37 states, selling jewelry, housewares, small appliances, giftware, silverware, cameras, luggage, radios, televisions and other home electronics, accessories for the patio, lawn, and garden, as well as sporting goods and toys. While most of the company's sales are generated through in-store purchases, Service Merchandise does publish several catalogs. In fact, the company focuses promotion efforts on the annual jewelry, gift, and home catalog, which is distributed to over 16 million households during the fall season. Over 600 pages, the catalog features mores than 8,500 items.

Company Origins

Founded in 1960, the company's beginnings can be traced to the variety store that Harry and Mary Zimmerman opened in 1934 in Pulaski, Tennessee. That enterprise grew into a chain of dime stores located in small Tennessee towns. Harry and Mary's son, Raymond Zimmerman, virtually grew up in the stores and began to work in one of them after attending the University of Miami and Memphis State University. After

the family sold most of the stores to Kuhn's, a variety store chain, the Zimmermans became variety store jobbers, a business in which they were still involved when they opened their catalog business in 1960. Their warehouse in downtown Nashville, Tennessee, became their first store. For ten years, the Zimmermans operated this single outlet before entering two additional markets: Memphis and Chattanooga, Tennessee. During those years of limited growth, the company developed its business strategy and management team.

Incorporation and Expansion in the 1970s

The company incorporated in Tennessee in 1970. Prior to that year, most catalog showroom businesses were privately held and were often family-owned companies operating locally. In 1971 Service Merchandise began to keep its stock in a warehouse connected to each store and to sell merchandise from samples only. By January 1972 the company was operating six showrooms. Later that year, it acquired Warco Supply Company in Indianapolis, Indiana, which operated a showroom, and it assumed the lease of an 80,000-square-foot discount store that it converted into a showroom.

In all, Service Merchandise opened eight new showrooms in 1972 and an additional nine the following year, expanding into 12 new markets. In April 1974 the company acquired seven showrooms from Malone & Hyde Inc., gaining access to that company's markets in Jackson, Tennessee; Little Rock, Arkansas; and Springfield, Missouri. By mid-1974, Service Merchandise had 27 showrooms in 11 states in the South and Midwest and was the nation's third-largest catalog showroom company. With most of its marketing dollars sunk into its catalog, the company distributed 1.9 million copies of the "annual book" catalog in 1974.

The early 1970s saw a shakeout in the catalog industry, with many operators, especially those new to the industry, expanding too quickly and finding themselves unable to pay their debts. The recession of 1973 and 1974 aggravated the situation, but the major catalog operators continued to fare well. In 1973 Raymond Zimmerman became Service Merchandise's president, while his father Harry assumed the post of chairman. Most

Company Perspectives:

"We are refocusing with the goal of strengthening our appeal to customers and adding shareholder value. Simply put, our goal is to renew Service Merchandise as a vital force in the retail industry."

company showrooms converted to point-of-sale electronic cash registers in the summer of 1973. The information recorded on each showroom's mini-computer could be transmitted via telephone wires to headquarters. Greater inventory control was the most important benefit of the new system.

With each expansion, Service Merchandise sought to achieve maximum visibility by locating in high traffic locations, often near regional shopping centers. In 1974 the company gained entry as an anchor tenant in two shopping malls. Each showroom's layout was similar, reflecting Service Merchandise's experience with the most profitable floor plan.

In 1975 Raymond Zimmerman told *Discount Merchandiser* that in Service Merchandise showrooms, while jewelry accounted for only three percent of the total square footage, it represented 25 percent of the sales volume. By that year the company had reduced the size of its prototype store from 60,000 to 50,000 square feet, which allowed it to enter smaller markets. By mid-1975 Service Merchandise had 38 catalog showrooms, and by 1978 it had 51. The company acquired 22 Value House showrooms in 1978, giving it a foothold in several New England markets.

The tremendous increase in gold prices in 1978 and 1979 wreaked havoc on the catalog showroom business. Since catalogs were printed as much as a year in advance, merchants were left with the dilemma of whether to raise prices or honor an advertised price and lose money. In one instance in 1978, Service Merchandise had printed flyers for the important months of November and December and chose to honor the stated prices rather than raise them.

Service Merchandise Publishes Its Own Catalog

The catalog showroom industry began to mature in the late 1970s. The three largest operators, Best Products Company, Modern Merchandising Inc., and Service Merchandise, had always avoided any direct competition in a single market, but this began to change in 1979 in major markets such as Miami and San Francisco.

Part of what precipitated this change was Service Merchandise's 1980 withdrawal from Creative Merchandising and Publishing, a Modern Merchandising subsidiary that published the catalogs for the three largest chains and for several smaller houses. By this time the largest of the three chains, Service Merchandise had sought the flexibility of being able to tailor its catalog to its own special needs. The move also saved money. From 1979 to 1982, the number of catalogs that the company mailed to customers remained constant at 6.5 million, thanks to Service Merchandise's tracking of its customers by zip code and

by telling those customers in the least productive zip codes that if they wished to receive the catalog, they would have to inform the company. By 1982 sales per catalog were $150, compared to $80 just a few years earlier.

Merchandising in the 1980s

Service Merchandise continued seeking new merchandising ideas. In 1980 and 1981 it was one of five retailers to experiment with allowing customers to order their wares via specially equipped color television sets. In 1981 the company developed a new computer program using information about demographics and an outlet's competitive characteristics to predict the market. Originally set up in 23 existing stores and in three new units, the program proved very accurate. By 1982 Service Merchandise had begun to experiment with "Silent Sam," an on-line cash register placed in the middle of the sales floor that allowed customers to check on product availability and to order their merchandise.

In the early 1980s the company made efforts at diversifying its operations, introducing a new retail establishment: The Toy Store. A total of six such stores were introduced, but when they proved unprofitable all were closed just a few years later.

Despite a recession, Service Merchandise managed to top the $1 billion mark in revenues in 1981. That year also marked the retirement of Harry Zimmerman as company chairman. He continued as honorary chairman and a company director, and son Raymond then began to serve as both chairman and president. By that time, Service Merchandise had 116 outlets.

Service Merchandise purchased the bankrupt Sam Solomon Company in 1982, adding the company's seven additional outlets in Charlotte, North Carolina, to its 118 units. The company also installed a computer system that allowed for checking current stock levels and making suggestions about alternatives for out-of-stock items.

Response to Changing Catalog Showroom Industry

As the catalog showroom industry matured, industry analysts criticized operators for getting away from the original concept that had made them so successful. Showrooms were often the size of more traditional mass marketers such as Kmart and J. C. Penney, and the leading catalog showroom operators had begun advertising on television. Industry analysts' prediction of a shakeout in the industry proved on target. Many of the smaller operators sold out or declared bankruptcy, and the larger showroom companies were forced to rethink their merchandising approach by making their stores more attractive, offering more upscale and trendy goods, and providing more customer service. The buying power of the large catalog showroom companies allowed them to operate on a lower margin than the smaller companies. Less than one-third of the catalog companies operating in 1971 remained in business just a dozen years later.

Service Merchandise's response to the changing market was aggressive. In 1981 it opened an upscale prototype unit in Novi, Michigan, and a jewelry store in Nashville, while also beginning to plan mini-showrooms of 30,000 square feet.

Attempting to diversify in 1983, Service Merchandise purchased Home-Owners Warehouse Inc., a company with a retail store in southern Florida that sold construction and home improvement products. Changing the company's name to Mr. How, the concept was used in establishing more such outlets as well. That same year, Service Merchandise also acquired a small chain called The Computer Shoppe.

Although he retained his position as chairman and chief executive officer, Raymond Zimmerman relinquished the company's presidency in late 1983 to James E. Poole, a career cement executive. Poole's tenure was short-lived, however, as he resigned suddenly just seven months later, with Zimmerman assuming the post again.

Service Merchandise began to move its corporate headquarters in 1983 from four main facilities in metropolitan Nashville to Brentwood, Tennessee, just outside of Nashville. However, it was not until 1990 that all corporate headquarters employees were under one roof in Brentwood.

Service Merchandise added 25 new units in 1984, with Chicago receiving its 17th outlet. At year's end, the company maintained 183 showrooms in 35 states. That year it remained the second-largest catalog showroom operator, behind Best Products Company, although it was far more profitable than the leader.

Two 1985 acquisitions added significant markets to the Service Merchandise fold, making it the industry leader in store units. The company acquired H. J. Wilson Company, which included apparel in its product mix in many of its 80 showrooms in 12 states, and Ellman's Inc., which offered jewelry and giftware in its seven units in two states. "We never wanted to be the largest, we just wanted to be the most profitable," Zimmerman told the *Atlanta Journal/Constitution* (August 18, 1985), "but of course, we don't mind having the most number of stores in operation, either."

By the mid-1980s catalog showroom operators were faced with increased price competition from department stores, mass merchants, and warehouse clubs. Service Merchandise experimented with new approaches and concepts to meet the competition. The company used in-store video promotions, a drive-through pick-up window, and a gift-wrapping department. "We'll try anything," Zimmerman told *Business Week* in 1985.

During this time, Service Merchandise had expanded The Computer Shoppe to ten units, had opened two jewelry stores under the Zimm's name, and had opened a single outlet called The Lingerie Store. The most expansion activity had to do with the Mr. How stores, with seven planned for 1985 and 18 for the following year.

In 1985 Service Merchandise installed a computerized inventory replenishment system that was designed to help reduce inventory costs, react immediately to marketplace demands, and avoid out-of-stock items. Company sales hit the $2 billion mark that year. In line with the firm's efforts to operate smarter was the 1986 opening of an automated, 752,000-square-foot warehouse in Montgomery, New York.

Mid-1980s Losses and Conflicts

The mid-1980s were difficult years for Service Merchandise. Both Harry and Mary Zimmerman died in 1986. The Mr. How stores proved to be a drain on the company, and after attempts to build the chain at a rapid pace failed, the line of stores was dismantled. Service Merchandise had discovered that the hardware business was tricky, with the warehouse format needing to turn over its inventory five or six times a year to maximize the profit margin. Such a turnover was approximately twice that of the average small hardware store. Moreover, the product mix that had worked in Florida was a failure in Chicago, one of the markets in which Service Merchandise had opened five Mr. How stores. Finally, the acquisition of H. J. Wilson and Ellman's had also been troublesome, with 60 percent of Wilson's inventory incompatible with that of Service Merchandise. The inventory had to be sold at a substantial loss.

These two problem areas seemed to divert management's attention from its main business. Sales per store had stopped growing and operating expenses began eating away at the company's narrow profit margin. Maximizing the number of in-stock items had always been one of Service Merchandise's foremost priorities, but the company found itself with a growing number of out-of-stock items, which sent customers shopping elsewhere.

Service Merchandise lost $47 million on sales of $2.5 billion in 1986, a rude dose of reality for a company accustomed to turning a respectable profit, no matter what the economic climate. That same year, Best Products Inc., the second-largest catalog showroom chain, lost $25 million. Industry analysts credited the discount store chains with offering customers wider selection of goods at the same low prices as the catalog showrooms and more amenities such as having to wait in line only to pay for goods, not to pick them up. The discounters also had more price flexibility, since they were not locked in on prices for an entire year, as are the catalog showrooms that publish annual catalogs.

Service Merchandise responded successfully by discontinuing some apparel lines, moving into selling more jewelry, and improving its inventory techniques. Efforts were also made to entice each customer to buy more, thus making each sales transaction more profitable.

However, many catalog showroom operators were unable to adjust to the changes in the market. McDade & Company filed for bankruptcy in late 1987, and Allied Wholesale Distributors and Wilkor Jewelry & Showroom closed in mid-1988.

In September 1988 several members of the company's senior management, headed by Raymond Zimmerman, who held the posts of chairman, president, and chief executive officer, announced they were considering taking the company private through a leveraged buyout. There was speculation that the move was announced simply to put the company into play, with the hope that other bidders would materialize. Four lawsuits, however, were brought by shareholders who felt Service Merchandise's management was failing to put shareholders' interests first, and this action stopped talk of a management buyout.

Also in September 1988 an unidentified party made an offer to buy Best Products Company. Securities analysts speculated that the offer, which Best rejected, might have been made by Service Merchandise, since there would have been only minimal duplication of the two stores' territories. This speculation was never confirmed.

Weathering the Late 1980s

Service Merchandise's 1988 sales surpassed the $3 billion mark. The company sold The Computer Shoppe chain in mid-1989. That same year, following two years of impressive growth and profits, it announced a $975 million recapitalization plan. Although the company denied it feared a takeover, such fears would not have been unwarranted, since three firms were said to have been interested. To avoid a hostile takeover, Best Products had gone private in 1988 after accepting a leveraged buyout led by New York-based investment firm Adler & Shaykin. The recapitalization plan provided for one-time cash dividend of $10 per share and a discontinuation of quarterly dividends.

Troubles ensued as in early 1990 Service Merchandise announced that two of its senior officers were targets of an Internal Revenue Service investigation. The two executives soon stepped aside. Less than a month later, a federal grand jury began to investigate the company for improper or illegal use of funds. Zimmerman appointed four of the company's five outside directors to conduct their own internal investigation. Unidentified sources told *Business Week* in 1990 that the investigation centered around whether improper payments had been made to judges and politicians.

The late 1980s and early 1990s were very difficult years for all retailers. In January 1991 Best Products sought protection from its creditors under Chapter 11 of the federal bankruptcy code. Service Merchandise seemed better equipped to weather the recession of the early 1990s. The company had consistently demonstrated an almost exuberant willingness to try any concept or technology that might further streamline its operation and maximize sales and customer satisfaction.

In 1990 Service Merchandise introduced a national gift registry, to which customers in all stores had access and which instantly updated all registries whenever purchases were made; by 1993, 90,000 engaged couples had used the service. Moreover, the company opened a store in the Mall of America, the world's largest shopping complex, in 1992. The company acquired two Dahlkemper's stores in Buffalo, New York during this time, and, having survived the worst of the economic recession, new Service Merchandise store openings proceed. In 1993, the company opened 27 new stores, bringing the company's store total to 391, with annual sales exceeding $3.8 billion.

New Management and Goals for a New Century

Gary M. Witkin, former vice-chairman and member of the board of directors at Saks Fifth Avenue, became president and chief operating officer of the company in 1994. Under his leadership, Service Merchandise focused on customer service and hired more sales staff at all stores. To provide better service and enhance efficiency, the company introduced an automated scheduling and productivity standards project. The Silent Sam computer service (a user-friendly computer allowing customers to inspect and order merchandise) was upgraded and renamed Service Express. In addition, the company focused on southern Florida and Texas markets, bringing the total number of stores to 406.

A new senior management team was organized in 1995. The store/field management group was reorganized as well, from 22 districts to 40, allowing more leadership and attention at the store level. Sales that year exceeded $4 billion.

In 1996 Raymond Zimmerman and Garry Witkin in the company's annual report noted that while the company had kept its $4 billion franchise and had turned a profit, the company's earnings and stock price were ultimately disappointing. In response, the company strove for improvements and set about upgrading merchandise quality with trendier and more branded products in stores and catalogs; implementing an efficient advertising strategy, including a television ad campaign financed at a savings; enhancing store interiors and merchandise arrangements, hoping to spur impulse purchasing; and gaining enhanced liquidity and long-term capital structure through the completion of a 15-year, $73.6 million mortgage financing.

In another move toward hands-on technology, Service Merchandise introduced a PC-based gift registry touch screen. The system allowed customers to register at a touch screen and, using radio frequency scanning guns, scan the UPC codes of their selected gifts. In late 1996, the store went on-line, offering a 7,000-item catalog at its web site.

In the spring of 1997 Gary Witkin became CEO, with Raymond Zimmerman remaining on as chairman. Change—at an accelerated pace—became a watchword. The year before the company had begun analyzing individual store performance. In early 1997 Service Merchandise announced plans to close about 60 underperforming stores as well as its Las Vegas distribution center. In addition, the company restructured management, getting rid of 1,200 to 1,500 positions at the assistant manager and "lead floor" levels. In the shopping environment Service Merchandise initiated an effort to physically enhance presentation. There was an effort to include thematic lifestyle displays. To reach even more customers, the company focused on expanded and targeted print advertising. The company also announced it would exit the personal computer business. The store anticipated implementing its new private label credit card program and testing a new co-branded credit card. Given its constant assessment of store performance, its openness to change, and its willingness to embrace new technology, Service Merchandise committed itself to succeed in the next century.

Further Reading

"Flying High with Catalog Showrooms," *Discount Merchandiser,* April, 1975.

Hisey, Pete, "Mining a Gem of a Category," *Discount Store News,* June 20, 1994, p. A32.

Hollow, Michele C., "Catalog Showroom Execs Mull Industry Future at NACSM," *Discount Store News,* February 7, 1994, pp. 3, 71.

Johnson, Jay L. "In this Corner" (profile of Raymond Zimmerman), *Discount Merchandiser,* April 1993, p. 8.

——, "Service Merchandise: A Survivor's Strategy," *Discount Merchandiser,* April 1993, pp. 22–29.

Konrad, Walecia, and Dean Foust, "Ray Zimmerman, Tightwad in a Tight Spot," *Business Week,* May 28, 1990.

Kuntz, Mary, "Catalog of Woes," *Forbes,* May 4, 1987.

——, "Reinventing the Store," *Business Week,* November 27, 1995.

Marcail, Gene G., "A New Catalog King Waiting in the Wings?" *Business Week,* February 8, 1993, p. 117.

Markowitz, Arthur, "Service Merchandise Set to Revamp Marketing Strategy, Test Teleshopping," *Discount Store News,* April 4, 1994, p. 4.

Miller, Paul, "Neither Mall nor Mail," *Catalog Age,* October 1992, pp. 5, 31.

Pellet, Jennifer, "Staying True to a $3 Billion Concept," *Discount Merchandiser,* March, 1990.

Starn, William, "I Screwed It Up," *Forbes,* December 6, 1993, p. 144.

Zimmerman, Raymond, "The Success of Service Merchandise," *Direct Marketing,* August 1992, pp. 42–45.

—Mary Sue Mohnke
—updated by Catherine Hamrick

Showboat, Inc.

2800 Fremont Street
Las Vegas, Nevada 89104
U.S.A.
(702) 385-9141

Public Company
Incorporated: 1960 as New Hotel Showboat Inc.
Employees: 5,700
Sales: $433.70 million (1996)
Stock Exchanges: New York
SICs: 7011 Hotels, Motels; 7933 Bowling Centers

Showboat, Inc. is an international operator of hotel and casino gaming and recreation centers. The company owns and operates the Showboat Casino, Hotel, and Bowling Center in Las Vegas, Nevada, opened in 1954; the Showboat Casino and Hotel in Atlantic City, New Jersey, opened in 1987; and 55 percent of the Showboat Mardi Gras riverboat casino in East Chicago, Indiana, opened in July 1997. The company is also the largest shareholder in and manager of the Sydney Harbor Casino hotel and casino complex in Sydney, Australia; in January 1997, Showboat announced an agreement with Publishing and Broadcasting Ltd. (PBL). of Australia to sell ten percent of Showboat's ownership position as well as management control of the Sydney operations, subject to approval of the sale by the New South Wales Casino Control Authority. In addition to its existing operations, Showboat has also been positioning itself to expand into other North American markets. The company has formed a partnership to develop a riverboat gaming complex in Lemay, Missouri. Showboat holds a minority investment in the Rockingham Park racetrack in Salem, New Hampshire. The company has also signed a contract to manage the casino operations of the Lummi Indian Nation located between Vancouver, Canada and Bellingham, Washington.

Showboat is led by J. Kell Houssels, chairman since 1988, and J. Kell Houssels III, president and chief executive officer since 1995. Traded on the New York Stock Exchange, Showboat's 1996 net revenues totaled $433 million, generating $75 million in EBITDA income (earnings before income taxes, depreciation, and amortization) and $6 million in net income. Showboat's more than 5,500 slot machines form the principal source of the company's revenues, producing more than 76 percent of sales in 1996.

The largest of Showboat's gaming holdings is the Showboat Hotel and Casino in Atlantic City. Located on 12 acres on the eastern end of the famed Atlantic City boardwalk, with another nine acres for parking, the Atlantic City showboat features 97,000 square feet of gaming space, including 3,600 slot machines, a 16-story hotel tower and a 24-story hotel tower, which together provide 800 rooms, and a 60-lane bowling center, as well as 27,000 square feet of meeting rooms and convention and exhibition space. Adjacent to the hotel casino complex is a nine-story parking garage, with space for 2,000 cars, a depot for 14 buses, and an underground, 500-car valet parking facility. In 1996, the Atlantic City operation produced $370 million of Showboat's total $433 million net revenues.

The oldest of Showboat's gaming holdings is its Las Vegas Showboat Casino, Hotel, and Bowling Center, located on 26 acres on Boulder Highway, approximately two and one-half miles from the downtown and Vegas Strip areas. For more than 40 years, the Las Vegas Showboat has catered especially to the local and family gaming customer; since a renovation and expansion in 1995, the complex consists of 75,000 square feet of casino space, an 18-story, 450-room hotel tower, a race and sports book, and 8,300 square feet of meeting room space. The Las Vegas Showboat also features a 106-lane bowling facility, making it the largest in North America and the second largest in the world, and one of the country's largest bingo parlors, with seating for some 1,300 people. In 1997, the company opened a recreational vehicle park on leased property adjacent to the hotel casino complex, with space for 80 campers. The Las Vegas Showboat, with nearly 1,500 slot machines, contributed $63 million to the company's 1996 net sales.

The newest of Showboat's gaming operations is its Mardi Gras-themed riverboat casino in East Chicago, Indiana, approximately 12 miles from Chicago, Illinois. The riverboat, built at a cost of $200 million, featured 53,000 square feet of gaming space on four levels, including nearly 1,800 slot machines and 90 gambling tables, with a total capacity of 3,750 people. Showboat received its preliminary license for the riverboat gaming operation in April 1997, with full operations expected to commence in July 1997.

In addition to these properties, the company has operated, since September 1995, an interim casino complex in Sydney, Australia. The interim complex features 500 slot machines and 150 table games; the permanent casino, operating under a 99-year license (the first 12 years of which grant it the exclusive right to operate a casino in all of New South Wales), was expected to open in late 1997 or early 1998 and would feature 1,500 slot machines, 200 gaming tables, a 352-room hotel, 139 serviced apartments, a lyric theater, a cabaret theater, convention and retail facilities, as well as a 2,500-car underground parking facility. In January 1997, Showboat agreed to sell 85 percent of its management control of the Sydney casino and ten percent of its ownership position to Publishing and Broadcasting Enterprises, owned by Australian magnate Kerry Packer.

Founded in the 1950s

When the Showboat appeared in the Nevada desert in 1954, its owners already held a long pedigree in Las Vegas's gaming history. Built for $2 million by William Moore, an architect and designer of one of the earliest Vegas casinos, the Last Frontier, together with partner J. Kell Houssels, the Desert Showboat Motor-Hotel featured 100 rooms and a casino housed in a Mississippi riverboat, complete with a paddlewheel and smokestacks, along the Boulder Highway, a couple of miles to the southeast of the growing Vegas Strip. Houssels, who had come to Las Vegas in the 1930s as gambling was being legalized in Nevada, had already struck his fortune at a blackjack table in Eli, Nevada in the 1920s and would soon become one of the city's most prominent citizens. In 1947, Houssels joined a group of investors, including Joseph Kelly, whose resume included working as a manager of an offshore gambling boat in Southern California, to purchase the city's first casino, the El Cortez Hotel, which had opened in 1941. By 1954, Houssels and Kelly had gained full ownership of that property. Four years earlier, Moe Dalitz, whose career included bootlegging during Prohibition, racketeering, and illegal gambling, had built the Desert Inn; Dalitz and the Desert Inn gang were brought in to run the casino operations of the Showboat, and the hotel itself was managed by Kelly.

The day before the Showboat's opening, a storm nearly washed the boat away; but the hotel casino celebrated its grand opening on September 3, 1954, with "Minsky's Follies of 1955" providing the entertainment. The Showboat fared poorly in its early years, finding it difficult to compete with the larger and flashier casinos on the Strip. In 1959, Houssels and Kelly formed an investor group to purchase the Showboat from the Desert Inn. Incorporating the company as New Hotel Showboat, Inc. and shortening the name of the hotel casino operation to the Showboat, Kelly and Houssels steered the hotel into a new direction. The new Showboat would not compete with the Vegas Strip for big-name, expensive entertainment and would abandon the Vegas tradition of attracting high-rollers with complementary rooms and credit. Instead, the Showboat turned to the local market and to the low-roller and family tourist trade. Key components in the hotel's new direction were the institution of a 49-cent breakfast and the construction of a 24-lane bowling center. At the same time, Showboat began its emphasis on high-margin slot machines over gaming tables. While Kelly ran the Showboat, Houssels branched out to manage the Tropicana hotel casino during the 1960s.

The hotel's bowling center proved to be a hit with the local crowd; by the early 1960s the bowling center had begun to organize bowling leagues, and in 1962, the Showboat teamed up with the Professional Bowlers Association to host that organization's televised tournaments. The Showboat made its first expansion in 1963, doubling the number of rooms and adding to its casino area. Five years later, the Showboat underwent a more extensive facelift, expanding its bowling center, adding a pool, and constructing an entirely new facade, emphasizing the Mississippi riverboat theme and featuring a two-story paddlewheel. To finance the expansion, Showboat went public, becoming the second Las Vegas casino to do so, and changed its name to Showboat, Inc.

By Las Vegas standards, the Showboat remained a small operation. But it was able to develop a strong core of repeat customers, and its popularity with locals and family tourists, enhanced by the addition of a bingo parlor, helped the hotel chart a steady course of profitability. The next major expansion occurred in 1973 with the addition of a nine-story, 250-room hotel tower. The company's stock began trading on the American Stock Exchange in that year. Two years later, Showboat added nine more stories to its hotel tower. These expansions, which boosted the casino to 40,000 square feet and more than 1,000 slot machines and enlarged the bingo parlor to 850 seats, making it one of the largest in the country, helped raise the company's revenues to $33 million by the end of the 1970s. Showboat had been consistently profitable, paying dividends since 1970.

Sailing to New Horizons in the 1980s and 1990s

Showboat continued to focus on Las Vegas in the early 1980s. The bowling center expanded to 106 lanes, placing it among the largest in the world and solidifying its status as a premiere site for professional tournaments. In 1981, the company added a 33,600-square-foot Sports Pavilion, with 5,500 seats, to provide a venue for boxing, wrestling, and other sports events. Showboat also added a race and sports book; in 1982, Showboat expanded its sports offerings when it purchased, for $2.6 million, an 18-hole championship golf course. These additions helped attract more and more customers to the heart of the company's operations, its casinos and, especially, its slot machines. By the mid-1980s, revenues had grown to nearly $50 million. In 1983, the company began listing on the New York Stock Exchange.

By then, Showboat was already looking toward a new horizon. The Atlantic City market seemed like a natural for the Showboat formula: with limited airport facilities, most of Atlantic City's gambling customers were day tourists arriving on buses or in cars. In 1985, the company began building its Ocean Showboat, leasing one of the last available boardwalk sites from Atlantic City pioneer Resorts International. The hotel casino structure, which would resemble an ocean liner, would be Showboat's most ambitious project ever, with an initial cost of $200 million (its final cost was $245 million). Unlike its Las Vegas predecessor, however, the new Showboat hotel would rival the largest of the Atlantic City casinos in size, featuring a 60,000-square-foot casino, more than 45,000 square feet of convention and meeting space, a 2,000-car parking garage, 500 hotel rooms, and a 60-lane bowling center. Like the Las Vegas operation, the new Showboat hotel casino would continue the company's policy of avoiding big-name entertainment, limiting credit, and focusing on slot machine players. In addition, the new Showboat was located at the most distant end of the boardwalk, far from the most active casinos.

Analysts were skeptical about Showboat's chances for success. Their gloom was fueled in part by a disappointing market, as Atlantic City's casino revenues slumped in the mid-1980s. Original plans to construct the new convention center next to the Showboat fell through; however, Showboat was soon joined by the even larger Taj Mahal, and the two casinos were linked by an aerial walkway. But Showboat also faced resistance from the New Jersey Division of Gaming Enforcement, which attempted to deny the company licensing to operate in the state. The division's chief source of concern was the presence of John Gaughan as a company director. Gaughan had admitted taking part in his family's illegal gambling operations as a teenager and also had held a three percent ownership in the Flamingo in Las Vegas during the mid-1960s, when that casino's profit-skimming activity was exposed. Nevertheless, the Casino Control Commission cleared Gaughan and granted Showboat the license. The opening of the Atlantic City Showboat in April 1987 helped the company more than double its sales, to $118 million, and by the end of the decade, the Atlantic City operation was producing some 80 percent of total company revenues.

It was not all smooth sailing for the company, however. To attract customers, the Atlantic City Showboat had begun to compete with the other casinos by booking top-name entertainment, extending credit, and giving away rooms and other perks to lure in the high-roller crowd. Revenues continued to soar, reaching $294 million in 1988. But the company's margins were thinning, dragging Showboat into the red, while the debt taken on to build the Atlantic City complex helped sink the company's stock. In 1988, Joe Kelly retired from the company and was replaced as chairman by Houssels.

Showboat refocused and returned to its roots: the local and low-roller crowd. The company stopped booking big-name entertainment and eliminated credit, while heightening the emphasis on slot machine revenues. The turnaround was swift. By 1989, company revenues swelled to $342 million and net income, aided by the $4.9 million sale of the Las Vegas golf course, topped $7 million. In 1990, the company completed a $28 million renovation of the Las Vegas Showboat, adding a parking garage, two new restaurants, a new, 1,500-seat bingo parlor, and expanding the casino area by some 78 percent, to 80,000 square feet.

Meanwhile, Showboat began looking to expand its gaming empire beyond the Vegas and Atlantic City markets. Riverboat gambling was beginning to spread across the United States, and Showboat entered the fray with a 1993 agreement to manage a new $42 million gambling boat, dubbed the Star Casino, to operate outside of New Orleans. By the end of 1993, Showboat had increased its participation in the Star Casino to 50 percent. The casino's revenues were disappointing, however, and the floating casino complex ran afoul of state gambling legislation that required gambling boats to cruise while conducting gaming operations. The Star Casino had ceased cruising after striking an obstruction in the waterway during the first month of operation. In late 1994, however, the state district attorney raised the threat of an indictment against the Star for violating the state's cruising requirement. Rather than face the possibility of an indictment, which would have led to a misdemeanor charge, Showboat sold the riverboat to Players International in January 1995. Indeed, Showboat was eager to avoid the taint of an indictment, even on a technicality, because it was already planning a far more ambitious move.

In May 1994, Showboat, together with the Australian construction group Leighton Holdings Ltd., won the right to develop Sydney's first casino operation. With the final structure slated at $1.2 billion and scheduled to open in 1998, the partnership opened an interim Sydney Harbor Casino in September 1995. Apart from its ownership interest, Showboat also took on management of the hotel casino. But revenues proved disappointing, in part because the Australian and Pacific Rim customers favored gaming tables over slot machines. In early 1997, Showboat agreed to sell its controlling interest in the casino complex to PBL.

Showboat once again focused on the domestic market. The Las Vegas Showboat underwent a new expansion in 1995, designed to help it compete against a number of new casino hotel complexes bent on attracting that Showboat's core local customer base. The Atlantic City Showboat also began a $53 million renovation and expansion. Meanwhile, Showboat's latest venture, a new, $200 million riverboat gambling complex, began operations in April 1997 in East Chicago, Indiana, tapping into the region's 6.9 million customer base. With J. Kell Houssels III taking over as president and CEO of the company in 1994, Showboat continued to chart its small but steady course in the gaming waters. Net revenues rose from $428 million in 1995 to $433 million in 1996.

Further Reading

"Casino Licensed Over State Objections," *The Record,* February 12, 1987, p. A39.

Chiang, Melissa, "Showboat Sets Up New Games on Both Sides of the Line," *Investor's Business Daily,* July 16, 1996, p. A27.

Franchine, Philip, "New East Chicago Boat Ups Gaming Ante," *Chicago Sun Times,* April 15, 1997, p. 10.

Wayne, Leslie, "Low Roller's High Stakes Bet," *New York Times,* October 15, 1985, p. D1.

——, "Showboat Finds Winning Formula," *New York Times,* June 18, 1991, p. D10.

Wickham, Shawne K., "Showboat Gambles on NH, Folds in Louisiana," *New Hampshire Sunday News,* January 22, 1995, p. A1.

—M.L. Cohen

Simon & Schuster Inc.

1230 Avenue of the Americas
New York, New York 10020
U.S.A.
(212) 698-7000
Fax: (212) 632-8090
Web site: http://www.simonandschuster.com

Wholly Owned Division of Viacom, Inc.
Incorporated: 1924
Employees: 10,200
Sales: $2.17 billion (1995)
Stock Exchanges: American
SICs: 7841 Books, Publishing Only; 2731 Textbooks
    Publishing Only, Not Printed On Site

Simon & Schuster Inc. became a division overseeing the publishing operation of Viacom, Inc., one of the world's largest entertainment and media companies, when it was acquired in 1994 as part of Paramount Communications. Simon & Schuster is the world's largest publisher of educational books, computer books, and books published in the English language. It has operations in 43 countries, and its book and multimedia products are distributed in 150 countries. The imprints of its educational publishing division include Allyn and Bacon, Computer Curriculum Corporation, Educational Management Group, Globe Fearon, Modern Curriculum, Modem Curriculum Press, Prentice Hall, Silver Burdett Ginn, and Simon & Schuster Custom Publishing.

Simon & Schuster is also a leader in publishing consumer, business, reference, and professional books under these imprints: Simon & Schuster, Pocket Books, The Free Press, Scribner, Jossey-Bass, The New York Institute of Finance, Prentice Hall Direct, Bureau of Business Practice, Simon & Schuster Children's Publishing, and Macmillan Publishing USA. In addition, the company is involved in electronic and customized publishing; it operates an online service for consumer books and an online subscription service for professional development of kindergarten through grade 12 teachers.

1920s Origins

Richard L. Simon and M. Lincoln Schuster founded the company in January 1924. Their first publication—at the suggestion of Simon's aunt, a crossword puzzle enthusiast—was *The Crossword Puzzle Book,* which came out in April. The book sold more than 100,000 copies, and Simon & Schuster followed it with three other crossword puzzle books in the company's first year. All four books were top nonfiction bestsellers, and by the end of the year Simon & Schuster had sold more than a million of them.

The puzzle books were highly profitable, but the craze eventually waned and Simon & Schuster had to diversify. Its first few efforts produced moderate successes, a tennis book by Bill Tilden and an investment guide by Merryle Stanley Rukeyser, and several failures, such as a novel called *Harvey Landrum* and a biography of Joseph Pulitzer. The company's first big success outside of the puzzle books was Will Durant's *The Story of Philosophy,* a bestseller in 1926 and 1927. The book established Simon & Schuster as a serious publishing company and led to Durant's authoring, with his wife, Ariel, the multivolume *Story of Civilization* series for Simon & Schuster over the next half-century.

Simon & Schuster quickly developed a reputation as a highly commercial publishing house (one successful project was a compilation of the ''Ripley's Believe It or Not'' newspaper cartoon features) but at the same time brought out many distinguished works. In its first two decades, Simon & Schuster output included Leon Trotsky's *History of the Russian Revolution,* Felix Salten's *Bambi,* Rachel Carson's *Under the Sea Wind,* Wendell Willkie's *One World,* and three volumes of the Durants' *Civilization* series. Simon & Schuster had a Pulitzer Prize winner in 1935, *Now in November* by Josephine Johnson. Other achievements of the early years were the publication of a collection of George Gershwin's songs, followed by similar compilations of the works of Noel Coward, Cole Porter, Jerome Kern, the team of Richard Rodgers and Lorenz Hart, and Rodgers's later teaming with Oscar Hammerstein II, as well as the *Treasury* series of oversized gift books, such as 1939's *A Treasury of Art Masterpieces,* followed by similar books on the theater, oratory, and the world's great letters. Aside from the founders, key figures in Simon & Schuster's early years were Leon Shimkin, the company's business manager, and Clifton Fadiman, editor-in-chief. While Fadiman left in the mid-1930s and achieved fame as a book reviewer and radio quiz-show host, Shimkin became an equal partner, financially and operationally. With the founders, he stayed on for many years and was highly influential in the company. In the late 1930s, he brought in two highly successful properties—Dale Carnegie's *How to Win Friends and Influence People* and J.K. Lasser's *Your Income Tax.*

In 1939 Simon, Schuster, and Shimkin put up 49 percent of the financing for Robert F. de Graff, an experienced publisher of hardcover reprints, to start Pocket Books, a line of inexpensive, mass-market paperback reprints. Although paperback books had appeared in the United States as far back as the 1770s, the format's full potential was not realized until the founding of Pocket Books, which was followed by several competitors. Initially priced at 25¢ a copy, Pocket Books became a great success—during World War II, various wartime agencies shipped 25 million Pocket Books overseas. Shimkin was able to weather wartime paper rationing by taking over the paper quotas of publishing companies that were not able to use their entire allotment.

Five of Pocket Books's initial 11 titles remain in print: William Shakespeare's *Five Great Tragedies,* Pearl S. Buck's *The Good Earth,* James Hilton's *Lost Horizon,* Agatha Christie's *The Murder of Roger Ackroyd,* and Felix Salten's *Bambi.* Eventually, Pocket Books published original titles as well as reprints of hardcover books; its most successful publication was Dr. Benjamin Spock's *Baby and Child Care,* first printed in 1946. Periodically updated, more than 33 million copies of this book had been printed by 1989. Pocket Books was merged into Simon & Schuster in 1966.

In 1942 Simon & Schuster started another line of inexpensive books, Little Golden Books, aimed at children. Full-color, high-quality children's books had not been available at such low prices—Little Golden Books, like Pocket Books, went for 25¢ a copy. Simon & Schuster was able to keep costs down by running 50,000 copies per title, an unheard of quantity. Simon & Schuster handled editorial, art, and sales functions for the books, and Western Printing and Lithographing Company took care of production and manufacturing. The venture was highly successful; by 1958 more than 400 million Little Golden Books had been sold, and the line had spawned such offshoots as Big Golden Books, Giant Golden Books, the *Golden Encyclopedia,* and Little Golden Records. Perhaps fearing a shakeout in the expanding children's book industry, or enticed by Western Printing's offer, Simon & Schuster sold its half interest in the venture to Western Printing in 1958.

Acquisition in the 1940s

In 1944 Field Enterprises, the Chicago communications company headed by Marshall Field, acquired Simon & Schuster from its principals—Simon, Schuster, and Shimkin—for about $3 million. The principals stayed on with long-term management contracts and operated quite independently of Field Enterprises. In 1957, shortly after Marshall Field's death, the executors of his estate were eager to get out of the book publishing business and sold Simon & Schuster back to the principals for $1 million.

Major titles published by Simon & Schuster in the 1940s and 1950s included William L. Shirer's *The Rise and Fall of the Third Reich,* Evan Hunter's *The Blackboard Jungle,* Meyer Levin's *Compulsion,* Kay Thompson's *Eloise,* Joseph Davies's *Mission to Moscow,* Mary McCarthy's story collection *The Company She Keeps,* Alexander King's *Mine Enemy Grows Older,* Herman Wouk's first book, *Aurora Dawn,* Laura Z. Hobson's *Gentleman's Agreement,* and Sloan Wilson's *The Man in the Gray Flannel Suit.* Humorous books also were important to the publishing house; these included cartoon collections by Walt Kelly, creator of "Pogo," and Al Capp of "Li'l Abner" fame, as well as verbal humor from James Thurber, P.G. Wodehouse, and S.J. Perelman. Moving into the 1960s, Simon & Schuster's popular authors included Harold Robbins, Jacqueline Susann, and Joseph Heller.

In 1957, Richard Simon, who was in poor health, retired from Simon & Schuster. He died in 1960, at which time Schuster and Shimkin each acquired half of his stock, making them equal partners of the company. When Schuster retired in 1966, he sold his share to Shimkin. Simon & Schuster subsequently went public, with its stock traded on the over-the-counter market and later listed on the American Stock Exchange.

Changing Leadership in the 1970s

In the next few years, Simon & Schuster negotiated with several potential acquirers. In May 1970, the company agreed in principle to be bought by Norton Simon Inc., a diversified company whose interests included magazine publishing; the deal fell apart two months later, however, in part because of the stock market's drop. In November of that year, Kinney National Service Inc. reached an agreement in principle to buy Simon & Schuster, but Shimkin became dissatisfied with the offer during the negotiation process. In 1974, Simon & Schuster agreed to a merger with Harcourt Brace Jovanovich, which had substantial textbook publishing operations but little in trade publishing, which was Simon & Schuster's strength. The deal was called off abruptly later that year; both parties cited the depressed stock market as a reason, but observers said Shimkin had been offended by certain public statements made by William Jovanovich: "He implied that his firm was taking over Simon & Schuster lock, stock, and barrel, and one got the impression that Leon Shimkin would be fortunate if he got a job in the mailroom," longtime Simon & Schuster executive Peter Schwed later wrote in his book, *Turning the Pages: An Insider's Story of Simon & Schuster, 1924–1984.*

A successful deal came through in 1975, when Gulf + Western Industries purchased Simon & Schuster through a swap of one share of Gulf + Western stock for every ten shares of the publishing company. Gulf + Western, which also owned Paramount Pictures, changed its name to Paramount Communications in 1989. As a condition of the deal, Richard E. Snyder, who had been executive vice-president of Simon & Schuster, moved up to the presidency; Snyder succeeded Seymour Turk, who had been named president in 1973 when Shimkin relinquished that role. Shimkin remained chairman of Simon & Schuster.

Under Snyder, Simon & Schuster expanded aggressively. It set up a dozen new imprints, or brand names, under which it published books, and its sales grew impressively, from $44 million at the time of the sale to Gulf + Western to $210 million in 1983. By 1989, revenues were up to $1.3 billion. One of the most financially successful new ventures was a line of romance novels called Silhouette Books. Simon & Schuster launched Silhouette in the early 1980s after it lost the U.S. distribution rights to the Harlequin Romances, published by Harlequin Enterprises Ltd. of Toronto. Silhouette soon rivaled Harlequin in popularity among romance readers, and Harlequin's parent, Torstar Corporation, bought Silhouette from Simon & Schuster for $10 million in 1984.

Simon & Schuster entered the textbook field in 1984 by buying Esquire Inc., which no longer owned *Esquire* magazine, for $170 million. The acquisition nearly doubled the Simon & Schuster staff, to 2,300, and lifted it to the nation's sixth largest book publisher, from thirteenth. Later that year, Gulf + Western bought Prentice Hall Inc., a major textbook publisher, for about $710 million and merged it into Simon & Schuster early in 1985, making Simon & Schuster the nation's largest book publisher. Ginn & Company, another educational publisher, came into the Simon & Schuster fold in 1982, after being bought by Gulf + Western for $100 million; in 1986, Gulf + Western bought Silver Burdett Company, an elementary textbook publisher, for about $125 million and combined its operations with Ginn. Software also became an important business for Simon & Schuster in the increasingly computerized decade of the 1980s, as did books on computers.

With the diversification into textbooks and information services, trade book publishing, which was Simon & Schuster's only business at the time of the sale to Gulf + Western, became only a small part of the business, or about six percent of sales in 1989. It remained a high-profile aspect of the company, however, which published both fiction and nonfiction books that ranged from highly commercial to highly prestigious efforts. Major titles in the 1970s and 1980s included Bob Woodward and Carl Bernstein's *All the President's Men* and *The Final Days,* Woodward's *Wired* and *VEIL: The Secret Wars of the CU, 1981–87,* Jackie Collins's *Hollywood Wives,* Taylor Branch's *Parting the Waters,* and former U.S. President Ronald Reagan's *An American Life.*

The 1990s and Beyond

By 1997, the publisher could boast that it had published 69 Pulitzer Prize winners. The trend in the publishing industry was not in traditional print publishing, however, but toward elec-

tronic publishing, or any computer-related materials. In 1996, President and CEO Jonathan Newcomb stated that the company's goal was to generate half of its revenues from electronic publishing, such as via CD-ROMS, videodisks, and the World Wide Web, by the year 2000. At the time, the percentage was 25 percent, but Newcomb set about achieving this goal by creating Corporate Digital Archive (CDA). CDA involved a reorganizing of the publisher's editing, production, and other processes so that everything could be categorized in databases. The archive then allowed material to be recalled and manipulated as desired by any division of the company.

With all of the editorial content owned by Simon & Schuster, the next step was to translate it into software. In 1997, Simon & Schuster Interactive, the consumer software publishing unit of Simon & Schuster Consumer Group opened in 1994, formed a joint venture with GT Interactive Software Corp. The aim was to develop PC titles derived from the interactive and electronic properties cited in the Consumer Group catalogue and market them globally.

In the same year, Simon & Schuster sold part of American Teaching Aids Inc., the unit that publishes teacher resource materials, to Frank Schaffer Publications. The development of new media for teachers continued, however. Simon & Schuster's Education Group announced the formation of an internet resource, Edscape (www.edscape.com), a subscription service that delivers interactive curriculum content for teachers of grades kindergarten through 12, as well as online professional development. College-level instructors were included in another venture formed by Prentice Hall and Xilinx, Inc., a supplier of programmable logic solutions. The agreement allowed the two companies to produce the Xilinx Student Edition, the first complete digital design learning environment for college-level instruction.

Principal Divisions

Education; Consumer Group; International and Business and Professional; Macmillan Publishing USA.

Further Reading

Schwed, Peter, *Turning the Pages: An Insider's Story of Simon & Schuster, 1924–1984,* New York: Macmillan, 1984.
Verity, John W., "A Model Paperless Library," *Business Week,* December 23, 1996, pp. 80–82.

—Trudy Ring
—updated by Dorothy Kroll

Sommer-Allibert S.A.

2, rue de l'Egalité
92748 Nanterre Cedex
France
(01) 41 20 40 40
Fax: (01) 47 21 49 09

Public Company
Incorporated: 1972
Employees: 18,000
Sales: Ffr 14.04 billion (1996)
Stock Exchanges: Paris
SICs: 6719 Holding Companies, Not Elsewhere
    Classified; 3069 Fabricated Rubber Products, Not
    Elsewhere Classified; 3089 Plastics Products, Not
    Elsewhere Classified; 2519 Household Furniture, Not
    Elsewhere Classified

Since the early 1990s, the European plastics giant Sommer-Allibert S.A. has transformed itself from a maker of primarily household-oriented products—such as resin outdoor furniture, plastic bathroom fixtures, and vinyl wall and floor coverings—into one of the leading plastic components suppliers to the worldwide automobile industry. In 1996, sales to the automotive industry accounted for more than 56 percent of Sommer-Allibert's total revenue of Ffr 14 billion, compared to just 38 percent at the start of the decade. The company's automotive division (except in France), grouped under publicly-traded German subsidiary SAI Automotive AG (formerly Sommer-Allibert Industries), is also its strongest performer, contributing 60.5 percent of the parent company's operating profit.

Sommer-Allibert designs and builds dashboards, door panels, floor coverings, sound-proofing and insulation installations, and other molded plastic parts for passenger car interiors for clients such as Renault, Peugeot, and Citroën in France, but also worldwide clients such as Volkswagen, Skoda, Toyota, BMW, Audi, Mercedes, Ford, General Motors, and Volvo. In the mid-1990s, Sommer-Allibert pioneered the development of interior cockpit modules—supplying everything but the seats—for early adopters such as the Volkswagen Polo, the BMW Z3, the Ford-Volkswagen line of minivans, and the Citroën Berlingo. A chief factor in the success of Sommer-Allibert's automobile products has been the company's willingness to locate its plants close to its clients' factories.

Through the 1990s, Sommer-Allibert pursued an aggressive international expansion program, building or acquiring production facilities throughout Europe and North America, as well as locations in the growing Asian and Latin American markets. In 1997, Sommer-Allibert began construction on a new facility in Pueblo, Mexico, to supply instrument panels for the much-anticipated return of the Volkswagen Beetle. The company operated 31 plastics production facilities supplying the automotive industry, as well as a number of joint-venture facilities, and approximately 20 additional facilities providing production, warehousing, and distribution for the company's other product divisions.

Despite the financial strength of its automotive products, Sommer-Allibert was perhaps best known to consumers for its wide range of household products, such as resin outdoor and garden furniture, storage products, and interior decoration accessories, categories upon which the company built much of its early growth. Yet by 1996, furniture sales had been scaled back to just under 8 percent of the total turnover; in early 1997 the company sold off its bathroom fixtures division—in part to ease the heavy debt load brought on by its aggressive expansion in the automotive market—and suggested the possibility of selling off not only its smaller Qualipac packaging division (1.7 percent of sales), but also its household furniture activities, either into a joint venture or as an outright sale.

If the sales came to fruition, Sommer-Allibert would continue to focus on automotive supplies and wall and floor coverings, and to a lesser degree on containers for industrial use. The company sold wall and floor coverings under the Sommer, Azrock, and other brand names and through partnerships with manufacturers, including Canada's Domco and Japan's Milliken. The wall and floor coverings division contributed nearly 30 percent of Sommer-Allibert's 1996 sales; this division's main strength is in vinyl coverings, which represents some 75 percent of the division's activity, compared to textiles, which accounted for approximately 25 percent of sales. The company's equipment sales, a segment in which the company has been active for more than three decades, included containers for fruit and vegetable distributors, industrial containers, palettes, and transport containers. During the 1990s, the company pushed into the growing rubbish bin market, selling recycling and other waste disposal containers to the community and private sectors.

In the 1990s, Sommer-Allibert was led by chairman Marc Assa, who took over the company's leadership from Bernard Deconninck. The longtime architect of the company's growth, Deconninck continued to hold more than 35 percent of Sommer-Allibert's shares, with nearly 48 percent of the voting rights through the holding company Société Industrie de Transformation (SIT).

Merging Two Businesses in the 1970s

Both Allibert, which specialized in plastic products, and Sommer, which specialized in floor and wall coverings, had been active for several decades when they merged in 1972 to form Sommer-Allibert. Since the late 1940s, Allibert's direction was led by Bernard Deconninck, who would remain at the head of the company into the 1990s. Originally, Deconninck had planned to enter medicine, but the war scuttled his plans. He instead entered manufacturing, making in-soles for shoes. While he manufactured these in-soles, he saw the future for plastics. As Deconninck told the *Financial Times,* "At the time we were buying plastic shoehorns from another manufacturer and I suddenly had a revelation about the possibilities which plastic processing could offer." Deconninck developed Allibert into three primary lines of business, developing plastics products for bathrooms, the automobile industry, and containers and packaging. In the early 1970s, Deconninck saw an opportunity to further diversify his company's operations by acquiring then-struggling Sommer's plastics, textile flooring, and wall covering operations. The merger was effected in 1972 and the company incorporated as Sommer-Allibert.

The merger presented a challenge to the company. Sommer had not kept up with capital investments and with development of new products, and the process of merging the two companies' operations and upgrading the combined company's floor and wall coverings arm would stretch into the next decade. As Deconninck told the *Financial Times,* "It took ten years to make Sommer recover as one of the leading manufacturers of plastic floors." Part of the recovery process involved heavy capital investment into new production facilities and equipment, including automating production processes, as well as modernizing the company's administration activities. By the mid-1980s, the company had invested some Ffr 1 billion on the renewal operation.

Meanwhile, Sommer-Allibert had begun a era of growth, principally through acquisition. "Our group was formed by a series of mergers and acquisitions of small- and medium-sized companies," Deconninck told the *Financial Times,* "The company today is in fact a federation of about 60 small- and medium-sized enterprises." By the early 1980s, that federation's sales had swelled to Ffr 3 billion. Nevertheless, the company was only marginally profitable, posting a net income

in 1981 of just Ffr 13.6 million, up from only Ffr 3.3 million the year before. And restructuring charges plagued the company's bottom line, dropping the company into the red with a loss of Ffr 89 million in 1984. With its restructuring largely completed by 1985, Sommer-Allibert was able to boast a strong recovery. Revenue for that year had climbed to Ffr 5 billion, and net profit soared to Ffr 103 million. Domestic sales accounted for about 60 percent of the company's sales. Sommer-Allibert operated through 43 subsidiaries with 8,700 employees in 16 countries.

Foreign development would become a prime factor in the company's strategic planning for its next growth phase. Primary targets in Europe included Germany and Spain, while the company also eyed expansion into the crucial North American market and into the booming Asian economies as well. One factor driving the company to globalized sales was its emphasis on household consumer products. The company's typically low-margin products necessitated heavy investment in automated production capacity to keep down costs, which in turn led the company to seek economies of scale in a wider, principally European market. Appealing to consumers presented its own challenges, however, as the company was forced to respond to country-specific consumer tastes, as well as to customize its marketing activities for each country. By the second half of the 1980s, European sales accounted for approximately 60 percent of the company's consumer products sales. In contrast, the company's industrial automotive sales remained primarily within the French market, accounting for 85 percent of these sales.

In 1986, Sommer-Allibert set up a new Netherlands-based subsidiary, Sommer-Allibert International, charged with raising the finances for a new phase of European acquisition and expansion. An early purchase was the acquisition of Compagnie Industrielle de Mecanismes (CIM), formerly part of the Rockwell Group, which made automobile arm rests and dashboards. Production of these products was moved into a newly established plant in the Lorraine valley. On the North American front, the company purchased a 30 percent stake in Domco Industries, the leading Canadian plastic flooring and coverings manufacturer, giving Sommer-Allibert a position from which to launch a drive into the U.S. market. By the following year, the company moved into the United States, building a 100,000 square-foot manufacturing facility in Stanley, North Carolina, for the company's U.S. subsidiary, Allibert, Inc.

Meanwhile, Sommer-Allibert also developed new product categories, including increasing its presence in the automobile plastic components industry, and expanding into the new category of resin-based outdoor furniture. As the European market for this new, more durable, and more easily maintained furniture expanded and then approached saturation, Sommer-Allibert, with the construction of its Stanley plant, moved to take advantage of the growing interest in the category in the North American market. In 1989, the company teamed up with Rubbermaid Inc. in the United States to form the joint venture Rubbermaid-Allibert Inc., headquartered at the Stanley facility, to dominate the booming U.S. resin-based furniture market. Sommer-Allibert brought its design and manufacturing expertise to the joint venture, while Rubbermaid supplied its brand name and sales and marketing experience for the U.S. market. Sales in 1988 had reached Ffr 8.7 billion, producing a net income of Ffr 363 million.

The company's attentions did not rest solely on its efforts in the United States. Sommer-Allibert had established two plants in Spain—still a protected market outside of the European Community—and expanded its floor coverings line with the acquisition of the rubber floor coverings line from Italy's Ilgagoma by 1987. After further investments in Spain, including the outright acquisitions of automobile parts specialists Gunasa, Garcia, and Moltex, Sommer-Allibert turned its attention to entering the British automotive market. The company's move into Germany began in earnest in 1988 when its publicly traded German subsidiary Sommer-Allibert Industrie acquired, for Ffr 320 million, Besmer Triangel, a maker of wall and floor coverings, but also a carpet and components supplier to the car industry. Following the acquisition, West German sales rose to more than 18 percent of Sommer-Allibert's total revenue, up from under 8.5 percent prior to the acquisition.

Transforming in the 1990s

Fears of a potential takeover prompted the company to re-structure its capital in 1989, placing 33 percent of the shares, and 45 percent of the voting rights, into the Deconninck family-owned SIT. Deconninck was named chairman of the new organizations, while Marc Assa prepared to take over the leadership of the company. Bigger changes were in store for Sommer-Allibert through the first half of the 1990s, however. The Besmer Triangel acquisition had already strengthened the company's position in the automotive market, aided by the addition of two new lines, Opel's Vectra and Ford Germany's Fiesta, in addition to products for Volkswagen's Golf, BMW's Series 3, and Audi. In 1989, the company began production on another German facility, in Peine, in order to supply components for the Volkswagen operations located there. By the end of that year, sales of automotive components topped sales of consumer and household products for the first time in the company's history, and Deconninck and Assa made plans for the company's automotive business rather than its consumer product lines to lead future growth. The plans soon came to fruition; in 1990, Sommer-Allibert entered into a joint-venture with Italy's Fimit, supplier of doors for Fiat, giving the company entry into that area of automotive components as well.

While the rest of the world slumped in the early 1990s, Germany's automobile industry, buoyed by the German reunification and the increased demand for cars from the former East Germany, saw major increases in production. Sommer-Allibert's growing position and investment in that country helped it reap the rewards of the German upturn, and Germany became the company's second-largest source of revenue, behind France. Sommer-Allibert also made plans to improve its position with the U.S. automotive industry, including forming a joint-venture with Milliken, a manufacturer of fabrics for car interiors. In addition the company expanded into the Pacific market, with a joint-venture in China, and sales and distribution activity in Hong Kong, Singapore, Korea, and Australia. As companies worldwide struggled through the recession of the 1990s, Sommer-Allibert's activities helped the company maintain a solid financial position. Sales neared Ffr 9.9 billion, for a net profit of more than Ffr 207 million in 1992.

With its focus on the automotive industry, Sommer-Allibert began to ease out of the consumer products business. In 1992, Rubbermaid and Sommer-Allibert amicably agreed to end their furniture joint-venture, with Rubbermaid buying out Sommer-Allibert's assets and the rights to use the Rubbermaid-Allibert brand name. Sommer-Allibert remained in the furniture industry, but only at the top end with its premium-priced Triconfort brand. And in light of a growing worldwide market, the company also returned to supplying the trash disposal container market (the company had previously been a minority partner in a joint-venture with industry leader Otto, of Germany).

Sommer-Allibert decided to build its own plants in the United States to improve its presence in the North American automotive supplies market. In response to a contract with General Motors, Sommer-Allibert began construction on a Ffr 80 million plant in Kansas in 1994, marking the first time the company had built a plant in the United States to supply a U.S. car maker. Until then sales to the United States, excluding the company's share of Domco, amounted to 2 percent of the company's total sales.

On the European front, the company built a new plant in Palmelo, Portugal, and two Luxembourg plants, one to produce floor and wall coverings, the second to produce interior car fittings for Ford Fiestas and Escorts in Luxembourg. By then, more than half of the company's revenues were generated outside of France, primarily in Europe, but with a growing percentage in North America and the Pacific. In 1994, the company passed the Ffr 10 billion mark, earning profits of Ffr 353 million. Of these revenues, more than half came from sales to the automotive industry.

The following year saw further increases in Sommer-Allibert's automotive capacity, including a thrust into the British market. In March 1995, the company formed a joint venture with U.S.-based Masland Corp. to supply interior trim and acoustic components for Nissan, Peugeot, and Saab, with plans to establish a second plant in order to supply parts for Jaguar. In October, the company formed a 50-50 joint venture with Siemens Automotive, integrating the latter company's instrument panels into Sommer-Allibert's cockpit modules to take advantage of the popularity of such modules in the automotive interior industry. Entering 1996, Sommer-Allibert acquired the plastic parts production plant of Mercedes-Benz in Woerth, Germany, while a joint venture with Japan's Inoac, formed in Greenville, South Carolina, began supplying BMW in the United States. The company's North American expansion was further enhanced as the company began construction on a plant in Pueblo, Mexico, to fulfill the newly awarded contract to supply the complete interiors—excluding seats—for the launching of the new Volkswagen Beetle.

Sommer-Allibert's aggressive expansion in the automotive industry saddled it with a heavy debt burden. In order to reduce debt, the company began plans to divest some of its operating divisions. The Salle de Bains bathroom fixtures division was sold off by the beginning of 1997, and the company began looking into either a joint venture or outright sale for its outdoor furniture segment. The future of the company seemed firmly focused on Sommer-Allibert's two main revenue generators: automotive interiors and floor and wall covering.

Principal Subsidiaries

Allibert Equipment; Allibert Inc. (United States); Allibert Triconfort; Sommer S.A.; SAI Automotive AG (Germany); Sommer-Allibert Ind. Mexico SA de CV (Mexico); Qualipac; Sommer Masland (United Kingdom; 50%); Allibert Contico (United States; 50%); Allibert Industries Ltd. (Montreal).

Further Reading

Betts, Paul, ''Sommer-Allibert Expands in Germany,'' *Financial Times,* June 6, 1988, p. 28.
——, ''Sommer-Allibert Sets Sights on U.S.,'' *Financial Times,* April 30, 1986, p. 32.
——, ''Why Sommer-Allibert Thinks of Variations on a Theme,'' *Financial Times,* October 21, 1987, p. 15

Chew, Edmund, ''Sommer-Allibert Securing Share of Growth,'' *Plastics News,* May 27, 1996, p. 9.
Duff, Mike, ''Mass Market Resin: The Hot New Niche,'' *HFD,* August 10, 1987, p. 1.
Mattei, Jacqueline, ''Sommer-Allibert Met le Cap au Nord,'' *Usine Nouvelle,* November 2, 1989, p. 56.
Monnot, Caroline, ''Sommer-Allibert Doit Revoir à la Baisse Ses Ambitions,'' *Le Monde,* April 16, 1990, p. 14.
''Sommer-Allibert Confident for 1997,'' *Les Echos,* April 4, 1997, p. 7.
''Sommer-Allibert Looks to Continue International Expansion,'' *Le Figaro Supplement du Lundi,* November 2, 1994, p. 3.

—M.L. Cohen

Southwest Gas Corporation

5241 Spring Mountain Road
PO Box 98510
Las Vegas, Nevada 89193-8510
U.S.A.
(702) 876-7237
Fax: (702) 365-2233

Public Company
Incorporated: 1931
Employees: 3,000
Sales: $644.06 million (1996)
Stock Exchanges: New York
SICs: 4924 Natural Gas Distribution

Southwest Gas Corporation is a natural gas utility serving one of the fastest growing regions of the United States. Southwest purchases, transports, and distributes natural gas to residential, commercial, and industrial customers in three states: Nevada, particularly the Las Vegas and northern Nevada areas; California, including the Lake Tahoe and San Bernardino County areas; and Arizona, in an area encompassing most of southern, central, and northwestern Arizona and including Phoenix and Tucson. Southwest is the largest natural gas utility in both Nevada and Arizona. In all, the company serves more than 1.1 million customers, of which 80 percent are residential customers, 14 percent are industrial customers, and six percent are small and large commercial and resale customers. The region's building boom, spurred by strong population growth in the 1990s, has also proved a boon to Southwest; in 1996 alone the company added 63,000 customers. Since 1990, the influx of new residents to the Las Vegas area alone has added more than 100,000 customers to Southwest. Despite this strong growth, Southwest has been able to maintain a healthy productivity ratio, with a customer-to-employee ratio of 691 to 1, compared with the industry average of 319 to 1.

The company's southwestern market may seem an unlikely growth market for a natural gas utility, which typically derives the bulk of revenues from heating systems and winter sales. In fact, the average winter temperature in the region served by Southwest Gas has been seen to be rising during the last decades of the 20th century. For this reason, Southwest has been active in encouraging the application of natural gas to other applications, specifically for combination air conditioning and heating systems, and for natural gas vehicles. The use of natural gas for air conditioning, particularly among industrial customers, is on the rise and provides more efficient and less expensive operation than traditional electric air conditioning systems. While Southwest contends with the trend toward milder winters, the company must also brace itself for the coming deregulation of the electric utility industry. Toward this end, the company has undergone a refocus of its operations. In 1996, Southwest sold off the last of its banking assets, a diversification move made by the company during the 1980s. In that same year, Southwest acquired Northern Pipeline Construction Co., based in Phoenix, for a stock swap valued at $24 million. Northern provides installation, replacement, and maintenance services for natural gas and other pipelines for some 25 utilities throughout the United States. Southwest had previously been one of Northern's largest competitors. The acquisition added Northern's $100 million in revenues to Southwest's annual sales, while positioning the company to extend its services beyond the Southwest region and its natural gas customers.

Southwest posted revenues of $644 million in 1996, for an operating profit of nearly $71.6 million and a net income of nearly $6.6 million. The company is led by Michael O. Maffie, who has served as president and chief executive officer since 1993.

Founded in 1931

Southwest Gas was founded in 1931 by Harold G. Laub, Joe Gray, Jr., and John Koeneman to provide butane gas distribution services to the small town of Barstow, California. Laub served as the company's first president, holding that position until 1964. Energy distribution, particularly the distribution of gas, was still in its infant stages as an industry, but the company was helped when the Santa Fe Railroad built a diesel locomotive repair facility in Barstow and later replaced its original roundhouse with a switching yard that would become the

West's largest such facility. The railroad's presence (Barstow was also served by the Union Pacific line) gave Southwest Gas a ready means of receiving gas supplies. Gas was brought in on tank cars and delivered to the company's nearby plant. From there, the gas was distributed through Southwest Gas's pipeline to its customers. In its first year, the company served some 160 customers. Soon after, Southwest Gas added a second California town, Victorville, servicing another 120 gas meters from a two-story structure that had once been used by the famed Wells Fargo company and by a western version of the Pony Express.

Despite its Depression-era roots, Southwest remained a thriving, if modest, operation, soon expanding to service other communities and installations in the Barstow area, including Apple Valley, Bicycle Lake, which later became Fort Irwin, and Victorville Airfield, later the site of the George Air Force Base. Then the construction of a pipeline bringing natural gas from Texas to California in the 1950s encouraged the company's evolution. The pipeline, owned by Pacific Gas & Electric, had been built to provide natural gas to that company's San Francisco service area. Southwest proposed to tap into the pipeline to route natural gas to its customers in Barstow and Victorville, replacing its tank car distribution system and the more volatile butane gas. Pacific Gas refused to allow Southwest Gas to feed off its pipeline. The intercession of the Federal Power Commission, however, opened the way to creating a natural gas pipeline network. In 1951, the company constructed a small pipeline and connected to Pacific Gas's 36-inch main.

The opening of private pipelines to third parties prompted Southwest Gas to expand its own operations. In 1953, the company moved into Nevada, forming Nevada Natural Gas Pipe Line Co. and building a 110-mile pipeline to connect to the Topock, Arizona pipeline owned by El Paso Natural Gas Company. Next, Southwest Gas created a new subsidiary, Nevada Southern Gas Company, which purchased the propane distribution business of Las Vegas Gas Company. Nevada Southern converted Las Vegas from propane to natural gas and began providing natural gas to industrial customers in Henderson, Nevada as well.

The company's move into Las Vegas proved to be the foundation of Southwest Gas's later growth. The first hotels had already appeared in Las Vegas during the 1940s, but the transformation of Las Vegas from a sleepy resort town into a national entertainment and gambling mecca began in earnest during the 1950s. Commercial customers such as the Last Frontier, the Desert Inn, the Golden Nugget, the Flamingo, the Thunderbird, the Sahara, and other casino hotels fashioned the famed Vegas Strip and stepped up the demand for natural gas, while also luring new residents to the area. By 1956, Southwest Gas counted 5,500 customers and had grown to more than $700,000 in annual revenues. To fuel its growth, the company went public that year, issuing some 44,000 shares of stock, and began trading on the OTC market. The following year, Southwest Gas merged Nevada Southern into the parent company's operations, and the expanded company struck out into new territory, acquiring Natural Gas Service of Arizona and that company's copper mining and cotton growing customers.

Southwest Gas moved its headquarters to Las Vegas in 1958, placing the company at the center of its three-state service area. The region was then undergoing its first population boom, and Southwest Gas set up a new subsidiary, Unity Financial Corp., to finance home mortgages and encourage the use of natural gas-burning equipment and appliances in new construction. The company's California base grew with the acquisition of a liquefied petroleum gas provider in the Big Bear Lake resort area. But Southwest Gas's largest growth would come first from Nevada. In 1961, the company bought the Carson Water Company, which supplied the water system to the state's capitol; the venture into water distribution did not last long, however, and the water system was later sold to the city. Meanwhile, the company had been granted certification to supply the natural gas requirements of some 16 towns in the Reno area, including that city. In 1963, Southwest Gas built a new, 230-mile pipeline that stretched from Idaho to Reno. From there, the company's customer base continued to expand, reaching the Lake Tahoe resort region. In 1964, Laub's son, William, took over as the company's president and chief executive officer, holding that position until 1987.

Fueling Growth from the 1970s

Strong population growth in Southwest Gas's service areas helped the company build its annual sales. Southern Nevada, including the Las Vegas area, was the nation's fastest growing region in terms of population. Arizona was also undergoing a population boom, as that state became a popular retirement region. As the 1970s began, Southwest Gas celebrated the addition of its 100,000th customer. The company had previously moved into the Colorado River region, with service to Bullhead City; in 1972, Southwest Gas extended its operations to Boulder City, next to the Hoover Dam, with the acquisition of Boulder Natural Gas Company. Two years later, the company moved into a new headquarters, combining its corporate and administrative operations under one roof. Designing the new headquarters brought the company into a new area—commercial design—and the company created a subsidiary, Design-Center Southwest, for that business. At the same time, Southwest Gas formed a gas exploration and development subsidiary, Energy Increments Inc., to lessen its reliance on third party natural gas suppliers. By 1976 the company's annual revenues had swelled to $110 million and by 1978 sales had grown to $133 million. One year later, however, Southwest Gas's sales more than doubled.

The Arab Oil Embargo of 1973 had prompted Washington to draft the Energy Act of 1978. As an offshoot of this legislation and the pervasive national fears that the country's energy resources were dwindling, the state of Arizona declared a three-year moratorium on new energy hookups. This move in turn led to the state-regulated breakup of Tucson Gas & Electric, which sold its gas system, and its 130,000 customers, to Southwest Gas. The company's revenues jumped to $275 million for 1979. In that year, Southwest Gas began trading on the New York Stock Exchange.

Entering the 1980s, the company added to its infrastructure, building a liquefied natural gas plant in Lovelock, Nevada and opening a liquid propane gas plant in Reno. The company also purchased a former cattle ranch near Spirit Mountain in Kingman, Arizona to begin developing a natural gas storage facility there. By 1981, revenues had grown again, reaching $315 million on a customer base of 335,000. Three years later, the company made its next major acquisition, paying $120 million to Arizona Public Service Company (APS) for its natural gas operations. The APS purchase added 339,000 customers. The purchase also brought Southwest Gas some 6,500 miles of pipeline, much of it in sore need of repair. While the deteriorated state of the APS pipeline system had been partially accounted for in the acquisition price, the cost of replacing the mains would far outrun the discount. The company had experienced a similar situation with the Tucson Gas & Electric gas system purchase; eventually, Southwest Gas won a court settlement that required the previous owner to repay nearly half of Southwest Gas's purchase price. No such relief was available to the company for the APS purchase, however, as the $30 million discount on that purchase included a provision that prohibited Southwest Gas from pursuing any legal action related to the sale.

Through the 1980s, however, the company's growth continued. Revenues grew to $611 million in 1985, and net income was also high, nearing $24 million. Flush with cash, the company joined in on a growing trend toward diversification among energy companies. In 1986, Southwest Gas dropped its "pure play" status when it paid $130 million for the stock of Nevada Savings and Loan Association, a Las Vegas-based thrift with $1.4 billion in assets. The move into banking proved to be a success initially and encouraged the company to expand the subsidiary's operations, which had grown to a chain of 28 branches and assets of $2.75 billion. In 1988, the banking operation's name was changed to PriMerit Bank (in part to distance itself from the developing savings and loan crisis), which then acquired Union Savings and Loan Association of Phoenix. The addition of the banking business helped raise Southwest Gas's revenues to more than $800 million by 1988. The banking operation also helped boost Southwest Gas's profitability: net earnings for that year were $41 million.

Sputtering in the 1990s

By the beginning of the 1990s, however, the troubles with the former APS pipeline system proved to be a severe drain on the company. Replacement costs had already topped $100 million by the late 1980s. The company sought relief from the Arizona Corporation Commission (ACC), charged with overseeing utility rates, asking for as much as a $52 million rate increase. The ACC, however, refused to pass the burden of pipeline replacement on to natural gas customers and, instead, shocked the company with a recommendation that its rates actually be lowered by $7 million.

At the same time, the savings and loan crisis was affecting the PriMerit subsidiary, dragging down its earnings. New federal regulations enacted in the wake of the crisis, which would bar PriMerit from the wholesale loan business and force the bank into more traditional, and less lucrative, banking operations, presented a bleak picture for PriMerit's future. By 1991, Southwest Gas was sputtering. Revenues fell to $794 million and, after net interest deductions of nearly $44.5 million, the company posted a loss of more than $14 million. In 1993, Southwest made its first move to exit the banking business, selling off its Arizona operations to World Savings and Loan,

based in Oakland, California. The rest of PriMerit followed in 1995, when Southwest Gas sold PriMerit's Nevada operations to Norwest Bank for $175 million in cash.

The gains from the sale helped Southwest Gas return to the black, despite a drop in revenues to $538 million in 1993. In addition, the company was undergoing a boom in new customer hookups, as the region, particularly the Las Vegas and Arizona areas, led the nation in population growth. The company also expanded its service in the Henderson and Needles, Nevada markets with the $16 million acquisition of CP National's gas operations in those communities. In 1995, Southwest Gas extended its operations to include the installation, replacement, and maintenance of pipelines with the $24 million stock-swap purchase of Northern Pipeline Construction Co., based in Phoenix. By then, however, the company was facing a new threat to its bottom line. A warming trend in the Southwest had been leading to milder winters in the past two decades; the winter of 1995 was particularly mild, cutting deeply into the company's sales. Revenues dropped from $599 million in 1994 to $563 million, and net income (not including a $17.5 million charge for discontinuing its PriMerit operations) sank to $2.7 million.

The company responded to the warming trend by promoting more heavily additional uses for natural gas, including new gas-driven air conditioning technology and natural gas vehicles. Southwest Gas also continued to add record numbers of new customers, including an estimated 66,000 in 1997. While the booming numbers of new customers helped to rebuild the company's revenues, which climbed again to $644 million in 1996, the cost of outfitting the new hookups, at least in the short term, would continue to place pressure on the company's bottom line. Nonetheless, the future appeared bright for the company as it neared its seventh decade. The coming deregulation of the electric utility industry spelled opportunity for natural gas suppliers. And the continuing population boom of its core Nevada and Arizona markets meant that Southwest Gas was likely to maintain its status as the nation's fastest growing utility for some time to come.

Principal Subsidiaries

PriMerit Bank.

Further Reading

Albrecht, Susan C., "Utility Aims for Jump in Customers," *Arizona Business Gazette,* July 4, 1988, p. 12.

Basch, Mark, "Gas Company Plans To Enter S&L Field with Nevada Buy," *American Banker,* March 26, 1986, p. 2.

Jarman, Max, "Utility's S&L Move a Winner," *Arizona Business Gazette,* September 8, 1989, p. 1.

Morrissey, John, "S&L Regulations, Arizona Ratemakers Burden '90 Earnings at Southwest Gas," *Las Vegas Business Press,* June 3, 1991, p. 3.

Timmons, Tony, "Southwest Gas Tries To Preserve Investment Grade Bond Rating," *Las Vegas Business Press,* January 13, 1997, p. 12.

Walker, Thom, "Cooling with Gas," *Arizona Daily Star,* June 9, 1996, p. G1.

—M.L. Cohen

SPARTECH *Corporation*
7733 Forsyth • Suite 1450 • Clayton, Missouri 63105-1817
®

Spartech Corporation

7733 Forsyth Boulevard
Suite 1450
Clayton, Missouri 63105-1817
U.S.A.
(314) 721-4242
Web site: http://www.spartech.com

Public Company
Incorporated: 1960 as Permaneer Corporation
Employees: 1,850
Sales: $391.35 million (1996)
Stock Exchanges: New York
SICs: 3083 Laminated Plastics Plate & Sheet; 3081
  Unsupported Plastics Film & Sheet

Spartech Corporation is everywhere. This company is the largest extruder of rigid plastic sheet and rollstock in the United States, and, with strategic partner and shareholder British Vita PLC, the largest rigid plastic sheet producer in the world. Spartech's 13 manufacturing facilities in the United States and Canada provide the plastic stock for such products as McDonald's golden arches, Shell service station signs, vehicle parts such as running boards, interiors and exteriors for recreational and other vehicles, spas, showers, bathtubs, burial vault liners, boats, refrigerators, and food and medical packaging. Sales of extruded sheet and rollstock account for approximately three-quarters of Spartech's revenues and capture more than one-third of this $1 billion domestic market. Spartech is also growing in two complementary plastics areas. The company's color and specialty compounds unit operates five plants in the United States and Canada and produces custom designed plastic alloys, compounds, color concentrates, and calendered film for footwear, lawn and garden equipment, cosmetics and medical product packaging, automotive equipment, loose-leaf binders, toys, fences, computer and computer cable housing, and many other products. Spartech's third and youngest operating division is its Molded Products group, which, with four plants in the United States and Canada, brings Spartech into thin-walled plastic food

packaging, such as yogurt containers and plastic lids, and industrial containers; thermoplastic tires and wheels for lawn and garden equipment, refuse containers, and toys; and a line of tableware and houseware products.

Since 1991, Spartech has been led by President and Chief Executive Officer Bradley B. Buechler, who previously served as controller and chief operating officer for the company. In September 1996, Spartech made a second public offering (its first since 1968) of six million shares. Revenues of $391 million for that year generated a net income of $18.3 million.

A Bumpy Road to Success Since the 1960s

Spartech originated as Permaneer Corporation in St. Louis, Missouri in 1960. Founded by Allen Portnoy, Permaneer manufactured doors, paneling, furniture, and other wood products. The company was successful through the decade, and it went public in 1968. Portnoy took Permaneer on an expansion spree in the early 1970s, borrowing heavily. By the mid-1970s, the company was collapsing under its debt load, and in 1975 Permaneer's creditors forced Portnoy's resignation. One year later, Permaneer declared bankruptcy.

Portnoy was not ready to give up, however. In 1977, Portnoy joined with Lawrence Powers, a Wall Street securities lawyer with a background in public offerings and acquisitions, to form Spartan Manufacturing Corporation. Spartan won bankruptcy court approval to take over Portnoy's former company. Portnoy took the titles of president and chief executive officer, Powers was named chairman, and, together with general counsel Martin Green, they controlled some 80 percent of Spartan's stock. The partners, determined to avoid Permaneer's fate, attempted to protect Spartan by taking it on the then-popular diversification route. Over the next several years, Spartan built itself into a conglomerate of nine separate businesses, ranging from plastics to computer equipment to oil well pipe couplings, and including store fixtures, precision machines, copper tubing, and a computer lease brokerage business. These acquisitions took the form of leveraged buyouts or were arranged through secured financing. In its initial years, Spartan enjoyed the tax breaks brought by Permaneer's financial problems, helping reduce the

---

Company Perspectives:

"Our commitment is: To meet the needs of our customers with the highest standards of value, service, integrity and ethics; to provide our employees with a safe and healthy work place where each has an equal opportunity to succeed; to operate our facilities in such a manner as to protect the environment around us; to aim for a consistent and superior return on equity for all shareholders."

---

income tax on Spartan's earnings. An early, yet troubled, centerpiece of the company was a plastic extrusion plant in Union, Missouri, a business that predated Spartan's formation. In 1980, the company acquired Alchem Plastics, with a plant in Los Angeles producing extruded custom sheet plastic, and a second plastics company, Koenig Plastics Co., a plastic scrap reprocessor, and bundled its plastics businesses under the Alchem name.

Spartan grew quickly. Starting with about $2 million in sales in 1977, Powers and Portnoy built annual revenues to $20 million in 1978, $56 million in 1979, and $79 million in 1980. And in those early years, Spartan's earnings appeared to keep pace, rising from $467,000 in 1978 to $1.5 million in 1979 and $1 million in 1980. Many of Spartan's businesses were already bleeding, however, when the company ran head on into the recession of the early 1980s. By 1982, Spartan was losing money—posting a loss of $4 million for the year despite sales topping $100 million—and Portnoy and Powers were besieged once again by creditors. Spartan began divesting its businesses as the company's fortunes continued to slide. Powers and Portnoy reorganized the company, renaming it Spartech, around its plastics and computer business. In 1983, the company posted a loss of $10 million. Relations between Portnoy and Powers also cooled. As Powers told the *St. Louis Post-Dispatch,* "I lost confidence in [Portnoy's] management of Spartech and he lost confidence in my willingness to follow his lead as we lurched from one dispute with creditors to another in 1982–83."

Portnoy and Powers agreed to split in 1983. Spartech, led by Powers, would keep its plastics business, while Portnoy would take control of the company's computer equipment business, spun off as Digitech. That company worked on technology that would allow computer speech recognition. But Digitech proved to be a money pit. Portnoy poured his personal savings and stock into the company to keep it afloat, but it finally went bankrupt in 1990.

Deja Vu in the 1980s

Powers, meanwhile, had been training as a manager, attending Harvard Business School's executive management program from 1982 to 1983. It was there that Powers hit upon the idea of restructuring Spartech around its plastics business to restore the company to profitability. Joined by Buechler, who took charge of the Alchem Plastics division, Spartech completed its divestiture of unrelated businesses and concentrated on rebuilding itself as a plastics manufacturer. The company started with

negative assets of some $2 million, with sales of $24.5 million and a net loss of nearly $11 million. By 1985, however, the company had turned itself around, raising revenues to nearly $33 million and posting a profit of nearly $1.3 million.

Buechler oversaw the day-to-day management of the company at its Missouri headquarters while Powers, working out of his New York office, led Spartech on a new buying spree (and into renewed losses by the end of the decade). During the mid-1980s, however, Spartech grew strongly, retaining its focus on the plastics industry. In May 1985 the company made its first new acquisition, of Southwest Converting for $2.5 million in cash and notes, adding that company's $7.5 million revenues. But Spartech was already preparing two more acquisitions that would double the company's size. The first acquisition, of Adams Industries, with revenues of $25 million, extended Spartech into a new area of plastics, polyethylene film manufacturing. The second acquisition followed in January 1986, adding the $30 million Franklin Plastics, a specialty plastics compounder, as a third Spartech division. At the same time, the company began paying attention to its internal growth, stepping up its capital expenditures. By 1986, the company's revenues had climbed to $70.6 million, providing a net income of $1.5 million. Spartech's stock, which had traded as low as 50 cents per share, was beginning to rise. Yet Spartech was only starting on its newest acquisition drive.

By 1988, Spartech had added seven more acquisitions, including rigid sheet producers Atlas Plastics and Eagle Plastics; specialty alloy and compounder The Resin Exchange; polyethylene film maker Favorite Plastics, for $18 million; the Burlington South compounding plant from Occidental Chemical Corp., for $6.2 million; and Koro Corp., a Boston-based rigid plastic sheet producer. The acquisitions helped boost Spartech's revenues to $138.4 million by 1987 and to $221.8 million in 1988 and gave Spartech the lead in the rigid sheet plastic market. The company was also profitable, generating $9.4 million in 1987. Financing for this activity came in part with a $12 million dollar investment by Trust Co. of the West subsidiary TCW Capital in 1986, which also helped to head off a hostile takeover attempt, followed by $40 million raised through a $25 million debenture offering and a $15 million subordinated financing agreement, the latter arranged through TCW Capital.

By 1988, however, Spartech's profits were beginning to slip beneath the weight of its debt load, which, at $100 million, had reached an 11 to 1 debt-to-equity ratio. Profits fell to $3.3 million for the year. The Koro unit was failing (the company sold it less than a year after its acquisition), as was its Favorite Plastics acquisition, leading Spartech to charge that company with inflating its revenues prior to its acquisition by Spartech. The company looked to selling its profitable Atlas-Alchem division to help maintain its profits. Instead, however, the company agreed to sell 28 percent of Spartech's stock to British Vita PLC, the largest rigid sheet plastic producer in Europe, which had seven plants to complement Spartech's six U.S. rigid sheet plants.

By 1989, Spartech was again seeing red, in the amount of $12.7 million on $185 million. The loss included the closing of Spartech's failing polyethylene film division, the disposition of which was completed only in 1991. Spartech's losses continued, reaching $17.7 million for 1991, which included a charge for $12 million against the closing of its polyethylene film plants. Under pressure from Spartech's major shareholders, British Vita and TCW, Powers resigned from the company in October 1991. He was replaced as chief executive by Buechler.

Third Time's the Charm in the 1990s

Under Buechler's leadership, Spartech again regrouped, now around its rigid sheet and rollstock division and its compound group. With the polyethylene unit's losses gone, and the company's overhead reduced (Spartech closed Powers's New York office and consolidated its headquarters in Clayton, after paying Powers a parachute of some $2.5 million) Spartech again returned to profitability, posting $4.2 million on 1982's $168.8 million in revenues. Buechler next turned to reducing the company's $75 million in debt. In April 1993, he reached agreement with the company's creditors to convert $30 million of subordinated debt into new shares of common and preferred stock, reducing the company's debt-to-equity ration to 1.2 to 1.

Meanwhile, Spartech returned to expansion through acquisition. In January 1993, the company purchased plastic custom extrusion equipment and related business from Penda Corp., adding $15 million to company sales. That purchase was followed in March of the next year by the $8 million acquisition of Product Components, Inc., adding two new manufacturing plants and extending Spartech's plastic sheet line. In September 1994, Spartech, which had been looking to expand its Midwest operations, bought up the extrusion and color concentrates units of Wichita, Kansas-based Pawnee Industries, Inc. These acquisitions helped Spartech boost its share of the rigid sheet market to 28 percent, while expanding its compounding capacity as well. The company's revenues rose to $256.6 million in 1994, for net earnings of nearly $11 million.

To prepare for further acquisitions as well as a second public offering, Spartech raised $50 million in a private share placement and arranged an unsecured credit line of $40 million. By January 1996, Spartech moved to grow again, purchasing Wisconsin-based Portage Industries Corp. for $16 million and adding that company's $35 million in sales and two sheet extrusion and light-gauge thermoforming plants. The Portage acquisition boosted Spartech's total production capacity to 450 million pounds per year.

Having entered the thin-wall thermoforming business with the Portage acquisition, Spartech moved to consolidate that capability, and also to enter a new market, injection molding. In June 1996, Spartech acquired Montreal-based Hamelin Group, Inc., and its sheet extrusion, color concentrate, and injection molding units. The purchase, for $55 million, brought Spartech into Canada for the first time and added some $80 million to Spartech's revenues, while boosting the company's production to 550 million pounds. The acquisition of Hamelin's injection molding business was also seen as a strategic move for the company, bringing it into the consumer market, which offered less volatility during economic downturns.

Spartech's sales continued to gain strongly due to its acquisition, rising from $352 million in 1995 to $391 million in 1996. The Hamelin addition was expected to swell Spartech's revenues to more than $475 million in its 1997 fiscal year. The company also reported continued strength in its earnings, with income of $14.5 million in 1995 and $18.3 million in 1996. In September 1996, Spartech posted a second public offering of six million shares. With its stock, which had slipped below $1 per share in the early 1990s, trading at $9.50 per share, Spartech finally appeared to have found its course.

Principal Divisions

Extruded Sheet & Rollstock (Spartech Plastics; GM-Plastics); Color & Specialty Compounds (Spartech Compounding; Korlin Concentrates; Spartech Vy-Cal Plastics); Molded Products (GenPak; Hamelin Industries; Hamelin Enterprises).

Further Reading

Allen, Leslie J., "Spartech Cuts Debt, Sees Growth Ahead," *St. Louis Post-Dispatch*, May 20, 1990, p. 1E.
Ezer, Andrew, "After False Starts, Spartech Achieving Steady Profit Climb," *St. Louis Business Journal*, March 23, 1987, p. 12A.
Lauzon, Michael, "Spartech Buying Hamelin," *Plastics News*, June 17, 1996, p. 1.
Manor, Robert, "Founder Gets $2.5 Million To Leave," *St. Louis Post-Dispatch*, October 13, 1991, p. 1E.
——, "Portnoy Had Faith in Firm," *St. Louis Post-Dispatch*, February 24, 1991, p. 1E.
Melnick, Robert, "Spartech Plans To Double Its Size with Two Acquisitions," *St. Louis Business Journal*, May 13, 1985, p. 10A.
"Spartech Corporation's Growing Role in the Plastics Business," *St. Louis Commerce*, November 1995, p. 28.

—M.L. Cohen

Spec's Music, Inc.

1666 North West 82nd Avenue
P.O. Box 520248
Miami, Florida 33126
U.S.A.
(305) 592-7288
Fax: (305) 592-1648

Public Company
Incorporated: 1948
Employees: 780
Sales: $77.5 million (1996)
Stock Exchanges: NASDAQ
SICs: 5735 Record & Prerecorded Tape Stores; 7841
    Video Tape Rental

One of the largest retailers of prerecorded music and related products in Florida and Puerto Rico, Spec's Music, Inc. operates a chain of stores that sell compact discs, cassettes, movies, and videos. During the late 1990s, as the company was moving away from an emphasis on retailing, Spec's Music operated 49 stores, including 20,000-square-foot "superstores" in Miami Beach and Sunrise, Florida. The company's stores were located in malls, strip centers, and free-standing locations throughout Florida. Four of the company's stores were located in malls in Puerto Rico.

Post-World War II Birth

When Martin W. Spector opened his first music store in 1948 he realized a lifelong dream. Forty years later he would tell a reporter from *Florida Trend* magazine, "Always in the back of my mind, I wanted to have a record store," but it took years before Spector gave in to his passion. For nearly 20 years before opening his first Spec's Music store, Spector labored in other lines of work, beginning his professional career in 1929 when he was admitted to the New York Bar. After practicing law for several years, the native Virginian decided to forego a life in law and entered the entertainment business. Spector worked as a talent agent, demonstrating enough talent on his own part to be tapped as head of talent for Universal Pictures. Spector sifted through the ranks of Hollywood hopefuls for two years after the end of World War II, but by the late 1940s, when Spector was in his early 40s, he decided to pursue his love of music in earnest. In 1948, he and his pregnant wife moved to Miami to be closer to family. There, in Miami, Spector embarked on a career that would fill his days for the next half century and inaugurate the inception of Spec's Music, Inc.

Spector's first store was a 1,500-square-foot structure in Coral Gables, Florida, situated along the South Dixie Highway on the outskirts of Miami. Inside the store was a collection of big-band melodies, recorded on then-standard 78 RPM vinyl discs, and other motley merchandise. Few record stores during the late 1940s could rely exclusively on the sale of recordings to generate sufficient revenue to stay alive, and Spector was no exception. The chain that would later dominate the Florida market began by selling a smattering of merchandise divorced from Spector's true passion. Intermingled among the 78s, were Kodak Brownie cameras, Magnavox television sets, washing machines, and refrigerators, all included in the store to give Spector the revenue-generating capability to feed his burgeoning family and keep his business alive.

Although the various appliances and products occupying retail space in the first store were necessary inclusions, Spector was wholly devoted to selling music. He played his favorite tunes over and over again inside the store, hoping to interest his patrons in purchasing the aired selections. Many did, as Spector focused on developing a strong reputation in customer service, one of the key ingredients to Spec's Music's success throughout its history. Spector's passion for music eventually became contagious, and his original store prospered, becoming the first link in a chain of retail outlets that would blanket Florida.

The days of having to stock washing machines and refrigerators ended forever with the birth of rock-and-roll, the popularity of which ignited the growth of the music industry on all fronts, including music retailers like Spector. In response, Spector opened a second and third store, renting retail space from local department stores. Expansion continued for the growing business, as two free-standing outlets were opened in Miami and Palm Beach. By the mid-1960s, roughly 20 years of business

Company Perspectives:

"Spec's is committed to maintaining its position as the dominant specialty retailer of prerecorded music and music-related products and offering the highest quality service to its customers. While all of our stores maintain a comprehensive selection of diverse music categories, our newly opened stores provide a unique opportunity for customers to interact with our products. Specifically, they can sample music at listening stations throughout the store and search on-line at information kiosks for product listings throughout Spec's network, as well as accessibility to more than 130,000 titles available via special order."

had engendered a compact network of five stores that were performing admirably, their emphasis on customer service and well-stocked inventories pushing sales forward. The decade also marked the arrival of Spec's Music's second generation of leadership, although the company's future leader was only in her teenage years.

Ann Spector (later Leiff) started working at her father's business during her off-hours from junior-high school. The third of four children, Ann's interest in the family business consumed nearly all of her free time. "I was there after classes, on weekends and on holidays," she remembered, "there was a pulse to the store—to the business—that hooked me early on." Though enchanted by the bustle within her father's store, Ann Spector Leiff opted to pursue her formal education outside of Florida and entered the University of Denver in 1970. After spending four years in Denver, where she majored in sociology, Leiff returned to Florida and joined the family business. Other job offers were there for the taking, but Martin Spector's promise to better any offer from any other prospective employer won Leiff over. Like her father, Leiff had found her life's work.

Although the daughter of the owner, Leiff did not benefit from any overt nepotism. She started as an eight-track-tape buyer, joining a company that had recorded encouraging growth during her four years away at college. When Leiff left for the University of Denver, annual sales stood at $962,000; when she returned the company's revenue volume had swelled to nearly $2.5 million, growth that necessitated deeper management. Spec's Music had quickly developed into an enterprise that Martin Spector could no longer effectively manage on his own, and his daughter Ann was quick to answer the call for managerial assistance. One year after her return, Leiff was promoted to supervisor in charge of nine stores; by 1980, at age 31, she had risen to the post of president, quickly scaling the ranks of a business that was flourishing in the southern Florida area. Under Leiff's directorship, Spec's Music would outstrip the growth achieved under her father's leadership in a few short years.

1980s Expansion

From 1968 into the 1980s, Spec's Music opened an average of two stores each year, all located in the southern region of Florida. Leiff would add to the company's store count quickly,

but not until she took the company public in the fall of 1985. The 1985 initial public offering occurred when the company was coming off recording $16.6 million in sales from its 16 stores. Although Spec's Music's financial and physical growth had been considerable since her first days as an eight-track-buyer, Leiff was intent on picking up the pace of growth on both fronts, and the public sale of stock was intended to generate the resources to fuel expansion. The company sold 660,000 shares at $6 per share, raising roughly $3.5 million for the expansion planned by Leiff, who along with her sister and her father maintained a majority stake in Spec's Music after the offering.

After opening an average of two stores per year for nearly two decades, Spec's Music grew robustly following the public offering, as clusters of stores were opened in Florida. Within two years, the number of stores composing the chain increased from 16 to 42, while annual sales climbed to $26.5 million. The two-year surge of growth was enough to make Spec's Music the largest retailer of pre-recorded music, videos, and related accessories in Florida, elevating the company atop an industry whose annual revenue volume was estimated at between $150 million and $200 million. For Leiff and Spector, the growth achieved during the months following the public offering fueled confidence for the future, leading to ambitious projections for expansion in the years ahead. In 1988, when the company was selected by *Forbes* magazine as one of the nation's 200 best-run small companies, Leiff announced plans to increase the chain's size to 100 stores by the early 1990s, giving the company a lofty goal to aim for as it moved past its 40th anniversary year.

By the beginning of the 1990s, Spec's Music's revenues had more than doubled since the 1985 public offering of stock, swelling from $16.6 million to more than $40 million. The number of employees had increased commensurately, tripling as the number of Spec's Music outlets increased to 50 statewide. Making its way through the economically recessive early 1990s, Spec's Music had to contend with forces equally as pernicious as the flagging retail industry. In August 1992, Hurricane Andrew swept through southern Florida, laying waste to homes and businesses that lay in its path. Among the victims of the tropical storm was Spec's Music. Two of the company's stores were destroyed and another 15 stores suffered disrupted business as a result of the storm, causing Spec's Music to lose nearly $1 million in revenue and to record an operating loss of $160,000. By the time the financial repercussions of Hurricane Andrew were being recorded, Spec's Music was entering its 45th year of business, the year Leiff had projected the company would be operating 100 retail outlets. At the time, there were only 59 stores composing the chain, but plans announced midway through 1993 once again pointed the company toward developing into a 100-unit chain.

In the summer of 1993, Leiff announced that Spec's Music was undertaking a $23-million, capital-expenditure program. In the renovation and expansion set to take place, 54 new stores were to be added to the chain and another 36 were slated to be refurbished, as Spec's Music executives struggled to find a formula that would beat back mounting competition from large, national chains. Blockbuster and Musicland were opening outlets in and around Spec's Music's markets, forcing the company to develop new strategies for the future. Aside from opening a prodigious number of new stores and renovating the majority of existing stores, the company's executives also planned to focus on music selections they felt were underserved by national competitors. This approach involved placing a greater emphasis on Latin music, classical music, and merchandise targeted for children. To provide room for a greater emphasis on these items, the company decided to remove many of its lackluster video rental departments. By mid-1993, 12 of the video rental departments had been closed and another eight were scheduled for removal in 1994.

Additional changes adopted in 1993 included new fixtures inside the stores that could house a combined stock of compact discs and cassettes, as well as listening "posts," each equipped with two headphones and programmed to play 10 compact discs, with featured titles rotating every several days or weeks. These new additions were showcased in a prototype, 7,000-square-foot store that opened in Tallahassee, Florida, in early 1994. However, a little more than a year later—in mid-1995—the company made a bold move in another direction by turning to the superstore format to help maintain its leading position in Florida, which was being threatened by increasing competition.

Mid-1990s Tumble

The two superstores—one in Coconut Grove and the other in South Beach—were massive, 23,000-square-foot, $2-million, two-story structures that each carried more than 70,000 titles. The superstores sported cafes, and offered weekend concerts, all in the hope that an entertaining environment would attract patrons away from competitors' stores. Despite the hoopla surrounding the grand opening of the Coconut Grove and South Beach stores, however, Spec's Music was beginning to show signs of anemic financial performance. Sales and earnings were slipping, forced downward by the stiff competition in Florida and by the lack of blockbuster music hits. Music sales were down nationwide, and Spec's Music was struggling. By the end of 1995, the company's annual sales stood at $79.6 million, a negligible increase over 1994's total of $78.4, but earnings slipped from $2.8 million to a meager $1 million. By the beginning of 1996, changes were needed, and those changes were to be effected by a new arrival to Spec's Music's headquarters.

In early 1996, Barry Gibbons was hired as the company's new chairman of the board, replacing Martin Spector who assumed the duties of chairman emeritus. Gibbons arrived at Spec's Music with a solid reputation as a corporate executive and an equally renowned reputation as an eccentric. When Gibbons left Burger King Corp., where he served as chairman and chief executive officer from 1989 to 1993, he blared opera music through the company's cafeteria sound system, making good on his promise to remain at Burger King until the "fat lady sings." Despite his penchant for the unconventional, British-born Gibbons was a hot commodity in the corporate world, having orchestrated the resurgence of Burger King, a feat that earned him the distinction of being named *Fortune* magazine's Turnaround Champ of 1990. Leiff, who was serving as the company's president and chief executive officer, was ecstatic about the addition, explaining to a reporter from *Billboard* magazine that Spec's Music "wants to get involved with other

facets of the music business besides retail, and Barry has a good strategic mind and is very good at brand marketing. He can help enhance and grow the company," she continued, "He seems to be a perfect fit." Martin Spector, then in his 90s, was less enthusiastic, declaring to the *St. Petersburg Times*, "I think about half of what he says is baloney, but I say give him a chance."

A little more than a month after Gibbons's arrival, Spec's Music announced the closure of its Coconut Grove superstore, an embarrassment that prompted Gibbons to yell at 50 of the company's store managers, "This company is on a slab in the morgue with a toe tag." Other retail outlets were shuttered during the year as well, causing a $4.5 million loss for the year. To recover, Gibbons led the company away from its dependence on its struggling stores and toward other lines of business in the music industry. In pursuit of this objective, a subsidiary was formed in 1996 to promote concerts and in early 1997 the company acquired Digital Sound Distributor, a distributor of Latin music in Florida, New York, Puerto Rico, and the Dominican Republic.

By 1997, the number of Spec's Music stores had been whittled down to 47, and more store closures were imminent as Gibbons strove to diversify within the entertainment and leisure industry. In the future, the retail sale of music was expected to play a lesser role in Spec's Music's business, while the company's involvement in other facets of the music industry increased. Whether or not this strategy would arrest the retrogressive financial slide occurring during the mid-1990s was to be determined in the late 1990s and the years beyond, as one of Florida's oldest music retailers struggled to reshape itself for the 21st century.

Principal Subsidiaries

Spec's Entertainment Services, Inc.

Further Reading

Albright, Mark, "Spec's Music Prepares to Compose a Comeback," *Knight-Ridder/Tribune Business News,* November 4, 1996, p. 11.
Christman, Ed, "Gibbons Named Chairman of Board at Spec's," *Billboard,* January 27, 1996, p. 5.
——, "Spec's Sees Profitability Downturn," *Billboard,* December 14, 1996, p. 53.
Jeffrey, Don, "Spec's Celebrates Opening of Prototype Store," *Billboard,* January 22, 1994, p. 55.
——, "Spec's Earmarks $23M for Upgrade, Expansion," *Billboard,* July 10, 1993, p. 40.
——, "Spec's Weathers Operating Loss: Says Hurricane Blew Away $900,000 in Revenue," *Billboard,* January 9, 1993, p. 54.
Matas, Alina, "Miami-Based Latin Music Distributor Acquired by Spec's Music," *Knight-Ridder/Tribune Business News,* February 13, 1997, p. 21.
Schulman, Sandra, "Spec's Ups the Ante in Florida with Pair of Miami Superstores," *Billboard,* September 30, 1995, p. 67.
Stevens, Mark, "How to Take a Good Business and Make It Better," *Working Woman,* March 1990, p. 38.
Wilson, Elizabeth, "Rockin' and Rollin' at Spec's Music," *Florida Trend,* February 1988, p. 74.

—Jeffrey L. Covell

Springs Industries, Inc.

205 North White Street
Fort Mill, South Carolina 29716
U.S.A.
(803) 547-1500
Fax: (803) 547-3805

Public Company
Incorporated: 1887 as Fort Mill Manufacturing Company
Employees: 20,000
Sales: $2.24 billion
Stock Exchanges: New York
SICs: 2211 Broadwoven Fabric Mills—Cotton; 2221
    Broadwoven Fabric Mills—Manmade

Springs Industries, Inc. is one of the world's largest producers of home furnishings and specialty fabrics. It has 39 manufacturing facilities in ten states, and a minority interest in a joint venture in Japan. Of the U.S. plants, 24 are in South Carolina. Springs' major brand names include Springmaid, Wamsutta, Dundee, Wabasso, Bali, Graber, Ultrasuede, and Ultraleather.

Company Origins

The company started in April 1887, when a group of 14 men and two women organized Fort Mill Manufacturing Company to produce cotton cloth. At that time, the Northeast and Midwest were booming, and cotton manufacturing was seen as a way to industrialize and revive the depressed South. Samuel Elliott White, a local planter and Civil War veteran, was elected the company's first president. Among the investors was Leroy Springs, a merchant who would become White's son-in-law and a key force in the company's development. The company produced its first yard of cotton cloth in February 1888. Its first annual report, in May 1888, stated that the plant had 200 looms and was producing 8,000 yards of cloth daily.

In 1892 many of the same investors started a second plant in Fort Mill. In 1895 Leroy Springs and others established another company, Lancaster Cotton Mills, of Lancaster, South Carolina.

Toward the end of the century, with the Lancaster mills flourishing, Springs acquired control of the Fort Mill plants, which were experiencing difficulties, and other troubled cotton mills in Chester, South Carolina. The Lancaster operation expanded in 1901 and again in 1913 and 1914, when it was said to be the largest cotton mill in the world under one roof. In 1914 Leroy Springs led the establishment of Kershaw Cotton Mills in Kershaw, South Carolina.

Leroy's son, Elliott White Springs, joined the company in 1919 after distinguished service as an aviator in World War I. According to the younger Springs's biographer, Burke Davis, Leroy Springs ordered Elliott to learn the business without pay. It took Elliott Springs a while to settle into the business; several times he quit and came back. In these early years, Elliott Springs was more interested in both writing—his best-known work is *War Birds, Diary of an Unknown Aviator*—and social life than in textile manufacturing.

Leroy Springs seemed to lose interest in the business himself during the 1920s. He ran up debt and let the equipment run down; he also speculated in the stock market. In 1928 a disgruntled cotton buyer shot Leroy Springs in the head on a street in Charlotte, North Carolina. Springs recovered physically, but became emotionally withdrawn. Shortly before Leroy Springs's death in 1931, Elliott Springs took over management of the company.

At this time, the family's textile operations consisted of six plants with 5,000 employees. Elliott Springs—until then considered a playboy and a dilettante—led a dramatic revitalization of the business, which was suffering from the Great Depression as well as from Leroy Springs's neglect. He negotiated with creditors to save the mills from foreclosure, went without salary for a period, and bought used but useful machinery at bargain prices to upgrade operations. In the fall of 1933, he bought a former J.P. Stevens plant in Chester, South Carolina. Also in 1933, Springs consolidated the various mill properties into a single company, Springs Cotton Mills.

In 1934 the United Textile Workers of America attempted to organize workers at the Springs mills. Elliott Springs allowed the union to address the workers at a company-owned baseball field

---

Company Perspectives:

"Springs people and the products and services they provide will represent the standard by which all others are measured. In partnership with our customers, suppliers and associates, we will continually investigate and define requirements to assure our products and services always provide total customer satisfaction. The road to continuous improvement is paved with seven values known as the 'The Springs of Achievement': Quality, Service, Creativity, Education, Personal and Family Well-Being, Respect for History, and Planning for the Future."

---

in Chester. After the organizers had spoken, Springs mounted the platform and told the workers that if they went on strike, he would close the plants and take his family to Europe. The workers later voted unanimously against union representation.

During the 1930s the Springs facilities had been expanded and modernized, despite the Depression. With the arrival of World War II, Elliott Springs turned over the company's entire production capacity to the military. Early in 1942 the company began manufacturing fabrics for a variety of military uses, including uniforms, tents, gas masks, and gun covers. All the Springs plants won awards from the U.S. Army and Navy for superior production.

The mills ran overtime, sometimes seven days a week, to keep up with wartime production. Elliott Springs feared this schedule would wear out the mills' machinery, so he instructed one of his plant managers to buy and store every replacement part available—an effort that paid off when the mills resumed normal operations in 1945. At the close of the war, Springs began construction of a bleaching plant and moved the company into the production of finished fabrics and consumer products, such as sheets and pillowcases. Also in 1945, the company established Springs Mills, Inc. in New York as the sales organization for its products.

The company's launch of the Springmaid brand of sheets and apparel fabrics in the late 1940s included a popular advertising campaign designed by Elliott Springs himself. Early ads included drawings of sexy, half-dressed young women and double-entendre copy. The best-remembered ad featured an American Indian brave lying exhausted in a hammock made of a sheet, with an Indian woman apparently rising from the same hammock. The caption read "A buck well spent on a Springmaid sheet." Some called the ads tasteless, but the campaign did focus attention on the Springmaid brand.

Springs at Mid-Century

Elliott Springs remained president of the company until his death in 1959. During his tenure, the assets of Springs Cotton Mills had grown to $138.5 million from $13 million. Sales had increased more than 19-fold, to $163 million, and the work force had nearly tripled, to 13,000. The company was the seventh largest in the U.S. textile industry, but was the most

profitable. H. William Close, Elliott Springs's son-in-law, succeeded him as president. Close expanded and modernized many Springs facilities and built a new headquarters for the sales organization in New York in 1962. In 1965 the company inaugurated carpet production with a plant in York, South Carolina.

In 1966 the sales group merged with the manufacturing company, with the resulting entity named Springs Mills, Inc. The same year, the merged company went public, selling 675,000 shares at $17 each. Late that year, Springs Mills shares were listed on the New York Stock Exchange.

In 1967 Springs considered a merger with another textile firm, Collins & Aikman Corporation, but abandoned the plan because of what the companies termed "operational difficulties." In 1968 Springs formed a new division to make and market knit fabrics; indeed, the 1960s and 1970s were a time of much diversification in Springs product lines. The company made a major conversion to production of cotton-synthetic blended fabrics, which had begun to outstrip cotton in popularity—in 1969, two major facilities were converted to blend production.

Springs hired its first nonfamily president, Peter G. Scotese, in 1969, with Close moving into the newly created post of chairman, which he held until he died in 1983. Scotese had been a vice-president of Federated Department Stores and, before that, a vice-president of another textile company, Indian Head, Inc. During Scotese's tenure, Springs expanded via numerous acquisitions, including, early in 1970, the finished-goods division of Indian Head.

Late in 1970 the Justice Department sued Springs and four other textile makers, charging that the manufacturers conspired with wholesalers and retailers to stabilize the prices of their prime lines of sheets and pillowcases, in violation of antitrust laws. Springs agreed to a consent decree in which the company agreed not to engage in such practices, without admitting that it ever had. Fifteen years later, the Justice Department agreed to terminate the decree, citing a 1977 Supreme Court ruling that price-fixing is illegal only when intended to curb competition and legal in other circumstances.

In 1972 Springs became a partner in a joint venture to start a textile plant in Indonesia, P.T. Daralon Manufacturing Co. Early in 1973 it entered the frozen foods business, acquiring Seabrook Foods Inc. of Great Neck, New York, for about $34.5 million. In 1974 Springs sold its three terry-cloth production plants to J.P. Stevens Inc. and discontinued operation of its carpet division at York, which had been unprofitable since its inception in 1965. Springs sold the facility to Cannon Mills Company in 1975. The Indonesian plant went into operation in 1975, but failed to generate enough revenue to maintain working capital; the unit's creditors had to defer interest and other payments. The following year, Springs sold its interest in the venture. Springs continued updating and modernizing its plants closer to home in the late 1970s, but also got out of another unprofitable business by closing the knit division in 1978. In 1979 Springs acquired Lawtex Industries, a maker of textile home furnishing products, for $15.4 million plus the assumption of $13.5 million in liabilities, and Graber Industries, Inc., a manufacturer of blinds, shades, and other window decorating products, for $38.5 million.

The 1980s: Diversification

Walter Y. Elisha succeeded Peter Scotese as president of Springs in 1981; like Scotese, Elisha came from the retail sector. After Close's death in 1983, Elisha became chairman of the company. In 1981 and 1982, Springs closed several Seabrook units and sold others. Also in 1982, the company adopted its present name, Springs Industries, Inc.

Springs made a major acquisition in 1985—M. Lowenstein Corporation, a New York textile maker that, like Springs, had been in business since the 19th century. The acquisition brought Springs the Wamsutta brand of household goods and an entry into the premium-priced bedding market and the industrial fabrics business through Lowenstein's Clark-Schwebel unit. The cost of the acquisition was about $265 million.

During the late 1980s Springs intensified its diversification away from the apparel-fabrics business, where foreign competition was strong, and instead refocused on industrial fabrics and home furnishings, purchasing the fiberglass-weaving and finishing operations of United Merchants & Manufacturers Inc. for about $60 million in 1988, and Carey-McFall Corporation, a maker of window shades and blinds, for about $35 million in 1989. Springs's finished nonindustrial fabrics business declined to 26 percent from 52 percent of total sales from 1980 to 1990; of these sales about half were to U.S. apparel manufacturers.

The 1990s: Acquisitions, Market Growth, Plant Closures

By 1990, company officials said they would continue to serve domestic apparel markets that provided adequate returns, but predicted that growth would come from the industrial fabrics and home furnishings businesses. In 1990 provisions for restructuring of operations—such as converting or closing finished fabrics plants—resulted in Springs reporting its first loss, 39¢ per share, in its 25 years as a public company. Springs officials noted, however, that earnings before restructuring charges were $2.07 per share, reflecting strength in certain areas of the business.

In 1991 Springs acquired the C.S. Brooks' Nashville plant, followed in 1992 by the acquisition of Finlayson Enterprises Ltd. along with two Canadian firms: C.S. Brooks Canada, Inc. and Griffiths-Kerr, which resulted in a new subsidiary called Springs Canada. As company officials had projected, by 1993 Springs derived 65 percent of its revenues from home furnishings sales, due in part to its acquisitions the previous year and to the growing North American market. A strong supporter of the North American Free Trade Agreement (NAFTA), Springs forecasted substantial long-term growth opportunities from the markets in Mexico and Canada. To promote the passage of NAFTA, the company ran a grass-roots campaign throughout 1993 in which 50,000 personal letters were written and innumerable phone calls were made to Congress. The formation of Springs Canada proved beneficial, expanding the company's North American market and making Springs one of the leading suppliers of sheets and pillowcases in Canada.

Through the mid-1990s Springs continued with its long-term marketing strategy of acquisitions and consolidations. In 1993 Clark-Schwebel contributed its European operations plus $8 million for an equity position in C.S.-Interglass A.G.; in 1994 the Clark-Schwebel Distribution was sold. In 1995 Springs acquired Dundee Mills (towels), Dawson Home Fashions (shower curtains), and Nanik (window coverings), combining Dundee & Dawson into a Bath Fashions Group division, while adding Nanik to its Window Fashions business. Moreover, Springs introduced a new line of Wamsutta towels to coordinate with products, such as rugs, ceramics and shower curtains, provided by the Bath Fashions Group. The Intek office panel business was sold by Springs in 1995, which was a record year for the company's net sales: over $2.26 billion.

1996 was marked both by the expansion of plants and the layoff of employees. As the high quality of technology for spinning and weaving steadily improved, the number of employees, the amount of space, and even the quantity of equipment needed for these tasks decreased. In order to reduce Springs' long-term debt and also to provide capital for acquisitions, the fiberglass division—Clark-Schwebel, Inc.—was sold for $193 million. Several older manufacturing plants were closed as well in 1996, their productivity taken over by the high-tech plants and by outsourcing.

Despite the closings and layoffs necessary in consolidating operations, Springs remained committed to its employees and to the communities in which they lived. Espousing seven values (quality, service, creativity, education, personal and family well-being, respect for history, and planning for the future), the company supported several plant and community improvement projects. Springs employees, known as associates at the company, were also encouraged to organize company and community activities that would further the seven core values. The company was named by *Fortune* magazine one of the "100 Best Companies to Work for in America" and one of the "Most Admired Companies in the United States."

In January 1997, Crandall Close Bowles was elected president and chief operating officer of Springs by the board of directors. Walter Y. Elisha continued as chairman and CEO. The great-great granddaughter of the company's founder, Captain Samuel Elliott White, Crandall Bowles had worked in Springs' finance department from 1973 to 1978, then joined her family's investment firm for 14 years, serving as president the last nine years there. In 1992 Bowles returned to Springs, first as vice-president of textile manufacturing, then as president of the Bath Group.

Although net sales did not manage to significantly top those of the previous year, the close of 1996 and early 1997 showed Springs to be well positioned in its industry, well-focused and intent on its market, with a strong capacity for continued growth.

Principal Subsidiaries

Graber Industries, Inc.; Carey-McFall Corp.; Dundee Acquisition Corp.; Fort Mill A, Inc.; Lancaster International Sales; Springmaid International, Inc.; Springs Canada, Inc. (Ontario);

Springs de Mexico, S.A. de C.(Mexico); Springs Industries (Asia) Inc.

Principal Divisions

Bath Fashions Group.

Further Reading

Andrews, Mildred Gwin, *The Men and the Mills,* Macon, Ga.: Mercer University Press, 1987.

Davis, Burke, *War Bird: The Life and Times of Elliott White Spring,* Chapel Hill: University of North Carolina Press, 1987.

Pettus, Louise, *The Springs Story, Our First Hundred Years,* Fort Mill, S.C.: Springs Industries, 1987.

Elisha, Walter Y., *Standing on the Shoulders of Visionaries: The Story of Springs Industries, Inc.,* Newcomen Publication Number 1403, N.J.: Princeton University Press, 1993.

"Springs to Shut Down 3 South Carolina Sites," *The Wall Street Journal,* July 1, 1996 p. B7F.

"Springs Agrees to Acquire Dundee," *New York Times,* January 14, 1995 p. A41.

"Springs to Sell Intek Assets," *Business Journal Serving Charlotte & the Metropolitan Area,* October 30, 1995 p. 21.

—Trudy Ring
—updated by K. CannCasciato

Stein Mart Inc.

1200 Riverplace Boulevard
Jacksonville, Florida 32207
U.S.A.
(904) 346-1500

Public Company
Incorporated: 1968
Employees: 7,600
Sales: $616.2 million (1996)
Stock Exchanges: NASDAQ
SICs: 5311 Department Stores

Stein Mart Inc. is an ''off-pricer''—a leading retail chain which sells upscale merchandise at 25–60 percent off of department store prices. Founded in 1902 in Greenville, Mississippi, as a general merchandise department store, it later developed into a discount store which purchased cancellations and over-productions from clothing mills. Stein Mart found increased success beginning in 1977, after opening up branches in Memphis and Nashville and has rapidly increased its number of branches since 1984 to a current total of 123 stores, which garnered sales in 1996 of $616 million. Stein Mart stores offer quality merchandise at discounted prices in a department store atmosphere and often serves as an anchor store at shopping malls.

Company Origins

Stein Mart was founded by Sam Stein, a Russian immigrant who opened his first store in Greenville, Mississippi in 1902. Under Stein, the store remained a general merchandise department store, providing basic goods to the residents of Greenville. Upon his death in 1932, Stein's son Jake, took over the store and redirected its focus toward discounted clothing. Jay Stein (Jake's son and head of the company in the 1990s) later recalled that his father Jake ''thought that to be a successful merchant, you had to do something special—either have a wider selection, or the prettiest store, or the cheapest price.'' Jake Stein's specialty would become men's and women's apparel at low prices.

A focus on discounted clothing was certainly timely as the country was at the height of the Great Depression of the 1930s. The original Stein Mart department store withstood the Depression and enjoyed moderate success during the postwar period, when a return to full employment increased the purchasing power of consumers and created a strong demand by consumers for goods.

In fact, the period from 1948 to 1962 has been called the ''retail revolution.'' During this time, retail rapidly expanded due to technological innovations and the growth of the middle class. The resulting marketplace was highly competitive, forcing institutions to innovate or fade away. A key development during this time was the growth of discount merchandising, such as practiced by Stein Mart. The concept had been established in the 1930s with the advent of supermarkets whose inexpensive locations, increased hours of operation, and advertising resulted in low margins; in the late 1940s discounting increased in popularity as consumers' distress over rising prices caused them to seek out bargains. In addition, consumer confidence in the quality of goods had increased thanks to advertising. And while incomes rose in the postwar boom, consumers resisted higher prices caused by inflation.

By purchasing cancellations and overproductions from clothing manufacturers (many of whom were also located in the South), Jake Stein was able to offer quality merchandise to his customers at a price they were able to afford. Stein achieved moderate success with this somewhat revolutionary concept, which rose in popularity throughout the country. However, the company remained a one-store operation in Greenville until Jay Stein took over operations in 1977 and began to pursue a plan of expansion.

Expansion in the 1970s and Onward

While traditional department stores serve as anchors in shopping malls and offer moderate to upscale merchandise at full price, discount clothiers generally offer brand-name merchandise in an informal atmosphere. Following the end of the Korean War, the production of retail goods began to meet or exceed consumer demand, resulting in a buyer's market. While yielding lower margins per item than department stores, discount retailers made up the difference by selling large quantities of merchandise rapidly.

Stein Mart straddled both concepts by offering customers the same ambience as a regular department store with discounted prices. In doing so, it helped to define "off-pricers" as a new category in retail. Stein Mart targeted customers who shopped department stores on a regular basis, inducing them to purchase Stein Mart goods by offering discounts of 25 to 60 percent off of department store prices. By the late 1970s, Stein Mart was the leading retailer of clothing for the family in the Mississippi Delta.

When Stein Mart expanded its original Greenville store during this time, several affluent women from the Greenville area offered to act as sales assistants during the store's liquidation sale of some designer clothing. At that time, Jay Stein noticed the women, "boutique ladies," as they came to be known, were able to provide an extraordinary level of service; they were knowledgeable on these more expensive brands given their own purchasing power and sophisticated taste.

Thus, when Stein Mart expanded into Memphis in 1977, Stein and his wife developed a designer boutique within the store and sought out local shopping mavens to operate it. Stein was quoted in *American Demographics* as saying "The boutique ladies are our secret weapon." The boutique lady concept would continue as a unique part of Stein Mart's strategy; they would consult with in-store clothing buyers to stock stores and ensure that Stein Mart kept abreast of trends. These women also tipped off friends and acquaintances when key new shipments arrived, ensuring that the merchandise would sell quickly.

Furthermore, when entering a new location, Stein Mart sought references for possible "bou ladies" from its ranks in other areas. The position became a status symbol in some Stein Mart locations, placing interested local women on waiting lists. In addition to the boutique ladies, Stein Mart stores also employed personal shoppers, referred to by the company as "agenda consultants."

Under Jay Stein, Stein Mart pursued a steady expansion program, growing from three stores in 1977 to 40 stores in 1990

and to 123 stores by the end of 1996. The chain first tackled new markets in the Southeast, establishing stores in Alabama, Georgia, Louisiana, and Texas. Later, Stein Marts began cropping up in the Midwest, with stores in Indiana, Ohio, and Missouri. In determining the prime locations for new Stein Mart stores, management targeted cities with populations of 125,000 or more and relied on demographic research regarding income, education, and occupation to help predict whether a community might support a discounter of designer merchandise.

In the 1990s Stein Marts generally served as anchor stores in neighborhood shopping centers. To enhance its image as an upscale clothier, Stein Mart initiated several marketing concepts, including store ambience, quality merchandise, and its "boutique ladies." A typical Stein Mart store averaged approximately 38,000 square feet in size. Plush carpeting, marble flooring, soft lighting and handsome furnishings all contributed to its department store ambience. Stein Mart also limited in-store "sale" signage and used discreet price tags to reduce any trace of the "discount store" appearance. Similarly, while Stein Mart kept costs in check through a centralized checkout system, it did not provide shopping carts. Another marketing tactic of Stein Mart was that their stores displayed merchandise in "lifestyle groupings" such as activewear, career apparel, etc. rather than the traditional size/age departments, believing this encouraged customers to make multiple purchases.

The Stein Mart store of the 1990s carried brand name merchandise including apparel, accessories, hosiery, costume jewelry, glassware, dishes, and cookware. While stores did carry private label merchandise to ensure selection, inventory was focused on designer apparel at discounted prices. Beginning in 1995, Stein Mart leased its shoe and fragrance departments to independent operators in order to provide customers with full-service without taking on additional stock.

The company relied on the efficient handling of inventory through drop shipments to each store rather than incurring the expenses of maintaining a distribution or warehouse center. Moreover, Stein Mart kept advertising costs low by relying primarily on limited print media ads and word-of-mouth to build a customer base. Unlike traditional discounters, who generally responded to unplanned buying opportunities of overstocked or returned merchandise, Stein Mart buyers simply waited about one month later than traditional department stores in order to negotiate lower prices from manufacturers, while still retaining access to a majority of that manufacturer's product line, ensuring that their selections would be timely and fashionable.

Stein Mart went public on NASDAQ in April 1992, and the company's stock doubled in value within 16 months. In the 1990s, Stein Mart stock has proved a good investment, with some fluctuations reflecting general trends in the retail industry. Stein Mart appeared to have been successful in pursuing investors. As of early 1997, company stock was cited as a good purchase by several brokers and received flattering coverage in a number of investor publications.

Stein Mart's Future

According to Stein Mart's early 1997 10K report, the company planned to open between 26 and 28 stores in 1997, some in states new to the company, such as California, Nevada, Iowa, and Wisconsin. After 75 years of existence as a single store, Stein Mart's accelerated growth between 1977 and the 1997 can only be regarded as phenomenal. By creating a new niche between discount and department stores while funding growth internally and keeping costs down, Stein Mart has been extremely successful. With its concept of upscale discounting, Stein Mart was poised to meet an internal goal of 600 stores, according to an article in *The Milwaukee Journal Sentinel,* by the end of the decade. Given the intense competition and fragmentation in the retail industry, reaching this goal would present a challenge, but Stein Mart has shown that after 75 years, it is never too late to make your presence known.

Further Reading

Carey, Bill, "Stein Mart's Growth Impressive," *Gannett News Service,* February 10, 1994.

Griffith, Jill, "Talk of the Town; Marketing Tools," *American Demographics,* October 1, 1995, p. 76.

Hajewski, Doris "Stein Mart's Lowbrow Name Misleading," *The Milwaukee Journal Sentinel,* March 18, 1997, p. 1.

Lloyd, Brenda "Stein Mart Takes Fashion/Value Formula On the Road; Florida-Based Retailer Builds 133-Unit Chain in 23 States," *Daily News Record,* April 21, 1997, p. 16.

Price, Joliene, " 'Bou Ladies' Coming to Peachtree City," *The Atlanta Journal and Constitution,* February 15, 1996, p. M03.

—Karen Troshynski-Thomas

STEINWAY & SONS

Steinway Musical Properties, Inc.

800 South Street
Waltham, Massachusetts 02154-1439
U.S.A.
(617) 894-9770
Fax: (617) 842-3395
Web site: http://www.g2g.com/steinway

Wholly Owned Subsidiary of Steinway Musical Instruments, Inc.
Founded: 1853 as Steinway & Sons
Employees: 1,000
Sales: $189.8 million (1995)
SICs: 3931 Musical Instruments

With a particular concentration on the production of concert grand pianos, Steinway Musical Properties, Inc. draws on a heritage of over 145 years in the painstaking business of piano manufacturing. Known for more than a century as Steinway & Sons, the company was founded by a family of German immigrants in the mid-19th century. Its innovations were key to the development of the modern acoustic piano, bringing the founding family prestige and prosperity. Factories in New York City and Hamburg, Germany, continue to create pianos in a highly labor-intensive process that remains largely unchanged since the early 20th century.

However, along with the rest of America's piano makers, Steinway endured a long, relentless, and painful decline in demand from the 1920s to the present. In 1963, the largely family-owned business was acquired by Columbia Broadcasting System, Inc. (now CBS, Inc.). Steinway traded hands again in 1985, when it was sold to a private group of investors. A third change in ownership came in 1996, when the venerable piano maker was sold to a Los Angeles investment group: The Selmer Company, Inc. operated Steinway as an independent interest with over $100 million in sales.

Roots in 19th-Century Germany

The Steinway firm traces its history to a small hamlet in Germany where founder and patriarch Heinrich Steinweg is said to have made his first piano as a wedding gift for his bride. Although his early years in the trade have been shrouded in familial folklore, it is known that Heinrich also made organs, guitars and zithers. Son Carl (known as Charles in the United States) was the first to emigrate to America in the 1840s. Heinrich, his wife Julianne, three daughters and four other sons departed for New York City in May 1850.

Like many immigrants, the family soon anglicized their surname and some given names; Steinweg (literally "stone road") became Steinway. Heinrich and his sons worked as apprentices with local piano manufacturers for about three years, building some pianos at home as well. They offered their first complete piano under the Steinway nameplate in 1853, and enjoyed virtually immediate success. To their initial retail outlet in New York City near Broadway they quickly added exclusive dealers in Baltimore, Maryland; Washington, D.C.; Louisville, Kentucky; and Savannah, Georgia. By 1856, when William formally joined his father and brothers Henry Jr. and Charles in the family enterprise, it had grown so fast the Steinways no longer had to work on the shop floor. All had advanced to managerial positions.

Development of the Modern Piano

The Steinways were quick to adopt technological innovations to the still-evolving instrument, a strategy that proved key to the company's early success. While there is no doubt that they possessed creative genius—Steinway & Sons accumulated over 50 patents from 1850 to 1890 alone—their particular aptitude was in adopting and combining others' breakthroughs. The earliest advances have been credited to Henry Jr., but when both he and brother Charles died in the spring of 1865, the family summoned Heinrich's youngest son, C. F. Theodore, from Germany, where he had been operating a struggling piano factory. Another son, Albert, also joined the firm as a minority partner at this time.

By all accounts a failure in his homeland, Theodore reluctantly came into his own in the United States. He originated the majority of the patented designs used in what came to be known as "the Steinway method" of piano building. Hallmarks of the design included the use of a one-piece iron frame to accommo-

Company Perspectives:

The Steinway & Sons piano company, in Astoria, Queens, is proud of the fact that 95 percent of piano soloists performing with major symphony orchestras choose to perform on Steinway pianos. One of the reasons is because Steinway & Sons still does a lot of things the old-fashioned way, such as cutting, bending, shaping and gluing the fine woods from which Steinway instruments are made, by hand, following a process developed and patented by the company over the past 143 years.

date the extremely high tension of the piano wires, overstringing of the bass wires for increased sound, and improvements in the power and responsiveness of the ''action,'' the mechanism that connects the keys to the hammer that strikes the string. As family chronicler D. W. Fostle emphasized in his 1995 book, *The Steinway Saga*, ''The design pioneered and popularized by the Steinways became the preferred way to build a piano and ultimately the only way.'' This highly labor-intensive process, involving over 12,000 moving parts and nearly as many painstaking steps, would continue to be used throughout the 20th century.

A steady stream of awards and commendations beginning in 1857 helped catapult sales from 12 units in 1853 to 400 in 1857, when the Steinways formalized their family partnership. By the end of the Civil War, Steinway & Sons had become the world's largest piano manufacturer, with more than 400 employees, $1 million in sales, and production of over 2,300 pianos per year. Unlike some of its largest competitors, Steinway did not reach this pinnacle by appealing to the market's lowest common denominator. In fact, its line included some of the world's most expensive instruments.

Second Generation of Leadership in the Late 1800s

While technical considerations as well as impeccable craftsmanship formed the core of Steinway's success, promotion also contributed greatly to the company's prosperity. Heinrich's son William proved the marketing genius of the family, guiding advertising and all manner of promotions. D. W. Fostle summarized the corporate strategy as ''prizes plus prestigious players plus patents equal high prices.'' The firm opened Steinway Hall, its first concert hall, in New York City in 1867. This musical and cultural forum, which featured a Steinway showroom, was just one factor in the public perception of the Steinway as the premier concert piano. The company also sponsored well-known European artists on tours throughout the United States. As Fostle posited, William ensured that ''from its earliest years the pianos of Steinway were conjoined with musical refinement and high aesthetic purpose.''

William succeeded his father as president of the company upon the latter's death in 1871. His first decade at the helm proved difficult, given the onset of the country's longest economic depression in 1873. In order to survive the downturn, which lasted into 1879, Steinway cut prices and wages. Squabbling within the family also made this a difficult period

for the company, but as the economy recovered, William began to expand the family interests. He bought 400 acres in Astoria, Queens, and built a factory, foundry, schools, a library, and a public bath. In 1880, William guided the establishment of a piano works in Hamburg, Germany. Production at this branch of the family enterprise would continue—albeit with interruptions—throughout the 20th century. William's reign peaked in 1891, when companywide sales totaled more than 3,000 pianos, and profits amounted to 30 percent of total dollar volume. Unbeknownst to his relatives and heirs, however, William died in 1896 bankrupt from dubious investments.

With sales declining to less than 2,000 units and the specter of William's insolvency hanging over the company in 1897, William's successor and nephew Charles (son of the elder Charles) tried to sell the struggling family firm to a group of British investors. The new president kept the family firm alive by slashing the prices of its top-line pianos and introducing lower-priced models in the early 1900s, nearly doubling sales by 1906. Three years later, when nationwide piano sales hit an all-time high of over 365,500 units, Steinway's own unit sales had recovered to 3,700 per year. However, industry consolidation and anti-German sentiment during the World War I years shrank Steinway's market share from 3.7 percent in 1909 to less than 1.5 percent by 1919.

Advertising Buoys Sales in 1920s

When Charles died that year, his brother Frederick T. Steinway took the helm. Although he had spent the previous 30 years directing manufacturing, Frederick's true forte would prove to be in another area. The new president had his work cut out for him; Steinway and all the world's piano manufacturers faced what D. W. Fostle called ''the four horsemen of the piano apocalypse: radio, depression, world war and television.'' The impact of radios alone diminished industrywide production from 348,000 in 1923 to 131,000 in 1929.

Fred successfully fought this battle by broadening Steinway's advertising presence from trade magazines to general publications. The strategy, which increased the company's ad budget to the heretofore unheard of level of nine percent of sales, brought a counter-cyclical increase in unit sales from 4,100 in 1921 to 6,300 by 1926. Fred also dramatically expanded the company's longstanding artist support system whereby Steinway supplied pianos and tuners for concert appearances without charge. This system endured, albeit in a much more limited form, throughout the remainder of the century, helping to equate the Steinway nameplate with professional musicianship in the public mind.

During this prosperous period, Fred fortuitously accumulated a multimillion dollar surplus account. It would prove to be a prime factor in Steinway's ability to endure the economic holocaust of the 1930s. Fred, however, would not witness this decline; when he died from a stroke in 1927, he was succeeded by William's son Theodore E. Steinway. His was not a happy tenure. The Depression further battered the piano industry, eliminating nearly two-thirds of the companies that had survived radio's onslaught. With thousands of warehoused pianos and no buyers, Steinway factories shut down for 20 months in the early 1930s. Theodore cut salaries across the board; executives (most of them family members) took the biggest cuts, at 66 percent. The surplus account lasted long enough for Steinway to launch its first baby grand in 1936. The company also resumed the manufacture of uprights two years later. Although Rothstein, writing for *Smithsonian* magazine, attributed the company's survival to "the integrity of the instrument," Theodore was willing to sacrifice some of that integrity for the sake of survival. For example, Steinway tried to make bargain-priced pianos in the late 1930s, but while output increased almost fourfold from 1935 to 1939, the company struggled to make a profit. Steinway even adopted an "if you can't beat 'em, join 'em" strategy, selling radios, records and record players out of Steinway Hall.

Even World War II couldn't pull the company out of its doldrums. Steinway only recorded profits in four of the 16 years from 1930 to 1945. Unlike some firms that benefitted from defense contracting, the piano company struggled to adapt to the new economic imperative. Steinway first applied its woodworking skills to the production of parts for Army gliders. Later in the conflict, it entered the rather morbid production of caskets. Despite a major campaign to honor the company's centenary, Steinway & Sons continued to struggle into the 1950s. The work week was cut in half at the end of 1953, and plants were shut down entirely for five weeks in 1954. Theodore Steinway resigned the presidency in 1955 and died two years later. He was succeeded by his son, Henry Z. Steinway.

Last Generation of Family Management in 1960s and 1970s

The new leader quickly recognized Steinway's immediate problems—a lack of skilled labor and an aging physical plant— and set out to rectify them. He sold off Steinway Hall and other parcels of real estate in order to raise funds for production, which he consolidated at a single plant. The new leader made considerable headway during his tenure, chalking up production increases of over ten percent in 1959 and 1960 and increasing Steinway & Sons' share of grand piano sales to 28 percent by 1963.

However, the 1960s brought new threats to the piano industry overall and Steinway in particular. Foremost among these was the penetration of imports into the domestic market. Led by Japan's Yamaha, imports of grand pianos grew from nil in 1960 to nearly 50 percent in 1969. Furthermore, the industry faced a continued population decline, which eroded its chief market, school age children. Budget cuts at schools and rising interest rates only exacerbated the problem.

Henry Z. sold the family firm via an exchange of shares to CBS, Inc. in 1972. Although the stock was never listed, it had started trading in the 1920s. Outside investors as well as some family factions had been clamoring for a sale for some time, and the company had in fact entertained more than 24 offers between 1955 and 1968. At the time, the broadcast television company seemed a logical parent for the piano maker. CBS CEO William Paley had already acquired several musical instrument companies and appeared dedicated to their care, but corporate ownership brought its own ills: bureaucracy, repeated reorganizations, and high management turnover. Moreover, Steinway was merely a tiny fraction of its overall operations. After Henry Z. was "promoted" to chairman—an empty title,

in this case—in 1977, the company operated under three more presidents in less than a decade. Production declined from over 5,400 in 1976 to less than 4,400 by 1982.

A Second Corporate Parent Adopts Steinway in Mid-1980s

In 1985, CBS sold Steinway to a Boston investment group that included brothers Robert and John Birmingham. The new owners approached the enterprise as strictly a manufacturing business, sometimes even slandering the storied past upon which Steinway's reputation was based. This new attitude raised fears, sometimes well founded, that the venerable piano and its quality would be corrupted. Writing for the *New Republic* in 1989, Edward Rothstein called their strategy "a philosophy entirely alien to a century of piano invention and craft," but in fact, with the support of a new marketing program, Steinway sold more grand pianos in North America from 1986 to 1991 than it had in the previous fifty years. In the early 1990s, the company supplemented its revenues with a reconditioning division. By this time, the number of Steinways that were rebuilt nationwide far surpassed the number of new Steinways produced.

An early 1990s recession diminished sales from $98.8 million in 1991 to $89.2 million in 1992, and the company suffered back-to-back losses totaling over $13 million in 1992 and 1993. Revenues increased over $100 million in 1994, when the pianomaker earned a $3.1 million profit.

Steinway Joins Selmer Musical Family in 1995

In 1995, an investment group owned by Kyle Kirkland and Dana Messina commenced acquisition of Steinway Musical Properties for over $100 million and merged it with The Selmer Company, Inc., a manufacturer of wind and percussion instruments that they had acquired two years earlier. In 1996, they sold 16 percent of the new holding company, Steinway Musical Instruments, Inc. to the public. They planned to use the estimated $60 million proceeds for debt reduction and capacity increases. Although the two subsidiaries were very similar in that they employed highly labor-intensive production methods and operated in a mature market, they were operated as distinct entities. The new owners hoped to increase Steinway's domestic market share via institutional sales, boost overseas sales via the German subsidiary, and improve manufacturing efficiency.

With combined total sales of over $230 million, Steinway and Selmer constituted the musical instrument industry's largest company.

Further Reading

Amato, Ivan, "The Finishing Touch: Robots May Lend a Hand in the Making of Steinway Pianos," *Science News,* February 18, 1989, pp. 108–09.

Fostle, D. W., "Henry Z. Steinway: A Grand Tradition," *Audio,* January 1993, pp. 52–63.

——, *The Steinway Saga: An American Dynasty,* New York: Scribner, 1995.

Goldenberg, Susan, *The House of Steinway,* New York: Dodd, Mead, 1988.

——, *Steinway from Glory to Controversy: An Unvarnished Portrait of the Family, the Business, and the Famous Piano,* Oakville, Ont.: Mosaic Press, 1996.

Halbfinger, David M., "Steinway Is Sold to Big Producer of Instruments," *Newsday,* April 19, 1995, p. A41.

Lieberman, Richard K., *Steinway & Sons,* New Haven: Yale University Press, 1995.

Matzer, Marla, "Playing Solo," *Forbes,* March 25, 1996, pp. 80–81.

McNamara, Victoria, "Piano Players Pull Strings in Race for Endorsements," *Houston Business Journal,* May 28, 1990, pp. 1–2.

Ratcliffe, Ronald V., *Steinway & Sons,* San Francisco: Chronicle Books, 1989.

Rothstein, Edward, "Don't Shoot the Piano," *New Republic,* May 1, 1989, pp. 32–35.

——, "To Make a Piano of Note It Takes More than Tools," *Smithsonian,* November 1988, pp. 142–51.

Singer, Aaron, *Labor Management Relations at Steinway & Sons, 1853–1896,* New York: Garland, 1986.

Solberg, Sara, and Dowling, Claudia Glenn, "Ain't It Grand: Steinway & Sons Celebrated 135 Years of Celestial Sound by Building Its 500,000th Classic Piano," *Life,* June 1988, pp. 99–103.

"Steinway & Sons Owner Agrees to Sell Company," *Wall Street Journal,* April 19, 1995, p. B9.

Winzeler, Megan, "Steinway Strikes a Chord," *Sales & Marketing Management,* August 1995, p. 16.

—April Dougal Gasbarre

Sturm, Ruger & Company, Inc.

Lacey Place
Southport, Connecticut 06490
U.S.A.
(203) 259-7843
Fax: (203) 254-2195
Web site: http://www.ruger-firearms.com

Public Company
Incorporated: 1949
Employees: 1,010
Sales: $223.3 million (1996)
Stock Exchanges: New York
SICs: 3484 Small Arms; 3324 Steel Investment
    Foundries

Sturm, Ruger & Company, Inc. is the leading independent producer of firearms in the United States. Sturm, Ruger designs, manufactures, and markets a full line of pistols, revolvers, rifles, and shotguns, primarily for sporting purposes, but also for law enforcement and military agencies. Products include the company's flagship .22 caliber target pistols, single-action revolvers, sporting carbines and target rifles, single-shot and bolt-action hunting rifles, lever action rifles, double-action revolvers, 9-millimeter and .40 and .45 caliber pistols, and over-and-under shotguns, as well as automatic rifles for the police and military markets. Sturm, Ruger, through its Pine Tree Casting, Uni-Cast, and Ruger Investment Casting divisions, is also engaged in ferrous, aluminum, and titanium precision investment casting for customers in the aerospace, sporting goods, and other industries, including production of the "Big Bertha" titanium golf club heads for the Callaway Golf Company. Sturm, Ruger is headquartered in Southport, Connecticut, site of the company's original manufacturing plant. The company operates four manufacturing and investment casting facilities in New Hampshire and Arizona. Founder William B. Ruger serves as chairman and chief executive officer. Ruger's son, William B. Ruger, Jr., is vice-chairman and senior executive officer. Sales for 1996 were $223.3 million, for a net income of $34.4 million.

A Firearms Fan in the 1930s

Bill Ruger's interest in firearms began while he was still a boy in Brooklyn, New York, and Ruger was already designing guns, as well as frequenting machine shops to learn about machining and manufacturing techniques, by the time he graduated from high school. In 1939, after spending two years studying liberal arts at the University of North Carolina, Ruger dropped out of college to pursue a career in firearms manufacturing. Ruger moved to New England, the seat of the country's firearms industry and headquarters of the some of the most famous names in firearms, including Colt, Smith & Weston, Winchester, Remington, and Savage. Ruger's search for work proved fruitless; nonetheless, he remained in Hartford, Connecticut, hoping for a job with Colt and, meanwhile, working on a design for a machine gun.

By late 1939, Ruger still had not found work, and he decided to move back to North Carolina, his wife's native state. Along the way, he stopped in Washington, D.C., and showed his machine gun design to Army Ordnance, which liked the design. Arriving in North Carolina, Ruger received an offer for work as a gun designer from the U.S. government's Springfield Armory in Massachusetts, the major supplier of small arms for the military services since the beginning of the century. Ruger worked in Springfield for several months; but his paycheck, $65 every two weeks, was not enough to support his wife and child, and Ruger brought his family back to North Carolina.

By then the country was preparing to enter the Second World War, and the military was seeking to replace its aging Browning machine guns. Ruger set to work designing a new machine gun to meet the government's specifications. He had a machine shop build a prototype of his machine gun, and he brought the prototype back to New England to shop it around the firearms manufacturers. He brought the prototype first to Remington, which turned it down. Smith & Weston and Winchester also rejected Ruger's design. But in late 1940, Ruger found work with Auto Ordnance Corporation of Bridgeport, Connecticut. Auto Ordnance had been founded in 1921 by General John Thompson, of "Tommy" submachine gun fame. Ruger spent the next three years perfecting his light machine gun design. His experience at Auto Ordnance also introduced

Company Perspectives:

" 'Arms Makers for Responsible Citizens.' More than just a motto, this simple statement has defined Sturm, Ruger since its founding in 1949. Variations of the phrase appear in some of our earliest product advertisements, right up to the present day. We are immensely proud of the fact that we have emerged as the leading American firearms manufacturer based upon the exemplary reputation our products enjoy with the honorable citizens of a great nation—one which cherishes the positive enjoyment of firearms in a free society."

him to a variety of manufacturing and machining techniques. Ruger's light machine gun was ready for prototype production and testing by 1944; however, with the war coming to an end, the government was no longer interested in new machine guns, and Ruger's machine gun never went into full production.

First Success in the 1950s

After the war, Ruger set out to build firearms on his own. In 1946, he formed the Ruger Corporation, a small shop in Southport, Connecticut, with the intention of designing and building sporting guns. To keep that end of the business afloat, Ruger took on subcontracts supplying parts to Auto Ordnance, which by then had branched out into manufacturing record players. Ruger's company thrived for the next two years. Then Ruger attempted to enter a new business, designing and producing high-end carpenter's tools. These proved too expensive to make, however, and by 1948, the 32-year-old Ruger was forced to close his business.

Down but not out, Ruger was determined to return to his original interest in firearms. He set to work perfecting one of his old designs, for a .22 caliber semiautomatic target pistol. With no cash of his own, Ruger turned to an acquaintance, Alexander Sturm, for financing. Sturm, then 26, came from a wealthy family, was a graduate of Yale Art School, a writer and artist, and a "student of heraldry," with an interest in firearms. Sturm and Ruger agreed to form Sturm, Ruger & Company in 1949 with $50,000 from Sturm's family. Ruger was in charge of designing and manufacturing; Sturm would provide the company's earliest advertising, including the company's trademark. The company started with six employees in Southport, Connecticut.

Sturm, Ruger brought out its first product after a year. Ruger combined his manufacturing and machining knowledge with his own intuitive sense of firearms design to produce Sturm, Ruger's low-cost, stamped-frame .22 caliber target pistol, which recalled the famous Colt pistols. Ruger's pistol sold at $37.50, compared with the Colt's $50 price, without sacrificing quality. Praised for being well-balanced and reliable, the .22 Ruger Standard also exhibited an aesthetic appeal that would become a Sturm, Ruger hallmark. An ad and an enthusiastic review in American Rifleman generated the company's first orders and, within a year, Sturm, Ruger had repaid the Sturm

family's $50,000 investment; this was the last money the company ever borrowed. The .22 Standard became one of the most popular handguns in the country and would remain a company mainstay for more than 50 years.

Sturm died in 1951 at the age of 29, of hepatitis. Ruger took over control of the company's management, while Sturm's estate retained its interest in the company. Sturm, Ruger turned to expanding its line of firearms. Unable to compete against the complete lines of the larger gun manufacturers, Sturm, Ruger instead concentrated on bringing handguns to the market, targeting the gun enthusiast, for whom firearms held an aesthetic appeal beyond their use for sport and hunting purposes. The company's next product was patterned after the famous Colt .45 Peacemaker, which had stopped production in 1940, but was produced as a .22 caliber revolver. The Ruger Single-Six revolver proved as successful as the company's .22 caliber pistol, helped by the booming popularity of the Western in the cinema and on television. By the mid-1950s, Sturm, Ruger's product line had expanded to include its centerfire single-action Blackhawk revolvers, which were available in a range of calibers, and the smaller Bearcat single-action handguns.

Ruger's long experience in manufacturing and machining techniques helped build the company's reputation and profits. From the start, Ruger had intended to produce his handguns using a new technique called precision investment casting. Precision investment casting used molds and patterns to shape molten steel, producing stronger components more efficiently than, and without the wastage of, traditional rough forging and machining techniques. By 1953, Sturm, Ruger was profitable enough to begin manufacturing its products using investment casting, adding to the company's reputation for high quality firearms and helping the company achieve higher profit margins. By the end of the decade, the company's revenues had grown to $3 million. It moved production to a larger plant, remaining in Southport. In 1960, Sturm, Ruger moved beyond handguns for the first time, introducing a semiautomatic hunting rifle, the Ruger .44 Magnum Carbine.

Expansion in the 1960s and 1970s

With the move into rifles, Sturm, Ruger added to its production capacity, opening a second manufacturing plant in Newport, New Hampshire. In 1963, the company, which had been subcontracting its casting work to other foundries, opened its own foundry, called Pine Tree Castings, also in Newport. The company continued to add to its firearms line, while maintaining production of its earlier firearms, adding a .22 caliber autoloading rifle in 1964, and, in 1967, opening a new trend in big game hunting with the introduction of a single-shot rifle, called the Number One. The following year, the company introduced its M-77, a bolt-action rifle. By then, the company's revenues had grown greater than $9 million, generating a net income of nearly $2 million.

Sturm, Ruger went public in 1969, in part to ease the company's entry into the law enforcement market with the introduction of .38 and .357 Magnum revolvers. Ruger was also eyeing a new market: automobiles. Sturm, Ruger actually produced two prototypes of automobiles and had lined up subcontractors and components suppliers. But as environmental and safety factors became more integral to car production, Ruger balked at the prospect of increasing government intervention in the automobile industry. Sturm, Ruger returned to its core business, producing firearms that were already beginning to achieve industry dominance. The company's line expanded to include a black powder "cap-and-ball" revolver and a line of single-action revolvers equipped with automatic safety features.

Awareness of safety issues was sweeping throughout U.S. industries, and the 1970s saw the rise of a new breed of product liability lawsuits. Firearms makers became a target for such lawsuits, and Sturm, Ruger was no exception. While revenues continued to rise, jumping to $33.8 million in 1975, Sturm, Ruger found itself the focus of growing numbers of lawsuits. To head off some of the suits against the company, Sturm, Ruger initiated a program to retrofit its handguns with new safety features. The liability suits, however, continued to pour in, and toward the late 1970s the company agreed to be purchased in a leveraged buyout by Forstmann, Little & Co. of New York. That deal fell through, however, and Ruger decided to maintain control of the company, spurning subsequent offers for Sturm, Ruger.

Surviving the 1980s

Sturm, Ruger entered the 1980s strongly, with revenues greater than $80 million in the 1980s and topping $100 million two years later. The company's income was also strong, returning a consistent ten percent on revenues. Ruger again showed his long-standing commitment to improved manufacturing techniques, converting production to CNC (computer numerically controlled) equipment in the early 1980s.

The company continued to introduce new models, feeding a growing gun collectors market, with products such as its Redhawk double-action revolvers and an expanding line of sporting rifles. The 1980s, however, saw the beginning of a downturn in the U.S. firearms industry, sparked in part by calls for increased gun control after the murder of John Lennon and the attempted assassination of President Reagan. Most of the major firearms manufacturers struggled through the decade; by the end of the 1980s, many of the famous names, such as Colt and Winchester, either faced bankruptcy or had been bought by larger corporations, or both.

As the 1990s began, Sturm, Ruger remained the sole independent among leading firearms manufacturers. The company's own revenues had slipped through much of the decade, but by 1990, sales had begun to climb again, reaching $122 million. At the same time, Sturm, Ruger continued its unbroken record of profitability. In 1990, Sturm, Ruger began trading on the New York Stock Exchange. The following year, Ruger's son, William Ruger, Jr., a Harvard graduate who had joined the company in 1964, was named the company's president. Ruger, Sr. remained as chairman and chief executive.

The company had also found a lucrative extension to its core firearms business: investment casting for manufacturers in other industries, such as the aerospace industry. Sturm, Ruger built on its existing capacity with the acquisition of Manchester, New Hampshire's American Metals and Alloys, Inc. for $3 million in 1985, adding, as the Uni-Cast Division, aluminum casting to the company's Pine Tree ferrous casting capability. Two years later, Sturm, Ruger expanded again, leasing a facility in Prescott, Arizona, adding manufacturing and casting capacity in the Southwest. By the mid-1990s, Sturm, Ruger's investment casting business represented more than ten percent of the company's annual sales.

One factor driving sales was, paradoxically, the increasing public pressure to ban or limit sales of semiautomatic rifles. Although Sturm, Ruger had long followed a policy of restricting sales of its own semiautomatic rifles exclusively to law enforcement and military agencies, fears of tightening government restrictions on purchases of firearms prompted gun enthusiasts to step up their firearms buying, including Sturm, Ruger's handguns and rifles. Sturm, Ruger was also helped by trends within the law enforcement community. Confronted by rising levels of handguns and other weapons on the street, police agencies turned from the traditional police revolver to new and more powerful semiautomatic pistols, including Sturm, Ruger's 9-millimeter pistols.

Sales reached $192.5 million in 1995, including $36.8 million from the company's casting business. The following year, after signing a $150 million agreement with Callaway Golf Company to produce that company's Big Bertha titanium golf club heads, Sturm, Ruger's sales jumped to $223 million. The agreement also called for the two companies to build a joint venture titanium foundry, in addition to Sturm, Ruger's existing Prescott, Arizona foundry, which came online in late 1996. Yet firearms continued to form the company's core and the focus of its future. Under the guidance of its chief and sole firearms designer, William Ruger, Sr., Sturm, Ruger had taken its place among the classic names of U.S. gunmakers.

Principal Divisions

Firearms Division (Newport, New Hampshire); Pine Tree Castings Division (Newport, New Hampshire); Firearms & Ruger Investment Casting Divisions (Prescott, Arizona); Uni-Cast Division (Manchester, New Hampshire).

Further Reading

"Bill Ruger's Gun Company Celebrates 45th Anniversary," *New Hampshire Business Review,* July 22, 1994, p. 1.

Calip, Roger, "William B. Ruger—Legendary Firearm Maker," *The Business Times,* September 1987, p. 7.

Greene, Richard, "Under the Gun," *Forbes,* March 2, 1981, p. 98.

Jones, John A., "Sturm, Ruger Flourishes as an Independent Firearms Firm," *Investor's Business Daily,* August 24, 1993, p. 36.

Millman, Joel, "Steady Finger on the Trigger," *Forbes,* November 9, 1992, p. 188.

Steadman, Nick, "For Sturm, Ruger It Was a Very Good Year," *International Defense Review,* February 1, 1990, p. 185.

Williams, Dick, "Ruger West," *Shooting Industry,* December 1993, p. 108.

Wilson, R.L., *Ruger & His Guns,* New York: Simon & Schuster, 1996.

—M.L. Cohen

Summit Family Restaurants Inc.

440 Lawndale Drive
Salt Lake City, Utah 84115-2917
U.S.A.
(801) 463-5500
Fax: (801) 463-5585

Wholly Owned Subsidiary of CKE Restaurants, Inc.
Incorporated: 1963 as JB's Big Boy Family Restaurants, Inc.
Employees: 5,000
Sales: $121 million
SICs: 5812 Eating Places

Summit Family Restaurants Inc., formerly known as JB's Restaurants Inc., is one of the nation's top 100 restaurant chains. Although at one time the chain included a few units in the East, in the 1990s it had about 100 restaurants in the western states of Utah and Arizona (its two main markets), New Mexico, Wyoming, Idaho, South Dakota, Colorado, Montana, and Washington. Summit serves hungry local residents and travelers in three kinds of establishments. Its core JB's Restaurants are designed to provide a wide variety of menu choices at a modest cost. Since about 1990, the firm had diversified to include two other types of restaurants as well. It operates several all-you-can-eat HomeTown Buffet restaurants and a few Galaxy Diners for those who enjoyed a nostalgic 1950s eating environment. Summit's history illustrates the difficulty of operating restaurants and making them profitable over the long term. The firm's leaders for over three decades have tried just about everything to remain competitive, investing in new menu choices, inside and outside remodeling, advertising, and even for the right to try new franchising concepts, as well as hiring managers from some of its main competitors. Some strategies worked and some did not. However, in the end the firm was not able to remain afloat as an independent corporation, so in 1996 it was acquired by a new owner, CKE Restaurants, Inc.

1960s Origins as a Big Boy Franchise

Summit Family Restaurants was founded as JB's Big Boy by Jack M. Broberg (JB), a graduate of the University of Southern California who had worked as a Lockheed sales engineer and sales account executive. In 1961 he opened the first JB's Big Boy in Provo, Utah, at 500 West 200 South. Later he gained the Big Boy franchise rights for Utah and opened his second Big Boy in Ogden, Utah. By 1965, the company operated its fourth store at 400 South State Street in Salt Lake City, which also contained its general office.

By 1967 the Marriott Corporation completed its purchase of Robert C. Wian Enterprises, the Los-Angeles based firm which owned or franchised more than 500 Big Boy restaurants. Marriott paid almost $9 million in stock for the Wian businesses, which brought in annually about $15 million in sales or franchise income. Marriott Corporation was run by its founder Bill Marriott, the CEO and board chairman, and his son Bill Marriott, Jr., president of the firm since 1964.

Jack Broberg continued to expand his particular Big Boy franchise in the late 1960s. By 1969, he had added JB's Big Boys in Idaho Falls and Twin Falls, Idaho, and Logan, Utah. The Broberg franchise in 1970 operated 18 Big Boy restaurants. This expansion was marked by a move in 1970 to new company headquarters at 3300 South West Temple in Salt Lake City.

In 1971, the growing chain celebrated its tenth anniversary by offering the public Big Boy Hamburgers for 25 cents. Also that year, Clark Jones joined the board of directors, an association that would continue into the 1990s.

After the company became a public corporation in 1972, it continued its expansion and also began diversifying in terms of different types of restaurants in different areas of the nation. In 1974 JB's acquired eight Big Boys in Arizona and two in Seattle, while also opening a new restaurant, called Scoreboard, in Glendale, California.

In 1975, with sales of $24.5 million at 57 restaurants, the company suffered its first financial setback in 14 years. Management attributed the losses largely to its unprofitable New England Big Boy. That year the firm's leaders sold its New Jersey Big Boy to the Marriott Corporation. Although the company generally named its eateries JB's Big Boy Restaurants, one exception was its three remaining New England stores, which operated in 1977 as Lobster Huts. Also during this time,

---

Company Perspectives:

"Summit Family Restaurants is committed to optimizing its value through continued growth in select family restaurant concepts and by continuously fine tuning its operations to maximize it operating efficiencies and unit margins. Summit is dedicated to increasing guest counts by assuring guests of the very best in family dining through consistently providing high quality food, great prices, and friendly and quick service."

---

to diversify, JB's introduced a specialty restaurant in Salt Lake City. Originally called Granny's Pies & Sandwiches, the name was changed to Apple Butter Farms, a family restaurant offering pricier menu selections than those of Big Boy's.

The ambiance of the Old West was the distinctive feature of the Old Salt City Jail, a restaurant purchased by JB's in 1980. Two years later the company opened a second Jail restaurant, this time in Tucson, Arizona. Furthermore, in 1981 it acquired Sun City, Arizona's Suntowner Restaurant, which catered to the many senior citizens in that community.

Downturn in the Late 1970s

Although the firm had diversified, in the late 1970s it experienced a serious decline. Quoted in an article on the firm in the January 1, 1983 issue of *Restaurant Business,* Clark Jones, who had been JB's financial vice-president in 1979, stated: "When the downturn came in the spring of 1979, we were not overly alarmed. From our contacts with other Big Boy operators around the country, we knew that nearly every operator was down. [At the end of September] for the first time in our history we did not exceed our prior year's sales volume. We realized then that it was not just the gasoline shortage that was causing our problems."

The nation's gasoline shortage caused by import restrictions especially hurt the 20 percent of JB's units that depended on tourists. Rising food costs and increasing competition also hurt JB's. Main competitors during this time included McDonald's, Pizza Hut, Denny's, Sizzler, Burger King, and others.

However, those external factors beyond JB's control were compounded by its own internal weaknesses. For example, its television advertising was spotty or even totally absent in some of its markets. In addition, JB's had not changed its basic menu in many years. It still featured the popular Big Boy hamburger, but relied heavily on fried foods, losing popularity among increasingly health-conscious diners. The lack of menu diversity, plus noisy cooking areas and inconsistent store policies, turned off some customers. In addition, Clark Jones stated that "While our outside signage said we were a family restaurant, we were really a coffee shop." In other words, Big Boy still catered to many lower-income singles who ordered just a cup of coffee and other low-cost items.

Retooling in the 1980s

Following this diagnosis, JB's management made some major changes. First, it consolidated its chain by eliminating 14

units in Nebraska, Nevada, Washington, and South Dakota. The cash derived from those sales allowed the firm to upgrade its remaining restaurants.

Moreover, the company's menu changed significantly. In 1980, all JB's units received charbroilers to cook for the first time New York strip steaks, in order to compete with budget steak houses like Sizzler. At the same time, JB's diversified its menu by offering all-you-can-eat salad bars that featured over 30 items. Several new salads, particularly taco salads, increased the menu's appeal to a wider audience. In the early 1980s, JB's also began offering its all-you-can-eat breakfast and fruit bar. To change from being a coffee shop to a family restaurant, it converted from plastic furnishings to all glass and chinaware, used better quality flatware, and made sure that its steak platters were hot and its salad bar plates were chilled.

Remodeling its remaining units inside and outside was another priority for JB's. The traditional outdoor signage featuring the Big Boy character holding a burger plate, which fit the old coffee shop image, was eliminated in the early 1980s. Improved landscaping and wood siding made more attractive the restaurants' exteriors. One major inside change was to remove all counter seats, which for years had been part of the coffee-shop decor. Other inside modifications included new carpeting, improved lighting, and room dividers to create more intimate dining spaces. JB's remodeled units cost an average of $150,000 per unit, but management found that such efforts increased their annual unit sales 40 to 80 percent.

In addition to the menu upgrades and remodeling, JB's made two other improvements in the late 1970s and early 1980s. First, it increased its promotional efforts with the help of Dave Asay, who in 1978 was the company's first formally trained marketing executive. Instead of focusing on discount coupons, Asay emphasized the chain's upgraded menu and value-added items, such as a free dessert added to a steak dinner. JB's concentrated its advertising in its five main markets: Salt Lake City, Tucson, Phoenix, Albuquerque, and Boise, while using spot ads in other markets.

Second, JB's implemented programs to help improve the knowledge and abilities of its managers and employees, while decreasing the company's high employee turnover rates. The four-step plan included better company benefits and pay, improved personnel screening, more growth opportunities, and formal training programs instead of the casual methods of the past.

The results of these various changes were dramatic. Between fiscal years 1978 and 1980 the company's revenues had declined 15 percent and net income decreased 53 percent. The following two years saw revenues rise 52 percent and incomes increase 175 percent, prompting one industry observer, in *Restaurant Business,* to write, "It is indeed impressive that JB's Restaurants. . .has been able to do what so many others have not—turn around in a down economy—which makes their achievement so much more noteworthy and newsworthy to us."

Challenges as an Independent Corporation

Bolstered by the success of their own management, JB's leaders soon became frustrated with the parentage of Marriott Corporation. In December 1984, JB's sued Marriott in Salt

Lake City's Federal District Court to end their franchising agreement. JB's cited Marriott's unwillingness to let it expand beyond its designated territory and Marriott's failure to adequately oversee and promote their restaurants. This lawsuit was a real threat to Marriott, which earlier had seen two of its franchises leave the system (Nashville-based Shoney's and Wheeling, West Virginia-based Elby's).

In February 1985 Marriott settled the lawsuit by agreeing to let JB's expand into five more states: Oregon, Washington, Hawaii, Nevada, and most of northern California. JB's committed to open 100 new restaurants over the next ten years. As part of this settlement, which cost JB's $7 million, JB's also purchased from Marriott 29 additional Big Boy Restaurants, mostly in California. In February 1985, the company became incorporated in Delaware under the name JB's Restaurants, Inc., thus distancing itself from the Big Boy name. That year JB's also sold its two Old City Jail restaurants.

In 1987, Marriott ended its control of the Big Boy system, selling the system to Elias Brothers, a franchisee operating 283 Big Boy's Restaurants at that time. The following year, for the first time in its history, JB's, with its 107 restaurants, became a company independent of the name Big Boy. Board chairman Clark Jones, in *Nation's Restaurant News,* explained that "The only benefit we'd obtain if we stayed in the system would be the Big Boy name. And now with Marriott saying it's pulling out, that's not as much of a plus anymore." JB's of course saved the annual franchise fees, which in 1987 ran about $1 million, based on one percent of its sales.

To diversify, JB's Restaurants in November 1990 announced that it had completed an agreement to become a franchisee of Sbarro eateries. Based in Commack, New York, Sbarro operated Italian fast-food outlets located mostly in shopping malls. JB's purchased two Sbarro units in Phoenix and Scotsdale, Arizona, and gained the right to start Sbarro outlets in Phoenix and Portland.

An even more significant diversification came in December 1991, when JB's announced it had agreed to invest $3.8 million in San Diego-based Americana Entertainment Group, Inc., the parent company of HomeTown Buffet, Inc. JB's thus gained HomeTown Buffet franchise rights for Utah, Arizona, Colorado, and New Mexico as a way of competing with other increasingly popular all-you-can-eat buffets.

In 1991, following a three-month trial run in Tucson, Arizona, JB's Restaurants began installing on-site bakeries in order to offer its customers several fresh baked items. By May the firm had added its Baker's Corner concept to 21 units. Cookies, muffins, and pies were baked on site, a practice also used and proven successful by Perkins, Baker's Square, and Denny's restaurant chains. In a 1991 issue of *Nation's Restaurant News,* JB's President Fred Gonzales explained that the on-site bakeries were one part of the company's strategy since leaving Big Boy. "We've been trying to broaden our image from the breakfast-coffee shop that we had when we were Big Boy and have customers consider us during dinner time, too." The company by 1991 had spent over $30 million to remodel its JB's Restaurants using such new concepts.

To finance its conversion of underperforming JB's Restaurants to the more profitable HomeTown Buffets, the company in 1992 sold 23 of its less profitable JB's Restaurants in Oregon and Washington. It received $4.5 million in this deal from IHOP Corporation, which intended to convert its new units into International House of Pancakes restaurants.

In June 1993 the firm announced that President/CEO Fred Gonzales was resigning. The company's board of directors had become frustrated with lack of progress in implementing the new HomeTown Buffet concept; by June, the third quarter of fiscal year 1993, the company had opened only one of the eight to ten new HomeTown Buffets it had planned for that year. Following several months during which Clark Jones served as interim president, in December 1993 the firm announced a new president and CEO: Don M. McComas, a former executive for the El Torito chain of Mexican restaurants.

Meanwhile, JB's made yet another shift in its attempt to remain competitive. In the fall of 1993 it decided to abandon its Sbarro franchise. Seven of its 13 outlets were sold back to the parent company, while its other six were simply closed. Because of limited resources, JB's felt it should concentrate on promoting the more profitable HomeTown Buffets. Outside analysts agreed with that decision, especially after HomeTown Buffet Inc. went public on September 22, 1993.

In 1994, after three straight years of losing money and also three consecutive years of declining sales at its JB's Restaurants, the company made several efforts to reverse the situation. While striving to improve its core JB's Restaurants' management, menu offerings, and marketing, the company attempted to expand the number of JB's Restaurants franchises, open new HomeTown Buffets, and convert some unprofitable JB's Restaurants into Galaxy Diners, which featured a nostalgic 1950s atmosphere complete with jukeboxes and soda fountains.

Toward the 21st Century

On April 4, 1995, the firm changed its name to Summit Family Restaurants Inc. to reflect the fact that it now oversaw not only the familiar JB's Restaurants (82 company-owned and 22 franchised), but also 14 HomeTown Buffets and four Galaxy Diners. The corporation's trading symbol on the NASDAQ exchange was changed from JBBB to SMFR.

When fiscal 1994 did not bring forth the anticipated reversal in JB's financial picture, Summit's directors hired Piper Jaffray, an investment banking firm with knowledge of the restaurant industry, to provide outside assessment and advice. The next month Piper Jaffray concluded that Summit could not continue as an independent public company and that it should seek a buyer.

In August 1995, Summit was first contacted by CKE Restaurants, Inc. about a possible acquisition. Based in Anaheim, California, CKE operated, franchised, and licensed a total of 667 Carl Jr.'s fast-food establishments in California, Nevada, Arizona, Oregon, Mexico, and the Pacific Rim. CKE had in 1994 become a holding company for Carl Karcher Enterprises, Inc., which was founded in California in 1966. By September 1995, CKE had offered what Summit considered the best acquisition terms, so Summit's attorneys drew up a draft merger agreement.

Meanwhile, in the fall of 1995, Summit was approached by another firm interested in acquiring the struggling restaurant chain. Stella Bella Corporation, USA, a coffee company based in San Diego, offered $7.25 per share to purchase Summit, but Summit turned down this and another Stella Bella offer a few months later. These failed attempts were significant, or at least quite interesting, because Stella Bella's president was Jack Broberg, JB's founder who had served as its chairman, president, and CEO until he retired in 1987. However, he was still a member of Summit's board of directors at the time of Stella Bella's attempted acquisition.

The CKE-Summit negotiations continued in 1996, and after Summit's stockholders approved an agreement at a special meeting in Salt Lake City on July 12, 1996, the merger was complete. Summit's stockholders received cash and CKE common stock after the merger.

CKE intended to gradually sell the HomeTown Buffet restaurants in order to raise cash to expand the Galaxy Diner units. CKE's chairman and CEO, William P. Foley, II, felt that Galaxy Diners had the potential to be successful, especially in rural areas. CKE also planned to sell or close poorly performing JB's Restaurants and upgrade the more profitable units.

One of the reasons for this merger was to save management expenses of running two firms. So during the negotiations in April 1996, Summit terminated its contracts with President/CEO Don M. McComas and four senior vice-presidents.

With this latest agreement, Summit Family Restaurants' history came full circle. Originally a franchise and part of a larger company, the original JB's Restaurants then became independent, but in 1996 the newly created Summit Family Restaurants again became part of a larger corporation. With CKE's resources and new leadership, Summit gained a chance at long-term success. But the restaurant industry's competitiveness and frequent acquisitions and mergers suggested that Summit's future would hold several challenges.

Further Reading

Berlinski, Peter, ''JB's Big Boys Bear Fruit: 1993 RB Turnaround Profile,'' *Restaurant Business,* January 1, 1983, p. 135.

Carlino, Bill, ''JB's Jumps into On-Premises Bakery Niche,'' *Nation's Restaurant News,* May 13, 1991, p. 7.

——, ''JB's Signs on as Sbarro Franchisee,'' *Nation's Restaurant News,* November 19, 1990, p. 1.

——, ''JB's Reins in Family Dining: Plans to Ride Growing Sbarro, HomeTown Units,'' *Nation's Restaurant News,* October 28, 1991, p. 1.

——, ''JB's Pledges to Develop HomeTown Buffet after CEO Resigns,'' *Nation's Restaurant News,* June 21, 1993, p. 3.

Liddle, Alan, ''IHOP to Acquire 23 JB's Units in Northwest,'' *Nation's Restaurant News,* August 3, 1992, p. 7.

''Marriott Vows to Fight JB's Lawsuit,'' *Nation's Restaurant News,* December 10, 1984, p. 1.

Prewitt, Milford, ''JB's Abandons Sbarro, Refocuses on HomeTown,'' *Nation's Restaurant News,* November 8, 1993, p. 7.

Romeo, Peter J., ''JB's Quits Big Boy: Strikes Out on Own in Wake of Marriott,'' *Nation's Restaurant News,* March 28, 1988, p. 1.

Zuckerman, David, ''J.B.'s Marriott Ink Franchise Deal,'' *Nation's Restaurant News,* February 25, 1985, p. 3.

—David M. Walden

Systems & Computer Technology Corp.

Great Valley Corporate Center
4 County View Road
Malvern, Pennsylvania 19355
U.S.A.
(610) 647-5930
Web site: http://www.sctcorp.com

Public Company
Incorporated: 1968
Employees: 2,200
Sales: $215.3 million (1996)
Stock Exchanges: NASDAQ
SICs: 7372 Prepackaged Software; 7376 Computer
    Facilities Management Services

Systems & Computer Technology Corp. (SCT) provides information-technology services and administrative-application software in the higher-education, local-government, utilities, and manufacturing/distribution markets. These systems operate on networks of desktop computers rather than on mainframes, thereby providing greater flexibility for users. By 1996 almost half of all college students in the United States were enrolled at institutions using SCT software.

Rise to Prominence, 1968–1984

SCT was founded as a consulting firm in November 1968 by 29-year-old Frederick A. Gross and four other young software specialists. Its first product was standardized software products for higher education, such as recordkeeping, registration, the grading of students, and staff payroll. "First we started as consultants," Gross told *Barron's* in 1984. "Then the colleges would ask us to stay." In 1972 the University of Maryland (Baltimore), a new campus, hired SCT to set up and run its total computer operation. The other segment of the company's business was software programs for state and local government. By 1973 it had its first major award, a federal contract as the technical project manager and cosystem/software contractor for

a prototype computer-based municipal information system to be developed in Reading, Pennsylvania.

In its early years SCT based itself in West Chester, Pennsylvania, a Philadelphia suburb. Interviewed in 1973 for *Computerworld,* Gross claimed the company, with 26 employees, was already profitable. "The areas we are in are national priorities: health, safety, law enforcement, education," he said. "By specializing in certain markets, we can communicate in the language of our customers."

In 1979 SCT revised and upgraded its applications software products to run in conjunction with database-management systems sold by such companies as IBM. Its revenues increased from $6.4 million in fiscal 1977 (the year ended September 30, 1977) to $43.8 million in fiscal 1983. Net income grew from $400,000 to $7.8 million during this period, and company headquarters moved to a corporate park in Malvern, another Philadelphia suburb. SCT went public in November 1982, raising about $30 million from the offering of a minority of its common stock at $16.50 a share. The stock reached as high as $38.25 a share the following year.

By this time SCT was the leader in both markets it served. Its client list of colleges and universities, originally confined to the Philadelphia area, now included Ohio State University, the Massachusetts Institute of Technology, and the University of Southern California. Governmental customers included Los Angeles County, Kalamazoo, Michigan, and Charleston County, South Carolina.

SCT had, in mid-1982, 35 contracts of 3 to 10 years for 94 separate clients, with annual fees ranging from about $300,000 to $5 million, to supply Computing Resource Management (CRT) services. Under these contracts SCT took full responsibility for all the client's computer-related activities. Its services included complete staffing and support of computer resources, development and implementation of software and hardware needs, and provision of the necessary technical and maintenance support. SCT was also separately offering its own proprietary software products, which the company typically licensed for a minimum of $110,000, not counting installation and training charges ranging from $170,000 to $200,000. Thirty-three software licensing agreements for 53 separate clients were in effect at this time, and the revenues typically generated operating profit margins of 50 percent or more.

Business boomed for the next two years. By late 1984 the company's higher-education client list had grown to include Harvard, New York, and Temple universities, the universities of Illinois, Pittsburgh, and Texas, and the California Institute of Technology. Its governmental clients now included San Francisco, New Orleans, Peoria, and Lincoln, Nebraska. Its backlog of orders had reached $135 million, and $34 million in cash was in its coffers, with virtually no long-term debt.

Scandal and Aftermath, 1985–1988

The first sign of a scandal that almost proved terminal for SCT became public in December 1984, when the company disclosed that its auditors had raised concerns over the use of licensing fees as revenue in its financial statements. SCT failed to release its annual 10K report to the U.S. Securities and Exchange Commission by the year-end deadline and was suspended by the National Association of Securities Dealers. ''Past management had cooked the books, and it was pretty hefty cooking,'' Gross's successor at SCT later told *OTC Review.* ''There were forged contracts and contracts that did not exist. The auditors became increasingly suspicious in 1984 and staged a midnight raid that found all sorts of bad things.''

In January 1985 Gross, SCT's president and chief executive officer, and Henry G. Simmons, vice-president and acting chief financial officer, resigned as officers and directors. Gross agreed to place his 16-percent stake in the company in a voting trust for three years. Michael J. Emmi was named chairman, president, and chief executive officer in May 1985. Gross and another former executive eventually were convicted on charges of insider trading and inflating the company's earnings in fiscal 1983 and 1984. The company paid $13 million in 1988 to settle a shareholder suit resulting from allegations of inflated earnings.

As soon as the improprieties of SCT management were exposed, the company immediately lost $18 million in business. There were no new accounts in 1986, a year in which SCT lost $14.8 million. A cost analysis of 66 pending contracts revealed that SCT would lose money on 44, and that the company's basic software was obsolete, couldn't be sold, and was written for the wrong hardware. Revenues fell to a low of $37.6 million in fiscal 1988, when the company lost $3.5 million. Emmi, a former General Electric Co. executive, scrapped Gross's freewheeling style in favor of clear chains of command and stronger financial controls. Nevertheless, he had to spend years assuring clients and investors that SCT would survive its difficulties, and during this period the company lost contracts with annual billing of about $31 million. The company's stock fell as low as $1.75 a share in 1988.

Renewed Growth in the 1990s

SCT regained profitability in fiscal 1989, with net income of $4.9 million (of which $1.9 million came from a tax-credit carryover) on revenues of $44.5 million. It began selling its new Banner software modules in 1988 to handle functions in higher education such as enrollment, scheduling, purchasing, and alumni development, and personnel and finance functions for both educational institutions and government bodies. In mid-1989 *OTC Review* called Banner ''so good it is almost selling itself overseas.'' SCT brought its backlog of business to nearly $100 million and in 1990 acquired Moore Cos., a privately held firm providing financial-management systems for government bodies, for cash and stock valued at $8 million.

SCT's revenues reached $65.4 million in fiscal 1991, when it lost $349,000, which occurred because of a $5.1-million charge for a change in accounting methods. In June 1991 the company won its biggest contract to date, a five-year, $42-million pact from George Washington University. It also bought two software units from Philadelphia Suburban Corp. for $3.5 million.

By 1992 SCT had licensed more than 370 Banner systems to over 140 institutions and government jurisdictions. That year the company acquired Dun & Bradstreet Software's Information Associates, Inc. subsidiary for $22.5 million. Information Associates was a leading supplier of administrative software to the higher-education market, with annual revenues of about $30 million. In 1993 SCT won a $35-million contract to manage computing systems in Dallas County, Texas.

By the end of 1993 SCT was again an investor favorite, after reporting revenues of $120.2 million and net earnings of $9.6 million in the fiscal year. Its software was used by 750 colleges and universities, 1,200 city and county governments, and 150 utility companies. The other half of its revenue (compared to 85 percent in 1988) came from managing computer facilities for 37 colleges and universities and local governments. In July 1993 SCT signed a 10-year, $50-million contract with the University of Medicine and Dentistry of New Jersey.

During fiscal 1994 SCT raised its revenues to $148.2 million and its net income to $11.6 million, both records. The following year it purchased Adage Systems International, Inc., a company with about $5 million in annual sales, for a minimum of about $1.7 million in stock. This acquisition gave SCT the Adage software system for manufacturing and distribution companies, a package so comprehensive that only one other company in the world was making one with as many functions. An updated version of Adage, with an easy-to-use graphic interface, was introduced in 1996.

Fiscal 1995 was not a good year for SCT. The company released a customer information-systems product for the utilities industry that analysts called flawed and earned only $3.1 million on revenues of $176.1 million. By contrast, SCT was back on track in fiscal 1996. Revenues increased to $215.3 million and net income to $9.1 million. During fiscal 1996, about 52 percent of SCT's revenues were derived from the higher-education market, about 25 percent from local government, about 18 percent from utilities, and about 5 percent from manufacturing/distribution. Foreign operations represented about eight percent of revenue. The long-term debt was $31.6 million, most of it incurred to purchase Information Associates.

SCT in 1996

SCT's OnSite (information-technology) services in 1996 were designed to assume total or partial control and responsibility of its clients' information resources, generally on a long-term basis. Besides Banner and Adage, its licensed software systems included IA-Plus, designed to meet the administrative computing needs of the higher-education market, and a limited-use Oracle Corp. system, which enabled a client to use Oracle with Banner at significantly lower cost than a full-use Oracle license. SCT's support services to its licensees included installation, training, and systems integration.

SCT occupied three adjacent buildings in the Great Valley Corporate Center in Malvern, two of them owned and one leased. It owned and occupied facilities in Rochester, New York, and Columbia, South Carolina, and leased a facility in Lexington, Kentucky. It also leased sales offices in Irvine and San Diego, California; Reston, Virginia; and Dallas, Texas; and leased office space in Basingstoke and Manchester, England.

Principal Subsidiaries

Adage Systems International (Australia) Pty. Ltd.; Adage Systems International (Europe) B.V.; ASI Australia Holding Co.; SCT Financial Corp.; SCT Government Systems, Inc.; SCT International Limited; SCT International Software & Services, Inc.; SCT Manufacturing & Distribution Systems, Inc.; SCT Property, Inc.; SCT Software & Resource Management Corp.; SCT Technologies (Canada) Inc.; SCT Utility Systems, Inc.; Systems & Computer Technology International S.A.R.L.

Further Reading

Armstrong, Michael W., "SCT Hopes 'Ups' Stay, 'Downs' Stay Away," *Philadelphia Business Journal,* November 18, 1991, p. 3.

Bergsman, Steve, "Systems and Computer Tech: The Turnaround Continues," *OTC Review,* March 1990, pp. 14–15.

Days, Michael, "Two Systems & Computer Officers Quit after Clash with Auditor over Revenue," *Wall Street Journal,* January 29, 1985, p. 18.

Helzner, Jerry, "Going to School," *Barron's,* March 19, 1984, pp. 47–48.

Knox, Andrea, "At SCT, It's Time to Find People," *Philadelphia Inquirer,* December 20, 1993, pp. 1C, 9C.

——, "Software Inspires SCT to Act," *Philadelphia Inquirer,* February 9, 1995, pp. 1C, 5C.

Leonard, Howard J., "Systems & Computer Technology," *Wall Street Transcript,* September 17, 1984, pp. 75257–75258.

Mulqueen, John, "Systems & Computer Tech: Turning Around a Fraud," *OTC Review,* February 1989, pp. 22–23.

——, "Systems & Computer Technology: 'We Have a Hot Product,' " *OTC Review,* July 1989, p. 19.

Myers, Nan, "CEO of the Year: Michael J. Emmi," *Business Philadelphia,* November 1995, p. 57.

"Software Company Says Specialization Key to Its Success," *Computerworld,* February 17, 1973, p. 23.

"Systems & Computer Technology Corp.," *Wall Street Transcript,* February 21, 1983, pp. 68829, 68832.

Wallace, David, "Despite Problems, SCT Pushing Ahead in Industry," *Philadelphia Business Journal,* July 30, 1990, p. 3B.

Wilen, John, "An 'Odd Duck' of Hi Tech Coming Back," *Philadelphia Business Journal,* June 14, 1996, p. 3.

—Robert Halasz

THERMADYNE®

Thermadyne Holding Corporation

101 South Hanley Road, Suite 300
Clayton, Missouri 63105
U.S.A.
(314) 721-5573
Fax: (314) 721-4822

Public Company
Incorporated: 1987
Employees: 3,005
Sales: $439.74 million (1996)
Stock Exchanges: NASDAQ
SICs: 3548 Welding Apparatus; 3549 Metalworking
     Machinery, Not Elsewhere Classified; 6719 Holding
     Companies, Not Elsewhere Classified

Thermadyne Holding Corporation is one of the world's largest suppliers of welding, cutting, and welding safety products. Thermadyne was founded in 1987 by James N. Mills when his company, Mills and Partners, acquired the Pacific Lumber Co. (Palco Industries). The core units of Thermadyne, including Victor Equipment Co., Stoody Co., Tweco Products, and Thermal Dynamics, date back as far as 1913. Each unit offers a different component to the welding industry and contributes a significant portion of the holding company's overall revenues. These units are marketed as brand names and separate divisions, and actually have a higher visibility than the holding company.

Victor Equipment Co.

The oldest portion of Thermadyne is the Victor Equipment Co. It was founded in San Francisco in 1913 by L.W. Stettner after he suffered a serious injury. A welder by trade, Stettner lost an eye during a welding accident, and following recovery, he was determined to design safer welding equipment and accessories.

Stettner was associated with Fred W. Clifford, owner of the Great Western Welding and Cutting Company. At this shop, Stettner began experimenting with many different equipment designs. His designs for welding equipment, cutting torches, and regulators were quickly adopted within the industry, and the welding shop soon became a manufacturer of welding equipment.

Under the name Victor Oxy-Acetylene Welding Equipment Company, Stettner became a leader in innovations and patent awards. These "firsts" included gooseneck nozzles, safety regulators, spiral mixers, water-cooled torches, bent cutting tips, and multiple-flame heating nozzles.

In 1928, the firm's name was shortened to Victor Welding Equipment Company. Two years later, it merged with Kimball Krogh Pump Company, which was founded in 1864, and the new name was shortened further to the Victor Equipment Co., a name still used into the 1990s.

By the 1960s, expansion was necessary, and the company moved its manufacturing from San Francisco to Denton, Texas. In Denton, the company experienced considerable growth, requiring additional plant expansions, fueled in part by the acquisition of Wingaersheck, originators of the Turbotorch air-fuel product line. A second Texas facility was built in Abilene, and the Turbotorch product was moved there. The Turbotorch line continued to be marketed to the public in the 1990s. Victor Equipment Co. was acquired by Palco Industries in the early 1980s, which was later purchased by Thermadyne.

The Stoody Co.

It never hurts to be in the right place at the right time, and that certainly was the case with the Stoody Co. This segment of Thermadyne had its origins in Whittier, California. In 1921, brothers Winston F. and Shelley M. Stoody opened up the Stoody Welding Co. to service the growing farm implement and tractor repair business. Right after opening their storefront, oil was discovered in nearby Santa Fe Springs, and soon a whole new business was born: repairing drill bits from the oil rigs.

But the Stoody brothers were not content to merely repair busted bits. They were convinced there could be a way to make the drill bits more durable, and to stay sharper longer. From their experiments begun in 1922, they developed a technique, called hardfacing, that would stay with the industry for many decades. Hardfacing is the overlaying of metal with a coating of abrasion-resistant alloys via a welding process. This overlay greatly extends the life of the equipment.

Winston and Shelley began applying hardfacing to drill bits, at first called the "Stoody Rod," then later the "Stoody Self-Hardening." They developed the first chromium-manganese alloy for this process. Two years later, they introduced the "Stoodite," a cast welding rod that would become the industry standard for the next 40 years. Their next breakthrough came in 1927, when they perfected the use of borium, a tungsten-carbide material that became one of the hardest commodities ever used.

With its success in alloy innovations, the Stoody Co. continued to pursue other metal combinations. During the 1930s and 1940s, the company expanded its product line of metal coatings to a wide variety of industries. In 1946, Stoody developed the industry's first application for submerged arc processing for hardfacing various types of equipment parts. By the 1950s, the company had a large line of long-wearing castings that had gained wide acceptance. In 1979, Stoody was acquired by Palco Industries, and six years later, Palco sold it to Polaris, a large metallurgical company. In 1988, Thermadyne acquired the Stoody Co.

Tweco Co.

Another key component of Thermadyne is the Tweco product line. Tweco stands for Townsend Welding Equipment Co., and was started in the basement of Ray Townsend, of Wichita, Kansas, in 1936. Townsend was known for his innovation called the "Redhead Ground Clamp," which was inspired by his belief that better ground connections would result in stronger, longer-lasting welds.

The next year, Townsend officially shortened the company name to Tweco, and launched a national advertising campaign. Growth came quickly for Townsend, as he moved his company out of his basement to its first storefront in 1938, and within a year, he bought some land and built his first factory, which he occupied in 1940.

World War II provided a boon for Tweco, as the demand for ships, tanks and armaments necessitated a huge supply of arc welding products. The product line included both metallic and carbon electrode holders (the part of the welding equipment held by the operator when welding.) He introduced "quick connect" type cable connectors. Truly, his advertising slogan captured the essence of his business: "If it goes on the end of a welding cable, Tweco makes it."

Prosperity continued following the war, and in 1950, he moved to a new manufacturing facility in Wichita. Although Tweco had always been an innovator, no inventions were more important than two introduced in the late 1960s. Tweco showed off its new MIG gun, a process using metal inert gas and electrodes for a faster weld, at the 1969 American Welding Society show. The firm also introduced a patented coaxial product called "Cablehoz." This innovation combined the power cable, control wires, and gas hose into a single cable. With these two new products, Tweco was propelled to the top as a leader in the industry. The company's growth spiraled, and soon it built its present-day facilities covering 188,000 square feet on a 21-acre tract in Wichita. The company has since sold more than 2,000,000 MIG guns, as well as cable, welding holders and other accessories. In 1981, Tweco was acquired by Palco Industries, which was purchased by Thermadyne in 1987.

Thermal Dynamics

Thermadyne is a leader in the area of plasma cutting and plasma welding, and its strength comes from its Thermal Dynamics unit. Plasma cutting is a method of using ionized-heated gas to cut materials, which is hotter and faster than the traditional usage of oxy-fuel technology.

Thermal Dynamics was started by two professors, James Browning and Merle Thorpe, from the Thayer School of Engineering at Dartmouth College in Hanover, New Hampshire. The two men developed the plasma torch in 1957 after experimenting with a high-temperature electric-arc torch. They started their business in a garage in Wilder, Vermont.

By 1960, sales of plasma cutting equipment had reached $1 million, and Browning and Thorpe moved the company to a plant in Lebanon, New Hampshire. The company became involved with NASA's Mercury space program, building systems that were used to simulate re-entry conditions. The firm continued its association with NASA through other early space programs.

Browning was founder and chairman of the company through 1968, when he sold his interest. Bradley Dewey Jr. then became chairman and CEO, and guided the company through its continued development of plasma cutting techniques. Dewey experienced catastrophe shortly after the purchase, as a huge fire destroyed the plant. Scrambling to keep the company together, he operated out of an abandoned automobile dealership in Vermont until the company could build a new plant in West Lebanon, New Hampshire, where it continued to produce equipment into the 1990s.

Dewey felt the market would eagerly support smaller equipment, and he began to focus research efforts in that direction. The move paid off, as in 1970, the company introduced the PAK 40, a 400-amp cutting system. Downsizing units seemed to be popular, so two years later, Thermal Dynamics introduced the PAK 20, a low-amp unit that was considered very affordable, and five years later brought out the PAK 10, the first plasma cutting unit that did not require a water-cooled torch.

These innovations made the company a popular purchasing target, and in 1977, it was acquired by Palco Industries. After Thermadyne acquired Palco in 1987, the company continued its trend toward smaller, more affordable plasma cutting units. In the early 1990s, Thermal Dynamics created a revolutionary product called the Stak Pak, the industry's first modular plasma cutting system.

Thermadyne's Formation

Although Thermadyne Holding Corporation has a relatively short history, it does not lack in the areas of growth and acquisition. Thermadyne started as a privately held company, with the expressed purpose of targeting other industrial companies for acquisition through leveraged buyouts (LBOs). When Mills and Partners purchased the Pacific Lumber Company, Palco owned Victor Equipment Co., Tweco Products, Thermal Dynamics, and Coyne Cylinder. The latter company was divested in 1996. Palco was changed to Thermadyne Industries Inc., and Thermadyne Holding Corporation was formed in 1989 to accommodate other diverse acquisitions.

In 1988, Thermadyne acquired the Stoody Co., which had become Stoody-Deloro Stellite through the acquisition of Deloro Stellite by its previous owner. In 1988, Thermadyne also acquired the Materials Applications Groups, known as MAG. From this, the company formed a unit called the "Wear Resistance Unit," which were divisions that produced alloys and coatings to help metal resist wear. As of the late 1980s, the holding company had three main components: 1) welding and cutting equipment; 2) wear resistance products; 3) floorcare products.

The floorcare products unit came about through the acquisition of Clarke Industries in 1986, one of James Mills' first acquisitions. This group manufactured floor buffers, waxers, sanders, and steam cleaners. Clarke Industries was divested in 1996.

Acquisition Campaign in the 1990s

The mid-1990s was a time of great change for Thermadyne. The large debt incurred through acquisitions plus high interest rates forced the company to briefly file for bankruptcy. It emerged several months later as a publicly held firm, trading on the NASDAQ stock exchange beginning in 1994. James Mills stayed active in the company for about another year after that date.

Acquisitions were plentiful in the mid-1990s, including: MECO, maker of gas regulators and other gas equipment; C & G Systems, makers of automated (computer-driven) cutting tables that move large units of metal on the tables to exact locations to be cut; Hard Metal Alloys, a hardfacing manufacturer whose products were merged into the Stoody line; CIGWELD, the top manufacturer in the Australian and the Pacific Rim market of general welding equipment and supplies; and GenSet, an Italian company started in 1974 to build low-power portable generators often used at construction sites.

Thermadyne's net sales reflected its many acquisitions. Revenues for 1992 and 1993, the last two years of its existence as a private company, were $243 million and $248 million, respec-tively. By 1995, net sales jumped to $316 million, and reached nearly $440 million in 1996.

New Focus for Thermadyne Holding Corp.

As the company entered the next century, it announced a new focus—one that is strictly on the welding market. To that end, it announced the divestiture of any companies that no longer fit directly in the welding market. The Deloro Stellite segment of Stoody-Deloro Stellite was put on the market since it was a metal coating unit, according to Randall E. Curran, the company's chairman, president and CEO. However, Thermadyne planned to keep the Stoody Co., which still manufactured hardfacing equipment and consumables, including welding alloys that mixed in with the weld to coat the metal materials. Thermadyne moved Stoody from its Californian roots to a new 180,000 square foot manufacturing facility in Bowling Green, Kentucky.

So the company that had three distinct operating units in 1989 trimmed itself down to just one—that being welding and cutting equipment. The various company names continued to be marketed as individual brand names, rather than under the Thermadyne umbrella, as they each had a rich history. When Mills formed Thermadyne, one of the principles was to always purchase a leader in a particular field. Each unit kept its leadership position, and therefore the individual company names continued to be extremely important.

As of 1997, the company "line-up" of businesses and brand names consisted of: Victor Equipment Co., oxy-fuel cutting equipment; Turbotorch, a unit of Victor Equipment Co., producing brazing and soldering materials; MECO, gas regulators; Thermal Dynamics, plasma cutting equipment; Thermal Arc, plasma welding equipment; Tweco, MIG and TIG (tungsten inert gas) welding guns, torches, and accessories; Arcair, a unit of Tweco, making air-carbon arc products, including systems widely used by fire and rescue personnel; Stoody Co., hardfacing equipment and consumables; CIGWELD, general welding and cutting supplies; C & G Systems, automated cutting tables; and GenSet, maker of generators.

As Thermadyne's focus was fixed solely on the welding market, it sought to expand its global position. The purchase of CIGWELD was prompted not only by its leadership position, but it opened the doors to the large Australian and Pacific Rim markets, as well as providing a foothold for entering China and other Asian countries. Focusing on a single market or industry has become the trend for many manufacturers in the 1990s, and Thermadyne Holding Corporation is positioned to hold on to its leadership role through its increasing global presence and marketing strength.

Principal Divisions

Victor Equipment Co.; Tweco; Stoody Co.; Thermal Dynamics; Thermal Arc; C & G Systems; CIGWELD; GenSet, MECO.

Further Reading

Allen, Leslie J., "HHM Group Forms Holding Company," *St. Louis Post-Dispatch,* March 14, 1989, Bus. Sec.

"NWSA 50 Years," Thermadyne and the Stoody Co. Salute the National Welding Supply Association, 1994, p. 50.

"NWSA 50 Years," Thermadyne and Tweco Salute the National Welding Supply Association, 1994, p. 59.

"NWSA 50 Years," Thermadyne and Victor Equipment Co. Salute the National Welding Supply Association, 1994, p. 44.

"NWSA 50 Years," Thermadyne and Thermal Dynamics Salute the National Welding Supply Association, 1994, p. 91.

Steyer, Robert, "TDII Gets OK to Reorganize as Public Firm," *St. Louis Post-Dispatch,* January 19, 1994, Bus. Sec.

"Thermadyne Industries Plan Approved," *St. Louis Post-Dispatch,* April 5, 1989, Bus. Sec.

"Thermadyne's President Gets New Titles, Duties," *St. Louis Post-Dispatch,* February 24, 1995, Bus. Sec.

—Gordon L. Heft

TJ International, Inc.

200 E. Mallard
Boise, Idaho 83706
U.S.A.
(208) 364-3300
Fax: (208) 364-3370
Web site: http://www.stockprofiles.com/tjco.htm

Public Company
Incorporated: 1960 as Trussdeck Corp.
Employees: 3,000
Sales: $577.2 million (1996)
Stock Exchanges: NASDAQ
SICs: 2439 Structural Wood Members, Not Elsewhere
    Classified

TJ International, Inc., through its Trus Joist MacMillan subsidiary, is the world's leading manufacturer of engineered lumber products. Having pioneered this field in the 1960s, TJ continues to hold a 60 percent share of the North American market and has taken the lead in the small, but growing, European and Asian markets as well. TJ's products are meant to replace traditional solid-sawn lumber for joists, trusses, and other areas of both commercial and residential construction. As the supply of old growth trees needed for solid-sawn lumber dwindles, TJ's products offer alternatives that are not only more readily available and more environmentally friendly, but also stronger, more reliable, and less labor intensive.

TJ markets its products to the commercial, residential, and industrial construction sectors. Products include trusses, I-joists for floors and roofs, rim joists, window and door headers, beams, construction columns, window and door cores, concrete forming and support members, and scaffolding planks. The company's products fall under three primary trademarks and technologies. The company markets its laminated veneer lumber under the Microlam trademark. The company pioneered the laminated veneer lumber (LVL) market, in which logs are cut into thin sheets of veneer, which are then dried, graded, and layered together with the grain parallel. This configuration is then processed using adhesives, heat, and pressure to create wood struts with thicknesses of three-quarters of an inch to 3.5 inches, widths from 24 to 48 inches, and lengths of up to 80 feet. The LVL process eliminates the natural defects of wood, such as knots and warping, reducing wastage. The LVL process is also capable of using up to 75 percent of a log. In addition, the struts are manufactured with knockout holes for wiring and piping, reducing construction site labor costs. Under the Parallam trademark, TJ markets its parallel strand lumber (PSL) products. Similar to LVL, PSL clips the veneer sheets taken from a log into five-eighths-inch-wide strands up to eight feet long. The strands are coated with adhesives, then subjected to pressure and microwave heating to cure the adhesives. The resulting billet, or block of lumber, can reach measurements up to 11 inches by 20 inches by 66 feet. The PSL process, which remains closely protected by patents, is capable of using a higher percentage of a log than traditional lumber techniques or LVL. TJ's youngest product line, marketed under the Timber-Strand trademark, uses a proprietary technology called laminated strand lumber (LSL). Unlike LVL and PSL, which typically use logs from larger trees such as pines, LSL uses small, cheaper, and faster-growing aspen, yellow poplars, and other species typically used as pulp logs. In the PSL process, logs are flaked into 12-inch-long strands, which are then coated with adhesives and pressed using steam-injection, which cures the adhesive and adds density to the wood. LSL boards range up to 5.5 inches thick, eight feet wide, and 48 feet long.

TJ's sales are gained primarily through its 51 percent share of Trus Joist MacMillan, a joint venture partnership established in 1991 with Canadian forest products giant MacMillan Bloedel. TJ acts as managing director of Trus Joist MacMillan. In 1996, the company posted sales of $577 million and net earnings of $16 million.

Pioneering Engineered Lumber in 1960

TJ was founded as Trussdeck Corporation by Art Troutner and Harold Thomas in 1960. Thomas provided $8,000 in start-up funds, but it was Troutner who supplied the tools, technology, and the ideas. Troutner, born in 1922, was raised on a farm in Pingree, Idaho, where he displayed a propensity for inventiveness at an early age. Recognizing that Pingree's two-year high school would not provide him with a proper education, Troutner set off for Boise at the age of 13 to live with his grandmother in a boarding house and attend high school in that community of 25,000. After high school, Troutner attended two semesters at Boise Junior College, then joined the Army Air Corps during the Second World War, where he became crew chief for such bombers as the B-17 Flying Fortress and the B-24 Liberator, while also helping to develop the B-29 Super Fortress. After the war, Troutner switched to architecture, receiving a degree in that field from the University of Idaho in 1949. Rather than apply for his architect's license, Troutner sought to combine his engineering skills with his architectural knowledge and his talent for invention. Over the next several decades, Troutner would design some 60 engineering/architectural projects, including the University of Idaho's Kibbie Dome, for which he received the American Society of Civil Engineers' Outstanding Structural Engineering Achievement Award in 1976, placing Troutner in the company of the designers of St. Louis's Gateway Arch, the World Trade Center, JFK International Airport, and the St. Lawrence Seaway.

Troutner and Thomas, a Boise native who studied forestry at the University of Idaho, first met in 1958. Thomas, a travelling wholesale lumber salesman, visited Troutner to sell him lumber for a theater Troutner was building. Instead, Troutner showed Thomas a truss he had been developing during the 1950s. The truss (called a joist when used in floors) featured an open web design, with two-by-fours fastened to overlaid steel tubing. As Troutner told *Forbes:* "It seemed to me there had to be a better way to build roofs and floors. So I invented this truss. It was lighter and it saved me time and money." Troutner had attempted to sell the idea to lumber manufacturers Boise Cascade and Potlatch, but found no takers. Thomas was impressed by the device, but suggested that Troutner was not using the proper glue and pressure to assemble the truss, at which suggestion Troutner threw Thomas out of his office.

Several months later, Thomas returned to Troutner and convinced the inventor to change the glue and pressure. Thomas next attempted to sell the truss to Weyerhaeuser, which turned it down. The two men decided to go into business for themselves, forming the Trussdeck Corporation in 1960 with $8,000 from Thomas matching Troutner's tools and equipment. Trussdeck's first home was in an old barn, which the company rented for $30 a month. Troutner would oversee the manufacturing, while Thomas acted as salesman and manager.

Trussdeck's truss slowly found acceptance from builders and the partners soon needed to expand the company's manufacturing capacity. The company needed capital to fund its growth, but, as a young start-up business with no real assets, was unable to arrange financing from banks. Instead, the partners turned to the growing fast food industry for inspiration and began to franchise the company's technology. Between 1962 and 1964, Trussdeck set up four franchises in different locations. The investors paid for the factory and equipment, which Troutner designed, and the right to use Trussdeck's patent, while Trussdeck took some two-thirds of each newly formed corporation. Investors were also responsible for sales and management of their franchises. Franchising in this way helped the company raise some $425,000. But, over the next several years, the partners found themselves buried in paperwork. Then one of the franchises, in Portland, Oregon, started failing, and Troutner and Thomas had to buy out the franchise and operate it themselves.

Meanwhile, Thomas was finding it difficult to act as the company's CEO and salesman while also running its marketing and finance operations. During the mid-1960s, he made a number of mistakes that slowed the company's growth. "We didn't raise prices fast enough in the boom years 1964–65," Thomas told *Forbes,* "so the company's sales went through the roof, but our margins shrank. Then in the bad years of 1966 and 1969, when demand dropped, we didn't drop prices and got hurt. We just weren't very good managers." Finally, in 1969, the company moved to merge its franchise operations into one company, renamed Trus Joist Corporation. Thomas and Troutner each took 20 percent of the new company, and 40 percent went to its franchise investors; the remaining 20 percent was purchased by private investors for $200,000. Next, Thomas brought in Peter Johnson, who held an MBA from Dartmouth's Amos Tuck School of Business Administration, to help run the company. Johnson started as the company's plant manager in 1968, was named president in 1971, and would help restructure the company to $102 million in sales by the end of that decade.

Trus Joist's revenues had reached $11 million by 1970. By then, however, the company was already finding it difficult to find the quality lumber it needed for its truss and joist products. Troutner went back to the drawing board and invented Microlam, the product that would fuel Trus Joist's growth through the 1970s. Microlam products cost some 50 percent more than traditional wood products, but could provide as much as 33 percent savings in labor costs. Microlam beams could also be made in lengths up to 80 feet, far longer than traditional beams. To bring these messages to the construction industry, Johnson began building Trus Joist's sales force to some 155 salesmen by the end of the decade. Total employment reached 1,000 by 1978, as sales grew to $56 million by 1977, $80 million by 1978, and $102 million by 1979, with net earnings for that year of $7.3 million.

From Vision 200 to Future 500 in the 1980s and 1990s

Johnson, who had also led Trus Joist through its initial public offering in 1973, left the company in 1979. He was replaced as president and COO by Walter Minnick, whose Harvard MBA had led him to work on President Nixon's White House staff, before quitting in disgust after Watergate and joining Trus Joist in 1974. As the 1980s began, however, Trus Joist faced the national recession and a suddenly stagnant building market. Thomas, a self-described penny-pincher (during the 1960s, he had a pay phone installed at the company's plant to cut down on employees' long distance phone charges), led the company into belt-tightening measures that included closing the company's Dubuque, Iowa plant, putting on hold plans to add a third West Coast plant, and cutting 13 percent of its salaried employees and 25 percent of its corporate staff. Executive pay cuts ranging from 5 to 15 percent were instituted as well. The result was an increase in profit margins and continued profitability. Despite a drop in revenues to $82 million in 1980, the company managed to earn $6.6 million.

Sales continued to falter during the early 1980s, dropping to $66 million by 1982, although the company continued to post profits. By 1983, construction picked up again, and the company's sales again began to grow. Meanwhile, the company's cash was building, and soon Trus Joist became an attractive takeover target. To head off that possibility, the company, which posted $96 million in 1984 revenues, developed a plan, dubbed "Vision 200," to double the company's size. Vision 200 proved to be easily attainable: by 1987, the company had increased its manufacturing facility from 13 plants in 1980 to 25 plants, plus 136 sales offices. The company's employee base also more than doubled, reaching 2,600. Revenues increased to $256.9 million, for net earnings of $13 million.

With this growth, Trus Joist next determined to double its size again, formulating its "Future 500" plan, which called for $500 million in annual sales and a spot on the Fortune 500. The first step toward achieving this goal was to diversify the company's operations. Future 500, however, was to prove more difficult to attain than Vision 200.

The company's first diversification move was into energy management systems, which cost Trus Joist some $2.5 million over 18 months in the mid-1980s. Abandoning that direction, in 1987 Trus Joist looked at a new area, acquiring Norco Windows of Hawkins, Wisconsin and Dashwood Industries, of Canada, both of which manufactured wood windows. The acquisitions helped raise annual sales to $351 million by 1989. But then the company, now reorganized as TJ International to include its Trus Joist and Norco subsidiaries, ran into a new recession. Residential housing starts collapsed, and the company's sales sank, to $327 million in 1990 and to $283 million in 1991. By 1991, the company suffered its first-ever loss, of nearly $11 million.

Meanwhile, the company's Trus Joint operation was coming under competitive pressure as other, larger lumber manufacturers, including Boise Cascade and Weyerhaeuser, sought to enter the engineered lumber market, which, given the shrinking old growth supply, was looking more and more attractive. One of these competitors was MacMillan Bloedel, which had spent some $100 million developing its Parallam technology to rival Trus Joist's Microlam. MacMillan, a $3 billion company, sought to expand its engineered lumber division and was considering buying TJ International. Instead, the two companies placed their engineered lumber subsidiaries into a joint venture partnership, named Trus Joist MacMillan. TJ held onto 51 percent of the joint venture, which continued to represent some

three-quarters of its annual sales, as well as maintaining the new company's management and direction. Taking charge of the new subsidiary was Trus Joist alum Tom Demig, as president and chief executive.

As the recession faded, TJ's revenues again began to climb, reaching $400 million in 1983. Its Norco Windows subsidiary was beginning to drag on the company's profits, however, and TJ faced a $8 million loss for the year. In 1994, TJ merged Norco with Oldach Window Corp. of Colorado Springs and SealRite Windows of Lincoln, Nebraska, forming the Outlook Window Partnership, with TJ as majority (64 percent) shareholder. The company's window losses continued, however, and in 1995, TJ discontinued its participation in Outlook.

Meanwhile, Trus Joist was looking at a bright new horizon. Environmental concerns were building pressure on the logging industry, leading to federal restrictions on old growth logging. As lumber resources began to dwindle, Trus Joist's engineered lumber products became more attractive, both in terms of environmental impact and in terms of the narrowing price gap. The addition of MacMillan's Parallam technology and the introduction of the new TimberStrand technology was also helping to enhance the engineered lumber market in general. TJ's sales entered a new growth phase, helped in part by a growing international market, especially in Japan and, more slowly, in Europe. By 1994, the company neared its long-desired $500 million mark (on sales of engineered lumber products). The following year, however, a lumber price drop caused the company's sales to sink back to $485 million. With a $40 million charge for the divestiture of its wood windows division, the company lost $36 million for the year. Minnick left the company that year, following disagreements with the board on the company's future direction. Minnick wanted to continue to diversify TJ, but the board chose to focus on growing the engineered lumber market. Minnick was replaced by Demig.

Under Demig, the company began looking toward expanding its international sales, and it opened sales offices in Japan, Australia, France, England, Belgium, Germany, and the Middle East. Trus Joist also built two new manufacturing plants, an $85 million plant in Buckhanon, West Virginia and a $106 million facility in Hazard, Kentucky. In 1996, the company at last reached its Future 500 goal, jumping to $577 million. With old growth lumber supplies continuing to shrink, TJ could look forward to the next milestone for its engineered lumber products—becoming a $1 billion company.

Principal Subsidiaries

Trus Joint MacMillan (51%).

Further Reading

Bailey, Julie, "Trus Joist Venture Heads Overseas," *Idaho Statesman,* November 5, 1995, p. 1E.

——, "What Does TJI Become?," *Idaho Statesman,* January 5, 1995, p. 5B.

Benoit, Ellen, "The Perils of Penny-Pinching," *Financial World,* October 20, 1987, p. 44.

R.L.F., "Spare That Old Tree!," *Forbes,* January 3, 1994, p. 156.

Galluccio, Nick, "Just a Different Glue," *Forbes,* November 24, 1980, p. 101.

"Knock on Wood," *Forbes,* October 30, 1978, p. 177.

Robertson, Lance, "Beneath TJ International's Wood Products Veneer Lies an Earth Friendly Approach," *Eugene Register-Guard,* May 20, 1993.

Tucker, John, "Boise Firm Grows with the Trees," *Idaho Statesman,* December 19, 1996, p. 5B.

Woodward, Tim, "Trus Joist Founder Still at Drawing Board," *Idaho Statesman,* March 27, 1997, p. 1A.

Yang, Dori Jones, "A Lumberman Goes Against the Grain," *Business Week,* March 29, 1993, p. 52.

—M.L. Cohen

The TJX Companies, Inc.

770 Cochituate Road
Framingham, Massachusetts 01701
U.S.A.
(508) 390-1000
Fax: (508) 390-3635

Public Company
Incorporated: 1962 as Zayre Corp.
Employees: 56,000
Sales: $7 billion (1996)
Stock Exchanges: New York
SICs: 5651 Family Clothing Stores; 5661 Women's
Shoes; 5944 Jewelry, Precious Stones, and Precious
Metals; 5261 Ready-to-Wear Apparel; 5632 Apparel,
Accessories; 5961 Women's Apparel, Mail Order

The TJX Companies, Inc. is the largest off-price apparel retailer in North America. Each of its operating divisions approaches off-price apparel retailing from a different perspective. T.J. Maxx, the largest retailer of its kind in the United States with 578 stores nationwide, offers brand-name family apparel, fine jewelry, house and gift wares, as well as women's shoes and accessories at prices 20 to 60 percent below department store regular prices. Marshall's is the nation's second largest off-price apparel retailer. Acquired by TJX in 1995, Marshall's operates over 450 stores nationwide, offering brand-name family apparel, giftware, domestics, and accessories, as well as shoes for the entire family and a broad assortment of menswear. Winners Apparel Ltd. and T.K. Maxx, each modeled after the T.J. Maxx concept, are leading off-price family apparel chains in Canada and the United Kingdom, respectively. Home-Goods, a chain of off-price home fashion stores, operated 21 stores at the end of 1996, offering giftware, bed and bath accessories, rugs, lamps, and seasonal merchandise.

Company Origins

The TJX Companies, Inc. traces its history to Zayre Corp., parent of the Zayre Store chain of discount department stores incorporated in 1962. The first Zayre—Yiddish for "very good"—store opened in Hyannis, Massachusetts, in 1956. Its founders were two cousins, Stanley and Sumner Feldberg. With sales doubling every second or third year, the Feldbergs were quick to establish new Zayre stores, which numbered more than 200 by the early 1970s. By then, the company had diversified into specialty retailing.

Among Zayre's early acquisitions was the Hit or Miss chain, which opened its first store in Natick, Massachusetts, in 1965. The store flourished and grew into a chain so quickly that within four years it had attracted the attention of a giant by comparison, Zayre. In 1969 Zayre bought the Hit or Miss chain and began its exploration of the upscale off-priced fashion market. Zayre's timing could not have been better. During the recession of the 1970s, Hit or Miss's results climbed so rapidly that Zayre began to think of expanding its off-priced upscale apparel merchandising.

The T.J. Maxx concept was also inspired in part by this recession. Bernard Cammarata, once a buyer himself and the future president and CEO of TJX, was hired by Zayre Corp. to capitalize on the potential for a chain offering off-priced upscale apparel for the whole family. In Auburn, Massachusetts, in March 1977, he opened the first T.J. Maxx.

Within six years of the opening of the first T.J. Maxx store, Zayre had found yet another avenue to the off-priced fashion market. In 1983 Chadwick's of Boston began to sell selected Hit or Miss items through mail-order catalogs. Hit or Miss and Chadwick's crossover operations allowed customers to handle products before ordering, and brought the frequent buyer the convenience of home shopping.

By the mid-1980s off-priced specialty retailing was becoming more important to Zayre. Hit or Miss and T.J. Maxx had brought in just 14 percent of the company's operating income in 1980; by the first half of 1983 these operations were producing nearly 45 percent of income. At the same time, however, Zayre was renovating its discount department stores and expanding its product mix. In 1984 Zayre entered the membership warehouse-club market, launching B.J.'s Wholesale Club, and also acquired Home Club, Inc., a chain of home improvement stores, the following year. While neither of these ventures was immediately profitable, Hit or Miss and T.J. Maxx continued to thrive.

Company Perspectives:

"TJX's staunch commitment to the communities in which we have a corporate and retail presence continues to be a cornerstone of our Company. Through The TJX Foundation and other corporate contributions, our philanthropic efforts center on those organizations that help needy families and children."

By 1986 the number of Hit or Miss stores in the United States had reached 420, and sales had climbed to $300 million. Some 70 percent of its inventory was made up of nationally known brands. The remaining 30 percent consisted of standard apparel, such as turtlenecks and corduroy pants, which were produced by Hit or Miss under its own private label. With such a merchandise mix, Hit or Miss was able to sell current fashion at 20 to 50 percent less than most specialty stores.

In 1986 profits of the Zayre chain, targeting low- to middle-income customers, dropped, although T.J. Maxx, Hit or Miss, and Chadwick's of Boston, targeting mid- to higher-income customers, continued to grow. That year alone, Zayre Corp. opened 35 more T.J. Maxx stores and 31 new Hit or Miss stores. In fact, Zayre Corp.'s off-priced retailing chains were so successful that by 1987 Zayre thought it prudent to organize them under one name and grant them autonomy from the decreasingly prosperous parent company.

TJX Companies is Established and Zayre is Sold

In June 1987 just ten years after its flagship chain, T.J. Maxx, opened its first store, The TJX Companies, Inc. was established as a subsidiary of Zayre. It sold 9.35 million shares of common stock in its initial public offering; Zayre owned 83 percent of the subsidiary.

During this time, Zayre was facing several challenges. In the first half of 1988, Zayre had operating losses of $69 million on sales of $1.4 billion. Observers blamed technological inferiority, poor maintenance, inappropriate pricing, and inventory pileups, and speculated Zayre was ripe for takeover. Throughout all this, subsidiary The TJX Companies continued to yield a profit.

In October 1988 the company decided to focus on TJX. It sold the entire chain of over 400 Zayre Stores to Ames Department Stores, Inc. In exchange, the company received $431.4 million in cash, a receivable note, and what was then valued at $140 million of Ames cumulative senior convertible preferred stock.

The company continued to hone in on its profitable new core business, selling unrelated operations. In June 1989 it spun off its warehouse club division, Waban, Inc., which owned B.J.'s and Home Club. Zayre gave shareholders one share of Waban for each two shares of Zayre they owned, as well as a $3.50 per share cash payment. The same month, the company acquired an outstanding minority interest in TJX. On the day it acquired the minority interest, the company merged with TJX. Later that month, the company changed its name from Zayre Corp. to The

TJX Companies, Inc. The newly named company began trading on the New York Stock Exchange.

The company's transition into an off-priced fashion business was relatively smooth, but the Ames preferred stock it received in the Zayre transaction had been a problem. This preferred stock was not registered and had no active market. While the stock was entitled to six percent annual dividends, Ames had the option of paying the first four semi-annual dividends with more Ames preferred stock rather than cash, an option that Ames exercised for each of the payments it had met. However, the value of Ames preferred stock was dubious, as Ames had been closing stores and experiencing losses.

In April 1990, TJX established a $185 million reserve against its Ames preferred stock and contingent lease liabilities on former Zayre stores as a result of Ames's announcement of continued poor performance. That same month, Ames filed for protection from creditors under Chapter 11 of the U.S. Bankruptcy Code.

The 1990s: Winners and Losers

On a bright note, TJX's operations remained solid. In 1991 T.J. Maxx, by far the company's largest division, posted record results for the 15th consecutive year since it opened. At the end of 1991 T.J. Maxx had 437 stores in 46 states. It planned to open many more stores, focusing primarily on the only scantily penetrated southwestern United States, as well as expanding several existing stores. T.J. Maxx also planned to follow up its success in jewelry and shoes by opening up these respective departments at locations that did not carry these items. It also planned to expand high-performance nonapparel categories, such as giftware and domestic items. T.J. Maxx also embarked on an effort to enlarge a number of stores to a larger format ranging from 30,000 to 40,000 square feet. This change facilitated expansion of all departments, especially giftware and housewares, as well as other nonapparel categories. T.J. Maxx opened 21 stores during 1996 and closed 30. The store recorded excellent sales in 1996, which increased five percent over the previous year.

The purchase of Marshalls from the Melville Corp. brought TJX a prize to complement T.J. Maxx. The immediate plan called for closing certain underperforming T.J. Maxx and Marshalls stores. Marshalls opened 11 stores in 1996 and closed 53. Sales at Marshalls rose ten percent in 1996. Fifteen openings and 50 closings were planned for 1997; more were not expected, since many of the existing stores had performed so well. TJX credited this success with its back-to-basics approach. The prior Marshall ownership had strayed from off-price strategies, so TJX refocused the business. It emphasized nonpromotional marketing, quality brand names at low prices, and timely markdowns—to draw customers back and strongly.

Success at T.J Maxx and Marshalls hinged on execution of the off-price concept, which demanded rapid inventory turnover at the store level. "Opportunistic buying" was done "in season," that is, close to customer need. Merchandise moved into warehouses and out to stores through state-of-the-art distribution centers and sophisticated inventory tracking systems. In effect, each of the 1,000-plus stores received two shipments of merchandise with a total of 10,000 items. Markdowns also played a major role, adding value for customers and clearing shelves. Despite the similarities in operations, TJX was determined that T.J. Maxx and Marshalls retain distinct identities.

TJX ventured into Canada in 1990 to acquire the five-store Winners Apparel Ltd. chain. Building on the off-price concept, similar to that of T.J. Maxx, Winners opened 13 stores in 1996, bringing its total to 65. Moreover, Winners planned on opening about 13 more stores in 1997. TJX viewed Winners as a meaningful way to expand over the next several years—about 12 new stores per year for the next several years. In fact, store sales posted an increase of 13 percent in 1996, plus an increase in operating income of 114 percent.

T.K. Maxx, also inspired by the T.J. Maxx concept, caught on in the United Kingdom in 1996. Comparable store sales increased by 30 percent, outperforming any predicted sales figures. This move abroad proved that further expansion was key to TJX's growth strategy.

Not all the news among TJX holdings was good. Despite concerted efforts to bolster merchandise assortment and value, sales at TJX's HomeGoods stores flagged. Moreover, Hit or Miss had a difficult time in the early 1990s, transitioning its business in a recessionary economy. After closing many nonperforming stores and renovating others, TJX sold this women's specialty division in 1995.

In late 1996 the company also sold its Chadwick's of Boston catalog division to Brylane L.P., owner of the Lane Bryant women's fashion chain. Proceeds from the sale totaled about $300 million, plus cash, a note, and certain receivables. The after-tax gain enabled TJX to repay about $500 million of debt, including the debt incurred in relation to the 1995 acquisition of Marshalls. The transaction left TJX with a stronger cash position and in a position of greater flexibility.

Overall, 1996 was a banner year for The TJX Companies. Sales from continuing operations hit $7 billion, up from $4 billion in 1995, fueled largely by the Marshalls acquisition and the economies of scale it allowed TJX to achieve. Focusing on containing expenses in order to pass greater values on to the customer and thereby increase sales volume, TJX expected to see continued earnings growth as the 20th century drew to a close. At the same time, the T.K. Maxx chain in England, planning on expansion onto the European Continent, represented another encouraging prospect for growth.

Principal Divisions

T.J. Maxx; HomeGoods; Marshalls; T.K. Maxx (United Kingdom); Winners Apparel Ltd. (Canada).

Further Reading

Mammarella, James, "TJX Diversifies, Adapts and Survives" *Discount Store News,* February 20, 1995, pp. 19–20.
Smith, Geoffrey, "Can TJX Turn Off-Price On?" *Business Week,* October 30, 1995, p. 44.
"T.J. Maxx/Marshalls Upsets Marketplace," *Discount Store News,* January 1, 1996, p. 3.
"TJX Adjusting Well to its Megachain Size," *Discount Store News,* June 17, 1996, p. 1

—Maya Sahafi
—updated by Catherine Hamrick

Town & Country Corporation

25 Union Street
Chelsea, Massachusetts
U.S.A.
(617) 884-8500
Fax: (617) 889-1473

Public Company
Incorporated: 1955 as Town & Country Jewelry
   Manufacturing Corporation
Employees: 2,200
Sales: $250.58 million (1996)
Stock Exchanges: American
SICs: 3911 Jewelry & Precious Metal

Town & Country Corporation is a noted designer, manufacturer, and marketer of fine jewelry. Some of its best known products include scholastic items, such as class rings and trophies; licensed sports commemoratives; and bracelets and charms. From its beginnings in 1955 as a tiny enterprise created by a teenager, Town & Country grew to become one of the nation's largest jewelry producers, with operations in the United States, the Caribbean, Hong Kong, and Bangkok. Following a period of expansion through acquisition in the late 1980s, when Town & Country purchased jewelry manufacturers Gold Lance Inc. and the L.G. Balfour Company, the company was in the late 1990s selling off such secondary interests, in an attempt to refocus its operations on the fine jewelry business and return to profitability.

Origins and Early History

Company founder C. William Carey, the son of a meatcutter, was 17 years old in 1955, sweeping floors in his uncle's jewelry store and studying jewelry repair and design at Boston's North Bennet Street Industrial School. During this time, based on his observations at his uncle's store, he came up with an idea for a start-up company: a wholesale company selling boys' silver rings and other jewelry under a unique system, a precursor to modern "just-in-time marketing" that monitored inventory by telephone in order to prevent overstocking. Armed with this idea, enumerated in a looseleaf notebook, and $500 in savings, Carey approached local banks and attempted to get a loan. He eventually persuaded a bank in his home town of Malden, Massachusetts, to loan him $25,000 in start-up capital, a loan for which his mother had to cosign. With this money in hand, Carey launched the Town & Country Jewelry Manufacturing Corporation and began his four-decade-long leadership of what would become one of the nation's leading jewelry suppliers and producers.

With profits unabated and a growing number of retailers comprising his clientele, Carey's operations expanded considerably and sales reached the million-dollar mark by 1960. At that time, because it had become impossible to buy enough inventory from independent manufacturers to fill his needs, Carey purchased a small New York jewelry manufacturing business and opened a factory in a Manhattan loft. This was the first in a series of many acquisitions to be made during Carey's leadership.

By 1972, sales had jumped to $5 million. Carey decided that it was time for his company to go public. However, the economic recession of the early 1970s would stall Carey's dreams of a public offering for several years. In the meantime, Carey began to travel to other countries in order to identify likely prospects for acquisition and expansion. He often personally visited international prospects and others within the United States, rather than relying on investment advisors. Moreover, unlike many executives of the time, he preferred friendly acquisitions in which existing management and employees were retained whenever possible. Town & Country's first international venture was launched in 1973, when the company built a plant in Hong Kong and began sales in Japan and other Pacific Rim countries through its subsidiary Anju Jewelry Ltd.

Rapid Expansion in the 1980s

Carey was travelling in the Caribbean in 1980 when he noticed a high-end retail chain of jewelry stores known as Little Switzerland, which catered to wealthy tourists. Convinced that the growing cruise ship business would make these shops a true gold mine, he went to the home of the chain's owner and persuaded him to sell him the business. Carey's instinct proved

---

Company Perspectives:

"The linchpin connecting everything we do is a well-designed, exciting array of fine jewelry to differentiate us from our competition and deliver a reasonable return to the Company. Our mission is to become the industry resource of choice for the product categories we manufacture, offering fine jewelry with broad consumer appeal. . . . Managing better, using our strengths and resources more intelligently, designing to create demand and, above all, providing superior customer service—these are the fundamentals that we believe will lead Town & Country to profitability."

---

correct, and within the next ten years sales at Little Switzerland grew from $5 million to $55 million.

In 1985 Town & Country finally went public, and then a rapid series of acquisitions and expansion began. A new subsidiary, Essex International Ltd., was established in 1985 to manufacture jewelry in Bangkok, Thailand, where labor costs were cheaper and the import-export trade was strongly encouraged. In the same year Town & Country purchased Gold Lance Inc. of Houston, thus entering the world of class ring manufacturing. The company then acquired another Texas company, Dallas-based Verilyte Gold, Inc., which added etched-gold jewelry to the Town & Country product line. By 1987 Little Switzerland had grown to a chain of 18 stores throughout the Caribbean (with ten more stores planned in 1996) and had acquired exclusive rights to sell Rolex watches in duty-free ports there.

Town & Country rounded off the 1980s with three major activities. First, it changed its name from Town & Country Jewelry Manufacturing Corporation to Town & Country Corporation in 1988, a change intended to reflect the broader range of the company's business and to anticipate its future growth. Second, the company acquired Feature Enterprises Inc., the nation's largest manufacturer of fashion diamond bridal ring sets. Finally, in the same busy year, Town & Country announced the acquisition of the L.G. Balfour Company, a major producer of jewelry and awards for corporations, plus high school, college, and championship sports rings. Just prior to the acquisition, Balfour had been awarded a three-year, $20 million contract with AT&T, said to be the largest corporate recognition program on record. With these acquisitions, financed by sales of $100 million raised through the sale of junk bonds, Town & Country hoped to double its annual sales from the $150 million figure reported for fiscal 1988. Town & Country was named the number one Massachusetts business of 1990 by Boston's leading newspaper.

However, for the first time Town & Country may have taken on more than it bargained for. In fiscal 1989 the company reported the first earnings drop in its history, and its stock fell sharply after this announcement. CEO Carey attributed this drop to weak sales at the newly-acquired Feature Enterprises and to operational disorganization at Balfour prior to its acquisition. The interest payments alone on its debt had soared to $23 million per year. Town & Country's management started talking about focusing on making its existing activities more profitable, rather than making further acquisitions.

The 1990s: Resizing the Corporation

At the onset of the 1990s, Town & Country was faced with financial challenges unknown in its earlier years. Carey, still heading the company, launched a strategy of consolidating operations, along with introducing licensed sports and celebrity jewelry products. In 1992, faced with actual losses and not just a drop in earnings, Carey announced consolidation of the Feature, Town & Country, and Verilyte domestic jewelry lines into a single Fine Jewelry Group, located at the company headquarters in Chelsea, Massachusetts.

A great deal of effort was put into marketing new products at the shaky Balfour subsidiary. The corporate awards and recognition program that had initially seemed so promising was terminated. In 1992 Balfour introduced a limited edition "commemorative" class ring and other jewelry based on the hugely popular television series, "Beverly Hills 90210." In 1994, Balfour also became the official licensee for Indianapolis 500 commemorative items (rings, belt buckles, plaques and desk ornaments) and for the newly-created Brickyard 400 stock car event. A ring honoring Richard Petty, the "King of Stock Car Racing," was designed as part of this new product line. Other new sports-related products were in the works, including 1996 Olympics commemorative pins and a commemorative flip coin to honor the National Football League's 75th anniversary.

At that time, Balfour was operating out of an antiquated plant in southeastern Massachusetts, and a modern facility was built nearby to accommodate the anticipated growth in business from licensed sports products. As usual, Carey had attempted to keep the current work force, and he was apologetic for having to build the plant in adjoining North Attleboro, rather than in the original plant's city of Attleboro.

Unfortunately, circumstances conspired to make the changes at Balfour less than profitable. Although sales at Town & Country rose in the early 1990s, severe losses ($47.3 million) were incurred in fiscal 1993 and only minimal profits were realized ($3.1 million) in fiscal 1994. Moreover, Zale Corporation, for many years Town & Country's largest customer, filed for bankruptcy reorganization in the early 1990s. Town & Country then began working to reach a final settlement of its claims against Zale's remaining assets, claims that were not finally resolved until fiscal 1996. While Balfour's scholastic division continued to be financially solid, sales of the newly-developed sports merchandise were dismal. Carey attributed much of the problem to the unfortunately timed baseball strike and the cancellation of the World Series, which had cooled the public's interest in licensed sports products.

Whatever the reason, investors had cause for great concern as Moody's Investment Service downgraded Town & Country's rating and projected a negative rating outlook for the company through the late 1990s, based largely on the size of its ongoing interest payments. As fiscal 1996 brought another year of losses ($1.87 million), it became clear that major changes were needed in the company's operations.

In his company's 1996 annual report, Carey set out what he saw as Town & Country's focus and direction through the remainder of the 1990s. The main priority was simply to restore profitability, through improved management, new product development, and innovative marketing. Specific strategies were also laid out: identification of cost control and cost cutting companywide; refocusing Balfour on the class ring business and making the licensed sports products a "pay-as-you-go" operation; introducing new technology in the Gold Lance class ring production process for improved delivery; developing more appealing products in the Fine Jewelry Group; and exploring Far East expansion opportunities. Carey noted that the Fine Jewelry Group was under unusual pressure from its commercial customers, who expected price concessions, more liberal return policies, and additional services such as more marketing support and exclusive product designs. All of these demands, if met, would erode profitability for the Group. He also noted the negative impact of lower-priced imported diamond merchandise and the disappointing post-Christmas sales of the prior year. Nevertheless, he believed that, with the changes being instituted as well as the adoption of a very conservative credit policy, Town & Country could become profitable again.

However, after this report was issued, profits in the first three quarters of fiscal 1997 plummeted, and sales also dropped by more than ten percent from the previous year. Even more drastic changes became inevitable, not necessarily in line with the goals expressed by Carey. In December 1996, Town & Country entered into an agreement to sell its Balfour class ring operations to Commemorative Brands Inc. of Texas for approximately $50 million. A month later, Town & Country founder C. William Carey tendered his resignation as chairman and chief executive officer, after over 41 years as the company's leader. Two company directors, William Schwabel and Charles Hill, were named as co-chairs of the board; Schwabel, CEO of Schwabel Corporation (a manufacturer of butane personal care appliances and hardware products), was named acting president as well.

The new company management announced that it was planning to concentrate on improving product design and upgrading the performance of manufacturing subcontractors. Focus was placed on the company's core operation, its fine jewelry business. Within three months after Carey's departure, the Gold Lance retail class ring business was sold for $11 million to Jostens Inc. of Minneapolis, the currently leading company in that segment of the jewelry market. Town & Country also continued the process of privatizing its Essex International operations in Thailand, after initiating a move out of Bangkok to the province of Chiang Mei in 1996, in order to take advantage of lower labor and operating costs. The possible impact on Town & Country's Anju Jewelry subsidiary of the return of Hong Kong to Chinese rule in 1997 was a consideration not publicly addressed by the new management.

A major internal reorganization was completed with the assistance of CSC Index, a management consulting firm. Town & Country reconfigured its product development process in order to bring new products to market more quickly. New teams were organized by product type and were made responsible for customer and market development activities. The company also hoped to reduce customer response time by implementing a customer team approach, in which team members would have varying skills designed to meet customer needs. Schwabel described the company's strategy as "a proven approach to improve customer service and accountability," in which the company "reduced the decision making cycle by eliminating two layers of management." He went on to note that "We expect that our response time in dealing with customers will be positively impacted."

Principal Subsidiaries

Anju Jewelry Ltd. (Hong Kong); Essex International Public Company Ltd. (Bangkok); Town & Country Fine Jewelry Group.

Further Reading

"Balfour Joins the Fast Track as Official Licensee for the INDY 500 and NASCAR's Brickyard 400," *Business Wire,* May 25, 1994.
"Balfour Move to Modern Facility Marks Beginning of New Era for 81-Year-Old Jewelry Giant," *Business Wire,* May 19, 1994.
Davey, Brett, "Balfour to Run Rings Around Sports-Licensing Business," *Providence Business News,* August 1, 1994, p. 9.
Edelman, Lawrence, "For Town & Country, Junk Is as Good as Gold," *Boston Globe,* June 12, 1990, p. 21.
"Jostens Acquires Gold Lance Business from Town & Country," *PR Newswire,* April 21, 1997.
Mehegan, David, "Jewelry King Takes a Little Stumble," *Boston Globe,* June 11, 1989, p. A1.
"Moody's Cuts Town & Country Notes," *Reuters Financial Service,* August 4, 1995.
"The Ring's the Thing," *Time,* May 26, 1997, p. 28.
Slack, Sarah, "Jewels for Chelsea; Town & Country Corp. To Consolidate U.S. Manufacturing Operations in Chelsea, Massachusetts," *Boston Business Journal,* February 10, 1992, p. 2.
Snyder, Sarah, "Chelsea Jewelry Firm to Buy Class Ringmaker, L.G. Balfour," *Boston Globe,* September 17, 1988, p. 12.
"Town & Country Announces Major Realignment of Its Domestic Fine Jewelry Operations," *Business Wire,* February 3, 1992.
"Town & Country Announces Sale of Its Gold Lance Subsidiary," *Business Wire,* April 21, 1997.
"Town & Country Changes Name to Reflect Broad Range of Business," *PR Newswire,* August 1, 1988.
"Town & Country Completes Acquisition of L.G. Balfour Company," *PR Newswire,* November 7, 1988.
"Town & Country's Little Switzerland Opens," *PR Newswire,* November 16, 1987.
"Trendy Becomes Traditional with Official 'Beverly Hills 90210' Class Ring," *PR Newswire,* July 9, 1992.

—Geraldine Azzata

Treadco, Inc.

1101 South 21st Street
Fort Smith, Arkansas 72901
P.O. Box 10048
Fort Smith, Arkansas 72917
U.S.A.
(501) 788-6400
Fax: (501) 788-6486
Web site: http://www.treadco.com

Public Company
Incorporated: 1958 as ABC Treadco, Inc.
Employees: 880
Sales: $144.2 million
Stock Exchanges: NASDAQ
SICs: 7534 Tire Retreading & Repair Shops; 5531
    Automobile & Home Supply Stores

Treadco, Inc. of Fort Smith, Arkansas is the nation's leading independent tire retreader and the country's second largest commercial truck tire dealer. Treadco operates 26 retreading production facilities and 28 facilities for its sales activities. The company owns 22 and leases 32 of these facilities. Treadco serves the South primarily, with the highest concentration of its facilities in Arkansas, Louisiana, and Texas, and facilities in Tennessee, Georgia, Kentucky, Oklahoma, Florida, and Mississippi. The company also serves the Southwest, West, and Midwest markets with facilities in Arizona, Las Vegas, Los Angeles, Missouri, and Columbus, Ohio. Although Treadco leads in truck tire retreading and new truck tire sales, its share of these highly fragmented markets is only 3.4 percent. No single company dominates either market. Of the 16 million retreads produced in the United States in 1996, Treadco sold approximately 570,000; of the 11.6 million new truck tires sold in that year, Treadco sold 399,000. Treadco's sales facilities feature most major brands of new truck tires, including Bridgestone, Michelin, General, Dunlop, and Kumho, among others.

In a difficult 1996, sales of retreaded truck tires slipped below half of Treadco's revenues, representing $62 million of the company's $144 million in revenues for the years, compared with $70.8 million of Treadco's 1995 revenues of $147.9 million. Much of Treadco's difficulty can be attributed to its soured relationship with long-time retread supplier, and that industry's leading supplier, Bandag, Inc. In 1996, Treadco ended its nearly 38-year relationship with Bandag and switched the bulk of its retreading franchises to Oliver Rubber Company, a subsidiary of Standard Products Company and the second largest supplier of retread rubber and related equipment and supplies. Treadco also operates a facility in Las Vegas that uses the Hercules/Cedco precure process, and, in a joint venture with Bridgestone/Firestone, a retreading production facility outside of St. Louis, which uses Bridgestone's Oncor mold-cure retreading system.

Although sales of retreads to the automobile market remain a small part of car tire sales, truck tire retreads generally outpace new truck tire sales. Prices for new truck tires range from $250 to $325 each, depending on their wheel placement; a retreaded truck tire costs from $80 to $110 and offers nearly the same mileage as a new tire. Truck tires are retreaded using one of two major processes: precure and mold cure. The precure process, as used by Bandag and Oliver, is the more widely used process in the United States. The first steps in the retreading production are similar for both retreading types. Used tires, called casings, are inspected both visually and electronically. Tires found to have punctures, ruptures, and other defects are rejected for retreading. Casings that pass the test are then inflated and the remaining tread is removed by buffing. In the precure process, the remaining undercasing is fitted with tread rubber according to the tire's placement—as a steering wheel, drive wheel, or trailer wheel—and then is sealed in a rubber envelope. This assembly is placed in a bonding chamber, which uses heat and air pressure to bond the tread to the undercasing. The mold cure process is more capital intensive. In this process, rubber is extruded onto the casing and is then placed in a mold that will form the tire's tread pattern when subjected to heat. Franchisees generally purchase the equipment and supplies, including tread rubber, from suppliers such as Bandag, Oliver, Bridgestone, and others.

In addition to its retreading and new truck tire sales operations, Treadco offers a variety of services to its customers. These include fleet evaluation and service scheduling, tire pickup and delivery, as well as 24-hour roadside assistance.

None of Treadco's customers accounted for more than two percent of the company's revenues. Former parent Arkansas Best Corporation and its ABF Freight System truck fleet remain Treadco's largest single customers, together representing 1.8 percent of Treadco's 1996 sales.

Treadco has been a publicly traded subsidiary since it was spun off in 1991 from Arkansas Best Corporation. Arkansas Best continues to hold 46 percent of Treadco's stock. Charles Young, son of Arkansas Best's founder, is chairman of Treadco. John R. Myers is Treadco's president and chief executive officer.

A Support Start-up in 1958

Treadco began as a single retreading shop in Little Rock, Arkansas to support Arkansas Best Corporation's growing ABF Freight System truck fleet. The Treadco subsidiary was one of the first shops franchised to use the recently introduced Bandag retreading system, which had been brought to the United States by Bandag's founder, Roy Carver, the previous year. Carver had discovered the retreading technique behind the Bandag system, which uses temperatures cooler than other precure retreading systems, on a trip to Germany in 1957. Carver procured the world rights to the system, which had originally been developed to support German vehicles during the Desert War of World War II. Retreads crafted with the original Bandag system suffered from a series of technical failures and almost sank Bandag. But Bandag continued to develop the technology and had perfected the system by 1962. Based on its retreading system, Bandag went on to become one of the top 1,000 companies in the country.

In 1969, Arkansas Best decided to expand its Treadco operations beyond its own fleet to service other trucking companies in the region. The company set up ABC Treadco as a subsidiary and was granted a second franchise for a plant in Fort Smith, Arkansas. Three years later, Treadco added a third Bandag plant, in Pine Bluff, Arkansas. In that year, the company also began selling new tires. Through the 1970s, the company continued to add retreading production plants, while opening satellite sales offices for sales of new tires as well as retreading services supported by the production facilities. By 1979, the Treadco subsidiary was producing nearly $12 million in revenues for its parent. By 1981, Treadco was operating 14 retreading production plants in several states, including newly opened facilities in Tyler and Beaumont, Texas. Treadco's retreading plants all used the Bandag system, making it the largest Bandag franchised retreader in the country. In that year, Treadco's revenues had grown to $22 million of its parent's $340 million. By then, Bandag's patents had expired and other retreaders had introduced similar, competing retreading systems. But Bandag continued to maintain more than half of the retreading market.

During the 1980s, Treadco continued to expand its facilities. In 1982, the company added a plant in Oklahoma City, and, by 1985, with the addition of three Texas plants, in Victoria, Amarillo, and San Antonio, the company operated a total of 23 plants in eight states. Revenues had continued to grow, to nearly $30 million in 1983 and topping $38 million by 1985. Treadco continued to use the Bandag system exclusively in its plants. The subsidiary was also posting consistent operating profits for

its parent. By 1985, Treadco's operating profit had reached $4 million. The following year, Treadco added three new Bandag production facility franchises and sales offices, in Corpus Christi, Texas and in Joplin and Lafayette, Missouri, bringing the company's total to 26 locations. Revenues increased to $47 million for that year. The following year, sales rose again, to $56 million, for operating profits of nearly $6.4 million. The addition of sales offices in Norcross, Georgia and Pharr, Texas and the construction of a production plant in Lubbock, Texas raised the Treadco chain to 19 production plants and eight sales offices. By then, Treadco was already among the top three tire retreaders in the country. In 1987, the company recapped some 350,000 tires, giving it 2.5 percent of the truck tire retreading market, while selling 135,000 new tires.

Over the next four years, Treadco concentrated on its sales satellites (a production plant could support two or more sales offices), adding 12 sales offices, while also opening four production plants during this period, including one serving the Phoenix, Arizona market. Treadco continued to use the Bandag system exclusively; by 1991, it was producing some 420,000 retreads per year. Meanwhile, Arkansas Best was fighting for survival: in 1988, Treadco's parent became the subject of a hostile takeover by Razorback Acquisitions, which had been formed by a group of Wall Street raiders. Arkansas Best, at the time led by brothers-in-law H.L. Hembree and Robert A. Young, resisted the takeover. When Razorback raised its bid to $24 per share, Arkansas Best sought, and found, a white knight in Kelso, the private merchant banking firm behind the leveraged buyouts of International House of Pancakes and American Standard, among others. Kelso led Arkansas Best's management into a leveraged buyout of $26 per share, thwarting the Razorback takeover. The leveraged buyout, however, left Arkansas Best, for the moment known as Best Holding Corporation, saddled with some $370 million in debt.

Arkansas Best was forced to reorganize, shedding several of its subsidiaries, including its Riverside Furniture and two truckload freight carrier subsidiaries in 1989. By 1991, Arkansas Best, now led by Young after Hembree's retirement, was pared down to its ABF Freight System trucking operation and its Treadco subsidiary. Treadco's 1990 sales had reached $83 million, posting a net income of nearly $1 million.

The War with Bandag in the 1990s

In a move to reduce its debt further, Arkansas Best spun off Treadco as a public company in 1991. Selling 2.5 million shares, Treadco's initial public offering raised $40 million for Arkansas Best, which retained a more than 46 percent interest in its former truck tire sales and retreading business. By then, Treadco had increased its number of locations to 36, including 20 retreading facilities. With an average 1,700 retreads per day and 430,000 retreads per year, Treadco maintained its leadership position as the industry's largest independent tire retreader, and second in the industry overall, behind Goodyear's in-house retreading operation. Treadco had also taken second place among leading new truck tire sellers and was the largest dealer of Bridgestone truck tires in the United States. Treadco continued to be led by James J. Seiter, named president and COO of the public company, and by Young as CEO.

The company continued its steady growth, raising revenues to $99 million in 1992 and to $113 million in 1993. The company's earnings were also steady, reaching $5.3 million and $5.8 million for those years. In October 1993, Treadco moved to expand into a new market, purchasing Trans-World Corp. and its five central Florida-based retreading and sales facilities, which included four Bandag system plants in Jacksonville, Orlando, Ocala, and Sarasota. The Trans-World acquisition raised the number of Treadco facilities to 45, including 26 retread production plants. By 1994, the acquisition's effect on Treadco's revenues was apparent, as sales jumped to $141 million, providing $11.1 million in operating profit and $6.5 million in net income for the year.

Treadco's production plants remained exclusively Bandag franchises, each bound under a separate multiyear agreement. These agreements gave Treadco the non-exclusive right to use the Bandag process, equipment, materials, and trademark, while requiring Treadco to purchase all of its tread rubber and other supplies from Bandag, at Bandag's prices. The agreements allowed Treadco to expand without any territorial restrictions; they did not, however, prevent competing Bandag franchises from operating in the areas Treadco served.

By the mid-1990s, the terms of these agreements, especially Bandag's control of the pricing of supplies, began to wear down Treadco. Over the 18 months between the beginning of 1994 and the middle of 1995, Bandag raised the price of tread rubber three times, for a total increase of nearly ten percent, while also raising the price of bonding cushion, another key ingredient in the retreading process. But Treadco, faced with an increasingly competitive trucking market, found itself unable to pass on the price increases to its customers.

In response, Treadco began looking beyond Bandag for the first time in its history. In April 1995, Treadco opened its first non-Bandag production plant, in Las Vegas, using the Hercules/ Cedco precure system. In that month, also, Treadco announced that it had reached an agreement to form a joint venture with Bridgestone, opening a retreading facility in St. Louis that would bring that company's mold cure process to the United States. Treadco informed Bandag of the new ventures in May, but received no response. As Seiter told *Tire Business,* "As time went on I got the feeling things were not going well with Bandag." In August 1995, Seiter received his answer. Bandag, in a statement saying that the company "believes that consistency and quality can best be delivered by independent tire dealers who are fully committed to the Bandag system," announced that it would not renew the franchises for eight of Treadco's plants that were coming up for renewal in June and July of 1996. Analysts suggested that the move was an attempt to force Treadco to back down from its ventures outside of the Bandag system. The announcement gave Treadco more than enough time, however, to line up a replacement retreading system. In September, Treadco announced that it had signed with Oliver Rubber Company to supply the eight plants with retreading equipment and supplies; the agreement with Oliver also included a provision for Oliver to take over supplying any

additional Treadco plants released from their Bandag agreements in the future.

A war was brewing between Bandag and Treadco. Indeed, one Bandag executive is reported to have donned an Indian headdress and war paint and to have declared war on Treadco at a Bandag sales meeting. By the beginning of October, Bandag informed Treadco that it would not renew the agreements for the remaining 18 Treadco plants unless Treadco agreed to abandon its use of other retreading systems. But Bandag lobbed its biggest salvo at the end of October, when three key Treadco executives, including Seiter, announced that they were leaving Treadco to join Bandag and set up a competing, Ft. Smith-based retreading franchise operation. A legal battle erupted soon after, with Treadco, claiming that Bandag was attempting to destroy its business, including luring away a number of Treadco's largest customers, seeking the court's permission to sever its remaining franchise agreements with Bandag.

Former Treadco Vice-President John R. Myers took over as president and CEO of Treadco in November 1995 and began the process of converting all of Treadco's production operations to Oliver's retreading system, a process that was completed by the end of 1996. Meanwhile, Treadco's Bridgestone-based mold cure plant had come on line by the end of 1995. The effects of the war with Bandag had already begun to show by then, with retreading revenues barely passing sales from the year before, for total revenues of $148 million over 1994's $140 million. By the end of 1996, retread revenues had slumped from nearly $71 million in 1995 to only $62 million; new tire sales formed the largest part of Treadco's sales for the first time, rising to $72.4 million of the company's revenues of $144 million for the year. In addition, Treadco sank into the red for the first time since becoming a public company, posting a net loss of $3.26 million. Nonetheless, with the completion of its plant conversions to the Oliver retreading system, Treadco could once again focus on its leadership position in the retreading industry. In July 1996, Treadco acquired Five Bros. Inc., a retreader with two sales offices and a production plant in Southern California, marking Treadco's entry into the Los Angeles market.

Further Reading

McCarron, Kathy, "Treadco Sues Bandag," *Tire Business,* November 13, 1995, p. 1.

Stewart, D.R., "3 Leave Treadco To Recruit for Rival," *Arkansas Democrat-Gazette,* October 24, 1995, p. 1D.

——, "Tire Scrap Takes Turn into Court," *Arkansas Democrat-Gazette,* November 3, 1995, p. 1D.

Tobler, Christopher, "Treadco, Bandag Fight Over Hiring Practices," *Arkansas Business,* December 11, 1995, p. 21.

Ulrich, Robert J., "The ABC's of Commercial Tire Dealing," *Modern Tire Dealer,* April 1991, p. 29.

——, "Retreading Revolution: Changes at Treadco May Be Far Reaching," *Modern Tire Dealer,* February 1996, p. 37.

Zielasko, Dave, and Kennedy, Gregory James, "Treadco To Lose 8 Bandag Franchises," *Tire Business,* September 4, 1995, p. 1.

—M.L. Cohen

Unitog Co.

1300 Washington Street
Kansas City, Missouri 64105
U.S.A.
(816) 474-7000
Fax: (816) 474-0699

Public Company
Incorporated: 1932
Employees: 4,400
Sales: $261.71 million (1997)
Stock Exchanges: NASDAQ
SICs: 2326 Men's/Boy's Work Clothing; 7213 Linen
   Supply; 7218 Industrial Launderers

Unitog Co. is a leading company in the uniform rental and laundering market, and a large manufacturer of uniforms, garments, and embroidered items. Through an aggressive acquisition campaign in the mid-1990s of nearly two dozen companies—mostly in the uniform rental and laundering service—the company has expanded its rental system locations to nearly 60, to go along with its seven manufacturing plants. It is especially dominant in providing uniforms for bottled beverage companies, the oil industry, and the U.S. Post Office.

Company Origins

Unitog was founded in November 1932 by Arthur Dutton Brookfield, known as A.D. The Great Depression was at its height, and like many companies of that time, its origins were very modest. Brookfield started the company in a small two-room office with a cardboard file cabinet and $3,500 in borrowed money. Brookfield's wife died six months prior following a lengthy illness, leaving him with three small children to feed. He had plenty of motivation to succeed.

The nucleus of Brookfield's idea for Unitog was this: Businesses needed to convey a professional image that would establish a company's identity and quality through well-groomed employees. Unitog would provide one-piece neatly tailored uniforms that would boost employee moral and increase visibility for the company.

Unitog's roots actually dated back to 1929. Brookfield was the vice-president for Cowden Manufacturing Co., a large industrial clothing firm with plants in several states. That year, Brookfield started a separate mail order division, called the Unitog Manufacturing Co., which specialized in one-piece "coveralls." The name Unitog was birthed from Brookfield's background as a former teacher of Latin. Unitog is a derivative of the Latin word "Unus," meaning one, and the Greek word "Toga," a Roman garment.

In 1932, Brookfield landed a huge account for Unitog, the Continental Oil Co. (Conoco). After signing the account, Cowden and Brookfield came to an amicable agreement in which Brookfield would get the Conoco account, purchase the Unitog name for $1, and go into business for himself. Conoco was a cornerstone for the fledgling Unitog during its first decade, and remained a key customer into the 1990s.

Struggling in the 1930s

In the early days, Brookfield could carry the company's inventory in the trunk of his car. He contracted out all of the cutting and sewing to various garment factories in Kansas City. Brookfield's offerings were remarkably small, consisting of just three items: a one-piece coverall, a grease coat for service station attendants, and a cap.

Brookfield continued the mail order method he had pioneered while at Cowden. He instituted a pre-pay policy for all orders, which kept cash flow steady during the lean years. At the time, Brookfield had four employees. One was Don Lockwood, a sweeper and shipping clerk. In the 50th anniversary booklet Unitog published in 1982, Lockwood described the early years: "When we had a $500 day, that was a red-letter occasion. And when we had a $1,000 week, we really hit it big."

During the late 1930s, Unitog's sales reached $500,000 annually, and it had branched out to produce other types of uniforms besides coveralls. During 1938 and 1939, the company scored some large accounts in the automobile dealer field, producing shop coats, white shirts, and work pants for employees in the service departments.

Unitog Becomes a Manufacturer

During Unitog's first decade, it was strictly a sales company, contracting out all manufacturing. However, that changed in 1941. At that time, Brookfield began shopping around for new manufacturers, and he met with Harry Garrison, president of Vitt, Mayes, Garrison Manufacturing Co. in Warrensburg, Missouri. Garrison had a good reputation for manufacturing quality clothing, and quality was a hallmark of Unitog. After the meeting, Garrison proposed a partnership between the two firms, so the Brookfield-Garrison Manufacturing Co. was incorporated that year, an equal partnership. Garrison was in charge of manufacturing, and Brookfield in charge of sales. In later years, Brookfield would take over the entire operation. In the mid-1990s, Unitog's largest uniform manufacturing plant was still located in Warrensburg.

The formation of the Brookfield-Garrison Manufacturing Co. could not have come at a better time. The U.S. entered World War II, and the demand for Army fatigues was tremendous. Brookfield served as head of the textile procurement section of the Mid Central War Resource Board, which proved a tremendous power base. He was also chairman of the Kansas City Union Manufacturers Association and went to Washington D.C. in July 1940 to seek contracts for his group. He came back with a $200,000 award for both his company and competitors H.D. Lee, Burlington, and J.A. Lamy. But Brookfield-Garrison Manufacturing Co. most certainly got its share of the business—20,000 coveralls out of the 62,000 contracted for. It was the first such large award to the textile industry west of Philadelphia.

In all, Brookfield-Garrison manufactured 150,000 fatigue suits and jackets for the defense program during the war. This growth prompted the company to open a second manufacturing facility in Concordia, Missouri. But despite the rush of business from the military, Unitog kept its eye on the civilian market. When the war ended, Unitog still had a solid base from the private sector. This foresight was key to its survival, as evidenced from a letter A.D. wrote to his son Dutton in 1945: "The day before the Japanese surrender, Hercules, the Army and everybody else were pushing us all just as hard as they could for increased production; but the day after, they all wanted to cancel."

Postwar Era

With the war over, Unitog focused on two related industries: automobiles and oil. By 1947, Conoco was still the breadwinner at Unitog, logging $237,600 in orders. However, car dealership business was quickly catching up, with Ford putting in orders worth $114,000, and Chevrolet $93,200. That year was also the first time Unitog surpassed the $1 million sales mark. It was during this time that Unitog landed another major coup; his name was Joe Curtis. Curtis retired from Conoco at the age of 66, and was extremely well known throughout the oil industry. Brookfield and Curtis had been close friends since their college days at the University of Michigan and naturally kept in touch through their business relationship. When Brookfield learned that Curtis was retiring, he immediately offered him a sales position. Curtis initially declined but then quickly became bored with retirement, and when A.D. contacted him 60 days later, he immediately took the offer and reported to work the next day.

At the age of 66, Curtis would start a sales career at Unitog that would last 20 years. He became known as Uncle Joe, and propelled Unitog to record sales. Don Lockwood, the former shipping clerk, by this time was a sales representative, and recalled that Curtis had so many connections, sales orders almost fell in his lap. "His name was like an 'open sesame' to formerly closed doors," Lockwood said.

1952 was a year of major change for Unitog, as A.D.'s son, Dutton, became president of the company. Dutton joined the company in 1939 after his graduation from the University of Missouri. Dutton served during World War II and returned to the company as a road salesman at a pay of $15 per week. He was promoted to sales manager by 1947 and quickly began rising through the ranks. By 1949, he was vice-president. A.D. decided it was time to turn the reins over to his son, so in 1952, A.D. became chairman, and Dutton was appointed president of Unitog and Brookfield Manufacturing. (Garrison retired in 1947, and the company became Brookfield Manufacturing.)

Insiders described A.D. and Dutton's style as night and day. A.D. founded the company during the Great Depression, when penny pinching was a way of life. He carried that throughout the company's prosperity. Dutton, on the other hand, believed in spending a dollar to make a dollar. He didn't mind borrowing money if it meant big payoffs down the road.

Post Office Provides Milestone in 1955

1955 was a year of mixed emotions for the Brookfield family. A.D. died on March 31 from a coronary occlusion while returning from Florida on a passenger train. Fortunately for the company, Dutton was firmly in charge of the company by that time. But 1955 also marked another milestone in Unitog's history: the Post Office announced it would establish a uniform allowance for many of its employees. Postal employees would receive $100 annually, and when multiplied times the 130,000 workers who were eligible, Brookfield immediately saw this as a golden opportunity. However, sales would not be a simple as calling on one person in a corporate office who would order hundreds of uniforms. Each uniform had to be sold directly to each Post Office employee, which required a completely different marketing method. In addition, the Post Office placed very strict requirements on the uniforms, stipulating they must be purchased from a licensed vendor.

To meet these new demands, Dutton Brookfield formed a new corporation in 1956, called Brookfield Uniforms. Dutton also borrowed a page from his father's game plan. Just as A.D. used Joe Curtis to help establish Unitog's presence in the oil industry, Dutton hired retired postal workers as sales representatives for the new Brookfield Uniform. These people immediately had connections to many former co-workers, and were also intimately familiar with the workings of the Post Office. Within four years, Brookfield Uniform had a 40-person sales force, and posted $1 million in sales. In 1961, Brookfield Uniforms and Brookfield Manufacturing were officially merged into Unitog.

1960s Ushers in Rental Services

As the company looks back on its history, no bigger decision was made than in 1960, when the company entered the rental and laundry business. That year the company formed Unitog Rental Services, Inc., and purchased its first industrial rental company, the Oak Park Laundry and Dry Cleaners in Kansas City, Missouri. Although the unit lost money its first three years, Dutton Brookfield was committed to seeing it become profitable. But even Dutton, at the time of the purchase, could not envision that someday the rental section would generate nearly 80 percent of the company's revenues.

In 1963, the company took out its first $1,000,000 loan in order to finance the acquisitions and expenses of the new rental unit. That year the company also developed the patented Transeal, which was a method of transferring company logos to uniforms, rather than sewing them on. In 1964, sales reached $6.5 million, with manufacturing plants in Warrensburg and Clinton, and sales and warehousing in Kansas City, Houston, Los Angeles, Minneapolis, Philadelphia, Portland, Oregon, and Columbus, Ohio.

The 1960s continued as a time of great growth for the firm. Larry Peoples, director of merchandising, recalled that Unitog had expanded its market presence to include soft drink bottlers, brewers, dairy products, and bakeries. "Business was kind of easy then," he was quoted as saying in the company's 50th Anniversary booklet. "We weren't pressured to ask those key questions because sales were increasing 15 percent a year whether we liked it or not," he added.

From 1964 through the early 1970s, additional manufacturing plants opened in Fort Smith, Arkansas, as well as in the Missouri cities of St. Louis, Warsaw, and Plattsburg. Moreover, the rental facilities expanded to Atlanta, San Diego, Santa Monica, Chicago, Toronto, Vancouver, and Montreal.

The 1970s

The 1970s was a time of maturing for the company, as well as taking some venture risks—which didn't all work out. One major change occurred in 1971, when the company went public. The company offered 250,000 shares and raised $2.9 million from the offering. It was during this time that Unitog attempted to establish a large presence in Canada. Unitog Canada Ltd. was formed in 1972, and the company invested $320,000 for a new facility in Vancouver which would house a rental laundry, dry cleaning plant, and a distribution center.

From the beginning, Unitog's entrance in the Canadian market was plagued with problems. Only half of a government financial grant came through, labor problems with unions surfaced, and a strike by Canadian postal workers and airline workers made it extremely difficult to fulfill orders. Salesmen were struggling to deliver orders themselves, but were unable to keep up with the demand. Management changes were instituted in an attempt to save the Canadian unit, but it was to no avail. The Canadian operations were eventually sold in 1977 to John Klymak and Randolph Rolf, the latter at the time a vice-president for Unitog. Rolf rejoined Unitog in 1985, and became president in 1987, then chairman of the board in 1991.

The early 1970s was also a time of maturing for the rental services unit. Although more than a decade old, it was still considered a "step child" compared to the manufacturing unit, and some conflict between the two divisions existed. By 1974, there were eight rental locations, but sales had hit an apex, and there was even discussion within the board that the rental division should be sold, since it was a drain on the company's focus.

However, 1974 was also a year of major change for the manufacturing side, as the oil embargo of the early 1970s was changing the way oil companies did business. Many service stations closed, or were converted to self-service, eliminating the need for uniforms. Sales hit a slump. It was during this time that the company's diversity into the rental business really began to pay off. Ernie Rylander and Jack Leisure were two men credited with building the rental unit into a major contributor to the company's pocketbook. By the mid-1970s, they were shaping the rental division into a major profit center.

The company decided on a course of growth through acquisition, although the price tags began to escalate. In 1978, Unitog bought Clean Rental Services, with operations in Birmingham, Alabama, and Nashville, Tennessee, for $2 million. In 1981, the company made its biggest acquisition, the Nuway Linen and Industrial Rental, in Long Beach, California, for $5 million. By the end of the decade, overall sales reached $50 million.

The decade ended in tragedy. Dutton Brookfield suffered severe injuries in a fire at his vacation home in May 1979 and died two months later at the age of 61. His son, Arthur Dutton Brookfield II, took over as president, the third generation Brookfield. He had started with the company in 1969 as a sales representative in Milwaukee, and had worked his way up the ladder, first as vice-president, then senior vice-president of operations. Like his father, he had been groomed for the position.

Brookfield Era Ends

The 1980s would see the end of the Brookfield family involvement in the business. In 1984, the firm went private, as company managers, including Arthur D. Brookfield II, bought Unitog for $36 million. However, within four years, Brookfield stepped down as vice-chairman, and soon was no longer involved in the operations of the company. As a private company, it continued its acquisition of rental units, and surpassed the $100 million in sales for the first time in its history in 1988. In May 1989, the company went public once again, ending its five-year stint as a private company.

Revenues Double in the 1990s

The 1990s was a time of expansion and contraction for Unitog. It opened its first overseas manufacturing plant in Honduras. Distribution centers were cut from 11 to only four. The Clinton, Missouri, plant was shut down. At a management meeting in 1991, 35 top managers huddled for a brainstorming session, and out of that meeting, two managers suggested their own positions were probably not necessary, and they left the company. But while the manufacturing side was downsizing, the rental side of the business was soaring. Unitog acquired three rental business in 1990, and the price tag for one company alone in 1992 was $30 million. Fiscal 1994 sales rose to $177 million.

During a five-year period in the mid-1990s, the company went on a rampage of acquisitions, completing 23 purchases which had an aggregate $99 million in annual revenues. That boosted fiscal 1997 revenues to $261.71 million, with net earnings of $12.12 million. The company had its strongest presence in the Midwest, portions of the South, and the auto corridor of Michigan, Illinois, Ohio, and Indiana. There were also many rental locations on the West Coast. The rental unit captured 78 percent of Unitog's revenues in fiscal 1997 and had become the dominate sector of the company.

Unitog competed with more than 1,000 other rental companies in the United States, but it was clearly in the top five firms going into the next century. In the mid-1990s CEO Randolph Rolf announced a campaign of additional acquisitions, and those plans, managed wisely, were expected to propel the company to continued strength as a major player in the uniform rental and manufacturing industry.

Further Reading

Bradley, Lenora K., *Unitog: A History of Corporate Growth,* 50th anniversary booklet, Kansas City: Unitog Co., April, 1982, p. 1–26.
Davis, Mark, "Unitog Investors Enjoy Turnaround," *Kansas City Star,* April 23, 1996, p. 27D.
DeAngelo, Dory, "Unitog Dresses America's Workers," All American Buyer's Guide, All American Publishers, Fall 1993, p. 26–28.
Heaster, William R., "Unitog Grows in Face of Changes," *Kansas City Times,* June 14, 1988, p. 7D.
Lee, Don, "Unitog's Reduction of Management Follows a Trend," *Kansas City Star,* September 24, 1991, p. 35E.
——, "Unitog to Sell Stock to Public," *Kansas City Times,* April 8, 1989, p. 1C.
Morgan, Ray, "Unitog to Celebrate Its 50th Birthday," *Kansas City Times,* April 29, 1982, p. 5C.
"Unitog, A Brief History," Unitog Co., April 1997, p. 1
"Unitog Completes Buyout," *Kansas City Star,* May 7, 1984, p. 5A.

—Gordon L. Heft

UPM

UPM-Kymmene Corporation

Snellmaninkatu 13
Post Office Box 203
FIN-00171 Helsinki
Finland
(358) 204 15 111
Fax: (358) 204 15 110
Web site: http://www.upm-kymmene.com

Public Company
Incorporated: 1872 as Kymmene Aktiebolag
Employees: 43,636
Sales: Fmk 51.76 billion (1996)
Stock Exchanges: Helsinki
SICs: 2611 Pulp Mills; 2621 Paper Mills

UPM-Kymmene Corporation, formerly the Kymmene Corporation, is Finland's leading forestry company and Europe's largest papermaking concern. It has 18 paper mills and six pulp mills in Finland, Germany, Britain, and France. The emphasis of the UPM-Kymmene group's operations is on the paper industry. Its chief products are publication and fine papers. The combined capacity of UPM-Kymmene's paper and board divisions was over 7 million metric tons in 1996. The company is Finland's market leader in the wood-based panel (chipboard, fiberboard, and plywood) industry and a major producer in the sawmill industry. UMP-Kymmene is self-sufficient in chemical pulp and derives part of its timber from its own forests.

Kymmene Corporation: From 1873 to the 1980s

The inception of Kymmene Corporation almost 120 years ago reflects the early stages of Finland's paper industry as a whole. The art of making groundwood pulp was discovered in 1846. Axel Wilhelm Wahren, one of the great Finnish industrialists, recognized the potential afforded by hydroelectric power, vast forests, and the proximity of the Russian market and in 1870 leased a section of the largest rapids on the River Kymi flowing through southeast Finland at Kuusankoski. At around the same time Count Carl Robert Mannerheim, father of Finland's military leader and president C.G.E. Mannerheim, pur-

chased an island in the same rapids and part of the riverbank. The founding meeting of Wahren's company, Kymmene Aktiebolag, was held on May 21, 1873. A company by the name of Kuusankoski Aktiebolag, established by Mannerheim, began operating in January 1872. In 1896 a third businessman, Rudolf Elving, purchased the Voikkaa Rapids farther upstream and over the next five years built four paper machines, a groundwood plant, and a sulfite pulp mill.

The founding of three large mills in the same area within a short period of time raised the prices of the local forest lands and timber, while the resulting competition reduced the prices of the end products. The rival enterprises soon became aware of the advantages of joining forces and in 1904 signed an agreement whereby Kymmene bought both the Kuusankoski company and the Voikkaa mill in exchange for shares in the company. The resulting company, the predecessor of today's Kymmene Corporation, was the largest limited company in Finland and the largest papermaker in the Nordic countries.

By the time of the merger, the individual companies had acquired 76,000 hectares of forest, an area that grew as more mergers took place. The purchase of Strömsdal Board Mill—the supplier of groundwood (used in paper manufacturing) to the company's paper mills—in 1915 increased the forest area by 21,000 hectares, and it increased by a further 119,300 with the purchase of the Halla sawmill. Halla also had some inland sawmills, and Kymmene became a major exporter of sawed goods.

During Rudolf Elving's four years as managing director beginning in 1904, Kymmene installed more production machinery than any other firm in Finland to that date. But a disastrous fire at the Voikkaa mill, in which three machines were destroyed, and a slump in prices on the paper market caused a setback from which the company recovered only under its next managing director, Gösta Serlachius.

The building of the railway from Helsinki to St. Petersburg in the early years opened up new prospects for Finnish groundwood, board, and paper on the Russian market. At the outset Kymmene sold goods on commission at certain points in Russia. The sales areas covered by the local agents were extended between 1910 and 1915, and the year 1916 saw the establishment in St. Petersburg of the Kauppaosakeyhtiö Kymmene Aktiebolag trading

company, registered as a Russian limited company, with sales
offices in Moscow, Nizni Novgorod, Rostov, Tiflis, Odessa,
Baku, Samara, St. Petersburg, Krakow, and Kiev.

Serlachius was followed as managing director by Gösta
Björkenheim. By that time World War I had broken out—
initially placing obstacles in the way of deliveries to Russia but
later increasing the demand for paper—Kymmene Corporation's leading position in the Russian paper market attracted
international attention. In October 1916 *The Times* of London,
in an article headed ''A Russian Paper King,'' wrote, ''the joint
stock company Kiummene is now regarded as the biggest
enterprise of the paper industry, not only in Russia, but in all
Europe.'' In 1917 paper exports to Russia were hindered by the
revolution. Lenin's rise to power put an end to private trade.

In the early decades of the 20th century Western Europe was
not regarded as a major market. Exports to the United Kingdom
were begun in the first decade, but the first major agreement, for
2,000 tons, was not signed until 1910.

Research into the potential of Western European markets
began to advance around 1910. That year Rafael Jaatinen, a
correspondence clerk in the company's sales office, traveled to
England to study trading methods. In 1919 the Finnish government sent a trade delegation to Western Europe and North
America. One of its members was Gösta Serlachius. In the
autumn of 1921 Kymmene laid the foundations for its own
export marketing organization. Its first new foreign agency
agreement was made with H. Reeve Angel & Co. of England.

Kymmene was one of the first Finnish companies to make
acquisitions abroad. Fearing that the United Kingdom would
levy customs duties to protect its own paper industry, Kymmene
acquired a majority stake in the Star Paper Mill Co. Ltd., which
had a paper mill at Blackburn. The following year Star took
over Yorkshire Paper Mills Ltd. at Barnsley.

Meanwhile, the company had increased its forest holdings in
Finland. The need to guarantee its supply of timber led Kymmene to purchase Högforsin Tehdas Osakeyhtiö, one of the
largest ironworks in Finland, in 1933. Kymmene Corporation
thus branched out into a completely new field—engineering.

By the end of 1935, Kymmene owned more land than at any
other time until its later mergers with Kaukas and Schauman. In
this year it bought Oy Läskelä Ab, which had 100,000 hectares of
forest and two paper mills, as well as a sulfite pulp mill situated
north of Lake Ladoga. Läskelä's mills and most of its forests
were, however, lost to the Soviet Union during World War II.

During the war the production of sawed timber, pulp, and
paper had to be curtailed to correspond to the reduction in

demand and work force. Some of the company's engineering
capacity was put toward making munitions, and its paper division made utility articles both for the Soviet front and for the
areas behind it. One-third of the war reparations paid by Finland
to the Soviet Union under the terms of the peace treaty ending
World War II consisted of products of the wood-processing
industry. Because of its size, Kymmene was the chief supplier.

The demand for forestry products remained brisk until the
late 1940s, but price controls imposed by the Finnish government at home reduced profitability. The company was also
forced to relinquish about 60,000 hectares, some of it land
expropriated by the Finnish government, for the resettlement of
evacuees from the parts of Karelia ceded to the Soviet Union.
Not until the late 1950s and early 1960s was the company again
in a position to extend its production, with a new newsprint
machine at Voikkaa. A new sulfate pulp mill went on line at
Kuusankoski in 1964.

By 1966 the company was ready to expand its operations
abroad. This time it joined forces with Oy Kaukas Ab to found a
German subsidiary, Nordland Papier. In the latter half of the
1960s, Kymmene was one of the partners in Finland's largest
forest industry project to date, Eurocan Pulp & Paper Ltd., in
British Columbia, Canada.

As one of the suppliers of chlorine for the petrochemical
industry, Kymmene decided to expand its chemical interests in
the late 1960s and early 1970s. The year 1970 also saw the
establishment of Oy Finnish Peroxides Ab—in collaboration
with the U.K. company Laporte Industries Ltd. and Solvay &
Cie S.A. in Belgium—for the manufacture of peroxide.

The output of the paper industry increased together with
expansion into other fields. A large machine making supercalendered paper grades went on stream at Voikkaa in 1968 and
was followed two years later at Kuusankoski by what was at
that time the largest fine-paper mill in Europe. Expansion was
also visible in the restructuring of the organization. In 1969, on
the appointment of Kurt Swanljung as managing director, the
company's industrial operations were divided into seven fields
of production: paper, pulp, conversion, chemicals, metal, sawmill, and board.

Kymmene purchased Soinlahti Sawmill and Brick Works in
1975, and with its subsidiary Star Paper Ltd. it acquired the
majority holding in the French company Papeteries Boucher
S.A. in 1977. The same year also saw the start-up of the
American company Leaf River Forest Products Inc. in Mississippi. There were also plans for building a pulp mill in Mississippi. In 1979 the company reorganized its foreign interests in
the forestry industry by selling its 50 percent holding in Eurocan
Pulp & Paper and buying all the shares in the Wolvercote Paper
Mill at Oxford in England.

By the 1970s Kymmene had steadily upgraded its range of
paper products. In order to establish closer contacts with its
customers and improve its marketing, it decided in 1975 to
resign from the Finnish Paper Mills' Association (Finnpap),
which it had rejoined in 1946 after having left it in 1920. The
main products not covered by its own sales organization were
the newsprint and magazine papers made by the Voikkaa mill.

The company cut down its range of activities in 1981. It discontinued its petrochemical manufacturing because of structural reorganization in the industry, and it closed the Barnsley paper mill, which was unprofitable. An agreement was made with the Great Northern Nekoosa Corporation for the building of a pulp mill in Mississippi (in which Kymmene would have a minority holding). In order to even out fluctuations in the forestry and metal industries, Kymmene at the end of 1982 purchased the majority holding in Strömberg, a company producing electrical equipment. The parent company was renamed the Kymmene-Strömberg Corporation. In mid-1985 Kymmene-Strömberg sold a major part of its engineering division, the Högfors foundry, and closed the Boucher mill in Calais, France.

The first in a chain of mergers resulting in the present Kymmene Corporation took place in 1985, when Kymmene procured 45 percent of the shares in Oy Kaukas Ab. Shareholders of the two companies approved the merger on January 7, 1986. The result was a highly integrated forestry concern. Casimir Ehrnrooth, chairman of the board of Kaukas, was appointed Kymmene-Strömberg's chairman of the board and chief executive officer at the end of 1985, and Fredrik Castrén continued as managing director.

In 1986 the company decided to concentrate exclusively on the forest industry. On June 19 the board of Kymmene-Strömberg approved an agreement selling Strömberg's business operations to ASEA A.B. The company took the name Kymmene Corporation.

Cooperation with Oy Wilh. Schauman Ab became increasingly close in the course of 1986. A Schauman-Kymmene merger was approved in 1987 and came into force in 1988. The company decided to concentrate on two major fields of production, and consequently Kymmene's Juankoski board mill, the printing works in Kouvola, and the self-copying paper mill were sold. The emergence of Kymmene Corporation in the late 1980s as Finland's largest wood-processing enterprise marked the joining of three companies, each dating from the 19th century.

Gösta Björkenheim had been managing director of both Kaukas and Kymmene. He was the son of Robert Björkenheim, the founder, director, and owner of Kaukaan Tehdas Osakeyhtiö—the name under which the Kaukas mill was originally established. Gösta Serlachius, nephew of Schauman's founder Wilhelm Schauman, had taken the helm of Kymmene Corporation at the beginning of this century.

Gösta Björkenheim was one of the first Finnish industrial leaders to recognize the vital need for employers to band together against growing unionism, and he invited the pulp and paper manufacturers to join him in founding an employers' association. Meanwhile, Gösta Serlachius was building up trade relations with the European and U.S. markets. At his suggestion the manufacturers set up three joint sales organizations: the Finnish Pulp Association, Finncell; the Finnish Paper Mills' Association, Finnpap; and the Finnish Paper Agency.

Oy Kaukas Ab: From 1873 to Its 1986 Merger with Kymmene

One of the pioneers in spotting the potential of birch wood was Robert Björkenheim, who had birch in his own forests in southern Finland. Being engaged in the sawmill industry, he saw machine bobbins being made in his father's homeland, Sweden, and went on to Glasgow to pursue the idea further. On February 6, 1873, Björkenheim and three others signed an agreement for the establishment of a bobbin factory at Mäntsälä on the banks of the Kaukas Rapids.

The first bobbin deliveries went to Scotland, where the largest buyer was Clark & Co. The production figures rose, but little profit was made, and it was 1882 before a dividend could be issued. The dwindling birch resources in the timber supply area, combined with the favorable outlook for this industry, prompted the decision to found a new factory near Lappeenranta in 1890. For 20 years the Kaukas mill struggled to produce bobbins before selling out to Hugo Standertskjöld in 1894. Gösta Björkenheim, later to take over the management of Kymmene, was chiefly instrumental in steering the company into clearer waters.

In 1903 Kaukas became a limited company. Gösta Björkenheim suggested that a pulp mill be built to use up the waste timber from the bobbin factory, and the mill began operating in March 1897. The customs duty levied on imported pulp was one reason for Kaukas's decision to build a new sulfite pulp mill in 1904. The first major extensions were carried out in 1912, after which Kaukas was for a time Finland's largest producer of sulfite pulp.

Initially more than half of the pulp was sold to Russia, while the rest went to the domestic market. On the completion of the second mill, it was necessary to look abroad for markets—first to Germany and later to the United States. The years 1895–1914 were a golden era for the bobbin factory. The number of customers rose to 100, but the bulk of production went to large, regular customers in Russia, Germany, Austria, France, England, and Belgium.

In 1916 Kaukas expanded further by buying up all the shares in the Kaltimon Puuhiomo groundwood plant, as well as a considerable area of good forest. Later in the year Kaukas purchased Osakeyhtiö T. & J. Salvesen, thereby acquiring four sawmills and 69,500 hectares of well-stocked forest. The most significant investment in terms of enlarging the company's forest reserves was the purchase of all the shares in Osakeyhtiö Gustaf Cederberg & Co. in 1920, which brought with it 105,000 hectares of forest.

The voice of Jacob von Julin, managing director of Kaukas between the two world wars, was frequently heard on the committees set up on behalf of the industry as a whole to further matters of industrial and economic policy and to boost exports. He was also the chairman of the trade delegation sent by the Finnish government to Western countries in 1919. World War I brought a slump in the bobbin industry, and Kaukas had to look around for other ways of converting timber.

A plywood industry had begun in Finland in 1912, with the start-up of the Jyväskylä mill belonging to Oy Wilh. Schauman Ab, which was later to merge with Kymmene Corporation. The decision to build a plywood mill at Kaukas was made in 1924, and it began production in 1926. The main product was plywood to produce chests for tea, meat, and tobacco transport.

The output of sulfate pulp tripled and that of sulfite pulp quadrupled in the period between the wars. Between 1933 and

1935 the sulfite pulp mill underwent major expansion. As a result of World War I, Kaukas lost many of its forests and timber procurement areas. During this period Kaukas evacuated many of its most valuable machines. The Kaukas bobbin factory was modernized after the war, and the American method was introduced. Production of bobbins came to an end in 1972.

Kaukas's plywood industry underwent modernization, including the addition of about 63,000 cubic meters of space, in the mid-1950s. New lathes and glue presses were installed in the early 1960s. These were followed in the 1970s by peeling and drying lines suitable for making spruce plywood. In the 1970s and 1980s the company placed emphasis on further processing of plywood.

The sawmills at Lappeenranta operated along traditional lines until the 1950s, when work began on a new mill, which would increase capacity to 330,000 cubic meters between 1967 and 1971. In 1977 a further, medium-sized sawmill was bought in the northern timber procurement area at Nurmes.

The pulp market was buoyant after World War II. Later the war in Korea sent raw materials prices skyrocketing. But this was followed by a cost crisis in the Finnish wood-processing industry, the result of fears of impending raw materials shortages and political conflict with the Soviet Union, a major buyer of dissolving pulp used for chemical conversion. The company debated whether to stop manufacturing dissolving pulp altogether, but capital investments brought about a rise in quality and demand.

In the early 1960s the company decided to build a new sulfate pulp mill, which went on line in 1964. With a view to the further development of pulp production, Casimir Ehrnrooth, managing director from 1967, proposed that the sulfite pulp mill be closed down and a second line producing long-fibered pine pulp be built at the sulfate pulp mill. This construction was done in the 1970s, and the mill was extended in two stages in the 1980s.

In order to diversify production, a paper mill was established at Dörpen in the Federal Republic of Germany. On the withdrawal of the Canadian company from the joint venture, its place was taken by Kymmene Corporation. Nordland Papier's first paper machine started up in 1969.

While paper production was starting up in the Federal Republic of Germany, Kaukas began to seek a suitable paper grade to be manufactured from its own bleached sulfate pulp. One of the central figures in the investigations and later in the start-up of production was Harri Piehl, who eventually became chief executive officer of Kymmene Corporation. The choice fell on lightweight coated (LWC) paper, a new type of magazine paper made from pulp, groundwood, and coating. The first production line at the mill started up in 1975 and the second in 1981. The choice of paper grade proved to be right because, with the steady increase in demand, a good price level could be maintained.

Oy Wilh. Schauman Ab: 1873 to the 1988 Kymmene Merger

Schauman, the company that merged with Kymmene in 1989, was likewise founded in the 19th century. Wilhelm Schauman, the founder of Oy Wilh. Schauman Ab, having left his job in a gun factory in St. Petersburg, settled in Pietarsaari and there began processing chicory in 1883.

In 1892 Schauman turned to timber, which soon overtook chicory in importance. In 1895, the year in which his sawmill started up, he started expanding in the Pietarsaari district. He ceased buying his timer ready cut in favor of standing timber. His exports of roundwood timber brought in good profits.

The second sawmill bought by Schauman in 1900 operated for many years at a loss, but his Pietarsaari sugar mill proved to be a profitable investment. His involvement with sugar nevertheless came to an end in 1919 with the merging of Finland's sugar mills.

Having sold its sugar interests, the company concentrated on projects that led to the establishment of what is now a market leader in plywood products. He began with boxboard and later added plywood. The Jyväskylä plywood mill represented a completely new departure. During the early years of World War I, the mill flourished. Sales were good, and profits large. Production in Savonlinna began in 1921, and in 1924 all the shares in a plywood mill at Joensuu were acquired.

Plywood was converted into chair bottoms, furniture, and board, and in 1931 a building joinery department was set up in Jyväskylä. Its main products were interior doors. Blockboard production began in Jyväskylä in 1933 and subsequently moved to Savonlinna. The mills at Jyväskylä, Savonlinna, and Joensuu merged in 1937 to form Oy Wilh. Schauman Ab.

During World War II the proportion of plywood products rose considerably. One of the most important products was a plywood tent for military use. In 1958 a chipboard mill was opened in Jyväskylä, in 1962 Schauman purchased a chipboard mill from Viiala Oy, and in 1969 a chipboard mill, built by Schauman, went into production at Joensuu.

By the early 1990s the company had chipboard mills in Joensuu, Ristiina (Pellos chipboard mill), and Kitee (Puhos chipboard mill). The chipboard mills in Jyväskylä and Viiala were no longer in operation, but Kymmene's subsidiary, Finnish Fiberboard Ltd., had a fiberboard mill in Heinola.

Schauman's second cornerstone was laid with the construction of a sulfite pulp mill in Pietarsaari begun in 1934 by a separate company, Ab Jakobstads Cellulosa-Pietarsaaren Selluloosa Oy. Pulp production doubled in the 1950s. The addition of a sulfate pulp mill, a paper mill, and a paper sack plant in the early 1960s meant a great increase in value-added products.

The next major investment in pulp manufacturing came in the first half of the 1970s, making Schauman the largest producer of market pulp in Finland. The Wisapak sack plant soon became the largest of its kind in Finland, and in 1969 Schauman purchased the Craf'Sac plant in Rouen, France. The establishment of an industrial wrappings unit raised the output considerably. All the former Schauman industrial divisions in Pietarsaari—sawn timer, pulp, paper, and packaging materials—were grouped together to form the Kymmene subsidiary, Wisaforest Oy Ab. The divisions were known as Wisatimber, Wisapulp, Wisapaper, and Wisapak.

Product development and the increase in plywood production continued at a brisk pace beginning in the 1960s. The most important technical innovations were in the field of plywood gluing and the development of a wide range of coated and processed plywood products, as well as the use of spruce as a raw material. Schauman became a world leader in plywood product development and the leading European plywood manufacturer.

Schauman at various points in its history also made furniture, along with more conventional converted panel products. Half a century of joinery production came to an end in 1969. In 1971 Schauman became a producer of large sailing yachts after buying Nautor, a boatyard near the Pietarsaari mills.

Among the advantages of the Kymmene-Kaukas-Schauman merger were greater financing potential and more effective operation and marketing. In order to exploit the advantages of a small company, Kymmene split up its five industrial divisions in Finland in 1990. The registered companies—Kaukas Oy, Kymi Paper Mills Ltd., Wisaforest Oy Ab, and Schauman Wood Oy—became fully owned subsidiaries of Kymmene Corporation. Similar status had already been granted to the subsidiaries abroad: Nordland Papier GmbH, Kymmene France S.A., Kymmene U.K. plc, and Caledonian Paper plc. This last mill project became the first and only one of its kind in the United Kingdom when it began LWC paper production in the spring of 1989. Kymmene U.K. plc's mills at Blackburn and Oxford were sold in the spring of 1990. Expansion through acquisition continued in 1990, when Kymmene bought the large French LWC and newsprint manufacturer Chapelle Darblay S.A.

The 1990s: The Establishment of UPM-Kymmene Corporation

In the early 1990s plans were made to merge Kymmene Corporation and Repola Ltd. The merger was approved by both companies' shareholders and the EU (European Union) Commission, and the two companies operated as a single unit beginning in November 1995. The merger officially took effect in April 1996.

As a result of its merger with Repola Ltd. and its United Paper Mills (UPM) subsidiary, Kymmene changed its name to UPM-Kymmene Corporation. On May 2, 1996, it began trading shares on the Helsinki Stock Exchange, but the company decided not to apply for a listing on the London Stock Exchange, opting instead to have its shares listed on the Stock Exchange Automated Quotations International System in London. The companies hoped eventually to save up to Fmk 2 billion in transportation, logistics, timber procurement, and sales as a result of the merger. Combined products of the merged companies made it the largest paper producer in Europe, with a capacity of over 7 million metric tons per year, and the second-largest producer worldwide to the International Paper Co. in the United States.

Shareholders chose Juha Niemala as UPM-Kymmene's president and chief executive officer once the merger was completed. Formerly he had been executive vice-president of UPM. His broad marketing background gave him the advantage over candidates with more substantial experience in the forestry industry. A strategic committee of three forest-industry veterans—Tauno Matomaki, Yrjo Niskanen, and Casimir Ehnrooth—was formed to act as a spending watchdog for the new president, but shareholders took much of its power away at their annual meeting in April 1997. Niemala did not take the shareholders' decision to mean he could go on a spending binge. Instead, he put several large investments on hold, though he continued with plant upgrading where necessary.

In May 1996 the UPM-Kymmene Kaipola plant began upgrading its paper machine number 6 (PM 6), which produced lightweight coated printing paper. Already the fastest and most-efficient machine of its kind, PM 6 produced in 1995 approximately 240,000 metric tons of paper, which amounted to 1,518 meters of paper per second. In July 1996 the company started up paper machine number 8 (PM 8), which produced release paper (used in the production of self-adhesive labels), at its Tervasaari mill in Valkeakoski, in the process increasing the production of release paper to 100,000 metric tons per year. Previously Tervasaari's capacity for release paper was only 55,000 metric tons per year.

In December 1996 UPM-Kymmene and Nokio Corporation each agreed to sell their 50 percent share of the joint venture Finnish Chemicals to Erikem Oy. Finnish Chemicals provided bleaching chemicals to the wood-processing industry. Including this transaction, UPM-Kymmene sold assets totaling Fmk 3.8 billion in 1996.

Principal Subsidiaries

UPM-Kymmene Magazine; UPM-Kymmene Newsprint; UPM Pack; UPM-Kymmene Timber; Schauman Wood Oy; UPM-Kymmene Tervasaari; Raflatac; UPM Stationery; Walkisoft; Oy Nautor Ab; UPM-Kymmene Forest; Rauma Corporation.

Further Reading

Ahvenainen, Jorma, *Paperitehtaista suuryhtiöksi, Kymin Osakeyhtiö vuosina 1918–1939,* Helsinki: Kymin Osakeyhtiö, 1972.
"Finnish Marketing Organizations Dissolve," *Pulp & Paper,* May 1996, p. 21.
Kaukas 1873–1944, Helsinki: Kaukas Oy, 1973.
"Kymmene, Repola Agree to Merger," *Pulp & Paper,* November 1995, p. 17.
Talvi, Veikko, *Kymin Osakeyhtiö-Kymmene Aktiebolag 1872–1972, The Pictorial Centenary Book,* Helsinki: Kymin Osakeyhtiö-Kymmene Aktiebolag, 1972.
——, *Pohjois-Kymenlaakson Teollistuminen, Kymin Osakeyhtiön historia 1872–1917,* Kouvola: Kymin Kymmene Corporation, 1979.
Schybergson, Per, *Juuret metsässä, Schauman 1883–1983,* Helsinki: Oy Wilh. Schauman Ab, 1983.
Standertskjöld, Johan, *Kaukas 1945–1985,* Espoo: Kaukas Oy, 1985.
Tiller, Alan, "Early Riser Reaches Top of the Tree," *The European,* April 17, 1997, p. 32.
"UPM-Kymmene Starts Up World's Largest Release Paper Machine," *Pulp & Paper,* September 1996, p. 29.

—Reijo Virta
updated by Terry Bain

Valhi, Inc.

Three Lincoln Centre
5430 LBJ Freeway
Suite 1700
Dallas, Texas 75240-2697
U.S.A.
(972) 233-1700
Fax: (972) 385-0586

Public Subsidiary of Contran Corporation
Incorporated: 1932
Employees: 7,950
Sales: $1.1 billion (1996)
Stock Exchanges: New York
SICs: 2063 Beet Sugar; 2493 Reconstituted Wood
    Products; 3429 Hardware, Not Elsewhere Classified;
    5812 Eating Places

Valhi, Inc. is one of the least known, but most successful, multinational conglomerates located in the United States. With just less than 8,000 employees, the company has continuing operations in four primary businesses, including component products, chemicals, hazardous waste management, and fast food. Valhi's four operating subsidiaries include: CompX International, Inc., one of the leading American manufacturers of ergonomic office workstation supplies and components, precision ball bearing drawer slides, and mechanical locks; NL Industries, Inc., ranked the fourth largest producer of titanium dioxide pigments in the world in 1996, with a reported 11 percent share of the worldwide sales volume of titanium dioxide pigments; Sybra, Inc. (which spells ''Arby's'' backwards), a franchisee of more than 150 Arby's restaurants in Florida, Texas, Pennsylvania, and Michigan; and Waste Control Specialists LLC, one of the fastest growing firms in the processing, treatment, storage, and disposal of hazardous waste materials in the United States.

Early History

Valhi, Inc. was a sleepy agricultural company with land holdings in California and Louisiana and sales totaling $21 million per year before it was transformed by Harold Clark Simmons into one of the most successful conglomerates within the United States. Simmons is one of those few people who knows how to read a financial report; in 1974 he skillfully negotiated the purchase of Valhi for approximately $8 million, although the assets turned out to be worth more than $100 million. With the purchase of Valhi, Simmons was on his way to becoming a billionaire.

Born in Golden, Texas, about 80 miles east of Dallas, Harold Simmons was raised by his schoolteacher parents in the midst of the Great Depression. Hardened by his experiences on the edge of the notorious dustbowls of the 1930s, Simmons was determined to make his fortune in the world. A lackadaisical student, yet with a photographic memory, he graduated from the University of Texas at Austin with a Bachelor's degree and Master's degree in Economics, and with his Phi Beta Kappa key dangling around his finger.

Following his graduation, Simmons first worked with the FDIC, and later with the Republic National Bank. The young man was less than ingratiating toward his superiors, however, and conflict arose with his boss at Republic National Bank. When Simmons suddenly quit his job, his wife was so distressed that he had thrown away a stable and lucrative future that she moved out of their home and left him with their two young daughters. Not knowing what to do, on a whim he gathered $5,000 of his own money and, with a note for $95,000, he purchased the University Pharmacy located directly across the way from Southern Methodist University.

While he managed the store and flipped burgers, Simmons also found time to read about James Ling, the force behind the famous conglomerate LTV. Impressed with the acquisition strategy that Ling had implemented to make LTV into the giant that it was, Simmons began to copy Ling's *modus operandi*. His first purchase was a 100 percent leveraged buyout for seven drugstores in Waco, Texas, soon followed by the acquisition of

30 more stores in Houston, and another 11 in eastern rural Texas. By the time the 1960s had come to a close, Simmons was managing the equivalent of a Texas oil well.

The Making of a Conglomerate

In 1973, Simmons sold all of his holdings for approximately $50 million to the Jack Eckerd Corporation. With his money, the ambitious but rather careless millionaire began to speculate in the financial services industry. In 1974, Simmons was indicted for mail and securities fraud in relation to one of the insurance companies he had purchased during this time. Although he was found not guilty by the judge, most of his money had been eaten up by court costs or spent in lavish living. As a result, his second wife also left him and, once again, he had two more daughters to take care of. Fortunately, he had learned his lessons well and retained just enough confidence to win control over Valhi, Inc.

After purchasing Valhi in 1974, Simmons established his own holding company, Contran Corporation, which controlled all Valhi's stock, and then began using Valhi to purchase companies. Soon he had the beginnings of a conglomerate. In 1982, he purchased Keystone Consolidated Industries, Inc. for the bargain price of $25 million. Keystone, a Dallas-based manufacturer of steel, wire, and hardware, was plagued with manufacturing cost overruns, labor problems, and disposing of hazardous waste materials. Simmons kept the management of Keystone, but implemented strict cost-cutting measures. Ever the business iconoclast, he also had no qualms about using approximately $15 million of Keystone's employee pension fund in his takeover bid for Amalgamated Sugar Company. Amalgamated Sugar, based in Utah, was a refiner and marketer of sugar and, most important to Simmons, had undervalued assets including $100 million in cash. Although Simmons had violated pension fund regulations and was required by the State Court of Utah to sell the Amalgamated shares owned by the fund, he remained undeterred and bought Amalgamated Sugar for $35 million worth of his own money.

The next major acquisition was NL Industries, a mismanaged firm with oil services and a titanium dioxide business worth more than $2 billion in sales annually. To prevent Simmons's takeover, management at NL Industries devised a poison pill defense that would dilute the shareholders' equity significantly if Simmons attacked and began buying stock. After studying the situation for approximately one-half hour, Simmons concluded that the poison pill of NL Industries was illegal and began buying the company's stock. When a federal judge agreed with Simmons that the poison pill was indeed illegal, Simmons rushed to buy the company the very same day. Upon conclusion of the purchase agreement, Simmons immediately split up the company into Baroid, an oilfield services operation, and NL Industries, Inc., a chemical company.

Although most corporate raiders like Simmons purchased companies for the specific reason of selling off their operating divisions at a higher cost than the value of the entire firm itself, thereby reaping a healthy and quick profit, Simmons himself was not a typical raider. In fact, when he purchased a company, he devoted a good deal of his time and energy into rehabilitating

its operating divisions. After having acquired Keystone Consolidated Industries, it took him seven years to revitalize it. By 1989, Keystone had opened a brand new steel mill worth $50 million, which boosted profits to $12 million on sales of $306 million. The year before, Keystone had reported a $6 million loss on sales of $257 million. Amalgamated Sugar Company was no different. After a hostile and extremely acrimonious takeover battle for control of the company, Simmons turned about face and asked its management to continue on at the company. For nearly eight years he invested more and more money to buy new sugar-processing equipment. After having spent nearly $70 million, productivity increased by 40 percent. Perhaps what is most impressive is that, although sugar prices increased only four percent from 1983 to 1989, Amalgamated Sugar saw its operating income jump to $38 million, a fourfold increase during those same years.

The best example of how Simmons exhibited an uncanny ability to understand and act upon industry basics was his turnaround of NL Industries. After buying the company in 1986, its oilfield services reported a loss of $324 million that same year since its managers had failed to downsize operations during the oil bust. Simmons immediately reorganized it into an independent company, Baroid, sold four units in the oilfield services that were losing money, including a long-standing oilfield equipment rental business, discontinued perks such as private corporate jets for management travel, and refocused on strengthening the company's main product of providing oilfield drilling fluids and measurement services. Finally, Simmons directed Baroid management to develop and introduce as quickly as possible new products to capitalize on the increased demand in horizontal drilling. In 1989, Baroid reported an unheralded increase of its operating income by 66 percent, to more than $30 million.

Simmons's careful and highly methodical analysis of financial statements enabled him to stay far away from the disastrous state of affairs in the oil, real estate, and banking sectors in Texas during the 1980s. By the end of the decade, Valhi owned and operated seven extremely profitable businesses, including NL Industries, which was involved in chemicals production, Baroid, a provider of petroleum services, Amalgamated Sugar, a producer of refined sugar, Medford, Inc., a manufacturer of forest products, Medite Corporation, a fiberboard company, Sybra, a large fast food chain of restaurants, and its Hardware Division, a manufacturer of locks and various metal products. Total revenues for Valhi at the end of fiscal 1989 were reported at $2.2 billion. Simmons had made himself into a billionaire.

The 1990s and Beyond

At the beginning of the 1990s, the trend toward takeovers and leveraged buyouts within the corporate world seemed to have run its course. Junk bonds, one of the ways enormously priced leverage buyouts were arranged throughout the 1980s, had been discredited as a long-term viable business strategy. Unfortunately, Harold Simmons, a man who was at his best during the takeover years, turned ice cold as an investor just when he most needed to infuse Valhi share earnings with another promising acquisition. In fact, during 1991 and 1992,

Simmons saw the value of his stock market holdings decline precipitously, to almost $1 billion in total value.

The one bright spot in his portfolio of companies was NL Industries, one of the country's leaders in the manufacture of titanium dioxide, or TiO2, a specialty chemical used as a brightener in paints, paper, fibers, ceramics, and also on the surface of many consumer appliances. Demand for titanium dioxide was growing at a much faster rate than could be supplied, especially in America where consumers wanted their appliances to have a "clean look." As demand continued to grow during the mid-1990s, NL Industries established its own subsidiary, Kronos, Inc., which constructed four new production facilities in Western Europe and one in Canada. By the end of 1995, Kronos had captured 18 percent of the total market share for titanium dioxide in Europe.

The success of NL Industries was not enough for Simmons, however, and in the mid-1990s he began to sell off companies he had previously purchased, to increase Valhi's liquidity and thereby concentrate on new investment opportunities. The first company to go was Baroid, the oilfield services firm that never reached the level of profitability Simmons desired. Quick to follow was Medite Corporation and Medford, Inc. Selling the fiberboard and lumber companies for $240 million gave Simmons some of the capital to begin looking for new investments. Yet the amount still was not enough to acquire a high quality firm. Consequently, Simmons disposed of Amalgamated Sugar Company for approximately $200 million in a deal with Snake River Sugar Company, an Oregon-based agricultural co-operative.

Satisfied that he had some of the funds needed for new investments, Simmons created Waste Control Specialists in November of 1995, to enter the rapidly growing market for the processing, treatment, storage, and disposal of hazardous waste materials in Texas. Money was provided for the construction of a facility in west Texas, which accepted its first waste materials for disposal in the winter of 1997. In the spring of 1997, Waste Control Specialists applied for authorization to treat, store, and dispose of low-level radioactive waste materials. In addition to the promise of high revenues from Waste Control Specialists, Simmons also reaped rewards from CompX, his components products company, created out of Valhi's Hardware Division. Having captured a well-defined niche market, CompX has grown into the largest supplier of ergonomic office workstation products in North America.

Simmons's fascination with the fast food industry had also run its course by the beginning of 1997. Sybra operated more than 150 Arby's restaurants over a four state area, including Michigan, Texas, Pennsylvania, and Florida. In fact, Sybra was the third biggest franchisee within Arby's operational network. A niche segment in the fast food industry, Arby's sells roast beef sandwiches, chicken sandwiches, and soft drinks. Yet sales increased only two percent from 1995 to 1996, primarily because of the highly competitive nature of the fast food industry. As a result of this disappointing performance, Simmons decided to dispose of his Sybra holdings and sold part of it to ICH Corporation and the remainder to Restaurant Property Master for a total of $84.7 million.

Valhi, Inc. will continue to act as a holding company for Harold Simmons. Simmons seems to be leaning toward a restructuring of Valhi's operations, with selloffs of companies that he has owned for years, and possible replacement firms undergoing intense financial scrutiny. Whether Simmons can keep the magic touch he had during the heyday of the takeover years and lead Valhi back to the preeminence it had during the 1980s still remains to be seen.

Principal Subsidiaries

NL Industries, Inc.; CompX International, Inc.; Waste Control Specialists LLC.

Further Reading

''Agreements Made To Sell Sybra Inc. for $84.7 Million,'' *The Wall Street Journal,* February 13, 1997, p. B8(E).

''Investor Harold Simmons: His Personal Takeover Philosophy,'' *Chemical and Engineering News,* May 28, 1990, pp. 11–15.

Kelly, Kevin, ''If Simmons Boards Lockheed, Can He Fly It?,'' *Business Week,* April 2, 1990, pp. 77–78.

Marcial, Gene, ''Buying a Stake in Harold Simmons,'' *Business Week,* September 22, 1986, p. 88.

Mason, Todd, ''Harold Simmons Is Coming Out To Play Again,'' *Business Week,* January 9, 1989, pp. 44–46.

Rowe Jr., Frederick E., ''The Harold Simmons Bet,'' *Forbes,* August 2, 1993, p. 148.

Serwer, Andrew Evan, ''The Whistling Billionaire,'' *Fortune,* April 10, 1989, pp. 102–106.

''A Takeover Artist Takes on the Teamsters,'' *Business Week,* October 22, 1984, p. 46.

''Valhi Sells Fiberboard Business,'' *The Wall Street Journal,* March 3, 1997, p. A6(E).

—Thomas Derdak

Valmont Industries, Inc.

P.O. Box 358
Valley, Nebraska 68064
U.S.A.
(402) 359-2201
Fax: (402) 343-0668
Web site: http//www.valmont.com

Public Company
Incorporated: 1967
Employees: 4,500
Sales: $644.5 million (1996)
Stock Exchanges: NASDAQ
SICS: 3441 Fabricated Structural Metal; 3523 Farm
    Machinery & Equipment; 3612 Transformers

Valmont Industries, Inc. is recognized as the world's leader in the design and production of mechanized agricultural irrigation equipment. They also lead globally in the manufacturing of a wide variety of metal products, consisting primarily of steel and aluminum poles and towers. Valmont is America's largest producer of lighting and traffic control poles. The company produces towers and structures for communication and utility applications, including various fabricated products for industrial and commercial uses, such as tubing for pneumatic conveyors, health fitness exercise equipment, and heat exchangers for energy generation and textile processing. Valmont operates 18 plants located in eight countries in North and South America, Europe, and Asia, and markets its products in more than 90 countries around the world.

A Post-World War II Investment

The company was founded by a young Marine, Robert B. Daugherty, who returned from World War II to the cornfields near Valley, Nebraska, and invested his life savings in a small farm equipment manufacturing business called Valley Manufacturing Company (renamed Valmont Industries, Inc. in 1967).

By the early 1950s a revolutionary field irrigation invention captured Daugherty's attention. Interested in diversifying his business, Daugherty purchased the patent rights to this unusual sprinkler irrigation contraption, which consisted of a long pipeline mounted on wheels that traveled in a circle and sprinkler-irrigated crops as it was propelled around a field. A small unit could cover an area of a quarter mile and could accommodate the spraying of fertilizers as well as water.

Traditional gravity-flow and flood-irrigation methods were untenable in certain regions of the country, where soil and water conditions were marginal. Land that could not previously be developed could be efficiently farmed with Valmont's rotating spray irrigation/fertilization system, known as a center pivot irrigator, efficiently supplying water and nutrients to the soil and consistently enhancing crop yields.

Along with their linear move irrigation system, which rolls in a straight line along the full length of a field, more than ten million acres of agricultural land would receive water from Valmont's irrigation systems by 1996. Large quantities of pipe were needed to produce the center pivot so the Valmont team began manufacturing it on their own. An outpouring of new applications for their pipe products led to a prominence in two markets: food production and infrastructure development.

Depressed Domestic Farm Market in the Early 1980s

The post World War II years of agricultural boom slowly but steadily gave way to an economic downturn in farming, which had reached a new low by the 1980s. As irrigation equipment was closely tied to the highly volatile agricultural economy, the company was operating $1.9 million in the red by 1985. Adding to the domestic farm depression, orders from the oil-rich Near East dried up as that region became more agriculturally self-sufficient.

Daugherty saw the need for establishing a new sector. Beginning as early as the 1960s machinery had been invented to produce metal tapered light and traffic signal poles for infrastructure development and light poles for outdoor commercial and industrial use. Valmont thus branched out from its core business and began to concentrate efforts on new product devel-

Company Perspectives:

"Valmont is committed to worldwide profitable growth and maximizing shareholder value, through a process of continuous improvement and superior management of capital and human resources. We will focus on agricultural irrigation and electrical construction products, where we have earned leadership positions."

opment and distribution. The company acquired Gate City Steel in 1981, a service center already marketing Valmont products, and by 1986 Gate City had purchased five producers of steel reinforcing bar to accommodate their street, highway, and electrical equipment market. Federal, state, and local governments found that by adding upgraded lighting, more signs and better signals to improve traffic flow, they could sometimes circumvent new road construction projects, increasing the demand for lighting and traffic signal poles.

In 1987 the U.S. Federal Highway Bill began a five-year, $70 million expenditure program, boosting Valmont's position. The company also expanded into producing poles for the transmission and distribution of electrical power and in 1987 paid General Electric $28 million to acquire and add a new subsidiary to its force, renamed Valmont Electric, a fluorescent and specialty lamp ballast business. According to Bill Birchard of *CFO, The Magazine for Senior Financial Executives,* "To enthusiastic Valmont managers in the late 1980s, the notion of diversifying into energy-saving lighting ballasts seemed like a great strategic opportunity, one worth pumping in another $10 million or so of capital to exploit."

Diversification Pays Off Into the 1990s

Discussing his strategy for success in an article in *Investment News & Views,* Daugherty cautioned, "New business development will occur only in those areas where we can capitalize on our existing channels of distribution, market knowledge, and investments." The company attributed much of its success to a dealer network and distribution system which offers its dealers continuous, extensive training in design, installation, and replacement parts.

The formation of another new subsidiary, a computer chain named ValCom demonstrated the creative flexibility of Daugherty's philosophy. Since Valmont already had a sizeable network of farm-equipment retailers, management decided to market IBM and other personal computers to farmers who already used Valmont irrigation systems. While farmers weren't as receptive to the idea as Valmont had hoped, the company did find a market among local businessmen who sought out the machines at local feed shops.

Valmont sold a 26 percent interest in ValCom to the public for $10 million shortly before the 1987 "October Crash." Shares dropped to ten percent below the offering price but by 1988 sales and profits rose about 50 percent, to $164 million and $3.6 million, respectively. By 1988 Valcom had recovered and

rose to rank fourth in the field of marketers of microcomputer hardware and software.

By the late 1980s overall company sales were improving. Daugherty told *Investment News & Views* that "the company enters into 1988 with the largest backlog in its history." Distressed farmers had been dumping used farm equipment on the market, and as the agricultural situation improved the demand grew for new irrigation systems. William Welsh II, the company president reported in May 1988 that gains in sales and profit spanned every major business unit.

Global Expansion and Reorganization in the 1990s

Valmont first entered the European market by acquiring a pole manufacturing company, SERMETO S.A., which held about ten percent of that market in France. In 1991 Valmont added to its holdings Nolte, a pole company in the Netherlands, further broadening their manufacturing capabilities. Near Montreal, Valmont acquired an 80 percent interest in Lampadaires Feralux, Inc., a Canadian manufacturer of aluminum lighting and traffic signal poles for the American market. During this period Valmont also successfully entered new markets in Eastern Europe, Africa, Asia, and South America.

New construction and redevelopment of cities and highways have always been important to the United States and Western European pole business. A severe recession in the commercial construction industry and political problems in the Middle East factored into a poor financial performance for Valmont in 1991. A restructuring charge of approximately $10 million contributed to the fall of Valmont stock into the mid-teens at a time when the stock market composite was booming.

Given also the losses from subsidiary Valmont Electric, CFO Terry J. McClain and CEO Mogens C. Bay decided to find a way to better assess and manage the entire company. McClain told Bill Birchard of *CFO, The Magazine for Senior Financial Executives* that "People were growing earnings, but weren't making the best choices about how and where to grow them. . . . Capital decisions were being made on the basis of too much emotion and too little analysis." Their problem was not with the concept of EVA per se, but in applying the concept to Valmont's particular needs. After extensive five-month discussions with a financial strategy consultant they came up with a unique concept, TVI, which simply computes Valmont's net operating profit after taxes minus a ten percent charge for capital employed. This method of simpler, asset-management emphasis and familiar accounting allowed managers to make better informed decisions, and more easily assess real performance, which worked in conjunction with an incentive program.

The reorganization also necessitated restructuring corporate information systems, as well as the closing of an irrigation manufacturing plant in Spain, moving production processes to lower cost areas (such as the move of Valmont Electric to Texas and Mexico).

Also in 1991 Valmont's successful computerized pivot control panel was improved allowing the farm manager to operate the system from his office, implement irrigation scheduling, and log data such as water applications and chemicals applied. ValCom, Inc. merged with Inacomp Computer Centers, Inc.

giving ValCom approximately 38 percent ownership of InaCom Corp., and offered investment flexibility in the microcomputer industry.

In 1993 the company named Mogens C. Bay, a native of Denmark with impressive global operating experience, president and chief executive officer. Valmont then created a new division, Valmont International, in response to NAFTA and GATT, in order to pursue the new market economies. According to the company's 1993 annual report, the new division was "responsible for developing business across business lines, identifying and capitalizing on opportunities wherever they may be, in whatever business."

Valmont utilized its fully owned subsidiaries, joint ventures, and licensing agreements to increase sales and reduce shipping costs. In their Saudi Arabian irrigation operations, for example, the company retained control of technological innovations by producing those components at home, while manufacturing structural components near the installation site, saving on shipping costs. Valmont opened a new metal structures business in Holland and eased into Asia by signing a joint venture agreement to build a plant in Shanghai, China, the largest and fastest-growing economy in the region.

Domestically, Valmont acquired Energy Steel Corporation of Tulsa, Oklahoma, to produce utility products and expanded plants in Salt Lake City, Utah, and in Brenham, Texas. Valmont's industrial production capacity was increased by about 25 percent from the domestic expansion and acquisitions.

Fearing that their aggressive growth could possibly spark interest in a takeover bid, the Valmont board of directors adopted a stockholders' rights plan, which, according to Scott Robertson of *American Metal Market,* "declared a dividend distribution of one right for each outstanding share of Valmont common stock. Upon becoming exercisable, each right would entitle its holder to buy one 1/1000th of a share of a new series of preferred stock at an exercise price of $100. The rights become exercisable if a person or group (other than certain exempt persons) acquires fifteen percent or more of Valmont's common stock." Dougherty owned approximately 27 percent of Valmont's outstanding common stock at the end of 1995 and was exempt from the rights plan as long as he owned no more than 35 percent of the company's common stock.

Cutting back to core businesses Valmont exited the steel reinforcing bar business, sold their interests in Inacom, their distributor and remarketer of personal computers, and sold Good-All Electric. They identified their new focus on metal manufacturing, marketing, engineering, coatings technology and on managing distribution worldwide. 1994 brought earnings up 30 percent on revenue growth of 7.5 percent, with record sales in the metal-poles-structure business due to the rapid expansion of cellular telephone networks and infrastructure investments in North America and Europe.

The company continued to invest heavily in new products, equipment and facilities around the world. Valmont reduced costs at its unprofitable lighting ballast business by $20 million, but continued to develop more energy-efficient ballast designs because the industry began a demand-inspired transition from traditional magnetic ballasts to more energy-efficient electronic ballasts.

1996 marked both the 50th anniversary of Valmont's beginnings and the retirement of its founder, Robert B. Daugherty, who remained on as a member of Valmont's board of directors. It was a banner year for the agricultural economy, bolstered by good prices and high yields as the worldwide demand for grain continued to increase. Agricultural equipment sales in South America and western Europe increased well above the previous year's level, with impressive gains in the North American market.

Tightening efforts to concentrate on their two primary businesses, the company sold its disappointing ballast operation, Valmont Electric, to Chicago Miniature Lamp, Inc. for approximately $25 million.

At the same time, the wireless communication market led in improved growth in the Industrial Products segment. In addition to manufacturing these communications structures, Valmont added the components needed to attach the antennas and wave guides to them, providing the product, installation and maintenance service worldwide. Sales of poles, towers, tubing and fabricated products increased in North America although profits were down in the European market resulting from unfavorable pricing pressures and weak markets in France and Germany. Valmont's aluminum pole facility near Lyons, France, was upgraded with a new spinner that expanded the product range and reduced costs. Valmont's strategy of enhancing it's production capabilities paid off by the first quarter of 1997, rewarded by climbing European orders for wireless communication poles, towers, and decorative light product lines.

Conserving Resources into the 21st Century

With 65 percent of the world's dwindling fresh water supply utilized by agriculture, leadership in creative and highly efficient irrigation systems continues to motivate Valmont's food production sector. Complicating the issue of fresh water resources are the estimates concerning the need to double the world's food production within the next 35 years to meet growing population/food demands.

According to Brian Stanley, writing in *Valmont News Release,* "Over half of the water pumped or diverted for irrigation is simply wasted due to inefficient irrigation techniques." The company is optimistic about the future of its center pivot which applies a precise amount of water, chemicals, and fertilizer to a predetermined height above the plants, feeding only the root zone. Simultaneous with heightened demand to meet efficient fertilization and water conservation requirements, many of the older irrigation systems installed during the 1970s were ready for replacement by the late 1990s. Finally, growth potential in major agricultural areas like South America, Australia, Europe, Africa and Asia offer further expansion opportunities for Valmont.

The first quarter of 1997 showed that Valmont sales of $165.4 million were up 28 percent from the previous first quarter. By April 1997 Mogens C. Bay announced at a shareholders meeting that the board declared a two-for one stock split, reflecting a continuous improvement in performance and the Board's confidence in the future. With its leadership position in irrigated agriculture both in the United States and overseas, such optimism appears well grounded. Moreover, that the world's demand for lighting and traffic structures will continue to grow seems likely, as developing countries invest in infrastructure. The conversion from wood to steel electrical distribution poles in the United States, and the rapid growth in the wireless communication industry worldwide also offer substantial opportunities for this company that grew from the cornfields.

Principal Subsidiaries

Energy Steel Corporation; Gibo-Conimast GmbH (Germany); Lampadaires Feralux, Inc. (Canada; 80%); Microflect Company; Nolte Mastenfabriek B.V. (Holland); Sermento (France; majority interest); Telec Centre S.A. (French; majority interest).

Further Reading

Abelson, Reed, "Valmont Industries (Companies to Watch)" *Fortune,* October 23, 1989, p. 134.

Brichard, Bill, "Do it Yourself: How Valmont Industries Implemented EVA," *CFO, The Magazine for Senior Financial Executives,* March, 1996, p. 34.

Cochran, Thomas, N., "Valmont Industries, Inc.: A Maker of Irrigation Pipe Finds Other Fertile Fields," *Barron's,* May 16, 1988, p. 85–87.

Dirrim, Craig, "The Nebraska Supreme Court Sounds the Death Knell for Recovery for Occupational Diseases Under the Nebraska Worker's Compensation Act," *Nebraska Law Review,* 1992, p. 964.

Painter, Steve, "New Irrigation Systems Refreshing for Farmers," *Journal of Commerce & Commercial,* June 10, 1993, p. 7A.

Robertson, Scott, "Valmont Industries Expanding Three Operations," *American Metal Market,* December 28, 1995, p. 4.

"Valmont Buys French Company," *American Metal Market,* June 3, 1996, p 4.

"Valmont Industries (Analyst's Report & Stock Information)," *Kansas City Business Journal,* January 8, 1990, p. 19.

"Valmont Industries, Inc.," *The Insider's Chronicle,* November 21, 1988, p. 3.

"Valmont Industries, Inc. (Who's News)," *Wall Street Journal,* August 3, 1993, p. B6.

"Valmont Industries Selling Lighting Equipment Unit," *New York Times,* January 7, 1997, p. 4N.

—Terri Burgman

Valores Industriales S.A.

Cuauhtemoc 400 Sur
64000 Monterrey, Nuevo Leon
Mexico
(528) 345-4400

Public Company
Incorporated: 1936
Sales: 15.52 billion pesos ($2.28 billion, 1995)
Stock Exchanges: Mexico City
SICs: 2082 Malt Beverages; 2086 Bottled and Canned
   Soft Drinks and Carbonated Waters; 2657 Folding
   Paperboard Boxes, Including Sanitary; 2671
   Packaging Paper and Plastics Film, Coated and
   Laminated; 3221 Glass Containers; 3411 Metal Cans;
   3581 Automastic Vending Machines; 5499
   Miscellaneous Food Stores; 6719 Offices of Holding
   Companies, Not Elsewhere Classified

The holding company Valores Industriales S.A. (better known in Mexico as Visa) is one of the largest businesses in Mexico. Through a subsidiary, Femsa, it is the nation's biggest brewer and producer of soft drinks. The company also, in 1995, operated 677 convenience stores in Mexico and engaged in the production and sale of packaging products to third parties.

Antecedents of Visa, 1890–1936

Cerveceria Cuauhtemoc, a Monterrey brewery, was founded in 1890 by Isaac Garza Garza, his brother-in-law Francisco Sada Muguerza, Jose Muguerza, and Jose Maria Schneider with capital of 150,000 pesos. In the beginning this brewery produced 1,500 bottles of beer and two tons of ice per day. Cerveceria Cuauhtemoc produced its first beer barrel in 1893 and made its mark in this period by winning first prize in the Chicago and Paris world fairs. A subsidiary, Cerveceria Central, was established in 1901 to supply Mexico City and the surrounding states.

In 1903 Cerveceria Cuauhtemoc was producing 80,000 bottles of beer a day and 100,000 barrels a year, and in 1909 it was producing 300,000 of each and employing 1,500 workers. By then the enterprise had expanded vertically, with factories to provide the glass, paper, cartons, and corks. Vidrios y Cristales de Monterrey S.A., established in 1899, became Vidriera Monterrey, S.A. in 1909, when it acquired the Owens patent for mechanical fabrication of glass bottles. Fabricas de Carton Monterrey was established in 1900 to produce boxes, bottle caps, and packaging materials of all kinds.

Cerveceria Cuauhtemoc suffered a potentially fatal blow when its founders backed Victoriano Huerta in the power struggle that followed the overthrow of Porfirio Diaz as president of Mexico in 1910. When the forces of Venustiano Carranza defeated Huerta in 1914 they seized the brewery, its owners having fled to Texas. The property was restored through the intervention of U.S. and Russian diplomats, but amid the anarchy of the revolution, the company's beer production fell from 16.5 million liters in 1912 to less than 3.4 million in 1914 and 1915 combined. The company's beer production did not fully recover until the mid-1920s.

Despite these problems, the founders and their children were contributing to the economic development of Monterrey. Isaac Garza's sons Eugenio and Roberto Garza Sada, graduates of the Massachusetts Institute of Technology, founded a technical school that became the precursor of Monterrey's Technological Institute. The brewery and its subsidiaries founded a civic association, a workers' group, and clinics, nurseries, and schools for the children of the workers. The Sociedad Cuauhtemoc, founded in 1918, established a one-stop familial service for workers that included company stores and a savings plan as well as the aforementioned benefits. The brewery's working day was reduced from 12 to nine hours in 1907.

During the 1920s a crown top was developed to replace the corks previously used for beer bottles. Responsibility for this function was turned over in 1929 to a new enterprise, Fabricas Monterrey S.A. (Famosa), which subsequently diversified into other products needed by the brewery, including metal containers and corrugated boxes, which had been introduced in 1926. Also in 1929, Malta, S.A. was established to produce malt for the brewery. Metal vats replaced wooden ones in 1930, making possible the pasteurization of beer.

Cerveceria Cuauhtemoc successfully adjusted to the Depression conditions of the 1930s and the leftist direction of the federal government under President Lazaro Cardenas. Beer shipments, after sinking to 14.4 million liters in 1932, reached 24.3 million in 1934—when the company was producing about 40 percent of the beer in Mexico—and 54.7 million in 1940. The Garza and Sada families were instrumental in the creation of a national employers' confederation. This group established a tame labor federation in order to forestall the development of a more militant group. In this way, and through its paternalistic welfare system, Cerveceria Cuauhtemoc avoided strikes.

Creation and Development of Visa, 1936–1974

By 1936 the holdings of the Garza and Sada families and their associates had been divided into two groups: the Cuauhtemoc (brewery) group and the Vidriera (glass) group. While descendants of Isaac Garza and Francisco Sada continued to hold shares within each group, management of the former was largely the responsibility of the Garza Sada family, particularly Eugenio and Roberto Garza Sada, while their cousins—sons of Francisco Sada Muguerza—were in charge of the latter. In that year the family's holdings were reorganized, with Valores Industriales S.A. (Visa) created as a holding company controlling the majority of shares of the firms formerly held by Cuauhtemoc, especially Cerveceria Cuauhtemoc and Famosa.

After two years of reorganization, the Visa group consisted of 12 companies, including Visa itself, Famosa, four breweries, Malta, a packaging company, a technical-services firm, a distribution company, and two financial agencies. One of the latter was Compania General de Aceptaciones, established in 1936 to facilitate financial transactions among the various companies controlled by the Garza and Sada families. Compania General de Aceptaciones took a large stake in one of Mexico's leading banks, the Banco de Londres y Mexico.

Hojalata y Lamina, S.A. (Hylsa) was founded by Visa in 1943 to produce steel sheet for metal bottletops during World War II, when supplies from the United States were cut. It subsequently expanded into a fully integrated steel complex, its activities ranging from iron-ore mining and processing to finished steel products. Hylsa became Mexico's second-largest steel producer and its largest private steel producer. In 1965 it was the second-largest private industrial company in Mexico, while Cerveceria Cuauhtemoc was third.

Cerveceria Cuauhtemoc introduced metal cans, the first in Mexico, in 1954. Another Visa subsidiary, Grafo Regia, S.A., was founded in 1957 to meet the company's needs for printing and other graphics materials. Visa dominated the bottling industry through its subsidiary Fomento Economico Mexicano S.A. de C.V. (Femsa). By 1970 Visa contained 90 subsidiaries and had 33,508 employees. By another count, it had 135 enterprises and 114 factories and branches.

Prosperous 1970s, Difficult 1980s

Eugenio Garza Sada was assassinated in 1973 in what was described as a botched kidnapping by left-wing guerrillas. Without his unifying influence, the Monterrey Group split from two to four units the following year: Visa, Grupo Industrial Alfa, Fomento de Industria y Comercio, or Fic (the former Vidriera Monterrey, soon to be renamed Vitro), and Cydsa, a chemicals complex formerly under Fic. Alfa received Hylsa, while Visa retained the brewery business and its stake in the Banco de Londres and its affiliated institutions. Eugenio Garza Laguera, a son of Eugenio Garza Sada, became chairman of Visa. Although the four holding companies were managed independently by different branches of the family, the Monterrey Group presented a united front in dealings with the Mexican government.

Visa grew mightily in the prosperous 1970s, a decade in which Mexico boomed because of sharply higher prices for its oil exports. Net sales rose from 4.15 billion pesos ($332 million) in 1974 to 17.82 billion pesos ($782 million) in 1979. Employment reached a peak of 34,859 in 1981, when net sales were 38.52 billion pesos ($1.57 billion). By this time Visa had no less than 174 subsidiaries. Having bought a chain of Hyatt hotels, its interests now included construction, real estate, tourism, animal feed, and plastics, besides its anchor beer and packaging enterprises and the soft-drink and mineral-water operations it began in 1979. The latter units enjoyed nearly half the cola sales in the greater Mexico City metropolitan area and more than half in Mexico's Southeast.

When oil prices fell in 1981, Mexico's economic boom, financed with borrowed money, came to a screeching halt. Visa found itself more than $1 billion in debt the following year, and the federal government nationalized Banca Serfin—the nation's third-largest bank—in which Visa held a 77 percent stake. The nondeposit banks and associated financial companies in Grupo Financiero Serfin, not nationalized, were reorganized into a new financial-services group called Valores de Monterrey (Vamsa). Vamsa's life-insurance subsidiary, Seguros Monterrey, was the largest in Mexico.

Visa reduced its holdings to pay its debts, falling to "only" 101 subsidiaries, but in 1986 it notified four major banks it would not be able to make further payments. Nevertheless, the company in 1985 acquired Cerveceria Moctezuma S.A., a rival brewer, in bankruptcy court. The transaction gave Visa at least 50 percent of the national beer market, although the federal government was a partner in the Moctezuma acquisition.

Adding to Visa's problems was dissatisfaction within the extended family. Javier Garza Calderon, who owned 45 percent of the holding company, tried unsuccessfully to wrest Visa from Eugenio, David, and Alejandro Garza Laguera, who controlled the rest. He filed several suits charging Eugenio with mishandling the administration of the conglomerate but was ultimately unsuccessful in winning control. In 1991 Garza Calderon's father, Javier Garza Sepulveda, tried to gain control of Visa through his Grupo Center. He also failed but made a big profit by selling his family's stock back to Visa for $428 million.

In 1988 Visa bought back $1.5 billion of its $1.7-billion foreign debt from 48 banks by paying an average of 30 cents on the dollar. The restructuring involved giving creditors about 20 percent of Femsa's equity. Visa offered 20 percent of the shares to the public and retained the other 60 percent. Visa also sold its hotels for $97 million and its share in a joint venture with Ford that was making plastic dashboards.

Visa in the 1990s

When Mexico's nationalized banks were fully reprivatized in 1991, a group of investors from Vamsa, headed by Eugenio Garza Laguera and Ricardo Guajardo, bought (through Grupo Financiero Bancomer) a 51 percent stake in Bancomer, Mexico's second-largest bank, and the stock-brokerage firm Acciones Bursatiles, for $2.55 billion, of which J.P. Morgan provided a $1-billion syndicated loan. Femsa took a 34 percent stake in Grupo Financiero Bancomer. Following this acquisition, Serfin regained most of Vamsa's subsidiaries, but Vamsa continued to be the parent company for Seguros Monterrey and Fianzas Monterrey.

Eugenio Garza Laguera became chairman of Bancomer, which was in far better financial shape than Visa's previous financial arm, Serfin, which was sold to another branch of the Garza Sada extended family. In 1995 Bancomer formed a partnership with GTE to compete in the Mexican long-distance telephone market, in association with AT&T and Spain's Telefonica, when the monopoly held by Telefonos de Mexico ended in 1997. Alfa subsequently also joined this partnership.

In 1992 Visa sold Femsa's mineral-waters business to Cadbury Schweeppes for $325 million and an 11 percent stake in Femsa for $215 million. It sold 30 percent of Femsa's soft-drink business to an indirect subsidiary of The Coca-Cola Co. in 1993 for $195 million. In 1994 it sold a 22 percent share of Femsa's beer business to John Labatt Ltd. of Canada and signed an agreement with Labatt to associate their respective companies in the United States. During 1992–93 Visa also opened 267 convenience stores in Mexico under the Oxxo name. By the end of 1995 there were 677 Oxxo stores in 17 of Mexico's largest cities. They were being administered by Femsa's retail division.

Femsa remained the heart of the Visa conglomerate. Publicly traded, this subsidiary accounted for nearly 60 percent of Visa's net sales in 1995. Its holdings included a publicly traded subsidiary of its own, Coca-Cola Femsa, whose net sales came to almost two-thirds of the parent Femsa company. (In 1994 Mexico's per-capita consumption of Coke was higher than that of any other country, even the United States.)

Femsa was producing and marketing beer under the brand names Superior, XX Lager, Tecate, Tecate Light, Indio, Heineken, Sol, Bohemia, and Carta Blanca, and soft drinks under the names Coke, Diet Coke, Fanta, Sprite, Sin Rival, and Extra Poma. It was exporting these beverages to 63 countries and also producing beer and food cans, crown caps, glass bottles, labels and wrappers, cardboard boxes, soft-drink cases, refrigerators,

and vending machines. Its Coca-Cola business held the franchise in the Mexico City metropolitan area, southeastern Mexico and, through a subsidiary, metropolitan Buenos Aires, Argentina.

During 1994, a year that ended in a new Mexican economic and financial crisis, Visa lost 775 million pesos ($221 million). In 1995 it posted net income of 204 million pesos ($30 million). Visa ended the year with 7.26 billion pesos ($1.06 billion) in long-term debt. The Garza Laguera family fortune, although considerably reduced by the economic crisis, was valued in 1996 at $1.1 billion. (In 1992 the family owned around 40 percent of Visa and 30 percent of Vamsa through Grupo Proa, a privately held holding company). Eugenio Garza Laguera was chairman of Visa, Vamsa, Femsa, and Coca-Cola Femsa, as well as Bancomer.

Principal Subsidiaries

Fomento Economico Mexicano, S.A. de C.V. (Femsa); Visa Bioindustrias, S.A. de C.V. (Bioindustrias).

Further Reading

Baker, Stephen, "Out from Under a Pile of Debt," *Business Week,* November 7, 1988, p. 54.

Concheiro, Elvira, et. al., *El poder de gran burgesia,* Mexico City: Ediciones de Cultura Popular, 1979, pp. 51–131.

Fuentes Mares, Jose, *Monterrey, una ciudad creadera y sus capitanes,* Mexico City: Editorial Jus, 1976, pp. 128–147.

Hamilton, Nora, *The Limits of State Autonomy: Post-Revolutionary Mexico,* Princeton, N.J.: Princeton University Press, 1982, pp. 307–316.

"Mexican Conglomerate Acquires Major Brewery," *Wall Street Journal,* July 22, 1985, p. 22.

"Mexico's Family Groups Struggle with Changes As New Powers Ascend," *Business Latin America,* May 4, 1987, pp. 138–139.

Morales, Miguel Angel, "El Grupo Monterrey vs. La Familia Revolucionaria," *Revista de Revistas,* December 22, 1982, pp. 14–17.

Moreno Hernandez, Wolfrano, *El Grupo Financiero Visa-Serfin,* unpublished thesis, Universidad Autonoma Metropolitana, Mexico City, 1986.

Palmeri, Christopher, and Kerry A. Dolan, "A Tough New World," *Forbes,* July 17, 1995, pp. 122–124.

Poole, Claire, "The Resurrection of Don Eugenio," *Forbes,* February 17, 1992, pp. 102, 106.

Saragoza, Alex N., *The Monterrey Elite and Mexican State, 1880–1940,* Austin: University of Texas Press, 1988.

Vizcaya Canales, Isidro, *Los origines de la industrialization de Monterrey,* Monterrey: Instituto Technologico y Estudios Superiores, 1971.

—Robert Halasz

Velcro Industries N.V.

15 Pietermaai
Willemstad, Curaçao
Netherlands Antilles
+31-(0) 603-669-4880
Fax: +31-(0) 603-669-1728
Web site: http://www.velcro.com

Public Company
Incorporated: 1957 as Velok Ltd.
Employees: 1,200
Sales: $177.1 million (1996)
Stock Exchanges: NASDAQ
SICs: 3965 Fasteners, Buttons, Needles & Pins

Velcro Industries N.V. was created in order to market one of the century's handiest inventions: hook and loop tape. The ubiquitous fastener has spawned almost innumerable applications, fastening blood pressure cuffs, sneakers, wallets, industrial lift belts, and prisoner leg restraints. Velcro products can be found around the world. The company also manufactures more conventional belts and fasteners. Ultra-Mate and Texacro are two of the company's other brands.

A 1940s Discovery

Walking is said to promote creativity, and this was literally true in the invention of Velcro hook and loop tape. As George de Mestral hiked with his dog along some alpine countryside one day in 1941, cockleburs continually fastened themselves to his trousers. Wondering what made the spiny seeds so tacky, he examined them under a microscope revealing thousands of tiny hooks on the surface of each one. His trousers, which he also examined, were essentially covered with loops of fabric. Although he appreciated the engineering implications of the discovery right away, it took eight years of tinkering for de Mestral to develop a usable product made out of nylon hooks and loops. The main challenge was perfecting the manufacturing process to ensure consistent results.

By the 1950s the inventor had created a company to market his novel product. The trademark "Velcro" was appropriately derived from the French words for velvet and hook: "velour" and "crochet." Although he earned less than $60 per week in his first years in business, de Mestral earned millions after he sold rights to the invention to a new company created by Jean Revaud, an American national.

Velcro S.A. was based in Switzerland. It entered a licensing agreement with Velok Ltd. of Canada in 1957. The agreement allowed Velok to produce Velcro tape in the Western Hemisphere as well as Asia and the Pacific. Velok agreed to give the Swiss company the rights to all patents it subsequently developed.

Velok changed its name to Velcro Industries Ltd. and eclipsed Velcro S.A. in innovations and growth. Velcro USA Inc. (originally American Velcro Inc.) and Velcro Canada Ltd. (Canadian Velcro Ltd.) were subsidiaries of Velcro Industries Ltd. The company eventually acquired the rights to the patent in the late 1960s.

In 1967, its sales were worth about $10 million a year and its stock $81 per share. C. Humphrey Cripps began acquiring shares of the company (through a Channel Islands holding company, Cohere Ltd.) when their price fell to around $5 each in the early 1970s. Cripps also took the post of company chairman and later installed two sons on the board.

Velcro was not the Cripps family's first foray into entrepreneurship. Humphrey's father, Cyril, established a factory to make piano frames in 1919; it later was a supplier for the automotive industry. Other holdings included private livestock and tourism investments. Known for its philanthropy (the Cripps Foundation gave Cambridge University £1 million in the 1960s), the family drew some scrutiny in the late 1980s after the company failed to offer a dividend in spite of healthy sales and cash reserves, prompting speculation about the family taking the company private. A minority shareholder, Alan Kahn, sued to prevent the transaction, and a U.S. judge ruled that the United States had jurisdiction in the case. Cripps canceled his plans. However, within five years, rumors of the chairman entertaining takeover offers were reported.

The company maintained a reputation for secrecy in financial matters and product development. The *New York Times* likened it to a private company. It held its annual meetings on the isolated Caribbean island of St. Maarten, meetings that, as reported in *Forbes* magazine, were not even attended by the board, who instead met with Cripps privately.

The Competitive 1980s

By the time the patent for the original Velcro tape expired in 1978, the word "Velcro" had become a synonym for hook and loop tape. The company launched a campaign to protect the brand name from falling into general use. A subsequent advertising campaign touted the product as "the first, the best."

The expiration of the patent opened the market to a slew of low-cost competitors. The French company Aplix (the leading European fastener supplier) and Japanese-owned YKK (a leading manufacturer of zippers for clothing) capitalized on the opportunity, particularly in the apparel and footwear industries. The demand for the fastener among shoe makers was so great that Velcro could not meet it alone, and it lost some business to foreign suppliers, some of whom had licensed the Velcro technology and name until 1978. However, when the fashion buzz wore off, excess capacity among hook and loop tape suppliers forced prices down.

Fashion designers, courted by the company since the 1960s, had finally begun to appreciate the possibilities. However, like the first Ford automobiles, Velcro tape was originally only available in black. Eventually the tape was formulated in sixteen different colors. An elastic version was also developed.

The company concentrated on supplying more stable, industrial markets after the shoe fad declined. Velcro products, the company explained, helped lower assembly costs in the automotive industry. The fastening devices were used to attach door panels among other things. The aerospace industry also appreciated the lightweight, rustproof fasteners that would not rattle. A standard component in jet planes since the 1960s, Velcro fasteners were used on aircraft ranging from small Pipers to the Space Shuttle. Medical supplies, which tended to be very expensive, provided a field in which Velcro could sell higher quality, more costly products, including the fasteners used on the Symbion Total artificial heart. Not only did the fasteners have to work perfectly, but they had to be immaculately clean as well, and, as in the fashion industry, the appearance of the products was often important as well.

The tape was enhanced to perform in different conditions. Flame resistant (Hi-Air), silver coated, electrically conductive (Hi-Meg), heat and corrosion resistant (Hi-Garde), fire retardant, and weather resistant polyester were among the formulations developed.

The hook side of the tape was available in differing densities and levels of durability; the loop side was also. However, the orientation of the loops made a difference in "peel strength." Randomly-oriented loops held more firmly, whereas orderly rows of loops had a somewhat more attractive appearance. The final, unsung layer, the adhesive, was also available in different formulations. Standard backed tape, meant to be sewn, had no adhesive at all. Most had peel-off backing and pressure-sensitive adhesives of different formulations for use in different applications and environments. The most durable involved a separate adhesive to be applied and activated by the user.

One-Wrap fasteners had a hook layer on one side and loops on the other and were used for wrapping purposes. Half and Half Tape featured hook tape with an adhesive backing and the opposite, with the loops, with a fabric backing that could be sewn onto other fabrics. Texacro, a less expensive brand of standard backed tape, was manufactured in Mexico. Velstick fasteners had a rigid plastic backing. The WrapStrap, an offering of Canada's WrapStrap Industries Inc., anchored two pieces of Velcro tape with an aluminum plate for securing cables and automotive and marine applications. Velcro tapes were available in a variety of widths, from ⅝″ to 12″, and were available cut into small circles, called "Velcoin" fasteners.

The fastener also proved handy for hanging displays at conventions and in retail stores. Inevitably, more whimsical applications for Velcro tape had to surface. At some bars, customers could don a suit covered with Velcro tape and fasten themselves to a wall covered with the complementary layer. Late-night talk show host David Letterman popularized this stunt. The more adventuresome could attempt to navigate a similarly fashioned inflatable obstacle course.

Expansion in the 1990s

Annual sales in fiscal year 1988 were $93 million. They had reached $115 million by 1992. In the mid-1990s, several factors sent the company's earnings and stock price downward. Velcro was forced to make a large tax payment to the Dutch government. Overseas expansion had to be funded, and the United States—where the company essentially runs its operations from Manchester, New Hampshire—required an increase in tax payments as well.

Velcro included hundreds of types of fasteners in its product offerings in the 1990s. It diversified into such conventional fasteners as screws and clips, which were usually custom engineered. Velcro began using stainless steel in manufacturing some of these new products, although nylon remained a component of some.

The company also developed variations of its original nylon hook and loop tape using less expensive materials. The Ultra-Mate brand HTH ("High Technology Hook") line was the pinnacle of this technology.

Ultra-Mate figured largely in a potentially lucrative co-branding exercise with Kimberly-Clark Corp., which used the fastener on its premium line of diapers, Huggies Supreme. Ultra-Mate's injection molding process made it more cost effective for this application than the traditional Velcro loop tape. However, the Velcro brand was featured on Huggies Supreme packaging because customers valued it. The venture was expected to increase Velcro USA's sales by $5 to $10 million per year.

New uses for traditional nylon-based Velcro tape continued to be developed. TacFast Systems Canada Limited developed the TacFast carpet fastening system based on Velcro tape. The system secured carpet effectively while allowing it to be easily moved if need arose. Velcro tape also anchored the artificial turf at the Toronto SkyDome and was employed to hold down toupees.

In 1996, earnings jumped nearly 20 percent to $16.3 million, while sales increased over 10 percent to $177.1 million. Although sales lagged in North America, Velcro Industries expected to benefit from the growth of markets in Asia and Latin America. A strong European presence remained a priority for the company, as evidenced by its acquisition of Ausonia S.r.l., the leading hook and loop producer in Italy.

Principal Subsidiaries

Velcro Hong Kong Limited; Velcro Australia Pty. Ltd.; Zhangjiagang Velcro Fastening Systems Co., Ltd. (China; 75%); Velcro Europe S.A. (Spain); Systemes de Fermeture S.A. (France); Velcro GmbH (Germany); Velcro Italia S.R.L.; Addey Milner Limited (Great Britain); Velcro Holdings B.V. (The Netherlands); Velcro USA Inc.; Velcro Laminates Inc. (USA); Velcro Canada Inc.; Velcromex S.A. de C.V. (Mexico); Velcro Finance Limited (Bermuda); Velcro Group Corporation (USA); Briole S.A. (Uruguay); Velcro de Costa Rica, S.A.; Velcro de Mexico, S.A. de C.V.; Velcro do Brasil LTDA.; Velcro Industries B.V. (Netherlands Antilles); Velcro Properties N.V. (Netherlands Antilles).

Principal Divisions

Automotive Division; Consumer Division; Industrial Division.

Further Reading

Berss, Marcia, " 'A Wacko Situation'," *Forbes,* May 23, 1994, p. 82.

Brush, Michael, "It Keeps Your Pants on, but Can It Fatten Your Wallet?" *New York Times,* April 14, 1996, p. F3.

Fastech of Jacksonville, http://www.fastech-velcro.com.

Giges, Nancy, "Velcro Faces Patent Problems by Diversifying Line," *Advertising Age,* November 7, 1977, p. 24.

Jancsurak, Joe, "Getting Hooked," *Appliance Manufacturer,* February 1994.

"Kimberly-Clark Revamps Huggies to Steal March on P&G's Pampers," *Marketing Week,* August 9, 1996, p. 10.

Krantz, K. Theodor, "How Velcro Got Hooked on Quality," *Harvard Business Review,* September/October 1989, pp. 34–40.

Marcial, Gene G., "Sticking with Velcro," *Business Week,* January 18, 1993, p. 74.

Meeks, Fleming, "Some Call It Greed," *Forbes,* October 3, 1988.

"There's No Such Thing as 'Velcro'," Manchester, New Hampshire: Velcro USA Inc., n.d.

"Velcro: A Success Story," *Magazine of Wall Street,* June 10, 1967, pp. 31–32, 40.

"Velcro's Stuck on Flying Disk Game," *Playthings,* April 1994.

"Velcro USA Inc.," *Automotive Industries,* June 1995.

—Frederick C. Ingram

Waldbaum, Inc.

Hemlock Street and Boulevard Avenue
Central Islip, New York 11722
U.S.A.
(516) 582-9300
Web site: http://www.waldbaums.com

*Wholly Owned Subsidiary of the Great Atlantic & Pacific
    Tea Co.*
Incorporated: 1921
Employees: 12,000
Sales: $1.4-$1.7 billion (1995 est.)
SICs: 5411 Grocery Stores

Waldbaum, Inc. is one of the leading supermarket chains in New York City and Long Island, with 98 stores in the Waldbaum network in 1996. After 82 years of control and management by the founding Waldbaum family, the company was sold to the Great Atlantic & Pacific Tea Co. in 1986 and became a subsidiary of this supermarket chain.

Private Enterprise, 1904–1961

Waldbaum's had its start in 1904, when Israel (Izzy) Waldbaum, an immigrant from Austria, began selling butter and eggs at 911 DeKalb Street in Brooklyn. "People used to stand three abreast to get into that little store," his widow recalled to *New York Times* reporter Judy Klemsrud in 1967. By 1938 there was a second Waldbaum's in Brooklyn's Coney Island section. In that year George and Ernest Brown, identical twins working as stock boys, were promoted to checkers. "It was unheard of then for a colored checker to be in a white neighborhood," Ernest Brown said three decades later. "It was even unheard of for a colored checker to be in a colored neighborhood." Both Browns later became store managers and, eventually, Waldbaum vice-presidents.

By the time Izzy Waldheim died in 1947 or 1948 at age 55, there were six or seven stores, all in Brooklyn. His son, Ira, left his studies at New York University to run the two appetizer stores and subsequently became president of the chain. The first Waldbaum's supermarket was opened in 1951 in Flushing, Queens. Net retail sales reached $55.2 million in 1960 and net income amounted to $660,000. The following year Waldbaum's went public by selling shares of common stock, mostly for the company's own account, at $14 a share, but the Waldbaum family retained 81 percent of the stock. At the time the company and its subsidiaries were operating 35 supermarkets in Brooklyn, Queens, and adjacent Nassau County, Long Island. It was also conducting wholesale food operations.

Expansion in the 1960s and 1970s

Waldbaum's acquired Michael's Fair-Mart Food Stores, Inc., a 13-unit chain with annual sales of more than $15 million, in 1962 for cash and stock. The company moved its headquarters from Brooklyn to Garden City, Long Island, in 1964 and the following year was operating 60 stores, including units in the borough of Staten Island and in Westchester County, north of New York City. Sales reached $197.4 million and net income totaled $2 million in 1967. By 1971 there were Waldbaum's in all of the New York City boroughs except Manhattan, in Nassau and Suffolk counties on Long Island, in four counties north of the city (as far away as Kingston, New York), and in northern New Jersey.

Manhattan remained unrepresented in the Waldbaum empire because of an unsuccessful eight-month venture in the early 1960s during which, Ira Waldbaum later said, "I heard people asking for *a* banana, *an* apple, *a* lamb chop. I knew that kind of volume wouldn't work for us, so I got out." New Jersey did not work out either, in part because the company could not compete on price with ShopRite and Pathmark. After only three years, Waldbaum's pulled out of the state in 1971.

Julia Waldbaum, Izzy's widow, remained active in management. Bearing the title of company secretary, she made surprise inspections of about 30 stores a month as self-appointed watchdog of the supermarket chain. Many of the customers recognized her because her picture appeared on almost all of the 400 food products sold under the Waldbaum label, although "they left me off the dog food and the bathroom tissue," she told a reporter in a tone hinting at disappointment. To the consternation of her family, she kept her telephone number listed in the book. "I like to have the customers to call me," she said, "because a lot of them think Julia Waldbaum is an imaginary person like Betty Crocker." She continued her inspections to an advanced age and died in 1996 at the age of 99.

In 1969 Waldbaum's acquired Holyoke Food Mart Inc., a privately held chain of 14 supermarkets in Connecticut and western Massachusetts with annual sales of $38 million. Most of these outlets continued to bear the Food Mart rather than Waldbaum name. Company sales quadrupled between 1960 and 1968, a period during which annual earnings declined only in 1965, when the company dropped trading stamps to reduce costs. Waldbaum's introduced a line of private-label foods and nonfood items in 1964. By the end of the decade the company was deriving about 20 percent of its grocery revenues from private-label merchandising. The establishment of stores as large as 30,000 square feet enabled Waldbaum's to stock a variety of nonfood merchandise, such as cosmetics, clothing, housewares, books, and magazines. Two stores had pharmacies. Waldbaum's also was participating in discount food merchandising through the operation of leased departments in six large discount stores on Long Island. These departments did not carry the Waldbaum name.

Waldbaum's moved its headquarters and distribution center farther east in 1974, to Central Islip, Long Island. Almost half of the 118 units that year were in Brooklyn and Queens. During 1978–1979 the company bought ten former Pantry Price/Hills Stores from the bankrupt Food Fair chain, bringing the total number of outlets to 138, compared with 80 in 1970. Net sales reached $1.1 billion in the last year of the decade, compared with $281 million in 1969, and net income was $7.8 million, compared with $2.7 million in 1969. By the end of the 1970s Waldbaum's was the second largest company in sales on Long Island and the third largest employer.

The Waldbaum's of the 1970s continued to gear its merchandising and advertising to its long-time base, the upper-middle-income Jewish customer. Many sources considered it to be the best appetizer and deli operation in the East. Its deli cases were being remerchandised to take advantage of the Italian, Greek, and Spanish trade in marketing areas where the population was not primarily Jewish. Waldbaum's seemed to be just as successful catering to these ethnic groups. Adhering to his mother's habits, Ira Waldbaum spent a great deal of time on the road, often visiting ten stores a day. "I don't like them [the employees] to think I'm sneaking around, but I never let them know in advance that I'm coming," he told a *New York Times* interviewer.

Challenges of the 1980s

In 1983 Waldbaum's opened its first "Megamart," a 55,000-square-foot store in Greenfield, Massachusetts. This was a significant departure because the extra space was filled with general merchandise—goods that the chain had generally avoided even though nonfood items yielded a higher profit margin. Another megamart was the remodeled, 52,000-square-foot outlet in Vails Gate, New York, which carried four to five times the amount of general merchandise it did previously,

including everything from cosmetics to a large selection of boxed toys.

The pace of movement toward megastores was a point of contention between the conservative Ira Waldbaum on one hand and his impatient-to-expand sons and son-in-law Aaron Malinksy, the company's executive vice-president, on the other. Technology was another sticking point. "It's hard to get the older people to use the computer data instead of just shooting from the hip," Martin Waldbaum told a *New York Times* reporter. "They are still in the butter-and-eggs philosophy."

Now the nation's twelfth largest supermarket chain, Waldbaum's earned a record $17.1 million on $1.76 billion in sales during 1985, its last year of independent operation. The enterprise was not without its problems, however. Profits had fallen in both 1983 and 1984. In the latter year Waldbaum's, along with three other supermarket chains, pleaded no-contest to a charge of conspiracy to fix prices by eliminating double-value coupons. It eventually paid $700,000 in fines and distributed $7.5 million worth of redeemable coupons to settle litigation. Early in 1986 a presidential commission charged that Waldbaum's and other supermarket chains were involved with organized crime in paying for various operating services.

A&P Subsidiary from 1986

In 1986 Waldbaum's was sold to the Great Atlantic & Pacific Tea Co. (A&P) for $50 a share, or $287.1 million. The Waldbaum family's stake in the company was more than 60 percent at this time. The family subsequently suffered embarrassment because Robert Chestman, a stockbroker who heard about the pending deal through a son-in-law of Ira Waldbaum, reaped profits of $250,000 in trades based on this information, part of which he shared with the son-in-law. Chestman was convicted on ten counts of insider trading.

Under A&P, Waldbaum's experienced a slide in market share in both New York City and Long Island (its New England stores having been turned over to Waldbaum's Foodmart, another A&P subsidiary). Despite initial promises that the chain would continue to be run as an independent unit, Ira Waldbaum was soon gone. Malinsky, who succeeded as president, eventually departed to run another A&P chain, leaving Ira's son Arthur the only family member remaining in management. Many other key employees also left and, according to a *Crain's New York Business* article, the chain's "low prices and ethnic merchandising savvy evaporated."

In 1993 one food broker described Waldbaum under A&P as "a typical story of taking a racehorse and turning it into a camel. While there was some off-the-cuff disorganized thinking at Waldbaum before A&P bought it, at least it had some spice." Three years later a supermarket competitor echoed the assessment that Waldbaum had lost its focus on ethnic foods, telling *Crain's*, "This was a traditionally Jewish chain and they brought in some guys from Detroit to run it."

Waldbaum's also was being faulted on other grounds. According to a New York state agency, the company failed 47 percent of its store inspections for sanitation in 1990, compared with an average of 26 percent for nine other major supermarket chains. During one inspection of a Brooklyn store two dead mice were found on the packaged-goods shelves. And in 1994 a federal court awarded 224 Waldbaum's employees more than $1.8 million in back wages due to violations of recordkeeping and overtime labor laws.

Waldbaum's, which dealt with 16 unions, had other labor problems in the 1990s. In 1992 a Teamsters local, representing the company's warehouse workers, urged a consumer boycott to win a contract. A union official said Waldbaum's pay scales were lower than other supermarket chains in the region because of "sweetheart" deals cut by an organized crime figure eventually forced to quit his Teamsters job by a court-appointed investigator. Subsequently hired by Waldbaum's as a labor contractor, this man lost his contract after Waldbaum's workers complained to federal authorities and the media. He was later found shot to death.

A&P attempted to improve Waldbaum's operations by relinquishing its responsibility for the chain's buying in 1995. This allowed Waldbaum's to establish better relations with its vendors. And A&P continued Waldbaum's policy of gradually replacing some of the older, smaller stores with superstores, such as the 52,000-square-foot Levittown unit, which included three aisles of health and beauty aids, a pharmacy, a flower shop, a bakery, a custom butcher, and a fresh fish counter. In 1991 a 60,000-square-foot Waldbaum's had opened in the South Bronx, only a few blocks from Yankee Stadium. A&P also provided Waldbaum's with capital to expand and upgrade its computer systems, thereby enabling the chain to track inventory and sales more swiftly.

A 1994 survey found that Waldbaum's 27 stores in New York City had 12 percent of the city's market share in its field and ranked first in the borough of Queens. It retained its No. 1 standing on Long Island (excluding the city), but was being hard pressed by King Kullen and Pathmark as well as warehouse clubs, discounters, convenience stores, and even drugstores. "Waldbaum's trades on its Jewish roots," an industry analyst told *Newsday.* "They have a higher-than-average pro-portion of different types of foods that would appeal to the Jewish market." He also noted that Waldbaum's was catering heavily to communities with large Italian-American populations, perhaps more than other big chains. Waldbaum'a also was marketing A&P's private-label food products, sold under the America's Choice and Master Choice brands. Nevertheless, the subsidiary was still said to be a drag on A&P's profits in 1996.

Further Reading

Barmash, Isadore, "A Family Feud Stays Friendly at Waldbaum," *New York Times,* April 13, 1986, Sec. 3, p. 12.

Fatsis, Stefan, "Family Firm Entangled in Insider Trading Scandal," *St. Louis Post Dispatch,* November 13, 1989, pp. 4BP, 6BP.

Fox, Bruce, "Waldbaum Settles Suit with Coupon Program," *Supermarket News,* July 27, 1987, p. 14.

Gilgoff, Harry, "Waldbaum's To Resolve Sanitation Complaints," *New York Newsday,* June 12, 1991, Sec. 1, p. 41.

Jaye, Daniel, "Higher Quality, Low Cost Foods Goal of Waldbaum Supermarkets," *Investment Dealers' Digest,* October 21, 1968, pp. 38–39.

Kagan, Paul F., "Fresh Growth in Store This Year for Rapidly Expanding Waldbaum," *Barron's,* July 21, 1969, pp. 27, 31.

Klemsrud, Judy, "When Julia Waldbaum Pinches the Fruit, Clerks Never Complain," *New York Times,* July 3, 1967, p. 34.

Lewis, Leonard, "Waldbaum Finds Success Based on 'Common Sense,' " *Supermarket News,* January 21, 1980, pp. 1, 34–35.

——, "Waldbaum, Suburb Star, Clinging to Ethnic Image," *Supermarket News,* January 14, 1980, pp. 1, 28.

Rigg, Cynthia, "A&P in Market To Fix Two Units," *Crain's New York Business,* March 29, 1993, p. 4.

Sheraton, Mimi, "A Supermarket Boss with a Mom-and-Pop Philosophy," *New York Times,* June 16, 1982, pp. C1, C19.

Sloane, Leonard, "Twins Attain Identical Success," *New York Times,* March 18, 1968, pp. 67, 73.

Temes, Judy, "A&P Seeks a Chain Reaction," *Crain's New York Business,* September 23, 1996, p. 49.

Wax, Alan J., "Leader of the Pack," *Newsday,* October 3, 1994, pp. C1, C6–C7.

—Robert Halasz

Walker Manufacturing Company

111 Pfingsten Road
Deerfield, Illinois 60015
U.S.A.
(847) 940-6013
Fax: (847) 267-8363

Wholly Owned Subsidiary of Tenneco Automotive
Incorporated: 1888 as Economy Spring Company
Employees: 11,500
Sales: $1.5 billion (1995)
SICs: 3714 Motor Vehicle Parts & Accessories

Celebrating more than a century of quality workmanship, Walker Manufacturing Company is the world's leading producer of original and aftermarket automotive exhaust systems. From horse-drawn carriages and Ford's Model T to Jaguar XJ6s and Ford Explorers, Walker's technology and success has matched the ongoing development of a society wholly dependent on motorized vehicles. The company operates three North American distribution centers, engineering facilities in the United States, Australia, Germany, and Japan, and 29 manufacturing operations around the globe (eight in the United States and 21 outside). By 1996 Walker's aftermarket exhaust components were utilized in an estimated 95 percent of all cars and trucks on the road, while its original exhaust parts equipped seven of the 10 best-selling passenger cars and nine of the top-selling light trucks sold nationwide.

From Farm to Auto Accessories, 1888 through the 1930s

In 1885 engineers Carl Benz and Gottlieb Daimler were independently building internal combustion engines in Germany. Some believe Siegfried Narkus constructed a four-wheeled motorized vehicle as early as 1875. Regardless, the late 1880s found many like-minded inventors perfecting "horseless" carriages—while a seemingly unrelated business, the Economy Spring Company, began operating in Racine, Wis-

consin, in 1888. Although there was no discernible connection between these events, their futures were inescapably linked.

At Economy Spring, four employees were occupied making springs for horse-drawn farm wagons and by year's end brought in $12,000 in sales. When the company introduced a new product—a harrow attachment for plows (for breaking up dirt, rooting up weeds, or covering seeds)—it proved so popular Economy Spring hired an additional 36 workers to keep up with demand. On the automotive front, Rudolf Diesel patented his internal combustion engine, Krebs designed the Panhard (a gasoline or petrol-powered auto), and Benz tested his four-wheeled motor car in Germany in 1894. In the United States, while Economy Spring's 40 workers continued to produce farm implements, the nation slipped into financial panic that lasted for four years. Untouched by the crisis, Economy Spring was generating revenue of over $75,000 annually.

After the turn of the century, demand for motorized automobiles grew worldwide. Economy Spring, meanwhile, was still thriving as a non-automotive company. When Henry Ford formed the Ford Motor Company with $100,000 in 1903 the workers at Economy Spring had no idea another crucial link in the company's evolution was put in place. Five years later, in 1908, as General Motors was formed and Ford sold its first Model T (15 million were later sold), William A. Walker, along with his twin sons, Willard and Warren, gained controlling interest in Economy Spring and were determined to make the growing company into what they called a "Walker Operation."

In 1912 Willard Walker met John Dwight of the Mitchell Motor Company on a Chicago-bound train. Before reaching the Windy City the two agreed that Walker's company would design and produce a "tire saver" to hold stored automobiles up off their slight tires during the winter when few were driven because of snow and ice. The "tire saver," which later became better known as a "jack," was Economy Spring's entry into the burgeoning automobile industry. Within four years the Walkers' jack factory employed 400 workers, and the company's name was officially changed from Economy Spring to Walker Manufacturing.

During the next decade, Henry Ford had revolutionized production by using an assembly line and sold his 10-millionth car, the United States entered and won the First World War, and Walker Manufacturing flourished selling jacks. In 1929 the company bought Ajax Auto Parts and became one of the nation's largest jack manufacturers. Yet suddenly Walker, like the rest of the country, was thrown into the Depression. To keep the company alive, Walker diversified into other automobile accessories, including a "silencer" to reduce back-pressure and bring exhaust noise to a minimum. To help design the new product, Walker hired an engineer named Earl Gunn away from the Nash Motor Company.

Previous silencers were thin tin contraptions barely worth their weight, but Walker and Gunn built one with a louvered or ventilated tube that churned exhaust fumes in one direction within the silencer. This effectively lowered back-pressure on the engine and muffled the auto's noise—earning the name "muffler." The louvered muffler was more than an industry first—for it not only put Walker Manufacturing in the forefront of exhaust system engineering, but was just the first of many innovations to come.

By 1931 world car production had reached 36 million, a virtually unlimited source of income for Walker. The following year, amidst rampant unemployment (13.7 million in the United States), Walker patented its technological marvel, the louvered muffler, and set out to equip the nation's many vehicles with them.

Mufflers Become a Way of Life, 1940s through the 1960s

The early 1940s brought World War II, gasoline rationing, and freezes on wages, salaries, and pricing—and a first for Walker with the debut of the company's stainless steel muffler. After the War, price controls were lifted, and Walker Manufacturing continued to modify and improve its automobile exhaust systems. The company's next breakthrough came in 1953 with the introduction of the first aluminized steel muffler, at a time when the United States accounted for a mere six percent of the world's population yet owned 60 percent of the world's automobiles.

Walker's success in making cars run smoother and better not only gave the company its mainstay, but helped automakers sell their wares to an increasingly four-wheel–bound society. After the aluminized steel muffler came further muffler tinkering, this

time an innovation called "Individual Tuning" which added specially designed sound chambers to the company's original mufflers. The technology that led to Individual Tuning soon evolved into "Precision" tuning for vehicles with higher compression, larger engines, and automatic transmissions.

The dawn of the 1960s found Americans and the rest of the world concerned about pollution, especially exhaust emissions from cars and trucks. The company initiated work on emission-control devices in conjunction with the California Motor Vehicle Pollution Control Board and in 1962 came out with crankcase parts, the forefather of catalytic converters. The following year Walker produced catalytic reactor systems for new vehicles and in 1964 perfected the devices while coming out with another industry first—the chambered pipe. Chambered pipes—pipes connecting the manifold to the exhaust outlet that were filled with small tuning cells at different intervals—greatly enhanced acoustical performance.

By 1966 U.S. passenger car registrations reached 78 million, along with 16 million trucks and buses. Walker's mechanical wizardry was a part of millions of vehicles and had attracted the attention of Tenneco Inc. A worldwide conglomerate primarily known for its gasoline stations throughout the United States, Tenneco acquired Walker in 1967. With Tenneco's backing and extensive resources, Walker's future seemed assured, and the company continued to place further emphasis on acoustical engineering and its relationship to automobile exhaust systems. To this end, Walker opened a new research facility in Grass Lake, Michigan, with state-of-the-art equipment and testing grounds.

Catalytic Converters and Beyond, 1970s and 1980s

In the late 1970s Walker's continued concern for pollution control led to the design of a reasonably priced catalytic converter to fit all car models. Parent company Tenneco made a move at this time to purchase Monroe Auto Equipment (ride control systems) as a complimentary business to Walker. The two were paired and spun off as Tenneco Automotive in 1977, and shortly thereafter Walker established a formal working relationship with the Environmental Protection Agency (EPA). This partnership helped produce the first universal catalytic converter in 1978, especially useful when emissions standards became more restrictive at the end of the decade.

In 1984 the company introduced the Walker Advantage muffler with Absorbite, and this product brought the Walker name firmly into the limelight. After trademarking its latest technology, Walker's design teams produced another breakthrough in 1987 with the debut of the DynoMax Performance Exhaust line. In 1988 Walker celebrated 100 years of business, marking its dominance of the design, engineering, production, and sales of automobile exhaust systems including catalytic converters, mufflers, tubular manifolds, pipes and entire stainless steel exhaust systems.

Onward and Upward, the 1990s

The early 1990s brought headway in Walker's design of an electronic muffler. In 1991 the company joined forces with NCTI (Noise Cancellation Technologies Inc.) to develop and produce electronic mufflers using NCTI's ''anti-noise'' sound waves. Twenty percent smaller than their predecessors, the electronic mufflers encouraged the formation of anti-noise sound waves to cancel out about 80 percent of the overall noise while simultaneously increasing fuel efficiency (up to six percent in the city). By the end of the year Walker's sales balanced out as 65 percent in aftermarket parts and accessories and 35 percent new products installation.

The company closed 1992 with sales of over $850 million and nearly 6,100 employees worldwide. Over the next few years Walker continued its worldwide expansion and experienced its share of triumphs and setbacks. One example of the latter came in 1994 when the company's plant in Hebron, Ohio, the largest of its 11 North American plants, was forced to close after Ford took its tailpipe and muffler needs in-house. On the upside, in 1994 Walker acquired Products for Power Inc. and Germany's Gillet Group (the Continent's largest exhaust system manufacturer and aftermarket supplier) and bought Perfection Automotive Products Corp. of Livonia, Michigan, and Spain's Manufacturas Fonos S.L. in 1995. Walker also began a 60,000-square-foot addition to its Litchfield, Michigan, plant in response to a higher volume of business from Honda and General Motors.

With international operations already established in Australia, Canada, China, Europe, Mexico, and South Africa, at the end of the summer of 1996, Walker was poised to conquer the South American automotive industry. South America's runaway inflation had reached its lowest point in 40 years, and new car and light truck sales were booming, when Walker took over Argentina's Minuzzi, headquartered in Buenos Aires, and renamed it Walker Argentina. Minuzzi's extensive exhaust operations, the second largest in the country, serviced several high profile customers including General Motors, Mercedes, and Volkswagen. Then Walker moved into sibling Monroe's facility in Mogi Mirim, Brazil, to manufacture and supply catalytic converters and exhaust systems for Volkswagen. Both South American operations, Walker Exhaust Systems do Brasil and Walker Argentina, joined the growing replacement market with plans to forge a combined 200 percent growth spurt by the year 2000.

Another boon came in the fall of 1996 when Walker's long relationship with Ford Motor Company took another upswing in the form of an exclusive contract to manufacture stainless steel exhaust pipes and mufflers for the auto giant. Ford also figured in Walker's international sales dominance, as Walker Australia, once in danger of losing its grip on the country's exhaust systems production, had come back with a vengeance to handle all exhaust systems manufacturing for Toyota and Mitsubishi, and a majority of Nissan's and Ford's as well. Another new agreement named Walker as the exhaust systems supplier for a new Saturn sedan, scheduled for introduction in 1999.

Additionally in 1996, Walker acquired the heavy duty truck exhaust operations of Stemco Inc. (a division of Coltec Industries) and entered into a joint venture with China's Jinzhou Automotive to gain a firmer hold of the Asian market. Walker's extensive international operations—including technical centers linked by a state-of-the-art computer system—now consisted of four facilities in the United Kingdom; three each in France and Germany; two in Australia; and one each in Argentina, Canada, China, the Czech Republic, Denmark, Japan, Mexico, Portugal, South Africa, and Sweden.

For the award-winning $1.5-billion exhaust systems manufacturer, the future seemed bright. Walker had conquered the auto exhaust systems market; one in every four mufflers sold worldwide was a Walker product. As the 21st century neared, the company continued to research acoustical performance, corrosion testing, and a host of other product line improvements to maintain its dominance.

Principal Divisions

AB-Starla Werken (Sweden); Dalian Walker Gillet Muffler Co. Ltd.; ETS R. Bellanger S.A. (France); Finnwalker OY (Finland); Harmo Industries Ltd. (U.K.); Lydex A/S (Denmark); Tenneco-Walker Ltd. (U.K.); Walker Argentina; Walker Australia Pty, Ltd.; Walker Deutschland GmbH (Germany); Walker Exhaust Systems do Brasil.

Further Reading

''Ford Selects Walker for Exhaust,'' *American Metal Market,* September 23, 1996, p. 4.
''On the Road to a Quieter Engine,'' *Construction Equipment,* September 15, 1991, p. 10.
''Tenneco Automotive Launches Major Expansion in South America,'' *PR Newswire,* August 20, 1996.
''Tenneco Unit in Argentina (Walker Manufacturing Acquires Minuzzi),'' *New York Times,* August 21, 1996, p. D2.
Vasilash, Gary S., ''Lessons from a Leader,'' *Production,* January 1993, pp. 32–40.
''Walker. . .100 Years of Leadership,'' Walker Manufacturing Company, 1989.

—Taryn Benbow-Pfalzgraf

Washington Gas

Washington Gas Light Company

1100 H Street N.W.
Washington, D.C. 20080
U.S.A.
(703) 750-1000
Fax: (703) 750-4440

Public Company
Incorporated: 1848
Employees: 2,274
Total Assets: $1.46 billion (1996)
Stock Exchanges: New York
SICs: 4924 Natural Gas Distribution

Washington Gas Light Company provides natural gas to the metropolitan Washington, D.C., area including segments of Maryland, Virginia, and West Virginia. It has provided gas service to customers in the District of Columbia since 1848 and has grown with the capital city as it changed from a sleepy southern town to an international metropolis. For Washington Gas Light (WGL), this meant acquiring smaller regional gas companies and broadening service to surrounding states as the population grew and suburbs extended. By 1996, more than 770,000 natural gas customers were served in Maryland (43 percent), Virginia (33 percent), West Virginia (two percent), and the District of Columbia (22 percent).

Formative Years

On July 8, 1848, four days after the cornerstone was laid for the Washington Monument, Washington Gas Light Co. received its charter from Congress. About 45,000 people lived in the rough hewn capital city with its chronically muddy streets and lackluster infrastructure. A few buildings were lit by gas produced by an apparatus fired by wood or coal that created water carbureted hydrogen gas. But this gas lighting was confined to large institutions such as Georgetown College, theaters, and a few hotels.

Washington's citizens were jealous of their counterparts in Baltimore and Philadelphia where gas lighting was available in many neighborhoods. To some extent, throughout its history, the administration of Washington, D.C., has been under the aegis of Congress. In order to effect change, Washington's citizens had to petition Congress to bring gas light to the city's streets. Though groups appealed to Congress several times during the 1840s, they did not meet with success.

Then in 1847, James Crutchett, an entrepreneur who had demonstrated gas lighting in Cincinnati, Wheeling, West Virginia, and other cities, proposed that Congress pay him to light up the Capitol and its grounds with gas. Crutchett's Capitol Hill gas lighting project was a success, but it was Benjamin B. French, Chief Clerk of the House of Representatives and friend to at least two Presidents, who had the connections to organize a gas company for Washington. French and a group of prominent local businessmen bought Crutchett's patent rights to produce gas and took over the business of supplying gas light to the Capitol. From there it was a short step to achieving incorporation and the Congressional charter. Washington Gas Light Company was thus the first Congressionally chartered gas company and is the first public utility so chartered that is still in operation.

During the 1850s, improvements and modern conveniences were introduced in this "gas light" era. But while street lights were installed in a few showcase neighborhoods where homes were illuminated, other districts remained dark and primitive. Running water and sanitary facilities were sparse, farm animals were penned in the alleys and grazed in the city's open spaces. Transportation was happenstance.

George W. Riggs, who had founded the Corcoran and Riggs bank with William W. Corcoran, become president of the WGL company in 1856. Riggs was a powerful, well-connected Washingtonian with the resources and allies to expand the fledgling gas company. In 1858 the West Station Gas Works were constructed at 26th Street and G Street N.W., while the company headquarters were at 514 Eleventh Street N.W. just above Pennsylvania Avenue. In 1860, the city corporation established the office of gas meter inspector and sealer, bringing public utility regulation under local authority.

With the outbreak of the Civil War in 1861 came disorder and heartbreak along with growth and activity. Troops were bivouacked on their way to the battlefields, purveyors of goods and services to the army flocked to the city. The work force expanded to support the military. The city experienced a brush with the Confederate forces when General Early's troops were engaged at Fort Stevens, but Washington itself was not burnt or bombarded. Parallel to the difficulties experienced by the city and the nation as a whole, a coal shortage during the war caused WGL's costs to increase, even as Congress reduced the gas rate by 17 percent.

President Grant in 1869 made the District of Columbia a Territorial Government, giving it a governor and council, a house of delegates and a delegate to Congress, a short-lived privilege that ended in 1874 when Congress established the Commission Government, putting the city more squarely under Congressional authority. Meanwhile WGL continued to expand and built a new headquarters at 413 Tenth Street N.W.

When Thomas Edison's invention, the incandescent lamp, hit the marketplace in 1878, the gas light industry considered it a serious competitive threat. The United States Electric Lighting Company of Washington tried to install electric lights along Pennsylvania Avenue in 1881, but just as gas lighting concerns had a difficult time getting established in the city, electric lighting was held at bay, and gas street lighting endured for several more decades. In 1888, WGL constructed its East Station Plant at 12th Street and N Street S.E. along the Anacostia River. Construction was seriously hampered by the marshy ground; walls would collapse and disappear into the river.

At the turn of the century, WGL had more than 54,000 gas meters in a thriving city of 330,000 people. Intending to secure a future site for a gas manufacturing plant, during 1913 WGL bought Analostan Island, in the Potomac River. The same year brought regulatory change. The Public Utilities Commission was created for Washington, D.C.; Congress would no longer directly regulate the city's utilities.

The First World War brought food rationing, fuel and labor shortages, even before the United States entered the war in 1917. During W.W. I, WGL expanded, by purchasing Rosslyn Gas Company in northern Virginia and adding it to the controlling interest already held in The Georgetown Gaslight Company. The expansion may have been too hasty, however. By the early 1930's, WGL was divesting real estate, selling Analostan Island to the Theodore Roosevelt Memorial Association and unloading the parcel of land that had been the Maryland Avenue Plant, a possession held since 1851.

The New Era

On January 31, 1931, President Hoover signaled from the White House to turn on a giant valve at the WGL's East Station

Plant to open the current of natural gas flowing from Kentucky and West Virginia. This gas was mixed with manufactured gas and distributed to customers. The New Deal brought population expansion which further intensified during World War II. Gas main lines were extended to Rockville, Maryland, nearly 20 miles out of the city. With the direct pipelines to the Appalachian region, thousands of new customers could be provided with gas. WGL grew out of its office building and purchased land at 11th Street and H Street for a new headquarters. Even through the years of the Great Depression, in fact during the first hundred years of the company's history, WGL sustained dividends every year since 1866.

From the beginning, WGL manufactured gas using a variety of methods. At first, the company made rosin gas. Later on, coal gas, oil gas, and carbureted water gas was processed until the introduction of natural gas in 1931 when gas from the Appalachian region became available to the Washington, D.C. area. Carbureted water gas was made by passing steam through hot coke or a mixture of coal and coke, then by adding oil gas, the water gas was enriched or carbureted. After World War II, natural gas supplies were augmented by sources of Texas gas sent via pipelines built or improved for war time emergency oil supply. During 1946–47, WGL adapted all customers' gas appliances to use natural gas, an enormous task involving some three million gas burners of domestic and commercial appliances.

From the post-W.W. II era onward, through the turbulent 1960s, Washington, D.C. enjoyed a steady population growth. In 1963, WGL's long term attempt to establish underground storage facilities for its natural gas came to a head. Land had been acquired in Brandywine, Maryland, in Prince George's County, an area that was then sparsely populated. The company wanted to stockpile gas purchased at uniform low rates for use during periods of peak demand. Safety concerns by residents close to the proposed site inflamed the legislative debate which turned on increased tax revenues for one county and threatened property values in a neighboring county. The underground storage project was stymied. During the summer of 1963, WGL announced a plan to acquire and operate a natural gas field in Hampshire County, West Virginia, some 125 miles northwest of Washington, D.C., and far from the safety concerns of suburban homeowners. The gas field would be owned by a new subsidiary, Hampshire Gas Co., with a view to providing gas to customers during the ever increasing demand, especially for winter peak loads.

Conservation efforts during the 1970s energy crisis and the usual customer attrition rate meant that less gas was being sold. As the economic times were inflationary, labor, construction, and interest costs were spiraling. Gas prices doubled from 1974 to 1977 and utility bills hit the ceiling. So did customers. But even during these tumultuous times, WGL continued to raise dividends for investors.

Competition in the 1980s

The 1980s ushered in an era of rapidly rising commercial and residential real estate values to the Washington, D.C. area. Construction boomed, but many of the new houses were designated for electric heating. WGL survived a series of potentially destructive events during this time—aggressive competition from the electric industry, changes in regulatory policy, and labor strikes.

In August 1985, aiming to improve competitiveness in the energy market, WGL created company divisions to serve Maryland, Virginia, and the District of Columbia. By decentralizing, the company hoped to counter heavy competition from aggressive electric companies promoting the merits of electric heat pumps for low cost home heating and from the oil industry which had been in a price slide.

Intending to stimulate competition and produce lower gas prices for consumers, federal energy regulators in the fall of 1985 changed policy regulations and established a voluntary rule requiring pipelines that had previously been buying and selling natural gas as well as transporting it, confine their activities to transporting the gas. In theory, this move would allow gas distribution companies such as WGL to purchase cheaper gas produced far away and pass the savings along to their customers. But large volume gas users such as hospitals and government agencies then sought avenues to cut their own deals with the producers, bypassing the local distributor, WGL.

In June 1986, 1,250 employees enrolled in the International Union of Gas Workers struck at WGL, the company's first strike in 25 years. Excessive overtime was the complaint, caused by staffing reductions, a policy the company had been implementing since 1982. Labor strife occurred again in 1995 when members of the International Union of Gas Workers objected to new contract terms that would allow the company to hire part time workers. A lockout of 109 days marked the acrimonious period.

Relations with the community, however, continue to be cordial. The Washington Area Fuel Fund initiated by WGL has raised $9 million since its inception in 1983 to provide fuel for poor families. Other community based programs supported by WGL included fixing up homes for senior citizens and disabled people, health care for needy children, and programs aimed to reduce infant mortality, a significant health problem in the District of Columbia.

The 1990s and Beyond

During the 1990s, the effects of deregulation of electric and gas utilities began to trickle down to the consumer level. The Federal Energy Regulatory Commission rewrote merger regulations, opening the utility company arena to acquisitions and mergers involving offshore and out of state utility companies. New entries in the gas utility business turned the heat up on WGL. Consolidation, improved marketing strategy, and focusing on new markets characterized WGL's response.

In the mid-1990s, competition was focused between natural gas and electricity in the lucrative residential market, the primary source of the company's net income. While WGL continued to enjoy a price advantage over electricity, the entry into the marketplace of other natural gas providers posed a threat to WGL's monopoly. During the fall of 1996, thousands of residents in Montgomery and Prince George's counties (suburbs of Washington, D.C.) received the option of buying natural gas from a supplier other than WGL, under a two-year pilot program ordered by state regulators. Horizon Energy, Broadstreet

Energyone, and BNG, Inc. offered savings plans, guaranteed caps on gas charges, rebates, and cash advances to lure customers from WGL.

As the electric utilities jostled for increased market share, WGL expected increased competition from that quarter. In an effort to garner some of the electricity market themselves, early in 1997, WGL announced that if regulators permitted, the company planned to market electricity to consumers in the Washington, D.C. area, using transmission lines of existing distribution companies. Fuel oil was also a noteworthy competitor in areas where clients required alternate fuel sources during peak demands.

During this time, WGL obtained the natural gas to meet its customer requirements through 13 long-term gas supply contracts scheduled to expire between 1998 and 2004. During periods of peak demand, such as the winter of 1996 when the Washington, D.C. area experienced record cold spells, WGL acquired extra gas supplies as needed, sometimes at higher prices than standard contracts. About 70 percent of WGL's gas supplies were transmitted through facilities of Columbia Gas System, a Reston, Virginia, based natural gas company that in 1997 announced plans to construct a pipeline to carry natural gas from western Canada, the Gulf of Mexico, and the Rocky Mountain region. These additional gas supplies were expected to help moderate prices in the future. With service agreements with eight interstate pipelines, WGL bought natural gas from more than 60 suppliers. Gas was also acquired under seasonal contracts or spot market purchases.

Another WGL savings strategy was to shift a certain amount of service and installation work to independent contractors. Consumer complaints about unsatisfactory, and at times unsafe, contractor work increased during the mid-1990s. In response, Washington Gas Watch: A Coalition to Protect the Public was established in 1997 by a group of community organizations to monitor contractors who work for WGL.

James H. DeGraffenreidt, Jr., president and chief operating officer of WGL, predicted in a late 1996 interview with *American Gas* that in the Company's future ''you will see continuing trends in consolidation. . . . You will see innovations, primarily in information technology, that will make it possible for customers to take greater control over the multiplicity of services.'' Indeed, throughout the last half of the 1990s, WGL was faced with transforming itself into a more consumer-oriented utility. Several new gas suppliers had entered the Washington, D.C. suburban marketplace. Competition required rethinking corporate marketing strategy. Winning back customers who switched to one of the other gas suppliers—EnergyOne, Enron, Horizon and BGE—was one aspect. Persuading customers who used another energy source to switch to gas was another strategy to improve market share. Moreover, since a competitive marketplace demands a responsive organization, WGL encouraged employees to work with greater autonomy to achieve objectives. Efforts to consolidate were underway. In 1996, Frederick Gas Company was merged into the parent company.

Principal Subsidiaries

Crab Run Gas Co.; Hampshire Gas Co.; Shenandoah Gas Co.; Advanced Marketing Concepts, Inc.; American Environmental

Products, Inc.; Brandywood Estates, Inc.; Davenport Insulation, Inc.; Universal Insulation, Inc.; Washington Gas Energy Systems, Inc.

Further Reading

Hershman, Robert R., and Edward T. Stafford, *Growing With Washington: The Story of Our First Hundred Years,* Washington Gas Light Company: Washington, D.C., 1948.

Petranek, Stephen, "The Power Brokers," *The Washington Post Magazine,* August 26, 1979., pp. 12–21.

Ryan, Karen, "Mind Over Marketing," *American Gas,* November 1996, pp. 28–38.

—L. Peat O'Neil

Watts Industries, Inc.

815 Chestnut Street
North Andover, Massachusetts 01845-6098
U.S.A.
(508) 688-1811
Fax: (508) 688-5841

Public Company
Incorporated: 1985 as Watts Regulator Company
Employees: 3,100
Sales: $518.5 million (1995)
Stock Exchanges: NASDAQ
SICs: 3492 Fluid Power Valves & Hose Fittings; 3494
 Valves & Pipe Fitting Not Elsewhere Classified

Watts Industries, Inc., is one of the country's leading designers, manufacturers, and sellers of valves that regulate air, gas, water, steam, and oil. It includes more than 40 wholly owned subsidiaries throughout the United States, Canada, Europe, and South America.

A New Frontier

When Joseph Edwin Watts was 17 years old, he emigrated from Cheshire, England, to the newly built town of Lawrence, Massachusetts. The town was founded in 1845 by a group of industrialists and entrepreneurs whose idea was to build "The Great Stone Dam" across the Merrimack River to harness the river's immense water power for industrial textile production.

The first records of Joseph Watts's employment were in 1867 as a machinist at the Pacific Mills in Lawrence. He worked there until 1874, when he left to go into business for himself. From his shop on Essex Street, he contracted work supplying parts and fittings for machinery at the nearby textile mills. He advertised himself in local trade publications as "Joseph E. Watts, Machinist and Brass Finisher, Manufacturer of Steam and Water Pressure Regulators." By 1893 Watts had constructed a block-long brick building on Lowell Street to house the Watts Regulator Company.

By that time Watts had become more than a machinist and manufacturer. He was also an inventor, and between 1881 and his death in 1894, he received 18 patents for valves that proved essential to almost every manufacturing concern in the area. Soon manufactures from all over the United States, Canada, and Europe were installing and using Watts valves.

After Watts's death the company was purchased by Robert E. Pickles and his partner, George W. Dodson. When Dodson left the company a few years later, Pickles brought in his brother Charles. Using advances in technology and improved materials, Robert Pickles was able to redesign many of Watts's valves so that they could be used not only for large industrial and municipal purposes but also for commercial household plumbing and heating.

1918–1945: A Family Business is Born

In 1918 Robert Pickles sold the Watts Regulator Company to a trio of investors who had each put up $25,000. They were Burchard Everett Horne, his uncle Herbert W. Horne, and their friend Norman Anderson. Within a year Burchard had bought out both his uncle's and Anderson's shares.

In the early 1860s the Horne family had moved from Lowell, Massachusetts, to Lawrence, where they had established the George W. Horne Roofing Company, which was eventually controlled by Burchard (better known as B.E.) Horne. By the time B.E. purchased the Watts Regulator Company, the textile industry, upon which the town of Lawrence had been founded, was in deep decline. The advent of steam power (as opposed to waterpower) meant that textile mills could be set up anywhere that fuel was available. Other technical advances, plus high labor costs and taxes in the North, drove the textile industry farther and farther south.

Robert Pickles had begun the diversification of the Watts Regulator Company, and B.E. Horne quickly capitalized on his emphasis on plumbing and heating uses for Watts valves. In fact, they were so determined to accentuate their flexibility that, in their 1919 catalog, the company stated, "We claim to be able to regulate and control any temperature or pressure of any fluid for any purpose and under any conditions."

Company Perspectives:

Watts's goals for the 1990s are to achieve growth of 15 percent each year and become a $1 billion company which responds to and anticipates the needs of customers all over the world.

A major development in Watts's expansion—and a major setback—came in the 1920s, when the company hired John G. Kelly, Inc., to handle its national distribution. Within a short period of time, Kelly landed the company a contract with Consolidated Gas of New York, manufacturers of mechanical refrigerators powered by gas. A Watts valve was installed in every Consolidated Gas refrigerator, which created a boom for the company. That boom lasted only a short time before Consolidated redesigned the refrigerator, eliminating the need for the Watts valve.

The company's breakthrough came in the late 1920s, when B.E. Horne and an inventor named Chetwood Smith developed and patented a combination temperature and pressure relief valve, which came to be known as the T&P Valve. The valve was an important development in the safety of hot-water supply tank systems. Overheated hot-water tanks (without these safety valves) had periodically exploded, causing extensive property damage and even fatalities. Although earlier valves had dealt with the problems of internal pressure building in the tanks, none had withstood the extremely high temperatures the water sometimes reached. The T&P Valve was not perfect, but it provided a level of safety never before reached in hot-water tanks. This valve became the staple of Watts's business; the company even licensed other manufacturers to make the valve and received a royalty for every valve sold.

By 1936 B.E. Horne was becoming dissatisfied with the national sales effort of the John G. Kelly company. When his son George graduated from college, B.E. appointed him head of marketing for Watts. It was George Horne's job to educate the plumbing and heating industries about the dangers of overheating hot-water systems and the relief provided by the T&P Valve. To that end he traveled the country setting up explosion demonstrations. He would mount a tank in a field, put it inside the shell of a house, and overheat the tank until it blew. This convinced people in the industry—who still thought that excess pressure was the only danger—of the necessity of the T&P Valve. As the word spread, sales at the company began to rise dramatically, despite the sluggish economy of the Depression. As a result, George Horne finally convinced his father to give up the roofing business, which he continued to run, and to devote himself solely to Watts. By the time World War II broke out, U.S. Army Engineers required T&P Valves on all Army hot-water supply tank installations.

1945–1972: The Great Expansion

After the war the Watts patents on the T&P Valve expired, and the company was forced to concentrate on developing and marketing new products. In 1951 B.E. Watts, always an avid

sportsman, set off on a fishing expedition from which he never returned. He suffered a gallbladder attack while fishing, fell in the lake, and drowned. Control of the Watts Regulator Company was passed on to his son George. At the time Watts sales totaled about $3.5 million a year.

Where B.E. Horne had been a conservative businessman, his son George was dedicated to progress and expansion. He expanded his sales force nationwide and often brought salespeople to Lawrence for training and new product education. He was constantly asking his sales force for ideas on new products. In the 1950s George Horne opened a fluid power division to make valves and control devices used on machine tools powered by air pressure.

In 1959 the company had outgrown its Lawrence premises, and George Horne opened a plant in Franklin, New Hampshire. The Lawrence plant continued to operate until 1970, but the workforce gradually shrank from 300 to 50. In addition to opening the Franklin plant, George Horne began to implement a professional management structure with two important hires. He brought in Robert Chaffee to take over the position of manager of sales, and he hired his son Tim as an all-around executive troubleshooter. In 1960 Watts, using an early generation IBM punch-card-operated computer, became one of the first companies to computerize its record keeping.

Robert Chaffee was in charge of revitalizing the sales force. He introduced regional company offices in Boston, Detroit, New York, San Francisco, Los Angeles, and Chicago. Another method Watts used for expansion in the 1960s was a "private label" program, which allowed companies to offer Watts products under their own names. One of the most successful aspects of the program was the relationship with Sears, Roebuck, in which valves, manufactured by Watts, were sold under the Sears name in their stores and catalogs.

By 1962 the company was expanding internationally, constructing a plant in Stroud, Gloucestershire, England, and another in Canada. In 1967 sales had risen to more than $17 million a year, and Tim Horne was promoted to vice-president and assistant general manager. Five years later Robert Chaffee resigned, and Tim Horne was named executive vice president.

1972–1984: New Products, New Markets

In the early 1970s Colorado state sanitation inspectors approached George Horne to help them find a solution to backflow problems. Backflow is the reversal of the normal flow of water in a system. For example, opening one water source might create a vacuum in another water-supply line, which could be dangerous if the water-supply line is connected to a contaminated source. These potentially hazardous "cross connections" occur everyday in such common areas as a garden hose connected to a tank of swimming-pool-treatment chemicals. Watts had already been manufacturing two simple, inexpensive backflow prevention connections, but they did not protect against high-pressure backflow conditions.

Watts then began an intensive period of research and development to design a more effective, less expensive valve than the ones that were already on the market. Within a year the company was producing the Watts Model 900 Backflow Preventer.

This marked the beginning of the company's move into the waterworks industry; Watts soon became a leader in the backflow prevention field, a position it maintained into the 1990s.

In 1976 Tim Horne became president of the company, and in 1978, when George Horne retired, Tim became both president and chief executive officer. One of Tim Horne's first moves was to sell off the fluid power division and to develop a line of industrial ball valves, which allowed the company to move into the chemical-processing industry. Although sales rose from $39.5 million in 1978 to more than $100 million in 1984, inroads into the chemical-processing industry were difficult to navigate, and it took the company more than ten years to establish itself in that field. That led Tim Horne to believe that the way of the future lay not only in new product development but in the acquisition of complementary companies.

Into the 1990s and Beyond

The year 1984 saw Watt's first acquisition—Spence Engineering, a manufacturer of steam regulators, which had $6.7 million in sales. Next came Hale Oilfield Products, a company that brought Watts into the oil and gas pipeline industry. Watts interrupted its acquisitions program in 1985 to prepare for its first public stock offering. In 1986 Tim Horne became chairman of the board and chief executive officer of Watts Industries, Inc., trading as WATTA on the NASDAQ exchange with shares offered at $16.50 each.

Throughout the 1980s and into the 1990s, Watts continued its strategy of acquiring small niche companies to fill out its product line. In the early 1990s Watts began acquiring companies in Europe. In the decade from 1985 to 1995, Watts Industries made 28 acquisitions.

The mid-1990s saw ups and downs for the company. According to a 1994 *Forbes* article, Watts suffered an economic downturn in 1993 mainly from a "sharp slump in aerospace and Navy contracts." By 1994, however, the company's annual report stated that Watts had achieved "another record year for both sales and earnings." And in October 1994 *Money* maga-zine chose Watts Industries as one of "Eight Small Stocks for Big Gains." In 1995 Watts announced a joint venture with the Suzhou Valve Factory of the People's Republic of China. One year later the company announced that Tyco International Ltd. had agreed to buy the waterworks valve business of Watts Industries. But in 1997 Watts was back in an acquisitions mode, acquiring the Ames Company, a leader in the design, manufacture, and marketing of backflow prevention valves.

In the company's 1994 annual report, Chairman of the Board Tim Horne stated, "We remain committed to our goal of double-digit growth with the ambitious objective of reaching $1 billion in sales by the end of the decade . . . With more financial resources allocated to new product development, the prospect of improving markets for more of our business segments, and our ongoing acquisition search, we are optimistic about future growth prospects."

Principal Subsidiaries

Watts Automatic Control Valve, Inc.; Watts International Sales Corp.; Watts Regulator Company; Watts Industries (Canada) Inc.; Watts Industries Europe B.V. (Netherlands); Watts Industries France S.A.; Watts Ocean GmbH (Germany).

Further Reading

Lyon, David, *The Watts Way,* North Andover, Massachusetts: Watts Regulator Company, 1994.
Mao, Phillipe, "We Are in a Mode to Create Jobs," *Forbes,* January 3, 1994, p. 113.
McAvoy, Kenneth J., "Watts Acquires Ames Co. Inc.," *Business Wire,* January 6, 1997.
Scherreik, Susan, "Eight Small Stocks for a Big Gain," *Money,* October 1994, p. 96.
"Watts Industries, Inc.," *Oil and Gas Journal,* May 22, 1995, p. 67.
"Watts Industries Sells Unit to Tyco International," *New York Times,* Sept. 6, 1996, p. D5.

—Sharyn Kolberg

Welbilt Corp.

225 High Ridge Road
Stamford, Connecticut 06905
U.S.A.
(203) 325-8300
Fax: (203) 325-9800
Web site: http://www.welbilt.com

Wholly Owned Subsidiary of Berisford International plc
Incorporated: 1929 as Welbilt Stove Co.
Employees: 2,200
Sales: $426.5 million (1993)
SICs: 3433 Heating Equipment, Except Electric & Warm
Air Furnaces; 3556 Food Products Machinery; 3585
Air Conditioning & Warm Air Heating Equipment &
Commercial & Industrial Refrigeration Equipment;
3589 Service Industry Machinery, Not Elsewhere
Classified; 5064 Electrical Appliances, Television &
Radio Sets

Welbilt Corp., through its subsidiaries, is the largest manufacturer of cooking and warming equipment in North America. Its customers include fast-food chains, institutional accounts such as schools and hospitals, full-service restaurants, and retail stores, including supermarkets and convenience stores. The company also distributes products in more than 65 countries. In the mid-1990s Welbilt had a dozen subsidiaries in the United States. It was acquired in 1995 by Berisford plc, a British firm. Welbilt's goal at that time was to increase its business to $1 billion by the year 2000.

The Years before 1955

Henry and Alexander Hirsch founded Welbilt Stove Co. in 1929, primarily to make residential gas ranges. The privately owned company's factory was in the New York City borough of Queens. Welbilt Stove added electric ranges, range hoods, household-incinerators, and home air conditioners in later years.

In 1955 the company acquired Detroit-Michigan Stove Co., a company with a much longer pedigree. Founded in 1864, incor-

porated in 1866, and reincorporated in 1907 as Detroit Stove Works, this closely held public corporation was, in 1920, manufacturing stoves and furnaces in Detroit under the "Jewel" name. W. T. Barbour was its president and J. A. Fry its secretary and general manager; later they advanced to chairman and president, respectively. In 1923 the company acquired Art Stove Co. and in 1925 Michigan Stove Co., changing its name to Detroit-Michigan Stove Co. The combined enterprise now, in addition to stoves and furnaces, made gas ranges for homes and heavy-duty heating and cooking appliances for hotels, clubs, restaurants, and institutions under the "Garland" and "Laurel" as well as "Jewel" and "Detroit Jewel" names. In 1927 the company placed a giant, 30-ton replica of an old-fashioned kitchen range on the roof of its factory near the approach to Detroit's Belle Isle Bridge. Originally built for the 1893 World's Fair in Chicago, this replica was billed as the "largest stove in the world."

Fiscal 1926 (ended July 31, 1926) was Detroit-Michigan Stove's best year for a long time, with net sales of $8.1 million and net profits of $1.2 million. During the Depression decade of the 1930s annual net sales fell as low as $2.3 million, and the company lost money each year from 1931 through 1934, and again in 1938. In fiscal 1940, however, when the firm had a net profit of $210,000 on net sales of $3.1 million, it was prosperous enough to begin paying dividends. The company dropped furnaces in the mid-1930s.

Detroit-Michigan Stove raised its revenues considerably by acquiring A-B Stoves, Inc. of Battle Creek, Michigan, in 1945. It also added a metal-fabricating division turning out parts for automotive and other manufacturers. Net sales reached a high of $21 million in 1948 and net profit nearly $2 million. By mid-century the company's Detroit plant consisted of 23 buildings, and its products included electric as well as gas ranges for homes. Sales dropped by nearly half in 1949, however, and did not rise significantly thereafter. The company lost more than $1 million in 1953 and more than $1.6 million in 1954 on sales of only $9 million.

Merged Company, 1955–1976

When Welbilt Stove acquired Detroit-Michigan Stove in 1955, the consolidated company became Welbilt Corp., a public corporation that inherited Detroit-Michigan's listing on the New York Stock Exchange. Net sales in 1955 were $22.8 million, and the company had net profit of $1.5 million. The Hirsches sold A-B Stoves in 1955 and closed the Detroit plant in 1957 but soon acquired four companies. The purchase of Consolidated Industries, Inc. in 1958 returned Welbilt to the furnace-making business, and that of Wedgewood-Holly Corp. in 1959, added a West Coast producer of higher-priced ranges. In 1960 the company acquired American Coils Co., an air-conditioning manufacturer, and Unagusta Manufacturing Co., a furniture maker. By the end of 1960 Welbilt had plants in four states and Canada as well as the Queens factory, where a new building was erected in 1964 for the manufacture of air-conditioning equipment as well as kitchen ranges.

Welbilt reached a peak of $56.8 million in sales in 1969 but lost money for the next five years: a total of $10.4 million. In 1971, 29-year-old Richard Hirsch succeeded his father Henry as president. It became clear to him that the company could not survive by making and marketing consumer goods. The biggest drain was Unagusta, which, after losing almost $6 million during 1971 and 1972, was sold for $5 million the following year. Wedgewood-Holly was sold in 1972. A lamp manufacturing operation that Welbilt had formed and the refrigeration-distributing division were scrapped in 1974. The following year Welbilt closed its Queens plant, transferring its production of cooking ranges, range hoods, air conditioners, and microwave ovens (introduced in 1973) to its remaining U.S. plants in Freeland, Pennsylvania, and Lafayette, Indiana.

Welbilt's stock fell as low as three cents a share in 1974. Stripped to the bone, its sales dropped to $15.8 million in 1975, yet it still lost $2.4 million that year. With total assets of only $6 million and an average $2.2–million loss for the previous three fiscal years, it lost its listing on the New York Stock Exchange. "The really dynamic growth of the company began in the late 1970s when the restructuring was completed and a decision made to expand our commitment to food service equipment," Hirsch told an *Appliance* editor in 1989. "We reviewed our goals and set new directions for the future. We had closed 12 divisions, retained Garland and shrunk the company to a critical mass."

A Star in the 1980s

Hirsch's downsizing enabled Welbilt to return to financial health. After three straight profitable years it ended 1979 with net sales of $32.5 million and net income of $2.8 million. The company resumed paying dividends in 1981 after a decade-long

drought. Hirsch and executive assistant Larry Gross—his old college roommate—now began acquiring manufacturers of products that could be sold to fast-food chains. In 1982 they bought four food-service Sunbeam Corp. subsidiaries, including Frymaster, Belshaw Brothers (a bakery equipment manufacturer) and Mile High, a producer of ice-making machines. New equipment was created for these firms, with an emphasis on reducing labor costs. Frymaster, for example, sold fryers for chicken and french fries that adjusted cooking time and temperatures, cleaned themselves, and shut themselves off. By 1989, largely due to other acquisitions, Belshaw systems were making about 65 percent of all the doughnuts in the world.

Company sales rose fourfold between 1982 and 1986. Between 1984 and 1988 Welbilt's compound annual earnings growth rate was 54 percent. During this period about 70 percent of Welbilt's sales and slightly more of its profits were coming from commercial food-service equipment, including not only ranges, ovens, and appliances, but also ventilators, grease filters and extractors, and exhaust fans. The remainder came from domestic appliances, including the manufacture and sale of residential gas-fired furnaces, the sale of residential ranges, the sale and distribution of refrigerators, and the distribution of freezers and oil-filled unit heaters. In 1984 Welbilt sold its Queens facility for $7.6 million and moved its executive offices to New Hyde Park, Long Island.

The company ended 1987 with net income of $12.8 million on revenues of $234.3 million. It had 16 subsidiaries, 11 factories (including plants in Canada and West Germany) and was doing business in almost 100 countries. The stock, once as low as 12 cents a share, traded for as high as $28.25 in 1988. Revenues came to $273.6 million and earnings to $6.2 million that year.

Private, then Public Again, 1988–1994

Welbilt went private in 1988, being acquired in a leveraged buy out by a group led by Kohlberg & Co. that included Richard Hirsch and his brother David (the company's treasurer and chief financial officer) for about $265 million. The new private company assumed a long-term debt of $187.7 million to help pay for the deal. While remaining as committed to Welbilt as ever, Hirsch espoused corporate autonomy. "The profit and loss centers are the responsibilities of the various divisional presidents," he told *Appliance*. Moses Shapiro, a director and one of the owners, added, "We're interventionist in terms of assistance and aid. We're hands off in terms of day-to-day activities. . . .The day-to-day operations are contained in a budget that then becomes the agreed-upon bible, which determines how the divisions work and are measured."

In April 1989 Welbilt acquired six divisions of Alco Standard Corp.'s Foodservice Equipment Group. These were Cleveland Range, a producer of steam-cooking equipment; Dean Industries, a manufacturer of gas and electric fryers and related equipment; Merco Products, a maker of food-warming equipment and broilers; Savory Equipment, a producer of countertop cooking appliances; U.S. Range, a manufacturer of commercial ranges, ovens, and broilers; and Alco World Trade, a marketer of food-service equipment.

Not all Welbilt products ignored the home consumer. Welbilt Appliance Inc., for example, was marketing several bread machines at retail and, according to industry sources, commanded almost half of this category by late 1991. This company also was producing other specialty kitchen appliances, compact refrigerators, and microwave ovens for the home, but only when the products dovetailed with the parent company's manufacturing and distribution of commercial food equipment. A company executive told *HFD,* for example, that such mainstream products as coffee-makers and toasters were not of interest "unless the product makes the coffee, toasts the bread, and fries an egg, all at the same time." Welbilt Appliance introduced just such a machine, called Breakfast Express, in 1993. In 1994, however, the parent company left the consumer-products field entirely by selling Welbilt Appliance to a Manhattan-based investment group.

Marion H. Antonini was appointed chairman and chief executive officer of Welbilt in the fall of 1990. He continued the corporate policy of allowing the subsidiaries to identify opportunities to enhance core product lines and develop their own new concepts. Company headquarters were moved from New Hyde Park to Stamford, Connecticut. Welbilt suffered a loss of $13.8 million on sales of $357 million in 1991 but returned to profitability the following year and had net income of $6.6 million on sales of $426.5 million in 1993.

In November 1993 Welbilt went public again, offering common stock at $18 a share. Some of the proceeds were used to reduce the long-term debt, which was $126.2 million at the end of the year. Investors responded favorably to the offering, and in 1994 the stock rose as high as $33.50 a share. That year the company acquired Lincoln Foodservice Products, a manufacturer of ovens, commercial kitchen supplies, and other food-service equipment. In January 1995 Berisford International plc, a British firm, acquired Welbilt for $33.75 a share. The Kohlberg family held almost 47 percent of the stock at this time.

Welbilt in the Mid-1990s

In 1996 Welbilt was essentially a holding company for 12 subsidiaries or lines: Belshaw, Cleveland, Dean, Frymaster, Garland, Ice-O-Matic, Lincoln, Merco, Savory, U.S. Range, Varimixer, and Vent Master. The Garland Group consisted of units making Garland-brand, premium-line cooking equipment and distributing Welbilt products abroad; U.S. Range produced low-cost ranges and ovens and such countertop equipment as broilers and griddles; Vent Master offered a product line including exhaust and recirculation systems. The Cleveland Group consisted of Cleveland, with a line of steamers and ovens, mixer kettles, tilting skillets, and cook/chill systems, and Merco/Savory, specializing in food-warming equipment, including toasters and rotisseries.

Frymaster was producing fryers and filtration systems and also overseeing Dean fryers and Varimixer mixing equipment. Lincoln, the world's largest manufacturer of commercial and institutional aluminum food-service utensils, also produced ovens, marketed kitchen cutlery, and imported and sold stainless-steel cookware with aluminum-clad bottoms. Belshaw was turning out 20 basic doughnut-making machines. Mile High was producing ice-makers under the Ice-O-Matic and Mile High brand names. Welbilt also had a center for developing new equipment.

The Garland Group had headquarters in Freeland, Pennsylvania, where it also operated a manufacturing plant. Additional plants were located in Gardena, California, and Mississauga, Ontario; it maintained a distribution center in Hayes, England. Merco/Savory was based in Lakewood, New Jersey. Frymaster and Varimixer were in Shreveport, Louisiana, and Dean in Gardena. Lincoln was in Fort Wayne, Indiana, and Belshaw in Seattle. Mile High was in Denver. The development center was in Tampa, Florida.

Principal Divisions

Belshaw; Cleveland Group; Frymaster; Garland Group; Lincoln; Mile High Equipment; Welbilt Development Center.

Principal Subsidiaries

Belshaw Bros., Inc.; Frymaster Corp.; Garland Catering Equipment, Ltd. (Great Britain); Garland Commercial Industries, Inc.; Garland Commercial Ranges, Ltd. (Canada); Lincoln Foodservice Products, Inc.; Merco/Savory; Mile High Equipment; U.S. Range, Inc.; Varimixer.

Further Reading

Babyak, Richard J., Jancsurak, Joe, and Remich, Norman C., Jr., "The Building of Welbilt," *Appliance Manufacturer,* February 1996, special section.

Barmash, Isadore, "Outsiders Invade Furniture Field," *New York Times,* July 31, 1966, Sec. 3, pp. 1, 11.

"Detroit Stove Plant to Close on June 30, Move to Maspeth, N.Y.," *Wall Street Journal,* April 23, 1957, p. 7.

Hollinger, Peggy, "Attractions of a Welbilt Deal," *Financial Times,* January 2, 1995, p. 16.

Leonard, Burr, "Rise and Fall and Rise," *Forbes,* February 9, 1987, pp. 98–99.

Malanga, Steve, "LBO: The Way It Was, the Way It Will Be," *Crain's New York Business,* March 19, 1990, pp. 27, 30.

Purpura, Linda, "The Welbilt Loaf," *HFD,* November 18, 1991, pp. 49, 68.

Stevens, James, "The Welbilt Story," *Appliance,* June 1989, pp. W5–W8, W25.

—Robert Halasz

Westvāco

Westvaco Corporation

Westvaco Building
299 Park Avenue
New York, New York 10171
U.S.A.
(212) 688-5000
Fax: (212) 688-5026

Public Company
Incorporated: 1899 as West Virginia Pulp and Paper
   Company
Employees: 15,110
Sales: $1.81 billion (1996)
Stock Exchanges: New York Midwest Pacific
SICs: 2621 Paper Mills; 2631 Paperboard Mills; 2656
   Sanitary Food Containers, Except Folding; 2657
   Folding Paperboard Boxes, Including Sanitary; 2671
   Coated & Laminated Paper & Plastic Film; 2674
   Uncoated Paper & Multiwall Bags; 2677 Envelopes;
   2821 Plastics Materials, Nonvulcanizable Elastomers
   & Synthetic Resins; 2843 Surface Active Agents,
   Finishing Agents & Sulfonated Oils & Assistants;
   2861 Gum & Wood Chemicals; 2869 Industrial
   Organic Chemicals, Not Elsewhere Classified; 2899
   Chemicals & Chemical Preparations, Not Elsewhere
   Classified

Westvaco Corporation is a major manufacturer of printing papers and envelopes, consumer and industrial packaging, and specialty chemicals that are by-products of the paper production process. The company began with the advent of automated papermaking, using wood instead of cotton as its raw material; it produced mainly printing paper for the domestic market until World War II. In the postwar era it integrated its production to make finished packaging products. Westvaco owns about 1.5 million acres of timberland in the United States and Brazil. Westvaco has intensified its international presence and currently serves customers in more than 70 countries. Nearly one-quarter of the company's income is now derived outside the United States. Westvaco spends heavily on research and marketing to locate markets worldwide.

Roots in Late 19th Century West Virginia

Born into a Scottish papermaking family, Westvaco founder William Luke came to the United States in 1852. Ten years later he began running a plant for Jessup & Moore Paper Company in Harper's Ferry, West Virginia. Although employed by Jessup & Moore until 1898, he set up a small plant of his own with his two sons in 1889. Originally established in Piedmont, West Virginia, a shift in the Potomac River and a 1922 municipal name change eventually put the same facility in Luke, Maryland, where Westvaco still operated a mill in the late 1990s.

The mill was one of many mills that, during the late 1800s, imported and developed automated wood-pulping technologies. Called the Piedmont Pulp and Paper Company, it became the first commercially successful sulfite pulp mill in the United States. Eventually U.S. makers used the sulfite process to make 83 percent of their paper. The Piedmont plant employed 60, and by 1891 it began production of printing paper under the name West Virginia Paper.

U.S. timber supply and automated processes lowered the price of paper and accelerated its consumption. In 1897 West Virginia Paper merged with West Virginia Pulp Company of Davis, West Virginia and became West Virginia Pulp and Paper Company (WVPP). It expanded along with the United States's growing demand, and it established a business headquarters in New York City. In addition to its white printing paper, it marketed pulp and chemical by-products. In 1904 William Luke relinquished the presidency of the company to his son John Luke, who held the position until 1921. William Luke died in 1912, at which time the company had four mills operating in West Virginia, Pennsylvania, Virginia, and New York.

Post-World War I Diversification

During the post-World War I recession, prices plummeted and strikes hit two-thirds of the industry, including WVPP.

Sales and earnings reached a record level, however, in 1920, which would be unequaled for 20 years.

While white paper production volume remained relatively constant, diversification accounted for virtually all growth after World War I. The company produced its first kraft paper in 1921, the first year of David Luke's tenure as president. David Luke was another son of the founder. Used in U.S. packaging since 1907, kraft paper replaced many wood and textile shipping containers. As trees in the southern states were more suitable for kraft, between the world wars kraft production in the region skyrocketed. West Virginia's kraft output grew steadily for 15 years but then leveled off.

In 1929 WVPP introduced containerboard, a heavier, corrugated paper used for boxes. Federally approved for shipping in 1914, use of this material grew tremendously during the world wars.

During the 1920s WVPP began purchasing woodlands to supply its own wood pulp, but self-sufficiency in fiber supply remained a long-term prospect. By the 1930s very little virgin timber remained in the southern states. WVPP continued to buy land close to its mills and eventually owned extensive woodlands. The immaturity of the trees in its holdings, however, forced it to rely on outside suppliers for its pulp supply and prevented diversification into finished wood products.

Another son of William Luke, Thomas Luke, became president in 1934, inheriting a company with young diversification attempts and old mills. Three years later the company built a new mill to produce kraft and containerboard. By 1939 all five mills operated 24 hours per day.

The company's mills continued to operate at capacity throughout World War II. Wartime allocations made scarce the materials for expansion and repair, however. Although its facilities produced 20 percent more volume by war's end, WVPP's facilities emerged from the war badly in need of modernization.

David L. Luke Initiates Series of Expansion Programs, 1945–1963

Ascending to president in 1945, David L. Luke, a grandson of the founder, established the company's modern growth pattern. He immediately began the first of many expansion programs, spending the $17.5 million the company had accumulated during the war. The company also used some of its cash surplus to acquire more land, selling the trees too mature for papermaking to provide additional financing.

Wartime research greatly expanded paper's uses, particularly in containers. Postwar demand continued to grow so explosively that only production volume and market share concerned papermakers. The industry enjoyed favorable prices, consolidating competition, and growing demand in all areas of paper products.

The industry set high prices, required more prompt payment, and used the cash influx to build new mills during the late 1940s. Capacity caught up with demand by the late 1940s, and surpassed it by the mid-1950s, creating the need for more development leading to automation, product consistency, and new uses for paperboard. Although still reliant on white paper, WVPP put much of its postwar development efforts into these areas.

Profit margins in the commodity-based paper industry remained slim during the 1950s, and a company's technological efficiency determined its success. The cyclicality of the industry meant that for the next 30 years papermakers invested in capacity additions. When they did so, they lowered prices precipitously. David L. Luke's expansion programs, however, coincided with the industry downturns. While occasionally requiring more debt than that to which the company was accustomed, automation allowed it to cut its work force for each of the next ten years.

The first major work stoppage since World War I occurred in 1952, when 4,000 employees struck. Labor relations flared up more frequently in the postwar era, decreasing earnings on occasion, well into the 1970s.

The company got more short-term use of its land in 1952 when it discovered a use for its hardwoods. Traditionally, only younger and softwood trees had been used for paper. Hardwoods on WVPP's land holdings used for paper allowed the company to reduce production costs.

Encouraged by the premature utility of its land, over two years the company aggressively increased its holdings 75 percent to 749,000 acres. Most of the money spent on expansion in the 1950s, however, went to equipment modifications required by the technology.

WVPP sold its output mainly to companies that converted it to finished products. Priced as a commodity, paper prices often changed dramatically, making earnings erratic. Demand, however, constantly increased, providing a greater cash flow.

Use of paperboard, a noncorrugated material for consumer product containers, grew explosively during David L. Luke's presidency. Just as kraft paper and containerboard accounted for the company's prewar growth, paperboard made up most postwar growth.

The 1953 acquisition of Hinde & Dauch Paper Company, a box maker, allowed WVPP to bypass distributors and represented the first major move toward integration. Hinde & Dauch (H&D) used WVPP's paperboard to produce its parent company's first finished paper products. Bleached paperboard was found to take colors as well as printing papers, making it highly adaptable to packaging uses. In 1955 WVPP purchased color presses to produce paperboard finished to client specifications.

West Virginia Pulp & Paper Company slowed expansion and improvement during the mid-1950s in its traditional sectors of printing papers, kraft, and containerboard, in favor of its new division. The company closed H&D's paper mills but built more than 20 new assembly plants for it during the next ten years, to make the most of H&D's knowledge of package design and experience with marketing finished products. These new plants allowed for the first increase in WVPP's work force since World War II. By constantly automating to reduce labor costs, its number of employees began to level off again by the early 1960s.

WVPP purchased a Brazilian paper box maker in 1953. By the end of the 1950s, the Brazilian subsidiary financed its own production expansion with fewer employees.

Demand for white printing papers began its first large increase in decades in 1954 as a population boom and renewed prosperity increased consumption of printed materials. Demand for all paper products grew so explosively in the 1950s that by 1956 the industry could not meet demand. WVPP's earnings increased out of proportion to sales, peaking at $16.3 million in 1956 after five successive years of gains.

The industry responded by rapidly expanding its capacity. WVPP typically upgraded one machine at a time, rather than building or buying new mills. This method slowly consolidated production into larger and fewer facilities. By 1959 WVPP completed its largest spending program, doubling capacity at the Luke mill; but when domestic growth slowed, prices collapsed. Despite annual sales records, for the next five years WVPP's earnings fluctuated wildly—at one point dropping to as low as $8 million. Other factors that depleted earnings included new technology that produced more pulp from harvested trees as well as price wars following the entry of forestry and container companies into paper. WVPP, which also sought to enter new markets, lowered prices as well.

Many companies waited for demand to catch up, but West Virginia Pulp & Paper continued its ten-year expansion plan. It focused on relatively inexpensive converting plants rather than mills, but its debt grew more sizable. The timing of the expansion speeded WVPP's recovery; by 1962 demand began to catch up to the capacity added in recent years. The spending program was completed and the company issued only $60 million in bonds.

The length of the industry's recession and the growth of H&D encouraged a renewed push toward finished products. In 1957 West Virginia purchased Virginia Folding Box Company, an assembler of cigarette packaging. It eagerly expanded the acquisition and reorganized itself into six divisions, four of which were in the business of converting: bleached boards, building boards, fine papers, H&D, kraft, and merchant paper. The company decentralized each division and provided each with its own sales force.

As new materials, particularly plastic, threatened to replace older forms of paper packaging, technical research intensified during the mid-1950s and the early 1960s. Higher than the industry average, WVPP's research expenditures enhanced its reputation for product development. Research and development spending quadrupled during the ten-year period, ending 1961 at $4 million annually.

WVPP pioneered several processes, including the use of electronic controls in production, the marketing of waste by-products in the chemicals division, the use of hardwoods, and the development of Clupak, a more elastic kraft paper. The company typically licensed or sold new technologies to pay for additional research.

By 1959 packaging grades of paper made up two-thirds of West Virginia's production volume. By 1960 the demand for office and printing papers (at one time WVPP's primary product) provided growth to the long-stagnant industry. Then oriented toward finished products and marketing, WVPP set up a separate sales force to sell directly to printers and paper converters.

When paper prices improved in the early 1960s, WVPP made the most of its recently completed investment program. The renewed efficiency and a change in its accounting method finally pushed 1965 earnings past the 1956 level. The downturn, however, had raised the competitive level of the industry. Like its competitors, WVPP came out of the late 1950s and early 1960s more diversified, integrated, and less production oriented.

WVPP exported negligibly until 1960, when three percent of sales went overseas. Although it did not pursue international markets actively for another 20 years, in 1962 it set up an international division to explore manufacturing possibilities abroad and established foreign subsidiaries in Europe and Australia.

David L. Luke retired in 1963. During his tenure the company had changed dramatically. At the end of World War II, West Virginia Pulp & Paper Company had produced commodity grades of paper for a few hundred customers, but by 1959 it had its own sales force selling a variety of finished paper products to a customer base of 11,000. The company had developed the marketing techniques and made the necessary acquisitions to get it started in finished conversion while keeping debt to a minimum.

Diversification and International Expansion, 1963–1988

Hesitant to join his family's company at first, David L. Luke's son David L. Luke III became CEO in 1963, after working 11 years for WVPP. He maintained the product development momentum initiated by his father and continued to upgrade efficiency with frequent spending programs. Like the rest of the industry, however, he reevaluated the use of debt in the coming decade. In 1962 the Luke family controlled 30 percent of the company's stock; by 1984 it controlled only two percent.

Still pursuing self-sufficiency in fiber supply, the company's land holdings were constantly becoming more productive. WVPP acquired its millionth acre in 1964. Research into forestry techniques produced hybrids that were not only more disease resistant but capable of growing three times the wood fiber per acre than the strains of 15 years earlier.

Shrinking timber reserves nationwide escalated land value further. Beginning in the late 1960s, WVPP developed land of commercial value and purchased additional timberland closer to its mills. Operating in 22 states, this latter strategy proved important when transportation costs inflated during the 1970s. Lower land values in the early 1970s allowed additional land purchases. Even though these lands provided only ten percent of its raw material requirements, in the long term they stood to raise the degree of self-sufficiency.

During the mid-1960s, the growth rate in earnings once again outpaced sales. Operating near capacity once again, the company was able to reduce the debt it had assumed to complete its expansion program. Most of this investment went to make its three main mills more efficient. Nearly half of sales in 1967 came from products introduced in the previous ten years. This success and resulting heavier cash flow tempted the company to offer consumer products, a segment profiting several of its competitors. WVPP purchased C.A. Reed Company in 1968, maker of disposable paper products. Although the disposables market soared in the 1960s and 1970s, WVPP sold it after only seven years.

White printing papers used by business systems also boosted sales. Although the industry began to see overruns again, WVPP began another expansion program in 1967. It included the building of a new white paper mill in Kentucky. At $90 million, it was the largest project ever attempted by the company. In 1969 the company changed its name to Westvaco Corporation. Growing dependence worldwide on North American pulp and timber helped make Westvaco less dependent on the health of the domestic economy, exporting ten percent of sales by the early 1970s.

Commodity-type production continued to plague the industry. In the early 1970s the industry suffered once again from too much capacity, higher production costs, and low prices. Tougher environmental standards and a weaker economy hastened closure of plants industrywide. Westvaco closed plants, but its frequent incremental upgrades kept shut-down costs low. Leaner by default, turnaround came quickly.

During the early 1970s the government kept paper prices and labor costs stable but put a freeze on earnings as well. U.S. paper production reached record levels. By 1972 the government loosened its restrictions on paper somewhat, but fierce price competition negated a four percent price increase approval in 1971.

Wage and price controls were lifted altogether in 1974, allowing the industry to pass on production costs. Like the industry's recession in the early 1960s, these price controls contributed to integration, as producers sought to increase earnings in areas outside federal control, particularly finished paper products.

The paper industry was now increasingly accountable to federal regulations. The Federal Energy Administration forced Westvaco and 12 other paper companies to convert certain plants to coal burning from oil. The Department of Justice blocked an attempt by Westvaco to acquire the remainder of U.S. Envelope, the largest domestic producer of envelopes, of which Westvaco owned 58 percent. The paper industry had

been investigated repeatedly for antitrust compliance and been named in private suits. Although Westvaco settled suits out of court it had never been indicted.

In the ten years ending 1975, Westvaco almost doubled sales, while simultaneously reducing its work force. During the mid-1970s demand in all sectors began to catch up with capacity, but growing production costs dampened earnings.

Energy shortages of the early 1970s prompted Westvaco to turn to its land holdings once again by mining coal for its own consumption. By 1974 it achieved 40 percent fuel self-sufficiency by burning its own waste from the production process. Such conservation efforts would help earnings substantially in the late 1970s.

The 1980s were turnaround years for papermakers. The industry started to spend on capacity once again. Although Westvaco now converted more than one-third of its paper production in its own plants, growth in the use of the personal computer and in the publishing industry gave way to rapid increases in demand for Westvaco's traditional printing papers.

By the mid-1980s, Westvaco emerged from one of the worst five-year periods for the industry with six straight earnings records. In addition, it had completed its spending program. These programs drained earnings, but at their conclusion the company earnings jumped dramatically, and the company produced more paper with larger, more efficient units and less labor. David Luke III began four such programs in his 24 years as CEO.

By employing its own sales force, Westvaco diversified not by acquisition, but by tailoring products for customers. Research and sales forces emphasized new uses for bleached board in microwave food packaging and liquids packaging.

During the mid-1980s, the company took a series of anti-takeover steps. Although at record levels, debt was lower than in most companies in the forest products and packaging industries. David Luke III's final spending program of $1.6 billion was financed 80 percent internally. Unlike those before it, the program intensified product development instead of production efficiency.

Westvaco set up trade offices in Tokyo and Hong Kong in the mid-1980s to tap the skyrocketing Asian and Pacific markets. Finished products paved the way for increased activity overseas, and by the late 1980s exports reached 15 percent of sales. The consistently profitable Brazil operations began to export, after holding 20 percent of Brazil's corrugated box market for decades.

Significant growth in the printing industry in the late 1980s led to capacity expansion. Westvaco emphasized heavier-weight printing papers, despite the industry's cyclicality, which forced buyers to cut costs occasionally.

Emphasis on "Differentiation" in the Late 1980s and Early 1990s

During David Luke III's 24 years as CEO, Westvaco did more than most papermakers to free itself from the cyclicality of commodity production. His program that accomplished this, "differentiation," continued under his successors—his brother John A. Luke, who became CEO in 1988, and John A. Luke Jr., whose attainment of the CEO position in 1992 represented the fifth generation of Lukes at the company helm. For Westvaco, differentiation meant manufacturing specialized products that met specific market segment needs. By lessening its reliance on commodity grade products, Westvaco would thus protect itself from the inevitable downturns of the cyclical paper industry; and, in practice, differentiation had proved to be a successful strategy for Westvaco through the mid-1990s.

Westvaco's specialty chemicals were a prime example of differentiated products. This business segment was bolstered in 1992 with the acquisition of North American Carbon. By 1995 Westvaco held a virtual monopoly of the U.S. market in carbons for automotive emission control devices, a sector that generated $15–$20 million each year. The company sought to strengthen its position further when it announced late in 1995 a plan to spend $80 million to build a new activated carbon plant near its Wickliffe, Kentucky fine papers mill, with operations scheduled to begin in mid-1997.

In the early 1990s differentiated products accounted for two-thirds of company sales, compared with only one-third a decade earlier. John A. Luke Jr. aimed to increase this further, to about three-quarters of overall sales. A major step toward this goal came in 1995 when Westvaco sold its corrugated container operations to Weyerhaeuser for an estimated $85 million, the rare occurrence in company history of an asset sale. Westvaco's exit from the corrugated container business promised to free up capacity at its Charleston, South Carolina mill for production of additional differentiated products, such as decorative laminates for kitchen countertops, which were made from saturating kraft paper.

Westvaco also continued to expand overseas as another basis for future growth. Subsidiaries were established in South Korea and Singapore in 1992 and in China, the Czech Republic, and India in 1995. Brazil, however, continued to be Westvaco's largest foreign beachhead, and the company's operations there were increased in 1996 with the opening of a new container plant in Pacujus and the purchase of a consumer packaging plant in Valinhos. Almost one-quarter of Westvaco's 1996 revenues were generated outside the United States, and John A. Luke Jr. set a goal to increase that figure to one-third within ten years.

Westvaco enjoyed an exceptionally strong year in 1995, fueled in part by a market upturn, with record revenue of $3.27 billion and record net income of $280.8 million. The company's stock split three for two that August. Meanwhile, environmental issues came to the fore when the Council on Economic Priorities placed Westvaco on its 1995 list of the country's eight worst corporate polluters, citing 1992 toxic emissions more than three times the industry average. For its part, Westvaco announced plans in early 1995 to spend $140 million to upgrade its bleached pulpmaking plants so as to eliminate the use of elemental chlorine. Environmental groups had been lobbying paper companies to eliminate this use of chlorine because of the creation of the highly toxic chemical dioxin as a by-product.

In early 1996, David L. Luke III retired from the Westvaco chairmanship, and John A. Luke Jr. added the post of chairman to his roles as president and CEO. In September of that same year Westvaco formed a joint venture with SCANA Corp. to build and operate a $160 million power cogeneration facility at Westvaco's North Charleston, South Carolina kraft paper mill. The new facility would enable Westvaco to make future expansions in its manufacturing operations at North Charleston. The company also announced plans to build a $20 million technical center in North Charleston with laboratories and offices for its specialty chemicals division.

From the late 1980s through the mid-1990s, Westvaco had been one of the steadiest-performing companies in the paper industry. Westvaco's emphasis on differentiated products and its reinvestment programs may have cut earnings over short-term periods, but it provided a sounder basis for long-term growth. The company was also well positioned to take advantage of an increasingly open world market, all of which added up to a promising future.

Principal Subsidiaries

Westvaco Development Corporation; Westvaco Latin America & Africa; Westvaco Pacific Pty. Ltd. (Australia); Westvaco Europe, S.A. (Belgium); Westvaco Foreign Sales Corporation (Belgium); Rigesa, Ltda. (Brazil); Westvaco do Brasil, Ltda. (Brazil); Westvaco Canada, Ltd.; Westvaco Quebec (Canada); Westvaco Shanghai (China); Westvaco Svitavy, spol. s r.o. (Czech Republic); Westvaco Hong Kong, Ltd.; Westvaco India; Westvaco Asia, K.K. (Japan); Westvaco Korea, Ltd.; Westvaco de México, S.A. de C.V. (Mexico); Westvaco Singapore Pte., Ltd; Westvaco Worldwide Distribution, S.A. (Switzerland); Westvaco Taiwan, Ltd.

Principal Divisions

Bleached Board Division; Chemical Division; Consumer Packaging Division; Envelope Division; Fine Papers Division; Kraft Division; Timberlands Division; Westvaco Worldwide.

Further Reading

Ferguson, Kelly, "Westvaco Corp.: 'Differentiation' Means Key to Success," *Pulp & Paper,* April 1995, pp. 36–37.

Parker, Marcia, "Quietly, Paper Giant Girds for Downturn," *Crain's New York Business,* March 18, 1991, pp. 3, 25.

Plishner, Emily S., "The Old Guard: Why Straitlaced Westvaco Should Interest Value-Minded Contrarians," *Financial World,* January 30, 1996, pp. 52, 54.

Westvaco 1888–1988: Centennial Recognition—The Early Years, New York: Westvaco Corporation, 1988.

—Ray Walsh
—updated by David E. Salamie

Wild Oats Markets, Inc.

1645 Broadway
Boulder, Colorado 80301-2602
U.S.A.
(303) 440-5220
Fax: (303) 581-9349
Web site: http://www.wildoats.com

Public Company
Incorporated: 1984
Employees: 2,900
Sales: $192.5 million (1996)
Stock Exchanges: NASDAQ
SICs: 5411 Grocery Stores; 5999 Miscellaneous Retail
    Stores, Not Elsewhere Classified

Wild Oats Markets, Inc., is the second largest natural foods grocery chain in the United States. With 2,900 employees, the company provides organic produce, steroid- and hormone-free meats, bulk foods, vitamins and herbal supplements, and other products in its 47 full-service grocery stores across the nation. Riding a wave of growth in the natural and health foods market, Wild Oats has expanded rapidly since its founding in 1984. Although the company has opened a significant number of new stores, its growth has come mainly through the acquisition of single health food stores or small grocery chains, most notably its purchase of rival Alfalfa's Markets in 1996.

Strong Growth from the Start in the 1980s

Wild Oats Markets was founded in 1984 by Michael Gilliland and his wife Elizabeth Cook. Most people who start natural or health food stores begin their businesses through their dedication to health foods and a commitment to the environment. Gilliland and Cook, however, had gotten their start in the food retail business with the purchase of a convenience store a few years earlier, which they had bought with cash advances on 17 credit cards and a second mortgage on Gilliland's mother's house. After the purchase of two other convenience stores, the pair decided to buy a natural foods market, which they felt would do well in health-conscious Boulder, Colorado. The $300,000 purchase thrust the couple into an environment quite different from the junk-food focus of convenience stores, an environment that gradually persuaded Gilliland and Cook to become semivegetarians themselves. In that first store, Gilliland worked the counter and Cook worked the deli. As the business expanded, Gilliland became chief executive officer and president and Cook became vice-president and in-house attorney.

The store grew steadily the first few years, and Gilliland and Cook opened two others in Colorado and two in Santa Fe, New Mexico, by the end of 1991. Another opened in Albuquerque in early 1992. The company had a stable base in the early 1990s that enabled them to take advantage of a boom in the consumption of natural and organic products. "It's happening everywhere," said Elizabeth Bertani, marketing director for *New Hope Communications,* a publisher of trade magazines for the industry. "There's been a phenomenal upswing in natural foods consumption." With $2 million in investor funds, Wild Oats expanded into Arizona and Missouri in 1992 and into California in 1993. With 650 employees and 1993 sales of $50 million, Wild Oats had become the third largest natural foods chain in the United States.

Wild Oats continued to exploit the phenomenal growth in what used to be considered a tiny niche. The *Natural Foods Merchandiser* reported that sales for the industry were up 18 percent in 1993, to more than $6 billion. And they continued to accelerate. By 1995, industry sales were at $9.17 billion, up 21.5 percent from the previous year. For comparison, all food sales grew 2.5 percent between 1993 and 1994. (With total food sales at $416 billion, however, natural foods still had plenty of room to grow.) Wild Oats paralleled this industry boom, growing at a rate of 544 percent between 1989 and 1993. In 1994, *Inc.* magazine included Wild Oats on its list of the 500 fastest growing small companies. As if to underscore the point, the company bought two Kathy's Ranch Markets in Las Vegas in July of that year, for a total of 16 stores in five states.

Wild Oats benefited not only from rapid growth in the industry, but also from the business savvy of Gilliland. Never a slave of the vegetarian ideology, Gilliland designed each store to cater to local tastes. For example, the market in Boulder was completely vegetarian and fostered a down-to-earth image, whereas the Santa Fe store sold meat and high-end, specialty items. In some places Wild Oats was advertised as a gourmet market rather than a natural foods market. "I'm a great believer in figuring out where customers are and walking with them," Gilliland said to Michele Conklin of the *Rocky Mountain News.* "It doesn't do you any good to put a hard-core vegetarian market in the middle of Pasadena because you're going to go out of business."

Despite its rapid expansion, Wild Oats in 1994 was still far behind the nation's top-selling natural foods grocery chain, Austin, Texas-based Whole Foods Markets. With sales of $300 million, Whole Foods also surpassed the next largest competitor, Fresh Fields, based in Rockville, Maryland. Wild Oats' most intense competition, however, challenged it much closer to home: Boulder, Colorado-based Alfalfa's Markets. After years of head-to-head competition, Wild Oats acquired Alfalfa's in 1996.

Alfalfa's Early History

Founded roughly the same time as Wild Oats, Alfalfa's had followed a similar fast growth curve. Mark Retzloff and Sahid Hass Hassan had cobbled together funds from investors, the Small Business Association, and themselves to open Alfalfa's Market in 1983. Retzloff told Claudia Ventura-Abbott that he "wanted to deliver high-quality, natural foods to people.... I was very environmentally conscious. It always seemed right to me to be involved in this business. It was a conscious type of work; it was making changes." The store shelved only products with no artificial additives, then looked for pesticide-free produce and steroid-free beef. The company worked directly with farmers and ranchers to encourage the production of and provide a market for natural products. This commitment led Alfalfa's to work with 1,000 suppliers, compared with the supermarket average of 60 suppliers. Not the usual tiny health food store, Alfalfa's became a full-service grocery store. "When we started out," Retzloff said to Ventura-Abbott, "we wanted to be a transition-type of market. We didn't want to be classified as a health-food store. We wanted to provide an atmosphere that people would feel comfortable in. We knew we'd have to carry a full line of products—produce, fish, meat, deli, and bakery, as well as convenience products, paper goods, and cleaning supplies." The company added an in-store cafe in 1985 and hosted a cooking school with professional cooks and guest chefs. By 1989 Alfalfa's was one of the top five natural food retail stores in the United States and had annual sales of $19 million.

In late the 1980s and early 1990s, Whole Foods tried to take over Alfalfa's Markets several times, culminating in a bid in July 1991 that was on the verge of acceptance when Alfalfa's stockholders balked at a condition that 51 percent of Alfalfa's stock be converted to Whole Foods. The company continued to grow, taking advantage of the same market wave that Wild Oats was riding. "There is a window here. You can't grow if the demand is not there, and now seems to be the time," Hass Hassan said to Jim Sheeler of the *Boulder Daily Camera,* "There is an opportunity now and within the next two years. Five years ago, there were few communities that would support a concept like this. Now there are hundreds." Alfalfa's reached sales of $30 million in 1991, with 500 employees; it then reached $48 million in sales in 1993. The company arranged additional financing to expand further, adding several stores in Colorado, including stores in Denver, Littleton, Fort Collins, and Vail. By 1994 Alfalfa's had six stores in Colorado and had acquired Vancouver, Canada-based Capers, with two stores and two more soon to open. Alfalfa's competition with Wild Oats then grew more fierce as it opened a store in Santa Fe, New Mexico, in 1995, where Wild Oats already had a store.

Major Acquisition

In addition to being based in Boulder, Colorado, Alfalfa's and Wild Oats had much in common. Their commitment to providing wholesome, natural foods was joined with their commitment to their employees and the community. Both stores had profit-sharing plans; at Wild Oats this took the form of bonuses if the employee's store hit its financial goals. Wild Oats also paid $200 annually to each employee toward a "wellness purchase," such as massages or a bike. Both companies were involved in the community: Wild Oats paid for one hour out of 40 of employee volunteering and gave 7.5 percent of pretax profits to environmental and social causes.

Despite their similarities, the two companies took pains to distinguish themselves, particularly in Boulder. Gilliland explained to Tammy Tierney of *Denver Business Journal,* "They take the high end; we take the low end. We have lower prices, are more low key, and are not so inclined to gourmet items." Elizabeth Cook expanded on the difference to Tierney, "We're a hard-core natural foods store. They concentrate on food service. We concentrate on bulk and mainstream grocery." In addition to competing for customers head-to-head in several cities in the West, the companies competed in their acquisitions. Both reportedly bid for the Kathy's Ranch stores in Las Vegas. "I think we both learn from each other," Gilliland said to Sheeler. "There's a certain amount of competitiveness that has kept us going, and if it were just us or them, I don't think we would have expanded so quickly."

However much Gilliland appreciated the competition, he was willing to forego it. In 1995 he began negotiations to acquire Alfalfa's. That year, Wild Oats had expanded to 21 stores and had reached sales of $100 million. Although Alfalfa's had only 11 stores that year, it reportedly had also reached $100 million in sales in 1995. The merger would make Wild Oats the second largest natural food chain, outpacing Fresh Fields. The potential merger ran into a couple of problems. New Mexico raised questions about whether the merger would violate antitrust regulations. It eventually recommended that Wild Oats sell one of its stores in New Mexico but did not actively challenge the merger. In addition, Whole Foods Markets reportedly renewed its own efforts to buy Alfalfa's, leading to rumors of a bidding war. Although Whole Foods had lost its previous three bids to buy Alfalfa's, it had the money to make a sweet offer. With 42 stores across the United States and sales of $500 million in 1995, it had the resources to out-muscle Wild Oats.

Wild Oats prevailed, however, and the merger went through. The final agreement stipulated that the company would be based in Boulder and take the name Wild Oats, although existing stores would operate under their original names. The merger created a company with $200 million in sales and 3,600 employees in 39 stores in the United States and Canada. Gilliland remained CEO and Hassan served as president of the new company. The merger was completed in July 1996, with Gilliland and Cook owners of 30 percent, investors owning approximately 50 percent, and Wild Oats and Alfalfa's officers owning the other 20 percent.

IPO in 1996

After the acquisition of Alfalfa's, Wild Oats concentrated on its next major goal, that of offering shares of the company on the public market. On October 23, 1996, the company achieved that goal, offering 1.69 million shares of stock on the NASDAQ. Speculation had been high that the stock would soar at the initial public offering, but with an offer price of $25, trading was low and the stock closed the first day at only $25.38. Jon Lieber, a broker at A.G. Edwards, considered the initial price too high, but also speculated that New York's biggest brokers did not understand Wild Oats' philosophy. "I'm from Manhattan," he said to John Accola of the *Rocky Mountain News,* "and, believe me, health food is definitely few and far between. You walk out of any exchange at noon, and they are inhaling hot dogs, pizzas, and gyros." Gilliland had expressed some concern about this to Conklin at the *Rocky Mountain News* before the IPO: "The biggest challenge will be balancing Wall Street but staying true to our mission. Is Wall Street going to appreciate that we have guest practitioners (such as nutritionists) on staff that we're not making money off of?"

The stock slipped after the IPO, coming to rest for the next few months around $17 to $18 a share. Then, in mid-January 1997, an analyst downgraded her rating of the company two notches based on information that Whole Foods intended to challenge Wild Oats by opening stores in Boulder, Denver, Santa Fe, and Salt Lake City—traditional Wild Oats territory. The stock fell 26 percent in one day, to $13.13.

Wild Oats ended 1996 with strong growth figures. Sales had risen to $192.5 million, largely because of the opening of seven new stores and the acquisition of 13 stores in 1996. The company did report a net loss for the year, however, of $4.5 million. The company attributed the loss to nonrecurring charges related to acquisitions, the closing of some stores, and the consolidation of corporate headquarters after the Alfalfa's acquisition. Without these nonrecurring charges of $7 million, company profits

would have been $2.5 million, up from $779,000 in 1995. In addition, same-store sales, which only measure sales from stores the company has owned for at least a full year, rose 3.8 percent, almost double the figure predicted by analysts.

These figures did not raise market confidence, however. The day Wild Oats announced its final quarter numbers, its stock actually fell $.25, to $13.88. Gilliland responded to continued concern about Whole Foods' proposed new stores by citing the double-digit gains in the natural foods market, which he felt assured Wild Oats room for continued growth, even in a more crowded marketplace. In addition, he was quoted by Lisa Greim in the *Rocky Mountain News* as saying, "We do very well against them in California. I think Whole Foods is going to be disappointed."

Despite the apparent lukewarm confidence of the stock market and the specter of increased competition from Whole Foods, Wild Oats continued its aggressive pattern of growth through acquisitions. The company completed a deal with Wholly Harvest in Florida in early 1997, trading stock for two stores. Wild Oats also moved into the Northwest, purchasing two natural food supermarkets in Eugene, Oregon, in March 1997. With the purchase of two stores in Memphis, Tennessee, the number of stores owned by Wild Oats rose to 47, a number the company planned to raise even higher in the coming months and, no doubt, in the coming years.

Further Reading

Accola, John, "On Wall Street, It's Mild Oats," *Rocky Mountain News,* October 24, 1996, pp. 1B, 16B.

Brown, Adrienne, "Real Deals," *Colorado Business,* March 1997, pp. 20–25.

Conklin, Michele, "Growing His Oats," *Rocky Mountain News,* July 7, 1996, pp. 1–2W, 11–14W.

Gonzalez, Erika, "Food Stores Merger Gets Scrutiny," *Boulder Daily Camera,* March 15, 1996.

——, "New Suitor in Grocery Merger," *Boulder Daily Camera,* January 18, 1996, p. 1B.

Greim, Lisa, "Wild Oats Gains, Stock Falls," *Rocky Mountain News,* January 25, 1997.

Lopez, Christopher, "Alfalfa's Natural Up North," *The Denver Post,* July 24, 1994.

Parker, Penny, "Wild Oats Sowing New Seeds," *The Denver Post,* November 18, 1994, pp. 1C, 5C.

Sheeler, Jim, "Wild Oats, Alfalfa's Become Power Players with Acquisition," *Boulder Daily Camera,* July 26, 1994.

Smith, Jerd, "Alfalfa's, Wild Oats Expanding Rapidly with Venture Funds," *Denver Business Journal,* January 24, 1992.

Smith, Kerri S., "Wild Oats Jarred," *The Denver Post,* January 15, 1997, pp. 1E, 8E.

Sutton, David, and Lindsey, Jennifer, "Specialty Food Partners Make Profit," *The Denver Post,* November 23, 1985, p. 2E.

Tierney, Tammy, "Markets Cash in on Buyers' Health Kick," *Denver Business Journal,* April 10, 1992.

Ventura-Abbott, Claudia, "Alfalfa's Laying Plans for Healthful Expansion," *Boulder County Business Report,* October 1989, pp. 18, 36.

—Susan Windisch Brown

Wolohan Lumber Co.

1740 Midland Road
Saginaw, Michigan 48605
U.S.A.
(517) 793-4532
Fax: (517) 793-4582

Public Company
Incorporated: 1964 as Wolohan Lumber Co.
Employees: 1,600
Sales: $418.0 million (1995)
Stock Exchanges: NASDAQ
SICs: 5031 Lumber, Plywood & Millwork; 5032 Brick,
   Stone & Related Materials; 5211 Lumber & Other
   Building Materials

A leading retailer in the lumber and building supply industry, Wolohan Lumber Co. sells a full-line of materials used mainly for new home construction and home-improvement projects. During the mid-1990s, Wolohan operated more than 60 stores, ranging between 20,000 square feet and 45,000 square feet in retail space, in seven Midwestern states, including Michigan, Wisconsin, Ohio, Illinois, Indiana, Missouri, and Kentucky. Although the company operated exclusively as a retailer during the 1990s, for decades it was involved in several different business lines. At the turn of the 20th century, Wolohan operated grain elevators, before entering the lumber business as a wholesaler. As the decades passed and numerous ownership changes were effected, Wolohan subsisted as a lumber-yard operator, deriving the bulk of its business from sales to professional contractors. Beginning in the early 1980s, the company embraced a new business strategy when it began targeting do-it-yourself customers and remolding its stores. Store expansion ensued, as the company developed into a regional chain that during the 1990s was deriving half of its total sales from do-it-yourself customers and professional contractors.

Early 20th-Century Origins

The Wolohan family's century-long legacy in the lumber business began with the patriarch of the family, Charles Wolo-

han, who founded Charles Wolohan Inc. at the turn of the 20th century. Located in Birch Run, Michigan, Charles Wolohan Inc. operated a granary elevator for local farmers and later added lumber as a sideline business. It was with lumber that the Wolohan family would score its greatest success, building an enterprise whose existence would span a century.

By the early 1920s, lumber had become a significant aspect of the Wolohan business, its growth fueled by an expanding home construction market. Partly because of the growth realized through the company's lumber business, Charles Wolohan Inc. was able to add a second elevator to its operations, establishing the granary in Hemlock, Michigan, in 1924. Over the course of the ensuing two decades, the Wolohan lumber and elevator operations steadily grew, expanding during years of economic depression and years of war. By 1950, there were seven elevators composing the company's operations, five of which where adjoined by lumber yards. At this point, in 1950, the company was acquired by Wickes Companies, marking the beginning of an era in Wolohan's history that saw it emerge as a pioneer in mill-direct buying and cash-and-carry retailing.

Two years after its acquisition of Wolohan, Wickes Cos. effected a company-wide reorganization that separated the lumber operations as a distinct entity. Named vice-president and general manager of the lumber operations was Richard Wolohan who joined the family business in 1932. While under Wolohan's stewardship, the Wickes-controlled family business began to experiment with then-novel retailing strategies, including cash-and-carry, which the company began testing at its Davison, Michigan, lumber yard in 1952. The most sweeping changes, however, were nearly three decades away. Their arrival signalled the creation of a distinctly different type of lumber retailer, one that held sway during the 1990s.

Independence Regained in the 1960s

A new business strategy was adopted during the late 1970s and early 1980s, but before the definitive changes reshaped the company for the 1990s several key developments occurred. In 1964—14 years after becoming part of the 50–lumber-yard Wickes enterprise—the Wolohan Lumber business struck out on its own once again. That year, Richard Wolohan and 10 managers left Wickes and formed Wolohan Lumber Co., the direct predecessor to the Wolohan lumber business that operated during the 1990s. Years after the split with Wickes, Richard Wolohan described Wolohan Lumber Co. at its outset, saying, "We were highly leveraged and undercapitalized—all the good and bad things that go along with that kind of enterprise," but aside from the company's financial vulnerability it stood strongly positioned in other respects. The management team in place had years of experience in the lumber business and possessed the purchasing, accounting, and operations expertise to make the eight-yard lumber company a winner.

Wolohan Lumber Co. generated $10.6 million in revenue during its first full year of operation. Six years later—in 1971—the company completed its initial public offering of stock, as it continued to expand during years of robust housing construction. Nearly all the company's growth during this period in its history was dependent on business derived from building contractors. Such would be the case throughout the 1960s and 1970s, a two-decade span during which Wolohan Lumber operated as a typical, builder-oriented lumber yard. By the end of the 1970s, however, a severe drop in the number of new housing construction starts prompted the company's management to re-evaluate its business strategy. It was a period in Wolohan Lumber's development that one industry observer described as a time of "serious soul-searching." After this introspective investigation, Wolohan Lumber management resolved to become a more retail-oriented company, that is, a lumber company whose focus was directed at the do-it-yourself (DIY) customer rather than exclusively at building contractors. By virtue of this decision, a new type of Wolohan Lumber began to take shape.

1980s: The "New" Wolohan Emerges

A number of steps were taken during the late 1970s and early 1980s to realize a shift in the company's business perspective, including the addition of a former K-Mart president to Wolohan Lumber's board of directors. By far the most influential addition, however, was an 18-year veteran of Wickes named David Wallace. Wallace joined Wolohan Lumber in 1980 and quickly made his influence felt, spearheading the metamorphosis that engendered an industry leader. "Dave Wallace was the key person from the outside in making the transition to a retail company," remembered a Wolohan family member. "He's a very strong executive who led our company through some difficult years and focused on the consumer side without losing the builder side of the business."

Wallace's inaugural years as president proved to be a crucible for both the company and its new leader. A nationwide

economic recession during the early 1980s devastated the automotive and steel industries in the Great Lakes region where many of Wolohan Lumber's markets were located, causing the lumber company's sales and profit levels to sink alarmingly. Wolohan Lumber's net income reached its nadir in 1982 when the company reported a meager $638,000 gain, but the program put into effect by Wallace already was underway, and more profitable years were quick to return.

The recovery orchestrated by Wallace greatly expanded Wolohan Lumber's customer base by targeting DIY customers. It also lessened the company's dependence on the frequently capricious home construction market. Wallace's aim was to increase the importance of consumer sales to Wolohan Lumber's bottom line, an objective that was accomplished by several key maneuvers. Advertising spending as a percentage of sales nearly doubled in the years following the early 1980s recession, as the company shifted its focus toward non-professionals. An extensive store renovation program also was put into effect, giving nearly every store a refurbished appearance and increased floor space. Further, those stores that did not meet profitability targets were shuttered. Perhaps most important, an employee training program was developed for everyone on the payroll, including sales clerks and corporate executives. The purpose of the employee training program was to stress the importance of DIY customers and how to meet their needs, the success of which proved instrumental to Wolohan Lumber's recovery during the 1980s.

By the late 1980s, there was tangible evidence that the strategy embraced during the early 1980s had produced positive results. The push to become a more retail-oriented company drove sales and profits upward at an encouraging rate, as the number of DIY transactions exponentially increased. The number of DIY transactions tripled between 1981 and 1988, pushing sales up 190 percent during the seven-year span. Annual profits recorded a much more prolific increase, soaring 1,659 percent between 1982 and 1988 to reach $11.22 million. By the end of the decade, the average square footage of Wolohan Lumber stores nearly had doubled to 24,000 square feet, making more room for the DIY customers who were patronizing the company's stores in droves. After several years of increased advertising spending and extensive remodeling, Wolohan Lumber executives had greatly increased the importance of the DIY customer. Total yearly sales were evenly divided between professional and DIY customers by the decade's conclusion, reaching a balance the company's management team had been aiming for since the early 1980s.

Growth Continues in the 1990s

Entering the 1990s, the Wolohan Lumber chain of building-supply and DIY centers comprised 50 stores scattered throughout seven Midwestern states, with the largest concentration of retail units located in the company's home state of Michigan. The early years of the decade witnessed another nationwide recession, but unlike the downturn during the early 1980s, the refocused Saginaw, Michigan, company was able to beat back the affects of a depressed economy more effectively thanks to its shift toward attracting DIY customers. Wolohan Lumber did not escape unscathed from the deleterious financial climate, however, struggling through what chief executive officer James

L. Wolohan described as a "disastrous" 1991. Although sales increased during the year, eclipsing $300 million for the first time, the company's net income slipped from nearly $12 million to $9.3 million. Compared to the ills suffered by other lumber retailers during the recession, however, the damage incurred by Wolohan Lumber was minimal, and by the end of 1992 the company was once again performing admirably.

Wolohan Lumber's recovery in 1992 took place while the nation was still in the thick of a pernicious recession, buoying hopes in Saginaw that the company's sales mix between professional and DIY customers would hold the company in good stead during cyclical downturns in the retail lumber industry. To keep the company moving in a positive direction, a chain-wide remodeling program was effected during the year that underscored management's attention to the needs of homeowners. As part of the remodeling effort, building materials and lawn and garden inventories were expanded. Higher profit margin, remodeler-oriented millwork and kitchen and bath presentations were also incorporated in the company's network of stores, helping sales for 1992 reach a record $344 million and net income rise above $10 million.

The encouraging financial figures posted in 1992 added vigor to Wolohan Lumber's expansion plans for the future. While retailers of all sorts continued to reel from the stifling economic climate, Wolohan Lumber increased its store count, opening two stores in 1993 and six stores—all in Michigan—in 1994. Sales surged ahead as a result, swelling to $380 million in 1993 and $449 million in 1994, marking the 13th consecutive year of record sales. Wolohan Lumber's enviable record of annual sales increases, which dated back to the recovery spearheaded by Wallace during the early 1980s, came to an end the following year, however, when the vagaries of the retail lumber industry negatively affected the 60-store chain. New home construction was down 12 percent during 1995, and lumber prices plummeted 20 percent, the combined affect of which crippled Wolohan Lumber's short-term profitability. Five new stores were added to the chain during the year, but four stores were closed because of weak profit performance, causing the company's net income for the year to plunge 66 percent from $11 million to $3.7 million. Sales, for the first time in 14 years, dropped as well, falling to $418 million as DIY sales dropped eight percent and contractor sales dipped six percent.

Although 1995 proved to be a difficult year, the retrogressive financial slide did not dampen hopes for the company's future, at least in the minds of management. Much of the blame for the year was attributed to factors outside of the company's control and to the four stores that fell below Wolohan's profitability standards—developments that did not dash hopes for a speedy recovery. Another store was added to the chain in early 1996, raising the total number of Wolohan stores to 62 and symbolizing the company's push forward during the late 1990s. As the company charted its course for the late 1990s and the celebration of its 35th year of independence, executives in Saginaw, led by chairman, president, and chief executive officer Jim Wolohan, were confident that the future would bring a continuation of the growth achieved during the 1980s and the first half of the 1990s.

Further Reading

Higgins, Kevin T., "Wolohan: The Quiet Giant's Fast Track," *Building Supply Home Centers,* June 1989, p. 66.

Palmer, Jay, "Nailing Down a Recovery," *Barron's,* August 10, 1992, p. 20.

Thompson, Boyce, "Steady Hands Keep Wolohan on the Upswing," *Building Supply Home Centers,* Summer 1988, p. 34.

"Wolohan Sales Surge, Store Openings on Tap," *Building Supply Home Centers,* June 1992, p. 46.

—Jeffrey L. Covell

The Yokohama Rubber Co., Ltd.

36-11, Shimbashi 5-chome
Minato-ku, Tokyo 105
Japan
+81 (3) 5400-4531
Web site: http://www.yokohamatire.com

Public Company
Incorporated: 1917
Employees: 14,316
Sales: ¥389.3 billion (US$3.67 billion)
Stock Exchanges: Tokyo
SICs: 3011 Tires and Inner Tubes; 3053 Gaskets,
   Packing and Sealing Devices; 3052 Rubber & Plastics
   Hose & Belting; 3728 Aircraft Parts and Equipment,
   Not Elsewhere Classified

With an estimated four percent of global tire and rubber sales in the early 1990s, The Yokohama Rubber Co., Ltd. ranked seventh among the world's top producers of tires and other rubber products. Yokohama Rubber's operations are divided into two primary segments: the Tire Group, which accounts for over 70 percent of total sales and is divided into three market categories: original equipment, replacement tires, and tires for export; and the Multiple Business Group, which encompasses all non-tire business including rubber industrial and engineered products like belts, hoses, sheeting, coatings, and even some sporting goods. Although for most of its history the company focused on its domestic Japanese business, an intense consolidation in the global tire and rubber industry prompted it to diversify geographically in the late 20th century. These international moves, coupled with an emphasis on research and development which is turning out a steady stream of new products, have strengthened the company's position in a competitive worldwide industry.

Company Origins

Formed in 1917, one of a number of Japanese industrial companies that emerged as a result of the opening of Japan to the outside world in the late 19th century, Yokohama Rubber developed during the 1920s by finding openings for innovation in Japan's growing industrial infrastructure. The company's most successful product during this period, providing the main basis for its growth, was the cord tire, which it began marketing in 1921. Until then, tires used in Japan were usually made of fabric, primarily canvas. Yokohama's Hamatown Cord, the first cord tire sold in Japan, was three times more durable than fabric tires and soon became popular on Japan's roads. At this time the company also developed products in the area of industrial systems, using rubber to improve the efficiency of transmission belts used in spinning and other industries. In 1921 the company began marketing rubber cut-edged transmission belts, which soon replaced leather transmission belts in a number of industries, and continued to improve on belt technology in 1929 when it produced Japan's first V-type belt which offered improved flexibility and transmission.

These early moves provided the basis for expansion in the 1930s, when accelerating economic activity in Japan created strong demand for rubber products both for vehicles and industrial applications. Yokohama developed balloon tires, tires designed specifically to prevent heat problems, giant tires for trucks, Y-shaped tread tires and, following a fashion started in the United States, tires with colored sidewalls. In 1930 the company developed a soft rubber lining designed for the chemical industry, to protect metals against corrosion and leaking, and also produced a hard rubber bearing to protect ships' propeller shafts. A crucial step in the company's growth occurred in 1935, when it began supplying tires to the major Japanese car producers, Nissan and Toyota, turning Yokohama Rubber into one of Japan's key rubber companies. Its growing reputation prompted the Department of the Imperial Household to ask the company to develop a set of tires for the Japanese Emperor's car, a contract that involved a year and a half of research and development and resulted in the production of 24 tires. The company stepped into the international market in 1934 when it patented, in Japan and the United States, a bandless hose for use in loading oil, followed in 1936 by Japan's first domestically produced hydraulic brake hose for cars. In 1939, the company made its strongest move to date in the growing synthetic rubber industry by developing its first synthetic rubber material.

Company Perspectives:

"The superior quality of our tires is recognized at the top, by world-class professional drivers competing in race and rally events in prestigious international and national series. Behind this recognition lie our capabilities in the development of advanced technologies, and evaluation and testing systems. This provides us with a strong base from which to go forward in further technological development. Our diversification strategy also distinguishes us from competitors. We have an enormous range of technologies and products, covering the fields of general industry, civil engineering, construction, marine business, aerospace, and sports and leisure. Take our originally developed technologies, based on our distinctive adhesive technologies and our environment-friendly technologies, our multifaceted business operations and global scope, and you have the 'Yokohama Advantage' in society."

World War II and Postwar Diversification

The outbreak of World War II prompted Yokohama Rubber to begin producing aircraft components, an area previously unexplored and, in 1941, fuel cells, flexible pipes, and tires for the Japanese army and navy's Zero and Hayabusa fighter aircraft. The strong wartime demand for these products led Yokohama, in 1944, to open a new plant at Mie to increase tire production for military aircraft. The desperate need for vehicle and industrial components in Japan's shattered postwar economy prompted the opening of another new plant at Mishima in 1946. Both of these plants remained crucial to Yokohama's production network into the early 1990s.

Like many areas of the Japanese economy, the rubber industry received a boost in the 1950s in the aftermath of the Korean War, from the U.S. Army's demand for military components. This allowed Yokohama Rubber, which was listed on the Tokyo Stock Exchange in 1950, to increase its involvement in the aircraft products market, in 1955 by beginning production of nylon cord aircraft tires and, over the next two years, aircraft fuel cells, hoses, and self-sealing couplings to meet U.S. military specifications. In 1957 the company began manufacturing and marketing tires for jet aircraft. Along with the expansion of aircraft components manufacturing, the company continued to develop and market new kinds of vehicle tires including, during the 1950s, rayon cord tires, Japan's first tubeless tires, butyl tires, snow tires, and nylon cord tires, as well as developing Hamaking all-weather tires, a basic design widely used in the early 1990s on buses and trucks in Japan. The company also began marketing its first synthetic rubber tires.

On the industrial side, the 1950s saw production of a rapidly growing range of components, including Japan's first cord conveyor belts using rubber insulated cord instead of canvas, material for use as rollers in iron works, an air spring for the Japanese National Railways Technical Research Institute, pneumatic rubber fenders for use by ships at docks, nuts resistant to loosening by vibrations, and rubber based adhesives for brake linings. The growth in the range and quantity of items being produced was helped by the increase in the company's productive capacity at two new large Yokohama Rubber plants, one at Ageo in 1950 and one at Hiratsuka in 1952.

Diversification Continues in 1960s

Notwithstanding its diversification into the areas of industrial products and aircraft components, vehicle tires remained the biggest part of Yokohama Rubber's activities and, during the 1960s, the company pushed ahead with a number of developments that ensured its position as one of the top tire manufacturers in the dynamic Japanese economy, which was growing at an average of 10 percent a year. The company began marketing all-steel radial tires for trucks and buses, studded tires, car racing tires, passenger car radials, and tubeless radials. In the aircraft area, Yokohama won a contract to supply tires to All Nippon Airways Co. Ltd.'s fleet of Boeing 727 jets. U.S. military contracts continued to provide important business, prompting the company to develop aircraft sealants and Teflon aircraft hoses and duct tubes. The company also developed a stream of fuel cells, tires, hose and tube assemblies, ferry tanks, insulation blankets, and de-icers for newly developing jet aircraft and, in 1970, honeycomb core and structural adhesives for aircraft.

Yokohama's diversification into innovative industrial products continued during the 1960s, as it developed more conveyor belt systems, including nylon and fire resistant belts, rubber highway joints to replace existing metal joints, rubber lining for atomic energy equipment, and a rubber fence for sports stadiums. The company also made shockproof pipe couplings for submarines, underwater soundproof materials for warships, dredging sleeves, high pressure hoses, liquid transportation tanks, and sheets for waterproofing roads, as well as developing new materials for use as sealants and lubricants. These continuing research based developments in all three of Yokohama Rubber's main areas of activity ensured that the company benefited from Japan's continued industrial growth. Far from remaining simply a tire company Yokohama had, by 1970, established itself as a major industrial group, with products to offer across the economy. The establishment of a new factory at Shinshiro in 1964 increased the company's productive capacity, enabling it to consolidate this versatility, while the opening of a Yokohama Rubber office in the United States in 1969, followed by a Canadian branch in 1970, marked the first move by the company to expand geographically as well as industrially.

Tire Innovations and Expanded Industrial Goods in the 1970s

Increasing sales in all of Yokohama's main product lines prompted it to undertake a major investment program in the early 1970s, including the establishment of two new factories designed for specific purposes. The Ibaraki plant, opened in 1973, was built to produce hydraulic hose, while the Onomichi plant, which began operating in 1974, specialized in making large off-road tires. Consolidation in all three product areas continued, with the company pushing ahead with new developments in the tire industry, producing steel belted radials for passenger cars, mud and snow radials and other off-road tires, aluminum wheels, and improving the kind of rubber used in its tires. During the 1970s Yokohama Rubber continued to extend its range of industrial goods, producing a rubber guard rail for highways, a rubber sheet to prevent adhesion of barnacles to ships, honeycomb sandwich structural material, new types of hose, rubber bags for oil spills at sea, all-weather paving material for tennis courts and athletic tracks, hot-melt type adhesives, soundproof rooms, sound- and vibration-proof materials for pianos, watertight floor assemblies, for ships' cargo holds, and many other products. Activity in the aircraft division also increased during this period, with the continued production of fuel cells, tube assemblies and other items developed over the previous two decades, as well as improving on the older designs and introducing new products. In 1972, the company developed an electric anti-icing device for helicopter rotor blades, and crash resistant fuel cells for aircraft, followed in later years by further developments in the areas of insulation blankets, honeycomb panels, and prepregs—semi-solid materials consisting of resin impregnated reinforcing fibers, used in the manufacture of aircraft primary structures, which need to be light and strong. Yokohama also began producing equipment for rockets, including heat exchangers and bellows. The company continued with its industrial diversification in 1983 when it moved into the sports products business in cooperation with ten specialist sports equipment manufacturers.

Global Competition Intensifies in the 1980s

The rapid consolidation of the global tire and rubber industry in the late 1980s and early 1990s compelled Yokohama to turn from its historical emphasis on the domestic market. It was ''buy or be bought'' in a market that shrunk from having 14 competitors splitting three-fourths of the sales to the ''big three''—Goodyear, Michelin and Bridgestone—controlling more than half the world's tire sales. Unlike many of its global competitors, Yokohama's strategy emphasized smaller-scale joint ventures and affiliations over mergers and acquisitions, though it has used these strategies as well. In 1984 the company separated its Canadian branch from its U.S. operation and, the following year, bought a 26 percent stake in a Malaysian tire company, IT International, in a deal involving the supply of Yokohama's technical assistance to the Malaysian company. Two years later, it launched an automotive equipment manufacturing and marketing venture, Aeroquip Automotive, in the United States, in partnership with Yokohama Aeroquip Co., and Aeroquip Co. of the United States. Later the same year, the company bought a ten percent stake in South Korea's largest tire maker, Hankook Tyre Manufacturing Company and, the following year, began cooperating with the Rubber Research Institute of Malaysia to develop extraction and pulverization technology for use in obtaining useful substances from natural rubber residue.

In 1987 Yokohama launched an expansion project for its aircraft parts plant at Hiratsuka, introducing the production of large motor parts for the H-11 rocket; bought a 40 percent stake in a maker of printed circuit boards for industrial machinery, Togoshi Co.; and signed a deal with a U.S. company, Technical Wire Products Inc., to produce and market its electromagnetic wave shielding materials in Japan. It also established a joint venture with another U.S. company, Morton Thiokol Inc., to manufacture and market polyurethane based automotive windscreen sealants in the United States. In the same year, Yokohama demonstrated its level of technical achievement by ending its agreements with a number of U.S. and European tire makers who had been supplying the company with technical expertise.

Following a share swap with another Japanese rubber company, Toyo Tyre and Rubber Co., Yokohama established a joint venture to sell passenger car tires and truck and bus steel radials in Germany with Marubeni Corp. in 1988. Later that year, the company made its biggest move to date into the huge U.S. tire market when, in a joint venture with Toyo Tyre and Rubber and the German industrial group Continental Aktiengesellschaft, Yokohama began construction of a plant to produce radial truck and bus tires in the United States. The plant, at Mount Vernon, Illinois, was designed to produce 880,000 tires per year at full capacity. Yokohama made another significant move into the U.S. market in 1989, when it bought a U.S. rubber company, Mohawk Rubber Co. Ltd., with a tire plant in Virginia, an industrial rubber products plant in Ohio, and retread shops in Alabama and California, for about US$150 million. It announced soon afterward that it intended to spend US$200 million over the next five to six years to raise production capacity at the plant. In the same year, Yokohama strengthened its assault on the U.S. market by launching its first television advertising campaign, and began a joint venture with Hankook in South Korea to produce tire tubes and flaps. The company's president, Kazuo Motoyama, summed up the direction of Yokohama's activity in 1989, when he said ''We have no intention whatsoever of remaining a local Japanese tire maker.''

Globalization, R&D Emphasized in 1990s

Given its relatively late entry into the global rubber fray, Yokohama Rubber set up an energetic expansion program encompassing both acquisitions and organic growth in the early 1990s. In 1990 alone, Yokohama bought 49 percent of a Taiwanese rubber hose maker, Shieh Chi Industrial Co.; launched its products in Portugal; signed a five-year technical agreement with another South Korean company, Bukdoo Chemical; and made moves to begin exporting radial motorcycle tires to Brazil. The company planned to expand from its Asian and North American strongholds into Europe by establishing factories and distribution centers throughout the continent. Increased penetration of Asian and Pacific Rim markets came with the creation of new production operations in the Philippines and Australia middecade. Along with this energetic geographic diversification, Yokohama continued to inject funds into its research and development program. This resulted in new products in a number of areas, including the development of electroconductive, antistatic flooring material, a printed wiring board that dissipates heat more efficiently than conventional ones, new prepregs for use as primary structural components for aircraft, new car window adhesives, and a radio-wave isolation room with smooth flat walls, which satisfy a strong demand from electronics and appliance manufacturers.

These extensions of Yokohama's geographic reach and product line were made against a backdrop of continued intense competition, especially from world market leader Michelin, which initiated a price war in the early 1990s. Hoping to seriously undermine its rivals, the French company timed its price cuts to coincide with the global recession then under way. Along with many of its competitors, Yokohama suffered declining sales and profits throughout the first half of the decade.

Revenues dropped from ¥441.4 billion in 1991 to ¥379.4 billion in 1994, and net income dropped from ¥5 billion to a loss of ¥207 million in 1993 before recovering to ¥2.1 billion during the period. A change in the company's fiscal year end shrunk fiscal 1995 to just three months (January 1, 1995 to March 31, 1995).

Although fiscal 1996 (ended March 31) sales showed the first year-over-year increase in the decade, net income resumed its downtrend, sliding to ¥563 million (US$5.3 million) from fiscal 1994. Company executives blamed the poor results on its U.S. subsidiary, Yokohama Tire Corp., which suffered a "one-two punch" of high debt service and raw materials expenses. A reorganization of the American operations mid-decade aimed to boost productivity by simultaneously increasing capacity, consolidating distribution, and decreasing employment levels.

Yokohama appeared mid-decade to have reconciled itself to a position outside the tire industry's "big three." Instead of concentrating its efforts on fighting for sales in the low-margin original equipment market, its strategy for the future included a continued emphasis on research and development with a particular focus on high-margin, niche products. Though the company wasn't likely to abandon its core tire business—which encompassed OEM, replacement, and specialty tires and continued to contribute more than two-thirds of sales in the mid-1990s—it expected sales of non-tire goods to grow fastest in the waning years of the 20th century.

Principal Subsidiaries

Yokohama Tire Corporation (U.S.A.); Yokohama Tire (Canada) Inc.; Yokohama Tyre Australia Pty. Ltd.; Yokohama Reifen GmbH (Germany); The Mohawk Rubber Company (U.S.A.).

Further Reading

"GTY Tire Plant May Lead to Other Joint Ventures," *Modern Tire Dealer,* August 1991, p. 5.
"This is Yokohama," Tokyo: The Yokohama Rubber Company, 1980.
Key Note Report: Rubber Manufacturing and Processing, Middlesex, Eng.: Key Note Publications Ltd., 1990.
Yamaguchi, Jack, "Unique Dry-Wet Tire from Yokohama," *Automotive Engineering,* October 1990, pp. 154–155.
"Yokohama Rubber Co. Ltd.," *Rubber World,* September 1992, p. 8.

—Richard Brass
—updated by April D. Gasbarre

Younkers, Inc.

P.O. Box 1495
Des Moines, Iowa 50397
U.S.A.
(515) 244-1112
Fax: (515) 247-7174

Wholly Owned Subsidiary of Proffitt's Inc.
Incorporated: 1904
Employees: 7,000 (2,700 full-time)
Sales: $613.4 million (fiscal 1995)
SICs: 5311 Department Stores

Younkers, Inc. is a Midwestern department store chain with, by early 1997, 48 stores in seven states. Most were in Iowa (18) or Wisconsin (17), but there were five each in Michigan and Nebraska, and one each in Illinois, Minnesota, and South Dakota. Younkers's stores were generally located in midsized to smaller cities where competition was more limited than in major metropolitan areas. In addition to apparel, Younkers's anchor line of business, the chain carried major cosmetic and fragrances lines, furniture, housewares, china, linens, gift items, and other merchandise. It also operated restaurants in certain of its stores. Younkers became a subsidiary and division of Proffitt's, Inc. in 1996.

An Iowa Institution, 1856–1978

Younkers (originally Younker & Brothers) was founded in Keokuk, Iowa, in 1856 by three young Polish-born brothers: Lipman, Samuel, and Marcus Younker. The general store was a base from which they strapped packs of merchandise on their backs that they carried into the neighboring countryside to farmers and others too busy or isolated to shop in town. They founded Iowa's first synagogue and closed the store on Saturdays, the Jewish Sabbath. Another brother, Herman, joined them in 1874 and opened a 1,320-square-foot dry goods store in Des Moines on their behalf with a $6,000 grubstake. "We have come here to live and mean to do what is right," the store declared in a newspaper advertisement taken out on its opening.

With the closing of the Keokuk store in 1879, Des Moines became headquarters for Younker Brothers. In 1881 it became the first Des Moines store to hire female sales clerks, and in 1900 this store moved to its present location at Seventh and Walnut Streets. Younker Brothers was a place to meet as well as to shop. Women lunched at the elegant Tea Room upstairs and teenagers took their dates there for dinner and dancing. Just about every organization in town met at the Tea Room. The store even had a knitting classroom. It installed Iowa's first escalator in 1939 and was the first department store in the United States to air condition its entire building.

Younker Brothers grew by acquiring Grand Department Store in 1912, Wilkins Department Store in 1923, and J. Mandelbaum & Sons in 1928. Originally incorporated in 1904, it merged with Harris-Emery Co. in 1927, thereby becoming the largest department store chain in Iowa, and reincorporated under Delaware law. Its net sales (excluding leased departments) rose from $8.4 million in 1938 to $26.4 million in fiscal 1948 (the year ended January 31, 1948). Net profit rose in this period from a low of $308,000 in 1939 to a high of nearly $2 million in fiscal 1947. At the end of 1947 it acquired a Sioux City, Iowa store from Davidson Brothers Co. and had, since 1941, opened branch stores in Ames, Fort Dodge, Marshalltown, and Mason City. Younker Brothers went public in December 1948 to retire bank loans, offering a minority of its common stock at $26 a share. Much of its stock remained in the hands of three Des Moines merchandising families: the Frankels, Mandelbaums, and Rosenfelds.

As the largest store in Iowa, the Younkers of this period carried the old adage that the customer is always right beyond the call of duty. A *Business Week* article cited the case of a lady who brought back her fur coat, complaining it didn't fit, after allowing her weight to balloon over the winter. The store remodeled it without argument. Morey Sostrin, president and general manager, said, "We figure that the advertising value of such cases in small towns in Iowa is worth far more than the adjustment cost." Younkers was known for liberal credit policies (including 60,000 charge accounts) and a mail-order service. It was also running three Des Moines restaurants.

During the 1950s Younker Brothers acquired another Sioux City store and opened branch stores in Iowa City, Oskaloosa, and Ottumwa, Iowa; Omaha, Nebraska; and Austin, Minnesota. The Omaha store, opened in 1955, was its first in a shopping center. Net sales, after reaching $45.5 million in fiscal 1956, slumped to $37.1 million the next year and did not surpass the 1956 figure until 1962. Net income dropped from $2.4 million in 1956 to $1.4 million in 1957 and did not top the 1956 figure until 1965. In 1961 the company acquired Kilpatrick's Department Store of Omaha.

Although the biggest downtown department store in Des Moines, the Younkers flagship retained a reputation for "small town friendliness." This six-story, 400,000-square-foot, block-long building was responsible for 42 percent of corporation sales in fiscal 1965. At the end of the decade, in addition to the main Des Moines and Sioux City stores, there were 16 Younkers branch stores in Iowa, more than half in major shopping centers. Net sales (including leased departments) reached a record $83.5 million in fiscal 1970, and net profit was a record $3.8 million. Apparel was accounting for nearly 80 percent of sales, with home furnishings, furniture, and appliances next in importance. Dividends had been paid each year since 1935. The long-term debt was $10 million.

Equitable of Iowa Subsidiary, 1979–1992

By 1978 Younkers had added branch stores in Des Moines and Davenport, Iowa; Moline, Illinois; and Sioux Falls, South Dakota, plus a main store in a Cedar Rapids shopping center and the Merle Hay Mall in Des Moines, which had a separate store for homes. This last store was destroyed by a fire that year in which ten employees were killed. Net sales came to $135.5 million in fiscal 1978, and net profit amounted to $5 million. In 1979 Equitable of Iowa purchased Younker Brothers for $72.2 million and made the retailer a subsidiary named Younkers. Des Moines breathed a sigh of relief, since Equitable was controlled by Iowa's first family, the Hubbells. "The loss of an independently-owned business always is sad," the *Des Moines Tribune* declared in an editorial. "But the acquisition of Younkers by another Des Moines-based firm avoids the drawbacks of absentee ownership and promises to be good for the community."

The Younkers chain of 29 stores—25 in Iowa—grew slowly during the next four years. Sales increased from $141.9 million in 1979 to $188.7 million in 1984. After net income slumped from $4.8 million in 1983 to only $723,000 in 1984, William Friedman, Jr.—a descendant of the group of families that had controlled Younkers since the 1920s—was ousted as president and chief executive officer, allegedly for alienating customers by turning Younkers into an upscale boutique. The Ottumwa store was closed, and 200 jobs were eliminated.

Under W. Thomas Gould, who first assumed the presidency and later became chief executive officer as well, Younkers shifted its focus back to the middle class. It updated its "Satisfaction Always" motto, adopted in 1936, to stress customer service even more than previously. Although not paying a commission on sales, the company adjusted wage rates every six months on a sales-per-hour basis. Salespeople were expected to acknowledge a customer within 30 seconds of arrival in a department at a distance of no more than 30 feet. Gould closed eight of the 37 Younkers stores that he felt were too small in markets that offered little growth opportunity, and he eliminated the chain's only furniture store.

Net income improved appreciably in 1986, and at the end of the year Younkers agreed to purchase a major competitor, Brandeis & Sons, which was operating 11 department stores in Iowa and Nebraska. This acquisition boosted Younkers's revenues by almost $100 million, and in 1988 the 37-store chain earned a record $8.3 million on revenues of $313.4 million. Gould and other Younkers managers chafed under Equitable's direction, however, because its profits were absorbed by the parent organization instead of being earmarked for expansion, which company managers felt was needed to generate the economies of scale needed to compete with the Kmarts and Wal-Marts on price. Between 1985 and 1992 Younkers paid Equitable about $63 million in dividends.

In June 1989 Equitable announced its intention to sell Younkers but rejected offers of about $90 million as inadequate. Sales grew slowly in subsequent years, but after the company earned a record $12.8 million on sales of $330 million in 1991, almost all of the common stock was put on the market at $12.50 a share. Some of the proceeds from the 6.17 million shares sold in 1992 were used to reduce Younkers's long-term debt from $104 million to $89 million.

Public Company Again, 1992–1995

Gould, who as chairman remained at the helm of Younkers, continued to stress customer service. Interviewed by *Daily News Record* [*DNR*] in 1992, he said, "The '80s were merchandise and marketing driven. The '90s are customer driven. . . . We have to totally reverse the hierarchy of the '80s where the buyers and merchandisers were on top and the sales associates were on the bottom." His philosophy was to stress basics rather than trendy but unsuitable merchandise. "Former management thought the American consumer had gotten thin and rich overnight," Gould told a *Business Week* reporter. In fact, the average female customer was consuming so many calories that Younkers was making one-quarter of its women's apparel sales in sizes 14 and higher and, therefore, was featuring large women in its catalog and fashion shows.

During fiscal 1992 (ended January 30, 1993) Younkers had net earnings of $17.6 million on net sales of $473.4 million. In April of that year Younkers purchased the department store division of financially troubled H.C. Prange Co., a privately owned chain with 25 stores, 18 of them in Wisconsin, for $67 million in cash and assumption of $9 million in debt. Prange proved harder to digest than expected, however, and although Younkers's sales rose to $597.9 million in fiscal 1993, net earnings fell to $12.2 million and, on an earnings-per-share basis, only half the previous year's level. During fiscal 1994 sales and earnings barely rose. The value of a share of Younkers stock fell from a high of $32.50 in 1993 to $12.25 in June 1994, making the company vulnerable to a takeover by a bigger store chain.

A battle royal for control of Younkers broke out in 1994, when Milwaukee-based retailer Carson Pirie Scott & Co. made an unsolicited $152 million ($17-a-share) takeover bid for the company. Carson's already held 12 percent of the stock. Younkers not only rejected the bid as inadequate but adopted a poison-pill defense intended to make the acquisition prohibitively expensive.

Undeterred, Carson's raised its bid to $19 a share in 1995 and won a nonbinding resolution from Younkers shareholders to put the company up for sale to the higher bidder, but Younkers's board voted not to sell. Carson's, which would have closed Younkers's headquarters and the downtown Des Moines store, then sued Younkers's directors for "gross breaches of fiduciary duty."

Sale to Proffitt's

By late 1995 Younkers's position was more attractive to alternative offers, because the former Prange stores had become an asset, accounting for more than 40 percent of the company's total sales. In February 1996 the company quickly accepted a $24-a-share, $216 million offer from Proffitt's, Inc., a department store chain based in Tennessee. Younkers, which became a Proffitt's subsidiary as well as a division, preserved its name and much of its independence, although about one-fifth of the jobs at Des Moines headquarters were eliminated. (The flagship Des Moines store, a money loser, remained open only because of a city financial aid package.) Even Carson's voted its shares in favor of the merger.

Gould became vice-chairman of Proffitt's, yielding the CEO position at Younkers to Robert Mosco. Mosco resigned in October 1996 to become president of Proffitt's newly formed Merchandising Group. Three "unproductive" Younkers stores were closed in 1996, and two others were sold to a third party. New Younkers units were scheduled to open, however, in Iowa City, Iowa, and Grandville, Michigan, in 1998. During fiscal 1997 (the year ended February 3, 1997) women's apparel accounted for 32 percent of Younkers's sales, men's apparel for 16 percent, home furnishings for 16 percent, and cosmetics for 11 percent. Children's apparel, accessories, leased departments, lingerie, and shoes accounted for the remainder of the division's sales, in that order.

Further Reading

Byrne, Harlan S., "Younkers," *Barron's,* September 13, 1995, pp. 35–36.

Chandler, Susan, "This Takeover Goes Way Past Hostile," *Business Week,* July 3, 1995, pp. 72–73.

"City Store Wins State Buyers," *Business Week,* May 28, 1949, pp. 56–58.

Couch, Mark P., "Peeking into Younkers' Executive Suite," *Business Record,* May 2, 1992, p. 1.

"Equitable of Iowa Says Friedman Removed as Younkers Chief," *Wall Street Journal,* January 4, 1985, p. 24.

"Equitable Puts Younkers Chain on the Block," *WWD (Women's Wear Daily),* June 1, 1989, pp. 1, 11.

Hartnett, Michael, "Younkers," *Stores,* March 1993, pp. 16, 18, 20.

"Insurance Firm Agrees To Buy Younker Bros.," *Daily News Record,* August 4, 1978, p. 3.

Kasler, Dale, "Surprise Bid Puts Younkers on the Market," *Des Moines Register,* October 29, 1994, 1A, 6A.

——, "Tom Gould, CEO," *Des Moines Register,* November 7, 1993, pp. 1G, 7G.

——, "Younkers," *Des Moines Register,* February 3, 1996, pp. 12S, 11S.

——, "Younkers Becomes a Part of Proffitt's," *Des Moines Register,* February 3, 1996, pp. 1A, 10A.

——, "Younkers Bid Caps Year of Troubles," *Des Moines Register,* October 30, 1994, pp. 1A, 7A.

——, "Younkers President Taking New Job," *Des Moines Register,* October 26, 1996, pp. 12S, 7S.

Oliver, Suzanne, "Milan Proposes, Des Moines Disposes," *Forbes,* July 19, 1993, pp. 88, 92.

Poxon, Jeffrey, "Younker Brothers, Inc.," *Wall Street Transcript,* January 10, 1972, p. 26,774.

Sharoff, Robert, "An Independent Voice in the Midwest," *DNR (Daily News Record),* February 3, 1992, p. 16.

Sloane, Leonard, "Iowa's Younkers: Friendly Store," *New York Times,* April 11, 1966, pp. 55, 59.

—Robert Halasz

Zytec Corporation

7575 Market Place Drive
Eden Prairie, Minnesota 55344
U.S.A.
(612) 941-1100
Fax: (612) 829-1837
Web site: http://www.zytec.com

Public Company
Incorporated: 1984
Employees: 2,300
Sales: $228 million (1996)
Stock Exchanges: NASDAQ
SICs: 3679 Electronic Components, Not Elsewhere
     Classified

Zytec Corporation is a leading designer and manufacturer of power supplies, which convert, distribute, and regulate the electricity needed to operate computers, peripherals, office equipment, and communications technology. The Minnesota-based company is one of the largest power supply producers in the United States and has earned a reputation for quality within the industry and with the high-tech original equipment manufacturers which are its customers. A smaller but growing portion of Zytec's business comes from its power supply service and logistics operation.

Roots with Control Data Corporation

In the mid-1960s, as part of its vertical integration strategy, Control Data Corporation (CDC) opened a power supply plant in Redwood Falls, Minnesota, a small town about 100 miles southwest of Minneapolis. The factory produced power supply units for CDC subsidiary Magnetic Peripherals Inc. (MPI), which manufactured large magnetic disk drives. Engineering, purchasing, inventory control, and production schedules for the Redwood Falls plant and other small-town ''feeder plants'' manufacturing components and subassemblies for CDC were centralized in the Twin Cities.

In the early 1980s, CDC was faced with rapidly advancing electronics technology and intense competition in the marketplace. In response, CDC implemented a new business strategy. The company began to sell off its low-tech manufacturing operations—such as power supply units, cables, and circuit boards—and turned its resources to product development. From a different perspective, the community of Redwood Falls was at risk of losing its largest employer (the plant had once employed more than 500 people), when the region was already being rocked by an agricultural crisis.

CDC offered to sell the plant to a long-time employee, peripheral products manager Ronald D. Schmidt. His initial response to the idea was negative, but he became interested in acquiring the company when he was assigned to work on a plan to jointly operate the power supply operation with another large computer company. When the joint venture failed to materialize and a buy out offer made by plant employees was rejected by CDC, Schmidt asked John M. Steel, another peripheral products manager, and Lawrence J. Matthews, head of component development at Magnetic Peripherals, to enter into a leveraged buy out of the plant.

CDC invested $500,000 for 22 percent of the company: an investment to be phased out over a three-year period through a discounted employee repurchase of stock. Schmidt, Steel, and Matthews raised $200,000, and CDC's financial subsidiary, Commercial Credit Co., kicked in $5.5 million in financing. Production would continue in Redwood Falls with the management and engineering offices located in the Twin Cities. Zytec was incorporated in January 1984 with Schmidt at the helm. Initially, CDC continued to provide Zytec with purchasing, inventory, and some corporate support services as well as orders for power supplies.

The Difficult Path to Independence

Schmidt, Steel, and Matthews planned to broaden their business by diversifying into other power supply markets, including minicomputers, engineering workstations, telephone switches, medical testing and diagnostic machines. The new owners also made a commitment to use Dr. W. Edward Deming's 14 points

---

Company Perspectives:

"We are a company that competes on value; is market driven; provides superior quality, service and value; builds strong relationships with our customers; and provides technical excellence in our products. We are action oriented and willing to innovate; foster integrity; autonomy and entrepreneurship; and believe in the importance of execution. We believe in a simple form and a lean staff; the importance of teamwork, mutual trust, involvement, and people as individuals; and the development of productive employees through training, education and capital investment. We focus on what we know best thereby making a fair profit on current operations to meet our obligations to all stakeholders and to perpetuate our continued growth."

---

for management—a philosophy which often received credit for reviving Japan's post–World War II economy—as a framework for making manufacturing changes. In the meantime, the newly independent company was operating under increased demand, while working to establish its own purchasing and production systems and building a warehouse for inventory. Nearly all of Zytec's first year revenues of $66 million were generated from its business with MPI.

The optimism associated with its initial surge of growth and plans for the future was squelched by a dramatic slump in the computer industry and existing manufacturing problems. Zytec began 1985 with $11 million in parts on its shelves and $6 million in unfinished product in the plant. Cycle times—the time from introduction of materials on the plant floor to shipment of product—were getting longer and cutting into already slim profit margins.

In the midst of the developing crisis, Schmidt worked to familiarize managers with Deming's concepts. He also brought on board people who were experienced in implementing Statistical Process Control (SPC) and Just-In-Time (JIT) manufacturing techniques: SPC involved the continuous monitoring of the production process in order to identify problems quickly, while JIT involved introducing and moving materials through the manufacturing process with maximum efficiency. Zytec also adopted a Total Quality Commitment (TQC) management approach which gave all employees some level of responsibility for establishing, tracking, and achieving production goals and objectives.

However, in June 1985, after several earlier cutbacks on new orders, MPI abruptly stopped all shipments. The computer industry had weakened, and sales on CDC's large disk drives had plummeted even further. Production at the Redwood Falls plant was completely shut down for two weeks. Zytec gradually resumed operation, with employees taking salary cuts of 10 to 20 percent. According to George Dixon in *Corporate Report Minnesota,* "Later that summer Control Data slowly began to place more orders. By then, however, Zytec had begun to get its ruinous inventory and work-in-progress problems under control." They survived the period, according to Schmidt, by living

off their inventory. Sales for 1985 had fallen to $48.5 million with losses of $2.3 million.

Reorganization and Renewal

Zytec's revamping was put into full gear in 1986. Employee training was accelerated. The factory was reorganized into manufacturing cells to streamline the production process. Quality control techniques were integrated into corporate areas as well as on the manufacturing floor and in the warehouse. Zytec returned to profitability in 1986, but revenues were still falling and the vast majority of orders were still coming from CDC.

San Francisco–based Micro-Tech Consultants, which served the power supply industry, estimated 1986 sales by independent producers to be more than $1.6 billion. With approximately $45 million in sales, Zytec was ranked seventh among U.S. firms. The industry consisted of many small producers with access to the same basic technology, operating under few industry standards, and most often producing custom made power supplies for a single large customer.

Power supplies, an essential element of electronic equipment, basically did the following: switch alternating current (AC) to the direct current (DC) used by electronic systems, provide various levels of DC voltage to subsystems and components, and monitor and regulate voltages to protect the equipment from power surges. However, the stress on the product caused by continuous use, the high level of manual construction, and the dearth of investment in technology had saddled the power supply industry with a reputation for product failure.

Recognition for Quality

By 1987, Zytec was gaining notice, not for its failures but for its successes. The manufacturer had become more competitive with overseas power supply producers in terms of cost, quality, scheduling and delivery times. Currency exchange rates had also started to favor domestic businesses. It gained such customers as Fujitsu America, Tandem Computers Inc., Unisys Corp., Abbott Laboratories, AT&T, IBM, Eastman Kodak, Network Systems, Sun Microsystems, and Storage Technology. Zytec continued to refine its operations, invest in technological advancements, and diversify its markets over the next few years.

In 1991, Zytec won the Malcolm Baldrige National Quality Award, the Minnesota Quality Award, and the IBM Market Driven Quality (MDQ) Gold Award. The privately held company's revenue grew by nearly 30 percent in spite of a recession. Zytec also expanded internationally with the acquisition of an Austrian power supply manufacturing plant.

By the beginning of 1992, Zytec had 21 customers; less than five percent of business was with CDC. Zytec planned to go public that year, but the initial public offering was canceled due to inconsistent earnings coupled with an unfavorable market for smaller companies. Zytec did win another honor: *Industry Week* magazine named the Redwood Falls plant one of "America's Ten Best Plants." David Altany of *Industry Week* said Schmidt's and Zytec's commitment to Deming's quality principles set them "apart from the pack." Nevertheless, the company's bottom line was still wavering: Austrian operations lost nearly $4.5 million and largely contributed to the year-end loss of $3.3 million.

Zytec finally went public in November 1993. The stock was sold at $10.375 for a total of $9.2 million. The Austrian plant still generated a small loss in 1993, but the company's earnings were on an upswing. Zytec-designed and collaborative power supplies, the product segment with the highest profit margin but the longest development time, brought in 78 percent of revenues in 1994. Customer-designed power supplies, a low-risk and low-margin segment of business, contributed 13 percent of revenues. The remaining nine percent was generated by the repair and service end of the business. Zytec's power supply repair operation was the largest in the United States: they handled the products of more than 200 manufacturers. The bulk of the service business was dedicated to one customer, Hewlett-Packard, via Zytec's California repair facility. Overall, Zytec's revenue for 1994 grew by 41 percent to $128 million.

Dynamic Forces Affect Zytec and the Industry

In the mid-1990s, the power supply market remained highly fragmented with over 350 manufacturers. According to a 1995 John G. Kinnard & Co. report, two industry trends were likely to benefit Zytec. Many original equipment manufacturers—which accounted for about half of the power supply market—were shutting down their internal power supply operations finding it more economical to purchase the product rather than to manufacture it themselves. In addition, as power supplies became more complex and the industry became more automated, increased design and capital costs made it more difficult for the smaller independent power supply manufacturers to be competitive. Only a small percentage of U.S. manufacturers—Zytec among them—had annual revenues of more than $100 million while the vast majority of U.S. power supply makers had annual sales of less than $10 million.

A different trend in the electronics industry, one of demand outstripping capacity, had a negative effect on Zytec in 1995. A shortage of power semiconductors shut down production on several key projects early in the year. Zytec compensated by seeking out additional suppliers and redesigning some products, but the supply problem kept year-end earnings down in spite of significant revenue growth.

Schmidt, Steel, and Matthews, the leaders of the buy out from CDC, still owned about 35 percent of the company in 1995; other employees owned an additional 10 percent. Since the IPO, Zytec stock had hovered around the initial offering price, but in 1996 the stock experienced some volatility: first, due to earnings estimates and then later because of an online bulletin board notice. Other activity included two stock splits and a postponed public offering.

The opening of a new manufacturing plant in Broomfield, Colorado, and an expansion of the plant in Redwood Falls helped alleviate Zytec's capacity problems. Zytec also acquired a magnetic components plant, the primary supplier for its Austrian operation, from the Hungarian government in 1996.

Zytec's 1996 revenues were $228 million. Net income rose 103 percent—if excluding a one time tax gain—to $7.9 million. In its 1996 10-K report, Zytec contributed its recent surge in sales to sole-provider opportunities with original equipment manufacturers for the Internet and data communications marketplace. Zytec also reported that its service and logistics business had been doubling each year, and the company was seeking additional customers in that growing area.

Future Directions

More complex electronics technology has driven the need for smaller and more efficient power supply systems such as the ones Zytec manufactures. They have hundreds of components and perform advanced diagnostic and power management functions. In 1996, Zytec established a distributed power architecture (DPA) office in Richardson, Texas, in 1996. DPA is a process which allows greater flexibility when adding electronic components or upgrading hardware. The developing technology had been commonly used in telecommunications and was finding expanded applications in data networking, large volume data storage, and high-end data processing markets. Based on industry forecasts, Zytec expected the DPA technology to be an important expansion of its business in the future.

Further Reading

Alexander, Steve, "Online Mention by Motley Fool Takes Zytec Stock on Wild Ride," *Star Tribune* (Minneapolis), May 9, 1996, p. 1D.
Altany, David, "America's Best Plants," *Industry Week,* October 19, 1992, p. 62.
"Corporate Capsule: Zytec Corp.," *Minneapolis/St. Paul CityBusiness,* July 12, 1996, p. 26.
Dixon, George, "Keizen!" *Corporate Report Minnesota,* December 1987, pp. 56–60.
Gross, Steve, "Pendulum Swings toward U.S. for Maker of Computer Parts," *Star Tribune* (Minneapolis), February 4, 1988, p. 1D.
——, "Zytec Cancels Offering, Cites Unsettled Market," *Star Tribune* (Minneapolis), June 23, 1992, p. 3D.
Jones, Jim, "A Quest for Quality," *Star Tribune* (Minneapolis), October 2, 1991, p. 1D.
Krause, Renhardt, "Plugging into Net to Jolt Power Supply Sales," *Investor's Business Daily* (Los Angeles), July 5, 1996.
Peterson, Susan E., "It's Easy to Miss Zytec's CEO, But Not His Success," *Star Tribune* (Minneapolis), February 24, 1992, p. 1D.
——, "Zytec Corp. Wins Baldrige National Quality Award," *Star Tribune* (Minneapolis), October 10, 1991, p. 1D.
"Quality with a Capital 'Z'," *Minnesota Enterprise,* January 1992, p. 6.
Rayner, Bruce C. P., "Zealous Zytec Takes On the World with JIT," *Electronic Business,* November 1, 1987, pp. 130–38.
"Serving Your Multinational Needs with Our Multinational Resources," *Zytec Corporation,* February 1997.
Youngblood, Dick, "Investment Is Key to Successful Global Competition," *Star Tribune* (Minneapolis), June 7, 1987, p. 1D.
——, "The Control Data Legacy: More Than 70 Businesses Trace Roots to Company," *Star Tribune* (Minneapolis), June 3, 1992, p. 2D.
——, "Zytec Puts Its Quality Effort on the Line and It Pays Off," *Star Tribune* (Minneapolis), June 13, 1994, p. 2D.
"Zytec '95 Sales Up 33%," *Electronic News,* March 4, 1996, p. 49.

—Kathleen Peippo

INDEX TO COMPANIES

Index to Companies

Listings in this index are arranged in alphabetical order under the company name. Company names beginning with a letter or proper name such as Eli Lilly & Co. will be found under the first letter of the company name. Definite articles (The, Le, La) are ignored for alphabetical purposes as are forms of incorporation that precede the company name (AB, NV). Company names printed in bold type have full, historical essays on the page numbers appearing in bold. Updates to entries that appeared in earlier volumes are signified by the notation (**upd.**). Company names in light type are references within an essay to that company, not full historical essays. This index is cumulative with volume numbers printed in bold type.

Groupe Ancienne Mutuelle, **III** 210–11
Groupe André, 17 210–12
Groupe Barthelmey, **III** 373
Groupe Bull, **10** 563–64; **12** 246. *See also* Compagnie des Machines Bull.
Groupe Casino. *See* Etablissements Economiques de Casino Guichard, Perrachon et Cie, S.C.A.
Groupe Danone, **14** 150
Groupe de la Cité, IV 614–16, 617
Groupe de la Financière d'Angers, **IV** 108
Groupe Jean Didier, **12** 413
Groupe Lagadère, **15** 293
Groupe Pinault, **19** 306, 309
Groupe Promodès S.A., 19 326–28
Groupe Salvat, **IV** 619
Groupe Victoire, **III** 394
Groupement des Exploitants Pétroliers, **IV** 545
Groupement Laitier du Perche, **19** 50
Groux Beverage Corporation, **11** 451
Grove Manufacturing Co., **I** 476–77; **9** 393
Grow Biz International, Inc., 18 207–10
Grow Group Inc., 12 217–19, 387–88
Growmark, **I** 421; **11** 23
Growth International, Inc., **17** 371
Gruene Apotheke, **I** 681
Gruma. *See* Grupo Industrial Maseca S.A.
Grumman Corp., I 58–59, **61–63**, 67–68, 78, 84, 490, 511; **7** 205; **8** 51; **9** 17, 206–07, 417, 460; **10** 316–17, 536; **11** **164–67 (upd.)**, 363–65, 428; **15** 285
Grün & Bilfinger A.G., **I** 560–61
Grundig, **I** 411; **II** 80, 117; **13** 402–03; **15** 514
Grundig Data Scanner GmbH, **12** 162
Grunenthal, **I** 240
Gruner + Jahr AG & Co., **IV** 590, 593; **7** 245; **15** 51
Gruntal and Co., **III** 263
Gruntal Financial Corp., **III** 264
Grupo Carso, **14** 489
Grupo Corvi S.A. de C.V., **7** 115
Grupo de Ingenieria Ecologica (GRIECO), **16** 260
Grupo Financiero Serfin, S.A., 19 188–90, 474
Grupo Herdez S.A., **18** 247
Grupo Industrial Alfa, S.A., **II** 262; **11** 386. *See also* Alfa, S.A. de C.V.
Grupo Industrial Bimbo, 19 191–93
Grupo Industrial Maseca S.A., **19** 192
Grupo Protexa, **16** 210
Grupo Quan, **19** 192–93
Grupo Televisa, S.A., 9 429; **18 211–14**; **19** 10
Grupo Tudor, **IV** 471
Grupo Zeta, **IV** 652–53; **7** 392
Gruppo IRI, **V** 325–27
GSG&T, **6** 495
GSI. *See* Geophysical Service, Inc.
GSI Acquisition Co. L.P., **17** 488
GSR, Inc., **17** 338
GSU. *See* Gulf States Utilities Company.
GT Interactive Software Corp., **19** 405
GTE Corporation, II 38, 47, 80; **III** 475; **V 294–98**; **9** 49, 171, 478–80; **10** 19, 97, 431; **11** 500; **14** 259, 433; **15** **192–97 (upd.)**; **18** 74, 111, 543. *See also* British Columbia Telephone Company.
GTO. *See* Global Transport Organization.
GTS Duratek, Inc., **13** 367–68
Guangzhou M. C. Packaging, **10** 130

Guaranty Bank & Trust Company, **13** 440
Guaranty Federal Savings & Loan Assoc., **IV** 343
Guaranty Properties Ltd., **11** 258
Guaranty Savings and Loan, **10** 339
Guaranty Trust, **16** 25
Guaranty Trust Co. of New York, **II** 329–32, 428; **IV** 20
Guardian, **III** 721
Guardian Bank, **13** 468
Guardian Federal Savings and Loan Association, **10** 91
Guardian Mortgage Company, **8** 460
Guardian National Bank, **I** 165; **11** 137
Guardian Royal Exchange Plc, III 350; **11 168–70**
Gubor Schokoladen, **15** 221
Guccio Gucci, S.p.A., 12 281; **15 198–200**
GUD Holdings, Ltd., **17** 106
Guelph Dolime, **IV** 74
Guernsey Banking Co., **II** 333
Guess, Inc., 15 201–03; **17** 466
Guest, Keen and Nettlefolds plc. *See* GKN plc.
Guest Supply, Inc., 18 215–17
Gueyraud et Fils Cadet, **III** 703
Guild Press, Inc., **13** 559
Guild Wineries, **13** 134
Guilford Industries, **8** 270–72
Guilford Mills Inc., 8 234–36
Guilford Transportation Industries, Inc., **16** 348, 350
Guinness Peat, **10** 277
Guinness plc, **I** 239, 241, **250–52**, 268, 272, 282; **II** 428–29, 610; **9** 100, 449; **10** 399; **13** 454; **18** 62, 501
Gujarat State Fertilizer Co., **III** 513
Gulco Industries, Inc., **11** 194
Güldner Aschaffenburg, **I** 582
Gulf + Western Inc., I 418, **451–53**, 540; **II** 147, 154–56, 177; **III** 642, 745; **IV** 289, 672; **7** 64; **10** 482; **13** 121, 169, 470
Gulf + Western Industries. *See* Paramount Communications.
Gulf Air, **6** 63
Gulf Canada Ltd., **I** 216, 262, 264; **IV** 495, 721; **6** 478; **9** 391; **13** 557–58
Gulf Caribbean Marine Lines, **6** 383
Gulf Engineering Co. Ltd., **IV** 131
Gulf Exploration Co., **IV** 454
Gulf Mobile and Northern Railroad, **I** 456
Gulf Mobile and Ohio Railroad, **I** 456; **11** 187
Gulf of Suez Petroleum Co., **IV** 412–14
Gulf Oil Chemical Co., **13** 502
Gulf Oil Corp., **I** 37, 584; **II** 315, 402, 408, 448; **III** 225, 231, 259, 497; **IV** 198, 287, 385–87, 392, 421, 450–51, 466, 470, 472–73, 476, 484, 508, 510, 512, 531, 538, 565, 570, 576; **17** 121–22
Gulf Plains Corp., **III** 471
Gulf Public Service Company, **6** 580
Gulf Resources & Chemical Corp., **15** 464
Gulf States Paper, **IV** 345
Gulf States Steel, **I** 491
Gulf States Utilities Company, 6 495–97; **12** 99
Gulf United Corp., **III** 194
Gulfstream Aerospace Corp., 7 205–06; **13** 358
Gulfstream Banks, **II** 336

Gulton Industries Inc., **7** 297; **19** 31
Gummi Werke, **I** 208
Gump's, **7** 286
Gunder & Associates, **12** 553
Gunderson, Inc. *See* The Greenbrier Companies.
Gunfred Group, **I** 387
The Gunlocke Company, **12** 299; **13** 269
Gunns Ltd., **II** 482
Gunpowder Trust, **I** 379; **13** 379
Gunter Wulff Automaten, **III** 430
Gunther, S.A., **8** 477
Gupta, **15** 492
Gurneys, Birkbeck, Barclay & Buxton, **II** 235
Gusswerk Paul Saalmann & Sohne, **I** 582
Gustav Schickendanz KG, **V** 165
Gustavus A. Pfeiffer & Co., **I** 710
Gustin-Bacon Group, **16** 8
Gutehoffnungshütte Aktienverein AG, **III** 561, 563; **IV** 104, 201
Guthrie Balfour, **II** 499–500
Gutta Percha Co., **I** 428
Gutzeit. *See* W. Gutzeit & Co.
Guy Carpenter & Co., **III** 282
Guy Motors, **13** 286
Guy Salmon Service, Ltd., **6** 349
GW Utilities Ltd., **I** 264; **6** 478
Gwathmey & Co., **II** 424; **13** 340
Gymboree Corporation, 15 204–06
Gypsum, Lime, & Alabastine Canada Ltd., **IV** 271

H & R Block, Incorporated, 9 268–70
H Curry & Sons. *See* Currys Group PLC.
H N Norton Co., **11** 208
H.A. Job, **II** 587
H&D. *See* Hinde & Dauch Paper Company.
H&H Craft & Floral, **17** 322
H.B. Claflin Company, **V** 139
H.B. Fuller Company, 8 237–40
H.B. Nickerson & Sons Ltd., **14** 339
H.B. Reese Candy Co., **II** 511
H.B. Tuttle and Company, **17** 355
H.B. Viney Company, Inc., **11** 211
H. Berlind Inc., **16** 388
H.C. Christians Co., **II** 536
H.C. Frick Coke Co., **IV** 573; **7** 550
H.C. Petersen & Co., **III** 417
H.C. Prange Co., **19** 511–12
H.D. Lee Company, Inc. *See* Lee Apparel Company, Inc.
H.D. Pochin & Co., **III** 690
H. Douglas Barclay, **8** 296
H.E. Butt Grocery Co., 13 251–53
H.F. Ahmanson & Company, II 181–82; **10 342–44 (upd.)**
H. Fairweather and Co., **I** 592
H.G. Anderson Equipment Corporation, **6** 441
H.H. Brown Shoe Company, **18** 60, **18** 62
H.H. Cutler Company, **17** 513
H.H. Robertson, Inc., **19** 366
H. Hackfeld & Co., **I** 417
H. Hamilton Pty, Ltd., **III** 420
H.I. Rowntree and Co., **II** 568
H.J. Green, **II** 556
H.J. Heinz Company, I 30–31, 605, 612; **II** 414, 480, 450, **507–09**, 547; **III** 21; **7** 382, 448, 576, 578; **8** 499; **10** 151; **11** **171–73 (upd.)**; **12** 411, 529, 531–32; **13** 383

Metromont Materials, **III** 740
Metroplitan and Great Western Dairies, **II** 586
Metropolitan Accident Co., **III** 228
Metropolitan Bank, **II** 221, 318; **III** 239; **IV** 644; **17** 323
Metropolitan Broadcasting Corporation, **7** 335
Metropolitan Clothing Co., **19** 362
Metropolitan Distributors, **9** 283
Metropolitan District Railway Company, **6** 406
Metropolitan Estate and Property Corp. Ltd., **IV** 710–11
Metropolitan Financial Corporation, **12** 165; **13 347–49**
Metropolitan Furniture Leasing, **14** 4
Metropolitan Gas Light Co., **6** 455
Metropolitan Life Insurance Company, **II** 679; **III** 265–66, 272, **290–94**, 313, 329, 337, 339–40, 706; **IV** 283; **6** 256; **8** 326–27; **11** 482
Metropolitan National Bank, **II** 284
Metropolitan Petroleum Corp., **IV** 180–81; **19** 319
Metropolitan Railway, **6** 407
Metropolitan Railways Surplus Lands Co., **IV** 711
Metropolitan Tobacco Co., **15** 138
Metropolitan Vickers, **III** 670
METSA, Inc., **15** 363
Metsä-Serla Oy, **IV 314–16**, 318, 350
Mettler United States Inc., **9** 441
Metzeler Kautschuk, **15** 354
Mexican Eagle Oil Co., **IV** 365, 531
Mexican Original Products, Inc., **II** 585; **14** 515
Mexofina, S.A. de C.V., **IV** 401
Meyer and Charlton, **IV** 90
Meyer Brothers Drug Company, **16** 212
Meyerland Company, **19** 366
Meyers & Muldoon, **6** 40
Meyers and Co., **III** 9
Meyers Parking, **18** 104
Meyrin, **I** 122
MFI, **II** 612
MFS Communications Company, Inc., **11 301–03**; **14** 253
MG Holdings. *See* Mayflower Group Inc.
MG Ltd., **IV** 141
MG&E. *See* Madison Gas & Electric.
MGM Grand Inc., **III** 431; **6** 210; **17 316–19**; **18** 336–37
MGM/UA Communications Company, **II** 103, **146–50**, 161, 167, 408; **IV** 676; **6** 172–73; **12** 323, 455; **15** 84. *See also* Metro-Goldwyn-Mayer.
mh Bausparkasse AG, **III** 377
MHI Group, Inc., **13** 356; **16** 344
MHT. *See* Manufacturers Hanover Trust Co.
Miami Power Corporation, **6** 466
Micamold Electronics Manufacturing Corporation, **10** 319
Michael Baker Corp., **14 333–35**
MICHAEL Business Systems Plc, **10** 257
Michael Joseph, **IV** 659
Michael Reese Health Plan Inc., **III** 82
Michael's Fair-Mart Food Stores, Inc., **19** 479
Michaels Stores, Inc., **17 320–22**, 360
MichCon. *See* MCN Corporation.

Michelin, **III** 697; **7** 36–37; **8** 74; **11** 158, 473
Michelin et Compagnie, **V** 236
Michiana Merchandising, **III** 10
Michie Co., **IV** 312; **19** 268
Michigan Automotive Compressor, Inc., **III** 593, 638–39
Michigan Bell Telephone Co., **14 336–38**; **18** 30
Michigan Carpet Sweeper Company, **9** 70
Michigan Consolidated Gas Company. *See* MCN Corporation.
Michigan Fruit Canners, **II** 571
Michigan General, **II** 408
Michigan International Speedway, **V** 494
Michigan Motor Freight Lines, **14** 567
Michigan National Corporation, **11 304–06**; **18** 517
Michigan Oil Company, **18** 494
Michigan Packaging Company, **15** 188
Michigan Plating and Stamping Co., **I** 451
Michigan Radiator & Iron Co., **III** 663
Michigan Shoe Makers. *See* Wolverine World Wide Inc.
Michigan Spring Company, **17** 106
Michigan State Life Insurance Co., **III** 274
Michigan Steel Corporation, **12** 352
Michigan Tag Company, **9** 72
Mickey Shorr Mobile Electronics, **10** 9–11
Micro D, Inc., **11** 194
Micro Decisionware, Inc., **10** 506
Micro Peripherals, Inc., **18** 138
Micro Power Systems Inc., **14** 183
Micro Switch, **14** 284
Micro Warehouse, Inc., **16 371–73**
Micro-Circuit, Inc., **III** 645
Micro-Power Corp., **III** 643
Micro/Vest, **13** 175
MicroAge, Inc., **16 367–70**
Microamerica, **12** 334
MicroBilt Corporation, **11** 112
MicroComputer Accessories, **III** 614
Microcomputer Asset Management Services, **9** 168
Microdot Inc., **I** 440; **8 365–68**, 545
Microfal, **I** 341
Microform International Marketing Corp., **IV** 642; **7** 312
Microfral, **14** 216
Micromedex, **19** 268
Micron Technology, Inc., **III** 113; **11 307–09**
Micropolis Corp., **10** 403, 458, 463
MicroPro International, **10** 556
Microprocessor Systems, **13** 235
Micros Systems, Inc., **18 335–38**
Microseal Corp., **I** 341
Microsoft Corporation, **III** 116; **6** 219–20, 224, 227, 231, 235, 254–56, **257–60**, 269–71; **9** 81, 140, 171, 195, 472; **10** 22, 34, 57, 87, 119, 237–38, 362–63, 408, 477, 484, 504, 557–58; **11** 59, 77–78, 306, 519–20; **12** 180, 335; **13** 115, 128, 147, 482, 509; **14** 262–64, 318; **15** 132–33, 321, 371, 483, 492, 511; **16** 4, 94, 367, 392, 394, 444; **18** 24, 64, 66, 306–7, 345, 349, 367, 541, 543; **19** 310
Microtel Limited, **6** 309–10
Microware Surgical Instruments Corp., **IV** 137
Microwave Communications, Inc., **V** 302
Mid-America Capital Resources, Inc., **6** 508

Mid-America Dairymen, Inc., **II** 536; **7 338–40**; **11** 24
Mid-America Industries, **III** 495
Mid-America Interpool Network, **6** 506, 602
Mid-America Packaging, Inc., **8** 203
Mid-America Tag & Label, **8** 360
Mid-Central Fish and Frozen Foods Inc., **II** 675
Mid-Continent Area Power Planner, **V** 672
Mid-Continent Computer Services, **11** 111
Mid-Continent Telephone Corporation. *See* Alltel Corporation.
Mid-Georgia Gas Company, **6** 448
Mid-Illinois Gas Co., **6** 529
Mid-Pacific Airlines, **9** 271
Mid-Packaging Group Inc., **19** 78
Mid-South Towing, **6** 583
Mid-States Development, Inc., **18** 405
Mid-Texas Communications Systems, **6** 313
Mid-Valley Dairy, **14** 397
Mid-West Drive-In Theatres Inc., **I** 245
Mid-West Paper Ltd., **IV** 286
MidAmerican Communications Corporation, **8** 311
Midas International Corporation, **I** 457–58; **10 414–15**, 554
MIDCO, **III** 340
Midcon, **IV** 481
Middle South Utilities, **V** 618–19
Middle West Corporation, **6** 469–70
Middle West Utilities Company, **V** 583–84; **6** 555–56, 604–05; **14** 227
Middle Wisconsin Power, **6** 604
Middleburg Steel and Alloys Group, **I** 423
Middlesex Bank, **II** 334
Middleton Packaging, **12** 377
Middleton's Starch Works, **II** 566
Middletown Manufacturing Co., Inc., **16** 321
Middletown National Bank, **13** 467
Midhurst Corp., **IV** 658
Midial, **II** 478
Midland Bank plc, **II** 208, 236, 279, 295, 298, **318–20**, 334, 383; **9** 505; **12** 257; **14** 169; **17 323–26 (upd.)**; **19** 198
Midland Brick, **14** 250
Midland Cooperative, **II** 536
Midland Counties Dairies, **II** 587
Midland Electric Coal Co., **IV** 170
Midland Enterprises Inc., **6** 486–88
Midland Gravel Co., **III** 670
Midland Industrial Finishes Co., **I** 321
Midland Insurance, **I** 473
Midland International, **8** 56–57
Midland Investment Co., **II** 7
Midland Linseed Products Co., **I** 419
Midland National Bank, **11** 130
Midland Railway Co., **II** 306
Midland Southwest Corp., **8** 347
Midland Steel Products Co., **13** 305–06
Midland United, **6** 556
Midland Utilities Company, **6** 532
Midland-Ross Corporation, **14** 369
Midlands Electricity, **13** 485
Midlands Energy Co., **IV** 83; **7** 188
Midlantic Corp., **13** 411
Midrange Performance Group, **12** 149
Midrex Corp., **IV** 130
Midvale Steel and Ordnance Co., **IV** 35, 114; **7** 48
Midway Airlines, **6** 105, 120–21

Mitsubishi Petrochemical Co., **I** 364; **III** 685

Mitsubishi Petroleum, **III** 760

Mitsubishi Pulp, **IV** 328

Mitsubishi Rayon Co. Ltd., **I** 330; **V** **369–71**; **8** 153

Mitsubishi Sha Holdings, **IV** 554

Mitsubishi Shipbuilding Co. Ltd., **II** 57; **III** 513, 577–78; **7** 348; **9** 349

Mitsubishi Shoji Trading, **IV** 554

Mitsubishi Shokai, **III** 577; **IV** 713; **7** 347

Mitsubishi Trading Co., **IV** 460

Mitsubishi Trust & Banking Corporation, **II** 323–24; **III** 289

Mitsui, **16** 84

Mitsui and Co., **I** 282; **IV** 18, 224, 432, 654–55; **V** 142; **6** 346; **7** 303; **13** 356

Mitsui Bank, Ltd., **II** 273–74, 291, **325–27**, 328, 372; **III** 295–97; **IV** 147, 320; **V** 142; **17** 556

Mitsui Bussan K.K., **I** 363, 431–32, 469, 492, 502–04, **505–08**, 510, 515, 519, 533; **II** 57, 66, 101, 224, 292, 323, 325–28, 392; **III** 295–96, 717–18; **IV** 147, 431; **9** 352–53

Mitsui Gomei Kaisha, **IV** 715

Mitsui Group, **9** 352

Mitsui House Code, **V** 142

Mitsui Light Metal Processing Co., **III** 758

Mitsui Marine and Fire Insurance Company, Limited, **III** 209, **295–96**, 297

Mitsui Mining & Smelting Co., Ltd., **IV** **145–46**, 147–48

Mitsui Mining Company, Limited, **IV** 145, **147–49**

Mitsui Mutual Life Insurance Company, **III** **297–98**

Mitsui O.S.K. Lines, Ltd., **I** 520; **IV** 383; **V** **473–76**; **6** 398

Mitsui Petrochemical Industries, Ltd., **I** 390, 516; **9** **352–54**

Mitsui Real Estate Development Co., Ltd., **IV** **715–16**

Mitsui Shipbuilding and Engineering Co., **III** 295, 513

Mitsui Toatsu, **9** 353–54

Mitsui Trading, **III** 636

Mitsui Trust & Banking Company, Ltd., **II** **328**; **III** 297

Mitsui-no-Mori Co., Ltd., **IV** 716

Mitsukoshi Ltd., **I** 508; **V** **142–44**; **14** 502

Mitsuya Foods Co., **I** 221

Mitteldeutsche Creditbank, **II** 256

Mitteldeutsche Energieversorgung AG, **V** 747

Mitteldeutsche Privatbank, **II** 256

Mitteldeutsche Stickstoff-Werke Ag, **IV** 229–30

Mitteldeutsches Kraftwerk, **IV** 229

Mixconcrete (Holdings), **III** 729

Miyoshi Electrical Manufacturing Co., **II** 6

Mizushima Ethylene Co. Ltd., **IV** 476

MJB Coffee Co., **I** 28

MK-Ferguson Company, **7** 356

MLC Ltd., **IV** 709

MLH&P. *See* Montreal Light, Heat & Power Company.

MMAR Group Inc., **19** 131

MML Investors Services, **III** 286

MNC Financial. *See* MBNA Corporation.

MNC Financial Corp., **11** 447

MND Drilling, **7** 345

MNet, **11** 122

Mo och Domsjö AB, **IV** 315, **317–19**, 340

Moa Bay Mining Co., **IV** 82; **7** 186

Mobay, **I** 310–11; **13** 76

Mobil Communications, **6** 323

Mobil Corporation, **I** 30, 34, 403, 478; **II** 379; **IV** 93, 295, 363, 386, 401, 403, 406, 423, 428, 454, **463–65**, 466, 472–74, 486, 492, 504–05, 515, 517, 522, 531, 538–39, 545, 554–55, 564, 570–71; **V** 147–48; **6** 530; **7** 171, **351–54 (upd.)**; **8** 552–53; **9** 546; **10** 440; **12** 348; **16** 489; **17** 363, 415; **19** 140, 225, 297

Mobile America Housing Corporation. *See* American Homestar Corporation.

Mobile and Ohio Railroad, **I** 456

Mobile Communications Corp. of America, **V** 277–78

Mobile One, **16** 74

Mobile Telecommunications Technologies Corp., **18** **347–49**

Mobira, **II** 69; **17** 353

Mobley Chemical, **I** 342

Mobù Company, **6** 431

Mobujidosha Bus Company, **6** 431

MOÇACOR, **IV** 505

Mocatta and Goldsmid Ltd., **II** 357

Mochida Pharaceutical Co. Ltd., **II** 553

Moctezuma Copper Co., **IV** 176–77

Modar, **17** 279

Modell's Shoppers World, **16** 35–36

Modern Equipment Co., **I** 412

Modern Furniture Rental, **14** 4

Modern Maid Food Products, **II** 500

Modern Merchandising Inc., **19** 396

Modern Patterns and Plastics, **III** 641

Modernistic Industries Inc., **7** 589

Modine Manufacturing Company, **8** **372–75**

MoDo. *See* Mo och Domsjö AB.

Moen Incorporated, **12** **344–45**

Moët-Hennessy, **I** 271–72; **10** 397–98

Mogul Corp., **I** 321; **17** 287

Mogul Metal Co., **I** 158

Mohasco Corporation, **15** 102

Mohawk & Hudson Railroad, **9** 369

Mohawk Airlines, **I** 131; **6** 131

Mohawk Industries, Inc., **19** **274–76**

Mohawk Rubber Co. Ltd., **V** 256; **7** 116; **19** 508

Mohr-Value Stores, **8** 555

Moilliet and Sons, **II** 306

Moist O'Matic, **7** 535

Mojo MDA Group Ltd., **11** 50–51

Mokta. *See* Compagnie de Mokta.

MOL. *See* Mitsui O.S.K. Lines, Ltd.

Molecular Biosystems, **III** 61

Molex Incorporated, **II** 8; **11** **317–19**; **14** 27

Moline National Bank, **III** 463

Molinos de Puerto Rico, **II** 493

Molinos Nacionales C.A., **7** 242–43

Molins Co., **IV** 326

Molkerie-Zentrak Sud GmbH, **II** 575

Moll Plasticrafters, L.P., **17** 534

Molloy Manufacturing Co., **III** 569

Mölnlycke, **IV** 338–39

Molson Companies Ltd., **I** **273–75**, 333; **II** 210; **7** 183–84; **12** 338; **13** 150, 199

Molycorp, **IV** 571

Mon-Dak Chemical Inc., **16** 270

Mon-Valley Transportation Company, **11** 194

MONACA. *See* Molinos Nacionales C.A.

Monarch Food Ltd., **II** 571

Monarch Marking Systems, **III** 157

MonArk Boat, **III** 444

Mond Nickel Co., **IV** 110–11

Mondadori. *See* Arnoldo Monadori Editore S.p.A.

Mondex International, **18** 543

Mondi Paper Co., **IV** 22

Monet Jewelry, **II** 502–03; **9** 156–57; **10** 323–24

Money Access Service Corp., **11** 467

Monfort, Inc., **13** **350–52**

Monheim Group, **II** 521

Monier Roof Tile, **III** 687, 735

Monis Wineries, **I** 288

Monk-Austin Inc., **12** 110

Monmouth Pharmaceuticals Ltd., **16** 439

Monochem, **II** 472

Monogram Aerospace Fasteners, Inc., **11** 536

Monogramme Confections, **6** 392

Monolithic Memories Inc., **6** 216; **16** 316–17, 549

Monon Corp., **13** 550

Monon Railroad, **I** 472

Monoprix, **V** 57–59

Monroe Auto Equipment, **I** 527

Monroe Calculating Machine Co., **I** 476, 484

Monroe Cheese Co., **II** 471

Monroe Savings Bank, **11** 109

Monrovia Aviation Corp., **I** 544

Monsanto Company, **I** 310, 363, **365–67**, 402, 631, 666, 686, 688; **III** 741; **IV** 290, 367, 379, 401; **8** 398; **9** 318, **355–57 (upd.)**, 466; **12** 186; **13** 76, 225; **16** 460–62; **17** 131

Monsanto Corp., **18** 112

Monsavon, **III** 46–47

Mont Blanc, **17** 5

Montabert S.A., **15** 226

Montan Transport GmbH, **IV** 140

Montana Enterprises Inc., **I** 114

Montana Power Company, **6** 566; **7** 322; **11** **320–22**

Montana Refining Company, **12** 240–41

Montana Resources, Inc., **IV** 34

Montana-Dakota Utilities Co., **7** 322–23

Montaup Electric Co., **14** 125

Montecatini, **I** 368; **IV** 421, 470, 486

Montedison SpA, **I** **368–69**; **IV** 413, 421–22, 454, 499; **14** 17

Montefibre, **I** 369

Montefina, **IV** 499

Monterey Mfg. Co., **12** 439

Monterey's Tex-Mex Cafes, **13** 473

Monterrey, Compania de Seguros sobre la Vida. *See* Seguros Monterrey.

Monterrey Group, **19** 10–11, 189

Montfort of Colorado, Inc., **II** 494

Montgomery Ward & Co., Incorporated, **III** 762; **IV** 465; **V** **145–48**; **7** 353; **8** 509; **9** 210; **10** 10, 116, 172, 305, 391, 393, 490–91; **12** 48, 309, 315, 335, 430; **13** 165; **15** 330, 470; **17** 460; **18** 477

Montiel Corporation, **17** 321

Montreal Bank, **II** 210

Montreal Engineering Company, **6** 585

Montreal Light, Heat & Power Consolidated, **6** 501–02

Montreal Mining Co., **17** 357

Montres Rolex S.A., **8** 477; **13** **353–55**; **19** 452

Montrose Chemical Company, **9** 118, 119

INDEX TO INDUSTRIES

Index to Industries

CONSTRUCTION

CONTAINERS

DRUGS

ELECTRICAL & ELECTRONICS

FINANCIAL SERVICES: BANKS

FINANCIAL SERVICES:
NON-BANKS

FOOD PRODUCTS

FOOD SERVICES & RETAILERS

HEALTH & PERSONAL CARE PRODUCTS

HEALTH CARE SERVICES

LEGAL SERVICES

MANUFACTURING

TOBACCO

TRANSPORT SERVICES

UTILITIES

WASTE SERVICES

NOTES ON CONTRIBUTORS

Notes on Contributors

AZZATA, Geraldine. Freelance writer.

BAIN, Terry. Freelance writer.

BODINE, Paul S. Freelance writer, editor, and researcher in Milwaukee, specializing in business subjects; contributor to the *Encyclopedia of American Industries, Encyclopedia of Global Industries, DISCovering Authors, Contemporary Popular Writers,* the Milwaukee *Journal Sentinel,* and the Baltimore *Sun.*

BOYER, Dean. Newspaper reporter and freelance writer in the Seattle area.

BROWN, Susan W. Freelance writer and editor.

BURGMAN, Teri. Iowa-based freelance writer specializing in profile essays and perennial gardening.

CANNCASCIATO, K. Freelance writer.

COHEN, M. L. Novelist and freelance writer living in France.

COVELL, Jeffrey L. Freelance writer and corporate history contractor.

DERDAK, Thomas. Freelance writer and adjunct professor of philosophy at Loyola University of Chicago; former executive director of the Albert Einstein Foundation.

FIERO, John W. Freelance writer, researcher, and consultant; Professor of English at the University of Southwestern Louisiana in Lafayette.

FUJINAKA, Mariko. Freelance writer.

GASBARRE, April Dougal. Archivist and freelance writer specializing in business and social history in Cleveland, Ohio.

HALASZ, Robert. Former editor in chief of *World Progress* and *Funk & Wagnalls New Encyclopedia Yearbook*; author, *The U.S. Marines* (Millbrook Press, 1993).

HAMRICK, Catherine. Freelance writer.

HEFT, Gordon. Freelance writer.

INGRAM, Frederick. Business writer living in Columbia, South Carolina; contributor to the *Encyclopedia of Business,* the *Encyclopedia of Consumer Brands,* and *Global Industry Profiles.*

KOHLBERG, Sharyn. Freelance writer.

KROLL, Dorothy. Business writer, journalist, and industry analyst.

JACOBSON, Robert R. Freelance writer and musician.

LEMIEUX, Gloria A. Freelance writer and editor living in Nashua, New Hampshire.

O'NEIL, L. Peat. Freelance writer and teacher based in Washington, D.C.; author of *Travel Writing: A Guide to Research, Writing, and Selling* (Writer's Digest Books, 1996).

PEIPPO, Kathleen. Minneapolis-based freelance writer.

PFALZGRAF, Taryn Benbow. Freelance editor, writer, and consultant in the Chicago area.

RICHMAN, Jordan. Freelance writer.

RICHMAN, Vita. Freelance writer.

SALAMIE, David E. Part-owner of InfoWorks Development Group, a reference publication development and editorial services company.

TROSHYNSKI-THOMAS, Karen. Freelance writer.

WALDEN, David. Freelance writer.

WHITELEY, Laura E. Freelance writer based in Kalamazoo, Michigan.